America Reads

ROBERT C. POOLEY, *General Editor*

The United

Introduction to Modern Poetry by **PAUL ENGLE,** *Professor of English and Director of Writers' Workshop, State University of Iowa.*

Composition Guide by **DON OTTO,** *Cerritos Junior College, Norwalk, California.*

Novel Discussion Guides by **KENNETH SICKAL,** *Cary Grove High School, Cary, Illinois.*

SCOTT, FORESMAN AND COMPANY

Chicago, Atlanta, Dallas, Palo Alto, Fair Lawn, N.J.

States *in* Literature

WALTER BLAIR *Professor of English, University of Chicago.*
Member of editorial boards of College English, American Literature,
and Publications of the Modern Language Association.
Author of Native American Humor *and* Mark Twain & "Huck Finn."

PAUL FARMER *Georgia Institute of Technology. Consultant in the teaching of English.*
Formerly Coordinator of Language Arts, Atlanta Public Schools, Atlanta, Georgia.

THEODORE HORNBERGER *Professor of English, University of Pennsylvania.*
Member of editorial board of American Literature. *Author of*
Benjamin Franklin *and* Scientific Thought in the American Colleges 1638-1800.

MARGARET WASSON *Director of Instruction,*
Highland Park Independent School District, Dallas, Texas.

The eagle shown on the title page was carved by Samuel McIntire, and is reproduced by courtesy of the Peabody Museum of Salem.

The following photographs were taken expressly for The United States in Literature by James Ballard, of Scott, Foresman and Company. Cover, title page, pages 96, 97, 98 (top, bottom middle and right), 109, 112, 120, 122, 124, 128, 130, 132, 133, 137, 139, 140 (bottom), 144, 159, 172, 175, 183, 184, 191, 192, 227, 229, 230, 234, 235, 247, 248, 249, 266, 267, 281, 282, 297, 298, 299, 309 (bottom right), 366, 386, 541, 626 (bottom right), 710.

Introducing American Literature

Contents

part two TWENTIETH-CENTURY AMERICAN LITERATURE

chapter nine

Article and Essay
612

GUIDES TO THE DISCUSSION
OF THE NOVEL

BETTER READING

SUPPLEMENTARY ARTICLES

The Magazine in America:

Introducing American Literature

From the time you closed the covers of your primer and said, "I've read a book," you have constantly been broadening your acquaintance with the printed word. As your skill in reading increased, your interests widened. You found yourself making journeys in time and space; you met the gods of Greek myth and the princesses of German fairy tales; you climbed the Alps, walked the roads of England, and traveled down the mighty Mississippi. You were unconcerned as to whether the story that you were reading was written by a Greek, an Englishman, an American, or a German. The important thing was the literature itself and its power to quicken your imagination, to arouse your mind, or to stir your feelings.

In this anthology, while literature itself will remain important, your approach to it will be different. In the first place, you will study only one segment of literature—the literature of the United States. In the second place, you will trace the development of this literature from the time of the early settlers to the present; you will discover that in its picturing of the American scene, its mirroring of the American way of life, its voicing of American ideals and aspirations, it has become a distinctive body of literature with characteristics which distinguish it from the literature of other nations; you will assess its unique qualities, its weaknesses, its strengths.

Compared with the literature of England, France, Italy, and other countries, American literature is young. In a scant three-and-a-half centuries it has progressed from a scattering of letters and journals to a body of writing read and admired the world over. The first chapter of this anthology is designed to give you a sampling of good modern American literature. It will serve another equally important purpose: it will acquaint you with ways of understanding and discussing authors and their works. With such a background, both the literature of the present day and the literature of the past will become more interesting.

The authors represented in this chapter have won acclaim testifying to their excellence. Each has won, in addition to smaller awards, a Pulitzer Prize in Letters[1]—the highest national literary honor. Two have also been awarded the Nobel Prize in Literature[2]—the most distinguished literary award in the world. As you read the short stories and poems, the one-act play, and the nonfiction, you will find that even a small sampling can be an indication of the variety, the qualities, and the excellence of twentieth-century American literature.

---

1. See Editorial Feature on page 51. 2. See Editorial Feature on page 22.

Conrad Richter now lives in Pine Grove, Pennsylvania, where he was born on October 13, 1890. His father was a minister, living and preaching in villages and mountain communities of northern and central Pennsylvania. As Conrad grew up, he came to know many families, like his own, descended from pioneers. Their tales and stories of early frontier days did much to shape his life and mind.

In 1928 Richter, his wife, and daughter went to New Mexico, where Richter tried to support his family by writing Western short stories for the cheaper magazines. The writing of "Early Marriage" marks a distinct change in his attitude toward his work. About it he writes:

EARLY

Conrad Richter

... Early in 1934 I determined to do only the best work of which I was capable, and in late January started "Early Marriage." We were broke and deeply in debt when George Horace Lorimer bought it and the rest of the stories in *Early Americana* which followed ....

But there had been more to it before that. In 1930 and 1931 we lived in a cabin in a Sandia Mountain village in an effort to make ends meet. Our daughter rode fifty miles round trip to and from school in Albuquerque with the son and daughter of the rancher who owned our cabin. While living here, a laundryman who came through to serve the summer folks, urged me to see his mother, the daughter of an early stage station keeper in the Estancia Valley and later the wife of a storekeeper at Ruidoso. He told me Billy the Kid had often stayed at their house and given him and his younger brothers rides on his horse. I was not interested in Billy the Kid but later on did stop to talk to her. She told me many details of her early life including trips in the wagon with her young brother to distant Santa Fe for post goods, and from that came much of the background of "Early Marriage."

This mountain village in the big pines at 7200 feet elevation was benevolent to us in another way. While we were there a neighbor originally from Ohio loaned and later gave me the volumes of Henry Howe's monumental work on early Ohio, and from reading these books came the resolve to do the Ohio trilogy of *The Trees, The Fields,* and *The Town.*

In 1951 *The Town* won for Conrad Richter the Pulitzer Prize in Letters (see page 51) for a "distinguished novel dealing with American life by an American author."

STEVE TURVILLE

MARRIAGE

For two days the leathery face of Asa Putman had been a document in cipher to anyone who could read the code. Since Saturday but one traveler had passed his solitary post,[1] a speck of adobe and picket corrals lost on the vast, sandy stretch of the Santa Ana Plain. Far as the eye could see from his doorway, the rutted El Paso Trail, unfenced, gutterless, innocent of grading, gravel, culverts, or telephone poles, imprinted only by iron tires, the hoofs of horses and oxen, sheep and cattle, and the paw of the loping lobo wolf lay with dust unraised.

Ordinarily, there were freighters with cracking whips and trailers rumbling on behind. Army trains to and from the forts set up their tents for the night beyond the springs. The private coaches of Santa Fe and Colorado merchants, of cattle kings and government officials, stopped long enough for the Putman children to admire the ladies, the magnificent woodwork and the luxurious cushions inside. Trail herds of gaunt red steers bawled for the water in the earthen tank, and pairs and companies of horsemen rode up and down.

But since Saturday not even a solitary buckboard from the far settlements in the Cedar Country had called for supplies or letters. Only a girl from the Blue Mesa had ridden in for her and her neighbors' mail. She had eaten dinner with the Putmans, refused to stay overnight, and started her long ride home.

A stranger from the East would have spoken about the stillness, the deadly waiting, and asked uneasily why Uncle Gideon hadn't come as promised. But in the Putman household it was not mentioned.

Asa deliberately busied himself about the post, filling the bin beneath the counter with navy beans and green coffee, leafing through the packet of letters in the drawer, and making a long rite out of feeding the occupants of the picket corrals—four horses of which were fresh for the next stage.

Rife, just turned fifteen, carried water and gathered cow chips in an old hide dragged by a rope to his saddle horn. Ignacita,[2] the Mexican housekeeper, spat sharply on her heavy irons in the torrid kitchen and kept glancing over her shoulder and out of the open door and windows.

And Nancy Belle, going on seventeen, packed and repacked the high, ironbound

"Early Marriage" is reprinted from *Early Americana* by Conrad Richter, by permission of Alfred A. Knopf, Inc., New York. Copyright 1935, 1936 by The Curtis Publishing Company.
1. *Since Saturday . . . post.* Because the distance between forts was so great, supply stations were established at intervals along the trail. The mail coaches changed horses at these stations; army pack trains camped overnight near them; and freight wagons stopped there to water their livestock. People who traveled by private coach could also use the post facilities and purchase supplies needed for their journeys. Asa Putman managed one of these stations.
2. Ignacita (ēg nä sē′tä), a Spanish name.

trunk that her father had bought for her at Santa Fe and sang softly to herself in the way that women sang fifty and sixty years ago.

Saturday she was being married at Gunstock, two hundred miles away—five days' journey in a wagon, four in a saddle or buckboard.

For six months she had thought of little else. The almanac fell apart at June as naturally as her mother's Bible did at the Twenty-third Psalm. So often had she run her finger down the page that anyone might tell from the worn line of type the very day she and Stephen Dewee would be man and wife. The Dewees lived four hundred miles west across the territory in the Beaverhead Country. She and Stephen were taking a mountain ranch near his people, and for the wedding they had compromised on Gunstock, nearly equidistant from both families and convenient to friends scattered up and down the Rio Grande.

She had lighted a candle in the dusk, when a figure appeared reluctantly in her doorway. Asa Putman had never been at ease in his daughter's bedroom. A tall, rawhide man in an unbuttoned, sagging vest, he was visibly embarrassed by any furnishings that suggested refinement. Invariably he kept his hat on in the house. He had it on now, a flat top and a flat brim, not so much like the Western hats you see now. Nancy Belle knew that her mother's people had never forgiven him for bringing his young wife and their two small children to this lonely post, at the mercy of outlaws and the worse Apaches.

Tonight she could see that something bothered him. He gave her a sidewise glance, so sharp and characteristic.

"I don't expect, Nancy Belle, you could put off your weddin'?"

The girl stood quietly gazing at him with a face like the tintype of her mother. But under her sedate gray dress, with tight waist and full skirts to the instep, she had frozen. She looked much older than her years. Her air of gentlefolk and her wide-apart gray eyes came from her mother. But the chin, tipped up with resolute fearlessness, was her father's.

"No, Papa!" Her two clear words held all the steady insistence of the desert.

"I figured how you'd feel," he nodded, avoiding her eyes. "I just wanted to put it up to you. I'd 'a' covered the *jornada*[3] on foot to be on time at my own weddin', but I didn't have to count on Gideon to hold me up."

"Are you telling me, Papa, that you can't go to Gunstock tomorrow?" Her voice remained quiet, but a coldness had seized her. Of all the people she had visualized at her wedding, the one next to Stephen she could least spare was the tall, grave figure of her father.

"I reckon I kind of can't, Nancy Belle," he said soberly. "Rife could tend to the stage all right and do the feedin'. But they's men come to this post no boy can handle." He shifted his position. "I figured once on closin' up the post till I got back. But the stage is comin' and the mail. And the freighters count on me for feed and grub. Then I got to protect my own property and the mail and freight for the Cedar Country that's in the storage room."

"I know," Nancy Belle said steadily. "I can get to Gunstock all right."

Far back in her father's assaying eyes, she fancied she saw a glint of pride.

"You're pretty nigh a woman now, Nancy Belle. And Rife's a good slice of a man. It's a straight trail to the Rio Grande, once you turn at the old post. Both you and Rife's been over it before. Of course, I'd like to be at the weddin', but the boy can tell me about it." He went to the window. "Rife!" he called.

Nancy Belle's brother came in presently. A slight boy, with his father's blue eyes, he seldom made a fuss over anything, even when he shot a stray duck on the tank or

---

3. *jornada* (hôr nä′dä), journey.

when they braked down the last cedar hill into Santa Fe with all the open doors of the plaza shops in sight. And when his father told him now, he showed neither enthusiasm nor regret—merely straightened.

"Sure. I can take you, Nancy Belle," he said.

Something pulled under his sister's tight basque. She remembered the long miles they would have in the wagon, the camps at lonely places, the ugly shadow ever hovering over the outposts of this frontier country and the blight that, since Saturday, seemed to have fallen on the trail. Her eyes swam. Now, at the last minute she yielded.

"If you'll let me ride, Papa, I'll wait another day for Uncle Gideon," she promised.

Her father's eyes moved to the ruffled red calico curtains at the shadeless windows.

"I don't hardly count on Gideon comin' any more, Nancy Belle. Besides, it's too long in the saddle to Gunstock—especially for a girl to get married. You'd be plumb wore out, and you wouldn't have your trunk. You couldn't get dressed for your weddin'."

He turned thoughtfully and went out, Rife close behind. Nancy Belle could hear her father's tones, slow and grave, coming from near one of the picket corrals.

It was too far to catch the words; but when they came in, she saw that her brother's features looked a little pale under the tan.

"You better get some sleep, Nancy Belle," her father said. "You and Rife are startin' before daylight. If Gideon comes, I'll ride after."

They had scarcely gone from the room when Ignacita came in from the kitchen, her black eyes glittering over a pile of freshly starched white in her arms.

"Nancy Belle, *chinita!*"[4] she whispered, plucking at the girl's sleeve. "You don't say to your *papacito*[5] I talk to you! I have promise I don't scare you. But I can't see you go so far in the wildness alone, *pobrecita!*[6] Sometimes people go safe from one place to the other, oh, *sí!* But sometimes, *chinita,*

they don't come back! You have not the oldness like Ignacita. Aye, I tell you these old eyes have seen men and women quartered from a tree like sheep or maybe tied over a stove like I don't have the words to say to you."

Nancy Belle did not answer except to lay, one by one, the ironed pieces in her trunk—a bride's muslin underwear trimmed with red-and-blue featherstitching; long petticoats stiffly flounced with ruffles, and nightgowns long in the sleeve and high in the neck, with ruffles at wrist and throat. The Mexican woman went on hoarsely. The girl folded away her winter's cashmere dress, buttoned up the front and with a white fichu. She unwrapped and wrapped again in crumpled white tissue the red slippers the old gentleman on the stage had sent her as a wedding present from Philadelphia.

When Ignacita had left, she opened her keepsake box covered with colored shells. The mirror on the inside lid turned back a face as calm as the little golden clouds that hung of an evening over the east to catch the desert sunset. But after she had undressed and put on her nightdress, for a long time she was aware of the soft pound of her heart faintly swaying the bed on its rawhide springs.

At the first sound of Ignacita's hand on the kitchen stove, Nancy Belle sprang out of bed. She dressed on the brown pool of burroskin, the only carpet on her adobe floor. Through the west window she could see the morning star burning like a brilliant candle. It hung, she told herself, over Gunstock and the Beaverhead, where Stephen at this moment, in their new log ranch house, lay thinking about her.

They ate in the kitchen by lamplight. She had never been so conscious of every detail—the great white cups and saucers, the familiar steel knives, the homey smell of the

---

4. chinita (chē nē′tä), a term of endearment. 5. papacito (pä pä sē′tō), daddy. 6. pobrecita (pō brä sē′tä), poor little thing. This term and the two preceding words are diminutives, a form often used in Spanish to express affection.

scorched paper shade, the unreadable eyes of her father, Rife, and Ignacita.

Asa Putman himself carried out the trunk. There was already hay in the wagon, a gunny sack of oats, food in a canned-tomato box and utensils in another, a water keg, bedroll tied in a wagon sheet, an ax, a bridle, and her own sidesaddle made to order over a man's tree. Her eyes caught the gleam of a rifle leaning up against the seat in the lantern light. Tethered to the rear of the wagon stood her saddle mare, Fancy, with pricked ears. She was going along to their new ranch home. Nancy Belle felt that she was still among intimate things, but outside the little circle of light lay darkness and the unknown.

When she said good-by to her father, he kissed her—something he had not done for years.

"You haven't changed your mind, Nancy Belle?" he asked.

She climbed quickly up over the wheel to the spring seat of the wagon before he might see that she was crying. Rife swung up like a monkey on the other side and pushed the rifle into the crevice behind the seat cushion. The lines tautened and the wagon lurched.

"Dios[7] go with you safe to your husband, Nancy Belle!" she heard Ignacita cry after her.

The morning star had set. They moved into a world of silent blackness. Nancy Belle could not see how the horses remained on the trail. When she looked back, the only light in all these square miles of black, unfriendly earth was the yellow window of her father's post.

It was almost a vision, golden and far away, like all beautiful things. She didn't trust herself to look again.

Two hours later the wagon was a lonely speck of boat rocking in an illimitable sage-green sea beneath the sun. The canvas wagon sheet fastened over the bows was a kind of sail, and eastward the sandy water did not stop rolling till it washed up at the foot of the faintly blue ramparts of the distant Espiritu[8] Range.

Just before they turned west on the cross trail to the Rio Grande, a heavy wagon with a yoke of oxen in front and a cow behind toiled around the crumbling adobe walls of the old, abandoned posthouse. A bearded man and a thin woman with a white face sat on the seat. She held a baby in her arms, and three black-eyed children peered from under the wagon sheet.

The bearded man saluted and stopped his willing team. Rife did likewise. The woman spoke first. Her tongue was swift and slightly acid.

"You better turn around and follow us if you want to save your hair!" she called. "Yesterday a sheepherder told us he saw—"

A sharp word from the bearded man caused her to relapse into sullen silence. He asked Rife where he might be going, then climbed down to the trail and said he wanted to talk to him a little. The boy followed reluctantly behind his wagon. Nancy Belle could hear the bearded man's tones coming slow and grave like her father's, while the woman made silent and horribly expressive lip language.

Rife came back, walking stiffly. The bearded man climbed up beside the woman.

"They got to go on," he told her in a low tone, then saluted with his whip. "Good luck, boy! And you, miss!"

Rife raised his whip in stiff acknowledgment. The wagons creaked apart. Nancy Belle saw in front of her the trail to the Rio Grande, little more than a pair of wheel tracks, that lost itself on the lonely plain. Rife seemed relieved that she did not ask what the bearded man had said. But it was enough for her not to be able to forget the woman's fearful signs and mouthings and the still horror in the curious eyes of the staring children.

Sister and brother talked very little. Nancy Belle saw her brother's eyes keep sweeping

---

7. *Dios* (dyōs), God. 8. *Espiritu* (es-pē'rē tü), a name meaning "spirit."

the country, scanning the horizons. Bunches of bear grass that might have been feathers pinioned his blue gaze, and clumps of cane cactus that seemed to hold pointing gun barrels. At arroyos thick with chamiso and Apache plume she could see his feet tighten on the footboard. Once he pulled out the rifle, but it was only a herd of antelopes moving across the desert page.

They camped for the night when the sun was still high. Nancy Belle asked no questions as the boy drove far off the trail into a grassy *cañada*.[9] She sang softly to herself as she fried the salt side bacon and put the black coffee pot to boil.

Rife hobbled Anton Chico and the Bar X horse and staked out Fancy close to the wagon.

She pretended not to notice when, before dark, he poured earth on the fire till not a spark or wisp of smoke remained. Out of one eye she watched him climb the side of the *cañada* and stand long minutes sweeping the country from the ridge, a slight, tense figure against the sullen glow of the sunset.

"It's all right," he said when he came down. "You can go to bed."

"What's all right?" she asked him.

"The horses," he said turning away, and Nancy Belle felt a stab of pain that so soon this boy must bear a man's responsibilities and tell a man's lies.

She prayed silently on her blankets spread on the hay in the wagon box, and lay down with her head on the sidesaddle, her unread Testament in her hand. She heard Rife unroll his camp bed on the ground beneath the wagon. It was all very strange and hushed without her father. Just to feel the Testament in her hand helped to calm her and to remember the day at the post when she had first met Stephen.

Her father had never let her come in contact with the men of the trail. Always, at the first sign of dust cloud on the horizon, he would tell both children to heap up the chip box, fill the water buckets, and carry

saddles and bridles into the house. But this day Asa Putman and Rife had gone to Fort Sumter. And to Nancy Belle, Uncle Gideon could seldom say no.

It had been a very hot day. She had been sitting in the shade of the earthen bank of the tank, moving her bare feet in the cool water, watching the ripples in the hot south wind. The leaves of the cottonwoods clashed overhead, and she heard nothing until she looked up, and there was a young man on a blue-gray horse with dust clinging to his hat brim and mustache. His eyes were direct as an eagle's. Firm lines modeled his lean face. But what she noticed most at the time was the little bow tie on his dark shirt.

Instantly she had tucked her bare, wet legs under her red dress. Her face burned with shame, but the young stranger talked to her about her father coolly, as if she, a girl of fifteen, had not been caught barefooted. Then he did what in her mind was a noble thing. When Uncle Gideon came out, he magnificently turned his back for her to run into the house and pull on shoes and stockings.

She thought of Stephen constantly next day and the next. She had grown a little used to the journey without her father now—the still, uncertain nights under the wagon sheet, sitting, lying, listening, waiting; the less uncertain days with the sun on the endless spaces; her never-quiet perch on the high spring seat under the slanted bow; the bumps, creaks, and lumberings of the wagon; the sand sifting softly over the red, turning wheels; all afternoon the sun in their faces; ahead the far haze and heat waves in which were still lost Gunstock and the Rio Grande. Almost she had forgotten the bearded man with the oxen and the curious, detached horror in the eyes of his children.

Since morning of the third day their prog-

---

9. *cañada* (căn yä'dä), small canyon or valley.

ress had been slower. The trail seemed level, except for the heavy breathing of the horses. But when Nancy Belle glanced back she could see the steady grade they had been climbing. Abruptly, in mid-afternoon, she found that the long, blue Espiritu Range had disappeared, vanished behind a high pine-clad hill which was its southernmost beginning. It was like the lizard that swallowed itself, a very real lizard. At this moment they were climbing over the lizard's tail.

"Cedars!" Rife said briefly, pointing with the whip to dark sprawling growths ahead.

"You breathe deep up here!" Nancy Belle drank in the light air.

Rife took a sniff, but his blue eyes never ceased to scan the high, black-thatched hill under whose frowning cliff they must pass.

"Soon we can see the Gunstock Mountains," Nancy Belle said.

"And Martin Cross' cabin," Rife nodded. "It's the last water to the Rio Grande."

"He's a nice old man," Nancy Belle ventured casually. "It would be nice to camp by his cabin tonight and talk."

The boy inclined his head. After a few moments he started to whistle softly. At the first cedar, Nancy Belle leaped off the moving wagon and climbed back with an evergreen branch. The twig, crushed in her hand, smelled like some store in Santa Fe.

They gained the summit. A breeze was sweeping here from the southwest, and the horses freshened. But Rife had suddenly stopped whistling and Nancy Belle's sprig of cedar lay on her lap. The frowning cliff of the pine-clad hill was still there. But Martin Cross' cabin had turned to a desolate mound of ashes. As they stared, a gust of wind sent wisps of smoke scurrying from the mound, and a red eye opened to watch them from the embers. Nancy Belle felt an uncontrollable twitching in the hair roots at the base of her scalp.

Where Martin Cross' eastbound wheel tracks met the trail, Rife reluctantly halted the horses and wet his air-dried lips.

"The water keg's dry, and the horses. If Papa was here, he'd drive over."

"I'm the oldest." Nancy Belle found her voice steady. "I'll ride over. There might be something we can do."

The boy rose quickly. His eyes seemed to remember something his father had said.

"You can drive the wagon over if I wave."

He had thrown her the lines and slipped back through the canvas-covered tunnel of wagon box, picking up Fancy's bridle and the rifle. Barebacked he rode toward the smoldering ashes at the foot of that frowning hill. The chestnut mare's tail and mane streamed like something gold in the wind.

When she looked back to the trail, her eyes were pinioned by a light object in the wheel track ahead of the Bar X horse. It was a long gray feather. Instantly she told herself that it had come from some wild turkey Martin Cross had shot, and yet never had air anywhere become so suddenly horrible and choking as in this canyon.

Rife did not signal her to drive over. She saw him come riding back at full speed. The mare was snorting. As he stopped her at the wagon, her chestnut head kept turning back toward what had once been a cabin. Rife slipped the lead rope about her neck and climbed into the seat with the rifle in his hands.

"The water—you wouldn't want it!" he said thickly. His cheeks, she noticed, were the color of yeso.[10]

"Rife"— Nancy Belle touched his arm when she had driven down the canyon— "what did you see at the cabin?"

The boy sat deaf and rigid beside her, eyes staring straight ahead. She saw that his young hands were still tortured around the barrel of his rifle.

Far down on the pitch-dark mesa she stopped the horses in the trail and listened. There were no stars, not a sound but the flapping of the wagon sheet in the wind and the clank of coffee pot and water bucket under the wagon. Half standing on the foot-

10. yeso (yā′sō), plaster or whitewash.

board, she guided the team off the trail in the intense blackness. Her swift hands helped the trembling boy stake out the mare and hobble the team. They did not light a lantern. Rife declined to eat. Nancy Belle chewed a few dry mouthfuls.

The wind came drawing out of the blackness with a great draft. It hissed through the grass, sucked and tore at the wagon sheet, and whistled through the spokes and brake rigging. Rife did not take his bedroll under the wagon tonight. He drew the ends of the wagon sheet together and lay down in the wagon box near his sister. For a long time they were silent. When she heard his heavy breathing, she lifted the rifle from his chest.

The storm grew. Sand began pelting against the canvas and sifted into the wagon box. An invisible cloud of choking dust found its way into eyes, mouth, ears, and lungs. Nancy Belle laid down the rifle a moment to pull a blanket over the face of the boy. He tossed and muttered pitifully, but he slept on.

Magically the rain, when it came, stopped the sand and dust. The girl drank in the clean-washed air. At daylight she slipped out to the ground. The mesa, stretching away in the early light, touched here and there with feathers of mist, would have been beautiful except for a sharp new loneliness. The horses were gone!

At her exclamation, Rife appeared from the wagon box. His shame at having slept through the night was quickly overshadowed by their misfortune.

Together they found where Fancy's stake had been pulled out and dragged. Yards farther on they could tell by Anton Chico's tracks that his hobbles had parted.

Nancy Belle made her brother come back to the wagon and stuff his pockets with cold biscuits and antelope jerky. She said she would have a hot breakfast ready when he returned. The horses, perhaps, were just down in some draw where they had drifted with the wind.

When he had gone with the rifle, she filled the coffee pot from a clearing water hole in the nearest arroyo. She fried potatoes and onions in the long-handled skillet. And when he did not come, she set fresh biscuits in the Dutch oven. Each biscuit held a square of salt side bacon in its top, and as it baked, the fat oozed down and incased it in a kind of glazed tastiness.

At noon she thought she heard a shot. Nowhere could she see him on the endless sweep of mesa. By late afternoon she was still alone. She read her Testament and wondered how many women over the world had read it in hours like this. Sitting in the shadow of the wagon, facing the direction he had gone, she looked up every few minutes. But all her eyes could find were cloud shadows racing across the lonely face of the mesa. All she could hear were the desolate cries from the unseen lark sparrows.

Darkness, stillness settled down on the empty land. She climbed back into the wagon and sat on the chuck-box, hands rigid on her knees. Again and again she convinced herself that the horses could not have been driven off or she would have seen the drivers' tracks. When wild, sharp barks shattered the stillness and set wires jerking in her limbs, she talked to herself steadily, but a little meaninglessly, of the post—on and on as the darkness was filled with the ringing and counter-ringing of shrill, cracked yappings—not long tones like a dog's, but incredibly short syllables rising, rising in a mad eternal scale and discord.

"I wish Papa had given me two of the chairs," she repeated. "Mamma said they were post oak from Texas. She said they had got white from scrubbing. I liked the laced rawhide seats with the hair left on. It made them soft to sit on. The seats in the parlor were black. And the ones in the kitchen were red. But I liked the brockle one in my room best."

The insane din around the wagon had become terrific. There were only two or three of the animals, Nancy Belle guessed, but they threw their voices and echoes together to make a score.

"When I was little I liked to go in the storage room," her voice went on, scarcely intelligible to her own ears. "It was dark and cool, and smelled of burlap and kerosene and whiskey and sweetish with brown sugar. I can see the fat sacks of green coffee. And the round tins of kerosene had boards on the side. The flour sacks were printed: 'Rough and Ready' in red letters. Mamma once used to make our underwear out of the sacking. I can smell the salt side bacon in the gunny sacks."

She could tell from the sounds that one of the animals was running insanely back and forth near the wagon tongue. She had never noticed before that they yelped both when breathing in and out. Suddenly came silence. It warned her. Instinctively she felt for the ax.

"Nancy Belle!" a boy's far, anxious voice called from the darkness.

She hallooed and leaned out over the tailboard. Three shadowy forms were coming across the mesa in the starlight. Never had horses looked so good.

"Were you scared?" Rife greeted. "Anything bother you?"

"Nothing," Nancy Belle said. "Just coyotes."

"I had to give Fancy her head after it got dark." He slid wearily to the ground. "She brought us straight back to the wagon."

Nancy Belle had wanted to put her arms around her brother. Now she hugged the mare instead. Rife ate fresh biscuits and a tin plate piled with cold potatoes. He drank several tin cups of coffee. Nancy Belle had slipped the oats-laden gunny-sack *morrales*[11] over the horses' heads.

"I had to walk halfway to the mountain," Rife said.

"Just help hitch up; then you can sleep all night," she promised.

It rained again heavily toward midnight. Flashes of lightning lit the drenched plain. For minutes at a time, quivering fingers of blue phosphorescence stood on the ears of the toiling horses. At dawn Nancy Belle still held the reins as the mud-splashed wagon crawled through a world bathed in early purple splendor.

Four days they had been crossing a hundred and seventy miles of desolate plain. Now the end waited in sight. To the west lay a land broken and tumbled by a mighty hand. Hill shouldered hill and range peered over range, all indescribably violet except where peaks tipped by the unseen sun were far-off flaming towers of copper.

It was a new land, her promised land, Stephen's land, Nancy Belle told herself, where nobody burned cow chips, but snapping cedar and pine, where cold water ran in the wooded canyons and the eye, weary of one flat circle the horizon round, had endless geometric designs to refresh the retina.

She sang softly as the wagon lumbered to the edge of a long, shallow valley, brown and uninhabited, running north and south, and desolate except for a winding ribbon that was white with sky and narrowly bordered with green.

"Rife!" Nancy Belle cried. "The Rio Grande!"

An hour afterward they pulled out of the sun into the shade of the long cottonwood *bosque*.[12] Nancy Belle wasn't singing now. Where she remembered wide sand bars glistening with sky and tracked by waterfowl, a chocolate red flood rolled. Where had been the island, tops of tule and scrub willow swung to and fro with the current.

Anton Chico and the Bar X horse stopped of their own accord in the trail, ears pricked forward at the swirling brown wash. While Rife turned the three horses loose to graze, Nancy Belle silently fried bacon and made coffee. When she had washed skillet and tin dishes in the river, the boy had wired the wagon box to the brake rigging. Now he was tying securely one end of his rope to

11. *morrales* (mō rä′läs), feedbags. 12. *bosque* (bōs′kä), grove; woods.

the center of the coupling pole under the wagon. The other end she knew he would fasten to the inadequate upper horn of the sidesaddle.

"I wouldn't mind the river if I just had my own saddle," he mourned.

They hitched up the team silently. Rife cinched the sidesaddle on Fancy and straddled it, the single stirrup useless to a man. Nancy Belle climbed into the wagon and picked up the lines. The other bank looked as far away as the Espiritu Range from the post. She wanted to say something to her brother—some last word, in case they didn't make it. But all she did was cluck her tongue to the horses.

Gingerly, one slow foot at a time, the team moved down the trail into the water.

"Give 'em their heads!" Rife called from the right rear.

Nancy Belle held a rein in each hand. The red channel water came to the wagon tongue, covered it, reached the horses' bellies. The team wanted to stop. Nancy Belle swung her whip, a stick tipped with a long rawhide lash. The wagon went on. The collars of both horses kept dipping, but never entirely out of sight. Still barely wading, the slow team reached the firmer footing of the island.

Two thirds of the river still rolled in front of the wagon. The west bank did not seem to have grown much closer, but the east bank behind them had moved far away. The team had to be whipped into the violent current. The water churned white through the wagon wheels. Suddenly both horses appeared to stumble and drop out of sight. Their heads came up wildly, spray blowing from their nostrils. The muddy water hid their legs, but by their bobbing motions Nancy Belle knew that they were swimming.

"Keep 'em pointed up the river!" Rife shouted.

Already she felt the wagon floating. It swung downstream with the current; then Rife's rope from Fancy's saddle snubbed it.

The team was snorting with every breath. The Bar X horse swam high in the water, his withers and part of his back out of the chocolate current. But all she could see of Anton Chico were his nose and ears.

Down between her ankles she saw water in the wagon box. She thought of the hem-stitched sheets at the bottom of her trunk, the towels and pillow cases crocheted with shell lace. Her blue velvet corduroy dress was probably wet already, and all the cunning print aprons with dust caps to match. River water couldn't hurt the little yellow creamer, sugar bowl, and covered butter dish that had been her mother's. And the gingham dresses could be washed. What worried her were her wedding dress and the keepsake box, especially the tintypes, one of which was Rife in a child's suit edged with black braid, his brand-new hat on his knee.

An older Rife was shouting something behind her now. She couldn't catch the words. Then she found what it was. The neck and withers of Anton Chico raised suddenly out of the water and both horses were scrambling up the steep bank below the ford. Only quick work with the lines saved the wagon from turning over. Safe and blowing on the high bank, the dripping horses shook themselves like puppies.

Nancy Belle couldn't go on until she had opened the trunk and appraised the damage. Rife unsaddled Fancy and drove on with the refreshed team. Behind his slight back in the wagon box, the girl changed to her blue velvet corduroy, which was hardly wet at all. Then she combed her hair and rolled into a cranny of her trunk the old felt hat that had been too large for her father.

A half-dozen riders met the wagon some miles down the Gunstock Canyon. All of them, Nancy Belle noticed, carried guns. Stephen wore a new white shirt and a gray hat with a curled brim she had not seen before. He stood in his stirrups, and swung her down in front of him on the saddle, where he kissed her. She had never felt his lips press into such a straight line.

"Papa couldn't come," she said. "So Rife brought me."

She felt Stephen's rigid arm around her. "We just got in from the Beaverhead ourselves."

"He means they never get any news out in the Beaverhead or he'd 'a' come further east to meet you!" Uncle Billy Williams put in. He had a lovable, squeaky voice. "The Apaches been breakin' loose again. Funny you didn't hear anything over in your country."

Nancy Belle gave him an inscrutable look with her gray eyes. Uncle Billy pulled out his bandanna and blew his nose.

"They got my old friend, Judge Hower, and his wife and kid in a buggy on the Upper Espiritu. The man that found what they did to 'em, they say, cried like a baby."

"That's all right, Uncle Billy," Stephen said in a gentle voice.

Nancy Belle glanced at Rife. Her brother's face looked gray and the eyes staring as when he had ridden in the late afternoon sunlight from the smoking ashes of Martin Cross' cabin.

Nearly fifty people, gathered in the big parlor upstairs at the hotel, greeted Nancy Belle. An old man whose young black eyes twinkled out of a bearded face said he was glad to see that she had her "hair on straight." Rife stopped with the trunk before driving to the livery, and Stephen's mother showed Nancy Belle to a room to dress.

The guests stopped talking when she came into the parlor in her white wedding dress. Her basque came to a point in the front and back. It fitted like a glove. The silk underskirt came to her instep and the ruffled overskirt to her knees. She had parted her hair from side to side and brushed the bangs down on her forehead. She felt very light-headed. The wagon still seemed to be jerking under her.

She glimpsed Rife gazing at her, a rapt expression in his reticent blue eyes. She was glad to see that he had brushed his hair. The brass swinging lamp had been lighted and the dark woodwork of the parlor festooned with evergreen branches. White streamers from the wall met in a papier-mâché bell in one corner. She noticed two children peering from the dark hall.

Stephen came to her, very straight in a long coat and stand-up collar with a black tie. He led her up beneath the papier-mâché bell. In a sibilant, churchlike whisper, the Gunstock preacher made sure of her full name. Then he coughed and began the ceremony. He had a deep voice, but Nancy Belle didn't hear all of the service. Her mind kept going back to a tall, grave man in a lonely adobe post on the wide Santa Ana Plain. And after she had said, "I do," her lips moved, but she was not praying for Stephen, her husband.

TO INCREASE UNDERSTANDING

1. The opening pages of the story deal with the danger surrounding the Putman family. (a) Give specific instances of ways in which the author intimates this danger. (b) At what point in the story is the cause of the danger actually stated? (c) What justification does the author have for withholding this information so long?

2. Explain how each of the following situations increases the awareness of danger on the part of Nancy Belle and Rife as well as the reader: (a) meeting the wagon and observing the behavior of the bearded man, his wife, and the children; (b) discovering the glowing ashes of Martin Cross' cabin; (c) seeing the gray feather lying on the trail ahead; (d) discovering that the horses are missing; (e) listening to the breathing and yelping of the coyotes; (f) crossing the Rio Grande.

3. (a) What details in the story bring out the mutual respect and love of Asa, Nancy Belle, and Rife? (b) How do these repeated revelations of affection increase the reader's concern about what happens to the girl and her brother?

4. (a) What qualities in Asa's character make him believe that he is justified in allowing Nancy Belle and Rife to go alone to Gunstock? (b) Is Nancy Belle justified in not postponing her trip?

Bernard De Voto was one of the few contemporary Americans fortunate enough to enjoy the freedoms of a frontier childhood. When he was born in Ogden, Utah, in 1897, the state had only recently been admitted to the Union. As a boy of eight he spent days playing in the foothills. A few years later he was climbing the nearer mountain peaks. Although he spent much of his adult life in the East, in his approach to life he remained a Western individualist. And his most enduring work as critic and historian deals with the period of Western expansion.

De Voto was a man of many talents and many interests. He was a fascinating teacher and a distinguished editor. Under his skillful pen "The Editor's Easy Chair," a feature of *Harper's Magazine* which he conducted from 1935 to 1952, became one of the magazine's most widely read departments. Above all he was a versatile writer who appealed to people of different backgrounds and interests. Readers of light fiction enjoyed the novels of "John August"—the pen name De Voto used in turning out the work that supported him and his family while he was doing research on more serious works. Students of literature knew him as an authority on Mark Twain and admired the scholarship of books like *Mark Twain at Work* (1942) and *Mark Twain's America* (1932). Not only historians but also the general public admired *The Year of Decision: 1846* (1943) and *Across the Wide Missouri* (1947), the winner of the Pulitzer Prize in history in 1948.

De Voto was a master of painstaking research. He studied all available sources—diaries, letters, old maps, army records, histories. He traveled widely to track down elusive documents and to see for himself the country crossed by westward-moving Americans. When he died in 1955, he left behind him a body of work that would help future Americans better understand their pioneer past.

Bernard De Voto

Crossing the Great Salt Desert

The tragic experiences of the Donner party typify the hardships endured by thousands in the movement westward to California and Oregon. Well-to-do people who had sold their property in Illinois, the Donners began their journey well equipped but poorly advised. They had been influenced by Lansford Hastings, an unscrupulous promoter of California real estate, whose lies about the passability of trails, distances, cutoffs, fuel and food supplies on the trail, and false promises of help were responsible for many of the tragedies connected with the expedition.

The selection that follows tells only a small part of the story of the Donner party—its crossing of the Wasatch Range and the Great Salt Desert in 1846. James Frazier Reed was in charge of the party during this crossing.

The Wasatch are one of the most beautiful of Rocky Mountain ranges, but not among the highest. Characteristic of them are small, narrow, twisting canyons which have no logic except the laws of flowing water. These canyons are adventurous for mountain climbers but their discouraging attribute for those who travel them seriously is the way they lead into one another. The Union Pacific Railroad takes the one direct pass through the north and south main chain of the Wasatch, Weber Canyon—but takes it by virtue of dynamite. All other passages of the Wasatch are circuitous, by small canyons which lead into other small canyons, sometimes widen into circular valleys off which a number of canyons lead (only one of which will be the right way onward), and by degrees take their streams westward round cliffs, the base of peaks, and the jutting ends of spinal ledges. Modern highways cross the Wasatch by such oblique routes now. The Donner party had to find such a route when, on the morning of August 12, they started out from their five-day encampment a little west of the mouth of Echo Canyon.

Fifteen days later, on August 27, they reached Salt Lake Valley, having covered a distance estimated, but probably underestimated, as thirty-six miles. In the meantime, Stanton and McCutchen, who had not been able to keep up with Reed, had rejoined the party,[1] and the Graves family,[2] thirteen altogether, with three wagons, had caught up with them from the east.

They had had to make a road for wagons, by a route which no wagon had ever taken before. With two of the able-bodied men absent and at least four other men disqualified by age or sickness, they had had to chop through aspen and popple and cottonwoods (and the underbrush that is just as bad) which choked the small canyons. They had to dig tracks and fell trees and level off centers high up on mountainsides, pry boulders out of their course, riprap swampy patches, sometimes bridge brooks that could not be crossed otherwise, grunt and strain and curse while the oxen heaved the wagons up inclines, over ridges, and around spurs of rock. Every ridge they topped showed a haze of further ridges beyond it. Every canyon that opened out closed in again. Every canyon that might be the last one ended in another one that might also be the last. Three times they found that they could go no farther, had to go back over part of the road they had built, and, abandoning it as wasted, try again, chopping and shoveling a new road. When they camped at the end of the fifteenth day they were almost out of the last canyon, the narrow defile which the Mormons were to call Parley's Canyon. The next morning they decided that they could not get through a tortuous place where the canyon walls almost met and the notch between was choked with loose rock. So they retraced their way up Parley's Canyon and the gulch by which they had entered it, and took the wagons straight up a mountain, over the ridge, and down into what is now called Emigration Canyon, and out, at last, into the valley of the lake.

Edwin Bryant,[3] who left Fort Bridger on

Reprinted from *The Year of Decision: 1846* by Bernard De Voto, by permission of Houghton Mifflin Company, Boston. Pages 342-346 slightly condensed and adapted. Copyright 1942, 1943 by Bernard De Voto.

1. *Stanton and McCutchen . . . party.* Stanton, McCutchen, and Reed had traveled ahead to find Hastings, who had promised to help them personally through the Wasatch, claiming he knew a better route. Reed had come back on August 11 without Stanton and McCutchen, whose horses had failed them. 2. *the Graves family.* Their own train having been dispersed by the Pawnee Indians, the Graves family had wandered aimlessly about for weeks, finally joining the Donners. 3. *Edwin Bryant.* Traveling with another party, Bryant had tried to warn the Donners of the difficulties of the crossing, but the messenger failed to give them his letter.

July 20, reached the valley of Great Salt Lake on July 26. The Donner party, leaving Fort Bridger on July 31, reached the valley on August 27. That difference in traveling time states the first circumstance of their disaster but does not reveal all that had happened to them in the Wasatch. Their morale had begun to break. The morale of any emigrant train can be judged by its success in solving a fundamental conflict. On one hand there is any American frontiersman's impulse to go his own way, make his own choices, reap the rewards of his own intelligence and skill, and pay the penalties for his own mistakes. On the other is the coöperation enforced by the wilderness, which requires choices to be made in the common interest, assesses against the group penalties for every mistake made by individuals, and pools intelligence and skill for the use of everyone. We have seen the wagon trains breaking up and re-forming. Every new grouping was an attempt to establish a small social system which would function effectively; a successful passage along the trail meant the creation of a group spirit.

The feeling of being members one of another cracked in the Wasatch. They had to have a scapegoat and Hastings was not enough. James Frazier Reed began to be the focus of blame. He was responsible, or could be thought responsible, for the route they took; also, he was now being paid back for his superior wealth and his aristocratic bearing. Furthermore, in fourteen days of heartbreaking labor some had begun to resent the weakness of companions who could not do their full share, and some had refused to do their share, accepting the common labor without putting into it all they had. The membrane that encloses the primordial inheritance[4] was thus wearing through, and an even more dangerous pressure had been put on it. They had thought that Big Mountain was the last ridge that they must cross, but Stanton and McCutchen rejoined them just as they got down

from it and told them that it was not. Then, Eliza Donner Houghton says, "Sudden fear of being lost in the trackless mountains almost precipitated a panic, and it was with difficulty that my father [George Donner] and other cool-headed persons kept excited families from scattering rashly into greater dangers." They had at last realized the danger they were in, and the realization was centrifugal, tending to drive them apart. It would dominate them from now on.

Overstrained and fearful but less exhausted than their stock, with the wagons jolted and shaken into a universal brittleness, they headed for the south end of Great Salt Lake and the Salt Desert beyond. There were eighty-six of them now, and twenty-three wagons. They toiled on, hurrying as fast as the condition of the oxen permitted, and in five days reached the last oasis east of the Salt Desert, Skull Valley. Here they found fragments of paper tacked to a board. Tamsen Donner gathered them up and pieced them together, and they proved to be a note from Hastings. The author of their ills was confessing another enthusiasm. He had originally said that the Salt Desert was no more than forty miles wide and could be crossed in one day. Now he was telling them that the crossing would take two days and nights.

It took them six days and they traveled all or most of every night.

Here is where the membrane broke, where the group was atomized to individuals. The blinding glare, the burning blue sky with the insolent peace of bellying clouds, the horizon of mountains blue and purple and amethyst, the reds of sunset and the greens of dawn—the cruel beauty of the death-giver could be observed in irony. Twisting whirlwinds or high walls of salt blew past them. Mirages offered them lakes and streams or showed them fields of

---

4. The membrane . . . primordial inheritance, the ability of the members of the Donner party to reason. The ability to reason is the outstanding quality that distinguishes man from the lower animals.

grass blowing in the wind. William Eddy[5] saw a file of men moving across the distance; they were himself repeated twenty times. Others saw similar processions and once some of them cried out, for this must be Hastings, the deliverer, coming back to help his victims. But none of this mattered, for fear and the pit were upon them. They might die...here...now. The social system disintegrated. Some drove their oxen to the uttermost exertion, some tried to conserve their strength, some merely went on. Following the tracks of Hastings' wagons, they strung out across the white hell, under sun or full moon, formless, disorganized, at random, the stock failing, men and women with death in their hearts, all of them forced to observe the stoic, uncomprehending agony of the children.

The heavily loaded outfits of Reed and the Donners fell to the rear, where shrewdness would have put them anyway in a crisis of *sauve qui peut*.[6] But too much had been required of the oxen in the Wasatch, and by the third night there was no water left in the casks. Men and stock must have water or die in the salt. Reed rode ahead, passing most of the others. Some had abandoned their wagons, driving the teams toward the water that was somewhere ahead. Others, frail, blackfaced, stolid, were trying to keep to the wheel tracks. At the end of the fourth day (if he had slept at all, it was during part of the first night) he got to Pilot Peak and its springs. William Eddy and the Graveses had got there before him, first of all. Eddy, taking water to an exhausted ox, went back a few miles with Reed, who again in the moon's unreality passed back down the frayed line of specters. He met his own teamsters, who had unhitched the oxen and were trying to get them and his horses to water in time. Then the Donners, driving their stock and some wagons. Then an abandoned Donner wagon and at last, toward dawn, his own wife and children and some employes. One of the employes took Reed's horse back for water. Reed and the others waited for the drivers and the oxen to return for them.

They sat there in the salt, under the sun, blistered by wind, all the next day. No oxen and no drivers came....The herd, maddened by thirst, had stampeded into the wasteland and would never be recovered....So at the end of the day, Reed carrying the three-year-old Tommy, the others packing some food from the wagons and the remaining gills of water, they started out to walk it. When the children could go no farther, they made a kind of camp. An insane ox charged them and they got up again and went on. They reached Jacob Donner's wagon, Reed heard that his own teams were lost, and, leaving his family, he hurried on toward Pilot Peak. Nearly everyone was getting to Pilot Peak now, some with their wagons, some with only their teams, some staggering in alone. The last day stretched out its agony, Jacob Donner came in bringing Reed's family, and, with no one dead, they had crossed the Salt Desert in six days.

---

5. *William Eddy.* Eddy and his family had been with the Donner party from the beginning. 6. *sauve qui peut* (sōv′kē pü′), a French phrase meaning "disorganized retreat"; literally, "save (himself) who can."

BETTER READING

Fact versus fiction

Of the two selections you have just read, one is classified as history, the other as a short story. Thus we have represented in "Crossing the Great Salt Desert" and "Early Marriage" examples of the two great branches of literature—factual prose and fiction. How does one differ from the other? We know, of course, that factual prose deals with facts—things known or believed to be true; and that fiction deals with things made up—the product of man's imagination. Beyond this basic difference there are other differences of which the careful reader should be aware.

Perhaps the most important difference to be noted in the comparison of factual writing and fiction is the author's purpose. The principal objective of the writer of factual prose is to inform the reader. To this end Bernard De Voto painstakingly collected every available fact about the Donner party's tragic journey westward. From historical records, from geographical data, and from observations and opinions based on personal knowledge of the region, he assembled his material. In the first sentence of "Crossing the Great Salt Desert" he expresses an opinion based on personal observation ("The Wasatch are one of the most beautiful of Rocky Mountain ranges") and a geographical fact (". . . but not among the highest"). In the last sentence of the first paragraph he draws a fact from historical records (". . . when, on the morning of August 12, they started out from their five-day encampment a little west of the mouth of Echo Canyon"). Assembling and weighing many facts, he draws conclusions, as when he writes, "The feeling of being members one of another cracked in the Wasatch" (page 17, column 1, paragraph 1). In short, "Crossing the Great Salt Desert" consists of (1) statements about the people, the places, and the events as they were actually observed and recorded by various individuals, and (2) statements of the author's logical conclusions based upon relating these various observations and records. If the reader cares to do so, he can verify or disprove any of these statements by going to the sources of the information.

How does the factual-prose writer's purpose of informing the reader differ from that of a fiction writer such as Richter? Certainly by reading "Early Marriage" one can learn much about the way people in the Southwest lived in early days. Obviously Richter had to do careful research on the way people dressed and lived, the construction of a covered wagon, the furnishings travelers carried across the empty plains. Richter himself gives us a clue to one source of his background material in the letter quoted in part on page 4. The reader can check the authenticity of Richter's facts about life in the early Southwest just as he can ascertain the truth of De Voto's facts. But in fiction factual information of this type is a means to an end, not the end itself. Richter's main purpose is to make the reader enter imaginatively into the lives of fictional characters. The details are so selected as to help the reader know Nancy Belle and Rife and share the emotions which they feel. From the very first sentence the author creates tenseness and an awareness of danger—"For

two days the leathery face of Asa Putman had been a document in cipher to anyone who could read the code." Detail upon detail adds to this implied danger: "Since Saturday but one traveler had passed his solitary post . . . Far as eye could see from his doorway, the rutted El Paso trail . . . lay with dust unraised . . . not even a solitary buckboard from the far settlements . . . had called for supplies or letters . . . the stillness . . . the deadly waiting." Throughout the story, by a careful chain of details, the author achieves a cumulative effect that communicates to the reader the danger, the fear, and the suspense that are evident in the reactions of everyone of the characters.

The reader may also react emotionally to factual prose. For example, as we read "Crossing the Great Salt Desert," we become emotionally involved in the fate of the Reeds and the Donners. But our reaction is seldom so intense because the author is necessarily more objective—more concerned with presenting facts. By contrast, the writer of fiction builds up our reactions by consciously involving us in the feelings, thoughts, and actions of the characters and situations he creates.

Answering the following questions will help clarify the differences between fact and fiction.

1. De Voto's chief purpose was to inform the reader. State specifically what he evidently wanted to inform him about.

2. (a) According to Bernard De Voto, upon what did the morale of an emigrant train depend? (b) Why did the morale of the Donner party crack in the Wasatch? (c) How did this loss of morale affect the crossing of the Salt Desert? (d) Justify De Voto's inclusion in a history of a passage dealing primarily with morale.

3. Richter has as his purpose "making the reader enter imaginatively into the lives of fictional characters." (a) Which character's thoughts does he tell us? Cite instances. (b) Why is the presentation of that character's thoughts particularly valuable in creating suspense?

4. (a) Why cannot De Voto tell us what members of the Donner party thought without becoming a writer of fiction rather than of history? (b) Point out places where, although he does not tell us the party's thoughts, De Voto helps the reader realize vividly their feelings. Explain how he accomplishes this. (c) Why are such passages proper for history?

Karl Shapiro

Auto Wreck

Born in Baltimore in 1913, Karl Shapiro grew up in a home with a large library. From his high-school days he wanted to write poetry. This interest was so strong that he neglected his studies at the University of Virginia to work on his verses. Against the advice of his family he left college, and for several years he wrote and rewrote his poems, worked at various jobs, went to Tahiti, and finally in 1937 resumed his studies at Johns Hopkins University.

In 1941 Shapiro entered the army. For three years he served in Australia and in New Guinea and the surrounding islands. These years were extremely valuable for the young poet. His poetry ripened and matured. *Person, Place, and Thing* (1942) was favorably received, and *V-Letter and Other Poems* (1944) was awarded a Pulitzer Prize.

Karl Shapiro has also won fame as critic and editor. From 1950 to 1956 he served as editor of *Poetry* (see the article on page 593) and at present he is editor of *Prairie Schooner*.

Prairie Schooner

December 24, 1960

Dear Mr. Farmer:

"Auto Wreck" seems to be my most popular poem. I don't mind really.

Its genesis is partly imaginary, partly composite, partly based on observation, like most poems. Notice that there are no sounds of pain or anguish in the poem. The people are silent, as in a silent film. Even the ambulance bell has a soft almost beautiful music. The accident is at night and the "arterial" light of the ambulance comes and goes through the darkness. And everything is somewhat in slow motion.

The bystander (the poet) is dissociated from the scene and merely wonders at its meaning and its horror. I watched the police wash the blood down the gutters and sweep away the broken glass, and the rest. I had a particular accident in mind, and the poem was written after witnessing a particularly bad one one midnight in Baltimore, but I drew upon similar scenes such as everyone has experienced from time to time.

The questions asked towards the end of the poem have a certain grisly banality, the very kind of question that loved ones would ask. <u>Why? Why?</u> For, given another second there would be no accident.

Incidentally, the first line is a deliberate wrenching of an iambic pentameter line, with two reversed feet at the end, "beating, beating". I think the device works well, considering the subject.

I hope these remarks will help.

Sincerely,

* victims

Karl Shapiro

105 Andrews Hall / University of Nebraska / Lincoln 8, Nebraska

Karl Shapiro

Its quick soft silver bell beating, beating,
And down the dark one ruby flare
Pulsing out red light like an artery,
The ambulance at top speed floating down
Past beacons and illuminated clocks   5
Wings in a heavy curve, dips down,
And brakes speed, entering the crowd.
The doors leap open, emptying light;
Stretchers are laid out, the mangled lifted
And stowed into the little hospital.   10
Then the bell, breaking the hush, tolls once,
And the ambulance with its terrible cargo
Rocking, slightly rocking, moves away,
As the doors, an afterthought, are closed. 14

We are deranged, walking among the cops
Who sweep glass and are large and
      composed.
One is still making notes under the light.
One with a bucket douches ponds of blood
Into the street and gutter.
One hangs lanterns on the wrecks that
      cling,   20
Empty husks of locusts, to iron poles.

Our throats were tight as tourniquets,
Our feet were bound with splints, but now
Like convalescents intimate and gauche,
We speak through sickly smiles and warn 25
With the stubborn saw of common sense,
The grim joke and the banal resolution.
The traffic moves around with care,
But we remain, touching a wound
That opens to our richest horror.   30

Already old, the question Who shall die?
Becomes unspoken Who is innocent?
For death in war is done by hands;
Suicide has cause and stillbirth, logic.
But this invites the occult mind,   35
Cancels our physics with a sneer,
And spatters all we knew of denouement
Across the expedient and wicked stones.

BETTER READING
The language of poetry

Poetry, like any other meaningful writing, is a communication from the writer to the reader—usually the communication of a feeling as well as of a thought. In conveying a feeling, poetry uses words that take on meaning in the context of sentences. To grasp this meaning, you will find it helpful to read poetry by sentences (which often do not correspond with lines), and to pay the same attention to punctuation within the sentence that you do in reading prose. If you do not observe such cautions, lines like the following from Tennyson's "Ulysses"

The long day wanes; the slow moon climbs; the deep
Moans round with many voices.

may become

The long day wanes the slow moon climbs the deep.
Moans round with many voices.

Since the poet usually compresses what he has to say in fewer words than the prose writer, his sentences often are difficult. He sometimes arranges the parts of a sentence in an order different from ordinary prose usage, and this causes another difficulty. The first sentence in the poem "Auto Wreck" illustrates these points. To get meaning here, the reader must find the subject and its verbs. The subject, *ambulance*, occurs in line 4; the verbs, *wings, dips,* and *brakes*, occur in lines 6 and 7. Only when the reader has read seven lines and located the four words that form the core of the sentence can he be certain of the meaning of the first three lines.

To pack as much meaning as possible into a few lines, the poet chooses words for their *connotations*, or the associations which they have for readers. Notice that in "Auto Wreck" as the ambulance approaches, the repetition of the word *beating* suggests urgency and the pulse of life; but when the ambulance moves away with its burden the same bell *tolls*, and that word connotes an end of urgency, and death.

Figures of speech are particularly useful for conveying emotion since they involve imaginative comparisons and identifications. In the first sentence of "Auto Wreck" what is literally a whirling red light on the top of an ambulance is figuratively described as "pulsing out red light like an artery," thereby suggesting a wound spurting blood and violence. This simile, especially when accompanied by lines which tell of beating and tolling bells, helps the poet communicate the anguish, horror, and mystery of sudden, accidental death.

The poet also uses devices such as meter, accent, rhyme, alliteration, and assonance to help communicate his thought and feeling. These are even more helpful in poetry than in prose, where, because the rhythm is less regular, less emphasis of these elements is possible.

Keeping the points made in this article in mind, use the following questions to further your understanding of "Auto Wreck."

1. Instead of the regular stanza form, Karl Shapiro uses stanzas much as one would use paragraphs in writing prose. Each stanza develops one idea. (a) Explain the idea developed in each stanza. (b) How are the stanzas related to one another?

2. Read again the third paragraph of Karl Shapiro's letter (page 20) and the second stanza of the poem. Explain why this stanza communicates the horror of the wreck more vividly than the corresponding paragraph of the letter does.

3. (a) What is the effect upon the reader of the figurative language in lines 22-30? (b) What comparison repeated by the figures of speech accounts for this effect?

The Nobel Prize in Literature

In 1888 an obituary appearing in a French newspaper reported the death of Alfred Nobel, Swedish inventor of dynamite. The obituary was a mistake; the newspaper had carelessly confused the name of very-much-alive Alfred Nobel with that of his recently dead brother, Ludwig. Reading it, however, Alfred must have been shocked at the disdainful picture given of himself as a man who had created his fortune from weapons of war. Although his long scientific career had been concerned with explosives, no one knew better than he the destructive potential of his handiwork.

It may be that Alfred Nobel hoped to be remembered as a promoter of peace, not as the "dynamite king" described in the false obituary. Whatever his reason, during the next eight years he formulated a unique plan which altered his reputation. When Nobel's real death notice was written in 1896, it could speak of his will and its benefits to mankind.

According to the terms of his will, Nobel established a fund of nine million dollars for the promotion of a peaceful and better world. He designated the income from the fund to be awarded annually in prizes in five categories —physics, chemistry, physiology or medicine, literature, and work promoting international peace.

The Nobel Prize in Literature, according to Nobel's will, is awarded to "the person who shall have produced in the field of literature the most distinguished work of an idealistic tendency." Since 1901 a committee of the Swedish Academy in Stockholm has annually reviewed recommendations submitted by universities and similar institutions. The award is made to a living author, regardless of nationality, for the entire body of his work and may be withheld during any given year if the Academy feels no living author is deserving of the distinction.

The Nobel Prize medal with its cash award of approximately $40,000 has been conferred on writers of many nationalities. Among those who have won this international distinction are six Americans: Sinclair Lewis, novelist, in 1930; Eugene O'Neill, dramatist, in 1936; Pearl Buck, novelist, in 1938; William Faulkner, novelist, in 1950; Ernest Hemingway, novelist, in 1954; and John Steinbeck, novelist, in 1962. You will find selections from each of these Nobel Prize writers in this anthology.

Pearl Buck has written over forty volumes of fiction and nonfiction, but she is popularly identified with a single book—*The Good Earth* (1931). This compassionate account of Chinese peasant life and its hardships won the Pulitzer Prize, was a best seller for nearly two years, has been translated into more than thirty languages, and was made into a successful motion picture. It was also the principal reason for the awarding of the Nobel Prize in Literature to Mrs. Buck in 1938.

The Good Earth grew out of Mrs. Buck's intimate knowledge of the Chinese land and people. Born in West Virginia, she was an infant when her parents, missionaries who had been in the United States on furlough, returned to China. Pearl grew up in Chinkiang on the Yangtse River. In the mornings she studied with her mother; in the afternoons she worked with a Chinese tutor. She was seventeen when she returned to the United States to attend Randolph Macon College in Virginia. After graduating in 1914, she went back to China. Several years later she married a young American agricultural missionary, and together they traveled to North China, the setting for *The Good Earth*. Later the Bucks moved to Nanking, where Mrs. Buck taught English literature at the University of Nanking and at Southeastern University. Since 1934 she has lived in Pennsylvania.

Pearl Buck's first book, *East Wind, West Wind* (1929), was published while she was living in Nanking. This was followed by *The Good Earth* and its sequels, *Sons* (1932) and *A House Divided* (1936), and by other novels of Chinese life. In the biographies of her mother and father—*The Exile* (1936) and *Fighting Angel* (1936)—she wrote warmly of the life of missionaries in a foreign land. This current of warmth and understanding runs through all her books and extends to people of all nations. In "The Enemy" (page 25), a story set in Japan, Pearl Buck affirms her faith that all men are brothers.

from My Several Worlds

Pearl Buck's autobiography, *My Several Worlds* (1953), is rich in memories of people, places, and events. One of the people she remembers fondly is Mr. Kung, an elderly Chinese scholar who had taught her as a young girl. Mr. Kung held to the strict literary standards which had shaped many centuries of Chinese writing. According to these standards, novels were not true literature. Influenced by Mr. Kung's rigid criteria for literature, Pearl Buck was overwhelmed upon learning that she, a novelist, had been awarded the Nobel Prize in Literature.

All this may explain my own small estimate of my powers, so that one day in the autumn of the year 1938, when I heard that I had been awarded the Nobel Prize in Literature for that year, I did not believe it, nor could I believe it until a telephone call to Stockholm confirmed it. My feelings then were still very confused. I could not understand why it should be given to me and I remember that I exclaimed, "Oh, I wish that it could have been given to Theodore Dreiser[1] instead!"

I did indeed so wish, for I admired Dreiser greatly as a writer. He was, to my mind, far more than a mere novelist. He had in his deep, ponderous, gigantic fashion got hold of something profoundly American, and if before twenty I read Charles Dickens, after twenty I read Dreiser and after Dreiser, Sinclair Lewis,[2] and of the two of them I felt Lewis the more brilliant but I knew Dreiser would be the more nearly permanent. And he was getting old, whereas I was still young, young enough to wait for future rewards.

If I had doubts about myself, they were doubled and tripled by my fellow writers who were men. The gist of such criticisms, and there were more than a few, was that no woman, except possibly the veteran writer, Willa Cather,[3] deserved the Nobel Prize, and that of all women I deserved it the least because I was too young, had written too few books of note, and was scarcely even to be considered an American, since I wrote about the Chinese and had lived only in their remote and outlandish part of the world. With my background and literary education, I was only too ready to agree with all this, and yet I did not know how to refuse the award without seeming even more presumptuous. In real distress, for it made me very unhappy to feel that my fellow writers were against the choice, I could only continue making melancholy preparations to go to Stockholm and accept the award which had been given me so unexpectedly and without any knowledge on my part that I was even considered a candidate.

It is only honest to say that I am sure the blast from my fellow writers fell upon me with a severity they had scarcely intended. I had for years worked so entirely alone in my writing, in such remote places in Asia, among people who could not understand my yearning to associate with others, especially Americans, who were writers and with whom I could communicate as kindred minds, that I was oversensitive to this American criticism which did indeed fall upon me too soon. And it must be confessed that I have never quite recovered, though years have passed, so that I have been too diffident, ever since, to mingle much with American writers or, perhaps, to undertake my proper responsibilities with them. To go among them even now revives painful memories of that autumn in 1938, when I was still new in my own country, still eager and hopeful and, as I can see now, absurdly worshipful toward my elders in the golden field of American letters.

And all this leads me to the kindly memory of Sinclair Lewis, himself a winner of the Nobel Prize in Literature. As I said, I met him at a P.E.N.[4] dinner, the only one, I think, which I have ever attended, and he sat next to me. I said very little because I felt reticent before so great a writer, and I listened with appreciation to what he said. He was already sad and disillusioned, and I felt a sort of reckless honesty in his words, his fine homely face turned away from me most of the time so that I had to listen carefully while he talked quickly on. Suddenly my turn came to make a little speech, and I got up, intensely mindful of the criticism from some of the very persons who sat that night before me, and looking back to what I had been taught in my Chinese childhood, I told them somehow, and I cannot remember exactly the words and I did not think them important

Reprinted from My Several Worlds by Pearl S. Buck. Copyright 1954 by Pearl S. Buck. Published by The John Day Company, New York.

1. Theodore Dreiser, twentieth-century American novelist. 2. Sinclair Lewis, see page 70. 3. Willa Cather, see page 38. 4. P.E.N., an abbreviation for The International Association of Poets, Playwrights, Editors, Essayists, and Novelists.

enough to write down, that I had long ago learned that a teller of tales is not to be considered a literary figure, and that my novels were only stories to amuse people and make a heavy hour pass a little more easily, and a few more sentences of the sort. Mr. Kung would have approved all I said.

Sinclair Lewis, however, did not approve. When I sat down again, he turned to me with an animation sparkling with anger. "You must not minimize yourself," he declared, and I remember every word because they fell like balm upon my wounded spirit. "Neither must you minimize your profession," he went on. "A novelist has a noble function." And then, as though he understood all I had been feeling, he went on to speak of that function, and how a writer must not heed what others say. I would weary, he said, of the very name of *The Good Earth,* for people would act as though it were the only book I had ever written, but never mind people, he said, never mind! He had often wished, he said, that he had never written *Main Street,* so sick did he get of hearing people speak of it as "your book."

"You must write many novels," he cried with an energy intense and inspiring. "And let people say their little say! They have nothing else to say."

What comfort that was from him, and how warmly I felt toward him ever after!

The Enemy

D r. Sadao Hoki's house was built on a spot of the Japanese coast where as a little boy he had often played. The low square stone house was set upon rocks well above a narrow beach that was outlined with bent pines. As a boy Sadao had climbed the pines, supporting himself on his bare feet, as he had seen men do in the South Seas when they climbed for coconuts. His father had taken him often to the islands of those seas, and never had he failed to say to the little grave boy at his side, "Those islands yonder, they are the stepping stones to the future for Japan."

"Where shall we step from them?" Sadao had asked seriously.

"Who knows?" his father had answered. "Who can limit our future? It depends on what we make it."

Sadao had taken this into his mind as he did everything his father said, his father who never joked or played with him but who spent infinite pains upon him who was his only son. Sadao knew that his education was his father's chief concern. For this reason he had been sent at twenty-two to America to learn all that could be learned of surgery and medicine. He had come back at thirty, and before his father died he had seen Sadao become famous not only as a surgeon but as a scientist. Because he was now perfecting a discovery which would render wounds entirely clean, he had not been sent abroad with the troops. Also, he knew, there was some slight danger that the old General might need an operation for a condition for which he was now being treated medically, and for this possibility Sadao was being kept in Japan.

Clouds were rising from the ocean now. The unexpected warmth of the past few days had at night drawn heavy fog from the cold waves. Sadao watched mists hide outlines of a little island near the shore and then come creeping up the beach below the house, wreathing around the pines. In a few minutes fog would be wrapped about the house too. Then he would go into the room where Hana, his wife, would be waiting for him with the two children.

But at this moment the door opened and she looked out, a dark-blue woolen *haori*[1] over her kimono. She came to him affectionately and put her arm through his as he stood, smiled, and said nothing. He had met Hana in America, but he had waited to fall in love with her until he was sure she was Japanese. His father would never have received her unless she had been pure in her race. He wondered often whom he would have married if he had not met Hana, and by what luck he had found her in the most casual way, by chance literally, at an American professor's house. The professor and his wife had been kind people anxious to do something for their few foreign students, and the students, though bored, had accepted this kindness. Sadao had often told Hana how nearly he had not gone to Professor Harley's house that night—the rooms were so small, the food so bad, the professor's wife so voluble. But he had gone and there he had found Hana, a new student, and had felt he would love her if it were at all possible.

Now he felt her hand on his arm and was aware of the pleasure it gave him, even though they had been married years enough to have the two children. For they had not married heedlessly in America. They had finished their work at school and had come home to Japan, and when his father had seen her the marriage had been arranged in the old Japanese way, although Sadao and Hana had talked everything over beforehand. They were perfectly happy. She laid her cheek against his arm.

It was at this moment that both of them saw something black come out of the mists. It was a man. He was flung up out of the ocean—flung, it seemed, to his feet by a breaker. He staggered a few steps, his body outlined against the mist, his arms above his head. Then the curled mists hid him again.

"Who is that?" Hana cried. She dropped Sadao's arm and they both leaned over the railing of the veranda. Now they saw him again. The man was on his hands and knees crawling. Then they saw him fall on his face and lie there.

"A fisherman perhaps," Sadao said, "washed from his boat." He ran quickly down the steps and behind him Hana came, her wide sleeves flying. A mile or two away on either side there were fishing villages, but here was only the bare and lonely coast, dangerous with rocks. The surf beyond the beach was spiked with rocks. Somehow the man had managed to come through them— he must be badly torn.

They saw when they came toward him that indeed it was so. The sand on one side of him had already a stain of red soaking through.

"He is wounded," Sadao exclaimed. He made haste to the man, who lay motionless, his face in the sand. An old cap stuck to his head soaked with sea water. He was in wet rags of garments. Sadao stooped, Hana at his side, and turned the man's head. They saw the face.

"A white man!" Hana whispered.

Yes, it was a white man. The wet cap fell away, and there was his wet yellow hair, long, as though for many weeks it had not been cut, and upon his young and tortured face was a rough yellow beard. He was unconscious and knew nothing that they did to him.

Now Sadao remembered the wound, and with his expert fingers he began to search for it. Blood flowed freshly at his touch. On the right side of his lower back Sadao saw that a gun wound had been reopened. The flesh was blackened with powder. Sometime, not many days ago, the man had been shot and had not been tended. It was bad chance that the rock had struck the wound.

"Oh, how he is bleeding!" Hana whispered again in a solemn voice. The mists screened them now completely, and at this time of day no one came by. The fisher-

1. *haori* (hä′ō ri), a loose outer garment.

men had gone home and even the chance beachcombers would have considered the day at an end.

"What shall we do with this man?" Sadao muttered. But his trained hands seemed of their own will to be doing what they could to stanch the fearful bleeding. He packed the wound with the sea moss that strewed the beach. The man moaned with pain in his stupor but he did not awaken.

"The best thing that we could do would be to put him back in the sea," Sadao said, answering himself.

Now that the bleeding was stopped for the moment, he stood up and dusted the sand from his hands.

"Yes, undoubtedly that would be best," Hana said steadily. But she continued to stare down at the motionless man.

"If we sheltered a white man in our house we should be arrested and if we turned him over as a prisoner, he would certainly die," Sadao said.

"The kindest thing would be to put him back into the sea," Hana said. But neither of them moved. They were staring with a curious repulsion upon the inert figure.

"What is he?" Hana whispered.

"There is something about him that looks American," Sadao said. He took up the battered cap. Yes, there, almost gone, was the faint lettering. "A sailor," he said, "from an American warship." He spelled it out: "U. S. Navy." The man was a prisoner of war!

"He has escaped," Hana cried softly, "and that is why he is wounded."

"In the back," Sadao agreed.

They hesitated, looking at each other. Then Hana said with resolution:

"Come, are we able to put him back into the sea?"

"If I am able, are you?" Sadao asked.

"No," Hana said. "But if you can do it alone..."

Sadao hesitated again. "The strange thing is," he said, "that if the man were whole I could turn him over to the police without difficulty. I care nothing for him.

He is my enemy. All Americans are my enemy. And he is only a common fellow. You see how foolish his face is. But since he is wounded..."

"You also cannot throw him back to the sea," Hana said. "Then there is only one thing to do. We must carry him into the house."

"But the servants?" Sadao inquired.

"We must simply tell them that we intend to give him to the police—as indeed we must, Sadao. We must think of the children and your position. It would endanger all of us if we did not give this man over as a prisoner of war."

"Certainly," Sadao agreed. "I would not think of doing anything else."

Thus agreed, together they lifted the man. He was very light, like a fowl that has been half starved for a long time until it is only feathers and skeleton. So, his arms hanging, they carried him up the steps and into the side door of the house. This door opened into a passage and down the passage they carried the man toward an empty bedroom. It had been the bedroom of Sadao's father and since his death it had not been used. They laid the man on the deeply matted floor. Everything here had been Japanese to please the old man, who would never in his own home sit on a chair or sleep in a foreign bed. Hana went to the wall cupboards and slid back a door and took out a soft quilt. She hesitated. The quilt was covered with flowered silk and the lining was pure white silk.

"He is so dirty," she murmured in distress.

"Yes, he had better be washed," Sadao agreed. "If you will fetch hot water I will wash him."

"I cannot bear for you to touch him," she said. "We shall have to tell the servants he is here. I will tell Yumi now. She can leave the children for a few minutes and she can wash him."

Sadao considered a moment. "Let it be so," he agreed. "You tell Yumi and I will tell the others."

But the utter pallor of the man's unconscious face moved him first to stoop and feel his pulse. It was faint but it was there. He put his hand against the man's cold breast. The heart too was yet alive.

"He will die unless he is operated on," Sadao said, considering. "The question is whether he will not die anyway."

Hana cried out in fear. "Don't try to save him! What if he should live?"

"What if he should die?" Sadao replied. He stood gazing down on the motionless man. This man must have extraordinary vitality or he would have been dead by now. But then he was very young—perhaps not yet twenty-five.

"You mean die from the operation?" Hana asked.

"Yes," Sadao said.

Hana considered this doubtfully, and when she did not answer Sadao turned away. "At any rate something must be done with him," he said, "and first he must be washed." He went quickly out of the room and Hana came behind him. She did not wish to be left alone with the white man. He was the first she had seen since she left America and now he seemed to have nothing to do with those whom she had known there. Here he was her enemy, a menace, living or dead.

She turned to the nursery and called, "Yumi!"

But the children heard her voice, and she had to go in for a moment and smile at them and play with the baby boy, now nearly three months old.

Over the baby's soft black hair she motioned with her mouth, "Yumi—come with me!"

"I will put the baby to bed," Yumi replied. "He is ready."

She went with Yumi into the bedroom next to the nursery and stood with the boy in her arms while Yumi spread the sleeping quilts on the floor and laid the baby between them.

Then Hana led the way quickly and softly to the kitchen. The two servants were frightened at what their master had just told them. The old gardener, who was also a house servant, pulled the few hairs on his upper lip.

"The master ought not to heal the wound of this white man," he said bluntly to Hana. "The white man ought to die. First he was shot. Then the sea caught him and wounded him with her rocks. If the master heals what the gun did and what the sea did, they will take revenge on us."

"I will tell him what you say," Hana replied courteously. But she herself was also frightened, although she was not superstitious as the old man was. Could it ever be well to help an enemy? Nevertheless she told Yumi to fetch the hot water and bring it to the room where the white man was.

She went ahead and slid back the partitions. Sadao was not yet there. Yumi, following, put down her wooden bucket. Then she went over to the white man. When she saw him her thick lips folded themselves into stubbornness. "I have never washed a white man," she said, "and I will not wash so dirty a one now."

Hana cried at her severely, "You will do what your master commands you!"

"My master ought not to command me to wash the enemy," Yumi said stubbornly.

There was so fierce a look of resistance upon Yumi's round dull face that Hana felt unreasonably afraid. After all, if the servants should report something that was not as it happened?

"Very well," she said with dignity. "You understand we only want to bring him to his senses so that we can turn him over as a prisoner?"

"I will have nothing to do with it," Yumi said. "I am a poor person and it is not my business."

"Then please," Hana said gently, "return to your own work."

At once Yumi left the room. But this left Hana with the white man alone. She might have been too afraid to stay had not her anger at Yumi's stubbornness now sustained her.

"Stupid Yumi," she muttered fiercely. "Is this anything but a man? And a wounded helpless man!"

In the conviction of her own superiority she bent impulsively and untied the knotted rags that kept the white man covered. When she had his breast bare she dipped the small clean towel that Yumi had brought into the steaming hot water and washed his face carefully. The man's skin, though rough with exposure, was of a fine texture and must have been very blond when he was a child.

While she was thinking these thoughts, though not really liking the man better now that he was no longer a child, she kept on washing him until his upper body was quite clean. But she dared not turn him over. Where was Sadao? Now her anger was ebbing, and she was anxious again and she rose, wiping her hands on the wrung towel. Then lest the man be chilled, she put the quilt over him.

"Sadao!" she called softly.

He had been about to come in when she called. His hand had been on the door and now he opened it. She saw that he had brought his surgeon's emergency bag and that he wore his surgeon's coat.

"You have decided to operate!" she cried.

"Yes," he said shortly. He turned his back to her and unfolded a sterilized towel upon the floor of the tokonoma² alcove, and put his instruments out upon it.

"Fetch towels," he said.

She went obediently, but how anxious now, to the linen shelves and took out the towels. There ought also to be old pieces of matting so that the blood would not ruin the fine floor covering. She went out to the back veranda where the gardener kept strips of matting with which to protect delicate shrubs on cold nights and took an armful of them.

But when she went back into the room,

she saw this was useless. The blood had already soaked through the packing in the man's wound and had ruined the mat under him.

"Oh, the mat!" she cried.

"Yes, it is ruined," Sadao replied, as though he did not care. "Help me to turn him," he commanded her.

She obeyed him without a word, and he began to wash the man's back carefully.

"Yumi would not wash him," she said.

"Did you wash him then?" Sadao asked, not stopping for a moment his swift concise movements.

"Yes," she said.

He did not seem to hear her. But she was used to his absorption when he was at work. She wondered for a moment if it mattered to him what was the body upon which he worked so long as it was for the work he did so excellently.

"You will have to give the anesthetic if he needs it," he said.

"I?" she repeated blankly. "But never have I!"

"It is easy enough," he said impatiently.

He was taking out the packing now and the blood began to flow more quickly. He peered into the wound with the bright surgeon's light fastened on his forehead. "The bullet is still there," he said with cool interest. "Now I wonder how deep this rock wound is. If it is not too deep it may be that I can get the bullet. But the bleeding is not superficial. He has lost much blood."

At this moment Hana choked. He looked up and saw her face the color of sulphur.

"Don't faint," he said sharply. He did not put down his exploring instrument. "If I stop now, the man will surely die." She clapped her hands to her mouth and leaped up and ran out of the room. Outside in the garden he heard her retching. But he went on with his work.

"It will be better for her to empty her

2. *tokonoma* (tō'kō nō'mä), a recess or alcove opening from the living room of a Japanese house, in which a picture drawn on silk may be hung.

stomach," he thought. He had forgotten that of course she had never seen an operation. But her distress and his inability to go to her at once made him impatient and irritable with this man who lay like dead under his knife.

"This man," he thought, "there is no reason under heaven why he should live."

Unconsciously this thought made him ruthless and he proceeded swiftly. In his dream the man moaned, but Sadao paid no heed except to mutter at him.

"Groan," he muttered, "groan if you like. I am not doing this for my own pleasure. In fact, I do not know why I am doing it."

The door opened and there was Hana again. She had not stopped even to smooth back her hair.

"Where is the anesthetic?" she asked in a clear voice.

Sadao motioned with his chin. "It is as well that you came back," he said. "This fellow is beginning to stir."

She had the bottle and some cotton in her hand.

"But how shall I do it?" she asked.

"Simply saturate the cotton and hold it near his nostrils," Sadao replied without delaying for one moment the intricate detail of his work. "When he breathes badly move it away a little."

She crouched close to the sleeping face of the young American. It was a piteously thin face, she thought, and the lips were twisted. The man was suffering whether he knew it or not. Watching him, she wondered if the stories they heard sometimes of the sufferings of prisoners were true. They came like flickers of rumor, told by word of mouth and always contradicted. In the newspapers the reports were always that wherever the Japanese armies went the people received them gladly, with cries of joy at their liberation. But sometimes she remembered such men as General Takima, who at home beat his wife cruelly, though no one mentioned it now that he had fought so victorious a battle in Manchuria. If a

man like that could be so cruel to a woman in his power, would he not be cruel to one like this, for instance?

She hoped anxiously that this young man had not been tortured. It was at this moment that she observed deep red scars on his neck, just under the ear. "Those scars," she murmured, lifting her eyes to Sadao.

But he did not answer. At this moment he felt the tip of his instrument strike against something hard, dangerously near the kidney. All thought left him. He felt only the purest pleasure. He probed with his fingers, delicately, familiar with every atom of this human body. His old American professor of anatomy had seen to that knowledge. "Ignorance of the human body is the surgeon's cardinal sin, sirs!" he thundered at his classes year after year. "To operate without as complete knowledge of the body as if you had made it—anything less than that is murder."

"It is not quite at the kidney, my friend," Sadao murmured. It was his habit to murmur to the patient when he forgot himself in an operation. "My friend," he always called his patients and so now he did, forgetting that this was his enemy.

Then quickly, with the cleanest and most precise of incisions, the bullet was out. The man quivered, but he was still unconscious. Nevertheless he muttered a few English words.

"Guts," he muttered, choking. "They got ...my guts..."

"Sadao!" Hana cried sharply.

"Hush," Sadao said.

The man sank again into silence so profound that Sadao took up his wrist, hating the touch of it. Yes, there was still a pulse so faint, so feeble, but enough, if he wanted the man to live, to give hope.

"But certainly I do not want this man to live," he thought.

"No more anesthetic," he told Hana.

He turned as swiftly as though he had never paused and from his medicines he chose a small vial and from it filled a hypodermic and thrust it into the patient's left arm. Then, putting down the needle, he took the man's wrist again. The pulse under his fingers fluttered once or twice and then grew stronger.

"This man will live in spite of all," he said to Hana and sighed.

The young man woke, so weak, his blue eyes so terrified when he perceived where he was, that Hana felt compelled to apology. She served him herself, for none of the servants would enter the room.

When she came in the first time she saw him summon his small strength to be prepared for some fearful thing.

"Don't be afraid," she begged him softly.

"How come...you speak English..." he gasped.

"I was a long time in America," she replied.

She saw that he wanted to reply to that, but he could not, and so she knelt and fed him gently from the porcelain spoon. He ate unwillingly, but still he ate.

"Now you will soon be strong," she said, not liking him and yet moved to comfort him.

He did not answer.

When Sadao came in the third day after the operation, he found the young man sitting up, his face bloodless with the effort.

"Lie down," Sadao cried. "Do you want to die?"

He forced the man down gently and strongly and examined the wound. "You may kill yourself if you do this sort of thing," he scolded.

"What are you going to do with me?" the boy muttered. He looked just now barely seventeen. "Are you going to hand me over?"

For a moment Sadao did not answer. He finished his examination and then pulled the silk quilt over the man.

"I do not know myself what I shall do with you," he said. "I ought of course to give you to the police. You are a prisoner of war—no, do not tell me anything." He put up his hand as he saw the young man about to speak. "Do not even tell me your name unless I ask it."

They looked at each other for a moment, and then the young man closed his eyes and turned his face to the wall.

"Okay," he whispered, his mouth a bitter line.

Outside the door Hana was waiting for Sadao. He saw at once that she was in trouble.

"Sadao, Yumi tells me the servants feel they cannot stay if we hide this man here any more," she said. "She tells me that they are saying that you and I were so long in America that we have forgotten to think of our own country first. They think we like Americans."

"It is not true," Sadao said harshly, "Americans are our enemies. But I have been trained not to let a man die if I can help it."

"The servants cannot understand that," she said anxiously.

"No," he agreed.

Neither seemed able to say more, and somehow the household dragged on. The servants grew daily more watchful. Their courtesy was as careful as ever, but their eyes were cold upon the pair to whom they were hired.

"It is clear what our master ought to do," the old gardener said one morning. He had worked with flowers all his life, and had been a specialist too in moss. For Sadao's father he had made one of the finest moss gardens in Japan, sweeping the bright green carpet constantly so that not a leaf or a pine needle marred the velvet of its surface. "My old master's son knows very well what he ought to do," he now said pinching a bud from a bush as he spoke. "When the man was so near death, why did he not let him bleed?"

"That young master is so proud of his skill to save life that he saves any life," the cook said contemptuously. She split a fowl's neck skillfully and held the fluttering bird and let its blood flow into the roots of a wistaria vine. Blood is the best of fertilizers, and the old gardener would not let her waste a drop of it.

"It is the children of whom we must think," Yumi said sadly. "What will be their fate if their father is condemned as a traitor?"

They did not try to hide what they said from the ears of Hana as she stood arranging the day's flowers in the veranda nearby, and she knew they spoke on purpose that she might hear. That they were right she knew too in most of her being. But there was another part of her which she herself could not understand. It was not sentimental liking of the prisoner. She had come to think of him as a prisoner. She had not liked him even yesterday when he had said in his impulsive way, "Anyway, let me tell you that my name is Tom." She had only bowed her little distant bow. She saw hurt in his eyes but she did not wish to assuage it. Indeed, he was a great trouble in this house.

As for Sadao, every day he examined the wound carefully. The last stitches had been pulled out this morning, and the young man would in a fortnight be nearly as well as ever. Sadao went back to his office and carefully typed a letter to the chief of police reporting the whole matter. "On the twenty-first day of February an escaped prisoner was washed up on the shore in front of my house." So far he typed and then he opened a secret drawer of his desk and put the unfinished report into it.

On the seventh day after that two things happened. In the morning the servants left together, their belongings tied in large square cotton kerchiefs. When Hana got up in the morning nothing was done, the house not cleaned and the food not prepared, and she knew what it meant. She was dismayed and even terrified, but her pride as a mistress would not allow her to show it. In-

stead, she inclined her head gracefully when they appeared before her in the kitchen, and she paid them off and thanked them for all that they had done for her. They were crying, but she did not cry. The cook and the gardener had served Sadao since he was a little boy in his father's house, and Yumi cried because of the children. She was so grieving that after she had gone she ran back to Hana.

"If the baby misses me too much tonight, send for me. I am going to my own house and you know where it is."

"Thank you," Hana said smiling. But she told herself she would not send for Yumi however the baby cried.

She made the breakfast and Sadao helped with the children. Neither of them spoke of the servants beyond the fact that they were gone. But after Hana had taken morning food to the prisoner she came back to Sadao.

"Why is it we cannot see clearly what we ought to do?" she asked him. "Even the servants see more clearly than we do. Why are we different from other Japanese?"

Sadao did not answer. But a little later he went into the room where the prisoner was and said brusquely, "Today you may get up on your feet. I want you to stay up only five minutes at a time. Tomorrow you may try it twice as long. It would be well that you get back your strength as quickly as possible."

He saw the flicker of terror on the young face that was still very pale.

"Okay," the boy murmured. Evidently he was determined to say more. "I feel I ought to thank you, doctor, for having saved my life."

"Don't thank me too early," Sadao said coldly. He saw the flicker of terror again in the boy's eyes—terror as unmistakable as an animal's. The scars on his neck were crimson for a moment. Those scars! What were they? Sadao did not ask.

In the afternoon the second thing happened. Hana, working hard on unaccustomed labor, saw a messenger come to the door in official uniform. Her hands went weak and she could not draw her breath. The servants must have told already. She ran to Sadao, gasping, unable to utter a word. But by then the messenger had simply followed her through the garden and there he stood. She pointed at him helplessly.

Sadao looked up from his book. He was in his office, the outer partition of which was thrown open to the garden for the southern sunshine.

"What is it?" he asked the messenger, and then he rose seeing the man's uniform.

"You are to come to the palace," the man said, "the old General is in pain again."

"Oh," Hana breathed, "is that all?"

"All?" the messenger exclaimed. "Is it not enough?"

"Indeed it is," she replied. "I am very sorry."

When Sadao came to say good-by, she was in the kitchen, but doing nothing. The children were asleep and she sat merely resting for a moment, more exhausted from her fright than from work.

"I thought they had come to arrest you," she said.

He gazed down into her anxious eyes. "I must get rid of this man for your sake," he said in distress. "Somehow I must get rid of him."

Of course," the General said weakly, "I understand fully. But that is because I once took a degree in Princeton. So few Japanese have."

"I care nothing for the man, Excellency," Sadao said, "but having operated on him with such success…"

"Yes, yes," the General said. "It only makes me feel you more indispensable to me. Evidently you can save anyone—you are so skilled. You say you think I can stand one more such attack as I have had today?"

"Not more than one," Sadao said.

"Then certainly I can allow nothing to happen to you," the General said with anxi-

ety. His long pale Japanese face became expressionless, which meant that he was in deep thought. "You cannot be arrested," the General said, closing his eyes. "Suppose you were condemned to death and the next day I had to have my operation?"

"There are other surgeons, Excellency," Sadao suggested.

"None I trust," the General replied. "The best ones have been trained by Germans and would consider the operation successful even if I died. I do not care for their point of view." He sighed. "It seems a pity that we cannot better combine the German ruthlessness with the American sentimentality. Then you could turn your prisoner over to execution and yet I could be sure you would not murder me while I was unconscious." The General laughed. He had an unusual sense of humor. "As a Japanese, could you not combine these two foreign elements?" he asked.

Sadao smiled. "I am not quite sure," he said, "but for your sake I would be willing to try, Excellency."

The General shook his head. "I had rather not be the test case," he said. He felt suddenly weak and overwhelmed with the cares of his life as an official in times such as these when repeated victory brought great responsibilities all over the south Pacific. "It is very unfortunate that this man should have washed up on your doorstep," he said irritably.

"I feel it so myself," Sadao said gently.

"It would be best if he could be quietly killed," the General said. "Not by you, but by someone who does not know him. I have my own private assassins. Suppose I send two of them to your house tonight—or better, any night. You need know nothing about it. It is now warm—what would be more natural than that you should leave the outer partition of the white man's room open to the garden while he sleeps?"

"Certainly it would be very natural," Sadao agreed. "In fact, it is so left open every night."

"Good," the General said yawning. "They are very capable assassins—they make no noise and they know the trick of inward bleeding. If you like I can even have them remove the body."

Sadao considered. "That perhaps would be best, Excellency," he agreed, thinking of Hana.

He left the General's presence then and went home, thinking over the plan. In this way the whole thing would be taken out of his hands. He would tell Hana nothing, since she would be timid at the idea of assassins in the house, and yet certainly such persons were essential in an absolute state such as Japan was. How else could rulers deal with those who opposed them?

He refused to allow anything but reason to be the atmosphere of his mind as he went into the room where the American was in bed. But as he opened the door, to his surprise he found the young man out of bed, and preparing to go into the garden.

"What is this!" he exclaimed. "Who gave you permission to leave your room?"

"I'm not used to waiting for permission," Tom said gaily. "Gosh, I feel pretty good again! But will the muscles on this side always feel stiff?"

"Is it so?" Sadao inquired surprised. He forgot all else. "Now I thought I had provided against that," he murmured. He lifted the edge of the man's shirt and gazed at the healing scar. "Massage may do it," he said, "if exercise does not."

"It won't bother me much," the young man said. His young face was gaunt under the stubby blond beard. "Say, doctor, I've got something I want to say to you. If I hadn't met a Jap like you—well, I wouldn't be alive today. I know that."

Sadao bowed but he could not speak.

"Sure, I know that," Tom went on warmly. His big thin hands gripping a chair were white at the knuckles. "I guess if all the Japs were like you there wouldn't have been a war."

"Perhaps," Sadao said with difficulty.

"And now I think you had better go back to bed."

He helped the boy back into bed and then bowed. "Good night," he said.

Sadao slept badly that night. Time and time again he woke, thinking he heard the rustling of footsteps, the sound of a twig broken or a stone displaced in the garden—a noise such as men might make who carried a burden.

The next morning he made the excuse to go first into the guest room. If the American were gone, he then could simply tell Hana that so the General had directed. But when he opened the door he saw at once that it was not last night. There on the pillow was the shaggy blond head. He could hear the peaceful breathing of sleep and he closed the door again quietly.

"He is asleep," he told Hana. "He is almost well to sleep like that."

"What shall we do with him?" Hana whispered her old refrain.

Sadao shook his head. "I must decide in a day or two," he promised.

But certainly, he thought, the second night must be the night. There rose a wind that night, and he listened to the sounds of bending boughs and whistling partitions.

Hana woke too. "Ought we not to go and close the sick man's partition?" she asked.

"No," Sadao said. "He is able now to do it for himself."

But the next morning the American was still there.

Then the third night of course must be the night. The wind changed to quiet rain, and the garden was full of the sound of dripping eaves and running springs. Sadao slept a little better, but he awoke at the sound of a crash and leaped to his feet.

"What was that?" Hana cried. The baby woke at her voice and began to wail. "I must go and see."

But he held her and would not let her move.

"Sadao," she cried, "what is the matter with you?"

"Don't go," he muttered, "don't go!"

His terror infected her and she stood breathless, waiting. There was only silence. Together they crept back into the bed, the baby between them.

Yet, when he opened the door of the guest room in the morning, there was the young man. He was very gay and had already washed and was now on his feet. He had asked for a razor yesterday and had shaved himself, and today there was a faint color in his cheeks.

"I am well," he said joyously.

Sadao drew his kimono round his weary body. He could not, he decided suddenly, go through another night. It was not that he cared for this young man's life. No, simply it was not worth the strain.

"You are well," Sadao agreed. He lowered his voice. "You are so well that I think if I put my boat on the shore tonight, with food and extra clothing in it, you might be able to row to that little island not far from the coast. It is so near the coast that it has not been worth fortifying. Nobody lives on it because in storm it is submerged. But this is not the season of storm. You could live there until you saw a Korean fishing boat pass by. They pass quite near the island because the water is many fathoms deep there."

The young man stared at him, slowly comprehending. "Do I have to?" he asked.

"I think so," Sadao said gently. "You understand—it is not hidden that you are here."

The young man nodded in perfect comprehension. "Okay," he said simply.

Sadao did not see him again until evening. As soon as it was dark he had dragged the stout boat down to the shore and in it he put food and bottled water that he had bought secretly during the day, as well as two quilts he had bought at a pawnshop. The boat he tied to a post in the water, for the tide was high. There was no moon and he worked without a flashlight.

When he came to the house he entered as though he were just back from his work, and so Hana knew nothing. "Yumi was here today," she said as she served his supper. Though she was so modern, still she did not eat with him. "Yumi cried over the baby," she went on with a sigh. "She misses him so."

"The servants will come back as soon as the foreigner is gone," Sadao said.

He went into the guest room that night before he went to bed and himself checked carefully the American's temperature, the state of the wound, and his heart and pulse. The pulse was irregular, but that was perhaps because of excitement. The young man's pale lips were pressed together and his eyes burned. Only the scars on his neck were red.

"I realize you are saving my life again," he told Sadao.

"Not at all," Sadao said. "It is only inconvenient to have you here any longer."

He had hesitated a good deal about giving the man a flashlight. But he had decided to give it to him after all. It was a small one, his own which he used at night when he was called.

"If your food runs out before you catch a boat," he said, "signal me two flashes at the same instant the sun drops over the horizon. Do not signal in darkness, for it will be seen. If you are all right but still there signal me once. You will find fish easy to catch but you must eat them raw. A fire would be seen."

"Okay," the young man breathed.

He was dressed now in the Japanese clothes which Sadao had given him, and at the last moment Sadao wrapped a black cloth about his blond head.

"Now," Sadao said.

The young American without a word shook Sadao's hand warmly, and then walked quite well across the floor and down the step into the darkness of the garden. Once—twice—Sadao saw his light flash to find his way. But that would not be suspected. He waited until from the shore there was one more flash. Then he closed the partition. That night he slept.

You say the man escaped?" the General asked faintly. He had been operated upon a week before, an emergency operation to which Sadao had been called in the night. For twelve hours Sadao had not been sure the General would live. The gall bladder was much involved. Then the old man had begun to breathe deeply again and to demand food. Sadao had not been able to ask about the assassins. So far as he knew they had never come. The servants had returned, and Yumi had cleaned the guest room thoroughly and had burned sulphur in it to get the white man's smell out of it. Nobody said anything. Only the gardener was cross because he had got behind with his chrysanthemums.

But after a week Sadao felt the General was well enough to be spoken to about the prisoner.

"Yes, Excellency, he escaped," Sadao now said. He coughed, signifying that he had not said all he might have said, but was unwilling to disturb the General farther. But the old man opened his eyes suddenly.

"That prisoner," he said with some energy, "did I not promise you I would kill him for you?"

"You did, Excellency," Sadao said.

"Well, well!" the old man said in a tone of amazement, "so I did! But you see, I was suffering a good deal. The truth is, I thought of nothing but myself. In short, I forgot my promise to you."

"I wondered, Your Excellency," Sadao murmured.

"It was certainly very careless of me," the General said. "But you understand it was not lack of patriotism or dereliction of duty." He looked anxiously at his doctor. "If the matter should come out, you would understand that, wouldn't you?"

"Certainly, Your Excellency," Sadao said. He suddenly comprehended that the General was in the palm of his hand and that as a consequence he himself was perfectly safe. "I can swear to your loyalty, Excellency," he said to the old General, "and to your zeal against the enemy."

"You are a good man," the General murmured and closed his eyes. "You will be rewarded."

But Sadao, searching the spot of black in the twilighted sea that night, had his reward. There was no prick of light in the dusk. No one was on the island. His prisoner was gone—safe, doubtless, for he had warned him to wait only for a Korean fishing boat.

He stood for a moment on the veranda, gazing out to the sea from whence the young man had come that other night. And into his mind, although without reason, there came other white faces he had known —the professor at whose house he had met Hana, a dull man, and his wife had been a silly talkative woman, in spite of her wish to be kind. He remembered his old teacher of anatomy, who had been so insistent on mercy with the knife, and then he remembered the face of his fat and slatternly landlady. He had had great difficulty in finding a place to live in America because he was a Japanese. The Americans were full of prejudice, and it had been bitter to live in it, knowing himself their superior. How he had despised the ignorant and dirty old woman who had at last consented to house him in her miserable home! He had once tried to be grateful to her because she had in his last year nursed him through influenza, but it was difficult, for she was no less repulsive to him in her kindness. But then, white people were repulsive, of course. It was a relief to be openly at war with them at last. Now he remembered the youthful, haggard face of his prisoner—white and repulsive.

"Strange," he thought, "I wonder why I could not kill him?"

Plot

In writing a short story, an author usually brings together events which form a significant pattern of action with a beginning, a middle, and an end —a *plot*. In many short stories this pattern involves one or more conflicts. *Conflict* may be of several types: (1) It may be based upon man's struggle against nature. In "The Enemy" the American sailor's efforts to survive against the sea and the rocks are an example of such a conflict. (2) It may pit man against man, as is shown by the enmity of Sadao and the Japanese people toward the sailor, who to them represents all Americans. (3) It may portray an interior struggle like Sadao's as his sense of patriotic duty fights his training as a doctor.

As a general rule, the more complex and rewarding plots are built around mental, emotional, and moral conflicts: Sadao's tangled relationship with the General; Hana's mixed emotions about the servants; Sadao's moral dilemma in which his feeling of duty to his country wars against his professional feeling about a human being who needs medical care. However, plots involving physical conflict—war, exploration, escapes— often contain more excitement and suspense.

In developing a conflict, the writer of a story may use a time arrangement, telling about the events in the order in which they occurred. Or, to bring in events which occurred earlier but are pertinent to the story, he may use the *flashback* technique. Thus by having Sadao's memory flash back to his past, Pearl Buck brings out both his extreme Japanese nationalism and his American education before she initiates her detailed account of the conflict central to this story. The author may also omit certain details, relying on information previously given to bridge the gap. For example, when Sadao is called to minister to the ailing General, the General's first speech reads, "Of course . . . I understand fully. But that is because I once took a degree in Princeton. So few Japanese have." The reader himself, realizing that Sadao has explained his dilemma to the General, supplies what has gone before.

Sometimes the plot of a story involves a *reversal*. During the first part, or *rising action,* one force is winning. Then there is a turning point—a climax—when the opposite force gains the ascendency. After the reversal comes the last division of the plot—the *falling action* or *denouement* (literally, the untying of the plot) which shows the victorious force triumphant. Upon finishing the story, the reader may look back and see that at the point of climax he can tell whether the main character will succeed or fail in his struggle with the opposing force. This climax in the action, which is called the *technical climax,* must not be confused with the *dramatic climax*—the point of greatest excitement to the reader—although in some stories the technical and the dramatic climaxes coincide.

When the writer arranges his sequence of events in an effective order, linked together in a chain of natural cause and effect consistent with the characters, and leading to a climax and a denouement that seem inevitable, we say that the plot has artistic unity—that it is a good plot.

The following questions will help you determine how well you understand plot.

1. What is the importance to the plot of "The Enemy" of each of the following: (a) Sadao's American training; (b) his intense nationalism; (c) the old General's illness?

2. In speaking of Japanese surgeons the General says, "The best ones have been trained by Germans and would consider the operation successful even if I died. . . . It seems a pity that we cannot better combine the German ruthlessness with the American sentimentality. Then you could turn your prisoner over to execution and yet I could be sure you would not murder me while I was unconscious." (a) What light does this statement throw on Sadao's attitude toward his American prisoner from the moment of finding him until his recovery? (b) How does it show that the General recognizes Sadao's dilemma? (c) What solution to the dilemma does the General offer?

3. (a) What is the technical climax of "The Enemy"? (b) What is the dramatic climax?

4. A short story, you have learned, may "be built upon one or more conflicts." Do you find one conflict, or more than one, in "Early Marriage"? Explain your answer, naming the conflict or conflicts.

5. (a) Indicate the technical climax of "Early Marriage." (b) What is the dramatic climax? Be prepared to justify your answers.

Born in Virginia in 1875, Willa Cather belonged to the fourth generation of an Anglo-Irish family. When she was eight years old, her family moved to a ranch in Nebraska. Since there were no schools near, Willa's two grandmothers instructed her in the English classics and in Latin. The children who lived on the neighboring ranches came from backgrounds far different from Willa's. Most of them were foreign born or the children of German, Swedish, Norwegian, Russian, or Bohemian parents. But differences in nationality and education counted little on the sparsely settled ranch lands. Willa lived the free and open life of the other children of the area, ranging wide on horseback, visiting her friends in their homes, learning at first hand how people of different cultures lived. Years later in such modern classics as *O Pioneers* (1913) and *My Antonia* (1918) she drew on memories of her Nebraska childhood.

The Cather family left the ranch in time for Willa to attend high school in Red Cloud, Nebraska. After graduating from the University of Nebraska, she did newspaper work in Pittsburgh and magazine editing in New York, and began to write poetry and short stories. Her first volume of poetry, *April Twilights*, appeared in 1903, and a book of short stories, *The Troll Garden*, was published in 1905. *O Pioneers* established her as a successful novelist. From 1913 until her death in 1947 she lived on the income from her books.

In 1923 Miss Cather was awarded the Pulitzer Prize for *One of Ours*, a story of World War I. *Death Comes for the Archbishop* (1927), one of her finest novels, is a quiet and moving story of early New Mexico. *Shadows on the Rock* (1931) reaches far into Quebec's past. In these novels of diversified settings Miss Cather shows the strong sense of place which is characteristic of her writing. Also characteristic is her ability to create characters of such sympathy, complexity, and interest that plot becomes relatively unimportant. Noteworthy also is Miss Cather's restrained and beautiful style, which imparts a sense of dignity and timelessness to all her work.

THE SCULPTOR'S FUNERAL

A group of the townspeople stood on the station siding of a little Kansas town, awaiting the coming of the night train, which was already twenty minutes overdue. The snow had fallen thick over everything; in the pale starlight the line of bluffs across the wide, white meadows south of the town made soft, smoke-colored curves against the clear sky. The men on the siding stood first on one foot and then on the other, their hands thrust deep into their trousers pockets, their overcoats open, their shoulders screwed up with the cold; and they glanced from time to time toward the southeast, where the railroad track wound along the river shore. They conversed in low tones and moved about restlessly, seeming uncertain as to what was expected of them. There was but one of the company who looked as though he knew exactly why he was there, and he kept conspicuously apart; walking to the far end of the platform, returning to the station door, then pacing up the track again, his chin sunk in the high collar of his overcoat, his burly shoulders drooping forward, his gait heavy and dogged. Presently he was approached by a tall, spare, grizzled man clad in a faded Grand Army suit, who shuffled out from the group and advanced with a certain deference, craning his neck forward until his back made the angle of a jacknife three-quarters open.

"I reckon she's a-goin' to be pretty late again tonight, Jim," he remarked in a squeaky falsetto. "S'pose it's the snow?"

"I don't know," responded the other man with a shade of annoyance, speaking from out an astonishing cataract of red beard that grew fiercely and thickly in all directions.

The spare man shifted the quill toothpick he was chewing to the other side of his mouth. "It ain't likely that anybody from the East will come with the corpse, I s'pose," he went on reflectively.

"I don't know," responded the other, more curtly than before.

"It's too bad he didn't belong to some lodge or other. I like an order funeral myself. They seem more appropriate for people of some reputation," the spare man continued, with an ingratiating concession in his shrill voice, as he carefully placed his toothpick in his vest pocket. He always carried the flag at the G.A.R.[1] funerals in the town.

The heavy man turned on his heel without replying and walked up the siding. The spare man shuffled back to the uneasy group. "Jim's ez full ez a tick, ez ushel," he commented commiseratingly.

Just then a distant whistle sounded, and there was a shuffling of feet on the platform. A number of lanky boys, of all ages, appeared as suddenly and slimily as eels wakened by the crack of thunder; some came from the waiting room, where they had been warming themselves by the red stove, or half asleep on the slat benches; others uncoiled themselves from baggage trucks or slid out of express wagons. Two clambered down from the driver's seat of a hearse that stood backed up against the siding. They straightened their stooping shoulders and lifted their heads, and a flash of momentary animation kindled their dull eyes at that cold, vibrant scream, the world-wide call for men. It stirred them like the note of a trumpet; just as it had often stirred the man who was coming home tonight, in his boyhood.

The night express shot, red as a rocket, from out the eastward marshlands and wound along the river shore under the long lines of shivering poplars that sentineled the meadows, the escaping steam hanging in gray masses against the pale sky and blotting out the Milky Way. In a moment the red glare from the headlight streamed up the snow-covered track before the siding and glittered on the wet, black rails. The burly man with the disheveled red

1. G.A.R., Grand Army of the Republic, an organization of those veterans who fought for the North during the Civil War.

beard walked swiftly up the platform toward the approaching train, uncovering his head as he went. The group of men behind him hesitated, glanced questioningly at one another, and awkwardly followed his example. The train stopped, and the crowd shuffled up to the express car just as the door was thrown open, the spare man in the G.A.R. suit thrusting his head forward with curiosity. The express messenger appeared in the doorway, accompanied by a young man in a long ulster and a traveling cap.

"Are Mr. Merrick's friends here?" inquired the young man.

The group on the platform swayed and shuffled uneasily. Philip Phelps, the banker, responded with dignity: "We have come to take charge of the body. Mr. Merrick's father is very feeble and can't be about."

"Send the agent out here," growled the express messenger, "and tell the operator to lend a hand."

The coffin was got out of its rough box and down on the snowy platform. The townspeople drew back enough to make room for it and then formed a close semicircle about it, looking curiously at the palm leaf[2] which lay across the black cover. No one said anything. The baggageman stood by his truck, waiting to get at the trunks. The engine panted heavily, and the fireman dodged in and out among the wheels with his yellow torch and long oilcan, snapping the spindle boxes. The young Bostonian, one of the dead sculptor's pupils who had come with the body, looked about him helplessly. He turned to the banker, the only one of that black, uneasy, stoop-shouldered group who seemed enough of an individual to be addressed.

"None of Mr. Merrick's brothers are here?" he asked, uncertainly.

The man with the red beard for the first time stepped up and joined the group. "No, they have not come yet; the family is scattered. The body will be taken directly to the house." He stooped and took hold of one of the handles of the coffin.

"Take the long hill road up, Thompson; it will be easier on the horses," called the liveryman as the undertaker snapped the door of the hearse and prepared to mount to the driver's seat.

Laird, the red-bearded lawyer, turned again to the stranger. "We didn't know whether there would be anyone with him or not," he explained. "It's a long walk, so you'd better go up in the hack." He pointed to a single battered conveyance, but the young man replied stiffly: "Thank you, but I think I will go up with the hearse. If you don't object," turning to the undertaker, "I'll ride with you."

They clambered up over the wheels and drove off in the starlight up the long, white hill toward the town. The lamps in the still village were shining from under the low, snow-burdened roofs; and beyond, on every side, the plains reached out into emptiness, peaceful and wide as the soft sky itself, and wrapped in a tangible, white silence.

When the hearse backed up to a wooden sidewalk before a naked, weather-beaten frame house, the same composite, ill-defined group that had stood upon the station siding was huddled about the gate. The front yard was an icy swamp, and a couple of warped planks, extending from the sidewalk to the door, made a sort of rickety footbridge. The gate hung on one hinge, and was opened wide with difficulty. Steavens, the young stranger, noticed that something black was tied to the knob of the front door.

The grating sound made by the casket, as it was drawn from the hearse, was answered by a scream from the house; the front door was wrenched open, and a tall, corpulent woman rushed out bareheaded into the snow and flung herself upon the

2. *the palm leaf.* The palm leaf is the traditional symbol of victory or triumph. As it is used here, it implies that the sculptor, Harvey Merrick, had been awarded a significant decoration for achievement in the arts.

coffin, shrieking: "My boy, my boy! And this is how you've come home to me!"

As Steavens turned away and closed his eyes with a shudder of unutterable repulsion, another woman, also tall, but flat and angular, darted out of the house and caught Mrs. Merrick by the shoulders, crying sharply: "Come, come, Mother; you mustn't go on like this!" Her tone changed to one of obsequious solemnity as she turned to the banker. "The parlor is ready, Mr. Phelps."

The bearers carried the coffin along the narrow boards, while the undertaker ran ahead with the coffin-rests. They bore it into a large unheated room that smelled of dampness and disuse and furniture polish, and set it down under a hanging lamp ornamented with jingling glass prisms and before a Rogers group[3] of John Alden and Priscilla, wreathed with smilax. Henry Steavens stared about him with the sickening conviction that there had been some horrible mistake and that he had somehow arrived at the wrong destination. He looked at the clover-green Brussels, the fat plush upholstery, among the hand-painted china plaques and panels and vases, for some mark of identification—for something that might once conceivably have belonged to Harvey Merrick. It was not until he recognized his friend in the crayon portrait of a little boy in kilts and curls, hanging above the piano, that he felt willing to let any of these people approach the coffin.

"Take the lid off, Mr. Thompson. Let me see my boy's face," wailed the elder woman between her sobs. This time Steavens looked fearfully, almost beseechingly into her face, red and swollen under its masses of strong, black, shiny hair. He flushed, dropped his eyes, and then, almost incredulously, looked again. There was a kind of power about her face—a kind of brutal handsomeness, even; but it was scarred and furrowed by violence, and so colored and coarsened by fiercer passions that grief seemed never to have laid a gentle finger

there. The long nose was distended and knobbed at the end, and there were deep lines on either side of it; her heavy black brows almost met across her forehead, her teeth were large and square and set far apart—teeth that could tear. She filled the room; the men were obliterated, seemed tossed about like twigs in an angry water, even Steavens felt himself being drawn into the whirlpool.

The daughter—tall, raw-boned woman in crepe, with a mourning comb in her hair which curiously lengthened her long face—sat stiffly upon the sofa, her hands, conspicuous for their large knuckles folded in her lap, her mouth and eyes drawn down, solemnly awaiting the opening of the coffin. Near the door stood a mulatto woman, evidently a servant in the house, with a timid bearing and an emaciated face pitifully sad and gentle. She was weeping silently, the corner of her calico apron lifted to her eyes, occasionally suppressing a long quivering sob. Steavens walked over and stood beside her.

Feeble steps were heard on the stairs, and an old man, tall and frail, odorous of pipe smoke, with shaggy, unkempt gray hair and a dingy beard, tobacco-stained about the mouth, entered uncertainly. He went slowly up to the coffin and stood rolling a blue cotton handkerchief between his hands, seeming so pained and embarrassed by his wife's orgy of grief that he had no consciousness of anything else.

"There, there, Annie, dear, don't take on so," he quavered timidly, putting out a shaking hand and awkwardly patting her elbow. She turned with a cry and sank upon his shoulder with such violence that he tottered a little. He did not even glance toward the coffin, but continued to look at her with a dull, frightened, appealing expression, as a spaniel looks at the whip. His sunken cheeks slowly reddened and burned with miserable shame. When his wife

---

3. Rogers group. A small piece of statuary executed by the American sculptor, John Rogers (1829-1904).

rushed from the room, her daughter strode after with set lips. The servant stole up to the coffin, bent over it for a moment, and then slipped away to the kitchen, leaving Steavens, the lawyer, and the father to themselves. The old man stood trembling and looking down at his dead son's face. The sculptor's splendid head seemed even more noble in its rigid stillness than in life. The dark hair had crept down upon the wide forehead; the face seemed strangely long, but in it there was not that repose we expect to find in the faces of the dead. The brows were so drawn that there were two deep lines above the beaked nose, and the chin was thrust forward defiantly. It was as though the strain of life had been so sharp and bitter that death could not at once wholly relax the tension and smooth the countenance into perfect peace—as though he were still guarding something precious and holy, which might even yet be wrested from him.

The old man's lips were working under his stained beard. He turned to the lawyer with timid deference: "Phelps and the rest are comin' back to set up with Harve, ain't they?" he asked. "Thank 'ee, Jim, thank 'ee." He brushed the hair back gently from his son's forehead. "He was a good boy, Jim; always a good boy. He was ez gentle ez a child and kindest of 'em all—only we didn't none of us ever onderstand him." The tears trickled slowly down his beard and dropped upon the sculptor's coat.

"Martin! Martin! Oh, Martin! come here," his wife wailed from the top of the stairs. The old man started timorously: "Yes, Annie, I'm coming." He turned away, hesitated, stood for a moment in miserable indecision; then reached back and patted the dead man's hair softly, and stumbled from the room.

"Poor old man, I didn't think he had any tears left. Seems as if his eyes would have gone dry long ago. At his age nothing cuts very deep," remarked the lawyer.

Something in his tone made Steavens glance up. While the mother had been in the room, the young man had scarcely seen anyone else; but now, from the moment he first glanced into Jim Laird's florid face and bloodshot eyes, he knew that he had found what he had been heartsick at not finding before—the feeling, the understanding that must exist in someone, even here.

The man was red as his beard, with features swollen and blurred by dissipation, and a hot, blazing blue eye. His face was strained—that of a man who is controlling himself with difficulty—and he kept plucking at his beard with a sort of fierce resentment. Steavens, sitting by the window, watched him turn down the glaring lamp, still its jangling pendants with an angry gesture, and then stand with his hands locked behind him, staring down into the master's face. He could not help wondering what link there could have been between the porcelain vessel and so sooty a lump of potter's clay.

From the kitchen an uproar was sounding; when the dining-room door opened, the import of it was clear. The mother was abusing the maid for having forgotten to make the dressing for the chicken salad which had been prepared for the watchers. Steavens had never heard anything in the least like it; it was injured, emotional, dramatic abuse, unique and masterly in its excruciating cruelty, as violent and unrestrained as had been her grief of twenty minutes before. With a shudder of disgust the lawyer went into the dining room and closed the door into the kitchen.

"Poor Roxy's getting it now," he remarked when he came back. "The Merricks took her out of the poorhouse years ago; and if her loyalty would let her, I guess the poor old thing could tell tales that would curdle your blood. She's the mulatto woman who was standing in here a while ago, with her apron to her eyes. The old woman is a fury; there never was anybody like her for demonstrative piety and ingenious cruelty. She made Harvey's life a hell for him when he lived at home; he was so sick ashamed of it. I never could see how he kept himself sweet."

"He was wonderful," said Steavens slowly, "wonderful; but until tonight I have never known how wonderful."

"That is the true and eternal wonder of it, anyway; that it can come even from such a dung heap as this," the lawyer cried, with a sweeping gesture which seemed to indicate much more than the four walls within which they stood.

"I think I'll see whether I can get a little air. The room is so close I am beginning to feel rather faint," murmured Steavens, struggling with one of the windows. The sash was stuck, however, and would not yield, so he sat down dejectedly and began pulling at his collar. The lawyer came over, loosened the sash with one blow of his red fist and sent the window up a few inches. Steavens thanked him, but the nausea which had been gradually climbing into his throat for the last half-hour left him with one desire—a desperate feeling that he must get away from this place with what was left of Harvey Merrick. Oh, he comprehended well enough now the quiet bitterness of the smile that he had seen so often on his master's lips!

He remembered that once, when Merrick returned from a visit home, he brought with him a singularly feeling and suggestive bas-relief of a thin, faded old woman, sitting and sewing something pinned to her knee; while a full-lipped, full-blooded little urchin, his trousers held up by a single gallows, stood beside her, impatiently twitching her gown to call her attention to a butterfly he had caught. Steavens, impressed by the tender and delicate modeling of the thin, tired face, had asked him if it were his mother. He remembered the dull flush that had burned up in the sculptor's face.

The lawyer was sitting in a rocking chair beside the coffin, his head thrown back and his eyes closed. Steavens looked at him earnestly, puzzled at the line of the chin, and wondering why a man should conceal a feature of such distinction under that disfiguring shock of beard. Suddenly, as though he felt the young sculptor's keen glance, Jim Laird opened his eyes.

"Was he always a good deal of an oyster?" he asked abruptly. "He was terribly shy as a boy."

"Yes, he was an oyster, since you put it so," rejoined Steavens. "Although he could be very fond of people, he always gave one the impression of being detached. He disliked violent emotion; he was reflective, and rather distrustful of himself—except, of course, as regarded his work. He was sure enough there. He distrusted men pretty thoroughly and women even more, yet somehow without believing ill of them. He was determined, indeed, to believe the best; but he seemed afraid to investigate."

"A burnt dog dreads the fire," said the lawyer grimly, and closed his eyes.

Steavens went on and on, reconstructing that whole miserable boyhood. All this raw, biting ugliness had been the portion of the man whose mind was to become an exhaustless gallery of beautiful impressions— so sensitive that the mere shadow of a poplar leaf flickering against a sunny wall would be etched and held there forever. Surely, if ever a man had the magic word in his finger tips, it was Merrick. Whatever he touched, he revealed its holiest secret; liberated it from enchantment and restored it to its pristine loveliness. Upon whatever he had come in contact with, he had left a beautiful record of the experience—a sort of ethereal signature; a scent, a sound, a color that was his own.

Steavens understood now the real tragedy of his master's life; neither love nor wine, as many had conjectured, but a blow which had fallen earlier and cut deeper than anything else could have done—a shame not his, and yet so unescapably his, to hide in his heart from his very boyhood. And without—the frontier warfare; the yearning of a boy, cast ashore upon a desert of newness and ugliness and sordidness, for all that is chastened and old, and noble with traditions.

At eleven o'clock the tall, flat woman in black crepe announced that the watchers were arriving, and asked them to "step into the dining room." As Steavens rose, the lawyer said dryly: "You go on—it'll be a good experience for you, doubtless; as for me, I'm not equal to that crowd tonight; I've had twenty years of them."

As Steavens closed the door after him he glanced back at the lawyer, sitting by the coffin in the dim light, with his chin resting on his hand.

The same misty group that had stood before the door of the express car shuffled into the dining room. In the light of the kerosene lamp they separated and became individuals. The minister, a pale, feeble-looking man with white hair and blond chin whiskers, took his seat beside a small side table and placed his Bible upon it. The Grand Army man sat down behind the stove and tilted his chair back comfortably against the wall, fishing his quill toothpick from his waistcoat pocket. The two bankers, Phelps and Elder, sat off in a corner behind the dinner table, where they could finish their discussion of the new usury law and its effect on chattel security loans. The real-estate agent, an old man with a smiling, hypocritical face, soon joined them. The coal and lumber dealer and the cattle shipper sat on opposite sides of the hard-coal burner, their feet on the nickelwork. Steavens took a book from his pocket and began to read. The talk around him ranged through various topics of local interest while the house was quieting down. When it was clear that the members of the family were in bed, the Grand Army man hitched his shoulders and, untangling his long legs, caught his heels on the rounds of his chair.

"S'pose there'll be a will, Phelps?" he queried in his weak falsetto.

The banker laughed disagreeably, and began trimming his nails with a pearl-handled pocketknife.

"There'll scarcely be any need for one, will there?" he queried in his turn.

The restless Grand Army man shifted his position again, getting his knees still nearer his chin. "Why, the ole man says Harve's done right well lately," he chirped.

The other banker spoke up. "I reckon he means by that Harve ain't asked him to mortgage any more farms lately, so as he could go on with his education."

"Seems like my mind don't reach back to a time when Harve wasn't bein' edycated," tittered the Grand Army man.

There was a general chuckle. The minister took out his handkerchief and blew his nose sonorously. Banker Phelps closed his knife with a snap. "It's too bad the old man's sons didn't turn out better," he remarked with reflective authority. "They never hung together. He spent money enough on Harve to stock a dozen cattle farms, and he might as well have poured it into Sand Creek. If Harve had stayed at home and helped nurse what little they had, and gone into stock on the old man's bottom farm, they might all have been well fixed. But the old man had to trust everything to tenants and was cheated right and left."

"Harve never could have handled stock none," interposed the cattleman. "He hadn't it in him to be sharp. Do you remember when he bought Sander's mules for eight-year-olds, when everybody in town knew that Sander's father-in-law give 'em to his wife for a wedding present eighteen years before, an' they was full-grown mules then?"

Everyone chuckled, and the Grand Army man rubbed his knees with a spasm of childish delight.

"Harve never was much account for anything practical, and he shore was never fond of work," began the coal and lumber dealer. "I mind the last time he was home; the day he left, when the old man was out to the barn helpin' his hand hitch up to take Harve to the train, and Cal Moots was patchin' up the fence; Harve, he come out on the step and sings out, in his ladylike voice, 'Cal Moots! Cal Moots! please come cord my trunk.'"

"That's Harve for you," approved the Grand Army man. "I kin hear him howlin' yet, when he was a big feller in long pants and his mother used to whale him with a rawhide in the barn for lettin' the cows get foundered in the cornfield when he was drivin' 'em home from pasture. He killed a cow of mine that-a-way onct—a pure Jersey and the best milker I had, an' the old man had to put up for her. Harve, he was watchin' the sun set acrost the marshes when the anamile got away; he argued that sunset was oncommon fine."

"Where the old man made his mistake was sending the boy East to school," said Phelps, stroking his goatee and speaking in a deliberate, judicial tone. "There was where he got his head full of trapseing to Paris and all such folly. What Harve needed, of all people, was a course in some first-class Kansas City business college."

The letters were swimming before Steavens' eyes. Was it possible that these men did not understand, that the palm on the coffin meant nothing to them? The very name of their town would have remained forever buried in the postal guide had it not been now and again mentioned in the world in connection with Harvey Merrick's. He remembered what his master had said to him on the day of his death, after the congestion of both lungs had shut off any probability of recovery, and the sculptor had asked his pupil to send his body home. "It's not a pleasant place to be lying while the world is moving and doing and bettering," he had said with a feeble smile, "but it rather seems as though we ought to go back to the place we came from, in the end. The townspeople will come in for a look at me; and after they have had their say, I

shan't have much to fear from the judgment of God!"

The cattleman took up the comment. "Forty's young for a Merrick to cash in; they usually hang on pretty well. Probably he helped it along with whiskey."

"His mother's people were not long-lived, and Harvey never had a robust constitution," said the minister mildly. He would have liked to say more. He had been the boy's Sunday-school teacher and had been fond of him; but he felt that he was not in a position to speak. His own sons had turned out badly, and it was not a year since one of them had made his last trip home in the express car, shot in a gambling house in the Black Hills.

"Nevertheless, there is no disputin' that Harve frequently looked upon the wine when it was red, also variegated, and it shore made an oncommon fool of him," moralized the cattleman.

Just then the door leading into the parlor rattled loudly and everyone started involuntarily, looking relieved when only Jim Laird came out. His red face was convulsed with anger, and the Grand Army man ducked his head when he saw the spark in his blue, bloodshot eye. They were all afraid of Jim; he was a drunkard but he could twist the law to suit his client's needs as no other man in all western Kansas could do, and there were many who tried. The lawyer closed the door gently behind him, leaned back against it, and folded his arms cocking his head a little to one side. When he assumed this attitude in the courtroom, ears were always pricked up, as it usually foretold a flood of withering sarcasm.

"I've been with you gentlemen before," he began in a dry, even tone, "when you've sat by the coffins of boys born and raised in this town; and, if I remember rightly, you were never any too well satisfied when you checked them up. What's the matter, anyhow? Why is it that reputable young men are as scarce as millionaires in Sand City? It might almost seem to a stranger that there was, some way, something the matter with your progressive town. Why did Reuben Sayer, the brightest young lawyer you ever turned out, after he had come home from the university as straight as a die, take to drinking and forge a check and shoot himself? Why did Bill Merrit's son die of the shakes in a saloon in Omaha? Why was Mr. Thomas' son, here, shot in a gambling house? Why did young Adams burn his mill to beat the insurance companies and go to the pen?"

The lawyer paused and unfolded his arms, laying one clenched fist quietly on the table. "I'll tell you why. Because you drummed nothing but money and knavery into their ears from the time they wore knickerbockers; because you carped away at them as you've been carping here to-night, holding our friends Phelps and Elder up to them for their models, as our grandfathers held up George Washington and John Adams. But the boys, worse luck, were young, and raw at the business you put them to; and how could they match coppers with such artists as Phelps and Elder? You wanted them to be successful rascals; they were only unsuccessful ones— that's all the difference. There was only one boy ever raised in this borderland between ruffianism and civilization who didn't come to grief, and you hated Harvey Merrick more for winning out than you hated all the other boys who got under the wheels. Lord! Lord, how you did hate him! Phelps, here, is fond of saying that he could buy and sell us all out any time he's a mind to; but he knew Harve wouldn't have given a tinker's damn for his bank and all his cattle farms put together; and a lack of appreciation, that way, goes hard with Phelps.

"Old Nimrod, here, thinks Harve drank too much; and this from such as Nimrod and me!

"Brother Elder says Harve was too free with the old man's money—fell short in filial consideration, maybe. Well, we can all remember the very tone in which brother Elder swore his own father was a liar, in the county court; and we all know that the old man came out of that partnership with his son as bare as a sheared lamb. But maybe I'm getting personal, and I'd better be driving ahead at what I want to say."

The lawyer paused a moment, squared his heavy shoulders, and went on: "Harvey Merrick and I went to school together, back East. We were dead in earnest, and we wanted you all to be proud of us someday. We meant to be great men. Even I, and I haven't lost my sense of humor, gentlemen, I meant to be a great man. I came back here to practice, and I found you didn't in the least want me to be a great man. You wanted me to be a shrewd lawyer—oh, yes! Our veteran here wanted me to get him an increase of pension, because he had dyspepsia; Phelps wanted a new county survey that would put the widow Wilson's little bottom farm inside his south line; Elder wanted to lend money at five per cent a month, and get it collected; old Stark here wanted to wheedle old women up in Vermont into investing their annuities in real-estate mortgages that are not worth the paper they are written on. Oh, you needed me hard enough, and you'll go on needing me!

"Well, I came back here and became the damned shyster you wanted me to be. You pretend to have some sort of respect for me; and yet you'll stand up and throw mud at Harvey Merrick, whose soul you couldn't dirty and whose hands you couldn't tie. Oh, you're a discriminating lot of Christians! There have been times when the sight of Harvey's name in some Eastern paper has made me hang my head like a whipped dog; and again, times when I liked to think of him off there in the world, away from all this hog wallow, climbing the big, clean upgrade he'd set for himself.

"And we? Now that we've fought and lied and sweated and stolen, and hated as only the disappointed strugglers in a bitter, dead little Western town know how to do, what have we got to show for it? Harvey Merrick wouldn't have given one sunset over your marshes for all you've got put together, and you know it. It's not for me to say why in the inscrutable wisdom of God, a genius should ever have been called from this place of hatred and bitter waters; but I want this Boston man to know that the drivel he's been hearing here tonight is the only tribute any truly great man could have from such a lot of sick, side-tracked, burnt-dog, land-poor sharks as the here-present financiers of Sand City—upon which town may God have mercy!"

The lawyer thrust out his hand to Steavens as he passed him, caught up his overcoat in the hall, and had left the house before the Grand Army man had had time to lift his ducked head and crane his long neck about at his fellows.

Next day Jim Laird was drunk and unable to attend the funeral services. Steavens called twice at his office, but was compelled to start East without seeing him. He had a presentiment that he would hear from him again, and left his address on the lawyer's table; but if Laird found it, he never acknowledged it. The thing in him that Harvey Merrick had loved must have gone underground with Harvey Merrick's coffin; for it never spoke again, and Jim got the cold he died of driving across the Colorado mountains to defend one of Phelps' sons who had got into trouble out there by cutting government timber.

BETTER READING

Character

One great merit of literature is that it acquaints us intimately with people of many kinds, from all countries and of all ages. It also improves our understanding even of people like those we know well. For while in the actual world we can only guess at our friends' or enemies' thoughts and feelings or speculate about their motives, from the storyteller, the dramatist, or the poet we can learn exactly what goes on in their minds and hearts. To learn why fictional beings act as they do, it is valuable to notice: (1) how the author acquaints us with his characters; (2) what their traits are; and (3) what their functions are in story, play, or poem.

(1) The author may acquaint us with characters in several ways. He may straightforwardly inform us about a character's habitual way of behaving, as Richter does when he says that Rife "seldom made a fuss over anything." The writer may so describe a character as to imply what sort of individual he or she is. Or an author may acquaint us with a character by showing us his dwelling. He may characterize by quoting typical speeches, by showing us how other characters react to a personality, by acquainting us with what goes on in the character's mind, and by showing the character in action. If a character is of some importance, the author will probably use several of these methods.

(2) Characters, depending on their importance, may have few or many traits. A minor character may display only one trait, for example, a hot temper. In developing more important characters the author will probably include many traits, and the reader needs to see both what these traits are and how they are interrelated. To understand "The Enemy," for instance, you must know that Sadao is a patriotic Japanese and an affectionate family man; that he is a surgeon dedicated to saving life and a Japanese citizen impelled to turn an enemy over to the proper authorities; and that therefore he is drawn in two opposite directions.

(3) The qualities which an author gives his characters may serve various functions. They may simply make the people more "lifelike" than they would be without such qualities. They may make them more attractive or more unattractive to the reader—an important matter since the reader's attitudes toward fictional figures "involve" him in his reading. Certain traits may motivate an incident which is part of the pattern of action; for example, the cowardice of Sadao's servants in "The Enemy" causes them to abandon their master and mistress. Or they may cause the whole plot in a narrative to take the form it does, as is the case when Nancy Belle's determination and courage in "Early Marriage" cause her to make her dangerous journey with Rife.

Characters and their development loom large in "The Sculptor's Funeral." Because the plot revolves around Henry Steavens' discovery that the townsfolk have completely failed to appreciate Merrick, that they have in fact hated him and placed every hindrance they could in his way, it is important that the author make us see the townsfolk and their attitudes. She introduces Merrick's father, the family servant, and the minister, all of whom are faintly sympathetic. She acquaints us with Jim Laird, the most sympathetic and understanding of all the villagers—a man who at the end of the story delivers a scornful speech which brings to its culmination Steavens' discovery and excoriates Merrick's neighbors. She also introduces a group of men who are important in the life of the town.

The questions which follow direct your attention to the characters and the characterization in this fierce narrative by one of the great writers of modern America.

1. (a) Which characters display a single trait each during the course of the story? (b) Why is each shown as having only a single trait? (c) Which characters have several or conflicting traits?

2. Read again the paragraph which describes the various ways an author may acquaint the reader with a character. Explain the means Willa Cather uses to characterize Jim Laird, citing instances of various methods from the text.

3. What justification is there for the author's including the detailed description of the Merrick parlor (page 41)?

4. (a) The sculptor's mother is shown weeping over her son's body; she is heard scolding the servant. Do these actions make her attractive or unattractive to the reader? Justify your answer. (b) List in the order of their attractiveness the following: Jim Laird, Harvey Merrick, Henry Steavens, the G.A.R. veteran. Justify your listing, and suggest why the story gains by making these characters likable or unlikable in this particular order.

5. The article states that Laird's scornful speech "brings to its culmination Steavens' discovery." Why is this true?

6. Would this story have been better if it had ended with the next to the last paragraph? Why, or why not?

PHOTO BY SALLY ROSS

Robert Penn Warren is one of the comparatively small group of writers who have received the praise of literary critics for both poetry and prose. His fame as a poet came first, and won for him several prizes. His widespread acceptance as a novelist was established by All the King's Men, a study of the rise and fall of a Southern political leader, which was awarded the Pulitzer Prize in 1947.

Warren was born in 1905 in Todd County, Kentucky, an area which furnished the background for the novel Night Rider. He went to school in Guthrie, Kentucky, until he was fifteen, and finished high school in Clarksville, Tennessee. While he was attending Vanderbilt University in Nashville, he found his interest shifting from studying chemistry to writing poetry. This interest grew while he studied for advanced degrees at the University of California, Yale, and Oxford. On his return to the United States from England, he turned to teaching and editing, while continuing to write. His first volume of poetry, XXXVI Poems, appeared in 1936; his first novel, Night Rider, was published in 1938.

Though Warren has lived in many places, in his poetry he often returns to the sights and sounds and incidents of Kentucky as he knew it in his childhood. His concrete images and graceful lines at times almost conceal the strength of his ideas. "Courtmartial," about which he writes in the letter on the opposite page, will give you a glimpse of the way in which he fuses memory and idea in moving, eloquent lines.

● ● ● In the summer of 1956 my family and I (wife, two small children) were living in a ruined fortress in Italy, on the Mediterranean -- the scene of a good many of the poems in the volume Promises, from which "Court-martial" comes. I wrote quite a few poems that summer -- in fact, fiddling with verse was about all I did for a long time. Some of the poems had to do with my children and the immediate scene, and some, by a natural association, had to do with my own early recollections. "Court-martial" is a recollection -- or a half-recollection, a reconstructed recollection, for the scene under the cedar tree and the small boy and the tales of the Civil War, including the taking of guerrillas, etc. is literal. The end is made-up, but it corresponds to a recollected feeling, some shock of reality that came from tales of what happened to bushwackers and that did not come, somehow, from the tales of mere battle, etc. The poem is about that I guess -- the discovery of some shock of human reality and pathos behind the facade of history. ● ● ●

Robert Penn Warren

Court-martial

Under the cedar tree,
He would sit, all summer, with me:
An old man and small grandson
Withdrawn from the heat of the sun.

Captain, cavalry, C.S.A.,[1]   5
An old man, now shrunken, gray,
Pointed beard clipped the classic way,
Tendons long gone crank and wry,
And long shrunken the cavalryman's thigh
Under the pale-washed blue jean.   10
His pipe smoke lifts, serene
Beneath boughs of the evergreen,

With sunlight dappling between.
I see him now, as once seen.

Light throbs the far hill.   15
The boughs of the cedar are still.

His years like landscape lie
Spread to the backward eye
In life's long irony.
All the old hoofbeats fade   20
In the calm of the cedar shade,
Where only the murmur and hum

"Court-Martial" is reprinted from Promises: Poems 1954-1956, by Robert Penn Warren, by permission of Random House, Inc., New York, and William Morris Agency, New York. Copyright © 1957 by Robert Penn Warren.
1. C.S.A., Confederate States of America.

Of the far farm, and summer, now come.
He can forget all—forget
Even mortgage and lien and debt,   25
Cutworm and hail and drouth,
Bang's disease, hoof-and-mouth,
Barn sagging and broken house—
For now in the shade, adrowse,
At last he can sit, or rouse   30
To light pipe, or say to me
Some scrap of old poetry—
Byron or Burns—and idly
The words glimmer and fade
Like sparks in the dark of his head.   35

In the dust by his chair
I undertook to repair
The mistakes of his old war.
Hunched on that toy terrain,
Campaign by campaign,   40
I sought, somehow, to untie
The knot of History,
For in our shade I knew
That only the Truth is true,
That life is only the act   45
To transfigure all fact,
And life is only a story
And death is only the glory
Of the telling of the story,
And the *done* and the *to-be-done*   50
In that timelessness were one,
Beyond the poor *being done*.

The afternoon stood still.
Sun dazzled the far hill.

It was only a chance word   55
That a chance recollection had stirred.
"Guerrilla—what's that?" I said.
"Bushwhackers, we called 'em," he said.
"Were they on the Yankee side?"
"Son, they didn't have any side.   60
Just out to plunder and ride
And hell-rake the pore countryside.
Just out for themselves, so, son,
If you happened to run across one,
Or better, laid hand to a passel,   65
No need to be squeamish, or wrestle
Too long with your conscience. But if—"

He paused, raised his pipe, took a whiff—
"If your stomach or conscience was queasy,
You could make it all regular, easy.   70

"By the road, find some shade, a nice patch.
Even hackberry does, at a scratch.
Find a spring with some cress fresh beside
    it,
Growing rank enough to nigh hide it.   74
Lord, a man can sure thirst when you ride.
Yes, find you a nice spot to bide.
Bide sweet when you can when you ride.
Order halt, let heat-daze subside.
Put out your pickets, vedettes out,
    dismount.
Water horses, grease gall, take count,   80
And while the men rest and jaw,
You and two lieutenants talk law.
Brevitatem justicia amat.[2]
Time is short—hell, a rope is—that's that."

That was that, and the old eyes were
    closed.   85
On a knee one old hand reposed,
Fingers crooked on the cob pipe, where
Last smoke raveled blue up the air.
Every tale has an end, has an end.
But smoke rose, did not waver or bend.   90
It unspooled, wouldn't stop, wouldn't end.

"By God—" and he jerked up his head.
"By God, they deserved it," he said.
"Don't look at me that way," he said.
"By God—" and the old eyes glared red.   95
Then shut in the cedar shade.

The head slept in that dusk the boughs
    made.
The world's silence made me afraid.
Then a July-fly, somewhere,
Like silk ripping, ripped the bright air.   100
Then stopped. Sweat broke in my hair.

I snatched my gaze away.
I swung to the blazing day.
Ruined lawn, raw house swam in light.

2. *Brevitatem justicia ·amat* (bre′vi tä′təm ūs tish′ə ä′mät), a Latin saying which means "justice loves brevity."

The far woods swam in my sight.   105
Throbbing, the fields fell away
Under the blaze of day.

Calmly then, out of the sky,
Blotting the sun's blazing eye,
He rode. He was large in the sky.   110
Behind, shadow massed, slow, and grew
Like cloud on the sky's summer blue.
Out of that shade-mass he drew.
To the great saddle's sway, he swung,
Not old now, not old now, but young,   115
Great cavalry boots to the thigh,
No speculation in eye.
Then clotting behind him, and dim,
Clot by clot, from the shadow behind him,
They took shape, enormous in air.   120
Behind him, enormous, they hung there:

Ornaments of the old rope,
Each face outraged, agape,
Not yet believing it true.
Each hairy jaw is askew,   125
Tongue out, out-staring eye,
And the spittle not yet dry
That was uttered with the last cry.

The horseman does not look back.
Blank-eyed, he continues his track,   130
Riding toward me there,
Through the darkening air.

The world is real. It is there.

TO INCREASE UNDERSTANDING

1. What methods does the poet use to characterize the grandfather? Cite examples.

2. (a) How does the grandfather defend the
lynching of the bushwhackers? (b) In what way
does he unconsciously reveal his sense of guilt?

3. Cite lines in which the poet's language
makes vivid (a) the summer day, (b) the grandfather's vision.

4. In the letter quoted on page 49, Robert Penn
Warren writes: "The poem is about . . . the discovery of some shock of human reality and pathos
behind the facade of history." Relate this statement to lines 39-52 and 101-132.

The Pulitzer Prizes in Letters

In 1864, when seventeen-year-old Joseph Pulitzer
came to the United States from Hungary, he
was just another unknown immigrant—yet by
the time he was forty, his energetic and successful career in journalism had changed the
entire philosophy of metropolitan newspaper
operation.

Pulitzer amassed a fortune as owner and
publisher of the St. Louis *Post-Dispatch* and
the New York *World*. Determined to exert a
lasting influence on American journalism and
letters, he bequeathed a generous amount of
his wealth to Columbia University. Pulitzer's
bequest made possible the establishment of the
School of Journalism at Columbia. It also provided an annual fund of $20,000, or more, part
to be awarded in prizes for superior accomplishments in journalism, letters, and music,
and the remainder in traveling scholarships in
journalism and art.

The Pulitzer Prizes in Letters have become
the most important literary awards made in
the United States. Announced on the first
Monday in May, the cash awards of $500 are
given for excellence in fiction, drama, American history, American biography or autobiography, general nonfiction, and verse. To be
eligible, a book or play must be the work of an
American author published during the year for
which it is nominated. Its subject matter should
deal, preferably, with American life.

Nominations come from many sources to
Columbia University. The trustees of the university, acting upon the recommendations of
the Advisory Board of the School of Journalism,
confer the awards.

The Pulitzer Prizes in Letters, first awarded
in 1917, have since become coveted marks of
literary success. Most of the twentieth-century
writers included in this anthology have won at
least one Pulitzer Prize.

Newspaper historians feel that Joseph Pulitzer exercised a remarkable influence on American journalism during his lifetime. It is possible that, through the Pulitzer Prizes, he has
exercised an even greater influence on American letters since his death.

Amy Lowell.

In 1874 Amy Lowell was born into one of the wealthiest and most distinguished families of Massachusetts. Her grandfather had founded the cotton-manufacturing town of Lowell. Her grandfather's cousin was the poet James Russell Lowell (see page 281). Her brothers were Percival Lowell, the astronomer, and Abbott Lawrence Lowell, for many years president of Harvard. Amy was educated privately and traveled widely. Years later the exotic sights and sounds of Greece, Egypt, Turkey, and other lands were reflected in the rich colors of her poetry.

Not until she was twenty-eight years old did Amy Lowell decide seriously to become a poet, and then she studied for eight years before publishing a line. Her first volume of poetry, *A Dome of Many-Colored Glass* (1912), was conventional, and echoed the melodies of older poets. Soon after its publication Miss Lowell joined the Imagists, a group of poets who believed in the use of free-verse forms, freedom to write about any subject, and, above all, the use of the exact word to create strong and concrete images. Miss Lowell's second volume of poetry, *Sword Blades and Poppy Seeds* (1914), brilliantly incorporated these beliefs; *Men, Women, and Ghosts* (1916), in which "Patterns" first appeared, showed that in addition to being a craftsman of note she was also a superb storyteller.

The "new poetry" of the Imagists was bitterly ridiculed. Miss Lowell traveled across the country for ten years, reading and lecturing. Gradually scorn gave way to acceptance, and by the time she died in 1925 her poetry held an honored place. She was posthumously awarded the Pulitzer Prize in 1926 for *What's O'Clock*.

Patterns

I walk down the garden-paths,
And all the daffodils
Are blowing, and the bright blue squills.
I walk down the patterned garden-paths
In my stiff, brocaded gown.
With my powdered hair and jeweled fan,
I too am a rare

"Patterns" is reprinted from *The Collected Poems of Amy Lowell*, by permission of Houghton Mifflin Company, Boston. Copyright 1944 by Ada D. Russell.
Miss Lowell's signature from The Berg Collection of the New York Public Library.

Pattern. As I wander down
The garden-paths.
My dress is richly figured,   10
And the train
Makes a pink and silver stain
On the gravel, and the thrift
Of the borders.
Just a plate of current fashion,   15
Tripping by in high-heeled, ribboned shoes.
Not a softness anywhere about me,
Only whalebone and brocade.
And I sink on a seat in the shade
Of a lime-tree. For my passion   20
Wars against the stiff brocade.
The daffodils and squills
Flutter in the breeze
As they please.
And I weep;   25
For the lime-tree is in blossom
And one small flower has dropped upon my bosom.

And the plashing of waterdrops
In the marble fountain
Comes down the garden-paths.   30
The dripping never stops.
Underneath my stiffened gown
Is the softness of a woman bathing in a marble basin,
A basin in the midst of hedges grown
So thick, she cannot see her lover hiding,   35
But she guesses he is near,
And the sliding of the water
Seems the stroking of a dear
Hand upon her.
What is Summer in a fine brocaded gown!   40
I should like to see it lying in a heap upon the ground.
All the pink and silver crumpled up on the ground.

I would be the pink and silver as I ran along the paths,
And he would stumble after,
Bewildered by my laughter.   45
I should see the sun flashing from his sword hilt and the buckles on his
        shoes.
I would choose
To lead him in a maze along the patterned paths,
A bright and laughing maze for my heavy-booted lover.
Till he caught me in the shade,   50
And the buttons of his waistcoat bruised my body as he clasped me
Aching, melting, unafraid.
With the shadows of the leaves and the sundrops,
And the plopping of the waterdrops,

All about us in the open afternoon—
I am very like to swoon
With the weight of this brocade,
For the sun sifts through the shade.

Underneath the fallen blossom
In my bosom,
Is a letter I have hid.
It was brought to me this morning by a rider from the Duke.[1]
"Madam, we regret to inform you that Lord Hartwell
Died in action Thursday se'nnight."[2]
As I read it in the white, morning sunlight,
The letters squirmed like snakes.
"Any answer, Madam," said my footman.
"No," I told him.
"See that the messenger takes some refreshment.
No, no answer."
And I walked into the garden,
Up and down the patterned paths,
In my stiff, correct brocade.
The blue and yellow flowers stood up proudly in the sun,
Each one.
I stood upright too,
Held rigid to the pattern
By the stiffness of my gown.
Up and down I walked,
Up and down.

In a month he would have been my husband.
In a month, here, underneath this lime,
We would have broke the pattern;
He for me, and I for him,
He as Colonel, I as Lady,
On this shady seat.
He had a whim
That sunlight carried blessing.
And I answered, "It shall be as you have said."
Now he is dead.

In Summer and in Winter I shall walk
Up and down
The patterned garden-paths
In my stiff, brocaded gown.
The squills and daffodils
Will give place to pillared roses, and to asters, and to snow.
I shall go

---

1. *the Duke,* probably John Churchill, Duke of Marlborough (1650-1722), commander of the united English and Dutch armies during the War of the Spanish Succession (1701-1714). The initial campaign was fought in Belgium and adjoining countries. **2.** *se'nnight,* an archaic word meaning a period of seven days and nights. Its meaning here is that Lord Hartwell died a week ago Thursday.

Up and down,
In my gown.
Gorgeously arrayed,
Boned and stayed.   100
And the softness of my body will be guarded from embrace
By each button, hook, and lace.
For the man who should loose me is dead,
Fighting with the Duke in Flanders,   105
In a pattern called a war.
Christ! What are patterns for?

BETTER READING

Setting

Since it helps us picture scenes and actions vividly, the setting—the representation of place and time in an imaginative work—can do much to make characters and actions real to us. And in handling setting, a skilled author can do far more than describe the physical background of a poem, drama, or short story. For setting can help shape the events that take place, aid the reader to understand the mood of a character or the twist of a plot, establish an emotional effect, and at times serve to underline the meaning of a story. Such uses of setting are called *functional*.

The selections you have previously read offer several examples of the functional use of setting. The plot of "The Enemy" gains plausibility through the setting of the story. Because on the particular evening on which the American appears from the sea there is a mist, because there is an island close to the shore, and because Sadao's home is isolated from the fishing villages, the reader finds it possible to believe that a wounded man could be washed ashore unseen by anyone but Sadao and his wife, and could later be helped to escape. In "Early Marriage" details of setting help create the atmosphere of tension in which Nancy Belle and Rife set off across the plains: "Bunches of bear grass that might have been feathers pinioned his blue gaze, and clumps of cane cactus that seemed to hold pointing gun barrels." Throughout the story the setting is described in words that echo the mood of the characters and help the reader share that mood.

Willa Cather handles her setting in "The Sculptor's Funeral" in such a way that Sand City is shown to be an entity that drives charity and integrity from this bleak huddle on the prairie. In a sense she almost makes the town a character—the *antagonist*. She heightens the sense of its ugliness by dwelling on the idyllic loveliness of the countryside: "The snow had fallen thick over everything; in the pale starlight the line of bluffs across the wide, white meadows south of the town made soft, smoke-colored curves against the clear sky." Again she writes, "the plains reached out into emptiness, peaceful and wide as the soft sky itself, and wrapped in a tangible, white silence." Contrasted with this is the town, which substitutes ugliness for beauty, raucousness for silence, and conflict for peace.

In "Patterns" details of setting are fused so intimately with the theme of the poem that they become an integral part of the whole.

1. This poem is laid in eighteenth-century England, a time when gardens laid out according to a formal pattern were very popular. (a) What descriptive details in the first stanza underline the fact that the woman speaking is walking in such a garden? (b) The speaker relates the patterned garden to herself by saying, "I too am a rare pattern." What does she mean?

2. (a) What is the season? (b) Why is this season most appropriate to the poem?

3. In line 83 the speaker says, "We would have broke the pattern." What does she mean?

4. Relate to the setting: (a) the message from the Duke; (b) the response of the lady to the rider from the Duke; (c) the war; (d) the lady's final exclamation.

5. "Patterns" is famous for the brilliance and clarity of its images, or word pictures. (a) Prepare to read to the class images you find particularly vivid. (b) What function does this word detail serve in making the poem believable?

● ● ● But what we really want to know is how I happened to write
the play: well, you must surely know there is no real answer,
an accurate answer isn't possible: a writer writes, period.
The rest is mystery, as the saying is. A man knows how to write
and he wants to write, or he must, and so he writes. The forms
vary, but it comes to the same thing: sitting there and putting
the stuff on paper. Among your students may be one or two who
are writers: they will write. And you may report to them if you
like that I don't even know grammar, since it is the truth.
I punctuate entirely on the basis of clarity, for instance.
Now, specific answers to your specific questions. (1) I happened
to write the play because I had a program of writing short plays
at that time. (2) It happened to be about a small town by the sea
because that's where I was living. (3) I frequently saw kids on
the beach excited about stuff they had found, and that may have
given me the idea of a kid finding an oyster, which in itself
is quite an event, although the California beaches have plenty
of mussels. I used to gather mussels off the rocks at low tide
and cook them and eat them. I once found an oyster myself, and
that may have figured in the play, for any oyster can mean the
hope of a pearl, since pearls come only from oysters. The barber
shop in the play is there because I like barber shops, and barbers,
and they figure in quite a few of my stories. The barber is a
kind of poet, and frequently slightly eccentric, certainly free
and independent when he owns and operates his own shop. The rest
is the consequence of the way I write in any case: the consequence
of myself. (4) The play took its own course, pretty much as all
of my writing does, once I have gone to work: a small boy, an
oyster, a barber, and soon a little of the whole world and all
of the human race is involved in the thing, somehow. I never knew
while I was writing precisely how the play was going to develop
and how it was going to end--because I was working, and I had
started and finished a lot of different pieces of work over the
years in precisely the same manner. Now, if there is an implication
here that something special and very important took place in the
writing of the little play, that is an accident entirely, and
the consequence of my trying to answer your questions. I do not
think it is astonishing that a writer writes. That's his work.
The astonishing thing is that he doesn't write better, most likely.
● ● ● I hope the foregoing proves useful to you, but most of all
to your students, and especially to the one or two who may be
writers. It's a good trade, in some ways almost as good as being
a barber.

William Saroyan

William Saroyan has won fame as short-story writer, novelist, and playwright. "The Daring Young Man on the Flying Trapeze" (1934) launched him on a successful career as a writer of short stories. His poignant story of family life, *The Human Comedy* (1942), established him as a successful novelist. And *The Time of Your Life* won a Pulitzer Prize for drama in 1940.

The son of Armenian parents, Saroyan was born in Fresno, California, in 1908. As a boy he was a voracious reader. At thirteen he left school and at one time or another worked as a telegraph messenger, newsboy, farm laborer, and office clerk. All of these experiences together with his reading supplied material for his short stories, novels, and plays. The excerpt from his letter on the preceding page sheds light on the writing of "The Oyster and the Pearl."

The Oyster and the Pearl

Characters

HARRY VAN DUSEN, *a barber*
CLAY LARRABEE, *a boy on Saturday*
VIVIAN MCCUTCHEON, *a new schoolteacher*
CLARK LARRABEE, CLAY'S *father*
MAN, *a writer*
ROXANNA LARRABEE, CLAY'S *sister*
GREELEY, CLAY'S *pal*
JUDGE APPLEGARTH, *a beachcomber*
WOZZECK, *a watch repairer*
ATTENDANT, *a man from the gasoline station*

"The Oyster and the Pearl" is reprinted from PERSPECTIVES 4, Summer 1953, by permission of the author. Copyright 1953 by William Saroyan. This play was first presented on February 4, 1953, on the TV-Radio Workshop's television program, OMNIBUS.

Scene: HARRY VAN DUSEN's *barbershop in O.K.-by-the-Sea, California, population 909. The sign on the window says:* Harry Van Dusen, Barber. *It's an old-fashioned shop, crowded with stuff not usually found in barbershops . . .* HARRY *himself, for instance. He has never been known to put on a barber's white jacket or to work without a hat of some sort on his head: a stovepipe, a derby, a western, a homburg, a skullcap, a beret, or a straw, as if putting on these various hats somewhat expressed the quality of his soul, or suggested the range of it.*

On the walls, on shelves, are many odds and ends, some apparently washed up by the sea, which is a block down the street: abalone and other shells, rocks, pieces of driftwood, a life jacket, rope, sea plants. There is one old-fashioned chair.

When the play begins, HARRY *is seated in the chair. A boy of nine or ten named* CLAY LARRABEE *is giving him a haircut.* HARRY *is reading a book, one of many in the shop.*

CLAY. Well, I did what you told me, Mr. Van Dusen. I hope it's all right. I'm no barber, though. *(He begins to comb the hair.)*

HARRY. You just gave me a haircut, didn't you?

CLAY. I don't know *what* you'd call it. You want to look at it in the mirror? *(He holds out a small mirror.)*

HARRY. No thanks. I remember the last one.

CLAY. I guess I'll never be a barber.

HARRY. Maybe not. On the other hand, you may turn out to be the one man hidden away in the junk of the world who will bring merriment to the tired old human heart.

CLAY. Who? Me?

HARRY. Why not?

CLAY. Merriment to the tired old human heart? How do you do that?

HARRY. Compose a symphony, paint a picture, write a book, invent a philosophy.

CLAY. Not me! Did you ever do stuff like that?

HARRY. I did.

CLAY. What did you do?

HARRY. Invented a philosophy.

CLAY. What's that?

HARRY. A way to live.

CLAY. What way did you invent?

HARRY. The *Take-it-easy way.*

CLAY. That sounds pretty good.

HARRY. All philosophies *sound* good. The trouble with mine was, I kept forgetting to take it easy. Until one day. The day I came off the highway into this barbershop. The barber told me the shop was for sale. I told him all I had to my name was eighty dollars. He sold me the shop for seventy-five, and threw in the haircut. I've been here ever since. That was twenty-four years ago.

CLAY. Before I was born.

HARRY. Fifteen or sixteen years before you were born.

CLAY. How old were you then?

HARRY. Old enough to know a good thing when I saw it.

CLAY. What did you see?

HARRY. O.K.-by-the-Sea, and this shop—the proper place for me to stop. That's a couplet. Shakespeare had them at the end of a scene, so I guess that's the end of this haircut. *(He gets out of the chair, goes to the hat tree, and puts on a derby.)*

CLAY. I guess I'd never get a haircut if you weren't in town, Mr. Van Dusen.

HARRY. Nobody would, since I'm the only barber.

CLAY. I mean, free of charge.

HARRY. I give you a haircut free of charge, you give me a haircut free of charge. That's fair and square.

CLAY. Yes, but you're a barber. You get a dollar a haircut.

HARRY. Now and then I do. Now and then I don't.

CLAY. Well, anyhow, thanks a lot. I guess I'll go down to the beach now and look for stuff.

HARRY. I'd go with you but I'm expecting a little Saturday business.

CLAY. This time I'm going to find something *real good*, I think.

HARRY. The sea washes up some pretty good things at that, doesn't it?

CLAY. It sure does, except money.

HARRY. What do you want with money?

CLAY. Things I need.

HARRY. What do you need?

CLAY. I want to get my father to come home again. I want to buy Mother a present...

HARRY. Now, wait a minute, Clay, let me get this straight. Where *is* your father?

CLAY. I don't know. He went off the day after I got my last haircut, about a month ago.

HARRY. What do you mean, he went off?

CLAY. He just picked up and went off.

HARRY. Did he say when he was coming back?

CLAY. No. All he said was, "Enough's enough." He wrote it on the kitchen wall.

HARRY. Enough's enough?

CLAY. Yeah. We all thought he'd be back in a day or two, but now we know we've got to *find* him and *bring* him back.

HARRY. How do you expect to do that?

CLAY. Well, we put an ad in *The O.K.-by-the-Sea Gull*...that comes out every Saturday.

HARRY *(opening the paper)*. This paper? But your father's not in town. How will he see an ad in this paper?

CLAY. He *might* see it. Anyhow, we don't know what else to do. We're living off the money we saved from the summer we worked, but there ain't much left.

HARRY. The summer you worked?

CLAY. Yeah. Summer before last, just before we moved here, we picked cotton in Kern County. My father, my mother, and me.

HARRY *(indicating the paper)*. What do you say in your ad?

CLAY *(looking at it)*. Well, I say...Clark Larrabee. Come home. Your fishing tackle's in the closet safe and sound. The fishing's good, plenty of cabezon, perch, and bass. Let bygones be bygones. We miss you. Mama, Clay, Roxanna, Rufus, Clara.

HARRY. That's a good ad.

CLAY. Do you think if my father reads it, he'll come home?

HARRY. I don't know, Clay. I hope so.

CLAY. Yeah. Thanks a lot for the haircut, Mr. Van Dusen.

(CLAY goes out. HARRY takes off the derby, lathers his face, and begins to shave with a straight-edge razor. A pretty girl in a swimming suit comes into the shop, closing a colorful parasol. She has long blond hair.)

HARRY. Miss America, I presume.

THE GIRL. Miss McCutcheon.

HARRY. Harry Van Dusen.

THE GIRL. How do you do.

HARRY *(bowing)*. Miss McCutcheon.

THE GIRL. I'm new here.

HARRY. You'd be new anywhere—brand-new, I might say. Surely you don't live here?

THE GIRL. As a matter of fact, I do. At any rate, I've been here since last Sunday. You see, I'm the new teacher at the school.

HARRY. You are?

THE GIRL. Yes, I am.

HARRY. How do you like it?

THE GIRL. One week at this school has knocked me for a loop. As a matter of fact, I want to quit and go home to San Francisco. At the same time I have a feeling I ought to stay. What do you think?

HARRY. Are you serious? I mean, in asking me?

THE GIRL. Of course I'm serious. You've been here a long time. You know everybody in town. Shall I go, or shall I stay?

HARRY. Depends on what you're looking for. I stopped here twenty-four years ago because I decided I wasn't looking for anything any more. Well, I was mistaken. I *was* looking, and I've found exactly what I was looking for.

THE GIRL. What's that?

HARRY. A chance to take my time. That's

why I'm still here. What are *you* looking for, Miss McCutcheon?

THE GIRL. Well…

HARRY. I mean, besides a husband…

THE GIRL. I'm not looking for a husband. I expect a husband to look for me.

HARRY. That's fair.

THE GIRL. I'm looking for a chance to teach.

HARRY. That's fair too.

THE GIRL. But this town!…The children just don't seem to care about anything—whether they get good grades or bad, whether they pass or fail, or anything else. On top of that, almost all of them are unruly. The only thing they seem to be interested in is games, and the sea. That's why I'm on my way to the beach now. I thought if I could watch them on a Saturday I might understand them better.

HARRY. Yes, that's a thought.

THE GIRL. Nobody seems to have any sensible ambition. It's all fun and play. How can I teach children like that? What can I teach them?

HARRY. English.

THE GIRL. Of course.

HARRY *(drying his face)*. Singing, dancing, cooking…

THE GIRL. Cooking?…I must say I expected to see a much older man.

HARRY. Well! Thank you!

THE GIRL. Not at all.

HARRY. The question is, Shall you stay, or shall you go back to San Francisco?

THE GIRL. Yes.

HARRY. The answer is, Go back while the going's good.

THE GIRL. Why? I mean, a moment ago I believed you were going to point out why I ought to stay, and then suddenly you say I ought to go back. Why?

HARRY *(after a pause)*. You're too good for a town like this.

THE GIRL. I am not!

HARRY. Too young and too intelligent. Youth and intelligence need excitement.

THE GIRL. There are *kinds* of excitement.

HARRY. Yes, there are. You need the big-city kind. There isn't an eligible bachelor in town.

THE GIRL. You seem to think all I want is to find a husband.

HARRY. But only to teach. You want to teach him to become a father, so you can have a lot of children of your own—to teach.

THE GIRL. *(She sits almost angrily in the chair and speaks very softly.)* I'd like a poodle haircut if you don't mind, Mr. Van Dusen.

HARRY. You'll have to get that in San Francisco, I'm afraid.

THE GIRL. Why? Aren't you a barber?

HARRY. I am.

THE GIRL. Well, this is your shop. It's open for business. I'm a customer. I've got money. I want a poodle haircut.

HARRY. I don't know how to give a poodle haircut, but even if I knew how, I wouldn't do it.

THE GIRL. Why not?

HARRY. I don't give women haircuts. The only women who visit this shop bring their small children for haircuts.

THE GIRL. I want a poodle haircut, Mr. Van Dusen.

HARRY. I'm sorry, Miss McCutcheon. In my sleep, in a nightmare, I would *not* cut your hair.

(The sound of a truck stopping is heard from across the street.)

THE GIRL *(softly, patiently, but firmly)*. Mr. Van Dusen, I've decided to stay, and the first thing I've got to do is change my appearance. I don't fit into the scenery around here.

HARRY. Oh, I don't know—if I were a small boy going to school, I'd say you look just right.

THE GIRL. You're just like the children. They don't take me seriously, either. They think I'm nothing more than a pretty girl who is going to give up in despair and go home. If you give me a poodle haircut I'll look more—well, plain and simple. I plan to dress differently, too. I'm determined to teach here. You've got to help me. Now, Mr. Van Dusen, the shears, please.

HARRY. I'm sorry, Miss McCutcheon. There's no need to change your *appearance* at all.

(CLARK LARRABEE *comes into the shop.*)

HARRY. You're next, Clark. (HARRY *helps* MISS MCCUTCHEON *out of the chair. She gives him an angry glance.*)

THE GIRL (*whispering*). I won't forget this rudeness, Mr. Van Dusen.

HARRY (*also whispering*). Never whisper in O.K.-by-the-Sea. People misunderstand. (*Loudly.*) Good day, Miss.

(MISS MCCUTCHEON *opens her parasol with anger and leaves the shop.* CLARK LARRABEE *has scarcely noticed her. He stands looking at* HARRY'S *junk on the shelves.*)

HARRY. Well, Clark, I haven't seen you in a long time.

CLARK. I'm just passing through, Harry. Thought I might run into Clay here.

HARRY. He was here a little while ago.

CLARK. How is he?

HARRY. He's fine, Clark.

CLARK. I been working in Salinas. Got a ride down in a truck. It's across the street now at the gasoline station.

HARRY. You've been home, of course?

CLARK. No, I haven't.

HARRY. Oh?

CLARK (*after a slight pause*). I've left Fay, Harry.

HARRY. You got time for a haircut, Clark?

CLARK. No thanks, Harry. I've got to go back to Salinas on that truck across the street.

HARRY. Clay's somewhere on the beach.

CLARK (*handing* HARRY *three ten-dollar bills*). Give him this, will you? Thirty dollars. Don't tell him I gave it to you.

HARRY. Why not?

CLARK. I'd rather he didn't know I was around. Is he all right?

HARRY. Sure, Clark. They're *all* O.K. I mean...

CLARK. Tell him to take the money home to his mother. (*He picks up the newspaper,* The Gull.)

HARRY. Sure, Clark. It came out this morning. Take it along.

CLARK. Thanks. (*He puts the paper in his pocket.*) How've things been going with *you*, Harry?

HARRY. Oh, I can't kick. Two or three haircuts a day. A lot of time to read. A few laughs. A few surprises. The sea. The fishing. It's a good life.

CLARK. Keep an eye on Clay, will you? I mean—well, I *had* to do it.

HARRY. Sure.

CLARK. Yeah, well...That's the first money I've been able to save. When I make some more, I'd like to send it here, so you can hand it to Clay, to take home.

HARRY. Anything you say, Clark.

(*There is the sound of the truck's horn blowing.*)

CLARK. Well...(*He goes to the door.*) Thanks, Harry, thanks a lot.

HARRY. Good seeing you, Clark.

(CLARK LARRABEE *goes out.* HARRY *watches him. A truck shifting gears is heard, and then the sound of the truck driving off.* HARRY *picks up a book, changes hats, sits down in the chair and begins to read. A* MAN *of forty or so, well dressed, rather swift, comes in.*)

THE MAN. Where's the barber?

HARRY. I'm the barber.

THE MAN. Can I get a haircut, real quick?

HARRY (*getting out of the chair*). Depends on what you mean by real quick.

THE MAN (*sitting down*). Well, just a haircut, then.

HARRY (*putting an apron around the* MAN). O.K. I don't believe I've seen you before.

THE MAN. No. They're changing the oil in my car across the street. Thought I'd step in here and get a haircut. Get it out of the way before I get to Hollywood. How many miles is it?

HARRY. About two hundred straight down the highway. You can't miss it.

THE MAN. What town is *this?*

HARRY. O.K.-by-the-Sea.

THE MAN. What do the people do here?

HARRY. Well, I cut hair. Friend of mine named Wozzeck repairs watches, radios, alarm clocks, and sells jewelry.

THE MAN. Who does he sell it to?

HARRY. The people here. It's imitation stuff mainly.

THE MAN. Factory here? Farms? Fishing?

HARRY. No. Just the few stores on the highway, the houses further back in the hills, the church, and the school. You a salesman?

THE MAN. No, I'm a writer.

HARRY. What do you write?

THE MAN. A little bit of everything. How about the haircut?

HARRY. You got to be in Hollywood to-night?

THE MAN. I don't have to be anywhere tonight, but that was the idea. Why?

HARRY. Well, I've always said a writer could step into a place like this, watch things a little while, and get a whole book out of it, or a play.

THE MAN. Or if he was a poet, a sonnet.

HARRY. Do you like Shakespeare's?

THE MAN. They're just about the best in English.

HARRY. It's not often I get a writer in here. As a matter of fact you're the only writer I've had in here in twenty years, not counting Fenton.

THE MAN. Who's he?

HARRY. Fenton Lockhart.

THE MAN. What's he write?

HARRY. He gets out the weekly paper. Writes the whole thing himself.

THE MAN. Yeah. Well...How about the haircut?

HARRY. O.K.

(HARRY *puts a hot towel around the man's head.* MISS MC CUTCHEON, *carrying a cane chair without one leg and without a seat, comes in. With her is* CLAY *with something in his hand, a smaller boy named* GREELEY *with a bottle of sea water, and* ROXANNA *with an assortment of shells.*)

CLAY. I got an oyster here, Mr. Van Dusen.

GREELEY. Miss McCutcheon claims there *ain't* a big pearl in it.

HARRY (*looking at* MISS MC CUTCHEON). Is she willing to admit there's a *little* one in it?

GREELEY. I don't know. I know I got sea water in this bottle.

MISS MC CUTCHEON. Mr. Van Dusen, Clay Larrabee seems to believe there's a pearl in this oyster he happens to have found on the beach.

CLAY. I didn't *happen* to find it. I went looking for it. You know Black Rock, Mr. Van Dusen? Well, the tide hardly ever gets low enough for a fellow to get around to the ocean side of Black Rock, but a little while ago it did, so I went around there to that side. I got to poking around and I found this oyster.

HARRY. I've been here twenty-four years, Clay, and this is the first time I've ever heard of anybody finding an oyster on our beach—at Black Rock, or anywhere else.

CLAY. Well, *I* did, Mr. Van Dusen. It's shut tight, it's alive, and there's a pearl in it, worth at least three hundred dollars.

GREELEY. A *big* pearl.

MISS MC CUTCHEON. Now, you children listen to me. It's never too soon for any of us to face the truth, which is supposed to set us free, not imprison us. The truth is, Clay, you want money because you need money. The truth is also that you have found an oyster. The truth is also that there is no pearl in the oyster.

GREELEY. How do you know? Did you look?

MISS MC CUTCHEON. No, but neither did Clay, and inasmuch as only one oyster in a million has a pearl in it, truth favors the probability that this is not the millionth oyster...the oyster with the pearl in it.

CLAY. There's a *big* pearl in the oyster.

MISS MC CUTCHEON. Mr. Van Dusen, shall we open the oyster and show Clay and his sister Roxanna and their friend Greeley that there is no pearl in it?

HARRY. In a moment, Miss McCutcheon. And what's that *you* have?

MISS MC CUTCHEON. A chair, as you see.

HARRY. How many legs does it have?

MISS MC CUTCHEON. Three of course. I can count to three, I hope.

HARRY. What do you want with a chair with only three legs?

MISS MC CUTCHEON. I'm going to bring things from the sea the same as everybody else in town.

HARRY. But everybody else in town *doesn't* bring things from the sea—just the children, Judge Applegarth, Fenton Lockhart, and myself.

MISS MC CUTCHEON. In any case, the same as the children, Judge Applegarth, Fenton Lockhart, and you. Judge Applegarth? Who's he?

HARRY. He judged swine at a county fair one time, so we call him Judge.

MISS MC CUTCHEON. Pigs?

HARRY. Swine's a little old-fashioned but I prefer it to pigs, and since both words mean the same thing——Well, I wouldn't care to call a man like Arthur Applegarth a pig judge.

MISS MC CUTCHEON. Did he actually judge swine, as you prefer to put it, at a county fair, one time? Did he even do *that*?

HARRY. Nobody checked up. He *said* he did.

MISS MC CUTCHEON. So that entitled him to be called Judge Applegarth?

HARRY. It certainly did.

MISS MC CUTCHEON. On that basis, Clay's oyster has a big pearl in it because he *says* so, is that it?

HARRY. I didn't say that.

MISS MC CUTCHEON. Are we living in the Middle Ages, Mr. Van Dusen?

GREELEY. No, this is 1953, Miss McCutcheon.

MISS MC CUTCHEON. Yes, Greeley, and to illustrate what I mean, that's water you have in that bottle. Nothing else.

GREELEY. *Sea* water.

MISS MC CUTCHEON. Yes, but there's nothing else in the bottle.

GREELEY. No, but there's little things in the water. You can't see them now, but they'll show up later. The water of the sea is full of things.

MISS MC CUTCHEON. Salt, perhaps.

GREELEY. No. *Living* things. If I look hard I can see some of them now.

MISS MC CUTCHEON. You can *imagine* seeing them. Mr. Van Dusen, are you going to help me or not?

HARRY. What do you want me to do?

MISS MC CUTCHEON. Open the oyster of course, so Clay will see for himself that there's no pearl in it. So he'll begin to face reality, as he should, as each of us should.

HARRY. Clay, do you mind if I look at the oyster a minute?

CLAY (*handing the oyster to* HARRY). There's a big pearl in it, Mr. Van Dusen.

HARRY (*examining the oyster*). Clay... Roxanna...Greeley...I wonder if you'd go down the street to Wozzeck's. Tell him to come here the first chance he gets. I'd rather he opened this oyster. I might damage the pearl.

CLAY, GREELEY, *and* ROXANNA. O.K., Mr. Van Dusen.

(*They go out*)

MISS MC CUTCHEON. What pearl? What in the world do you think you're trying to do to the minds of these children? How am I ever going to teach them the principles of truth with an influence like yours to fight against?

HARRY. Miss McCutcheon. The people of O.K.-by-the-Sea are all poor. Most of them can't afford to pay for the haircuts I give them. There's no excuse for this town at all, but the sea is here, and so are the hills. A few people find jobs a couple of months every year North or South, come back half dead of homesickness, and live on next to nothing the rest of the year. A few get pensions. Every family has a garden and a few chickens, and they make a few dollars selling vegetables and eggs. In a town of almost a thousand people there isn't one rich man. Not even one who is well-off. And yet these people are the richest I have ever known. Clay doesn't really want money, as you seem to think. He wants his father to come home, and he thinks money will help get his father home. As a matter of fact his father is the man who stepped in here just as you were leaving. He left thirty dollars for me to give to Clay, to take home. His father and his mother haven't been getting along. Clark Larrabee's a fine man. He's not the town drunk or anything like that, but having four kids to provide for he gets to feeling ashamed of the showing he's making, and he starts drinking. He wants his kids to live in a good house of their own, wear good clothes, and all the other things fathers have always wanted for their kids. His wife wants these things for the kids, too. They don't have these things, so they fight. They had one too many fights about a month ago, so Clark went off—he's working in Salinas. He's either going to keep moving away from his family, or he's going to come back. It all depends on— well, I don't know what. This oyster maybe. Clay maybe. (*Softly.*) You and me maybe.

(*There is a pause. He looks at the oyster. MISS MC CUTCHEON looks at it, too.*)

HARRY. Clay believes there's a pearl in this oyster for the same reason you and I believe whatever *we* believe to keep *us* going.

MISS MC CUTCHEON. Are you suggesting we play a trick on Clay, in order to carry out your mumbo-jumbo ideas?

HARRY. Well, maybe it *is* a trick. I know Wozzeck's got a few pretty good-sized cultivated pearls.

MISS MC CUTCHEON. You plan to have Wozzeck pretend he has found a pearl in the oyster when he opens it, is that it?

HARRY. I plan to get three hundred dollars to Clay.

MISS MC CUTCHEON. Do you *have* three hundred dollars?

HARRY. Not quite.

MISS MC CUTCHEON. What about the other children who need money? Do you plan to put pearls in oysters for them, too? Not just here in O.K.-by-the-Sea. Everywhere. This isn't the only town in the world where people are poor, where fathers and mothers fight, where families break up.

HARRY. No, it isn't, but it's the only town where I live.

MISS MC CUTCHEON. I give up. What do you want me to do?

HARRY. Well, could you find it in your heart to be just a little less sure about things when you talk to the kids—I mean, the troubled ones? You can get Clay around to the truth easy enough just as soon as he gets his father home.

(ARTHUR APPLEGARTH *comes in.*)

HARRY. Judge Applegarth, may I present Miss McCutcheon?

THE JUDGE (*removing his hat and bowing low*). An honor, Miss.

MISS MC CUTCHEON. How do you do, Judge.

HARRY. Miss McCutcheon's the new teacher at the school.

THE JUDGE. We are honored to have you. The children, the parents, and—the rest of us.

MISS MC CUTCHEON. Thank you, Judge. (*To HARRY, whispering.*) I'll be back as soon as I change my clothes.

HARRY (*whispering*). I told you not to whisper.

MISS MC CUTCHEON (*whispering*). I shall expect you to give me a poodle haircut.

HARRY (whispering). Are you out of your mind?

MISS MC CUTCHEON (aloud). Good day, Judge.

THE JUDGE (bowing). Good day, Miss. (While he is bent over he takes a good look at her knees, calves, ankles, and bow-tied sandals.)

(MISS MC CUTCHEON goes out. JUDGE APPLEGARTH looks from the door to HARRY.)

THE JUDGE. She won't last a month.

HARRY. Why not?

THE JUDGE. Too pretty. Our school needs an old battle-ax, like the teachers we had when we went to school, not a bathing beauty. Well, Harry, what's new?

HARRY. Just the teacher, I guess.

THE JUDGE. You know, Harry, the beach isn't what it used to be—not at all. I don't mind the competition we're getting from the kids. It's just that the quality of the stuff the sea's washing up isn't good any more. (Goes to door.)

HARRY. I don't know. Clay Larrabee found an oyster this morning.

THE JUDGE. He did? Well, one oyster don't make a stew, Harry. On my way home I'll drop in and let you see what I find.

HARRY. O.K., Judge.

(The JUDGE goes out. HARRY comes to life suddenly and becomes businesslike.)

HARRY. Now, for the haircut! (He removes the towel he had wrapped around the WRITER's head.)

THE WRITER. Take your time.

HARRY. (He examines the shears, clippers, and combs.) Let's see now.

(The WRITER turns and watches. A gasoline station ATTENDANT comes to the door.)

THE ATTENDANT (to the WRITER). Just wanted to say your car's ready now.

THE WRITER. Thanks.

(The ATTENDANT goes out.)

THE WRITER. Look. I'll tell you what. How much is a haircut?

HARRY. Well, the regular price is a dollar.

It's too much for a haircut, though, so I generally take a half or a quarter.

THE WRITER (getting out of the chair). I've changed my mind. I don't want a haircut after all, but here's a dollar just the same. (He hands HARRY a dollar, and he himself removes the apron.)

HARRY. It won't take a minute.

THE WRITER. I know.

HARRY. You don't have to pay me a dollar for a hot towel. My compliments.

THE WRITER. That's O.K. (He goes to the door.)

HARRY. Well, take it easy now.

THE WRITER. Thanks. (He stands a moment, thinking, then turns.) Do you mind if I have a look at that oyster?

HARRY. Not at all.

(The WRITER goes to the shelf where HARRY has placed the oyster, picks it up, looks at it thoughtfully, puts it back without comment, but instead of leaving the shop he looks around at the stuff in it. He then sits down on a wicker chair in the corner, and lights a cigarette.)

THE WRITER. You know, they've got a gadget in New York now like a safety razor that anybody can give anybody else a haircut with.

HARRY. They have?

THE WRITER. Yeah, there was a full-page ad about it in last Sunday's Times.

HARRY. Is that where you were last Sunday?

THE WRITER. Yeah.

HARRY. You been doing a lot of driving.

THE WRITER. I like to drive. I don't know, though—those gadgets don't always work. They're asking two-ninety-five for it. You take a big family. The father could save a lot of money giving his kids a haircut.

HARRY. Sounds like a great idea.

THE WRITER. Question of effectiveness. If the father gives the boy a haircut the boy's ashamed of, well, that's not so good.

HARRY. No, a boy likes to get a professional-looking haircut all right.

THE WRITER. I thought I'd buy one, but I don't know.

HARRY. You got a big family?

THE WRITER. I mean for myself. But I don't know—there's something to be said for going to a barbershop once in a while. No use putting the barbers out of business.

HARRY. Sounds like a pretty good article, though.

THE WRITER (getting up lazily). Well, it's been nice talking to you.

(WOZZECK, carrying a satchel, comes in, followed by CLAY, ROXANNA, and GREELEY.)

WOZZECK. What's this all about, Harry?

HARRY. I've got an oyster I want you to open.

WOZZECK. That's what the kids have been telling me.

ROXANNA. He doesn't believe there's a pearl in the oyster, either.

WOZZECK. Of course not! What foolishness!

CLAY. There's a big pearl in it.

WOZZECK. O.K., give me the oyster. I'll open it. Expert watch repairer, to open an oyster!

HARRY. How much is a big pearl worth, Louie?

WOZZECK. Oh, a hundred. Two hundred, maybe.

HARRY. A very big one?

WOZZECK. Three, maybe.

THE WRITER. I've looked at that oyster, and I'd like to buy it. (To CLAY.) How much do you want for it?

CLAY. I don't know.

THE WRITER. How about three hundred?

GREELEY. Three hundred dollars?

CLAY. Is it all right, Mr. Van Dusen?

HARRY. (He looks at the WRITER, who nods.) Sure it's all right.

(The WRITER hands CLAY the money.)

CLAY (looking at the money and then at the WRITER). But suppose there ain't a pearl in it?

THE WRITER. There is, though.

WOZZECK. Don't you want to open it first?

THE WRITER. No, I want the whole thing. I don't think the pearl's stopped growing.

CLAY. He says there is a pearl in the oyster, Mr. Van Dusen.

HARRY. I think there is, too, Clay; so why don't you just go on home and give the money to your mother?

CLAY. Well...I knew I was going to find something good today!

(The children go out. WOZZECK is bewildered.)

WOZZECK. Three hundred dollars! How do you know there's a pearl in it?

THE WRITER. As far as I'm concerned, the whole thing's a pearl.

WOZZECK (a little confused). Well, I got to get back to the shop, Harry.

HARRY. Thanks for coming by.

(WOZZECK goes out. The WRITER holds the oyster in front of him as if it were an egg, and looks at it carefully, turning it in his fingers. As he is doing so, CLARK LARRABEE comes into the shop. He is holding the copy of the newspaper that HARRY gave him.)

CLARK. We were ten miles up the highway when I happened to see this classified ad in the paper. (He hands the paper to HARRY and sits down in the chair.) I'm going out to the house, after all. Just for the weekend of course, then back to work in Salinas again. Two or three months, I think I'll have enough to come back for a long time. Clay come by?

HARRY. No. I've got the money here.

CLARK. O.K., I'll take it out myself, but first let me have the works—shave, haircut, shampoo, massage.

HARRY (putting an apron on CLARK). Sure thing, Clark. (He bends the chair back, and begins to lather CLARK's face.)

(MISS MC CUTCHEON, dressed neatly, looking like another person almost, comes in.)

MISS MC CUTCHEON. Well?

HARRY. You look fine, Miss McCutcheon.

MISS MCCUTCHEON. I don't mean that. I mean the oyster.

HARRY. Oh, that! There *was* a pearl in it.

MISS MCCUTCHEON. I don't believe it.

HARRY. A *big* pearl.

MISS MCCUTCHEON. You might have done me the courtesy of waiting until I had come back before opening it.

HARRY. Couldn't wait.

MISS MCCUTCHEON. Well, I don't believe you, but I've come for my haircut. I'll sit down and wait my turn.

HARRY. Mr. Larrabee wants the works. You'll have to wait a long time.

MISS MCCUTCHEON. Mr. Larrabee? Clay's father? Roxanna's father?

(CLARK *sits up.*)

HARRY. Clark, I'd like you to meet our new teacher, Miss McCutcheon.

CLARK. How do you do.

MISS MCCUTCHEON. How do you do, Mr. Larrabee. (*She looks bewildered.*) Well, perhaps some other time, then, Mr. Van Dusen.

(*She goes out.* CLARK *sits back.* JUDGE APPLEGARTH *stops at the doorway of the shop.*)

THE JUDGE. Not one thing on the beach, Harry. Not a blessed thing worth picking up and taking home.

(JUDGE APPLEGARTH *goes on. The* WRITER *looks at* HARRY.)

HARRY. See what I mean?

THE WRITER. Yeah. Well...so long. (*He puts the oyster in his coat pocket.*)

HARRY. Drop in again any time you're driving to Hollywood.

THE WRITER. Or away.

(*He goes out.*)

CLARK (*after a moment*). You know, Harry, that boy of mine, Clay . . . well, a fellow like that, you can't just go off and leave him.

HARRY. Of course you can't, Clark.

CLARK. I'm taking him fishing tomorrow morning. How about going along, Harry?

HARRY. Sure, Clark. Be like old times again. (*There is a pause.*)

CLARK. What's all this about an oyster and a pearl?

HARRY. Oh, just having a little fun with the new teacher. You know, she came in here and asked me to give her a poodle haircut? A poodle haircut! I don't believe I remember what a poodle *dog* looks like, even.

BETTER READING
Theme

Sometimes years after we have read a story, a poem, or a play, it again flashes into mind. With most of the details erased by time, a strong general impression still remains. In recalling "The Enemy," for example, we may find that we have forgotten the names of the characters and the intricacies of the plot, but we remember that in this story an individual shows that the healing code of a doctor is more important than national prejudice. Similarly, a poem like "Auto Wreck" may leave in our memories only a feeling of the horror and apparent futility of sudden death. What we are recalling is the *theme*, the basic idea that underlies a piece of imaginative literature and gives it a meaning larger than the work itself.

Some imaginative works written purely to entertain, to suggest a single impression, or to create a mood or an emotion may be said not to have a theme. But many literary works have a purpose deeper than the mere telling—a theme, a concept which is developed memorably.

Neither poet nor prose writer ever regards the expression of a theme as his total purpose in writing. In fact, as far as poetry is concerned, probably only a very poor poet would start with a theme and try to weave a poem around it. Karl Shapiro's account of the writing of "Auto Wreck" (page 20) and Robert Penn Warren's letter on the composition of "Court-Martial" (page 48) probably come close to expressing the manner in which most poems develop. From a startling impact, from an unexpected glimpse of beauty, from any aspect of living that awakens the imagination and arouses the emotions, the poem grows with the theme as its core. The reader, shocked into awareness by the poet's emotion, perceives the general idea behind the specific details, and so grasps the theme.

How does theme develop in a story or a play? In some cases the author has a comment on life to make. He feels this comment to be significant and true. To communicate it to the reader, he creates in his imagination a segment of life so appealing to our senses, our emotions, and our imaginations that we too may feel its significance and truth. But not all themes develop in this way. Sometimes an author creates a character who seems to grow just as a living person does, and from the personality of this imaginative character the theme develops. Occasionally a setting may suggest a theme. From reading Conrad Richter's letter (page 4), can you gain any idea of how the theme of "Early Marriage" developed?

The theme of a story or play may be thought of as its skeleton; the setting, characters, and action as its living flesh and blood. Sometimes the reader confuses *plot* with *theme*, forgetting that plot has relation only to a particular story while theme is the basic idea to be abstracted from the fusion of plot, characters, and setting. In many stories the theme is relatively easy to find. But sometimes, as in William Saroyan's "The Oyster and the Pearl," the reader is left wondering just what meaning the author is trying to bring out. Using the following questions, try your skill at figuring out the theme of this play.

1. In the opening scene Harry Van Dusen tells Clay that he "may turn out to be the one man hidden away in the junk of the world who will bring merriment to the tired old human heart." Explain how this description actually characterizes Van Dusen himself.

2. *(a)* Contrast Miss McCutcheon's and Mr. Van Dusen's attitudes toward life, pointing out specific speeches throughout the play which express their philosophies. *(b)* How does the oyster bring these two philosophies into focus? *(c)* What additional viewpoints are revealed by the attitudes of Wozzeck, the Judge, Greeley, and the Writer?

3. Why does the author never reveal whether or not there is an actual pearl in the oyster?

4. Use the clues you have gained from answering the preceding questions to work out your own statement of the theme of "The Oyster and the Pearl." The excerpt from Saroyan's letter on page 56 may give you additional help.

Conrad Aiken was born in Savannah, Georgia, in 1889. When he was nine years old, he went to Massachusetts to live with a great aunt. He attended Harvard University, and several years later his first book of poetry, *Earth Triumphant and Other Tales in Verse* (1914), was published. In all the years from that time to the present he has exerted a strong influence on American letters. In 1929 he was awarded the Pulitzer Prize for *Selected Poems*. In 1950-1951 he held the Library of Congress Chair of Poetry. In 1953 his *Collected Poems* won the National Book Award.

In answer to a question about "One Star Fell and Another," Aiken writes: "... it is No. LVII of a series of poems, *Preludes for Memnon*, and only acquired a title when it was anthologized. But I have no particular recollection about the composition of this particular unit of the sixty-three that composed the book—after all, that was thirty years ago! And anyway, what one feels before or after writing a poem seems to me immaterial: to the extent that a poem is successful, isn't it self-explanatory?"

One Star Fell and Another

One star fell and another as we walked.
Lifting his hand toward the west, he said—
—How prodigal that sky is of its stars!
They fall and fall, and still the sky is sky.
Two more have gone, but heaven is heaven still.   5

Then let us not be precious of our thought,
Nor of our words, nor hoard them up as though
We thought our minds a heaven which might change
And lose its virtue when the word had fallen.
Let us be prodigal, as heaven is;   10
Lose what we lose, and give what we may give,—
Ourselves are still the same. Lost you a planet—?
Is Saturn gone? Then let him take his rings
Into the Limbo of forgotten things.

O little foplings of the pride of mind,   15
Who wrap the phrase in lavender, and keep it
In order to display it: and you, who save our loves
As if we had not worlds of love enough—!

Let us be reckless of our words and worlds,
And spend them freely as the tree his leaves;   20
And give them where the giving is most blest.
What should we save them for,—a night of frost? . . .
All lost for nothing, and ourselves a ghost.

TO INCREASE UNDERSTANDING

1. (a) State in your own words the theme of the poem. (b) What comparisons does the poet use to develop this theme?

2. The article "The Language of Poetry" (page 21) states that a poem is usually "the communication of a feeling as well as of a thought" and that to express both thought and feeling the poet makes use of figurative language and of words rich in connotation. (a) Cite words or phrases from the poem which are rich in connotation. (b) Cite examples of figurative language which help you understand the poet's mood or meaning.

"One Star Fell and Another" is reprinted from Collected Poems by Conrad Aiken, by permission of Oxford University Press, New York. Copyright 1953 by Conrad Aiken.

CONRAD AIKEN 69

In 1930 Sinclair Lewis became the first American to receive the Nobel Prize—"for his powerful and vivid art of description, and his ability to use wit and humor in the creation of original characters." Thus Lewis rounded out a decade during which he was acknowledged the foremost man of letters in the United States. He had risen to sudden fame ten years earlier with the publication of *Main Street* (1920), a novel that satirized the stupidity and ignorance of the typical American small town. *Babbitt* (1922), a satirical portrait of George Follansbee Babbitt, realtor extraordinary, added to his fame. *Arrowsmith* (1925), the story of a young doctor who struggles against the quacks and charlatans of science and medicine, won him the Pulitzer Prize in 1926. Several other novels including *Dodsworth* (1929) were published during this ten years of magnificent production. Although Lewis continued to write until his death in 1951, he never again attained the peak he had reached in the 1920's.

Sinclair Lewis was born in Sauk Center, Minnesota, the son of a country doctor. Restless and energetic, he interrupted his studies at Yale University to free lance in New York. Later he wandered about the country working on various newspapers and continuously trying to write. He had published five conventional and mediocre novels before *Main Street* showed for the first time his great gifts: his storytelling ability, his flair for mimicry of speech, his powers of photographic description, and humor which ranged from gentle irony to biting satire.

The Hack Driver

I dare say there's no man of large affairs, whether he is bank president or senator or dramatist, who hasn't a sneaking love for some old rum-hound in a frightful hat, living back in a shanty and making his living by ways you wouldn't care to examine too closely. (It was the Supreme Court justice speaking. I do not pretend to guarantee his theories or his story.) He may be a Maine guide, or the old garageman who used to keep the livery stable, or a perfectly useless innkeeper who sneaks off to shoot ducks when he ought to be sweeping the floors, but your pompous big-city man will contrive to get back and see him every year, and loaf with him, and secretly prefer him to all the highfalutin leaders of the city.

There's that much truth, at least, to this Open Spaces stuff you read in advertisements of wild and woolly Western novels. I don't know the philosophy of it; perhaps it means that we retain a decent simplicity, no matter how much we are tied to Things, to houses and motors and expensive wives. Or again it may give away the whole game of civilization; may mean that the apparently civilized man is at heart nothing but a hobo who prefers flannel shirts and bristly cheeks and cussing and dirty tin plates to all the trim, hygienic, forward-looking life our womenfolks make us put on for them.

When I graduated from law school, I suppose I was about as artificial and idiotic and ambitious as most youngsters. I wanted to climb, socially and financially. I wanted to be famous, and dine at large houses with men who shuddered at the Common People who don't dress for dinner. You see, I hadn't learned that the only thing duller than a polite dinner is the conversation afterward; when the victims are digesting the dinner

and accumulating enough strength to be able to play bridge. Oh, I was a fine young calf! I even planned a rich marriage. Imagine then how I felt when, after taking honors and becoming fifteenth assistant clerk in the magnificent law firm of Hodgins, Hodgins, Berkman, and Taupe, I was set not at preparing briefs but at serving summonses! Like a cheap private detective! Like a mangy sheriff's officer! They told me I had to begin that way and, holding my nose, I feebly went to work. I was kicked out of actresses' dressing rooms, and from time to time I was righteously beaten by large and indignant litigants. I came to know, and still more to hate, every dirty and shadowy corner of the city. I thought of fleeing to my home town, where I could at once become a full-fledged attorney at law. I rejoiced one day when they sent me out forty miles or so to a town called New Mullion, to serve a summons on one Oliver Lutkins. This Lutkins had worked in the Northern Woods, and he knew the facts about a certain timberland boundary agreement; we needed him as a witness, and he had dodged service.

When I got off the train at New Mullion, my sudden affection for sweet and simple villages was dashed by the look of the place, with its mud-gushing streets and its rows of shops either paintless or daubed with a sour brown. Though it must have numbered eight or nine thousand inhabitants, New Mullion was as littered as a mining camp. There was one agreeable-looking man at the station—the expressman. He was a person of perhaps forty, red-faced, cheerful, thick; he wore his overalls and denim jumper as though they belonged to him; he was quite dirty and very friendly, and you knew at once that he liked people and slapped them on the back out of pure easy affection.

"I want," I told him, "to find a fellow named Oliver Lutkins."

"Him? I saw him 'round here 'twa'n't an hour ago. Hard fellow to catch, though—always chasing around on some phony business or other. Probably trying to get up a poker game in the back of Fritz Beineke's harness-shop. I'll tell you, boy—Any hurry about locating Lutkins?"

"Yes. I want to catch the afternoon train back." I was as impressively secret as a stage detective.

"I'll tell you. I've got a hack. I'll get out the old boneshaker, and we can drive around together and find Lutkins. I know most of the places he hangs out."

He was so frankly friendly, he so immediately took me into the circle of his affection, that I glowed with the warmth of it. I knew, of course, that he was drumming up business, but his kindness was real, and if I had to pay hack fare in order to find my man, I was glad that the money would go to this good fellow. I got him down to two dollars an hour; he brought from his cottage, a block away, an object like a black piano-box on wheels.

He didn't hold the door open, certainly he didn't say: "Ready, sir." I think he would have died before calling anybody "sir." When he gets to Heaven's gate he'll call St. Peter "Pete," and I imagine the good saint will like it. He remarked, "Well, young fellow, here's the handsome equipage," and his grin—well, it made me feel that I had always been his neighbor. They're so ready to help a stranger, those villagers. He had already made it his own task to find Oliver Lutkins for me.

He said, and almost shyly: "I don't want to butt in on your private business, young fellow, but my guess is that you want to collect some money from Lutkins—he never pays anybody a cent; he still owes me six bits on a poker game I was fool enough to get into. He ain't a bad sort of Yahoo, but he just naturally hates to loosen up on coin of the realm. So if you're trying to collect any money off him, we better kind of, you might say, creep up on him and surround him. If you go asking for him—anybody can tell you come from the city, with that trick fedora of yours—he'll suspect something and take a sneak. If you want me to, I'll go into Fritz Beineke's and ask for him, and you can keep out of sight behind me."

I loved him for it. By myself I might never have found Lutkins. Now, I was an army with reserves. In a burst I told the hack driver that I wanted to serve a summons on Lutkins; that the fellow had viciously refused to testify in a suit where his knowledge of a certain conversation would clear up everything. The driver listened earnestly—and I was still young enough to be grateful at being taken seriously by any man of forty. At the end he pounded my shoulder (very painfully) and chuckled: "Well, we'll spring a little surprise on Br'er Lutkins."

"Let's start, driver."

"Most folks around here call me Bill. Or Magnuson. William Magnuson, fancy carting and hauling."

"All right, Bill. Shall we tackle this harness-shop—Beineke's?"

"Yes, jus' likely to be there as anywheres. Plays a lot of poker, and a great hand at bluffing—damn him!" Bill seemed to admire Mr. Lutkins' ability as a scoundrel; I fancied that if he had been sheriff he would have caught Lutkins with fervor and hanged him with affection.

At the somewhat gloomy harness-shop we descended and went in. The room was odorous with the smell of dressed leather. A scanty sort of man, presumably Mr. Beineke, was selling a horse collar to a farmer.

"Seen Nolly Lutkins around today? Friend of his looking for him," said Bill, with treacherous heartiness.

Beineke looked past him at my shrinking alien self; he hesitated, and owned: "Yuh, he was in here little while ago. Guess he's gone over to the Swede's to get a shave."

"Well, if he comes in, tell him I'm looking for him. Might get up a little game of poker. I've heard tell that Lutkins plays these here immoral games of chance."

"Yuh, I believe he's known to sit in on Authors,"[1] Beineke growled.

We sought the barbershop of "the Swede." Bill was again good enough to take the lead, while I lurked at the door. He asked not only the Swede but two customers if they had seen Lutkins. The Swede decidedly had not; he raged: "I ain't seen him, and I don't want to, but if you find him you can just collect the dollar thirty-five he owes me!" One of the customers thought he had seen Lutkins "hiking down Main Street, this side of the hotel."

"Well, then," Bill concluded, as we labored up into the hack, "his credit at the Swede's being *ausgewent*,[2] he's probably getting a scrape at Heinie Gray's. He's too darn lazy to shave himself."

At Gray's barbershop we missed Lutkins by only five minutes. He had just left—presumably for the poolroom. At the poolroom it appeared that he had merely bought a pack of cigarettes and gone on. Thus we pursued him, just behind him but never catching him, for an hour, till it was past one and I was hungry. Village born as I was and in the city often lonely for good coarse country wit, I was so delighted by Bill's cynical opinions on the barbers and clergymen and doctors and draymen of New Mullion that I scarcely cared whether I found Lutkins or not.

"How about something to eat?" I suggested. "Let's go to a restaurant and I'll buy you a lunch."

"Well, ought to go home to the old woman. And I don't care much for these restaurants—ain't but four of 'em and they're all rotten. Tell you what we'll do. Like nice scenery? There's an elegant view from Wade's Hill. We'll get the old woman to put us up a lunch—she won't charge you but half a dollar, and it'd cost you that for a greasy feed at the caif—and we'll go up there and have a Sunday-school picnic."

I knew that my friend Bill was not free from guile; I knew that his hospitality to the Young Fellow from the City was not altogether a matter of brotherly love. I was paying him for his time; in all I paid him for six hours (including the lunch hour!) at what was then a terrific price. But he was no more dishonest than I, who charged the whole thing up to the Firm, and it would have been worth paying him myself to have his presence.

His country serenity, his natural wisdom, was a refreshing bath to the city-twitching youngster. As we sat on the hill-top, looking across orchards and a creek which slipped among the willows, he talked of New Mullion, gave a whole gallery of portraits. He was cynical yet tender. Nothing had escaped him, yet there was nothing, no matter how ironically he laughed at it, which was beyond his understanding and forgiveness. In ruddy color he painted the rector's wife who, when she was most in debt, most loudly gave the responses of what he called the "Episcopalopian church." He commented on the boys who came home from college in "ice-cream pants," and on the lawyer who, after years of torrential argument with his wife, would put on either a linen collar or a necktie, but never both. He made them live. In that day I came to know New Mullion better than I did the city, and to love it better.

If Bill was ignorant of universities and of urban ways, yet much had he traveled in the realm of jobs. He had worked on railroad section gangs, in harvest fields and contractors' camps, and from his adventures he had brought back a philosophy of simplicity and laughter. He strengthened me. Nowadays, thinking of Bill, I know what

_____

1. Authors, a card game for children. 2. ausgewent, an expression meaning "gone out" or "exhausted."

people mean (though I abominate the simpering phrase) when they yearn over "real he-men."

We left that placid place of orchards and resumed the search for Oliver Lutkins. We could not find him. At last Bill cornered a friend of Lutkins and made him admit that "he guessed Oliver's gone out to his ma's farm, three miles north."

We drove out there, mighty with strategy. "I know Oliver's ma. She's a terror. She's a cyclone." Bill sighed. "I took a trunk out for her once, and she pretty near took my hide off because I didn't treat it like it was a crate of eggs. She's somewheres about nine feet tall and four feet thick and quick's a cat, and she sure manhandles the Queen's English. I'll bet Oliver has heard that somebody's on his trail, and he's sneaked out there to hide behind ma's skirts. Well, we'll try bawling her out. But you better let me do it, boy. You may be great at Latin and geography, but you ain't educated in cussing." We drove into a poor farmyard; we were faced by an enormous and cheerful old woman. My guardian stockily stood before her and snarled, "Remember me? I'm Bill Magnuson, the expressman. I want to find your son Oliver. Friend of mine here from the city got a present for him."

"I don't know anything about Oliver, and I don't want to," she bellowed.

"Now you look here. We've stood for just about enough plenty nonsense. This young man is the attorney general's provost, and we got legal right to search any and all premises for the person of one Oliver Lutkins."

Bill made it sound terrific, and the Amazon seemed impressed. She retired into the kitchen and we followed. From the low old range, turned by years of heat into a dark silvery gray, she snatched a sadiron, and she marched on us, clamoring, "You just search all you want to—providin' you don't mind getting burnt to a cinder." She bellowed, she swelled, she laughed at our nervous retreat.

"Let's get out of this. She'll murder us," Bill groaned and, outside: "Did you see her grin? She was making fun of us. Can you beat that for nerve?"

I agreed that it was *lèse-majesté*.[3]

We did, however, make adequate search. The cottage had but one story. Bill went round it, peeking in at all the windows. We explored the barn and the stable; we were reasonably certain that Lutkins was not there. It was nearly time for me to catch the afternoon train, and Bill drove me to the station. On the way to the city I worried very little over my failure to find Lutkins, I was too absorbed in the thought of Bill Magnuson. Really, I considered returning to New Mullion to practice law. If I had found Bill so deeply and richly human, might I not come to love the yet uncharted Fritz Beineke and the Swede barber and a hundred other slow-spoken, simple, wise neighbors? I saw a candid and happy life beyond the neat learnings of universities and law firms. I was excited, as one who has found a treasure.

But if I did not think much about Lutkins, the office did. I found them in a state, next morning; the suit was ready to come to trial; they had to have Lutkins; I was a disgrace and a fool. That morning my eminent legal career almost came to an end. The Chief did everything but commit mayhem; he somewhat more than hinted that I would do well at ditch-digging. I was ordered back to New Mullion, and with me they sent an ex-lumber-camp clerk who knew Lutkins. I was rather sorry, because it would prevent my loafing again in the gorgeous indolence of Bill Magnuson.

When the train drew in at New Mullion, Bill was on the station platform, near his dray. What was curious was that the old dragon, Lutkins' mother, was there talking to him, and they were not quarreling but laughing.

From the car steps I pointed Bill out to

3. *lèse-majesté* (lez′mä′jes′tā′), a crime against the dignity of a ruler. [French]

the lumber-camp clerk, and in young hero worship I murmured: "There's a fine fellow, a real man."

"Meet him here yesterday?" asked the clerk.

"I spent the day with him."

"He help you hunt for Oliver Lutkins?"

"Yes, he helped me a lot."

"He must have! He's Lutkins himself!"

But what really hurt was that when I served the summons, Lutkins and his mother laughed at me as though I were a bright boy of seven, and with loving solicitude they begged me to go to a neighbor's house and take a cup of coffee.

"I told 'em about you, and they're dying to have a look at you," said Lutkins joyfully. "They're about the only folks in town that missed seeing you yesterday."

BETTER READING

Tone

A skilled craftsman blends plot, setting, characters, and language in a literary work to form a unified whole. But because the writer, like all other individuals, is a personality with his own likes and dislikes, the stamp of his emotional reactions will affect all these elements. This attitude of an author as evident in his work is called *tone*.

The author's attitude toward characters, action, settings, and feelings may be revealed explicitly or implicitly. It is *explicit* when he states it directly to the reader, *implicit* when he conveys his attitude indirectly. Many modern writers of narrative use implicit rather than explicit methods to suggest emotional reactions. In "The Sculptor's Funeral" Willa Cather does not say directly that the boys who appear when the evening train comes in are a shiftless, sinister group. Rather, she writes that they "appeared as suddenly and slimily as eels wakened by the crack of thunder" and "uncoiled themselves from baggage trucks or slid out of express wagons." The connotative words convey the tone.

In many cases the writer of lyric poetry explicitly states his attitude. The "I" he creates may be an idealized version of the person he actually

is or may differ in various ways, but the tone of the poem will reflect to some extent his own emotional reaction. In "Auto Wreck" we feel that Karl Shapiro is voicing a personal reaction to unnecessary and sudden death. And even though Conrad Aiken attributes the idea of "One Star Fell and Another" to an unidentified "he," the reader senses that the reaction expressed is that of the poet himself.

To grasp the full meaning of a work of literature, the reader must learn to sense its tone. Is it comic, tragic, witty, satirical, sentimental, disillusioned, disinterested, idealistic, or a combination of several of these? How would you characterize the dominant tone of the following: "The Sculptor's Funeral," "Early Marriage," "The Oyster and the Pearl," "One Star Fell and Another," "Auto Wreck"?

It is not difficult to grasp that an author's tone is tragic, comic, or idealistic, but an *ironic* tone is by its very nature more difficult to detect. The word *irony* comes from the Greek *eiron*—a type character in ancient comedy. This character was a wise person who assumed the guise of a simpleton. By extension, irony has come to refer to writing in which a wise author plays at being stupid. This author has his tongue in his cheek; he says one thing while actually meaning another. The clues to what he really means are to be found in the way he uses language, portrays character, describes events, or expresses attitudes. His intent may be to shock or to amuse, to hide a grim comment on life under a light tone, or through banter to provoke a reform; but the approach is indirect. Sinclair Lewis brilliantly sustains an ironic tone throughout "The Hack Driver."

1. The narrator of "The Hack Driver" is a Supreme Court justice recalling an experience he had as a young man. Why is this a good situation for the use of an ironic tone?

2. (a) In describing his meeting with the hack driver, the narrator comments, "They're so ready to help a stranger, those villagers" (page 72, column 1, paragraph 6). At what point did you realize that this comment and the passage from which it is taken are ironic? (b) Locate similar passages throughout the story and explain why they are ironic.

3. How do these passages prepare for the ending of the story?

One of the foremost colonial
silversmiths painted by one
of the foremost colonial artists:
Paul Revere, with the tools and
a product of his craft, in a
portrait by John Singleton
Copley (1738-1815).

Paul Revere - Esther Forbes -

I had been working on a novel
(for I always think of myself
primarily as a novelist) about
Boston, as the discontent of the
colonists was seething up into the
American Revolution. My central
character was a tolerant man
who could see the good and bad
in both the Whig and Tory point of
view. Hitler's Germany and the
beginning of World War II made
me so intolerant I felt I had
lost all contact with the central
theme the incipient novel demanded.
It was my publisher who suggested
writing a biography about one man,
as non-fiction does require so
much less emotional involvement
than fiction. I picked Paul Revere
partly because I knew there was
a great collection of his personal
papers in existence, partly because
so little had been written about
the artizan or almost average
man of this period. He was not
a political philosopher, but

primarily a man of action. Without
innumerable men of his general
type the American Revolution could
hardly have been won. Such men
were often of great ingenuity, and
like Revere, men of integrity,
self sacrifice, willing to risk
everything for a cause they thought
right. The fact his father was a
child refugee from religious
persecutions in France, and that
he himself so well exemplified
the old American success story
also attracted me. The two magnificent
portraits of him, one by Copley painted
in his early middle years and in his
work clothes, the other painted by
Stuart when Revere was an old
man gave me visual proof of
what he looked like. His letters
surely would prove the manner of
man he was and how he felt.
The Boston of the period, because of
the earlier work on the novel, I already
knew pretty well, and had read
the best diaries and general sources.
I also knew where I would be apt to
find material I did not already
have

Esther Forbes was born in Massachusetts, where her family had lived for generations. Growing up in an atmosphere rich in the lore of earlier days, Esther Forbes became interested in New England's past, and she also became interested in writing.

Her first book, O Genteel Lady! (1926), tells of a woman's struggle against the artificial restrictions of Victorian times. In A Mirror for Witches (1928) Miss Forbes brought the spirit of a still earlier New England—the New England of the witchcraft trials—alive by using the style of the great diarists of that day. Paradise was a historical novel which, instead of treating the Puritans romantically or symbolically, as had earlier novels, presented them with a matter-of-fact realism based on Miss Forbes' careful research.

To the writing of Paul Revere and the World He Lived In—her first venture into biography—Miss Forbes brought the warmth, vividness, and pace she had developed as a writer of historical novels, as well as meticulous research. As the title suggests, it is history as well as biography, and it was as history that it was awarded the Pulitzer Prize in 1943. In later novels, like Johnny Tremain, a prize-winning book for children and The Running of the Tide, a novel of New England's great sailing days which won the Metro-Goldwyn-Mayer prize in 1948, Esther Forbes continues to create the illusion of a living and vital past, a quality that is outstanding in her fiction and nonfiction alike.

Esther Forbes

Paul Revere and the Alarum

By early spring of 1775 tension between England and her American colonies was high. Word came to General Gage in Boston that the colonists were collecting powder and arms at Concord. He also learned that John Hancock and Samuel Adams, two leaders of the colonial cause, were at nearby Lexington. They were in hiding at the parsonage of Reverend Jonas Clark, a relative of Hancock. Gage decided the time to act had come and made ready to move against Concord.

Word of the British plans filtered through to Dr. Joseph Warren and the other patriotic Sons of Liberty, among them Paul Revere. Revere, a prosperous silversmith, had several times carried messages for the patriots.

This was the situation on Tuesday, April 18, 1775. In describing the events, the author quotes from several eyewitness accounts.

On Tuesday afternoon Gage sent out a group of picked officers. It was for them to block the roads leading toward Concord so no rebel express could ride through and warn the town. They were to pretend to be merely a pleasure party riding out to Cambridge for a dinner in the country. Their arms would be hidden by their cloaks. If questioned closely, they could admit that they were out after their own deserters. At Cambridge some of these men would turn toward Charlestown and after dark hide in the bushes to waylay any messenger who might cross the river and try to reach Concord by that route. The other officers were to do their intercepting closer to Concord. These men knew Paul Revere's name, but not his face. Of these two nets spread out to catch him or any other man who attempted to go through that night, Paul Revere knew nothing. Of the third precaution all Boston knew. The man-of-war *Somerset* was moved into the very mouth of the Charles River, commanding the expanse of water any boat headed for Charlestown must cross.

At dusk, Lord Percy left General Gage at the Province House and went quietly to the Common, where the boats were drawn up and troops already lined up waiting to embark. The townspeople stood about watching these preparations. The Earl was not recognized and listened to their comments. He heard a voice say:

"The British troops have marched, but will miss their aim."

"What aim?" asked Percy.

"Why, the cannon at Concord."

Percy went back to Gage. In some way their secret was known.

At Joseph Warren's, the plans were perfected. As soon as it was definitely known whether the British went by land or sea, Robert Newman would be notified and the lanterns in Christ's[1] hung. This he had already agreed to do. He was twenty-three at the time. His older brother was organist at Christ's and he was sexton. He did not like the work, but had taken the job "because," as he said, "times are so hard." Not only did he have the keys to the church, but lived just across the street from it. The only drawback was that his mother's house was full of British officers billeted on the family.

These lanterns would give the warning, but no detail, of the expedition. Farther upstream the British boats would be ferrying over the troops. There was a chance Paul Revere could get past the *Somerset*—but only a chance. He was ready to take it.

William Dawes, the young cordwainer, would attempt to ride out through the British sentries on the Neck. He lived near North Square and his father was a silversmith. Undoubtedly Revere knew him well. He had played no conspicuous part in the brewing revolution, as had Revere, and was not a marked man, although he had recently knocked down a soldier for insulting his pretty wife. "Billy" Dawes was a born actor. Later, during the siege of Boston, he used to go in and out almost at will, disguised as a drunken farmer, thoroughly enjoying himself and the risks he took. In the portrait painted of him in middle age, when he could write *Major* in front of his name and the proud word *merchant* after it, he is still a comical-looking fellow, with his close-set eyes, long nose, and humorous mouth. If anyone could allay suspicion of the sentries, act the part of an inebriated farmer or a half-witted bumpkin, it would be Billy Dawes. Paul Revere looked as clever as he was. Billy Dawes did not. He would have farther to go than Revere and about an equally poor chance of getting through. He passed the gates by pretending great innocence and with the connivance of a British soldier.

Now that the troops were actually at the bottom of the Common, Joseph Warren started Billy Dawes over the Neck and sent for Paul Revere. The time had come.

"About ten o'clock Dr. Warren sent in great haste for me, and begged that I would immediately set off for Lexington, where Messre. Hancock and Adams were, and acquaint them of the movement, and that it was thought they were the objects. When I got to Dr. Warren's house, I found he had sent an express by land to Lexing-

---

1. *lanterns in Christ's hung.* The *Somerset* guarded the channel between Boston and Charlestown which Paul Revere had to cross before he could start his ride. The signal had been arranged since there was a possibility that under the *Somerset's* watch Paul Revere might not reach Charlestown. Two lanterns would be hung in the church spire if the British moved on Concord by water, one if they moved by land. Christ's Church, after 1776, acquired the nickname "Old North." At the time of Revere's ride it was still commonly known as Christ's.

ton—a Mr. William Dawes."[2] As is often pointed out, Paul Revere never got to Concord; it is noteworthy that it was only Lexington he originally started out to warn. Yet he definitely had Concord in mind as well.

The two friends parted. When, if ever, they would meet again they could not know. Joseph Warren would chance staying inside the lines a little longer for the sake of the information he might pick up. But any moment he might hear the rap on his door and see a corporal's guard, an officer with the warrant for his arrest in his hand— wanted in London for treason. Paul Revere also risked all he had and life as well. General Gage had handled the insurrection thus far with kid gloves, but no country has ever hesitated to drop with a bullet, if necessary, a man caught exciting to armed revolt.

First Paul sought out Robert Newman, who, knowing that it might be awkward for a prominent Son of Liberty and express rider to rap at his mother's door and call him out, had pretended to go to bed early, leaving the officers in the living rooms, then slipped out an upper window, over a roof, and was already in the dark street waiting for any orders. One of the vestrymen at Christ's, John Pulling, went with Newman, as probably did Revere's neighbor, Thomas Barnard. The door was locked after him and the guard stood in the street as the young fellow took the lanterns from the closet and softly mounted the wooden stairs. Higher and higher, feeling his way in the darkness, he climbed, past the eight great bells, silent in the bell loft, until he came to the highest window of the belfry. To the north he could see, over the shoulder of Copp's Hill, the mouth of the Charles, the black hull of the *Somerset*, the glimmer of her riding lights. Beyond was Charlestown, and there he knew men were waiting, watching for his signal. He lit the lanterns, hung them, and felt his way back to the floor of the church. Probably Newman displayed his lanterns for a moment only. He

certainly could not wish to warn the *Somerset*. They were out by the time Paul Revere had crossed into Charlestown. In spite of the poem,[3] they were not a signal *to* Paul Revere, but *from* him. The Sunday before he had told Colonel Conant[4] to watch for them. When the men in Charlestown saw "a glimmer and then a gleam of light," Paul Revere was still in Boston.

Something must have happened in the street while Newman was inside, for he dared not leave by the way he had come. Instead he climbed out of a window at the rear of the church, circled about, and entered his mother's house by the roofs and the upper window. Lying awake, he might hear below him the laughter of the officers over their cards. That much of the deed was done.

Having started Robert Newman on his ascent to fame, Paul Revere went to his own house in North Square. In all directions, marching in full battle gear, small groups of redcoats were leaving their barracks and billets, heading for the Common. Troops were lined up in North Square. No one was allowed to enter it or leave. Somehow Paul Revere got through them. He put on his short surtout and heavy riding boots. Perhaps Rachel[5] tried to argue him out of this dangerous ride, for he seems to have been curiously absent-minded for so competent a man. He forgot two things. His spurs and some cloth with which to muffle the oars of his rowboat. So he left the house, and his dog followed him.

Joshua Bentley, a boatbuilder, and Thomas Richardson were ready to row him across. He picked them up at some prearranged place and the three started for the part of North Boston where that winter Paul Revere had kept his boat hidden. Then

2. "About ten o'clock . . . Mr. William Dawes." The author quotes Paul Revere, who wrote three accounts of his adventure. These three accounts are the most significant of the eyewitness reports used by the author. 3. the poem, "Paul Revere's Ride," by Henry Wadsworth Longfellow. 4. Colonel Conant. William Conant was a Son of Liberty who lived in Charlestown. Revere had explained the lantern signal to him. 5. Rachel, wife of Paul Revere.

the matter of muffling the oars came up. None of them wished to return to his own house, but one of them had a girl friend. He gave a peculiar whistle outside her window, at the corner of North and North Centre streets. The window went up. There was a whispered conversation and a flannel petticoat was tossed down. Then Revere remembered his spurs. He wrote a note to Rachel, tied it to his dog's collar. Soon the dog was back again with the spurs. This story he also told his children, but perhaps only to amuse them. So at last he was booted and spurred, but a long way yet from being ready to ride.

The *Somerset* blocked the shortest route, forcing them to keep rather well out to sea. She was a great frigate of sixty-four guns and was stationed there for but one purpose--to keep men like Paul Revere in Boston. A cry to heave to or even a spatter of shot was expected. Beyond her, upstream, the British boats were going back and forth already, carrying the regulars to Cambridge.

All winter it had been abnormally warm and spring had come almost ahead of itself. Fruit trees were in bloom; the fields already ploughed. That night, however, was chill, and "it was young flood, the ship was winding and the moon was rising," as Paul Revere noticed. The muffled oars softly eased his little rowboat closer and closer to the Charlestown side. There had been neither hail nor shot from the *Somerset*. So he leaped to dry land close to the old Battery. Richardson and Bentley had done their work. Revere went on alone.

At Colonel Conant's he found a group waiting for him. Had they seen his signals? They had. He told them "what was acting" and learned to his surprise that the roads toward Cambridge and on to Concord were already patrolled by British officers who had left Boston in the afternoon.

Richard Devens, of the Committee of Safety, said he had left Menotomy in his chaise around sunset. And he had seen "a great number of B.O. [British officers] and

their servants on horseback." As they were behaving in a suspiciously nonchalant manner and had asked where "Clark's tavern[6] was," Devens had sent word to the Clark parsonage. It might be they were out to arrest the two rebel chiefs housed there. He knew this messenger might be picked up, as he was. Paul Revere himself might have better luck. He would need a good horse to slip through the cordon. Probably he had as fine a mount as the luxurious town of Charlestown could produce. John Larkin was one of the wealthiest citizens. It was his best horse that was now turned over to Revere. Twenty-three years later, he gratefully remembered how good, how "very good," was this Larkin horse. It would be slender and nervous in the Yankee manner, small by modern standards, sure-footed, tireless. Now for the remainder of the night Revere's success, perhaps his life and the lives of others, would depend upon this horse. He would adjust the stirrups carefully to his own length, test with a forefinger the snugness of the girths. They must be tight, but not binding. The bit must hang exactly right. In that unhurried moment before mounting, he could measure the courage and stamina of his companion, catch the flash of white in the wild, soft eye, note the impatient stamp of the small hooves, feel under his hand the swelling of muscle along the neck, the strength in withers and loin, his touch and voice assuring the sensitive animal that he was his friend.

And now it was eleven o'clock. Only an hour before, he had stood in Joseph Warren's parlor knowing that the time had come. Then, by the bright cold moonlight everyone noticed that night, he swung to the saddle.

So away, down the moonlit road, goes Paul Revere and the Larkin horse, gallop-

---

6. *Clark's tavern.* The Clark parsonage in Lexington was close to Buckman's Tavern. Since the British officers were unfamiliar with the locality, they apparently confused the parsonage with the tavern.

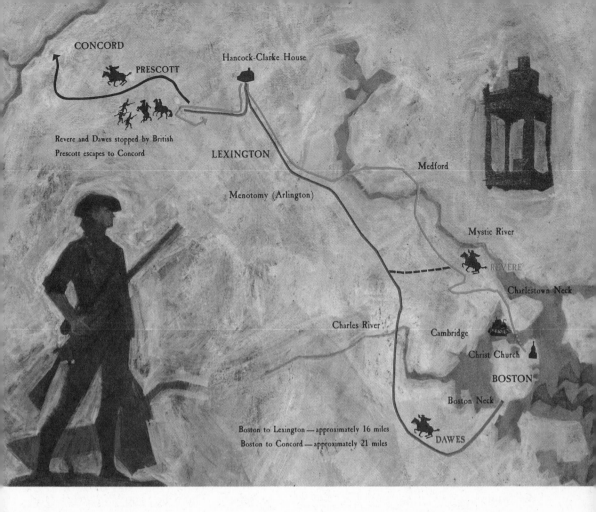

ing into history, art, editorials, folklore, poetry; the beat of those hooves never to be forgotten. The man, his bold, dark face bent, his hands light on the reins, his body giving to the flowing rhythm beneath him, becoming, as it were, something greater than himself—not merely one man riding one horse on a certain lonely night of long ago, but a symbol to which his countrymen can yet turn.

Paul Revere had started on a ride which, in a way, has never ended.

Charlestown like Boston was a promontory attached to the mainland by a slender neck. Paul Revere rode over this neck. The Charles River was on his left and the Mys-

tic upon his right. He was now in a sparsely settled, desolate stretch of salt marsh, moors, claypits, and scrub. In his day this was the "common" of Charlestown and now is Somerville. Of the two roads traversing this dreary expanse, he took the one to his left which led directly into Cambridge and was the shortest way to Lexington. Only two days before he had traveled this road and knew it well.

"The moon shone bright," he remembered. "I had got almost over Charlestown Common toward Cambridge when I saw two Officers on Horseback, standing under the shade of a Tree, in a narrow part of the roade. I was near enough to see their Holsters & cockades. One of them started his horse toward me and the other up the road, as I supposed to head me should I escape the first. I turned my horse short about, and rid upon a full gallop for Mistick Road." In this brief, slippery, cross-country race the heavier British charger (handsome enough for parade) was no match for the light-footed Yankee horse. Out of the tail of his eye Paul Revere could see how he was outdistancing his pursuer in three hundred yards. And next the clumsy animal had "got into a clay-pond." No shots were fired and, if any words were spoken, Paul Revere did not record them.

As the road to Cambridge was blocked, he quickly came down on that other road (now Broadway), followed the Mystic River, which he crossed, and entered Medford over a plank bridge. Here "I awaked the Captain of the minutemen: and after that I alarumed almost every house till I got to Lexington."

Bells rang, drums beat—"The regulars are out!" Women gathered children and silver and fled to swamps. Men seized muskets and powder horns. Other men mounted and rode off to other towns to carry the warning—"The regulars are out." "The horror of that midnight cry" was not quickly forgotten in Middlesex County.

Paul Revere recrossed the Mystic, went through Menotomy (as Arlington was called at that time—Lieutenant Sutherland[7] calls it "Anatomy"), and so was back on the route he had planned to take before the officers forced him to detour. Cambridge, now behind him, did not need any express rider to tell them the British had marched. Colonel Smith had already landed his men at Phipps' farm in East Cambridge. With that curious disregard for the privates' comfort and health so many of the British officers showed, he left his men drawn up and shivering until two o'clock. They had waded up to their middles in salt water to get ashore. If only they had marched immediately, they would have been in Lexington and Concord before any sizable force could have been raised to oppose them.

Close upon midnight Paul Revere came into Lexington. And here was the meeting house casting its moonstruck shadow across the Green where so soon men were to die. Close by it was Buckman's Tavern from which he might have heard the voices of men, laughter even, or the clink of tankards. Captain Parker had called out the local minutemen that afternoon when word first came that a handful of unexplainable British officers were abroad and might be after Adams and Hancock. It does not seem to have been known in Lexington that a considerable force of the regulars were coming until Revere arrived. As it was cold standing about outdoors, the militiamen had retired to Buckman's. The Yankee soldier had as strong a regard for his own comfort as the British officers had disregard for their men. Colonel Smith's forces freezing in their disciplined ranks in the salt marshes of East Cambridge, and Captain Parker's men so cozy and undisciplined at the same moment at Buckman's, make a characteristic contrast.

Paul Revere went straight to the Clark parsonage. There he found Sergeant Monroe and seven men guarding the house. Revere demanded to be admitted, in so loud a voice the sergeant reproved him. The ladies and gentlemen had gone to bed and had "requested not to be disturbed by any noise that night" (this sounds more like Hancock than Adams).

"Noise!" shouted Revere. "You'll have noise enough before long! The regulars are out."

He knocked loudly on the door.

The Reverend Mr. Clark opened a window and thrust out his granite head. Paul Revere demanded to see John Hancock. But the clergyman, "ever deliberate and watchful," not recognizing the man in the dark,

---

7. *Lieutenant Sutherland,* a British officer serving under Lieutenant Colonel Francis Smith, who commanded the British troops at Lexington and Concord.

said he could not be admitting strangers at that time of night without knowing who they were and what they wanted. John Hancock had "retired to rest, but not to sleep." He recognized Revere's voice.

"Come in, Revere, we are not afraid of you."

So he went in and told his story. It was not merely a patrol of British officers that was out this night, but probably "over a thousand light troops." He had seen them crossing the Charles at ten. They might be here any moment now. There was no doubt but their destination was Lexington to pick up the rebel leaders, and Concord for the stores. This was thundering news and all was commotion.

John Hancock was demanding his sword and gun. He was determined to take his place with the minutemen if they opposed the march of the British. Sam Adams tried to persuade him against such foolishness. These two men had just been elected Massachusetts delegates to the Second Continental Congress in Philadelphia. They argued about the matter, and then, half an hour after Revere, Dawes came in.

The two expresses ate and drank, and once more mounted. The countryside as well as Hancock and Adams had been warned. Three days before, Revere had got word to Concord that the British might seize the stores there and by now they were pretty well hidden. However, the two men decided to go over to Concord, alarming the minutemen as they went.

As they moved out of Lexington, they were joined by Samuel Prescott, a young doctor from Concord, who had been over to Lexington courting a Miss Millikan. As it was now after one o'clock, he was hardly keeping the early hours credited to our forebears. When he heard what was happening, he offered to ride with them, for being a local man and a high Son of Liberty, he pointed out that the people would "give more credit" to what he said than to strangers. Paul Revere says:

...when we had got about half way from Lexington to Concord, the other two, stopped at a House to awake the man. I kept along, when I had got about 200 yards ahead of them, I saw two officers under a tree as before [not far from Hartwell Farm, North Lincoln]. I immediately called to my company to come up, saying here was two of them (for I had told them what Mr. Devens told me, and of my being stopped) in an instant I saw four officers, who rode up to me, with their pistols in their hands & said G—D d—m you stop, if you go an inch further you are a dead Man. Immeditly Mr. Prescot came up he turned the butt of his whipp we attempted to git thro them, but they kept before us, and swore if we did not turn into that pasture, they would blow our brains out. They had placed themselves opposite a pair of Barrs, and had taken the Barrs down. They forced us in. The Doctor jumped his horse over a low stone wall, and got to Concord. I observed a wood at a small distance and made for that intending when I gained that to jump my Horse & run afoot, just as I reached it out started six officers, siesed my bridle, put their pistols to my Breast, ordered me to dismount, which I did. One of them, who appeared to have command there, and much of a Gentleman, asked where I came from; I told him. he asked what time I left it; I told him, he seemed much surprised, He said Sir may I crave your name? I answered my name is Revere. What said he Paul Revere? I answered yes; the other abused me much; but he told me not to be afraid, no one should hurt me. I told him they would miss their Aim. [This seems to have been a common catch-phrase that night.] He said they should not, they were only after some Deserters they expected down the Road. I told him I knew better, I knew what they were after; that I had alarumed the country all the way up, that their Boats had catch'd aground, and I should have 500 men there soon; one of them said they had 1500 coming.

...Major Mitchel of the 5th Reg't clap'd a pistol to my head and said if I did not tell the truth, he would blow my brains out....I gave him much the same answers; after he and two more had spoke together in a low voice he then ordered me to mount, and the Major rode up to me and took the reins. G—d sir you are not to ride with reins I assure you; and gave them to the officer on my right to lead me. I asked him to let me have the reins & I would not run from him, he said he would not trust me. He then Ordered 4 men out of the Bushes, and to mount their horses they were countrymen which they had stopped who were going home; they ordered us to march. He came up to me and said "We are now going toward your friends, and if you attempt to run or we are insulted, we will blow your Brains out." I told him he might do as he pleased.

Major Mitchell had reason to worry. They must join Colonel Smith's columns before the country was aroused and they themselves were cut off. He also wished to warn Colonel Smith that, in spite of General Gage's confidence that the "damned rebels" would not fight, it looked to him as though they would. He would now ride as fast as he could go to join the British marching out. There was no more time to bother with prisoners.

Although he had caught one of the three riders headed for Lexington, two had escaped him.

William Dawes (always the actor) made his dash for freedom, flapping his leather breeches and yelling, "Haloo, boys, I've got two of 'em." But he pulled up his horse so short, he not only fell off, but lost his watch, and presumably his horse as well. A few days later, he retraced his steps and found the watch. It was only Doctor Prescott who got through to Concord that night.

The British officers formed a circle about Paul Revere and the four countrymen. The little cavalcade "rid down toward Lexington, a pretty smart pace. I was often insulted by the officers calling me dammed Rebel, etc. etc. The officer who led me said I was in a d—m—d critical situation. I told him I was sensible of it. After we had got about a mile. I was given to the Sarjant to lead, who was Ordered to take out his pis-

tol and if I should run to execute the Major's sentence."

There was the soft thudding of horses' hooves, the clink of bits, spur-chains, military accoutrement. So they rode through the chilly silence of those darkest hours before the dawn. Sometimes at such an hour a cock will crow, a watchdog bark. And now there came another sound, for "when we got within about half a mile of Lexington Meeting house we heard a gun fired. The Major asked me what that was for. I told him to alarm the country."

There was no time to lose. Major Mitchell ordered the girths and bridles on the four countrymen's horses to be cut and the horses to be driven off. These men might now go home as best they might on foot. Paul asked the Major to dismiss him too. At first he would not, but admitted he could not "carry me let the consequence be what it will." More alarm guns were heard from Lexington. "The Major ordered us to a halt he asked me how far it was to Cambridge and many more questions which I answered. He then asked the Sarjant, if his horse was tired, he said yes"; Paul Revere noticed in the dark it was a small horse; "he Ordered him to take my horse. I dismounted, the Sarjant mounted my horse, they cutt the Bridle and Saddle off the Sarjant's horse & they told me they should make use of my horse for the night and rode off down the road."

Paul Revere saw the last of the "good" Larkin horse with a British grenadier sergeant on top of him. Although the Major promised to make use of it for only the one night, it disappeared completely into the British army and that was the end of him.

The mounted patrol drifted away. The four countrymen had already departed. Revere was alone. Either Billy Dawes or Doctor Prescott would surely get through to Concord. As he was less than a mile from Lexington, he decided to look in on Hancock and Adams and find out, as he would say, "what was acting." Fearing to be picked up again, he left the road and made his way cross-lots over stone walls and pastures. The riding boots of the period were amazingly heavy once you were dismounted, with spurs making it almost impossible to walk over rough ground without tripping. He did not know the environs of Lexington, but when he found himself in a graveyard, stumbling over the stones, he knew the parsonage was close at hand.

At the Jonas Clarks' the same argument was going on that he had left perhaps an hour before. Hancock was still anxious to take his place with the armed farmers who would challenge the movements of the regulars. It was with very great difficulty that he was dissuaded from it by Mr. Clark and Mr. Adams. The latter, clapping him on the shoulder, said to him "that it is not our business; we belong to the cabinet; It was not till break of day that Mr. H. could be persuaded that it was improper for him to expose himself against such a powerful force."

Paul Revere says that Hancock and Adams "concluded to go from that house toward Woburn. I went with them." But soon Revere's curiosity, restlessness, or patriotism got the better of him. He and Hancock's clerk, John Lowell, returned to Lexington. Reports were coming in fast: The British had not marched. The British are almost here. The British even this moment are "coming up the rocks." Lowell asked Revere to go with him to Buckman's Tavern and help him carry away the trunk containing Hancock's papers. He did not wish them to fall into British hands. Revere went.

And now the night was over. The strange, unearthly, gray, and dewy hour of dawn. The belfry bell still tolling, the rub-a-dub of William Diamond's drum called the minutemen to take their historic places. Revere crossed the Green, where in the unreal light of dawn some fifty or sixty men, farmers mostly and dressed as such, were forming ranks. Women and children and others stood at open doors and windows to gaze. Was it true? Was it these men, their sons, fathers, husbands, brothers, friends, who would oppose the march of the British? The King had forbidden all such military organizations as these. Any moment now the King's regulars would be upon them. This handful could not give battle—only serve as martyrs. Some of the minutemen preferred to live and fight another day, but even as these "poltroons" dropped out of the ranks, more and more men took their places, lining up between the meeting house and Buckman's Tavern. Revere silently passed through them.

He and Lowell found Hancock's trunk in an upper chamber at the tavern. And from that window Revere looked down "and saw the British very near upon a full march." Here were the orderly scarlet ranks of the marching grenadiers, the glitter of the just-risen sun glowing on pipe-clayed baldrics, brass buttons, gold lace, and satin coats of horses, steel bayonets. All as fine and orderly as a pack of playing cards—at least from the waist up. They may have been a bit bedraggled from there down, after their struggles in the salt marsh of East Cambridge. The officer in command was Revere's North Square neighbor of the last year—"fiery and profane," "amiable and gallant," Major Pitcairn himself. Near him was Major Mitchell and his officers—perhaps one of them on the Larkin horse.

Colonel Smith had landed his men as quietly as he could, but kept them standing around until two in the morning, which was about the time Paul Revere was captured. They moved rapidly into Cambridge proper without drums, ensigns, or breakfast.

When Major Mitchell had joined the main body of troops, the soldiers gathered about him to hear his story. It was "between 3 & 4 in the morning," Lieutenant Sutherland says, "he told us the whole country was Alarmed & had Galloped for their lives, or words to that purpose, that they had taken Paul Revierre but was obliged to lett him go after having cutt his girths and Stirrups."

Colonel Smith on Mitchell's advice immediately sent back to General Gage for Percy and the eight hundred men held as reinforcements, for it looked like bloody work ahead. He also ordered Major Pitcairn to go ahead quickly with six light companies and seize the two bridges at Concord. The patrolling officers went back over the road they had just galloped down "for their lives," probably acting as guides.

So it was Pitcairn, the British officers, and these six companies Paul Revere now saw from the upper window of Buckman's Tavern. What would happen when this orderly flood of scarlet and steel met the frail lines on the Green was not his business. He was to rescue John Hancock's trunk.

He and John Lowell carried it through the militiamen, who waited for they hardly knew what, stonily staring at the approaching redcoats. At one hundred and fifty feet the regulars came to a smart halt. Pitcairn himself and at least two officers galloped toward the provincials to disband them with words—if possible.

In this pause Revere passed close to Captain Parker, a good man already close to his fatal sickness. He heard him say, "Let the troops pass by and don't molest them without they begin first," and then Revere was off the Green. "A gun was fired. I heard the report and turned my head," but by then some shed or shrub cut off his view of the minutemen. He could only see the regulars: "and saw smoke in front of the troops, they immediately gave a great shout, ran a few paces and then the whole fired." But he went on with Hancock's trunk, toward the Clark parsonage, with that simple absorption in what was to be done at the moment which characterizes the whole man. Embattled farmers might stand and shots be fired that would be heard round the world. He gave them one glance and went on with his job. How it began, who fired the first shot, he does not pretend to know. Nor did he hear Major Pitcairn's famous "Disperse ye rebels, ye villains, disperse...Lay down your arms. Why don't ye lay down your arms?" Seventy-seven men are still on the Green, Captain Parker's words ringing in their ears:

"Don't fire unless fired on, but if they mean to have a war let it begin here."

Major Pitcairn also had commanded his men not to fire—yet someone did. The evidence seems to be that it was one of the provincials, not in the ranks upon the Green, but well hidden behind a stone wall or (as Lieutenant Sutherland swears), someone from an upper window in Buckman's Tavern did take that first shot and the British immediately answered with a volley.

Parker ordered his men to withdraw. One British private and Pitcairn's horse had been wounded. The regulars broke ranks to pursue the flying militia, killing a few more of them. They had been shut up in Boston for almost a year and were wild to get out and after this enemy. Their officers could hardly make themselves heard above the huzzahing of the exultant troops, and had difficulty in re-forming them again upon the Green. In the middle of all this, Colonel Smith arrived with the rest of the soldiers. Eight of the provincials had been killed and ten wounded. The engagement was quickly over and the British on their march to Concord.

Sam Adams and John Hancock were back once more in their carriage, moving still farther away to safety than Woburn, where Revere had left them. They, too, heard the rattle of musketry. Adams felt his soul swell with uncontrollable joy as he contemplated the mighty future, and with prophetic utterance of his country's dawning independence he exclaimed:

"O! What a glorious morning is this!"

But Hancock mistook the prophecy for a mere comment upon the weather. The nineteenth of April was (in one sense of the word) a very nice day.

COMPARING AND CONTRASTING

Speaking of Paul Revere's ride, Esther Forbes writes: "So away, down the moonlit road, goes Paul Revere and the Larkin horse, galloping into history, art, editorials, folklore, poetry." The following exercise calls on you to locate and read two other literary works in which Paul Revere figures largely—Henry Wadsworth Longfellow's poem, "Paul Revere's Ride," and Stephen Vincent Benét's short story, "A Tooth for Paul Revere"—and to compare and contrast them with the biographical selection by Esther Forbes. Whenever possible bring into the discussion other materials in which Revere plays a part; for example, *Johnny Tremain*, by Esther Forbes. Remember to keep in mind the various things about fiction and nonfiction you have learned from the "Better Reading" articles in this chapter. If a point is disputed, consult the appropriate article.

1. *(a)* What types of factual information does Esther Forbes make use of in "Paul Revere and the Alarum"? *(b)* Which source of information do you think re-creates the most vivid picture of the man and his time? *(c)* What device does the author use to suggest a conjecture, as in the case of Revere's forgetting both his spurs and a cloth to muffle the oars (page 79)?

2. Although in writing biography an author usually concentrates on a single figure, he must also present information about people who affect the personality or actions of the major figure. Explain the kinds of information Esther Forbes uses in her development of each of the following: *(a)* Robert Newman; *(b)* William Dawes; *(c)* Sam Adams; *(d)* Lieutenant Sutherland.

3. *(a)* When revising "A Tooth for Paul Revere," Benét said he "soft-pedaled the actual magic, tried to prepare for it, and tried to build up... incidental touches so as to make...it convincing." Why would changes of the sort Benét describes make this a better story? *(b)* Benét said that the silver box is a "symbol," a concrete image which stands for a concept or idea. State this concept or idea and relate it to the theme.

4. *(a)* How did Longfellow's purpose in writing "Paul Revere's Ride" presumably differ from Esther Forbes' purpose in writing the historical account? *(b)* What do you think was Benét's purpose in writing "A Tooth for Paul Revere"?

5. *(a)* Point out ways in which Longfellow's poem differs in factual information from Esther Forbes' historical study. *(b)* How do you account for these differences? *(c)* Does Benét's account of Revere's actions on the night of the famous ride agree more nearly with Longfellow's or Esther Forbes' version? Why do you think this is so?

6. Both Esther Forbes and Stephen Vincent Benét present vivid pictures of Paul Revere as an individual. *(a)* According to the biography, what sort of man was Revere? Cite specific phrases or passages to prove your point. *(b)* On what kinds of evidence does Esther Forbes presumably base her portrait of the man? *(c)* Explain and illustrate some of the methods Benét uses to characterize Revere. *(d)* How does Benét's interpretation differ from Esther Forbes'? *(e)* In "Paul Revere's Ride" does Longfellow present a complete portrait of Revere or develop only one trait? Explain your answer.

7. *(a)* Explain Esther Forbes' statement, "Paul Revere had started on a ride which, in a way, has never ended." *(b)* Read aloud the lines from "Paul Revere's Ride" which express the same idea. *(c)* In what way are "Paul Revere's Ride" and "A Tooth for Paul Revere" similar in theme?

8. *(a)* Describe the tone of "Paul Revere and the Alarum," "Paul Revere's Ride," and "A Tooth for Paul Revere." *(b)* Which of these seems closest in tone to Grant Wood's attitude in the painting (below) of Paul Revere's ride?

BIBLIOGRAPHY

BUCK, PEARL, *The Good Earth*. (Day •Pocket Books) Mrs. Buck's deep understanding of China is revealed in this absorbing and realistic novel of birth, marriage, and death in the Wang family.

CATHER, WILLA, *Death Comes for the Archbishop*. (Knopf) This is a beautiful story about an urbane and scholarly bishop and a fiery and energetic priest. A thoughtful novel, it captures completely the pioneer spirit of the Southwest.

CATHER, WILLA, *O Pioneers*. (Houghton) With dignity and compassion, the author tells of a young girl on a Nebraska farm. Alexandra's life becomes a series of disappointments and tragedies from which she emerges a warm and selfless woman.

DE VOTO, BERNARD, *Across the Wide Missouri*. (Houghton) This magnificently exciting book chronicles the lives of the mountain men during the great days of the Rocky Mountain fur trade.

DE VOTO, BERNARD, *Year of Decision*. (••Houghton) The most vivid imagination would fail to conceive the plot of a tale more exciting than this true account of the sufferings and hardships endured by westward-moving settlers in 1846.

FERBER, EDNA, *So Big*. (Doubleday •Avon) This novel bears out Edna Ferber's reputation as a natural-born storyteller. The story of Salina and her son concerns her struggles to make their small farm a success.

HERSEY, JOHN, *A Bell for Adano*. (Knopf •Avon) Portrayal of character is the author's greatest achievement in this outstanding novel about an Italian-American major who tries to rebuild an Italian town that has been under Fascist rule.

KENNEDY, JOHN F., *Profiles in Courage*. (Harper •Pocket Books) This is a tribute to the moral courage of Americans in politics from John Quincy Adams to Robert Taft. It relates the stories of men who took stands they thought right, regardless of the consequences.

LA FARGE, OLIVER, *Laughing Boy*. (Houghton •Pocket Books) Told here is the tragic story of Laughing Boy and Slim Girl, young Navahos who shared a deep love for each other and for their people.

LEWIS, SINCLAIR, *Arrowsmith*. (Harcourt) Arrowsmith, doctor and idealist, makes an important discovery in bacteriology that, with crushing irony, leads to personal tragedy.

LEWIS, SINCLAIR, *Main Street*. (Harcourt) In one of the first realistic portrayals of small-town life in America, Sinclair Lewis tells of Carol Kennicott and her efforts to uplift the citizens of Gopher Prairie.

MARQUAND, JOHN, *The Late George Apley*. (Little •Pocket Books) Recorded herein are the habits and sayings of two generations of Boston Brahmins whose lives are rigidly controlled by caste and tradition. This is satire at its best.

MICHENER, JAMES, *Bridges at Toko-ri*. (Random) This fast-paced novel concerns the men of a naval task force in Korea, and their assignment —to destroy the heavily guarded bridge at Toko-Ri to prevent the moving of supplies to the Communist forces.

RAWLINGS, MARJORIE, *The Yearling*. (••Scribner) If you have not read this rural classic of the Florida backwoods, do so. It is a very human story of a fawn, a boy called Jody, and that boy's efforts to understand the world he lives in.

RICHTER, CONRAD, *The Trees*. (Knopf) This is the first of a trilogy about the Ohio frontier which includes *The Fields* and *The Town*. The story follows a family through its escape into the wilderness seeking isolation, and its eventual return to the city. These are truly great novels, alive with the atmosphere of the forest and with color and warm humanity.

SAROYAN, WILLIAM, *The Human Comedy*. (Harcourt) People are more important than plot in this short but tender novel of a family whose son is killed in World War II.

TARKINGTON, BOOTH, *Seventeen*. (Grosset •Bantam) There is nothing weighty, nothing sublime in the telling of the ups and downs of Willie Baxter; but there is everything foolish and delightful.

WILDER, THORNTON, *The Bridge of San Luis Rey*. (Grosset •Washington Square) In 1714 an Inca bridge in Peru fell, killing five people. Wilder reconstructs their lives in this skillful and powerful novel. Thoughtful students will gain much from the reading of this modern classic.

WOUK, HERMAN, *The Caine Mutiny*. (••Doubleday) Action-story fans will rank this intriguing book by one of America's most popular writers among the best. The action takes place on the minesweeper "Caine" during World War II.

•paperback ••paperback and hard-cover.

part one THREE
CENTURIES
of AMERICAN
LITERATURE
1607-1900

Founding of
Jamestown, Virginia

Champlain
founds
Quebec

1600   1610

A Graphic Chronology
of American literature and life

Compared to the long chronology of literature in England, France, and various other countries around the world, the history of literature in the United States is very short. A scant three hundred and fifty years separates the first sparse journals of discovery and exploration from today's wealth of literature of all types. The graphic chronology to the year 1900 on the following six pages, with its continuation into the twentieth century on pages 442-443, traces the swift and splendid rise of American literature from John Smith's *True Relation* to the present day.

Illustrations used for landing of the pilgrims, founding of Harvard, and Salem trials photographed by James Ballard. The Battle of Naseby courtesy of The British Museum. All other illustrations from Culver Pictures, Inc.

• John Smith,
  A True Rela

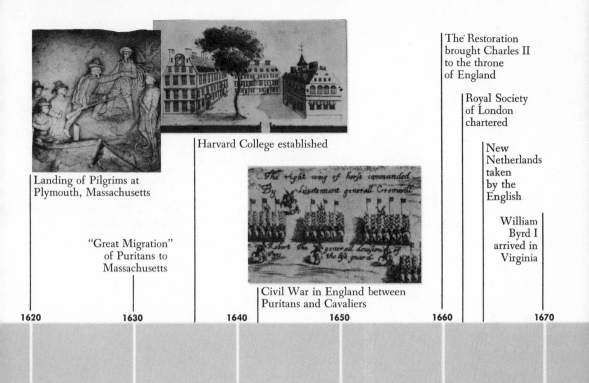

The Restoration brought Charles II to the throne of England

Royal Society of London chartered

New Netherlands taken by the English

William Byrd I arrived in Virginia

Harvard College established

Landing of Pilgrims at Plymouth, Massachusetts

"Great Migration" of Puritans to Massachusetts

Civil War in England between Puritans and Cavaliers

| 1620 | 1630 | 1640 | 1650 | 1660 | 1670 |

CAPTAIN JOHN SMITH 1579-1631
WILLIAM BRADFORD 1590-1657
ANNE BRADSTREET c1612-1672

TAYLOR

• John Smith, *The Generall Historie of Virginia, New England, and the Summer Isles*

• *The Bay Psalm Book*

• William Bradford, *A History of Plymouth Plantation*

• Anne Bradstreet, *The Tenth Muse Lately Spring Up in America*

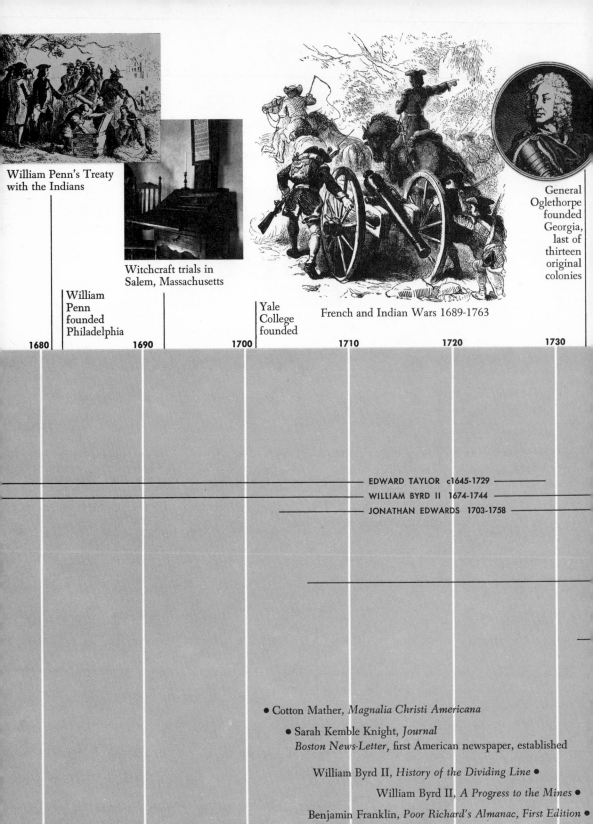

William Penn's Treaty
with the Indians

Witchcraft trials in
Salem, Massachusetts

William
Penn
founded
Philadelphia

Yale
College
founded

French and Indian Wars 1689-1763

General
Oglethorpe
founded
Georgia,
last of
thirteen
original
colonies

| 1680 | 1690 | 1700 | 1710 | 1720 | 1730 |

EDWARD TAYLOR c1645-1729 ————

WILLIAM BYRD II 1674-1744 ————

JONATHAN EDWARDS 1703-1758 ————

• Cotton Mather, *Magnalia Christi Americana*

• Sarah Kemble Knight, *Journal*
Boston News-Letter, first American newspaper, established

William Byrd II, *History of the Dividing Line* •

William Byrd II, *A Progress to the Mines* •

Benjamin Franklin, *Poor Richard's Almanac, First Edition* •

Franklin's kite experiment

General Braddock defeated by
French and Indians

Battle of
Lexington

Declaration of Independence

First ascent of men
in a free balloon

Constitutional
Convention in
Philadelphia

1740   1750   1760   1770   1780   1790

IRVING

BENJAMIN FRANKLIN 1706-1790
THOMAS PAINE 1737-1809
THOMAS JEFFERSON 1743-1826
PHILIP FRENEAU 1752-1832
GEORGE WASHINGTON 1732-1799

• Jonathan Edwards, *Sinners in the Hands of an Angry God*

• Benjamin Franklin, *The Way to Wealth*

Benjamin Franklin, *Autobiography* (first part) •

• Thomas Paine, *Common Sense*

Philip Freneau, *The British Prison-Ship* •

Thomas Jefferson, *Notes on the State of Virginia* •

Alexander Hamilton, *The Federalist* •

Louisiana Purchase

War of 1812

Andrew Jackson
inaugurated
seventh President

Mexican War
began

U.S. Census:
population
nearly
5,500,000

Erie Canal
completed

U.S. Census:
population
17,000,000

California
Gold Rush

1800	1810	1820	1830	1840	1850

WASHINGTON IRVING 1783-1859
WILLIAM CULLEN BRYANT 1794-1878
JAMES FENIMORE COOPER 1789-1851
EDGAR ALLAN POE 1809-1849
HENRY DAVID THOREAU 1817-1862
RALPH WALDO EMERSON 1803-1882
OLIVER WENDELL HOLMES 1809-1894
HENRY WADSWORTH LONGFELLOW 1807-1882
JAMES RUSSELL LOWELL 1819-1891
JOHN GREENLEAF WHITTIER 1807-1892
NATHANIEL HAWTHORNE 1804-1864
HERMAN MELVILLE 1819-1891

PAINE
JEFFERSON
FRENEAU
WASHINGTON

Washington Irving,
Knickerbocker's History

Edgar Allan Poe, *Tales of the Grotesque and Arabesque* ●

Henry David Thoreau
Walden

James Fenimore Cooper, *The Deerslayer* ●

Walt Whitman
Leaves of Grass

William Cullen Bryant, "Thanatopsis" ●

Ralph Waldo Emerson, *Essays* ●

Washington Irving, *Sketch Book* ●

Henry Wadsworth Longfellow, *Evangeline* ●

James Russell Lowell, *The Biglow Papers, First Series* ●

Herman Melville, *Redburn* ●

Nathaniel Hawthorne, *The Scarlet Letter* ●

War Between the States

Bell telephone patented

Edison invented
incandescent lamp

U.S. Census:
population 50,000,000

coln
ted
sident

Union Pacific Railroad
completed

Early automobile
made in America

Spanish-American War

| 1860 | 1870 | 1880 | 1890 | 1900 | 1910 |

HEMINGWAY

FAULKNER

FROST

SANDBURG

WALT WHITMAN 1819-1892

PAUL HAMILTON HAYNE 1830-1886

HENRY TIMROD 1828-1867

ABRAHAM LINCOLN 1809-1865

SAMUEL CLEMENS 1835-1910

BRET HARTE 1836-1902

SARAH ORNE JEWETT 1849-1909

STEPHEN CRANE 1871-1900

SIDNEY LANIER 1842-1881

EMILY DICKINSON 1830-1886

• *Atlantic Monthly* established

• Oliver Wendell Holmes,
  Autocrat of the Breakfast-Table

• Henry Timrod, "Ethnogenesis"

• John Greenleaf Whittier, *Snow-Bound*

• Bret Harte, *The Luck of Roaring Camp and Other Stories*

• Sidney Lanier, "The Marshes of Glynn"

• Samuel Clemens, *Adventures of Huckleberry Finn*

• Sarah Orne Jewett, *A White Heron and Other Stories*

• Stephen Crane,
  The Red Badge of Courage

chapter one Planters and Puritans

That the speech, laws, and institutions of the United States are so largely English is a miracle. They might easily, had two or three events turned out differently, have been Spanish or French. Both Spain and France were active in America earlier and on a larger scale than England. Large and powerful nations, they left many traces of their presence in vast segments of North America—the Great Lakes region, the Mississippi Valley, the Southwest, the Gulf Coast, and Florida. American place names tell the story of a land once occupied predominantly by non-English peoples: the Indians, the French, and the Spaniards.

Right: Mayflower II in Plymouth Harbor.
Next page: A closer view of her high stern.

Nevertheless, the dominant force in the development of the United States turned out to be the folk of an island not quite so large as the present state of Oregon. They, the English, were not much interested in North America until a century and a half after Columbus had discovered it. In the reign of Elizabeth I (1558-1603), however, thanks largely to war with Spain and a great expansion of sea trade, a few Englishmen began to point out the advantages of establishing colonies in the New World. Colonies, they argued, would put money into English pockets, provide land and opportunity for the poor and the idle, strengthen England by ending its dependence upon rivals for timber, ship stores, and the materials of war. Furthermore, was it not England's plain duty to save the American savages from the unreformed religion of Spain and France? Such appeals—to love of money, love of country, and love of Protestantism—at length persuaded the English to colonize. Today the effects of that decision may be seen around the world, but most remarkably, perhaps, in the United States.

No conscious planning or general enthusiasm was involved. The profit motive, which was behind several sixteenth-century attempts to establish permanent colonies in America, finally brought a lasting settlement at Jamestown in Virginia in 1607. Its success was based on a growing European craving for tobacco, which the Virginia colonists quickly learned to raise and market.

Religious motives, as well as economic, lay behind the other early settlements, those of the Pilgrims and the Puritans in New England. The Pilgrims, a small religious group which had left the state Church of England and lived for a time in Holland, landed at Plymouth in Massachu-

setts in 1620. United by their faith and by earnest leaders, they learned to cultivate Indian corn and the other food plants of a northern land and to take a modest part in the North Atlantic fisheries. Before long, however, the Pilgrims were surrounded and absorbed by the Puritans of the "Great Migration" of 1628-1640. In the space of twelve years, about 25,000 persons moved from England to the colonies of Massachusetts, Rhode Island, New Haven, and Hartford. They were called Puritans because their leaders, many of them wealthy and well educated, had wished to reform further, or "purify," the Church of England. Having failed to get their way, they decided to found commonwealths in America in which they could have what they felt to be the most desirable relation between church and state: a theocracy, or a state whose head would be God and whose laws would be those of God's word, the Holy Bible. The Puritans did not achieve a theocracy, but they did establish quickly and firmly a diversified economy under which New England grew and prospered. Agriculture, light industry, trade, fishing, shipbuilding, and seafaring soon made life in New England much like that in the island from which the settlers came.

By the end of the seventeenth century the two most important colonies were Virginia and Massachusetts. They typify two distinct ways of life in the period of settlement. The differences resulted from climate, geography, economic opportunity, and the nature and ambitions of the people who chose the one colony or the other for their homes.

In Virginia, tobacco had created the plantation way of life, with its great and beautiful houses for the fortunate few and its desire to perpetuate in America the traditions of the English landed aristocracy. Because it involved Negro slavery, this way of life had elements of danger, but generations of Virginians loved it, and its traditions of hospitality, good manners, taste, and learning have remained one part of American civilization.

In Massachusetts, more diversified occupations had produced the town or village way of life. Agriculture was less important—and, considering New England's rocky soil, much more difficult—than a number of other ways of making a living. Puritan emphasis on religion, especially on read-

ing the Bible, made education of more general concern in Massachusetts than in Virginia. Slavery was not yet a moral issue (indeed, some of the Puritan clergymen owned slaves), but, except for the Yankee slave traders, it was not profitable. Massachusetts town life, centering around the meeting house, was less aristocratic than that of the plantation.

For many years, Virginia and Massachusetts were closer to England than they were to each other. The one looked to the England of squires and country houses, the other to the England of tradesmen and mariners. In time, Virginia and Massachusetts were drawn together, along with the colonies settled later, by a common opposition to increased control by Parliament and the King's ministers. Each has a claim, however, to be called the cradle of American independence. Each provided heroes of our national history when the descendants of the Puritans and the descendants of the Planters were brought together in the Revolutionary War.

Planter and Puritan, in short, have each a place in American history and in present-day attitudes toward life in the United States. To understand them better we turn to the early colonial writers—to the men and women who, somehow, found the time to write. The demands and hazards of a raw wilderness left the colonist little leisure: when he did write, his pen served a practical purpose. Because of this utilitarian approach, early colonial literature consists largely of travel narratives, sermons, and a vast amount of autobiographical writing in the form of diaries, journals, histories, and some poems. In each instance we see the colonist writing to inform or instruct his reader.

We shall first consider the writer who best exemplifies the culture of each section of the new country: William Byrd II, the most articulate Virginian of the early eighteenth century, and Jonathan Edwards, the embodiment of the American Puritan tradition. Then we shall turn back further into early American life to see how people of different occupations used their pens for various purposes. There is Captain John Smith writing his *True Relation* to urge Englishmen to try life in the New World, and William Bradford recording the history of Plymouth for his family and friends. There is Anne Bradstreet, Puritan housewife, who sent her poems to England to be published, and Edward Taylor, Puritan minister, whose religious poems were a well-kept secret for over two hundred years. Reading from the works of these early Americans will round out our idea of the writings of Planter and Puritan.

Opposite: An Indian village as it looked in 1590 (left). Photographs showing the outside and inside of a reconstructed wigwam, Pioneer Village, Salem (center).
The Jabez Howland House (right), built in 1666, the only house still existing in Plymouth used by one of the Pilgrims.
Right: A tobacco wharf shown in a detail from an eighteenth-century map.

COLONIAL WILLIAMSBURG

William Byrd II

1674-1744

William Byrd II was born into the planter aristocracy of Virginia. His father, as a youth of eighteen, had come from London in 1670 to inherit an uncle's estate. Three years after his arrival he married a young widow of some social standing, the daughter of Colonel Horsmanden, an English soldier and country gentleman. Like many of his fellow colonists, Colonel Horsmanden had come to Virginia when the forces of King Charles I were defeated by the Puritans in the Civil War that devastated England in mid-seventeenth century. Soon after his daughter's wedding he returned to England to live. His country house in Essex, northeast of London, became the transatlantic base of the Byrd family. William Byrd II and his three sisters were all educated in England under the eye of the Horsmanden family.

In the Virginia Colony the first William Byrd prospered. With a talent for buying and selling, he dealt in land, furs, slaves, tobacco, and imported goods of every kind. When he died in 1704 he left his only son and namesake, then a man of thirty, 26,000 acres and all that went with them.

VIRGINIA GENTLEMAN

William Byrd II lived for thirty of his seventy years in England. He was first taken there as an infant, to be out of danger of an Indian attack. At the age of seven he left Virginia again, this time to be educated at Felsted Grammar School, a few miles from the Horsmanden home. He learned Latin, Greek, and Hebrew, and for the rest of his life felt it was his duty to read something each day in one of the ancient languages. At sixteen he was in Holland briefly, to observe Dutch ways of doing business. After a short time with an English business firm, he entered the Middle Temple[1] to study law, and in 1695, aged twenty-one, he was admitted to the bar.

Among his friends in the Middle Temple were two famous dramatists, William Congreve and William Wycherley, who perhaps gave him his lifelong interest in the theater. The chief evidence of Byrd's unusual charm and promise, however, is his adoption as a protégé by Sir Robert Southwell (1633-1702), who was Secretary of State for Ireland and, between 1690 and 1696, President of the Royal Society of London for the Advancement of Science, the oldest and most renowned scientific organization in Great Britain. Southwell introduced Byrd to many famous and influential men in political and scientific circles, some of whom were very useful to him

---

1. *Middle Temple*, one of the four Inns of Court in London that prepare students for a legal career.

in diplomatic missions he later undertook for the Virginia Colony. In 1696 Byrd was elected a Fellow of the Royal Society.

Except for brief periods in Virginia, Byrd spent his time in England until after his father's death in 1704. Soon after receiving his inheritance he married, in May 1706, Lucy Parke, daughter of a Virginian landowner and soldier who at that time was governor of the Leeward Islands. With his bride he settled at Westover on the James River, the house his father had built and which he was soon to rebuild and enlarge. Here in the Virginia Tidewater, not far from the capital at Williamsburg, he began to lead the life of a Virginia plantation owner. But Byrd was not just another wealthy planter. Much of the interest in him today is based on the fact that for a good part of his life he kept a "secret" or shorthand diary, which provides the best picture that we have of the day-by-day life of a Virginian of the ruling class. Since 1941 three portions of the diary have been decoded and published. The first covers the years between 1709 and 1712, and is the most important in understanding the planter. The second and third are the diaries of 1717-1721, when for the most part he was in London, and of 1739-1741, near the end of his life. A typical entry is that of February 4, 1711:

4. I rose at 5 o'clock and read a chapter in Hebrew and some Greek in Lucian. I said my prayers and ate boiled milk for breakfast. I gave my necessary orders

Opposite: Old capitol, Williamsburg. Right: Portrait of William Byrd II, painted in London between 1715 and 1720.

to Tom Turpin and he went away about 10 o'clock. About 11 we walked to church and heard a good sermon of Mr. Anderson. After church we ate some toast and drank some mead and went over the creek with our horses where the water was very high and I was very wet and got a violent cold. Mrs. Dunn[2] returned home and we rode to my brother Duke's[3] where we found all well. My sister did not ask us to eat till my brother came home and then I got some milk and potatoes. My cold grew worse. About 9 o'clock we went to bed. I said a short prayer and had good thoughts, good humor, and indifferent good health, thank God Almighty.[4]

Byrd's diary is filled with minutiae of everyday living as well as with larger concerns. In it he comments on his health and that of his family and "people" (that is, his slaves), on his reading, his visitors, his trips and his business, and other matters.

His personal life had its tragedies. Lucy bore him two sons, both of whom died in infancy, and two daughters. Byrd returned to England in 1715, staying until 1719. Lucy joined him there late in 1716; a few months later she died of smallpox. The 1717-1721 diary describes Byrd's courtship of several different women. In 1724 he married Maria Taylor, took her back to Virginia, and rounded out his life in domestic tranquillity.

That Byrd should regard London rather than Williamsburg as the center of his life is not surprising. His writings sometimes suggest that life in Virginia was dull by comparison with that in England; he even used "banishment" to describe his situation. More often, however, he made the best of things and expressed himself satisfied with his native land. The letter printed below, written to his friend Charles Boyle, the Earl of Orrery, is a bright picture.

---

2. *Mrs. Dunn*, a friend of Mrs. Byrd's.   3. *my brother Duke's*. Byrd refers to James Duke and his wife as "brother" and "sister." They may have been distantly related to the Byrd family.   4. *The Secret Diary of William Byrd of Westover, 1709-1712*, ed. Louis B. Wright and Marion Tinling. Copyright 1941 by Louis B. Wright and Marion Tinling. The Dietz Press, Richmond, p. 296.

Byrd's Westover Plantation as it appears today.

Letter to Charles Boyle

July 5, 1726

Besides the advantage of a pure air, we abound in all kinds of provisions without expense (I mean we who have plantations). I have a large family of my own, and my doors are open to everybody, yet I have no bills to pay and half-a-crown will rest undisturbed in my pocket for many moons together. Like one of the patriarchs, I have my flocks and my herds, my bondmen and bondwomen, and every sort of trade amongst my own servants so that I live in a kind of independence of everyone but Providence. However this sort of life is without expense, yet it is attended with a great deal of trouble. I must take care to keep all my people in their duty, to set all the springs in motion and to make every one draw his equal share to carry the machine forward. But then 'tis an amusement in this silent country and a continual exercise of our patience and economy. Another thing, My Lord, that recommends this country very much: we sit securely under our vines and our fig trees without any danger to our property. We have neither public robbers nor private, which your Lordship will think very strange when we have often needy governors and pilfering convicts sent amongst us. . . . Thus, My Lord, we are very happy in our Canaans if we could but forget the onions and fleshpots of Egypt.[1]

"Letter to Charles Boyle" by William Byrd, from *The Virginia Magazine of History and Biography*. Virginia Historical Society, Richmond, 1924.

1. *we are very happy in our Canaans . . . Egypt.* Using Biblical references to convey his meaning, Byrd states that the Virginia planters, like himself, would be very happy in their lands of promise (Canaans) if they could forget the pleasures of England (Egypt). Byrd implies that the Israelites, long held captive in Egypt, may have yearned for the comforts of Egypt after they had reached their Promised Land, Canaan.

MAN OF AFFAIRS Sir Robert Southwell's influence in shaping the life of his young protégé was strong and beneficial. In his respect for learning and in his sense of civic responsibility Byrd did his best to live like Southwell. A character sketch written by Byrd years later (see page 104) shows Southwell was the Virginian's ideal. As a very young man Byrd was elected to Virginia's House of Burgesses. In 1709 he was made a member of the King's Council, the highest governing body in the colony, a position he held until his death. On several occasions he served in England as an agent for Virginia. In 1728 he was one of the commissioners in charge of running the dividing line between Virginia and North Carolina.

William Byrd was continually acquiring more land; at the time of his death he held title to almost 180,000 acres. The fact that much of this land was on the frontier led to his increasing interest in the rich, unsettled lands to the west. Decades before the French penetrated into the Ohio Valley, Byrd was warning Williamsburg of this danger. He laid out the city of Richmond and is honored as its founder.

Amid all the business of public affairs, Byrd never lost the interest in learning and in books that his fine education had awakened. He gradually collected the finest library in the colonies. He corresponded with fellow

Illustration from a book on tobacco growing (1800) showing method of rolling tobacco.

COLONIAL WILLIAMSBURG

103

members in the Royal Society. He not only kept a detailed diary and wrote numerous letters notable for their wit and urbanity, but he also wrote a number of things intended for publication. While a number of pamphlets were published during his lifetime, he spent much time, obviously, on three manuscripts which were not printed until 1841. Called the Westover Manuscripts, they were essays or travel sketches. *History of the Dividing Line, Run in the Year 1728,* which exists in two quite different forms, describes his experiences as one of the commissioners for surveying the Virginia-North Carolina boundary, part of which ran through the Great Dismal Swamp. *A Journey to the Land of Eden in the Year 1723* and *A Progress to the Mines in the Year 1732* (see page 105) tell of trips he made into the back country to inspect lands which he had purchased and to evaluate industrial possibilities. In all three pieces he tried to use his literary knowledge, and he shows a contempt for the ignorance and "piggishness" of the frontier worthy of the most untraveled Londoner.

Men like Byrd had little sympathy with the frontier and the small farm. Their world was that of civilization, as represented by the landed gentry of England. Yet they resisted royal governors and centralized control as vigorously as any Yankee tradesman or back-country "poor white." In the generation after Byrd's, the planter aristocracy was to make Virginia the "mother of Presidents."

COLONIAL WILLIAMSBURG

Kasitzky's Beft Virginia *LONDON.*

Top: Detail of a tobacco plant.
Above: Label for tobacco grown in Virginia to be sold in London.

Sir Robert Southwell

He had the happiness of an early virtue in spite of the ignorance of childhood, and the vanity and madness of youth. He had from his cradle an infirm constitution, which, however, was made up to him by a sound and vigorous mind. But for all this, the frequent interruptions of his health had no unkind influence on the sweetness and serenity of his temper. He had alone the secret of giving pleasure to others, at the very moment he felt pain himself. While he was young, he was wise enough to instruct the old, and when he came to be old, he was agreeable enough to please the young. All that had the honor of his conversation confessed that he had a peculiar talent of mixing delight with information. Religion appeared in all her charms when he was practicing it; he had zeal without bitterness, devotion without hypocrisy, and charity without ostentation. His principles were so

"Sir Robert Southwell" from *Another Secret Diary of William Byrd of Westover,* ed. Maude H. Woodfin and Marion Tinling. The Dietz Press, Inc., Richmond, 1942. Modernized. By permission of the publishers and authors.

firmly riveted that he was able to converse in a corrupt court[1] above thirty years, without any prejudice to his integrity. During that whole time, he signalized his fidelity to his Prince without forfeiting his duty to his country. And though he was all that while a courtier, and in eminent stations, yet he improved his virtue and his understanding more abundantly than his estate. Nobody had ever a more powerful knack of education, for he knew how to infuse his own bright qualities into all that had the happiness of his tuition, and could give virtue so many graces as to make it irresistible. He was so great a master of persuasion that he could charm people into their duty, without the harsh methods of discipline and severity. He devoted most of his time and his thoughts to the glorious and generous design of doing good, and was at once the friend and favorite of mankind. Whatever he undertook was forecast with so much prudence and sagacity that he left no room for repentance. He had a mighty fund of knowledge, and was always the wiser and better for what he knew. He was so uncorrupt, so untainted with vice and folly, that whoever was intimate with him had the nearest prospect of innocence that he can ever meet with out of Paradise.

FROM *A Progress to the Mines in the Year 1732*

In the fall of 1732, Byrd made an extended trip to inspect his frontier mining properties and to collect what information he could about the manufacture of iron. He stopped to visit with various planters along his way; on September 27 he reached the home of Colonel Alexander Spotswood, the owner and operator of some iron mines. Colonel Spotswood had formerly been colonial governor of Virginia (1710-1722), and in his attempt to limit the power of the Council had been vigorously opposed by Byrd. Judging from Byrd's description of their visit, the controversy in which the two men had engaged did not affect their mutual respect and friendship.

27th. ... I came into the main country road that leads from Fredericksburg to Germanna, which last place I reached in ten miles more. This famous town consists of Colonel Spotswood's enchanted castle on one side of the street, and a baker's dozen of ruinous tenements on the other, where so many German families had dwelt some years ago; but are now removed ten miles higher, in the fork of Rappahannock, to land of their own. There had also been a chapel about a bowshot from the Colonel's house, at the end of an avenue of cherry trees, but some pious people had lately burnt it down, with intent to get another built nearer to their own homes. Here I arrived about three o'clock, and found only Mrs. Spotswood at home, who received her old acquaintance with many a gracious smile. I was carried into a room elegantly set off with pier glasses, the largest of which came soon after to an odd misfortune. Amongst other favorite animals that cheered this lady's solitude, a brace of tame deer ran familiarly about the house, and one of them came to stare at me as a stranger. But unluckily spying his own figure in the glass, he made a spring over the tea table that stood under it and shattered the glass to pieces, and falling back upon the tea table, made a terrible fracas among the china. This exploit was so sudden and accompanied with such a noise that it surprised me, and perfectly frightened Mrs. Spotswood. But 'twas worth all the damage to show the moderation and good humor with which she bore this disaster.

In the evening the noble Colonel came home from his mines, who saluted me very civilly, and Mrs. Spotswood's sister, Miss Theky, who had been to meet him *en cavalier*,[1] was so kind too as to bid me welcome. We talked over a legend[2] of old stories, supped about nine, and then prattled with the ladies till it was time for a traveler to retire. In the meantime I observed my old friend to be very uxorious, and exceedingly fond of his children. This was so opposite to the maxims he used to preach up before he was married that I could not forbear rubbing up the memory of them.

SIR ROBERT SOUTHWELL   1. *corrupt court*, the court of Charles II.

A PROGRESS TO THE MINES   1. *en cavalier* (äɴ kä vä lyä′), on horseback.   2. *legend*, legion, or great number.

But he gave a very good-natured turn to his change of sentiments, by alleging that whoever brings a poor gentlewoman into so solitary a place, from all her friends and acquaintance, would be ungrateful not to use her and all that belongs to her with all possible tenderness.

28th. We all kept snug in our several apartments till nine, except Miss Theky, who was the housewife of the family. At that hour we met over a pot of coffee, which was not quite strong enough to give us the palsy. After breakfast the Colonel and I left the ladies to their domestic affairs and took a turn in the garden, which has nothing beautiful but three terrace walks that fall in slopes one below another. I let him understand that besides the pleasure of paying him a visit I came to be instructed by so great a master in the mystery of making of iron, wherein he had led the way, and was the Tubal Cain of Virginia.[3] He corrected me a little there, by assuring me he was not only the first in this country,[4] but the first in North America, who had erected a regular furnace.[5] That they ran altogether upon bloomeries in New England and Pennsylvania,[6] till his example had made them attempt greater works. But in this last colony, they have so few ships to carry their iron to Great Britain that they must be content to make it only for their own use, and must be obliged to manufacture it when they have done. That he hoped he had done the country very great service by setting so good an example. That the four furnaces now at work in Virginia circulated a great sum of money for provisions and all other necessaries in the adjacent counties. That they took off a great number of hands from planting tobacco and employed them in works that produced a large sum of money in England to the persons concerned, whereby the country is so much the richer.

Then I inquired after his own mines, and hoped, as he was the first engaged in this great undertaking, that he had brought them to the most perfection. He told me he had iron in several parts of his great tract of land, consisting of 45,000 acres. But that the mine he was at work upon was thirteen miles below Ger-

manna. That his ore (which was very rich) he raised a mile from his furnace, and was obliged to cart the iron, when it was made, fifteen miles to Massaponox, a plantation he had upon Rappahannock River; but that the road was exceeding good, gently declining all the way, and had no more than one hill to go up in the whole journey. For this reason his loaded carts went it in a day without difficulty. He said it was true his works were of the oldest standing, but that his long absence in England, and the wretched management of Mr. Greame, whom he had entrusted with his affairs, had put him back very much. . . . That his furnace stood still a great part of the time, and all his plantations ran to ruin. That indeed he was rightly served for committing his affairs to the care of a mathematician, whose thoughts were always among the stars.

Our conversation on this subject continued till dinner, which was both elegant and plentiful. The afternoon was devoted to the ladies, who showed me one of their most beautiful walks. They conducted me through a shady lane to the landing, and by the way made me drink some very fine water that issued from a marble fountain and ran incessantly. Just behind it was a covered bench, where Miss Theky often sat and bewailed her maiden state. Then we proceeded to the river, which is the south branch of Rappahannock, about fifty yards wide, and so rapid that the ferry-boat is drawn over by a chain, and therefore called the Rapidan. At night we drank prosperity to all the Colonel's projects in a bowl of rack punch, and then retired to our devotions.

29th. Having employed about two hours in retirement, I sallied out at the first summons to breakfast, where our conversation with the ladies, like whip sillabub, was very pretty, but

3. *the Tubal Cain* (tū′bəl kān) *of Virginia.* Tubal Cain is mentioned in the Bible (Genesis 4:22) as "an instructor of artificers in brass and iron." He is regarded as the inventor of the metal-working arts. 4. *country,* colony. 5. *a regular furnace,* a real plant for removing the iron from the ore and for reheating it for shaping into various forms. 6. *they ran altogether upon bloomeries in New England and Pennsylvania.* A bloomery was the first forge in an ironworks where the metal, already separated from the ore, was made into lumps of iron. The manufacturers of New England and Pennsylvania had only bloomeries as contrasted with Colonel Spotswood's more modern furnace.

had nothing in it. This it seems was Miss Theky's birthday, upon which I made her my compliments, and wished she might live twice as long a married woman as she had lived a maid. I did not presume to pry into the secret of her age, nor was she forward to disclose it, for this humble reason, lest I should think her wisdom fell short of her years.

Then the Colonel and I took another turn in the garden, to discourse farther on the subject of iron. He was very frank in communicating all his dear-bought experience to me, and told me very civilly he would not only let me into the whole secret, but would make a journey to James River, and give me his faithful opinion of all my conveniences. For his part he wished there were many more ironworks in the country, provided the parties concerned would preserve a constant harmony among themselves, and meet and consult frequently, what might be for their common advantage.

30th. The sun rose clear this morning, and so did I, and finished all my little affairs by breakfast. It was then resolved to wait on the ladies on horseback, since the bright sun, the fine air, and the wholesome exercise, all invited us to it. We forded the river a little above the ferry, and rode six miles up the neck to a fine level piece of rich land, where we found about twenty plants of ginseng with the scarlet berries growing of the top of the middle stalk. The root of this is of wonderful virtue in many cases, particularly to raise the spirits and promote perspiration, which makes it a specific in colds and coughs. The Colonel complimented me with all we found, in return for my telling him the virtues of it. We were all pleased to find so much of this king of plants so near the Colonel's habitation, and growing too upon his own land; but were, however, surprised to find it upon level ground, after we had been told it grew only upon the north side of stony mountains. I carried home this treasure, with as much joy, as if every root had been a graft of the Tree of Life,[7] and washed and dried it carefully.

---

7. *Tree of Life*, a tree in the Garden of Eden. According to its description in the Book of Genesis, the food of this tree gave everlasting life.

This airing made us as hungry as so many hawks, so that between appetite and a very good dinner, 'twas difficult to eat like a philosopher. In the afternoon the ladies walked me about amongst all their little animals, with which they amuse themselves, and furnish the table; the worst of it is, they are so tenderhearted, they shed a silent tear every time any of them are killed. At night the Colonel and I quitted the threadbare subject of iron, and changed the scene to politics. . . . Our conversation was interrupted by a summons to supper, for the ladies, to show their power, had by this time brought us tamely to go to bed with our bellies full, though we both at first declared positively against it. So very pliable a thing is frail man when women have the bending of him.

 TO INCREASE UNDERSTANDING

1. Cite specific details from either the biography of William Byrd or from his writing that indicate the wealth, culture, and leisure of a gentleman planter.

2. (a) What admirable qualities did Sir Robert Southwell possess according to Byrd's character sketch of him? (b) How did Byrd's life reflect his influence?

3. In *A Progress to the Mines* Byrd writes, ". . . I came to be instructed by so great a master in the mystery of making of iron." (a) What information on industrial beginnings in the colonies do you gain from this selection? (b) How did Colonel Spotswood show himself to be proud of his standing in the iron industry? (c) What was his attitude in giving the information requested by Byrd?

4. Byrd's writing style has been described as witty, polished, and vivacious. (a) What influences shaped his writing? (b) Cite three or four passages which you feel justify this description.

EXTENDING INTERESTS

A round-table discussion group might be formed to investigate the reasons for the growth of an aristocratic class in Virginia and the effect of this class on economic life, architecture, literature, education, and clothing in the colony. Before holding the discussion, a chairman should be appointed, the subject divided into its various aspects, and each member of the group made responsible for reading up on one phase of the problem.

Jonathan Edwards

1703-1758

Jonathan Edwards' ancestors had arrived in New England during the Great Migration, settling near Hartford, Connecticut, about 1640. For two generations the Edwardses were merchants; but Jonathan Edwards' father, Timothy, displayed a fondness for books and was sent to Harvard College. Here, in 1691, he received two degrees in one day: the B.A. in the morning and the M.A. in the afternoon. Continuing his studies, he was soon licensed to preach, and in 1694 he was ordained as pastor of a newly organized congregation at East Windsor, a few miles north of Hartford. Six months later he married Esther, daughter of the Reverend Solomon Stoddard of Northampton, Massachusetts, a minister of such force that he was called "Pope Stoddard" behind his back. Esther proved to be an ideal wife, her husband's superior in practicality. She managed all the family finances as well as the household, while Timothy spent long hours in his study working on his sermons and preparing young men for college entrance examinations. Timothy and Esther lived together for sixty-three years. Of their eleven children, the fifth child and the only boy was Jonathan.

A PURITAN BOYHOOD

Little is known of Jonathan Edwards' childhood. He is said to have begun to study Latin at six and was soon proficient in it and the other exercises set by his father. A fragment of autobiography (page 110) explains that at the age of seven he had the first of many "concerns and exercises" about his soul.

Since both Jonathan's father and grandfather were Congregationalist[1] ministers, the boy was very early trained in the beliefs of the Puritans. One of these was Calvin's doctrine of election. John Calvin, a sixteenth-century French leader of the Protestant Reformation, had taught that God chose only certain persons, "the elect," to be saved. As Jonathan Edwards grew older and began to ponder this idea, he found himself disliking the thought that God could choose whom He would for eternal life, rejecting others and leaving them to perish and be tormented for eternity in hell. Not until he was sixteen or seventeen and about to be graduated from Yale College did this Calvinistic doctrine satisfy him. A serious illness, followed by a period of great inward turmoil, finally led to his full acceptance of his complete dependence upon God. From then on he began to have what he called an "inward, sweet delight in God and divine things," as well as a new understanding of Christ, and redemption and salvation through Him. Such serenity, assurance, and a sense of beautiful unity were the enviable gifts which the Puritan faith gave to deeply religious men like Edwards. Not all Puritans received them, but they were what the preachers promised.

Opposite: Pulpit of the Old Ship Church, Hingham, Massachusetts, built in 1681.

---

1. *Congregationalist.* Two principal forms of church government developed in New England: Congregationalism in which each church governed itself, and Presbyterianism in which the church was governed by elected elders. In 1649, the Puritans agreed upon a form of church government which was partly Congregational and partly Presbyterian.

FROM *Personal Narrative*

I had a variety of concerns and exercises about my soul[1] from my childhood; but I had two more remarkable seasons of awakening, before I met with that change by which I was brought to those new dispositions, and that new sense of things, that I have since had. The first time was when I was a boy, some years before I went to college, at a time of remarkable awakening in my father's congregation. I was then very much affected for many months, and concerned about the things of religion, and my soul's salvation, and was abundant in religious duties. I used to pray five times a day in secret, and to spend much time in religious conversation with other boys, and used to meet with them to pray together.

I experienced I know not what kind of delight in religion. My mind was much engaged in it, and had much self-righteous pleasure; and it was my delight to abound in religious duties. I with some of my schoolmates joined together, and built a booth in a swamp, in a very retired spot, for a place of prayer. And besides, I had particular secret places of my own in the woods, where I used to retire by myself; and was from time to time much affected. My affections[2] seemed to be lively and easily moved, and I seemed to be in my element when engaged in religious duties. And I am ready to think, many are deceived with such affections, and such a kind of delight as I then had in religion, and mistake it for grace.

But in process of time, my convictions and affections wore off and I entirely lost all those affections and delights and left off secret prayer at least as to any constant performance of it. . . .

From my childhood up, my mind had been full of objections against the doctrine of God's sovereignty, in choosing whom He would to eternal life, and rejecting whom He pleased; leaving them eternally to perish, and be everlastingly tormented in hell. It used to appear like a horrible doctrine to me. But I remember the time very well, when I seemed to be convinced, and fully satisfied, as to this sovereignty of God, and His justice in thus eternally disposing of men, according to His sovereign pleasure. But I never could give an account how, or by what means, I was thus convinced, not in the least imagining at the time, nor a long time after, that there was any extraordinary influence of God's Spirit in it; but only that now I saw further, and my reason apprehended the justice and reasonableness of it. However my mind rested in it; and it put an end to all those cavils and objections. And there has been a wonderful alteration in my mind, with respect to the doctrine of God's sovereignty, from that day to this; so that I scarce ever have found so much as the rising of an objection against it, in the most absolute sense, in God showing mercy to whom He will show mercy, and hardening whom He will. God's absolute sovereignty and justice, with respect to salvation and damnation, is what my mind seems to rest assured of, as much as of any thing that I see with my eyes; at least it is so at times. But I have often, since that first conviction, had quite another kind of sense of God's sovereignty than I had then. I have often since had not only a conviction, but a delightful conviction. The doctrine has very often appeared exceeding pleasant, bright, and sweet. Absolute sovereignty is what I love to ascribe to God. But my first conviction was not so.

Not long after I first began to experience these things, I gave an account to my father of some things that had passed in my mind. I was pretty much affected by the discourse we had together; and when the discourse was ended, I walked abroad alone, in a solitary place in my father's pasture, for contemplation. And as I was walking there, and looking upon the sky and clouds, there came into my mind so sweet a sense of the glorious majesty and grace of God, as I know not how to express. I seemed to see them both in a sweet conjunction; majesty and meekness joined together; it was a sweet, and gentle, and holy majesty; and also

---

1. *exercises about my soul.* Edwards means that he undertook various practices to strengthen his spiritual life.
2. *affections,* disposition of mind.

a majestic meekness; an awful sweetness; a high, and great, and holy gentleness.

After this my sense of divine things gradually increased, and became more and more lively, and had more of that inward sweetness. The appearance of everything was altered; there seemed to be, as it were, a calm, sweet cast, or appearance of divine glory, in almost everything. God's excellency, His wisdom, His purity and love, seemed to appear in everything; in the sun, moon, and stars; in the clouds and blue sky; in the grass, flowers, trees; in the water, and all nature; which used greatly to fix my mind. I often used to sit and view the moon for a long time; and in the day spent much time in viewing the clouds and sky, to behold the sweet glory of God in these things; in the meantime singing forth, with a low voice, my contemplations of the Creator and Redeemer. And scarce anything, among all the works of nature, was so sweet to me as thunder and lightning; formerly, nothing had been so terrible to me. Before, I used to be uncommonly terrified with thunder, and to be struck with terror when I saw a thunderstorm rising; but now, on the contrary, it rejoiced me. I felt God, if I may so speak, at the first appearance of a thunderstorm; and used to take the opportunity, at such times, to fix myself in order to view the clouds and see the lightning play, and hear the majestic and awful voice of God's thunder, which oftentimes was exceedingly entertaining, leading me to sweet contemplations of my great and glorious God. While thus engaged, it always seemed natural to me to sing, or chant forth my meditations; or, to speak my thoughts in soliloquies with a singing voice.

MINISTER   That Edwards should enter the ministry was natural, once he had found great satisfaction in religion. After he was graduated from Yale in 1720 (he was barely seventeen), he spent two years in the study of theology. He preached briefly at a Presbyterian church in New York in 1722-1723, returning to Yale as a tutor in 1724-1726. In the autumn of 1726 he was settled as his grandfather's colleague in the Congregational church at Northampton. The following year he married Sarah Pierpont of New Haven, a girl of seventeen noted for her religious fervor.

When his grandfather Stoddard died early in 1729, Edwards became sole minister at Northampton. Here he remained for over twenty years, during which time his fame as a preacher constantly grew greater. In fact, the image of Edwards as a stern and powerful preacher is so strong that one forgets that he lived a full family life. He and his wife had eleven children, three sons and eight daughters. According to F. B. Dexter,[1] during the later half of his ministry, Edwards wrote down his sermon outlines on scraps of paper, some of it the thin soft paper used by his wife and daughters to make fans. One sermon outline is on the back of a bill for "a Gold Locket and Chane" for Mrs. Edwards, another on the back of a stationer's bill which includes "1 childs plaything, four and sixpence."

Edwards' published sermons show that much of his effectiveness resulted from the logical, orderly, and artistic qualities of his presentation. His parishioners were deeply affected by his sermons, and in the winter and spring of 1734-1735 Northampton experienced a religious revival such as New England had never seen before. More than three hundred persons declared themselves converted, and religious fervor spread through the vicinity. For six months or more everyone talked of religion and of little else. Although Edwards was aware that not all those who believed that they had had a genuine religious experience could be trusted, he was convinced

1. *Proceedings of the Massachusetts Historical Society,* 1901-1902, pp. 14-16.

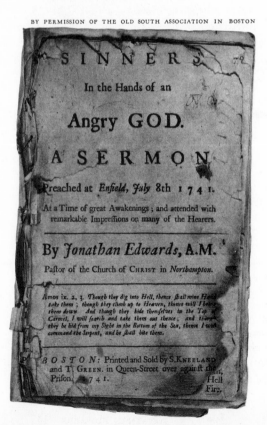

that God had wrought a great work. To describe it he wrote *A Faithful Narrative of the Surprising Work of God . . . in Northampton* (first draft 1736), many times printed in England and translated into German and Dutch.

The Northampton affair was the prelude to the "Great Awakening" of 1740-1742, in which the leader was an English Methodist preacher and evangelist, George Whitefield. The Great Awakening took religion to the masses and established revivalism as a characteristic feature of some American Protestant sects. In the midst of this religious enthusiasm Edwards preached a sermon which is a classic example of stirring a religious meeting by an appeal to fear. Although he delivered it unemotionally, *Sinners in the Hands of an Angry God* (page 113), because of the force, rhythm, and vividness of its language, so powerfully affected his hearers that they screamed out in pain as he spoke, some falling to the floor in emotional torment. Strong medicine as this sermon is, it is wholly consistent with Edwards' lifelong insistence on deep and genuine religious experience. In tone, however, it is much less appealing than his account of the sweetness of acknowledging God's sovereignty in a thunderstorm. And in justice to Edwards, one must remember that his "hellfire" sermon is not typical. It illustrates his faith in revivalism, but is not his most thoughtful writing on the problem of saving grace. That came in *A Treatise Concerning Religious Affections* (1746). Here he pleaded that a person should strive for "that sense of divine things, that apprehension of the truth, importance, and excellency of the things of religion, which then sways and prevails, and governs his heart and hands." He told his listeners that assurance of grace comes through a constant renewal of the initial religious experience. What Edwards demanded was a continuous, although humble, search for mystical experience like his own.

Had Edwards lived a hundred years earlier, he would have found a more general acceptance of his belief that individuals must be willing to describe publicly to the congregation their spir-

Above: A portrait of Jonathan Edwards. Below: Title page from the first printing of his "hellfire" sermon.

itual experiences. But in a period wherein the Puritan was changing into a Yankee and things other than religion became important, people were more reticent. Since Edwards wanted in his congregation only those who could offer some evidence of saving grace, a struggle developed between him and the most powerful members of the congregation. The outcome of the conflict was Edwards' dismissal from Northampton in 1750. His farewell sermon emphasized his future meeting with his congregation on the day of judgment, with the implication that he was more likely to be cleared than they.

Edwards lived for nearly eight years after his Northampton ministry ended. Most of the time he was at Stockbridge, where he had charge of a missionary church among the Massachusetts Indians. There he found time to write a number of impressive theological treatises on such subjects as the freedom of the will, original sin, redemption, the nature of true virtue, and God's purpose in creating the world.

In September 1757 Edwards was elected president of the College of New Jersey, now Princeton University. Although doubtful about his decision, he accepted and took up his duties early in 1758. Inoculated against smallpox, he developed a fever and died on March 22, less than three months after going to Princeton. His world-wide reputation as a theologian came for the most part after his death, as the books written at Stockbridge were printed and read.

Edwards obviously was an exceptional man, an outstanding representative of the Puritan way of life. In him may be seen its fiery core of mysticism as well as its fondness for theological disputation and its stern and uncompromising logic. He shows also Puritanism's high regard for education and learning and the Bible.

The Puritan gave to New England a God-centered universe and a gnawing conscience. This conscience was strongly for independence, as the only way of assuring religious independence, and in the late eighteenth and early nineteenth centuries it weighed heavily in such reform movements as abolition, temperance, pacifism, and equal rights for women.

FROM *Sinners in the Hands of an Angry God*

The wrath of God is like great waters that are dammed for the present; they increase more and more and rise higher and higher, till an outlet is given; and the longer the stream is stopped, the more rapid and mighty is its course when once it is let loose. 'Tis true that judgment against your evil work has not been executed hitherto; the floods of God's vengeance have been withheld; but your guilt in the meantime is constantly increasing, and you are every day treasuring up more wrath; the waters are continually rising and waxing more and more mighty; and there is nothing but the mere pleasure of God that holds the waters back, that are unwilling to be stopped, and press hard to go forward. If God should only withdraw his hand from the floodgate it would immediately fly open, and the fiery floods of the fierceness and wrath of God would rush forth with inconceivable fury, and would come upon you with omnipotent power; and if your strength were ten thousand times greater than it is, yea, ten thousand times greater than the strength of the stoutest, sturdiest devil in hell, it would be nothing to withstand or endure it.

The bow of God's wrath is bent, and the

arrow made ready on the string, and justice bends the arrow at your heart and strains the bow, and it is nothing but the mere pleasure of God, and that of an angry God, without any promise or obligation at all, that keeps the arrow one moment from being made drunk with your blood.

Thus are all you that never passed under a great change of heart by the mighty power of the Spirit of God upon your souls; all that were never born again and made new creatures, and raised from being dead in sin to a state of new and before altogether unexperienced light and life (however you may have reformed your life in many things, and may have had religious affections, and may keep up a form of religion in your families and closets and in the house of God, and may be strict in it), you are thus in the hands of an angry God; 'tis nothing but his mere pleasure that keeps you from being this moment swallowed up in everlasting destruction.

However unconvinced you may now be of the truth of what you hear, by and by you will be fully convinced of it. Those that are gone from being in the like circumstances with you, see that it was so with them; for destruction came suddenly upon most of them; when they expected nothing of it, and while they were saying, Peace and Safety. Now they see that those things that they depended on for peace and safety were nothing but thin air and empty shadows.

The God that holds you over the pit of hell much as one holds a spider or some loathsome insect over the fire, abhors you, and is dreadfully provoked; his wrath toward you burns like fire; he looks upon you as worthy of nothing else but to be cast into the fire; he is of purer eyes than to bear to have you in his sight; you are ten thousand times so abominable in his eyes as the most hateful and venomous serpent is in ours. You have offended him infinitely more than ever a stubborn rebel did his prince; and yet it is nothing but his hand that holds you from falling into the fire every moment. 'Tis ascribed to nothing else, that you did not go to hell the last night; that you were suffered to awake again in this world after you closed your eyes to sleep and there is no

other reason to be given why you have not dropped into hell since you arose in the morning, but that God's hand has held you up. There is no other reason to be given why you have not gone to hell since you have sat here in the house of God, provoking his pure eyes by your sinful wicked manner of attending his solemn worship. Yea, there is nothing else that is to be given as a reason why you don't this very moment drop down into hell.

O sinner! Consider the fearful danger you are in. 'Tis a great furnace of wrath, a wide and bottomless pit, full of the fire of wrath, that you are held over in the hand of that God whose wrath is provoked and incensed as much against you as against many of the damned in hell. You hang by a slender thread, with the flames of divine wrath flashing about it, and ready every moment to singe it and burn it asunder; and you have no interest in any Mediator, and nothing to lay hold of to save yourself, nothing to keep off the flames of wrath, nothing of your own, nothing that you ever have done, nothing that you can do, to induce God to spare you one moment....

❧ TO INCREASE UNDERSTANDING

1. In "Personal Narrative," Edwards writes, "I had a variety of concerns and exercises about my soul from my childhood." (a) Describe these childhood exercises. (b) What aspects of Edwards' upbringing account for such a serious religious interest in one so young?

2. (a) Judging from "Personal Narrative," why did Calvin's doctrine of election seem "horrible" to Jonathan Edwards? (b) How did he come to accept the doctrine? (c) Cite examples of how his "delightful" conviction changed the appearance of everything for him.

3. (a) Describe Edwards' Northampton ministry. (b) What qualities made Edwards stand out among the ministers of New England? (c) Explain the combination of circumstances that resulted in his dismissal.

4. (a) What images describe the wrath of God in Sinners in the Hands of an Angry God? (b) What qualities in Edwards' prose contribute to the effect this sermon had on his congregation?

5. Both of the selections you have read affirm Edwards' belief in God's sovereignty. How, then, do they differ?

A COLONIAL BEST SELLER

The Whole Booke of Psalmes Faithfully Translated into English Metre came off the press of Stephan Daye in Cambridge, Massachusetts in 1640. A slender calf-bound volume with sturdy brass clasps, it was the first book to be printed in British America. We know it as the "Bay" Psalm Book because of its immediate adoption, as a hymnal, by the churches in Massachusetts Bay Colony.

We do not usually associate the Puritans with music, but the singing of the Psalms was an integral part of their worship and a matter of grave concern. The Bay Psalm Book was the colonial Puritan's contribution to the long history of English versions of the Psalms, or Psalters. Beginning with a few Psalms translated into prose (which could be chanted) and then into meter (which could be sung), the English, by 1562, had a complete Psalter of the one hundred fifty Psalms of the Old Testament together with sixty-five tunes. It was this edition which the Puritans carried with them to New England. However, like other aspects of religious worship which had offended them, the New England Puritans felt this Psalter needed to be "purified." To their way of thinking, the early translators had sacrificed the sense of the Biblical text in order to achieve rhyme or graceful expression. The New England Puritan wanted to sing a more literal translation—one which clearly respected the meaning of the Hebrew text. This demand for accuracy rather than elegance shaped the translation undertaken by three Puritan divines about 1636. The following lines from the Twenty-third Psalm illustrate how these men "respected rather a plain translation, than to smooth our verses with the sweetness of any paraphrase."

> The Lord to mee a shepheard is,
>   want therefore shall not I.
> Hee in the folds of tender-grasse,
>   doth cause mee downe to lie:
> To waters calme me gently leads
>   Restore my soule doth hee:
> he doth in paths of righteousness:
>   for his names sake leade mee.

The Bay Psalm Book, selling at twenty pence a copy, was a colonial best seller. It was revised and enlarged, went through fifty editions, and for over a century the New England Puritan carried it with him to worship. It even found adherents in England and Scotland. Only ten of the original seventeen hundred copies printed by Stephan Daye are known to be in existence. One sold for $151,000 in 1947. The Bay Psalm Book, once a commonplace of Puritan life, is today a collector's item.

Title page from the first edition of the "Bay" Psalm Book.

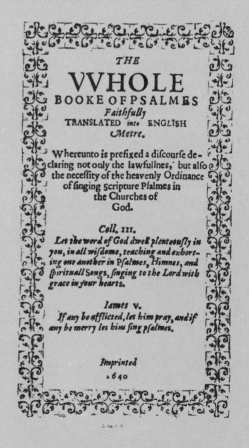

Captain John Smith 1579-1631

Over fifty years before William Byrd II was born, Captain John Smith, a soldier of fortune distinguished by much of the daring that had marked English adventurers in the reign of Queen Elizabeth I, landed with a band of adventurers near the mouth of a river on the Virginia coast. Of the 143 men who had sailed from England late in 1606, 105 survived the voyage. Impoverished gentlemen, tradesmen, and servingmen, interested only in finding gold and ignorant of the hazards of the new land, they were unlikely colonizers. Only John Smith, a member of the governing Council by appointment in sealed orders from London, seemed to have the vigor, determination, and imagination necessary to deal with food shortages, disease, and hostile Indians.

*John White, artist and cartographer for Raleigh's first
expedition to settle Virginia, drew this map of the southern coast. Red dots
along the Virginia coast show where settlers landed. The drawing
is remarkably accurate by sixteenth-century standards.*

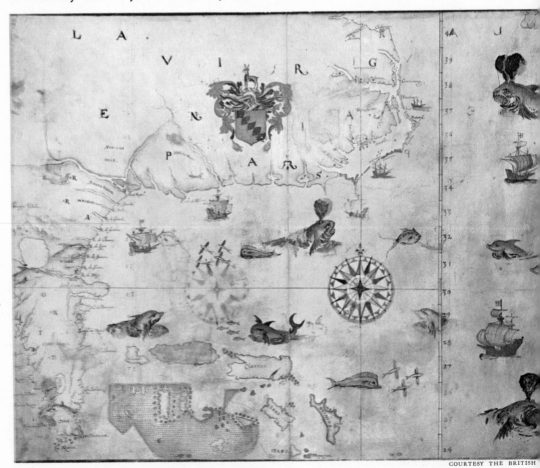

Smith remained in Virginia until October 1609. During this time he provided for the defense of the colony, procured food from the Indians, gave wise counsel, and led explorations into the surrounding country. He also became a vigorous promoter of colonization and wrote the first of his books urging emigration to the new land—*A True Relation* (1607). Later, after his explorations along the coast of New England, he published several other books, including *The Generall Historie of Virginia, New England, and the Summer Isles* (1624).

Captain Smith's books were read carefully by all who contemplated sailing for the colonies. They found in them vivid glimpses of an unknown land and of forest warfare with the redskins. Moreover, the Captain's style revealed his swashbuckling personality and enlivened his narrative. His most famous story is undoubtedly that of his capture by the Indians and his rescue by Pocahontas, the lovely Indian princess who later married another Englishman. Captain Smith wrote of his capture both in *A True Relation* (1607) and in *The Generall Historie* (1624), but only in the latter did he include the story of Pocahontas. This fact has led some scholars to doubt its authenticity. The selection which follows is taken from *The Generall Historie*.

Captain Smith Among the Indians

The winter [of 1607] approaching, the rivers became so covered with swans, geese, ducks, and cranes, that we daily feasted with good bread, Virginia peas, pumpkins, putchamins, fish, fowl, and diverse sorts of wild beasts as fat as we could eat them, so that none of our tuftaffety humorists[1] desired to go for England.

But our comedies never endured long without a tragedy; some idle exceptions being muttered against Captain Smith for not discovering the head of Chickahamania River, and taxed by the Council to be too slow in so worthy an attempt. The next voyage he proceeded so far that with much labor by cutting of trees asunder he made his passage; but when his barge could pass no farther, he left her in a broad bay out of danger of shot, commanding none should go ashore till his return: himself with two English and two savages went up higher in a canoe, but he was not long absent but[2] his men went ashore, whose want of government gave both occasion and opportunity to the savages to surprise one George Cassen, whom they slew, and much failed not[3] to have cut off the boat and all the rest.

Smith, little dreaming of that accident, being got to the marshes at the river's head, twenty miles in the desert, had his two men slain (as is supposed) sleeping by the canoe, whilst himself by fowling sought them victual; who, finding he was beset with two hundred savages, two of them he slew, still defending himself with the aid of a savage his guide, whom he bound to his arm with his garters and used him as a buckler; yet he was shot in his thigh a little and had many arrows that stuck in his clothes but no great hurt, till at last they took him prisoner.

When this news came to Jamestown, much was their sorrow for his loss, few expecting what ensued.

Six or seven weeks those barbarians kept him prisoner, many strange triumphs and conjurations they made of him, yet he so demeaned himself amongst them, as he not only diverted them from surprising the fort, but procured his own liberty, and got himself and

1. *tuftaffety humorists*, critical, elegant gentlemen who prided themselves on following their whims (humors) and behaving in an unusual or eccentric fashion. Tuftaffeta was a fashionable silk fabric which had a pattern formed by tufts. 2. *but*, until. 3. *much failed not*, almost succeeded.

his company such estimation amongst them, that those savages admired him more than their own Quiyouckosucks.[4] The manner how they used and delivered him is as follows.

The savages having drawn from George Cassen whither Captain Smith was gone, prosecuting that opportunity they followed him with three hundred bowmen, conducted by the King of Pamaunkee, who in divisions searching the turnings of the river, found Robinson and Emry[5] by the fireside; those they shot full of arrows and slew. Then finding the Captain, as is said, that used the savage that was his guide as his shield (three of them being slain and divers others so galled) all the rest would not come near him. Thinking thus to have returned to his boat, regarding them as he marched more than his way, slipped up to the middle in an oozy creek and his savage with him; yet durst they not come to him till being near dead with cold, he threw away his arms. Then according to their composition[6] they drew him forth and led him to the fire, where his men were slain. Diligently they chafed his benumbed limbs.

He demanding for their captain, they showed him Opechankanough, King of Pamaunkee, to whom he gave a round ivory double compass dial.[7] Much they marveled at the playing of the fly and needle, which they could see so plainly, and yet not touch it because of the glass that covered them. But when he demonstrated by that globelike jewel the roundness of the earth, the skies, the sphere of the sun, moon, and stars, and how the sun did chase the night round about the world continually; the greatness of the land and sea, the diversity of nations, variety of complexions, and how we were to them antipodes, and many other suchlike matters, they all stood as amazed with admiration. Notwithstanding, within an hour after they tied him to a tree, and as many as could stand about him prepared to shoot him, but the King holding up the compass in his hand, they all laid down their bows and arrows, and in a triumphant manner led him to Orapaks, where he was after their manner kindly feasted and well used.

At last they brought him to Meronocomoco,

where was Powhatan, their emperor. Here more than two hundred of these grim courtiers stood wondering at him, as he had been a monster; till Powhatan and his train had put themselves in their great braveries. Before a fire upon a seat like a bedstead, he sat covered with a great robe, made of raccoonskins, and all the tails hanging by. On either hand did sit a young wench of sixteen or eighteen years, and along on each side the house, two rows of men, and behind them as many women, with all their heads and shoulders painted red; many of their heads bedecked with the white down of birds; but every one with something.

At his entrance before the King, all the people gave a great shout. The Queen of Appamatuck was appointed to bring him water to wash his hands, and another brought him a bunch of feathers, instead of a towel, to dry them. Having feasted him after their best barbarous manner they could, a long consultation was held; but the conclusion was, two great stones were brought before Powhatan: then as many as could laid hands on him, dragged him to them, and thereon laid his head, and being ready with their clubs to beat out his brains, Pocahontas, the King's dearest daughter, when no entreaty could prevail, got his head in her arms, and laid her own upon his to save him from death: whereat the emperor was contented he should live to make him hatchets, and her bells, beads, and copper; for they thought him as well of all occupations as themselves. For the King himself will make his own robes, shoes, bows, arrows, pots; plant, hunt, or do anything so well as the rest.

Two days after, Powhatan having disguised himself in the most fearfullest manner he could, caused Captain Smith to be brought forth to a great house in the woods, and there upon a mat by the fire to be left alone. Not long after, from behind a mat that divided the house, was made the most dolefullest noise he

4. *Quiyouckosucks* (kwē youk′ō suks), god before whose images the Indians of this region made offerings for rain. 5. *Robinson and Emry*, the two men mentioned as slain in a preceding paragraph. Smith was hunting nearby. 6. *composition*, agreement. 7. *round ivory double compass dial.* This primitive type of compass was a ball containing liquid on which a magnetic needle floated.

ever heard; then Powhatan, more like a devil than a man, with some two hundred more as black as himself, came unto him and told him now they were friends and presently he should go to Jamestown to send him two great guns and a grindstone, for which he would give him the country of Capahowosick, and forever esteem him as his son Nantaquoud.

So to Jamestown with twelve guides Powhatan sent him. That night they quartered in the woods, he still expecting (as he had done all this long time of his imprisonment) every hour to be put to one death or other, for all their feasting. But almighty God, by His divine providence, had mollified the hearts of those stern barbarians with compassion. The next morning betimes they came to the fort, where Smith having used the savages with what kindness he could, he showed Rawhunt, Powhatan's trusty servant, two demi-culverins and a millstone to carry Powhatan: they found them somewhat too heavy; but when they did see him discharge them, being loaded with stones, among the boughs of a great tree loaded with icicles, the ice and branches came so tumbling down that the poor savages ran away half dead with fear. But at last we regained some conference with them, and gave them such toys; and sent to Powhatan, his women, and children such presents, and gave them in general full content.

❧ TO INCREASE UNDERSTANDING

1. (a) What was Captain John Smith's chief purpose in writing his books? (b) Cite details in "Captain Smith Among the Indians" that would have been of interest to an English reader of the seventeenth century.

2. (a) Why were the Jamestown adventurers unlikely colonists? (b) Indicate those passages in this selection which illustrate the attitude of his colleagues toward Captain Smith.

3. (a) Judging from this selection, what qualities of leadership did Captain Smith possess? (b) In what ways does he show an understanding of his captors?

4. A critic has written: "Of all the Indian tales of early America, that of Captain John Smith's rescue by Pocahontas is the most famous and the most symbolic. That Smith probably made it up matters little; it tells us still what the English wanted to think about themselves and about the people they were to displace." (a) In what way is the tale symbolic? (b) What does the second sentence of the statement mean? (c) Do you agree or disagree with the statement? Explain.

 WORDS!

Had the British failed to make good their claim to the New World, you would learn English as a foreign language. As it happened, however, Americans speak and write English—not the King's English you associate with a British subject, but American-English. What is American-English? Simply stated, it is the English language enriched by loan-words— words Americans have borrowed from non-English sources. One source of loan-words was the American Indian. When you read "Captain Smith Among the Indians," you probably recognized *Powhatan* and *Pocahontas* as Indian words. But when Smith states that Powhatan "sat covered with a great robe, made of raccoonskins," did you recognize *raccoon* as a word the early colonists borrowed from the Indians?

The following paragraph contains eighteen words which were adopted into English either directly from an Indian language or as a result of the early settlers' encounters with the Indians.

1. Identify the eighteen words. Consult your dictionary to verify your identification.

2. What features of the frontier do these words suggest?

The powwow had reached the height of its noise and frenzy. With tomahawks slashing the empty air, Delaware warriors circled and recircled an orange-bright fire of hickory boughs. Their jerking figures cast twisted shadows across watchful squaws and empty wigwams. Now and again a papoose awakened, its whimpers drowned in the deafening cadence. Braves who could stalk the moose in perfect silence now beat their moccasins against the earth as if it were a drum. It was the savage cadence of the frontier, for when the Indian no longer met the paleface in solemn caucus, when he no longer traded wampum or the skins of the deer and the skunk—and chose the warpath instead—then the frontier shook with its beat. The frontier moved westward to this rhythm. Before it could be silenced, the sound would carry to the far side of the Appalachians and into the Ohio country. Fort Dearborn would hear it before Chicago could be built. It would cross the Mississippi to be heard by Custer in the Dakota Territory. Before the savage beat could be silenced, it would echo in Wyoming—and beyond. Indian moccasins beat the rhythm of the frontier.

William Bradford 1590-1657

Below: Massasoit (great chief), powerful leader of the Wampanoags. Lower right: Grave of John Howland on Burial Hill, Plymouth, where many Pilgrims lie.

The group of earnest Pilgrims with whom William Bradford sailed in the *Mayflower* in 1620 differed greatly from the adventurers who had been Captain John Smith's companions. But like the Jamestown colonists they faced problems with the Indians and the rigors of keeping alive in a strange and inhospitable land. William Bradford, a veteran of the Pilgrims' eleven years of exile in Holland, rapidly became one of the leaders of the Plymouth Colony and its governor for most of the rest of his life. His earnest faith and sober acceptance of responsibility in the most perilous circumstances are apparent in *The History of Plymouth Plantation* (written about 1644), the earliest and most reliable record of the hardships and triumphs of the Pilgrims. Bradford's literary style, obviously influenced by his reading and rereading of the English Bible, has long been admired.

The excerpt from Bradford's *History* beginning on the next page describes the Pilgrims' first alliance with the Indians. During the first fearful winter (1620-1621) nearly half of the 102 colonists had died, and Captain Miles Standish had met the Indians in a brief skirmish; but with spring came hope.

The Pilgrims Meet the Indians

All this while the Indians came skulking about them, and would sometimes show themselves aloof off, but when any approached near them, they would run away. And once they stole away their tools where they had been at work, and were gone to dinner. But about the 16 of March, a certain Indian came boldly amongst them, and spoke to them in broken English, which they could well understand but marveled at it. At length they understood by discourse with him, that he was not of these parts, but belonged to the eastern parts where some English ships came to fish, with whom he was acquainted and could name sundry of them by their names, amongst whom he had got his language. He became profitable to them in acquainting them with many things concerning the state of the country in the east parts where he lived, which was afterwards profitable unto them; as also of the people here, of their names, number, and strength, of their situation and distance from this place, and who was chief amongst them. His name was Samoset; he told them also of another Indian whose name was Squanto, a native of this place, who had been in England and could speak better English than himself. Being, after some time of entertainment and gifts, dismissed, a while after he came again, and 5 more with him, and they brought again all the tools that were stolen away before, and made way for the coming of their great sachem, called Massasoit; who, about 4 or 5 days after, came with the chief of his friends and other attendance, with the aforesaid Squanto. With whom, after friendly entertainment, and some gifts given him, they made a peace with him (which hath now continued this 24 years) in these terms.

1. That neither he nor any of his should injure or do hurt to any of their people.

2. That if any of his did any hurt to any of theirs, he should send the offender, that they might punish him.

3. That if anything were taken away from any of theirs, he should cause it to be restored; and they should do the like to him.

4. If any did unjustly war against him, they would aid him; if any did war against them, he should aid them.

5. He should send to his neighbors confederates to certify them of this, that they might not wrong them, but might be likewise comprised in the conditions of peace.

6. That when their men came to them, they should leave their bows and arrows behind them.

After these things he returned to his place called Sowans, some 40 miles from this place, but Squanto continued with them, and was their interpreter, and was a special instrument sent of God for their good beyond their expectation. He directed them how to set their corn, where to take fish, and to procure other commodities, and was also their pilot to bring them to unknown places for their profit, and never left them till he died. He was a native of this place, and scarce any left alive besides himself. He was carried away with divers others by one Hunt, a master of a ship, who thought to sell them for slaves in Spain. But he got away for England, and was entertained by a merchant in London, and employed to Newfoundland and other parts, and lastly brought hither into these parts by one Mr. Dermer, a gentleman employed by Sir Ferdinando Gorges[1] and others for discovery and other designs in these parts.

1. *Sir Ferdinando Gorges* (gôr′jəs), a man instrumental in forming the Plymouth Company. Before the Pilgrims left England, he had sent exploratory parties to America.

 TO INCREASE UNDERSTANDING

1. How would you compare William Bradford and Captain John Smith as historians? Studying the article "Fact Versus Fiction" (page 18) will help you answer this question.

2. How did the hazards encountered by the Pilgrims in Massachusetts compare with the hazards the Jamestown adventurers faced in Virginia?

3. Why do you think William Bradford regarded Squanto as "a special instrument sent of God"?

4. In spite of the fact that Bradford's *History* was probably not intended for publication, his prose style has been highly praised by critics. What points of excellence can you find in this selection?

Anne Bradstreet c.1612-1672

Ten years after the Pilgrims had found a refuge at Plymouth, Anne
Bradstreet arrived in Massachusetts with the thousands of Puritans who
composed the Great Migration. As a child in England she had had a
more careful education than girls commonly received at that time. At sixteen she married a young graduate of Cambridge University, Simon
Bradstreet, and two years later, in 1630, made the long voyage westward
at his side.

Puritan housewives as a rule worked hard, finding little time for other
than the household arts; Anne Bradstreet was the outstanding exception.
Her poems first appeared in *The Tenth Muse Lately Sprung Up in
America*, published in London in 1650. A second and larger collection,
for which she herself made some revisions, was printed in Boston in 1678.

*Center of colonial "household arts." This New England fireplace, preserved as it was in the seven-
teenth century, is in the Howland House (see picture, page 98).*

Many of her verses are bookish, but a handful are personal, revealing both a charmingly feminine mind and the firm faith which sustained the Puritans through dislocation, illness, and bereavement. Such a poem is that which describes her eight children. It was written about 1658, after her eldest son had gone to England to study medicine. Samuel was the "chief of the brood." The "second bird" was Dorothy, who married the Reverend Seaborn Cotton in 1654 and lived first in Connecticut and later in New Hampshire. Sarah, the "third, of color white," had married Richard Hubbard of Ipswich. Simon was at Harvard College, "the academy." The "fifth," actually the seventh, was probably her third son, Dudley. Hannah, Mercy, and John were still at home. Despite the triteness of the chief metaphor, the birds in the nest, and of the "literary" diction and allusions, the poem conveys the warmth of a large family with a remarkable and loving mother. Puritanism has seldom been more attractively fused with universal human emotion.

In Reference to Her Children

I had eight birds hatched in one nest;
Four cocks there were, and hens the rest.
I nursed them up with pain and care,
Nor cost nor labor did I spare,
Till at the last they felt their wing,   5
Mounted the trees, and learned to sing.
Chief of the brood then took his flight
To regions far, and left me quite;
My mournful chirps I after send
Till he return or I do end: 10
Leave not thy nest, thy dam, and sire;
Fly back and sing admidst this choir.
My second bird did take her flight,
And with her mate flew out of sight;
Southward they both their course did bend,   15
And seasons twain they there did spend,
Till after, blown by southern gales,
They northward steered with fillèd sails.
A prettier bird was nowhere seen
Along the beach, among the treen.   20
I have a third, of color white,
On whom I placed no small delight;
Coupled with mate loving and true,
Hath also bid her dam adieu,
And where Aurora first appears   25
She now hath perched, to spend her years.
One to the academy flew
To chat among that learnèd crew;
Ambition moves still in his breast
That he might chant above the rest,   30

Striving for more than to do well—
That nightingales he might excel.
My fifth, whose down is yet scarce gone,
Is 'mongst the shrubs and bushes flown,
And as his wings increase in strength   35
On higher boughs he'll perch at length.
My other three still with me nest
Until they're grown; then, as the rest,
Or here or there they'll take their flight;
As is ordained, so shall they light.   40
If birds could weep, then would my tears
Let others know what are my fears
Lest this my brood some harm should catch
And be surprised for want of watch:
Whilst pecking corn, and void of care,   45
They fall unawares in fowler's snare;
Or whilst on trees they sit and sing,
Some untoward boy at them do fling;
Or whilst allured with bell and glass,
The net be spread, and caught, alas!   50
Or lest by lime twigs they be foiled,
Or by some greedy hawks be spoiled.
Oh, would, my young, ye saw my breast,
And knew what thoughts there sadly rest.
Great was my pain when I you bred,   55
Great was my care when I you fed;
Long did I keep you soft and warm,
And with my wings kept off all harm.
My cares are more, and fears, than ever,
My throbs such now as 'fore were never.   60

Alas, my birds, you wisdom want;
Of perils you are ignorant—
Ofttimes in grass, on trees, in flight,
Sore accidents on you may light.
Oh, to your safety have an eye; 65
So happy may you live and die.
Meanwhile my days in tunes I'll spend
Till my weak lays with me shall end;
In shady woods I'll sit and sing,
Things that are past to mind I'll bring— 70
Once young and pleasant, as are you.
But former toys—no joys—adieu!
My age I will not once lament,
But sing my time so near is spent,
And from the top bough take my flight 75
Into a country beyond sight,
Where old ones instantly grow young,
And there with seraphims set song.
No seasons cold nor storms they see,
But spring lasts to eternity. 80
When each of you shall in your nest
Among your young ones take your rest,
In chirping language oft them tell
You had a dam that loved you well,

That did what could be done for young, 85
And nursed you up till you were strong;
And 'fore she once would let you fly
She showed you joy and misery,
Taught what was good, and what was ill,
What would save life, and what would kill. 90
Thus gone, amongst you I may live,
And dead, yet speak, and counsel give.
Farewell, my birds, farewell, adieu!
I happy am if well with you.

❧ TO INCREASE UNDERSTANDING

1. (*a*) Describe Mistress Bradstreet's attitude toward her children. (*b*) In your opinion does it differ in any significant way from the attitude of mothers today? Explain.

2. How does the simple diction contribute to the effect of the poem?

3. In the biography of Anne Bradstreet you read that her verses reveal "both a charmingly feminine mind and the firm faith which sustained the Puritans." Cite examples of both of these attributes in this poem.

View of the ancient Buildings belonging to Harvard College.

Drawn by Nathaniel Dearborn, Boston, March 24
1798

Edward Taylor c.1645-1729

In 1668 Edward Taylor at the age of twenty-two or twenty-three arrived from England in Massachusetts Bay. He found a well-established colony, proud of the erudition of its ministers and of Harvard College. Taylor was admitted to Harvard, from which he was graduated in 1671. Following his graduation, he became pastor of the church in the frontier village of Westfield, Massachusetts. Here he lived during the remaining fifty-eight years of his life, quietly serving the people of his village. Since his poems were not written for publication and only a few people knew of their existence, Taylor's parishioners in Westfield were unaware that their pious minister was, all unknown, the greatest poet in colonial America.

In the two centuries after Taylor's death the existence of his poems was almost forgotten; but since 1929, when a selection from his manuscripts was first published, he has been recognized by critics as the greatest American poet before the nineteenth century. Like Jonathan Edwards, Taylor was an orthodox Puritan who believed in the Calvinistic doctrine of election. But he dwelt by preference on the elect rather than on the damned, and his poems show a loving Christ and a joy in Puritanism. As a poet he is distinguished for his sincerity of thought and feeling and for his use of metaphors drawn straight from personal religious experience. In the poem which follows, Edward Taylor visualizes the Puritan congregation as a Coach transporting the elect (the Saints) to their salvation (Glory). Each of the five stanzas elaborates this image.

The Joy of Church Fellowship Rightly Attended

In Heaven soaring up, I dropped an Ear
  On Earth: and oh! sweet Melody:
And listening found it was the Saints who
    were
    Encoached for Heaven that sang for Joy.
    For in Christ's Coach they sweetly sing,   5
    As they to Glory ride therein.

Oh! joyous hearts! Enfired with holy Flame!
  Is Speech thus tasseled with praise?
Will not your inward fire of Joy contain,
  That it in open flames doth blaze?   10
    For in Christ's Coach Saints sweetly sing,
    As they to Glory ride therein.

And if a string do slip, by Chance, they soon
  Do screw it up again: whereby
They set it in a more melodious Tune   15
  And a Diviner Harmony.
    For in Christ's Coach they sweetly sing
    As they to Glory ride therein.

In all their Acts, public and private, nay,
  And secret too, they praise impart.   20
But in their Acts Divine and Worship, they
  With Hymns do offer up their Heart.
    Thus in Christ's Coach they sweetly sing
    As they to Glory ride therein.

Some few not in; and some whose Time and
    Place   25
  Block up this Coach's way do go
As Travelers afoot: and so do trace
  The Road that gives them right thereto;
    While in this Coach these sweetly sing
    As they to Glory ride therein.   30

"The Joy of Church Fellowship Rightly Attended" from *The Poetical Works of Edward Taylor*, edited by Thomas H. Johnson. Copyright 1939, Rockland Editions. Copyright 1943, Princeton University Press. (The spelling has been modernized for this anthology by permission of the publishers.

Upon What Base?

Upon what base was fixed the lathe wherein
He turned this globe and rigolled it[1] so trim?
Who blew the bellows of His furnace vast?
Or held the mold wherein the world was cast?
Who laid its cornerstone? Or whose
      command?   5
Where stand the pillars upon which it stands?
Who laced and filleted[2] the earth so fine
With rivers like green ribbons smaragdine?[3]
Who made the seas its selvage,[4] and its locks
Like a quilt ball within a silver box?[5]   10
Who spread its canopy? Or curtains spun?
Who in this bowling alley bowled the sun?

"Upon What Base?" from *The Poetical Works of Edward Taylor*, edited by. Thomas H. Johnson. Copyright 1939. Rockland Editions. Copyright 1943, Princeton University Press. (The spelling has been modernized for this anthology by permission of the publishers.)
1. *rigolled* (rig'əld) *it*, shaped and grooved it so that its various parts fitted snugly together. 2. *filleted*, edged. 3. *smaragdine* (smä rag'din), having the deep green color of emeralds. 4. *Who made . . . selvage* (sel'vij)? Who made the seas the edges or borders of the earth? 5. *locks . . . box*, landlocked lakes or arms of the sea that look like balls of quilting materials in a silver-colored sewing box.

❧ TO INCREASE UNDERSTANDING

1. (*a*) How did Edward Taylor's attitude toward Puritanism differ from Jonathan Edwards'? (*b*) How is this difference in attitude reflected in the writings of these two clergymen?

2. (*a*) What is Taylor's theme in "The Joy of Church Fellowship Rightly Attended"? (*b*) Explain the meaning of those images which seem especially vivid to you.

3. Edward Taylor is known for his use of homely metaphors drawn from personal experience. (*a*) State the central image in "Upon What Base?" (*b*) To what kinds of earthly craftsmen does Taylor refer to reinforce his central image?

4. (*a*) In "Upon What Base?" what particular aspects of the beauty of the earth does Taylor select for comment in lines 7-11? (*b*) What do *canopy* and *curtains* suggest to you?

5. In what ways does reading Taylor's poetry increase your understanding of everyday life in colonial New England?

THE LARGER VIEW

A. Two of the paragraphs below were written by Virginians; two were written by Puritans. On a sheet of paper, identify the author of each paragraph as representative of either the Planter or Puritan culture; then list all the clues on which you base your decision.

I believe it is as healthy a country as any under heaven; but the extraordinary pleasantness of the weather, and plenty of the fruit, lead people into many temptations. Here they enjoy all the benefits of a warm sun, and by their shady trees are protected from its inconvenience. Here all their senses are entertained with an endless succession of native pleasures. The merry birds too, join their pleasing notes to this rural comfort, especially the mock birds, who love society so well, that often when they see mankind, they will perch upon a twig very near them, and sing the sweetest wild airs in the world. Men's taste is regaled with the most delicious fruits, which, without art, they have in great variety and perfection. And then their smell is refreshed with an eternal fragrancy of flowers and sweets, with which nature perfumes and adorns the woods and branches almost the whole year round.

Robert Beverley

Lamentable deaths and destruction amongst men have been oftentimes presaged by "blazing stars" in heaven. Especially destructions by mortal and contagious diseases. Especially that which is, of all diseases miserable mortals are subject unto, the most terrible—I mean the plague of pestilence. Such sights are heaven's alarm to a sinful world, to give notice that God hath bent His bow and made His arrows ready and that if sinners turn not, the arrows of pestilence and death shall fall down upon them speedily. We cannot but remember the blazing star that was seen but sixteen years ago, and a terrible plague followed. And it is reported that immediately after that great blazing star which appeared above threescore years ago God sent the plague amongst the natives in this land, which swept them away in such multitudes as that the living were not enough to bury the dead. So did the Lord cast out the heathen before this His people.

Increase Mather

October 7, 1704.—About two o'clock in the afternoon we arrived. Here I informed myself of the manners and customs of the place. They are governed by the same laws as we (or little differing) throughout the whole colony, and much the same way of church government, and many of them good, sociable people and I hope religious too; but a little too much independent in their principles and, as I have been told, were formerly in their zeal very rigid in their administrations toward such as their laws made offenders—even to a harmless kiss or innocent merriment among young people. Whipping being frequent and counted an easy punishment and about which the judges are absolute in their sentences. They are generally very plain in their dress throughout the colony that you may know where they belong, especially the women, meet them where you will. There are everywhere a number of Indians and they are the most savage of all the savages of that kind I have ever seen.

Sarah Kemble Knight

The common planters do not much admire labor or any manly exercise, except horse racing, nor diversion, except cockfighting in which some greatly delight. This easy way of living and the heat of the summer make some very lazy, who are then said to be climate-struck. They are such lovers of riding that almost every ordinary person keeps a horse; and I have known some to spend the morning in ranging several miles in the woods to find and catch their horses only to ride two or three miles to church, to the courthouse, or to a horse race where they generally appoint to meet on business. No people can entertain their friends with better cheer and welcome, and strangers and travelers are here treated in the most free, plentiful and hospitable manner; so that a few inns on the road are sufficient.

Hugh Jones

B. Early colonial literature is described as utilitarian. With the following questions to guide you, evaluate the practical nature of Planter and Puritan writing.

1. What purposes were served by the travel narratives, the sermons, and the diaries?
2. Account for the fact that the colonists produced a relatively small amount of imaginative writing.

BIBLIOGRAPHY

BENÉT, STEPHEN VINCENT, *Western Star*. (Rinehart) Planters and Puritans come to life in this long narrative poem, which catches not only the satisfactions and hardships of the pioneers but also the spirit which drove them West.

BRADFORD, WILLIAM, *Of Plymouth Plantation*. (•Capricorn) An introduction by Editor Harvey Wise helps set the background for this abridged edition of Bradford's classic account of the struggles and achievements of the Pilgrims in New England. The original manuscript has been cut to eliminate repetition.

BRADSTREET, ANNE, *The Works of Anne Bradstreet in Prose and Verse*. (Smith, Peter) Anne Bradstreet's poems are often whimsical and dramatic. Included in this collection is "An Author to Her Book," one of her best poems.

FINNEY, GERTRUDE, *Is This My Love?* (Longmans) Beatrice Whitman journeys to the raw Jamestown settlement in a bridal ship. Her gradual acceptance of pioneer life and her love for an unpolished young settler are realistically portrayed in this novel of the very old South.

ROBINSON, GERTRUDE, *Catch a Falling Star*. (Dutton) Love and hardship blend in an exciting romantic novel about a young English girl's decision to marry a colonist and begin a new life in the New York wilderness.

SETON, ANYA, *The Winthrop Woman*. (Houghton •Pocket Books) Based on the life of Elizabeth Winthrop, this exciting novel tells of Elizabeth's girlhood in England, her three marriages, and her rebellions against bigotry. Readers will find this unconventional woman of New England a memorable character.

SMITH, BRADFORD, *Captain John Smith, His Life and Legend*. (Lippincott) In this realistic recreation of a great historic period, Bradford Smith tells the story of a man whose legend has outlived his reality. Smith's *Bradford of Plymouth* is equally interesting.

WINSLOW, OLA, *Jonathan Edwards*. (•Collier Books) Miss Winslow's Pulitzer prize-winning biography of Edwards presents a vivid impression of this important early American. No glamour relieved Edwards' character in life and Miss Winslow has inserted none. Written with clarity and simplicity, the book is full of information that the mature student will find engrossing.

•paperback

chapter two Founders of the Nation

Less than one hundred and fifty years after John Smith landed at Jamestown, thirteen colonies, all under the rule of England, fringed the Atlantic coast. In New England a cluster of Puritan colonies surrounded the original settlements in Massachusetts. The Southern colonies followed the pattern of life established by the planters in Virginia. New York and New Jersey, after forty years of Dutch rule, were taken over by the English in 1664. The English Quakers under William Penn had colonized Pennsylvania, and welcomed members of various German sects, attracted by Penn's assurance of complete religious tolerance. The ultimate attainment of unity by these colonies is almost incredible, for many factors tended to disunite them. By present-day standards they were amazingly self-dependent and isolated. What few roads connected them were passable only on horseback or in uncomfortable horse-drawn carriages. Trade and commerce were almost wholly by sailing ships, and probably less intercolonial than with England, the West Indies, and even Africa. Religious differences were frequent and often bitter. Many communities did not even use the English language. The center of what cultural life there was lay three thousand miles away in London, not in Boston or New York or Philadelphia or Williamsburg.

*Elfreth's Alley, an eighteenth-century
Philadelphia street preserved as it appeared
in Franklin's time.*

129

Yet, when all the differences have been noted, the colonies had some things in common. People everywhere were busy making a living in a new environment in the hope that they and their children might have a better and more rewarding life than that attainable back in Europe. All were engaged in the task of adapting European customs and institutions, especially those of England, to this new environment. And all shared what is perhaps most important, a magnificent dream. They spoke of this vision as "the future greatness of America," by which they meant that over the mountains lay a vast rich continent which it was their destiny and that of their children and their children's children to possess. Colonial Americans accepted without question a phrase of George Berkeley, an English philosopher who lived for a time in Rhode Island: "Westward the course of Empire takes its way." Their continent was to be a new Garden of Eden.

Two obstacles lay between the colonists and their realization of the American dream. The first was that Spain and France claimed and occupied the lands beyond the Appalachian Mountains. The second was that English government officials failed to share the Americans' vision; they thought the colonies ought primarily to be useful and profitable to the mother country.

The first of these obstacles was largely removed when in 1763 the victory of the English in the French and Indian War opened to settlement by the colonists the land west to the Mississippi. The American Revolution disposed of the second obstacle. Thereafter Americans were free to manage their own affairs and to try to make their dream come true.

Philadelphia as it appeared about 1752.

The men who lived through the French and Indian War and the long struggle for political self-determination constitute one of the most remarkable generations in all history. Three of them—George Washington, John

PHILADELPHIA; taken by *GEORGE HEAP* from the *JERSEY SHORE*, under the Direction of *NICHOLAS SCULL* Surv

To the Honourable Thomas Penn and Richard Penn, true and absolute Proprietors of the Province of Pennsylvania and Counties of NEWCASTLE, KENT and SUSSEX on DELAWARE, this Perspective View is humbly Dedicated by Nicholas Scull

Adams, and Thomas Jefferson—became the first three presidents of the United States. Others—Patrick Henry, Alexander Hamilton, and Thomas Paine—have a secure place in our national gallery of heroes. All of them were men of many talents—broad-visioned, forward-looking, and articulate. They not only fought for freedom but they expressed their beliefs in clear, forceful prose. By general agreement, however, the most representative man of that generation was a self-made man known variously as a home-spun philosopher, a scientist, a political leader, a diplomat, and, not least of all, a writer. His name was Benjamin Franklin.

Benjamin Franklin

1706-1790 Franklin's long and active life very nearly spans the eighteenth century. Already a successful businessman when Washington, Jefferson, and other founders of the nation were born, he brought a realistic and mature out-look to the deliberations that finally welded an independent nation from thirteen English colonies. He had an early grasp of the continental destiny of the colonies, although right up to the Declaration of Independence, which he helped draft, he regarded the colonists as Englishmen. His polit-ical judgments were mixed with economic realism, both of which he had arrived at through experience and observation. Born the son of a candle-maker, he is one of the earliest examples of the American creed that a poor boy with ambition and intelligence can rise to any position in the land.

WORKMAN Benjamin Franklin was born in Boston in 1706. Had his family not been
AND poor, he might have gone to Harvard College and shared in the tradition
PHILOSOPHER which produced Jonathan Edwards. But he was the tenth child of an artisan who could give him only two years of formal education, and that in a "writing school" designed to teach boys enough to be useful in busi-ness. His basic training came from life in a large family, and led to a somewhat more directly practical morality than was taught more fervent Puritans. Franklin himself attests to this in essays such as "The Whistle" (page 134), written in 1779, when he had achieved wealth and fame.

From the first Franklin was educated by experience. At ten or eleven he was helping his father in the shop, and at twelve he was apprenticed to his older brother James, who had just brought back a press from Eng-land and opened a printshop. There Benjamin cleaned up, delivered papers, learned to set type and operate a flat-bed press. What was most important, he developed a passion for reading and an ambition to write.

In 1721 James Franklin established a weekly newspaper, the *New Eng-land Courant*. He had the help of some Boston gentlemen who were criti-cal of the group in political power, and the *Courant* became the first "opposition" paper in American journalism. Politics, however, was not its only feature. One of its models was the *Spectator,* a London sheet written by Joseph Addison and Richard Steele, which commented with humor and satire on people and events. The *Courant* asked its readers to con-tribute "short Pieces, Serious, Sarcastic, Ludicrous, or other ways amusing."

Benjamin, aged sixteen, and already well acquainted with the satirical methods of the *Spectator,* accepted the invitation, and slipped his first essay under the door at night so that his brother would not know who had written it. Signed "Silence Dogood," it was followed by thirteen others, in which a fictitious widow with no education but much common sense commented on Boston attitudes. Silence Dogood was an ancestor of a long and popular line of "horse-sense philosophers," among them Mark Twain and Will Rogers. In "A Receipt to Make a New England Funeral Elegy" (page 135) she successfully satirizes the pompous verses with which Puritans had long been accustomed to pay tribute to their departed friends and heroes.

The political comments of the *Courant* got James Franklin into trouble —into jail, as a matter of fact. For a month in 1722 Benjamin ran the paper by himself. A year later the authorities forbade James to "print or publish" his newspaper. To keep it going, he trickily made Benjamin the printer and publisher, canceling the apprenticeship papers but drawing up others to be kept secret between them. At that point Benjamin, now master of his trade and perhaps a little proud of himself as a writer, made a decision which he afterward regarded as morally wrong. Knowing that James would not dare reveal the true facts, he assumed that he was free of his obligations and ran away.

Seventeen-year-old Benjamin got to Philadelphia on a Sunday morning in October 1723 with his pockets stuffed with dirty shirts and stockings, and, for capital, a Dutch dollar and a shilling in copper. In his famous *Autobiography,* written between 1771 and 1790 for the guidance of his son, Franklin looked back over long years to his arrival in the city with which he would always be identified:

I walked toward the top of the street, gazing about till near Market Street, where I met a boy with bread. I had often made a meal of dry bread, and, inquiring where he had bought it, I went immediately to the baker's he directed me to. I asked for biscuits, meaning such as we had at Boston; that sort, it seems, was not made in Philadelphia. I then asked for a three-penny loaf, and

Opposite: A printing press used in the shop founded by Franklin (left) and similar to the one he used to print the first Poor Richard's Almanack *(right). Left: One of the publications from Franklin's press.*

was told they had none. Not knowing the different prices, nor the names of the different sorts of bread, I told him to give me three-penny worth of any sort. He gave me accordingly three great puffy rolls. I was surprised at the quantity, but took it, and having no room in my pockets, walked off with a roll under each arm, and eating the other. Thus I went to Market Street as far as Fourth Street, passing by the door of Mr. Read, my future wife's father; when she, standing at the door, saw me, and thought I made, as I certainly did, a most awkward, ridiculous appearance.

So came to Philadelphia her greatest man. There he was to make his way up in the world on his own, a new man in a new settlement.

Although his trade provided quick employment, Franklin's success was not instantaneous. However, within a few years he had his own printshop, where he bought and sold almost everything that seemed profitable, his own newspaper (the *Pennsylvania Gazette*), and his own almanac (*Poor Richard's*). Before long he was public printer, first for Pennsylvania and then for New Jersey and Maryland as well, which meant a good income from printing official documents, legal reports, and paper currency. He invested wisely in real estate, and provided the capital for young printers in other centers, some of them as far away as the West Indies. With the help of his wife Deborah, a good manager, money rolled in, and Franklin put it to good use. In 1748, when he was forty-two, he was able to retire from business and live upon the income from his investments.

Franklin's success story is associated in the public mind with the creation of another character who, like Silence Dogood, spoke the language of the

THE FRANKLIN INSTITUTE, PHILADELPHIA

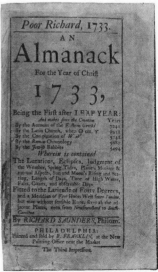

HISTORICAL SOCIETY OF PENNSYLVANIA

common people and shared their simple philosophy of life. Realizing that an almanac was likely to sell even in rural homes where the only other book might be a Bible, Franklin decided to publish one. His almanac purported to be the publication of a certain Richard Saunders, who came to be known as Poor Richard. For twenty-five years after 1732, Poor Richard spoke out between the dull matter of tides, weather, and astronomical tables. His proverbs and aphorisms were borrowed from many sources but rephrased in a homespun way. The almanacs also printed earthy sayings: Fish and visitors smell in three days. Let thy maidservant be faithful, strong, and homely. There's more old drunkards than old doctors. . . . What caught the public fancy, however, were Franklin's praises of the simple, get-ahead-in-life virtues.

In 1757 Franklin made a collection of Poor Richard's sayings under the guise of a lay sermon entitled *The Way to Wealth*. Supposedly delivered by Father Abraham, a "plain, clean, old man," it exhorts the reader to practice industry, pay attention to business, exercise frugality, and cultivate prudence. *The Way to Wealth* became Franklin's most popular work, reprinted dozens of times and translated into almost every living language. The familiar praises of industry it contains have long been identified with Franklin, although few of them were original with him. You will recognize some of them as you read the selection on page 135.

FROM *The Whistle*

When I was a child of seven years old, my friends, on a holiday, filled my pocket with coppers. I went directly to a shop where they sold toys for children; and, being charmed with the sound of a *whistle,* that I met by the way in the hands of another boy, I voluntarily offered and gave all my money for one. I then came home, and went whistling all over the house, much pleased with my *whistle,* but disturbing all the family. My brothers, and sisters, and cousins, understanding the bargain I had made, told me I had given four times as much for it as it was worth; put me in mind what good things I might have bought with the rest of the money; and laughed at me so much for my folly, that I cried with vexation; and the reflections gave me more chagrin than the *whistle* gave me pleasure.

This however was afterward of use to me, the impression continuing on my mind; so that often, when I was tempted to buy some unnecessary thing, I said to myself, *Don't give too much for the whistle;* and I saved my money.

As I grew up, came into the world, and observed the actions of men, I thought I met with many, very many, who *gave too much for the whistle.*

When I saw one too ambitious of court favor, sacrificing his time in attendance on levees, his repose, his liberty, his virtue, and perhaps his friends, to attain it, I have said to myself, *This man gives too much for his whistle.*

When I saw another fond of popularity, constantly employing himself in political bustles, neglecting his own affairs, and ruining them by that neglect, *He pays, indeed,* said I, *too much for his whistle.*

If I knew a miser, who gave up every kind of comfortable living, all the pleasures of doing good to others, all the esteem of his fellow citizens, and the joys of benevolent friendship, for the sake of accumulating wealth, *Poor man,* said I, *you pay too much for your whistle.*

A Receipt to Make a New England Funeral Elegy

For the Title of your Elegy. Of these you may have enough ready made to your Hands; but if you should chuse to make it your self, you must be sure not to omit the Words *Aetatis Suae* [of his age], which will Beautify it exceedingly.

For the Subject of your Elegy. Take one of your Neighbors who has lately departed this Life; it is no great matter at what Age the Party dy'd, but it will be best if he went away suddenly, being *Kill'd, Drown'd,* or *Froze to Death.*

Having chose the Person, take all his Virtues, Excellencies, &c., and if he have not enough, you may borrow some to make up a sufficient Quantity: To these add his last Words, dying Expressions, &c., if they are to be had; mix all these together, and be sure you *strain* them well. Then season all with a Handful or two of Melancholly Expressions, such as, *Dreadful, Deadly, cruel cold Death, unhappy Fate, weeping Eyes,* &c. Have mixed all these Ingredients well, put them into the empty Scull of some young *Harvard;* (but, in Case you have ne'er a One at Hand, you may use your own); there let them Ferment for the Space of a Fortnight, and by that Time they will be incorporated into a Body, which take out, and having prepared a sufficient Quantity of double Rhimes, such as, *Power, Flower; Quiver, Shiver; Grieve us, Leave us; tell you, excel you; Expeditions, Physicians; Fatigue him, Intrigue him;* &c., you must spread all upon Paper, and if you can procure a Scrap of Latin to put at the End, it will garnish it mightily; then having affixed your Name at the Bottom, with a *Maestus Composuit,*[1] you will have an Excellent Elegy.

N.B.[2] This Receipt will serve when a Female is the Subject of your Elegy, provided you borrow a greater Quantity of Virtues, Excellencies, &c.

Silence Dogood

FROM *The Way to Wealth*

It would be thought a hard government that should tax its people one-tenth part of their time, to be employed in its service. But idleness taxes many of us much more, if we reckon all that is spent in absolute sloth, or doing of nothing, with that which is spent in idle employments or amusements that amount to nothing. Sloth, by bringing on diseases, absolutely shortens life. *Sloth, like rust, consumes faster than labor wears; while the used key is always bright,* as Poor Richard says. *But dost thou love life, then do not squander time, for that's the stuff life is made of,* as Poor Richard says. How much more than is necessary do we spend in sleep, forgetting, that *The sleeping fox catches no poultry,* and that *There will be sleeping enough in the grave,* as Poor Richard says.

If time be of all things the most precious, *wasting time* must be, as Poor Richard says, *the greatest prodigality;* since, as he elsewhere tells us, *Lost time is never found again;* and what we call *time enough, always proves little enough.* Let us then be up and doing, and doing to the purpose; so by diligence we do more with less perplexity. *Sloth makes all things difficult, but industry all easy;* and *He that riseth late must trot all day, and shall scarce overtake his business at night;* while *Laziness travels so slowly, that Poverty soon overtakes him. Drive thy business, let not that drive thee;* and *Early to bed, and early to rise, makes a man healthy, wealthy, and wise,* as Poor Richard says.

So what signifies wishing and hoping for better times? We may make these times better, if we bestir ourselves. *Industry need not wish,* and *He that lives upon hope will die fasting. There are no gains without pains;* then *Help, hands, for I have no lands;* or, if I have, they are smartly taxed. *He that hath a trade hath an estate;* and *He that hath a calling hath an*

A RECEIPT 1. *Maestus Composuit* (mĭs′təs kəm pō′sü it), a Latin expression meaning "a mourner composed." Franklin is suggesting that in signing his elegy the author identify himself as a mourner. 2. *N.B.,* the abbreviation of the Latin *nota bene,* meaning "note well."

office of profit and honor, as Poor Richard says; but then the trade must be worked at, and the calling well followed, or neither the estate nor the office will enable us to pay our taxes. If we are industrious, we shall never starve; for, *At the workingman's house hunger looks in, but dares not enter.* Nor will the bailiff or the constable enter, for *Industry pays debts, while despair increaseth them.* What though you have found no treasure, nor has any rich relation left you a legacy. *Diligence is the mother of good luck, and God gives all things to industry. Then plough deep while sluggards sleep, and you shall have corn to sell and to keep.* Work while it is called today, for you know not how much you may be hindered tomorrow. *One today is worth two tomorrows,* as Poor Richard says; and further, *Never leave that till tomorrow, which you can do today.* If you were a servant, would you not be ashamed that a good master should catch you idle? Are you then your own master? *Be ashamed to catch yourself idle,* when there is so much to be done for yourself, your family, your country, and your king. Handle your tools without mittens; remember, that *The cat in gloves catches no mice,* as Poor Richard says. It is true there is much to be done, and perhaps you are weak-handed; but stick to it steadily, and you will see great effects; for *Constant dropping wears away stones;* and *By diligence and patience the mouse ate in two the cable;* and *Little strokes fell great oaks.*

Methinks I hear some of you say, "Must a man afford himself no leisure?" I will tell thee, my friend, what Poor Richard says, *Employ thy time well, if thou meanest to gain leisure;* and, *Since thou art not sure of a minute, throw not away an hour.* Leisure is time for doing something useful; this leisure the diligent man will obtain, but the lazy man never; for *A life of leisure and a life of laziness are two things. Many, without labor, would live by their wits only, but they break for want of stock;* whereas industry gives comfort, and plenty, and respect. *Fly pleasures, and they will follow you. The diligent spinner has a large shift;* and *Now I have a sheep and a cow, everybody bids me good morrow;* all of which is well said by Poor Richard.

SCIENTIST From his youth Franklin showed a considerable interest in science, and one of the chief reasons for his anxiety to retire from business was his eagerness to devote himself to scientific studies. In this area his bent was toward the practical, although, oddly enough, he is best remembered for his theoretical contributions to the subject of electricity. Between 1747 and 1750 he was constantly making experiments with the electrical apparatus he imported from Europe (the Leyden jar, ancestor of our storage battery, had just been invented); he experimented also with apparatus he himself devised. Many of his friends shared his enthusiasm for the popular novelty of electricity, and he reported their findings to Peter Collinson, a London merchant and a member of the Royal Society, with whom he had long had business dealings. Collinson saw that these findings were published, and from the time *Experiments and Observations on Electricity* was printed in 1751, Franklin was a famous man in Europe.

Franklin merited his fame in this branch of physics on two counts. First, he developed the "one fluid" hypothesis, which accounted for more of the observed facts than did any theories of his predecessors. He invented for the explanation of his hypothesis such familiar terms as *positive, negative, battery, conductor.* Second, by his suggestion that pointed iron rods might protect buildings from lightning, which his most famous experiment showed was just a form of electricity, he gave to his work the appeal of practicality and usefulness.

While Franklin did his most important scientific work in electricity, his interests embraced areas as divergent as the progress of cyclonic storms across the eastern United States and the cause of the common cold. Most of Franklin's scientific contributions were made before 1752, although in later years he continued occasionally to conduct experiments in areas in which he was interested or to make suggestions in letters to correspondents scattered across the world. It is no wonder that he was regarded as the leading scientist of the Western Hemisphere, and was honored, as William Byrd II had been honored, by election to the exclusive Royal Society.

Portrait of Franklin by Charles W. Peale, most famous for his many portraits of Washington.

First Aerial Voyage by Man

In 1783, the year in which the treaty of peace between England and the new United States was signed, the people of France were greatly excited by a considerable number of balloon ascensions. The first successful balloon, a linen globe inflated over a fire fed by bundles of straw, had been tried out near Lyons by the Montgolfier (môn′gôl′fyā′) brothers in June 1783. Other experiments followed this first one, including several in which a man, protected by guide ropes, went up in a balloon.

Franklin, who was living at Passy, near Paris, followed these experiments with interest and sent reports on them to his friend Sir Joseph Banks, a member of the Royal Society. In the following extract from one of these letters, Franklin first refers to his earlier correspondence and then gives an eyewitness account of the first ascent of men in a free balloon.

TO SIR JOSEPH BANKS

Passy, Nov. 21, 1783

Dear Sir,

I received your friendly letter of the 7th instant. I am glad my letters respecting the aerostatic experiment were not unacceptable. But as more perfect accounts of the construction and management of that machine have been and will be published before your transactions,[1] and from which extracts may be made that will be more particular and therefore more satisfactory, I think it best not to print those letters. I say this in answer to your question, for I did not indeed write them with a view of their being inserted. M. Faujas de St. Fond[2] acquainted me yesterday that a book on the subject, which has been long expected, will be published in a few days, and I shall send you one of them. Enclosed is a copy of the *procès verbal*[3] taken of the experiment made yesterday in the garden of the queen's palace, la Muette, where the Dauphin[4] now resides, which being near my house I was present. This paper was drawn up hastily, and

may in some places appear to you obscure; therefore I shall add a few explanatory observations.

This balloon was larger than that which went up from Versailles and carried the sheep, etc.[5] Its bottom was open, and in the middle of the opening was fixed a kind of basket grate in which fagots and sheaves of straw were burnt. The air, rarefied in passing through this flame, rose in the balloon, swelled out its sides, and filled it.

The persons, who were placed in the gallery made of wicker and attached to the outside near the bottom, had each of them a port through which they could pass sheaves of straw into the grate to keep up the flame, and thereby keep the balloon full. When it went over our heads, we could see the fire, which was very considerable. As the flame slackens, the rarefied air cools and condenses, the bulk of the balloon diminishes and it begins to descend. If these in the gallery see it likely to descend in an improper place, they can, by throwing on more straw and renewing the flame, make it rise again, and the wind carries it farther.

La Machine poussée par le Vent s'est dirigée sur une des Allées du Jardin.[6] That is, against the trees of one of the walks. The gallery hitched among the top boughs of those trees which had been cut and were stiff, while the body of the balloon leaned beyond and seemed likely to overset. I was then in great pain for the men, thinking them in danger of being thrown out or burnt, for I expected that the

---

1. *your transactions.* In its yearly publication called *Transactions*, the Royal Society carried accounts of new scientific developments. Certain of Franklin's letters, such as his letter to Peter Collinson containing the account of the electric kite, had been published in *Transactions*. Banks had suggested to Franklin that his previous letters on aerial voyages might be inserted in the forthcoming volume. 2. *Monsieur Faujas de St. Fond* (mə syœ′ fō zhäs′ də saɴ fôn′), a French geologist who had set on foot the subscription to finance the ascent of the first hydrogen-filled balloon. 3. *procès verbal* (prô sā′ vėr bäl′), written report. 4. *the Dauphin* (dô′fən), the eldest son of the king of France by traditional title. The Dauphin at this time was a two-year-old boy. 5. *that which went up from Versailles* (vär sī′) . . . *sheep, etc.* On September 19 Joseph Montgolfier sent up a balloon carrying a sheep, a cock, and a duck—the first aerial travelers. 6. *La Machine . . . Allées du Jardin.* The machine, driven by the wind, blew against one of the walls of the garden.

balloon being no longer upright, the flame would have laid hold of the inside that leaned over it. But by means of some cords that were still attached to it, it was soon brought upright again, made to descend, and carried back to its place. It was, however, much damaged.

Planant sur l'Horizon.[7] When they were as high as they chose to be, they made less flame and suffered the machine to drive horizontally with the wind, of which, however, they felt very little, as they went with it, and as fast. They say they had a charming view of Paris and its environs, the course of the river, etc., but that they were once lost, not knowing what part they were over, till they saw the Dome of the Invalids,[8] which rectified their ideas. Probably while they were employed in keeping up the fire, the machine might turn, and by that means they were *désorienté*,[9] as the French call it.

There was a vast concourse of gentry in the garden, who had great pleasure in seeing the adventurers go off so cheerfully, and applauded them by clapping, etc., but there was at the same time a good deal of anxiety for their safety. Multitudes in Paris saw the balloon passing, but did not know there were men with it, it being then so high that they could not see them.

Développant du Gaz.[10] That is, in plain English, *burning more straw;* for though there is a little mystery made concerning the kind of air with which the balloon is filled, I conceive it to be nothing more than hot smoke or common air rarefied—though in this I may be mistaken; . . .

Ayant encore dans leur Galerie le deux tiers de leur approvisionment.[11] That is, their provision of straw, of which they carried up a great quantity. It was well that, in the hurry of so hazardous an experiment, the flame did not happen by any accidental mismanagement to lay hold of this straw; though each had a bucket of water by him by way of precaution.

One of these courageous philosophers, the Marquis d'Arlandes, did me the honor to call upon me in the evening after the experiment, with Mr. Montgolfier, the very ingenious inventor. I was happy to see him safe. He informed me they lit gently without the least shock, and the balloon was very little damaged. . . .

With great and sincere esteem, I am, dear sir, your most obedient and humble servant,

B. Franklin

---

7. *Planant sur l'Horizon,* hovering on the horizon. 8. *the Dome of the Invalids,* the dome of the Hôtel des Invalides (ō tel′ dä zän vä lēd′), a hospital for old or sick soldiers in Paris. 9. *they were "désorienté"* (dā zô′rē än tā′), they had lost their sense of direction. 10. *Développant du Gaz,* developing gas. 11. *Ayant encore . . . approvisionment,* still having in their gallery two thirds of their provisions.

CITIZEN AND PATRIOT

HISTORICAL SOCIETY OF PENNSYLVANIA

Leather fire bucket used by a volunteer company.

Franklin's business success was no doubt due in part to his discovery that it was useful to have friends. He was unquestionably a "joiner," sometimes from financial motives. In 1727, for example, he and other young tradesmen and artisans formed the Junto, or Leather Apron Club, in order to exchange information likely to prove profitable, as well as to debate questions of philosophy and politics.

The Junto, however, was more than a means of getting new business. It became the seedbed for public projects which were increasingly dear to Franklin's heart, and in which he exerted himself with modesty and with no more private interest than that of his fellow citizens. A paid night watch, or police force; a volunteer fire company; an academy and college; a hospital for the poor of the city; a subscription library; the paving of Philadelphia streets—these are a few of the public enterprises in which Franklin, with the help of the Junto members and other associates, engaged. Many of the organizations which he helped to form were the first of their kind in America. Not the least of the reasons for their establishment was Franklin's skill as a propagandist. A circular letter, *A Proposal for Promoting Useful Knowledge Among the British Plantations in America* (1743), led to the formation of the first American scientific society, the American Philosophical Society. His *Proposals Relating to the Education of Youth in Pennsylvania* (1749) led to the establishment of the College of Philadelphia, later the University of Pennsylvania. The proposal concludes with a typical statement of Franklin's social ideals:

The Idea of what is *true Merit* should also be often presented to Youth, explain'd and impress'd on their Minds, as consisting in an *Inclination* join'd with an *Ability* to serve Mankind, one's Country, Friends, and Family; which *Ability* is (with the Blessing of God) to be acquir'd or greatly increas'd by *true Learning*; and should indeed be the great *Aim* and *End* of all Learning.

It was natural that a man like Franklin should be sought out for public office. He began on the local level as justice of the peace, Philadelphia postmaster, and clerk of the General Assembly of Pennsylvania. In the troubled years before the French and Indian War he wrote numerous tracts, such as *Plain Truth* (1747) and *Plan for Settling the Western Colonies* (1756), which dealt with Pennsylvania problems. In 1757 Franklin was sent to England to serve as agent of the Pennsylvania legislature. He remained there, except for a year's respite in 1763-1764, until 1775. During these years he became agent for several colonies; gradually he came to be regarded as chief spokesman for all the colonies. To the English he was as close to an American ambassador as there was. Best known of his many writings seeking to reconcile the difficulties between England and America are his satires of 1773: "An Edict by the King of Prussia" and "Rules by Which a Great Empire May be Reduced to a Small One." During the seventeen years Franklin served in England, his attitudes changed from those of a Pennsylvanian to those of a man serving all the colonies.

The final phase of Franklin's public service was the most spectacular. After his return to America he was elected to the Second Continental Congress and served with Jefferson and John Adams on the committee which drafted the Declaration of Independence. Then, in 1776, he was appointed one of three commissioners to seek military and naval assistance from France. For nearly ten years Paris was his center of operations, and, in large part be-

THE FRANKLIN INSTITUTE, PHILADELPHIA

Above: First American political cartoon, published by Franklin in 1754. Below: Congress Voting Independence, *painted in 1788 by Pine and Savage. Samuel Adams is seated, far left; John Adams is standing, center, facing Franklin (seated center); Jefferson is handing a paper to Hancock.*

HISTORICAL SOCIETY OF PENNSYLVANIA

cause of his personal popularity, he secured the much-needed support of France and Spain and eventually helped negotiate the Treaty of Paris (1783), by which England recognized American independence. When he returned to America in 1785 he was old and ill, yet he found strength to serve as a delegate to the Constitutional Convention and to continue his work with many humanitarian and scientific societies.

The successive stages in Franklin's life as public-spirited citizen and as statesman reveal both the growth of an American and the varied ways in which a skillful writer can influence public opinion. As a writer he was, in the first place, convinced of the rightness of the causes for which he wrote, and he carried conviction to his readers. He wrote clearly and logically, developing his points step by step, patiently leading his readers to the inevitable conclusion. Above all, he was a man whose personality colored everything he wrote. His readers delighted in his personal touches, his little laughs at his own mistakes and weaknesses, his ready wit, and his clever satire. Despite the fact that he wrote of serious and sometimes crucial matters, he was fair in his judgments, humane in his treatment of others, seldom dull, and frequently amusing.

Few writings of Franklin are better evidence of his knowledge of diplomacy and practical politics and of the human touch in everything he wrote than his concluding speech at the Constitutional Convention, which is printed on page 142.

Speech in the Convention, at the Conclusion of Its Deliberations, September 17, 1787

Mr. President,

I confess, that I do not entirely approve of this Constitution at present; but, Sir, I am not sure I shall never approve it; for, having lived long, I have experienced many instances of being obliged, by better information or fuller consideration, to change opinions even on important subjects, which I once thought right, but found to be otherwise. It is therefore that, the older I grow, the more apt am I to doubt my own judgment of others. Most men, indeed, as well as most sects in religion, think themselves in possession of all truth, and that wherever others differ from them it is so far error. Steele,[1] a Protestant, in a dedication, tells the Pope, that the only difference between our two churches in their opinions of the certainty of their doctrine, is, the Romish Church is *infallible,* and the Church of England is *never in the wrong.* But, though many private persons think almost as highly of their own infallibility as of that of their sect, few express it so naturally as a certain French lady, who, in a little dispute with her sister, said, "But I meet with nobody but myself that is always in the right." *"Je ne trouve que moi qui aie toujours raison."*

In these sentiments, Sir, I agree to this Constitution, with all its faults—if they are such, because I think a general government necessary for us, and there is no *form* of government but what may be a blessing to the people, if well administered; and I believe, further, that this is likely to be well administered for a course of years, and can only end in despotism, as other forms have done before it, when the people shall become so corrupted as to need despotic government, being incapable of any other. I doubt, too, whether any other convention we can obtain, may be able to make a better constitution; for, when you assemble a number of men, to have the advantage of their joint wisdom, you inevitably assemble with those men all their prejudices, their passions, their errors of opinion, their local interests, and their selfish views. From such an assembly can a *perfect* production be expected? It therefore astonishes me, Sir, to find this system approaching so near to perfection as it does; and I think it will astonish our enemies, who are waiting with confidence to hear that our counsels are confounded like those of the builders of Babel,[2] and that our States are on the point of separation, only to meet hereafter for the purpose of cutting one another's throats. Thus I consent, Sir, to this Constitution, because I expect no better, and because I am not sure that it is not the best. The opinions I have had of its *errors* I sacrifice to the public good. I have never whispered a syllable of them abroad. Within these walls they were born, and here they will die. If every one of us, in returning to our constituents, were to report the objections he has had to it, and endeavor to gain partisans in support of them, we might prevent its being generally received, and thereby lose all the salutary effects and great advantages resulting naturally in our favor among foreign nations, as well as among ourselves, from any real or apparent unanimity. Much of the strength and efficiency of any government, in procuring and securing happiness to the people, depends on *opinion,* on the general opinion of the goodness of that government, as well as of the wisdom and integrity of its governors. I hope, therefore, for our own sakes, as a part of the people, and for the sake of our posterity, that we shall act heartily and unanimously in recommending this Constitution, wherever our influence may extend, and turn our future thoughts and endeavors to the means of having it *well administered.*

On the whole, Sir, I cannot help expressing a wish, that every member of the con-

---

1. *Steele.* The reference is probably to Richard Steele, the English essayist, who joined with Joseph Addison in writing the *Spectator.* 2. *builders of Babel.* According to the Bible (Genesis 11:1-9), builders in the ancient city of Babylon decided to construct a tower which would reach to heaven. God punished them by changing their language into several new and different languages. Unable to understand one another, they had to leave the tower unfinished.

vention who may still have objections to it, would with me on this occasion doubt a little of his own infallibility, and, to make *manifest* our *unanimity,* put his name to this instrument.

 WORDS!

Franklin's Speech in the Convention fairly rolls with words derived from Latin. When, for example, he pleads for *unanimity* of action, he is asking that the delegates be of one mind (*unus animus*).

Show how the original meaning of each Latin word below has been retained in the sentences that follow it.

fallere, to deceive
1. Franklin asked the delegates to doubt a little of their own *infallibility.*

2. In thinking the colonists wouldn't fight, the British held a *fallacious* belief.

salus, good health
1. Franklin pointed out that a unanimous decision would have *salutary* effects.
2. The Southern delegates enjoyed a *salubrious* climate.

efficere, to accomplish
1. Franklin declared that the *efficiency* of any government depended upon opinion.
2. The British believed in the *efficacy* of the redcoats.

integer, whole
1. Franklin relied upon the *integrity* of his fellow delegates.
2. Volunteer militia were *integrated* with professional soldiers in the Revolutionary army.

MAN OF THE WORLD Neither his financial success, nor his scientific fame, nor his remarkable public service tells the whole story of Benjamin Franklin as man and as writer. Mention must be made of his enjoyment of the crowded social life of the eighteenth century, his pleasure in reading, and his writing of light, graceful essays far removed in subject and tone from political tracts or scientific papers.

When Franklin was in London as agent for the American colonies, his worldly wisdom, wit, and humor made him a favorite member of the groups which gathered in the new coffee houses for evenings of amusing talk. Later, in Paris, his official business brought him into daily contact with the brilliant society surrounding the court of the French king. In this assemblage of clever men and women Dr. Franklin, as he was then called, occupied a unique place as a scientist of international fame, the American minister to France, a philosopher out of the New World, and a brilliant conversationalist famous for his quickness in witty exchanges. A widely circulated story is illustrative: At a Paris banquet, the diplomats present were asked to toast their respective countries. The British ambassador said, "To England!—the Sun, whose warm beneficent rays encourage the growth of industry and assist in the expansion of labor in every form throughout the world!" The French minister said, "To France!—the Moon, whose soft glow encourages the flowering of literature and the mellowing of the arts!" When Franklin stood, the audience tittered, for it appeared that he was left with nothing important to claim. But unhesitatingly he said, "To the United States!—the Joshua at whose command the sun and the moon stand still!"

As a boy in his brother's printshop, Franklin had become interested in books, and this interest stayed with him throughout his long life. His favorite authors ranged from the ancient Greeks and Romans to his own contemporaries in England and France. Addison and Steele, whose *Spectator* had long ago inspired Franklin's *Dogood Papers,* remained prime favorites.

Not surprisingly, the man who shone among the brilliant assemblies of England and France and who was conversant with the literature of several countries was as at home writing as a sophisticated man of the world as in assuming the rôle of a Mistress Dogood or a Poor Richard. For the friends who gathered at his home at Passy outside Paris he wrote little essays, called *bagatelles*. He set up a press to amuse himself and his friends by printing them. These bagatelles, better than any of Franklin's earlier writings, show his worldly wisdom, his light humor, and his graceful style. One of them, "The Whistle" (page 134), you have already read. Others are "The Morals of Chess," "Dialogue Between Franklin and the Gout," and "The Ephemera." The last of these, addressed to his friend Madame Brillon, is a brilliant summation of the views of a noted man on human life and fame.

Top: A view of Christ Church Burial Ground, where Franklin is buried. Bottom: One of Franklin's wills, written in his own hand.

The Ephemera

An Emblem of Human Life

You may remember, my dear friend, that when we lately spent that happy day in the delightful garden and sweet society of the Moulin Joly,[1] I stopped a little in one of our walks and stayed some time behind the company. We had been shown numberless skeletons of a kind of little fly, called an ephemera, whose successive generations, we were told, were bred and expired within the day. I happened to see a living company of them on a leaf, who appeared to be engaged in conversation. You know I understand all the inferior animal tongues. My too great application to the study of them is the best excuse I can give for the little progress I have made in your charming language. I listened

1. *Moulin Joly* (mü lăn′ zhô lē′), the name of the home of a friend of Franklin on an island in the Seine (săn). Here in the summer of 1778 Franklin spent a day with Madame Brillon and other friends. Later in the selection Franklin uses *Moulin Joly*, which means "pretty mill," to represent the whole world.

through curiosity to the discourse of these little creatures; but as they, in their national vivacity, spoke three or four together, I could make but little of their conversation. I found, however, by some broken expressions that I heard now and then, they were disputing warmly on the merit of two foreign musicians, one a *cousin,* the other a *moscheto*[2]*;* in which dispute they spent their time, seemingly as regardless of the shortness of life as if they had been sure of living a month. Happy people! thought I, you are certainly under a wise, just, and mild government, since you have no public grievances to complain of, nor any subject of contention but the perfections and imperfections of foreign music! I turned my head from them to an old gray-headed one, who was single on another leaf, and talking to himself. Being amused with his soliloquy, I put it down in writing, in hopes it will likewise amuse her to whom I am so much indebted for the most pleasing of all amusements, her delicious company and heavenly harmony.

"It was," said he, "the opinion of learned philosophers of our race, who lived and flourished long before my time, that this vast world, the Moulin Joly, could not itself subsist more than eighteen hours; and I think there was some foundation for that opinion, since, by the apparent motion of the great luminary[3] that gives life to all nature, and which in my time has evidently declined considerably toward the ocean at the end of our earth, it must then finish its course, be extinguished in the waters that surround us, and leave the world in cold and darkness, necessarily producing universal death and destruction. I have lived seven of those hours, a great age, being no less than four hundred and twenty minutes of time. How very few of us continue so long! I have seen generations born, flourish, and expire. My present friends are the children and grandchildren of the friends of my youth, who are now, alas, no more! And I must soon follow them; for, by the course of nature, though still in health, I cannot expect to live above seven or eight minutes longer. What now avails all my toil and labor in amassing honeydew on this leaf, which I can-

not live to enjoy! What the political struggles I have been engaged in for the good of my compatriot inhabitants of this bush, or my philosophical studies for the benefit of our race in general! for in politics, what can laws do without morals? Our present race of ephemerae will in a course of minutes become corrupt, like those of other and older bushes, and consequently as wretched. And in philosophy how small our progress! Alas! art is long, and life is short! My friends would comfort me with the idea of a name they say I shall leave behind me; and they tell me I have lived long enough to nature and to glory. But what will fame be to an ephemera who no longer exists? And what will become of all history in the eighteenth hour, when the world itself, even the whole Moulin Joly, shall come to its end, and be buried in universal ruin?"

To me, after all my eager pursuits, no solid pleasures now remain but the reflection of a long life spent in meaning well, the sensible conversation of a few good lady ephemerae, and now and then a kind smile and a tune from the ever amiable *Brillante.*[4]

B. Franklin

---

2. *two foreign musicians . . . cousin* (kü zaɴ′) *. . . moscheto* (mō skāt′tō). At the time Franklin wrote "The Ephemera," Parisians were disputing about the relative merits of a German and an Italian musician. Franklin satirizes this argument by having the insects discuss the music of the *cousin* (the French word for a gnat) and the *moscheto* (the Italian word for a mosquito). 3. *the great luminary,* the sun. 4. *Brillante* (bri yaɴt′), shining one. Franklin is punning on Madame Brillon's name, the pronunciation of which is similar to that of *Brillante.*

❧ TO INCREASE UNDERSTANDING
The Whistle, A Receipt, The Way to Wealth

1. (*a*) How does the essay, "The Whistle," illustrate the statement, "Franklin was educated by experience"? (*b*) Cite examples of the way Franklin here applies a boyhood experience to illustrate mature concepts.

2. (*a*) Describe how working on his brother's paper, the *New England Courant,* led Franklin to make his first venture into journalism. (*b*) How did this experience affect his viewpoint in much of his later writing?

3. (*a*) What conventions of the Puritan elegy does Franklin ridicule in "A Receipt to Make a New England Funeral Elegy"? (*b*) Why do you

think this and other *Dogood Papers* were popular with the *Courant's* readers?

4. (*a*) What circumstances led to the creation of Poor Richard? (*b*) In what ways are Poor Richard, Silence Dogood, and Father Abraham alike?

5. (*a*) What is the underlying theme of *The Way to Wealth*? (*b*) How did this theme contribute to the interest of almanac readers in Poor Richard's sayings?

6. What indications can you find that "The Whistle" and *The Way to Wealth* were written by the same man?

The First Aerial Voyage by Man

1. (*a*) Which details in "The First Aerial Voyage by Man" show Franklin's interest in balloon ascension as a scientific experiment? (*b*) Which details would have no place in a purely scientific paper? (*c*) Why do you think Franklin included in his letter details which had no bearing on the scientific aspects of the experiment?

2. It has been stated that Franklin's experience as a newspaperman increased his value as a scientist. (*a*) Using "The First Aerial Voyage" as an example, give reasons to support this statement. (*b*) How did his experience in writing help him gain fame for his discoveries in electricity?

Speech in the Convention

1. Discuss as fully as possible the following factors that made Franklin the ideal person to deliver the closing speech at the Constitutional Convention: (*a*) his experiences in public life; (*b*) his personality; (*c*) his career as man of letters.

2. Cite specific examples in the speech of (*a*) Franklin's knowledge of diplomacy, (*b*) his sense of practical politics, and (*c*) his mastery of the human touch.

3. If you had been a delegate to the Constitutional Convention who was reluctant to approve the Constitution as it had been drafted, would Franklin's statements have influenced you to change your mind? Why or why not?

The Ephemera

1. Franklin's writings aided his influence both as a public servant and as a scientist. Show how his pen was also of value to him as a man of the world.

2. What is the basic idea of "The Ephemera"? In stating this idea, use an adjective that is derived from the word *ephemera*.

3. (*a*) Why did Franklin choose "an old gray-headed" ephemera to deliver the soliloquy? (*b*) What points of comparison with the world in general and with Franklin's own life do you find in the soliloquy?

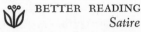 BETTER READING
Satire

In England, the eighteenth century was the age of satire. The poets Dryden and Pope, the essayists Addison, Steele, and Swift, the novelist Fielding were all satirists—men who used their pens to attack or ridicule human folly. With sharp shafts of irony, sarcasm, or wit they mocked the pretensions of society, probed the inequalities of social justice, and sought to show men the frailties of human institutions. Together they made satire a dominant note in the literature of the early eighteenth century; and even after the last of this famous group had died, their influence continued to affect the writing and conversation of their successors.

Franklin, the American, shared to some extent the satirical view of life popular in England—in fact, his early literary tastes had been partially formed by reading the *Spectator* essays of Addison and Steele. Young Franklin modeled his *Dogood Papers* on these essays. The vein of satire crops out occasionally in the writing Franklin did throughout his life, but is particularly noticeable in the work of his later years.

Consider "The Ephemera." How does the very idea of the piece show Franklin's satirical bent? What particular habits and ideas of man does he satirize? Is the satire biting or relatively mild?

Think again about "A Receipt to Make a New England Funeral Elegy." In what ways does its purpose differ from that of "The Ephemera"? How does this purpose affect its tone?

 EXTENDING INTERESTS

Modern space travel began with the balloon ascension Franklin witnessed in November 1783. Your class may be interested in an article entitled, "When Man First Left the Earth" in *Horizon* magazine (September 1958). In it you will find illustrations of the early balloons and a history of the ascensions. Several members of the class might read the article and each report on one phase of early balloon ascension—the significant first flights, the appearance of the balloons, the aeronauts, and the scientific purpose involved.

An entertaining, informative account of Franklin's interest in balloon ascensions may be found at the beginning of Chapter 24 of *Benjamin Franklin*, by Carl Van Doren.

THE MAGAZINE IN AMERICA: Introduction

In an age of no radios, television, newsreels, telephones, or telegraph systems, Franklin and his contemporary writers relied upon newspapers, magazines, and pamphlets to carry their ideas to the public. Every great issue, from the Stamp Act to the Declaration, from the Revolution to the ratification of the Constitution, was debated in the periodical press. The best political essays of Franklin, Paine, Jefferson, Hamilton, and Freneau first appeared in periodicals.

Unlike the newspapers, which circulated in a single city or a single colony, the magazines sought to influence readers in all thirteen colonies. From their beginnings in 1741 with the *American Magazine* and Franklin's *General Magazine,* colonial magazines contained articles which interested, alike, a planter in Williamsburg and a merchant in Boston.

Usually selling for a shilling, and always short-lived, the magazines dealt with timely issues briefly and pointedly. They were the kind of publication a man could take home, read, and discuss with his neighbors by the fireside or at a tavern. Through such publications, the colonists acquired the magazine-reading habit characteristic of Americans today.

More than two thirds of all adult Americans are regular magazine readers. They have their choice of seven thousand periodicals, including at least one specializing in every vocation, every hobby, every interest or need in American life. In subsequent chapters of this anthology you will read about some of the oldest and some of the most influential magazines, and about the part their editors have played in shaping American literature.

On August 4, 1821, Philadelphians had in their hands the first issue of the *Saturday Evening Post.* Published in the same office which had formerly housed Franklin's *Pennsylvania Gazette,* the new four-page *Post* contained attractive tidbits for almost everyone. Its news, editorials, and essays kept the sober-minded citizen abreast of his time. Farmers scanned its almanac—merchants consulted its shipping schedules. The ladies of Philadelphia wept over its obituaries or delighted in its uplifting, if sentimental, verse. In serving the diverse interests of its readers, the *Post* became one of the important weeklies of its time.

By 1850 the *Post* had become much broader in its coverage; now imaginative literature found a place beside factual or informative writings. Stories and poems by such first-rate writers as Poe, Bryant, Cooper, Emerson, Hawthorne, and Lowell graced its pages.

When an American buys the *Saturday Evening Post* at his newsstand today, he expects the same kind of informed comment and entertainment which has always characterized the magazine. Six million weekly purchasers find within its highly illustrated pages short stories and serial installments by unknown or established writers. Willa Cather, Bret Harte, Stephen Crane, O. Henry, and Sinclair Lewis —to name only a few of the authors who appear in this anthology—have all been *Post* contributors.

In nonfiction articles by poets and prize fighters, businessmen and humorists, statesmen and teachers, the *Saturday Evening Post* mirrors every diverse facet of American life and is truly a magazine for every American.

Thomas Paine 1737-1809

Political independence from Great Britain, the idea which Franklin accepted only reluctantly, was whole-heartedly urged by Thomas Paine, the greatest propagandist of the Revolution. Born in England, Paine left school at thirteen and worked unhappily at a variety of jobs. After a meeting with Franklin in London, Paine determined to try life in the colonies. Although he did not arrive in America until 1774, he so fully accepted the American vision of a continental destiny that within the next two years he persuaded great numbers of his fellow countrymen, including George Washington, that the time had come for separation from Britain.

Paine's *Common Sense* appeared in January 1776, when Washington was in command of the American army, which had bottled up the British in Boston. Like Franklin, most Americans still hoped for some kind of resolution, short of an open break, of their quarrel with Britain. Paine's pamphlet, asserting that "nothing can settle our affairs so expeditiously as an open and determined DECLARATION FOR INDEPENDENCE," was widely read (125,000 copies were printed within three months), and the Declaration was drawn up and signed in the following summer.

Like all propagandists, Paine sought to arouse men's emotions. He was not content merely to present an argument, even though the argument might be based, as Washington put it, on "sound doctrine and unanswerable reasoning." What he wanted was action, and to achieve that he appealed to the self-interest and idealism of all who shared the American dream of the future.

Paine's later writings are also important: (1) *The American Crisis*, a series of essays which appeared irregularly throughout the war, especially at points when the patriots' cause seemed to be faltering; (2) *The Rights of Man* (1791-1792), which linked the American Revolution to the one that soon followed in France; and (3) *The Age of Reason* (1794-1795), intended to free the minds of men from what Paine regarded as false religion. The last of these aroused great bitterness among pious Americans and severely damaged Paine's reputation.

Although Paine's later writings lost him the regard he had gained during the Revolutionary War, no one can dispute his skill as a master of persuasion. He presented his arguments with brilliance, clarity, and force. He understood the power of language to move men to action, and he used this power with never failing skill. The selection from *Common Sense* beginning on the next page shows Paine's ability to put in vivid, persuasive language the ideals which prompted the founding of the nation.

FROM *Common Sense*

I n the following pages I offer nothing
more than simple facts, plain arguments,
and common sense; and have no other
preliminaries to settle with the reader,
than that he will divest himself of prejudice and prepossession, and suffer his reason
and his feeling to determine for themselves:
that he will put on, or rather that he will not
put off, the true character of a man, and generously enlarge his views beyond the present
day.

Volumes have been written on the subject
of the struggle between England and America. Men of all ranks have embarked in the
controversy, from different motives, and with
various designs; but all have been ineffectual,
and the period of debate is closed. Arms as
the last resource decide the contest; the appeal
was the choice of the King, and the Continent
has accepted the challenge.

It has been reported of the late Mr. Pelham[1]
(who though an able minister was not without his faults) that on his being attacked in
the House of Commons on the score that his
measures were only of a temporary kind, replied, "They will last my time." Should a
thought so fatal and unmanly possess the Colonies in the present contest, the name of
Ancestors will be remembered by future generations with detestation.

1. *Mr. Pelham.* Henry Pelham was prime minister of Great
Britain, 1744-1754.

The Sun never shone on a cause of greater worth. 'Tis not the affair of a City, a County, a Province, or a Kingdom; but of a continent—of at least one eighth part of the habitable globe. 'Tis not the concern of a day, a year, or an age; posterity are virtually involved in the contest, and will be more or less affected even to the end of time by the proceedings now. Now is the seedtime of continental union, faith, and honor. The least fracture now, will be like a name engraved with the point of a pin on the tender rind of a young oak; the wound would enlarge with the tree, and posterity read it in full-grown characters.

By referring the matter from argument to arms, a new era for politics is struck—a new method of thinking has arisen. All plans, proposals, &c., prior to the nineteenth of April,[2] i.e., to the commencement of hostilities, are like the almanacs of last year; which though proper then, are superseded and useless now. Whatever was advanced by the advocates on either side of the question then, terminated in one and the same point, viz., a union with Great Britain; the only difference between the parties was the method of effecting it; the one proposing force, the other friendship; but it has so far happened that the first has failed, and the second has withdrawn her influence. . . .

Much has been said of the united strength of Britain and the Colonies, that in conjunction they might bid defiance to the world. But this is mere presumption; the fate of war is uncertain; neither do the expressions mean anything, for this continent would never suffer itself to be drained of inhabitants to support the British arms in either Asia, Africa, or Europe.

Besides, what have we to do with setting the world at defiance? Our plan is commerce, and that, well attended to, will secure us the peace and friendship of all Europe; because it is the interest of all Europe to have America a *free port*. Her trade will always be a protection, and her barrenness of gold and silver secure her from invaders.

I challenge the warmest advocate of reconciliation to show a single advantage that this continent can reap by being connected with Great Britain. I repeat the challenge—not a single advantage is derived. Our corn will fetch its price in any market in Europe, and our imported goods must be paid for, buy them where we will.

But the injuries and disadvantages which we sustain by that connection are without number; and our duty to mankind at large, as well as to ourselves, instructs us to renounce the alliance, because any submission to, or dependence on, Great Britain, tends directly to involve this continent in European wars and quarrels, and sets us at variance with nations who would otherwise seek our friendship, and against whom we have neither anger nor complaint. As Europe is our market for trade, we ought to form no partial connection with any part of it. 'Tis the true interest of America to steer clear of European contentions, which she can never do while by her dependence on Britian she is the makeweight in the scale of British politics.

Europe is too thickly planted with kingdoms to be long at peace, and whenever a war breaks out between England and any foreign power, the trade of America goes to ruin, *because of her connection with Britain*. The next war may not turn out like the last,[3] and should it not, advocates for reconciliation now will be wishing for separation then, because neutrality in that case would be a safer convoy than a man-of-war. Everything that is right or reasonable pleads for separation. The blood of the slain, the weeping voice of nature cries, 'TIS TIME TO PART. Even the distance at which the Almighty has placed England and America is a strong and natural proof that the authority of the one over the other was never the design of heaven. The time likewise at which the continent was discovered adds weight to the argument, and the manner in which it was peopled increases the force of it. The Reformation[4] was preceded by the discovery of America, as if the Almighty graciously meant to open a sanctuary to the per-

---

2. *nineteenth of April.* The date the minutemen engaged the British at Lexington. 3. *The next war . . . like the last.* The English had only recently defeated the French in the French and Indian War (1754-1763). 4. *The Reformation.* The religious movement in sixteenth-century Europe that led to the establishment of Protestantism.

secuted in future years, when home should afford neither friendship nor safety. . . .

'Tis repugnant to reason, to the universal order of things, to all examples from future ages, to suppose that this continent can long remain subject to any external power. The most sanguine in Britain do not think so. The utmost stretch of human wisdom cannot, at this time, compass a plan, short of separation, which can promise the continent even a year's security. Reconciliation is *now* a fallacious dream. Nature has deserted the connection, and art cannot supply her place. For, as Milton wisely expresses, "never can true reconcilement grow where wounds of deadly hate have pierced so deep."[5]

Every quiet method for peace has been ineffectual. Our prayers have been rejected with disdain; and have tended to convince us that nothing flatters vanity or confirms obstinacy in kings more than repeated petitioning—and nothing has contributed more than that very measure to make the kings of Europe absolute. Witness Denmark and Sweden.[6] Wherefore, since nothing but blows will do, for God's sake let us come to a final separation, and not leave the next generation to be cutting throats under the violated unmeaning names of parent and child.

To say they[7] will never attempt it again is idle and visionary; we thought so at the repeal of the Stamp Act,[8] yet a year or two undeceived us; as well as may we suppose that nations which have been once defeated will never renew the quarrel.

As to government matters, 'tis not in the power of Britain to do this continent justice: the business of it will soon be too weighty and intricate to be managed, with any tolerable degree of convenience, by a power so distant from us, and so very ignorant of us; for if they cannot conquer us they cannot govern us. To be always running three or four thousand miles with a tale or a petition, waiting four or five months for an answer, which, when obtained, requires five or six more to explain it in, will in a few years be looked upon as folly and childishness. There was a time it was proper, and there is a proper time for it to cease.

Small islands not capable of protecting themselves are the proper objects for government to take under their care; but there is something absurd in supposing a continent to be perpetually governed by an island. In no instance has nature made the satellite larger than its primary planet; and as England and America, with respect to each other, reverse the common order of nature, it is evident that they belong to different systems. England to Europe: America to itself.

I am not induced by motives of pride, party, or resentment to espouse the doctrine of separation and independence; I am clearly, positively, and conscientiously persuaded that 'tis the true interest of this continent to be so; that everything short of *that* is mere patchwork, that it can afford no lasting felicity—that it is leaving the sword to our children, and shrinking back at a time when a little more, a little further, would have rendered this continent the glory of the earth. . . .

5. *For, as Milton . . . pierced so deep.* Paine is quoting from *Paradise Lost,* written by the English poet John Milton (1608-1674). 6. *Witness Denmark and Sweden.* Quarrels among the nobles had led to the establishment of an absolute monarchy in Denmark under Frederick III in 1660 and in Sweden under Gustavus III in 1772. 7. *they,* the British government. 8. *the Stamp Act.* In order to raise revenue in the American colonies, the British Parliament passed an act requiring the use of stamps or stamped paper for certain official documents and commercial writings. Although the act went into effect in November 1765, intense colonial opposition forced its repeal the next year.

TO INCREASE UNDERSTANDING

1. Although Thomas Paine had been in America less than two years when he wrote *Common Sense,* he wholeheartedly embraced the American cause. How did his attitude toward separation from England differ from the attitude of most Americans, including Franklin?

2. What arguments does Paine give for "referring the matter from argument to arms"?

3. Point out passages in *Common Sense* that indicate Paine's grasp of America's continental destiny.

4. On page 148 you read: "Like all propagandists, Paine sought to arouse men's emotions." (*a*) Cite passages from *Common Sense* that in your opinion demonstrate this fact. (*b*) Do you agree that propaganda is necessary in situations such as that in which Paine wrote his pamphlet? Why, or why not?

Thomas Jefferson 1743-1826

Thomas Jefferson is rated among the greatest of all Americans. A Virginia planter and aristocrat, a graduate of William and Mary College, a lawyer by profession, he had little to gain and everything to lose by taking his place among the champions of independence. Yet from the first motions in the Virginia House of Burgesses for separation from Britain, this brilliant and versatile man took his place with the fighters for freedom. After independence was won, he served the infant Republic, becoming the third President of the United States and eventually a symbol of American democracy.

Jefferson was only thirty-three when he was made chairman of the committee appointed by the Second Continental Congress to draft a suitable statement of the American cause for freedom. The document which resulted, the Declaration of Independence, is, more than most state papers, the work of a single man. In it Jefferson said little or nothing that had not

Jefferson, painted by Rembrandt Peale, son of Charles W. Peale, and Jefferson's own manuscript of the Declaration.

been said before, but his ringing sentences, at once a statement of American principles and a review of the causes of the quarrel with Britain, presented the American view to the world with classic dignity. In this document Jefferson also showed himself a skillful propagandist, laying most of the blame for the conflict upon King George III rather than upon Parliament or the English people.

Although Jefferson as a writer is chiefly known for the Declaration of Independence, he is also the author of other great state papers. A man of varied interests, he wrote on practically every subject, from agriculture to architecture. The projected fifty-two volume edition of *The Papers of Thomas Jefferson,* which will embrace everything Jefferson ever wrote, will include eighteen thousand letters written by him. The tone of Jefferson's diverse writings varies as his purpose varies; in them we find light and charming correspondence, carefully composed scientific theories, and the formal but inspiring phrases of the state papers. But whatever the tone, the reader is always aware that Jefferson understood the power and beauty of words and used them magnificently.

The Declaration of Independence

When, in the course of human events, it becomes necessary for one people to dissolve the political bands which have connected them with another, and to assume, among the Powers of the earth, the separate and equal station to which the Laws of Nature and of Nature's God entitle them, a decent respect to the opinions of mankind requires that they should declare the causes which impel them to the separation.

We hold these truths to be self-evident: that all men are created equal; that they are endowed by their Creator with certain inalienable Rights; that among these are Life, Liberty, and the pursuit of Happiness. That, to secure these Rights, Governments are instituted among Men, deriving their just powers from the consent of the governed—That, whenever any Form of Government becomes destructive of these ends, it is the Right of the People to alter or abolish it, and to institute new Government, laying its foundation on such Principles, and organizing its Powers in such form, as to them shall seem most likely to effect their Safety and Happiness. Prudence, indeed, will dictate that Governments long established should not be changed for light and transient causes; and, accordingly, all experience hath shown that mankind are more disposed to suffer, while evils are sufferable, than to right themselves by abolishing the forms to which they are accustomed. But, when a long train of abuses and usurpations, pursuing invariably the same Object, evinces a design to reduce them under absolute Despotism, it is their right, it is their duty, to throw off such Government, and to provide new Guards for their future security. Such has been the patient sufferance of these Colonies, and such is now the necessity which constrains them to alter their former Systems of Government. The history of the present King of Great Britain is a history of repeated injuries and usurpations, all having in direct object the establishment of an absolute Tyranny over these States. To prove this, let Facts be submitted to a candid world:

He has refused his Assent to Laws the most wholesome and necessary for the public good.

He has forbidden his Governors to pass Laws of immediate and pressing importance, unless suspended in their operation till his Assent should be obtained; and, when so suspended, he has utterly neglected to attend to them.

He has refused to pass other Laws for the accommodation of large districts of people, unless those people would relinquish the rights of Representation in the Legislature; a right inestimable to them, and formidable to tyrants only.

He has called together legislative bodies at places unusual, uncomfortable, and distant from the depository of their Public Records, for the sole purpose of fatiguing them into compliance with his measures.

He has dissolved Representative Houses repeatedly for opposing, with manly firmness, his invasions on the rights of the people.

He has refused for a long time after such dissolutions to cause others to be elected; whereby the Legislative Powers, incapable of Annihilation, have returned to the People at large for their exercise; the State remaining, in the meantime, exposed to all the dangers of invasions from without, and convulsions within.

He has endeavored to prevent the Population of these States; for that purpose obstructing the Laws for Naturalization of Foreigners; refusing to pass others to encourage their migrations hither, and raising the conditions of new Appropriations of Lands.

He has obstructed the Administration of Justice by refusing his Assent to Laws for establishing Judiciary Powers.

He has made Judges dependent on his Will alone for the tenure of their offices, and the amount and Payment of their salaries.

He has erected a multitude of New Offices, and sent hither swarms of Officers to harass our People and eat out their substance.

He has kept among us, in times of Peace, Standing Armies, without the Consent of our legislatures.

He has affected to render the Military independent of and superior to the Civil Power.

He has combined with others to subject us to a jurisdiction foreign to our constitution, and unacknowledged by our laws: giving his Assent to their Acts of pretended Legislation:

For quartering large bodies of armed troops among us;

For protecting them, by a mock Trial, from Punishment for any Murders which they should commit on the Inhabitants of these States;

For cutting off our Trade with all parts of the world;

For imposing Taxes on us without our Consent;

For depriving us, in many cases, of the benefits of Trial by Jury;

For transporting us beyond Seas to be tried for pretended offences;

For abolishing the free System of English Laws in a neighboring Province,[1] establishing therein an Arbitrary government, and enlarging its Boundaries, so as to render it at once an example and fit instrument for introducing the same absolute rule into these Colonies;

For taking away our Charters, abolishing our most valuable Laws, and altering, fundamentally, the Forms of our Governments;

For suspending our own Legislatures, and declaring themselves invested with Power to legislate for us in all cases whatsoever.

He has abdicated Government here by declaring us out of his Protection, and waging War against us.

He has plundered our seas, ravaged our Coasts, burnt our towns, and destroyed the Lives of our People.

He is, at this time, transporting large Armies of foreign Mercenaries to complete the works of death, desolation, and tyranny, already begun with circumstances of Cruelty and Perfidy scarcely paralleled in the most barbarous ages, and totally unworthy the Head of a civilized nation.

He has constrained our fellow Citizens, taken Captive on the high Seas, to bear Arms against their Country, to become the executioners of their friends and Brethren, or to fall themselves by their Hands.

He has excited domestic insurrections amongst us, and has endeavored to bring on

1. *a neighboring Province,* Quebec, which England had acquired as a result of the French and Indian War. According to the Quebec Act of 1774, French Civil Law was established, a royal governor was appointed, and the boundaries were enlarged to include much of the country between the Ohio and the Mississippi rivers.

the inhabitants of our frontiers the merciless Indian Savages, whose known rule of warfare is an undistinguished destruction of all ages, sexes, and conditions.

In every stage of these Oppressions, We have Petitioned for Redress, in the most humble terms: Our repeated Petitions have been answered only by repeated injury. A Prince, whose character is thus marked by every act which may define a Tyrant, is unfit to be the ruler of a free People.

Nor have We been wanting in attentions to our British brethren. We have warned them, from time to time, of attempts by their legislature to extend an unwarrantable jurisdiction over us. We have reminded them of the circumstances of our emigration and settlement here. We have appealed to their native justice and magnanimity, and we have conjured them, by the ties of our common kindred, to disavow these usurpations, which would inevitably interrupt our connections and correspondence. They, too, have been deaf to the voice of justice and of consanguinity. We must, therefore, acquiesce in the necessity which denounces our Separation, and hold them, as we hold the rest of mankind—Enemies in War—in Peace, Friends.

WE, THEREFORE, the REPRESENTATIVES of the UNITED STATES OF AMERICA, in GENERAL CONGRESS Assembled, appealing to the Supreme Judge of the world for the rectitude of our intentions, Do, in the Name and by the Authority of the good People of these Colonies, solemnly PUBLISH and DECLARE, That these United Colonies are, and of Right ought to be, FREE AND INDEPENDENT STATES; that they are Absolved from all Allegiance to the British Crown, and that all political connection between them and the State of Great Britain is, and ought to be, totally dissolved; and that, as FREE AND INDEPENDENT STATES, they have full Power to levy War, conclude Peace, contract Alliances, establish Commerce, and to do all other Acts and Things which INDEPENDENT STATES may of right do. And, for the support of this Declaration, with a firm reliance on the Protection of Divine Providence, we mutually pledge to each other our Lives, our Fortunes, and our Sacred Honor.

 TO INCREASE UNDERSTANDING

1. How do you account for Jefferson's being among the champions of independence?

2. (a) Under what circumstances did the signers of the Declaration of Independence believe men are justified in setting up a new government? (b) What did they give as their reason for making this document public?

3. (a) Why is the second paragraph of the Declaration considered its most important passage? (b) To what rights does it say all men are entitled? (c) What is the significance of the phrase, "pursuit of happiness"?

4. (a) Why was it shrewd to lay most of the blame for the conflict with England on George III? (b) Name some of the abuses of which the makers of the Declaration declared him guilty.

5. In *Common Sense*, Paine urged a "Declaration for Independence"; Jefferson wrote it. (a) How does the writing of these two men differ in tone? (b) Explain why you think the language each man used is best suited to his particular purpose.

 WORDS!

Few of the founders of American liberty were primarily interested in producing literature. They were concerned with the problems of winning and establishing a sound and lasting government. Nevertheless, because these men recognized the power of appropriate language to influence action, they made every effort to write clearly and forcefully. In keeping with the seriousness of their themes, they wrote in a dignified, formal manner.

One of the marks of formal English is its vocabulary, the use of words that belong to the written rather than to the commonly spoken language. In the Declaration, Jefferson uses many long, formal words, such as *inalienable, annihilation, usurpations.* These words, like most formal vocabulary, are based on Latin roots. Also, he uses many words which would not ordinarily appear in informal talk. For example, he says *invariably* instead of *always, relinquish* instead of *give up,* and *consanguinity* instead of *blood ties.*

1. Run through the Declaration and list several words and phrases that you would label as formal.

2. Explain the meaning of each word or phrase, and suggest an informal substitute for each.

3. What effect do your substitutions have on the famous document?

Philip Freneau 1752-1832

Of the many poets who wrote of the issues and events of the Revolutionary War period, Philip Freneau is the best known. While a student at Princeton he showed two of the interests that dominated his life: he began writing poems based on English models, and he became interested in politics. During the war he saw active service as a ship's officer, running the British blockade from the West Indies. In the course of this dangerous work he was captured and thrust into a prison so horrible that his ardent nature flamed out in hatred of the British. Out of this experience grew "The British Prison Ship" (1781), followed by a long series of satires and ballads in which he expressed the hopes and fears of his countrymen. "On the Memorable Victory" (page 157) belongs to this series. It is an excellent example of Freneau's combination of first-hand knowledge of the sea, patriotism, and eighteenth-century poetic form and diction.

After the war ended, Freneau spent some years in coastwise shipping. Later he became an editor, eventually founding a paper of his own. The prime purpose of Freneau's *National Gazette* was to oppose the policies of the Federalists. Into this battle Freneau threw the same fierce energy he had earlier displayed against the British. His bitter partisanship incurred the wrath of Washington and other leading Federalists, but he was supported by Jefferson and the Republicans. Through his paper he was instrumental in the development of the two-party system in American politics.

This man who hated the British and mercilessly baited the Federalists had his gentler side. In addition to satiric ballads and scathing editorials, throughout his life he wrote lyrics extolling his love of the sea and his feeling for the American countryside. Although he imitated English models, yet he paved the way for Bryant, Lowell, and other writers who from the American scene wrought a truly American poetry.

The Serapis *(right) and the* Bon Homme Richard, *from a painting by William Elliott.*

On the Memorable Victory

*Obtained by the Gallant Captain John Paul Jones,
of the* Bon Homme Richard, *over the* Seraphis,
under the command of Captain Pearson

This poem is an account of the best-known and most
bitterly fought naval action of the Revolutionary
War.

Jones, in the converted and poorly equipped mer-
chantman he had renamed to honor Franklin's Poor
Richard, led a raiding force on the British Isles. On
September 23, 1779, the American raiders—the *Bon
Homme Richard,* the *Pallas,* the *Vengeance,* and
the *Alliance*—encountered the Baltic merchant fleet
under convoy of the British *Serapis* and *Countess of
Scarborough* just off the east coast of England. The
Bon Homme Richard engaged the *Serapis* (Freneau
spells it *Seraphis*), and for more than three moonlit hours the two ships fought at close quarters. Surprisingly, Freneau fails to use the famous reply by
Jones to Pearson's demand that he surrender: "I
have not begun to fight."

O'er the rough main, with flowing sheet,
The guardian of a numerous fleet,
   Seraphis from the Baltic came;
A ship of less tremendous force
Sail'd by her side the self-same course,   5
   Countess of Scarb'ro' was her name.

And now their native coasts appear,
Britannia's hills their summit rear
   Above the German main:
Fond to suppose their dangers o'er,   10
They southward coast along the shore,
   Thy waters, gentle Thames, to gain.

Full forty guns *Seraphis* bore,
And *Scarb'ro's Countess* twenty-four,
   Mann'd with Old England's boldest tars—
What flag that rides the Gallic seas   16
Shall dare attack such piles as these,
   Design'd for tumults and for wars!

Now from the topmast's giddy height
A seaman cry'd—"Four sail in sight   20
   "Approach with favoring gales,"
Pearson, resolv'd to save the fleet,
Stood off to sea, these ships to meet,
   And closely brac'd his shivering sails.

With him advanc'd the *Countess* bold,   25
Like a black tar in wars grown old:
   And now these floating piles drew nigh;
But, muse, unfold, what chief of fame
In the other warlike squadron came,
   Whose standards at his masthead fly.   30

'Twas JONES, brave JONES, to battle led
As bold a crew as ever bled
   Upon the sky-surrounded main;
The standards of the western world
Were to the willing winds unfurl'd,   35
   Denying Britain's tyrant reign.

The *Good-Man-Richard* led the line;
The *Alliance* next: with these combine
   The Gallic ship they *Pallas* call,[1]
The *Vengeance,* arm'd with sword and flame;
These to attack the Britons came—   41
   But *two* accomplish'd all.

Now Phoebus[2] sought his pearly bed:
But who can tell the scenes of dread,
   The horrors of that fatal night!   45
Close up those floating castles came;
The *Good-Man-Richard* bursts in flame;
   Seraphis trembled at the sight.

She felt the fury of *her* ball:
Down, prostrate, down the Britons fall;   50
   The decks were strew'd with slain:
JONES to the foe his vessel lash'd;
And, while the black artillery flash'd,
   Loud thunders shook the main.

Alas! that mortals should employ   55
Such murdering engines, to destroy
   That frame by heaven so nicely join'd;
Alas! that e'er the god decreed
That brother should by brother bleed,
   And pour'd such madness in the mind.   60

But thou, brave JONES, no blame shalt bear;
The rights of men demand your care:
   For *these* you dare the greedy waves—

---

1. *The Gallic ship they* Pallas *call.* The *Pallas* as well as
the *Bon Homme Richard* and the *Vengeance* were French
ships. The French government had turned them over to
Jones for use in his raiding expedition. They flew the
American flag. 2. *Phoebus,* the sun.

No tyrant, on destruction bent,
Has plann'd thy conquests—thou art sent   65
   To humble tyrants and their slaves.

See!—dread *Seraphis* flames again—
And art thou, JONES, among the slain,
   And sunk to Neptune's caves below—[3]
He lives—though crowds around him fall,   70
Still he, unhurt, survives them all;
   Almost alone he fights the foe.

And can thy ship these strokes sustain?
Behold thy brave companions slain,
   All clasped in ocean's dark embrace.   75
STRIKE, OR BE SUNK—the Briton cries—
SINK IF YOU CAN—the chief replies,
   Fierce lightnings blazing in his face.

Then to the side three guns he drew,
(Almost deserted by his crew)   80
   And charg'd them deep with woe:
By Pearson's flash he aimed hot balls;
His mainmast totters—down it falls—
   O'erwhelming half below.

Pearson had yet disdain'd to yield,   85
But scarce his secret fears conceal'd
   And thus was heard to cry—
"With hell, not mortals, I contend;
"What art thou—human or a fiend,
   "That dost my force defy?   90

"Return, my lads, the fight renew!"—
So call'd bold Pearson to his crew;
   But call'd, alas, in vain;
Some on the decks lay maim'd and dead;
Some to their deep recesses fled,   95
   And more were shrouded in the main.

Distress'd, forsaken, and alone,
He haul'd his tattered standard down,
   And yielded to his gallant foe;
Bold *Pallas* soon the *Countess* took—   100
Thus both their haughty colors struck,
   Confessing what the brave can do.

But, JONES, too dearly didst thou buy
These ships possest so gloriously,
   Too many deaths disgrac'd the fray: 105

Thy barque that bore the conquering flame,
That the proud Briton overcame,
   Even she forsook thee on thy way;

For when the morn began to shine,
Fatal to her, the ocean brine   110
   Pour'd through each spacious wound;
Quick in the deep she disappear'd,
But JONES to friendly Belgia[4] steer'd,
   With conquest and with glory crown'd.

Go on, great man, to scourge the foe,   115
And bid the haughty Britons know
   They to our *Thirteen Stars* shall bend;
The *Stars* that, veil'd in dark attire,
Long glimmer'd with a feeble fire,
   But radiant now ascend.   120

Bend to the Stars that flaming rise
On western worlds, more brilliant skies.
   Fair Freedom's reign restor'd—
So when the Magi,[5] come from far,
Beheld the God-attending Star,   125
   They trembled and ador'd.

---

3. *And sunk to Neptune's caves below.* Neptune was the Roman god of the sea. 4. *Belgia.* Jones took his prizes to the largest of the West Frisian Islands, a chain of islands in the North Sea just off the northeast coast of the Netherlands. 5. *the Magi,* the wise men from the East who found the Infant Jesus in Bethlehem.

TO INCREASE UNDERSTANDING

1. How does the poem reflect (*a*) Freneau's first-hand knowledge of the sea, (*b*) his patriotism, and (*c*) his hatred of the British?

2. What devices does the poet use to make the story of the battle vivid to his readers?

3. (*a*) Cite passages in which Freneau describes Jones' heroism. (*b*) What is Freneau's attitude toward Pearson, the British commander?

4. Compare the ideals expressed in "On the Memorable Victory" with the ideals Freneau's contemporaries expressed in prose.

 EXTENDING INTERESTS

Freneau is as famous for his nature lyrics as for his patriotic poems. You may enjoy reading and talking over "The Wild Honeysuckle" and "The Indian Burying Ground," both in *The Home Book of Verse,* edited by Burton Stevenson.

George Washington 1732-1799

Above: Portrait of Washington from life by Rembrandt Peale. Right: Procession in Philadelphia commemorating Washington's death.

Our national capital, one of our states, and dozens of counties and towns are named after George Washington, the hero of the Revolution and our first President. No other American, probably, has been so idolized by his countrymen while he lived and so honored after death. A Virginia planter with a strong sense of duty, he served his country long and faithfully, at considerable sacrifice of his fortune and his tastes.

His first biographer, Mason L. Weems, called him "the greatest man that ever lived," and invented anecdotes to prove that even as a boy he had been a model youth with almost superhuman strength. (The cherry-tree story, for which there is no authority whatsoever, still survives. That Washington threw a silver dollar across the Potomac is as doubtful as the little-hatchet tale.) Legend made Washington almost too good to be true, and biographers even in the present day find it hard to make him a warm human personality. An austere

HIGH STREET, From the Country Market-place PHILADELPHIA.

with the procession in commemoration of the Death of GENERAL GEORGE WASHINGTON, *December 26th 1799.*

yet humble man, driven more by an aristocrat's sense of social responsibility than by personal ambition or democratic convictions, he strides through our history and our folklore like a mysterious colossus.

As a writer, Washington is remarkable for clarity rather than imagination. His state papers, of which the Farewell Address is the best known, were often in part composed by his aides, notably by Alexander Hamilton. As the following excerpt from the Address shows, Washington erred in some of his conjectures about the future the country faced under the recently adopted Constitution. He underestimated the strength of sectional differences, as the War Between the States was to reveal. He recognized the evils of the two-party system, but he did not grasp its inevitability. His concept of American isolation from the rest of the world was destroyed by the airplane even before there were jets and intercontinental missiles. Upon one important point, however, Washington's wisdom still prevails: his belief that only by orderly processes of change, as provided for in the Constitution of 1787, would the nation survive. The Address remains a key to vast segments of American thought and a guide to the chief snags in American political life. It also shows Washington's grasp of the realities of the American situation at a time when critics and enemies freely predicted an early collapse of the new nation.

FROM *Farewell Address to the People of the United States, September 17th, 1796*

In contemplating the causes which may disturb our Union, it occurs as a matter of serious concern, that any ground should have been furnished for characterizing parties by *Geographical* discriminations—*Northern* and *Southern*—*Atlantic* and *Western;* whence designing men may endeavor to excite a belief that there is a real difference of local interests and views. One of the expedients of Party to acquire influence, within particular districts, is to misrepresent the opinions and aims of other districts. You cannot shield yourselves too much against the jealousies and heartburnings which spring from these misrepresentations; they tend to render alien to each other those who ought to be bound together by fraternal affection. . . .

To the efficacy and permanency of your Union, a government for the whole is indispensable. No alliances however strict between the parts can be an adequate substitute. They must inevitably experience the infractions and interruptions which all alliances in all times have experienced. Sensible of this momentous truth, you have improved upon your first essay,[1] by the adoption of a Constitution of Government, better calculated than your former for an intimate Union, and for the efficacious management of your common concerns. This government, the offspring of our own choice uninfluenced and unawed, adopted upon full investigation and mature deliberation, completely free in its principles, in the distribution of its powers, uniting security with energy, and containing within itself a provision for its own amendment, has a just claim to your confidence and support. Respect for its authority, compliance with its laws, acquiescence in its measures, are duties enjoined by the fundamental maxims of true liberty. The basis of our political systems is the right of the people to make and to alter their constitutions of government. But the constitution which at any time exists, till changed by an explicit and authentic act of the whole people, is sacredly obligatory upon all. The very idea of the power and the right of the people

1. *your first essay,* the Articles of Confederation, a constitution adopted by the thirteen original states in 1781, and replaced by the present Constitution in 1788.

to establish government, presupposed the duty of every individual to obey the established government.

All obstructions to the execution of the laws, all combinations and associations, under whatever plausible character, with the real design to direct, control, counteract, or awe the regular deliberation and action of the constituted authorities, are destructive of this fundamental principle and of fatal tendency. They serve to organize faction, to give it an artificial and extraordinary force—to put in the place of the designated will of the nation, the will of a party—often a small but artful and enterprising minority of the community—and, according to the alternate triumphs of different parties, to make the public administration the mirror of the ill-concerted and incongruous projects of faction, rather than the organ of consistent and wholesome plans digested by common councils, and modified by mutual interests. However combinations or associations of the above description may now and then answer popular ends, they are likely, in the course of time and things, to become potent engines by which cunning, ambitious, and unprincipled men will be enabled to subvert the power of the people and to usurp for themselves the reins of government, destroying afterward the very engines which have lifted them to unjust dominion.

Toward the preservation of your government and the permanency of your present happy state, it is requisite not only that you steadily discountenance irregular oppositions to its acknowledged authority, but also that you resist with care the spirit of innovation upon its principles, however specious the pretexts. One method of assault may be to effect, in the forms of the Constitution, alterations which will impair the energy of the system, and thus to undermine what cannot be directly overthrown. In all the changes to which you may be invited, remember that time and habit are at least as necessary to fix the true character of governments, as of other human institutions—that experience is the surest standard by which to test the real tendency of the existing constitution of a country—that facility in changes upon the credit of mere hypothesis and opinion exposes to perpetual change, from the endless variety of hypothesis and opinion: and remember, especially, that, for the efficient management of your common interests, in a country so extensive as ours, a government of as much vigor as is consistent with the perfect security of liberty is indispensable. Liberty itself will find in such a government, with powers properly distributed and adjusted, its surest guardian....

It is important, likewise, that the habits of thinking in a free country should inspire caution in those entrusted with its administration, to confine themselves within their respective constitutional spheres; avoiding in the exercise of the powers of one department to encroach upon another. The spirit of encroachment tends to consolidate the powers of all the departments in one, and thus to create, whatever the form of government, a real despotism. A just estimate of that love of power, and proneness to abuse it, which predominates in the human heart, is sufficient to satisfy us of the truth of this position. The necessity of reciprocal checks in the exercise of political power, by dividing and distributing it into different depositories, and constituting each the guardian of the public weal against invasions by the others, has been evinced by experiments ancient and modern, some of them in our country and under our own eyes. To preserve them must be as necessary as to institute them. If in the opinion of the people, the distribution or modification of the constitutional powers be in any particular wrong, let it be corrected by an amendment in the way which the Constitution designates. But let there be no change by usurpation; for though this, in one instance, may be the instrument of good, it is the customary weapon by which free governments are destroyed. The precedent must always greatly overbalance in permanent evil any partial or transient benefit which the use can at any time yield.

Of all the dispositions and habits which lead to political prosperity, religion and morality are indispensable supports. In vain would that man claim the tribute of patriotism, who should labor to subvert these great pillars of human happiness, these firmest props of the duties of men and citizens. The mere politician, equally with the pious man, ought to respect and to cherish them. A volume could not trace all their connections with private and public felicity. Let it simply be asked where is the security for property, for reputation, for life, if the sense of religious obligation *desert* the oaths, which are the instruments of investigation in Courts of Justice? And let us with caution indulge the supposition that morality can be maintained without religion. Whatever may be conceded to the influence of refined education on minds of peculiar structure, reason and experience both forbid us to expect that national morality can prevail in exclusion of religious principle. . . .

Promote, then, as an object of primary importance, institutions for the general diffusion of knowledge. In proportion as the structure of a government gives force to public opinion, it is essential that public opinion should be enlightened.

As a very important source of strength and security, cherish public credit. One method of preserving it is to use it as sparingly as possible—avoiding occasions of expense by cultivating peace, but remembering also that timely disbursements to prepare for danger frequently prevent much greater disbursements to repel it—avoiding likewise the accumulation of debt, not only by shunning occasions of expense, but by vigorous exertions in time of peace to discharge the debts which unavoidable wars may have occasioned, not ungenerously throwing upon posterity the burden which we ourselves ought to bear. The execution of these maxims belongs to your representatives, but it is necessary that public opinion should coöperate. To facilitate to them the performance of their duty, it is essential that you should practically bear in mind that toward the payment of debts there must be revenue—that to have revenue there must be taxes—that no taxes can be devised which are not more or less inconvenient and unpleasant. . . .

The great rule of conduct for us, in regard to foreign nations, is, in extending our commercial relations, to have with them as little *political* connection as possible. So far as we have already formed engagements, let them

be fulfilled with perfect good faith. Here let us stop.

Europe has a set of primary interests, which to us have none, or a very remote relation. Hence she must be engaged in frequent controversies, the causes of which are essentially foreign to our concerns. Hence therefore it must be unwise in us to implicate ourselves, by artificial ties in the ordinary vicissitudes of her politics, or the ordinary combinations and collisions of her friendships or enmities.

Our detached and distant situation invites and enables us to pursue a different course. If we remain one people, under an efficient government, the period is not far off when we may defy material injury from external annoyance; when we may take such an attitude as will cause the neutrality we may at any time resolve upon to be scrupulously respected; when belligerent nations, under the impossibility of making acquisitions upon us will not lightly hazard the giving us provocation; when we may choose peace or war, as our interest guided by our justice shall counsel.

Why forego the advantages of so peculiar a situation? Why quit our own to stand upon foreign ground? Why, by interweaving our destiny with that of any part of Europe, entangle our peace and prosperity in the toils of European ambition, rivalship, interest, humor, or caprice?

'Tis our true policy to steer clear of permanent alliances, with any portion of the foreign world. . . .

Taking care always to keep ourselves, by suitable establishments, on a respectably defensive posture, we may safely trust to temporary alliances for extraordinary emergencies. . . .

 TO INCREASE UNDERSTANDING

1. (*a*) Locate and read the passage in which Washington speaks specifically of the two-party system. (*b*) Explain his reasons for objecting to it.

2. What is Washington's attitude toward making changes in the Constitution?

3. What advice does Washington offer his fellow citizens regarding (*a*) public credit, (*b*) commercial relations, and (*c*) foreign alliances?

4. Why do you think Washington's Farewell Address is regarded as an outstanding state paper?

THE LARGER VIEW

A. With the points listed below to guide you, discuss the major differences between the Founders of the Nation and the Planters and Puritans.

1. What was the dominant interest of Franklin and his contemporaries? Did you find a similar interest in Edwards? In Byrd? Explain.

2. Were Edwards and Byrd more concerned or less concerned with national issues than were Franklin, Jefferson, and Washington?

3. Are the writings of Franklin, Paine, and Jefferson in their tone and purpose closer to William Bradford or to Captain John Smith? Explain.

B. Explain why you think Franklin's Speech in the Convention, Paine's *Common Sense,* and Washington's Farewell Address may be said to continue the utilitarian tradition of Planter and Puritan writing.

BIBLIOGRAPHY

BOWERS, CLAUDE, *Young Jefferson.* (Houghton) Dealing primarily with the "human" Jefferson, the author recaptures the personality and ideals of this outstanding American statesman.

BROWN, MARION, *Young Nathan.* (Westminster) Better understanding of what made Nathan Hale the courageous patriot he was is found in this fictionalized biography.

CARSON, JULIA, *Son of Thunder.* (Longmans) This fictional account of Patrick Henry's career includes interesting scenes of home and family life.

CUNLIFFE, MARCUS, *Washington, Man and Monument.* (Little •Mentor) The author tears away the myths surrounding Washington and comes up with a perceptive biography of the true man.

DESMOND, ALICE, *Martha Washington, Our First Lady.* (Dodd) Girls will enjoy the romantic story of the young Virginia girl who married the President.

EATON, JEANETTE, *Leader by Destiny.* (Harcourt) This dignified and arresting biography stresses the development of Washington's character and his great contributions to history.

FRANKLIN, BENJAMIN, *Autobiography.* (Dutton •Dolphin) The lively memoirs of one of the great founders of the nation are written in a simple, direct, idiomatic manner that has continued to attract readers through many years.

FRANKLIN, BENJAMIN, *Benjamin Franklin: Selected Writings,* edited by Chester E. Jorgenson and Frank L. Mott. (•Hill & Wang) Whether he was writing to inform or to entertain, Franklin's work is always worth reading. As an added bonus, the editors have included useful critical and biographical material.

LANCASTER, BRUCE, *Secret Road.* (Little •Permabooks) You will enjoy this stirring story of the secret servicemen and their exposure of Benedict Arnold.

LISITZKY, GENE, *Thomas Jefferson.* (Viking) This excellent biography skillfully points out Jefferson's influence on his country's history.

NORTON, ANDRÉ, *Yankee Privateer.* (World Pub.) This colorful yarn of a Maryland landlubber captured by the British and forced to prove his mettle as a sailor will appeal to all.

PAGE, ELIZABETH, *Tree of Liberty.* (Holt, Rinehart & Winston) Three generations of an American family play their parts in great national events in this novel which covers the vast panorama of the beginnings of American national life and national philosophy.

PAINE, THOMAS, *Common Sense and the Crisis.* (•Dolphin) Paine translated his high ideals and principles into brilliant journalistic terms. These essays are among his most powerful.

ROBERTS, KENNETH, *Oliver Wiswell.* (Doubleday) All the bitterness of a war within a war is powerfully and dramatically told in this fictional account of the war's effect on the Tories.

SCHACHNER, NATHAN, *Alexander Hamilton.* (•Barnes, A. S.) Hamilton's relationships with other great men of the times are pointed out in this frank, well-written biography.

TURNBULL, AGNES, *Day Must Dawn.* (Macmillan) The experiences of a Scotch-Irish pioneer family in Pennsylvania at the time of the Revolutionary War make an absorbing story.

VAN DOREN, CARL, *Benjamin Franklin.* (Viking) While the *Autobiography* covers only a small segment of Franklin's life, Van Doren's book is an authoritative account of all the aspects of this complex American's long life.

VAN DOREN, CARL, *Great Rehearsal.* (Viking •Compass) The makings of the Constitution are followed step by step in terms of personalities who took part and conflicts of interest which had to be reconciled.

•paperback

National Period

Thomas Jefferson was in his early thirties when he drafted the Declaration of Independence. When he died at eighty-three, the nation which he had helped establish was well on the way to achieving the continental destiny of which the Founding Fathers had dreamed. The Louisiana Purchase had pushed the territory of the United States westward to the Rocky Mountains. The vast frontier wilderness beyond the Appalachians lay open to settlement. The West beckoned and the pioneers followed. Trappers, Indian fighters, traders, and settlers—on foot or by Conestoga wagon—they moved west. As the Cumberland Road stretched into Ohio and barges went the length of the Erie Canal, the westward surge accelerated.

The generation which founded the nation had been born citizens of the British Empire. The generation which followed grew up as Americans. They thought in terms of national, not colonial, achievement. They were manufacturers building small factories all over New England, soldiers and sailors repelling the British in the War of 1812, frontiersmen glorying in the fact that "common men" could elect Jackson to the presidency. And they were the generation of writers who put the American scene and the American spirit into literature.

The roll call of great American writers begins with the writers of this Early National Period—Washington Irving, William Cullen Bryant, James Fenimore Cooper, and Edgar Allan Poe. Unlike Franklin, Paine, Jefferson, and their contemporaries, whose chief purpose in writing was utilitarian, the object of these later writers was to entertain. Their best writings were imaginative. Instead of factual articles and speeches meant to persuade the reader, for the most part they wrote short stories, poetry, and novels.

The careers of the writers of the Early National Period differed in a second important way from the careers of the late eighteenth-century writers. All of these, including Franklin, wrote in the manner of British authors who had flourished in the past. Irving and Bryant started as imitators of older English writers, and Irving to some extent always echoed his early British teachers. In time, however, these early nineteenth-century writers caught up with the contemporary parade. Together they won for American writing an honored place in the literature of the world.

Portrait of Irving at twenty-seven by one of his friends, the nationally famous painter, John Wesley Jarvis.

Washington Irving

1783-1859 Washington Irving's mother suggested his name. "George Washington's work is ended," she is reported to have said, "and the child shall be named for him."

Mrs. Irving's words underline the fact that her son's birth came at an important moment in our history. It occurred in New York, April 3, 1783, five months before peace was proclaimed between Great Britain and the colonies. Washington Irving was to live all but the first few months of his long life not as a British colonist but as a citizen of a young republic. His best writings appeared in the Early National Period.

NEW YORK Although the general trend in the young republic was away from the stern
AMATEUR religiousness of colonial days, Washington Irving's father, a zealous Scotch Presbyterian, held that everything enjoyable was wicked. For family reading he prescribed the Bible, the catechism, and that Puritan masterpiece by John Bunyan, *Pilgrim's Progress*. He made a great effort to pass along his harsh beliefs, his strict rules for living, to his son.

But Irving's mother, an Englishwoman, was tender and kind, and four brothers and three sisters—all older than Washington—already had rebelled against their father's dour faith. Moreover, the boy's environment seemed to encourage play rather than piety. The town of New York, so travelers said, was the gayest in all the country. There the fashionably dressed belles and beaux enjoyed the society of the drawing room and the ballroom and knew the excitement of the arts—music, literature, and the drama. And a New York boy in the upper middle class was bound to feel the influence of his surroundings.

In a series of schools he attended before leaving classrooms for good, he learned as little as his teachers allowed. He wandered around New York and its fringes, sailing boats in the straits of Hell Gate, standing by the harbor and watching ships move seaward, exploring nearby farms, or hunting squirrels in the woods along the Hudson. He took drawing lessons and learned to play the flute. In time, he discovered the fascination of the playhouse. Whenever he could afford it, he went in the evening to a nearby theater. There he watched the actors until nine, when he hurried home for family prayers. After prayers, he quickly climbed to his room, slipped through his window, clambered down the roof, and ran to the theater so that he might enjoy the last part of the show. And his favorite books were not religious tomes but accounts of travel to far countries and adventure stories such as *Robinson Crusoe* and *Sinbad the Sailor*.

Washington's father wished him to study for the ministry, but instead, after some family counsels, he followed the example of his brother John and entered a law office to study law. His easygoing life had not prepared him for what he called "the dull routine of a lawyer's office." Moreover, his health, never robust, caused him to discontinue his studies, and from 1804 until 1806 he traveled in Europe. Eventually he passed his bar examinations, but he never did much with his legal training. With an indulgent family eager to satisfy his every whim, he drifted into a gay life which happened to furnish the first impetus toward literature.

Curly-haired, handsome, pleasant in manner and with a fine spontaneous smile, young Irving had a talent for good fellowship. He became a consistent theatergoer. He became a boon companion of the gallants of the town. A group of them which he joined had gay times when their informal club got together. It called itself "The Nine Worthies" or "The Lads of Kilkenny." It dined in the most fashionable or the most picturesque public houses; then the members chatted and sang for hours on end.

Irving's interests and those of his friends led him to try his hand at writing. His first published pieces, which he wrote when nineteen and twenty, were jocose newspaper essays about fashions, marriage customs, dueling, and the theater. In 1807 and 1808, Irving, his brother William, and his friend James K. Paulding wrote and published a series of papers in which the talk of the Worthies figured largely. The periodical was called *Salmagundi*, after a spicy appetizer, and it was put out at intervals—whenever its easygoing editors managed to write out enough material to fill an issue. They offered satirical sketches of social climbers, politicians, military men, critics, and, of course, the belles whose company they so enjoyed. The society folk of New York read the magazine with delight and amusement.

Irving's next book pushed the satire of his native city into the past. He and his brother Peter started to write *A History of New York* as a parody of a pompous and dull book by S. L. Mitchell, *The Picture of New York*, published in 1807. When Irving's brother withdrew from the collaboration, Irving, as he put it, "altered the plan of the work." "Discarding all idea of parody," he said, "I determined that what had been originally intended as an introductory sketch should comprise the whole work, and afford a comic history of the city." The result, published in 1809, was a playful account of New York (as the title page modestly proclaimed) "from the Beginning of the World to the End of the Dutch Dynasty . . . being the only Authentic History of the Times that has ever been, or ever will be Published." Supposedly written by an antiquarian named Diedrich Knicker-bocker, it told hilarious stories about the old-time Dutch governors and playfully spoofed some of the leading Dutch families. Descendants of those families at first did not appreciate the humor very well. An old lady in Albany, for instance, misplaced her elegant manners long enough to say, with fervor, that she wished she could horsewhip the author. "It was a confounded impudent thing," Irving said years later, "in such a youngster as I was to be meddling in this way with old family names." But New Yorkers who were not so touchy and folk outside of New York, some of them in Great Britain, thought the book very funny. The great contemporary novelist Sir Walter Scott said that he laughed at it until his sides ached, and, years later, Charles Dickens read and reread his copy until he wore it to pieces.

The selection on the next page is from *A History of New York.*

Broadway, New York, in 1818 as painted by Axel Klinckowstrom.

Early Life in Manhattan

In those good days of simplicity and sunshine, a passion for cleanliness was the leading principle in domestic economy, and the universal test of an able housewife—a character which formed the utmost ambition of our unenlightened grandmothers. The front door was never opened, except on marriages, funerals, New Year's days, the festival of St. Nicholas,[1] or some such great occasion. It was ornamented with a gorgeous brass knocker, curiously wrought, sometimes in the device of a dog, and sometimes of a lion's head, and was daily burnished with such religious zeal that it was ofttimes worn out by the very precautions taken for its preservation. The whole house was constantly in a state of inundation, under the discipline of mops and brooms and scrubbing brushes; and the good housewives of those days were a kind of amphibious animal, delighting exceedingly to be dabbling in water—insomuch that a historian of the day gravely tells us that many of his townswomen grew to have webbed fingers like unto a duck; and some of them, he had little doubt, could the matter be examined into, would be found to have the tails of mermaids—but this I look upon to be a mere sport of fancy, or, what is worse, a willful misrepresentation.

The grand parlor was the sanctum sanctorum,[2] where the passion for cleaning was indulged without control. In this sacred apartment no one was permitted to enter, excepting the mistress and her confidential maid, who visited it, once a week, for the purpose of giving it a thorough cleaning, and putting things to rights—always taking the precaution of leaving their shoes at the door, and entering devoutly on their stocking feet. After scrubbing the floor, sprinkling it with fine white sand, which was curiously stroked into angles and curves and rhomboids with a broom—after washing the windows, rubbing and polishing the furniture, and putting a new bunch of evergreens in the fireplace—the window shutters were again closed to keep out the flies, and the room carefully locked up until the revolution of time brought round the weekly cleaning day.

As to the family, they always entered in at the gate, and most generally lived in the kitchen. To have seen a numerous household assembled round the fire, one would have imagined that he was transported back to those happy days of primeval simplicity, which float before our imaginations like golden visions. The fireplaces were of a truly patriarchal magnitude, where the whole family, old and young, master and servant, black and white, nay, even the very cat and dog, enjoyed a community of privilege and had each a right to a corner. Here the old burgher would sit in perfect silence, puffing his pipe, looking in the fire with half-shut eyes and thinking of nothing for hours together; the *goede vrouw*,[3] on the opposite side, would employ herself diligently in spinning yarn, or knitting stockings. The young folks would crowd around the hearth, listening with breathless attention to some old crone of a Negro, who was the oracle of the family, and who, perched like a raven in a corner of the chimney, would croak forth for a long winter afternoon a string of incredible stories about New England witches—grisly ghosts, horses without heads—and hairbreadth escapes, and bloody encounters among the Indians.

In those happy days a well-regulated family always rose with the dawn, dined at eleven, and went to bed at sunset. Dinner was invariably a private meal, and the fat old burghers showed incontestable signs of disapprobation and uneasiness at being surprised by a visit from a neighbor on such occasions. But though our worthy ancestors were thus singularly averse to giving dinners, yet they kept up the social bands of intimacy by occasional banquetings, called tea parties.

These fashionable parties were generally confined to the higher classes, or *noblesse*,[4]

---

1. *festival of St. Nicholas*, December 6. On this day the Dutch children of New Amsterdam received gifts from St. Nicholas. 2. *sanctum sanctorum* (sangk′təm sangk tō′rəm), holy of holies. Irving means that the parlor was considered too fine to be used. 3. *goede vrouw* (ʜü′də vrou), good woman. 4. *noblesse* (nō bles′), persons of noble birth. Irving here borrows the word from the French language and humorously applies it to the wealthier citizens of New Amsterdam.

that is to say, such as kept their own cows and drove their own wagons. The company commonly assembled at three o'clock, and went away about six, unless it was in wintertime, when the fashionable hours were a little earlier, that the ladies might get home before dark. The tea table was crowned with a huge earthen dish, well stored with slices of fat pork, fried brown, cut up into morsels, and swimming in gravy. The company being seated around the genial board, and each furnished with a fork, evinced their dexterity in launching at the fattest pieces in this mighty dish—in much the same manner as sailors harpoon porpoises at sea, or our Indians spear salmon in the lakes. Sometimes the table was graced with immense apple pies, or saucers full of preserved peaches and pears; but it was always sure to boast an enormous dish of balls of sweetened dough, fried in hog's fat, and called doughnuts, or olykoeks[5]—a delicious kind of cake, at present scarce known in this city, except in genuine Dutch families.

The tea was served out of a majestic Delft teapot, ornamented with paintings of fat little Dutch shepherds and shepherdesses tending pigs, with boats sailing in the air, and the houses built in the clouds, and sundry other ingenious Dutch fantasies. The beaux distinguished themselves by their adroitness in replenishing this pot from a huge copper tea-kettle, which would have made the pygmy macaronies of these degenerate days sweat merely to look at it. To sweeten the beverage, a lump of sugar was laid beside each cup, and the company alternately nibbled and sipped with great decorum, until an improvement was introduced by a shrewd and economic old lady, which was to suspend a large lump directly over the tea table, by a string from the ceiling, so that it could be swung from mouth to mouth—an ingenious expedient, which is still kept up by some families in Albany, but which prevails without exception in Communipaw, Bergen, Flatbush, and all our uncontaminated Dutch villages.

At these primitive tea parties the utmost propriety and dignity of deportment prevailed. No flirting nor coquetting—no gambling of old ladies, nor hoyden chattering and romping of young ones—no self-satisfied struttings of wealthy gentlemen, with their brains in their pockets, nor amusing conceits and monkey divertissements[6] of smart young gentlemen, with no brains at all. On the contrary, the young ladies seated themselves demurely in their rush-bottom chairs, and knit their own woolen stockings; nor even opened their lips excepting to say yah Mynheer,[7] or yah ya Vrouw, to any question that was asked them; behaving in all things like decent, well-educated damsels. As to the gentlemen, each of them tranquilly smoked his pipe, and seemed lost in contemplation of the blue and white tiles with which the fireplaces were decorated; wherein sundry passages of Scripture were piously portrayed: Tobit and his dog[8] figured to great advantage; Haman swung conspicuously on his gibbet[9]; and Jonah appeared most manfully bouncing out of the whale, like Harlequin through a barrel of fire.

The parties broke up without noise and confusion. They were carried home by their own carriages, that is to say, by the vehicles nature had provided them, excepting such of the wealthy as could afford to keep a wagon. The gentlemen gallantly attended their fair ones to their respective abodes, and took leave of them with a hearty smack at the door: which, as it was an established piece of etiquette, done in perfect simplicity and honesty of heart, occasioned no scandal at that time, nor should it at the present—if our great-grandfathers approved of the custom, it would argue a great want of deference in their descendants to say a word against it.

In this dulcet period of my history, when the beauteous island of Manna-hata[10] presented a scene, the very counterpart of those glowing pictures drawn of the golden reign of

5. olykoeks (ol′i kukz′). 6. divertissements (dē ver tēs-mäŋ′), amusements. [French] 7. yah Mynheer (yä mĭn-här′ or mĭn hēr′), yes, Sir. Mynheer is the Dutch word for Sir or Mr. 8. Tobit (tō′bit) and his dog. The book of Tobit is an ancient story relating the trials of an Old Testament Jew held captive in Nineveh. When his son Tobias (tō bī′əs) undertakes a journey for him, he is aided by the angel Raphael. A dog accompanies Tobias and the angel. 9. Haman (hā′mən) . . . on his gibbet. Haman, an enemy of the Jews, was hanged on a gallows about seventy-five feet high. (Esther, Chapters 5-7.) 10. Manna-hata (ma′nə-hat′ə), the Indian name for Manhattan.

Saturn,[11] there was, as I have before observed, a happy ignorance, an honest simplicity prevalent among its inhabitants, which, were I even able to depict, would be but little understood by the degenerate age for which I am doomed to write. Even the female sex, those arch innovators upon the tranquillity, the honesty, and gray-beard customs of society, seemed for a while to conduct themselves with incredible sobriety and comeliness.

Their hair, untortured by the abominations of art, was scrupulously pomatumed back from their foreheads with a candle,[12] and covered with a little cap of quilted calico, which fitted exactly to their heads. Their petticoats of linsey-woolsey were striped with a variety of gorgeous dyes—though I must confess these gallant garments were rather short, scarce reaching below the knee, but then made up in the number, which generally equaled that of the gentleman's smallclothes; and what is still more praiseworthy, they were all of their own manufacture—of which circumstance, as may well be supposed, they were not a little vain.

I cannot say much in vindication of the shortness of the petticoats; it doubtless was introduced for the purpose of giving the stockings a chance to be seen, which were generally of blue worsted, with magnificent red clocks—or, perhaps, to display a well-turned ankle, and a neat, though serviceable foot, set off by a high-heeled leathern shoe, with a large and splendid silver buckle. Thus we find that the gentle sex in all ages have shown the same disposition to infringe a little upon the laws of decorum, in order to betray a lurking beauty, or gratify an innocent love of finery.

From the sketch here given, it will be seen that our good grandmothers differed considerably in their ideas of a fine figure from their scantily dressed descendants of the present day. A fine lady, in those times, waddled under more clothes, even on a fair summer's day, than would have clad the whole bevy of a modern ballroom. Nor were they the less admired by the gentlemen in consequence thereof. On the contrary, the greatness of a lover's passion seemed to increase in proportion to the magnitude of its object—and a volu-minous damsel, arrayed in a dozen of petticoats, was declared by a Low Dutch sonneteer[13] of the province to be radiant as a sunflower, and luxuriant as a full-blown cabbage. Certain it is, that in those days the heart of a lover could not contain more than one lady at a time; whereas the heart of a modern gallant has often room enough to accommodate half a dozen. The reason of which I conclude to be, that either hearts of the gentlemen have grown larger, or the persons of the ladies smaller: this, however, is a question for the physiologists to determine.

But there was a secret charm in these petticoats, which, no doubt, entered into the consideration of the prudent gallants. The wardrobe of a lady was in those days her only fortune; and she who had a good stock of petticoats and stockings was as absolutely an heiress as is a Kamchatka damsel with a score of bearskins, or a Lapland belle with a plenty of reindeer. The ladies, therefore, were very anxious to display these powerful attractions to the greatest advantage; and the best rooms in the house, instead of being adorned with caricatures of Dame Nature, in water colors and needlework, were always hung round with abundance of homespun garments, the manufacture and the property of the females—a piece of laudable ostentation that still prevails among the heiresses of our Dutch villages.

The gentlemen, in fact, who figured in the circles of the gay world in these ancient times corresponded, in most particulars, with the beauteous damsels whose smiles they were ambitious to deserve. True it is, their merits would make but a very inconsiderable impression upon the heart of a modern fair: they neither drove their curricles, nor sported their tandems, for as yet those gaudy vehicles were not even dreamt of; neither did they distinguish themselves by their brilliancy at the

11. *golden reign of Saturn.* Saturn, a character of ancient mythology, was banished from his throne by his son Jupiter. He fled to Italy, where he civilized the people and taught them agriculture. Because of his wise and mild rule his reign is called the Golden Age. 12. *pomatumed* (pō mā′-tǝmd) . . . *with a candle.* To keep their hair pulled smoothly back from their foreheads as was fashionable at that time, the Dutch belles used candle wax as a hair dressing (pomatum). 13. *Low Dutch sonneteer,* a poet, probably a poor one.

table, and their consequent rencounters with watchmen, for our forefathers were of too pacific a disposition to need those guardians of the night, every soul throughout the town being sound asleep before nine o'clock. Neither did they establish their claims to gentility at the expense of their tailors, for as yet those offenders against the pockets of society, and the tranquillity of all aspiring young gentlemen, were unknown in New Amsterdam; every good housewife made the clothes of her husband and family, and even the *goede vrouw* of Van Twiller[14] himself thought it no disparagement to cut out her husband's linsey-woolsey galligaskins.

Not but what there were some two or three youngsters who manifested the first dawning of what is called fire and spirit; who held all labor in contempt; skulked about docks and market places; loitered in the sunshine; squandered what little money they could procure at hustlecap and chuck farthing[15]; swore, boxed, fought cocks, and raced their neighbors' horses; in short, who promised to be the wonder, the talk, and abomination of the town, had not their stylish career been unfortunately cut short by an affair of honor with a whipping post.

Far other, however, was the truly fashionable gentleman of those days: his dress, which served for both morning and evening, street and drawing room, was a linsey-woolsey coat, made, perhaps, by the fair hands of the mistress of his affections, and gallantly bedecked with abundance of large brass buttons; half a score of breeches heightened the proportions of his figure; his shoes were decorated by enormous copper buckles; a low-crowned broad-rimmed hat overshadowed his burly visage; and his hair dangled down his back in a prodigious queue of eelskin.

Thus equipped, he would manfully sally forth, with pipe in mouth, to besiege some fair damsel's obdurate heart—not such a pipe, good reader, as that which Acis did sweetly tune in praise of his Galatea,[16] but one of true Delft manufacture, and furnished with a charge of fragrant tobacco. With this would he resolutely set himself down before the fortress, and rarely failed, in the process of

time, to smoke the fair enemy into a surrender, upon honorable terms.

Such was the happy reign of Wouter Van Twiller, celebrated in many a long-forgotten song as the real golden age, the rest being nothing but counterfeit copper-washed coin. In that delightful period, a sweet and holy calm reigned over the whole province. The burgomaster smoked his pipe in peace; the substantial solace of his domestic cares, after her daily toils were done, sat soberly at the door, with her arms crossed over her apron of snowy white, without being insulted with ribald strollers or vagabond boys—those unlucky urchins who do so infest our streets, displaying, under the roses of youth, the thorns and briers of iniquity. Then it was that the lover with ten breeches, and the damsel with petticoats of half a score, indulged in all the innocent endearments of virtuous love, without fear and without reproach; for what had that virtue to fear, which was defended by a shield of good linsey-woolseys, equal at least to the seven bullhides of the invincible Ajax?[17]

14. *Van Twiller* (van twil′ər), director general of New Amsterdam from 1633 to 1637. 15. *hustlecap and chuck farthing*, ancient gambling games played with coins. 16. *pipe . . . in praise of his Galatea* (gal′ə tē′ə). Acis (ā′sis), a Sicilian shepherd, loved the sea nymph Galatea. With his shepherd's pipe he played melodies to show his love. 17. *seven bullhides . . . Ajax* (ā′jaks). According to Greek mythology, Ajax, one of the greatest of the Greek heroes, had a shield made of seven layers of bullhide and an outside fold of brass.

Illustration by the great American illustrator Felix Darley for the History, *1835.*

IRVING AND ROMANTICISM *A History of New York* won wide recognition for its author. It hardly would have been surprising if its reception had caused its author to decide, once and for all, to earn his living by writing. But nothing of the sort happened. For one thing, the family was enjoying good times financially, and Irving's brothers were happy to share the large returns from their importing business with their favorite. For another thing, Irving was still lamenting—as indeed he had been while writing his history—the recent death of a young woman, Matilda Hoffman, to whom he had been engaged. The tragic end of a romance which he was to remember to his dying day (he was never to marry) had weakened his initiative.

So there were still more years of indecision and inaction. Then the beginning of a new stage in his career was marked by his going to Europe for a stay which, unexpectedly, lasted for seventeen years.

In 1815, as Irving was making plans for a pleasant tour of Europe, a real need arose for him to go to England. As a result of the War of 1812, the Irving family's importing business was in a bad tangle and there seemed to be a chance that Irving might be of assistance in straightening out the firm's affairs. But even such a greenhorn as he soon saw that the task was hopeless. Irving did everything in his power to postpone the crash; in spite of his best efforts, in 1818 the Irving firm was forced into bankruptcy. It was only at this time that Irving made up his mind that, if possible, he would use his pen to earn a living.

England at that time was quite unfriendly to Americans and critical of American writing. Travelers and critics agreed that the United States lagged woefully behind the world in art and literature. In February 1819, the *British Critic* said:

The Americans have no national literature, and no learned men. . . . The talents of our transatlantic brethren show themselves chiefly in political pamphlets. The Americans are too young to rival in literature the old nations of Europe. They have neither history, nor romance, nor poetry, nor legends on which to exercise their genius and kindle their imagination. The inhabitants of the United States will never have to boast of a native poetry, or a native music. . . .

Shortly after this, Sydney Smith, English wit and critic, was asking in *The Edinburgh Review:* "In the four quarters of the globe, who reads an American book? or goes to an American play? or looks at an American picture?" Some writers went so far as to suggest that life in the wilds of the North American continent had brutalized the inhabitants and had finally produced a degenerate race of men.

It was in this hostile atmosphere that Irving again turned to writing. In his earlier works his style had not been very different from that of Franklin and the other eighteenth-century writers. His first papers had been signed with the pseudonym Jonathan Oldstyle; and he was an oldstyle writer—one who echoed the voices of British authors such as Addison, Steele, and Goldsmith, all of whom had died before he was born. Now he turned from the outmoded tradition that *Salmagundi* and *A History of New York* represented and embraced the spirit of the new Romantic Movement. Many trends made up this movement, but we may note three in particular: (1) An emphasis upon emotion in literature—emotion ranging from sentimentality to deep feeling. (2) A great interest in the picturesque elements of the past. (3) An enthusiasm about portraying national life and character—such an enthusiasm as is evident, for example, in Scott's narrative poems and in his historical novels.

Various influences had turned Irving toward this literary movement which was underway in several parts of the Old World. As far back as 1810 Sir Walter Scott's thrilling narrative poem about old-time Scotland, *The Lady of the Lake,* had come into Irving's hands, and he had read it with great pleasure. This had been followed by Byron's poetic romances, *Childe Harold, The Corsair,* and others, which also pleased him. During his years in England, Irving had met many British authors, and talked with them about their new enthusiasms.

More important, during a holiday late in the August of 1817, he paid a visit to Sir Walter Scott. He rode up to Scott's home, Abbotsford, in a post chaise, and sent in a letter of introduction. Soon, Scott's hunting dogs came barking out to the road, and then the famous author himself, wearing "an old green shooting coat, with a dog-whistle at the button hole," came out and hospitably greeted him. Scott had admired *A History of New York,* and he found Irving attractive personally. Therefore he welcomed his visitor warmly, put him up for four days, rambled around the countryside with him, and just about talked Irving's arm off.

Irving discovered that his host was the very embodiment of what he admired—an author who, in a light-hearted spirit, wrote of the lore of his own countryside. "I never met with an antiquarian so delightful, either in his writings or his conversation," said Irving, "and the quiet subacid humor that was prone to mingle with his disquisitions gave them, to me, a peculiar and exquisite flavor." What is more, Scott probably told Irving that treasures of the kind he sought might be found in German literature; for soon the American author plunged into the study of German. In May 1818, he wrote a friend, "I have been for some time past engaged in the study of the German language and have got so far as to be able to read and splutter a little. It is a severe task, and has required hard study; but the rich mine of German literature holds forth abundant reward."

The Sketch Book, issued in installments in 1819 and 1820, shows how well Irving had learned the lessons Scott and the other romantic writers had taught him. Most of this series of papers consisted of charming essays on English life and manners, but it is chiefly remembered today for two short stories, "Rip Van Winkle" and "The Legend of Sleepy Hollow."

The Sketch Book appeared in America first, and Irving waited impatiently in England for news of its reception to make its slow way across the ocean. He had sent off the first number in March 1819. At the end of July he was still waiting—"a little nervous," he said. He received no word until September 9, a few days before the third number appeared in the United States.

The news, when it finally came, was wonderful. Irving said that he was so "overwhelmed" by the praise that he feared "it could not be real." The later numbers as well as the first were hailed by American critics and readers alike as masterpieces. English publishers, who had been cool when Irving first offered them the pieces in the collection, now were willing to print the entire volume. The English public joined the American public in making it a success. British readers were very pleased with Irving's pictures of England. Here, they said, was an American who appreciated them—one who at times portrayed English life as well as their own best authors had. The *British Critic,* which had been so harsh in February 1819, said in November 1820:

We would gladly believe, and will take our author's word for the fact, that a country in which the author of these Sketches received his education and formed his opinions, cannot be deserving of all the bitter sarcasm and reproach which writers in this island have heaped upon it. For our own parts, we hope to see the day when all animosities and mean jealousies between this country and that of our author will be sunk in oblivion. A few such writers as this before us, on both sides of the Atlantic, would do more to promote this happy consummation than could be effected, possibly, by events of apparently much greater moment.

Irving's genial writing also improved the feelings of Americans toward the British. He showed his countrymen the charm of British life, and he helped them appreciate the real virtues of the English. Professor Henry Seidel Canby, a twentieth-century American critic, pictures Irving as "an American Marco Polo, bringing home the romance of other countries, bearing their gifts of suavity, detachment, ease, and beauty to a raw country

Sleepy Hollow country.

dependent upon its vulgar strength, stronger in brains than in manners, yet not devoid in a craving for civility."[1]

Publication of *The Sketch Book* was the turning point in Irving's career. Other books written during the period—*Bracebridge Hall* (1822) and *Tales of a Traveller* (1824)—were also successful. These books also were shaped by the romantic influence. As Irving wrote of England or of other countries, he showed that he loved, as he said, "to loiter about the ruined castle, to meditate on the falling tower, to escape, in short, from the commonplace realities of the present, and lose myself among the shadowy grandeurs of the past." In his most successful short stories—"Rip Van Winkle" and "The Legend of Sleepy Hollow" in *The Sketch Book* and "The Devil and Tom Walker" in *Tales of a Traveller*—he did these things: (1) Like Scott, he told legendary and historical narratives about his own native countryside. (2) Like Scott, he treated his legendary lore lightly or semi-humorously. (3) He drew upon German literature for the suggestion of legends, which he adapted to the American scene. (4) Like most romantic writers, he so wrote as to express emotion and to create an emotional effect. Thus this famous author allied himself with the leaders of the world-wide Romantic Movement, and, by his example, helped American writers fall into step with the writers of their day.

1. Henry Seidel Canby, *Classic Americans*. (New York: Russell & Russell, Inc., 1959), page 92

The Devil and Tom Walker

A few miles from Boston in Massachusetts, there is a deep inlet, winding several miles into the interior of the country from Charles Bay, and terminating in a thickly wooded swamp or morass. On one side of this inlet is a beautiful dark grove; on the opposite side the land rises abruptly from the water's edge into a high ridge, on which grow a few scattered oaks of great age and immense size.

Under one of these gigantic trees, according to old stories, there was a great amount of treasure buried by Kidd the pirate. The inlet allowed a facility to bring the money in a boat secretly and at night to the very foot of the hill; the elevation of the place permitted a good lookout to be kept that no one was at hand; while the remarkable trees formed good landmarks by which the place might easily be found again. The old stories add, moreover, that the devil presided at the hiding of the money, and took it under his guardianship; but this, it is well known, he always does with buried treasure, particularly when it has been ill-gotten. Be that as it may, Kidd never returned to recover his wealth, being shortly after seized at Boston, sent out to England, and there hanged for a pirate.

About the year 1727, just at the time that earthquakes were prevalent in New England, and shook many tall sinners down upon their knees, there lived near this place a meager, miserly fellow, of the name of Tom Walker. He had a wife as miserly as himself; they were so miserly that they even conspired to cheat each other. Whatever the woman could lay hands on, she hid away; a hen could not cackle but she was on the alert to secure the new-laid egg. Her husband was continually prying about to detect her secret hoards, and many and fierce were the conflicts that took place about what ought to have been common property.

They lived in a forlorn-looking house that stood alone, and had an air of starvation. A few straggling savin trees, emblems of sterility, grew near it; no smoke ever curled from its chimney; no traveler stopped at its door. A miserable horse, whose ribs were as articulate as the bars of a gridiron, stalked about a field, where a thin carpet of moss, scarcely covering the ragged beds of pudding stone, tantalized and balked his hunger; and sometimes he would lean his head over the fence, look piteously at the passer-by, and seem to petition deliverance from this land of famine.

The house and its inmates had altogether a bad name. Tom's wife was a tall termagant, fierce of temper, loud of tongue, and strong of arm. Her voice was often heard in wordy warfare with her husband; and his face sometimes showed signs that their conflicts were not confined to words. No one ventured, however, to interfere between them. The lonely wayfarer shrunk within himself at the horrid clamor and clapper-clawing,[1] eyed the den of discord askance; and hurried on his way, rejoicing, if a bachelor, in his celibacy.

One day that Tom Walker had been to a distant part of the neighborhood, he took what he considered a short cut homeward, through the swamp. Like most short cuts, it was an ill-chosen route. The swamp was thickly grown with great gloomy pines and hemlocks, some of them ninety feet high, which made it dark at noonday and a retreat for all the owls of the neighborhood. It was full of pits and quagmires, partly covered with weeds and mosses, where the green surface often betrayed the traveler into a gulf of black, smothering mud; there were also dark and stagnant pools, the abodes of the tadpole, the bullfrog, and the water snake, where the trunks of pines and hemlocks lay half-drowned, half-rotting, looking like alligators sleeping in the mire.

Tom had long been picking his way cautiously through this treacherous forest, stepping from tuft to tuft of rushes and roots, which afforded precarious footholds among deep sloughs; or pacing carefully, like a cat, along the prostrate trunks of trees, startled now and then by the sudden screaming of the bittern, or the quacking of wild duck rising on the wing from some solitary pool. At length he arrived at a firm piece of ground, which

ran out like a peninsula into the deep bosom of the swamp. It had been one of the strongholds of the Indians during their wars with the first colonists. Here they had thrown up a kind of fort, which they had looked upon as almost impregnable, and had used as a place of refuge for their squaws and children. Nothing remained of the old Indian fort but a few embankments, gradually sinking to the level of the surrounding earth and already overgrown in part by oaks and other forest trees, the foliage of which formed a contrast to the dark pines and hemlocks of the swamp.

It was late in the dusk of evening when Tom Walker reached the old fort, and he paused there awhile to rest himself. Anyone but he would have felt unwilling to linger in this lonely, melancholy place, for the common people had a bad opinion of it, from the stories handed down from the time of the Indian wars, when it was asserted that the savages held incantations here and made sacrifices to the evil spirit.

Tom Walker, however, was not a man to be troubled with any fears of the kind. He reposed himself for some time on the trunk of a fallen hemlock, listening to the boding cry of the tree toad, and delving with his walking staff into a mound of black mold at his feet. As he turned up the soil unconsciously, his staff struck against something hard. He raked it out of the vegetable mold, and lo! a cloven skull, with an Indian tomahawk buried deep in it, lay before him. The rust on the weapon showed the time that had elapsed since this deathblow had been given. It was a dreary memento of the fierce struggle that had taken place in this last foothold of the Indian warriors. "Humph!" said Tom Walker as he gave it a kick to shake the dirt from it.

"Let that skull alone!" said a gruff voice. Tom lifted up his eyes and beheld a great black man seated directly opposite him, on the stump of a tree. He was exceedingly surprised, having neither heard nor seen anyone approach; and he was still more perplexed on observing, as well as the gathering gloom would permit, that the stranger was neither

---

1. *clapper-clawing*, an argument accompanied by scratching and slapping.

Negro nor Indian. It is true he was dressed in a rude half-Indian garb, and had a red belt or sash swathed round his body; but his face was neither black nor copper color, but swarthy and dingy, and begrimed with soot, as if he had been accustomed to toil among fires and forges. He had a shock of coarse black hair that stood out from his head in all directions, and bore an ax on his shoulder.

He scowled for a moment at Tom with a pair of great red eyes.

"What are you doing on my grounds?" said the black man, with a hoarse, growling voice.

"Your grounds!" said Tom, with a sneer, "no more your grounds than mine; they belong to Deacon Peabody."

"Deacon Peabody be damned," said the stranger, "as I flatter myself he will be, if he does not look more to his own sins and less to those of his neighbors. Look yonder, and see how Deacon Peabody is faring."

Tom looked in the direction that the stranger pointed and beheld one of the great trees, fair and flourishing without, but rotten at the core, and saw that it had been nearly hewn through, so that the first high wind was likely to blow it down. On the bark of the tree was scored the name of Deacon Peabody, an eminent man who had waxed wealthy by driving shrewd bargains with the Indians. He now looked around, and found most of the tall trees marked with the name of some great man of the colony, and all more or less scored by the ax. The one on which he had been seated, and which had evidently just been hewn down, bore the name of Crowninshield; and he recollected a mighty rich man of that name, who made a vulgar display of wealth, which it was whispered he had acquired by buccaneering.

"He's just ready for burning!" said the black man, with a growl of triumph. "You see I am likely to have a good stock of firewood for winter."

"But what right have you," said Tom, "to cut down Deacon Peabody's timber?"

"The right of a prior claim," said the other. "This woodland belonged to me long before one of your white-faced race put foot upon the soil."

"And pray, who are you, if I may be so bold?" said Tom.

"Oh, I go by various names. I am the wild huntsman in some countries; the black miner in others. In this neighborhood I am known by the name of the black woodsman. I am he to whom the red men consecrated this spot, and in honor of whom they now and then roasted a white man, by way of sweet-smelling sacrifice. Since the red men have been exterminated by you white savages, I amuse myself by presiding at the persecutions of Quakers and Anabaptists[2]; I am the great patron and prompter of slave dealers, and the grand master of the Salem witches."[3]

"The upshot of all which is, that, if I mistake not," said Tom, sturdily, "you are he commonly called Old Scratch."

"The same, at your service!" replied the black man, with a half-civil nod.

Such was the opening of this interview, according to the old story; though it has almost too familiar an air to be credited. One would think that to meet with such a singular personage, in this wild, lonely place, would have shaken any man's nerves; but Tom was a hard-minded fellow, not easily daunted, and he had lived so long with a termagant wife that he did not even fear the devil.

It is said that after this commencement they had a long and earnest conversation together, as Tom returned homeward. The black man told him of great sums of money buried by Kidd the pirate, under the oak trees on the high ridge, not far from the morass. All these were under his command, and protected by his power, so that none could find them but such as propitiated his favor. These he offered to place within Tom Walker's reach, having conceived an especial kindness for him; but they were to be had only on certain conditions. What these conditions were may be easily surmised, though Tom never disclosed them publicly. They must have been very hard, for he required time to think of them, and he was

---

2. *Anabaptists* (an'ə bap'tists), members of a Protestant sect which originated in Switzerland in the sixteenth century. Quakers and Anabaptists were persecuted in the Massachusetts colony. 3. *Salem witches*, old women accused of witchcraft in the Salem witch trials of 1692.

not a man to stick at trifles when money was in view.

When they had reached the edge of the swamp, the stranger paused. "What proof have I that all you have been telling me is true?" said Tom. "There's my signature," said the black man, pressing his finger on Tom's forehead. So saying, he turned off among the thickest of the swamp, and seemed, as Tom said, to go down, down, down, into the earth, until he totally disappeared.

When Tom reached home, he found the black print of a finger burned, as it were, into his forehead, which nothing could obliterate.

The first news his wife had to tell him was the sudden death of Absalom Crowninshield, the rich buccaneer. It was announced in the papers with the usual flourish that "A great man had fallen in Israel."[4]

Tom recollected the tree which his black friend had just hewn down and which was ready for burning. "Let the freebooter roast," said Tom; "who cares!" He now felt convinced that all he had heard and seen was no illusion.

He was not prone to let his wife into his confidence; but as this was an uneasy secret, he willingly shared it with her. All her avarice was awakened at the mention of hidden gold, and she urged her husband to comply with the black man's terms, and secure what would make them wealthy for life. However Tom might have felt disposed to sell himself to the devil, he was determined not to do so to oblige his wife; so he flatly refused, out of the mere spirit of contradiction. Many were the quarrels they had on the subject; but the more she talked, the more resolute was Tom not to be damned to please her.

At length she determined to drive the bargain on her own account, and if she succeeded, to keep all the gain to herself. Being of the same fearless temper as her husband, she set off for the old Indian fort toward the close of a summer's day. She was many hours absent. When she came back, she was reserved and sullen in her replies. She spoke something of a black man, whom she met about twilight hewing at the root of a tall tree. He was sulky, however, and would not come to terms; she

was to go again with a propitiatory offering, but what it was she forbore to say.

The next evening she set off again for the swamp, with her apron heavily laden. Tom waited and waited for her, but in vain; midnight came, but she did not make her appearance; morning, noon, night returned, but still she did not come. Tom now grew uneasy for her safety, especially as he found she had carried off in her apron the silver tea pot and spoons, and every portable article of value. Another night elapsed, another morning came; but no wife. In a word, she was never heard of more.

What was her real fate nobody knows, in consequence of so many pretending to know. It is one of those facts which have become confounded by a variety of historians. Some asserted that she lost her way among the tangled mazes of the swamp, and sank into some pit or slough; others, more uncharitable, hinted that she had eloped with the household booty, and made off to some other province; while others surmised that the tempter had decoyed her into a dismal quagmire, on the top of which her hat was found lying. In confirmation of this, it was said a great black man, with an ax on his shoulder, was seen late that very evening coming out of the swamp, carrying a bundle tied in a check apron, with an air of surly triumph.

The most current and probable story, however, observes that Tom Walker grew so anxious about the fate of his wife and his property that he set out at length to seek them both at the Indian fort. During a long summer's afternoon he searched about the gloomy place, but no wife was to be seen. He called her name repeatedly, but she was nowhere to be heard. The bittern alone responded to his voice, as he flew screaming by; or the bullfrog croaked dolefully from a neighboring pool. At length, it is said, just in the brown hour of twilight, when the owls began to hoot, and the bats to flit about, his attention was attracted by the clamor of carrion crows hovering about a cypress tree. He looked up and beheld a bundle tied in a check apron and

4. *Israel*, Massachusetts. The Puritans of Massachusetts regarded their colony as the Promised Land (Israel).

hanging in the branches of the tree, with a great vulture perched hard by, as if keeping watch upon it. He leaped with joy; for he recognized his wife's apron and supposed it to contain the household valuables.

"Let us get hold of the property," said he consolingly to himself, "and we will endeavor to do without the woman."

As he scrambled up the tree, the vulture spread its wide wings and sailed off screaming into the deep shadows of the forest. Tom seized the checked apron, but, woeful sight! found nothing but a heart and liver tied up in it!

Such, according to this most authentic old story, was all that was to be found of Tom's wife. She had probably attempted to deal with the black man as she had been accustomed to deal with her husband; but though a female scold is generally considered a match for the devil, yet in this instance she appears to have had the worst of it. She must have died game, however; for it is said Tom noticed many prints of cloven feet deeply stamped upon the tree, and found handfuls of hair that looked as if they had been plucked from the coarse black shock of the woodsman. Tom knew his wife's prowess by experience. He shrugged his shoulders as he looked at the signs of a fierce clapper-clawing. "Egad," said he to himself, "Old Scratch must have had a tough time of it!"

Tom consoled himself for the loss of his property with the loss of his wife, for he was a man of fortitude. He even felt something like gratitude toward the black woodsman, who, he considered, had done him a kindness. He sought, therefore, to cultivate a further acquaintance with him, but for some time without success; the old blacklegs played shy, for whatever people may think, he is not always to be had for calling for; he knows how to play his cards when pretty sure of his game.

At length, it is said, when delay had whetted Tom's eagerness to the quick, and prepared him to agree to anything rather than not gain the promised treasure, he met the black man one evening in his usual woodsman's dress, with his ax on his shoulder, sauntering along the swamp and humming a tune. He affected to receive Tom's advances with great indifference, made brief replies, and went on humming his tune.

By degrees, however, Tom brought him to business, and they began to haggle about the terms on which the former was to have the pirate's treasure. There was one condition which need not be mentioned, being generally understood in all cases where the devil grants favors; but there were others about which, though of less importance, he was inflexibly obstinate. He insisted that the money found through his means should be employed in his service. He proposed, therefore, that Tom should employ it in the black traffic; that is to say, that he should fit out a slave ship. This, however, Tom resolutely refused; he was bad enough in all conscience, but the devil himself could not tempt him to turn slave trader.

Finding Tom so squeamish on this point, he did not insist upon it, but proposed, instead, that he should turn usurer; the devil being extremely anxious for the increase of usurers, looking upon them as his peculiar people.

To this no objections were made, for it was just to Tom's taste.

"You shall open a broker's shop in Boston next month," said the black man.

"I'll do it tomorrow, if you wish," said Tom Walker.

"You shall lend money at two per cent a month."

"Egad, I'll charge four!" replied Tom Walker.

"You shall extort bonds, foreclose mortgages, drive the merchants to bankruptcy—"

"I'll drive them to the devil," cried Tom Walker.

"You are the usurer for my money!" said blacklegs with delight. "When will you want the rhino?"[5]

"This very night."

"Done!" said the devil.

"Done!" said Tom Walker. So they shook hands and struck a bargain.

A few days' time saw Tom Walker seated behind his desk in a counting house in Boston.

His reputation for a ready-moneyed man,

---

5. *rhino* (rī'nō), money. [*Slang*]

who would lend money out for a good consideration, soon spread abroad. Everybody remembers the time of Governor Belcher,[6] when money was particularly scarce. It was a time of paper credit.[7] The country had been deluged with government bills, the famous Land Bank[8] had been established; there had been a rage for speculating; the people had run mad with schemes for new settlements, for building cities in the wilderness; land jobbers[9] went about with maps of grants, and townships, and El Dorados, lying nobody knew where, but which everybody was ready to purchase. In a word, the great speculating fever which breaks out every now and then in the country had raged to an alarming degree, and everybody was dreaming of making sudden fortunes from nothing. As usual the fever had subsided; the dream had gone off, and the imaginary fortunes with it; the patients were left in doleful plight, and the whole country resounded with the consequent cry of "hard times."

At this propitious time of public distress did Tom Walker set up as usurer in Boston. His door was soon thronged by customers. The needy and adventurous, the gambling speculator, the dreaming land jobber, the thriftless tradesman, the merchant with cracked credit—in short, everyone driven to raise money by desperate means and desperate sacrifices hurried to Tom Walker.

Thus Tom was the universal friend of the needy, and acted like a "friend in need"; that is to say, he always exacted good pay and good security. In proportion to the distress of the applicant was the hardness of his terms. He accumulated bonds and mortgages; gradually squeezed his customers closer and closer; and sent them at length, dry as a sponge, from his door.

In this way he made money hand over hand; became a rich and mighty man, and exalted his cocked hat upon 'Change.[10] He built himself, as usual, a vast house, out of ostentation; but left the greater part of it unfinished and unfurnished, out of parsimony. He even set up a carriage in the fullness of his vainglory, though he nearly starved the horses which drew it; and as the ungreased wheels

groaned and screeched on the axletrees, you would have thought you heard the souls of the poor debtors he was squeezing.

As Tom waxed old, however, he grew thoughtful. Having secured the good things of this world, he began to feel anxious about those of the next. He thought with regret on the bargain he had made with his black friend, and set his wits to work to cheat him out of the conditions. He became, therefore, all of a sudden, a violent churchgoer. He prayed loudly and strenuously, as if heaven were to be taken by force of lungs. Indeed, one might always tell when he had sinned most during the week by the clamor of his Sunday devotion. The quiet Christians who had been modestly and steadfastly traveling Zionward,[11] were struck with self-reproach at seeing themselves so suddenly outstripped in their career by this new-made convert. Tom was as rigid in religious as in money matters; he was a stern supervisor and censurer of his neighbors, and seemed to think every sin entered up to their account became a credit on his own side of the page. He even talked of the expediency of reviving the persecution of Quakers and Anabaptists. In a word, Tom's zeal became as notorious as his riches.

Still, in spite of all this strenuous attention to forms, Tom had a lurking dread that the devil, after all, would have his due. That he might not be taken unawares, therefore, it is said he always carried a small Bible in his coat pocket. He had also a great folio Bible on his counting-house desk, and would frequently be found reading it when people called on business; on such occasions he would lay his green spectacles in the book, to mark the place, while he turned round to drive some usurious bargain.

Some say that Tom grew a little crack-

6. *Governor Belcher*, Jonathan Belcher, who governed Massachusetts from 1730 to 1741. 7. *paper credit*, assets that existed on paper but were actually of no value. 8. *Land Bank*, a scheme to relieve the shortage of gold in Massachusetts by establishing a bank whose resources rested on real-estate mortgages. 9. *land jobbers*, men who bought tracts of undeveloped land as a speculation and sold them to others. 10. *'Change*, the Exchange, or the financial center of Boston, where merchants, traders, and brokers do business. 11. *Zionward*, toward heaven. Zion, originally the hill in Jerusalem on which the temple stood, is often used to typify heaven.

brained in his old days, and that, fancying his end approaching, he had his horse new shod, saddled and bridled, and buried with his feet uppermost; because he supposed that at the last day the world would be turned upside down in which case he should find his horse standing ready for mounting, and he was determined at the worst to give his old friend a run for it. This, however, is probably a mere old wives' fable. If he really did take such a precaution, it was totally superfluous; at least so says the authentic old legend, which closes his story in the following manner.

One hot summer afternoon in the dog days, just as a terrible black thundergust was coming up, Tom sat in his counting house in his white cap and India silk morning gown. He was on the point of foreclosing a mortgage, by which he would complete the ruin of an unlucky land speculator for whom he had professed the greatest friendship. The poor land jobber begged him to grant a few months' indulgence. Tom had grown testy and irritated, and refused another day.

"My family will be ruined and brought upon the parish,"[12] said the land jobber.

"Charity begins at home," replied Tom; "I must take care of myself in these hard times."

"You have made so much money out of me," said the speculator.

Tom lost his patience and his piety. "The devil take me," said he, "if I have made a farthing!"

Just then there were three loud knocks at the street door. He stepped out to see who was there. A black man was holding a black horse, which neighed and stamped with impatience.

"Tom, you're come for," said the black fellow, gruffly. Tom shrank back, but too late. He had left his little Bible at the bottom of his coat pocket, and his big Bible on the desk buried under the mortgage he was about to foreclose; never was sinner taken more unawares. The black man whisked him like a child into the saddle, gave the horse the lash, and away he galloped, with Tom on his back, in the midst of the thunderstorm. The clerks stuck their pens behind their ears, and stared after him from the windows. Away went Tom Walker, dashing down the streets, his white

cap bobbing up and down, his morning gown fluttering in the wind, and his steed striking fire out of the pavement at every bound. When the clerks turned to look for the black man, he had disappeared.

Tom Walker never returned to foreclose the mortgage. A countryman, who lived on the border of the swamp, reported that in the height of the thundergust he had heard a great clattering of hoofs and a howling along the road, and running to the window caught sight of a figure, such as I have described, on a horse that galloped like mad across the fields, over the hills, and down into the black hemlock swamp toward the old Indian fort; and that shortly after, a thunderbolt falling in that direction seemed to set the whole forest in a blaze.

The good people of Boston shook their heads and shrugged their shoulders, but had been so much accustomed to witches and goblins and tricks of the devil in all kinds of shapes, from the first settlement of the colony, that they were not so much horror-struck as might have been expected. Trustees were appointed to take charge of Tom's effects. There was nothing, however, to administer upon. On searching his coffers, all his bonds and mortgages were found reduced to cinders. In place of gold and silver, his iron chest was filled with chips and shavings; two skeletons lay in his stable instead of his half-starved horses, and the very next day his great house took fire and burned to the ground.

Such was the end of Tom Walker and his ill-gotten wealth. Let all griping money brokers lay this story to heart. The truth of it is not to be doubted. The very hole under the oak trees whence he dug Kidd's money is to be seen to this day; and the neighboring swamp and old Indian fort are often haunted on stormy nights by a figure on horseback, in morning gown and white cap, which is doubtless the troubled spirit of the usurer. In fact, the story has resolved itself into a proverb, and is the origin of that popular saying, so prevalent throughout New England, of "The Devil and Tom Walker."

---

12. *brought upon the parish,* forced to depend upon public charity for support.

HISTORIAN AND
BIOGRAPHER
In 1826 romantic associations drew Irving to Spain. As he wrote, "From earliest boyhood, when, on the banks of the Hudson, I first pored over the pages of an old Spanish history about the wars of Granada,[1] that city has ever been a subject of my waking dreams." He now turned to the writing of history and biography, each tinged, naturally enough, with romantic coloration. He was more imaginative than scholarly, and his emotions were more involved in what he wrote than the emotions of an impartial historian would be. The play of his fancy and feeling over the accounts which he wrote gave them their chief appeal. His books included *The Life and Voyages of Columbus* (1828), *Conquest of Granada* (1829), and *The Alhambra*[2] (1832)—all imaginative handlings of materials gathered in Spain.

In 1832, Irving returned to the United States, and the welcome he received showed clearly that his countrymen appreciated his books and the world-wide recognition which they had received. He spent a year reacquainting himself with his homeland, covering the country pretty thoroughly from New England to the prairies, and spending a year in Wash-

1. *wars of Granada* (grə nä′də). Granada, in southern Spain, was ruled by the Moors throughout the Middle Ages. In 1492 the Christians under Ferdinand and Isabella conquered Granada and drove the Moors from Spain. 2. *The Alhambra* (al ham′brə), a book concerned with the history and legends of the Alhambra, the palace near Granada of the Moorish kings in Spain.

Irving's study at Sunnyside, where he wrote his life of Washington.

SLEEPY HOLLOW RESTORATIONS

ington, where he observed the workings of our government at close range. Then he bought an old stone cottage at Tarrytown on the Hudson, and remodeled it into Sunnyside, the home where he remained the rest of his days, with the exception of the years 1842-1846, which he spent in Madrid as Minister to Spain.

His important books during this period fall into two classes. One group, based upon his own travels in the West and upon various documents, deals with aspects of Western life and history. *A Tour on the Prairies* (1835) shows Irving as a visitor to a part of the country in which, even as he watched, a new phase of our history was developing. *Astoria* (1836) and *The Adventures of Captain Bonneville* (1837) recount the adventures of fur traders and explorers in the Far West. The second group includes two biographies, one—*Oliver Goldsmith* (1849)—of an eighteenth-century English writer who was one of Irving's literary idols, and the other—*Life of Washington* (1855-1859)—of the American patriot for whom Irving was named.

All these books showed that Irving, in his last years, was still a master stylist; but only the volume which sets forth the legends and the romance of the Alhambra and a few passages which give vivid pictures of life in the West compete in interest or importance with his writings before 1826.

Yet the career which ended in mid-nineteenth century had been, as a whole, both admirable and important. During its course, Irving reëstablished links between the Old World and the new nation which had come into being about the time he was born; he proved that an American writer could be a fine artist; and he brought the spirit of romance to American letters.

Sunnyside as it appears today after restoration.

The Camp of the Wild Horse

Through a chance meeting in 1832 with Henry L. Ellsworth, a government commissioner of Indian affairs, Irving had an opportunity to explore the Indian country in what is now the state of Oklahoma. Escorted by a hundred Rangers from the army, Ellsworth, Irving, and their party went deep into the land of the Indians. The following selection, from *A Tour on the Prairies,* describes a camp along the Arkansas River.

We had encamped in a good neighborhood for game, as the reports of rifles in various directions speedily gave notice. One of our hunters soon returned with the meat of a doe, tied up in the skin, and slung across his shoulders. Another brought a fat buck across his horse. Two other deer were brought in, and a number of turkeys. All the game was thrown down in front of the Captain's fire, to be portioned out among the various messes. The spits and camp kettles were soon in full employ, and throughout the evening there was a scene of hunters' feasting and profusion.

We had been disappointed this day in our hopes of meeting with buffalo, but the sight of the wild horse had been a great novelty, and gave a turn to the conversation of the camp for the evening. There were several anecdotes told of a famous gray horse which has ranged the prairies of this neighborhood for six or seven years, setting at naught every attempt of the hunters to capture him. They say he can pace and rack (or amble) faster than the fleetest horses can run. Equally marvelous accounts were given of a black horse on the Brassos, who grazed the prairies on that river's banks in the Texas. For years he outstripped all pursuit. His fame spread far and wide; offers were made for him to the amount of a thousand dollars; the boldest and most hardriding hunters tried incessantly to make prize of him, but in vain. At length he fell a victim to his gallantry, being decoyed under a tree by a tame mare, and a noose dropped over his head by a boy perched among the branches.

The capture of the wild horse is one of the most favorite achievements of the prairie tribes; and, indeed, it is from this source that the Indian hunters chiefly supply themselves. The wild horses which range those vast grassy plains, extending from the Arkansas to the Spanish settlements,[1] are of various forms and colors, betraying their various descents. Some resemble the common English stock, and are probably descended from horses which have escaped from our border settlements. Others are of a low but strong make, and are supposed to be of the Andalusian breed, brought out by the Spanish discoverers.

Some fanciful speculatists have seen in them descendants of the Arab stock, brought into Spain from Africa, and thence transferred to this country; and have pleased themselves with the idea that their sires may have been of the pure coursers of the desert, that once bore Mahomet and his warlike disciples[2] across the sandy plains of Arabia.

The habits of the Arab seem to have come with the steed. The introduction of the horse on the boundless prairies of the Far West changed the whole mode of living of their inhabitants. It gave them that facility of rapid motion, and of sudden and distant change of place, so dear to the roving propensities of man. Instead of lurking in the depths of gloomy forests, and patiently threading the mazes of a tangled wilderness on foot, like his brethren of the North, the Indian of the West is a rover of the plain; he leads a brighter and more sunshiny life, almost always on horseback, on vast flowery prairies and under cloudless skies.

I was lying by the Captain's fire, late in the evening, listening to stories about those coursers of the prairies, and weaving speculations of my own, when there was a clamor of voices and a loud cheering at the other end of the camp; and word was passed that Beatte, the half-breed,[3] had brought in a wild horse.

In an instant every fire was deserted; the whole camp crowded to see the Indian and his prize. It was a colt about two years old, well grown, finely limbed, with bright prominent eyes and a spirited yet gentle demeanor. He gazed about him with an air of mingled stupefaction and surprise at the men, the horses, and the campfires; while the Indian stood before him with folded arms, having hold of the other end of the cord which noosed his captive, and gazing on him with a most imperturbable aspect. If the horse, however, manifested the least restiveness, Beatte would immediately worry him with the lariat, jerking him first on one side, then on the other, so as almost to throw him on the ground; when he had thus rendered him passive, he would resume his statuelike attitude and gaze at him in silence.

The whole scene was singularly wild: the

---

1. *from the Arkansas . . . Spanish settlements,* from the territory which became the state of Arkansas to the towns founded by the Spanish among the Indians of New Mexico and southwestern Texas. 2. *Mahomet* (mə hom′it) *and his warlike disciples.* Mohammed (Mahomet) founded Islam (is′ləm), or the Mohammedan religion, in Arabia in the seventh century and encouraged his disciples to use force against those who would not accept its doctrines. 3. *Beatte* (bā ät′), *the half-breed,* an interpreter hired by the party. Irving says that Beatte was of French and Osage Indian parentage, and often refers to him as "the Indian," but Beatte himself claimed to be all French.

tall grove, partially illuminated by the flashing fires of the camp, the horses tethered here and there among the trees, the carcasses of deer hanging around, and in the midst of all, the wild huntsman and his wild horse, with an admiring throng of rangers, almost as wild.

In the eagerness of their excitement, several of the young Rangers sought to get the horse by purchase or barter, and even offered extravagant terms; but Beatte declined all their offers. "You give great price now," said he; "tomorrow you be sorry, and take back."

The young men importuned him with questions about the mode in which he took the horse, but his answers were dry and laconic; he evidently looked down upon them with contempt as greenhorns, little versed in the noble science of woodcraft.

Afterwards, however, when he was seated by our fire, I readily drew from him an account of his exploit; for, though taciturn among strangers and little prone to boast of his actions, yet his taciturnity, like that of all Indians, had its times of relaxation.

He informed me that on leaving the camp he had returned to the place where we had lost sight of the wild horse. Soon getting upon its track, he followed it to the banks of the river. Here, the prints being more distinct in the sand, he perceived that one of the hoofs was broken and defective, so he gave up the pursuit.

As he was returning to the camp, he came upon a gang of six horses, which immediately made for the river. He pursued them across the stream, left his rifle on the river bank, and, putting his horse to full speed, soon came up with the fugitives. He attempted to noose one of them, but the lariat hitched on one of his ears, and he shook it off. The horses dashed up a hill, he followed hard at their heels, when, of a sudden, he saw their tails whisking in the air, and they plunging down a precipice. It was too late to stop. He shut his eyes, held in his breath, and went over with them—neck or nothing. The descent was between twenty and thirty feet, but they all came down safe upon a sandy bottom.

He now succeeded in throwing his noose around a fine young horse. As he galloped alongside of him, the two horses passed each side of a sapling, and the end of the lariat was jerked out of his hand. He regained it, but an intervening tree obliged him again to let it go. Having once more caught it, and coming to a more open country, he was enabled to play the young horse with the line until he gradually checked and subdued him, so as to lead him to the place where he had left his rifle.

He had another formidable difficulty in getting him across the river, where both horses stuck for a time in the mire, and Beatte was nearly unseated from his saddle by the force of the current and the struggles of his captive. After much toil and trouble, however, he got across the stream, and brought his prize safe into camp.

For the remainder of the evening, the camp remained in a high state of excitement; nothing was talked of but the capture of wild horses. Every youngster of the troop was for this harum-scarum kind of chase; everyone promised himself to return from the campaign in triumph, bestriding one of these wild coursers of the prairies. Beatte had suddenly risen to great importance; he was the prime hunter, the hero of the day. Offers were made him by the best-mounted Rangers to let him ride their horses in the chase provided he would give them a share of the spoil. Beatte bore his honors in silence, and closed with none of the offers. Our stammering, chattering, gasconading little Frenchman,[4] however, made up for his taciturnity, by vaunting as much upon the subject as if it were he that had caught the horse. Indeed he held forth so learnedly in the matter, and boasted so much of the many horses he had taken, that he began to be considered an oracle; and some of the youngsters were inclined to doubt whether he were not superior even to the taciturn Beatte.

The excitement kept the camp awake later than usual. The hum of voices, interrupted by occasional peals of laughter, was heard from the groups around the various fires, and the

---

4. *Frenchman,* Antoine Deshetres (än twän′ dez etr′), whom Irving usually refers to as "Tonish." He had been hired by the party in St. Louis to act as guide and interpreter.

night was considerably advanced before all had sunk to sleep.

With the morning dawn the excitement revived, and Beatte and his wild horse were again the gaze and talk of the camp. The captive had been tied all night to a tree among the other horses. He was again led forth by Beatte, by a long halter or lariat, and, on his manifesting the least restiveness, was, as before, jerked and worried into passive submission. He appeared to be gentle and docile by nature, and had a beautifully mild expression of the eye. In his strange and forlorn situation, the poor animal seemed to seek protection and companionship in the very horse which had aided to capture him.

Seeing him thus gentle and tractable, Beatte, just as we were about to march, strapped a light pack upon his back, by way of giving him the first lesson in servitude. The native pride and independence of the animal took fire at this indignity. He reared, and plunged, and kicked, and tried in every way to get rid of the degrading burden. The Indian was too potent for him. At every paroxysm he renewed the discipline of the halter, until the poor animal, driven to despair, threw himself prostrate on the ground, and lay motionless, as if acknowledging himself vanquished. A stage hero, representing the despair of a captive prince, could not have played his part more dramatically. There was absolutely a moral grandeur in it.

The imperturbable Beatte folded his arms, and stood for a time looking down in silence upon his captive; until seeing him perfectly subdued, he nodded his head slowly, screwed his mouth into a sardonic smile of triumph, and, with a jerk of the halter, ordered him to rise. He obeyed, and from that time forward offered no resistance. During that day he bore his pack patiently, and was led by the halter; but in two days he followed voluntarily at large among the supernumerary horses of the troop.

I could not but look with compassion upon this fine young animal, whose whole course of existence had been so suddenly reversed. From being a denizen of these vast pastures, ranging at will from plain to plain and mead to mead, cropping of every herb and flower, and drinking of every stream, he was suddenly reduced to perpetual and painful servitude, to pass his life under the harness and the curb, amid, perhaps, the din and dust and drudgery of cities. The transition in his lot was such as sometimes takes place in human affairs and in the fortunes of towering individuals—one day, a prince of the prairies—the next day, a pack horse!

❧ TO INCREASE UNDERSTANDING
Early Life In Manhattan

1. (*a*) In what ways is "Early Life in Manhattan" representative of the sort of person Irving was when he wrote *A History of New York*? (*b*) Illustrate the statement that Irving was a "playful amateur" in his first period as a writer.

2. (*a*) What great contrasts does Irving note in the behavior of the early dwellers in Manhattan and in that of his own time? (*b*) Cite passages in which Irving satirizes society by means of these contrasts.

3. *A History of New York* is often described as a "comic history." Do you find this selection humorous? Select passages to justify your answer.

The Devil and Tom Walker

1. In 1819 the *British Critic* commented: "The talents of our transatlantic brethren show themselves chiefly in political pamphlets." (*a*) Explain why at the time it was written this statement might have been justified. (*b*) How did Irving change the situation?

2. (*a*) What were some of the important trends in the Romantic Movement? (*b*) Explain ways in which "The Devil and Tom Walker" shows the influence of this movement.

3. (*a*) Why do you think in "The Devil and Tom Walker" Irving describes the events as if they were true? (*b*) How does he maintain the elaborate pretense that the story is fact, not fiction?

4. This story ends with Tom's death. Is it, therefore, a tragic story? Explain.

5. (*a*) What elements of the supernatural do you find in this story? (*b*) How do these elements contribute to the story?

6. (*a*) What do you learn about Irving's attitudes from reading this story? (*b*) How is this revelation of character in line with romanticism?

7. Irving by means of stories like "The Devil and Tom Walker" changed the hostile opinion of American letters abroad. If you had been a European reader in those days, what qualities would you have found to admire in this story?

The Camp of the Wild Horse

1. (a) In what ways do the books of Irving's last period reflect his life and interests at this time? (b) What are Irving's strong points as historian and biographer? (c) What are his weaknesses?
2. (a) Select the descriptions in "The Camp of the Wild Horse"* that give you the most vivid pictures of Beatte; of the captured horse. (b) How do Irving's personality and feelings become evident through these descriptions? (c) Would you say Irving is still the romantic writer? Explain your answer.
3. Compare Irving's use of legend in this selection with that in "The Devil and Tom Walker."
4. How do Irving's narrative style and purpose in this selection differ from those in "Early Life in Manhattan"?

BETTER READING
Washington Irving's humor

The distinctive quality of Washington Irving's humor lies not so much in *what* he says as in *how* he says it. He delights in exaggerating with a straight face, and in making ironic, tongue-in-cheek remarks which say just the opposite of what he means.

Consider Irving's language. He takes the eighteenth-century habit of using long sentences and many words of Latin derivation, and exaggerates it grandly. For example, there is nothing amusing in the statement, "The whole house was constantly being cleaned." But when, in "Early Life in Manhattan," Irving rolls out, "The whole house was constantly in a state of inundation, under the discipline of mops and brooms and scrubbing brushes," the dignified words produce a half-mocking, ironic effect.

Irving also creates humor by exaggerating the seriousness of situations. He pretends that the weekly cleaning of the Dutch parlor is a grave ritual. Accordingly, he transforms the parlor into a "sanctum sanctorum" or "sacred apartment" and has the Dutch women enter it "devoutly" as they would a church. By inflating the weekly cleaning with such unmerited seriousness, Irving makes it appear humorously ridiculous.

The reader becomes so conditioned to Irving's overblown language and exaggerated seriousness that a simple statement of fact has comic force. For example, in introducing the wealthy members of the Dutch community, Irving elevates them to the *noblesse*. The reader at this point expects an equally lofty description to follow, but Irving does not comply. Instead, he deflates the *noblesse* by defining them as "such as kept their own cows and drove their own wagons." This sudden literal description takes the reader off guard and creates a species of humor which holds its charm even for present-day readers.

Select four or five sentences from "Early Life in Manhattan" or "The Devil and Tom Walker" that represent Irving's distinctive type of humor. In each case point out the words and phrases which help create the ironic, tongue-in-cheek effect. Then consider whether or not Irving abandons this technique in "The Camp of the Wild Horse."

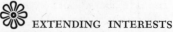 WORDS!

As you have learned, Washington Irving's humor is based partially on the use of many rather difficult words, like the adjectives from "The Devil and Tom Walker" in the first column below. Copy each of these adjectives on a sheet of paper. Then choose antonyms from the second column and write them after the correct adjectives.

parsimonious	simple
propitiatory	rare
ostentatious	squeamish
inflexible	begrimed
superfluous	pliant
ill-gotten	antagonistic
melancholy	false
authentic	generous
testy	necessary
prevalent	joyous
	patient
	honest
	expedient

EXTENDING INTERESTS

"Rip Van Winkle," "The Spectre Bridegroom," and "The Legend of Sleepy Hollow" are other romantic tales by Washington Irving. You will find them in *The Sketch Book.* Irving also wrote excellent supernatural tales which appear in *The Bold Dragoon and Other Ghostly Tales,* edited by A. C. Moore. Read one of these stories by Irving and then prepare to discuss, in class, the romantic elements it contains.

THE HUDSON RIVER SCHOOL

The Romantic Movement that inspired Irving and other authors of the Early National Period to include so much native landscape in their writings also reawakened the interest of American artists in nature. To these romantic spirits, the untamed landscape of the new United States was a fresh means of expressing nature as a revelation of God. Asher B. Durand, Thomas Cole, and other artists, now known as the Hudson River School of painters, pro-duced paintings that show broad vistas of the Hudson River region, the Catskills, and the West. "Kindred Spirits," painted by Durand in 1848, pictures Thomas Cole and William Cullen Bryant on a high rock ledge, perhaps musing upon the natural majesty that surrounds them. Highly detailed and stretching into vast distances, "Kindred Spirits" is typical of American landscape painting at its romantic best.

William Cullen Bryant 1794-1878

Born, like Irving, late in the eighteenth century, William Cullen Bryant began as a writer in the older mode, but in time learned to use the subject matter and the techniques of contemporary literary men.

In 1808 Cullen (as he was called), age thirteen, graduated from the little Cummington township school. Seated on wooden benches and hearing him read the poem he had written for the occasion, his teacher, his pastor, and his family, as Tremaine McDowell[1] suggests, must have been proud of him. For he had absorbed their ideas and expressed those ideas in verse which they greatly admired.

The Yankees of the isolated village in the hills of western Massachusetts where Cullen had been born and raised were partial to old-fashioned beliefs and ways. They admired the boy's graduation poem because it expressed the religious views of orthodox Puritanism. They had admired his recently published poem, "The Embargo," because it championed the political beliefs of the waning Federalist Party. His elders had influenced not only his religious and political attitudes but also his style of writing. When Cullen was eight his grandfather had given him a ninepenny coin for turning into rhymes part of the Bible—the gloomy Book of Job—and his father had patiently pointed out faults in versification. His father had introduced him to his own favorites among eighteenth-century English writers—Joseph Addison, Alexander Pope, and Samuel Johnson—and it was on their poetry the youngster had modeled his graduation verse. His composition, like the best poems of this trio, was written in polished heroic couplets—rhyming lines with five accents in each line. Unaware of the Romantic Movement underway in England, he wished to write poetry, as he said,

> With classic purity, unstudied ease,
> To sense instructive, pleasing to the ear,
> Correct yet flowing, elegant and clear.

For two years after his graduation Bryant prepared for college under an uncle's direction, spent a year at Williams College, studied for law, and from 1815 to 1825 practiced law. During these years he was writing poetry. Most of "Thanatopsis," perhaps his most famous poem, was written when he was seventeen, although it was not published until six years later. In 1821 he published a slim volume called simply *Poems;* containing only eight pieces, it remains a landmark in American literary history.

In 1825 Bryant left New England for New York. After editing a couple of magazines, he became associated with the *Evening Post,* a newspaper which had been founded by Alexander Hamilton. In 1829 he began a career as editor-in-chief which lasted until his death in 1878.

By the time Bryant moved to New York he had discarded his Puritan beliefs to become a Unitarian, his Federalist convictions to become a Democrat—in time a champion of the very democratic Andrew Jackson.

---

1. [George] *Tremaine McDowell*, a twentieth-century American scholar who has edited William Cullen Bryant's work.

And although he had not cast off all his habits of using old-fashioned phrasings, he had become a romantic writer.

Bryant's life and his reading had wrought the changes. As a boy he had explored the green Massachusetts hillsides. His father, a country doctor who collected herbs for his own drugs, had taught him botany; he became as he said "a passionate botanist"; and when later as a lawyer in Great Barrington he hiked through the surrounding countryside, he boasted that he could name "every tree, flower, and spire of grass" in the Berkshires.

He had more than a scientific interest in nature. Always, as he once wrote, he had found exciting "the first snowfall," "a winter daybreak over the wide wastes of snow," "the return of spring, with its flowers," thunderstorms followed by "sunshine and rainbows," the flame-colored leaves which came with autumn—pasture lands, forests, crags, streams.

One favorite eighteenth-century Scottish poet whom Bryant had known when a boy had put into his poetry perceptions and feelings something like Bryant's. James Thomson, in *The Seasons* (1726-1730), had accurately pictured British scenery, often communicating some of the enjoyment he felt when viewing it. Looking back, historians now see that Thomson was a harbinger of the romantic poets who became prominent in England during Cullen's childhood. These poets gave Nature a larger place in their writings and in their lives than Addison, Pope, and Johnson had done. William Wordsworth, who lived in the beautiful Lake District, was the chief figure in the group.

Bryant's discovery of Wordsworth in 1811 or 1812 was a thrilling experience. "The Face of Nature," he said, "of a sudden seemed to change into a strange freshness and life." Wordsworth had revealed to the young American how his experiences and feelings could be made the stuff of great poetry. Soon, like the leading Lake poet and his associates, Bryant was showing Nature vividly and movingly as a source of counsel, reverie, and delight. Also since he was picturing the American scene which he knew intimately—something practically no one had done before—he was determined to capture its unique details. He once scolded his brother for putting a skylark into a poem: "The skylark is an English bird, and an American who has never visited England has no right to be in raptures about it." Trees, flowers, a zooful of birds and animals in Bryant's poems were none of them imported. "It is his proper praise," said Ralph Waldo Emerson, "that he first and he only made known to mankind our northern landscape."

The romantic poets also taught Bryant to make his verse forms less regular. Complaining that the heroic couplet of his boyhood verses "condemned" the poet "to tinkle the same eternal tune with its fetters," he experimented with blank verse. Although by modern standards the resulting lines were still quite regular, his use of pauses in all sorts of places (but not often at line ends) made his rhythms much less singsong. Also he experimented with rhymed quatrains such as the Lake poets had adapted from popular ballad measures, and these experiments too gave him added freedom. And to express his fresh insights he abandoned much of the more formal language of the older poetry and like Wordsworth tried to approach "the real language of men."

Bryant's contribution, therefore, to the literature of the Early National Period was the picturing of previously unrecorded aspects of the New England landscape in forms and words which were novel and moving.

Thanatopsis

The word *thanatopsis* is a combination of Greek words meaning "a view of death." As you read, try to determine what attitude toward death Bryant is presenting.

To him who in the love of Nature holds
    Communion with her visible forms, she speaks
A various language; for his gayer hours
She has a voice of gladness, and a smile
And eloquence of beauty, and she glides   5
Into his darker musings, with a mild
And healing sympathy that steals away
Their sharpness ere he is aware. When thoughts
Of the last bitter hour come like a blight
Over thy spirit, and sad images   10

Of the stern agony, and shroud, and pall,
And breathless darkness, and the narrow house[1]
Make thee to shudder and grow sick at heart—
Go forth, under the open sky, and list
To Nature's teachings, while from all around—   15
Earth and her waters, and the depths of air—
Comes a still voice—
               Yet a few days, and thee
The all-beholding sun shall see no more
In all his course; nor yet in the cold ground,
Where thy pale form was laid with many tears,   20
Nor in the embrace of ocean shall exist
Thy image. Earth, that nourished thee, shall claim

1. *the narrow house,* the grave.

Thy growth, to be resolved to earth again,
And, lost each human trace, surrendering up
Thine individual being, shalt thou go   25
To mix forever with the elements,
To be a brother to the insensible rock
And to the sluggish clod which the rude swain
Turns with his share and treads upon. The oak
Shall send his roots abroad and pierce thy
    mold.   30
Yet not to thine eternal resting place
Shalt thou retire alone; nor couldst thou wish
Couch more magnificent. Thou shalt lie down
With patriarchs of the infant world—with
    kings,   34
The powerful of the earth—the wise, the good,
Fair forms, and hoary seers of ages past,
All in one mighty sepulcher. The hills
Rock-ribbed and ancient as the sun; the vales
Stretching in pensive quietness between;
The venerable woods; rivers that move   40
In majesty; and the complaining brooks
That make the meadows green; and, poured
    round all
Old Ocean's gray and melancholy waste—
Are but the solemn decorations all
Of the great tomb of man. The golden sun,   45
The planets, all the infinite host of heaven,
Are shining on the sad abodes of death
Through the still lapse of ages. All that tread
The globe are but a handful to the tribes
That slumber in its bosom. Take the wings   50
Of morning, pierce the Barcan wilderness,[2]
Or lose thyself in the continuous woods
Where rolls the Oregon,[3] and hears no sound
Save his own dashings—yet the dead are there;
And millions in those solitudes, since first   55
The flight of years began, have laid them
    down

In their last sleep—the dead reign there alone.
So shalt thou rest, and what if thou withdraw
In silence from the living, and no friend   59
Take note of thy departure? All that breathe
Will share thy destiny. The gay will laugh
When thou art gone, the solemn brood of
    care
Plod on, and each one as before will chase
His favorite phantom; yet all these shall leave
Their mirth and their employments, and shall
    come   65
And make their bed with thee. As the long
    train
Of ages glides away, the sons of men,
The youth in life's green spring, and he who
    goes
In the full strength of years, matron and maid,
The speechless babe, and the gray-headed
    man—   70
Shall one by one be gathered to thy side,
By those who in their turn shall follow them.
  So live, that when thy summons comes to
    join
The innumerable caravan which moves
To that mysterious realm, where each shall
    take   75
His chamber in the silent halls of death,
Thou go not, like the quarry slave at night,
Scourged to his dungeon, but, sustained and
    soothed
By an unfaltering trust, approach thy grave   79
Like one who wraps the drapery of his couch
About him, and lies down to pleasant dreams.

---

2. *Barcan wilderness*, the desert land of Cyrenaica (sir'i-
nā'i kə), which was formerly the ancient kingdom of Barca,
in northern Africa. 3. *the Oregon*, the old name for the
Columbia River, which flows between the states of Oregon
and Washington.

To a Whither, midst falling dew
Waterfowl While glow the heavens with the last steps of day,
         Far, through their rosy depths, dost thou pursue
             Thy solitary way?

             Vainly the fowler's eye   5
         Might mark thy distant flight to do thee wrong,
         As, darkly seen against the crimson sky,
             Thy figure floats along.

Seek'st thou the plashy brink
Of weedy lake, or marge of river wide,   10
Or where the rocking billows rise and sink
    On the chafed oceanside?

There is a Power whose care
Teaches thy way along that pathless coast—
The desert and illimitable air—   15
    Lone wandering, but not lost.

All day thy wings have fanned,
At that far height, the cold, thin atmosphere,
Yet stoop not, weary, to the welcome land,
    Though the dark night is near.   20

And soon that toil shall end;
Soon shalt thou find a summer home, and rest,
And scream among thy fellows; reeds shall bend,
    Soon, o'er thy sheltered nest.

Thou'rt gone, the abyss of heaven   25
Hath swallowed up thy form; yet, on my heart
Deeply hath sunk the lesson thou hast given,
    And shall not soon depart.

He, who, from zone to zone,
Guides through the boundless sky thy certain flight,   30
In the long way that I must tread alone,
    Will lead my steps aright.

 TO INCREASE UNDERSTANDING

1. The best way to grasp the meaning of "Thana-topsis" as a whole is to consider first the ideas developed in its various parts. (*a*) *Lines 1-17.* What does the poet suggest that man do when he is oppressed by thoughts of death? (*b*) *Lines 17-57.* What comfort does Nature offer the man facing death? (*c*) *Lines 58-72.* Why is dying unmourned not important? (*d*) *Lines 73-81.* What is important?

2. When Bryant published his volume *Poems* (1821), he added to "Thanatopsis" lines 1-17 (to "Yet a few days") and the last sixteen lines (beginning with "As the long train"). (*a*) What function does the addition at the beginning of the poem serve? (*b*) What is the purpose of the last sixteen lines?

3. Do you find the ideas expressed in "Thanatop-sis" consoling or disturbing? Explain your answer.

4. In "Thanatopsis" Bryant uses archaic words such as *thee, thou, list,* and *couldst.* Do you feel this archaic wording enhances the moral tone of the poem? Why?

5. What are the qualities of "Thanatopsis" that anticipate Bryant's later romanticism?

6. How do "Thanatopsis" and "To a Waterfowl" reflect Bryant's Puritan background?

7. (*a*) What is the theme of "To a Waterfowl"? (*b*) Do you find the same inspiration in the message of the waterfowl as Bryant did? Why or why not?

8. Prepare to read aloud to the class lines from "Thanatopsis" and "To a Waterfowl" that show Bryant's acute observation of nature.

9. How does Bryant's use of the American landscape differ from Irving's?

James Fenimore Cooper 1789-1851

James Fenimore Cooper was born five years before Bryant, six years after Irving. Until he was past thirty he lived an active life in which authorship had no part. Yet once he had taken up his pen, like Bryant and Irving he found new materials for literature in a youthful nation. And he surpassed both in national and world-wide fame.

When Fenimore was a year old, his family moved from his birthplace, Burlington, New Jersey, to the new settlement of Cooperstown, which his father had laid out on the shore of Otsego Lake in New York. Though the boy lived in a fine manor house on a thousand-acre tract, his home was surrounded by wilderness, and in many ways his was the life of a frontier boy. He learned to use the bow and arrow, to ride horseback, to fish, to shoot. He heard much about Indians who not long before had lived in the forests and had paddled canoes on the lake. He often came upon remnants of old blockhouses once used to fight the Indians; he heard reminiscences of hot skirmishes; and he encountered some members of the Oneida tribe who still camped in the woods.

At thirteen—not an unusual age for college freshmen at the time—he entered Yale. Studies were not attractive to him. Not surprisingly he was expelled during his second year for a prank; the story is that he tied a donkey to his tutor's chair. Next he was sent to sea for a year on a merchant ship, and on his return he was commissioned as a midshipman in the Navy. After three years he left the sea to marry. Since his bride did not cherish the rôle of a sailor's wife, he settled down as a gentleman farmer. During nine years he moved back and forth between Cooperstown and the Westchester home of his wife's family.

This outdoor man with his craggy tanned features was living in a newly built farmhouse in Scarsdale when, surprisingly, he turned author—surprisingly because he was a contented country squire, he had trouble writing even a letter, and he had shown no interest in creative authorship. One evening he flung aside a dull English novel and told his wife he could write a better novel himself. To the astonishment of both his wife and

Otsego Lake.

Portrait of Cooper by John Wesley Jarvis.

daughter (and perhaps even himself) he did write a novel, *Precaution,* which was published in 1820.

It is questionable that he had made good his boast, for it would be hard to find many novels duller than this one. It had English characters and settings and an English plot, and Cooper was handicapped by the fact that he knew nothing about England at first hand. The book made hardly any impression.

Instead of being discouraged, Cooper set his jaw and started another novel. (He was a hot-tempered man who over the years spent much time, energy, and money in legal battles.) Luckily, this time he hit upon a congenial subject. He had always loved history, especially that of New York State. He had frequently heard an old neighbor retell his experiences as a fighter in the New York highlands during the Revolutionary War. Another neighbor and long-time family friend, the statesman John Jay, told him about a secret agent whom he had employed to spy upon the British. Writing *The Spy* (1821), Cooper, as he said, "chose patriotism for his theme" and selected his hero "as the best illustration of his subject." The story of Harvey Birch's adventures as a secret agent during the American Revolution succeeded both in America and abroad, and launched its author upon a very successful career in fiction writing.

Cooper wrote thirty-three novels as well as volumes of social comment, naval history, and travel. Some novels, *The Pilot* (1823), for example, used his knowledge of life at sea and won him fame as an early creator of sea stories. But the best and most famous group of books he wrote derived authority from his boyhood memories of life in a frontier settlement. This was the Leatherstocking Series, so called from one of the names applied to their frontiersman hero, Natty Bumppo, one of the most memorable characters in American fiction. There are five books in the series: (1) *The Pioneers* (1823); (2) *The Last of the Mohicans* (1826); (3) *The Prairie* (1827); (4) *The Pathfinder* (1840); and (5) *The Deerslayer* (1841).[1] To read the story of Natty Bumppo from youth to old age one must read these novels not in the order of composition but, following the numbering above, in this order: 5, 2, 4, 1, 3.

The order in which the books were written shows that they were started without a plan and composed at random, sometimes after long intervals. Not until after publication did Cooper notice that he had changed the name of a character midway through a novel and that at one point he had aged his hero two years in a few paragraphs. There were other signs that the impetuous Cooper had been hasty and careless about details. His style was far from polished, and at times his characters seemed to be reading their lines instead of talking them. Also he followed other writers of the day in making the "gentlemen" in his novels stuffy—"clothes upon sticks," as James Russell Lowell put it. His "ladies" (or "females"), again in Lowell's words,

> . . . from one model don't vary,
> All sappy as maples and flat as the prairie.

Despite these faults, his books, the Leatherstocking Series in particular,

---

1. See the selection from *The Deerslayer* beginning on page 198. A guide to discussion of the complete novel will be found on page 205.

are great achievements. Cooper learned much about writing historical adventure stories from Sir Walter Scott, and he wrote with great gusto, probably because his narratives were a sort of outlet for a man of action who had turned to writing. Dealing as Scott and other romantic writers had with historical or legendary characters and happenings, Cooper, in his tales about Natty Bumppo, unfolded an epic account. Leatherstocking is clearly a product unique to America, a frontiersman whose character and actions are shaped by the forest in which he lives. The Indians, too, as Natty is fond of saying, have their own "gifts and natur' and trainin'," their codes, their ways of fighting, of treating their captives. They are firmly placed in unmistakably American settings.

Though modern readers may squirm as they read Cooper's long descriptions, the author should be credited for doing something similar to Bryant—putting into fiction our own mountains, forests, lakes, streams, and prairies. Moreover, he was a magnificent storyteller, and the stories he told, though based on history, are full of danger, hairbreadth escapes, brave deeds. Cooper is widely regarded as the first great American novelist.

View of Otsego Hall, from an early engraving.

FROM *The Deerslayer*

The events of *The Deerslayer,* from which the following selection is taken, take place between 1740 and 1745. Natty Bumppo, at this time a young man, has been reared by the Delaware Indians. He therefore has been trained in the ways of the forest and of the Indians. His closest friend is a young Delaware chief, Chingachgook, who is engaged to an Indian girl named Hist. This girl has been stolen by the Hurons and adopted into their tribe. In attempting her rescue, Deerslayer has himself been captured by the Hurons.

It was one of the common expedients of the savages, on such occasions, to put the nerves of their victims to the severest proofs. On the other hand, it was a matter of Indian pride to betray no yielding to terror or pain, but for the prisoner to provoke his enemies to such acts of violence as would soonest produce death. Many a warrior had been known to bring his own sufferings to a more speedy termination, by taunting reproaches and reviling language, when he found that his physical system was giving way under the agony of sufferings produced by a hellish ingenuity that might well eclipse all that has been said of the infernal devices of religious persecution. This happy expedient of taking refuge from the ferocity of his foes in their passions was denied Deerslayer, however, by his peculiar notions of the duty of a white man; and he had stoutly made up his mind to endure everything in preference to disgracing his color.

No sooner did the young men understand that they were at liberty to commence than some of the boldest and most forward among them sprang into the arena, tomahawk in hand. Here they prepared to throw that dangerous weapon, the object being to strike the tree as near as possible to the victim's head without absolutely hitting him. This was so hazardous an experiment that none but those who were known to be exceedingly expert with the weapon were allowed to enter the lists[1] at all, lest an early death might interfere

with the expected entertainment. In the truest hands, it was seldom that the captive escaped injury in these trials; and it often happened that death followed even when the blow was not premeditated. In the particular case of our hero, Rivenoak[2] and the older warriors were apprehensive that the example of the Panther's fate[3] might prove a motive with some fiery spirit suddenly to sacrifice his conqueror, when the temptation of effecting it in precisely the same manner, and possibly with the identical weapon with which the warrior had fallen, offered. This circumstance, of itself, rendered the ordeal of the tomahawk doubly critical for the Deerslayer.

It would seem, however, that all who now entered what we shall call the lists were more disposed to exhibit their own dexterity than to resent the deaths of their comrades. Each prepared himself for the trial with the feelings of rivalry rather than with the desire for vengeance; and for the first few minutes the prisoner had little more connection with the result than grew out of the interest that necessarily attached itself to a living target. The young men were eager, instead of being fierce, and Rivenoak thought he still saw signs of being able to save the life of the captive when the vanity of the young men had been gratified, always admitting that it was not sacrificed to the delicate experiments that were about to be made.

The first youth who presented himself for the trial was called the Raven, having as yet had no opportunity of obtaining a more warlike sobriquet. He was remarkable for high pretension rather than for skill or exploits, and those who knew his character thought the captive in imminent danger when he took his stand and poised the tomahawk. Nevertheless, the young man was good-natured, and no thought was uppermost in his mind other than the desire to make a better cast than any of his fellows. Deerslayer got an inkling of this warrior's want of reputation by the injunc-

1. *enter the lists*, join in the contest. This is a phrase borrowed from the tournaments of the Middle Ages.   2. *Rivenoak* (rĭv′ən ōk′), a Huron chief who wanted Deerslayer to join his tribe.   3. *the Panther's fate.* Deerslayer had killed the Panther, a Huron warrior, with his tomahawk.

tions that he had received from the seniors, who, indeed, would have objected to his appearing in the arena at all but for an influence derived from his father, an aged warrior of great merit, who was then in the lodges of the tribe.[4] Still, our hero maintained an appearance of self-possession. He had made up his mind that his hour was come, and it would have been a mercy, instead of a calamity, to fall by the unsteadiness of the first hand that was raised against him.

After a suitable number of flourishes and gesticulations that promised much more than he could perform, the Raven let the tomahawk quit his hand. The weapon whirled through the air with the usual evolutions, cut a chip from the sapling to which the prisoner was bound, within a few inches of his cheek, and stuck in a large oak that grew several yards behind him. This was decidedly a bad effort, and a common sneer proclaimed as much, to the great mortification of the young man. On the other hand, there was a general but suppressed murmur of admiration at the steadiness with which the captive stood the trial. The head was the only part he could move, and this had been purposely left free, that the tormentors might have the amusement, and the tormented endure the shame, of dodging and otherwise attempting to avoid the blows. Deerslayer disappointed these hopes by a command of nerve that rendered his whole body as immovable as the tree to which he was bound. Nor did he even adopt the natural and usual expedient of shutting his eyes, the firmest and oldest warrior of the red men never having more disdainfully denied himself this advantage, under similar circumstances.

The Raven had no sooner made his unsuccessful and puerile effort than he was succeeded by Le Daim-Mose,[5] or the Moose, a middle-aged warrior, who was particularly skillful in the use of the tomahawk, and from whose attempt the spectators confidently looked for gratification. This man had none of the good nature of the Raven, but he would gladly have sacrificed the captive to his hatred of the palefaces generally, were it not for the greater interest he felt in his own success as one particularly skillful in the use of this weapon. He took his stand quietly but with an air of confidence, poised his little ax but a single instant, advanced a foot with a quick motion, and threw. Deerslayer saw the keen instrument whirling toward him, and believed all was over; still he was not touched. The tomahawk had actually bound the head of the captive to the tree by carrying before it some of his hair, having buried itself deep beneath the soft bark. A general yell expressed the delight of the spectators, and the Moose felt his heart soften a little toward the prisoner, whose steadiness of nerve alone enabled him to give this evidence of his consummate skill.

Le Daim-Mose was succeeded by the Bounding Boy, or Le Garçon qui Bondi,[6] who came leaping into the circle like a hound or a goat at play. This was one of those elastic youths whose muscles seemed always in motion, and who either affected or who from habit was actually unable to move in any other manner than by showing the antics just mentioned. Nevertheless he was both brave and skillful, and had gained the respect of his people by deeds in war as well as success in the hunts. A far nobler name would long since have fallen to his share had not a Frenchman of rank inadvertently given him this sobriquet, which he religiously preserved as coming from his great father who lived beyond the wide salt lake. The Bounding Boy skipped about in front of the captive, menacing him with his tomahawk, now on one side and now on another and then again in front, in the vain hope of being able to extort some sign of fear by this parade of danger. At length Deerslayer's patience became exhausted by all this mummery, and he spoke for the first time since the trial had actually commenced.

"Throw away, Huron!" he cried, "or your tomahawk will forget its arr'nd.[7] Why do you

---

4. *in the lodges of the tribe*, at home with the main body of Hurons. The Indians who were torturing Deerslayer belonged to a group who had come within the English boundaries for hunting and fishing. 5. *Le Daim-Mose* (lə daṅ'mōz'), a French name meaning "the moose-deer." The Hurons made friends with the French, and many of them were called by names the French had given them. 6. *Le Garçon qui Bondi* (lə gär sōṅ' kē bōṅ di'), French for "the boy who bounds." 7. *arr'nd*, errand.

keep loping about like a fa'an[8] that's showing its dam how well it can skip, when you're a warrior grown, yourself, and a warrior grown defies you and all your silly antics? Throw, or the Huron gals will laugh in your face."

Although not intended to produce such an effect, the last words aroused the "Bounding" warrior to fury. The same nervous excitability which rendered him so active in his person made it difficult to repress his feelings, and the words were scarcely past the lips of the speaker than the tomahawk left the hand of the Indian. Nor was it cast without good will, and a fierce determination to slay. Had the intention been less deadly, the danger might have been greater. The aim was uncertain, and the weapon glanced near the cheek of the captive, slightly cutting the shoulder in its evolutions. This was the first instance in which any other object than that of terrifying the prisoner and of displaying skill had been manifested; and the Bounding Boy was immediately led from the arena and was warmly rebuked for his intemperate haste, which had come so near defeating all the hopes of the band.

To this irritable person succeeded several other young warriors, who not only hurled the tomahawk but who cast the knife, a far more dangerous experiment, with reckless indifference; yet they always manifested a skill that prevented any injury to the captive. Several times Deerslayer was grazed, but in no instance did he receive what might be termed a wound. The unflinching firmness with which he faced his assailants, more especially in the sort of rally with which this trial terminated, excited a profound respect in the spectators; and when the chiefs announced that the prisoner had well withstood the trials of the knife and the tomahawk, there was not a single individual in the band who really felt any hostility toward him, with the exception of Sumach[9] and the Bounding Boy. These two discontented spirits got together, it is true, feeding each other's ire; but, as yet, their malignant feelings were confined very much to themselves, though there existed the danger that the others, ere long, could not fail to be excited by their own efforts into that demoniacal state which usually accompanied all similar scenes among the red men.

Rivenoak now told his people that the paleface had proved himself to be a man. He might live with the Delawares, but he had not been made woman with that tribe. He wished to know whether it was the desire of the Hurons to proceed any further. Even the gentlest of the females, however, had received too much satisfaction in the late trials to forego their expectations of a gratifying exhibition; and there was but one voice[10] in the request to proceed. The politic chief, who had some such desire to receive so celebrated a hunter into his tribe as a European minister had to devise a new and available means of taxation, sought every plausible means of arresting the trial in season; for he well knew if permitted to go far enough to arouse the more ferocious passions of the tormentors, it would be as easy to dam the waters of the great lakes of his own region as to attempt to arrest them in their bloody career. He therefore called four or five of the best marksmen to him and bid them put the captive to the proof of the rifle, while, at the same time, he cautioned them touching the necessity of their maintaining their own credit by the closest attention to the manner of exhibiting their skill.

When Deerslayer saw the chosen warriors step into the circle with their arms prepared for service, he felt some such relief as the miserable sufferer who had long endured the agonies of disease feels at the certain approach of death. Any trifling variance in the aim of this formidable weapon would prove fatal, since the head being the target, or rather the point it was desired to graze without injury, an inch or two of difference in the line of projection must at once determine the question of life or death.

In the torture by the rifle there was none of the latitude permitted that appeared in the case of even Gessler's apple,[11] a hair's-breadth

---

8. *fa'an*, fawn. 9. *with the exception of Sumach* (sü′mak or shü′mak). Sumach was the sister of the Panther. 10. *there was but one voice*, all of the Hurons spoke together in agreement. 11. *in the case of even Gessler's apple*. According to legend, Gessler was the Austrian tyrant who forced William Tell to shoot the apple from the head of his little son.

being, in fact, the utmost limits that an expert marksman would allow himself on an occasion like this. Victims were frequently shot through the head by too eager or unskillful hands; and it often occurred that, exasperated by the fortitude and taunts of the prisoner, death was dealt intentionally in a moment of ungovernable irritation. All this Deerslayer well knew, for it was in relating the traditions of such scenes, as well as of the battles and victories of their people, that the old men beguiled the long winter evenings in their cabins. He now fully expected the end of his career, and experienced a sort of melancholy pleasure in the idea that he was to fall by a weapon as much beloved as the rifle. . . .

The warriors prepared to exhibit their skill, as there was a double object in view: that of putting the constancy of the captive to the proof, and that of showing how steady were the hands of the marksmen under circumstances of excitement. The distance was small, and, in one sense, safe. But in diminishing the distance taken by the tormentors, the trial to the nerves of the captive was essentially increased. The face of Deerslayer, indeed, was just removed sufficiently from the ends of the guns to escape the effects of the flash, and his steady eye was enabled to look directly into their muzzles, as it might be, in anticipation of the fatal messenger that was to issue from each. The cunning Hurons well knew this fact; and scarce one leveled his piece without first causing it to point as near as possible at the forehead of the prisoner, in the hope that his fortitude would fail him, and that the band would enjoy the triumph of seeing a victim quail under their ingenious cruelty. Nevertheless, each of the competitors was still careful not to injure, the disgrace of striking prematurely being second only to that of failing altogether in attaining the object.

Shot after shot was made, all the bullets coming in close proximity to the Deerslayer's head, without touching it. Still, no one could detect even the twitching of a muscle on the part of the captive, or the slightest winking of an eye. This indomitable resolution, which so much exceeded everything of its kind that any present had before witnessed, might be referred to three distinct causes. The first was resignation to his fate, blended with natural steadiness of deportment, for our hero had calmly made up his mind that he must die, and preferred this mode to any other; the second was his great familiarity with this particular weapon, which deprived it of all the terror that is usually connected with the mere form of the danger; and the third was this familiarity carried out in practice, to a degree so nice as to enable the intended victim to tell, within an inch, the precise spot where each bullet must strike, for he calculated its range by looking in at the bore of the piece. So exact was Deerslayer's estimation of the line of fire that his pride finally got the better of his resignation, and, when five or six had discharged their bullets into the trees, he could not refrain from expressing his contempt.

"You may call this shooting, Mingos,"[12] he exclaimed, "but we've squaws among the Delawares, and I have known Dutch gals on the Mohawk, that could outdo your greatest indivors. Ondo these arms of mine; put a rifle into my hands; and I'll pin the thinnest war lock in your party to any tree you can show me, and this at a hundred yards—aye, or at two hundred, if the object can be seen—nineteen shots in twenty—or, for that matter, twenty in twenty, if the piece is creditable and trusty!"

A low, menacing murmur followed this cool taunt; the ire of the warriors kindled at listening to such a reproach from one who so far disdained their efforts as to refuse even to wink when a rifle was discharged as near his face as could be done without burning it. Rivenoak perceived that the moment was critical; and, still retaining his hope of adopting so noted a hunter into his tribe, the politic old chief interposed in time, probably, to prevent an immediate resort to that portion of the torture which must necessarily have produced death, through extreme bodily suffering if in no other manner. Moving into the center of the irritated group, he addressed them with his usual wily logic and plausible manner, at

12. *Mingos* (ming′gōz), a name scornfully applied by the Delawares to their enemies.

once suppressing the fierce movement that had commenced.

"I see how it is," he said. "We have been like the palefaces when they fasten their doors at night, out of fear of the red man. They use so many bars that the fire comes and burns them before they can get out. We have bound the Deerslayer too tight; the thongs keep his limbs from shaking, and his eyes from shutting. Loosen him; let us see what his own body is really made of."

It is often the case when we are thwarted in a cherished scheme that any expedient, however unlikely to succeed, is gladly resorted to, in preference to a total abandonment of the project. So it was with the Hurons. The proposal of the chief found instant favor; and several hands were immediately at work cutting and tearing the ropes of bark from the body of our hero. In half a minute Deerslayer stood free from bonds. Some time was necessary that he should recover the use of his limbs, the circulation of the blood having been checked by the tightness of the ligatures; and this was accorded to him by the politic Rivenoak under the pretense that his body would be more likely to submit to apprehension if its true tone were restored, though really with a view to give time to the fierce passions which had been awakened in the bosoms of his young men to subside. This ruse succeeded; and Deerslayer, by rubbing his limbs, stamping his feet, and moving about, soon regained the circulation, recovering all his physical powers as if nothing had occurred to disturb them.

It is seldom men think of death in the pride of their health and strength. So it was with Deerslayer. Having been helplessly bound, and, as he had every reason to suppose, so lately on the very verge of the other world, to find himself so unexpectedly liberated, in possession of his strength, and with a full command of limb, acted on him like a sudden restoration to life, reanimating hopes that he had once absolutely abandoned. From that instant all his plans changed. In this he simply obeyed a law of nature; for while we have wished to represent our hero as being resigned to his fate, it has been far from our intention to represent him as anxious to die. From the instant that his buoyancy of feeling revived, his thoughts were keenly bent on the various projects that presented themselves as modes of evading the designs of his enemies; and he again became the quick-witted, ingenious, and determined woodsman, alive to all his own powers and resources. The change was so great that his mind resumed its elasticity; and, no longer thinking of submission, it dwelt only on the devices of the sort of warfare in which he was engaged.

As soon as Deerslayer was released, the band divided itself in a circle around him in order to hedge him in; and the desire to break down his spirit grew in them, precisely as they saw proofs of the difficulty there would be in subduing it. The honor of the band was now involved in the issue; and even the female sex lost all its sympathy with suffering, in the desire to save the reputation of the tribe. The voices of the girls, soft and melodious as nature had made them, were heard mingling with the menaces of the men; and the wrongs of Sumach suddenly assumed the character of injuries inflicted on every Huron female. Yielding to this rising tumult the men drew back a little, signifying to the females that they left the captive, for a time, in their hands, it being a common practice on such occasions for the women to endeavor to throw the victim into a rage by their taunts and revilings, and then to turn him suddenly over to the men in a state of mind that was little favorable to resisting the agony of bodily suffering. Nor was this party without the proper instruments for effecting such a purpose. Sumach had a notoriety as a scold; and one or two crones had come out with the party, most probably as the conservators of its decency and moral discipline, such things occurring in savage as well as civilized life. It is unnecessary to repeat all that ferocity and ignorance could invent for such a purpose, the only difference between this outbreaking of feminine anger and a similar scene among ourselves consisting in the figures of speech and the epithets, the Huron women calling their prisoner by the names of the lower and least respected animals that were known to themselves.

But Deerslayer's mind was too much occupied to permit him to be disturbed by the abuse of excited hags; and their rage necessarily increasing with his indifference, as his indifference increased with their rage, the furies soon rendered themselves impotent by their own excesses. Perceiving that the attempt was a complete failure, the warriors interfered to put a stop to this scene, and this so much the more because preparations were now seriously making for the commencement of the real tortures, or that which would put the fortitude of the sufferer to the test of severe bodily pain. . . . Fragments of dried wood were rapidly collected near the sapling; the splinters which it was intended to thrust into the flesh of the victim, previously to lighting, were all collected; and the thongs were already produced to bind him to the tree. . . .

Suddenly a young Indian came bounding through the Huron ranks, leaping into the very center of the circle in a way to denote the utmost confidence or a temerity bordering on foolhardiness. Five or six sentinels were still watching the lake at different and distant points; and it was the first impression of Rivenoak that one of these had come in with tidings of import. Still, the movements of the stranger were so rapid, and his war dress, which scarcely left him more drapery than an antique statue, had so little distinguishing about it, that, at the first moment, it was impossible to ascertain whether he were friend or foe. Three leaps carried this warrior to the side of Deerslayer. Not till this was effected did the stranger bestow a glance on any other object; then he turned and showed the astonished Hurons the noble brow, fine person, and eagle eye of a young warrior in the paint and panoply of a Delaware. He had a rifle in each hand, the butts of both resting on the earth, while from one dangled its proper pouch and horn. This was Killdeer,[13] which even as he looked boldly and in defiance on the crowd around him, he suffered to fall back into the hands of the proper owner. The presence of two armed men, though it was in their midst, startled the Hurons. Their rifles were scattered about against the different trees and their only weapons were their knives and tomahawks. Still, they had too much self-possession to betray fear. It was little likely that so small a force would assail so strong a band; and each man expected some extraordinary proposition to succeed so decisive a step. The stranger did not seem disposed to disappoint them; he prepared to speak.

"Hurons," he said, "this earth is very big. The great lakes are big, too; there is room beyond them for the Iroquois; there is room for the Delawares on this side. I am Chingachgook, the son of Uncas, the kinsman of Tamenund. That paleface is my friend. My heart was heavy when I missed him. Come, let us say farewell, and go on our path."

"Hurons, this is your mortal enemy, the Great Serpent[14] of them you hate!" cried Briarthorn.[15] "If he escape, blood will be in your moccasin prints from this spot to the Canadas.[16] I am *all* Huron."[17]

As the last words were uttered, the traitor cast his knife at the naked breast of the Delaware. With a quick movement Chingachgook avoided the blow, the dangerous weapon burying its point in a pine. At the next instant a similar weapon glanced from the hand of the Serpent, and quivered in the recreant's heart. A minute had scarcely elapsed from the moment in which Chingachgook bounded into the circle, and that in which Briarthorn fell, like a dog, dead in his tracks. The rapidity of events prevented the Hurons from acting; but this catastrophe permitted no further delay. A common exclamation followed, and the whole party was in motion. At this instant a sound unusual to the woods was heard, and every Huron, male and female, paused to listen with ears erect and faces filled with expectation. The sound was regular and heavy, as if the earth were struck with beetles. Objects became visible among the trees of the background, and a body of troops was seen advancing with measured tread. They came upon the charge, the scarlet of the King's livery shin-

13. *Killdeer*, Deerslayer's rifle. 14. *the Great Serpent*, Chingachgook. He was so called for his wisdom, cunning, and prudence. 15. *Briarthorn*, a Delaware warrior, traitor to his tribe, who had joined the Hurons. 16. *the Canadas*, Canada. 17. *I am all Huron*. Briarthorn, the traitor, is asserting that he is more loyal than are the Hurons themselves.

ing among the bright green foliage of the forest.

The scene that followed is not easily described. It was one in which wild confusion, despair, and frenzied efforts were so blended as to destroy the unity and distinctness of the action. A general yell burst from the enclosed Hurons; it was succeeded by the hearty cheers of England. Still, not a musket or rifle was fired, though that steady, measured tramp continued, and the bayonet was seen gleaming in advance of a line that counted nearly sixty men. The Hurons were taken at a fearful disadvantage. On three sides was the water, while their formidable and trained foes cut them off from flight on the fourth. Each warrior rushed for his arms, and then all on the point, man, woman, and child, eagerly sought cover. In this scene of confusion and dismay, however, nothing could surpass the discretion and coolness of Deerslayer. He threw himself on a flank of the retiring Hurons, who were inclining off toward the southern margin of the point, in the hope of escaping through the water. Deerslayer watched his opportunity, and finding two of his recent tormentors in range, his rifle first broke the silence of the terrific scene. The bullet brought down both at one discharge. This drew a general fire from the Hurons, and the rifle and war cry of the Serpent were heard in the clamor. Still the trained men returned no answering volley, if we except the short, prompt word of authority, and that heavy, measured, and menacing tread. Presently, however, the shrieks, groans, and denunciations that usually accompany the use of the bayonet followed. That terrible and deadly weapon was glutted in vengeance. The scene that succeeded was one of those of which so many have occurred in our own times, in which neither age nor sex forms an exemption to the lot of a savage warfare.

 TO INCREASE UNDERSTANDING

1. Critics consider Cooper the first great American novelist. (*a*) On what qualities of Cooper's work do they base this judgment? (*b*) Give examples from the selection that illustrate some of these characteristics. (*c*) What romantic qualities does the selection reveal?

2. Cooper's phraseology may seem old-fashioned, even quaint, to the modern reader. But this stylistic fault does not diminish the excitement Cooper creates in his novels. One reason for this is his organization—the arrangement of events by a born storyteller. (*a*) Examine the selection for old-fashioned phraseology such as "our hero" or "female sex." (*b*) Explain how Cooper arranged his plot to create suspense.

3. Examine Cooper's portrayal of Deerslayer. (*a*) What methods does Cooper use to characterize Deerslayer? (*b*) How do the attitudes of Rivenoak, the Moose, and the Bounding Boy reinforce Cooper's characterization of Deerslayer? (Rereading the "Better Reading" article on page 47 will help you answer these questions.)

4. In your opinion, are the events of the story believable? Explain your answer.

5. Does Deerslayer represent the *true* or the *ideal* frontiersman? Justify your answer.

 WORDS!

In *The Deerslayer* Cooper writes: "The first youth who presented himself for the trial was called the Raven, having as yet had no opportunity of obtaining a more warlike *sobriquet*." A sobriquet (so′brə kā) is a secondary name which is so descriptive of a person (or a place or a thing) that it identifies him as effectively as his primary or proper name.

1. Referring to an unabridged dictionary, determine the origin of the word *sobriquet*. What was its original meaning?

2. List the various sobriquets which Cooper employs in the selection from *The Deerslayer*. In what ways are they effective?

Sobriquets are not confined to fiction. You frequently meet them in other context. For example, you may have a fanciful nickname or call a friend by his. The sportscaster you heard during the World Series may have called the baseball a "pill." You may have seen a cartoon picturing the United States as "Uncle Sam," a New Mexico license plate boasting the "Land of Enchantment," or a travel poster proclaiming Rome as the "Eternal City."

1. Substitute the primary name for each sobriquet listed below.

2. Select one sobriquet and explain its effectiveness.

paleface	Old Glory
Deerslayer	Bard of Avon
redcoat	iron horse
John Bull	Jolly Roger
alma mater	staff of life

DISCUSSION GUIDE

The Deerslayer, by James Fenimore Cooper

In discussing The Deerslayer *emphasis should be focused primarily on Cooper's storytelling genius, his creation in Deerslayer of an epic American figure, and his romanticism.*

SUSPENSE. *In its several plot strands, The Deerslayer anticipates three types of novel widely popular today: the detective story, the love story, and the adventure story.*

What elements of the detective story do you find? How is the mystery unraveled?

Trace the love stories of Hist and of Judith. Explain the relationship between the love stories and the adventure strand of the novel. From a practical viewpoint in the Leatherstocking Tales, what complications would have arisen had Deerslayer accepted Judith's proposal? (Remember the sequence in which these novels were written.) Is Deerslayer's rejection of Judith in character? Why, or why not?

In narrating adventure Cooper employs several techniques to develop suspense and hold the reader's interest:

1. *He arranges episodes in an order of increasing tension.* Discuss the important adventure sequences in the novel and explain how each further complicates the action.

2. *He gains variety in handling adventure by basing episodes on four aspects of danger: discovering the nature of danger, going into danger, fighting danger, and escaping danger.* Give examples of each of these.

3. *He makes the outcome important to the reader by treating of serious matters.* Explain how international affairs enter the novel. In what instances does life or death hang on a venture?

4. *He creates reality and a consequent involvement of the reader by use of detail.* Select a particular incident and explain how Cooper's use of specific detail makes it come alive.

Which of the plot strands—mystery, romance, or adventure—plays the largest part? Explain.

CHARACTERIZATION. *In his preface to the novel Cooper states that in Deerslayer he wishes to portray "the highest principles of civilization as they are exhibited in the uneducated" and "all of savage life that is not incompatible with...great rules of conduct."*

Summarize Deerslayer's traits. What physical characteristics does he possess? Are these physical characteristics or moral traits emphasized? In what ways does Deerslayer embody "the highest principles of civilization"? How, in this character, is "savage life" reconciled with the "great rules of conduct"? How does Cooper account for high moral principles in one raised by the Delawares? Does Natty's character develop during the course of the novel?

Cooper further explains in the preface that in order to make Deerslayer a believable and sympathetic character he has mixed with his ideal characteristics "traits derived from the prejudices, tastes, and even weaknesses of his [Cooper's] youth." In your opinion does Cooper succeed in his attempt to make Deerslayer real rather than ideal? In discussing this question consider: (a) Deerslayer's moralizing in talks with Judith; (b) his treatment of his enemies; (c) his return from furlough; (d) his behavior in face of torture; (e) his rejection of Judith.

Cooper endows Hutter and March with common traits that contrast strikingly with Deerslayer's. What are those traits? Why does Natty disapprove of their desire for scalps but accept it in Chingachgook? Is the conflict between Deerslayer and the frontiersmen primarily physical, emotional, or moral?

Cooper contrasts the Delawares and the Hurons. Cite incidents that dramatize this contrast.

What rôles do the frontiersmen and Chingachgook play in furthering the reader's sympathetic reaction to Deerslayer?

COOPER'S ROMANTICISM. *In* The Deerslayer *and the other Leatherstocking Tales, Cooper gave to his countrymen an American equivalent of Scott's romantic novels.*

What is romantic about Cooper's handling of action in *The Deerslayer?* Consider the various plot strands, the suspense, the ending.

Why is Deerslayer considered a romantic character? Can Chingachgook be regarded as a romantic figure? Explain your answer.

What is Deerslayer's attitude toward nature? How does it reflect Cooper's romanticism?

Summarize the elements of setting (time and place), plot, character, theme, and tone that make *The Deerslayer* a romantic novel.

Edgar Allan Poe 1809-1849

Unlike Irving, Bryant, and Cooper, Poe was born in the nineteenth century. But his work fell in the same period as theirs: his first book appeared in 1827, less than a decade after Irving's *Sketch Book*, Bryant's *Poems*, and Cooper's *Spy*. And he died before any of the trio did.

Edgar Poe was born in Boston on January 19, 1809. When his mother, an actress herself and the widow of an actor, died in Richmond, Virginia, in 1811, wealthy Mrs. Allan of that city took the boy into her home and bestowed upon him his second name. Abroad with Mrs. Allan and her husband from 1815 to 1820, Edgar attended English schools. Back in Virginia he studied in a Richmond academy and under private tutors. A fine athlete, handsome, winning, intelligent, talented as a flutist and writer of verses, he was doted upon and spoiled by the childless Allans. This pampering, the constant changes of his earliest years with wandering actors, his uncertain status in the Allan home (he never was adopted), all have been suggested as unfortunate influences upon his sensitive, nervous, and explosive temperament. His make-up played a part in shaping an unhappy life.

Entering the University of Virginia at seventeen, Poe did well in classes. As the foster son of one of the state's wealthiest men, though, he took up with some of his school's high-stepping, aristocratic students. He drank —and for this tense youth even a little drink was disastrous; he played cards recklessly; he piled up formidable "debts of honor." Allan sternly refused to pay such debts, withdrew Edgar from the university, and set him to work in the family firm. The boy promptly ran away—to Boston.

Although the break between Edgar and his foster father was partially mended for a few years, the old relationship had been destroyed. Poe served for a time in the army. His foster father secured his admission to West Point; but a disciplined military life was not the career for one so proud and hot-tempered, and he was soon expelled. The death of Mrs. Allan, who had never ceased to love her erratic but brilliant foster son, led ultimately to the final break in 1832 between Edgar and Mr. Allan.

Edgar was forced to try to make a living with his pen. In the preceding five years he had published three volumes of poetry, but they had made very little money. Now he turned first to writing tales, and, after some success, to work as an editor, in those days a hard means of earning a livelihood for even the steadiest of men. In 1836 he married his cousin, fragile, thirteen-year-old Virginia Clemm. She was constantly ill, and, until her death in 1847, Poe worried about her health and the medical bills. Over the years his life followed a pattern: again and again he made a good start and did well for some time. Then his erratic temperament, his poverty, and his frustrations caused him to lose control of himself, perhaps to turn to drink. He resigned or was discharged from his position and had to start anew. He was in a depressed mood, when late in September 1849, he stopped in Baltimore during a trip. Some days later he was found in a bar-room, battered and semiconscious, and was taken to a hospital. He died there October 7.

Poe's harassing experiences led many in his time and later to connect his life with the strangeness and terror characterizing many of his poems and tales. His appearance encouraged this: his slender dark-clad figure, his abundant black hair, his nobly proportioned forehead, his luminous eyes, and his twisted mouth gave him the look of one of his own unworldly, harried heroes. And like every other author he did make use of his experiences.

But more important than personal experiences, he himself claimed when he discussed his writing, was craftsmanship—artistry. Poe had a wonderfully logical mind. It enabled him to analyze brilliantly literary works in magazines he edited and to win a name as one of the best critics of his day.

Poe's logical mind also enabled him to hit upon a sure-fire formula for writing tales. The chief aim of a tale writer, he reasoned, should be to create an effect upon the reader's mind and feelings. The writer, therefore, should start by deciding what effect he wanted to create and then should make every happening and word help achieve it. Two kinds of stories, the detective story and the supernatural tale, which Poe wrote according to this formula, were chiefly responsible for his fame.

Poe really was the inventor of the detective story, which he called the "ratiocinative" tale. Here believing the effect intended was "to perplex the reader and whet his desire for elucidation," he originated two devices useful to this day. One might be called "the device of the baffled friend": he gave his brilliant detective a companion not good at solutions and had him tell the story. Viewing the happenings through this narrator's eyes, the reader shares his growing puzzlement. Poe used his second device at the tale's end: he had the detective disclose his surprising solution and then "elucidate" step by step the reasoning which led to it. "The Purloined Letter" (page 208) demonstrates Poe's use of these two devices in a detective story.

Poe's supernatural tales were more clearly related to the Romantic Movement. Everywhere "Gothic stories" emphasizing the weird and chilling readers' spines were popular. Having studied magazines, Poe knew this. He surpassed contemporaneous writers by starting with the effect—terror—in mind, then devising incidents and ordering them so they mounted to a frightening climax. He showed, reacting to these incidents, a char-

The cottage at Fordham, N. Y., where Poe lived his last three years.

acter or a group of characters with whom readers identified themselves, whose increasing horror they shared. Consciously, too, he carefully chose words with emotional freightings which helped develop his effect. "The Masque of the Red Death" (page 218) shows Poe's short-story formula in a supernatural tale.

Poe's interest in writing poetry was lifelong. Until the year of his death he found time between writing stories and critical articles to compose poems. His first consideration was, "Of the innumerable effects, or impressions, ... what one shall I ... select?" Believing as other romantic poets did that beauty was (as he said) "the essence of the poem," he considered what emotion was associated with it. Questioning the *tone* of beauty's "highest manifestation," he concluded: "... all experience has shown that this tone is one of *sadness*. Beauty of whatever kind, in its supreme development, invariably excited the sensitive soul to tears. Melancholy is thus the most legitimate of all the poetic tones." Poe therefore "looked within" himself for incidents or details, he chose words for their suggestive powers and, with his effect in mind, arranged them in musical patterns. The finest creations, he believed, saddened the reader in part because they hinted meanings which no earthling could formulate. Only a supernatural being such as Poe's Israfel (page 222) could convey the meanings suggested by the poet's beautiful, musical, and sad songs.

The Purloined Letter

Nil sapientiae odiosius acumine nimio.
—Seneca[1]

At Paris, just after dark one gusty evening in the autumn of 18–, I was enjoying the twofold luxury of meditation and a meerschaum, in company with my friend C. Auguste Dupin, in his little back library, or book closet, *au troisième*,[2] No. 33 Rue Dunôt,[3] Faubourg St. Germain.[4] For one hour at least we had maintained a profound silence; while each, to any casual observer, might have seemed intently and exclusively occupied with curling eddies of smoke that oppressed the atmosphere of the chamber. For myself, however, I was mentally discussing certain topics which had formed matter for conversation between us at an earlier period of the evening; I mean the affair of the Rue Morgue and the mystery attending the murder of Marie Rogêt.[5] I looked upon it, therefore, as something of a coincidence, when the door of our apartment was thrown open and admitted our old acquaintance, Monsieur G—, the Prefect of the Parisian police.[6]

We gave him a hearty welcome; for there was nearly half as much of the entertaining as of the contemptible about the man, and we had not seen him for several years. We had been sitting in the dark, and Dupin now arose for the purpose of lighting a lamp. But he sat down again, without doing so, upon G—'s saying that he had called to ask the opinion of my friend about some official business which had occasioned a great deal of trouble.

"If it is any point requiring reflection," observed Dupin, as he forbore to enkindle the

1. "*Nil sapientiae ... nimio*," nothing is so odious to wisdom as too great shrewdness. Seneca (sen′ə kə), the author of this saying, was a Roman philosopher who lived at about the time of Christ.   2. *au troisième* (ō trwä′zē yem), on the third floor. Actually this was the fourth floor, as the French begin their count above the ground floor.   3. *No. 33 Rue Dunôt* (rü′ dy nō′). This is the street address. *Rue* is the French word for "street."   4. *Faubourg St. Germain* (fō bür′ saN zhèr′maN′), a section of Paris.   5. *the affair of the Rue Morgue* (rü môrg′) ... *Marie Rogêt* (rō zhä′). The reference is to two of Poe's own stories, "The Murders in the Rue Morgue" and "The Mystery of Marie Rogêt."   6. *a coincidence ... the Prefect of the Parisian police.* Monsieur G— had vainly attempted to solve both the murders in the Rue Morgue and the murder of Marie Rogêt. Dupin had solved both cases.

wick, "we shall examine it to better purpose in the dark."

"That is another of your odd notions," said the Prefect, who had a fashion of calling everything "odd" that was beyond his comprehension, and thus lived amid an absolute legion of "oddities."

"Very true," said Dupin, as he supplied his visitor with a pipe and rolled toward him a comfortable chair.

"And what is the difficulty now?" I asked. "Nothing more in the assassination way, I hope?"

"Oh, no; nothing of that nature. The fact is, the business is *very* simple indeed, and I make no doubt that we can manage it sufficiently well ourselves; but then I thought Dupin would like to hear the details of it, because it is so excessively *odd*."

"Simple and odd," said Dupin.

"Why, yes; and not exactly that, either. The fact is, we have all been a good deal puzzled because the affair *is* so simple, and yet baffles us altogether."

"Perhaps it is the very simplicity of the thing which puts you at fault," said my friend.

"What nonsense you *do* talk!" replied the Prefect, laughing heartily.

"Perhaps the mystery is a little *too* plain," said Dupin.

"Oh, good heavens! who ever heard of such an idea?"

"A little *too* self-evident."

"Ha! ha! ha!—ha! ha! ha!—ho! ho! ho!" roared our visitor, profoundly amused. "Oh, Dupin, you will be the death of me yet!"

"And what, after all, *is* the matter on hand?" I asked.

"Why, I will tell you," replied the Prefect, as he gave a long, steady, and contemplative puff, and settled himself in his chair. "I will tell you in a few words; but, before I begin, let me caution you that this is an affair demanding the greatest secrecy, and that I should most probably lose the position I now hold were it known that I confided it to anyone."

"Proceed," said I.

"Or not," said Dupin.

"Well, then. I have received personal information from a very high quarter that a certain document of the last importance has been purloined from the royal apartments. The individual who purloined it is known. This beyond a doubt; he was seen to take it. It is known, also, that it still remains in his possession."

"How is this known?" asked Dupin.

"It is clearly inferred," replied the Prefect, "from the nature of the document, and from the nonappearance of certain results which would at once arise from its passing *out* of the robber's possession; that is to say, from his employing it as he must design in the end to employ it."

"Be a little more explicit," I said.

"Well, I may venture so far as to say that the paper gives its holder a certain power in a certain quarter where such power is immensely valuable."

"Still I do not quite understand," said Dupin.

"No? Well, the disclosure of the document to a third person, who shall be nameless, would bring in question the honor of a personage of most exalted station; and this fact gives the holder of the document an ascendancy over the illustrious personage whose honor and peace are so jeopardized."

"But this ascendancy," I interposed, "would depend upon the robber's knowledge of the loser's knowledge of the robber. Who would dare—"

"The thief," said G—, "is the Minister D—,[7] who dares all things, those unbecoming, as well as those becoming, a man. The method of the theft was not less ingenious than bold. The document in question—a letter,[8] to be frank—had been received by the personage robbed while alone in the royal boudoir. During its perusal she was suddenly interrupted by the entrance of the other exalted personage, from whom especially it was her wish to conceal it. After a hurried and vain endeavor to thrust it in a drawer, she was forced to place it, open as it was, upon a table.

---

7. *the Minister D——.* This man was the head (minister) of a department in the government. 8. *a letter.* At the time of the story, letters were written on one side of a sheet of paper, which was then folded and sealed with wax. The address was written upon the outside, no envelope being used.

The address, however, was uppermost, and, the contents thus unexposed, the letter escaped notice. At this juncture enters the Minister D——. His lynx eye immediately perceives the paper, recognizes the handwriting of the address, observes the confusion of the personage addressed, and fathoms her secret. After some business transactions, hurried through in his ordinary manner, he produces a letter somewhat similar to the one in question, opens it, pretends to read it, and then places it close to the other. Again he converses for some fifteen minutes upon the public affairs. At length in taking leave he takes also from the table the letter to which he had no claim. Its rightful owner saw, but of course dared not call attention to the act, in the presence of the third personage, who stood at her elbow. The Minister decamped, leaving his own letter—one of no importance—upon the table."

"Here, then," said Dupin to me, "you have precisely what you demand to make the ascendancy complete—the robber's knowledge of the loser's knowledge of the robber."

"Yes," replied the Prefect; "and the power thus attained has, for some months past, been wielded, for political purposes, to a very dangerous extent. The personage robbed is more thoroughly convinced every day of the necessity of reclaiming her letter. But this, of course, cannot be done openly. In fact, driven to despair, she has committed the matter to me."

"Than whom," said Dupin, amid a perfect whirlwind of smoke, "no more sagacious agent could, I suppose, be desired, or even imagined."

"You flatter me," replied the Prefect; "but it is possible that some such opinion may have been entertained."

"It is clear," said I, "as you observe, that the letter is still in possession of the Minister, since it is this possession—and not any employment of the letter—which bestows the power. With the employment the power departs."

"True," said G——; "and upon this conviction I proceeded. My first care was to make thorough search of the Minister's *hôtel*[9]; and here my chief embarrassment lay in the necessity of searching without his· knowledge. Beyond all things, I have been warned of the

danger which would result from giving him reason to suspect our design."

"But," said I, "you are quite *au fait*[10] in these investigations. The Parisian police have done this thing often before."

"Oh, yes; and for this reason I did not despair. The habits of the Minister gave me, too, a great advantage. He is frequently absent from home all night. His servants are by no means numerous. They sleep at a distance from their master's apartment, and, being chiefly Neapolitans, are readily made drunk. I have keys, as you know, with which I can open any chamber or cabinet in Paris. For three months a night has not passed, during the greater part of which I have not been engaged, personally, in ransacking the D—— *hôtel*. My honor is interested, and, to mention a great secret, the reward is enormous. So I did not abandon the search until I had become fully satisfied that the thief is a more astute man than myself. I fancy that I have investigated every nook and corner of the premises in which it is possible that the paper can be concealed."

"But is it not possible," I suggested, "that although the letter may be in possession of the Minister, as it unquestionably is, he may have concealed it elsewhere than upon his own premises?"

"This is barely possible," said Dupin. "The present peculiar condition of affairs at court, and especially of those intrigues in which D—— is known to be involved, would render the instant availability of the document—its susceptibility of being produced at a moment's notice—a point of nearly equal importance with its possession."

"Its susceptibility of being produced?" said I.

"That is to say, of being *destroyed*," said Dupin.

"True," I observed; "the paper is clearly then upon the premises. As for its being upon the person of the Minister, we may consider that as out of the question."

"Entirely," said the Prefect. "He has been twice waylaid, as if by footpads, and his per-

9. *hôtel* (ō tel′), home. *Hôtel* is the French word for "private residence." 10. *au fait* (ō fe′), expert. [French]

son rigorously searched under my own inspection."

"You might have spared yourself this trouble," said Dupin. "D——, I presume, is not altogether a fool, and, if not, must have anticipated these waylayings as a matter of course."

"Not *altogether* a fool," said G——, "but then he's a poet, which I take to be only one remove from a fool."

"True," said Dupin, after a long and thoughtful whiff from his meerschaum, "although I have been guilty of certain doggerel myself."

"Suppose you detail," said I to the Prefect, "the particulars of your search."

"Why, the fact is, we took our time, and we searched *everywhere*. I have had long experience in these affairs. I took the entire building, room by room, devoting the nights of a whole week to each. We examined, first, the furniture of each apartment. We opened every possible drawer; and I presume you know that, to a properly trained police agent, such a thing as a *secret* drawer is impossible. Any man is a dolt who permits a *secret* drawer to escape him in a search of this kind. The thing is *so* plain. There is a certain amount of bulk—of space—to be accounted for in every cabinet. Then we have accurate rules. The fiftieth part of a line could not escape us. After the cabinets we took the chairs. The cushions we probed with the fine, long needles you have seen me employ. From the tables we removed the tops."

"Why so?"

"Sometimes the top of a table, or other similarly arranged piece of furniture, is removed by the person wishing to conceal an article. Then the leg is excavated, the article deposited within the cavity, and the top replaced. The bottoms and tops of bedposts are employed in the same way."

"But could not the cavity be detected by sounding?" I asked.

"By no means, if, when the article is deposited, a sufficient wadding of cotton be placed around it. Besides, in our case we were obliged to proceed without noise."

"But you could not have removed—you could not have taken to pieces *all* articles of furniture in which it would have been possible to make a deposit in the manner you mention. A letter may be compressed in a thin spiral roll, and in this form it might be inserted into the rung of a chair, for example. You did not take to pieces all the chairs?"

"Certainly not; but we did better. We examined the rungs of every chair in the *hôtel*, and, indeed, the jointings of every description of furniture, by the aid of a most powerful microscope. Had there been any traces of recent disturbance, we should not have failed to detect it instantly. A single grain of gimlet dust, for example, would have been as obvious as an apple. Any disorder in the gluing—any unusual gaping in the joints—would have sufficed to insure detection."

"I presume you looked to the mirrors, be-

THE CONSTRUCTION OF A TALE

A skillful literary artist has constructed a tale. If wise, he has not fashioned his thoughts to accommodate his incidents; but having conceived, with deliberate care, a certain unique or single *effect* to be wrought out, he then invents such incidents—he then combines such events as may best aid him in establishing this preconceived effect. If his very initial sentence tend not to the outbringing of this effect, then he has failed in his first step. In the whole composition there should be no word written, of which the tendency, direct or indirect, is not to the one preëstablished design. And by such means, with such care and skill, a picture is at length painted which leaves in the mind of him who contemplates it with a kindred art, a sense of the fullest satisfaction. The idea of the tale has been presented unblemished, because undisturbed; and this is an end unattainable by the novel. Undue brevity is just as exceptionable here as in the poem, but undue length is yet more to be avoided.

From Poe's review
of Hawthorne's *Twice-Told Tales*,
in *Graham's Magazine*,
May 1842

tween the boards and the plates, and you probed the beds and the bedclothes, as well as the curtains and carpets?"

"That, of course; and when we had absolutely completed every particle of furniture in this way, then we examined the house itself. We divided its entire surface into compartments, which we numbered, so that none might be missed; then we scrutinized each individual square inch throughout the premises, including the two houses immediately adjoining, with the microscope, as before."

"The two houses adjoining!" I exclaimed. "You must have had a great deal of trouble."

"We had; but the reward offered is prodigious."

"You include the *grounds* about the houses?"

"All the grounds are paved with brick. They gave us comparatively little trouble. We examined the moss between the bricks, and found it undisturbed."

"You looked among D—'s papers, of course, and into the books of the library?"

"Certainly; we opened every package and parcel. We not only opened every book, but we turned over every leaf in each volume, not contenting ourselves with a mere shake, according to the fashion of some of our police officers. We also measured the thickness of every book *cover,* with the most accurate admeasurement, and applied to each the most jealous scrutiny of the microscope. Had any of the bindings been recently meddled with, it would have been utterly impossible that the fact should have escaped observation. Some five or six volumes, just from the hands of the binder, we carefully probed, longitudinally, with the needles."

"You explored the floors beneath the carpets?"

"Beyond doubt. We removed every carpet, and examined the boards with the microscope."

"And the paper on the walls?"

"Yes."

"You looked into the cellars?"

"We did."

"Then," I said, "you have been making a miscalculation, and the letter is *not* upon the premises, as you suppose."

"I fear you are right there," said the Prefect. "And now, Dupin, what would you advise me to do?"

"To make a thorough re-search of the premises."

"That is absolutely needless," replied G—. "I am not more sure that I breathe than I am that the letter is not at the *hôtel.*"

"I have no better advice to give you," said Dupin. "You have, of course, an accurate description of the letter?"

"Oh, yes." And here the Prefect, producing a memorandum book, proceeded to read aloud a minute account of the internal, and especially of the external, appearance of the missing document. Soon after finishing the perusal of this description, he took his departure, more entirely depressed in spirits than I had ever known the good gentleman before.

In about a month afterwards he paid us another visit, and found us occupied very nearly as before. He took a pipe and a chair, and entered into some ordinary conversation. At length I said, "Well, but G—, what of the purloined letter? I presume you have at last made up your mind that there is no such thing as overreaching the Minister?"

"Confound him, say I—yes. I made the re-examination, however, as Dupin suggested—but it was all labor lost, as I knew it would be."

"How much was the reward offered, did you say?" asked Dupin.

"Why, a very great deal—a *very* liberal reward. I don't like to say how much precisely; but one thing I *will* say, that I wouldn't mind giving my individual check for fifty thousand francs[11] to anyone who could obtain me that letter. The fact is, it is becoming of more and more importance every day; and the reward has been lately doubled. If it were trebled, however, I could do no more than I have done."

"Why, yes," said Dupin, drawlingly, between the whiffs of his meerschaum, "I really —think, G—, you have not exerted yourself— to the utmost in this matter. You might—do a little more, I think, eh?"

11. *fifty thousand francs,* almost $10,000 at the time Poe wrote his story.

"How? In what way?"

"Why (puff, puff), you might (puff, puff) employ counsel in the matter, eh (puff, puff, puff)? Do you remember the story they tell of Abernethy?"[12]

"No; hang Abernethy!"

"To be sure! Hang him and welcome. But, once upon a time, a certain rich miser conceived the design of sponging upon this Abernethy for a medical opinion. Getting up, for this purpose, an ordinary conversation in a private company, he insinuated his case to the physician as that of an imaginary individual.

" 'We will suppose,' said the miser, 'that his symptoms are such and such; now, doctor, what would *you* have directed him to take?'

" 'Take!' said Abernethy, 'why, take *advice, to be sure.*' "

"But," said the Prefect, a little discomposed, "I am *perfectly* willing to take advice, and to pay for it. I would *really* give fifty thousand francs to anyone who would aid me in the matter."

"In that case," replied Dupin, opening a drawer and producing a checkbook, "you may as well fill me up a check for the amount mentioned. When you have signed it, I will hand you the letter."

I was astounded. The Prefect appeared absolutely thunderstricken. For some minutes he remained speechless and motionless, looking incredulously at my friend with open mouth and eyes that seemed starting from their sockets. Then, apparently recovering himself in some measure, he seized a pen, and after several pauses and vacant stares, finally filled up and signed a check for fifty thousand francs, and handed it across the table to Dupin. The latter examined it carefully and deposited it in his pocketbook; then, unlocking an escritoire, took thence a letter and gave it to the Prefect. This functionary grasped it in a perfect agony of joy, opened it with a trembling hand, cast a rapid glance at its contents, and then, scrambling and struggling to the door, rushed at length unceremoniously from the room and from the house.

When he had gone, my friend entered into some explanations.

"The Parisian police," he said, "are exceedingly able in their way. They are persevering, ingenious, cunning, and thoroughly versed in the knowledge which their duties seem chiefly to demand. Thus, when G— detailed to us his mode of searching the premises at the *Hôtel* D—, I felt entire confidence in his having made a satisfactory investigation—so far as his labors extended."

"So far as his labors extended?" said I.

"Yes," said Dupin. "The measures adopted were not only the best of their kind, but carried out to absolute perfection. Had the letter been deposited within the range of their search, these fellows would, beyond a question, have found it."

I merely laughed—but he seemed quite serious in all that he said.

"The measures, then," he continued, "were good in their kind, and well executed. Their defect lay in their being inapplicable to the case, and to the man. A certain set of highly ingenious resources are, with the Prefect, a sort of Procrustean bed to which he forcibly adapts his designs.[13] But he perpetually errs by being too deep or too shallow for the matter in hand; and many a schoolboy is a better reasoner than he. I knew one about eight years of age, whose success at guessing in the game of 'even and odd' attracted universal admiration. This game is simple, and is played with marbles. One player holds in his hand a number of these toys, and demands of another whether that number is even or odd. If the guess is right, the guesser wins one; if wrong, he loses one.

"The boy to whom I allude won all the marbles of the school. Of course he had some principle of guessing; and this lay in mere observation and admeasurement of the astuteness of his opponents. For example, an arrant simpleton is his opponent, and, holding up his closed hand, asks, 'Are they even or odd?' Our schoolboy replies, 'Odd,' and loses. But upon

---

12. *Abernethy* (ab′ər nē′thi *or* ab′ər neth′i), a famous but eccentric English surgeon who lived from 1764 to 1831.
13. *A certain set . . . designs.* The Procrustean bed takes its name from Procrustes (prō krus′tēz), a robber in Greek mythology, who either stretched his victims, or cut off their legs to make them fit the length of his bed. Just as Procrustes tried to make all men fit one bed, so the Prefect tried to use the same devices to solve all problems.

the second trial he wins, for he then says to himself, 'The simpleton had them even upon the first trial, and his amount of cunning is just sufficient to make him have them odd upon the second; I will therefore guess odd.' He guesses odd, and wins. Now, with a simpleton a degree above the first he would have reasoned thus: 'This fellow finds that in the first instance I guessed odd, and in the second he will propose to himself, upon the first impulse, a simple variation from even to odd, as did the first simpleton. But then a second thought will suggest that this is too simple a variation, and finally he will decide upon putting it even as before. I will therefore guess even,' He guesses even, and wins. Now, this mode of reasoning in the schoolboy, whom his fellows termed 'lucky'—what, in its last analysis, is it?"

"It is merely," I said, "an identification of the reasoner's intellect with that of his opponent."

"It is," said Dupin.

"And the identification," I said, "of the reasoner's intellect with that of his opponent's, depends, if I understand you right, upon the accuracy with which the opponent's intellect is admeasured."

"For its practical value it depends upon this," replied Dupin. "The Prefect and his cohort fail so frequently, first, by default of this identification, and secondly, by ill-admeasurement of the intellect with which they are engaged. They consider only their *own* ideas of ingenuity; and, in searching for anything hidden they advert only to the modes in which *they* would have hidden it. They are right in this much—that their own ingenuity is a faithful representative of that of *the mass*; but when the cunning of the individual is diverse in character from their own, the felon foils them, of course. This always happens when the felon's cunning is above their own, and very usually when it is below. They have no variation of principle in their investigations. What, for example, in this case of D——, has been done to vary the principle of action? What is all this boring, and probing, and sounding, and scrutinizing with the microscope, and dividing the surface of the building into reg-

istered square inches? What is it all but *the application* of the one principle or set of principles of search, principles which are based upon the one set of notions regarding human ingenuity, to which the Prefect has long been accustomed? Do you not see he has taken it for granted that *all* men proceed to conceal a letter—not exactly in a gimlet hole bored in a chair leg—but, at least in *some* out-of-the-way hole or corner? And do you not see, also, that such *recherché*[14] nooks for concealment are adapted only for ordinary occasions and would be adopted only by ordinary intellects? You will now understand why, had the purloined letter been hidden anywhere within the limits of the Prefect's examination, its discovery would have been a matter altogether beyond question. This functionary, however, has been thoroughly mystified; and the remote source of his defeat lies in the supposition that the Minister is a fool because he has acquired renown as a poet. All fools are poets; this the Prefect *feels,* and he is merely guilty of a *non distributio medii*[15] in thence inferring that all poets are fools."

"But is this really the poet?" I asked. "There are two brothers, I know; and both have attained reputation in letters. The Minister, I believe, has written learnedly on the differential calculus. He is a mathematician and no poet."

"You are mistaken; I know him well; he is both. As poet *and* mathematician he would reason well; as mere mathematician he could not have reasoned at all, and thus would have been at the mercy of the Prefect. I know him as courtier, too, and as a bold *intrigant.*[16] Such a man, I considered, could not fail to be aware of the ordinary policial modes of action. He could not have failed to anticipate—and events have proved that he did not fail to anticipate—the waylayings to which he was subjected. He must have foreseen, I reflected, the secret in-

---

14. *recherché* (re shär shä′ *or* rə shär′shä), carefully thought up; hidden. [*French*] 15. *non distributio medii* (nōn dis′tri bü′tē ō me′di ē), a Latin phrase meaning a mistake in reasoning known as the undistributed middle term. In this case it means that because the Prefect believes all fools are poets, in his mind it follows that all poets are fools. 16. *a bold intrigant* (in′tri gənt), intriguer or schemer. [*French*]

vestigations of his premises. His frequent absences from home at night, which were hailed by the Prefect as certain aids to his success, I regarded only as ruses, to afford opportunity for thorough search to the police, and thus the sooner to impress them with the conviction to which G—, in fact, did finally arrive—the conviction that the letter was not upon the premises. I felt, also, that G—'s whole train of thought would necessarily pass through the mind of the Minister. It would imperatively lead him to despise all the ordinary *nooks* of concealment. *He* could not, I reflected, be so weak as not to see that the most intricate and remote recess of his *hôtel* would be as open as his commonest closets to the eyes, to the probes, to the gimlets, and to the microscopes of the Prefect. I saw, in fine, that he would be driven, as a matter of course, to *simplicity*. You will remember, perhaps, how desperately the Prefect laughed when I suggested, upon our first interview, that it was just possible this mystery troubled him so much on account of its being so *very* self-evident."

"Yes," said I, "I remember his merriment well. I really thought he would have fallen into convulsions."

"There is a game of puzzles," continued Dupin, "which is played upon a map. One party playing requires another to find a given word—the name of town, river, state, or empire—any word, in short, upon the motley and perplexed surface of the chart. A novice in the game generally seeks to embarrass his opponents by giving them the most minutely lettered names; but the adept selects such words as stretch in large characters, from one end of the chart to the other. These, like overlarge street signs over shops, escape observation by dint of being excessively obvious. But this is a point, it appears, somewhat above or beneath the understanding of the Prefect. He never once thought it probable, or possible, that the Minister had deposited the letter immediately beneath the nose of the whole world by way of best preventing any portion of that world from perceiving it.

"But the more I reflected upon the daring, dashing, and discriminating ingenuity of the Minister—upon the fact that the document must always have been at *hand,* if he intended to use it to good purpose, and upon the decisive evidence, obtained by the Prefect, that it was not hidden within the limits of that dignitary's ordinary search—the more satisfied I became that, to conceal this letter, the Minister had resorted to the comprehensive and sagacious expedient of not attempting to conceal it at all.

"Full of these ideas, I prepared myself with a pair of green spectacles, and called one fine morning, quite by accident, at the Ministerial *hôtel.* I found D— at home, yawning, lounging, and dawdling, as usual, and pretending to be in the last extremity of ennui. He is perhaps, the most really energetic human being now alive—but that is only when nobody sees him.

"To be even with him, I complained of my weak eyes and lamented the necessity of the spectacles, under cover of which I cautiously and thoroughly surveyed the whole apartment, while seemingly intent only upon the conversation of my host.

"I paid especial attention to a large writing table near which he sat, and upon which lay confusedly some miscellaneous letters and other papers, with one or two musical instruments and a few books. Here, however, after a long and very deliberate scrutiny, I saw nothing to excite particular suspicion.

"At length my eyes, in going the circuit of the room, fell upon a trumpery filigree card rack of pasteboard, that hung, dangling by a dirty blue ribbon, from a little brass knob just beneath the middle of the mantelpiece. In this rack, which had three or four compartments, were five or six visiting cards and a solitary letter. This last was much soiled and crumpled. It was torn nearly in two, across the middle—as if a design, in the first instance, to tear it entirely up as worthless had been altered, or stayed, in the second. It had a large black seal, bearing the D— cipher[17] *very* conspicuously, and was addressed, in a diminutive female hand, to D—, the Minister himself. It was thrust carelessly, and even, as it seemed, con-

17. *black seal . . . cipher.* The seal of black sealing wax, which had been used to fasten the letter, was imprinted with the monogram (cipher) of the D—— family.

temptuously, into one of the upper divisions of the rack.

"No sooner had I glanced at this letter than I concluded it to be that of which I was in search. To be sure, it was, to all appearance, radically different from the one of which the Prefect had read us so minute a description. Here, the seal was large and black, with the D— cipher; there, it was small and red, with the ducal arms of the S— family. Here, the address, to the Minister, was diminutive and feminine; there, the superscription, to a certain royal personage, was markedly bold and decided. The size alone formed a point of correspondence. But, then, the *radicalness* of these differences, which was excessive—the dirt, the soiled and torn condition of the paper, so inconsistent with the *true,* methodical habits of D—, and so suggestive of a design to delude the beholder into an idea of the worthlessness of the document—these things, together with the hyperobtrusive situation of this document, full in the view of every visitor, were exactly in accordance with the conclusions to which I had previously arrived.

"I protracted my visit as long as possible, and while I maintained a most animated discussion with the Minister, upon a topic which I knew well had never failed to interest and excite him, I kept my attention really riveted upon the letter. In this examination, I committed to memory its external appearance and arrangement in the rack; and I also fell, at length, upon a discovery which set at rest whatever trivial doubt I might have entertained. In scrutinizing the edges of the paper, I observed them to be more *chafed* than seemed necessary. They presented the *broken* appearance which is manifested when a stiff paper, having been once folded and pressed with a folder, is refolded in a reversed direction, in the same creases or edges which had formed the original fold. This discovery was sufficient. It was clear to me that the letter had been turned, as a glove, inside out, redirected, and resealed. I bade the Minister good morning, and took my departure at once, leaving a gold snuffbox upon the table.

"The next morning I called for the snuffbox, when we resumed, quite eagerly, the con-versation of the preceding day. While thus engaged, however, a loud report, as if of a pistol, was heard immediately beneath the windows of the *hôtel,* and was succeeded by a series of fearful screams and the shoutings of a mob. D— rushed to a casement, threw it open, and looked out. In the meantime, I stepped to the card rack, took the letter, put it in my pocket, and replaced it by a facsimile, so far as regards externals—which I had carefully prepared at my lodgings—imitating the D— ·cipher very readily by means of a seal formed of bread.

"The disturbance in the street had been occasioned by the frantic behavior of a man with a musket. He had fired it among a crowd of women and children. It proved, however, to have been without ball, and the fellow was suffered to go his way as a lunatic or a drunkard. When he had gone, D— came from the window, whither I had followed him immediately upon securing the object in view. Soon afterwards I bade him farewell. The pretended lunatic was a man in my own pay."

"But what purpose had you," I asked, "in replacing the letter by à facsimile? Would it not have been better, at the very first, to have seized it openly and departed?"

"D—," replied Dupin, "is a desperate man, and a man of nerve.· His *hôtel,* too, is not without attendants devoted to his interest. Had I made the wild attempt you suggest, I might never have left the Ministerial presence alive. The good people of Paris might have heard of me no more. But I had an object apart from these considerations. You know my political prepossessions. In this matter I act as a partisan of the lady concerned. For eighteen months the Minister has had her in his power. She has now him in hers—since, being unaware that the letter is not in his possession, he will proceed with his exactions as if it was. Thus will he inevitably commit himself at once to his political destruction. His downfall, too, will not be more precipitate than awkward. It is all very well to talk about the *facilis descensus Averni*[18]; but in all kinds

18. *facilis descensus Averni* (fä′ki lis dā skän′səs ə wėr′nē), easy is the descent to Avernus (the Lower World). This famous saying is from Virgil's *Aeneid.*

of climbing, as Catalani[19] said of singing, it is far more easy to get up than to come down. In the present instance I have no sympathy—at least no pity—for him who descends. He is that *monstrum horrendum,*[20] an unprincipled man of genius.

"I confess, however, that I should like very well to know the precise character of his thoughts, when, being defied by her whom the Prefect terms 'a certain personage,' he is reduced to opening the letter which I left for him in the card rack."

"How? Did you put anything particular in it?"

"Why—it did not seem altogether right to leave the interior blank—that would have been insulting. D— at Vienna once, did me an evil turn, which I told him, quite good-humoredly, that I should remember. So, as I knew he would feel some curiosity in regard to the identity of the person who had out-witted him, I thought it a pity not to give him a clue. He is well acquainted with my manu-script, and I copied into the middle of the blank sheet the words:

> —Un dessein si funeste,
> S'il n'est digne d'Atrée, est digne de Thyeste.[21]

They are to be found in Crébillon's *Atrée.*"[22]

---

19. *Catalani* (kä'tä lä'nē), a famous Italian soprano, who lived from 1779 to 1849. 20. *monstrum horrendum* (mōn'strum hôr ren'dum), dreadful monster. The Latin words are from Virgil's *Aeneid.* 21. *"Un dessein . . . digne de Thyeste,"* so evil a plan, if not worthy of Atreus (ā'trüs or ā'tri əs), is worthy of Thyestes (thī es'tēz). In Greek mythology the brothers Atreus and Thyestes are symbols of savagery and treachery. 22. *They are to be found in Crébillon's* (krā'bē yonz') Atrée (ä trā'). *Atrée,* which tells the story of Atreus, was written by the French tragic poet, Prosper J. de Crébillon (1674-1762).

THE MAGAZINE IN AMERICA

Poe and Magazine Criticism

Edgar Allan Poe called himself a "magazinist." He edited magazines in both the South and the North, received much of his meager income from the sale of magazine contributions, and even moved to Philadelphia, the center of magazine publication in the United States in the 1830's and 1840's.

Poe was not alone among American writers in devoting much of his energy to writing for magazines. Since international copyright laws did not exist, book publishers made it a practice to pirate the novels and poems of distinguished English writers which they could reprint in America without payment of royalties. Forced to compete with this vast source of "free" material, American writers had only a slim chance of seeing their work in book form. They turned, therefore, to the magazines, which offered a better source of income.

The magazines drew freely upon native talent, but often published inferior work as readily as they did the best work of American writers. The sure voice of a discerning critic was needed to condemn poor writing for its deficiencies and praise good writing for its merits. Edgar Allan Poe, for a time, became that critic; in fact, Poe earned a reputation as a critic long before he was recognized as poet and short-story writer.

Poe was one of the first Americans to develop a systematic philosophy of literary art, which he expounded while editor of several now extinct magazines such as the *Southern Literary Messenger, Graham's Magazine,* and *Burton's Gentleman's Magazine.* Unlike earlier critics who followed personal prejudice in judging American writers as either "great geniuses" or "silly amateurs," Poe measured writers according to specific literary standards. On the whole, these standards were shaped by romanticism. Poe's statements in "The Construction of a Tale" (page 211) show how precisely he expressed his theories.

American literature found its first real critic in Poe. He led the way in making the magazine a suitable vehicle for criticism, a function many American magazines continue to perform in their reviews of books, drama, music, and art.

The Masque of the Red Death Edgar Allan Poe

The Red Death had long devastated the country. No pestilence had ever been so fatal, or so hideous. Blood was its avatar and its seal—the redness and the horror of blood. There were sharp pains, and sudden dizziness, and then profuse bleeding at the pores, with dissolution. The scarlet stains upon the body and especially upon the face of the victim were the pest ban which shut him out from the aid and from the sympathy of his fellow men. And the whole seizure, progress, and termination of the disease were the incidents of half an hour.

But the Prince Prospero was happy and dauntless and sagacious. When his dominions were half depopulated, he summoned to his presence a thousand hale and light-hearted friends from among the knights and dames of his court, and with these retired to the deep seclusion of one of his castellated abbeys. This was an extensive and magnificent structure, the creation of the Prince's own eccentric yet august taste. A strong and lofty wall girdled it in. This wall had gates of iron. The courtiers, having entered, brought furnaces and massy hammers and welded the bolts. They resolved to leave means neither of ingress nor egress to the sudden impulses of despair or of frenzy from within. The abbey was amply provisioned. With such precautions the courtiers might bid defiance to contagion. The external world could take care of itself. In the meantime it was folly to grieve, or to think. The Prince had provided all the appliances of pleasure. There were buffoons, there were *improvvisatori*,[1] there were ballet dancers, there were musicians, there was Beauty, there was wine. All these and security were within. Without was the Red Death.

It was toward the close of the fifth or sixth month of his seclusion, and while the pestilence raged most furiously abroad, that the Prince Prospero entertained his thousand friends at a masked ball of the most unusual magnificence.

It was a voluptuous scene, that masquerade. But first let me tell of the rooms in which it was held. There were seven—an imperial suite. In many palaces, however, such suites form a long and straight vista, while the folding doors slide back nearly to the walls on either hand, so that the view of the whole extent is scarcely impeded. Here the case was very different, as might have been expected from the Prince's love of the bizarre. The apartments were so irregularly disposed that the vision embraced but little more than one at a time. There was a sharp turn at every twenty or thirty yards, and at each turn a novel effect. To the right and left, in the middle of each wall, a tall and narrow Gothic window looked out upon a closed corridor which pursued the windings of the suite. These windows were of stained glass whose color varied in accordance with the prevailing hue of the decorations of the chamber into which it opened. That at the eastern extremity was hung, for example, in blue—and vividly blue were its windows. The second chamber was purple in its ornaments and tapestries, and here the panes were purple. The third was green throughout and so were the casements. The fourth was furnished and lighted with orange, the fifth with white, the sixth with violet. The seventh apartment was closely shrouded in black velvet tapestries that hung all over the ceiling and down the walls, falling in heavy folds upon a carpet of the same material and hue. But in this chamber only, the color of the windows failed to correspond with the decorations. The panes here were scarlet—a deep blood-color. Now in no one of the seven apartments was there any lamp or candelabrum, amid the profusion of golden ornaments that lay scattered to and fro or depended from the roof. There was no light of any kind emanating from lamp or candle within the suite of chambers. But in the corridors that followed the suite there stood, oppo-

---

1. *improvvisatori* (im′prŏv vē′zä tō′rē), composers and singers of extemporary songs. [*Italian*]

site to each window, a heavy tripod, bearing a brazier of fire, that projected its rays through the tinted glass and so glaringly illumined the room. And thus were produced a multitude of gaudy and fantastic appearances. But in the western or black chamber the effect of the firelight that streamed upon the dark hangings through the blood-tinted panes was ghastly in the extreme, and produced so wild a look upon the countenances of those who entered that there were few of the company bold enough to set foot within its precincts at all.

It was in this apartment, also, that there stood against the western wall a gigantic clock of ebony. Its pendulum swung to and fro with a dull, heavy, monotonous clang; and when the minute hand made the circuit of the face, and the hour was to be stricken, there came from the brazen lungs of the clock a sound which was clear and loud and deep and exceedingly musical, but of so peculiar a note and emphasis that, at each lapse of an hour, the musicians of the orchestra were constrained to pause, momentarily, in their performance, to hearken to the sound; and thus the waltzers[2] perforce ceased their evolutions; and there was a brief disconcert of the whole gay company; and, while the chimes of the clock yet rang, it was observed that the giddiest grew pale, and the more aged and sedate passed their hands over their brows as if in confused revery or meditation. But when the echoes had fully ceased, a light laughter at once pervaded the assembly; the musicians looked at each other and smiled as if at their own nervousness and folly, and made whispering vows, each to the other, that the next chiming of the clock should produce in them no similar emotion; and then, after the lapse of sixty minutes (which embrace three thousand and six hundred seconds of the Time that flies) there came yet another chiming of the clock, and then were the same disconcert and tremulousness and meditation as before.

But, in spite of these things, it was a gay and magnificent revel. The tastes of the Prince were peculiar. He had a fine eye for colors and effects. He disregarded the *decora*[3] of mere fashion. His plans were bold and fiery,

and his conceptions glowed with barbaric luster. There are some who would have thought him mad. His followers felt that he was not. It was necessary to hear and see and touch him to be *sure* that he was not.

He had directed, in great part, the movable embellishments of the seven chambers, upon occasion of this great fete; and it was his own guiding taste which had given character to the masqueraders. Be sure they were grotesque. There were much glare and glitter and piquancy and phantasm—much of what has been since seen in *Hernani*.[4] There were arabesque figures with unsuited limbs and appointments. There were delirious fancies such as the madman fashions. There was much of the beautiful, much of the wanton, much of the bizarre, something of the terrible, and not a little of that which might have excited disgust. To and fro in the seven chambers there stalked, in fact, a multitude of dreams. And these—the dreams—writhed in and about, taking hue from the rooms, and causing the wild music of the orchestra to seem as the echo of their steps. And, anon, there strikes the ebony clock which stands in the hall of the velvet. And then, for a moment, all is still, and all is silent save the voice of the clock. The dreams are stiff frozen as they stand. But the echoes of the chime die away—they have endured but an instant—and a light, half-subdued laughter floats after them as they depart. And now again the music swells, and the dreams live, and writhe to and fro more merrily than ever, taking hue from the many tinted windows through which stream the rays from the tripods. But to the chamber which lies most westwardly of the seven, there are now none of the maskers who venture; for the night is waning away, and there flows a ruddier light through the blood-colored panes; and the blackness of the sable drapery appalls; and to him whose foot falls upon the sable carpet, there comes from the near clock of ebony a muffled peal more solemnly emphatic than any which reaches *their* ears who in-

2. *the waltzers*. At the time Poe wrote his story, the waltz was considered an immoral dance. Poe's use of it depicts the wild nature of the revelry.   3. *decora* (di kô′ra), proprieties. [Latin]   4. *Hernani* (er nä′nē), a romantic play by the French author, Victor Hugo (1802-1885).

dulge in the more remote gaieties of the other apartments.

But these other apartments were densely crowded, and in them beat feverishly the heart of life. And the revel went whirlingly on, until at length there commenced the sounding of midnight upon the clock. And then the music ceased, as I have told; and the evolutions of the waltzers were quieted; and there was an uneasy cessation of all things as before. But now there were twelve strokes to be sounded by the bell of the clock; and thus it happened, perhaps, that more of thought crept, with more of time, into the meditations of the thoughtful among those who reveled. And thus, too, it happened, perhaps, that before the last echoes of the last chime had utterly sunk into silence, there were many individuals in the crowd who had found leisure to become aware of the presence of a masked figure which had arrested the attention of no single individual before. And the rumor of this new presence having spread itself whisperingly around, there arose at length from the whole company a buzz, or murmur, expressive of disapprobation and surprise—then, finally, of terror, of horror, and of disgust.

In an assembly of phantasms such as I have painted, it may well be supposed that no ordinary appearance could have excited such sensation. In truth the masquerade license of the night was nearly unlimited; but the figure in question had out-Heroded Herod,[5] and gone beyond the bounds of even the Prince's indefinite decorum. There are chords in the hearts of the most reckless which cannot be touched without emotion. Even with the utterly lost, to whom life and death are equally jests, there are matters of which no jest can be made. The whole company, indeed, seemed now deeply to feel that in the costume and bearing of the stranger neither wit nor propriety existed. The figure was tall and gaunt, and shrouded from head to foot in the habiliments of the grave. The mask which concealed the visage was made so nearly to resemble the countenance of a stiffened corpse that the closest scrutiny must have had difficulty in detecting the cheat. And yet all this might have been endured, if not approved, by the mad revelers around. But

the mummer had gone so far as to assume the type of the Red Death. His vesture was dabbled in *blood*—and his broad brow, with all the features of the face, was besprinkled with the scarlet horror.

When the eyes of Prince Prospero fell upon this spectral image (which, with a slow and solemn movement, as if more fully to sustain its rôle, stalked to and fro among the waltzers) he was seen to be convulsed, in the first moment with a strong shudder either of terror or distaste; but, in the next, his brow reddened with rage.

"Who dares?" he demanded hoarsely of the courtiers who stood near him—"who dares insult us with this blasphemous mockery? Seize him and unmask him—that we may know whom we have to hang at sunrise, from the battlements!"

It was in the eastern or blue chamber in which stood the Prince Prospero as he uttered these words. They rang throughout the seven rooms loudly and clearly—for the Prince was a bold and robust man, and the music had become hushed at the waving of his hand.

It was in the blue room where stood the Prince, with a group of pale courtiers by his side. At first, as he spoke, there was a slight rushing movement of this group in the direction of the intruder, who at the moment was also near at hand, and now, with deliberate and stately step, made closer approach to the speaker. But from a certain nameless awe with which the mad assumptions of the mummer had inspired the whole party, there were found none who put forth hand to seize him; so that, unimpeded, he passed within a yard of the Prince's person; and while the vast assembly, as if with one impulse, shrank from the centers of the rooms to the walls, he made his way uninterruptedly, but with the same solemn and measured step which had distinguished him from the first, through the blue chamber to the purple—through the purple to the green—through the green to the orange—through this again to the white—and even

5. *out-Heroded Herod* (her'əd). A quotation from Hamlet's speech to the players in Shakespeare's *Hamlet*. In this reference, Poe means that the masked figure had gone beyond the extremes of the masquerade.

thence to the violet, ere a decided movement had been made to arrest him. It was then, however, that the Prince Prospero, maddening with rage and the shame of his own momentary cowardice, rushed hurriedly through the six chambers, while none followed him on account of a deadly terror that had seized upon all. He bore aloft a drawn dagger, and had approached, in rapid impetuosity, to within three or four feet of the retreating figure, when the latter, having attained the extremity of the velvet apartment, turned suddenly and confronted his pursuer. There was a sharp cry—and the dagger dropped gleaming upon the sable carpet, upon which, instantly afterward, fell prostrate in death the Prince Prospero. Then, summoning the wild courage of despair, a throng of the revelers at once threw themselves into the black apartment, and, seizing the mummer, whose tall figure stood erect and motionless within the shadow of the ebony clock, gasped in unutterable horror at finding the grave cerements and corpselike mask, which they handled with so violent a rudeness, untenanted by any tangible form.

And now was acknowledged the presence of the Red Death. He had come like a thief in the night. And one by one dropped the revelers in the blood-bedewed halls of their revel, and died each in the despairing posture of his fall. And the life of the ebony clock went out with that of the last of the gay. And the flames of the tripods expired. And Darkness and Decay and the Red Death held illimitable dominion over all.

Poems by Poe

Annabel Lee This poem, which was the last one Poe wrote, is an idealized account of his wife, Virginia Clemm, who died in 1847.

It was many and many a year ago,
   In a kingdom by the sea,
That a maiden there lived whom you may know
   By the name of Annabel Lee;
And this maiden she lived with no other thought   5
   Than to love and be loved by me.

I was a child and *she* was a child,
   In this kingdom by the sea,
But we loved with a love that was more than love—
   I and my Annabel Lee;   10
With a love that the wingèd seraphs of heaven
   Coveted her and me.

And this was the reason that, long ago,
   In this kingdom by the sea,
A wind blew out of a cloud, chilling   15
   My beautiful Annabel Lee;
So that her highborn kinsmen came
   And bore her away from me,
To shut her up in a sepulcher
   In this kingdom by the sea.   20

The angels, not half so happy in heaven,
    Went envying her and me—
Yes! that was the reason (as all men know,
    In this kingdom by the sea)
That the wind came out of the cloud by night,   25
    Chilling and killing my Annabel Lee.

But our love it was stronger by far than the love
    Of those who were older than we,
    Of many far wiser than we;
And neither the angels in heaven above,   30
    Nor the demons down under the sea,
Can ever dissever my soul from the soul
    Of the beautiful Annabel Lee;

For the moon never beams, without bringing me dreams
    Of the beautiful Annabel Lee;   35
And the stars never rise, but I feel the bright eyes
    Of the beautiful Annabel Lee;
And so, all the night-tide, I lie down by the side
Of my darling—my darling—my life and my bride,
    In the sepulcher there by the sea,   40
    In her tomb by the sounding sea.

Israfel

To the Mohammedans, Israfel (iz′rə fel) is the angel of music, the one who will sound the trumpet at the resurrection of all men from their graves. Although speaking of the music of Israfel, this poem stands so well for Poe's own beliefs about the function of poetry that biographers have often applied the name "Israfel" to him.

And the angel Israfel, whose heartstrings are a lute, and who has the sweetest voice of all God's creatures.
        —The Koran[1]

In heaven a spirit doth dwell
"Whose heartstrings are a lute";
None sing so wildly well
As the angel Israfel,
And the giddy stars (so legends tell),   5
Ceasing their hymns,[2] attend the spell
    Of his voice, all mute.

Tottering above
    In her highest noon,[3]
    The enamored moon   10

Blushes with love,
    While, to listen, the red levin[4]
(With the rapid Pleiads, even,
    Which were seven[5])
Pauses in Heaven.   15

And they say (the starry choir
    And the other listening things)
That Israfeli's fire
Is owing to that lyre
    By which he sits and sings,   20
The trembling living wire
Of those unusual strings.

But the skies that angel trod,
    Where deep thoughts are a duty,

1. *The Koran* (kô rän′ or kō′ran), the sacred book of the Mohammedans. 2. *And the giddy stars . . . ceasing their hymns.* It was an ancient belief that the stars gave forth heavenly music as they moved in their courses. 3. *her highest noon,* the position at which the moon is highest in the sky. 4. *levin* (lev′in), lightning. 5. *Pleiads* (plē′adz or plī′adz) . . . *seven,* a group of seven stars usually called the Pleiades (plē′ə dēz or plī′ə dēz). According to Greek mythology these stars were once the seven daughters of Atlas, the giant who supported the world on his shoulders.

Where Love's a grown-up god,   25
    Where the Houri[6] glances are
Imbued with all the beauty
    Which we worship in a star.

Therefore thou are not wrong,
    Israfeli, who despisest   30
An unimpassioned song;
    To thee the laurels belong,
    Best bard, because the wisest!
Merrily live, and long!

The ecstasies above   35
    With thy burning measures suit;
Thy grief, thy joy, thy hate, thy love,
    With the fervor of thy lute—
    Well may the stars be mute!

Yes, Heaven is thine; but this   40
    Is a world of sweets and sours;
Our flowers are merely—flowers,
And the shadow of thy perfect bliss
    Is the sunshine of ours.

If I could dwell   45
Where Israfel
    Hath dwelt, and he where I,
He might not sing so wildly well
    A mortal melody,
While a bolder note than this might swell   50
    From my lyre within the sky.

To Helen

Poe's boyhood idol, Mrs. Jane Stanard, was the
Helen to whom this tribute is addressed. Like Helen
of Troy, she suggests to the poet all the haunting
beauty of the legendary past. He sees himself a
wanderer, like Ulysses, until her inspiring beauty,
which he likens to an ancient (Nicean) ship, carries him after fruitless voyagings to a safe harbor.
By referring to Mrs. Stanard in the third stanza as
Psyche, he suggests her beauty of soul.

Helen, thy beauty is to me
    Like those Nicean barks of yore,
That gently, o'er a perfumed sea,
    The weary, wayworn wanderer bore
    To his own native shore.   5

On desperate seas long wont to roam,
    Thy hyacinth hair, thy classic face,
Thy Naiad airs, have brought me home
    To the Glory that was Greece
And the grandeur that was Rome.   10

Lo! in yon brilliant window niche
    How statuelike I see thee stand,
    The agate lamp within thy hand!
Ah, Psyche, from the regions which
    Are Holy Land!   15

ISRAFEL. 6. *Houri* (hŭ′ri *or* hou′ri), a beautiful spirit of
the Mohammedan paradise.

❧ TO INCREASE UNDERSTANDING
The Purloined Letter

1. You will recall that in writing the ratiocinative
tale, Poe frequently made use of two devices. (*a*)
What are these devices? (*b*) How does Poe make
use of them in this tale?

2. In many stories the author sets down happenings according to their order in time. Poe once
pointed out, however, that in a ratiocinative tale the
author may deliberately perplex the reader by *not*
presenting incidents in the order of their occurrence.
(*a*) List the main events in the story in the order
in which they actually occurred. (*b*) Point out how
Poe changed this order and explain how the changes
contribute to the effect he wished to create.

3. (*a*) At what point in the story did you realize

that neither Dupin nor the narrator thinks highly of
the Prefect's ability? (*b*) Why, according to Dupin,
is the Prefect unable to find the missing letter?

4. (*a*) Early in the story Dupin suggests to the
Prefect that the mystery is "a little *too* self-evident."
What clue does this statement provide to Dupin's
reasoning in solving the mystery? (*b*) Trace the
steps in his reasoning process from the time he first
hears of the missing letter until the time he recovers
it.

The Masque of the Red Death

1. In what way does "The Masque of the Red
Death" reflect the romantic influence?

2. Read carefully Poe's views given in "The Construction of a Tale" (page 211). With this material
and the facts you learned in reading Poe's biography

in mind, consider how well he observes his tenets in "The Masque of the Red Death." Discuss the following points. (*a*) Does the initial sentence tend to set the tone of the entire tale? (*b*) Trace Poe's organization of events and cite details which you feel are most important in building up the preconceived effect. (*c*) Select a passage in which Poe's wording has significant emotional connotation. (*d*) Do you feel the length of the tale is satisfactory?

3. (*a*) What is the theme of "The Masque of the Red Death"? (*b*) Cite details which symbolize the theme.

Poems by Poe

1. Cite lines which indicate that "Annabel Lee" may be considered an idealized account of Poe's wife, Virginia Clemm.

2. (*a*) How does this poem illustrate the timelessness of love? (*b*) How do you interpret the last four lines of the last stanza?

3. (*a*) What qualities of "Annabel Lee" remind you of a ballad? (*b*) Point out words and phrases that give the poem its unreal atmosphere.

4. (*a*) From his description of Israfel's song, what characteristics of poetry do you think Poe most admires? (*b*) Can you find passages showing these characteristics?

5. What biographical meaning do you find in the last stanza of "Israfel"?

6. What elements of romantic poetry does "Israfel" share with "Annabel Lee"?

7. Poe's meaning in "To Helen" depends upon the classical imagery in which it is expressed. (*a*) What likeness does Poe draw between Helen and the Nicean barks in the first stanza? (*b*) How does this simile serve to characterize the poet? (*c*) Explain how the metaphors in stanzas two and three enhance Poe's meaning.

8. What would you say the theme of "To Helen" is?

9. Judging from this poem, how would you describe Mrs. Stanard's influence upon Poe?

✳ EXTENDING INTERESTS

Read another of Poe's famous short stories such as "The Fall of the House of Usher," "The Murders in the Rue Morgue," "The Pit and the Pendulum," "The Gold-Bug," "The Mystery of Marie Rogêt," "The Black Cat," or "The Tell-Tale Heart." Then tell the class (1) whether you would classify it as a supernatural or a ratiocinative tale, and (2) how well, in your opinion, the story fulfills Poe's standards for the prose tale.

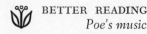

BETTER READING
Poe's music

The magic which Poe's poetry has exerted over several generations of readers lies principally in its matchless melody. Reviewing some of the devices which Poe has used to haunt the ear and to create a mood appropriate to his theme will add to your appreciation of his artistry.

(*a*) *Rhyme.* The end *rhyme,* or rhyme at the end of a line, is only one of the rhyming devices Poe has used. Far more unusual and elaborate is his use of *internal rhyme* within the lines. Read the last stanza of "Annabel Lee" slowly. Notice that *beams* in line 34 rhymes with *dreams* at its end, that the word *rise* in line 36 rhymes with *eyes* at the end of the line, and that *night-tide* and *side* in line 38 rhyme with each other and with *bride* at the end of line 39.

(*b*) *Alliteration,* the repetition of the initial sound of two or more closely related words or accented syllables, is frequently used by Poe. Again referring to the last stanza of "Annabel Lee," notice the alliterative effect of *sepulcher* and *sea* in line 40, and of *sounding* and *sea* in line 41.

(*c*) *Assonance,* the resemblance in the sound of the vowel in two or more accented syllables, adds greatly to the musical effect of the poetry. The last stanza of "Annabel Lee" is an excellent example of how Poe mingles assonance and internal rhyme. The long *e* sound of the internally rhymed words *beams* and *dreams* (line 34) is repeated in *me* in the same line, in *Lee* (lines 35 and 37), in *feel* (line 36), and in *sea* (lines 40 and 41). Also, the long *i* sound of the internally rhymed words *rise* and *eyes* (line 36), *night-tide* and *side* (line 38), and *bride* (line 39) is repeated in *bright* (line 36), in *lie* (line 38), in *my* and *life* (line 39), and in *by* (lines 38, 40, and 41). Notice that the *o* sound in *moon* (line 34) is repeated in *tomb* (line 41) and is closely related to the *o* sound in *beautiful* (lines 35 and 37).

(*d*) *Repetition,* the deliberate repeating of a word or phrase, is particularly striking in Poe's poetry. Notice, for example, how Poe has repeated in "Annabel Lee" the phrase, *kingdom by the sea* (lines 2, 8, 14, 20, and 24). Poe's use of *love* in slightly varied phrases (lines 6, 9, 11, and 27) also achieves a subtle effect of repetition.

Choose a stanza of "Israfel" or "To Helen" that you find exceptionally musical and prepare to read it aloud to the class. Be ready to point out whatever examples of rhyme, alliteration, assonance, or repetition it may contain. Would you agree that "To Helen" produces a more restrained effect than "Annabel Lee" and "Israfel"? Why?

THE LARGER VIEW

The writers of the Early National Period were all affected by the Romantic Movement, but personality and background caused each man to express romantic qualities in a different way and to a different degree. Keeping in mind the selections you have studied, answer the following questions.

1. Which writer or writers do you think typify the romantic interest in native legend and history? Would you agree that personality and background influenced this interest? Explain.

2. Which author best demonstrates the humorous treatment of legend? Why do you think so?

3. In your opinion which author was most influenced by the romantic emphasis upon emotion and emotional effect? Explain your answer.

4. Compare or contrast the way in which Irving, Bryant, Cooper, and Poe used nature in their writing.

5. Explain why you would or would not describe a Puritan writer, such as Jonathan Edwards, or a colonial writer, such as Benjamin Franklin, as a romantic.

6. Like other literary trends, romanticism is not confined to one period. Contemporary American writers often reflect its influence. What romantic elements do you find in the selections included in the chapter "Introducing American Literature" (pages 2-88)?

BIBLIOGRAPHY

BROOKS, VAN WYCK, *The World of Washington Irving*. (Dutton) Not only Irving but also Bryant, Cooper, Audubon, and other Americans of the period are presented here. Brooks' careful research as well as his insight make this an outstanding literary history.

COOPER, JAMES FENIMORE, *The Deerslayer*. (Dodd •Dolphin) Natty Bumppo's initiation into the wilderness is told in this epic novel, one of five adventure stories dealing with a backwoodsman of early America.

COOPER, JAMES FENIMORE, *The Leatherstocking Saga*, edited by Allen Nevins. (Pantheon) Mr. Nevins has deleted irrelevant passages to make these classic tales more attractive to readers.

COOPER, JAMES FENIMORE, *The Spy*. (Dodd •Dolphin) The spy is a cool, shrewd, fearless man employed by General Washington in a service which involves great personal danger and little glory.

FORBES, ESTHER, *Rainbow on the Road*. (Houghton) This novel is the very humorous odyssey through New England of Jude Rebough, an itinerant portrait painter, and Eddy, his companion. Much of the book's excitement is caused by Jude's resemblance to the legendary Robin Hood.

FORESTER, CECIL, *The Captain from Connecticut*. (Little) The hazardous voyage of the ship "Delaware" and its captain, Josh Peabody, is told with spirit and pace in an adventure-packed sea story.

GROSSMAN, JAMES, *James Fenimore Cooper*. (Sloane) The author's excellent analysis of Cooper's complex personality is as interesting reading as fiction.

IRVING, WASHINGTON, *Knickerbocker's History of New York*, edited by Anne Carroll Moore. (Ungar) If you enjoyed the selection in the text, you will want to read all of this irreverent parody on the history of New York.

IRVING, WASHINGTON, *The Sketch Book*. (Dodd •Signet) All will enjoy these witty, original, and sometimes impossibly unrealistic sketches and essays by Irving at his best.

POE, EDGAR ALLAN, *Complete Tales and Poems*. (Modern Library) The thrilling, ingenious twists of Poe's work have fascinated readers through the years.

POE, EDGAR ALLAN, *Portable Poe*, edited by Phillip Van Doren Stern. (•Viking) a well-edited edition of Poe's work, this book contains all the brilliance of Poe at his best. Included are stories, poems, articles, and letters.

SPERRY, ARMSTRONG, *Danger to Windward*. (Winston) Lovers of sea stories will enjoy this novel of the whaling business after the War of 1812.

TULLY, ANDREW, *When They Burned the White House*. (Simon & Schuster) Newspaperman Tully covers the major phases of the War of 1812 in spirited, colorful stories with careful attention to facts.

WINWAR, FRANCES, *Haunted Palace; A Life of Edgar Allan Poe*. (Harper) Miss Winwar's objective yet affectionate portrayal of Poe will give added insight into his writings.

•paperback

On August 31, 1837, an American poet, essayist, and philosopher named Ralph Waldo Emerson made a remarkable speech at Harvard University. In it he said, "We [Americans] will walk on our own feet; we will work with our own hands; we will speak our own minds." In these words Emerson voiced the feelings not only of a new generation of writers, rapidly rising to prominence, but of the American public as well. For the nation, spurred on and excited by the growth of democracy during the recently concluded presidency of Andrew Jackson, felt the need to cast off the last traces of dependence on Europe. The Declaration of Independence had declared our political freedom. Emerson's words were a cultural declaration of independence, a ringing notice to the world that culturally as well as politically the United States had come of age.

Emerson voiced the pride of a nation that had achieved fifty years of independence, of physical growth, of progress toward democracy. In these decades just preceding the Civil War, the frontier had moved far to the West. Railroads and canals linked the growing towns. Manhood suffrage was almost universal, and property qualifications for voting had been abolished. Industry was rapidly becoming more important, particularly in New England. There the abundance of skilled labor and water power promoted the opening of factories. As the factories grew, their owners prospered. With the accumulation of wealth came an increasing interest in higher education, in travel, and in culture generally. This fortunate combination of circumstances produced a literary outpouring of such vigor and variety that literary historians have labeled the period "America's Golden Day."

chapter four America's Golden Day

Van Wyck Brooks, an American critic, called his book about our outstanding literature in those decades, *The Flowering of New England*. The title underlines the fact that New England was at its height as the literary and cultural capital of America. A surprisingly large number of our best authors were living and writing in New England—Henry David Thoreau, Ralph Waldo Emerson, Henry Wadsworth Longfellow, James Russell Lowell, Oliver Wendell Holmes, Nathaniel Hawthorne, John Greenleaf Whittier, Richard Henry Dana, Jr., and Francis Parkman, to name only a few. Among these writers were poets, essayists, philosophers, historians, short-story writers, and novelists. Although their types of writing and subject matter differed, two great interests dominated much of their thinking: the world of nature and the world of human affairs. In New England, as throughout the world, men were discovering new attractions and new meanings in the physical world and examining society and social institutions anew.

Henry David Thoreau

1817-1862

Henry David Thoreau was a cantankerous and eccentric but very interesting writer. No man's roots dug deeper into Yankee earth, and no man was a more complete down-Easter than he. Yet eccentric and individualistic as he was, he shared the interest in nature and in man typical of this period. No one enjoyed fields, forests, mountains, and streams more—or learned more from them—than Thoreau did. And no one scrutinized more carefully or spoke more honestly about what he considered the weaknesses in our social and political structure than did the thin, wiry man from Concord.

CRAFTSMAN, WOODSMAN, PHILOSOPHER

Concord, Massachusetts, Thoreau's birthplace and his home during his whole lifetime, was a little country village. Thoreau was fond of it from the start. "I," he wrote at least half-seriously, "have never got over my surprise that I should have been born in the most estimable place in all the world, and in the very nick of time, too." Thoreau was particularly fond of the world of nature that was an easy distance from any Concord doorway. In his boyhood, he enjoyed exploring the thick woods and the old orchards nearby. He enjoyed hunting hares, partridges, and wild pigeons in the forests, shore birds in the water meadows and swamps, muskrats and ducks along the rivers. Swimming and boating by day, spearing fish by torchlight at night, he appreciated the rivers which flowed through the town. In winter, he liked to skate on the streams and ponds, and he enjoyed sledding so much that he once said he would miss it in heaven.

Four years of study at Harvard followed by graduation in 1837 did not lessen Thoreau's affection for the out-of-doors or for the home town to which he promptly returned. Now a somewhat more scientific interest in nature supplemented his instinctive enjoyment of it. His sister, Sophia, the family botanist, introduced him to the study of plants. His brother, John, who over the years had compiled a long list of Concord birds, passed along the list for Henry to study. Thus started the growth of a knowledge of the flowers, birds, and animals around Concord which in time was to surpass that of both Sophia and John.

This interest in the world of nature was important in the new school which John and Henry Thoreau founded in Concord in 1838. The school was a most unusual one for those strict times, because its two teachers did not think that children should be flogged. ("I," said Thoreau, "have always

228 AMERICA'S GOLDEN DAY

regarded cowhide as a nonconductor.") The hope was that students would like school so well that discipline would not be necessary—and the hope was realized. The brothers took part in the sports of the students, and led them on field trips during which they studied flowers, birds, and animals, and even at times did some surveying. The school closed in 1841 because of John's poor health (he died shortly after), but it was long remembered as a pioneering experiment pointing the way toward twentieth-century ideas about education.

Thoreau, looking for a new way to earn a livelihood, sought for one which would give him as much time out-of-doors as possible. College graduate though he was, he liked white-collar work less than open-air manual labor. Further, he had real talent for such work. A friend and neighbor, Ralph Waldo Emerson, himself awkward with any tools, never could stop admiring Thoreau's amazing skills. "There was a wonderful fitness," he wrote, "of body and mind. He could pace sixteen rods more accurately than another man could measure them with rod and chain.... He could estimate the measure of a tree very well by his eye; he could estimate the weight of a calf or a pig, like a dealer. From a box containing a bushel or more of loose pencils, he could take up with his hands fast enough just a dozen pencils at every grasp."

Such a gifted worker found that he could get all the work he wanted, but he did not work steadily at any one chore. To gain money for his

The spareness of Thoreau's way of living may be judged from this collection of his personal possessions. The desk (center) and the flute and bedstead (far right) are known to have been in his hut at Walden.

simple wants he worked in many different capacities. To cite a few examples: Surveyor Thoreau marked off boundaries and drew several good maps of Concord which still survive. Mason Thoreau built walls, some of which stand today. Pencil maker Thoreau manufactured a product which won prizes at an exposition. Carpenter and Gardener Thoreau was a handy man around the Emerson household.

But this versatile workman dropped his tools and became his own master whenever he could afford it, in order that he might have afternoons, nights, or whole days at a time to study and enjoy the world of nature. He carried a box in which to press and preserve plants; he had a field glass and a magnifying glass and a big knife. Although he was a thin little man, he was tough and muscular: his hands were strong and nimble, and his legs were sturdy. "When he walked to get over the ground," said a neighbor, "one thought of a tireless machine." There was an almost animal-like sharpness to his senses. His gray-blue eyes, peering out from under bushy brows, were unusually keen. They could distinguish the tiniest insects among the plants and dead leaves on the ground. He had a giant Roman nose which was as efficient as it was impressive. Whenever he picked a plant, he liked to sniff it long enough to make its scent a part of his acquaintance with it. His sense of hearing and his sense of touch were equally keen.

Emerson, impressed though he was by Thoreau's "most adapted and serviceable body," was equally impressed—as others were—by the wisdom he acquired on his wide-ranging explorations. "He knew the country like a fox or a bird," said Emerson, "and passed through it as freely by paths of his own." Emerson told how, in the spring, Thoreau could predict to the day when each wild flower would be in bloom. "Snakes coiled around his leg," Emerson testified; "the fishes swam into his hand, and he took them out of the water; he pulled the woodchuck out of his hole by the tail and took the foxes under his protection from the hunters."

But Thoreau's study of nature did not end with his merely perceiving and recording details in the lives of plants and animals; he had other interests. "All science," he wrote, "is merely a makeshift, a means to an end. All nature is to be regarded as it concerns man."

This attitude was one which many poets and philosophers shared in Thoreau's day and which many share in our day. The men of that time had a renewed interest in nature because they felt that if they could truly understand the deeper meaning of it, they could learn great philosophical truths. They tried as William Blake (1757-1827), the English poet, had recently tried,

> To see a world in a grain of sand,
> And a heaven in a wild flower;

or they believed, as Alfred Tennyson (1809-1892), another English poet, did, that one who understood "a flower in a crannied wall" would "know what God and man is." God, they reasoned, is everywhere. Therefore if a small detail were really apprehended, great insights would result. So Thoreau was interested in deeper meanings. "It is the subject of the vision, the truth alone, that concerns me," he wrote. "The philosopher for whom rainbows can be explained away never saw them. With regard to such objects, I find that it is not they themselves (with which the men of science deal) that concern me; the point of interest is somewhere *between* me and the rainbows."

Thoreau, in other words, was rather more a philosopher than he was a scientist. Like most good philosophers, he had some ideas which were hard to communicate. Chiefly these ideas concern the relationship between nature and goodness and truth. These difficult ideas are not unusual ones: they are shared by many people who believe that God is everywhere—in the world of mountains, forests, rivers, and lakes as well as in men's hearts.

But though Philosopher Thoreau had as hard a time as anybody else explaining these mystical ideas, he managed to make many of his unusual ideas extraordinarily easy (for philosophical ideas) to understand. He made a special effort to write clearly: he hated big words and sloppy sentences. "It is on the whole better," he wrote, "as it is simpler, to use the common language." He was also helped as a writer by the fact that there was a lurking humor in almost all that he wrote. This humor emphasized important points, added interest, and helped clarify his ideas. Furthermore, because this Yankee craftsman and woodsman was such a practical man, he hardly ever disappeared from the view of the ordinary reader in a cloud of generalities. Even his most profound writings were those of a man who planted his hobnail boots firmly on the Concord earth and refused to try to fly.

The selection beginning on the following page, which is from *Walden*, Thoreau's most famous book, is a typical example of Thoreau's keen and detailed observation of nature.

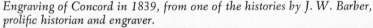

Engraving of Concord in 1839, from one of the histories by J. W. Barber, prolific historian and engraver.

The Battle of the Ants

One day when I went out to my woodpile, or rather my pile of stumps, I observed two large ants, the one red, the other much larger, nearly half an inch long, and black, fiercely contending with one another. Having once got hold, they never let go, but struggled and wrestled and rolled on the chips incessantly. Looking farther, I was surprised to find the chips were covered with such combatants—that it was not a *duellum,* but a *bellum,*[1] a war between two races of ants, the red always pitted against the black, and frequently two red ones to one black. The legions of these Myrmidons[2] covered all the hills and vales in my woodyard, and the ground was already strewn with the dead and dying, both red and black.

It was the only battle which I have ever witnessed, the only battlefield I ever trod while the battle was raging; internecine war; the red republicans on the one hand, and the black imperialists[3] on the other. On every side they were engaged in deadly combat, yet without any noise that I could hear, and human soldiers never fought so resolutely.

I watched a couple that were fast locked in each other's embraces, in a little sunny valley amid the chips, now at noonday prepared to fight till the sun went down, or life went out. The smaller red champion had fastened himself like a vise to his adversary's front, and through all the tumblings on that field never for an instant ceased to gnaw at one of his feelers near the root, having already caused the other to go by the board; while the stronger black one dashed him from side to side, and, as I saw on looking nearer, had already divested him of several of his members. They fought with more pertinacity than bulldogs. Neither manifested the least disposition to retreat. It was evident that their battle cry was "Conquer or die."

In the meanwhile there came along a single red ant on the hillside of this valley, evidently full of excitement, who either had dispatched his foe or had not yet taken part in the battle (probably the latter, for he had lost none of his limbs); whose mother had charged him to return with his shield or upon it.[4] Or perchance he was some Achilles, who had nourished his wrath apart, and had now come to avenge or rescue his Patroclus.[5] He saw this unequal combat from afar. He drew near with rapid pace till he stood on his guard within half an inch of the combatants; then, watching his opportunity, he sprang upon the black warrior, and commenced his operations near the root of his right foreleg, leaving the foe to select among his own members.

And so there were three united for life, as if a new kind of attraction had been invented which put all other locks and cements to shame. I should not have wondered by this time to find that they had their respective musical bands stationed on some eminent chip, and playing their national airs the while, to excite the slow and cheer the dying combatants. I was myself excited somewhat even as if they had been men. The more you think of it, the less the difference. And certainly there is not the fight recorded in Concord history,[6] at least, if in the history of America, that will bear a moment's comparison with this, whether for the numbers engaged in it, or for the patriotism and heroism displayed. For numbers and for carnage it was an Austerlitz[7]

---

1. *not a "duellum"* (dü el′əm) *but a "bellum"* (bel′əm), not merely a duel between two contestants but a war between two armies.   2. *Myrmidons* (mẻr′mi donz), warriors of ancient Thessaly, according to Greek legend.   3. *red republicans . . . black imperialists.* At the time this selection was published in 1854, Europe had recently undergone several revolutions in which the people of a number of countries had rebelled against their rulers.   4. *whose mother . . . with his shield or upon it.* According to tales of ancient Greece, this was the command given by Spartan mothers to their sons when the sons went off to war. It means: Die rather than surrender.   5. *Achilles* (ə kil′ēz) . . . *Patroclus* (pə trō′kləs). Because of a quarrel with Agamemnon (ag′ə mem′non), the Greek commander in chief in the Trojan War, Achilles sulked in his tent. But when he heard that his friend Patroclus had been killed, he hurried into the battle to avenge him.   6. *the fight recorded in Concord history,* the second battle of the Revolutionary War, on April 19, 1775.   7. *Austerlitz* (ôs′tər lits), battle fought in old Austria (now Czechoslovakia) during the Napoleonic Wars. Here in 1805 Napoleon defeated the Russians and Austrians. Many thousands were killed.

or Dresden.[8] Concord Fight! Two killed on the patriots' side,[9] and Luther Blanchard wounded! Why, here every ant was a Buttrick[10]—"Fire, for God's sake fire!"—and thousands shared the fate of Davis and Hosmer. There was not one hireling there. I have no doubt that it was a principle they fought for, as much as our ancestors, and not to avoid a threepenny tax on their tea[11]; and the results of this battle will be as important and memorable to those whom it concerns as those of the battle of Bunker Hill, at least.

I took up the chip on which the three I have particularly described were struggling, carried it into my house, and placed it under a tumbler on my window sill, in order to see the issue. Holding a microscope to the first-mentioned red ant, I saw that, though he was assiduously gnawing at the near foreleg of his enemy, having severed his remaining feeler, his own breast was all torn away, exposing what vitals he had there to the jaws of the black warrior, whose breastplate was apparently too thick for him to pierce; and the dark carbuncles of the sufferer's eyes shone with ferocity such as war only could excite. They struggled half an hour longer under the tumbler, and when I looked again the black soldier had severed the heads of his foes from their bodies, and the still living heads were hanging on either side of him like ghastly trophies at

his saddlebow, still apparently as firmly fastened as ever, and he was endeavoring with feeble struggles, being without feelers and with only the remnant of a leg, and I know not how many other wounds, to divest himself of them; which after half an hour more he accomplished.

I raised the glass, and he went off over the window sill in that crippled state. Whether he finally survived that combat, and spent the remainder of his days in some Hôtel des Invalides,[12] I do not know; but I thought that his industry would not be worth much thereafter. I never learned which party was victorious, nor the cause of the war; but I felt for the rest of that day as if I had had my feelings excited and harrowed by witnessing the struggle, the ferocity and carnage, of a human battle before my door.

---

8. *Dresden*, the last of Napoleon's great victories, in which he defeated the Russian, Austrian, and Prussian forces in 1813. Dresden is in Germany.   9. *Two killed on the patriots' side.* Thoreau is writing of the midmorning fight at the North Bridge when the militia advanced and attacked the British on guard there. Two Americans, Captain Isaac Davis and a man named Hosmer (both mentioned below), were killed. 10. *Buttrick*, the major in command of the Concord militia in the fight at the North Bridge.   11. *a threepenny tax on their tea,* a reference to the Boston Tea Party and the colonists' objections to taxation without representation.   12. *Hôtel des Invalides* (ō tel′ dā zän vä lēd′), a beautiful monument in Paris founded by Louis XIV as a residence for old and wounded veterans of the French armies.

THE
WALDEN IDEA

The *Walden, or Life in the Woods,* was published in 1854. This book, which has become an American classic, is interesting because of the insight it gives the reader into Thoreau's attitude toward life. It is interesting also because it tells us Thoreau's solution for a problem which was becoming important in his day and is even more important in ours—the rapid growth of science and industry in the United States. In New England a man with such sharp eyes as Thoreau's could see early signs of coming change. Not far from Concord, two factory villages, Lowell and Lawrence, were growing like mushrooms. Nearer at hand railway tracks and telegraph wires were changing the look of the landscape; train whistles which Thoreau heard by day and by night screamed news of the growing importance of the machine. Americans were beginning to struggle with the changes brought into their lives by the machine age.

Different groups offered varied solutions. One group urged American laborers to band together in a political party: in one election in New York City, such a party polled 30% of the vote. Another group favored trade unions: in 1837 delegates from such unions in a dozen different cities met and formed a National Trades Union. Several groups tried living in communities which embodied new social and economic organizations. One of the first of these was New Harmony, founded on a thirty-thousand-acre tract in Indiana by Robert Owen, an English reformer. Some thousand eager colonists made the long journey west to try life in a community where property was held jointly and labor shared, but after four years under seven different constitutions or plans of government the project failed in 1829. At Fruitlands in Harvard, Massachusetts, Amos Bronson Alcott[1] founded another community based on the sharing of labor, but this project lasted only a short time. The most famous of the experimental communities was Brook Farm, founded in 1841 at West Roxbury near Boston by George Ripley and a group of earnest social reformers. Authors and laborers, Harvard students and farmers, even men from foreign lands, came to try life in this coöperative community where everyone must work and where the pay was the same for all kinds of work. Men who worked in the dairy barn received about the same wages as the scholars who taught in the excellent school. The social life—picnics and dances, concerts and lectures—was open to all. But after six years this project, too, failed.

Thoreau also tried his experiment: he set up his model community. It was a one-man community located by Walden Pond, about a mile from Concord, out beyond the poorhouse. "Experiment" might seem to some to be too high-falutin a name to apply to Thoreau's unpretentious stay out in a hut by a pond, and it would have astonished Thoreau's fellow townsmen if they had heard that his report on that stay was to be an American literary masterpiece. Here are the simple facts:

Emerson, who had bought some ground alongside Walden Pond, gave Thoreau permission to go out there and live. In return, Thoreau was to clear the briar bushes from part of the property. In March 1845, Thoreau went out to Emerson's lot, carrying a borrowed ax. He cut a good share of his own timber, and bought a laborer's shack for the boards and nails in it. He built a hut so small that a friend called it a "sentry box." Beginning July 4, 1845, Thoreau lived in his pondside hut for two years and two months. Often he heard passers-by saying incredulously, "Does he *live* here?" He was not living in the wilds away from his fellow men: he walked into town whenever he felt like it, and sometimes invited himself for dinner at friends' houses; and his friends frequently called on him. Thoreau found that by doing day labor now and then, and by selling farm produce, he could spend only a small part of his time working and get along easily. This left a large share of his time for studying nature, visiting friends, and writing a book. When he finished writing his book, Thoreau left his hut on Walden Pond forever.

Above: Plant life on Walden's shore. Opposite: Walden Pond.

That was all there was to the "experiment" which Thoreau told about in *Walden*. The chief reasons for the lasting importance of this book are these: (1) Since much of this book is written in Thoreau's typical humorous style, many have found it amusing. (2) The descriptions of plant and animal life as he observed them at Walden are as fascinating as any Thoreau ever wrote (for instance, "The Battle of the Ants," page 232).

1. *Amos Bronson Alcott*, educator and philosopher. He was the father of Louisa May Alcott, the author of *Little Women*.

(3) The account by Thoreau, the fine craftsman, of his way of building his hut and living in the woods has an interest not unlike that of such a book, say, as *Robinson Crusoe*. (4) The book set forth what might be called "the Walden Idea"—its author's suggestion about what a man might do to cope with the problems of the machine age.

Thoreau, like many others who have thought about the results of the machine in our lives, noticed that possible luxuries were multiplied. The bare necessities of life were four—food, shelter, clothing, and fuel. If these were reduced to a bare minimum, they were pretty easy to get. As for luxuries, such as great accumulations of property or money, or travel by train, one could easily get along without them. Everything beyond the bare necessities was a luxury for which you spent part of your precious lifetime. Thoreau, practical Yankee that he was, wanted to consider what kind of bargain he was getting. The question he asked was, "How much of your energy should you spend to buy unimportant luxuries?" His answer was, "None at all."

His idea was simple enough. It was that the less time you spend doing what is unimportant, the more time you can spend in doing what is important. For Thoreau, the important things of life were exploring nature, reading books, thinking, and writing. His simple way of living gave him plenty of time for all these activities. In his day and in ours, many people spend so much time acquiring luxuries that they never have time to live. Thoreau would claim that their luxuries cost too much. The following excerpts from *Walden* set forth the idea very well.

Why I Went to the Woods

I went to the woods because I wished to live deliberately, to front only the essential facts of life, and see if I could not learn what it had to teach, and not, when I came to die, discover that I had not lived I did not wish to live what was not life, living is so dear; nor did I wish to practice resignation, unless it was quite necessary. I wanted to live deep and suck out all the marrow of life, to live so sturdily and Spartanlike as to put to rout all that was not life, to cut a broad swath and shave close, to drive life into a corner, and reduce it to its lowest terms, and, if it proved to be mean, why then to get the whole and genuine meanness of it, and publish its meanness to the world; or if it were sublime, to know it by experience, and be able to give a true account of it in my next excursion.[1] For most men, it appears to me, are in a strange uncertainty about it, whether it is of the devil or of God, and have *somewhat hastily* concluded that it is the chief end of man here to "glorify God and enjoy Him forever."[2]

Still we live meanly, like ants, though the fable tells us that we were long ago changed into men[3]; like pygmies we fight with cranes[4]; it is error upon error, and clout upon clout,

---

1. *my next excursion*, my next or future life. 2. "*glorify God and enjoy Him forever*," the answer in the Westminster Catechism of the Presbyterian Church to the question, "What is the chief end of man?" A catechism is a book of questions and answers about religion. 3. *like ants . . . changed into men*. According to Hopi (hō'pē) Indian lore, the first people were ants. 4. *like pygmies we fight with cranes*. Homer and other ancient writers believed that the pygmies, dwarf inhabitants of Africa, carried on warfare with the cranes.

and our best virtue has for its occasion a superfluous and evitable wretchedness. Our life is frittered away by detail. An honest man has hardly need to count more than his ten fingers or in extreme cases he may add his ten toes, and lump the rest.

Simplicity, simplicity, simplicity! I say, let your affairs be as two or three, and not a hundred or a thousand; instead of a million count half a dozen, and keep your accounts on your thumbnail. In the midst of this chopping sea of civilized life, such are the clouds and storms and quicksands and thousand-and-one items to be allowed for, that a man has to live, if he would not founder and go to the bottom and not make his port at all, by dead reckoning,[5] and he must be a great calculator indeed who succeeds. Simplify, simplify. Instead of three meals a day, if it be necessary eat but one; instead of a hundred dishes, five; and reduce other things in proportion. Our life is like a German Confederacy, made up of petty states,[6] with its boundary forever fluctuating, so that even a German cannot tell you how it is bounded at any moment. The nation itself, with all its so-called internal improvements, which, by the way, are all external and superficial, is just such an unwieldy and overgrown establishment, cluttered with furniture and tripped up by its own traps, ruined by luxury and heedless expense, by want of calculation and a worthy aim, as the million households in the land; and the only cure for it as for them is in a rigid economy, a stern and more than Spartan simplicity of life and elevation of purpose. It lives too fast. Men think that it is essential that the *Nation* have commerce, and export ice, and talk through a telegraph, and ride thirty miles an hour, without a doubt, whether *they* do or not; but whether we should live like baboons or like men is a little uncertain. If we do not get out sleepers, and forge rails, and devote days and nights to the work, but go to tinkering upon our *lives* to improve them, who will build railroads? And if railroads are not built, how shall we get to heaven in season? But if we stay at home and mind our business, who will want railroads? We do not ride on the railroad; it rides upon us.

My House by Walden Pond

The exact cost of my house, paying the usual price for such materials as I used, but not counting the work, all of which was done by myself, was as follows; and I give the details because very few are able to tell exactly what their houses cost, and fewer still, if any, the separate cost of the various materials which compose them.

Boards	$8.03½,	mostly shanty boards.
Refuse shingles for roof and sides. .	4.00	
Laths	1.25	
Two second-hand windows with glass	2.43	
One thousand old brick	4.00	
Two casks of lime .	2.40	That was high.
Hair	.31	More than I needed.
Mantel-tree iron[1] .	.15	
Nails	3.90	
Hinges and screws	.14	
Latch	.10	
Chalk	.01	
Transportation . . .	1.40	I carried a good part
In all	$28.12½	on my back.

These are all the materials excepting the timber, stones, and sand, which I claimed by squatter's right. I have also a small woodshed adjoining, made chiefly of the stuff which was left after building the house. I intend to build

WHY I WENT TO THE WOODS. 5. *dead reckoning*, calculation of a ship's position by using a compass and studying the record of the voyage, and without using observations of the sun and stars. 6. *a German Confederacy, made up of petty states.* At the time Thoreau wrote *Walden*, Germany as a nation did not exist. Until the rise of Napoleon at the end of the eighteenth century, there had been a German emperor, but he was a mere figurehead; in each of the several hundred German states the real ruler was its prince or duke. At the Congress of Vienna (1814-1815), which met to reorganize Europe after Napoleon's defeat at the Battle of Waterloo, the German states were reduced in number from several hundred to thirty-eight and a loose German Confederation was formed. However, the real power remained with the heads of the states rather than in the confederation. In 1871 Bismarck, a statesman from Prussia, the strongest of the German states, welded Germany into an empire.

MY HOUSE BY WALDEN POND. 1. *Mantel-tree iron*, a piece of iron across the top of a fireplace to support the masonry above.

me a house which will surpass any on the main street in Concord in grandeur and luxury, as soon as it pleases me as much and will cost me no more than my present one.

I thus found that the student who wishes for a shelter can obtain one for a lifetime at an expense not greater than the rent which he now pays annually. If I seem to boast more than is becoming, my excuse is that I brag for humanity rather than for myself; and my shortcomings and inconsistencies do not affect the truth of my statement. Notwithstanding much cant and hypocrisy—chaff which I find it difficult to separate from my wheat, but for which I am as sorry as any man—I will breathe freely and stretch myself in this respect, it is such a relief to both the moral and physical system; and I am resolved that I will not through humility become the devil's attorney.[2] I will endeavor to speak a good word for the truth. At Cambridge College[3] the mere rent of a student's room, which is only a little larger than my own, is thirty dollars each year, though the corporation[4] had the advantage of building thirty-two side by side and under one roof, and the occupant suffers the inconvenience of many and noisy neighbors, and perhaps a residence in the fourth story. . . . Of the present economical and social arrangements I was more independent than any farmer in Concord, for I was not anchored to a house or farm, but could follow the bent of my genius, which is a very crooked one, every moment. . . .

By surveying, carpentry, and day labor of various other kinds in the village in the meanwhile, for I have as many trades as fingers, I had earned $13.34. The expense of food for eight months, namely, from July 4 to March 1, the time when these estimates were made, though I lived there more than two years—not counting potatoes, a little green corn, and some peas, which I had raised, nor considering the value of what was on hand at the last date, was:

Rice	$1.73½	
Molasses	1.73	{ Cheapest form of the saccharine.
Rye meal	1.04¾	
Indian meal	.99¾	Cheaper than rye.
Pork	.22	
Flour	.88	{ Costs more than Indian meal, both money and trouble.
Sugar	.80	
Lard	.65	
Apples	.25	
Dried apples	.22	
Sweet potatoes	.10	
One pumpkin	.06	
One watermelon	.02	
Salt	.03	

All experiments which failed

Yes, I did eat $8.74, all told; but I should not thus unblushingly publish my guilt, if I did not know that most of my readers were equally guilty with myself, and their deeds would look no better in print. The next year I sometimes caught a mess of fish for my dinner, and once I went so far as to slaughter a woodchuck which ravaged my beanfield—effect his transmigration, as a Tartar would say[5]—and devour him, partly for experiment's sake; but though it afforded me a momentary enjoyment, notwithstanding a musky flavor, I saw that the longest use would not make that a good practice, however it might seem to have your woodchucks ready dressed by the village butcher.

Clothing and some incidental expenses within the same dates, though little can be inferred from this item, amounted to	$8.40¾
Oil and some household utensils	2.00

So that all the pecuniary outgoes, excepting for washing and mending, which for the most part were done out of the house, and their bills have not yet been received—and these are all and more than all the ways by which money necessarily goes out in this part of the world—were:

2. *the devil's attorney*, a liar. 3. *Cambridge College*, Harvard University, which is located in Cambridge, Massachusetts. 4. *the corporation*, the governing board of the college. 5. *effect his transmigration, as a Tartar would say.* Tartars were a horde of Mongols and Turks who overran parts of Europe during the Middle Ages. Thoreau is saying that like many primitive people they believed that at death the soul passed into another body (transmigration).

House	$28.12½
Farm, one year[6]...................	14.72½
Food, eight months................	8.74
Clothing, etc., eight months........	8.40¾
Oil, etc., eight months.............	2.00
In all	$61.99¾

I address myself now to those of my readers who have a living to get. To meet this I have:

For farm produce sold...............	$23.44
Earned by day labor................	13.34
In all........................	$36.78

which subtracted from the sum of the outgoes leaves a balance of $25.21¾ on the one side—this being very nearly the means with which I started, and the measure of expenses to be incurred—and on the other, besides the leisure and independence and health thus secured, a comfortable house for me as long as I choose to occupy it.

These statistics, however accidental and therefore uninstructive they may appear, as they have a certain completeness, have a certain value also. Nothing was given me of which I have not rendered some account. It appears from the above estimate that my food alone cost me in money about twenty-seven cents a week. It was, for nearly two years after this: rye and Indian meal without yeast, potatoes, rice, a very little salt pork, molasses, and salt and my drink—water. It was fit that I should live on rice, mainly, who loved so well the philosophy of India. To meet the objec-tions of some inveterate cavilers, I may as well state that if I dined out occasionally, as I always had done, and I trust shall have opportunities to do again, it was frequently to the detriment of my domestic arrangements. But the dining out, being, as I have stated, a constant element, does not in the least affect a comparative statement like this.

I learned from my two years' experience that it would cost incredibly little trouble to obtain one's necessary food, even in this latitude; that a man may use as simple a diet as the animals, and yet retain health and strength. I have made a satisfactory dinner, satisfactory on several accounts, simply off a dish of purslane (*Portulaca oleracea*) which I gathered in my cornfield, boiled, and salted. I give the Latin on account of the savoriness of the trivial name. And pray what more can a reasonable man desire, in peaceful times, in ordinary noons, than a sufficient number of ears of green sweet corn boiled, with the addition of salt? Even the little variety that I used was a yielding to the demands of appetite, and not of health. Yet men have come to such a pass that they frequently starve, not for want of necessaries, but for want of luxuries; and I know a good woman who thinks that her son lost his life because he took to drinking water only....

---

6. *Farm, one year.* This item covers the expenses incurred by Thoreau in his planting and cultivating of a 2½-acre farm.

REBEL One evening in July 1846, Thoreau walked from Walden to Concord to pick up a mended shoe at the cobbler's shop. In town, he was met by Sam Staples, the sheriff and tax collector. Sam arrested him.

The reason was that Thoreau had not paid his poll tax, and the reason for his refusing to pay it was this: that he did not want to support certain activities of the government. Back in 1838, he had refused to pay taxes which had been levied to support a church which he did not attend. In 1846, he refused to pay his poll tax because, like many others, he was opposed to the Mexican War for which he could find no justification.

Sam felt awkward about arresting this man whom he had known for many years, this man with whom he'd had many pleasant conversations. He said, "I'll pay your tax, Henry, if you're hard up." Thoreau apparently said that he had the $1.50 needed to pay the tax, but he just refused to pay, anyhow. Why, he reasoned, should he support a government whose actions he believed immoral? So Sam regretfully locked Thoreau up in jail.

A story that is told in Concord to this day is that while Thoreau was in jail, his friend, Ralph Waldo Emerson, visited him. Emerson believed as Thoreau did, but he had paid the poll tax. The story has it that their talk went this way: Emerson said, "Henry, why are you here?" And the prisoner answered, "Waldo, why are you *not* here?"

The next morning, much to Thoreau's disgust, someone in his family—his Aunt Maria, probably—sneaked over to the jail and paid the tax and the fees. But the visitor to Concord from Walden had made known his principles and had spent a night in jail to show that he believed in them.

Thoreau's experiences in jail as well as his beliefs concerning government are considered in an essay called "Civil Disobedience," published in 1849. In this essay Thoreau adopted an extreme attitude toward the long-admired American quality of self-reliance. That quality had been bred especially by life on the frontier, where the rugged individual chafed against controls of every sort. Relatively few Americans, however, had gone so far as Thoreau now did in believing that a man should refuse to let his rights as an individual be interfered with in any way by the government, and by the time Thoreau died, in 1862, the belief in such extreme individualism was even less general.

It is doubtful if Thoreau influenced very many Americans of his day—or later times—to adopt the ideas for which he willingly went to jail. But in the twentieth century in far-off India the great leader Mahatma Gandhi was to read Thoreau's essay and put his ideas into practice in what was an extraordinarily successful rebellion against the British Empire.

A summary of Thoreau's attitude toward the relations between the individual and the state is contained in the motto quoted by him in the opening sentence of the selection beginning on the following page.

Opening paragraphs of the manuscript of Thoreau's essay on walking.

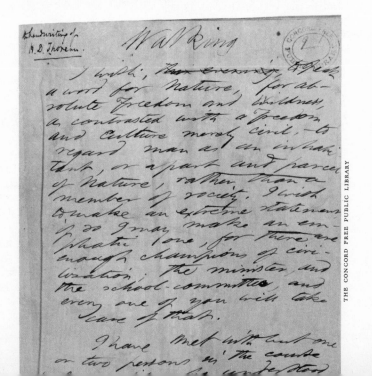

FROM *Civil Disobedience*

I heartily accept the motto, "That government is best which governs least"; and I should like to see it acted up to more rapidly and systematically. Carried out, it finally amounts to this, which also I believe—"That government is best which governs not at all"; and when men are prepared for it, that will be the kind of government which they will have. Government is at best but an expedient; but most governments are usually, and all governments are sometimes, inexpedient. The objections which have been brought against a standing army, and they are many and weighty, and deserve to prevail, may also at last be brought against a standing government. The standing army is only an arm of the standing government. The government itself, which is only the mode which the people have chosen to execute their will, is equally liable to be abused and perverted before the people can act through it. Witness the present Mexican War, the work of comparatively a few individuals using the standing government as their tool; for, in the outset, the people would not have consented to this measure.

This American government—what is it but a tradition, though a recent one, endeavoring to transmit itself unimpaired to posterity, but each instant losing some of its integrity? It has not the vitality and force of a single living man, for a single man can bend it to his will. It is a sort of wooden gun to the people themselves. But it is not the less necessary for this; for the people must have some complicated machinery or other, and hear its din, to satisfy that idea of government which they have. Governments show thus how successfully men can be imposed on, even impose on themselves, for their own advantage. It is excellent, we must all allow. Yet this government never of itself furthered any enterprise, but by the alacrity with which it got out of its way. *It* does not keep the country free. *It* does not settle the West. *It* does not educate. The character inherent in the American people has done all that has been accomplished; and it would have done somewhat more if the government had not sometimes got in its way. For government is an expedient by which men would fain succeed in letting one another alone; and, as has been said, when it is most expedient, the governed are most let alone by it. Trade and commerce, if they were not made of India rubber, would never manage to bounce over the obstacles which legislators are continually putting in their way; and, if one were to judge these men wholly by the effects of their actions and not partly by their intentions, they would deserve to be classed and punished with those mischievous persons who put obstructions on the railroads.

But, to speak practically and as a citizen, unlike those who call themselves no-government men, I ask for, not at once no government, but *at once* a better government. Let every man make known what kind of government would command his respect, and that will be one step toward obtaining it....

I have paid no poll tax for six years. I was put into jail once on this account, for one night; and, as I stood considering the walls of solid stone, two or three feet thick, and the iron grating which strained the light, I could not help being struck with the foolishness of that institution which treated me as if I were mere flesh and blood and bones, to be locked up. I wondered that it should have concluded at length that this was the best use it could put me to, and had never thought to avail itself of my services in some way. I saw that, if there was a wall of stone between me and my townsmen, there was a still more difficult one to climb or break through before they could get to be as free as I was. I did not for a moment feel confined, and the walls seemed a great waste of stone and mortar. I felt as if I alone of all my townsmen had paid my tax. They plainly did not know how to treat me, but behaved like persons who are underbred. In every threat and in every compliment there was a blunder; for they thought that my chief desire was to stand on the other side of that stone wall. I could not but smile to see how industriously they locked the door on my meditations, which followed them out again without let or hindrance, and *they* were really all that was dangerous. As they could not reach me, they had resolved to punish my body; just as boys, if they cannot come at some person against whom they have a spite, will abuse his dog. I saw that the State was half-witted, that it was timid as a lone woman with her silver spoons, and that it did not know its friends from its foes, and I lost all my remaining respect for it, and pitied it.

Thus the State never intentionally confronts a man's sense, intellectual or moral, but only his body, his senses. It is not armed with superior wit or honesty, but with superior physical force. I was not born to be forced. I will breathe after my own fashion. Let us see who is the strongest. What force has a multitude? They only can force me who obey a higher law than I. They force me to become like themselves. I do not hear of *men* being *forced* to live this way or that by masses of men. What sort of life were that to live? When I meet a government which says to me, "Your money or your life," why should I be in haste to give it my money? It may be in a great strait, and not know what to do: I cannot help that. It must help itself; do as I do. It is not worth the while to snivel about it. I am not responsible for the successful working of the machinery of society. I am not the son of the engineer. I perceive that, when an acorn and a chestnut fall side by side, the one does not remain inert to make way for the other, but both obey their own laws, and spring and grow and flourish as best they can, till one, perchance, overshadows and destroys

the other. If a plant cannot live according to its nature, it dies; and so a man.

The night in prison was novel and interesting enough. The prisoners in their shirt sleeves were enjoying a chat and the evening air in the doorway when I entered. But the jailer said, "Come, boys, it is time to lock up"; and so they dispersed, and I heard the sound of their steps returning into the hollow apartments. My roommate was introduced to me by the jailer as "a first-rate fellow and a clever[1] man." When the door was locked, he showed me where to hang my hat, and how he managed matters there. The rooms were whitewashed once a month; and this one, at least, was the whitest, most simply furnished, and probably the neatest apartment in the town. He naturally wanted to know where I came from, and what brought me there; and, when I had told him, I asked him in my turn how he came there, presuming him to be an honest man, of course; and, as the world goes, I believe he was. "Why," said he, "they accuse me of burning a barn; but I never did it." As near as I could discover, he had probably gone to bed in a barn when drunk, and smoked his pipe there; and so a barn was burnt. He had been there some three months waiting for his trial to come on, and would have to wait as much longer; but he was quite domesticated and contented, since he got his board for nothing, and thought that he was well treated.

He occupied one window, and I the other; and I saw that if one stayed there long, his principal business would be to look out the window. I had soon read all the tracts that were left there, and examined where former prisoners had broken out, and where a grate had been sawed off, and heard the history of the various occupants of that room; for I found that even here there was a history and a gossip which never circulated beyond the walls of the jail. Probably this is the only house in the town where verses are composed, which are afterward printed in a circular form, but not published. I was shown quite a long list of verses which were composed by some young

---

1. *clever*, honest, kind, obliging. The word *clever* was used colloquially in this sense in New England in Thoreau's time.

men who had been detected in an attempt to escape, who avenged themselves by singing them.

I pumped my fellow prisoner as dry as I could, for fear I should never see him again; but at length he showed me which was my bed, and left me to blow out the lamp.

It was like traveling into a far country, such as I had never expected to behold, to lie there for one night. It seemed to me that I never had heard the town clock strike before, nor the evening sounds of the village; for we slept with the windows open, which were inside the grating. It was to see my native village in the light of the Middle Ages, and our Concord was turned into a Rhine stream, and visions of knights and castles passed before me. They were the voices of old burghers that I heard in the streets. I was an involuntary spectator and auditor of whatever was done and said in the kitchen of the adjacent village inn—a wholly new and rare experience to me. It was a closer view of my native town. I was fairly inside of it. I never had seen its institutions before. This is one of its peculiar institutions; for it is a shire town.[2] I began to comprehend what its inhabitants were about.

In the morning, our breakfasts were put through the hole in the door, in small oblong-square tin pans, made to fit, and holding a pint of chocolate, with brown bread, and an iron spoon. When they called for the vessels again, I was green enough to return what bread I had left; but my comrade seized it, and said that I should lay that up for lunch or dinner. Soon after he was let out to work at haying in a neighboring field, whither he went every day, and would not be back till noon; so he bade me good day, saying that he doubted if he should see me again.

When I came out of prison—for someone interfered, and paid that tax—I did not perceive that great changes had taken place on the common, such as he observed who went in a youth and emerged a tottering and gray-headed man[3]; and yet a change had to my eyes come over the scene—the town, and State, and country—greater than any that mere time could effect. I saw yet more distinctly the State in which I lived. I saw to what extent the people among whom I lived could be trusted as good neighbors and friends; that their friendship was for summer weather only; that they did not greatly propose to do right; that they were a distinct race from me by their prejudices and superstitions, as the Chinamen and Malays are; that in their sacrifices to humanity they ran no risks, not even to their property; that after all they were not so noble but they treated the thief as he had treated them, and hoped, by a certain outward observance and a few prayers, and by walking in a particular straight though useless path from time to time, to save their souls. This may be to judge my neighbors harshly; for I believe that many of them are not aware that they have such an institution as the jail in their village.

It was formerly the custom in our village, when a poor debtor came out of jail, for his acquaintances to salute him, looking through their fingers, which were crossed to represent the grating of a jail window, "How do ye do?" My neighbors did not thus salute me, but first looked at me, and then at one another, as if I had returned from a long journey.

I was put in jail as I was going to the shoemaker's to get a shoe which was mended. When I was let out the next morning, I proceeded to finish my errand, and, having put on my mended shoe, joined a huckleberry party, who were impatient to put themselves under my conduct; and in half an hour—for the horse was soon tackled—was in the midst of a huckleberry field, on one of our highest hills, two miles off, and then the State was nowhere to be seen.

This is the whole history of "My Prisons."[4] . . .

The authority of government, even such as I am willing to submit to—for I will cheerfully obey those who know and can do better than I, and in many things even those who neither know nor can do so well—is still an impure

2. *a shire town*, a county seat. The jail in which Thoreau was confined in Concord was the county jail. 3. *who went in a youth . . . gray-headed man*. This is a reference to Silvio Pellico (sēl'vē ō pel'lē kō), an Italian poet and dramatist, whose health had been broken by his sufferings in prison. The record of his experiences, entitled *My Prisons*, was translated into many languages. 4. "*My Prisons*," the title of Pellico's book. (See footnote 3.)

one: to be strictly just, it must have the sanction and consent of the governed. It can have no pure right over my person and property but what I concede to it. The progress from an absolute to a limited monarchy,[5] from a limited monarchy to a democracy, is a progress toward a true respect for the individual. Even the Chinese philosopher[6] was wise enough to regard the individual as the basis of the empire. Is a democracy, such as we know it, the last improvement possible in government? Is it not possible to take a step further toward recognizing and organizing the rights of man? There will never be a really free and enlightened State until the State comes to recognize the individual as a higher and independent power, from which all its own power and authority are derived, and treats him accordingly. I please myself with imagining a State at last which can afford to be just to all men, and to treat the individual with respect as a neighbor; which even would not think it inconsistent with its own repose if a few were to live aloof from it, not meddling with it, nor embraced by it, who fulfilled all the duties of neighbors and fellow men. A State which bore this kind of fruit, and suffered it to drop off as fast as it ripened, would prepare the way for a still more perfect and glorious State, which also I have imagined, but not yet anywhere seen.

---

5. *an absolute . . . limited monarchy.* An absolute monarchy is one in which the ruler has unlimited power; a limited monarchy is one in which the ruler's powers are limited by the laws of the nation.   6. *the Chinese philosopher,* Confucius (cən fū′shəs), who lived about five hundred years before Christ.

TO INCREASE UNDERSTANDING
Selections from Walden

1. (*a*) What social and economic problems disturbed thoughtful people in Thoreau's day? (*b*) Describe some of the attempts to solve these problems. (*c*) What was Thoreau's way of attacking such problems?

2. Why is *Walden* considered an important book?

3. (*a*) Point out passages in "The Battle of the Ants" in which Thoreau compares ants to men. (*b*) What does the nature of the comparison imply about men? (*c*) How does this comparison help Thoreau to convey his message effectively?

4. In the first paragraph of "Why I Went to the Woods" Thoreau explains exactly the reasons back of his experiment. Tell in your own words what he means by each of the following sentences, paying particular attention to the italicized words and expressions.

(*a*) I went to the woods because I wished *to live deliberately, to front* only the essential facts of life, and see if I could not learn what it had to teach, and not, when I came to die, *discover that I had not lived.*

(*b*) I did not wish *to live what was not life,* living is so *dear.*

(*c*) I wanted *to live deep and suck out all the marrow of life,* to live so sturdily and Spartanlike as *to put to rout all that was not life, to cut a broad swath and shave close, to drive life into a corner,* and *reduce it to its lowest terms,* and, if it proved to be *mean,* why then to get the whole and genuine meanness of it.

5. (*a*) State Thoreau's idea of simplicity as it is developed in the third paragraph of this selection (page 237, column 1, paragraph 1). (*b*) Comment on the aptness of his comparison of modern life to a German Confederacy. (*c*) Is there a conflict between simplicity, as Thoreau understood it, and progress? Explain. (*d*) What virtue, if any, do you find in Thoreau's viewpoint?

6. (*a*) What does Thoreau mean by writing, "We do not ride on the railroad; it rides upon us" (page 237, column 1, paragraph 1)? (*b*) Relate this paradox to his ideas about simplicity.

7. Triumphantly Thoreau records the total cost of his house by Walden Pond as being only $28.12½. What, in your opinion, was his chief reason for wishing to keep down the cost?

8. (*a*) What qualities and abilities did Thoreau possess that made it possible for him to make a success of the experiment at Walden Pond? (*b*) Do you think his plan would prove successful for the average man today? Explain your answer.

9. Thoreau was a scholar as well as a woodsman. What evidence of this do you find in these selections?

10. (*a*) What did Thoreau mean by writing, "The philosopher for whom rainbows can be explained away never saw them"? (*b*) How is this statement related to his general attitude toward nature? (*c*) How does Thoreau's interest in nature differ from that of Washington Irving or James Fenimore Cooper?

Civil Disobedience

1. (*a*) Why may Thoreau be considered a rebel? (*b*) What circumstances in early nineteenth-century

life had fostered attitudes like Thoreau's? (c) What has been the importance of Thoreau's idea of civil disobedience in the twentieth century?

2. In the first paragraph of this selection Thoreau writes: "Government is at best but an expedient; but most governments are usually, and all governments are sometimes, inexpedient." (a) Explain this statement. (b) Trace the arguments in the first two paragraphs by which Thoreau seeks to prove his point. (c) What points can you advance to support or refute his argument?

3. On his being put in jail Thoreau commented: "I could not help being struck with the foolishness of that institution which treated me as if I were mere flesh and blood and bones, to be locked up" (page 241, column 2, paragraph 2). (a) What did he mean? (b) What did he consider the essential elements of a man's make-up? (c) The unessential elements? (d) Why did he consider himself to be more free inside the jail than his fellow men who were outside?

4. (a) Judging from the last paragraph of the selection, what was Thoreau's idea of the "free and enlightened State"? (b) To what extent do your ideas on this subject agree or disagree with his?

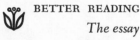

BETTER READING
The essay

The term *essay* describes most of the nonfictional prose we read. Washington Irving's chatty descriptions of New Amsterdam, Poe's criticism of *Twice-Told Tales,* and Thoreau's "Civil Disobedience"—all are essays. The prose essay has such a broad range because it is the least restricted and the most adaptable of all literary forms. Moderate length and freedom of expression are its chief characteristics.

Imagine, for example, that two men take a walk on a fine spring day and then return to their desks to write about it. The first essayist tells us, almost conversationally, why he likes to walk. His personality illuminates the subject—length, structure, and style evolve naturally from his feelings about walking. Because the writer's personality controls his essay, we say it represents the *informal* essay pattern. The second essayist adopts a different approach. In a series of logical arguments, he persuades us that walking is good exercise. We say his essay represents the *formal* essay pattern because its structure and style are tightly organized. These traditions of formality and informality have marked the essay since its beginnings.

Although essays had undoubtedly been written earlier, the form was unnamed and its pattern unrecognized until the Frenchman, Montaigne (mon tān'), called his brief prose pieces *essais* or "attempts." Montaigne, writing in 1580, set down his comments on the passing scene so informally that his wit and charm illumined every line. His English contemporary, Francis Bacon, adopted the formal essay when writing his tightly organized practical guides to conduct. Both men incorporated aphorisms or wise sayings into their work, but Bacon's essays were as serious, dignified, and logical as Montaigne's were personal, rambling, and unconventional.

Flexible in its range and expression, the essay is so capable of variation that each age has adapted it to fresh needs. Eighteenth-century periodicals made it an excellent vehicle for satire and humor: Addison and Steele, in particular, polished the essay until it was as witty and sophisticated as they were themselves. Franklin followed their lead in his *Dogood Papers* and then, like Paine, Hamilton, and Freneau, shaped the essay to political purposes. Irving brought the informal essay to perfection in his *Sketch Book.* Poe adapted the formal essay to literary criticism.

The writers of America's Golden Day found the essay admirably suited to an age that was probing the behavior of man and searching for new patterns to live by. Emerson, Lowell, Holmes, and others turned to the essay to express their ideas. Thoreau was essentially an essayist. His greatest book, *Walden,* is in reality a collection of related essays.

Consider Thoreau as an essayist. Is the excerpt from *Walden* entitled "Why I Went to the Woods" (page 236) formal or informal in tone and organization? What points of similarity do you find between Thoreau's "Civil Disobedience" and the selection from Paine's *Common Sense?* How does "Civil Disobedience" differ from Irving's "Early Life in Manhattan"?

 WORDS!

Since Thoreau often uses a common word in an unusual sense, we are likely to miss his meaning. Examine the sentence on page 232 in which he tells us that the three battling ants were "united for life, as if a new kind of *attraction* had been invented which put all other locks and cements to shame." Obviously, Thoreau is not using *attraction* in its usual sense of "that which allures." Turn to the Glossary or a dictionary and select the definition that does fit the context. Then reword the sentence, without using the word *attraction,* in such a way as to make it clear. Explain, too, why the following words are particularly appropriate in the sentence: *united, locks,* and *cement.*

THE FACTORY GIRLS OF LOWELL

Lowell, Massachusetts, close to Thoreau's beloved Concord, mushroomed in his lifetime from a sleepy country village into one of the major cotton-manufacturing centers of New England. The Concord and Merrimack rivers, where Thoreau fished and boated and which he knew so intimately, furnished the power that drove the looms and spinning machines. Although Thoreau feared the industrialization he saw around him, for a while at least, Lowell was an industrial Utopia. Prominent visitors such as Andrew Jackson, Charles Dickens, and Davy Crockett came to admire the new factories and the good working conditions; they left praising the remarkable factory girls of Lowell.

In mid-nineteenth century it was unusual to find women working in factories. Married ladies and young girls alike were expected to busy themselves in the home, within their family circle. But because women were ideally suited to keeping bobbin and loom threads unbroken and unsnarled, the mill owners of Lowell had sought out local farm girls for their factories. The mill owners had their hands full persuading them to come. No God-fearing Yankee farmer was willing to send his daughter, young and respectable as she was, away from home and family. It was unheard of! Faced with such dour reluctance, the mill

owners had no choice but to provide the moral atmosphere and protection young ladies required. They did so by building company-owned boarding houses where the girls could live under the chaperoning eye of a stern matron.

Then the girls flocked to Lowell from the country. They were capable and literate young women trained for the arduous and varied tasks of farmlife. For the princely sum of $3.50 a week, they watched the bobbins, tended the looms, and often packed the finished product. They remained in Lowell long enough to bank a suitable dowry and then returned home to the farm and marriage.

Working the same twelve-hour day they had been accustomed to on the farm, these country girls still had the energy to pursue a variety of intellectual interests. In full-skirted dresses, with parasols over their arms, they crowded the lecture halls to hear men like Emerson speak; they listened to church sermons with equal enthusiasm. Their reading was extensive for they shared books with one another—often smuggling copies into the factory, to their overseers' dismay.

The most remarkable thing about the factory girls, however, was their writing. The light verse, original stories, and moral essays, which they wrote for their church literary circles, eventually were collected and published in their own periodical, the *Lowell Offering*. Written and edited by the factory girls, and financed by the mill owners, four issues of the *Offering* appeared in 1840 and in 1841, and several more issues after 1842. The *Lowell Offering*, it is true, was the work of amateur writers; but if its literary quality was not of the highest caliber, neither can it be dismissed as inferior.

When all the industrial abuses Thoreau feared came into being, the country girls left Lowell. We remember them today for their short-lived *Offering*, which shows us dramatically that the New England factory worker shared the same literary interests as his better known American contemporaries did.

Ralph Waldo Emerson 1803-1882

Ralph Waldo Emerson was fourteen years Thoreau's senior and during his lifetime far more famous. In the lectures and writings which established his reputation he expressed beliefs similar to the younger man's; in fact, he helped Thoreau arrive at some of his ideas. But because Emerson was more of a bookman and more interested in generalizations, he expressed such beliefs, and others, with different emphases.

Emerson was born in Boston. His New England ancestors included many ministers and learned men. His father, who died when Waldo was eight, was a Unitarian minister; and his Aunt Mary Moody Emerson, who lived with the family, was an avid reader. As a boy Waldo was encouraged to make use of books, and he became fond of them. Daily he recited lessons, as did his brothers, to members of the family. At church instead of listening to sermons he read books which he had brought along. Nighttimes, blankets pulled up to his chin to warm him in his chilly bedroom, he read the ancient Greek philosopher, Plato, so that years after when he thought of this favorite philosopher he recalled the smell of wool.

Waldo went to Harvard, where he worked for his room and board. After his graduation in 1821 he taught school for a time, then attended Harvard Divinity School. In 1829 he became minister of a Unitarian church and married Miss Ellen Tucker. After years of hard work and financial difficulty the young minister seemed at last secure and contented: he was happily married, his congregation liked him, and he seemed destined to continue in his pastorate for many years.

But two events changed this. In 1831 his wife died, and the following year he resigned from his church because even that liberal Unitarian congregation held to some forms of worship in which Emerson did not believe. He went abroad, traveling in Italy and Great Britain. His journals show that unlike most travelers he found sightseeing less interesting than intellectual discussions with famous men such as the romantic poets William Wordsworth and Samuel Taylor Coleridge. But the adventure most important to him was his meeting on a lonely Scotch farm and a long conversation with Thomas Carlyle, an author then practically unknown. This meeting helped Emerson work out his own philosophy. Carlyle preached a doctrine toward which Emerson had been moving, a belief akin to that of Plato, which had won followers throughout the world. This belief was that the whole material universe is an emblem of a deeper reality—Carlyle called it "a garment of the spirit." As Thoreau would hold later, Carlyle held that since God is everywhere, the true comprehension of any detail offers a key to the comprehension of everything. This first meeting between Carlyle and Emerson began a friendship which was kept alive by letters throughout the course of their long lives.

When Emerson returned to New England in 1833, he bought a house and two acres of land in Concord, and remarried. As he became part of the intellectual life of Concord and nearby Boston, he found a great interest in a philosophy much like that which he and Carlyle had talked about. In 1836 he published his first volume, *Nature,* which outlined this philosophy, known as *Transcendentalism.*

*erson's house,
ncord.*

Transcendentalism has been defined as "the recognition in man of the capacity of knowing truth intuitively, or of attaining knowledge transcending [going beyond] the reach of the senses." Emerson became the chief spokesman for Transcendentalism. In his lectures and writings he distinguished between the *understanding*, by which he meant the rational faculty, and *reason*, which to him signified a suprarational or intuitive faculty. Like Carlyle he was a mystic in his belief that in his best moments man could see beneath the surfaces of things to their inner meaning. This reliance on intuition as a guide led to Emerson's feeling that intuition was more trustworthy than all standards and laws imposed by religion or society. In "Self-Reliance" (page 250), his best-known and most quoted essay, he states this belief: "Nothing is at last sacred but the integrity of your own mind."

Self-reliant, Emerson did not follow slavishly even so dear a friend as Carlyle. An optimist like most Americans in that hopeful era, he could not share the dour Scotchman's bitterness of spirit. Steeped in democracy like others who held village offices and took part in Concord's town meetings, he could not accept Carlyle's aristocratic attitudes. Emerson believed that even the humblest man should be allowed to help run the village and the nation because his intuition would lead him to see deep meanings beneath surfaces. Delighting, like Thoreau, in the outdoor world, he gave

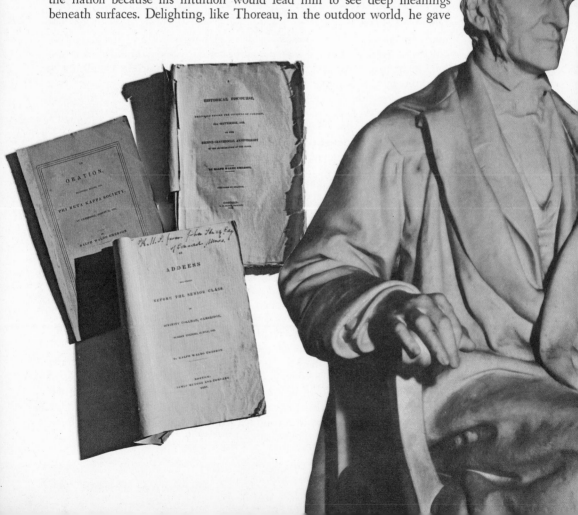

nature a more important place in his life and thought than Carlyle did in his.

Emerson's environment influenced him in other ways. His ancestors had included hard-headed businessmen as well as ministers and scholars; his family's poverty had taught him the value of money. He lectured widely, describing the process thus:

"I'll bet you fifty dollars a day," said lecture committees, "that you will not leave your library, and wade and ride and suffer all manner of indignities and stand up for an hour each night reading in a hall"; and I answered, "I'll bet I will." I do it and win the $900 [each season].

So to the culture-hungry audiences of the 1840's and 1850's Emerson lectured. By train and horse and buggy he traveled through New England, south to the Middle Atlantic states, west to Wisconsin, Michigan, and even the Pacific coast. He secured income too by publishing essays first in magazines and later in book form: *Essays* (1841), *Essays: Second Series* (1844), *Representative Men* (1850), *The Conduct of Life* (1860), and others.

A practical Yankee for all his mysticism, Emerson made a vital part of his philosophy what he called "the actual horizon of life." As he explained in his essay "Experience," he believed every man was driven by two forces —practical considerations and intuition—and concluded, "The mid-world

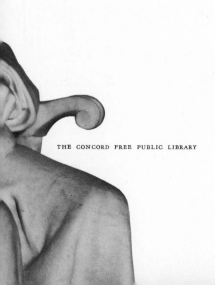

Left: Statue of Emerson and some of his printed speeches, both in the Concord Public Library. Right: A handbill advertising, among other things, Emerson's participation in a community event.

THE CONCORD FREE PUBLIC LIBRARY

April 19th, 1861.   April 19th, 1867.

MONUMENT CELEBRATION.

THE MONUMENT,

Recently erected to the memory of the Soldiers of Concord, who fell in the War of the Rebellion, will be dedicated

ON FRIDAY, APRIL 19th, 1867,

With appropriate exercises, in which all residents of the town and those interested in the occasion are cordially invited to participate.

All are requested to meet on the Common, in front of the Church of the First Parish, at 1 1-2 o'clock, P. M., promptly, where a Procession will be formed and proceed to the Town Hall, under the escort of the

CONCORD ARTILLERY.

CAPT. RICHARD BARRETT,

ACCOMPANIED BY

GILMORE'S FULL BAND.

AT THE TOWN HALL.

A Report will be made by the Hon. E. R. HOAR,
Chairman of the Monument Committee;

An Address delivered by R. W. EMERSON;

And a Poem by F. B. SANBORN;

WITH SINGING, AND MUSIC BY THE BAND.

☞ Seats will be reserved in the Town Hall for the families of those whose names are upon the Monument.

HON. JOHN S. KEYES, President of the Day.

Committee of Arrangements:

GEO. KEYES,   HENRY J. HOSMER,
GEO. M. BROOKS,   LORENZO EATON,   RICHARD BARRETT.

ANDREW J. HARLOW, Chief Marshal.

is best." In viewing the universe he tried to follow Plato because he was "a balanced soul . . . perceptive of the two elements." The "two elements" to which Emerson refers are concrete things and the spirit pervading them.

In his poetry and prose Emerson stresses the relationship between concrete things and the pervading spirit in two ways: (1) He generalizes—discusses the overall scheme of things so as to underline both the One and the Many as part and parcel of it. "We unite all things," he explains, "by seeing the law which pervades them; by perceiving the superficial differences and the profound resemblances." (2) He particularizes—shows concrete details in such a way as to point out the meaning of the whole reflected in them.

Most readers find it hard to follow Emerson's generalizations, his complex explanations, through long essays. But they can more easily take in particularizations in sentences and brief poems. His sentences, "The drop is a small ocean" and "The world globes itself in a drop of dew," for instance, both say in concrete ways that, rightly understood, even a drop of water can represent a profound idea. His poem, "The Snowstorm" (page 265), describes so common a phenomenon as a heavy snowfall in such a way as to make it symbolize a contrast between man's limited capacities and the power of God. In such writings Emerson's philosophy finds striking artistic expression.

Self-Reliance

Probably the most famous essay written by an American, "Self-Reliance" is both longer and more difficult than most essays of the present day. Its difficulty arises both from its wealth of related ideas and from the fact that these ideas are in themselves difficult. You will gain more from a first reading of "Self-Reliance" if you pause occasionally to review the ideas Emerson has presented. To help you do this, the essay has been divided into three parts, and questions provided after each.

I read the other day some verses written by an eminent painter which were original and not conventional. The soul always hears an admonition in such lines, let the subject be what it may. The sentiment they instill is of more value than any thought they may contain. To believe your own thought, to believe that what is true for you in your private heart is true for all men—that is genius. Speak your latent conviction, and it shall be the universal sense; for the inmost in due time becomes the outmost, and our first thought is rendered back to us by the trumpets of the Last Judgment. Familiar as the voice of the mind is to each, the highest merit we ascribe to Moses, Plato, and Milton is that they set at naught books and traditions, and spoke not what men, but what *they* thought. A man should learn to detect and watch that gleam of light which flashes across his mind from within, more than the luster of the firmament of bards and sages. Yet he dismisses without notice his thought, because it is his. In every work of genius we recognize our own rejected thoughts; they come back to us with a certain alienated majesty. Great works of art have no more affecting lesson for us than this. They teach us to abide by our spontaneous impression with good-humored inflexibility when the whole cry of voices is on the other side. Else tomorrow a stranger will say with masterly good sense precisely what we have thought and felt all the time, and we shall be forced to take with shame our own opinion from another.

There is a time in every man's education when he arrives at the conviction that envy is ignorance; that imitation is suicide; that he must take himself for better, for worse, as his portion; that though the wide universe is full of good, no kernel of nourishing corn can come to him but through his toil bestowed on that plot of ground which is given to him to till. The power which resides in him is new in nature, and none but he knows what that is which he can do, nor does he know until he has tried. Not for nothing one face, one character, one fact, makes much impression on him and another none. This sculpture in the memory is not without preëstablished harmony. The eye was placed where one ray should fall, that it might testify of that particular ray. We but half express ourselves, and are ashamed of that divine idea which each of us represents. It may be safely intrusted as proportionate and of good issues, so it be faithfully imparted, but God will not have his work made manifest by cowards. A man is relieved and gay when he has put his heart into his work and done his best; but what he has said or done otherwise shall give him no peace. It is a deliverance which does not deliver. In the attempt his genius deserts him; no muse befriends; no invention, no hope.

Trust thyself: every heart vibrates to that iron string. Accept the place the Divine Providence has found for you, the society of your contemporaries, the connection of events. Great men have always done so, and confided themselves childlike to the genius of their age, betraying their perception that the absolutely trustworthy was seated at their heart, working through their hands, predominating in all their being. And we are now men, and must accept in the highest mind the same transcendent destiny; and not minors and invalids in a protected corner, not cowards fleeing before a revolution, but guides, redeemers, and benefactors, obeying the Almighty effort and advancing on Chaos and the Dark.

What pretty oracles nature yields us on this text in the face and behavior of children, babes, and even brutes! That divided and rebel mind, that distrust of a sentiment because our arithmetic has computed the strength and means opposed to our purpose, these have not. Their mind being whole, their eye is as yet unconquered, and when we look in their faces we are disconcerted. Infancy conforms to nobody; all conform to it; so that one babe commonly makes four or five out of the adults who prattle and play to it. So God has armed youth and puberty and manhood no less with its own piquancy and charm, and made it enviable and gracious and its claims not to be put by, if it will stand by itself. Do not think the youth has no force, because he cannot speak to you and me. Hark! in the next room his voice is sufficiently clear and emphatic. It seems he knows how to speak to his contemporaries. Bashful or bold then, he will know how to make us seniors very unnecessary.

The nonchalance of boys who are sure of a dinner, and would disdain as much as a lord to do or say aught to conciliate one, is the healthy attitude of human nature. A boy is in the parlor what the pit is in the playhouse[1]: independent, irresponsible; looking out from his corner on such people and facts as pass by, he tries and sentences them on their merits, in the swift, summary way of boys, as good, bad, interesting, silly, eloquent, troublesome. He cumbers himself never about consequences, about interests; he gives an independent, genuine verdict. You must court him; he does not court you. But the man is as it were clapped into jail by his consciousness. As soon as he has once acted or spoken with éclat he is a committed person, watched by the sympathy or the hatred of hundreds, whose affections must now enter into his account. There is no Lethe[2] for this. Ah, that he could pass again into his neutrality! Who can thus avoid all pledges and, having observed, observe again from the same unaffected, unbiased, unbribable, unaffrighted innocence must always be formidable. He would utter opinions on all passing affairs, which being seen to be not private but necessary, would sink like darts into the ear of men and put them in fear.

These are the voices which we hear in solitude, but they grow faint and inaudible as we enter into the world. Society everywhere is in conspiracy against the manhood of every one of its members. Society is a joint-stock com-

1. *what the pit is in the playhouse.* In Elizabethan theaters the pit, or ground floor, was the cheapest location because it had no seats. The members of the audience who stood in the pit heckled the actors and made loud outspoken criticisms of the performance. 2. *Lethe* (lē'thi), the river of forgetfulness in Greek mythology.

pany, in which the members agree, for the better securing of his bread to each shareholder, to surrender the liberty and culture of the eater. The virtue in most request is conformity. Self-reliance is its aversion. It loves not realities and creators, but names and customs.

Whoso would be a man, must be a nonconformist. He who would gather immortal palms must not be hindered by the name of goodness, but must explore if it be goodness. Nothing is at last sacred but the integrity of your own mind. Absolve you to yourself, and you shall have the suffrage of the world. I remember an answer which when quite young I was prompted to make to a valued adviser who was wont to importune me with the dear old doctrines of the church. On my saying, "What have I to do with the sacredness of traditions, if I live wholly from within?" my friend suggested—"But these impulses may be from below, not from above." I replied, "They do not seem to me to be such; but if I am the Devil's child, I will live then from the Devil." No law can be sacred to me but that of my nature. Good and bad are but names very readily transferable to that or this; the only right is what is after my constitution; the only wrong what is against it. A man is to carry himself in the presence of all opposition as if everything were titular and ephemeral but he. I am ashamed to think how easily we capitulate to badges and names, to large societies and dead institutions. Every decent and well-spoken individual affects and sways me more than is right. I ought to go upright and vital, and speak the rude truth in all ways. If malice and vanity wear the coat of philanthropy, shall that pass? If an angry bigot assumes this bountiful cause of Abolition, and comes to me with his last news from Barbados,[3] why should I not say to him, "Go love thy infant; love thy woodchopper; be good-natured and modest; have that grace; and never varnish your hard, uncharitable ambition with this incredible tenderness for black folk a thousand miles off. Thy love afar is spite at home." Rough and graceless would be such greeting, but truth is handsomer than the affectation of love. Your goodness must have some edge to it, else it is

none. The doctrine of hatred must be preached, as the counteraction of the doctrine of love, when that pules and whines. I shun father and mother and wife and brother when my genius calls me. I would write on the lintels of the doorpost, *Whim.* I hope it is somewhat better than whim at last, but we cannot spend the day in explanation. Expect me not to show cause why I seek or why I exclude company. Then again, do not tell me, as a good man did today, of my obligation to put all poor men in good situations. Are they *my* poor? I tell thee, thou foolish philanthropist, that I grudge the dollar, the dime, the cent I give to such men as do not belong to me and to whom I do not belong. There is a class of persons to whom by all spiritual affinity I am bought and sold; for them I will go to prison if need be; but your miscellaneous popular charities; the education at college of fools; the building of meeting houses to the vain end to which many now stand; alms to sots, and the thousand-fold relief societies—though I confess with shame I sometimes succumb and give the dollar, it is a wicked dollar, which by and by I shall have the manhood to withhold.

Virtues are, in the popular estimate, rather the exception than the rule. There is the man *and* his virtues. Men do what is called a good action, as some piece of courage or charity, much as they would pay a fine in expiation of daily nonappearance on parade. Their works are done as an apology or extenuation of their living in the world, as invalids and the insane pay a high board. Their virtues are penances. I do not wish to expiate, but to live. My life is for itself and not for a spectacle. I much prefer that it should be of a lower strain, so it be genuine and equal, than that it should be glittering and unsteady. I wish it to be sound and sweet, and not to need diet and bleeding.[4] I ask primary evidence that you are a man, and refuse this appeal from the man to his actions. I know that for myself it makes no difference whether I do or forbear those actions which are reckoned excellent. I cannot

3. *Barbados* (bär bä′dōz), a British island in the West Indies where slavery was abolished in 1834. 4. *diet and bleeding.* In Emerson's time doctors treated certain diseases by prescribing special foods and by taking quantities of blood from the patient.

consent to pay for a privilege where I have intrinsic right. Few and mean as my gifts may be, I actually am, and do not need for my own assurance or the assurance of my fellows any secondary testimony.

What I must do is all that concerns me, not what the people think. This rule, equally arduous in actual and in intellectual life, may serve for the whole distinction between greatness and meanness. It is the harder because you will always find those who think they know what is your duty better than you know it. It is easy in the world to live after the world's opinion; it is easy in solitude to live after our own; but the great man is he who in the midst of the crowd keeps with perfect sweetness the independence of solitude.

The objection to conforming to usages that have become dead to you is that it scatters your force. It loses your time and blurs the impression of your character. If you maintain a dead church, contribute to a dead Bible society, vote with a great party either for the government or against it, spread your table like base housekeepers—under all these screens I have difficulty to detect the precise man you are: and of course so much force is withdrawn from all your proper life. But do your work, and I shall know you. Do your work, and you shall reinforce yourself. A man must consider what a blindman's buff is this game of conformity. If I know your sect I anticipate your argument. I hear a preacher announce for his text and topic the expediency of one of the institutions of his church. Do I not know beforehand that not possibly can he say a new and spontaneous word? Do I not know that with all this ostentation of examining the grounds of the institution he will do no such thing? Do I not know that he is pledged to himself not to look but at one side, the permitted side, not as a man, but as a parish minister? He is a retained attorney, and these airs of the bench[5] are the emptiest affectation. Well, most men have bound their eyes with one or another handkerchief, and attached themselves to some one of these communities of opinion. This conformity makes them not false in a few particulars, authors of a few lies, but false in all particulars. Their every truth is not quite true. Their two is not the real two, their four not the real four; so that every word they say chagrins us and we know not where to begin to set them right. Meantime nature is not slow to equip us in the prison uniform of the party to which we adhere. We come to wear one cut of face and figure, and acquire by degrees the gentlest asinine expression. There is a mortifying experience in particular, which does not fail to wreak itself also in the general history; I mean the "foolish face of praise," the forced smile which we put on in company where we do not feel at ease, in answer to conversation which does not interest us. The muscles, not spontaneously moved but moved by a low usurping willfulness, grow tight about the outline of the face, with the most disagreeable sensation.

For nonconformity the world whips you with its displeasure. And therefore a man must know how to estimate a sour face. The bystanders look askance on him in the public street or in the friend's parlor. If this aversion had its origin in contempt and resistance like his own he might well go home with a sad countenance; but the sour faces of the multitude, like their sweet faces, have no deep cause, but are put on and off as the wind blows and a newspaper directs. Yet is the discontent of the multitude more formidable than that of the senate and the college. It is easy enough for a firm man who knows the world to brook the rage of the cultivated classes. Their rage is decorous and prudent, for they are timid, as being very vulnerable themselves. But when to their feminine rage the indignation of the people is added, when the ignorant and the poor are aroused, when the unintelligent brute force that lies at the bottom of society is made to growl and mow,[6] it needs the habit of magnanimity and religion to treat it godlike as a trifle of no concernment.

The other terror that scares us from self-trust is our consistency; a reverence for our past act or word because the eyes of others have no other data for computing our orbit than our past acts, and we are loth to disappoint them.

5. bench, the judge, who sits on the "bench." 6. mow (mō), grimace, make faces.

But why should you keep your head over your shoulder? Why drag about this corpse of your memory, lest you contradict somewhat you have stated in this or that public place? Suppose you should contradict yourself? what then? It seems to be a rule of wisdom never to rely on your memory alone, scarcely even in acts of pure memory, but to bring the past for judgment into the thousand-eyed present, and live ever in a new day. In your metaphysics you have denied personality to the Deity, yet when the devout motions of the soul come, yield to them heart and life, though they should clothe God with shape and color. Leave your theory, as Joseph his coat in the hand of the harlot,[7] and flee.

A foolish consistency is the hobgoblin of little minds, adored by little statesmen and philosophers and divines. With consistency a great soul has simply nothing to do. He may as well concern himself with his shadow on the wall. Speak what you think now in hard words and tomorrow speak what tomorrow thinks in hard words again, though it contradict everything you said today.—"Ah, so you shall be sure to be misunderstood."—Is it so bad then to be misunderstood? Pythagoras was misunderstood, and Socrates, and Jesus, and Luther, and Copernicus, and Galileo, and Newton,[8] and every pure and wise spirit that ever took flesh. To be great is to be misunderstood.

I suppose no man can violate his nature. All the sallies of his will are rounded in by the law of his being, as the inequalities of [the] Andes and Himalayas are insignificant in the curve of the sphere. Nor does it matter how you gauge and try him. A character is like an acrostic of an Alexandrian stanza—read it forward, backward, or across, it still spells the same thing. In this pleasing contrite wood-life which God allows me, let me record day by day my honest thought without prospect or retrospect, and, I cannot doubt, it will be found symmetrical, though I mean it not and see it not. My book should smell of pines and resound with the hum of insects. The swallow over my window should interweave that thread or straw he carries in his bill into my web also. We pass for what we are. Character teaches

above our wills. Men imagine that they communicate their virtue or vice only by overt actions, and do not see that virtue or vice emit a breath every moment.

There will be an agreement in whatever variety of actions, so they be each honest and natural in their hour. For of one will, the actions will be harmonious, however unlike they seem. These varieties are lost sight of at a little distance, at a little height of thought. One tendency unites them all. The voyage of the best ship is a zigzag line of a hundred tacks. See the line from a sufficient distance, and it straightens itself to the average tendency. Your genuine action will explain itself and will explain your other genuine actions. Your conformity explains nothing. Act singly, and what you have already done singly will justify you now. Greatness appeals to the future. If I can be firm enough today to do right and scorn eyes, I must have done so much right before as to defend me now. Be it how it will, do right now. Always scorn appearances and you always may. The force of character is cumulative. All the foregone days of virtue work their health into this. What makes the majesty of the heroes of the senate and the field, which so fills the imagination? The consciousness of a train of great days and victories behind. They shed a united light on the advancing actor. He is attended as by a visible escort of angels. That is it which throws thunder into Chatham's voice,[9] and dignity into Washington's port, and America into Adams' eye.[10] Honor is venerable to us

7. *Joseph . . . of the harlot.* This is a reference to an episode in the Bible (Genesis 39:12) which relates the difficulties Joseph experienced while a slave in the house of an Egyptian master. 8. *Pythagoras was misunderstood . . . Newton.* To illustrate his meaning, Emerson cites several great leaders who were misunderstood in their lifetimes. He names the Greek philosophers, Pythagoras (pə thag′ə rəs) and Socrates (sok′rə tēz); and the religious leaders, Jesus and Martin Luther (lü′thər). Among misunderstood scientists, he cites Copernicus (kə pėr′nə kəs), the Polish astronomer (1473-1543) who held that the earth revolves on its axis and that the planets move around the sun; and Galileo (gal′ə lē′ō), the Italian astronomer (1564-1642), the first to prove that the earth goes around the sun; and Isaac Newton (1642-1727), the English scientist who discovered the law of gravitation. 9. *Chatham's voice.* William Pitt, the first earl of Chatham (1708-1778), was a prominent English statesman. 10. *Adams' eye.* Samuel Adams (1722-1803) was an American leader at the time of the Revolutionary War.

because it is no ephemera. It is always ancient virtue. We worship it today because it is not of today. We love it and pay it homage because it is not a trap for our love and homage, but is self-dependent, self-derived, and therefore of an old immaculate pedigree, even if shown in a young person.

I hope in these days we have heard the last of conformity and consistency. Let the words be gazetted and ridiculous henceforward. Instead of the gong for dinner, let us hear a whistle from the Spartan fife. Let us never bow and apologize more. A great man is coming to eat at my house. I do not wish to please him; I wish that he would wish to please me. I will stand here for humanity, and though I would make it kind, I would make it true. Let us affront and reprimand the smooth mediocrity and squalid contentment of the times, and hurl in the face of custom and trade and office, the fact which is the upshot of all history, that there is a great responsible Thinker and Actor working wherever a man works; that a true man belongs to no other time or place, but is the center of things. Where he is there is nature. He measures you and all men and all events. Ordinarily, everybody in society reminds us of somewhat else, or of some other person. Character, reality, reminds you of nothing else; it takes place of the whole creation. The man must be so much that he must make all circumstances indifferent. Every true man is a cause, a country, and an age; requires infinite spaces and numbers and time fully to accomplish his design—and posterity seems to follow his steps as a train of clients. A man Caesar is born, and for ages after we have a Roman Empire. Christ is born, and millions of minds so grow and cleave to his genius that he is confounded with virtue and the possible of man. An institution is the lengthened shadow of one man; as, Monachism, of the Hermit Anthony[11]; the Reformation, of Luther; Quakerism, of Fox[12]; Methodism, of Wesley[13]; Abolition, of Clarkson.[14] Scipio, Milton called "the height of Rome"[15]; and all history resolves itself very easily into the biography of a few stout and earnest persons.

Let a man then know his worth, and keep things under his feet. Let him not peep or steal, or skulk up and down with the air of a charity boy, or an interloper in the world which exists for him. But the man in the street, finding no worth in himself which corresponds to the force which built a tower or sculptured a marble god, feels poor when he looks on these. To him a palace, a statue, or a costly book have an alien and forbidding air, much like a gay equipage, and seem to say like that, "Who are you, Sir?" Yet they all are his, suitors for his notice, petitioners to his faculties that they will come out and take possession. The picture waits for my verdict; it is not to command me, but I am to settle its claims to praise. That popular fable of the sot who was picked up dead drunk in the street, carried to the duke's house, washed and dressed and laid in the duke's bed, and, on his waking, treated with all obsequious ceremony like the duke, and assured that he had been insane, owes its popularity to the fact that it symbolizes so well the state of man, who is in the world a sort of sot, but now and then wakes up, exercises his reason and finds himself a true prince.[16]

Our reading is mendicant and sycophantic. In history our imagination plays us false. Kingdom and lordship, power and estate, are a gaudier vocabulary than private John and Edward in a small house and common day's work; but the things of life are the same to both; the sum total of both is the same. Why all this deference to Alfred and Scanderbeg and Gustavus?[17] Suppose they were virtuous;

---

11. *Monachism, of the Hermit Anthony.* Monachism (mon′ə-kiz əm) is a system of living according to fixed rules in groups shut off from the world and devoted to religion. This system was founded by the Egyptian hermit-monk, St. Anthony (251-356? A.D.). **12.** *Quakerism, of Fox.* George Fox (1624-1691), the English religious leader, founded the Society of Friends, or Quakers, about 1650. **13.** *Methodism, of Wesley.* John Wesley (1703-1791), English clergyman, founded the Methodist church. **14.** *Abolition, of Clarkson.* Thomas Clarkson (1760-1846) was a well-known English abolitionist. **15.** *Scipio* (sip′i ō) . . . *height of Rome.* Scipio was the Roman general who destroyed Carthage in 146 B.C. **16.** *That popular fable . . . a true prince.* Such a story is told in the "Induction" to Shakespeare's *Taming of the Shrew.* **17.** *Why all this deference to Alfred and Scanderbeg and Gustavus?* Emerson is referring to Alfred the Great (849-899 A.D.), king of the West Saxons; Scanderbeg (skan′dər beg), Albanian patriot (1403-1468) who opposed the Turks; and Gustavus Adolphus (ə dol′fəs), king of Sweden from 1611 to 1632.

did they wear out virtue? As great a stake depends on your private act today as followed their public and renowned steps. When private men shall act with original views, the luster will be transferred from the actions of kings to those of gentlemen.

The world has been instructed by its kings, who have so magnetized the eyes of nations. It has been taught by this colossal symbol the mutual reverence that is due from man to man. The joyful loyalty with which men have everywhere suffered the king, the noble, or the great proprietor to walk among them by a law of his own, make his own scale of men and things and reverse theirs, pay for benefits not with money but with honor, and represent the law in his person, was the hieroglyphic by which they obscurely signified their consciousness of their own right and comeliness, the right of every man.

 Pause to Reflect

1. One of Emerson's most quoted lines is: "Trust thyself: every heart vibrates to that iron string." Cite passages in the first three paragraphs of the essay which give Emerson's reasons for his belief in self-reliance, and explain each passage.

2. Using the following quotations as a guide, explain why Emerson believes that *conformity* is an enemy to self-reliance.

(*a*) Infancy conforms to nobody; all conform to it (page 251).

(*b*) Society everywhere is in conspiracy against the manhood of every one of its members (page 251).

(*c*) Whoso would be a man, must be a nonconformist (page 252).

(*d*) Nothing is at last sacred but the integrity of your own mind (page 252).

(*e*) The great man is he who in the midst of the crowd keeps with perfect sweetness the independence of solitude (page 253).

3. According to Emerson, the other great enemy of self-reliance is *consistency*. Explain how he develops each of the following statements to advance his argument:

(*a*) A foolish consistency is the hobgoblin of little minds (page 254).

(*b*) To be great is to be misunderstood (page 254).

(*c*) An institution is the lengthened shadow of one man (page 255).

The magnetism which all original action exerts is explained when we inquire the reason of self-trust. Who is the Trustee? What is the aboriginal Self, on which a universal reliance may be grounded? What is the nature and power of that science-baffling star, without parallax, without calculable elements, which shoots a ray of beauty even into trivial and impure actions, if the least mark of independence appear? The inquiry leads us to that source, at once the essence of genius, of virtue, and of life, which we call Spontaneity or Instinct. We denote this primary wisdom as Intuition, whilst all later teachings are tuitions. In that deep force, the last fact behind which analysis cannot go, all things find their common origin. For the sense of being which in calm hours rises, we know not how, in the soul, is not diverse from things, from space, from light, from time, from man, but one with them and proceeds obviously from the same source whence their life and being also proceed. We first share the life by which things exist and afterward see them as appearances in nature and forget that we have shared their cause. Here is the fountain of action and of thought. Here are the lungs of that inspiration which giveth man wisdom and which cannot be denied without impiety and atheism. We lie in the lap of immense intelligence, which makes us receivers of its truth and organs of its activity. When we discern justice, when we discern truth, we do nothing of ourselves, but allow a passage to its beams. If we ask whence this comes, if we seek to pry into the soul that causes, all philosophy is at fault. Its presence or its absence is all we can affirm. Every man discriminates between the voluntary acts of his mind and his involuntary perceptions, and knows that to his involuntary perceptions a perfect faith is due. He may err in the expression of them, but he knows that these things are so, like day and night, not to be disputed. My willful actions and acquisitions are but roving; the idlest reverie, the faintest native emotion, command my curiosity and respect. Thoughtless people contradict as readily the statement of perceptions as of opinions, or rather much more readily; for they do not distinguish between perception and notion. They fancy that I choose to see this or that thing. But perception is not whimsical, but fatal. If I see a trait, my children will see it after me, and in course of time all mankind—although it may chance that no one has seen it before me. For my perception of it is as much a fact as the sun.

The relations of the soul to the divine spirit are so pure that it is profane to seek to interpose helps. It must be that when God speaketh he should communicate, not one thing, but all things; should fill the world with his voice; should scatter forth light, nature, time, souls from the center of the present thought; and new date and new create the whole. Whenever a mind is simple and receives a divine wisdom, old things pass away; means, teachers, texts, temples fall; it lives now, and absorbs past and future into the present hour. All things are made sacred by relation to it—one as much as another. All things are dissolved to their center by their cause, and in the universal miracle petty and particular miracles disappear. If therefore a man claims to know and speak of God and carries you backward to the phraseology of some old moldered nation in another country, in another world, believe him not. Is the acorn better than the oak which is its fullness and completion? Is the parent better than the child into whom he has cast his ripened being? Whence then this worship of the past? The centuries are conspirators against the sanity and authority of the soul. Time and space are but physiological colors which the eye makes, but the soul is light: where it is, is day; where it was, is night; and history is an impertinence and an injury if it be anything more than a cheerful apologue or parable of my being and becoming.

Man is timid and apologetic; he is no longer upright; he dares not say "I think," "I am," but quotes some saint or sage. He is ashamed before the blade of grass or the blowing rose. These roses under my window make no reference to former roses or to better ones; they are for what they are; they exist with God today. There is no time to them. There is simply the rose; it is perfect in every moment of its exist-

ence. Before a leaf bud has burst, its whole life acts; in the full-blown flower there is no more; in the leafless root there is no less. Its nature is satisfied and it satisfies nature in all moments alike. But man postpones or remembers; he does not live in the present, but with reverted eye laments the past, or, heedless of the riches that surround him, stands on tiptoe to foresee the future. He cannot be happy and strong until he too lives with nature in the present, above time.

This should be plain enough. Yet see what strong intellects dare not yet hear God himself unless he speak the phraseology of I know not what David, or Jeremiah, or Paul.[18] We shall not always set so great a price on a few texts, on a few lives. We are like children who repeat by rote the sentences of grandames and tutors, and, as they grow older, of the men of talents and character they chance to see, painfully recollecting the exact words they spoke. Afterward, when they come into the point of view which those had who uttered these sayings, they understand them and are willing to let the words go; for at any time they can use words as good when occasion comes. If we live truly, we shall see truly. It is as easy for the strong man to be strong, as it is for the weak to be weak. When we have new perception, we shall gladly disburden the memory of its hoarded treasures as old rubbish. When a man lives with God, his voice shall be as sweet as the murmur of the brook and the rustle of the corn.

And now at last the highest truth on this subject remains unsaid; probably cannot be said; for all that we say is the far-off remembering of the intuition. That thought by what I can now nearest approach to say it, is this. When good is near you, when you have life in yourself, it is not by any known or accustomed way; you shall not discern the footprints of any other; you shall not see the face of man; you shall not hear any name—the way, the thought, the good, shall be wholly

18. *I know not what David, or Jeremiah* (jer′ə mī′ə), *or Paul.* David, second king of Israel, was noted as a singer and poet; Jeremiah was a Hebrew prophet who in powerful language denounced the evils of his time; Paul was the apostle who wrote many of the Epistles in the New Testament.

strange and new. It shall exclude example and experience. You take the way from man, not to man. All persons that ever existed are its forgotten ministers. Fear and hope are alike beneath it. There is somewhat low even in hope. In the hour of vision there is nothing that can be called gratitude, nor properly joy. The soul raised over passion beholds identity and eternal causation, perceives the self-existence of Truth and Right, and calms itself with knowing that all things go well. Vast spaces of nature, the Atlantic Ocean, the South Seas; long intervals of time, years, centuries, are of no account. This which I think and feel underlay every former state of life and circumstances, as it does underlie my present, and what is called life and what is called death.

Life only avails, not the having lived. Power ceases in the instant of repose; it resides in the moment of transition from a past to a new state, in the shooting of the gulf, in the darting to an aim. This one fact the world hates; that the soul *becomes;* for that forever degrades the past, turns all riches to poverty, all reputation to a shame, confounds the saint with the rogue, shoves Jesus and Judas equally aside. Why then do we prate of self-reliance? Inasmuch as the soul is present there will be power not confident but agent.[19] To talk of reliance is a poor external way of speaking. Speak rather of that which relies because it works and is. Who has more obedience than I masters me, though he should not raise his finger. Round him I must revolve by the gravitation of spirits. We fancy it rhetoric when we speak of eminent virtue. We do not yet see that virtue is Height, and that a man or a company of men, plastic and permeable to principles, by the law of nature must overpower and ride all cities, nations, kings, rich men, poets, who are not.

This is the ultimate fact which we so quickly reach on this, as on every topic, the resolution of all into the ever-blessed ONE. Self-existence is the attribute of the Supreme Cause, and it constitutes the measure of good by the degree in which it enters into all lower forms. All things real are so by so much virtue as they contain. Commerce, husbandry, hunt-

ing, whaling, war, eloquence, personal weight, are somewhat, and engage my respect as examples of its presence and impure action. I see the same law working in nature for conservation and growth. Power is, in nature, the essential measure of right. Nature suffers nothing to remain in her kingdoms which cannot help itself. The genesis and maturation of a planet, its poise and orbit, the bended tree recovering itself from the strong wind, the vital resources of every animal and vegetable, are demonstrations of the self-sufficing and therefore self-relying soul.

Thus all concentrates: let us not rove; let us sit at home with the cause. Let us stun and astonish the intruding rabble of men and books and institutions by a simple declaration of the divine fact. Bid the invaders take the shoes from off their feet, for God is here within. Let our simplicity judge them, and our docility to our own law demonstrate the poverty of nature and fortune beside our native riches.

But now we are a mob. Man does not stand in awe of man, nor is his genius admonished to stay at home, to put itself in communication with the internal ocean, but it goes abroad to beg a cup of water of the urns of other men. We must go alone. I like the silent church before the service begins, better than any preaching. How far off, how cool, how chaste the persons look, begirt each one with a precinct or sanctuary! So let us always sit. Why should we assume the faults of our friend, or wife, or father, or child, because they sit around our hearth, or are said to have the same blood? All men have my blood and I all men's. Not for that will I adopt their petulance or folly, even to the extent of being ashamed of it. But your isolation must not be mechanical, but spiritual, that is, must be elevation. At times the whole world seems to be in conspiracy to importune you with emphatic trifles. Friend, climate, child, sickness, fear, want, charity, all knock at once at thy closet door and say, "Come out unto us." But keep thy state; come not into their confusion. The power men possess to annoy me I give them

19. *not confident but agent,* not overbold (confident) but acting to exert itself (agent).

by a weak curiosity. No man can come near me but through my act. "What we love that we have, but by desire we bereave ourselves of the love."

If we cannot at once rise to the sanctities of obedience and faith, let us at least resist our temptations; let us enter into the state of war and wake Thor and Woden, courage and constancy, in our Saxon breasts.[20] This is to be done in our smooth times by speaking the truth. Check this lying hospitality and lying affection. Live no longer to the expectation of these deceived and deceiving people with whom we converse. Say to them, "O father, O mother, O wife, O brother, O friend, I have lived with you after appearances hitherto. Henceforward I am the truth's. Be it known unto you that henceforward I obey no law less than the eternal law. I will have no covenants but proximities. I shall endeavor to nourish my parents, to support my family, to be the chaste husband of one wife—but these relations I must fill after a new and unprecedented way. I appeal from your customs. I must be myself. I cannot break myself any longer for you, or you. If you can love me for what I am, we shall be the happier. If you cannot, I will still seek to deserve that you should. I will not hide my tastes or aversions. I will so trust that what is deep is holy, that I will do strongly before the sun and moon whatever inly rejoices me and the heart appoints. If you are noble, I will love you; if you are not, I will not hurt you and myself by hypocritical attentions. If you are true, but not in the same truth with me, cleave to your companions; I will seek my own. I do this not selfishly but humbly and truly. It is alike your interest, and mine, and all men's, however long we have dwelt in lies, to live in truth. Does this sound harsh today? You will soon love what is dictated by your nature as well as mine, and if we follow the truth it will bring us out safe at last." But so may you give these friends pain. Yes, but I cannot sell my liberty and my power, to save their sensibility. Besides, all persons have their moments of reason, when they look out into the region of absolute truth; then will they justify me and do the same thing.

The populace think that your rejection of popular standards is a rejection of all standard, and mere antinomianism[21]; and the bold sensualist will use the name of philosophy to gild his crimes. But the law of consciousness abides. There are two confessionals, in one or the other of which we must be shriven. You may fulfill your round of duties by clearing yourself in the *direct* or in the *reflex* way. Consider whether you have satisfied your relations to father, mother, cousin, neighbor, town, cat, and dog—whether any of these can upbraid you. But I may also neglect this reflex standard and absolve me to myself. I have my own stern claims and perfect circle. It denies the name of duty to many offices that are called duties. But if I can discharge its debts it enables me to dispense with the popular code. If anyone imagines that this law is lax, let him keep its commandment one day.

And truly it demands something godlike in him who has cast off the common motives of humanity and has ventured to trust himself for a taskmaster. High be his heart, faithful his will, clear his sight, that he may in good earnest be doctrine, society, law, to himself, that a simple purpose may be to him as strong as iron necessity is to others.

If any man consider the present aspects of what is called by distinction *society*, he will see the need of these ethics. The sinew and heart of man seem to be drawn out, and we are become timorous, desponding whimperers. We are afraid of truth, afraid of fortune, afraid of death, and afraid of each other. Our age yields no great and perfect persons. We want men and women who shall renovate life and our social state, but we see that most natures are insolvent, cannot satisfy their own wants, have an ambition out of all proportion to their practical force and do lean and beg day and night continually. Our housekeeping is mendicant, our arts, our occupations, our marriages, our religion we have not chosen, but society has chosen for us. We are parlor

20. *Thor . . . our Saxon breasts.* Thor (thôr) and Woden (wō'dən) were ancient Norse gods worshiped by the Saxons, one of the Germanic tribes that conquered Britain in the fifth century. 21. *antinomianism* (an'ti nō'mi en iz‑ əm), the doctrine that the moral law may be set aside on the ground that faith alone is necessary to salvation.

soldiers. We shun the rugged battle of fate, where strength is born.

If our young men miscarry in their first enterprises they lose all heart. If the young merchant fails, men say he is *ruined*. If the finest genius studies at one of our colleges and is not installed in an office within one year afterward in the cities or suburbs of Boston or New York, it seems to his friends and to himself that he is right in being disheartened and in complaining the rest of his life. A sturdy lad from New Hampshire or Vermont, who in turn tries all the professions, who *teams it, farms it, peddles,* keeps a school, preaches, edits a newspaper, goes to Congress, buys a township, and so forth, in successive years, and always like a cat falls on his feet, is worth a hundred of these city dolls. He walks abreast with his days and feels no shame in not "studying a profession," for he does not postpone his life, but lives already. He has not one chance, but a hundred chances. Let a Stoic[22] open the resources of man and tell men they are not leaning willows, but can and must detach themselves; that with the exercise of self-trust, new powers shall appear; that a man is the word made flesh, born to shed healing to the nations; that he should be ashamed of our compassion, and that the moment he acts from himself, tossing the laws, the books, idolatries, and customs out of the window, we pity him no more but thank and revere him; and that teacher shall restore the life of man to splendor and make his name dear to all history.

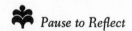 *Pause to Reflect*

1. Read again the explanation of Transcendentalism on page 248. (*a*) What does Emerson mean by the terms *understanding* and *reason*? (*b*) To which of these is *intuition* related? (*c*) Explain what Emerson means by intuition.

2. (*a*) Is Emerson's *intuition* the same thing as *conscience*? (*b*) If not, how does it differ?

3. (*a*) What does Emerson seem to think the relation between God and man should be? (*b*) To what extent would a Puritan like Jonathan Edwards have agreed with Emerson's view? (*c*) Do you regard Emerson's view of religion as orthodox? Explain.

4. What, in general, seems to be Emerson's attitude toward the past?

5. Emerson says: "The populace think that your rejection of popular standards is a rejection of all standard" (page 259). (*a*) Explain how Emerson refutes this idea. (*b*) Cite passages to illustrate whether Emerson regards living by one's own standards an easy or a difficult course to follow.

It is easy to see that a greater self-reliance must work a revolution in all the offices and relations of men: in their religion; in their education; in their pursuits; their modes of living; their association; in their property; in their speculative views.[23]

1. In what prayers do men allow themselves! That which they call a Holy Office is not so much as brave and manly. Prayer looks abroad and asks for some foreign addition to come through some foreign virtue, and loses itself in endless mazes of natural and supernatural, and mediatorial, and miraculous. Prayer that craves a particular commodity, anything less than all good, is vicious. Prayer is the contemplation of the facts of life from the highest point of view. It is the soliloquy of a beholding and jubilant soul. It is the spirit of God pronouncing his works good. But prayer as a means to effect a private end is meanness and theft. It supposes dualism and not unity in nature and consciousness. As soon as the man is at one with God, he will not beg. He will then see prayer in all action. The prayer of the farmer kneeling in his field to weed it, the prayer of the rower kneeling with the stroke of his oar, are true prayers heard throughout nature, though for cheap ends. Caratach, in Fletcher's *Bonduca*, when ad-

22. *Stoic* (stō'ik). A Stoic was a member of a school of philosophy founded in ancient Greece by Zeno (zē'nō). This school of philosophy taught that virtue is the highest good and that men should be free from passion and unmoved by life's happenings. The term *stoic* has come to be applied to a person who remains calm, represses his feelings, and is indifferent to either pleasure or pain. 23. In this part of "Self-Reliance" Emerson treats these areas of human conduct in four main divisions which he numbered for emphasis.

monished to inquire the mind of the god Audate, replies[24]:

His hidden meaning lies in our endeavors;
Our valors are our best gods.

Another sort of false prayers are our regrets. Discontent is the want of self-reliance: it is infirmity of will. Regret calamities if you can thereby help the sufferer; if not, attend your own work and already the evil begins to be repaired. Our sympathy is just as base. We come to them who weep foolishly and sit down and cry for company, instead of imparting to them truth and health in rough electric shocks, putting them once more in communication with their own reason. The secret of fortune is joy in our hands. Welcome evermore to gods and men is the self-helping man. For him all doors are flung wide; him all tongues greet, all honors crown, all eyes follow with desire. Our love goes out to him and embraces him because he did not need it. We solicitously and apologetically caress and celebrate him because he held on his way and scorned our disapprobation. The gods love him because men hated him. "To the persevering mortal," said Zoroaster, "the blessed Immortals are swift."[25]

As men's prayers are a disease of the will, so are their creeds a disease of the intellect. They say with those foolish Israelites, "Let not God speak to us, lest we die. Speak thou, speak any man with us, and we will obey." Everywhere I am hindered of meeting God in my brother, because he has shut his own temple doors and recites fables merely of his brother's, or his brother's brother's God. Every new mind is a new classification. If it prove a mind of uncommon activity and power, a Locke, a Lavoisier, a Hutton, a Bentham, a Fourier,[26] it imposes its classification on other men, and lo! a new system! In proportion to the depth of the thought, and so to the number of the objects it touches and brings within reach of the pupil, is his complacency. But chiefly is this apparent in creeds and churches, which are also classifications of some powerful mind acting on the elemental thought of duty and man's relation to the Highest. Such is Calvanism, Quakerism, Swedenborgianism.[27]

The pupil takes the same delight in subordinating everything to the new terminology as a girl who has just learned botany in seeing a new earth and new seasons thereby. It will happen for a time that the pupil will find his intellectual power has grown by the study of his master's mind. But in all unbalanced minds the classification is idolized, passes for the end and not for a speedily exhaustible means, so that the walls of the system blend to their eye in the remote horizon with the walls of the universe; the luminaries of heaven seem to them hung on the arch their master built. They cannot imagine how you aliens have any right to see—how you can see; "It must be somehow that you stole the light from us." They do not yet perceive that light, unsystematic, indomitable, will break into any cabin, even into theirs. Let them chirp awhile and call it their own. If they are honest and do well, presently their neat new pinfold will be too strait and low, will crack, will lean, will rot and vanish, and the immortal light, all young and joyful, million-orbed, million-colored, will beam over the universe as on the first morning.

2. It is for want of self-culture that the superstition of traveling, whose idols are Italy, England, Egypt, retains its fascination for all educated Americans. They who made England, Italy, or Greece venerable in the imagination, did so by sticking fast where they were, like an axis of the earth. In manly hours we feel that duty is our place. The soul is no traveler; the wise man stays at home, and when his necessities, his duties, on any occasion call him from his house, or into foreign

24. *Caratach . . . replies.* Emerson quotes from the drama *Bonduca* (1647) written by the English playwright John Fletcher. 25. *"To the . . . swift."* Zoroaster (zō′rō as′tər) was the founder of the ancient religion of the Persians. The quotation means that the gods of mythology (Immortals) were quick to answer the prayers of self-reliant men. 26. *a Locke, a Lavoisier* (lä vwä zyā′) . . . *Fourier* (fü ryā′). John Locke (1632-1704) was an English philosopher; Antoine Lavoisier (1743-1794), was the French chemist who discovered oxygen; James Hutton (1726-1797) was an English geologist; Jeremy Bentham (1748-1832) was an English philosopher and political scientist; and François Fourier (1772-1837) was a noted French political scientist who advocated a society along the lines of Brook Farm. 27. *Swedenborgianism* (swē′dən bôr′ji en iz əm), the religious doctrine formulated by Emanuel Swedenborg, a Swedish philosopher.

lands, he is at home still and shall make men sensible by the expression of his countenance that he goes, the missionary of wisdom and virtue, and visits cities and men like a sovereign and not like an interloper or a valet.

I have no churlish objection to the circumnavigation of the globe for the purposes of art, of study, and benevolence, so that the man is first domesticated, or does not go abroad with the hope of finding somewhat greater than he knows. He who travels to be amused, or to get somewhat which he does not carry, travels away from himself, and grows old even in youth among old things. In Thebes, in Palmyra,[28] his will and mind have become old and dilapidated as they. He carries ruins to ruins.

Traveling is a fool's paradise. Our first journeys discover to us the indifference of places. At home I dream that at Naples, at Rome, I can be intoxicated with beauty and lose my sadness. I pack my trunk, embrace my friends, embark on the sea and at last wake up in Naples, and there beside me is the stern fact, the sad self, unrelenting, identical, that I fled from. I seek the Vatican and the palaces. I affect to be intoxicated with sights and suggestions, but I am not intoxicated. My giant goes with me wherever I go.

3. But the rage of traveling is a symptom of a deeper unsoundness affecting the whole intellectual action. The intellect is vagabond, and our system of education fosters restlessness. Our minds travel when our bodies are forced to stay at home. We imitate; and what is imitation but the traveling of the mind? Our houses are built with foreign taste; our shelves are garnished with foreign ornaments; our opinions, our tastes, our faculties lean, and follow the Past and the Distant. The soul created the arts wherever they have flourished. It was in his own mind that the artist sought his model. It was an application of his own thought to the thing to be done and the conditions to be observed. And why need we copy the Doric or the Gothic model? Beauty, convenience, grandeur of thought, and quaint expression are as near to us as to any, and if the American artist will study with hope and love the precise thing to be done by him, con-

sidering the climate, the soil, the length of the day, the wants of the people, the habit and form of the government, he will create a house in which all these will find themselves fitted, and taste and sentiment will be satisfied also.

Insist on yourself; never imitate. Your own gift you can present every moment with the cumulative force of a whole life's cultivation; but of the adopted talent of another you have only an extemporaneous half possession. That which each can do best, none but his Maker can teach him. No man yet knows what it is, nor can, till that person has exhibited it. Where is the master who could have taught Shakespeare? Where is the master who could have instructed Franklin, or Washington, or Bacon,[29] or Newton? Every great man is a unique. The Scipionism of Scipio is precisely that part he could not borrow. Shakespeare will never be made by the study of Shakespeare. Do that which is assigned you, and you cannot hope too much or dare too much. There is at this moment for you an utterance brave and grand as that of the colossal chisel of Phidias,[30] or trowel of the Egyptians, or the pen of Moses or Dante,[31] but different from all these. Not possibly will the soul, all rich, all eloquent, with thousand-cloven tongue, deign to repeat itself; but if you can hear what these patriarchs say, surely you can reply to them in the same pitch of voice; for the ear and the tongue are two organs of one nature. Abide in the simple and noble regions of thy life, obey thy heart, and thou shalt reproduce the Foreworld again.

4. As our Religion, our Education, our Art look abroad, so does our spirit of society. All men plume themselves on the improvement of society, and no man improves.

Society never advances. It recedes as fast on one side as it gains on the other. It undergoes continual changes; it is barbarous, it is civilized, it is Christianized, it is rich, it is scientific; but this change is not amelioration. For

---

28. *In Thebes* (thēbz) *in Palmyra* (pal mī'ra), ancient ruined cities. Thebes is in Greece, Palmyra in Syria.   29. *Bacon*. Emerson may be referring to either of two English scientists, Roger Bacon (1214?-1294) or Francis Bacon (1561-1626). 30. *Phidias* (fid'i as), Greek sculptor who lived in the fifth century B.C.   31. *Dante*. See the reference to Dante on page 271.

everything that is given, something is taken. Society acquires new arts and loses old instincts. What a contrast between the well-clad, reading, writing, thinking American, with a watch, a pencil, and a bill of exchange in his pocket, and the naked New Zealander, whose property is a club, a spear, a mat, and an undivided twentieth of a shed to sleep under! But compare the health of the two men and you shall see that the white man has lost his aboriginal strength. If the traveler tell us truly, strike the savage with a broadax and in a day or two the flesh shall unite and heal as if you struck the blow into soft pitch, and the same blow shall send the white to his grave.

The civilized man has built a coach, but has lost the use of his feet. He is supported on crutches, but lacks so much support of muscle. He has a fine Geneva watch, but he fails of the skill to tell the hour by the sun. A Greenwich nautical almanac he has, and so being sure of the information when he wants it, the man in the street does not know a star in the sky. The solstice he does not observe; the equinox he knows as little; and the whole bright calendar of the year is without a dial in his mind. His notebooks impair his memory; his libraries overload his wit; the insurance office increases the number of accidents; and it may be a question whether machinery does not encumber; whether we have not lost by refinement some energy, by a Christianity entrenched in establishments and forms, some vigor of wild virtue. For every Stoic was a Stoic; but in Christendom where is the Christian?

There is no more deviation in the moral standard than in the standard of height or bulk. No greater men are now than ever were. A singular equality may be observed between the great men of the first and of the last ages; nor can all the science, art, religion, and philosophy of the nineteenth century avail to educate greater men than Plutarch's heroes,[32] three or four and twenty centuries ago. Not in time is the race progressive. Phocion, Socrates, Anaxagoras, Diogenes,[33] are great men, but they leave no class. He who is really of their class will not be called by their name,

but will be his own man, and in his turn the founder of a sect. The arts and inventions of each period are only its costume and do not invigorate men. The harm of the improved machinery may compensate its good. Hudson and Bering accomplished so much in their fishing boats as to astonish Parry and Franklin,[34] whose equipment exhausted the resources of science and art. Galileo, with an opera glass, discovered a more splendid series of celestial phenomena than any one since. Columbus found the New World in an undecked boat. It is curious to see the periodical disuse and perishing of means and machinery which were introduced with loud laudation a few years or centuries before. The great genius returns to essential man. We reckoned the improvements of the art of war among the triumphs of science, and yet Napoleon conquered Europe by the bivouac,[35] which consisted of falling back on naked valor and disencumbering it of all aids. The Emperor held it impossible to make a perfect army, says Las Cases,[36] "without abolishing our arms, magazines, commissaries, and carriages, until, in imitation of the Roman custom, the soldier should receive his supply of corn, grind it in his hand-mill, and bake his bread himself."

Society is a wave. The wave moves onward, but the water of which it is composed does not. The same particle does not rise from the valley to the ridge. Its unity is only phenomenal. The persons who make up a nation today, next year die, and their experience dies with them.

And so the reliance on Property, including the reliance on governments which protect it,

32. *Plutarch's heroes.* Plutarch (plü′tärk) was a first-century Greek biographer who wrote the lives of famous Greeks and Romans. 33. *Phocion* (fō′shi ŏn) . . . *Anaxagoras* (an′ak sag′ə rəs), *Diogenes* (dī oj′ə nēz), philosophers of ancient Greece. 34. *Hudson and Bering . . . as to astonish Parry and Franklin.* Henry Hudson was a seventeenth-century English navigator who explored Canada. Vitus Jonassen Bering (1680-1741) was the Danish navigator who explored the Bering Sea. Sir William Parry (1790-1855) and Sir John Franklin (1786-1847) were English explorers who went into the Arctic. 35. *Napoleon . . . by the bivouac.* Napoleon forced his armies to camp outdoors without shelter and to live off the country. By so doing, the troops could move very quickly without having to wait for supply vans. 36. *Las Cases* (läs käz′), the Marquis de Las Cases (1766-1842), who recorded his conversations with Napoleon at St. Helena.

is the want of self-reliance. Men have looked away from themselves and at things so long that they have come to esteem the religious, learned, and civil institutions as guards of property, and they deprecate assaults on these, because they feel them to be assaults on property. They measure their esteem of each other by what each *has,* and not by what each *is.* But a cultivated man becomes ashamed of his property, out of new respect for his nature. Especially he hates what he has if he sees that it is accidental—came to him by inheritance, or gift, or crime; then he feels that it is not having; it does not belong to him, has no root in him and merely lies there because no revolution or no robber takes it away. But that which a man is, does always by necessity acquire; and what the man acquires, is living property, which does not wait the beck of rulers, or mobs, or revolutions, or fire or storm, or bankruptcies, but perpetually renews itself wherever the man breathes. "Thy lot or portion of life," said the Caliph Ali,[37] "is seeking after thee; therefore be at rest from seeking after it." Our dependence on these foreign goods leads us to our slavish respect for numbers. The political parties meet in numerous conventions; the greater the concourse and with each new uproar of announcement, "The delegation from Essex![38] The Democrats from New Hampshire! The Whigs of Maine!" the young patriot feels himself stronger than before by a new thousand of eyes and arms. In like manner the reformers summon conventions and vote and resolve in multitude. Not so, O friends! will the God deign to enter and inhabit you, but by a method precisely the reverse. It is only as a man puts off all foreign support and stands alone that I see him to be strong and to prevail. He is weaker by every recruit to his banner. Is not a man better than a town? Ask nothing of men, and, in the endless mutation, thou only firm column must presently appear the upholder of all that surrounds thee. He who knows that power is inborn, that he is weak because he has looked for good out of him and elsewhere, and, so perceiving, throws himself unhesitatingly on his thought, instantly rights himself, stands in the erect position, commands his

limbs, works miracles; just as a man who stands on his feet is stronger than a man who stands on his head.

So use all that is called Fortune. Most men gamble with her, and gain all, and lose all, as her wheel rolls. But do thou leave as unlawful these winnings, and deal with Cause and Effect, the chancellors of God. In the Will work and acquire, and thou hast chained the wheel of Chance, and shall sit hereafter out of fear from her rotations. A political victory, a rise of rents, the recovery of your sick, or the return of your absent friend, or some other favorable event raises your spirits, and you think good days are preparing for you. Do not believe it. Nothing can bring you peace but yourself. Nothing can bring you peace but the triumph of principles.

---

37. *Caliph Ali* (kä′lif ä′li), the son-in-law of Mohammed ruler of Mecca in the seventh century. 38. *Essex,* a county in eastern Massachusetts.

❧ TO INCREASE UNDERSTANDING

1. In the last section of "Self-Reliance" Emerson expresses some rather unconventional opinions on various areas of living. Explain the thought surrounding each of the following statements and express your personal reaction to Emerson's idea.

(*a*) Prayer that craves a particular commodity, anything less than all good, is vicious (page 260).

(*b*) Traveling is a fool's paradise (page 262).

(*c*) We imitate; and what is imitation but the traveling of the mind (page 262)?

(*d*) Society never advances (page 262).

2. As a public lecturer, Emerson was afraid of weakening the effect of his statements by introducing qualifications. For example, he says ". . . if I am the Devil's child, I will live then from the Devil" (page 252). (*a*) What other examples do you find of Emerson's shockingly unqualified assertions? (*b*) How did they affect you as you read the essay? (*c*) Do you imagine your reaction was the kind Emerson intended?

3. Do you find any similarity of idea between the paragraphs beginning "The civilized man has built a coach, but has lost the use of his feet" (page 263) and Thoreau's thoughts on simplicity? Explain your answer.

4. Judging from your own knowledge and experience, to what extent are Emerson's ideas on self-reliance practical?

Poems by Emerson

The Snowstorm

Announced by all the trumpets of
    the sky,
      Arrives the snow, and, driving
      o'er the fields,
Seems nowhere to alight. The whited air
Hides hills and woods, the river, and the
    heaven,
And veils the farmhouse at the garden's end. 5
The sled and traveler stopped, the courier's
    feet
Delayed, all friends shut out, the housemates
    sit
Around the radiant fireplace, enclosed
In a tumultuous privacy of storm.

    Come see the north wind's masonry.   10
Out of an unseen quarry evermore
Furnished with tile, the fierce artificer
Curves his white bastions with projected roof
Round every windward stake, or tree, or door.
Speeding, the myriad-handed, his wild work 15
So fanciful, so savage, nought cares he
For number or proportion. Mockingly,
On coop or kennel he hangs Parian wreaths;
A swanlike form invests the hidden thorn,
Fills up the farmer's lane from wall to wall, 20
Maugre the farmer's sighs; and at the gate
A tapering turret overtops the work.
And when his hours are numbered, and the
    world
Is all his own, retiring, as he were not,
Leaves, when the sun appears, astonished   25
    Art
To mimic in slow structures, stone by stone,
Built in an age, the mad wind's night work,
The frolic architecture of the snow.

The Rhodora
On Being Asked, Whence Is the Flower?

In May, when sea winds pierced our solitudes,
I found the fresh rhodora in the woods,
Spreading its leafless blooms in a damp nook,
To please the desert and the sluggish brook.
The purple petals, fallen in the pool,   5
Made the black water with their beauty gay;

Here might the redbird come his plumes to
    cool,
And court the flower that cheapens his array.
Rhodora! if the sages ask thee why
This charm is wasted on the earth and sky, 10
Tell them, dear, that if eyes were made for
    seeing,
Then Beauty is its own excuse for being:
Why thou wert there, O rival of the rose!
I never thought to ask, I never knew;
But, in my simple ignorance, suppose   15
The selfsame Power that brought me there
    brought you.

Each and All

Little thinks, in the field, yon red-cloaked
    clown,
Of thee from the hill-top looking down;
The heifer that lows in the upland farm,
Far-heard, lows not thine ear to charm;
The sexton, tolling the bell at noon,   5
Dreams not that great Napoleon
Stops his horse, and lists with delight,
Whilst his files sweep round yon Alpine
    height;
Nor knowest thou what argument
Thy life to thy neighbor's creed has lent. 10
All are needed by each one;
Nothing is fair or good alone.

I thought the sparrow's note from heaven,
Singing at dawn on the alder bough;
I brought him home, in his nest, at even; 15
He sings the song, but it cheers not now,
For I did not bring home the river and sky;
He sang to my ear, they sang to my eye.

The delicate shells lay on the shore;
The bubbles of the latest wave   20
Fresh pearls to their enamel gave,
And the bellowing of the savage sea
Greeted their safe escape to me.
I wiped away the weeds and foam,
I fetched my sea-born treasures home;   25
But the poor, unsightly, noisome things
Had left their beauty on the shore
With the sun and the sand and the wild
    uproar.

The lover watched his graceful maid,
As 'mid the virgin train she strayed,   30
Nor knew her beauty's best attire
Was woven still by the snow-white choir.
At last she came to his hermitage,
Like the bird from the woodlands to the
    cage—
The gay enchantment was undone;   35
A gentle wife, but fairy none.

Then I said, "I covet Truth;
Beauty is unripe childhood's cheat—
I leave it behind with the games of youth."
As I spoke, beneath my feet   40
The ground-pine curled its pretty wreath,
Running over the club-moss burrs;
I inhaled the violet's breath;
Around me stood the oaks and firs;
Pine cones and acorns lay on the ground;   45
Over me soared the eternal sky,
Full of light and deity;
Again I saw, again I heard,
The rolling river, the morning bird;—
Beauty through my senses stole,   50
I yielded myself to the perfect whole.

❧ TO INCREASE UNDERSTANDING

1. (a) How does the picture in the opening stanza of "The Snowstorm" suggest that nature is superior to man? (b) According to Emerson's description in stanza 2, how does the north wind's masonry differ from that of man?

2. "The Snowstorm," according to the biography of Emerson (page 250), so describes the storm "as to make it symbolize a contrast between man's limited capacities and the power of God." Explain.

3. (a) What is the question Emerson raises in "The Rhodora"? (b) Read the question aloud and explain Emerson's answers.

4. (a) What is the theme of "Each and All"? (b) What examples does Emerson advance to develop the theme? (c) Relate the poem to transcendental doctrines.

5. Do you find in these poems by Emerson any of the ideas he expresses in "Self-Reliance"? Explain your answer.

6. In writing a poem, "Poe 'looked within' himself for incidents or details, he chose words for their suggestive powers and, with his effect in mind, arranged them in musical patterns" (page 208). Do the poems by Emerson that you have read seem to show that he proceeded in the same manner? Support your answer.

Henry Wadsworth Longfellow 1807-1882

Thoreau and Emerson were Concord men. Nearby lived "the Cambridge group"—Henry Wadsworth Longfellow, Oliver Wendell Holmes, and James Russell Lowell—active as writers at about the same time. All three were descendants of old New England families; all were scholars who received training abroad; all were Harvard professors who won fame as men of letters far beyond Cambridge. Though, like the Concord men, they were influenced by European literature, with them this influence took a different form.

Although Henry Wadsworth Longfellow spent his adult years largely in Cambridge, he was born in Portland, Maine. In "My Lost Youth" he recalled his native city fondly as

> . . . the beautiful town
> That is seated by the sea.

The sea, which he had known and loved as a boy, became a favorite subject in his later poetry.

Longfellow's house, Cambridge.

Longfellow attended Bowdoin College. After his graduation, he was offered a professorship of modern languages there on condition of further study. He studied and traveled abroad for three years. Later, when Harvard offered him a similar position, he went abroad for more study.

Below left: Entrance hall of the Longfellow house. Below right: Longfellow's study, preserved as it was when he died. The collection of art work, books, and mementos shows his international tastes.
Left: The study as reflected in the convex mirror over the fireplace.

Europe was tremendously important to him. Having been almost smothered as a youth by an overaffectionate mother, he first achieved and enjoyed freedom by crossing the ocean. The Old World—its traditions, its culture, its beauty—delighted him as it had Irving, in whose works he had previously glimpsed its appeal. Longfellow's first wife accompanied him abroad, but died in Rotterdam in 1836. The next year, still abroad, he met the woman who after a long courtship was to become his second wife. Europe therefore had many emotional associations for him, and these were augmented by his discovery there of his pleasure in reading and studying Old World literature.

This pleasure he passed along to Bowdoin and Harvard students. Students at Harvard long recalled his striking appearance. When he began to teach in Cambridge he was a handsome young man with long brown hair, a high forehead, large expressive blue eyes, a large well-chiseled nose, a sensitive mouth, a square chin. His dress had been somewhat influenced by European fashions: he wore a jauntily tilted wide-brimmed hat, a well-fitted frock coat, a wine-colored waistcoat, lavender gloves. After some years he cultivated an abundant beard which in time grew white, setting off features which by contrast remained young, and his dress became more conservative.

This portrait of Longfellow was painted by his son Ernest in 1876. It is a detail of the portrait seen in the photograph of the study (center) on the preceding page.

Longfellow communicated his enthusiasm about European peoples and their literature to readers outside his classes by writing travel books in which he distilled the essence of his foreign experiences. He also made translations of European poems which embodied the emotions of the originals and echoed their music. This practice in translation aided him greatly in perfecting his poetic technique. His first book of original poems, *Voices of the Night* (1839), showed this skill in deceptively simple verses which won him national fame.

In January 1840 he wrote a friend that in his ballad, "The Wreck of the Hesperus," he had naturalized a form which had long flourished abroad. He continued: "The *national ballad* is a virgin soil here in New England; and there are great materials." Several such compositions, notably "The Skeleton in Armor," appeared in *Ballads and Other Poems* (1841).

Longfellow's adaptation of the ballad to American materials illustrates his chief literary achievement. One might say that he "Americanized" European forms or that he "Europeanized" American materials. *Evangeline* (1847), *The Song of Hiawatha* (1855), and *The Courtship of Miles Standish* (1858), were long narrative poems in the manner of similar European poems but treating American legends. *The Golden Legend* (1851) brought to America poetry like that of Europe in the Middle Ages. *Tales of a Wayside Inn* (1863) collected a series of stories, most of them of American origin, in a poem constructed in the manner of Chaucer's *Canterbury Tales*.

The poems on pages 269-272 all show Longfellow, the master technician, at work. In several he demonstrates his ability to handle the intricate pattern of the Italian sonnet with great artistry. In others, such as "The Tide Rises, the Tide Falls," he writes in simple stanzas but chooses his words with such regard for sound and meaning that each syllable plays an important part in creating the desired tone.

The Arsenal at Springfield

The arsenal at Springfield, Massachusetts, which was established by the Continental Congress in Revolutionary War days, is one of the oldest in the United States. Longfellow's visit to this arsenal brought forth the question—still unanswered today —"Why must there be war?"

This is the Arsenal. From floor to ceiling,
    Like a huge organ, rise the burnished arms;
But from their silent pipes no anthem pealing
    Startles the villages with strange alarms.

Ah! what a sound will rise, how wild and dreary,   5
    When the death-angel touches those swift keys!
What loud lament and dismal Miserere[1]
    Will mingle with their awful symphonies!

I hear even now the infinite fierce chorus,
    The cries of agony, the endless groan,   10
Which, through the ages that have gone before us,
    In long reverberations reach our own.

On helm and harness rings the Saxon hammer,[2]
    Through Cimbric forest roars the Norseman's song,[3]
And loud, amid the universal clamor,   15
    O'er distant deserts sounds the Tartar gong.

I hear the Florentine, who from his palace
    Wheels out his battle bell[4] with dreadful din,
And Aztec priests upon their teocallis[5]
    Beat the wild war drum made of serpent's skin;   20

The tumult of each sacked and burning village:
    The shout that every prayer for mercy drowns;
The soldiers' revels in the midst of pillage;
    The wail of famine in beleaguered towns;

The bursting shell, the gateway wrenched asunder,   25
    The rattling musketry, the clashing blade;
And ever and anon, in tones of thunder,
    The diapason of the cannonade.

---

1. *Miserere* (miz′ə rā′rā), a prayer of petition in time of trouble. *Miserere* is the first word of the Latin version of the Psalm which begins "Have mercy upon me, O Lord." 2. *On helm and harness ... Saxon hammer.* This refers to the forging of helmets (helms) and other armor (harness) by the ancient inhabitants of Germany. In this and the following stanza Longfellow suggests the sounds made as various nations of the past prepared for warfare. 3. *Cimbric* (sim′brik) *forest ... Norseman's song.* The reference is probably to Jutland, a peninsula of Denmark. Jutland is believed to have been the original home of the Cimbri, a warlike northern tribe who invaded Roman territory and were destroyed in northern Italy in 101 B.C. 4. *the Florentine ... battle bell.* During the thirteenth century the soldiers of Florence, an Italian city, wheeled the battle bell onto the battlefield itself and placed it close to the battle flag. 5. *teocallis* (tē′ō kal′iz), flat-topped pyramids built for worship by the Aztecs, the Indians who ruled Mexico before the coming of the Spaniards in 1519.

Is it, O man, with such discordant noises,
　　With such accursed instruments as these,　　　　　30
Thou drownest Nature's sweet and kindly voices,
　　And jarrest the celestial harmonies?

Were half the power, that fills the world with terror,
　　Were half the wealth, bestowed on camps and courts,
Given to redeem the human mind from error,　　　　35
　　There were no need of arsenals nor forts—

The warrior's name would be a name abhorrèd!
　　And every nation, that should lift again
Its hand against a brother, on its forehead
　　Would wear forevermore the curse of Cain![6]　　40

Down the dark future, through long generations,
　　The echoing sounds grow fainter and then cease;
And like a bell, with solemn, sweet vibrations,
　　I hear once more the voice of Christ say, "Peace!"

Peace! and no longer from its brazen portals　　　　45
　　The blast of War's great organ shakes the skies!
But beautiful as songs of the immortals,
　　The holy melodies of love arise.

The Tide Rises,
the Tide Falls

The tide rises, the tide falls,
　　The twilight darkens, the curlew calls;
Along the sea-sands damp and brown
The traveler hastens toward the town,
　　And the tide rises, the tide falls.　　　　　　　　5

Darkness settles on roofs and walls,
But the sea in the darkness calls and calls;
The little waves, with their soft, white hands,
Efface the footprints in the sands,
　　And the tide rises, the tide falls.　　　　　　　　10

The morning breaks; the steeds in their stalls
Stamp and neigh, as the hostler calls;
The day returns, but nevermore
Returns the traveler to the shore,
　　And the tide rises, the tide falls.　　　　　　　　15

---

6. *on its forehead . . . the curse of Cain.* After Cain had killed his brother Abel, the Lord placed a mark upon him to protect him from the vengeance of others. He was branded as a murderer. (Genesis 4: 8-15.)

Divina Commedia

In July of 1861 Longfellow's second wife met with a fatal household accident. A match ignited her dress, and despite Longfellow's desperate attempt to extinguish the flames, she died the next day. Longfellow, overcome by the tragedy, sought solace for his grief in work. The difficult task he set for himself was the translation into English of the *Divina Commedia* (di vē'nä kōm mä'dyä), or *Divine Comedy*, by Dante Alighieri (dän'tä ä'li gyär'i), one of the greatest of Italian poets. This epic poem consists of three parts, which describe Dante's imaginary journey to Hell, Purgatory, and Paradise. In his translation, Longfellow prefaced each part with two sonnets. In these sonnets the cathedral represents Dante's epic, a majestic "edifice" of poetry. Although Longfellow's purpose apparently is to describe the cathedral, he is actually commenting both on Dante's poem and the comfort it offered him in his grief. Sonnets One and Two, which follow, prefaced "Inferno," the first part of the *Divine Comedy*.

One

Oft have I seen at some cathedral door
 A laborer, pausing in the dust and heat,
 Lay down his burden, and with reverent feet
 Enter, and cross himself, and on the floor
Kneel to repeat his paternoster[1] o'er;   5
 Far off the noises of the world retreat;
 The loud vociferations of the street
 Become an undistinguishable roar.
So, as I enter here from day to day,
 And leave my burden at this minster gate,[2]   10
 Kneeling in prayer, and not ashamed to pray,
The tumult of the time disconsolate
 To inarticulate murmurs dies away,
 While the eternal ages watch and wait.

Two

How strange the sculptures that adorn these towers!
 This crowd of statues, in whose folded sleeves
 Birds build their nests; while canopied with leaves
 Parvis[1] and portal bloom like trellised bowers,
And the vast minster seems a cross of flowers![2]   5
 But fiends and dragons on the gargoyled eaves
 Watch the dead Christ between the living thieves,
 And, underneath, the traitor Judas lowers!
Ah! from what agonies of heart and brain,
 What exultations trampling on despair,   10
 What tenderness, what tears, what hate of wrong,
What passionate outcry of a soul in pain,
 Uprose this poem of the earth and air,
 This medieval miracle of song!

ONE. **1.** *paternoster* (pat'ər nos'tər), the Lord's Prayer, so called because the opening words are "Pater Noster" in Latin. **2.** *minster gate*, the cathedral door.
TWO. **1.** *Parvis*, church porch. **2.** *the vast minster . . . cross of flowers.* Most European cathedrals were built in the shape of a cross. To the poet, the carved and ornamented cathedral seen from above suggests a cross of flowers.

Nature

As a fond mother, when the day is o'er,
Leads by the hand her little child to bed,
Half willing, half reluctant to be led,
And leave his broken playthings on the floor,
Still gazing at them through the open door,   5
Nor wholly reassured and comforted
By promises of others in their stead,
Which, though more splendid, may not please him more;
So Nature deals with us, and takes away
Our playthings one by one, and by the hand   10
Leads us to rest so gently, that we go
Scarce knowing if we wish to go or stay,
Being too full of sleep to understand
How far the unknown transcends the what we know.

The Sound of the Sea

The sea awoke at midnight from its sleep,
And round the pebbly beaches far and wide
I heard the first wave of the rising tide
Rush onward with uninterrupted sweep;
A voice out of the silence of the deep,   5
A sound mysteriously multiplied
As of a cataract from the mountain's side,
Or roar of winds upon a wooded steep.
So comes to us at times, from the unknown
And inaccessible solitudes of being,   10
The rushing of the sea-tides of the soul;
And inspirations, that we deem our own,
Are some divine foreshadowing and foreseeing
Of things beyond our reason or control.

 TO INCREASE UNDERSTANDING

1. (*a*) What detail of the arsenal at Springfield makes Longfellow think of an organ? (*b*) Trace his use of this figure throughout the poem.

2. (*a*) Read aloud the lines from "The Arsenal at Springfield" that offer Longfellow's solution to the threat of war. (*b*) Mention instances of progress in attempting to follow this idea.

3. (*a*) State the poet's theme in "The Tide Rises, the Tide Falls." (*b*) What do you think the "traveler" and the "tide" represent?

4. (*a*) What is the theme of "Divina Commedia One"? (*b*) Trace the comparison Longfellow makes between himself and the laborer.

5. (*a*) Describe in your own words the cathedral as Longfellow pictures it in the first eight lines of "Divina Commedia Two." (*b*) What double reference do you understand in the words "medieval miracle of song" (line 14)?

6. (*a*) To what is nature compared in the poem of this name? (*b*) Through what details does Longfellow work out his analogy? (*c*) What is the theme of the poem?

7. How would you describe the tone of "Nature"? Read aloud several lines to illustrate your answer.

8. What details in the first eight lines of "The Sound of the Sea" show that Longfellow has first-hand knowledge of the sea?

9. How do "The Tide Rises, the Tide Falls" and "The Sound of the Sea" compare in their treatment of the sea?

10. Like many other writers of his day, Longfellow felt that literature ought to embody moral instruc-

tion. How do "The Arsenal at Springfield" and "The Sound of the Sea" illustrate this belief?

11. Through his years of study and travel abroad, Longfellow became well acquainted with European literature and history. Cite lines from the poems which show the influence of this background.

12. The biography of Longfellow speaks of this poet as a "master technician" (page 268). Using any poem or part of a poem as an example, explain as fully as possible why he deserves this description. Take into consideration the use of appropriate imagery, figurative language, alliteration, assonance, and rhyme.

 BETTER READING
The sonnet

Among the major New England poets, the one most influenced by European verse patterns was Longfellow. One of the verse forms which challenged his poetic ability, as it had challenged poets before him, was the sonnet.

A sonnet is a lyric poem of fourteen lines written in iambic pentameter, a meter with five accents in each line. Originated by Italian poets during the thirteenth century, it reached perfection a century later in the work of Petrarch (pē'trärk), and came

to be known as the Petrarchan or Italian sonnet. The fourteen lines of the Italian sonnet impose a rigid rhyme scheme: the first eight lines, called the *octave*, rhyme *abbaabba* and present the poet's subject; the concluding six lines, or *sestet*, rhyme *cdecde* and indicate the significance of the facts set forth, or resolve the problem posed, in the octave.

When English poets of the sixteenth century discovered Petrarch, they were challenged by the demands the Italian sonnet made upon a poet's artistry. In experimenting with the verse form they often altered its original rhyme scheme—the most notable variation being the English sonnet which rhymes *abab/cdcd/efef/gg*.

Thus, when he attempted the sonnet, Longfellow had both the Italian and the English tradition to draw upon. It is typical of his interest in Old World literature that he chose the older Italian form, and a tribute to his artistry that he mastered its difficult discipline.

Which of the poems by Longfellow that you have studied are sonnets? Choose your favorite among these sonnets and be prepared to explain the following points: (*a*) the rhyme scheme; (*b*) the subject presented in the octave; (*c*) the relationship of the octave to the sestet. Tell also why you like this particular sonnet best.

Oliver Wendell Holmes 1809-1894

BETTMANN ARCHIVE

Caricature of Holmes by Spy, a British satirist.

The birthplace of Oliver Wendell Holmes in Cambridge was the ancient house in which the defense of Bunker Hill had been planned. Except for trips abroad Holmes lived all his life in Cambridge and the old Beacon Hill neighborhood in Boston. Tradition, locale, and family were important to Holmes both as a boy and as a man; he often commented on and joked about the importance of these things to him.

Holmes went to a private school, then to Harvard. There he was a gay student whose scholastic achievement was average, though he did exhibit literary gifts by writing and selling several poems. For all his amiability he held firm convictions. This he proved in 1829 when his father, a preacher in the older tradition, was forced by a liberal congregation to leave his church. Faced with a choice between family loyalty and personal convictions, the twenty-year-old son sided with the parishioners. Again, a year later, he made another independent choice when he decided not to enter the ministry, the law, or teaching in the humanities—the chief avenues for college-trained men of his social class—but medicine, which in those days was not considered as dignified as the other professions.

Since the best training in medicine was then offered abroad, Holmes

*Above right: Boston
in 1860. Right:
Holmes delivering
address at Harvard
Medical School in
1882. Below: Some
of the Harvard
buildings as they
appeared in 1840.*

studied in Edinburgh, then Paris, before returning home to receive his M.D. from the Harvard Medical School. After practicing a very short time he taught medicine at Dartmouth (1838-1840), then at Harvard (1847-1882). He was a devoted teacher: Medicine and "Science" were always of tremendous seriousness and importance for him.

His light-hearted ways at times led some people to mistake his true attitude toward his work. When he became a practicing physician at the age of twenty-seven, his youth and his tiny stature made it hard for people to take him seriously, nor were they attracted when word got around that he had said "small fevers will be gratefully received." In medical school, lecturing on anatomy, he was under severe handicaps: the room was small and poorly ventilated; his classes met late in the day after hours of work had wearied them. But he kept his students alert and helped them master the subject. He illustrated everything he said with carefully prepared "exhibits"; he compared bodily organs to familiar objects; he made puns and told witty stories.

In addition to a devotion to science, Holmes' years of study in Europe had given him a love for the light-hearted gaiety of the Continent. This spirit is evident not only in the imagination and wit which enlivened his classes, but also in his best-loved writings. He modeled himself on men like Ambroise Paré, a sixteenth-century French surgeon and author, whom he described as "good, wise, quaint, shrewd, chatty." In both his poetry and prose he strove for the light informal tone, the charm and the humor, of French men of the world or of eighteenth-century British authors.

Many of his verses were "occasional"; that is, they were composed for reading aloud on certain festive occasions—at a college class reunion, on an anniversary, at a celebration. They gracefully referred to the occasion and commented upon it in polished lines which sparkled with wit. For decades banquet committees in New England felt they just had to have Holmes come and read some timely verses; as he wrote

Caricature of Holmes as a medical student, drawn by Holmes himself.

> I'm a florist in verse, and what would people say
> If I came to a banquet without my bouquet?

Many of his poems were so full of allusions to the events they celebrated that as the events were forgotten the poems lost their meaning. Some, however, like "The Last Leaf" (page 277), deal with subjects of lasting interest, and in addition to precision and wit have touches of pathos which add to their appeal. Holmes could also write serious moralistic poems in the Longfellow vein. "The Chambered Nautilus" (page 276), inspired typically enough by a subject interesting to a scientist, is an example.

The same sprightliness, vigor, wisdom, and charm that are displayed in the poems are apparent also in Holmes' essays and make them delightful reading. *The Autocrat of the Breakfast-Table* (1858), *The Professor at the Breakfast-Table* (1860), *The Poet at the Breakfast-Table* (1872), and *Over the Teacups* (1891), each composed of papers which appeared originally in the *Atlantic Monthly*, won Holmes a wide and appreciative audience. Each essay is an imaginary conversation in which little Dr. Holmes, thinly disguised as "autocrat," "professor," or "poet," leads an animated conversation with a group of people gathered around a boarding-house table.

The Chambered Nautilus

This poem was first published in *The Autocrat of the Breakfast-Table*. In introducing the poem, Holmes wrote: "I will read you a few lines ... suggested by ... one of those chambered shells to which is given the name of pearly nautilus. ... The name [*nautilus* from the Greek *naus*, "ship"] shows that it has long been compared to a ship." In describing the shell itself Holmes wrote of "the series of enlarging compartments successively dwelt in by the animal that inhabits the shell, which is built in a widening spiral." From this "widening spiral" the poet draws his lesson.

This is the ship of pearl, which, poets feign,
    Sails the unshadowed main—
    The venturous bark that flings
      On the sweet summer wind its purpled wings
In gulfs enchanted,[1] where the Siren sings,[2]   5
    And coral reefs lie bare,
Where the cold sea-maids[3] rise to sun their streaming hair.

Its webs of living gauze[4] no more unfurl;
    Wrecked is the ship of pearl!
    And every chambered cell,   10
Where its dim dreaming life was wont to dwell,
As the frail tenant shaped his growing shell,
    Before thee lies revealed—
Its irised[5] ceiling rent, its sunless crypt unsealed!

Year after year beheld the silent toil   15
    That spread his lustrous coil;
    Still, as the spiral grew,
He left the past year's dwelling for the new,
Stole with soft step its shining archway through,
    Built up its idle door,   20
Stretched in his last-found home, and knew the old no more.

Thanks for the heavenly message brought by thee,
    Child of the wandering sea,
    Cast from her lap, forlorn!
From thy dead lips a clearer note is born   25
Than ever Triton[6] blew from wreathèd horn!
    While on mine ear it rings,
Through the deep caves of thought I hear a voice that sings:

Build thee more stately mansions, O my soul,
    As the swift seasons roll!   30
    Leave thy low-vaulted past!
Let each new temple, nobler than the last,
Shut thee from heaven with a dome more vast,
    Till thou at length art free,
Leaving thine outgrown shell by life's unresting sea!   35

---

1. *gulfs enchanted*. The chambered nautilus lives in the South Pacific and Indian oceans. 2. *the Siren sings*. According to Greek mythology the sirens were nymphs who by their sweet singing lured sailors to destruction. 3. *sea-maids*, mermaids. 4. *webs of living gauze*, tentacles. 5. *irised*, containing the colors of the rainbow as pearl does. 6. *Triton* (tri'tən), the mythological Greek god of the sea. His horn makes the roaring of the ocean.

The Last Leaf

This poem was suggested to Holmes by the sight of the aged Major Thomas Melville, Herman Melville's grandfather. This "venerable relic of the Revolution," as Holmes called him, had been one of the "Indians" who participated in the Boston Tea Party (1774).

I saw him once before,
As he passed by the door,
  And again
The pavement stones resound,
As he totters o'er the ground   5
  With his cane.

They say that in his prime,
Ere the pruning-knife of Time
  Cut him down,
Not a better man was found   10
By the Crier on his round
  Through the town.

But now he walks the streets,
And he looks at all he meets
  Sad and wan,   15
And he shakes his feeble head,
That it seems as if he said,
  "They are gone."

The mossy marbles rest
On the lips that he has pressed   20
  In their bloom,
And the names he loved to hear
Have been carved for many a year
  On the tomb.

My grandmamma has said—   25
Poor old lady, she is dead
  Long ago—
That he had a Roman nose,
And his cheek was like a rose
  In the snow.   30

But now his nose is thin,
And it rests upon his chin
  Like a staff,
And a crook is in his back,
And a melancholy crack   35
  In his laugh.

I know it is a sin
For me to sit and grin
  At him here;
But the old three-cornered hat,   40
And the breeches, and all that,
  Are so queer!

And if I should live to be
The last leaf upon the tree
  In the spring,   45
Let them smile, as I do now,
At the old forsaken bough
  Where I cling.

My Last Walk with the
Schoolmistress (A Parenthesis)

The selection which follows forms part of one of the last papers in *The Autocrat of the Breakfast-Table.* The schoolmistress mentioned in the title is one of the group which gathers with the Autocrat each morning at the boarding-house table. She has gradually assumed a more and more important rôle as the Autocrat discovers her charms. In describing his last walk with her, the Autocrat frequently interrupts his narration to address the reader directly, to muse at length on various subjects, or to ponder remarks made by his friend, the Professor.

I can't say just how many walks she and I had taken together before this one. I found the effect of going out every morning was decidedly favorable on her health. Two pleasing dimples, the places for which were just marked when she came, played, shadowy, in her freshening cheeks when she smiled and nodded good morning to me from the schoolhouse steps.

I am afraid I did the greater part of the talking. At any rate, if I should try to report all that I said during the first half-dozen walks we took together, I fear that I might receive a gentle hint from my friends the publishers, that a separate volume, at my own risk and expense, would be the proper method of bringing them before the public.

—I would have a woman as true as Death. At the first real lie which works from the heart outward, she should be tenderly chloroformed into a better world, where she can have an angel for a governess, and feed on strange fruits which will make her all over again, even to her bones and marrow.—Whether gifted with the accident of beauty or not, she should have been molded in the rose-red clay of Love, before the breath of life made a moving mortal of her. Love-capacity is a congenital endowment; and I think, after a while, one gets to know the warm-hued natures it belongs to from the pretty pipe-clay counterfeits of it.—Proud she may be, in the sense of respecting herself; but pride, in the sense of contemning others less gifted than herself, deserves the two lowest circles of a vulgar woman's Inferno, where the punishments are Smallpox and Bankruptcy.—She who nips off the end of a brittle courtesy, as one breaks the tip of an icicle, to bestow upon those whom she ought cordially and kindly to recognize, proclaims the fact that she comes not merely of low blood, but of bad blood. Consciousness of unquestioned position makes people gracious in proper measure to all; but if a woman puts on airs with her real equals, she has something about herself or her family she is ashamed of, or ought to be. Middle-, and more than middle-aged people, who know family histories, generally see through it. An official of standing was rude to me once. "Oh, that is the maternal grandfather," said a wise old friend to me, "he was a boor." —Better too few words, from the woman we love, than too many: while she is silent, Nature is working for her; while she talks, she is working for herself.—Love is sparingly soluble in the words of men; therefore they speak much of it; but one syllable of woman's speech can dissolve more of it than a man's heart can hold.

—Whether I said any or all of these things to the schoolmistress, or not—whether I stole them out of Lord Bacon—whether I cribbed them from Balzac—whether I dipped them from the ocean of Tupperian wisdom[1]—or whether I have just found them in my head, laid there by that solemn fowl, Experience (who, according to my observation, cackles oftener than she drops real live eggs), I cannot say. Wise men have said more foolish

things—and foolish men, I don't doubt, have said as wise things. Anyhow, the schoolmistress and I had pleasant walks and long talks, all of which I do not feel bound to report.

—You are a stranger to me, Ma'am.—I don't doubt you would like to know all I said to the schoolmistress.—I sha'n't do it;—I had rather get the publishers to return the money you have invested in this. Besides, I have forgotten a good deal of it. I shall tell only what I like of what I remember.

—My idea was, in the first place, to search out the picturesque spots which the city[2] affords a sight of, to those who have eyes. I know a good many, and it was a pleasure to look at them in company with my young friend. There were the shrubs and flowers in the Franklin Place front yards or borders; Commerce is just putting his granite foot upon them. Then there are certain small seraglio gardens, into which one can get a peep through the crevices of high fences—one in Myrtle Street, or backing on it—here and there one at the North and South Ends. Then the great elms in Essex Street. Then the stately horse chestnuts in that vacant lot in Chambers Street, which hold their outspread hands over your head (as I said in my poem the other day), and look as if they were whispering, "May grace, mercy, and peace be with you!"—and the rest of that benediction. Nay, there are certain patches of ground, which, having lain neglected for a time, Nature, who always has her pockets full of seeds, and holes in all her pockets, has covered with hungry plebeian growths, which fight for life with each other, until some of them get broad-leaved and succulent, and you have a coarse vegetable tapestry which Raphael[3] would not have disdained to spread over the foreground of his masterpiece. The Professor pretends that he found such a one in Charles Street, which, in its daredevil impudence of rough-and-tumble vegetation, beat the pretty-behaved flower beds of the Public Garden as ignominiously as a group of young tatterde-

1. *the ocean of Tupperian wisdom.* M. F. Tupper, a nine-teenth-century English author, was known for his trite and uninspired moralizing. 2. *the city,* Boston. 3. *Raphael* (rafʹi əl *or* rāʹfi əl), one of the most famous Italian painters (1483-1520).

malions playing pitch-and-toss beats a row of Sunday-school boys with their teacher at their head.

But then the Professor has one of his burrows in that region, and puts everything in high colors relating to it. That is his way about everything.—"I hold any man cheap," he said, "of whom nothing stronger can be uttered than that all his geese are swans."— "How is that, Professor?" said I; "I should have set you down for one of that sort."— "Sir," said he, "I am proud to say, that Nature has so far enriched me, that I cannot own so much as a *duck* without seeing in it as pretty a swan as ever swam the basin in the garden of Luxembourg."[4] And the Professor showed the whites of his eyes devoutly, like one returning thanks after a dinner of many courses.

I don't know anything sweeter than this leaking in of Nature through all the cracks in the walls and floors of cities. You heap up a million tons of hewn rocks on a square mile or two of earth which was green once. The trees look down from the hillsides and ask each other, as they stand on tiptoe—"What are these people about?" And the small herbs at their feet look up and whisper back, "We will go and see." So the small herbs pack themselves up in the least possible bundles, and wait until the wind steals to them at night and whispers—"Come with me." Then they go softly with it into the great city—one to a cleft in the pavement, one to a spout on the roof, one to a seam in the marbles over a rich gentleman's bones, and one to the grave without a stone where nothing but a man is buried— and there they grow, looking down on the generations of men from moldy roofs, looking up from between the less trodden pavements, looking out through iron cemetery-railings. Listen to them, when there is only a light breath stirring, and you will hear them saying to each other, "Wait awhile." The words run along the telegraph of those narrow green lines that border the roads leading from the city, until they reach the slope of the hills, and the trees repeat in low murmurs to each other, "Wait awhile!" By and by the flow of life in the streets ebbs and the old leafy inhabitants—the smaller tribes always in front—

saunter in, one by one, very careless seemingly, but very tenacious, until they swarm so that the great stones gape from each other with the crowding of their roots, and the feldspar begins to be picked out of the granite to find them food. At last the trees take up their solemn line of march, and never rest until they have encamped in the market place. Wait long enough and you will find an old doting oak hugging a huge worn block in its yellow underground arms; that was the cornerstone of the State House. Oh, so patient she is, this imperturbable Nature!

—Let us cry!—

But all this has nothing to do with my walks and talks with the schoolmistress. I did not say that I would not tell you something about them. Let me alone, and I shall talk to you more than I ought to, probably. We never tell our secrets to people that pump for them.

Books we talked about, and education. It was her duty to know something of these, and of course she did. Perhaps I was somewhat more learned than she, but I found that the difference between her reading and mine was like that of a man's and a woman's dusting a library. The man flaps about with a bunch of feathers; the woman goes to work softly with a cloth. She does not raise half the dust, nor fill her own eyes and mouth with it—but she goes into all the corners and attends to the leaves as much as the covers.—Books are the *negative* pictures of thought, and the more sensitive the mind that receives their images, the more nicely the finest lines are reproduced. A woman (of the right kind) reading after a man, follows him as Ruth followed the reapers of Boaz,[5] and her gleanings are often the finest of the wheat.

But it was in talking of Life that we came most nearly together. I thought I knew some-

---

4. *swam the basin in the garden of Luxembourg* (luk′səm-bĕrg). The Luxembourg is an art museum in Paris, where the Senate of France meets. It was formerly a palace and its gardens are now a park. 5. *A woman ... follows him as Ruth followed the reapers of Boaz.* According to the Bible, Ruth met her future husband, Boaz (bō′az), while working in his fields during the grain harvest. She followed the reapers as they cut the barley and wheat and gleaned, or gathered, the grain into sheaves.

thing about that—that I could speak or write about it somewhat to the purpose.

To take up this fluid earthly being of ours as a sponge sucks up water—to be steeped and soaked in its realities as a hide fills its pores lying seven years in a tan pit—to have winnowed every wave of it as a mill wheel works up the stream that runs through the flume upon its floatboards—to have curled up in the keenest spasms and flattened out in the laxest languors of this breathing-sickness, which keeps certain parcels of matter uneasy for three- or fourscore years—to have fought all the devils and clasped all the angels of its delirium—and then, just at the point where the white-hot passions have cooled down to cherry-red, plunge our experience into the ice-cold stream of some human language or other, one might think would end in a rhapsody with something of spring and temper in it. All this I thought my power and province.

The schoolmistress had tried life, too. Once in a while one meets with a single soul greater than all the living pageant that passes before it. As the pale astronomer sits in his study with sunken eyes and thin fingers, and weighs Uranus or Neptune as in a balance, so there are meek, slight women who have weighed all that this planetary life can offer, and hold it like a bauble in the palm of their slender hands. This was one of them. Fortune had left her, sorrow had baptized her; the routine of labor and the loneliness of almost friendless city-life were before her. Yet, as I looked upon her tranquil face, gradually regaining a cheerfulness that was often sprightly, as she became interested in the various matters we talked about and places we visited, I saw that eye and lip and every shifting lineament were made for love—unconscious of their sweet office as yet, and meeting the cold aspect of Duty with the natural graces which were meant for the reward of nothing less than a Great Passion.

—I never spoke one word of love to the schoolmistress in the course of these pleasant walks. It seemed to me that we talked of everything but love on that particular morning. There was, perhaps, a little more timidity and hesitancy on my part than I have commonly shown among our people at the boarding house. In fact, I considered myself the master at the breakfast-table; but, somehow, I could not command myself just then so well as usual. The truth, is I had secured a passage to Liverpool in the steamer which was to leave at noon—with the condition, however, of being released in case circumstances occurred to detain me. The schoolmistress knew nothing about all this, of course, as yet.

It was on the Common that we were walking. The *mall* or boulevard of our Common, you know, has various branches leading from it in different directions. One of these runs downward from opposite Joy Street southward across the whole length of the Common to Boylston Street. We called it the long path, and were fond of it.

I felt very weak indeed (though of a tolerably robust habit) as we came opposite the head of this path on that morning. I think I tried to speak twice without making myself distinctly audible. At last I got out the question,—"will you take the long path with me?" —"Certainly," said the schoolmistress, "with much pleasure." —"Think," I said, "before you answer; if you take the long path with me now, I shall interpret it that we are to part no more!"—The schoolmistress stepped back with a sudden movement, as if an arrow had struck her.

One of the long granite blocks used as seats was hard by—the one you may still see close by the Ginkgo tree. "Pray, sit down," I said. —"No, no," she answered, softly, "I will walk the *long path* with you!"

—The old gentleman who sits opposite met us walking, arm in arm, about the middle of the long path, and said, very charmingly, "Good morning, my dears!"

TO INCREASE UNDERSTANDING
Poems by Holmes

1. (a) In "The Chambered Nautilus" why does Holmes compare the chambered shell to a ship? (b) Where does this figure of speech end? (c) What does the chambered nautilus symbolize?

2. Compare stanzas 3 and 5 of "The Chambered Nautilus." (a) What information does the

poet give you in stanza 3? (b) What use does he make of this factual information in stanza 5?

3. (a) What is Holmes' attitude toward the aged gentleman he is describing in "The Last Leaf"? (b) How does his use of figurative language contribute to the expression of this attitude?

4. (a) How does the tone of "The Last Leaf" differ from the tone of "The Chambered Nautilus"? (b) Which poem do you like better? (c) Does the tone have an important influence upon your preference? Explain.

My Last Walk with the Schoolmistress

1. Holmes makes several statements about women in this selection from *The Autocrat of the Breakfast-Table*. (a) Select passages which illustrate his views.

(b) What admirable qualities does he find in the schoolmistress?

2. As the Autocrat describes his walk with the schoolmistress, he often pauses to muse over other subjects. What are some of these subjects?

3. If you had been one of the boarders seated around the breakfast table, at what point would you have interrupted the Autocrat to disagree? Explain.

4. Would you classify this selection as an informal or a formal essay? Name specific qualities to justify your answer. (Rereading "The Essay," page 245, will help you answer this question.)

5. It may be said of Dr. Holmes that in wit, polish, and cleverness he stood high among the writers of his time. How do "The Last Leaf" and "My Last Walk with the Schoolmistress" illustrate this description?

James Russell Lowell 1819-1891

Like Longfellow and Holmes, Lowell was descended from an aristocratic New England family, was a Harvard professor, and became a famous author. But because he was born twelve years after Longfellow, ten after Holmes, he was subject to somewhat different influences.

From his youth Lowell was impressionable and quick to respond to new ideas. As a Harvard undergraduate he was stirred when he heard Emerson lecture on his so-called "radical" doctrines. In his senior year as the result of a prank he was "rusticated," or sent to the country as punishment for six weeks. By good fortune he was sent to Concord, where he met Emerson. A few years after graduation he fell in love with and married Maria White, a Transcendentalist, an admirer of Emerson and Carlyle, and an enthusiast about some of the social reforms being urged at this time.

As a result of such influences, Lowell became active as a reformer, writing fervent editorials and poems championing numerous social causes, including the abolition of slavery. In 1846, he wrote a very popular series of poems strongly opposing the war with Mexico. "Thinking the Mexican War . . . a national crime committed in behalf of slavery," he explained, "and wishing to put the feelings of those who thought as I did in a way that would tell, I imagined myself . . . an upcountry man . . . always instinctively falling back into the natural stronghold of his homely dialect when heated. . . ." The "upcountry man" whom Lowell created to voice his feelings was Hosea Biglow. His anti-Mexican War and antislavery poems in Yankee dialect were collected in book form in 1848 as *The Biglow Papers*. In the tradition of homespun humor, dating back to Franklin's *Dogood Papers* and Poor Richard's pithy sayings, these poems showed that the aristocratic Lowell had aligned himself with rising democratic groups in a way his Harvard colleagues had not. During the War Between the

States, he revived his rustic oracle for a second series of *Biglow Papers*, which appeared in the *Atlantic Monthly* between 1862 and 1866. These poems, his greatest popular success, are all remarkable for their ability to use homespun dialect to create people and places. "The Courtin'" (page 283) is today the most popular of them. Most of the others now make hard reading because they are concerned with forgotten disputes and outdated political preachments.

Lowell proved his versatility by publishing two books totally different from *The Biglow Papers* in 1848, the year in which the first series of *Papers* made its appearance. One of these works, *A Fable for Critics*, was published anonymously. In rollicking verse it wittily commented on the leading authors of the day, as in this sample:

> There's Holmes, who is matchless among you for wit;
> A Leyden-jar always full-charged, from which flit
> The electrical tingles of hit after hit . . .
> His are just the fine hands, too, to weave you a lyric
> Full of fancy, fun, feeling, or spiced with satiric
> In measure so kindly, you doubt if the toes
> That are trodden upon are your own or your foes'.

Lowell's house in Cambridge.

The other work, *The Vision of Sir Launfal,* like *The Idylls of the King* by the contemporary British poet, Tennyson, made use of Arthurian legends.

Lowell's life also proved that he was versatile. In 1855, when Longfellow retired from his professorship at Harvard, Lowell took his place, teaching there until 1876. At Harvard he was known as a fascinating teacher. Many former students, years after, vividly recalled his rambling but engrossing lectures and his discussions of authors when he talked informally with class members during evening visits to his book-lined study. In 1857 Lowell helped found the *Atlantic Monthly* and edited it until 1861. Like Washington Irving, Lowell was appointed to diplomatic posts in Spain and England; he was minister to Spain from 1877 to 1880 and minister to England from 1880 to 1885. In these fields also his keen perception, his lively wit, and his wide scholarship made him a success.

Throughout his life, Lowell continued to create literature, sometimes commenting upon political controversies, sometimes writing criticism, sometimes composing lyrics or long poems. As editor of the *Atlantic* and as contributor to other periodicals he wrote telling reviews of contemporary books. He discussed brilliantly in a series of volumes most of the world's great authors, from Dante's day to his own. In his poems he showed a mastery, comparable with that of Longfellow, of melodic language and verse. One of his best poems was a long one written in 1865 for the memorial occasion indicated by its full title, "Ode Recited at the Commemoration of the Living and Dead Soldiers of Harvard University." Although the "Ode" referred to the conflict between the North and the South in which the dead soldiers had served, it rose above partisan politics, particularly in the tribute to Lincoln printed on page 286. This represents Lowell's democratic faith; it shows also his skill as a versifier who shaped his irregular lines to conform with his thought and employed meaningful and musical words to evoke emotion.

The Courtin'

God makes sech nights, all white an'
    still
  Fur 'z you can look or listen,
Moonshine an' snow on field an' hill,
  All silence an' all glisten.

Zekle crep' up quite unbeknown   5
  An' peeked in thru' the winder,
An' there sot Huldy all alone,
  'ith no one nigh to hender.

A fireplace filled the room's one side
  With half a cord o' wood in—   10
There warn't no stoves (tell[1] comfort
    died)
  To bake ye to a puddin'.

The wa'nut logs shot sparkles out
  Towards the pootiest,[2] bless her,
An' leetle flames danced all about   15
  The chiny on the dresser.

Agin the chimbley crook-necks[3] hung,
  An' in amongst 'em rusted
The ole queen's-arm[4] thet Gran'ther Young
  Fetched back from Concord busted.   20

The very room, coz she was in,
  Seemed warm from floor to ceilin',

---

1. *tell,* until. 2. *pootiest,* prettiest. 3. *crook-necks,* squashes with crooked necks. 4. *queen's-arm,* a musket which takes its name from Queen Anne, who ruled England from 1702 to 1714.

An' she looked full ez rosy agin
  Ez the apples she was peelin'.

'Twas kin' o' kingdom-come[5] to look   25
  On sech a blessed cretur,
A dog rose[6] blushin' to a brook
  Ain't modester nor sweeter.

He was six foot o' man, A-1,
  Clear grit an' human natur';   30
None couldn't quicker pitch a ton[7]
  Nor dror a furrer[8] straighter.

He'd sparked it with full twenty gals,
  Had squired 'em, danced 'em, druv 'em,
Fust this one, an' then thet, by spells—   35
  All is, he couldn't love 'em.

But long o' her his veins 'ould run
  All crinkly like curled maple,
The side she breshed felt full o' sun
  Ez a south slope in Ap'il.   40

She thought no v'ice had sech a swing
  Ez hisn in the choir;
My! when he made Ole Hunderd[9] ring,
  She *knowed* the Lord was nigher.

An' she'd blush scarlit, right in prayer,   45
  When her new meetin'-bunnet
Felt somehow thru' its crown a pair
  O' blue eyes sot upun it.

Thet night, I tell ye, she looked *some!*
  She seemed to've gut a new soul,   50
For she felt sartin-sure he'd come,
  Down to her very shoe sole.

She heered a foot, an' knowed it tu,
  A-raspin' on the scraper—
All ways to once her feelin's flew   55
  Like sparks in burnt-up paper.

He kin' o' l'itered on the mat
  Some doubtfle o' the sekle,[10]
His heart kep' goin' pity-pat
  But hern went pity Zekle.   60

An' yet she gin her cheer a jerk
  Ez though she wished him furder,

An' on her apples kep' to work
  Parin' away like murder.

"You want to see my Pa, I s'pose?"   65
  "Wal...no....I come dasignin'—"
"To see my Ma? She's sprinklin' clo'es
  Agin tomorrer's i'nin'."

To say why gals acts so or so,
  Or don't, 'ould be presumin';   70
Mebby to mean *yes* an' say *no*
  Comes nateral to women.

He stood a spell on one foot fust,
  Then stood a spell on t'other,
An' on which one he felt the wust   75
  He couldn't ha' told ye nuther.

Says he, "I'd better call agin";
  Says she, "Think likely, Mister";
Thet last word pricked him like a pin,
  An' .... Wal, he up an' kist her.   80

When Ma bimeby upon 'em slips,
  Huldy sot pale ez ashes,
All kin' o' smily roun' the lips
  An' teary roun' the lashes.

For she was jes' the quiet kind   85
  Whose naturs never vary,
Like streams that keep a summer mind
  Snowhid in Jenooary.

The blood clost roun' her heart felt glued
  Too tight for all expressin',   90
Tell mother see how metters stood,
  An' gin 'em both her blessin'.

Then her red come back like the tide
  Down to the Bay o' Fundy,[11]
An' all I know is they was cried   95
  In meetin'[12] come nex' Sunday.

---

5. *kingdom-come*, as if one had already arrived in heaven.
6. *dog rose*, the common wild rose. 7. *pitch a ton*, pitch a
ton of hay. 8. *dror a furrer*, draw (plow) a furrow. 9. *Ole
Hunderd*, the hymn, "Praise God from Whom All Blessings
Flow," which is regularly sung as a part of many Protestant
church services. 10. *sekle*, sequel, or outcome. 11. *Bay o'
Fundy*, an inlet of the Atlantic Ocean, separating New
Brunswick from Nova Scotia. 12. *cried in meetin'*. The
marriage banns, signifying their intention to wed, were
announced by the minister at church service.

THE MAGAZINE IN AMERICA

The Atlantic Monthly

During the nineteenth century, American writers looked to the growing magazines for their best chance of gaining publication. Editors of a general magazine, like the *Saturday Evening Post,* or a woman's magazine, like *Godey's Lady's Book,* were swamped by the flood of short stories, essays, and poems that crossed their desks every day. The writers of America's Golden Day were so productive that literary monthlies, magazines devoted solely to the best of American letters, appeared on the scene. The *North American Review, Graham's Magazine, Knickerbocker Magazine,* and the *Southern Literary Messenger* were among the first to enjoy success. But to a group of distinguished New Englanders, even these magazines were not enough.

Seated around a Boston dinner table one evening in 1857, Emerson, Longfellow, and Lowell, among others, discussed the organization of a new literary monthly. Holmes suggested its name, the *Atlantic Monthly,* and Lowell was appointed its first editor. With such a galaxy of supporters how could any magazine fail to succeed! The first issue of the *Atlantic* appeared in November of 1857 and featured unsigned contributions by Emerson, Harriet Beecher Stowe, Lowell, and Holmes. Although writers for the religious press were shocked by some of Holmes' views in *The Autocrat,* his humorous sketches and poems were a staple of the early years of publication. Whittier and Hawthorne were contributors, but Thoreau, infuriated at the way Lowell had edited his first contribution to the *Atlantic,* refused to contribute as long as Lowell sat in the editor's chair.

For more than a hundred years the *Atlantic Monthly* has succeeded in presenting much of the best of American letters while gradually broadening its scope. Current issues of the magazine include, in addition to fiction and poetry, book reviews and articles on science, education, and contemporary affairs. The writers no longer are Holmes and Lowell, of course, but the high standards of the old New England writers remain in a magazine for today's readers who reject formula fiction, sensational articles, and sentimental verse.

Perhaps one of the most impressive tributes was paid to the *Atlantic* by President Woodrow Wilson. Wilson gave his final public expression about world coöperation for peace, "The Road Away from Revolution," to the *Atlantic* for a relatively small fee. Wilson could have commanded a considerable price for the article from magazines of wider circulation, but he felt that his development of a theme so close to his heart should be presented to Americans in the pages of the magazine he regarded most highly.

Title page of Vol. I, No. 1.

THE

ATLANTIC MONTHLY.

A MAGAZINE OF

LITERATURE, ART, AND POLITICS.

BOSTON:
PHILLIPS, SAMPSON AND COMPANY,
13 Winter Street.

LONDON: TRÜBNER AND COMPANY.

On July 21, 1865, friends and alumni of Harvard College gathered to pay tribute to the Harvard men who had served during the recently concluded War Between the States. Lowell wrote his "Ode Recited at the Harvard Commemoration" for this occasion. The sixth section of the poem, given below, is Lowell's famous tribute to Lincoln, who had been assassinated a few months earlier on April 14, 1865.

VI

S uch was he, our Martyr-Chief,
    Whom late the Nation he had led,
    With ashes on her head,
    Wept with the passion of an angry grief:
Forgive me, if from present things I turn   5
To speak what in my heart will beat and burn,
And hang my wreath on his world-honored urn.
    Nature, they say, doth dote,
    And cannot make a man
    Save on some worn-out plan,   10
    Repeating us by rote:
For him her Old World molds aside she threw,
    And, choosing sweet clay from the breast
    Of the unexhausted West,
With stuff untainted shaped a hero new,   15
Wise, steadfast in the strength of God, and true.
    How beautiful to see
Once more a shepherd of mankind indeed,
Who loved his charge but never loved to lead;
One whose meek flock the people joyed to be,   20
    Not lured by any cheat of birth,
    But by his clear-grained human worth,
And brave old wisdom of sincerity!
    They knew that outward grace is dust;
    They could not choose but trust   25
In that sure-footed mind's unfaltering skill,
    And supple-tempered will
That bent like perfect steel to spring again and thrust.
    His was no lonely mountain-peak of mind,
    Thrusting to thin air o'er our cloudy bars,   30
    A sea-mark now, now lost in vapors blind;
    Broad prairie rather, genial, level-lined,
    Fruitful and friendly for all human kind,
Yet also nigh to heaven and loved of loftiest stars.
    Nothing of Europe here,   35
Or, then, of Europe fronting mornward still,
    Ere any names of Serf and Peer[1]

---

1. *Europe fronting mornward ... Serf and Peer.* Lowell contrasts Europe and its adherence to the old tradition of social classes with America and its classless society.

Could Nature's equal scheme deface
And thwart her genial will;
Here was a type of the true elder race,   40
And one of Plutarch's men talked with us face to face.[2]
I praise him not; it were too late;
And some innative weakness there must be
In him who condescends to victory
Such as the Present gives, and cannot wait,   45
Safe in himself as in a fate.
So always firmly he:
He knew how to bide his time,
And can his fame abide,
Still patient in his simple faith sublime,   50
Till the wise years decide.
Great captains, with their guns and drums,
Disturb our judgment for the hour,
But at last silence comes;
These are all gone, and, standing like a tower,   55
Our children shall behold his fame,
The kindly-earnest, brave, foreseeing man,
Sagacious, patient, dreading praise, not blame,
New birth of our new soil, the first American.

---

2. *one of Plutarch's men . . . face to face.* Lowell is saying that Lincoln is worthy of comparison with the heroic Greeks and Romans celebrated by the first-century Greek biographer, Plutarch, in his *Lives.*

 TO INCREASE UNDERSTANDING

1. Lowell's poem, "The Courtin'," appeared in his second series of *Biglow Papers.* (*a*) Explain why "The Courtin'," unlike the other *Biglow Papers,* continues to be a popular poem. (*b*) What was Lowell's reason for writing *The Biglow Papers* in Yankee dialect?

2. (*a*) What devices does Lowell use to create humor in "The Courtin'"? (*b*) Does Lowell make Zekle and Huldy seem ridiculous? (*c*) What is his attitude toward them? Prove your statement.

3. The biographical essay describes *The Biglow Papers* as belonging to "the tradition of homespun humor dating back to Franklin's *Dogood Papers* and Poor Richard's pithy sayings." How does "The Courtin'" illustrate this relationship?

4. (*a*) In the passage from "Ode Recited at the Harvard Commemoration" what qualities does Lowell admire in Lincoln? (*b*) Cite passages in which figurative language is employed. What purpose does this language serve?

5. (*a*) What does Lowell mean when he calls Lincoln the "first American"? (*b*) What significance does Lowell attach to Lincoln's frontier origins?

6. Explain how this poem illustrates Lowell's faith in democratic ideals.

 BETTER READING
Meter in poetry

Sometimes the rhythm of a poem makes an important contribution to the pleasure with which we read it. We take it for granted that all poems have rhythm, regular or irregular, and that many poems use rhyme. However, some knowledge of the regular rhythms, called *meters,* that are used in all but free verse, will add to our enjoyment of poetry by helping us see precisely how the poet uses them.

The basis of meter is the *foot.* Each foot contains one accented syllable and one or more unaccented syllables. The arrangement of accented and unaccented syllables in a foot gives us four basic meters:

(*a*) *The iamb.* This metrical foot, which consists of an unaccented syllable followed by an accented syllable ($\smile$ /), as in the word *delight,* is the measure most commonly used in verse written in the English language. Notice how the accents fall in the lines from Freneau's poem "The Wild Honeysuckle":

No rov | ing foot | shall crush | thee here,|

No bus | y hand | pro voke | a tear. |

(b) *The trochee.* This two-syllabled metrical foot is the opposite of the iamb. Here the accented syllable precedes the unaccented syllable (´˘), as in the word *golden.* Longfellow used this meter in *Hiawatha:*

Out of | child hood | in to | man hood |

Now had | grown my | Hi a | wath a. |

(c) *The anapest.* This three-syllabled measure consists of two short or unaccented syllables followed by one long or accented syllable (˘˘´), as in the word *introduce.* It is seldom sustained throughout an entire poem, but many poets gain variety and a swift-moving effect by combining anapestic with iambic feet. The following lines from "Sandolphon," by Longfellow, illustrate this meter:

From the spir | its on earth | that a dore |

From the souls | that en treat | and im plore. |

(d) *The dactyl.* Like the anapest, the dactyl is a three-syllabled foot, but in the dactyl the long or accented syllable precedes the two unaccented syllables (´˘˘), as in the word *happiness.* Few poems are written entirely in dactylic feet, but Longfellow used this meter frequently in *The Courtship of Miles Standish:*

Noth ing was | heard in the | room but the |

hur ry ing | pen of the | strip ling. |

Few poems are written in metrical feet of a single kind. Poets worth their salt tend to avoid the monotony of a completely regular beat by using *substitute feet.* For example, *strip'ling* is a trochee at the end of a dactylic line by Longfellow quoted above. Poets may also use *spondees,* poetic feet composed of two accented syllables. Most spondees, like the words *sweet clay* in line 13 of Lowell's "Commemoration Ode" (page 286), are made up of two monosyllabic words, both of which receive emphasis. Departures from regular rhythm not only destroy monotony; they also may emphasize important words.

In the excerpt from Lowell's "Ode" (page 286) lines 19 and 21 are in completely regular iambic meter. Between them, by contrast, is the line, "One

whose meek flock the people joyed to be." Here the dactylic "One whose" stresses *One,* and since *meek flock* is a spondee these words also are emphasized.

In some instances a poet may so use substitute feet as to make rhythms echo the thought being expressed. In each stanza of Longfellow's "The Tide Rises, the Tide Falls" (page 270), the opening four lines move rapidly; then the fifth line, much slower in movement, imitates the everlasting relentless tide.

Poetry varies not only in meter but also in the number of feet in a line. A line of poetry containing only one foot is said to be written in *monometer;* a line of two feet is called *dimeter;* a line of three feet gives us *trimeter.* Thus, the lines from "Sandolphon" scanned in the preceding column are said to be written in *anapestic trimeter.*

Tetrameter, a line of four metrical feet, is frequently used by poets. "The Wild Honeysuckle" is written in *iambic tetrameter* and the meter of *Hiawatha* is *trochaic tetrameter.*

Pentameter is a line of five metrical feet. *Iambic pentameter* is used in sonnets such as Longfellow's "Divina Commedia One and Two" (page 271). Iambic pentameter is also used in the dignified unrhymed lines we call *blank verse.* Bryant's "Thanatopsis" (page 192) and Emerson's "The Snowstorm" (page 265) are written in blank verse.

How, in "The Snowstorm" does the poet manage the rhythm to stress the fact that the farm folk's movement is halted while, outside, the storm continues to move? Compare the verse structure of "The Snowstorm" with that of "The Courtin'" (page 283) and "The Last Leaf" (page 277). How is the verse pattern of each related to the mood and feeling of the poem?

Examine the meters of some of the other poems you have studied in this chapter. Indicate on the blackboard the scansion of several lines from various poems. Can you find substitute feet or spondees used for emphasis? To imitate the action being described? Can you find examples of more than one meter in a single poem? Which meter predominates?

 EXTENDING INTERESTS

James Russell Lowell's "Commemoration Ode" was the first of many poetic tributes to Lincoln. In *The Home Book of Verse,* edited by Burton Stevenson you will find Vachel Lindsay's poem, "Abraham Lincoln Walks at Midnight" and Edwin Markham's poem, "Lincoln, Man of the People." Read these two modern tributes to Lincoln and then compare Lindsay and Markham with Lowell as interpreters of Lincoln.

John Greenleaf Whittier 1807-1892

If any great author in the New England of the period resembled Lowell's farmer-poet, Hosea Biglow, it was John Greenleaf Whittier. Born and reared on a farm in the township of Haverhill, Massachusetts, educated in two brief terms at Haverhill Academy paid for with money he had scraped to save, Whittier used in his poems the simple words of a man with little schooling. Sometimes, as when he rhymed *staff* and *scarf* or *Eva* and *leave her,* unwittingly he did so in conformity with the dialect pronunciations of his district. Again like Hosea, Whittier during his young manhood and middle age used his pen to attack slavery. Dark, erect, and slender, Whittier had the burning eyes of a zealot; he often defiantly faced mobs, and on occasion his black frock coat was spattered with eggs. His fervent spirit gave fire to his antislavery writings, and he first became famous as a leader in the abolition movement.

The bitterness of Whittier's partisan verses and the fact that they were inspired by the controversy of a particular age marred most of them for those who read them only after the argument had ended. Historically important though they were, they are less admired today than the quieter verses of the years when, stooped and white-bearded, a venerable old Quaker, Whittier had left the battle arena.

One aspect of Whittier's turbulent years, however, had prepared him

CULVER PICTURES

for the themes and tone of his later writing. He had lived through these years (as he would live to the end of his long life) in rural Essex County, first in his birthplace, later in Amesbury. Always he had been strongly attached to the soil of his district, to its people, and to its traditions. With his battles behind him, it was natural that he should write about what he knew and loved. So he vividly and affectionately described New England scenery, or retold legends of the seacoast, of Indians, of witchcraft, or of his Quaker forebears. His use of such lore, of course, related him to other users of similar material such as Irving and Longfellow and made his works, like theirs, attractive to nineteenth-century readers.

Snow-Bound (page 291), the best of Whittier's long poems, was written in 1866, a year after the ending of the Civil War. Recalling as it does winter evenings during the poet's childhood, it captures the scene perfectly and portrays with sympathetic understanding and gentle humor the members of the family seated around the fireside as the snow piles up outside. From an early age Whittier had been influenced by another farmer-poet, Robert Burns (1759-1796), and *Snow-Bound* did for the New England countryman what "The Cotter's Saturday Night" had done for the poor Scotch farmer. Both extol the dignity of simple people and the pleasures of humble life. But although the themes are similar, Whittier's poem is not derivative. It is unmistakably a Yankee idyl catching the essence of life in nineteenth-century New England.

Ichabod

In 1850, the Senate of the United States was debating whether slavery should be permitted in the new territories acquired as a result of the Mexican War. Northern abolitionists expected Daniel Webster, the Massachusetts senator and the most famous orator of his day, to take a strong antislavery position. In his speech on March 7, however, Webster supported compromise proposals which extended slavery into these new territories. Webster's speech was a bitter disappointment to the abolitionists, particularly to Whittier, who admired Webster greatly. In protest, Whittier wrote "Ichabod." The poem takes its title from the Bible (I Samuel 4:21): "And she named the child Ichabod, saying, the glory is departed from Israel."

So fallen! so lost! the light withdrawn
   Which once he wore!
The glory from his gray hairs gone
   Forevermore!

Revile him not—the Tempter hath   5
   A snare for all;
And pitying tears, not scorn and wrath,
   Befit his fall!

Oh, dumb be passion's stormy rage,
   When he who might   10
Have lighted up and led his age,
   Falls back in night.

Scorn! would the angels laugh, to mark
   A bright soul driven,
Fiend-goaded, down the endless dark,   15
   From hope and heaven!

Let not the land once proud of him
   Insult him now,
Nor brand with deeper shame his dim,
   Dishonored brow.   20

But let its humbled sons, instead,
   From sea to lake,
A long lament, as for the dead,
   In sadness make.

Of all we loved and honored, naught   25
   Save power remains—
A fallen angel's pride of thought,
   Still strong in chains.

All else is gone; from those great eyes
   The soul has fled: 30
When faith is lost, when honor dies,
   The man is dead!

Then, pay the reverence of old days
   To his dead fame;
Walk backward, with averted gaze,
   And hide the shame!

FROM *Snow-Bound*

A Winter Idyl

In a note on the poem, Whittier wrote: "In my boyhood, in our lonely farmhouse, we had scanty sources of information: few books and only a small weekly newspaper .... Under such circumstances storytelling was a necessary resource in the long winter evenings. My father, when a young man, had traversed the wilderness to Canada, and could tell us of his adventures with Indians and wild beasts .... My uncle was ready with his record of hunting and fishing and, it must be confessed, with stories of witchcraft and apparitions. My mother, who had been born in the Indian-haunted region of Somersworth, New Hampshire, told us of the inroads of the savages and the narrow escapes of her ancestors."

The sun that brief December day
Rose cheerless over hills of gray,
And, darkly circled, gave at noon
A sadder light than waning moon.
Slow tracing down the thickening sky   5
Its mute and ominous prophecy,
A portent seeming less than threat,
It sank from sight before it set.
A chill no coat, however stout,
Of homespun stuff could quite shut out,   10
A hard, dull bitterness of cold,
That checked, mid-vein, the circling race
Of lifeblood in the sharpened face,
The coming of the snowstorm told.
The wind blew east; we heard the roar   15
Of Ocean on his wintry shore
And felt the strong pulse throbbing there
Beat with low rhythm our inland air.

Meanwhile we did our nightly chores—
Brought in the wood from out of doors,   20
Littered the stalls, and from the mows

Raked down the herd's-grass for the cows,
Heard the horse whinnying for his corn;
And, sharply clashing horn on horn,
Impatient down the stanchion rows   25
The cattle shake their walnut bows;
While, peering from his early perch
Upon the scaffold's pole of birch,
The cock his crested helmet bent
And down his querulous challenge sent.   30

Unwarmed by any sunset light
The gray day darkened into night,
A night made hoary with the swarm
And whirl-dance of the blinding storm,
As zigzag wavering to and fro   35
Crossed and recrossed the wingèd snow;
And ere the early bedtime came,
The white drift piled the window frame,
And through the glass the clothesline posts
Looked in like tall and sheeted ghosts.   40

So all night long the storm roared on;
The morning broke without a sun....
And, when the second morning shone,
We looked upon a world unknown,

Whittier's birthplace, scene of Snow-Bound.

BROWN BROTHERS

On nothing we could call our own.　　45
Around the glistening wonder bent
The blue walls of the firmament,
No cloud above, no earth below—
A universe of sky and snow! . . .

A prompt, decisive man, no breath　　50
Our father wasted: "Boys, a path!"
Well pleased (for when did farmer boy
Count such a summons less than joy?),
Our buskins on our feet we drew;
　With mittened hands, and caps drawn low, 55
　To guard our necks and ears from snow,
We cut the solid whiteness through;
And, where the drift was deepest, made
A tunnel walled and overlaid
With dazzling crystal; we had read　　60
Of rare Aladdin's wondrous cave,
And to our own his name we gave,
With many a wish the luck were ours
To test his lamp's supernal powers.
We reached the barn with merry din,　　65
And roused the prisoned brutes within.
The old horse thrust his long head out,
And grave with wonder gazed about;
The cock his lusty greeting said,
And forth his speckled harem led;　　70
The oxen lashed their tails, and hooked,
And mild reproach of hunger looked. . . .

As night drew on, and, from the crest
Of wooded knolls that ridged the west
The sun, a snow-blown traveler, sank　　75
From sight beneath the smothering bank,
We piled with care our nightly stack
Of wood against the chimney back—
The oaken log, green, huge, and thick,
And on its top the stout back stick;　　80
The knotty forestick laid apart,
And filled between with curious art
The ragged brush; then, hovering near,
We watched the first red blaze appear,
Heard the sharp crackle, caught the gleam　85
On whitewashed wall and sagging beam,
Until the old, rude-furnished room
Burst, flower-like, into rosy bloom;
While radiant with a mimic flame
Outside the sparkling drift became;　　90
And through the bare-boughed lilac tree
Our own warm hearth seemed blazing free. . . .

Shut in from all the world without,
We sat the clean-winged hearth about,
Content to let the north wind roar　　95
In baffled rage at pane and door,
While the red logs before us beat
The frost line back with tropic heat;
And ever, when a louder blast
Shook beam and rafter as it passed,　　100
The merrier up its roaring draft
The great throat of the chimney laughed,
The house dog on his paws outspread
Laid to the fire his drowsy head,
The cat's dark silhouette on the wall　　105
A couchant tiger's seemed to fall;
And, for the winter fireside meet,
Between the andirons' straddling feet,
The mug of cider simmered slow;
The apples sputtered in a row;　　110
And, close at hand, the basket stood
With nuts from brown October's wood.

What matter how the night behaved?
What matter how the north wind raved?
Blow high, blow low, not all its snow　　115
Could quench our hearthfire's ruddy glow. . . .

We sped the time with stories old;
Wrought puzzles out, and riddles told;
Or stammered from our schoolbook lore
"The chief of Gambia's golden shore."[1] . . . 120
Our father rode again his ride
On Memphremagog's[2] wooded side;
Sat down again to moose and samp[3]
In trapper's hut and Indian camp;
Lived o'er the old idyllic ease　　125
Beneath St. François'[4] hemlock trees;
Again for him the moonlight shone
On Norman cap[5] and bodiced zone[6];
Again he heard the violin play
Which led the village dance away,　　130
And mingled in its merry whirl
The grandam and the laughing girl.

---

1. "*The chief of Gambia's golden shore.*" Whittier is quoting
a line from "The African Chief," a popular poem of the
time.　2. *Memphremagog* (mem frə mä′gog), a lake in
Vermont and Canada.　3. *samp*, corn-meal mush.　4. *St.
François* (san′ frän′swä′), the St. Francis River, in eastern
Canada. Because the river is located in the French-speaking
section of Canada, it is known by both its French and its
English names.　5. *Norman cap,* a cap originally worn in
France, with square corners turned back from the face.
6. *bodiced zone,* waist.

Or, nearer home, our steps he led
Where Salisbury's[7] level marshes spread
   Mile-wide as flies the laden bee;   135
Where merry mowers, hale and strong,
Swept, scythe on scythe, their swaths along
   The low green prairies of the sea.
We shared the fishing off Boar's Head,[8]
   And round the rocky Isles of Shoals[9]   140
   The hake-broil on the driftwood coals;
The chowder on the sand beach made,
Dipped by the hungry, steaming hot,
With spoons of clamshell from the pot. . . .

Our mother, while she turned her wheel   145
Or ran the new-knit stocking heel,
Told how the Indian hordes came down
At midnight on Cochecho town,[10]
And how her own great-uncle bore
   His cruel scalp mark to fourscore.   150
Recalling, in her fitting phrase,
   So rich and picturesque and free
   (The common unrhymed poetry
Of simple life and country ways),
The story of her early days—   155
She made us welcome to her home;
Old hearths grew wide to give us room;
We stole with her a frightened look
At the gray wizard's conjuring book,[11]
The fame whereof went far and wide   160
Through all the simple countryside;
We heard the hawks at twilight play
The boat horn on Piscataqua,[12]
The loon's weird laughter far away;
We fished her little trout brook; knew   165
What flowers in wood and meadow grew;
What sunny hillsides autumn-brown
She climbed to shake the ripe nuts down;
Saw where in sheltered cove and bay
The ducks' black squadron anchored lay;   170
And heard the wild geese calling loud
Beneath the gray November cloud. . . .

Our uncle,[13] innocent of books,
Was rich in lore of fields and brooks,
The ancient teachers never dumb   175
Of Nature's unhoused lyceum.
In moons and tides and weather wise,
He read the clouds as prophecies;
And foul or fair could well divine
By many an occult hint and sign,   180

Holding the cunning-warded keys[14]
To all the woodcraft mysteries;
Himself to Nature's heart so near
That all her voices in his ear
Of beast or bird had meaning clear. . . .   185

Next, the dear aunt,[15] whose smile of cheer
And voice in dreams I see and hear—
The sweetest woman ever Fate
Perverse denied a household mate— . . .
Called up her girlhood memories,   190
The huskings and the apple bees,
The sleigh rides and the summer sails,
Weaving through all the poor details
And homespun warp of circumstance
A golden woof-thread of romance. . . .   195

There, too, our elder sister[16] plied
Her evening task the stand beside;
A full, rich nature, free to trust,
Truthful and almost sternly just,
Impulsive, earnest, prompt to act,   200
And make her generous thought a fact,
Keeping with many a light disguise
The secret of self-sacrifice. . . .

As one who held herself a part
Of all she saw, and let her heart   205
   Against the household bosom lean,
Upon the motley-braided mat
Our youngest[17] and our dearest sat. . . .
The chill weight of the winter snow
   For months upon her grave has lain;   210
And now, when summer south winds blow
   And brier and harebell bloom again,
I tread the pleasant paths we trod,

---

7. *Salisbury*, a town in Massachusetts. 8. *Boar's Head*, headland on the New Hampshire coast. 9. *Isles of Shoals*, a group of islands off the southeastern coast of New Hampshire. 10. *Cochecho* (kō chē′kō) *town*, in New Hampshire. 11. *gray wizard's conjuring book*. The Whittiers owned a copy of a book of magic used by Bantam the sorcerer, a dealer in "evil spirits," who lived in the region where Mrs. Whittier had spent her childhood. 12. *Piscataqua* (here pronounced pis kat′ə kwä), a river forming the boundary line between Maine and New Hampshire. 13. *our uncle*, Moses Whittier, a bachelor. 14. *cunning-warded keys*. A "ward" is a notch in a key. The meaning is that the uncle's knowledge was like a cleverly notched key which "unlocked" the mysteries of the woods. 15. *aunt*, Mercy Evans Hussey, a sister of Whittier's mother. 16. *elder sister*, Mary Whittier Caldwell. 17. *Our youngest*, Elizabeth Whittier, the poet's younger sister, who was his closest friend and companion until her death in 1864.

I see the violet-sprinkled sod,
Whereon she leaned, too frail and weak   215
The hillside flowers she loved to seek,
Yet following me wher'er I went
With dark eyes full of love's content.
The birds are glad; the brier rose fills
The air with sweetness; all the hills   220
Stretch green to June's unclouded sky;
But still I wait with ear and eye
For something gone which should be nigh,
A loss in all familiar things,
In flower that blooms, and bird that sings. 225
And yet, dear heart! remembering thee
    Am I not richer than of old? . . .

Brisk wielder of the birch and rule,
The master of the district school[18]
Held at the fire his favored place;   230
Its warm glow lit a laughing face,
Fresh-hued and fair, where scarce appeared
The uncertain prophecy of beard. . . .
Born the wild Northern hills among,
From whence his yeoman father wrung   235
By patient toil subsistence scant,
Not competence and yet not want,
He early gained the power to pay
His cheerful, self-reliant way;
Could doff at ease his scholar's gown   240
To peddle wares from town to town;
Or through the long vacation's reach
In lonely lowland districts teach,
Where all the droll experience found
At stranger hearths in boarding round,   245
The moonlit skater's keen delight,
The sleigh drive through the frosty night,
The rustic party, with its rough
Accompaniment of blindman's buff,
And whirling plate, and forfeits paid,   250
His winter task a pastime made.
Happy the snow-locked homes wherein
He tuned his merry violin,
Or played the athlete in the barn,
Or held the good dame's winding yarn,   255
Or mirth-provoking versions told
Of classic legends rare and old,
Wherein the scenes of Greece and Rome
Had all the commonplace of home. . . .

At last the great logs, crumbling low,   260
Sent out a dull and duller glow;

The bull's-eye watch that hung in view,
Ticking its weary circuit through,
Pointed with mutely warning sign
Its black hand to the hour of nine.   265
That sign the pleasant circle broke:
My uncle ceased his pipe to smoke,
Knocked from its bowl the refuse gray,
And laid it tenderly away;
Then roused himself to safely cover   270
The dull red brand with ashes over.
And while, with care, our mother laid
The work aside, her steps she stayed
One moment, seeking to express
Her grateful sense of happiness   275
For food and shelter, warmth and health,
And love's contentment more than wealth,
With simple wishes (not the weak,
Vain prayers which no fulfillment seek,
But such as warm the generous heart,   280
O'erprompt to do with Heaven its part)
That none might lack, that bitter night,
For bread and clothing, warmth and light.

Within our beds awhile we heard
The wind that round the gables roared,   285
With now and then a ruder shock,
Which made our very bedsteads rock.
We heard the loosened clapboards tossed,
The board-nails snapping in the frost;
And on us, through the unplastered wall,   290
Felt the light-sifted snowflakes fall;
But sleep stole on, as sleep will do
When hearts are light and life is new;
Faint and more faint the murmurs grew,
Till in the summer land of dreams   295
They softened to the sound of streams,
Low stir of leaves, and dip of oars,
And lapsing waves on quiet shores.

Next morn we wakened with the shout
Of merry voices high and clear;   300
And saw the teamsters drawing near
To break the drifted highways out.
Down the long hillside treading slow
We saw the half-buried oxen go,
Shaking the snow from heads uptossed,   305
Their straining nostrils white with frost.

18. *The master . . . school*, George Haskell, the district schoolmaster, who boarded with the Whittiers.

Before our door the straggling train
Drew up, an added team to gain.
The elders threshed their hands a-cold,
    Passed, with the cider mug, their jokes   310
    From lip to lip; the younger folks
Down the loose snowbanks, wrestling, rolled;
Then toiled again the cavalcade
    O'er windy hill, through clogged ravine,
    And woodland paths that wound between   315
Low-drooping pine boughs winter-weighed.
From every barn a team afoot;
At every house a new recruit;
Where, drawn by Nature's subtlest law,
Haply the watchful young men saw   320
Sweet doorway pictures of the curls
And curious eyes of merry girls,
Lifting their hands in mock defense
Against the snowballs' compliments,
And reading in each missive tossed   325
The charm which Eden never lost.

We heard once more the sleigh bells' sound;
    And, following where the teamsters led,
The wise old Doctor went his round,
Just pausing at our door to say,   330
In the brief, autocratic way
Of one who, prompt at Duty's call,
Was free to urge her claim on all,
    That some poor neighbor sick abed
At night our mother's aid would need.   335
For, one in generous thought and deed,
    What mattered in the sufferer's sight
    The Quaker matron's inward light,[19]
The Doctor's mail of Calvin's creed?[20]
All hearts confess the saints elect   340
    Who, twain in faith, in love agree,
And melt not in an acid sect
    The Christian pearl of charity!

So days went on; a week had passed
Since the great world was heard from last.   345
The Almanac we studied o'er;
Read and reread our little store
Of books and pamphlets, scarce a score;
One harmless novel, mostly hid
From younger eyes, a book forbid,   350
And poetry (or good or bad,
A single book was all we had)....
At last the floundering carrier bore
The village paper to our door.

Lo! broadening outward as we read,   355
To warmer zones the horizon spread;
In panoramic length unrolled
We saw the marvel that it told....
We felt the stir of hall and street,
The pulse of life that round us beat;   360
The chill embargo of the snow
Was melted in the genial glow;
Wide swung again our ice-locked door,
And all the world was ours once more! ...

Telling the Bees

This poem, written in 1858 before Whittier had
ended his career as an abolitionist, is based upon a
superstition which he thus explained: "A remarkable custom, brought from the Old Country, formerly prevailed in the rural districts of New England. On the death of a member of the family, the
bees were at once informed of the event, and their
hives dressed in mourning. This ceremonial was
supposed to prevent the swarms from leaving their
hives and seeking a new home." In this poem the
ballad stanzas, the evocation of the scene, the use of
a tradition are typical of Whittier at his best.

Here is the place; right over the hill
    Runs the path I took;
You can see the gap in the old wall still,
And the stepping-stones in the shallow
    brook.

There is the house, with the gate red-barred,   5
    And the poplars tall;
And the barn's brown length, and the
    cattle-yard,
    And the white horns tossing above the wall.

There are the beehives ranged in the sun;
    And down by the brink   10
Of the brook are her poor flowers,
    weed-o'errun,
    Pansy and daffodil, rose and pink.

SNOW-BOUND.   19. inward light, religious convictions.
20. mail of Calvin's creed, strict belief in the principles of
John Calvin, a French religious reformer.

A year has gone, as the tortoise goes,
    Heavy and slow;
And the same rose blows, and the same sun
    glows,   15
    And the same brook sings of a year ago.

There's the same sweet clover-smell in the
    breeze;
    And the June sun warm
Tangles his wings of fire in the trees,
    Setting, as then, over Fernside farm.   20

I mind me how with a lover's care
    From my Sunday coat
I brushed off the burs, and smoothed my hair,
    And cooled at the brookside my brow and
    throat.

Since we parted, a month had passed—   25
    To love, a year;
Down through the beeches I looked at last
    On the little red gate and the well-sweep
    near.

I can see it all now—the slantwise rain
    Of light through the leaves,   30
The sundown's blaze on her windowpane,
    The bloom of her roses under the eaves.

Just the same as a month before—
    The house and the trees,
The barn's brown gable, the vine by
    the door—   35
    Nothing changed but the hives of bees.

Before them, under the garden wall,
    Forward and back,
Went drearily singing the chore-girl small,
    Draping each hive with a shred of black.

Trembling, I listened: the summer sun   41
    Had the chill of snow;
For I knew she was telling the bees of one
    Gone on the journey we all must go!

Then I said to myself, "My Mary weeps   45
    For the dead today:
Haply her blind old grandsire sleeps
    The fret and the pain of his age away."

But her dog whined low; on the doorway sill,
    With his cane to his chin,   50
The old man sat; and the chore-girl still
    Sung to the bees stealing out and in.

And the song she was singing ever since
    In my ear sounds on:—
"Stay at home, pretty bees, fly not hence!   55
    Mistress Mary is dead and gone!"

 TO INCREASE UNDERSTANDING

1. What circumstances caused Whittier to write "Ichabod"?

2. Describe Whittier's attitude toward Daniel Webster. Point out lines that illustrate the attitude.

3. Why is the title of the poem appropriate to the theme?

4. It has been said that Whittier saw things through the eyes of the common man. (*a*) How does this statement apply to *Snow-Bound* and "Telling the Bees"? (*b*) Would you agree that this point of view is one of the reasons for the enduring appeal of Whittier's poetry? Explain.

5. As he portrays his scenes and characters in *Snow-Bound,* Whittier catches the mood of each moment he describes. (*a*) Select three or four stanzas, summarize each, and describe the mood Whittier creates. (*b*) Which portrait appeals to you most? Explain.

6. (*a*) Point out similarities between lines 31-49 of *Snow-Bound* and Emerson's poem, "The Snowstorm" (page 265). (*b*) Cite examples from each poem that illustrate the power of both poets to evoke vivid images.

7. (*a*) Summarize the story of "Telling the Bees." (*b*) What is the climax of the poem?

8. A poet whose work embodies many characteristics of a section is called a *local colorist.* Do *Snow-Bound* and "Telling the Bees" justify calling Whittier by this term? Explain your answer.

 EXTENDING INTERESTS

Taken as a group, no American poets have been more popular or better loved than those who flourished in New England during America's Golden Day. Your parents and your grandparents memorized many of their poems. Ask an older member of your family to name a favorite poem by one of these writers. Find the poem and practice reading it aloud. Then arrange with your teacher for a poetry-reading hour at which these favorite poems may be read and the reasons for their popularity discussed.

Nathaniel Hawthorne 1804-1864

This crayon portrait of Hawthorne by Eastman Johnson may be seen hanging in the corner of Longfellow's study in the photograph on page 267.

Hawthorne, like Whittier, was neither a Concord nor a Cambridge man, though he spent some years in Concord. He differed from his great New England contemporaries in writing fiction rather than essays and poems. But he joined Longfellow and Whittier in drawing upon history and legends in his works; like them he agreed that literature should point a moral. However, Hawthorne often transmuted legends of the past into allegory or symbolism and used it to develop the moral. In this way he imparted a poetic quality to his stories and novels.

Hawthorne was born in Salem, Massachusetts, the son of a shipmaster who died when the boy was four. After graduation from Bowdoin in 1825, he returned to Salem to live with his widowed mother and two sisters. Theirs was an unsocial household which even during his early years had prevented his making friends his own age. Now for twelve years he lived in relative seclusion with results he described in a letter of 1837 to Longfellow, formerly a Bowdoin classmate: "I have been carried apart from the main current of life, and find it impossible to get back again.... I have secluded myself from society ... put me in a dungeon; and now I cannot find the key...."

In his solitary room, though, Hawthorne read much and wrote a great deal. He began to end his isolation in 1836 by serving as a magazine editor. The following year several of his stories were published as *Twice-Told Tales*. He worked as a "weigher and gauger" in the Boston Custom House in 1839-1840, and at Brook Farm for nearly a year (1841-1842). Meanwhile he had fallen in love with Sophia Peabody of Salem. He married her in 1842 and they moved to the Old Manse in Concord. Hawthorne believed that his courtship, marriage, and family life more than anything else helped him reëstablish membership in society. How happy his early married life was he indicated in the preface to his second collection of tales, *Mosses from an Old Manse*, published in 1846 after he and Sophia had returned to Salem. He worked in the Salem Custom House until 1849, then turned to the writing of novels—*The Scarlet Letter* (1850),[1] *The House of the Seven Gables* (1851), and *The Blithedale Romance* (1852), each set in New England. From 1853 to 1857 Hawthorne was consul at Liverpool. Next he went to Italy, the background for his last completed novel, *The Marble Faun* (1860). In the year of its publication he returned to Concord, his home when he died.

Hawthorne's life and personality shaped his fiction. Remembering his dangerous tendency to break with the world, he constantly dealt with man's relations with his fellows. Often he pictured the difficulties of individuals cut off from society by oversensitiveness or aggressiveness. His Puritan ancestry and his deep interest in New England history led him to dwell also on man's consciousness of sin.

Hawthorne made an important discovery when he was "a secluded man" in Salem attempting "to open an intercourse with the world" by writing stories. It was that he wrote best if he gave his narratives "a certain remoteness" from actuality by placing them in the past or in scenes removed from

---

1. See the discussion guide for *The Scarlet Letter* on page 315.

ordinary experience, "under circumstances, to a great extent, of the author's own choosing or creation." He did well, also, to use characters "of the author's own making, or . . . of his own mixing." By so doing, he found, he could attach symbolical or allegorical meanings to his tales, thus strengthening the underlying idea or theme. "In all my stories, I think," he wrote, "there is one idea running through them like an iron rod, to which all other ideas are referred or subordinate."

But Hawthorne had a side which impelled him to give his stories reality, too. This Salem skipper's son was a tall, well-built, vigorous man—a masculine man with warmth and humor which won friends in college who continued affectionate relationships with him for decades. His appearance was anything but delicate. In his youth dark, abundant, wavy hair topped a massive, well-shaped head; heavy eyebrows shadowed sparkling dark blue eyes. He had a streak of practicality which drove him into the world to earn a living and stirred a lively interest in politics and people. He sized up men and women he met on his travels and jotted down shrewd observations about them in his notebooks. Realizing that if a story was

THE HOUSE OF SEVEN GABLES

"too remote, too shadowy, and unsubstantial," people found it unattractive, he tried to embody enough actuality, warmth, and humor in his fiction to win sympathetic readers. So he infused imaginative narratives with sufficient reality to place them in "a neutral territory, somewhere between the real world and fairyland, where the Actual and the Imaginary may meet and each imbue itself with the nature of the other."

"The Maypole of Merry Mount" (page 300) embodies both aspects. As the author's prefatory remarks show, it draws its allegory from a historical incident, and adds imaginative detail to information about "the manners of the age" in developing a theme. "Jollity and gloom," says he, "were contending for an empire." The Merry Mount colonists he associates with color, light silky textures, with the result that in this conflict they stand for Jollity. The Puritans he associates with darkness, blackness, iron; consequently, they stand for Gloom. The bridal couple in the end mark a reconciliation between these two extremes which represents Hawthorne's belief about the balanced way of living, the idea running through this tale like an "iron rod."

Opposite: Hawthorne's desk (right), now in the House of Seven Gables, Salem. Chestnut Street (left), Salem, famous for its houses, many of which were built by shipmasters in Hawthorne's time. Left: Other houses on Chestnut Street showing the work and influence of the famous architect Samuel McIntire. Below: The Old Manse, Concord, where, at different times, both Emerson and Hawthorne lived.

The Maypole of Merry Mount

There is an admirable foundation for a philosophic romance in the curious history of the early settlement of Mount Wollaston, or Merry Mount. In the slight sketch here attempted, the facts, recorded on the grave pages of our New England annalists, have wrought themselves, almost spontaneously, into a sort of allegory. The masques, mummeries, and festive customs, described in the text, are in accordance with the manners of the age. Authority on these points may be found in Strutt's *Book of English Sports and Pastimes*.

Bright were the days at Merry Mount, when the Maypole was the banner staff of that gay colony! They who reared it, should their banner be triumphant, were to pour sunshine over New England's rugged hills, and scatter flower seeds throughout the soil. Jollity and gloom were contending for an empire. Midsummer Eve[1] had come, bringing deep verdure to the forest, and roses in her lap, of a more vivid hue than the tender buds of Spring. But May, or her mirthful spirit, dwelt all the year round at Merry Mount, sporting with the Summer months, and reveling with Autumn, and basking in the glow of Winter's fireside. Through a world of toil and care she flitted with a dreamlike smile, and came hither to find a home among the lightsome hearts of Merry Mount.

Never had the Maypole been so gaily decked as at sunset on Midsummer Eve. This venerated emblem was a pine tree, which had preserved the slender grace of youth, while it equaled the loftiest height of the old wood monarchs. From its top streamed a silken banner, colored like the rainbow. Down nearly to the ground the pole was dressed with birchen boughs, and others of the liveliest green, and some with silvery leaves, fastened by ribbons that fluttered in fantastic knots of twenty different colors, but no sad ones. Garden flowers, and blossoms of the wilderness, laughed gladly forth amid the verdure, so fresh and dewy that they must have grown by magic on that happy pine tree. Where this green and flowery splendor terminated, the shaft of the Maypole was stained with the seven brilliant hues of the banner at its top. On the lowest green bough hung an abundant wreath of roses, some that had been gathered in the sunniest spots of the forest, and others, of still richer blush, which the colonists had reared from English seed. O, people of the Golden Age,[2] the chief of your husbandry was to raise flowers!

But what was the wild throng that stood hand in hand about the Maypole? It could not be that the fauns and nymphs, when driven from their classic groves and homes of ancient fable, had sought refuge, as all the persecuted did, in the fresh woods of the West. These were Gothic monsters, though perhaps of Grecian ancestry. On the shoulders of a comely youth uprose the head and branching antlers of a stag; a second, human in all other points, had the grim visage of a wolf; a third, still with the trunk and limbs of a mortal man, showed the beard and horns of a venerable he-goat. There was the likeness of a bear erect, brute in all but his hind legs, which were adorned with pink silk stockings. And here again, almost as wondrous, stood a real bear of the dark forest, lending each of his forepaws to the grasp of a human hand, and as ready for the dance as any in that circle. His inferior nature rose half way, to meet his companions as they stooped. Other faces wore the similitude of man or woman, but distorted or extravagant, with red noses pendulous before their mouths, which seemed of awful depth, and stretched from ear to ear in an eternal fit of laughter. Here might be seen the Salvage Man, well known in heraldry,[3] hairy as a baboon, and girdled with green leaves. By his

---

1. *Midsummer Eve*, a time around June 21.   2. *the Golden Age*, a legendary age, long past, of perfect human happiness and innocence.   3. *the Salvage Man, well known in heraldry*. The figure of a man wreathed in foliage was a device used on coats of arms to represent an uncivilized man. In referring to this device as the "Salvage Man," heraldry retains the obsolete spelling of *savage*.

side, a noble figure, but still a counterfeit, appeared an Indian hunter, with feathery crest and wampum belt. Many of this strange company wore fool's caps, and had little bells appended to their garments, tinkling with a silvery sound, responsive to the inaudible music of their gleesome spirits. Some youths and maidens were of soberer garb, yet well maintained their places in the irregular throng by the expression of wild revelry upon their features. Such were the colonists of Merry Mount, as they stood in the broad smile of sunset round their venerated Maypole.

Had a wanderer, bewildered in the melancholy forest, heard their mirth, and stolen a half-affrighted glance, he might have fancied them the crew of Comus,[4] some already transformed to brutes, some midway between man and beast, and the others rioting in the flow of tipsy jollity that foreran the change. But a band of Puritans, who watched the scene, invisible themselves, compared the masques to those devils and ruined souls with whom their superstition peopled the black wilderness.

Within the ring of monsters appeared the two airiest forms that had ever trodden on any more solid footing than a purple and golden cloud. One was a youth in glistening apparel, with a scarf of the rainbow pattern crosswise on his breast. His right hand held a gilded staff, the ensign of high dignity among the revelers, and his left grasped the slender fingers of a fair maiden, not less gaily decorated than himself. Bright roses glowed in contrast with the dark and glossy curls of each, and were scattered round their feet, or had sprung up spontaneously there. Behind this lightsome couple, so close to the Maypole that its boughs shaded his jovial face, stood the figure of an English priest, canonically dressed, yet decked with flowers, in heathen fashion, and wearing a chaplet of the native vine leaves. By the riot of his rolling eye, and the pagan decorations of his holy garb, he seemed the wildest monster there, and the very Comus of the crew.

"Votaries of the Maypole," cried the flower-decked priest, "merrily, all day long, have the woods echoed to your mirth. But be this your merriest hour, my hearts! Lo, here stand the Lord and Lady of the May, whom I, a clerk of Oxford,[5] and high priest of Merry Mount, am presently to join in holy matrimony. Up with your nimble spirits, ye morris dancers,[6] green men, and glee maidens, bears and wolves, and horned gentlemen! Come; a chorus now, rich with the old mirth of Merry England, and the wilder glee of this fresh forest; and then a dance, to show the youthful pair what life is made of, and how airily they should go through it! All ye that love the Maypole, lend your voices to the nuptial song of the Lord and Lady of the May!"

This wedlock was more serious than most affairs of Merry Mount, where jest and delusion, trick and fantasy, kept up a continual carnival. The Lord and Lady of the May, though their titles must be laid down at sunset, were really and truly to be partners for the dance of life, beginning the measure that same bright eve. The wreath of roses, that hung from the lowest green bough of the Maypole, had been twined for them, and would be thrown over both their heads, in symbol of their flowery union. When the priest had spoken, therefore, a riotous uproar burst from the rout of monstrous figures.

"Begin you the stave,[7] reverend Sir," cried they all; "and never did the woods ring to such a merry peal as we of the Maypole shall send up!"

Immediately a prelude of pipe, cithern, and viol, touched with practiced minstrelsy, began to play from a neighboring thicket, in such a mirthful cadence that the boughs of the Maypole quivered to the sound. But the May Lord, he of the gilded staff, chancing to look into his Lady's eyes, was wonder-struck at the almost pensive glance that met his own.

"Edith, sweet Lady of the May," whispered he reproachfully, "is yon wreath of roses a garland to hang above our graves, that you look so sad? O, Edith, this is our golden time!

---

4. *Comus* (kō'məs), a young Greek and Roman god of revelry. 5. *clerk of Oxford*, a clergyman trained at Oxford University in England. 6. *morris dancers*. The morris dance was a folk dance imported from Spain in medieval times. It was originally performed by five men whose costumes were decorated with beautifully tuned bells. By the sixteenth century, these dancers were costumed as Robin Hood and his men and performed on May Day. 7. *stave*, stanza of a song.

Tarnish it not by any pensive shadow of the mind; for it may be that nothing of futurity will be brighter than the mere remembrance of what is now passing."

"That was the very thought that saddened me! How came it in your mind too?" said Edith, in a still lower tone than he, for it was high treason to be sad at Merry Mount. "Therefore do I sigh amid this festive music. And besides, dear Edgar, I struggle as with a dream, and fancy that these shapes of our jovial friends are visionary, and their mirth unreal, and that we are no true Lord and Lady of the May. What is the mystery in my heart?"

Just then, as if a spell had loosened them, down came a little shower of withering rose leaves from the Maypole. Alas, for the young lovers! No sooner had their hearts glowed with real passion than they were sensible of something vague and unsubstantial in their former pleasures, and felt a dreary presentiment of inevitable change. From the moment that they truly loved, they had subjected themselves to earth's doom of care and sorrow, and troubled joy, and had no more a home at Merry Mount. That was Edith's mystery. Now leave we the priest to marry them, and the masquers to sport round the Maypole, till the last sunbeam be withdrawn from its summit, and the shadows of the forest mingle gloomily in the dance. Meanwhile, we may discover who these gay people were.

Two hundred years ago, and more, the Old World and its inhabitants became mutually weary of each other. Men voyaged by thousands to the West: some to barter glass beads, and suchlike jewels, for the furs of the Indian hunter; some to conquer virgin empires; and one stern band to pray. But none of these motives had much weight with the colonists of Merry Mount. Their leaders were men who had sported so long with life, that when Thought and Wisdom came, even these unwelcome guests were led astray by the crowd of vanities which they should have put to flight. Erring Thought and perverted Wisdom were made to put on masques, and play the fool. The men of whom we speak, after losing the heart's fresh gaiety, imagined a wild phi-

losophy of pleasure, and came hither to act out their latest daydream. They gathered followers from all that giddy tribe whose whole life is like the festal days of soberer men. In their train were minstrels, not unknown in London streets; wandering players, whose theaters had been the halls of noblemen; mummers, ropedancers, and mountebanks,[8] who would long be missed at wakes, church-ales,[9] and fairs; in a word, mirthmakers of every sort, such as abounded in that age, but now began to be discountenanced by the rapid growth of Puritanism. Light had their footsteps been on land, and as lightly they came across the sea. Many had been maddened by their previous troubles into a gay despair; others were as madly gay in the flush of youth, like the May Lord and his Lady; but whatever might be the quality of their mirth, old and young were gay at Merry Mount. The young deemed themselves happy. The elder spirits, if they knew that mirth was but the counterfeit of happiness, yet followed the false shadow willfully, because at least her garments glittered brightest. Sworn triflers of a lifetime, they would not venture among the sober truths of life not even to be truly blest.

All the hereditary pastimes of Old England were transplanted hither. The King of Christmas was duly crowned, and the Lord of Misrule[10] bore potent sway. On the Eve of St. John, they felled whole acres of the forest to make bonfires,[11] and danced by the blaze all night, crowned with garlands, and throwing flowers into the flame. At harvesttime, though their crop was of the smallest, they made an image with the sheaves of Indian corn, and wreathed it with autumnal garlands, and bore it home triumphantly. But what chiefly characterized the colonists of Merry Mount was their veneration for the Maypole. It has made their true history a poet's tale. Spring decked the hallowed emblem with young blossoms and fresh green boughs; Summer brought

---

8. *mountebanks*, performers who deceived their audiences with tricks, stories, and jokes.   9. *church-ales*, feasts held in the churchyard to raise money for the church.   10. *Lord of Misrule*, the master of festival revelry.   11. *the Eve of St. John . . . bonfires*. On the Eve of St. John, or Midsummer Eve, bonfires were lighted to celebrate the summer solstice.

roses of the deepest blush and the perfected foliage of the forest; Autumn enriched it with that red and yellow gorgeousness which converts each wildwood leaf into a painted flower; and Winter silvered it with sleet, and hung it round with icicles, till it flashed in the cold sunshine, itself a frozen sunbeam. Thus each alternate season did homage to the Maypole, and paid it a tribute of its own richest splendor. Its votaries danced round it, once, at least, in every month; sometimes they called it their religion, or their altar; but always, it was the banner staff of Merry Mount.

Unfortunately, there were men in the New World of a sterner faith than these Maypole worshipers. Not far from Merry Mount was a settlement of Puritans, most dismal wretches, who said their prayers before daylight, and then wrought in the forest or the cornfield till evening made it prayertime again. Their weapons were always at hand to shoot down the straggling savage. When they met in conclave, it was never to keep up the old English mirth, but to hear sermons three hours long, or to proclaim bounties on the heads of wolves and the scalps of Indians. Their festivals were fast days, and their chief pastime the singing of psalms. Woe to the youth or maiden who did but dream of a dance! The selectman nodded to the constable; and there sat the light-heeled reprobate in the stocks; or if he danced, it was round the whipping post, which might be termed the Puritan Maypole.

A party of these grim Puritans, toiling through the difficult woods, each with a horseload of iron armor to burden his footsteps, would sometimes draw near the sunny precincts of Merry Mount. There were the silken colonists, sporting round their Maypole; perhaps teaching a bear to dance, or striving to communicate their mirth to the grave Indian; or masquerading in the skins of deer and wolves, which they had hunted for that especial purpose. Often, the whole colony were playing at blindman's buff, magistrates and all, with their eyes bandaged, except a single scapegoat, whom the blinded sinners pursued by the tinkling of the bells at his garments. Once, it is said, they were seen following a flower-decked corpse, with merri-

THE ENGLISH MAYPOLE

May Day was a great public festival in the towns and villages of old England. Beginning in medieval times, old and young alike went "a-maying" to celebrate the coming of spring. Before dawn the villagers went into nearby woods to gather May flowers and hawthorn branches and to find a likely tree which they fashioned into a gaily ribboned, flower-wreathed maypole. Teams of oxen hauled the maypole in triumphant procession to the center of town where sturdy lads hoisted it into position. Merrymaking and folk dancing went on around the glorious maypole all day: a newly crowned May Queen ruled the festivities; masked and costumed figures (some impersonating animals) mingled with the morris dancers; a Lord of Misrule played his pranks. These innocent May Day pleasures gradually became wild and riotous; and the Puritans, who regarded the maypole as a pagan symbol, banned such festivities in 1644. With the return of the Stuart kings to the English throne in 1660, however, May Day traditions were revived and are still observed in modern England. The delightful maypole custom never took root in America, possibly because John Endicott wielded his sword so well at Merry Mount.

ment and festive music, to his grave. But did the dead man laugh? In their quietest times, they sang ballads and told tales, for the edification of their pious visitors; or perplexed them with juggling tricks; or grinned at them through horse collars; and when sport itself grew wearisome, they made game of their own stupidity, and began a yawning match. At the very least of these enormities, the men of iron shook their heads and frowned so darkly that the revelers looked up, imagining that a momentary cloud had overcast the sunshine, which was to be perpetual there. On the other hand, the Puritans affirmed that, when a psalm was pealing from their place of worship, the echo which the forest sent them back seemed often like the chorus of a jolly catch, closing with a roar of laughter. Who but the fiend, and his bond slaves, the crew of Merry Mount, had thus disturbed them? In due time, a feud arose, stern and bitter on one side, and as serious on the other as anything could be among such light spirits as had sworn allegiance to the Maypole. The future complexion of New England was involved in this important quarrel. Should the grizzly saints establish their jurisdiction over the gay sinners, then would their spirits darken all the clime, and make it a land of clouded visages, of hard toil, of sermon and psalm forever. But should the banner staff of Merry Mount be fortunate, sunshine would break upon the hills, and flowers would beautify the forest, and late posterity do homage to the Maypole.

After these authentic passages from history, we return to the nuptials of the Lord and Lady of the May. Alas! we have delayed too long, and must darken our tale too suddenly. As we glance again at the Maypole, a solitary sunbeam is fading from the summit, and leaves only a faint, golden tinge blended with the hues of the rainbow banner. Even that dim light is now withdrawn, relinquishing the whole domain of Merry Mount to the evening gloom, which has rushed so instantaneously from the black surrounding woods. But some of these black shadows have rushed forth in human shape.

Yes, with the setting sun, the last day of mirth had passed from Merry Mount. The ring of gay masquers was disordered and broken; the stag lowered his antlers in dismay; the wolf grew weaker than a lamb; the bells of the morris dancers tinkled with tremulous affright. The Puritans had played a characteristic part in the Maypole mummeries. Their darksome figures were intermixed with the wild shapes of their foes, and made the scene a picture of the moment, when waking thoughts start up amid the scattered fantasies of a dream. The leader of the hostile party stood in the center of the circle, while the rout of monsters cowered around him, like evil spirits in the presence of a dread magician. No fantastic foolery could look him in the face. So stern was the energy of his aspect, that the whole man, visage, frame, and soul, seemed wrought of iron, gifted with life and thought, yet all of one substance with his headpiece and breastplate. It was the Puritan of Puritans; it was Endicott[12] himself!

"Stand off, priest of Baal![13]" said he, with a grim frown, and laying no reverent hand upon the surplice. "I know thee, Blackstone![14] Thou art the man who couldst not abide the rule even of thine own corrupted church, and hast come hither to preach iniquity, and to give example of it in thy life. But now shall it be seen that the Lord hath sanctified this wilderness for his peculiar people. Woe unto them that would defile it! And first, for this flower-decked abomination, the altar of thy worship!"

And with his keen sword Endicott assaulted the hallowed Maypole. Nor long did it resist his arm. It groaned with a dismal sound; it showered leaves and rosebuds upon the remorseless enthusiast; and finally, with all its green boughs and ribbons and flowers, symbolic of departed pleasures, down fell the banner staff of Merry Mount. As it sank, tradition says, the evening sky grew darker, and the woods threw forth a more somber shadow.

---

12. *Endicott*, John Endicott (1588?-1665) first English colonial governor of Massachusetts Bay Colony.   13. *Baal* (bā′əl or bāl), a false god.   14. *Blackstone*. Hawthorne takes liberties with history when he identifies the priest of Merry Mount as William Blackstone (1595-1675). Blackstone, it is true, had his differences with the Puritans, but was a devout Anglican minister who worked with the Indians near Boston.

"There," cried Endicott, looking triumphantly on his work, "there lies the only Maypole in New England! The thought is strong within me that, by its fall, is shadowed forth the fate of light and idle mirthmakers, amongst us and our posterity. Amen, saith John Endicott."

"Amen!" echoed his followers.

But the votaries of the Maypole gave one groan for their idol. At the sound, the Puritan leader glanced at the crew of Comus, each a figure of broad mirth, yet, at this moment, strangely expressive of sorrow and dismay.

"Valiant captain," quoth Peter Palfrey, the Ancient of the band, "what order shall be taken with the prisoners?"

"I thought not to repent me of cutting down a Maypole," replied Endicott, "yet now I could find in my heart to plant it again, and give each of these bestial pagans one other dance round their idol. It would have served rarely for a whipping post!"

"But there are pine trees enow," suggested the lieutenant.

"True, good Ancient," said the leader. "Wherefore, bind the heathen crew, and bestow on them a small matter of stripes apiece, as earnest of our future justice. Set some of the rogues in the stocks to rest themselves, so soon as Providence shall bring us to one of our own well-ordered settlements, where such accommodations may be found. Further penalties, such as branding and cropping of ears, shall be thought of hereafter."

"How many stripes for the priest?" inquired Ancient Palfrey.

"None as yet," answered Endicott, bending his iron frown upon the culprit. "It must be for the Great and General Court to determine, whether stripes and long imprisonment, and other grievous penalty, may atone for his transgressions. Let him look to himself! For such as violate our civil order, it may be permitted us to show mercy. But woe to the wretch that troubleth our religion!"

"And this dancing bear," resumed the officer. "Must he share the stripes of his fellows?"

"Shoot him through the head!" said the energetic Puritan. "I suspect witchcraft in the beast."

"Here be a couple of shining ones," continued Peter Palfrey, pointing his weapon at the Lord and Lady of the May. "They seem to be of high station among these misdoers. Methinks their dignity will not be fitted with less than a double share of stripes."

Endicott rested on his sword, and closely surveyed the dress and aspect of the hapless pair. There they stood, pale, downcast, and apprehensive. Yet there was an air of mutual support, and of pure affection, seeking aid and giving it, that showed them to be man and wife, with the sanction of a priest upon their love. The youth, in the peril of the moment, had dropped his gilded staff, and thrown his arm about the Lady of the May, who leaned against his breast, too lightly to burden him, but with weight enough to express that their destinies were linked together, for good or evil. They looked first at each other, and then into the grim captain's face. There they stood, in the first hour of wedlock, while the idle pleasures, of which their companions were the emblems, had given place to the sternest cares of life, personified by the dark Puritans. But never had their youthful beauty seemed so pure and high as when its glow was chastened by adversity.

"Youth," said Endicott, "ye stand in an evil case, thou and thy maiden wife. Make ready presently, for I am minded that ye shall both have a token to remember your wedding day!"

"Stern man," cried the May Lord, "how can I move thee? Were the means at hand, I would resist to the death. Being powerless, I entreat! Do with me as thou wilt, but let Edith go untouched!"

"Not so," replied the immitigable zealot. "We are not wont to show an idle courtesy to that sex, which requireth the stricter discipline. What sayest thou, maid? Shall thy silken bridegroom suffer thy share of the penalty, besides his own?"

"Be it death," said Edith, "and lay it all on me!"

Truly, as Endicott had said, the poor lovers stood in a woeful case. Their foes were triumphant, their friends captive and abased, their home desolate, the benighted wilderness around them, and a rigorous destiny, in the shape of the Puritan leader, their only guide. Yet the deepening twilight could not altogether conceal that the iron man was softened; he smiled at the fair spectacle of early love; he almost sighed for the inevitable blight of early hopes.

"The troubles of life have come hastily on this young couple," observed Endicott. "We will see how they comport themselves under their present trials ere we burden them with greater. If, among the spoil, there be any garments of a more decent fashion, let them be put upon this May Lord and his Lady, instead of their glistening vanities. Look to it, some of you."

"And shall not the youth's hair be cut?" asked Peter Palfrey, looking with abhorrence at the lovelock and long glossy curls of the young man.

"Crop it forthwith, and that in the true pumpkinshell fashion," answered the captain. "Then bring them along with us, but more gently than their fellows. There be qualities in the youth, which may make him valiant to fight, and sober to toil, and pious to pray; and in the maiden, that may fit her to become a mother in our Israel,[15] bringing up babes in better nurture than her own hath been. Nor think ye, young ones, that they are the happiest, even in our lifetime of a moment, who misspend it in dancing round a Maypole!"

And Endicott, the severest Puritan of all who laid the rock foundation of New England, lifted the wreath of roses from the ruin of the Maypole, and threw it, with his own gauntleted hand, over the heads of the Lord and Lady of the May. It was a deed of prophecy. As the moral gloom of the world overpowers all systematic gaiety, even so was their home of wild mirth made desolate amid the sad forest. They returned to it no more. But as their flowery garland was wreathed of the brightest roses that had grown there, so, in the tie that united them, were intertwined all the purest and best of their early joys. They went heavenward, supporting each other along the difficult path which it was their lot to tread, and never wasted one regretful thought on the vanities of Merry Mount.

Drowne's Wooden Image
Nathaniel Hawthorne

The following story occurs in a specific place which is described with some vividness; characters with Yankee names (Hunnewell, Hobart, and Copley—the last an actual artist) dwell there; and Drowne engages in a commonplace trade. Yet the period is "in the good old times"—remote and indefinite enough so that Hawthorne can embody meaningful details in a story set in that era. As a result, the carver's usual figureheads with their "wooden aspect" can stand for the workaday achievements of a man merely blessed with talent; the image for the ship *Cynosure,* for an inspired work of art. The story thus can richly embody the author's ideas about the nature of art and the artist.

One sunshiny morning, in the good old times of the town of Boston, a young carver in wood, well known by the name of Drowne, stood contemplating a large oaken log, which it was his purpose to convert into the figurehead of a vessel. And while he discussed within his own mind what sort of shape or similitude it were well to bestow upon this excellent piece of timber, there came into Drowne's workshop a certain Captain Hunnewell, owner and commander of the good brig called the *Cynosure,* which had just returned from her first voyage to Fayal.[1]

"Ah! that will do, Drowne, that will do!" cried the jolly captain, tapping the log with his rattan. "I bespeak this very piece of oak for the figurehead of the *Cynosure.* She has shown herself the sweetest craft that ever floated, and I mean to decorate her prow with the handsomest image that the skill of man can cut out of timber. And, Drowne, you are the fellow to execute it."

"You give me more credit than I deserve,

MAYPOLE OF MERRY MOUNT. **15.** *Israel,* Massachusetts, the Promised Land of the Puritans.

DROWNE'S WOODEN IMAGE. **1.** *Fayal* (fī äl′), one of the islands of the Azores (ə zôrz′) in the Atlantic Ocean near Portugal. Yankee ships called on many such distant ports during their long voyages.

Captain Hunnewell," said the carver, modestly, yet as one conscious of eminence in his art. "But, for the sake of the good brig, I stand ready to do my best. And which of these designs do you prefer? Here"—pointing to a staring, half-length figure, in a white wig and scarlet coat—"here is an excellent model, the likeness of our gracious king. Here is the valiant Admiral Vernon. Or, if you prefer a female figure, what say you to Britannia with the trident?"

"All very fine, Drowne; all very fine," answered the mariner. "But as nothing like the brig ever swam the ocean, so I am determined she shall have such a figurehead as old Neptune never saw in his life. And what is more, as there is a secret in the matter, you must pledge your credit not to betray it."

"Certainly," said Drowne, marveling, however, what possible mystery there could be in reference to an affair so open, of necessity, to the inspection of all the world as the figurehead of a vessel. "You may depend, captain, on being as secret as the nature of the case will permit."

Captain Hunnewell then took Drowne by the button, and communicated his wishes in so low a tone that it would be unmannerly to repeat what was evidently intended for the carver's private ear. We shall, therefore, take the opportunity to give the reader a few desirable particulars about Drowne himself.

He was the first American who is known to have attempted—in a very humble line, it is true—that art in which we can now reckon so many names already distinguished, or rising to distinction. From his earliest boyhood he had exhibited a knack—for it would be too proud a word to call it genius—a knack, therefore, for the imitation of the human figure in whatever material came most readily to hand. The snows of a New England winter had often supplied him with a species of marble as dazzlingly white, at least, as the Parian or the Carrara, and if less durable, yet sufficiently so to correspond with any claims to permanent existence possessed by the boy's frozen statues. Yet they won admiration from maturer judges than his schoolfellows, and were indeed, remarkably clever, though destitute of the native

warmth that might have made the snow melt beneath his hand. As he advanced in life, the young man adopted pine and oak as eligible materials for the display of his skill, which now began to bring him a return of solid silver as well as the empty praise that had been an apt reward enough for his productions of evanescent snow. He became noted for carving ornamental pump heads, and wooden urns for gateposts, and decorations, more grotesque than fanciful, for mantelpieces. No apothecary would have deemed himself in the way of obtaining custom without setting up a gilded mortar, if not a head of Galen or Hippocrates,[2] from the skillful hand of Drowne.

But the great scope of his business lay in the manufacture of figureheads for vessels. Whether it were the monarch himself, or some famous British admiral or general, or the governor of the province, or perchance the favorite daughter of the shipowner, there the image stood above the prow, decked out in gorgeous colors, magnificently gilded, and staring the whole world out of countenance, as if from an innate consciousness of its own superiority. These specimens of native sculpture had crossed the sea in all directions, and had been not ignobly noticed among the crowded shipping of the Thames and wherever else the hardy mariners of New England had pushed their adventures. It must be confessed that a family likeness pervaded these respectable progeny of Drowne's skill; that the benign countenance of the king resembled those of his subjects, and that Miss Peggy Hobart, the merchant's daughter, bore a remarkable similitude to Britannia, Victory, and other ladies of the allegoric sisterhood; and, finally, that they all had a kind of wooden aspect which proved an intimate relationship with the unshaped blocks of timber in the carver's workshop. But at least there was no inconsiderable skill of hand, nor a deficiency of any attribute to render them really works of art, except that deep quality, be it of soul or intellect, which bestows life upon the lifeless

2. *mortar . . . Hippocrates.* A mortar is a bowl of hard material in which substances are pounded to a powder. Its likeness, or that of one of the ancient Greek physicians Galen (gā'lən) and Hippocrates (hi pok'rə tēz), indicated a place where medicine was prepared.

and warmth upon the cold, and which, had it been present, would have made Drowne's wooden image instinct with spirit.

The captain of the *Cynosure* had now finished his instructions.

"And Drowne," said he, impressively, "you must lay aside all other business and set about this forthwith. And as to the price, only do the job in first-rate style, and you shall settle that point yourself."

"Very well, captain," answered the carver, who looked grave and somewhat perplexed, yet had a sort of smile upon his visage; "depend upon it, I'll do my utmost to satisfy you."

From that moment the men of taste about Long Wharf and the Town Dock who were wont to show their love for the arts by frequent visits to Drowne's workshop, and admiration of his wooden images, began to be sensible of a mystery in the carver's conduct. Often he was absent in the daytime. Sometimes, as might be judged by gleams of light from the shop windows, he was at work until a late hour of the evening; although neither knock nor voice, on such occasions, could gain admittance for a visitor, or elicit any word of response. Nothing remarkable, however, was observed in the shop at those hours when it was thrown open. A fine piece of timber, indeed, which Drowne was known to have reserved for some work of especial dignity, was seen to be gradually assuming shape. What shape it was destined ultimately to take was a problem to his friends and a point on which the carver himself preserved a rigid silence. But day after day, though Drowne was seldom noticed in the act of working upon it, this rude form began to be developed until it became evident to all observers that a female figure was growing into mimic life. At each new visit they beheld a larger pile of wooden chips and a nearer approximation to something beautiful. It seemed as if the hamadryad of the oak had sheltered herself from the unimaginative world within the heart of her native tree, and that it was only necessary to remove the strange shapelessness that had incrusted her, and reveal the grace and loveliness of a divinity. Imperfect as the design, the attitude, the costume, and especially the face of the image

still remained, there was already an effect that drew the eye from the wooden cleverness of Drowne's earlier productions and fixed it upon the tantalizing mystery of this new project.

Copley, the celebrated painter, then a young man and a resident of Boston, came one day to visit Drowne; for he had recognized so much of moderate ability in the carver as to induce him, in the dearth of professional sympathy, to cultivate his acquaintance. On entering the shop, the artist glanced at the inflexible image of king, commander, dame, and allegory, that stood around, on the best of which might have been bestowed the questionable praise that it looked as if a living man had here been changed to wood, and that not only the physical, but the intellectual and spiritual part, partook of the stolid transformation. But in not a single instance did it seem as if the wood were imbibing the ethereal essence of humanity. What a wide distinction is here! And how far would the slightest portion of the latter merit have outvalued the utmost degree of the former!

"My friend Drowne," said Copley, smiling to himself, but alluding to the mechanical and wooden cleverness that so invariably distinguished the images, "you are really a remarkable person! I have seldom met with a man in your line of business that could do so much; for one other touch might make this figure of General Wolfe,[3] for instance, a breathing and intelligent human creature."

"You would have me think that you are praising me highly, Mr. Copley," answered Drowne, turning his back upon Wolfe's image in apparent disgust. "But there has come a light into my mind. I know, what you know as well, that the one touch which you speak of as deficient is the only one that would be truly valuable, and that without it these works of mine are no better than worthless abortions. There is the same difference between them and the works of an inspired artist as between a signpost daub and one of your best pictures."

"This is strange," cried Copley, looking him in the face, which now, as the painter fancied, had a singular depth of intelligence, though

---

3. *General Wolfe*, James Wolfe (1727-1759), an English general killed at the battle of Quebec.

hitherto it had not given him greatly the advantage over his own family of wooden images. "What has come over you? How is it that, possessing the idea which you have now uttered, you should produce only such works as these?"

The carver smiled, but made no reply. Copley turned again to the images, conceiving that the sense of deficiency which Drowne had just expressed, and which is so rare in a merely mechanical character, must surely imply a genius, the tokens of which had heretofore been overlooked. But no; there was not a trace of it. He was about to withdraw when his eyes chanced to fall upon a half-developed figure which lay in a corner of the workshop, surrounded by scattered chips of oak. It arrested him at once.

"What is here? Who has done this?" he broke out, after contemplating it in speechless astonishment for an instant. "Here is the divine, the life-giving touch. What inspired hand is beckoning this wood to arise and live? Whose work is this?"

"No man's work," replied Drowne: "The figure lies within that block of oak, and it is my business to find it."

"Drowne," said the true artist, grasping the carver fervently by the hand, "you are a man of genius!"

As Copley departed, happening to glance backward from the threshold, he beheld Drowne bending over the half-created shape, and stretching forth his arms as if he would have embraced and drawn it to his heart; while, had such a miracle been possible, his countenance expressed passion enough to communicate warmth and sensibility to the lifeless oak.

"Strange enough!" said the artist to himself. "Who would have looked for a modern Pygmalion in the person of a Yankee mechanic!"

As yet, the image was but vague in its outward presentment; so that, as in the cloud shapes around the western sun, the observer rather felt, or was led to imagine, than really saw what was intended by it. Day by day, however, the work assumed greater precision, and settled its irregular and misty outline into distincter grace and beauty. The general de-

sign was now obvious to the common eye. It was a female figure, in what appeared to be a foreign dress; the gown being laced over the bosom, and opening in front so as to disclose a skirt or petticoat, the folds and inequalities of which were admirably represented in the oaken substance. She wore a hat of singular gracefulness, and abundantly laden with flowers, such as never grew in the rude soil of New England, but which, with all their fanciful luxuriance, had a natural truth that it seemed impossible for the most fertile imagination to have attained without copying from real prototypes. There were several little appendages to this dress, such as a fan, a pair of earrings, a chain about the neck, a watch in the bosom, and a ring upon the finger, all of which would have been deemed beneath the dignity of sculpture. They were put on, however, with as much taste as a lovely woman might have shown in her attire, and could

A figurehead carved
in Boston.

therefore have shocked none but a judgment spoiled by artistic rules.

The face was still imperfect; but gradually, by a magic touch, intelligence and sensibility brightened through the features, with all the effect of light gleaming forth from within the solid oak. The face became alive. It was a beautiful, though not precisely regular and somewhat haughty aspect, but with a certain piquancy about the eyes and mouth, which, of all expressions, would have seemed the most impossible to throw over a wooden countenance. And now, so far as carving went, this wonderful production was complete.

"Drowne," said Copley, who had hardly missed a single day in his visits to the carver's workshop, "if this work were in marble it would make you famous at once; nay, I would almost affirm that it would make an era in the art. It is as ideal as an antique statue, and yet as real as any lovely woman whom one meets at a fireside or in the street. But I trust you do not mean to desecrate this exquisite creature with paint, like those staring kings and admirals yonder?"

"Not paint her!" exclaimed Captain Hunnewell who stood by; "not paint the figurehead of the *Cynosure!* And what sort of a figure should I cut in a foreign port with such an unpainted oaken stick as this over my prow! She must, and she shall, be painted to the life, from the topmost flower in her hat down to the silver spangles on her slippers."

"Mr. Copley," said Drowne, quietly, "I know nothing of marble statuary, and nothing of the sculptor's rules of art; but of this wooden image, this work of my hands, this creature of my heart"—and here his voice faltered and choked in a very singular manner—"of this—of her—I may say that I know something. A wellspring of inward wisdom gushed within me as I wrought upon the oak with my whole strength, and soul, and faith. Let others do what they may with marble, and adopt what rules they choose. If I can produce my desired effect by painted wood, those rules are not for me, and I have a right to disregard them."

"The very spirit of genius," muttered Copley to himself. "How otherwise should this carver feel himself entitled to transcend all rules, and make me ashamed of quoting them?"

He looked earnestly at Drowne, and again saw that expression of human love which, in a spiritual sense, as the artist could not help imagining, was the secret of the life that had been breathed into this block of wood.

The carver, still in the same secrecy that marked all his operations upon this mysterious image, proceeded to paint the habiliments in their proper colors, and the countenance with Nature's red and white. When all was finished he threw open his workshop, and admitted the townspeople to behold what he had done. Most persons, at their first entrance, felt impelled to remove their hats, and pay such reverence as was due to the richly dressed and beautiful young lady who seemed to stand in a corner of the room, with oaken chips and shavings scattered at her feet. Then came a sensation of fear; as if, not being actually human, yet so like humanity, she must therefore be something preternatural. There was, in truth, an indefinable air and expression that might reasonably induce the query, Who and from what sphere this daughter of the oak should be? The strange, rich flowers of Eden on her head; the complexion, so much deeper and more brilliant than those of our native beauties; the foreign, as it seemed, and fantastic garb, yet not too fantastic to be worn decorously in the street; the delicately wrought embroidery of the skirt; the broad gold chain about her neck; the curious ring upon her finger; the fan, so exquisitely sculptured in open work, and painted to resemble pearl and ebony;—where could Drowne, in his sober walk of life, have beheld the vision here so matchlessly embodied! And then her face! In the dark eyes, and around the voluptuous mouth, there played a look made up of pride, coquetry, and a gleam of mirthfulness, which impressed Copley with the idea that the image was secretly enjoying the perplexing admiration of himself and other beholders.

"And will you," said he to the carver, "permit this masterpiece to become the figurehead of a vessel? Give the honest captain yonder figure of Britannia—it will answer his purpose far better—and send this fairy queen to England, where, for aught I know, it may bring you a thousand pounds."

"I have not wrought it for money," said Drowne.

"What sort of a fellow is this!" thought Copley. "A Yankee, and throw away the chance of making his fortune! He has gone mad; and thence has come this gleam of genius."

There was still further proof of Drowne's lunacy, if credit were due to the rumor that he had been seen kneeling at the feet of the oaken lady, and gazing with a lover's passionate ardor into the face that his own hands had created. The bigots of the day hinted that it would be no matter of surprise if an evil spirit were allowed to enter this beautiful form, and seduce the carver to destruction.

The fame of the image spread far and wide. The inhabitants visited it so universally, that after a few days of exhibition there was hardly an old man or a child who had not become minutely familiar with its aspect. Even had the story of Drowne's wooden image ended here, its celebrity might have been prolonged for many years by the reminiscences of those who looked upon it in their childhood, and saw nothing else so beautiful in afterlife. But the town was now astounded by an event, the narrative of which has formed itself into one of the most singular legends that are yet to be met with in the traditionary chimney corners of the New England metropolis, where old men and women sit dreaming of the past, and wag their heads at the dreamers of the present and the future.

One fine morning, just before the departure of the *Cynosure* on her second voyage to Fayal, the commander of that gallant vessel was seen to issue from his residence in Hanover Street. He was stylishly dressed in a blue broadcloth coat, with gold lace at the seams and buttonholes, an embroidered scarlet waistcoat, a triangular hat, with a loop and broad binding of gold, and wore a silver-hilted hanger at his side. But the good captain might have been arrayed in the robes of a prince or the rags of a beggar, without in either case attracting notice, while obscured by such a companion as now leaned on his arm. The people in the street started, rubbed their eyes, and either leaped aside from their path, or stood as if transfixed to wood or marble in astonishment.

"Do you see it?—do you see it?" cried one, with tremulous eagerness. "It is the very same!"

"The same?" answered another, who had arrived in town only the night before. "Who do you mean? I see only a sea captain in his shore-going clothes, and a young lady in a foreign habit, with a bunch of beautiful flowers in her hat. On my word, she is as fair and bright a damsel as my eyes have looked on this many a day!"

"Yes; the same!—the very same!" repeated the other. "Drowne's wooden image has come to life!"

Here was a miracle indeed! Yet, illuminated by the sunshine, or darkened by the alternate shade of the houses, and with its garments fluttering lightly in the morning breeze, there passed the image along the street. It was exactly and minutely the shape, the garb, and

PYGMALION'S IVORY STATUE

Greek mythology has always been a rich source of legend for writers to draw upon. One of the favorite myths is the story of Pygmalion (pigmā′li ən) and Galatea (gal′ə tē′ə).

Pygmalion, king of Cyprus, amused himself by carving statues from ivory. One day he began to sculpture an especially fine piece of ivory. As his chisel made cut after cut in the smooth white surface, the figure of a young woman took shape. The completed statue was so beautiful that Pygmalion fell in love with it. Wishing for a wife as beautiful as the statue, he prayed to Aphrodite (af′rə dī′ti), the goddess of love. Aphrodite answered his prayer by transforming the statue into a real woman, Galatea, whom Pygmalion married.

George Bernard Shaw's play, *Pygmalion*, and the musical based upon it, *My Fair Lady*, are very popular modern uses of this legend.

the face which the townspeople had so recently thronged to see and admire. Not a rich flower upon her head, not a single leaf, but had had its prototype in Drowne's wooden workmanship, although now their fragile grace had become flexible, and was shaken by every footstep that the wearer made. The broad gold chain upon the neck was identical with the one represented on the image, and glistened with the motion imparted by the rise and fall of the bosom which it decorated. A real diamond sparkled on her finger. In her right hand she bore a pearl and ebony fan, which she flourished with a fantastic and bewitching coquetry, that was likewise expressed in all her movements as well as in the style of her beauty and the attire that so well harmonized with it. The face with its brilliant depth of complexion had the same piquancy of mirthful mischief that was fixed upon the countenance of the image, but which was here varied and continually shifting, yet always essentially the same, like the sunny gleam upon a bubbling fountain. On the whole, there was something so airy and yet so real in the figure, and withal so perfectly did it represent Drowne's image, that people knew not whether to suppose the magic wood etherealized into a spirit or warmed and softened into an actual woman.

"One thing is certain," muttered a Puritan of the old stamp, "Drowne has sold himself to the devil; and doubtless this gay Captain Hunnewell is a party to the bargain."

"And I," said a young man who overheard him, "would almost consent to be the third victim, for the liberty of saluting those lovely lips."

"And so would I," said Copley, the painter, "for the privilege of taking her picture."[4]

The image, or the apparition, whichever it might be, still escorted by the bold captain, proceeded from Hanover Street through some of the cross lanes that make this portion of the town so intricate, to Ann Street, thence into Dock Square, and so downward to Drowne's shop, which stood just on the water's edge. The crowd still followed, gathering volume as it rolled along. Never had a modern miracle occurred in such broad daylight, nor in the presence of such a multitude of witnesses. The airy image, as if conscious that she was the object of the murmurs and disturbance that swelled behind her, appeared slightly vexed and flustered, yet still in a manner consistent with the light vivacity and sportive mischief that were written in her countenance. She was observed to flutter her fan with such vehement rapidity that the elaborate delicacy of its workmanship gave way, and it remained broken in her hand.

Arriving at Drowne's door, while the captain threw it open, the marvelous apparition paused an instant on the threshold, assuming the very attitude of the image, and casting over the crowd that glance of sunny coquetry which all remembered on the face of the oaken lady. She and her cavalier then disappeared.

"Ah!" murmured the crowd, drawing a deep breath, as with one vast pair of lungs.

"The world looks darker now that she has vanished," said some of the young men.

But the aged, whose recollections dated as far back as witch times, shook their heads, and hinted that our forefathers would have thought it a pious deed to burn the daughter of the oak with fire.

"If she be other than a bubble of the elements," exclaimed Copley, "I must look upon her face again."

He accordingly entered the shop; and there, in her usual corner, stood the image, gazing at him, as it might seem, with the very same expression of mirthful mischief that had been the farewell look of the apparition when, but a moment before, she turned her face toward the crowd. The carver stood beside his creation mending the beautiful fan, which by some accident was broken in her hand. But there was no longer any motion in the lifelike image, nor any real woman in the workshop, nor even the witchcraft of a sunny shadow, that might have deluded people's eyes as it flitted along the street. Captain Hunnewell, too, had vanished. His hoarse sea-breezy tones, however, were audible on the other side of a door that opened upon the water.

---

4. *taking her picture.* Hawthorne means that Copley would like to draw her likeness.

"Sit down in the stern sheets, my lady," said the gallant captain. "Come, bear a hand, you lubbers, and set us on board in the turning of a minuteglass."

And then was heard the stroke of oars.

"Drowne," said Copley with a smile of intelligence, "you have been a truly fortunate man. What painter or statuary[5] ever had such a subject! No wonder that she inspired a genius into you, and first created the artist who afterward created her image."

Drowne looked at him with a visage that bore the traces of tears, but from which the light of imagination and sensibility, so recently illuminating it, had departed. He was again the mechanical carver that he had been known to be all his lifetime.

"I hardly understand what you mean, Mr. Copley," said he, putting his hand to his brow. "This image! Can it have been my work? Well, I have wrought it in a kind of dream; and now that I am broad awake I must set about finishing yonder figure of Admiral Vernon."

And forthwith he employed himself on the stolid countenance of one of his wooden progeny, and completed it in his own mechanical style, from which he was never known afterward to deviate. He followed his business industriously for many years, acquired a competence, and in the latter part of his life attained to a dignified station in the church, being remembered in records and traditions as Deacon Drowne, the carver. One of his productions, an Indian chief, gilded all over, stood during the better part of a century on the cupola of the Province House, bedazzling the eyes of those who looked upward, like an angel of the sun. Another work of the good deacon's hand—a reduced likeness of his friend Captain Hunnewell, holding a telescope and quadrant —may be seen to this day, at the corner of Broad and State streets, serving in the useful capacity of sign to the shop of a nautical instrument maker. We know not how to account for the inferiority of this quaint old figure, as compared with the recorded excellence of the Oaken Lady, unless on the supposition that in every human spirit there is imagination, sensibility, creative power, genius, which, according to circumstances, may either be developed in this world, or shrouded in a mask of dullness until another state of being. To our friend Drowne there came a brief season of excitement, kindled by love. It rendered him a genius for that one occasion, but, quenched in disappointment, left him again the mechanical carver in wood, without the power even of appreciating the work that his own hands had wrought. Yet who can doubt that the very highest state to which a human spirit can attain, in its loftiest aspirations, is its truest and most natural state, and that Drowne was more consistent with himself when he wrought the admirable figure of the mysterious lady, than when he perpetrated a whole progeny of blockheads?

There was a rumor in Boston, about this period, that a young Portuguese lady of rank, on some occasion of political or domestic disquietude, had fled from her home in Fayal and put herself under the protection of Captain Hunnewell, on board of whose vessel, and at whose residence, she was sheltered until a change of affairs. This fair stranger must have been the original of Drowne's Wooden Image.

---

5. *statuary,* sculptor.

 TO INCREASE UNDERSTANDING
The Maypole of Merry Mount

1. (*a*) Describe some of the festive customs Hawthorne weaves into "The Maypole of Merry Mount." (*b*) How did the inclusion of these conform to his theories about fiction?

2. (*a*) What two extremes do the Puritans and the colonists at Merry Mount represent? (*b*) Relate to Hawthorne's contrasting of these extremes the following passages: the destruction of the maypole (page 304); the costumes of the Merry Mount dancers (page 300); the description of the Puritans (page 303); Endicott's speech (page 304).

3. Hawthorne portrays Endicott and the priest as single-trait characters. (See the "Better Reading" article, page 47.) What are their respective traits? Why does the author give them such traits?

4. What idea runs through this tale like an "iron rod"? Point out passages in which the idea is stated.

5. What do you think Hawthorne means by calling this story a "philosophic romance"?

6. In his review of *Twice-Told Tales,* Edgar Allan

Poe praised Hawthorne highly. Poe wrote, "Of Mr. Hawthorne's Tales we would say, emphatically, that they belong to the highest region of Art . . . ." Reread Poe's statements in "The Construction of a Tale" (page 211) and then describe the qualities of "The Maypole of Merry Mount" that you think fulfill Poe's requirements for a successful tale.

Drowne's Wooden Image

1. (a) What is the setting of "Drowne's Wooden Image"? (b) Cite some details which give the setting its sense of reality. (c) What echoes of the Puritan past do you find in the story?

2. What is the purpose of the flashback on page 307?

3. What methods of characterization does Hawthorne employ in creating Drowne?

4. In his frequent visits to the carver's shop, Copley observes Drowne closely. (a) How does Drowne change while he works on his figurehead? (b) What causes the change? (c) Is the change temporary or permanent? (d) Why does Hawthorne have Copley refer to Drowne as "a modern Pygmalion"?

5. Hawthorne is careful to draw a contrast between Drowne's "wooden" images and his "inspired" image. (a) In what ways do the figureheads differ? (b) What qualities does the inspired image possess that make it a work of art?

6. In relating the conversations between Copley and Drowne, Hawthorne says several things about the nature of art and the artist. (a) What are Hawthorne's theories about art? (b) How do these theories relate to his theme in this story?

7. State why you feel that "Drowne's Wooden Image," like "The Maypole of Merry Mount," is a good example of Hawthorne's theory of the short story.

BETTER READING
Hawthorne's allegory

Hawthorne, always fascinated by New England's Puritan past, again and again made it the subject of his novels and short stories. He frequently turned to the dusty pages of the early annalists for historical facts which he could fuse with imaginative details to produce an *allegory*, or a tale whose underlying meaning differs from the surface meaning. One story that kindled his imagination was the brief history of Mount Wollaston or Merry Mount.

In 1625 Captain Wollaston arrived in New England with a large number of indentured servants and an English adventurer, Thomas Morton. The Captain founded his settlement, Mount Wollaston, and

then quickly moved on to Virginia. Wollaston left some of his servants behind with Thomas Morton, who took possession of the colony and renamed it Ma-re-Mount. Because of his lax morals and his gun trade with the Indians, Morton soon incurred the Pilgrims' wrath. They sent Miles Standish to arrest him and disperse the Merry Mount colonists. Standish was only partially successful in his mission: Morton was sent to England under arrest, but a few colonists remained at Merry Mount. Their lingering presence was as distasteful to the newly arrived Puritans as it had been to the Pilgrims. John Endicott, the first Puritan governor of Massachusetts Bay Colony, visited Merry Mount in 1629. He rebuked the colonists, and when he struck down their maypole the colony of Merry Mount ceased to exist.

Perhaps Hawthorne found his idea for a symbolic story in William Bradford's *History of Plymouth Plantation*, for Bradford says that the colonists of Merry Mount "fell to great licenciousnes. . . . And Morton became lord of misrule, and maintained (as it were) a schoole of Athisme. . . . They allso set up a May-pole, drinking and dancing aboute it many days togeather. . . ." Or, in reading Thomas Morton's *New English Canaan*, Hawthorne may have been struck by the contrast between Morton's gay irreverence (he calls Miles Standish "Captaine Shrimp") and Endicott's stern righteousness.

Whatever sparked his imagination, Hawthorne sensed that by combining the historical facts with imaginative details, he could give the story of Merry Mount a meaning deeper than the histories did.

To transform history into allegory, Hawthorne used some facts and invented others. How much historical fact did Hawthorne retain in "The Maypole of Merry Mount"? What characters and situations did he invent? Why do you think he ignored the gun trade but emphasized the maypole?

An allegory has two levels of meaning—one in its plot, the other in its moral. State the plot of *The Maypole of Merry Mount*. What symbols, such as light and darkness, convey the moral meaning?

 EXTENDING INTERESTS

Now that you have the background to appreciate Hawthorne's skill as a writer you will enjoy reading more of his tales. You will find "The Minister's Black Veil," "Dr. Heidegger's Experiment," and "The Ambitious Guest" in *Twice-Told Tales*. *Mosses from an Old Manse* contains "Young Goodman Brown," "The Artist of the Beautiful," and "Rappaccini's Daughter." Members of the class interested in Hawthorne might read one of these stories and then report on it to the class.

DISCUSSION GUIDE

The Scarlet Letter, by Nathaniel Hawthorne[1]

In discussing this novel, emphasis should be upon the author's use of setting, characters, plot, and imagery to develop his meaning.

HAWTHORNE'S WAY OF WRITING A STORY *is discussed on pages 297-299. Among other things he says that he wished to locate his stories in "a neutral territory, somewhere between the real world and fairyland." Cite instances of "the real world" in The Scarlet Letter. How does "The Custom House" stress "fairyland," or the remoteness of the events in the novel? Some happenings in The Scarlet Letter are truly in "a neutral territory." For instance, how does Hawthorne in "The Custom House" make it impossible for the reader to be sure whether the story he tells about Hester is merely a factual account or largely an imaginative one? How does he make sure that the reader will be unable to say with certainty whether the scarlet letter appearing in the sky is "a revelation from a supernatural source" or "a natural phenomenon"? Cite other happenings that the author places in "a neutral territory."*

PLOT AND MEANING. *Hawthorne spoke of The Scarlet Letter as "turning different sides of the same dark idea to the reader's eye." The idea, stated briefly, is that a terrible result of sin is to estrange and isolate those touched by it from society, from their true selves, or from God; and that the individuals will suffer until they have reëstablished the ties which have been broken. To do this each individual must accept full responsibility, truly recognize and regret his misdeeds, and openly proclaim them. Point out passages in which Pearl, Chillingworth, Hester, and Dimmesdale are shown to be estranged and isolated.*

The novel shows how each character reëstablishes or fails to reëstablish what Hawthorne calls "the electric chain of human sympathy." The stories of the four characters show different sides of this concept.

CHILLINGWORTH, as he himself says, has sinned in marrying Hester without loving her. How does he sin against Dimmesdale? Why is this a greater sin? How does this behavior affect

Chillingworth himself? How does his story end, and why is the ending appropriate?

PEARL, because she is a child, is incapable of sinning and takes her "moral coloration" from her mother; she herself "lacks reference and adaptation to the world." How do her adventures with the birds and beasts of the forest allegorically illustrate this fact? "She wanted," says Hawthorne in Chapter XVI, "a grief that should touch her, and thus humanize and make her capable of sympathy." At what point does her "humanization" occur? What causes it? How does the rest of her life prove that she has become a dweller in the mature world? How does her story complement that of Chillingworth? How does Pearl perform the same office for Hester that Chillingworth performs for the minister?

"I pity thee," says Chillingworth to HESTER, "for the good that has been wasted in thy nature." What would Hester's true nature have been in normal circumstances? What has led to her isolation from the community? Why does the community in time feel that she has made amends for her sin? Why does Hawthorne say, "The scarlet letter had not done its office" (Chapter XIII)? When does it do its office? How does Hawthorne show that it has?

DIMMESDALE accepts full responsibility for sinning and deeply regrets it. What details stress his spiritual qualities? Why does he not confess his sin publicly? Why are his sermons and his appearance on the scaffold "mockeries of penitence"? How does Hawthorne show that his decision to flee with Hester is another avoidance of his duty? When does Dimmesdale determine to confess his sin publicly? How does his story end? How does his story complement Hester's?

COLOR, LIGHT, AND SHADOW. *One of Hawthorne's chief ways of suggesting meaning is his use of color, light or shadow for the purpose of indicating the moral state of a character.* Describe Chillingworth's eyes when he is first presented. How does the color of his eyes change as his sin grows greater? How are light and color used in describing Pearl? What ideas of the child does this imagery foster? Comment on the use of imagery in interpreting the stories of Hester and Dimmesdale.

---

1. This Guide was prepared by Walter Blair.

Above: Portrait of Melville by Richard Chase. Left: The venerable whaler Charles W. Morgan, now preserved at Mystic Seaport, Connecticut. Below: A whaler's log.

m Baker of Warren.

nesday Nov 21ᵗʰ 1838.
... with light winds from the N. W. heading
...tward saw right whales and chased starboard
...h waist boat killed and about sunset took
...de and took in sail, and shortly after the
...d to the S. W. middle and latter part fresh
...daylight commenced cutting and after we got
...to the N. W.
...hese 24 hours.   Lat. By obs. 36.11.
*   Long. By ct 23.30.*

Thursday Nov 22ᵈ 1838.
...s with fine breezes from the Westward at
...5 P.M. saw a large sperm whale lowered
...ared but did not strike, whale bound to the West
...almost nearly calm saw a right whale.

In the South Atlantic

Sunday Nov 25ᵗʰ ...
Commences with light ...
saw plenty of whales low...
struck and he stove the b...
line and let him go. m...
...breezes saw whales and chased waist boa...
So ends there 24 hours.

W. B.   T. B.

Monday Nov 26ᵗʰ 18...
Begins with very light
...hale, middle part nearly
from the Northward saw
...success, and caught two po...
So ends there 24 h...

L. B.

Herman Melville 1819-1891

Herman Melville was the one great writer of America's Golden Day who was not a New Englander; he was born in New York City. Yet he had close ties with the section which was producing so much fine literature. He had New England (as well as New York) ancestors; he was strongly influenced by Hawthorne and he wrote fiction similar to Hawthorne's; and when he wrote his masterpiece, *Moby-Dick,* and for some years after, he lived in New England.

His background, though, differed tremendously from those of most authors. His formal schooling in Albany Academy was brief. At twenty he signed as a sailor on a merchant ship bound to Liverpool; at twenty-one he began voyages on whalers and a United States frigate which carried him to the South Seas and did not return him to these shores until after his twenty-fifth birthday. Life aboard ship, he therefore said later, was "his Harvard and his Yale." And through the rest of his days, muscular, bearded Melville had the sturdy bearing of a man who has been an ocean-roving sailor.

His best books, moreover, fictionized his sea-going adventures, though not in the order of their occurrence. *Typee* (1846) told how, after deserting his ship, he lived among cannibals in the Taipi Valley until another ship carried him away. *Omoo* (1847) told of his wanderings in the South Seas. *Mardi* (1849) made a fanciful use of other South Seas experiences. *Redburn* (1849) went back to his first voyage and fictionized it. *White-Jacket* (1850) made use of his life in the Navy. *Moby-Dick* (1851) told of a whaling voyage.

Still, much more than a knowledge of the sea figured in this author's writings. Though he had little formal schooling and felt that ships were his best teachers, Melville carried on graduate work, one might say, by ranging widely through the books of the world. In writing even novels which seemed wholly autobiographical, he made much use of his reading.

Among American authors Melville liked Hawthorne best: upon discovering him in 1850 he proclaimed that Hawthorne "almost alone among his generation" merited comparison with even Shakespeare. At precisely that time Hawthorne happened to be living in Lenox a few miles from Mel-

Detail from a piece of scrimshaw—art work carved by whalers on pieces of whalebone or whale ivory.

NEW BEDFORD WHALING MUSEUM

ville's Pittsfield home. The two writers became friends and during the next year drove and walked country roads or sat by firesides, talking at length (as Hawthorne said) "about time and eternity, things of this world and the next, and books, and publishers, and all possible and impossible matters." The friendship lasted even after Hawthorne had gone to Liverpool as consul; in 1856 Melville visited him there.

One reason for Melville's enthusiasm about Hawthorne's writings was that he and his friend were concerned with similar problems. Both were eager to embody meanings in stories by mingling actuality and the imagined. Discussing Hawthorne's *Mosses from an Old Manse,* Melville praised one story for the "mystical depth of its meaning," another for its "profound moral," still another for its "wonderful symbolizing of the secret workings in men's souls." Like Hawthorne—much more urgently, indeed, than Hawthorne—Melville was impelled to base settings, characterizations, and plots upon counterparts in the real world. At the same time he was eager so to diffuse these and his writing about them with imagination as to interpret them—to give them moral meanings. Like Hawthorne, therefore, Melville at his best made much use of allegorical and symbolic details.

Moby-Dick is full of details from reality. It is so packed with Melville's perceptions recalled from whaling days and with facts that it provides an accurate treatise on whaling. Members of the ship's crew are realistically portrayed. But Captain Ahab, whose leg has been sheared off by the white whale Moby-Dick, has become crazed by his desire for revenge and obsessed with the belief that the whale is the emblem of the malice and the evil of the universe. The attitude of Ahab and the differing attitudes of the crew as they pursue the whale all have symbolic or allegorical meanings. Understandably when Hawthorne read this novel he was able to comment on the "part and parcel allegoricalness of the whole"; and modern critics have discussed at great length the philosophical themes and the way Melville developed them.

A similar (though less complex) mingling of reality and of imaginative details occurs in *Redburn,* a selection from which follows.[1] Wellingborough Redburn, the narrator, is a youth who, like the Melville of 1839, takes his first voyage from New York to Liverpool. The sailors Redburn meets and the experiences he has are like those recalled by his creator, but this hero is made much more boyish than Melville had been, and his experiences are more shattering. As a result the story can develop, as its theme, innocence becoming aware of the hardness and wickedness of the world. Young Redburn, nurtured on romantic tales of the sea, learns that much shipboard life is unglamorous. Unaware of life's darker aspects, he encounters the depraved seaman Jackson, sees cruelty, sickness, and death on ship and on visits ashore. One symbol of the change he undergoes is the fine gray shooting jacket which his brother gives him and which he proudly dons as he starts his adventures. Soon he finds that it is as unsuitable for a voyage as are his romantic ideas for life.

The cutting printed here opens on the day Redburn's ship, the *Highlander,* is making ready to sail. Redburn, immaculate in his new shooting jacket but hungry, tired, and homesick, has just come on board.

This wood carving of the "Little Navigator" was used as an advertisement by a New Bedford nautical instrument maker in the 1820's.

NEW BEDFORD WHALING MUSEUM

---

1. A guide to the discussion of the entire novel may be found on page 328.

FROM *Redburn*

As I was standing looking round me, the chief mate approached in a great hurry about something, and seeing me in his way, cried out, "Ashore with you, you young loafer! There's no stealings here; sail away, I tell you, with that shooting jacket!"

Upon this I retreated, saying that I was going out in the ship as a sailor.

"A sailor!" he cried, "a barber's clerk, you mean; *you* going out in the ship? What, in that jacket? Hang me, I hope the old man hasn't been shipping any more greenhorns like you—he'll make a shipwreck of it if he has. But this is the way nowadays; to save a few dollars in seamen's wages, they think nothing of shipping a parcel of farmers and clodhoppers and baby boys. What's your name, Pillgarlic?"

"Redburn," said I.

"A pretty handle to a man, that; scorch you to take hold of it; haven't you got any other?"

"Wellingborough," said I.

"Worse yet. Who had the baptizing of ye? Why didn't they call you Jack, or Jill, or something short and handy. But I'll baptize you over again. D'ye hear, sir, henceforth your name is 'Buttons.' And now do you go, Buttons, and clean out that pigpen in the longboat; it has not been cleaned out since last voyage. And bear a hand about it, d'ye hear; there's them pigs there waiting to be put in; come, be off about it, now."

Was this then the beginning of my sea career? Set to cleaning out a pigpen, the very first thing?

But I thought it best to say nothing; I had bound myself to obey orders, and it was too late to retreat. So I only asked for a shovel, or spade, or something else to work with.

"We don't dig gardens here," was the reply; "dig it out with your teeth!"

After looking round, I found a stick and went to scraping out the pen, which was awkward work enough, for another boat called the "jolly boat," was capsized right over the longboat, which brought them almost close together. These two boats were in the middle of the deck. I managed to crawl inside of the longboat; and after barking my shins against the seats, and bumping my head a good many times, I got along to the stern, where the pigpen was.

While I was hard at work a drunken sailor peeped in, and cried out to his comrades, "Look here, my lads, what sort of a pig do you call this? Hallo! Inside there! What are you 'bout there? Trying to stow yourself away to steal a passage to Liverpool? Out of that! Out of that, I say." But just then the mate came along and ordered this drunken rascal ashore.

The pigpen being cleaned out, I was set to work picking up some shavings, which lay about the deck, for there had been carpenters at work on board. The mate ordered me to throw these shavings into the longboat at a particular place between two of the seats. But as I found it hard work to push the shavings through in that place, and as it looked wet there, I thought it would be better for the shavings as well as myself, to thrust them where there was a larger opening and a dry spot. While I was thus employed, the mate observing me, exclaimed with an oath, "Didn't I tell you to put those shavings somewhere else? Do what I tell you, now, Buttons, or mind your eye!"

Stifling my indignation at his rudeness, which by this time I found was my only plan,

I replied that that was not so good a place for the shavings as that which I myself had selected, and asked him to tell me *why* he wanted me to put them in the place he designated. Upon this, he flew into a terrible rage, and without explanation reiterated his order like a clap of thunder.

This was my first lesson in the discipline of the sea, and I never forgot it. From that time I learned that sea officers never gave reasons for anything they order to be done. It is enough that they command it, so that the motto is, "Obey orders, though you break owners."

I now began to feel very faint and sick again, and longed for the ship to be leaving the dock; for then I made no doubt we would soon be having something to eat. But as yet, I saw none of the sailors on board, and as for the men at work in the rigging, I found out that they were riggers, that is, men living ashore, who worked by the day getting ships ready for sea. . . . At last I watched my chance, and while people's backs were turned, I seized a carrot from several bunches lying on deck, and clapping it under the skirts of my shooting jacket, went forward to eat it; for I had often eaten raw carrots, which taste something like chestnuts. This carrot refreshed me a good deal, though at the expense of a little pain in my stomach. Hardly had I disposed of it, when I heard the chief mate's voice crying out for "Buttons." I ran after him, and received an order to go aloft and "Slush down the maintopmast."

This was all Greek to me, and after receiving the order, I stood staring about me, wondering what it was that was to be done. But the mate had turned on his heel, and made no explanations. At length I followed after him, and asked what I must do.

"Didn't I tell you to slush down the maintopmast?" he shouted.

"You did," said I, "but I don't know what that means."

"Green as grass! A regular cabbagehead!" he exclaimed to himself. "A fine time I'll have with such a greenhorn aboard. Look you, youngster. Look up to that long pole there— d'ye see it? That piece of a tree there, you timberhead—well—take this bucket here, and go up the rigging—that rope ladder there—do you understand?—and dab this slush all over the mast, and look out for your head if one drop falls on deck. Be off now, Buttons."

The eventful hour had arrived; for the first time in my life I was to ascend a ship's mast. Had I been well and hearty, perhaps I should have felt a little shaky at the thought; but as I was then, weak and faint, the bare thought appalled me.

But there was no hanging back; it would look like cowardice, and I could not bring myself to confess that I was suffering for want of food; so rallying again, I took up the bucket.

It was a heavy bucket, with strong iron hoops, and might have held perhaps two gallons. But it was only half full now of a sort of thick lobbered gravy, which I afterward learned was boiled out of the salt beef used by the sailors. Upon getting into the rigging, I found it was no easy job to carry this heavy bucket up with me. The rope handle of it was so slippery with grease that although I twisted it several times about my wrist, it would be still twirling round and round, and slipping off. Spite of this, however, I managed to mount as far as the top,[1] the clumsy bucket half the time straddling and swinging about between my legs, and in momentary danger of capsizing. Arrived at the top, I came to a dead halt, and looked up. How to surmount that overhanging impediment completely posed me for the time. But at last, with much straining, I contrived to place my bucket in the top; and then, trusting to Providence, swung myself up after it. The rest of the road was comparatively easy; though whenever I incautiously looked down toward the deck, my head spun round so from weakness, that I was obliged to shut my eyes to recover myself. I do not remember much more. I only recollect my safe return to the deck.

In a short time the bustle of the ship increased; the trunks of cabin passengers arrived, and the chests and boxes of the steerage passengers, besides baskets of wine and fruit for the captain.

---

1. *top*, a platform around the top of a lower mast.

At last we cast loose, and swinging out into the stream, came to anchor, and hoisted the signal for sailing. Everything, it seemed, was on board but the crew; who in a few hours after, came off, one by one, in Whitehall boats, their chests in the bow, and themselves lying back in the stern like lords; and showing very plainly the complacency they felt in keeping the whole ship waiting for their lordships.

"Ay, ay," muttered the chief mate, as they rolled out of their boats and swaggered on deck, "it's your turn now, but it will be mine before long. Yaw about while you may, my hearties, I'll do the yawing after the anchor's up." . . .

While we sat eating our beef and biscuit [the next morning], two of the men got into a dispute, about who had been seafaring the longest; when Jackson called upon them in a loud voice to cease their clamor, for he would decide the matter for them. Of this sailor, I shall have something more to say, as I get on with my narrative; so, I will here try to describe him a little.

Did you ever see a man, with his hair shaved off, and just recovered from yellow fever? Well, just such a looking man was this sailor. He was as yellow as gamboge, had no more whisker on his cheek, than I have on my elbows. His hair had fallen out, and left him very bald, except in the nape of his neck, and just behind the ears, where it was stuck over with short little tufts, and looked like a worn-out shoebrush. His nose had broken down in the middle, and he squinted with one eye, and did not look very straight out of the other. He dressed a good deal like a Bowery boy; for he despised the ordinary sailor rig, wearing a pair of great overall blue trousers, fastened with suspenders, and three red woolen shirts, one over the other; for he was subject to rheumatism, and was not in good health, he said; and he had a large white wool hat, with a broad rolling brim. He was a native of New York City, and had a good deal to say about highbinders, and rowdies,[2] whom he denounced as only good for the gallows; but I thought he looked a good deal like a highbinder himself.

His name, as I have said, was Jackson, and he told us, he was a near relation of General Jackson of New Orleans,[3] and swore terribly, if anyone ventured to question what he asserted on that head. In fact he was a great bully, and being the best seaman on board, and very overbearing in every way, all the men were afraid of him, and durst not contradict him, or cross his path in anything. And what made this more wonderful was, that he was the weakest man, bodily, of the whole crew; and I have no doubt that young and small as I was then, compared to what I am now, I could have thrown him down. But he had such an overawing way with him; such a deal of brass and impudence, such an unflinching face, and withal was such a hideous-looking mortal, that Satan himself would have run from him. And besides all this, it was quite plain, that he was by nature a marvelously clever, cunning man, though without education; and understood human nature to a kink, and well knew whom he had to deal with; and then, one glance of his squinting eye was as good as a knockdown, for it was the most deep, subtle, infernal-looking eye, that I ever saw lodged in a human head. I believe, that by good rights it must have belonged to a wolf, or starved tiger; at any rate, I would defy any oculist, to turn out a glass eye, half so cold, and snaky, and deadly. It was a horrible thing; and I would give much to forget that I have ever seen it, for it haunts me to this day.

It was impossible to tell how old this Jackson was, for he had no beard, and no wrinkles, except small crow's-feet about the eyes. He might have seen thirty, or perhaps fifty years. But according to his own account, he had been to sea ever since he was eight years old, when he first went as a cabin boy in an Indiaman,[4] and ran away to Calcutta. And according to his own account, too, he had

---

2. *highbinders, and rowdies.* Jackson, who had sailed to China, knew about the secret Chinese societies whose members, known as "highbinders," were hired assassins. He denounced highbinders and ruffians (rowdies) alike.
3. *General Jackson of New Orleans*, Andrew Jackson, who was the hero of the Battle of New Orleans during the War of 1812. 4. *Indiaman*, a ship in the trade with India.

passed through every kind of dissipation and abandonment in the worst parts of the world. . . .

He would tell of lying in Batavia during a fever, when his ship lost a man every few days, and how they went reeling ashore with the body, and got still more intoxicated by way of precaution against the plague. He would talk of finding a *cobra de capello,* or hooded snake, under his pillow in India, when he slept ashore there. He would talk of sailors being poisoned at Canton with drugged shampoo,[5] for the sake of their money; and of the Malay ruffians, who stopped ships in the Strait of Gaspar, and always saved the captain for the last, so as to make him point out where the most valuable goods were stored.

His whole talk was of this kind, full of piracies, plagues, and poisonings. And often he narrated many passages in his own individual career, which were almost incredible, from the consideration that few men could have plunged into such infamous vices, and clung to them so long, without paying the death penalty.

But in truth, he carried about him the traces of these things, and the mark of a fearful end nigh at hand, like that of King Antiochus[6] of Syria, who died a worse death, history says, than if he had been stung out of the world by wasps and hornets.

Nothing was left of this Jackson but the foul lees and dregs of a man; he was thin as a shadow; nothing but skin and bones; and sometimes used to complain that it hurt him to sit on the hard chests. And I sometimes fancied, it was the consciousness of his miserable, broken-down condition, and the prospect of soon dying like a dog, in consequence of his sins, that made this poor wretch always eye me with such malevolence as he did. For I was young and handsome, at least my mother so thought me, and as soon as I became a little used to the sea, and shook off my low spirits somewhat, I began to have my old color in my cheeks, and, spite of misfortune, to appear well and hearty; whereas *he* was being consumed by an incurable malady, that was eating up his vitals, and was more fit for a hospital than a ship. . . .

I well remember the first time I saw him, and how I was startled at his eye, which was even then fixed upon me. He was standing at the ship's helm, being the first man that got there, when a steersman was called for by the pilot[7]; for this Jackson was always on the alert for easy duties, and used to plead his delicate health as the reason for assuming them, as he did; though I used to think that, for a man in poor health, he was very swift on the legs, at least when a good place was to be jumped to; though that might only have been a sort of spasmodic exertion under strong inducements, which everyone knows the greatest invalids will sometimes show.

And though the sailors were always very bitter against anything like sogering, as they called it; that is, anything that savored of a desire to get rid of downright hard work; yet I observed that, though this Jackson was a notorious old soger the whole voyage (I mean, in all things not perilous to do, from which he was far from hanging back), and in truth was a great veteran that way, and one who must have passed unhurt through many campaigns; yet, they never presumed to call him to account in any way; or to let him so much as think, what they thought of his conduct. But I often heard them call him many hard names behind his back; and sometimes, too, when, perhaps, they had just been tenderly inquiring after his health before his face. They all stood in mortal fear of him; and cringed and fawned about him like so many spaniels; and used to rub his back, after he was undressed and lying in his bunk; and used to run up on deck to the cookhouse, to warm some cold coffee for him; and used to fill his pipe, and give him chews of tobacco, and mend his jackets and trousers; and used to watch, and tend, and nurse him every way.

5. *poisoned . . . shampoo.* Sailors, ashore in Canton, often had themselves massaged or "shampooed." The Chinese poisoned them by drugging the substance they rubbed into the sailors' bodies. **6.** *King Antiochus* (an tī′ə kəs). The death of Antiochus, a Syrian ruler of the second century B.C., is graphically described in Maccabees 2, one of the books of the Apocrypha, those fourteen books of the Old Testament not universally accepted. According to this version, Antiochus suffered internal tortures, his body swarmed with worms, and his flesh rotted away. **7.** *pilot,* a man whose business is to guide ships in or out of harbor.

And all the time, he would sit scowling on them, and found fault with what they did; and I noticed, that those who did the most for him, and cringed the most before him, were the very ones he most abused; while two or three who held more aloof, he treated with a little consideration.

It is not for me to say, what it was that made a whole ship's company submit so to the whims of one poor miserable man like Jackson. I only know that so it was; but I have no doubt, that if he had had a blue eye in his head, or had had a different face from what he did have, they would not have stood in such awe of him. And it astonished me, to see that one of the seamen, a remarkably robust and good-humored young man from Belfast in Ireland, was a person of no mark or influence among the crew; but on the contrary was hooted at, and trampled upon, and made a butt and laughingstock; and more than all, was continually being abused and snubbed by Jackson, who seemed to hate him cordially, because of his great strength and fine person, and particularly because of his red cheeks.

But then, this Belfast man, although he had shipped for an able-seaman, was not much of a sailor; and that always lowers a man in the eyes of a ship's company; I mean, when he ships for an able-seaman, but is not able to do the duty of one. For sailors are of three classes — able-seaman, ordinary seaman, and boys; and they receive different wages according to their rank. Generally, a ship's company of twelve men will only have five or six able-seamen, who if they prove to understand their duty every way (and that is no small matter either, as I shall hereafter show, perhaps), are looked up to, and thought much of by the ordinary seamen and boys, who reverence their very pea jackets, and lay up their sayings in their hearts.

But you must not think from this, that persons called "boys" aboard merchant ships are all youngsters, though to be sure, I myself was called a boy, and a boy I was. No. In merchant ships, a boy means a greenhand, a landsman on his first voyage. And never mind if he is old enough to be a grandfather, he is still called a boy; and boys' work is put upon him.

But I am straying off from what I was going to say about Jackson's putting an end to the dispute between the two sailors in the forecastle after breakfast. After they had been disputing some time about who had been to sea the longest, Jackson told them to stop talking; then bade one of them open his mouth; for, said he, "I can tell a sailor's age just like a horse's—by his teeth." So the man laughed, and opened his mouth; and Jackson made him step out under the scuttle, where the light came down from the deck; and then made him throw his head back, while he looked into it, and probed a little with his jackknife, like a baboon peering into a junk bottle. I trembled for the poor fellow, just as if I had seen him under the hands of a crazy barber, making signs to cut his throat, and he all the while sitting stock-still, with the lather on, to be shaved. For I watched Jackson's eye and saw it snapping, and a sort of going in and out, very quick, as if it were something like a forked tongue; and somehow, I felt as if he were longing to kill the man; but at last he grew more composed, and after concluding his examination, said, that the first man was the oldest sailor, for the ends of his teeth were the evenest and most worn down; which, he said, arose from eating so much hard sea biscuit; and this was the reason he could tell a sailor's age like a horse's.

At this, everybody made merry, and looked at each other, as much as to say— "come boys, let's laugh"; and they did laugh; and declared it was a rare joke.

This was always the way with them. They made a point of shouting out, whenever Jackson said anything with a grin; that being the sign to them that he himself thought it funny; though I heard many good jokes from others pass off without a smile; and once Jackson himself (for to tell the truth, he sometimes had a comical way with him, that is, when his back did not ache) told a truly funny story, but with a grave face; when, not knowing how he meant it, whether for a laugh or otherwise, they all sat still, waiting what to do, and looking perplexed enough; till at last Jackson roared out upon them for a parcel of fools and idiots; and told them to their beards, how it was; that he had purposely put on his grave face, to see whether they would not look grave too; even when he was telling something that ought to split their sides. And with that, he flouted, and jeered at them, and laughed them all to scorn; and broke out in such a rage, that his lips began to glue together at the corners with a fine white foam.

He seemed to be full of hatred and gall against everything and everybody in the world; as if all the world was one person, and had done him some dreadful harm that was rankling and festering in his heart. Sometimes I thought he was really crazy; and often felt so frightened at him, that I thought of going to the captain about it, and telling him Jackson ought to be confined, lest he should do some terrible thing at last. But upon second thoughts, I always gave it up; for the captain would only have called me a fool, and sent me forward again. . . .

The second day out of port, the decks being washed down and breakfast over, the watch[8] was called, and the mate set us to work.

It was a very bright day. The sky and water were both of the same deep hue; and the air felt warm and sunny; so that we threw off our jackets. I could hardly believe that I was sailing in the same ship I had been in during the night, when everything had been so lonely and dim; and I could hardly imagine that this was the same ocean, now so beautiful and blue, that during part of the night watch had rolled along so black and forbidding.

There were little traces of sunny clouds all over the heavens; and little fleeces of foam all over the sea; and the *Highlander* made a strange, musical noise under her bows, as she glided along, with her sails all still. . . .

I had now completely got over my seasickness, and felt very well; at least in my body, though my heart was far from feeling right; so that I could now look around me, and make observations.

And truly, though we were at sea, there was much to behold and wonder at, to me, who was on my first voyage. What most amazed me was the sight of the great ocean itself, for we were out of sight of land. All round us, on both sides of the ship, ahead and astern, nothing was to be seen but water—water—water; not a single glimpse of green shore, not the smallest island, or speck of moss anywhere. Never did I realize till now what the ocean was: how grand and majestic, how solitary, and boundless, and beautiful, and blue; for that day it gave no tokens of squalls or hurricanes, such as I had heard my father tell of; nor could I imagine how anything that seemed so playful and placid, could be lashed into rage, and troubled into rolling avalanches of foam and great cascades of waves, such as I saw in the end. . . .

I felt as if in a dream all the time; and when I could shut the ship out, almost thought I was in some new, fairy world, and expected to hear myself called to, out of the clear blue air, or from the depths of the deep blue sea. But I did not have much leisure to indulge in such thoughts; for the men were now getting some stunsails ready to hoist aloft, as the wind was getting fairer and fairer for us; and these stunsails are light canvas which are spread at such times, away out beyond the ends of the yards, where they overhang the wide water, like the wings of a great bird. . . .

At last we hoisted the stunsails up to the topsail yards, and as soon as the vessel felt them, she gave a sort of bound like a horse, and the breeze blowing more and more, she went plunging along, shaking off the foam from her bows, like foam from a bridle bit. Every mast and timber seemed to have a pulse in it that was beating with life and joy; and I felt a wild exulting in my own heart, and felt as if I would be glad to bound along so round the world.

Then was I first conscious of a wonderful thing in me that responded to all the wild commotion of the outer world; and went reeling on and on with the planets in their orbits, and was lost in one delirious throb at the center of the All. A wild bubbling and bursting was at my heart, as if a hidden spring had just gushed out there; and my blood ran tingling along my frame, like mountain brooks in spring freshets. . . .

---

8. *the watch*, the time of duty of one group of a ship's crew. A watch usually lasts four hours.

But how soon these raptures abated, when after a brief idle interval, we were again set to work, and I had a vile commission to clean out the chicken coops, and make up the beds of the pigs in the longboat. . . .

I must now tell of my first going aloft at sea.

It happened on the second night out of port, during middle watch, when the sea was quite calm, and the breeze was mild.

The order was given to loose the main skysail, which is the fifth and highest sail from the deck. It was a very small sail, and from the forecastle looked no bigger than a cambric pocket handkerchief. But I have heard that some ships carry still smaller sails above the skysail, called moonsails, and skyscrapers, and cloud-rakers. But I shall not believe in them till I see them; a skysail seems high enough in all conscience, and the idea of anything higher than that, seems preposterous. Besides, it looks almost like tempting heaven, to brush the very firmament so, and almost put the eyes of the stars out; when a flaw of wind, too, might very soon take the conceit out of these cloud-defying cloud-rakers.

Now, when the order was passed to loose the skysail, an old Dutch sailor came up to me, and said, "Buttons, my boy, it's high time you be doing something; and it's boy's business, Buttons, to loose de royals, and not old men's business, like me. Now d'ye see dat leetle fellow way up dare? *Dare,* just behind dem stars dare. Well tumble up, now, Buttons, I zay, and looze him; way you go, Buttons."

All the rest joining in, and seeming unanimous in the opinion that it was high time for me to be stirring myself, and doing boy's business, as they called it, I made no more ado, but jumped into the rigging. Up I went, not daring to look down, but keeping my eyes glued, as it were, to the shrouds, as I ascended.

It was a long road up those stairs, and I began to pant and breathe hard, before I was half way. But I kept at it till I got to the Jacob's ladder; and they may well call it so, for it took me almost into the clouds; and at last, to my own amazement, I found myself hanging on the skysail yard, holding on might and main to the mast; and curling my feet round the rigging, as if they were another pair of hands.

For a few moments I stood awe-stricken and mute. I could not see far out upon the ocean, owing to the darkness of the night; and from my lofty perch, the sea looked like a great, black gulf, hemmed in, all round, by beetling black cliffs. I seemed all alone, treading the midnight clouds; and every second, expected to find myself falling—falling—falling, as I have felt when the nightmare has been on me.

I could but just perceive the ship below me, like a long narrow plank in the water; and it did not seem to belong at all to the yard, over which I was hanging. A gull, or some sort of seafowl, was flying around the truck over my head, within a few yards of my face; and it almost frightened me to hear it; it seemed so much like a spirit, at such a lofty and solitary height.

Though there was a pretty smooth sea, and little wind; yet, at this extreme elevation, the ship's motion was very great; so that when the ship rolled one way, I felt something as a fly must feel, walking the ceiling; and when it rolled the other way, I felt as if I was hanging along a slanting pine tree.

But presently I heard a distant, hoarse noise from below; and though I could not make out anything intelligible, I knew it was the mate hurrying me. So in a nervous, trembling desperation, I went to casting off the gaskets, or lines tying up the sail; and when all was ready, sung out as I had been told, to "hoist away!" And hoist they did, and me too along with the yard and sail; for I had no time to get off, they were so unexpectedly quick about it. It seemed like magic; there I was, going up higher and higher; the yard rising under me, as if it were alive, and no soul in sight. Without knowing it at the time, I was in a good deal of danger, but it was so dark that I could not see well enough to feel afraid—at least on that account; though I felt frightened enough in a promiscuous way. I only held on hard, and made good the saying of old sailors, that the last person to fall overboard from the rigging is a landsman, because he grips the ropes so fiercely; whereas old tars are less careful, and sometimes pay the penalty.

After this feat, I got down rapidly on deck, and received something like a compliment from Max the Dutchman. . . .

[It was on a Sunday we made the Banks of Newfoundland; a drizzling, foggy, clammy Sunday.]

We were still on the Banks, when a terrific storm came down upon us, the like of which I had never before beheld, or imagined. The rain poured down in sheets and cascades; the scupper holes could hardly carry it off the decks; and in bracing the yards we waded about almost up to our knees; everything floating about, like chips in a dock.

This violent rain was the precursor of a hard squall, for which we duly prepared, taking in our canvas to double-reefed topsails.

The tornado came rushing along at last, like a troop of wild horses before the flaming rush of a burning prairie. But after bowing and cringing to it awhile, the good *Highlander* was put off before it; and with her nose in the water, went wallowing on, ploughing milk-white waves, and leaving a streak of illuminated foam in her wake.

It was an awful scene. It made me catch my breath as I gazed. I could hardly stand on my feet, so violent was the motion of the ship. But while I reeled to and fro, the sailors only laughed at me; and bade me look out that the ship did not fall overboard; and advised me to get a handspike, and hold it down hard in the weather scuppers, to steady her wild motions. But I was now getting a little too wise for this foolish kind of talk; though all through the voyage, they never gave it over.

This storm past, we had fair weather until we got into the Irish Sea.

The morning following the storm, when the sea and sky had become blue again, the man aloft sung out that there was a wreck on the lee beam. We bore away for it, all hands looking eagerly toward it, and the captain in the mizzen-top with his spyglass. Presently, we slowly passed alongside of it.

It was a dismantled, water-logged schooner, a most dismal sight, that must have been drifting about for several long weeks. The bulwarks were pretty much gone; and here and there the bare stanchions, or posts, were left standing, splitting in two the waves which broke clear over the deck, lying almost even with the sea. . . .

Lashed, and leaning over sideways against the taffrail, were three dark, green, grassy objects, that slowly swayed with every roll, but otherwise were motionless. I saw the captain's glass directed toward them, and heard him say at last, "They must have been dead a long time." These were sailors, who long ago had lashed themselves to the taffrail for safety; but must have famished.

Full of the awful interest of the scene, I surely thought the captain would lower a boat to bury the bodies, and find out something about the schooner. But we did not stop at all; passing on our course, without so much as learning the schooner's name, though everyone supposed her to be a New Brunswick lumberman.

On the part of the sailors, no surprise was shown that our captain did not send off a boat to the wreck. For me, I could not but feel amazed and shocked at his indifference; but my subsequent sea experiences have shown me that such conduct as this is very common, though not, of course, when human life can be saved.

So away we sailed, and left her—drifting, drifting on; a garden spot for barnacles and a playhouse for the sharks.

"Look there," said Jackson, hanging over the rail and coughing—"look there; that's a sailor's coffin. Ha! ha! Buttons? Wouldn't you like to take a sail with them 'ere dead men? Wouldn't it be nice?" And then he tried to laugh, but only coughed again.

"Don't laugh at dem poor fellows," said Max, looking grave; "don' you see dar bodies, dar souls are farder off dan de Cape of Dood Hope."

"Dood Hope, Dood Hope," shrieked Jackson, with a horrid grin, mimicking the Dutchman, "dare is no dood hope for dem, old boy; dey are drowned and d—d, as you and I will be, Red Max, one of dese dark nights."

"No, no," said Blunt,[9] "all sailors are saved; they have plenty of squalls here below, but fair weather aloft."

"Don't talk of heaven to me—it's a lie—I know it—and they are all fools that believe in it," howled Jackson through a cough. "Do you think, you Greek, that there's any heaven for *you?* Will they let *you* in there, with that tarry hand, and that oily head of hair? Avast! When some shark gulps you down his hatchway one of these days, you'll find, that by dying, you'll only go from one gale of wind to another; mind that, you Irish cockney!" And so saying, he went off, holding his hands to his chest, and coughing, as if his last hour was come.

Every day this Jackson seemed to grow worse and worse, both in body and mind. He seldom spoke, but to contradict, deride, or curse; and all the time, though his face grew thinner and thinner, his eyes seemed to kindle more and more, as if he were going to die out at last, and leave them burning like tapers before a corpse.

Though he had never attended churches, and knew nothing about Christianity—no more than a Malay pirate; and though he could not read a word, yet he was spontaneously an atheist and an infidel; and during the long night watches, would enter into arguments to prove there was nothing worth living for; but everything to be hated, in the wide world. He was a horrid desperado; and like a wild Indian, whom he resembled in his tawny skin and high cheekbones, he seemed to run amuck at heaven and earth. He was a Cain afloat; branded on his yellow brow with some inscrutable curse; and going about corrupting and searing every heart that beat near him.

But there seemed to be even more woe than wickedness about the man; and his wickedness seemed to spring from his woe; and for all his hideousness, there was that in his eye at times, that was ineffably pitiable and touching; and though there were moments when I almost hated this Jackson, yet I have pitied no man as I have pitied him.

---

9. *Blunt,* one of the ship's crew.

TO INCREASE UNDERSTANDING

1. (*a*) Describe Redburn during his first day aboard the *Highlander.* (*b*) Point out passages which indicate how his shipboard experiences affected him.

2. (*a*) What methods does Melville use to characterize Jackson? (See "Better Reading," page 47.) (*b*) Is Jackson realistically or symbolically portrayed? Explain. (*c*) Does Redburn's attitude toward Jackson remain unchanged? Cite passages to support your answer.

3. (*a*) What did Melville mean by saying life aboard ship was "his Harvard and his Yale"? (*b*) Explain how Melville used his sea-going experiences in his novels. (*c*) Point out instances of Melville's knowledge of the sea in this selection. (*d*) Point out vivid descriptions of the sea in *Redburn.* In each case explain how the details help establish the mood.

4. Like Hawthorne, Melville was eager "to embody meanings in stories by mingling actuality and the imagined." Cite passages from *Redburn* that illustrate this.

WORDS!

As you imaginatively accompanied Redburn on his first voyage aboard the *Highlander,* you met one nautical word after another. Melville knew the language of the sea would be unfamiliar to most readers and for this reason he defined his nautical words in the context of the story. For example, Melville writes: "...the sailors were always very bitter against anything like *sogering*...that is, anything that savored of a desire to get rid of downright hard work."

The following list contains several more nautical words which Melville defines in context. Copy this list on a sheet of paper. Using the context clues Melville supplies, write down, opposite each word, what you think its meaning is. When you have completed the list, check your definitions with the Glossary.

riggers (page 320, column 1, paragraph 2)
boy (page 323, column 1, paragraph 3)
able-seaman (page 323, column 1, paragraph 2)
stunsails (page 324, column 2, paragraph 1)
main skysail (page 325, column 1, paragraph 4)
gaskets (page 325, column 2, paragraph 4)
stanchions (page 326, column 2, line 4)

See Redburn *Discussion Guide on next page.*

DISCUSSION GUIDE

Redburn, by Herman Melville

Like Hawthorne, Melville desired his novels to partake of the real and the imaginary. Drawing settings, characterizations, and plots from his own experiences, he infused them with imagination to produce a moral meaning. These are the ideas on which the discussion should be centered.

FACT AND FICTION. *On page 318 you read about Moby-Dick:* "It is so packed with Melville's perceptions recalled from whaling days and with facts that it provides an accurate treatise on whaling." Redburn *contains much source material on Liverpool in the first half of the nineteenth century.* What kinds of information does Melville include? What evidence is there that this is first-hand information? Is this material merely a collection of facts or is the author's attitude indicated? If so, how? Does any of it seem to be "diffused...with imagination"? On what other subjects might *Redburn* serve as a source book?

In the discussion of Redburn *(page 318) you read that* "the narrator is a youth who, like the Melville of 1839, takes his first voyage from New York to Liverpool...but this hero is made much more boyish than Melville had been." What advantages are gained by writing the story in the first person? What reasons are there for making the narrator younger than Melville was? What devices does Melville use to keep the reader's sympathy with the narrator? How does Redburn develop during the course of the novel?

Since in the plot of Redburn *it is the interaction between the narrator and a group of sailors that is important, it is unnecessary for the author to develop fully each member of this group.* Characterize the sailors as a group. Which men stand out from the group? What methods does Melville use to develop these minor characters? (See the article on methods of developing character on page 47.) As the story progresses, the captain and the first mate show characteristics somewhat different from what their initial speech and actions would suggest. What is the final impression created by each?

Harry Bolton enters the plot only in the last third of the novel. Why does his entrance develop an element of suspense? How does he serve as a foil for Redburn? What does his story add to the novel as a whole?

THEME AND MORAL MEANINGS. *The theme of* Redburn *is stated on page 318 as* "innocence becoming aware of the hardness and wickedness of the world." This theme is worked out largely through the use of symbols. The shooting jacket, which symbolizes Redburn's innocence of the world and his romanticism, is introduced in the first sentence of the first paragraph of Chapter I. What does this placement suggest as to Melville's idea of the importance of the jacket in interpreting the meaning of the story? Describe the jacket as it looks when Redburn receives it. What is there about it that again and again causes Redburn unhappiness? How does it change as the voyage progresses? What mental and emotional changes in Redburn do the physical changes in the jacket symbolize?

In Chapter I "an old-fashioned glass ship" *is also introduced.* What does it symbolize? What significance is there in the fact that the ship is glass? What happens to the ship? How does Redburn intimate that he regards the present state of the ship as symbolic of his own experience?

On the return voyage, when fever is raging among the steerage passengers, Redburn speaks of Jackson as "The only true leper among us." What does this mean? Why did Jackson's most virulent hatred seem to fix upon the physically able or the morally good? Why does the small English stowaway pull away when Jackson tries to befriend him? Why is Jackson the only one of all the sailors not superstitiously afraid of the "living corpse"? Does the manner of Jackson's death seem appropriate? How does it affect the crew? Contrast the weather the day Jackson dies with that of the following morning. What is the importance of Jackson in working out the theme of the novel?

The use of a narrator makes it possible for Melville to offer digressions—actually brief essays—on his attitude toward various aspects of life apart from but complementary to the theme. What opinions are expressed in *Redburn* about poverty in Liverpool, the claims made by ship-sailing and recruiting posters, the methods used to get emigrants to take a particular ship, steerage passage? Name other subjects upon which a moral judgment is made and comment upon the attitude expressed.

THE LARGER VIEW

Imagine that someone unfamiliar with American literature has asked you to characterize the writing of Thoreau, Emerson, Longfellow, Holmes, Lowell, Whittier, Hawthorne, and Melville. Begin by writing Thoreau's name on a sheet of paper. Indicate alongside his name whether he was a prose writer, a poet, or both. Then select from the following list the literary form, or forms, characteristic of Thoreau and the themes he was interested in. Jot down your selections. Continue in this way with each writer of America's Golden Day. When your list is complete, use your notations to write a thumbnail description of each writer in this chapter.

sea	social abuses
common man	allegory
war	individualism
essay	sonnet
nature	Puritan past
Europe	ode
local color	science
short story	Transcendentalism
industrialism	novel

BIBLIOGRAPHY

BROOKS, VAN WYCK, *The Flowering of New England.* (••Dutton) Covering the years 1815 through 1865, the author recaptures the atmosphere of the period, attractively portrays the leading figures, and gives good summaries of their works.

EMERSON, RALPH WALDO, *The Portable Emerson,* edited by Mark Van Doren. (••Viking) Mature students will want to read more of Emerson's ideas and views. This book contains some of his best writing.

GREENSLET, FERRIS, *The Lowells and Their Seven Worlds.* (Houghton) A fine multiple biography, this book traces with humor and affection what seven generations of Lowells have contributed to America.

HAWTHORNE, HILDEGARDE, *Romantic Rebel: The Story of Nathaniel Hawthorne.* (Appleton) The skill of a storyteller and an intimate knowledge of her grandfather's life have enabled Miss Hawthorne to write a biography that is as interesting as a novel.

HAWTHORNE, NATHANIEL, *The House of the Seven Gables.* (Dodd •Dolphin) In this novel filled with sinister happenings an old, inherited curse rests on the house of the seven gables, and an air of tragedy haunts the Pyncheon family, its occupants.

HAWTHORNE, NATHANIEL, *The Scarlet Letter.* (Dodd •Dolphin) The classic story of Hester Prynne, condemned by the townspeople of Puritan Boston, is a searching study of conscience and of the workings of the heart.

HOLMES, OLIVER WENDELL, *Autocrat of the Breakfast-Table.* (Dutton •Dolphin) The setting for these witty, imaginary conversations is the table of a boarding house.

HOLMES, OLIVER WENDELL, *Complete Poetical Works.* (Houghton) Here is a collection of poems that generations of Americans have loved. Included are "Old Ironsides," "My Aunt," and "The Deacon's Masterpiece."

LONGFELLOW, HENRY WADSWORTH, *The Poems of Longfellow.* (Modern Library) Longfellow's poems range from rhythmic ballads to long narrative poems to thoughtful melodious lyrics. There is something here to suit every taste.

LOWELL, JAMES RUSSELL, *Complete Poetical Works.* (Houghton) Lowell's versatility is clearly demonstrated in this collection. Be sure to read the witty *Fable for Critics,* the Yankee-dialect poem *The Biglow Papers,* and the romantic *Vision of Sir Launfal.*

MELVILLE, HERMAN, *Redburn.* (Farrar-Straus •Anchor) If you have enjoyed the representative selection in the text, you will want to read the remainder of this realistic portrayal of life at sea.

THARP, LOUISE HALL, *The Peabody Sisters of Salem.* (Little) The Peabody sisters numbered three: Elizabeth, forceful and intellectual, started the first kindergarten in America; Mary, the kind and gentle-mannered schoolteacher, became the wife of Horace Mann, the educator; and Sophia, the lovely and artistic invalid, married Nathaniel Hawthorne.

THOREAU, HENRY DAVID, *Walden.* (Harper •Dolphin) If you have enjoyed the selections from *Walden* in your anthology, you will want to learn more of Thoreau's solitary sojourn of two years in a cabin on Walden Pond.

WHITTIER, JOHN GREENLEAF, *Snowbound and Other Poems,* edited by Bliss Perry. (Houghton) Whittier expresses ideas and events in words alive with emotion. He is at his best in this well-edited collection.

•paperback ••paperback and hard-cover

chapter five Conflict

When Thoreau was sent to Concord jail in 1846 for refusing to pay his poll tax, he was protesting against the Mexican War— a war in which Ulysses S. Grant and Robert E. Lee fought side by side. Fifteen years later these same men were ranged on opposite sides, and the nation which Emerson had exhorted to greatness was riven by the War Between the States.

All during the second quarter of the nineteenth century, tension had been slowly mounting between the North and the South. Even as the nation achieved its continental destiny and embraced all the lands westward to the Pacific, while industrial towns multiplied in the North and cotton became king in the South, a developing antagonism flawed the relations between sections. The threat of secession hung in the air. On the floor of the United States Senate, the country's great orators—Daniel Webster, Henry Clay, and John C. Calhoun—debated the burning issues. "Liberty *and* Union, one and inseparable, now and forever," urged Webster of Massachusetts. "The South asks for justice, simple justice, and less she ought not to take," countered Calhoun of South Carolina. As the 1850's wore on, the struggle for men's minds and loyalties intensified. This struggle was waged not only in the oratory of statesmen but also in the homely dialect of frontiersmen, and in a steady stream of verse, stories, and editorials. Then in April of 1861 debate was drowned by the guns of Fort Sumter and the nation found itself at war.

The poet Walt Whitman, writing soon after the Battle of Chancellorsville in the fateful days of 1863, raised the question: "What history, I say, can ever give—for who can know—the mad, determin'd tussle of the armies, in all their separate large and little squads ... ? Who knows the conflict, hand-to-hand—the many conflicts in the dark, those shadowy-tangled, flashing-moonbeam'd woods—the writhing groups and squads—the cries, the din, the cracking guns and pistols—the distant cannon—the cheers and calls and threats ... the flash of the naked sword, and rolling flame and smoke ... ? Of scenes like these, I say, who writes—whoe'er can write the story?" Yet Walt Whitman himself and other writers like Henry Timrod, Paul Hamilton Hayne, and Abram Ryan did record in poetry the ideals, the glory, and the anguish of those days. And among others Robert E. Lee and Abraham Lincoln in their prose bore witness to the honor and the compassion that sustained men of both sides throughout the conflict.

Walt Whitman

1819-1892

Although Walt Whitman was born in the same year as Lowell and only two years after Thoreau, there are reasons for considering him a writer of the Period of Conflict rather than a representative of America's Golden Day. He was profoundly influenced by the war years 1861-1865. His living and his writing showed the growing importance of the city, of industry and science, in American life. He used new forms for his poetry. His ideas about democracy, internationalism, and immortality were molded by the thinking of his times. And it was not until long after the New England group of writers had passed their prime that he won acceptance as a towering figure in American poetry.

THE EARLY WHITMAN

Walter Whitman, born May 31, 1819, on a farm at West Hills, Long Island, moved to Brooklyn with his family when he was four, and lived there until he was well-grown. He was, nevertheless, a child of the country. Brooklyn itself in the poet's youth was really a quiet little village. While living there, he roamed the nearby countryside, and frequently he paid long visits to his grandparents on their Long Island farms. His youth, too, was associated with the country. After learning the printer's trade, he not

only set type but also reported for little local newspapers. He ranged through the farm districts to collect news from the farmers. Between 1836 and 1841, when the printing business was slack, he taught in a number of schools. He "boarded out" with the families of his students, and found his acquaintance with farm people (as he said later) "one of my best experiences and deepest lessons in human nature."

As Whitman grew older, he felt the pull of the rapidly expanding cities. Work of the sort he wanted and living of the sort he appreciated were to be found in nearby New York. So between 1839 and 1848 he worked on newspapers in New York as well as in Brooklyn, and he greatly enjoyed the big city.

He was fascinated by the crowds on the ferryboats. He went regularly to theaters, concert halls, and opera houses. He dined and chatted with a Bohemian group of authors in Pfaff's basement restaurant under the Broadway sidewalks. He found pleasure in the sight of the moving Broadway crowds. On that great street, as he said, there was "always something novel or inspiriting."

WALT WHITMAN HOUSE

He was particularly fond of riding the Broadway omnibuses and talking with their colorful drivers. These men were, he felt, "a strange, natural, quick-eyed and wondrous race." "How many hours," he wrote, "forenoons and afternoons—how many exhilarating nighttimes I have had ... riding the whole length of Broadway, listening to some yarn ... or perhaps I declaiming some stormy passage from *Julius Caesar* or *Richard*[1] (you could roar as loudly as you chose in that heavy, dense, uninterrupted street bass). Yes, I knew all the drivers then: Broadway Jack, Dressmaker, Balky Bill, George Storms, Old Elephant, his brother Young Elephant (who came afterward), Tippy, Pop Rice, Big Frank, Yellow Frank, Yellow Joe, Pete Callahan, Patsey Dee, and dozens more...."

Whitman, country-bred though he was, apparently tried to show that he was at home in the city by becoming a good deal of a dandy. Descriptions of him at the time picture him as a graceful six-footer with a neatly trimmed pointed beard and dressed in the height of fashion. He wore a stylish beaver hat at an angle; he had a boutonniere on the lapel of his frock coat; he carried a cane. His trousers were immaculate and fashion-

---

1. "*Richard.*" The reference may be to either *Richard II* or *Richard III*, both historical plays by Shakespeare.

Broadway in 1857.

able, and his boots were brightly polished. A picture of him in this period reminds us of an old-time fashion plate.

And just as his clothes resembled those turned out by the most popular tailors, his writings at this time resembled those of the most popular authors. As yet, Whitman had not learned how to turn his own life and his own thoughts into literature. Practically none of his knowledge and feeling—about farms and farmers, about city streets and their teeming life —came into what he wrote. In a period during which sentimentalism and moralizing were the mode, Walter Whitman wrote and published pathetic stories, a hectic and preachy "temperance novel," and poems which were trite in their wording and sentimental in their feeling.

Young Grimes

When old Grimes died, he left a
    son—
    The graft of worthy stock;
In deed and word he shows himself
    A chip of the old block.

In youth, 'tis said, he liked not school— 5
    Of tasks he was no lover;
He wrote sums in a ciphering book,
    Which had a pasteboard cover.

Young Grimes ne'er went to see the girls
    Before he was fourteen; 10
Nor smoked, nor swore, for that he knew
    Gave Mrs. Grimes much pain.

He never was extravagant
    In pleasure, dress, or board;
His Sunday suit was of blue cloth, 15
    At six and eight a yard.[1]

But still there is, to tell the truth,
    No stinginess in him;
And in July he wears an old
    Straw hat with a broad brim. 20

No devotee in fashion's train
    Is good old Grimes' son;
He sports no cane—no whiskers wears,
    Nor lounges o'er the town.

He does not spend more than he earns 25
    In dissipation's round;

But shuns with care those dangerous rooms
    Where vice and sin abound.

It now is eight and twenty years
    Since young Grimes saw the light; 30
And no house in the land can show
    A fairer, prouder sight.

For there his wife, prudent and chaste,
    His mother's age made sweet,
His children trained in virtue's path, 35
    The gazer's eye will meet.

Upon a hill, just off the road
    That winds the village side,
His farmhouse stands, within whose door
    Ne'er entered Hate or Pride. 40

But Plenty and Benevolence
    And Happiness are there—
And underneath that lowly roof
    Content smiles calm and fair.

Reader, go view the cheerful scene— 45
    By it how poor must prove
The pomp, and tinsel, and parade,
    Which pleasure's followers love.

Leave the wide city's noisy din—
    The busy haunts of men— 50
And here enjoy a tranquil life,
    Unvexed by guilt or pain.

---

1. At six and eight a yard, at six shillings and eight pence, or about $1.60, a yard. At the time Whitman wrote the poem (1839), most woolens were imported from England and their prices were quoted in English money.

It is safe to say that if Whitman had continued to write the sort of verse he turned out in the first years of his career no one would be likely to remember him today. But in the late 1840's and the early 1850's, something changed the man, and the change showed in his work. Some revolution in his personality, in his way of thinking and feeling, in his way of writing, made him a different—and a great—poet. Most important of all, he became a poet of vast and expanding horizons, encompassing in his vision the entire nation.

The results of the change were shown in a book which Whitman published at his own expense in 1855. This was the first edition of *Leaves of Grass*. Even the portrait of Whitman on the title page provided a sharp contrast with the elegant dandy pictured earlier. Here was a man with a rough, untrimmed beard. His hat was battered. He was in shirt sleeves, and the open collar of his shirt revealed the top of flannel underwear. His trousers, far from being elegant, were the dungarees of a laboring man. This, the book revealed, was not *Walter* Whitman but *Walt* Whitman—a seemingly new personality.

The poems differed as much from the earlier poems as Walt differed from Walter. Here, for instance, was the opening of a new poem:

There was a child went forth every day,
And the first object he looked upon and received with wonder or pity or love
    or dread, that object he became,
And that object became part of him for the day or a certain part of the day . . .
    or for many years or stretching cycles of years.

The early lilacs became part of the child,
And grass, and white and red morning-glories, and white and red clover, and
    the song of the phoebe bird,
And the March-born lambs, and the sow's pink-faint litter, and the mare's foal,
    and the cow's calf, and the noisy brood of the barnside or by the mire of
    the pondside . . . and the fish suspending themselves so curiously below
    there . . . and the beautiful curious liquid . . . and the water plants with
    their graceful flat heads . . . all became part of him.

Notice that rhyme has disappeared, and that the rhythm is quite different from that of the conventional poetry of the period. Notice too that instead of echoing the ideas and words of other poets—instead of writing what he now called "a poem distilled from poems"—Whitman is talking, in a new manner, of life as he himself has known it. He is giving a very personal interpretation of his Long Island boyhood. He expresses himself in language which is more like common talk, more simple and idiomatic, than most poets were using at that time. And this poem represents the whole book of poems which Printer Whitman set up in type and printed with his own hands.

Readers of the present day see *Leaves of Grass* as the book in which Whitman's poetic powers became evident; but when the book first appeared, reviewers either ignored it or sternly criticized it. Workers in a New York newspaper office listened to excerpts and roared with laughter. The poet Whittier read a little in the copy which Walt had sent him and then disgustedly flung the book into the blazing grate. But Whitman, serenely sure that he spoke for all America and that in time his poetry would be appreciated, prepared a second edition, with several new poems, in 1856, and a third in 1860. And as the years passed, Whitman continued to revise and enlarge *Leaves of Grass,* weaving new poems from new experiences until he came to think of the book as a kind of autobiography.

What changed Walter Whitman to Walt Whitman, and replaced the conventional verse and hackneyed ideas of "Young Grimes" with the free rhythms and new ideas of *Leaves of Grass?* Whitman himself thought that he had grown up. "I found myself possessed," he wrote, "at the age of thirty-one to thirty-three, with a special desire and conviction . . . a desire that had been flitting through my previous life, or hovering on the flanks, most indefinitely hitherto, had steadily advanced to the front, defined itself, and finally dominated everything else."

Students of Whitman find that several other influences were at work. They notice, for instance, that Whitman was a great reader of the Bible, and that some of his rhythms are much like those of the poetic parts of that book. They point out that Whitman was, like many in his day, much interested in oratory. It was a time when many of the greatest leaders were great public speakers, too—Daniel Webster, Wendell Phillips, Henry Clay, Edward Everett, and others. In New York, Whitman had haunted the law courts and had heard great speakers in many meetings. He was to write enviously of the power of the public speaker:

O the orator's joys!
To inflate the chest—to roll the thunder of the voice from the ribs and throat,
To make the people rage, weep, desire, with yourself,
To lead America—to quell America with a great tongue.

The passages from Shakespeare which Whitman intoned on omnibuses were declamatory speeches. It was not strange, therefore, such critics claim, that the form—the organization and the rhythm—of Whitman's new poetry resembled that of oratory. Whitman always believed that his poems should be read much as orations were, that they should be chanted and intoned.

Critics also point out that various earlier poets had prepared the way for the new verse form, which is of a type commonly called *free verse.* During the first part of the nineteenth century, quite a few poets in England and the United States had experimented with verse forms which broke away from the regular rhythms of the older poetry. In England, there had been Coleridge and Blake; in America, Emerson, Thoreau, and Lowell—and in both countries there had been experimenters less famous than these. Whitman, therefore, in writing his free verse, merely pushed to an extreme what others had done on a smaller scale.

So much for the new form of Whitman's poetry. But what of the new substance, the new attitudes, the new feelings which it presented? Probably the substance was drawn in part from life itself, in part from the influence of certain books which the poet read.

Whitman's work, it happened, introduced him to some aspects of American living and thinking which were important in his new songs. As a newspaper reporter and as a schoolteacher, he had come to know how farmers lived, how they felt about many subjects. In 1848, having been employed by a New Orleans newspaper, he journeyed for the first time beyond Long Island and New York. By coach he followed the trail of the

Title page of the first edition.

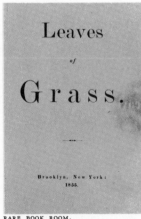

pioneers through Cumberland Gap to Wheeling, then went by boat down the Ohio and the Mississippi. When his work in New Orleans was completed, he traveled home again by way of the pioneer highway first used by the early French explorers—the Mississippi River and the Great Lakes. During his journeys of five thousand miles he became aware of the vast unsettled expanses of the country and caught the frontier point of view. He witnessed the struggle of farmers, frontiersmen, and workmen to gain further social and economic rights. They wanted equality of opportunity, so that they might flourish in what they believed was a great land of opportunity. When Whitman returned to Brooklyn, he himself became a laborer, working as a carpenter on houses his father was erecting in the fast-growing city. Thus Whitman, in fact and in sympathy, as the costume he wore in his new picture showed, aligned himself with the toilers.

And it happened that Whitman's reading, in this period of his development, emphasized similar ideas. Very important to him were the writings of Ralph Waldo Emerson, who was urging his fellow countrymen to do their own thinking, to be independent and self-sufficient, to be democratic. Whitman spoke of Emerson's importance to his own development: "I was simmering, simmering. Emerson brought me to a boil."

So the new Whitman, employing the new verse form which he had developed, preached the individualistic ideas about democracy prevalent in the swaggering new country. The long, loosely organized "Song of Myself," sections from which are printed on the next page, is often considered the most thoroughly democratic poem ever written. Although it is entitled "Song of Myself," Whitman imagines himself as speaking through it for all Americans.

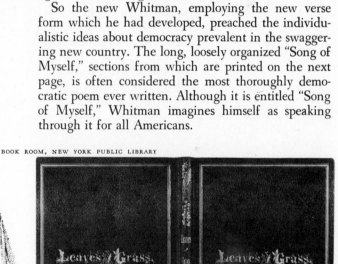

RARE BOOK ROOM, NEW YORK PUBLIC LIBRARY

Left: The "new" Walt Whitman as he appeared on the frontispiece of the first edition of Leaves of Grass. *Above: The binding of the first edition.*

FROM *Song of Myself*

16

I am of old and young, of the foolish as much as the wise,
Regardless of others, ever regardful of others,
Maternal as well as paternal, a child as well as a man,
Stuff'd with the stuff that is coarse and stuff'd with the stuff that is fine,
One of the Nation of many nations, the smallest the same and the largest the same,   5
A Southerner soon as a Northerner, a planter nonchalant and hospitable down by the
    Oconee[1] I live,
A Yankee bound my own way ready for trade, my joints the limberest joints on earth
    and the sternest joints on earth,
A Kentuckian walking the vale of the Elkhorn[2] in my deerskin leggings, a Louisianian
    or Georgian,
A boatman over lakes or bays or along coasts, a Hoosier, Badger, Buckeye[3];
At home on Canadian snowshoes or up in the bush, or with fishermen off
    Newfoundland,   10
At home in the fleet of iceboats, sailing with the rest and tacking,
At home on the hills of Vermont or in the woods of Maine, or the Texan ranch,
Comrade of Californians, comrade of free North-Westerners (loving their big
    proportions),
Comrade of raftsmen and coalmen, comrade of all who shake hands and welcome to
    drink and meat,
A learner with the simplest, a teacher of the thoughtfulest,   15
A novice beginning yet experient of myriads of seasons,
Of every hue and caste am I, of every rank and religion,
A farmer, mechanic, artist, gentleman, sailor, Quaker,
Prisoner, fancy-man, rowdy, lawyer, physician, priest.

I resist any thing better than my own diversity,   20
Breathe the air but leave plenty after me,
And am not stuck up, and am in my place.

(The moth and the fish eggs are in their place,
The bright suns I see and the dark suns I cannot see are in their place,
The palpable is in its place and the impalpable is in its place.)   25

17

These are really the thoughts of all men in all ages and lands, they are not original
    with me,
If they are not yours as much as mine they are nothing, or next to nothing,
If they are not the riddle and the untying of the riddle they are nothing,
If they are not just as close as they are distant they are nothing.

This is the grass that grows wherever the land is and the water is,   30
This the common air that bathes the globe.

---

1. *Oconee* (ō kō′nē), a river in Georgia.   **2.** *Elkhorn*, a creek in northern Kentucky.   **3.** *Hoosier, Badger, Buckeye*, names popularly applied to inhabitants of Indiana, Wisconsin, and Ohio, respectively.

To the patriotic Whitman the debates and political events which threatened to embroil the nation in civil war were profoundly disturbing. He
loved the South as much as the North, and he distrusted the political
leaders of both sections. He believed that slavery would in time disappear,
and he had little sympathy with the extreme abolitionists. The war,
when it came, was a bitter disillusion to him; he had hoped for better
things from American democracy. Once war came, however, his devotion
to the Union led him to identify himself with this section rather more
fully than his earlier philosophy might lead one to expect. Yet he was
not a poet of hatred. His war poems ring more with the personal dis-
locations of war than with martial music, although "Beat! Beat! Drums!"
(page 340) accepts the challenge of combat.

Whitman's mother's family had been Quakers, and it was perhaps because of this Quaker background that Whitman did not enlist. His first-
hand experience of the war began in 1862, when he went to Virginia to
care for his brother George, who had been wounded. His brother had
almost recovered when the poet arrived, but Whitman worked in the field
hospital, helped convoy some of the wounded to a Washington hospital,
and volunteered as a male nurse.

Until late in 1864 Whitman served in the various hospitals and in
nearby army camps. He visited the wards and tried to supply what the
wounded and sick men needed—sweets, perhaps, or tobacco, or writing
paper, or money. He read to some, wrote letters for others. His chief
service, in his opinion, however, was simply indicating a personal interest
in the men. "The American soldier," he wrote, "is full of affection and
the yearning for affection. And it comes wonderfully grateful to him to
have this yearning gratified when he is laid up with painful wounds or
illness, far away from home, among strangers." Again, he wrote in a
letter: "Mother, I have real pride in telling you that I have the consciousness of saving quite a number of lives by saving the soldiers from
giving up—and being a good deal with them. The men say it is so, and
the doctors say it is so—and I will candidly confess I can see it is true,
though I say it of myself. I know you will like to hear it, so I tell
you." Our knowledge of psychology helps us understand that Whitman
probably was reporting accurately on his achievements. His friendliness
was an antidote for shock and stimulated the will to live.

*Carver Hospital,
similar to those in
which Whitman
served. The
photograph is
by Mathew Brady,
the first man
to make extensive
coverage of a
war in photo-
graphs.*

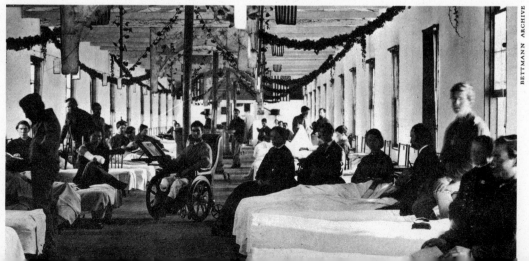

Beat! Beat! Drums!

Beat! beat! drums!—blow! bugles! blow!
Through the windows—through doors—burst like a ruthless force,
Into the solemn church, and scatter the congregation,
Into the school where the scholar is studying;
Leave not the bridegroom quiet—no happiness must he have now with his bride,   5
Nor the peaceful farmer any peace, plowing his field or gathering his grain,
So fierce you whirr and pound you drums—so shrill you bugles blow.

Beat! beat! drums!—blow! bugles! blow!
Over the traffic of cities—over the rumble of wheels in the streets;
Are beds prepared for sleepers at night in the houses? no sleepers must sleep in those   10
      beds,
No bargainers' bargains by day—no brokers or speculators—would they continue?
Would the talkers be talking? would the singer attempt to sing?
Would the lawyer rise in the court to state his case before the judge?
Then rattle quicker, heavier drums—you bugles wilder blow.

Beat! beat! drums!—blow! bugles! blow!   15
Make no parley—stop for no expostulation,
Mind not the timid—mind not the weeper or prayer,
Mind not the old man beseeching the young man,
Let not the child's voice be heard, nor the mother's entreaties,
Make even the trestles to shake the dead where they lie awaiting the hearses,   20
So strong you thump O terrible drums—so loud you bugles blow.

Cavalry Crossing a Ford

A line in long array where they wind betwixt green islands,
They take a serpentine course, their arms flash in the sun—hark to the musical clank,
Behold the silvery river, in it the splashing horses loitering stop to drink,
Behold the brown-faced men, each group, each person a picture, the negligent rest on
      the saddles,
Some emerge on the opposite bank, others are just entering the ford—while,   5
Scarlet and blue and snowy white,
The guidon flags flutter gaily in the wind.

As Toilsome I Wander'd Virginia's Woods

As toilsome I wander'd Virginia's woods,
To the music of rustling leaves, kick'd by my feet (for 'twas autumn),
I mark'd at the foot of a tree the grave of a soldier,
Mortally wounded he, and buried on the retreat (easily all could I understand)

The halt of a mid-day hour, when up! no time to lose—yet this sign left,   5
On a tablet scrawl'd and nail'd on the tree by the grave,
Bold, cautious, true, and my loving comrade.

Long, long I muse, then on my way go wandering;
Many a changeful season to follow, and many a scene of life;
Yet at times through changeful season and scene, abrupt, alone, or in the crowded
    street,   10
Comes before me the unknown soldier's grave—comes the inscription rude in Virginia's
    woods,
Bold, cautious, true, and my loving comrade.

When Lilacs Last in the Dooryard Bloomed

Walt Whitman first saw Lincoln in 1861, and was much impressed by his appearance. Later, working with the wounded in Washington, and seeing the President almost daily, Whitman came to have great faith in him and love for him.

Lincoln was assassinated April 14, 1865, and Whitman heard the news the next day in Brooklyn. "There were many lilacs in full bloom," said Whitman later. "I find myself always reminded of the great tragedy of that day by the sight and odor of these blossoms. It never fails."

This memory went into the poem which Whitman wrote about Lincoln's death. Like most elegies, it begins with lamentation (sections 1-12), and after a transition (section 13) concludes with consolation (sections 14-16).

1

When lilacs last in the dooryard bloomed,
And the great star early drooped in the western sky in the night,
I mourned, and yet shall mourn with ever-returning spring.

Ever-returning spring, trinity sure to me you bring,
Lilac blooming perennial and drooping star in the west,   5
And thought of him I love.

2

O powerful western fallen star!
O shades of night—O moody, tearful night!
O great star disappeared—O the black murk that hides the star!
O cruel hands that hold me powerless—O helpless soul of me!   10
O harsh surrounding cloud that will not free my soul.

3

In the dooryard fronting an old farmhouse near the whitewashed palings,
Stands the lilac bush tall-growing with heart-shaped leaves of rich green,
With many a pointed blossom rising delicate, with the perfume strong I love,
With every leaf a miracle—and from this bush in the dooryard,   15
With delicate-colored blossoms and heart-shaped leaves of rich green,
A sprig with its flower I break.

4

In the swamp in secluded recesses,
A shy and hidden bird is warbling a song.
Solitary the thrush,   20
The hermit withdrawn to himself, avoiding the settlements,
Sings by himself a song.

Song of the bleeding throat,
Death's outlet song of life (for well dear brother I know,
If thou wast not granted to sing thou would'st surely die).   25

5

Over the breast of the spring, the land, amid cities,
Amid lanes and through old woods, where lately the violets peeped from the ground,
        spotting the gray debris,
Amid the grass in the fields each side of the lanes, passing the endless grass,
Passing the yellow-speared wheat, every grain from its shroud in the dark brown fields
        uprisen,
Passing the apple-tree blows[1] of white and pink in the orchards,   30
Carrying a corpse to where it shall rest in the grave,
Night and day journeys a coffin.

6

Coffin that passes through lanes and streets,
Through day and night with the great cloud darkening the land,
With the pomp of the inlooped flags with the cities draped in black,   35
With the show of the States themselves as of crape-veiled women standing,
With processions long and winding and the flambeaus of the night,
With the countless torches lit, with the silent sea of faces and the unbared heads,
With the waiting depot, the arriving coffin, and the somber faces,
With dirges through the night, with the thousand voices rising strong and solemn,   40
With all the mournful voices of the dirges poured around the coffin,
The dim-lit churches and the shuddering organs—where amid these you journey,
With the tolling tolling bells' perpetual clang,
Here, coffin that slowly passes,
I give you my sprig of lilac.   45

7

(Nor for you, for one alone,
Blossoms and branches green to coffins all I bring,
For fresh as the morning, thus would I chant a song for you O sane and sacred death.

All over bouquets of roses,
O death, I cover you over with roses and early lilies,   50
But mostly and now the lilac that blooms the first,
Copious I break, I break the sprigs from the bushes,
With loaded arms I come, pouring for you,
For you and the coffins all of you O death.)

---

1. *blows*, blossoms.

O western orb sailing the heaven, 55
Now I know what you must have meant as a month since I walked,
As I walked in silence the transparent shadowy night,
As I saw you had something to tell as you bent to me night after night,
As you drooped from the sky low down as if to my side (while the other stars all
     looked on),
As we wandered together the solemn night (for something I know not what kept me
     from sleep), 60
As the night advanced, and I saw on the rim of the west how full you were of woe,
As I stood on the rising ground in the breeze in the cool transparent night,
As I watched where you passed and was lost in the netherward black[2] of the night,
As my soul in its trouble dissatisfied sank, as where you sad orb,
Concluded, dropt in the night, and was gone. 65

Sing on there in the swamp,
O singer bashful and tender, I hear your notes, I hear your call,
I hear, I come presently, I understand you,
But a moment I linger, for the lustrous star has detained me,
The star my departing comrade holds and detains me. 70

O how shall I warble myself for the dead one there I loved?
And how shall I deck my song for the large sweet soul that has gone?
And what shall my perfume be for the grave of him I love?

Sea-winds blown from east and west,
Blown from the Eastern sea and blown from the Western sea, till there on the prairies
     meeting, 75
These and with these and the breath of my chant,
I'll perfume the grave of him I love.

O what shall I hang on the chamber walls?
And what shall the pictures be that I hang on the walls,
To adorn the burial-house of him I love? 80

Pictures of growing spring and farms and homes,
With the Fourth-month[3] eve at sundown, and the gray smoke lucid and bright,
With floods of the yellow gold of the gorgeous, indolent, sinking sun, burning,
     expanding the air,
With the fresh sweet herbage under foot, and the pale green leaves of the trees prolific,
In the distance the flowing glaze, the breast of the river, with a wind-dapple here and
     there, 85
With ranging hills on the banks, with many a line against the sky, and shadows,
And the city at hand with dwellings so dense, and stacks of chimneys,
And all the scenes of life and the workshops, and the workmen homeward returning.

---

2. *netherward black*, the darkness that seems to hug the region near the horizon. 3. *Fourth-month*, April, the month in which Lincoln was assassinated.

Lo, body and soul—this land,
My own Manhattan with spires, and the sparkling and hurrying tides, and the ships, ⁹⁰
The varied and ample land, the South and the North in the light, Ohio's shores and
      flashing Missouri,
And ever the far-spreading prairies covered with grass and corn.

Lo, the most excellent sun so calm and haughty,
The violet and purple morn with just-felt breezes,
The gentle soft-born measureless light,   95
The miracle spreading bathing all, the fulfilled noon,
The coming eve delicious, the welcome night and the stars,
Over my cities shining all, enveloping man and land.

13

Sing on, sing on you gray-brown bird,
Sing from the swamps, the recesses, pour your chant from the bushes,   100
Limitless out of the dusk, out of the cedars and pines.

Sing on dearest brother, warble your reedy song,
Loud human song, with voice of uttermost woe.

O liquid and free and tender!
O wild and loose to my soul—O wondrous singer!   105
You only I hear—yet the star holds me (but will soon depart),
Yet the lilac with mastering odor holds me.

14

Now while I sat in the day and looked forth,
In the close of the day with its light and the fields of spring, and the farmers preparing
      their crops,
In the large unconscious scenery of my land with its lakes and forests,   110
In the heavenly aerial beauty (after the perturbed winds and the storms),
Under the arching heavens of the afternoon swift passing, and the voices of children
      and women,
The many-moving sea tides, and I saw the ships how they sailed,
And the summer approaching with richness, and the fields all busy with labor,
And the infinite separate houses, how they all went on, each with its meals and minutia
      of daily usages,   115
And the streets how their throbbings throbbed, and the cities pent—lo, then and there,
Falling upon them all and among them all, enveloping me with the rest,
Appeared the cloud, appeared the long black trail,
And I knew death, its thought, and the sacred knowledge of death.

Then with the knowledge of death as walking one side of me,   120
And the thought of death close-walking the other side of me,
And I in the middle as with companions, and as holding the hands of companions,
I fled forth to the hiding receiving night that talks not,
Down to the shores of the water, the path by the swamp in the dimness,
To the solemn shadowy cedars and ghostly pines so still.   125

And the singer so shy to the rest received me,
The gray-brown bird I know received us comrades three,
And he sang the carol of death, and a verse for him I love.
From deep secluded recesses,
From the fragrant cedars and the ghostly pines so still,   130
Came the carol of the bird.

And the charm of the carol rapt me,
As I held as if by their hands my comrades in the night,
And the voice of my spirit tallied the song of the bird.

Come lovely and soothing death,   135
Undulate round the world, serenely arriving, arriving,
In the day, in the night, to all, to each,
Sooner or later delicate death.

Praised be the fathomless universe,
For life and joy, and for objects and knowledge curious,   140
And for love, sweet love—but praise! praise! praise!
For the sure-enwinding arms of cool-enfolding death.

Dark mother always gliding near with soft feet,
Have none chanted for thee a chant of fullest welcome?
Then I chant it for thee, I glorify thee above all,   145
I bring thee a song that when thou must indeed come, come unfalteringly.

Approach strong deliveress,
When it is so, when thou hast taken them I joyously sing the dead,
Lost in the loving floating ocean of thee,
Laved in the flood of thy bliss O death.   150

From me to thee glad serenades,
Dances for thee I propose saluting thee, adornments and feastings for thee,
And the sights of the open landscape and the high-spread sky are fitting,
And life and the fields, and the huge and thoughtful night.

The night in silence under many a star,   155
The ocean shore and the husky whispering wave whose voice I know,
And the soul turning to thee O vast and well-veiled death,
And the body gratefully nestling close to thee.

Over the treetops I float thee a song,
Over the rising and sinking waves, over the myriad fields and the prairies wide,   160
Over the dense-packed cities all and the teeming wharves and ways,
I float this carol with joy, with joy to thee O death.

15

To the tally of my soul,
Loud and strong kept up the gray-brown bird,
With pure deliberate notes spreading, filling the night.   165

Loud in the pines and cedars dim,
Clear in the freshness moist and the swamp perfume,
And I with my comrades there in the night.

While my sight that was bound in my eyes unclosed,
As to long panoramas of visions.   170

And I saw askant the armies,
I saw as in noiseless dreams hundreds of battleflags,
Borne through the smoke of the battles and pierced with missiles I saw them,
And carried hither and yon through the smoke, and torn and bloody,
And at last but a few shreds left on the staffs (and all in silence),   175
And the staffs all splintered and broken.

I saw battle corpses, myriads of them,
And the white skeletons of young men, I saw them,
And I saw the debris and debris of all the slain soldiers of the war,
But I saw they were not as was thought,   180
They themselves were fully at rest, they suffered not,
The living remained and suffered, the mother suffered,
And the wife and the child and the musing comrade suffered,
And the armies that remained suffered.

16

Passing the visions, passing the night,   185
Passing, unloosing the hold of my comrades' hands,
Passing the song of the hermit bird and the tallying song of my soul,
Victorious song, death's outlet song, yet varying ever-altering song,
As low and wailing, yet clear the notes, rising and falling, flooding the night,
Sadly sinking and fainting, as warning and warning, and yet again bursting with
          joy,   190
Covering the earth and filling the spread of the heaven,
As that powerful psalm in the night I heard from recesses,
Passing, I leave thee lilac with heart-shaped leaves,
I leave thee there in the dooryard, blooming, returning with spring.

I cease from my song for thee,   195
From my gaze on thee in the west, fronting the west, communing with thee,
O comrade lustrous with silver face in the night.
Yet each to keep and all, retrievements out of the night,
The song, the wondrous chant of the gray-brown bird,
And the tallying chant, the echo aroused in my soul,   200
With the lustrous and drooping star with the countenance full of woe,
With the holders holding my hand nearing the call of the bird,
Comrades mine and I in the midst, and their memory ever to keep, for the dead I
          loved so well,
For the sweetest, wisest soul of all my days and lands—and this for his dear sake,
Lilac and star and bird twined with the chant of my soul,   205
There in the fragrant pines and the cedars dusk and dim.

The experiences Whitman had as a nurse could not but influence him as a poet. He learned the importance of suffering and the importance of good relationships between human beings. He became more humane, more coöperative, aware not only of freedom but also of responsibility.

Doubtless Whitman's own physical suffering also had its influence. An accidental wound in his hand in August 1863 was followed by blood poisoning. He suffered from malaria. And he worked harder than he should have in the hospitals. Eventually Whitman, who had never been sick, was forced to go to bed for several days at a time. He had "spells of deathly faintness." Finally, he was forced to end his hospital work and return home to Brooklyn. After partial recovery, he returned to Washington in 1865, and worked in various government departments. But he was never to recover his health. In 1869, he was having his "spells" again, and

Portrait by Thomas Eakins, one of America's foremost painters. Of him Whitman said: I never knew of but one artist and that's Tom Eakins who could resist the temptation to see what they think they ought to see rather than what is.

the use of his limbs was impaired. In 1873, he suffered a paralytic stroke which left him partially crippled. He left Washington for Camden, New Jersey, where he lived during the final years of his life.

Whitman, between 1865 and his death, was no longer proclaiming himself "one of the roughs." He was called by his friends "the good gray poet." Admirers who traveled from many parts of the country or even across the ocean to visit him felt that this epithet was appropriate. He sat in an upper room of his house with books, newspapers, galley proofs, and manuscripts littering the floor about him. But visitors forgot their chaotic surroundings as they looked at the poet sitting motionless in his chair. His complexion was a healthy pink. But the face showed the effects of age and suffering; the heavy-lidded blue eyes, glazed and thoughtful, looked into the distance; and the magnificent white beard seemed to emphasize the poet's dignity. There was a spiritual quality in his appearance. Painters, sculptors, and photographers found him a wonderful subject. His songs lacked the vigor, the brutal force, of his earliest songs. They were more pensive and more serene. And his thoughts of men and of life led him to develop new themes.

In Whitman's thinking there was a growing recognition of the dependence of man upon man—a theme which had been only briefly developed in his earlier poems. The war, naturally enough, emphasized Whitman's love for the United States as a nation. Now in the years after the War Between the States, as America became more and more of a force in world affairs, Whitman looked beyond the boundaries of his own country. He wrote a poem to France in 1871, to Brazil—newly made a republic—in the same year, to Spain in 1873. The poet who had believed that America must break away from the Old World ways now emphasized the fact that our country could learn much from the older nations. His "Passage to India" (page 349) is a moving plea for the physical, intellectual, and spiritual unity of all the nations of the world.

Another developing theme concerned death. In the early years of his career, Whitman had thought little of this subject. In 1855, when he first published *Leaves of Grass*, death to him had simply meant that the physical body returned to nature:

> I bequeath myself to the dirt to grow from the grass I love,
> If you want me again look for me under your boot soles.

But Whitman's experiences in caring for the wounded during the Civil War had caused him to see death as an important element in the whole career of man. The tragic death of Lincoln had strengthened this feeling. Whitman's own illness, too, had forced him to come face to face with the problems of man's mortality. Long before, like Emerson and Thoreau, Whitman had seen the significance and importance of all material things. Now he came to see that even death was a part of the total scheme. He became convinced that "the untold want by life and land ne'er granted" could be satisfied only when the voyager reached the land of death. The only true life, he said in his songs, must be that which follows death. And so Whitman became a great poet of immortality.

He faced death with serene confidence. His doctor, Richard Maurice Bucke, wrote: "I watched for years . . . in his sick-room, when from day to day and month to month his life was scarcely worth a week's purchase, and he knew it well; and I learned there for the first time in what spirit a truly heroic soul confronted death. Equally removed from fear and bravado; maintaining absolute equanimity; patient and forbearing; at times suffering but never complaining—so far from it, indeed, that he would rarely acknowledge he was in pain—for many weary, lingering months he awaited with calmness and resignation the inevitable end. He never for a moment lost the sweetness and charm of his habitual manner." The end came March 26, 1892.

During his last years, Whitman began to win solid recognition. A number of the leading literary men of England praised and published his work, and more and more Americans came to admire it. After his death, his reputation continued to grow, and today he is generally classed among the greatest American poets.

FROM *Passage to India*

1

Singing my days,
Singing the great achievements of the present,
Singing the strong light works of engineers,
Our modern wonders (the antique ponderous Seven[1] outvied):
In the Old World the east, the Suez Canal,[2]   5
The New by its mighty railroad[3] spanned. . . .

2

Passage to India!
Lo soul, seest thou not God's purpose from the first?
The earth to be spanned, connected by network, . . .
The oceans to be crossed, the distant brought near,   10
The lands to be welded together.

A worship new I sing,
You captains, voyagers, explorers, yours,
You engineers, you architects, machinists, yours,
You, not for trade or transportation only,   15
But in God's name, and for thy sake O soul.

3

Passage to India!
Lo soul for thee of tableaus twain.
I see in one the Suez Canal initiated, opened,
I see the procession of steamships, the Empress Eugenie's leading the van,[4]   20

---

1. *Seven*, the seven wonders of the ancient world. These were the Pyramids of Egypt, the great lighthouse at Alexandria in Egypt, the hanging gardens of Babylon, the temple of Diana at Ephesus (ef'ə səs) in Asia Minor, the statue of Jupiter by Phidias (fid'i əs), the Mausoleum (magnificent tomb) at Halicarnassus (hal'ə kär nas'əs) in Asia Minor, and the Colossus of Rhodes, a huge statue of the god Apollo.   2. *Suez* (sü ez' *or* sü'ez) *Canal*, completed in 1867 and formally opened two years later. It separated Asia and Africa by cutting through the Isthmus of Suez, and shortened the passage to India from Europe by thousands of miles.   3. *mighty railroad*, the Union Pacific, the first railroad linking East and West. It was completed in 1869.   4. *the Empress Eugenie's leading the van*. Since the Suez Canal had been constructed by a French company, the honor of leading the ships of various countries through it at the formal opening fell to a French ship. Guest of honor on this ship was Empress Eugénie (œ zhä në'), wife of Napoleon III, emperor of France.

I mark from on deck the strange landscape, the pure sky, the level sand in the distance,
I pass swiftly the picturesque groups, the workmen gathered,
The gigantic dredging machines.

In one again, different (yet thine, all thine, O soul, the same),
I see over my own continent the Pacific railroad surmounting every barrier,   25
I see continual trains of cars winding along the Platte[5] carrying freight and passengers,
I hear the locomotives rushing and roaring, and the shrill steam whistle,
I hear the echoes reverberate through the grandest scenery in the world,
I cross the Laramie plains,[6] I note the rocks in grotesque shapes, the buttes,
I see the plentiful larkspur and wild onions, the barren, colorless, sage deserts,   30
I see in glimpses afar or towering immediately above me the great mountains, I see the
       Wind River and the Wasatch Mountains,[7]
I see the Monument Mountain[8] and the Eagle's Nest,[9] I pass the Promontory,[10] I
       ascend the Nevadas,[11]
I scan the noble Elk Mountain[12] and wind around its base,
I see the Humboldt Range,[13] I thread the valley and cross the river,
I see the clear waters of Lake Tahoe,[14] I see forests of majestic pines,   35
Or crossing the great desert, the alkaline plains, I behold enchanting mirages of waters
       and meadows,
Marking through these and after all, in duplicate slender lines,
Bridging the three or four thousand miles of land travel,
Tying the Eastern to the Western sea,
The road between Europe and Asia.   40
(Ah Genoese, thy dream![15] thy dream!
Centuries after thou art laid in thy grave,
The shore thou foundest verifies thy dream.)

4

Passage to India!
Struggles of many a captain, tales of many a sailor dead,   45
Over my mood stealing and spreading they come,
Like clouds and cloudlets in the unreached sky.

Along all history, down the slopes,
As a rivulet running, sinking now, and now again to the surface rising,
A ceaseless thought, a varied train—lo, soul, to thee, thy sight, they rise,   50
The plans, the voyages again, the expeditions;
Again Vasco da Gama[16] sails forth,

---

5. *the Platte*, a river flowing into the Missouri. The Union Pacific follows it across Nebraska. Footnotes 5-14 identify places Whitman mentions as being visible from the Union Pacific. However, since at the time this poem was written Whitman had never traveled west of the Mississippi, he was uncertain of his geography, and several of the places are mentioned in incorrect order. 6. *Laramie plains*, level uplands in eastern Wyoming. 7. *the Wind River and the Wasatch* (wô′sach) *Mountains*. The Wind River Mountains are in western Wyoming; the Wasatch Mountains in Utah. 8. *Monument Mountain*, probably Monument Peak near Elko in northeastern Nevada. 9. *Eagle's Nest*, possibly a reference to Eagle Peak, located in western Nevada, just east of Reno. 10. *the Promontory*, the point near Salt Lake, Utah, at which the railroad gangs laying the track west met those coming east from California. 11. *the Nevadas*, the Sierra Nevada Mountains on the Nevada-California border. 12. *Elk Mountain*, a peak in the Medicine Bow Range in Wyoming. 13. *Humboldt Range*, a mountain range in western Nevada. 14. *Lake Tahoe* (tä′hō or tä′hō), a mountain lake in California and Nevada. 15. *Genoese* (jen′ō ēz′), *thy dream*. Columbus, who was born in Genoa, Italy, was seeking a route to India when he discovered America. 16. *Vasco da Gama* (väs′kō də gä′mə), Portuguese navigator who rounded the Cape of Good Hope and made the first journey by sea from Europe to India in 1497-1498.

Again the knowledge gained, the mariner's compass,
Lands found and nations born, thou born America.
For purpose vast, man's long probation filled,
Thou rondure[17] of the world at last accomplished.

5

O vast Rondure, swimming in space,
Covered all over with visible power and beauty,
Alternate light and day and the teeming spiritual darkness,
Unspeakable high processions of sun and moon and countless stars above,
Below, the manifold grass and waters, animals, mountains, trees,
With inscrutable purpose, some hidden prophetic intention,
Now first it seems my thought begins to span thee. . . .

6

Year at whose wide-flung door I sing!
Year of the purpose accomplished!
Year of the marriage of continents, climates, and oceans! . . .
O sun and moon and all you stars! Sirius and Jupiter![18]
Passage to you!

Passage, immediate passage! the blood burns in my veins!
Away O soul! hoist instantly the anchor!
Cut the hawsers—haul out—shake out every sail!
Have we not stood here like trees in the ground long enough?
Have we not groveled here long enough, eating and drinking like mere brutes?
Have we not darkened and dazed ourselves with books long enough?

Sail forth—steer for the deep waters only,
Reckless O soul, exploring, I with thee, and thou with me,
For we are bound where mariner has not yet dared to go,
And we will risk the ship, ourselves and all.

O my brave soul!
O farther farther sail!
O daring joy, but safe! are they not all the seas of God?
O farther, farther, farther sail!

Joy, Shipmate, Joy!

Joy, shipmate, joy!
(Pleased to my soul at death I cry);
Our life is closed, our life begins,
The long, long anchorage we leave,
The ship is clear at last, she leaps!
She swiftly courses from the shore,
Joy, shipmate, joy.

---

17. *rondure* (ron'jər), roundness. In the next line Whitman addresses the world as "the round earth" (Rondure).
18. *Sirius* (sir'i əs) *and Jupiter*, the brightest fixed star and the largest planet.

Young Grimes

1. In the biography of the early Whitman you read, "Practically none of his knowledge and feeling ...came into whàt he wrote." (a) How does "Young Grimes" illustrate this statement? (b) How does Young Grimes, as Whitman pictures him, compare with Whitman himself at this period?

2. Most young poets show that they are beginners by using faulty rhymes, limping rhythms, and awkward phrasings. Point out examples of any or all of these.

3. Would you agree that "Young Grimes" is (a) "trite" in its wording, and (b) "sentimental" in its feeling? Account for your answer by pointing to specific passages.

Song of Myself

1. What ideas does Emerson express in "Self-Reliance" that would account for Whitman's comment, "Emerson brought me to a boil"?

2. The picture of Whitman in the first edition of *Leaves of Grass* showed him dressed as a workman rather than as the dandy he had earlier been. (a) Explain how this change in appearance indicates a change in the poet. (b) What circumstances had probably changed Whitman's outlook on life?

3. (a) How does "Song of Myself" differ from "Young Grimes" in language, rhythm, and rhyme? (b) How is Whitman's manner of writing in "Song of Myself" typical of the new Whitman? (c) Compare this poem with contemporary poems of this period and estimate to what extent the unfavorable reception of *Leaves of Grass* was based on the form of the poetry.

4. Whitman expresses the theme of "Song of Myself" in a series of *paradoxes*, or seemingly contradictory statements. For example, he writes, "I am of old and young, of the foolish as much as the wise." Point out other paradoxes in the poem.

5. What evidence do you find that "Song of Myself" was influenced by oratory?

Three Short Poems of War

1. (a) What do the drums symbolize in "Beat! Beat! Drums!"? (b) Mention some of the kinds of people who hear the beating drums. (c) Why does the poet tell of the sound reaching so many different kinds of people?

2. The effects of the drums differ from stanza to stanza. In stanza 1, for instance, the drums are merely heard. (a) What are their effects, by contrast, in stanzas 2 and 3? (b) How does the poem mount to a climax in stanza 3?

3. Point out details in "Cavalry Crossing a Ford" that illustrate Whitman's ability to picture military scenes as sharply as a camera.

4. (a) What is the theme of "As Toilsome I Wander'd Virginia's Woods"? (b) Why do you think Whitman found the inscription unforgettable?

5. (a) Characterize the tone of these war poems. (b) How do they differ from many poems of war?

When Lilacs Last in the Dooryard Bloomed

1. What is the trinity Whitman mentions in the first section as returning with every spring?

2. What does the "powerful western fallen star" (line 7) symbolize?

3. The lilac symbolizes human love and memory. What lines in sections 3 and 7 develop this symbolism?

4. The bird's song symbolizes immortality. Cite lines that you feel best make this symbolism clear, and explain the reasons why these lines suggest immortality.

5. (a) What details are stressed in the description of the funeral procession (sections 5-6)? (b) In what way is section 5 contrasted with section 6? (c) What reason can you give for the poet's use of this contrast?

6. (a) What idea does Whitman introduce in section 7? (b) Why is this section placed in parenthesis?

7. Sections 10-12 are Whitman's lamentations for Lincoln. (a) What is his particular concern in section 10? (b) Are the first three lines of section 11 to be understood literally or figuratively? Explain them. (c) How do the remainder of this section and section 12 elaborate the idea introduced in these lines? (d) Why is Whitman's lament appropriate for Lincoln?

8. (a) Notice that section 13 seems a continuation of section 9. Why is this so? (b) Why is section 13 considered a transitional section?

9. (a) Summarize the thought of section 14, lines 108-115. (b) What is the cloud referred to in line 118? (c) How do you interpret lines 120-125?

10. (a) What is the feeling toward death in the lyric which begins "Come lovely and soothing death" (line 135)? (b) How do this lyric and the succeeding sections vary in tone and mood from the earlier portions of the poem?

11. What resemblances can you cite between this poem and the selection from "Song of Myself"?

Passage to India and Joy, Shipmate, Joy!

1. (a) What is the theme of "Passage to India"? (b) How does this theme reflect Whitman's concerns in his later years?

2. (a) What two specific historical events are

commemorated in "Passage to India"? (b) Why were these events important to Whitman?

3. (a) What is the poet's meaning in lines 69-82? (b) What is their relationship to the poem as a whole? (c) What resemblance do you find between these lines and "Joy, Shipmate, Joy!"?

4. Why is Whitman considered a great poet of immortality?

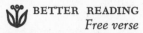 BETTER READING
Free verse

Although the type of verse that Walt Whitman used in *Leaves of Grass* differed greatly from that which Longfellow, Holmes, and Whittier were writing at the same time, yet it was not something completely new. Free verse, as distinguished from conventional verse, had appeared in the Psalms of David and the Song of Solomon centuries before Christ; Frenchmen and Germans had experimented with the form. But it remained for Whitman to make the modern world aware that poetry need possess neither rhyme nor conventional meter.

The term *free verse* explains itself—it is free: free of the demands of rhyme, free of the necessity of following the stresses of regular metric feet. Free verse must have rhythm, but this rhythm is less regular than that of conventional verse and is achieved by the poet through a subtle handling of the cadences of words, phrases, and lines.

The very absence of regular meter and rhyming lines forces certain problems upon the writer of free verse. In conventional verse the poet determines in what meter a particular idea can best be developed; this meter prescribes the number of feet in each line. How does the free-verse writer decide when a line should end? In Whitman's poetry the determining factor in line length is the unit of expression, or the material that lies naturally between pauses. In rhymed verse the rhyme holds the stanza together and makes evident how many lines comprise a stanza. The writer of free verse must use other devices to gain unity in a stanza. Whitman sometimes makes the stanza a grammatical unit; at other times the stanza is developed as a paragraph would be in prose. Whitman often uses parallel constructions in succeeding lines, sometimes beginning these consecutive lines with the same words.

Free verse makes extensive use of some of the poetic devices used in conventional poetry. Imagery is widely used, and the use of a recurring image, such as the leaf image in section 3 of "When Lilacs Last in the Dooryard Bloomed," is frequent. Alliteration and assonance add to the musical effect of much free verse.

Point out uses of alliteration and assonance in the following lines from "Passage to India."

Lo soul, seest thou not God's purpose from the first?
The earth to be spanned, connected by network, . . .
The oceans to be crossed, the distant brought near,
The lands to be welded together.

Because free verse lacks some of the elements of conventional verse, you will probably find it more difficult to analyze than, for example, a sonnet by Longfellow or a lyric by Poe. For your first attempt choose one stanza of free verse by Whitman. Explain as well as you can the devices the poet has used in achieving rhythm and melody.

 WORDS!

Walt Whitman enjoyed using words of French origin in his poems. *Flambeau, debris,* and *bouquet,* all of which occur in "When Lilacs Last in the Dooryard Bloomed," are such words. Many French words have kept some of the characteristics of French pronunciation. For this reason it is necessary to check carefully the pronunciation of words derived from the French language. Give the correct pronunciation and meaning of *flambeau, debris,* and *bouquet.* (Consult the Glossary to make sure you are right.)

Determine the pronunciation of the italicized words below by consulting the Glossary. Then be prepared (1) to read the sentence aloud as it stands, and (2) to read the sentence, substituting another word or words for the italicized word.

1. Our host at the annual dinner was considered a real *gourmet.*

2. The trappers' usual *rendezvous* was a low bluff beside the river.

3. The *ingénue* wore clothes of a type well suited to a *petite* person.

4. His *ennui* disappeared as he learned that the task would require all his ingenuity.

5. People rushed out of the burning house in various kinds of *dishabille.*

6. A series of *tableaus* representing the growth of the United States concluded the program given by the students.

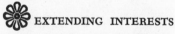 EXTENDING INTERESTS

"Passage to India" expresses Whitman's belief in the need for coöperation among men of all nations. If Whitman were alive today, what do you think would be his viewpoint toward the various agencies designed to promote accord among nations and to secure a better living standard for all peoples? Be as specific as possible in your discussion.

THE MAGAZINE IN AMERICA

Harper's Weekly

During the four momentous years of the War Between the States, *Harper's Weekly* correspondents marched with the armies. From battlefield and army camp they wrote on-the-scene and behind-the-scene stories that made Shiloh and Bull Run, Vicksburg and Malvern Hill vivid to the reader. Even more vivid were the sketches by the magazine's artists—Alfred and William Waud, Thomas Nast, and Winslow Homer—whose pencils captured the horror of battle, the humor of camp, the youthful poignancy of drummer boys. The photographer, Mathew Brady, was a familiar figure to the soldiers as he darted here and there with camera poised to immortalize more than one battlefield and most of the Union generals. *Har-*

CULVER PICTURES

THE ATTACK ON FREDERICKSBURG—THE FORLORN HOPE SCALING THE HILL.—[See Page 827.]

per's Weekly reported the war so completely that official complaint came from the North that the South could learn too much about Union fortifications from the weekly's pages!

The war came at a time when *Harper's Weekly,* America's first news magazine, had created national readership for itself. Founded in 1857 as a "journal of civilization," the weekly gave its readers the one thing they were unable to find in any other magazine—accurate and highly illustrated news coverage. Full-page pictures that told a story were its hallmark. Thus, from the first clash of Union and Confederate arms at Fort Sumter, *Harper's Weekly* had the necessary staff and an ideal format to report the war more completely and graphically than its competitors could.

When the war was over, *Harper's Weekly* turned its vigorous attention to the Tweed Ring, long notorious for its vicious grip on New York politics. One strong editorial after another urged reform, but it was Thomas Nast's cartoons, not words, that aroused public opinion. A cartoon captioned "Let Us Prey," caricaturing the members of the Tweed Ring as vultures, was typical of Nast's attack and proved how cartoons could affect public opinion. At a later date, Nast created the elephant and the donkey as symbols for the Republican and Democratic parties.

Americans today expect to receive almost instantaneous news of war and catastrophe through television, radio, and newspapers. But they also expect to find expert news coverage and analysis in the pages of *Time, Newsweek, U.S. News & World Report,* and the *Reporter,* and picture-stories in *Life, Look,* and *Ebony.* In their reports, cartoons, and illustrations, the modern news magazines have followed the lead of the magazine that "watched" the Civil War—*Harper's Weekly.*

A GROUP OF VULTURES WAITING FOR THE STORM TO "BLOW OVER."—"LET US PREY."

Above: The famous Nast cartoon
on the Tweed ring. Left above:
One of the special reporters for
Harper's Weekly "on his journey-
ings." Left below: A sketch
by one of America's most famous
realist painters, Winslow Homer.

The Southern Cause

Without some sense of the intense devotion of the Southerner to the land in which he lived one cannot understand the Civil War. The land itself was, and is, beautiful, offering almost infinite delights to the senses. Its seacoasts are varied, its plains fertile, and its tree-clad mountains have in the spring an undergrowth of rhododendrons and dogwood. In the generally mild climate flowers bloom in profusion.

In the half century before the Civil War, moreover, the South had a sense of destiny which has seldom been matched in American history. The textile mills of England and the North were insatiable in their demand for cotton, with which to clothe a good part of the world. In producing the cotton, the Southern planters could rightly feel that they were serving a vitally useful function. Not all of them were wealthy, but most aspired to be, and to justify the pursuit of wealth they had the conviction that what they were doing was well worth reward. To most white Southerners, the South was a land apart, a kind of modern Garden of Eden.

Their view of the Negro was essentially patriarchal. Someone, they argued, had to see that the basic needs and the religious instruction of the Negroes were provided for; someone had to care for the uneducated. Such a man as Jefferson Davis seems to have had a deep and humble sense of responsibility, and to have followed what he felt to be his duty as best he could. Men like Davis, and many more whose attitudes are more in question, resented interference from outside and were ready to defend the Southern way of life as, on the whole, the best there was, slavery or no slavery.

Oak Alley, a plantation home in Louisiana overlooking the Mississippi.

Paul Hamilton Hayne 1830-1886

No one of the Southern poets of the Civil War period has better expressed
the physical beauty of the land or more successfully evoked the romantic
mood of the Old South than Paul Hamilton Hayne. He was born and
educated in Charleston, South Carolina. Before the war changed the
course of his life, he had published three volumes of poetry and had won
generous praise from the New England group of poets. During the war his
Charleston home was burned, his library destroyed, his income ended. He
retired to Augusta, Georgia, built himself a simple cottage in a pine grove,
and began to write his best poetry. "Aspects of the Pines" shows the poet's
warm appreciation of nature and explains why he is often called "the poet
of the pines."

Aspects of the Pines

Tall, somber, grim, against the morning sky
 They rise, scarce touched by melancholy airs,
Which stir the fadeless foliage dreamfully,
 As if from realms of mystical despairs.

Tall, somber, grim, they stand with dusky gleams   5
 Brightening to gold within the woodland's core,
Beneath the gracious noontide's tranquil beams—
 But the weird winds of morning sigh no more.

A stillness, strange, divine, ineffable,
 Broods round and o'er them in the wind's surcease, 10
And on each tinted copse and shimmering dell
 Rests the mute rapture of deep-hearted peace.

Last, sunset comes—the solemn joy and might
 Borne from the west when cloudless day declines—
Low, flutelike breezes sweep the waves of light,   15
 And, lifting dark green tresses of the pines,

Till every lock is luminous—gently float,
 Fraught with hale odors up the heavens afar.
To faint when twilight on her virginal throat
 Wears for a gem the tremulous vesper star.   20

Henry Timrod 1828-1867

Southern-born and Southern-educated, Henry Timrod of Charleston is often called "the Laureate of the Confederacy." His "Ethnogenesis" (which may be roughly translated as "the birth of a people") was written in February 1861, while the Southern Congress at Montgomery, Alabama, was framing a constitution for the Confederate States of America. Probably the best expression of the views of the Southern whites at the moment of secession, it combines effectively the Southern love of the South, the Southern sense of the righteousness of the Confederate cause, and the Southern conviction that the Southern way of life should be considered as a model rather than as a shame.

Timrod enlisted in the Confederate army, but because of ill health was able to serve less than a year. Although the remaining years of his short life were a constant struggle against poverty and disease, he managed to produce exquisite poetry in which romantic ardor was balanced by restraint. "Ode Sung on the Occasion of Decorating the Graves of the Confederate Dead, at Magnolia Cemetery, Charleston, S.C." (see page 361), which was written in the last year of his life, is his most famous poem. In its quiet lines sorrow for the destruction of the old way of life replaces the fervor of "Ethnogenesis."

Ethnogenesis

Written During the Meeting of the First Southern Congress, at Montgomery, February 1861

I

Hath not the morning dawned with added light?
And shall not evening call another star
Out of the infinite regions of the night,
To mark this day in Heaven? At last, we are
A nation among nations; and the world   5
Shall soon behold in many a distant port
   Another flag unfurled!
Now, come what may, whose favor need we court?
And, under God, whose thunder need we fear?
   Thank Him who placed us here   10
Beneath so kind a sky—the very sun
Takes part with us; and on our errands run
All breezes of the ocean; dew and rain
Do noiseless battle for us; and the Year,
And all the gentle daughters in her train,   15
March in our ranks, and in our service wield
Long spears of golden grain!
A yellow blossom as her fairy shield,
June flings her azure banner to the wind,
   While in the order of their birth   20
Her sisters pass, and many an ample field

Grows white beneath their steps, till now, behold,
    Its endless sheets unfold
THE SNOW OF SOUTHERN SUMMERS![1] Let the earth
Rejoice! beneath those fleeces soft and warm   25
    Our happy land shall sleep
    In a repose as deep
As if we lay entrenched behind
Whole leagues of Russian ice and Arctic storm!

II

And what if, mad with wrongs themselves have wrought,   30
    In their own treachery caught,
    By their own fears made bold,
    And leagued with him of old,
Who long since in the limits of the North[2]
Set up his evil throne, and warred with God—   35
What if, both mad and blinded in their rage,
Our foes should fling us down their mortal gage,
And with a hostile step profane our sod!
We shall not shrink, my brothers, but go forth
To meet them, marshaled by the Lord of Hosts,   40
And overshadowed by the mighty ghosts
Of Moultrie and Eutaw—who shall foil
Auxiliars such as these?[3] Nor these alone,
    But every stock and stone[4]
    Shall help us; but the very soil,   45
And all the generous wealth it gives to toil,
And all for which we love our noble land,
Shall fight beside, and through us; sea and strand,
    The heart of woman, and her hand,
Tree, fruit, and flower, and every influence,   50
    Gentle, or grave, or grand;
    The winds in our defense
Shall seem to blow; to us the hills shall lend
    Their firmness and their calm;
And in our stiffened sinews we shall blend   55
    The strength of pine and palm!

III

Nor would we shun the battleground,
    Though weak as we are strong;
Call up the clashing elements around,
    And test the right and wrong!   60
On one side, creeds that dare to teach
What Christ and Paul refrained to preach[5];

---

1. *The snow of southern summers*, cotton. 2. *with him . . . of the North*. According to John Milton's epic poem, *Paradise Lost*, Satan retired to the North after revolting against God in Heaven. 3. *mighty ghosts . . . Auxiliars such as these?* Timrod is suggesting that Revolutionary War patriots who fought the British at Fort Moultrie and Eutaw Springs will be allies (Auxiliars) of the South. 4. *every stock and stone*, every senseless (inanimate) thing. 5. *creeds . . . to preach*. Timrod asserts that the creed of the abolitionists has no Biblical authority.

Codes built upon a broken pledge,[6]
And Charity that whets a poniard's edge;
Fair schemes that leave the neighboring poor[7]
To starve and shiver at the schemer's door,
While in the world's most liberal ranks enrolled,
He turns some vast philanthropy to gold;
Religion, taking every mortal form
But that a pure and Christian faith makes warm,
Where not to vile fanatic passion urged,
Or not in vague philosophies submerged,
Repulsive with all Pharisaic leaven,[8]
And making laws to stay the laws of Heaven!
And on the other,[9] scorn of sordid gain,
Unblemished honor, truth without a stain,
Faith, justice, reverence, charitable wealth,
And, for the poor and humble, laws which give,
Not the mean right to buy the right to live,
   But life, and home, and health!
To doubt the end were want of trust in God,
   Who, if He has decreed
   That we must pass a redder sea
Than that which rang to Miriam's holy glee,[10]
   Will surely raise at need
   A Moses with his rod!

65

70

75

80

85

IV

But let our fears—if fears we have—be still,
And turn us to the future! Could we climb
Some mighty Alp, and view the coming time,
The rapturous sight would fill
   Our eyes with happy tears!
Not only for the glories which the years
Shall bring us; not for lands from sea to sea,
And wealth, and power, and peace, though these shall be;
But for the distant peoples we shall bless,
And the hushed murmurs of a world's distress:
For, to give labor to the poor,
   The whole sad planet o'er,
And save from want and crime the humblest door,
Is one among the many ends for which
   God makes us great and rich!
The hour perchance is not yet wholly ripe

90

95

100

---

6. *pledge*, a reference to the protection of slavery under the Constitution. 7. *the neighboring poor*. This refers to the underpaid workers in Northern factories. 8. *Pharisaic* (far'ə sāʹik) *leaven*. The Pharisees were members of an ancient Jewish sect whom Jesus condemned because they made a great outward show of religion without a real sense of spiritual belief. Jesus told his disciples to beware the "Pharisaic leaven." (Luke 18 : 10-14.) By this he meant that a hypocritical outward show of religion alters the true substance of spiritual belief just as leaven, a fermenting agent like yeast, changes the original nature of dough. 9. *And on the other*. The first part of this contrast begins with line 61. 10. *a redder sea . . . Miriam's holy glee*. This is a reference to the crossing of the Red Sea by the Israelites and their subsequent rejoicing. (Exodus 14:15.) Miriam was a sister of Moses.

When all shall own it, but the type
Whereby we shall be known in every land
Is that vast gulf[11] which lips our Southern strand,   105
And through the cold, untempered ocean pours
Its genial streams, that far off Arctic shores
May sometimes catch upon the softened breeze
Strange tropic warmth and hints of summer seas.

Ode

Sleep sweetly in your humble graves,
  Sleep, martyrs of a fallen cause;
Though yet no marble column[1] craves
  The pilgrim here to pause.

In seeds of laurel in the earth,   5
  The blossom of your fame is blown,
And somewhere, waiting for its birth,
  The shaft is in the stone!

Meanwhile, behalf[2] the tardy years
  Which keep in trust your storied tombs,   10
Behold! your sisters bring their tears,
  And these memorial blooms.

Small tributes! but your shades will smile
  More proudly on these wreaths today,
Than when some cannon-molded pile   15
  Shall overlook this bay.

Stoop, angels, hither from the skies!
  There is no holier spot of ground
Than where defeated valor lies,
  By mourning beauty crowned!   20

ETHNOGENESIS. **11.** *that vast gulf*, the Gulf Stream.

ODE. **1.** *no marble column*. At the time Timrod wrote his "Ode," no monument had been erected in Charleston to the soldiers of the Confederacy. Later, as Timrod prophesies in stanzas 3 and 4, a fine monument was erected. **2.** *behalf*, in behalf of.

Abram Joseph Ryan 1838-1886

A Roman Catholic priest, Abram Joseph Ryan served as chaplain with a Southern regiment from 1862 until the end of the war. His grief at the death of a younger brother in battle and the defeat of the cause in which he so strongly believed inspired his best poetry. Poems like "The Conquered Banner" are notable for dignity as well as pathos, and restrained but deep emotion. Because he expressed so well the spirit of the South in defeat, Ryan is called "the poet of the Lost Cause."

The Conquered Banner

Furl that Banner, for 'tis weary;
  Round its staff 'tis drooping dreary;
    Furl it, fold it—it is best;
    For there's not a man to wave it,
And there's not a sword to save it,   5
And there's not one left to lave it
In the blood which heroes gave it;
And its foes now scorn and brave it;
  Furl it, hide it—let it rest!

Take that Banner down! 'tis tattered;   10
Broken is its staff and shattered;
And the valiant hosts are scattered,
  Over whom it floated high.
Oh, 'tis hard for us to fold it,
Hard to think there's none to hold it,   15
Hard that those who once unrolled it
  Now must furl it with a sigh!

Furl that Banner—furl it sadly!
Once ten thousand hailed it gladly,
And ten thousands wildly, madly,   20
  Swore it should forever wave—
Swore that foeman's sword should never
Hearts like theirs entwined dissever,
Till that flag should float forever
  O'er their freedom or their grave!   25

Furl it! for the hands that grasped it,
And the hearts that fondly clasped it,
  Cold and dead are lying low;
And that Banner—it is trailing,
While around it sounds the wailing   30
  Of its people in their woe.

For, though conquered, they adore it—
Love the cold, dead hands that bore it,
Weep for those who fell before it,
Pardon those who trailed and tore it—   35
But, oh, wildly they deplore it,
  Now who furl and fold it so!

Furl that Banner! True, 'tis gory,
Yet 'tis wreathèd round with glory,
And 'twill live in song and story   40
  Though its folds are in the dust!

For its fame on brightest pages,
Penned by poets and by sages,
Shall go sounding down the ages—
  Furl its folds though now we must.   45

Furl that Banner, softly, slowly,
Treat it gently—it is holy,
  For it droops above the dead.
Touch it not—unfold it never;
Let it droop there, furled forever—   50
  For its people's hopes are fled!

 TO INCREASE UNDERSTANDING
Paul Hamilton Hayne

1. (*a*) In "Aspects of the Pines" at what times of day does Hayne describe the trees? (*b*) What effect does the mention of the wind in each stanza have on the tone of the poem as a whole?
2. Much of this poem's continuing fame rests on its vivid imagery and skillful use of figurative language. Point out examples which appeal to you.

Henry Timrod

1. (*a*) What circumstances inspired Timrod to write "Ethnogenesis"? (*b*) Explain why the title is appropriate.
2. (*a*) Cite lines in sections I and II of "Ethnogenesis" indicating that Timrod felt nature itself was allied with the Southern cause. (*b*) Trace the contrast Timrod draws between the North and the South in section III. (*c*) Cite lines that illustrate Timrod's belief in the righteousness of the Southern cause.
3. What great destiny does Timrod predict for the South? Explain his reasons for his belief.
4. What is the theme of the "Ode"?
5. How does the tone of "Ethnogenesis" differ from the tone of the "Ode"?
6. Explain why Timrod is often called "the Laureate of the Confederacy," basing your answer on "Ethnogenesis" and the "Ode."

Abram Joseph Ryan

1. State the theme of "The Conquered Banner."
2. (*a*) How are "The Conquered Banner" and Timrod's "Ode" related in the circumstances under which they were composed? (*b*) Would you say that the poems are similar? Explain your answer. (*c*) Which one do you think is the better poem? Be ready to justify your opinion.
3. How does the poetry of Hayne, Timrod, and Ryan reflect their intense devotion to the South?

Robert E. Lee 1807-1870

Of the many Southern heroes, none has grown in stature as the years have passed to compare with Robert E. Lee, who in 1862, at the age of fifty-five, assumed command of the Army of Northern Virginia. From that moment until he surrendered that army to Ulysses S. Grant at Appomattox Court House on April 9, 1865, Lee was the chief field commander of the Confederate forces. His military genius has never been disputed. Lee came, as a matter of fact, very close to winning the war, and the exploits of his lieutenants and his men continue to astound students of military science. Yet it is Lee the man, rather than Lee the general, who has come to typify the idealism and heroism of the South in wartime. His modest acceptance of his great responsibilities, both before and after the conflict; his quiet dignity; and, most of all, the simplicity and depth of his religious faith have impressed all thoughtful Americans. He hated war; he sided with his native Virginia only after profound searching of soul; and no one who reads the following letter, written several months after the surrender which ended the war, can doubt his honesty and sincerity.

General G. T. Beauregard, to whom the letter which follows is addressed, was, like Lee, a West Point graduate and a veteran of the Mexican War. On the outbreak of war he resigned his commission in the United States Army, as Lee did, and took up arms for the Confederate cause.

Photograph of Lee by Mathew Brady made shortly after the surrender at Appomattox.

Letter to G. T. Beauregard

Lexington, Va.
October 3, 1865

y dear General: I have received your letter of the 1st ult.,[1] and am very sorry to learn that the papers of yourself and Johnston[2] are lost, or at least beyond your reach, and I hope they may be recovered. Mine never can be, though some may be replaced. ... I hope both you and Johnston will write the history of your campaigns. Every one should do all in his power to collect and disseminate the truth, in the hope that it may find a place in history and descend to posterity.

I am glad to see no indication in your letter of an intention to leave the country. I think the South requires the aid of her sons now

1. *ult.*, abbreviation for Latin *ultimo*, "in the last month."
2. *Johnston*, Joseph E. Johnston, a Confederate general.

more than at any period of her history. As you ask my purpose, I will state that I have no thought of abandoning her unless compelled to do so.

After the surrender of the Southern armies in April, the revolution in the opinions and feelings of the people seemed so complete and the return of the Southern States into the Union of all the states so inevitable, that it became in my opinion the duty of every citizen, the contest being virtually ended, to cease opposition and place himself in a position to serve the country ... I need not tell you that true patriotism sometimes requires of men to act exactly contrary at one period to that which it does at another, and the motive that impels—the desire to do right—is precisely the same. The circumstances which govern their actions change and their conduct must conform to the new order of things. History is full of illustrations of this. Washington himself is an example: at one time he fought against the French, under Braddock in the service of the King of Great Britain; at another he fought with the French at Yorktown, under the orders of the Continental Congress of America, against the King. He has not been branded by the world with reproach for this, but his course has been applauded.

 TO INCREASE UNDERSTANDING

1. Many of Lee's former soldiers seriously considered leaving the country after their surrender. (*a*) According to his "Letter to Beauregard," what was Lee's attitude toward such action? (*b*) Cite his reasons for believing as he did. (*c*) Do you think his attitude was an unusual one for a defeated general? Explain.

2. What action does Lee hope Beauregard will take with his military records? Why?

3. What aspects of Lee's personality do you find reflected in his "Letter to Beauregard"?

Spirituals

Lincoln reluctantly accepted war as the only way to save the Union, and no doubt divergent interpretations of the rights of the states under the Constitution were in part the cause of the conflict. Differences in economic interests likewise played a part. To the mass of the Northern people, however, the appeal to arms was the final stage of a moral crusade to abolish Negro slavery. A generation of militant reformers, prominent among them William Lloyd Garrison, founder of the weekly *Liberator* (1831), and Harriet Beecher Stowe, author of *Uncle Tom's Cabin* (1852), had convinced them that slavery was wrong.

Many Southern writers insisted, with some justice, that the evils of the slave system were exaggerated by the abolitionists. They believed that many Negroes were better off in servitude than they would be as free laborers. Nevertheless enslaved men and women clearly longed for liberty and expressed their longing in a number of the sad and lovely spirituals— religious songs with haunting melodies. The origins of the spirituals have been disputed, but their vivid imagery and emotional power have appealed to even the most sophisticated listeners and have given them an honored place in art music as well as in folk song.

Favorite materials of the spirituals are the stories told dramatically in Exodus, Numbers, and Joshua, those books of the Bible which describe the captivity of the Jews in Egypt and their deliverance from bondage under the leadership of Moses.

Go Down, Moses

When Israel was in Egypt's land,
  Let my people go!
Oppress'd so hard dey could not stand,
  Let my people go!

Chorus
Go down, Moses,   5
  Way down in Egypt's land.
Tell ole Pha-raoh,
  Let my people go!

Thus say de Lord, bold Moses said,
  Let my people go!   10
If not I'll smite your first-born dead,
  Let my people go!

Chorus
Go down, Moses,
  Way down in Egypt's land.
Tell ole Pha-raoh,   15
  Let my people go!

No more shall dey in bondage toil,
  Let my people go!
Let dem come out wid Egypt's spoil,
  Let my people go!   20

Chorus
Go down, Moses,
  Way down in Egypt's land.
Tell ole Pha-raoh,
  Let my people go!

Deep River

Deep river, my home is over Jordan.
Deep river, Lord, I want to cross over into
    Campground.
Oh, chillun, oh, don't you want to go
To that gospel feast, that promised land,
That land where all is peace?   5
Walk into heaven and take my seat
And cast my crown at Jesus' feet. Lord,
Deep river, my home is over Jordan.
Deep river, Lord, I want to cross over into
    Campground.

Joshua Fit de Battle ob Jericho

Joshua fit de battle ob Jericho—[1]
  Jericho—Jericho—
Joshua fit de battle ob Jericho,
  And de walls came a-tumblin' down.

You may talk about yo' King ob Gideon,[2]
You may talk about yo' man of Saul,[3]   5
Dere's none like good ole Joshua,
  At de battle ob Jericho.

Up to de walls ob Jericho
He marched wid spear in han',
"Go blow dem ram horns," Joshua cried,   10
"Kase de battle am in my han'."

Den de lam' ram sheep-horns begin to blow,
Trumpets begin to soun',
Joshua commanded de chillun to shout,
An' de walls came a-tumblin' down.   15

Dat mornin'—
Joshua fit de battle ob Jericho—Jericho—
  Jericho,
Joshua fit de battle ob Jericho,
An' de walls came a-tumblin' down.

---

1. *Joshua . . . Jericho.* According to Chapter 6 of the Book of Joshua, the Lord commanded Joshua to have his people march for seven days around Jericho, a city in Canaan, the land the Lord had promised to the Israelites. On the seventh day as the priests blew on the rams' horn trumpets, the city walls fell and the city was taken. 2. *King ob Gideon,* a Hebrew hero who delivered the Israelites from the Midianites and other desert raiders. (Judges, Chapters 6-8.) 3. *Saul,* first king of Israel.

EXTENDING INTERESTS

With your teacher's permission, devote a class period to playing recordings of Negro spirituals. Albums that might be included are: *Marian Anderson Spirituals* (Victor LM2032); *God's Trombones and Other Spirituals,* sung by Fred Waring's Pennsylvanians (Decca DL8047); and *Old Time Religion,* sung by the Johnson Family Singers (Victor LPM1128). Your classmates may suggest other excellent recordings of spirituals to be included in the program.

Singers in Blue and Gray

Huddled around campfires or marching into battle, soldiers in Blue and Gray sang to lift their spirits or their courage. Just as the soldiers of the Revolution had treasured "Yankee Doodle," the soldier-singers of the War Between the States favored certain unforgettable tunes.

The Union man probably volunteered for service to the stirring strains of "The Battle Cry of Freedom," while the Confederate heard his call to arms in "The Bonnie Blue Flag." Once in uniform, the fighting man had little recreation; singing was the one way he could relieve the interminable drills and marches, the waiting to fight and the fear of fighting. On a day of high spirits, the tune of "Goober Peas" might float above a Southern encampment or "Grafted into the Army" might ring out in Union trenches. A soldier's longing for the girl back home was echoed in "Aura Lea" and "Lorena." The soldier-singers of the Civil War paid scant attention to the origin of the songs they sang; Southerners, for example, sang "My Darling Nellie Gray" without changing the abolitionist lyrics. As the war went on and on, Yankee and Confederate alike poured their weariness and homesickness into the sentimental ballads "Tenting on the Old Camp Ground" and "Just Before the Battle, Mother."

The two great marching songs of the Civil War, "Dixie" and "The Battle Hymn of the Republic," have interesting histories. "Dixie" was first sung on Broadway by Bryant's Minstrels in 1859. The nonsense words and lively tune made it immediately popular all over the country.

I wish I was in de land ob cotton,
Old times dar am not forgotten;
   Look away! Look away! Look away! Dixie Land!
In Dixie Land whar I was born in,
Early on one frosty mornin',
   Look away! Look away! Look away! Dixie Land!

Chorus
Den I wish I was in Dixie! Hooray! Hooray!
In Dixie's Land we'll take our stand, to lib an'
   die in Dixie.
Away! away! away down South in Dixie.
Away! away! away down South in Dixie.

The song was introduced to the South in a New Orleans production of *Pocahontas* just

before the war began. Confederate regiments in Louisiana took it up; soon it was widely used in the Southern armies. Several literary "improvements" of "Dixie" were written, but the original song by Northern-born and pro-Union Daniel Decatur Emmett became, ironically, the rallying song of the Confederacy.

The martial and resounding lyrics of "The Battle Hymn of the Republic" were written by a well-known reform leader of the time, Julia Ward Howe. On a visit to a Union camp near Washington, D.C., Mrs. Howe had heard the soldiers singing the popular "John Brown's Body," a doggerel song which had fitted its words to an old Southern revival hymn. Inspired by the music and the scene, Mrs. Howe returned home to compose fresh lyrics for the old hymn. Her version was first published in the *Atlantic Monthly* in February 1862. "The Battle Hymn of the Republic" quickly became the great marching song of the North.

Mine eyes have seen the glory of the coming of
    the Lord:
He is trampling out the vintage where the grapes
    of wrath are stored:
He hath loosed the fateful lightning of His
    terrible swift sword;
  His truth is marching on.

Chorus
Glory! glory! Hallelujah!
Glory! glory! Hallelujah!
Glory! glory! Hallelujah!
  His truth is marching on!

Contemporary view of Union soldiers singing "McClellan is Our Man."

Abraham Lincoln 1809-1865

So remote was Lincoln from the traditional man of past ages that James Russell Lowell, reading his "Commemoration Ode" (page 286) at Harvard in 1865, called him "the first American." A hundred years later he still remains "the first American," without any doubt the foremost figure in the national mythology. Homely, largely self-educated, faced with the greatest crisis that his country had yet had to meet, Lincoln was hated as well as loved, and he suffered patiently through setback after setback before the Union he loved was finally saved. Then he died at the hands of an assassin, calling forth the national mourning so vividly described in Whitman's "When Lilacs Last in the Dooryard Bloomed" (page 341). Six weeks before he died, Lincoln delivered the speech printed on the next page. His forgiving spirit and his vision of a nation once more united shine through the simple words.

A considerably enlarged detail from a photo by Brady of Lincoln delivering his Second Inaugural Address.

Second Inaugural Address, March 4, 1865

Fellow Countrymen: At this second appearing to take the oath of the presidential office, there is less occasion for an extended address than there was at the first. Then a statement, somewhat in detail, of a course to be pursued, seemed fitting and proper. Now, at the expiration of four years, during which public declarations have been constantly called forth on every point and phase of the great contest which still absorbs the attention and engrosses the energies of the nation, little that is new could be presented. The progress of our arms, upon which all else chiefly depends, is as well known to the public as to myself; and it is, I trust, reasonably satisfactory and encouraging to all. With high hope for the future, no prediction in regard to it is ventured.

On the occasion corresponding to this four years ago, all thoughts were anxiously directed to an impending civil war. All dreaded it—all sought to avert it. While the inaugural address was being delivered from this place, devoted altogether to saving the Union without war, insurgent agents were in the city seeking to destroy it without war—seeking to dissolve the Union, and divide effects, by negotiation. Both parties deprecated war; but one of them would make war rather than let the nation survive; and the other would accept war rather than let it perish. And the war came.

One eighth of the whole population were colored slaves, not distributed generally over the Union, but localized in the southern part of it. These slaves constituted a peculiar and powerful interest. All knew that this interest was, somehow, the cause of the war. To strengthen, perpetuate, and extend this interest was the object for which the insurgents would rend the Union, even by war; while the government claimed no right to do more than to restrict the territorial enlargement of it.

Neither party expected for the war the magnitude or the duration which it has already attained. Neither anticipated that the cause of the conflict might cease with, or even before, the conflict itself should cease. Each looked for an easier triumph and a result less fundamental and astounding. Both read the same Bible, and pray to the same God; and each invokes His aid against the other. It may seem strange that any man should dare to ask a just God's assistance in wringing their bread from the sweat of other men's faces; but let us judge not, that we be not judged.[1] The prayers of both could not be answered—that of neither has been answered fully.

The Almighty has His own purposes. "Woe unto the world because of offenses! for it must needs be that offenses come; but woe to that man by whom the offense cometh."[2] If we shall suppose that American slavery is one of those offenses which in the providence of God, must needs come, but which, having continued through His appointed time, He now wills to remove, and that He gives to both North and South this terrible war, as the woe due to those by whom the offense came, shall we discern therein any departure from those divine attributes which the believers in a living God always ascribe to Him? Fondly do we hope—fervently do we pray—that this mighty scourge of war may speedily pass away. Yet, if God wills that it continue until all the wealth piled by the bondman's two hundred and fifty years of unrequited toil shall be sunk, and until every drop of blood drawn with the lash shall be paid by another drawn with the sword, as was said three thousand years ago, so still it must be said, "The judgments of the Lord are true and righteous altogether."[3]

With malice toward none; with charity for all; with firmness in the right, as God gives us to see the right, let us strive on to finish the work we are in; to bind up the nation's wounds; to care for him who shall have borne the battle, and for his widow and his orphan—to do all which may achieve and cherish a just and lasting peace among ourselves, and with all nations.

---

1. *judge not . . . judged.* Matthew 7:1. 2. *"Woe unto the world . . . the offense cometh."* Matthew 18:7. 3. *"The judgments . . . righteous altogether."* Psalms 19:9.

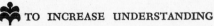 TO INCREASE UNDERSTANDING

1. What does Lincoln say was the purpose of the North in the war?

2. What, judging from this address, was his own attitude toward slavery?

3. How did Lincoln feel about the preservation of the Union?

4. How are the quotations from the Bible useful in developing the point made in the final paragraph?

5. Why is this speech regarded as a great piece of literature? Consider such points as: (*a*) word choice; (*b*) word order; (*c*) variation in sentence structure; (*d*) figures of speech; (*e*) tone.

 WORDS!

The adjective *inaugural* is formed from the verb *inaugurate*, which has a very interesting history. Look up its origin in an unabridged dictionary and be prepared to explain how it came to have its present meaning. Be ready, too, to use *inaugurated, inaugural,* and *inauguration* in three sentences each

beginning with the name of a President of the United States.

 EXTENDING INTERESTS

It has become a tradition in American political life for the newly inaugurated President to speak to the nation. These inaugural addresses are important state documents; many are also cherished as fine literature. Members of your class might be assigned to read the first inaugural addresses of Jefferson, Lincoln, Roosevelt, Eisenhower, and Kennedy, and then report to the class on the public issues they reflect and the elements of literary style they reveal. You will find the speeches most readily in a volume published by the U.S. Congress entitled *Inaugural Addresses of the Presidents of the United States from George Washington 1789 to Harry S. Truman 1949,* and in the supplements, *Inaugural Address of Dwight D. Eisenhower,* January 20, 1953, and *Inaugural Address of John Fitzgerald Kennedy,* January 20, 1961. If your school library does not contain this publication, consult your school librarian for other sources.

THE LARGER VIEW

A. Explain how the following passages reflect the favorite themes of Southern writers during the Period of Conflict.

1. Low, flutelike breezes sweep the waves of
    light,
    And, lifting dark green tresses of the
    pines,
    Till every lock is luminous. . . .

2.   . . . At last, we are
    A nation among nations; and the world
    Shall soon behold in many a distant port
    Another flag unfurled!

3. Furl that Banner, softly, slowly,
    Treat it gently—it is holy,
       For it droops above the dead.
    Touch it not—unfold it never;
    Let it droop there, furled forever—
       For its people's hopes are fled!

B. Whitman was a contemporary of Emerson, Longfellow, Holmes, Lowell, and Whittier, but the subject matter and form of his poetry differ greatly from that written by the great New Englanders.

1. (*a*) Summarize the ways in which Whitman stands apart from the poetic mainstream of his time. (*b*) What influences shaped Whitman's unique viewpoint?

2. Both Lowell and Whitman expressed their grief for Lincoln's death in moving elegies. Reread Lowell's "Commemoration Ode" (page 286), and then explain how it differs from "When Lilacs Last in the Dooryard Bloomed" in (*a*) verse form, (*b*) images, (*c*) description of Lincoln, and (*d*) description of the mourning nation. Which poem do you feel is the more effective expression of grief? Account for your answer.

BIBLIOGRAPHY

ALLAN, MERRIT, *Blow, Bugles, Blow.* (Longmans) The reader senses the confusion, the boredom, and the thunder of war in this story of Rick O'Shay, a volunteer in the Union army. When Rick enters the army, he is an eager, raw recruit; he leaves the service a hardened trooper. *Johnny Reb* presents another attractive character caught up in the problems of a war-torn nation.

BROOKS, VAN WYCK, *The Times of Melville and Whitman.* (Dutton) Whitman and his contemporaries are vividly portrayed in this account of literary happenings and historical events in the last half of the nineteenth century.

CATTON, BRUCE, *This Hallowed Ground.* (Doubleday •Pocket Books) With dramatic awareness of the times and the problems, Mr. Catton here presents the entire scope of the Civil War from Fort Sumter to the Union victory. In *A Stillness at Appomattox,* which won the Pulitzer Prize for history in 1954, Mr. Catton concentrates on the period from the battle of Gettysburg to Lee's surrender at Appomattox. Anyone especially interested in this period of history will find both books good reading.

DEUTSCH, BABETTE, *Walt Whitman; Builder for America.* (Messner) As full of vigor as Whitman himself, this book richly records the life of an American who spent his lifetime speaking the truth that was in him.

EDMONDS, WALTER DUMAUX, *Cadmus Henry.* (Dodd) Cadmus Henry joins the army prepared to perform heroically at General Lee's side. Instead he is assigned to desk detail and later to scout duty, floating over enemy territory in a balloon. The book has marvelous undercurrents of humor.

GARTH, DAVID, *Gray Canaan.* (Putnam) A lovely girl with Northern sympathies is suspected of being a Northern agent by a young Southern general. It is a well-told tale.

KANE, HARTNETT, *Gallant Mrs. Stonewall.* (Doubleday) This is a well-documented and extremely interesting account of the life of General Stonewall Jackson and his wife.

KEITH, HAROLD, *Rifles for Watie.* (Crowell) There is never a dull moment in this top-notch account of the war as fought in the West. The story concerns a Kansas farm boy assigned to espionage duty.

LANCASTER, BRUCE, *No Bugles Tonight.* (Little) All will enjoy this yarn of the adventures and misadventures of Whipple Sheldon, a secret agent in the heart of the South.

MITCHELL, MARGARET, *Gone With the Wind.* (••Macmillan) Led by an unscrupulous determination to save herself from poverty, Scarlett O'Hara is matched only by Rhett Butler, a blockade runner and an engaging scoundrel, in Miss Mitchell's prize-winning novel of Georgia during the Civil War and the Reconstruction days.

NOBLE, HOLLISTER, *Woman With a Sword.* (Doubleday) You will find fascinating reading and vivid impressions of the Civil War tensions in the fictional biography of Anna Ella Carroll, journalist, lawyer, and Lincoln's personal investigator.

STEVENSON, JANET, *Weep No More.* (Viking) Elizabeth Van Lew, known as Crazy Bet, seems to be nothing more than a harmless old Confederate woman who passes out Bibles, but beneath the disguise is a brilliant Union agent. This story, which is based on fact, is full of suspense.

TUCKER, GLENN, *Chicamauga: Bloody Battle in the West.* (Dobbs) War buffs will want to read this absorbing account of one of the most fiercely fought battles of the Civil War. Vivid personality sketches add to the author's presentation of this famous battle.

WHITMAN, WALT, *Leaves of Grass.* (Doubleday •Dolphin) Students who enjoy Whitman's smooth-flowing and idiomatic poetry will want to read more of this famous book.

WHITMAN, WALT, *The Portable Walt Whitman,* edited by Mark Van Doren. (••Viking) Although the emphasis in this collection is on *Leaves of Grass,* the prose writings in which Whitman explained and justified his poetry as well as some of his other prose writings have been included.

•paperback   ••paperback and hard-cover

New Outlooks

Writing shortly after the end of the War Between the States, Whitman expressed his hope of soon seeing again "the United States hand in hand in one unbroken circle." This hope of unity and a desire to see the United States assume its place among the great nations affected the thinking of Americans in all sections and spurred a tremendous growth in all areas of living. Railroads began to span the continent. Prewar factories, small before the war, growing into industrial giants, drew more people to the cities. The frontier, constantly pushing farther west, filled with people whose democratic spirit had a greater impact on American life than ever before. The arts, including literature, took on a new significance. This period of growth and change may appropriately be called the period of New Outlooks.

Understandably, the authors living in the new America of factory and city, of westering frontiers and transcontinental railroads, differed in important ways from authors of the prewar era. Before the war, for example, most important writers had lived on the Eastern seacoast, particularly in New England; now a great many were from the South, the Middle West, and even the Far West. Previously, most prominent writers had been aristocrats; now, like Stephen Crane and Sidney Lanier, most were from middle-class or poor families. Most authors of earlier times had been educated in some Eastern college—a large share of them in Harvard; now some leading authors like Bret Harte, Sarah Orne Jewett, Emily Dickinson, and William Dean Howells were not college educated, and others, like Samuel Clemens, did not have even a high-school education.

It would be strange if these new authors with such different backgrounds had not produced literature quite different from that of a younger America. The new writings, in general, were less scholarly, less genteel, than the earlier ones. Some had less polish. But the newer writings were likely to be more robust, more full of life. Finally, postwar authors were likely to be less influenced by Europe and more influenced by the new American nation which was becoming a force in the world.

Samuel Clemens

1835-1910

In his place of birth, family, education, and writing, Sam Clemens—or, to use his pen name, Mark Twain[1]—is a good representative of the postwar authors. Born and reared in the Middle West, the son of a day-dreaming storekeeper and lawyer, he never finished grade school. In fact, at twelve he began to work for a living. He got his education chiefly in the school of experience, garnering his knowledge in a number of trades in various parts of the country. What he wrote had the gusto of the West, and it was full of the picturesque life he had known intimately.

JOURNALIST Sam Clemens was born in Florida, Missouri, in 1835. His parents were pioneers who, shortly before his birth, had moved westward from Tennessee. From the age of four, Sam was reared in Hannibal, a sleepy town perched above the mile-wide Mississippi. His informal schooling, gained from personal experience in a riverside town with wild country on three sides of it, probably was more valuable than his six years of formal education. He learned how to observe keenly and minutely—a necessary skill on the frontier. A man who met him years later wrote, "He has the peculiar Indianlike or American faculty of observing innumerable little things which no European would ever think of. There is, I think, a great deal of 'hard old Injun' in him." He acquired a thirst for information, for facts and figures—fine equipment for a journalist.

In 1847, when the death of his father left the family in bad financial circumstances, Sam became a printer's apprentice. After his apprenticeship, he went to work as a printer for his brother Orion, publisher of the *Hannibal Journal*. In the print shop Sam set in type stories of all sorts, including, probably, humorous stories culled from newspapers. From such models he doubtless learned a great deal about writing. At about sixteen, Sam began to publish in the *Journal* some pieces of his own—comic poems about the girls he had been courting, jesting comments on the news, jibes at fellow townsfolk.

Sam was seventeen when he left Hannibal and set out to see the world. He wandered eastward as far as New York, picking up printing jobs in several cities, sending back travel letters to Orion, who printed them as contributions from "Our Traveling Correspondent." He returned West to work for Orion, now located in Iowa. Then the lure of the great river beside which he had grown up asserted itself, and Sam realized an old ambition by becoming first, a pilot's apprentice on a Mississippi River steamboat, then, after eighteen months, a full-fledged pilot. The selection

Photographs of Twain and his boyhood home in Hannibal.

1. *Mark Twain,* a cry meaning "two fathoms deep," used by a leadsman on a Mississippi River steamboat.

from *Life on the Mississippi* (page 377), describes his boyhood desire to become a steamboatman and gives a vivid picture of the rôle the river steamer played in American life for many years.

Sam's happy years of piloting ended in 1861 when the war closed river traffic. Briefly he served with a group of Confederate volunteers. When Orion was appointed secretary of Nevada Territory—an area rich in silver and gold—Sam determined to go West also and to earn his fortune as a miner. But he had no luck. The year 1862 found him living in a flimsy cabin in the Esmerelda mining settlement, suffering from the cold and harassed by the high price of mining-camp food. Invited to become a reporter for the *Territorial Enterprise*, published in Virginia City, a hundred and thirty miles away, he walked half the distance to the new job. While working in Virginia City, Clemens adopted his pen name, Mark Twain. Although he found the job of reporting in a lively mine town

Lithograph by Currier and Ives. Millions of prints by this famous company were sold during the last decades of the nineteenth century at prices from fifteen cents to three dollars. In this century they have become a collector's item, one selling for as much as $3000.

JBLISHED BY CURRIER & IVES.   125 NASSAU ST. NEW YOR

THE GREAT MISSISSIPPI STEAMBOAT RACE.

FROM NEW ORLEANS TO ST. LOUIS, JULY 1870.

The Boats left the Wharf at w Orleans June 30th 1870 at 55 P.M. The Lee reached the Wharf at at St. Louis July 4th at 11.25 AM.

Between the R.E.Lee, Capt. John W. Cannon and Natchez Capt. Leathers.
WON BY THE R.E.LEE. TIME: 3 DAYS 18 HOURS AND 30 MINUTES; DISTANCE 1210 MILES.

The Natchez reached the Whar Boat at St Louis July 4th at 5.58 P.M.S hours & thirty three min. behind the Lee, h ing been detained six hrs by a fog at Devils

fascinating, in 1864 he left for San Francisco and worked there as reporter or correspondent.

In 1867 Twain went abroad for the first time—to France, Italy, Spain, and Palestine. Newspaper stories about this trip were revised and published as *The Innocents Abroad* (1869), his first important book. With the proceeds, Clemens bought a Buffalo newspaper which he published during 1870 and 1871. When he sold the *Express,* his associations with newspapers ended, but he continued to write for magazines and, until the last years of his long life, to write such journalistic books as *Roughing It* (1872), *A Tramp Abroad* (1880), *Life on the Mississippi* (1883), and *Following the Equator* (1897). All these books are made up of the sorts of things he had been writing for years as a newspaperman, or journalist.

Several things made Mark a fine journalist. For one thing, his good luck at being on the spot when interesting things were happening made possible *Life on the Mississippi,* an account of the liveliest days of steamboating, and *Roughing It,* Mark's chronicle of the West in its most zestful and interesting years.

For another thing, he had an eye for details. Whether he was describing a miner's hut or a volcano, a jack rabbit or the Egyptian Sphinx, he could notice and record precisely those elements which brought them plainly before the reader's eyes.

Finally, he was effective as a journalist because he could consistently interest the reader by recording his own highly individual reactions and ideas. *The Innocents Abroad* became immediately and lastingly popular, less for its descriptions of foreign scenes than for Twain's scornful accounts of idiotic sightseers unable to form their own opinions of what they saw, his observations of foreign manners and customs, and his exaggerated claims for the superiority of American scenes over foreign scenes. From a sharp-tongued mother, he had inherited a keen sense of humor, and this gift was nurtured by his work as a printer, his work as a pilot, and his life among fun-loving miners. Hence he could see humorous elements in almost any situation, and he could write humor ranging from subtle satire to broad slapstick. Like a good talker who has interesting things to say on any subject, Twain could constantly interest the reader.

FROM *Life on the Mississippi*

When I was a boy, there was but one permanent ambition among my comrades in our village on the west bank of the Mississippi River. That was, to be a steamboatman. We had transient ambitions of other sorts, but they were only transient. When a circus came and went, it left us all burning to become clowns; the first Negro minstrel show that ever came to our section left us all suffering to try that kind of life;

now and then we had a hope that if we lived and were good, God would permit us to be pirates. These ambitions faded out, each in its turn; but the ambition to be a steamboatman always remained.

Once a day a cheap, gaudy packet arrived upward from St. Louis, and another downward from Keokuk.[1] Before these events, the

---

1. *Keokuk* (kē'ə kuk), a Mississippi River town in the southeastern corner of Iowa, about fifty miles above Hannibal.

day was glorious with expectancy; after them, the day was a dead and empty thing. Not only the boys, but the whole village, felt this. After all these years I can picture that old time to myself now, just as it was then: the white town drowsing in the sunshine of a summer's morning; the streets empty, or pretty nearly so; one or two clerks sitting in front of the Water Street stores, with their splint-bottomed chairs[2] tilted back against the walls, chins on breasts, hats slouched over their faces, asleep—with shingle-shavings enough around to show what broke them down; a sow and a litter of pigs loafing along the sidewalk, doing a good business in watermelon rinds and seeds; two or three lonely little freight piles scattered about the levee; a pile of skids on the slope of the stone-paved wharf, and the fragrant town drunkard asleep in the shadow of them; two or three wood flats[3] at the head of the wharf, but nobody to listen to the peaceful lapping of the wavelets against them; the great Mississippi, the majestic, the magnificent Mississippi, rolling its mile-wide tide along, shining in the sun; the dense forest away on the other side; the point above the town, and the point below, bounding the river-glimpse and turning it into a sort of sea, and withal a very still and brilliant and lonely one. Presently a film of dark smoke appears above one of those remote points: instantly a Negro drayman, famous for his quick eye and prodigious voice, lifts up the cry, "S-t-e-a-m-boat a-comin'!" and the scene changes! The town drunkard stirs, the clerks wake up, a furious clatter of drays follows, every house and store pours out a human contribution, and all in a twinkling the dead town is alive and moving. Drays, carts, men, boys, all go hurrying from many quarters to a common center, the wharf. Assembled there, the people fasten their eyes upon the coming boat as upon a wonder they are seeing for the first time. And the boat *is* rather a handsome sight, too. She is long and sharp and trim and pretty; she has two tall, fancy-topped chimneys, with a gilded device of some kind swung between them; a fanciful pilot house, all glass and gingerbread, perched on top of the texas deck[4] behind them; the paddle boxes[5] are gorgeous with a picture or

with gilded rays above the boat's name; the boiler deck, the hurricane deck,[6] and the texas deck are fenced and ornamented with clean white railings; there is a flag gallantly flying from the jack staff[7]; the furnace doors are open and the fires glaring bravely; the upper decks are black with passengers; the captain stands by the big bell, calm, imposing, the envy of all; great volumes of the blackest smoke are rolling and tumbling out of the chimneys—a husbanded grandeur created with a bit of pitch pine just before arriving at a town; the crew are grouped on the forecastle; the broad stage[8] is run far out over the port bow, and a deck hand stands picturesquely on the end of it with a coil of rope in his hand; the pent steam is screaming through the gauge cocks; the captain lifts his hand, a bell rings, the wheels stop; then they turn back, churning the water to foam, and the steamer is at rest. Then such a scramble as there is to get aboard, and to get ashore, and to take in freight and to discharge freight, all at one and the same time; and such a yelling and cursing as the mates facilitate it all with! Ten minutes later the steamer is under way again, with no flag on the jack staff and no black smoke issuing from the chimneys. After ten more minutes the town is dead again, and the town drunkard asleep by the skids once more.

My father was a justice of the peace, and I supposed he possessed the power of life and death over all men, and could hang anybody that offended him. This was distinction enough for me as a general thing; but the desire to be a steamboatman kept intruding, nevertheless. I first wanted to be a cabin boy, so that I could come out with a white apron on and shake a tablecloth over the side, where all my

---

2. *splint-bottomed chairs,* chairs with seats woven of thin strips (splints) of wood. (Chairs of this sort are frequently called *split-bottomed* chairs.) 3. *wood flats,* small flat-bottomed boats. 4. *texas deck.* The texas was a range of staterooms adjacent to the pilot house reserved for officers. The texas deck adjoined these living quarters. 5. *paddle boxes,* the wooden coverings built over the upper part of the paddle wheels which propelled the steamer. On a side-wheel steamer the paddle wheels were located one at each side. 6. *the boiler deck, the hurricane deck.* The boiler deck is that part of the upper deck situated immediately over the boilers; the hurricane deck is the topmost deck. 7. *jack staff,* a short pole erected at the front of the vessel. 8. *stage,* stage-plank, or gangplank.

old comrades could see me; later I thought I would rather be the deck hand who stood on the end of the stage-plank with the coil of rope in his hand, because he was particularly conspicuous. But these were only daydreams —they were too heavenly to be contemplated as real possibilities.

By and by one of our boys went away. He was not heard of for a long time. At last he turned up as apprentice engineer or "striker" on a steamboat. This thing shook the bottom out of all my Sunday-school teachings. That boy had been notoriously worldly, and I just the reverse; yet he was exalted to this eminence, and I left in obscurity and misery. There was nothing generous about this fellow in his greatness. He would always manage to have a rusty bolt to scrub while his boat tarried at our town, and he would sit on the inside guard[9] and scrub it, where we all could see him and envy him and loathe him. And whenever his boat was laid up he would come home and swell around the town in his blackest and greasiest clothes, so that nobody could help remembering that he was a steamboatman; and he used all sorts of steamboat technicalities in his talk, as if he were so used to them that he forgot common people could not understand them. He would speak of the "labboard"[10] side of a horse in an easy, natural way that would make one wish he was dead. And he was always talking about "St. Looy" like an old citizen; he would refer casually to occasions when he was "coming down Fourth Street," or when he was "passing by the Planter's House," or when there was a fire and he took a turn on the brakes of "the old Big Missouri"; and then he would go on and lie about how many towns the size of ours were burned down there that day. Two or three of the boys had long been persons of consideration among us because they had been to St. Louis once and had a vague general knowledge of its wonders, but the day of their glory was over now. They lapsed into a humble silence, and learned to disappear when the ruthless cub engineer approached. This fellow had money, too, and hair oil. Also an ignorant silver watch and a showy brass watch chain. He wore a leather belt and used no suspenders. If ever a youth was cordially admired and hated by his comrades, this one was. No girl could withstand his charms. He "cut out" every boy in the village. When his boat blew up at last, it diffused a tranquil contentment among us such as we had not known for months. But when he came home the next week, alive, renowned, and appeared in church all battered up and bandaged, a shining hero, stared at and wondered over by everybody, it seemed to us that the partiality of Providence for an undeserving reptile had reached a point where it was open to criticism.

This creature's career could produce but one result, and it speedily followed. Boy after boy managed to get on the river. The minister's son became an engineer. The doctor's and the postmaster's sons became mud clerks[11]; the wholesale liquor dealer's son became a barkeeper on a boat; four sons of the chief merchant, and two sons of the county judge, became pilots. Pilot was the grandest position of all. The pilot, even in those days of trivial wages, had a princely salary—from a hundred and fifty to two hundred and fifty dollars a month, and no board to pay. Two months of his wages would pay a preacher's salary for a year. Now some of us were left disconsolate. We could not get on the river—at least our parents would not let us.

So, by and by, I ran away. I said I would never come home again till I was a pilot and could come in glory. But somehow I could not manage it. I went meekly aboard a few of the boats that lay packed together like sardines at the long St. Louis wharf, and humbly inquired for the pilots, but got only a cold shoulder and short words from mates and clerks. I had to make the best of this sort of treatment for the time being, but I had comforting daydreams of a future when I should be a great and honored pilot, with plenty of money, and could kill some of these mates and clerks and pay for them.

9. *inside guard*, part of the steamboat's deck which curved out over the paddle wheel. 10. "*labboard*," larboard, the left or port side of a ship looking forward from the stern. 11. *mud clerks*, second clerks on river steamers. They were so called because it was their duty to go ashore at unimportant stops, often mere mudbanks, to receive or check off freight.

YARNSPINNER During many periods of his life, Clemens found vast entertainment in listening to yarnspinners. Storytelling was a chief form of amusement on the frontier, and even as a boy Sam heard many fireside yarns. As printer's devil and printer, he probably put into type many a story which its author had told in the fashion of an oral storyteller. Still later, on Mississippi steamboats moving up and down the river, he enjoyed yarns spun by fellow pilots or passengers. Even later, in the Far West, he loved to listen to and to swap stories.

Clemens' country-wide fame began when, after hearing one story which was going the rounds, he retold it in print. In the winter of 1864-1865, he and some companions were staying at Jim Gillis' cabin on Jackass Hill in the central California mining district adjoining Calaveras County. When the weather was good, the author and his friends engaged in pocket mining, or searching for pockets of gold. When the weather was bad—and many days were rainy—they gathered around Gillis' fireplace and told yarns, or they joined yarnspinning sessions in the nearby Angel's Camp Hotel. One story was told by Ben Coon, a solemn, rather stupid fellow who saw nothing humorous about it. Clemens and Gillis listened with great solemnity, but when they left the hotel, they repeated bits of the story and howled with laughter. In a notebook which he was keeping at the time, Clemens wrote the main details:

Coleman with his jumping frog—bet stranger $50.00—stranger had no frog, and C. got him one; in the meantime stranger filled C.'s frog full of shot and he couldn't jump. The stranger's frog won.

Mark later told the story to Artemus Ward, a famous humorist, who urged him to write it so that it might be printed. Published in an Eastern magazine in 1865, "The Celebrated Jumping Frog of Calaveras County" (page 382) was an overnight literary sensation. Newspapers all over the United States published the story, and Americans everywhere read it with delight.

From then on, Mark Twain frequently introduced stories of the oral type into accounts of personal experiences. As Bernard De Voto, in *Mark Twain's America,* has said, "He took the humorous anecdote, combined it with autobiographical reminiscence, and so achieved the narrative form best adapted to his mind." Many of his books thus became accounts of the author's life or his travels interspersed with anecdotes. In *The Innocents Abroad, Roughing It, A Tramp Abroad, Life on the Mississippi,* and *Following the Equator,* he used such a pattern of autobiography combined with anecdotes. Since these volumes were published over a long period—1869 to 1897—we can see that Mark Twain's skill as a yarnspinner was important to him throughout the major part of his writing career.

"The humorous story," Mark Twain once said, "is strictly a work of art—high and delicate art—and only an artist can tell it." He might have added that *reading* the humorous story is also a high and delicate art.

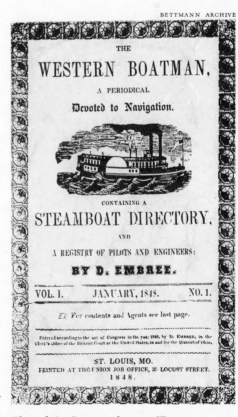

THE
WESTERN BOATMAN,
A PERIODICAL
Devoted to Navigation.

CONTAINING A
STEAMBOAT DIRECTORY,
AND
A REGISTRY OF PILOTS AND ENGINEERS:
BY D. EMBREE.

VOL. 1.   JANUARY, 1848.   NO. 1.

For contents and Agents see last page.

Entered according to the act of Congress in the year 1846, by D. EMBREE, in the Clerk's Office of the District Court of the United States, in and for the District of Ohio,

ST. LOUIS, MO.
PRINTED AT THE UNION JOB OFFICE, 35 LOCUST STREET.
1848.

Above left: Cartoon showing Twain riding to fame and fortune on his "Jumping Frog." Below left: A typical river town in Mark Twain's time.

The Celebrated Jumping Frog of Calaveras County

In compliance with the request of a friend of mine, who wrote me from the East, I called on good-natured, garrulous old Simon Wheeler, and inquired after my friend's friend, Leonidas W. Smiley, as requested to do, and I hereunto append the result. I have a lurking suspicion that *Leonidas W.* Smiley is a myth; that my friend never knew such a personage; and that he only conjectured that if I asked old Wheeler about him, it would remind him of his infamous *Jim* Smiley, and he would go to work and bore me to death with some exasperating reminiscence of him as long and as tedious as it should be useless to me. If that was the design, it succeeded.

I found Simon Wheeler dozing comfortably by the barroom stove of the dilapidated tavern in the decayed mining camp of Angel's, and I noticed that he was fat and baldheaded, and had an expression of winning gentleness and simplicity upon his tranquil countenance. He roused up, and gave me good day. I told him a friend of mine had commissioned me to make some inquiries about a cherished companion of his boyhood named *Leonidas W.* Smiley—Rev. *Leonidas W.* Smiley, a young minister of the Gospel, who he had heard was at one time a resident of Angel's Camp. I added that if Mr. Wheeler could tell me anything about this Rev. Leonidas W. Smiley, I would feel under many obligations to him.

Simon Wheeler backed me into a corner and blockaded me there with his chair, and then sat down and reeled off the monotonous narrative which follows this paragraph. He never smiled, he never frowned, he never changed his voice from the gentle-flowing key to which he tuned his initial sentence, he never betrayed the slightest suspicion of enthusiasm; but all through the interminable narrative there ran a vein of impressive earnestness and sincerity which showed me plainly that, so far from his imagining that there was anything ridiculous or funny about his story, he regarded it as a really important matter, and admired its two heroes as men of transcendent genius in finesse. I let him go on in his own way, and never interrupted him once.

"Rev. Leonidas W. H'm, Reverend Le—well, there was a feller here once by the name of *Jim* Smiley, in the winter of '49—or maybe it was the spring of '50—I don't recollect exactly, somehow, though what makes me think it was one or the other is because I remember the big flume wasn't finished when he first came to the camp. But anyway, he was the curiousest man about always betting on anything that turned up you ever see, if he could get anybody to bet on the other side; and if he couldn't, he'd change sides. Any way that suited the other man would suit *him*—any way just so's he got a bet, *he* was satisfied. But still he was lucky, uncommon lucky; he most always come out winner. He was always ready and laying for a chance; there couldn't be no solit'ry thing mentioned but that feller'd offer to bet on it, and take any side you please, as I was just telling you. If there was a horse race, you'd find him flush or you'd find him busted at the end of it; if there was a dog fight, he'd bet on it; if there was a cat fight, he'd bet on it; if there was a chicken fight, he'd bet on it. Why, if there was two birds setting on a fence, he would bet you which one would fly first; or if there was a camp meeting,[1] he would be there reg'lar to bet on Parson Walker, which he judged to be the best exhorter about there, and so he was too, and a good man. If he even see a straddlebug[2] start to go anywheres, he would bet you how long it would take him to get wherever he was going to, and if you took him up, he would foller that straddlebug to Mexico but what he would[3] find out where he was bound for and how long he was on the road.

"Lots of the boys here has seen Smiley, and can tell you about him. Why, it never made no difference to *him*—he'd bet on *anything*—the dangdest feller. Parson Walker's wife laid

---

1. *camp meeting*, religious meeting held outdoors or in a tent, usually lasting several days. 2. *straddlebug*, any one of several species of long-legged beetles. 3. *but what he would*, in order to.

very sick once, for a good while, and it seemed as if they warn't going to save her; but one morning he come in, and Smiley asked how she was, and he said she was considerable better—thank the Lord for His inf'nite mercy —and coming on so smart that with the blessing of Prov'dence she'd get well yet; and Smiley, before he thought, says, 'Well, I'll resk two-and-a-half that she don't anyway.'

"Thish-yer Smiley had a mare—the boys called her the fifteen-minute nag, but that was only in fun, you know, because of course she was faster than that—and he used to win money on that horse, for all she was so slow and always had the asthma, or the distemper, or the consumption, or something of that kind. They used to give her two or three hundred yards' start, and then pass her under way; but always at the fag end of the race she'd get excited and desperate-like, and come cavorting and straddling up, and scattering her legs around limber, sometimes in the air, and sometimes out to one side among the fences, and kicking up m-o-r-e dust and raising m-o-r-e racket with her coughing and sneezing and blowing her nose—and *always* fetch up at the stand just about a neck ahead, as near as you could cipher it down.

"And he had a little small bull pup, that to look at him you'd think he wan't worth a cent but to set around and look ornery and lay for a chance to steal something. But as soon as money was up on him he was a different dog; his under jaw'd begin to stick out like the fo'castle of a steamboat, and his teeth would uncover and shine like the furnaces. And a dog might tackle him and bullyrag him, and bite him, and throw him over his shoulder two or three times, and Andrew Jackson— which was the name of the pup—Andrew Jackson would never let on but what *he* was satisfied, and hadn't expected nothing else—and the bets being doubled and doubled on the other side all the time, till the money was all up; and then all of a sudden he would grab that other dog jest by the j'int of his hind leg and freeze to it—not chaw, you understand, but only just grip and hang on till they throwed up the sponge, if it was a year.

"Smiley always come out winner on that

pup, till he harnessed a dog once that didn't have no hind legs, because they'd been sawed off by a circular saw, and when the thing had gone along far enough, and the money was all up, and he come to make a snatch for his pet holt, he saw in a minute how he'd been imposed on, and how the other dog had him in the door,[4] so to speak, and he 'peared surprised, and then he looked sorter discouraged-like, and didn't try no more to win the fight, and so he got shucked out[5] bad. He give Smiley a look, as much as to say his heart was broke, and it was *his* fault, for putting up a dog that hadn't no hind legs for him to take holt of, which was his main dependence in a fight, and then he limped off a piece and laid down and died. It was a good pup, was that Andrew Jackson, and would have made a name for hisself if he'd lived, for the stuff was in him and he had genius—I know it, because he hadn't had no opportunities to speak of, and it don't stand to reason that a dog could make such a fight as he could under them circumstances if he hadn't no talent. It always makes me feel sorry when I think of that last fight of his'n, and the way it turned out.

"Well, thish-yer Smiley had rat terriers, and chicken cocks, and tomcats and all them kind of things, till you couldn't rest, and you couldn't fetch nothing for him to bet on but he'd match you. He ketched a frog one day, and took him home, and said he calk'lated to edercate him; and so he never done nothing for three months but set in his back yard and learn that frog to jump. And you bet he *did* learn him, too. He'd give him a little punch behind, and the next minute you'd see that frog whirling in the air like a doughnut—see him turn one summer-set, or maybe a couple, if he got a good start, and come down flatfooted and all right, like a cat. He got him up so in the matter of catching flies, and kep' him in practice so constant, that he'd nail a fly every time as far as he could see him.

"Smiley said all a frog wanted was education, and he could do 'most anything—and I believe him. Why, I've seen him set Dan'l Webster down here on this floor—Dan'l Web-

---

4. *had him in the door*, had him at a disadvantage. 5. *shucked out*, beaten.

ster was the name of the frog—and sing out, 'Flies, Dan'l, flies!' and quicker'n you could wink he'd spring straight up and snake a fly off'n the counter there, and flop down on the floor ag'in as solid as a gob of mud, and fall to scratching the side of his head with his hind foot as indifferent as if he hadn't no idea he'd been doin' any more'n any frog might do. You never see a frog so modest and straightfor'ard as he was, for all he was so gifted. And when it come to fair and square jumping on a dead level, he could get over more ground at one straddle than any animal of his breed you ever see. Jumping on a dead level was his strong suit, you understand; and when it come to that, Smiley would ante up money on him as long as he had a red.[6] Smiley was monstrous proud of his frog, and well he might be, for fellers that had traveled and been everywheres all said he laid over any frog that ever *they* see.

"Well, Smiley kept the beast in a little lattice box, and he used to fetch him downtown sometimes and lay for a bet. One day a feller —a stranger in the camp, he was—come across him with his box, and says:

" 'What might it be that you've got in the box?'

"And Smiley says, sorter indifferent-like, 'It might be a parrot, or it might be a canary, maybe, but it ain't—it's only just a frog.'

"And the feller took it, and looked at it careful, and turned it round this way and that, and says, 'H'm—so 'tis. Well, what's *he* good for?'

" 'Well,' Smiley says, easy and careless, 'he's good enough for *one* thing, I should judge—he can outjump ary frog in Calaveras County.'

"The feller took the box again, and took another long, particular look, and give it back to Smiley, and says, very deliberate, 'Well, I don't see no p'ints about that frog that's any better'n any other frog.'

" 'Maybe you don't,' Smiley says. 'Maybe you understand frogs and maybe you don't understand 'em; maybe you've had experience, and maybe you ain't only a amature, as it were. Anyways, I've got *my* opinion, and I'll resk forty dollars that he can outjump any frog in Calaveras County.'

"And the feller studied a minute, and then says, kinder sad-like, 'Well, I'm only a stranger here, and I ain't got no frog; but if I had a frog, I'd bet you.'

"And then Smiley says, 'That's all right— that's all right—if you'll hold my box a minute, I'll go and get you a frog.' And so the feller took the box, and put up his forty dollars along with Smiley's, and set down to wait.

"So he set there a good while thinking and thinking to himself, and then he got the frog out and prized his mouth open and took a teaspoon and filled him full of quail shot— filled him pretty near up to his chin—and set him on the floor.

"Smiley he went to the swamp and slopped around in the mud for a long time, and finally he ketched a frog, and fetched him in, and give him to this feller, and says:

" 'Now, if you're ready, set him alongside of Dan'l, with his forepaws just even with Dan'l's, and I'll give the word.' Then he says, 'One—two—three—jump!' and him and the feller touched up the frogs from behind, and the new frog hopped off, but Dan'l give a heave and hysted up his shoulders—so—like a Frenchman, but it wan't no use—he couldn't budge; he was planted as solid as an anvil, and he couldn't no more stir than if he was anchored out. Smiley was a good deal surprised, and he was disgusted too, but he didn't have no idea what the matter was, of course.

"The feller took the money and started away; and when he was going out at the door, he sorter jerked his thumb over his shoulder—this way—at Dan'l, and says again, very deliberate, 'Well, *I* don't see no p'ints about that frog that's any better'n any other frog.'

"Smiley he stood scratching his head and looking down at Dan'l a long time, and at last he says, 'I do wonder what in the nation that frog throw'd off for—I wonder if there ain't something the matter with him—he 'pears to look mighty baggy, somehow.' And he ketched Dan'l by the nap of the neck, and lifted him up, and says, 'Why blame my cats if he don't weigh five pound!' and turned him upside

---

6. *a red*, a red cent, or any money at all.

down, and he belched out a double handful of shot. And then Smiley see how it was, and he was the maddest man—he set the frog down and took out after that feller, but he never ketched him. And—"

[Here Simon Wheeler heard his name called from the front yard, and got up to see what was wanted.] And turning to me as he moved away, he said: "Just set where you are, stranger, and rest easy—I ain't going to be gone a second."

But, by your leave, I did not think that a continuation of the history of the enterprising vagabond *Jim* Smiley would be likely to afford me much information concerning the Rev. *Leonidas W.* Smiley, and so I started away.

At the door I met the sociable Wheeler returning, and he buttonholed me and recommenced:

"Well, thish-yer Smiley had a yaller one-eyed cow that didn't have no tail, only just a short stump like a bannanner, and—"

However, lacking both time and inclination, I did not wait to hear about the afflicted cow, but took my leave.

FICTION WRITER Mark Twain won his greatest fame and his high position among American men of letters, not for journalistic reports or imaginative yarns, but for his two best-known novels—*The Adventures of Tom Sawyer* (1876) and *The Adventures of Huckleberry Finn* (1884).[1] Like Twain's journalistic reports, these novels were crammed with concrete details which he had observed, remembered fully, and set down. Sometimes historians quote passages from his books to show clearly what life of the sort he portrayed had been like. *Tom Sawyer,* for instance, offered a fine picture of the town of Hannibal (St. Petersburg in the book) in the days of Twain's boyhood—the houses, the church, the school—and the green countryside and the river. *Huckleberry Finn* pictured an even broader scene—the river and the towns alongside the river from Missouri to Arkansas. Twain seems to have tried to get into this novel as many classes of people and as many customs and scenes as possible. The result was a panorama of life in the Mississippi Valley in the mid-nineteenth century.

Like Twain's yarns, his best fiction was full of the characteristic talk of Americans. A note which he placed in the opening pages of *Huckleberry Finn* shows how much care he took to render American speech accurately:

In this book a number of dialects are used, to wit: the Missouri Negro dialect; the extremest form of the backwoods Southwestern dialect; the ordinary 'Pike County' dialect; and four modified varieties of this last. The shadings have not been done in a haphazard fashion, or by guesswork; but painstakingly, and with the trustworthy guidance and support of personal familiarity with these several forms of speech.

Yet though his novels resemble his journalistic stories and his yarns, they differ greatly in some respects. For one thing, when Twain was writing a first-rate novel, he could give its episodes

1. See the selection from *Huckleberry Finn* beginning on page 387. A guide to discussion of the complete novel will be found on page 400.

or even the whole book a well-rounded plot structure. In *Tom Sawyer*, several threads of narrative told how Tom moved from childhood to the threshold of maturity. Again, running throughout the whole of *Huckleberry Finn* is the boy's growing affection and respect for his Negro companion, Jim.

Also different from the journalistic reports and yarns is the tone of Mark's best fiction—one of longing for "the good old days." In the years between 1871 and 1891, when he wrote his two masterpieces, Twain was living in a big, elaborate mansion in Hartford, Connecticut, a great rambling house which he had built with the returns from his writings. He and his family had a coachman and several servants; they entertained lavishly; they frequently took trips to Europe. He was on friendly terms with great financial and literary figures. But it often seemed to him that the past had been the best time after all, and often he could not recall the old days without being homesick for them. When he heard from an old Hannibal schoolmate in 1870, he wrote: "The fountains of my great deep are broken up and I have rained reminiscences for four-and-twenty hours. The old life has swept before me like a panorama; the old days have trooped by in their old glory again; the old faces have looked out of the mists of the past; old footsteps have sounded in my listening ears; old hands have clasped mine; old voices have greeted me...."

Two views of the house Twain built in Hartford. The Hartford Daily Times called it "one of the oddest looking buildings in the state."

It was in such a spirit of tenderness and longing that Twain often wrote of the America of his boyhood. His feeling colored what he wrote, and the scenes he pictured frequently had more charm, more beauty, or more comedy than had the actual scenes upon which they were based. They were lifelike, to be sure, but they showed life in a rather more idyllic form than it had ever managed to achieve. Yet Twain, grown to manhood, knew about the tragedy of life, too, and he also stressed the faults, the troubles and sorrows of the men and women and children whom he portrayed. The result was a rich depiction of America during Twain's boyhood and youth.

Contemporary photo of the Blankenship House, reputedly Huck Finn's home.

FROM *The Adventures of Huckleberry Finn*

Mark Twain said of his greatest novel that it "is a story which details some passages in the life of an ignorant village boy, Huck Finn, son of the town drunkard....He has run away from his persecuting father, and from a persecuting good widow who wishes to make a nice, truth-telling, respectable boy of him; and with him a slave... has also escaped. They have found a fragment of a lumber raft, and are floating down the river by night, and hiding in the willows by day." Twilight is falling as the following incident begins. Huck Finn is the narrator.

We went along during three hours and more. Well, the night got gray and ruther thick, which is the next meanest thing to fog. You can't tell the shape of the river, and you can't see no distance. It got to be very late and still, and then along comes a steamboat up the river. We lit the lantern, and judged she would see it. Upstream boats didn't generly come close to us; they go out and follow the bars and hunt for easy water under the reefs; but nights like this they bull right up the channel against the whole river.

We could hear her pounding along, but we didn't see her good till she was close. She aimed right for us. Often they do that and try to see how close they can come without touching; sometimes the wheel bites off a sweep, and then the pilot sticks his head out and laughs, and thinks he's mighty smart. Well, here she comes, and we said she was going to try and shave us; but she didn't seem to be sheering off a bit. She was a high one, and she was coming in a hurry, too, looking like a black cloud with rows of glowworms around it; but all of a sudden she bulged out, big and scary, with a long row of wide-open furnace doors shining like red-hot teeth, and her monstrous bows and guards[1] hanging right over us. There was a yell at us, and a jingling of bells to stop the engines, a powwow of cussing, and whistling of steam—and as Jim went overboard on one side and I on the other, she came smashing straight through the raft.

I dived—and I aimed to find the bottom, too, for a thirty-foot wheel had got to go over me, and I wanted it to have plenty of room. I could always stay under water a minute; this time I reckon I stayed under a minute and a half. Then I bounced for the top in a hurry, for I was nearly busting. I popped out to my armpits and blowed the water out of my nose, and puffed a bit. Of course there was a booming current; and of course that boat started her engines again ten seconds after she stopped them, for they never cared much for raftsmen; so now she was churning along up the river, out of sight in the thick weather, though I could hear her.

I sung out for Jim about a dozen times, but I didn't get any answer; so I grabbed a plank that touched me while I was treading water, and struck out for shore, shoving it ahead of me. But I made out to see that the drift of the current was toward the left-hand shore, which meant that I was in a crossing[2]; so I changed off and went that way.

It was one of those long, slanting, two-mile crossings; so I was a good long time in getting over. I made a safe landing, and clumb up the bank. I couldn't see but a little ways, but I went poking along over rough ground for a quarter of a mile or more, and then I run across a big old-fashioned double log house before I noticed it. I was going to rush by and get away, but a lot of dogs jumped out and went to howling and barking at me, and I knowed better than to move another peg.

In about a minute somebody spoke out a window without putting his head out, and says: "Be done, boys! Who's there?"

I says: "It's me."

"Who's me?"

"George Jackson, sir."

"What do you want?"

"I don't want nothing, sir. I only want to go along by, but the dogs won't let me."

"What are you prowling around here this time of night for—hey?"

"I warn't prowling around, sir: I fell overboard off of the steamboat."

"Oh, you did, did you? Strike a light there, somebody. What did you say your name was?"

"George Jackson, sir. I'm only a boy."

"Look here, if you're telling the truth you needn't be afraid—nobody'll hurt you. But don't try to budge; stand right where you are. Rouse out Bob and Tom, some of you, and fetch the guns. George Jackson, is anybody with you?"

"No, sir, nobody."

I heard people stirring around the house now, and see a light. The man sung out:

"Snatch that light away, Betsy, you old fool —ain't you got any sense? Put it on the floor behind the front door. Bob, if you and Tom are ready, take your place."

"All ready."

"Now, George Jackson, do you know the Shepherdsons?"

"No, sir; I never heard of them."

"Well, that may be so, and it mayn't. Now, all ready. Step forward, George Jackson. And mind, don't you hurry—come mighty slow. If there's anybody with you, let him keep back— if he shows himself, he'll be shot. Come along now. Come slow; push the door open yourself —just enough to squeeze in, d'you hear?"

I didn't hurry; I couldn't if I'd wanted to. I took one slow step at a time and there warn't a sound, only I thought I could hear my heart. The dogs were as still as the humans, but they followed a little behind me. When I got to the three log doorsteps, I heard them unlocking and unbarring and unbolting. I put my hand on the door and pushed it a little and a little more till somebody said, "There, that's enough —put your head in." I done it, but I judged they would take it off.

The candle was on the floor, and there they all was, looking at me, and me at them, for about a quarter of a minute: Three big men with guns pointed at me, which made me

---

1. guards, the parts of the boat's deck which curved out over the paddle wheels at each side of the ship. 2. a crossing, a place in a river at which the channel, which follows the current, shifts from one side of the river to the other.

wince, I tell you; the oldest, gray and about sixty, the other two thirty or more—all of them fine and handsome—and the sweetest old gray-headed lady, and back of her two young women which I couldn't see right well. The old gentleman says:

"There; I reckon it's all right. Come in."

As soon as I was in, the old gentleman he locked the door and barred it and bolted it, and told the young men to come in with their guns, and they all went in a big parlor that had a new rag carpet on the floor, and got together in a corner that was out of the range of the front windows—there warn't none on the side. They held the candle, and took a good look at me, and all said, "Why, *he* ain't a Shepherdson—no, there ain't any Shepherdson about him." Then the old man said he hoped I wouldn't mind being searched for arms, because he didn't mean no harm by it—it was only to make sure. So he didn't pry into my pockets, but only felt outside with his hands, and said it was all right. He told me to make myself easy and at home, and tell all about myself; but the old lady says:

"Why, bless you, Saul, the poor thing's as wet as he can be; and don't you reckon it may be he's hungry?"

"True for you, Rachel—I forgot."

So the old lady says: "Betsy, you fly around and get him something to eat as quick as you can, poor thing; and one of you girls go and wake up Buck and tell him—oh, here he is himself. Buck, take this little stranger and get the wet clothes off from him and dress him up in some of yours that's dry."

Buck looked about as old as me—thirteen or fourteen or along there, though he was a little bigger than me. He hadn't on anything but a shirt, and he was very frowzy-headed. He came in gaping and digging one fist into his eyes, and he was dragging a gun along with the other one. He says: "Ain't they no Shepherdsons around?"

They said, no, 'twas a false alarm.

"Well," he says, "if they'd 'a' ben some, I reckon I'd 'a' got one."

They all laughed, and Bob says: "Why, Buck, they might have scalped us all, you've been so slow in coming."

"Well, nobody came after me, and it ain't right. I'm always kept down; I don't get no show."

"Never mind, Buck, my boy," says the old man, "you'll have show enough, all in good time, don't you fret about that. Go 'long with you now, and do as your mother told you."

When we got upstairs to his room, he got me a coarse shirt and a roundabout and pants of his, and I put them on. While I was at it he asked me what my name was, but before I could tell him he started to tell me about a bluejay and a young rabbit he had catched in the woods day before yesterday, and he asked me where Moses was when the candle went out. I said I didn't know; I hadn't heard about it before, no way.

"Well, guess," he says.

"How'm I going to guess," says I, "when I never heard tell of it before?"

"But you can guess, can't you? It's just as easy."

"*Which* candle?" I says.

"Why, any candle," he says.

"I don't know where he was," says I; "where was he?"

"Why, he was in the *dark!* That's where he was!"

"Well, if you knowed where he was, what did you ask me for?"

"Why, blame it, it's a riddle, don't you see? Say, how long are you going to stay here? You got to stay always. We can just have booming times—they don't have no school now. Do you own a dog? I've got a dog—and he'll go in the river and bring out chips that you throw in. Do you like to comb up Sundays, and all that kind of foolishness? You bet I don't, but Ma she makes me. Confound these ole britches! I reckon I'd better put 'em on, but I'd rather not, it's so warm. Are you all ready? All right. Come along, old hoss."

Cold corn pone, cold corn-beef, butter, and buttermilk—that is what they had for me down there, and there ain't nothing better that ever I've come across yet. Buck and his ma and all of them smoked cob pipes, except Betsy, who was gone, and the two young women. They all smoked and talked, and I eat and talked. The young women had quilts around them, and their hair down their backs. They all asked me questions, and I told them how Pap and me and all the family was living on a little farm down at the bottom of Arkansaw, and my sister Mary Ann run off and got married and never was heard of no more, and Bill went to hunt them and he warn't heard of no more, and Tom and Mort died, and then there warn't nobody but just me and Pap left, and he was just trimmed down to nothing, on account of his troubles; so when he died I took what there was left, because the farm didn't belong to us, and started up the river, deck passage,[3] and fell overboard; and that was how I come to be here. So they said I could have a home there as long as I wanted it. Then it was most daylight and everybody went to bed.

I went to bed with Buck, and when I waked up in the morning, drat it all, I had forgot what my name was. So I laid there about an hour trying to think, and when Buck waked up I says: "Can you spell, Buck?"

"Yes," he says.

"I bet you can't spell my name," says I.

"I bet you what you dare I can," says he.

"All right," says I, "go ahead."

"G-e-o-r-g-e- J-a-x-o-n—there now," he says.

"Well," says I, "you done it, but I didn't think you could. It ain't no slouch of a name to spell—right off without studying."

I set it down, private, because somebody might want *me* to spell it next, and so I wanted to be handy with it and rattle it off like I was used to it.

It was a mighty nice family, and a mighty nice house, too. I hadn't seen no house out in the country before that was so nice and had so much style. It didn't have an iron latch on the front door, nor a wooden one with a buckskin string, but a brass knob to turn, the same as houses in town. There warn't no bed in the parlor, nor a sign of a bed; but heaps of parlors in towns has beds in them. There was a big fireplace that was bricked on the bottom, and the bricks was kept clean and red by pouring water on them and scrubbing them with another brick; sometimes they wash them over with red water paint that they call Spanish brown, same as they do in town. They had

big brass dog irons that could hold up a saw log. There was a clock on the middle of the mantelpiece, with a picture of a town painted on the bottom half of the glass front, and a round place in the middle of it for the sun, and you could see the pendulum swinging behind it. It was beautiful to hear that clock tick; and sometimes when one of these peddlers had been along and scoured her up and got her in good shape, she would start in and strike a hundred and fifty before she got tuckered out. They wouldn't took any money for her.

Well, there was a big outlandish parrot on each side of the clock, made out of something like chalk, and painted up gaudy. By one of the parrots was a cat made of crockery, and a crockery dog by the other; and when you pressed down on them they squeaked, but didn't open their mouth nor look different nor interested. They squeaked through underneath. There was a couple of big wild-turkey-wing fans spread out behind those things. On the table in the middle of the room was a kind of a lovely crockery basket that had apples and oranges and peaches and grapes piled up in it, which was much redder and yellower and prettier than real ones is, but they warn't real because you could see where pieces had got chipped off and showed the white chalk, or whatever it was, underneath.

This table had a cover made out of beautiful oilcloth, with a red and blue spread eagle painted on it, and a painted border all around. It came all the way from Philadelphia, they said. There was some books, too, piled up perfectly exact, on each corner of the table. One was a big family Bible full of pictures. One was *Pilgrim's Progress*, about a man that left his family, it didn't say why. I read considerable in it now and then. The statements was interesting, but tough. Another was *Friendship's Offering*, full of beautiful stuff and poetry; but I didn't read the poetry. Another was Henry Clay's speeches, and another was Dr. Gunn's *Family Medicine*, which told you all about what to do if a body was sick or dead. There was a hymnbook, and a lot of

---

3. *deck passage*, traveling on the deck of a steamboat. This was the cheapest way to travel.

other books. And there was nice, split-bottom chairs, and perfectly sound, too—not bagged down in the middle and busted, like an old basket.

They had pictures hung on the walls—mainly Washingtons and Lafayettes, and battles, and Highland Marys,[4] and one called "Signing the Declaration." There was some that they called crayons, which one of the daughters which was dead made her own self when she was only fifteen years old. They was different from any pictures I ever see before—blacker, mostly, than is common. One was a woman in a slim black dress, belted small under the armpits, with bulges like a cabbage in the middle of the sleeves, and a large black scoop-shovel bonnet with a black veil, and white slim ankles crossed about with black tape, and very wee black slippers, like a chisel, and she was leaning pensive on a tombstone on her right elbow, under a weeping willow, and her other hand hanging down her side holding a white handkerchief and a reticule, and underneath the picture it said "Shall I Never See Thee More Alas." Another one was a young lady with her hair all combed up straight to the top of her head, and knotted there in front of a comb like a chair back, and she was crying into a handkerchief and had a dead bird laying on its back in her other hand with its heels up, and underneath the picture it said "I Shall Never Hear Thy Sweet Chirrup More Alas." There was one where a young lady was at a window looking up at the moon, and tears running down her cheeks; and she had an open letter in one hand with black sealing wax showing on one edge of it, and she was mashing a locket with a chain to it against her mouth, and underneath the picture it said "And Art Thou Gone Yes Thou Art Gone Alas."

These was all nice pictures, I reckon, but I didn't somehow seem to take to them, because if ever I was down a little they always give me the fantods.[5] Everybody was sorry the girl died, because she had laid out a lot more of these pictures to do, and a body could see by what she had done what they had lost. But I reckoned that with her disposition she was having a better time in the graveyard. She was at work on what they said was her greatest picture when she took sick, and every day and every night it was her prayer to be allowed to live till she got it done, but she never got the chance. It was a picture of a young woman in a long white gown, standing on the rail of a bridge all ready to jump off, with her hair all down her back, and looking up to the moon, with the tears running down her face, and she had two arms folded across her breast, and two arms stretched out in front, and two more reaching up toward the moon—and the idea was to see which pair would look best, and then scratch out all the other arms; but, as I was saying, she died before she got her mind made up and now they kept this picture over the head of the bed in her room, and every time her birthday come they hung flowers on it. Other times it was hid with a little curtain. The young woman in the picture had a kind of a nice sweet face, but there was so many arms it made her look too spidery, seemed to me.

This young girl kept a scrapbook when she was alive, and used to paste obituaries and accidents and cases of patient suffering in it out of the *Presbyterian Observer,* and write poetry after them out of her own head. It was very good poetry. This is what she wrote about a boy by the name of Stephen Dowling Bots that fell down a well and was drownded:

ODE TO STEPHEN DOWLING BOTS, DEC'D.

And did young Stephen sicken,
   And did young Stephen die?
And did the sad hearts thicken,
   And did the mourners cry?

No; such was not the fate of
   Young Stephen Dowling Bots;
Though sad hearts round him thickened,
   'Twas not from sickness' shots.

No whooping cough did rack his frame,
   Nor measles drear with spots;
Not these impaired the sacred name
   Of Stephen Dowling Bots.

---

4. *Highland Marys,* pictures of beautiful girls. The name "Highland Mary" refers to Mary Campbell, to whom the Scotch poet Robert Burns wrote some of his finest poetry.
5. *the fantods,* the fidgets. [*Slang*]

Despised love struck not with woe
  That head of curly knots,
Nor stomach troubles laid him low,
  Young Stephen Dowling Bots.

O no. Then list with tearful eye,
  Whilst I his fate do tell,
His soul did from this cold world fly
  By falling down a well.

They got him out and emptied him;
  Alas it was too late;
His spirit was gone for to sport aloft
  In the realms of the good and great.

If Emmeline Grangerford could make poetry like that before she was fourteen, there ain't no telling what she could 'a' done by and by. Buck said she could rattle off poetry like nothing. She didn't ever have to stop to think. He said she would slap down a line, and if she couldn't find anything to rhyme with it would just scratch it out and slap down another one, and go ahead. She warn't particular; she could write about anything you choose to give her to write about just so it was sadful. Every time a man died, or a woman died, or a child died, she would be on hand with her "tribute" before he was cold. She called them tributes. The neighbors said it was the doctor first, then Emmeline, then the undertaker—the undertaker never got in ahead of Emmeline but once, and then she hung fire on a rhyme for the dead person's name, which was Whistler. She warn't ever the same after that; she never complained, but she kinder pined away and did not live long.

Poor thing, many's the time I made myself go up to the little room that used to be hers and get out her poor old scrapbook and read in it when her pictures had been aggravating me and I had soured on her a little. I liked all that family, dead ones and all, and warn't going to let anything come between us. Poor Emmeline made poetry about all the dead people when she was alive, and it didn't seem right that there warn't nobody to make some about her now she was gone; so I tried to sweat out a verse or two myself, but I couldn't seem to make it go somehow. . . .

It was a double house, and the big open place betwixt them was roofed and floored, and sometimes the table was set there in the middle of the day, and it was a cool, comfortable place. Nothing couldn't be better. And warn't the cooking good, and just bushels of it too!

Col. Grangerford was a gentleman, you see. He was a gentleman all over; and so was his family. He was wellborn, as the saying is, and that's worth as much in a man as it is in a horse, so the Widow Douglas[6] said.

Col. Grangerford was very tall and very slim, and had a darkish-paly complexion, not a sign of red in it anywheres; he was clean-shaved every morning all over his thin face, and he had the thinnest kind of lips, and the thinnest kind of nostrils, and a high nose, and heavy eyebrows, and the blackest kind of eyes, sunk so deep back that they seemed like they was looking out of caverns at you, as you may say. His forehead was high, and his hair was gray and straight and hung to his shoulders. His hands was long and thin, and every day of his life he put on a clean shirt and a full suit from head to foot made out of linen so white it hurt your eyes to look at it; and on Sundays he wore a blue tailcoat with brass buttons on it. He carried a mahogany cane with a silver head to it. There warn't no frivolishness about him, not a bit, and he warn't ever loud. He was as kind as he could be—you could feel that, you know, and so you had confidence. Sometimes he smiled and it was good to see; but when he straightened himself up like a liberty pole, and the lightning begun to flicker out from under his eyebrows, you wanted to climb a tree first, and find out what the matter was afterwards.

When him and the old lady come down in the morning, all the family got out of their chairs and give them good day, and didn't set down again till they had set down. . . .

Bob was the oldest and Tom next—tall, beautiful men with very broad shoulders and brown faces, and long black hair and black eyes. They dressed in white linen from head to foot, like the old gentleman, and wore broad Panama hats.

---

6. *the* Widow Douglas, the good widow from whose home Huck has run away.

Then there was Miss Charlotte; she was twenty-five, and tall and proud and grand, but as good as she could be when she warn't stirred up; but when she was, she had a look that would make you wilt in your tracks, like her father. She was beautiful.

So was her sister, Miss Sophia, but it was a different kind. She was gentle and sweet like a dove, and she was only twenty.

Each person had somebody to wait on them —Buck too. My boy had a monstrous easy time, because I warn't used to having anybody do anything for me, but Buck's was on the jump most of the time.

This was all there was of the family now, but there used to be more—three sons; they got killed; and Emmeline that died.

Sometimes a stack of people would come there, horseback, from ten or fifteen miles around, and stay five or six days, and have such junketings round about and on the river, and dances and picnics in the woods daytimes, and balls at the house nights. These people was mostly kinfolks of the family. The men brought their guns with them. It was a handsome lot of quality, I tell you.

There was another clan of aristocracy around there—five or six families—mostly of the name of Shepherdson. They was as high-toned and wellborn and rich and grand as the tribe of Grangerfords. The Shepherdsons and Grangerfords used the same steamboat landing, which was about two mile above the Grangerfords' house; so sometimes when I went up there with a lot of our folks, I used to see a lot of the Shepherdsons there on their fine horses.

One day Buck and me was away out in the woods hunting, and heard a horse coming. We was crossing the road. Buck says: "Quick! Jump for the woods!"

We done it, and then peeped down the woods through the leaves. Pretty soon a splendid young man came galloping down the road, setting his horse easy and looking like a soldier. He had his gun across his pommel. I had seen him before. It was young Harney Shepherdson. I heard Buck's gun go off at my ear, and Harney's hat tumbled off from his head. He grabbed his gun and rode straight to the place where we was hid. But we didn't wait. We started through the woods on a run. The woods warn't thick, so I looked over my shoulder to dodge the bullet, and twice I seen Harney cover Buck with his gun; and then he rode away the way he come—to get his hat, I reckon, but I couldn't see. We never stopped running till we got home. The old gentleman's eyes blazed a minute—'twas pleasure, mainly, I judged—then his face sort of smoothed down, and he says, kind of gentle: "I don't like that shooting from behind a bush. Why didn't you step into the road, my boy?"

"The Shepherdsons don't, Father. They always take advantage."

Miss Charlotte she held her head up like a queen while Buck was telling his tale, and her nostrils spread and her eyes snapped. The two young men looked dark, but never said nothing. Miss Sophia she turned pale, but the color came back when she found the man warn't hurt.

Soon as I could get Buck down by the corn-cribs under the trees by ourselves, I says: "Did you want to kill him, Buck?"

"Well, I bet I did."

"What did he do to you?"

"Him? He never done nothing to me."

"Well, then, what did you want to kill him for?"

"Why, nothing—only it's on account of the feud."

"What's a feud?"

"Why, where was you raised? Don't you know what a feud is?"

"Never heard of it before—tell me about it."

"Well," says Buck, "a feud is this way: A man has a quarrel with another man, and kills him; then that other man's brother kills *him*; then the other brothers, on both sides, goes for one another; then the *cousins* chip in—and by and by everybody's killed off, and there ain't no more feud. But it's kind of slow, and takes a long time."

"Has this one been going on long, Buck?"

"Well, I should *reckon!* It started thirty years ago, or some'ers along there. There was trouble 'bout something, and then a lawsuit to settle it; and the suit went agin one of the men, and so he up and shot the man that won the suit—which he would naturally do, of course. Anybody would."

"What was the trouble about, Buck?—land?"

"I reckon maybe—I don't know."

"Well, who done the shooting? Was it a Grangerford or a Shepherdson?"

"Laws, how do I know? It was all long ago."

"Don't anybody know?"

"Oh, yes, Pa knows, I reckon, and some of the other old people; but they don't know now what the row was about in the first place."

"Has there been many killed, Buck?"

"Yes; right smart chance of funerals. But they don't always kill. Pa's got a few buckshot in him; but he don't mind it, 'cuz he don't weigh much anyway. Bob's been carved up some with a bowie, and Tom's been hurt once or twice."

"Has anybody been killed this year, Buck?"

"Yes; we got one, and they got one. 'Bout three months ago my cousin Bud, fourteen year old, was riding through the woods on t'other side of the river, and didn't have no weapon with him, which was blame' foolishness, and in a lonesome place he hears a horse a-coming behind him, and sees old Baldy Shepherdson a-linkin' after him with his gun in his hand and his white hair a-flying in the wind; and 'stead of jumping off and taking to the brush, Bud 'lowed he could outrun him; so they had it, nip and tuck, for five mile or more, the old man a-gaining all the time. So at last Bud seen it warn't any use, so he stopped and faced around so as to have the bullet holes in front, you know, and the old man he rode up and shot him down. But he didn't get much chance to enjoy his luck, for inside of a week our folks laid him out."

"I reckon that old man was a coward, Buck."

"I reckon he warn't a coward. Not by a blame' sight. There ain't a coward amongst them Shepherdsons—not a one. And there ain't no cowards amongst the Grangerfords either. Why, that old man kep' up his end in a fight one day for half an hour against three Grangerfords, and come out winner. They was all a-horseback; he lit off of his horse and got behind a little woodpile, and kep' his horse before him to stop the bullets; but the Grangerfords stayed on their horses and capered around the old man, and peppered away at him, and he peppered away at them. Him and his horse went home pretty leaky and crippled, but the Grangerfords had to be *fetched* home—and one of 'em was dead, and another died the next day. No, sir; if a body's out hunting for cowards, he don't want to fool anytime amongst them Shepherdsons, becuz they don't breed any of that *kind*."

Next Sunday we all went to church, about three mile, everybody a-horseback. The men took their guns along, so did Buck, and kept them between their knees or stood them handy against the wall. The Shepherdsons done the same. It was pretty ornery preaching—all about brotherly love, and suchlike tiresomeness; but everybody said it was a good sermon, and they all talked it over going home, and had such a powerful lot to say about faith and good works and free grace and preforeordestination,[7] and I don't know what all, that it did seem to me to be one of the roughest Sundays I had run across yet.

About an hour after dinner everybody was dozing around, some in their chairs and some in their rooms, and it got to be pretty dull. Buck and a dog was stretched out on the grass in the sun sound asleep. I went up to our room, and judged I would take a nap myself. I found that sweet Miss Sophia standing in her door, which was next to ours, and she took me in her room and shut the door very soft, and asked me if I liked her, and I said I did; and she asked me if I would do something for her and not tell anybody, and I said I would. Then she said she'd forgot her Testament, and left it in the seat at church between two other books, and would I slip out quiet and go there and fetch it to her, and not say nothing to nobody. I said I would. So I slid out and slipped off up the road, and there warn't anybody at the church, except maybe a hog or two, for there warn't any lock on the door, and hogs likes a puncheon floor in summertime because

---

7. *preforeordestination*. Huck is combining *predestination* and *foreordination*, both of which mean "that which has been determined by God from all eternity."

it's cool. If you notice, most folks don't go to church only when they've got to; but a hog is different.

Says I to myself, something's up; it ain't natural for a girl to be in such a sweat about a Testament. So I give it a shake, and out drops a little piece of paper with *"Half past two"* wrote on it with a pencil. I ransacked it, but couldn't find anything else. I couldn't make anything out of that, so I put the paper in the book again, and when I got home and upstairs there was Miss Sophia in her door waiting for me.

She pulled me in and shut the door; then she looked in the Testament till she found the paper, and as soon as she read it, she looked glad; and before a body could think she grabbed me and give me a squeeze and said I was the best boy in the world, and not to tell anybody. She was mighty red in the face for a minute, and her eyes lighted up, and it made her powerful pretty. I was a good deal astonished, but when I got my breath, I asked her what the paper was about, and she asked me if I had read it, and I said no, and she asked me if I could read writing, and I told her no, only coarse hand,[8] and then she said the paper warn't anything but a bookmark to keep her place, and I might go and play now.

I went off down to the river, studying over this thing, and pretty soon I noticed that my boy was following along behind. When we was out of sight of the house, he looked back and around a second, and then comes a-running, and says: "If you'll come down into de swamp, I'll show you a whole stack o' water moccasins."

Thinks I, that's mighty curious; he said that yesterday. He oughter know a body don't love water moccasins enough to go around hunting for them. What is he up to, anyway?

So I says: "All right; trot ahead."

I followed a half a mile; then he struck out over the swamp and waded ankle-deep as much as another half mile. We come to a little flat piece of land which was dry and very thick with trees and bushes and vines, and he says: "You shove right in dah jist a few steps; dah's whah dey is. I's seed 'm befo'; I don't k'yer to see 'em no mo'."

Then he slopped right along and went away, and pretty soon the trees hid him. I poked into the place a ways and come to a little open patch as big as a bedroom all hung around with vines, and found a man laying ther asleep—and, by jings, it was my old Jim!

I waked him up, and I reckoned it was going to be a grand surprise to him to see me again, but it warn't. He nearly cried he was so glad, but he warn't surprised. Said he swum along behind me that night, and heard me yell every time, but dasn't answer, because he didn't want nobody to pick *him* up and take him into slavery again. Says he: "I got hurt a little, en couldn't swim fas', so I wuz a considerable ways behine you towards de las'; when you landed, I reck'ned I could ketch up wid you on de lan' 'dout havin' to shout at you, but when I see dat house, I begin to go slow. I 'uz off too fur to hear what dey say to you— I wuz 'fraid o' de dogs; but when it 'uz all quiet ag'in, I knowed you's in de house, so I struck out for de woods to wait for day. Early in de mawnin' some er de hands come along, gwyne to de field, en dey tuk me en showed me dis place, whah de dogs can't track me on account o' de water, en dey brings me truck to eat every night, en tells me how you's a-gittin' along."

"Why didn't you tell my Jack to fetch me here sooner, Jim?"

"Well, 'twarn't no use to 'sturb you, Huck, tell we could do sumfn—but we's all right now. I ben a-buyin' pots en pans en vittles, as I got a chanst, en a-patchin' up de raf' nights when——"

"*What* raft, Jim?"

"Our ole raf'."

"You mean to say our old raft warn't smashed all to flinders?"

"No, she warn't. She was tore up a good deal—one en' of her was; but dey warn't no great harm done, only our traps[9] was mos' all los'. Ef we hadn' dive' so deep en swum so fur under water, en de night hadn't been so dark, en we warn't so sk'yered, en ben sich punkinheads, as de sayin' is, we'd a seed de

---

8. *coarse hand,* a clumsy handwriting.   9. *traps,* equipment.

raf'. But it's jis' as well we didn't, 'kase now she's all fixed up ag'in mos' as good as new, en we's got a new lot o' stuff, in de place o' what us los'."

"Why, how did you get hold of the raft again, Jim—did you catch her?"

"How I gwyne to ketch her en I out in de woods? No; some er de hands foun' her ketched on a snag along heah in de ben', en dey hid her in a crick 'mongst de willows, en dey wuz so much jawin' 'bout which un 'um she b'longs to de mos' dat I come to heah 'bout it pretty soon, so I ups en settles de trouble by tellin' 'um she don't b'long to none uv 'um, but to you en me; en I ast 'm if dey gwyne to grab a young genlman's propaty, en git a hid'n[10] for it? Den I gin 'm ten cents apiece, en dey 'uz mighty well satisfied, en wisht some mo' raf's 'ud come along en make 'm rich ag'in. Dey's mighty good to me, dese folks is, en whatever I wants 'm to do fur me I doan' have to ast 'm twice, honey. Dat Jack's a good boy."

"Yes, he is. He ain't ever told me you was here; told me to come, and he'd show me a lot of water moccasins. If anything happens, *he* ain't mixed up in it. He can say he never seen us together, and it'll be the truth."

I don't want to talk much about the next day. I reckon I'll cut it pretty short. I waked up about dawn, and was a-going to turn over and go to sleep again when I noticed how still it was—didn't seem to be anybody stirring. That warn't usual. Next I noticed that Buck was up and gone. Well, I gets up, a-wondering, and goes downstairs—nobody around; everything as still as a mouse. Just the same outside. Thinks I, what does it mean?

Down by the woodpile I comes across my Jack, and says: "What's it all about?"

Says he: "Don't you know?"

"No," says I, "I don't."

"Well, den, Miss Sophia's run off! 'deed she has. She run off in de night some time—nobody don't know jis' when—run off to get married to dat young Harney Shepherdson, you know—leastways, so dey 'spec. De fambly foun' it out 'bout half an hour ago—maybe a little mo'—en I *tell* you, dey warn't no time los'. Sich another hurryin' up guns en hosses

you never see! De women folks has gone for to stir up de relations, en ole Mars Saul en de boys tuck dey guns en rode up de river road for to try to ketch dat young man en kill him 'fo' he kin git acrost de river wid Miss Sophia. I reck'n dey's gwyne to be mighty rough times."

"Buck went off 'thout waking me up."

"Well, I reck'n he *did*! Dey warn't gwyne to mix you up in it. Mars Buck he loaded up his gun en 'lowed he's gwyne to fetch home a Shepherdson or bust. Well, dey'll be plenty un 'm dah, I reck'n, en you bet you he'll fetch one."

I took up the river road as hard as I could put. By and by I begin to hear guns a good ways off. When I come in sight of the log store and the woodpile where the steamboats land, I worked along under the trees and brush till I got to a good place, and then I clumb up into the forks of a cottonwood that was out of reach, and watched. There was a wood rank[11] four foot high a little ways in front of the tree, and first I was going to hide behind that; but maybe it was luckier I didn't.

There was four or five men cavorting around on their horses in the open place before the log store, cussing and yelling, and trying to get at a couple of young chaps that was behind the wood rank alongside of the steamboat landing; but they couldn't come it. Every time one of them showed himself on the river side of the woodpile, he got shot at. The two boys was squatting back to back behind the pile, so they could watch both ways.

By and by the men stopped cavorting around and yelling. They started riding toward the store; then up gets one of the boys, draws a steady bead over the wood rank, and drops one of them out of his saddle. All the men jumped off of their horses and grabbed the hurt one and started to carry him to the store; and that minute the two boys started on the run. They got halfway to the tree I was in before the men noticed. Then the men see them, and jumped on their horses and took out after them. They gained on the boys, but it didn't do no good, the boys had too good a

10. hid'n, hiding, or whipping. 11. *wood rank*, one length of corded wood, or a pile eight feet long.

start; they got to the woodpile that was in front of my tree, and slipped in behind it, and so they had the bulge[12] on the men again. One of the boys was Buck, and the other was a slim young chap about nineteen years old.

The men ripped around awhile, and then rode away. As soon as they was out of sight, I sung out to Buck and told him. He didn't know what to make of my voice coming out of the tree at first. He was awful surprised. He told me to watch out sharp and let him know when the men come in sight again; said they was up to some devilment or other.

I wished I was out of that tree, but I dasn't come down. Buck begun to cry and rip, and 'lowed that him and his cousin Joe (that was the other young chap) would make up for this day yet. He said his father and his two brothers was killed and two or three of the enemy. Said the Shepherdsons laid for them in ambush. Buck said his father and brothers ought to waited for their relations—the Shepherdsons was too strong for them. I asked him what was become of young Harney and Miss Sophia. He said they'd got across the river and was safe. I was glad of that; but the way Buck did take on because he didn't manage to kill Harney that day he shot at him—I hain't ever heard anything like it.

All of a sudden, bang! bang! bang! goes three or four guns—the men had slipped around through the woods and come in from behind without their horses! The boys jumped for the river—both of them hurt—and as they swum down the current the men run along the bank shooting at them and singing out, "Kill them, kill them!" It made me so sick I most fell out of the tree. I ain't a-going to tell *all* that happened—it would make me sick again. I wished I hadn't ever come ashore that night to see such things. I ain't ever going to get shut of them—lots of times I dream about them.

I stayed in the tree till it begun to get dark, afraid to come down. Sometimes I heard guns away off in the woods; and twice I seen little gangs of men gallop past the log store with guns; so I reckoned the trouble was still a-going on. I was mighty downhearted; so I made up my mind I wouldn't ever go anear the house again, because I reckoned I was to blame, somehow. I judged that that piece of paper meant that Miss Sophia was to meet Harney somewheres at half past two and run off; and I judged I ought to told her father about that paper and the curious way she acted, and then maybe he would 'a' locked her up, and this awful mess wouldn't ever happened.

When I got down out of the tree I crept along down the river bank a piece, and found the two bodies laying in the edge of the water, and tugged at them till I got them ashore; then I covered up their faces, and got away as quick as I could. I cried a little when I was covering up Buck's face, for he was mighty good to me.

It was just dark now. I never went near the house, but struck through the woods and made for the swamp. Jim warn't on his island, so I tramped off in a hurry for the crick, and crowded through the willows, red-hot to jump aboard and get out of that awful country. The raft was gone! My souls, but I was scared! I couldn't get my breath for most a minute. Then I raise a yell. A voice not twenty-five foot from me says: "Good lan'! is dat you, honey? Doan' make a noise."

It was Jim's voice—nothing ever sounded so good before. I run along the bank a piece and got aboard, and Jim he grabbed me and hugged me, he was so glad to see me. He says: "Laws bless you, chile, I 'uz right down sho' you's dead ag'in. Jack's been heah; he says he reck'n you's been shot, kase you didn' come home no mo'; so I's jes' dis minute a'startin' de raf' down towards de mouf er de crick, so's to be all ready for to shove out en leave soon as Jack comes ag'in en tells me for certain you *is* dead. Lawsy, I's mighty glad to get you back ag'in, honey."

I says: "All right—that's mighty good; they won't find me, and they'll think I've been killed and floated down the river—there's something up there that'll help them think so—so don't you lose no time, Jim, but just shove off for the big water as fast as ever you can."

I never felt easy till the raft was two mile

---

12. *had the bulge*, had the advantage or upper hand.

below there and out in the middle of the Mississippi. Then we hung up our signal lantern, and judged that we was free and safe once more. I hadn't had a bite to eat since yesterday, so Jim he got out some corn dodgers and buttermilk, and pork and cabbage and greens —there ain't nothing in the world so good when it's cooked right—and whilst I eat my supper we talked and had a good time. I was powerful glad to get away from the feuds, and so was Jim to get away from the swamp. We said there warn't no home like a raft, after all. Other places do seem so cramped up and smothery, but a raft don't. You feel mighty free and easy and comfortable on a raft.

Two or three days and nights went by; I reckon I might say they swum by, they slid along so quiet and smooth and lovely. Here is the way we put in the time. It was a monstrous big river down there—sometimes a mile and a half wide. We run nights, and laid up and hid daytimes; soon as night was most gone we stopped navigating and tied up—nearly always in the dead water under a towhead[13]; and then cut young cottonwoods and willows, and hid the raft with them. Then we set out the lines.[14] Next we slid into the river and had a swim, so as to freshen up and cool off; then we set down on the sandy bottom where the water was about knee-deep, and watched the daylight come.

Not a sound anywhere—perfectly still—just like the whole world was asleep, only sometimes the bullfrogs a-cluttering, maybe. The first thing to see, looking away over the water, was a kind of dull line—that was the woods on t'other side; you couldn't make nothing else out; then a pale place in the sky; then more paleness spreading around; then the river softened up away off, and warn't black any more, but gray; you could see little dark spots drifting along ever so far away—trading scows, and such things; and long black streaks—rafts; sometimes you could hear a sweep screaking; or jumbled-up voices, it was so still, and sounds come so far; and by and by you could see a streak on the water which you know by the look of the streak that there's a snag there

in a swift current which breaks on it and makes that streak look that way; and you see the mist curl up off of the water, and the east reddens up, and the river, and you make out a log cabin in the edge of the woods, away on the bank on t'other side of the river, being a woodyard, likely, and piled by them cheats so you can throw a dog through it anywheres[15]; then the nice breeze springs up, and comes fanning you from over there, so cool and fresh and sweet to smell on account of the woods and the flowers; but sometimes not that way, because they've left dead fish laying around, gars and such, and they do get pretty rank; and next you've got the full day, and everything smiling in the sun, and the songbirds just going it!

---

13. *towhead*, a sand bar covered with cottonwoods. 14. *set out the lines*, set out fishing lines. 15. *woodyard . . . throw a dog through it anywheres.* Huck means that at the woodyard, a place at which firewood for steamboats was sold, the wood was piled loosely so that the purchaser got less than he paid for.

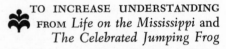 TO INCREASE UNDERSTANDING FROM *Life on the Mississippi* and *The Celebrated Jumping Frog*

1. (*a*) In what ways was Clemens, in background, rearing, and experience, typical of American writers of his period? (*b*) How did his various experiences prove of value to him as a writer? (*c*) Explain in detail the relation of the selection from *Life on the Mississippi* and "The Celebrated Jumping Frog" to Clemens' own life.

2. In the selection from *Life on the Mississippi* Twain mentions three transient or passing ambitions of the boys of Hannibal. (*a*) What were these transient ambitions? (*b*) What was Twain's purpose in mentioning them?

3. Paragraph 2 is a very long one, but it is not difficult to follow if you notice Twain's careful arrangement of his materials. (*a*) What simple fact does he state in sentence 1? (*b*) In sentence 2 what contrast does he indicate that he is going to show? (*c*) Where does he start and end the "before" picture? (*d*) The "after" picture? (*e*) What does he place between the "before" and "after" pictures? (*f*) Point out some of the details that are most helpful to you in sensing the mood of each section of the paragraph.

4. In what ways does Twain introduce humor into the story of the local boy who became an apprentice engineer?

5. How did Mark Twain happen to write "The Celebrated Jumping Frog of Calaveras County"?

6. To capture the flavor of the oral yarn in writing, it is necessary for an author to make it possible for his readers (1) to see the narrator and (2) to hear him speak. (a) What parts of "The Celebrated Jumping Frog" are devoted to acquainting the reader with Simon Wheeler, the narrator of the yarn? (b) What kinds of information does Twain give about Wheeler? (c) How does this information add to the humor of the story? (d) Why does Twain use peculiar sentence patterns, misspellings, and grammatical errors in the yarn itself? (e) Why does he italicize certain words?

7. (a) Point out particularly comic passages in Wheeler's monologue and suggest why they are comic. (b) Explain why "The Celebrated Jumping Frog" was probably much funnier to readers a hundred years ago than it is to us today.

From The Adventures of Huckleberry Finn

1. How does Twain arrange Huck's arrival at the Grangerfords?

2. Point out episodes in the early portion of the selection that show Huck's ingenuity and ability to fend for himself.

3. Twain uses a vast amount of detail to describe the Grangerford home. (a) How does Twain characterize Huck in showing his reactions to the furnishings? (b) What attitudes of Twain's toward the Grangerfords are indicated by this description?

4. (a) What comic elements do you find in Huck's description of Emmeline Grangerford? (b) In what ways is Emmeline like other members of her family?

5. (a) Describe Buck, Colonel Grangerford, and Sophia. (b) How do their characteristics and past history set the stage for what happens later?

6. Like other writers, Twain not only pictures life in his books, but he also comments upon life. (a) What is his attitude toward feuding? (b) How, exactly, is that attitude indicated by Huck's telling of the Grangerford episode?

7. Compared with the early portion of the selection, Twain's description of the skirmish is sparse. (a) Why do you think Twain didn't go into considerable detail? (b) How does his wording give the effect of rapid action?

8. What is your opinion of the Grangerfords at the conclusion of the selection?

9. (a) How does the tone of the concluding river passage differ from that of other portions of the selection? (b) What effect is achieved as a result of placing this passage so close to the account of the feud?

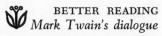

BETTER READING
Mark Twain's dialogue

No one knew better than Mark Twain the various uses of dialogue and the importance of dialogue to journalistic writing, yarns, and fiction. Good dialogue serves three purposes: (1) It can make a character real to the reader by reproducing the way he talks and by showing through what he says the kind of person he is. (2) It can provide background information that the reader needs to know in order to understand a particular episode. And (3) it can advance the action of the story.

In the selection from *Huckleberry Finn*, Mark Twain uses dialogue skillfully for each of these purposes. Sometimes one purpose is dominant, but all three are often combined. Locate each of the dialogues listed below and point out what purpose or purposes each dialogue serves.

1. Huck's initial dialogue with Colonel Grangerford (pages 388-389).

2. Huck's dialogue with Buck at the corncribs (pages 393-394).

3. Huck's conversation with Jim (pages 395-396).

4. Huck's conversation with his boy Jack (page 396).

 WORDS!

On a sheet of paper answer each of the following questions. Be ready to explain why you decided as you did. Use the Glossary if necessary.

1. If the drayman on the steamboat called out in a *prodigious* voice, did he (a) speak clearly, (b) call out loudly, or (c) swear?

2. If the steamboat was *husbanding* its pitch pine, was it (a) using it sparingly, (b) wasting it, or (c) using it to make a grand effect?

3. When the "striker" used steamboat *technicalities* in his talk, was he (a) swearing in the fashion of rivermen, (b) using terms that applied especially to steamboats, or (c) bragging about his adventures?

4. If old Simon Wheeler was a *garrulous* man, was he (a) reticent, (b) enthusiastic, or (c) talkative?

5. As a genius in *finesse*, did Jim Smiley have (a) a talent for losing wagers, (b) a skill in handling delicate situations, or (c) a tendency to cheat?

6. When Huck *ransacked* Miss Sophia's Testament, did he (a) search through it, (b) hide it, or (c) catalogue its contents?

7. If the Shepherdsons *cavorted* around on their horses, were they (a) taking flight, (b) prancing about, or (c) trying to hide?

DISCUSSION GUIDE

The Adventures of Huckleberry Finn, by Mark Twain[1]

The discussion may well center around characters in relation to plot and in relation to theme; the ending of the book; and the style.

CHARACTERS AND PLOT. *In paragraph 2 of Chapter I Huck is unhappy because he can't adapt himself to "dismal regular and decent ways" at the widow's; so, says he, "when I couldn't stand it no longer I lit out." This pattern recurs throughout the book: (1) he remains somewhere for a time; (2) he finds he can't stand it any longer; (3) he lights out.* What qualities in Huck's character make probable *each* of these three stages in flights from (a) Pap, (b) the Walter Scott, (c) the Grangerfords, (d) the King and the Duke, (e) the Wilkses? Relate the pattern to the rhythms of pause and movement in the novel.

How does Jim happen to join Huck on Jackson's Island? Why do Huck and Jim leave the island and go downstream? Why do they continue downstream after passing Cairo?

As the story progresses what changes take place in Huck's attitude toward Jim, and why do they occur? Trace these changes from Huck's initial attitude to his comment in Chapter XL, "I knowed he was white inside."

CHARACTERS AND THEME. *Huck's accounts of shore folk encountered on the river, in towns, and on plantations convey the theme of the novel—Twain's view of the majority of mankind.* Why do Huck's background and character make him a trustworthy observer? *In Chapter XXI Huck calls the white trash of Bricksville "a mighty ornery lot," and in Chapter XXXII he applies the same words to kings.* What facts about these groups at opposite ends of the scale justify his claim? Speaking of kings, he says they are what they are because of their nature and environment. Show how, on the basis of Huck's picturing of them, the same things may be said of (a) Pap, (b) the Grangerfords, (c) Sherburn, (d) the Wilkses' townsfolk, (e) the lynchers of the King and the Duke, (f) the Phelpses' neighbors. Colonel Sherburn in his speech to the mob (Chapter XXII) restates Huck's claim. How has his background qualified

1. This Guide was prepared by Walter Blair, author of *Mark Twain & "Huck Finn."*

him to be Twain's spokesman? How does he picture mankind?

Review Huck's struggle with his conscience when he decides to notify Miss Watson about Jim's whereabouts. *Twain says this struggle shows that "in a crucial emergency a sound heart is a safer guide" than "a deformed conscience," that is, a conscience that acts according to training.* How does this statement reflect Twain's belief about society in general? Relate it to Huck's struggle. Cite other instances in which Huck and Jim act independently of their upbringing. How does the contrast between this pair and the shore dwellers develop Twain's theme?

CHARACTERS, THEME, AND THE ENDING. *Many critics consider the chapters beginning with Tom Sawyer's romantic plan to free Jim (Chapters XXXIV and following) the weakest part of the book. They hold that in them both Huck and Jim are degraded, that the plot strands ravel out, and that the theme developed earlier is lost in a welter of wild happenings. Several critics, by contrast, hold that these happenings fittingly conclude the story.* Taking into account all the accusations of the former group of critics, argue for either stand.

STYLE AND TONE. *Huck's style, all critics agree, is one of Twain's great triumphs.* Study the style of the descriptions of Pap (Chapter V); the storm (Chapter IX); Buck's death (Chapter XVIII, page 397 in this text); life on the river (Chapter XIX, page 398 in this text); and the circus riders (Chapter XXII). What words would you use to characterize each? How do they differ in tone? Is the language such as Huck would use? What are the signs in the contrasting phrasings of Emmeline, the King, and the Duke which would indicate that they are insincere or hypocritical?

The tone of Twain's best fiction is described on page 386 as "one of longing for 'the good old days.'" In what portions or scenes of *Huck Finn* is this tone most evident? In what scenes is there more comedy than the event pictured would normally suggest? How does Twain reconcile his pessimistic view of mankind in general with "a spirit of tenderness and longing"?

THE MAGAZINE IN AMERICA

The Editor As Counselor

When young William Dean Howells (1837-1920) exclaimed, "Ah! if I only could write something worthy of the *Atlantic*," he couldn't foresee that he would not only become an *Atlantic* contributor, but its editor as well. Ohio-born and largely self-taught, Howells aspired to share the front rank of American letters with the distinguished, Harvard-educated New Englanders he so admired. While working in his father's printing shop or as a reporter on the *Ohio State Journal*, Howells may have thought his chances were slim; but in 1860 three of his poems were accepted by the *Atlantic* and he made a pilgrimage to New England, where he was warmly received by Longfellow, Holmes, and Lowell. A campaign biography of Lincoln earned him an appointment as consul at Venice in 1861; upon his return from Italy five years later, he resumed his association with the *Atlantic*, be-

coming its editor-in-chief in 1871. The prestige and influence Howells enjoyed as *Atlantic* editor were further enhanced by his association, which began in the late 1880's, with another distinguished literary magazine, *Harper's New Monthly Magazine*—now known as *Harper's Magazine*. For twenty years he wrote *Harper's* best-known feature, "The Editor's Easy Chair." One of Howells' successors in the editor's chair at *Harper's* was Bernard De Voto, whom you met on page 15.

Howells knew most of the important writers from the Golden Day of Hawthorne and Lowell to the dawn of the twentieth century. American men of letters respected him as a poet, essayist, critic, biographer, playwright, and novelist; much of the new realism we find in American writing at the turn of the century was stimulated by realistic novels like Howells' *The Rise of Silas Lapham* (1885). As the editor of two influential literary monthlies, Howells was in a unique position to guide American authors of the new literary era: Henry James, Stephen Crane, Frank Norris, and Samuel Clemens were only four of the many writers who sought and respected his counsel.

Of these postwar authors, Howells knew Sam Clemens best. After introducing the American humorist to *Atlantic* readers in his review of *The Innocents Abroad* (1869), Howells frequently met with Clemens, who accepted many suggestions the editor made. Clemens, encouraged by Howells' interest in Western themes, wrote a series about piloting on the Mississippi for the *Atlantic*. "Old Times on the Mississippi" appeared in six installments between January and July of 1875; in 1883 these articles were augmented and published as *Life on the Mississippi*.

Poe, while a magazine editor, had recognized and encouraged new talent but had had little direct association with authors. Howells made the relationship between a writer and his editor closer and more personal. Modern magazine editors, following his example, exercise a vital influence on American writing today.

Folk Songs of the West

The people exploring and settling the lonely stretches of the West made endurable many of their hardships and heartaches by spinning yarns such as the ones Mark Twain enjoyed. The frontiersmen's thoughts and feelings also found expression in their songs. As others all over the world have done, the pioneers composed songs about people, situations, and happenings that appealed most strongly to their feelings and imagination. They fitted the only kinds of words they knew to the only kind of music with which they were familiar. The songs they composed, sang, and learned by heart retained many ballad qualities: repetition and refrain, dramatic ways of unfolding happenings, and ways of leaping over some details and of presenting others with minute care.

The folk songs that follow vary as widely as the interests and circumstances of those who sang them. "The Old Chisholm Trail" is one of many cowboy songs that tell of the cowboy's work tending cattle. "The Little Old Sod Shanty on the Claim" is a typical song of the homesteaders who built their sod houses on the wide plains of Kansas and Nebraska.

The Old Chisholm Trail

Come along, boys, and listen to my tale,
I'll tell you of my troubles on the old
    Chisholm trail.[1]

Chorus
Come ti yi youpy, youpy yea, youpy yea,
Coma ti yi youpy, youpy yea.

I started up the trail October twenty-third,   5
I started up the trail with the 2-U herd.

Oh, a ten-dollar hoss and a forty-dollar
    saddle,
And I'm goin' to punchin' Texas cattle.

I woke up one morning on the old Chisholm
    trail,
Rope in my hand and a cow by the tail.   10

I'm up in the mornin' afore daylight
And afore I sleep the moon shines bright.

My hoss throwed me off at the creek called
    Mud,
My hoss throwed me off round the 2-U herd.

Last time I saw him he was going 'cross the
    level   15
A-kicking up his heels and a-running like the
    devil.

Last night I was on guard and the leader
    broke the ranks,
I hit my horse down the shoulders and I
    spurred him in the flanks.

The wind commenced to blow, and the rain
    began to fall,
It looked, by grab, like we was goin' to lose
    'em all.   20

My slicker's in the wagon and I'm gittin'
    mighty cold,
And these longhorn sons-o'-guns are gittin'
    hard to hold.

Saddle up, boys, and saddle up strong
For I think these cattle have scattered along.

---

1. *Chisholm* (chiz′əm) *trail*, a famous cattle trail which extended from the Red River in eastern Texas to southern Kansas.

With my blanket and my gun and my rawhide rope,   25
I'm a-slidin' down the trail in a long, keen lope.

I don't give a hoot if they never do stop;
I'll ride as long as an eight-day clock.

We rounded 'em up and put 'em on the cars,
And that was the last of the old Two Bars.   30

Oh, it's bacon and beans most every day—
I'd as soon be a-eatin' prairie hay.

I went to the boss to draw my roll,
He had it figgered out I was nine dollars in the hole.

I'll sell my outfit just as soon as I can,   35
I won't punch cattle for no other man.

With my knees in the saddle and my seat in the sky,
I'll quit punching cows in the sweet by-and-by.

Fare you well, old trail-boss, I don't wish you any harm,
I'm quittin' this business to go on the farm.   40

The Little Old Sod Shanty on the Claim

I am looking rather seedy now while holding down my claim,[1]
And my victuals are not always of the best;
And the mice play shyly round me as I nestle down to rest,
In my little old sod shanty in the West.
Yet I rather like the novelty of living in this way,   5
Though my bill of fare is always rather tame,
But I'm happy as a clam on the land of Uncle Sam,
In my little old sod shanty on my claim.

Chorus
The hinges are of leather and the windows have no glass,

While the board roof lets the howling blizzards in,   10
And I hear the hungry kiyote as he slinks up through the grass,
Round my little old sod shanty on my claim.

O when I left my Eastern home, a bachelor so gay,
To try and win my way to wealth and fame,
I little thought that I'd come down to burning twisted hay[2]   15
In the little old sod shanty on my claim.
My clothes are plastered o'er with dough, I'm looking like a fright,
And everything is scattered round the room,
But I wouldn't give the freedom that I have out in the West   19
For the table of the Eastern man's old home.

Still I wish that some kind-hearted girl would pity on me take,
And relieve me from the mess that I am in;
The angel, how I'd bless her if this her home she'd make
In the little old sod shanty on my claim.
And we would make our fortunes on the prairies of the West,   25
Just as happy as two lovers we'd remain;
We'd forget the trials and troubles we endured at the first,
In the little old sod shanty on our claim.

And if kindly fate should bless us with now and then an heir,
To cheer our hearts with honest pride of fame,   30
O then we'd be contented for the toil that we had spent
In the little old sod shanty on our claim.
When time enough had lapsed and all of those little brats
To noble man- and womanhood had grown,
It wouldn't seem half so lonely as around us we should look,   35
And see the little old sod shanty on our claim.

---

1. *I am looking rather seedy now while holding down my claim.* According to the Homestead Act of 1862, a settler might claim up to 160 acres of public land by living on it for five years. 2. *I little thought . . . burning twisted hay.* Because of the scarcity of trees, the early settlers on the plains twisted hay into ropes and burned it.

Bret Harte 1836-1902

Although he was born in the East—in Albany, New York—Bret Harte, like Mark Twain, in several ways represented the breed of authors who won fame after the Civil War. He had a sketchy education before he went to the Pacific Coast. There he taught school, worked briefly in the gold mines, served as a Wells Fargo Express messenger, became a printer and then an editor and an author. Though he was in the West only from 1854 to 1871, he became renowned as "the writer of the epic of the gold rush."

Harte's success was partly the result of good luck, partly of skill. The ending of the war had awakened the interest of the reunited nation in learning how people lived in every section—a fascination that in part accounts for the success of Mark Twain's vivid pictures of the Midwest and the South and of Whittier's *Snow-Bound* (page 291). When Harte started to write his clever stories about Far Western mining camps, he soon discovered that he had struck literary gold.

"The Luck of Roaring Camp" (page 406) was first published in a California magazine in 1868. Like Twain's "Celebrated Jumping Frog," it was reprinted everywhere and quickly won acclaim for its author. Other stories and poems about Western life, and a book, *The Luck of Roaring Camp and Other Stories* (1870), established Harte as a sensationally popular author. When the *Atlantic Monthly* offered him a generous contract, he departed for the East. Dapperly dressed, his handsome features set off by curly locks streaked with silver, he traveled triumphantly, stopping frequently to play the social and literary lion.

Above: A woodcut of 1854 showing miners "cradle-rocking" for gold.
Right: Typical gambling saloon in a western mining town.

Unfortunately, the rest of Harte's life was an anticlimax. A few additional stories such as "How Santa Claus Came to Simpson's Bar" (1872) and "An Ingénue of the Sierras" (1893) and a few poems were up to his earlier standards, but much of his work became thin, repetitious, and unexciting. In 1878 he went to Germany on a consular appointment. From 1888 until his death in 1902 he lived in England, his reputation fading.

Even though Harte's period of glory was short-lived, the impact of his stories was sufficient to develop a new trend in American fiction, and, in fact, to found a new school of writers. The chief ingredients of his stories were not new, although his combination of them was. He was greatly influenced by Charles Dickens (1812-1870), the British novelist who in the 1850's and 1860's was more popular in the United States than any American novelist. From Dickens, Harte learned to make characters individual by caricaturing them—giving them a few exaggerated traits, often grotesque ones. From Dickens he learned also to describe settings in such a way that they corresponded with the character's emotions or foreshadowed certain happenings. The critic Van Wyck Brooks suggests a third effect of Dickens' influence on Harte when he writes: "Dickens had prepared the way for [Harte] in his treatment of outcasts and rough men in vividly drawn surroundings of slum and country, together with a feeling for the goodness of heart that so often exists in the rudest."[1] Harte's outcasts, too, have hearts of gold. For example, John Oakhurst, the gambler in "The Outcasts of Poker Flat," hard-boiled though he is at the gaming table, is impelled by his nobility to give his life for others.

Harte's technique, like that of Twain, was also greatly influenced by a group of American humorists who had flourished before the Civil War. These storytellers wrote tales of the type then being told around campfires and in country stores. Harte mentioned that these humorists "often ... gave a striking photograph of a community or a section" and "voiced not only the dialect, but the habits of thought of a people or locality." Harte's materials and style were often much like those of such writers.

But although Harte made use of certain methods developed by Dickens and the American humorists, his application of them to portray the fabulous and picturesque life of the Far West was new. New also was Harte's evocation of a postwar nostalgia which the writer shared with many of his countrymen and which made glamorous the recent past.

Soon writers in every section of the nation had joined the group of which Harte was the acknowledged founder. Like Harte, these *local colorists* stressed sectional backgrounds, characters, actions, and dialect. They too looked longingly back at the color-drenched period which the Civil War had ended. They too pictured this past with vividness, sentiment, and humor.

In addition to founding a vigorous school of regionalists, Harte invented the *Western.* He was the discoverer of its stock characters—badmen, gamblers, the sheriff and his posse, the dance-hall girl with a good heart. He discovered too the appeal of the barroom fracases, lynchings, holdups, and shy courtships by masculine Westerners which still delight readers and television viewers.

1. Van Wyck Brooks, *The Times of Melville and Whitman,* (New York: E. P. Dutton & Co., 1947), page 270.

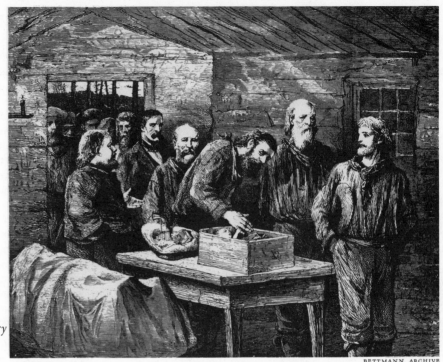

A contemporary
illustration for
Harte's story.

The Luck of Roaring Camp

There was commotion in Roaring Camp. It could not have been a fight, for in 1850 that was not novel enough to have called together the entire settlement. The ditches and claims were not only deserted, but "Tuttle's grocery" had contributed its gamblers, who, it will be remembered, calmly continued their game the day that French Pete and Kanaka Joe shot each other to death over the bar in the front room. The whole camp was collected before a rude cabin on the outer edge of the clearing. Conversation was carried on in a low tone, but the name of a woman was frequently repeated. It was a name familiar enough in the camp—"Cherokee Sal."

Perhaps the less said of her the better. She was a coarse, and it is to be feared, a very sinful woman. But at that time she was the only woman in Roaring Camp, and was just then lying in sore extremity, when she most needed the ministration of her own sex. Dissolute, abandoned, and irreclaimable, she was yet suffering a martyrdom hard enough to bear even when veiled by sympathizing womanhood, but now terrible in her loneliness. The primal curse[1] had come to her in that original isolation which must have made the punishment of the first transgression so dreadful. It was, perhaps, part of the expiation of her sin, that, at a moment when she most lacked her sex's intuitive tenderness and care, she met only the half-contemptuous faces of her masculine associates. Yet a few of the spectators were, I think, touched by her suffer-

1. *The primal curse.* This is a reference to God's words to Eve after she and Adam had sinned: "In sorrow thou shalt bring forth children." (Genesis 3:16.)

ings. Sandy Tipton thought it was "rough on Sal," and, in the contemplation of her condition, for a moment rose superior to the fact that he had an ace and two bowers in his sleeve.[2]

It will be seen also, that the situation was novel. Deaths were by no means uncommon in Roaring Camp, but a birth was a new thing. People had been dismissed from the camp effectively, finally, and with no possibility of return; but this was the first time that anybody had been introduced *ab initio*.[3] Hence the excitement.

"You go in there, Stumpy," said a prominent citizen known as Kentuck, addressing one of the loungers. "Go in there, and see what you kin do. You've had experience in them things."

Perhaps there was a fitness in the selection. Stumpy, in other climes, had been the putative head of two families; in fact, it was owing to some legal informality in these proceedings that Roaring Camp—a city of refuge—was indebted to his company. The crowd approved the choice, and Stumpy was wise enough to bow to the majority. The door closed upon the extempore surgeon and midwife, and Roaring Camp sat down outside, smoked its pipe, and awaited the issue.

The assemblage numbered about a hundred men. One or two of these were actual fugitives from justice, some were criminal, and all were reckless. Physically, they exhibited no indication of their past lives and character. The greatest scamp had a Raphael face,[4] with a profusion of blond hair; Oakhurst, a gambler, had the melancholy air and intellectual abstraction of a Hamlet[5]; the coolest and most courageous man was scarcely over five feet in height, with a soft voice and an embarrassed timid manner. The term *roughs* applied to them was a distinction rather than a definition. Perhaps in the minor details of fingers, toes, ears, etc., the camp may have been deficient, but these slight omissions did not detract from their aggregate force. The strongest man had but three fingers on his right hand; the best shot had but one eye.

Such was the physical aspect of the men that were dispersed around the cabin. The camp lay in a triangular valley, between two hills and a river. The only outlet was a steep trail over the summit of a hill that faced the cabin, now illuminated by the rising moon. The suffering woman might have seen it from the rude bunk whereon she lay—seen it winding like a silver thread until it was lost in the stars above.

A fire of withered pine boughs added sociability to the gathering. By degrees the natural levity of Roaring Camp returned. Bets were freely offered and taken regarding the result. Three to five that "Sal would get through with it"; even, that the child would survive; side bets as to the sex and complexion of the coming stranger. In the midst of an excited discussion an exclamation came from those nearest the door, and the camp stopped to listen. Above the swaying and moaning of the pines, the swift rush of the river, and the crackling of the fire rose a sharp, querulous cry—a cry unlike anything heard before in the camp. The pines stopped moaning, the river ceased to rush, and the fire to crackle. It seemed as if Nature had stopped to listen too.

The camp rose to its feet as one man! It was proposed to explode a barrel of gunpowder, but, in consideration of the situation of the mother, better counsels prevailed, and only a few revolvers were discharged; for, whether owing to the rude surgery of the camp, or some other reason, Cherokee Sal was sinking fast. Within an hour she had climbed, as it were, that rugged road that led to the stars, and so passed out of Roaring Camp, its sin and shame forever. I do not think that the announcement disturbed them much, except in speculation as to the fate of the child. "Can he live now?" was asked of Stumpy. The answer was doubtful. The only other being of Cherokee Sal's sex and maternal condition in

---

2. *an ace and two bowers in his sleeve.* In some card games the bowers, which are two of the jacks, are the two highest cards in the game. Cheating gamblers hid high extra cards in their sleeves to substitute for the poor cards in their hands. **3.** *ab initio* (äb in ish′ i ō), from the very beginning. [*Latin*] **4.** *a Raphael* (raf′i al) *face*, a beautiful and sweet face such as those of the Biblical characters painted by Raphael, a great Italian artist who lived from 1483 to 1520. **5.** *Hamlet*, the principal character in the tragedy of the same name by William Shakespeare. Hamlet was a melancholy, intellectual man who pondered deeply on the tragic problem he faced.

the settlement was a donkey. There was some conjecture as to fitness, but the experiment was tried. It was less problematical than the ancient treatment of Romulus and Remus,[6] and apparently as successful.

When these details were completed, which exhausted another hour, the door was opened, and the anxious crowd, who had already formed themselves into a queue, entered in single file. Beside the low bunk or shelf, on which the figure of the mother was starkly outlined below the blankets, stood a pine table. On this a candle box was placed, and within it, swathed in staring red flannel, lay the last arrival at Roaring Camp. Beside the candle box was placed a hat. Its use was soon indicated. "Gentlemen," said Stumpy, with a singular mixture of authority and ex officio complacency[7]—"Gentlemen will please pass in at the front door, round the table, and out at the back door. Them as wishes to contribute anything toward the orphan will find a hat handy." The first man entered with his hat on; he uncovered, however, as he looked about him, and so, unconsciously, set an example to the next.

In such communities good and bad actions are catching. As the procession filed in, comments were audible—criticisms addressed, perhaps, rather to Stumpy, in the character of showman—"Is that him?" "Mighty small specimen"; "Hasn't more'n got the color"; "Ain't bigger nor a derringer." The contributions were as characteristic: a silver tobacco box; a doubloon; a navy revolver, silver mounted; a gold specimen; a very beautifully embroidered lady's handkerchief (from Oakhurst the gambler); a diamond breastpin; a diamond ring (suggested by the pin, with the remark from the giver that he "saw that pin and went two diamonds better"); a slung shot[8]; a Bible (contributor not detected); a golden spur; a silver teaspoon (the initials, I regret to say, were not the giver's); a pair of surgeon's shears; a lancet; a Bank of England note for £5[9]; and about $200 in loose gold and silver coin. During these proceedings Stumpy maintained a silence as impassive as the dead on his left— a gravity as inscrutable as that of the newly born on his right.

Only one incident occurred to break the monotony of the curious procession. As Kentuck bent over the candle box half curiously, the child turned, and in a spasm of pain, caught at his groping finger, and held it fast for a moment. Kentuck looked foolish and embarrassed. Something like a blush tried to assert itself in his weather-beaten cheek. "The d—d little cuss!" he said, as he extricated his finger, with, perhaps, more tenderness and care than he might have been deemed capable of showing. He held that finger a little apart from its fellows as he went out, and examined it curiously. The examination provoked the same original remark in regard to the child. In fact, he seemed to enjoy repeating it. "He rastled with my finger," he remarked to Tipton, holding up the member, "the d—d little cuss!"

It was four o'clock before the camp sought repose. A light burnt in the cabin where the watchers sat, for Stumpy did not go to bed that night. Nor did Kentuck. He drank quite freely and related with great gusto his experience, invariably ending with his characteristic condemnation of the newcomer. It seemed to relieve him of any unjust implication of sentiment, and Kentuck had the weaknesses of the nobler sex. When everybody else had gone to bed, he walked down to the river, and whistled reflectingly. Then he walked up the gulch, past the cabin, still whistling with demonstrative unconcern. At a large redwood tree he paused and retraced his steps, and again passed the cabin. Halfway down to the river's bank he again paused, and then returned and knocked at the door. It was opened by Stumpy.

"How goes it?" said Kentuck, looking past Stumpy toward the candle box.

"All serene," replied Stumpy.

"Anything up?"

6. *It was less problematical than the ancient treatment of Romulus and Remus.* According to Roman myth, Romulus (rom′ū ləs), the founder and first king of Rome, and his brother Remus (rē′məs) were nourished by a wolf. 7. *ex officio* (eks ə fish′i ō) *complacency*, self-satisfaction deriving from the office held. 8. *a slung shot*, a weapon made of a piece of metal or stone fastened to a short strap or chain. 9. *a Bank of England note for £5*, a piece of paper money worth five pounds drawn on the Bank of England. At the time of the story a five-pound note was worth about $25 in United States money.

"Nothing."

There was a pause—an embarrassing one—Stumpy still holding the door. Then Kentuck had recourse to his finger, which he held up to Stumpy. "Rastled with it—the d——d little cuss," he said, and retired.

The next day Cherokee Sal had such rude sepulture as Roaring Camp afforded. After her body had been committed to the hillside, there was a formal meeting of the camp to discuss what should be done with her infant. A resolution to adopt it was unanimous and enthusiastic. But an animated discussion in regard to the manner and feasibility of providing for its wants at once sprung up. It was remarkable that the argument partook of none of those fierce personalities with which discussions were usually conducted at Roaring Camp. Tipton proposed that they should send the child to Red Dog—a distance of forty miles—where female attention could be procured. But the unlucky suggestion met with fierce and unanimous opposition. It was evident that no plan which entailed parting from their new acquisition would for a moment be entertained. "Besides," said Tom Ryder, "them fellows at Red Dog would swap it, and ring in somebody else on us." A disbelief in the honesty of other camps prevailed at Roaring Camp as in other places.

The introduction of a female nurse in the camp also met with objection. It was argued that no decent woman could be prevailed to accept Roaring Camp as her home, and the speaker urged that "they didn't want any more of the other kind." This unkind allusion to the defunct mother, harsh as it may seem, was the first spasm of propriety—the first symptom of the camp's regeneration. Stumpy advanced nothing. Perhaps he felt a certain delicacy in interfering with the selection of a possible successor in office. But when questioned, he averred stoutly that he and Jinny—the mammal before alluded to—could manage to rear the child. There was something original, independent, and heroic about the plan that pleased the camp. Stumpy was retained. Certain articles were sent for to Sacramento. "Mind," said the treasurer, as he pressed a bag of gold dust into the expressman's hand, "the best that can be got—lace, you know, and filigreework and frills—d——n the cost!"

Strange to say, the child thrived. Perhaps the invigorating climate of the mountain camp was compensation for material deficiencies. Nature took the foundling to her broader breast. In that rare atmosphere of the Sierra foothills—that air pungent with balsamic odor, that ethereal cordial, at once bracing and exhilarating, he may have found food and nourishment, or a subtle chemistry that transmuted donkey's milk to lime and phosphorus. Stumpy inclined to the belief that it was the latter and good nursing. "Me and that donkey," he would say, "has been father and mother to him! Don't you," he would add, apostrophizing the helpless bundle before him "never go back on us."

By the time he was a month old, the necessity of giving him a name became apparent. He had generally been known as "the Kid," "Stumpy's boy," "the Cayote" (an allusion to his vocal powers), and even by Kentuck's endearing diminutive of "the d——d little cuss." But these were felt to be vague and unsatisfactory, and were at last dismissed under another influence. Gamblers and adventurers are generally superstitious, and Oakhurst one day declared that the baby had brought "the luck" to Roaring Camp. It was certain that of late they had been successful. "Luck" was the name agreed upon, with the prefix of Tommy for greater convenience. No allusion was made to the mother, and the father was unknown. "It's better," said the philosophical Oakhurst, "to take a fresh deal all round. Call him Luck, and start him fair." A day was accordingly set apart for the christening. What was meant by this ceremony the reader may imagine, who has already gathered some idea of the reckless irreverence of Roaring Camp. The master of ceremonies was one "Boston," a noted wag, and the occasion seemed to promise the greatest facetiousness. This ingenious satirist had spent two days in preparing a burlesque of the church service, with pointed local allusions. The choir was properly trained and Sandy Tipton was to stand godfather. But after the procession had marched to the grove with music and banners, and the child had been deposited before a mock altar, Stumpy stepped before the expectant crowd.

"It ain't my style to spoil fun, boys," said the little man, stoutly, eyeing the faces around him, "but it strikes me that this thing ain't exactly on the squar. It's playing it pretty low down on this yer baby to ring in fun on him that he ain't goin' to understand. And ef there's going to be any godfathers round, I'd like to see who's got any better rights than me."

A silence followed Stumpy's speech. To the credit of all humorists be it said that the first man to acknowledge its justice was the satirist, thus stopped of his fun. "But," said Stumpy, quickly, following up his advantage, "we're here for a christening, and we'll have it. I proclaim you Thomas Luck, according to the laws of the United States and the State of California, so help me God." It was the first time that the name of the Deity had been uttered otherwise but profanely in the camp. The form of christening was perhaps even more ludicrous than the satirist had conceived; but strangely enough, nobody saw it and nobody laughed. Tommy was christened as seriously as he would have been under a Christian roof, and cried and was comforted in as orthodox fashion.

And so the work of regeneration began in Roaring Camp. Almost imperceptibly a change came over the settlement. The cabin assigned to Tommy Luck—or The Luck, as he was more frequently called—first showed signs of improvement. It was kept scrupulously clean and whitewashed. Then it was boarded, clothed, and papered. The rosewood cradle—packed eighty miles by mule—had, in Stumpy's way of putting it, "sorter killed the rest of the furniture." So the rehabilitation of the cabin became a necessity. The men who were in the habit of lounging in at Stumpy's to see "how The Luck got on" seemed to appreciate the change, and, in self-defense, the rival establishment of "Tuttle's grocery" bestirred itself, and imported a carpet and mirrors. The reflections of the latter on the appearance of Roaring Camp tended to produce stricter habits of personal cleanliness. Again Stumpy imposed a kind of quarantine upon those who

aspired to the honor and privilege of holding The Luck. It was a cruel mortification to Kentuck—who, in the carelessness of a large nature and the habits of frontier life, had begun to regard all garments as a second cuticle, which, like a snake's, only sloughed off through decay—to be debarred this privilege from certain prudential reasons. Yet such was the subtle influence of innovation that he thereafter appeared regularly every afternoon in a clean shirt, and face still shining from his ablutions. Nor were moral and social sanitary laws neglected. Tommy, who was supposed to spend his whole existence in a persistent attempt to repose, must not be disturbed by noise. The shouting and yelling which had gained the camp its infelicitous title were not permitted within hearing distance of Stumpy's. The men conversed in whispers, or smoked with Indian gravity. Profanity was tacitly given up in these sacred precincts, and throughout the camp a popular form of expletive, known as "D—n the luck!" and "Curse the luck!" was abandoned, as having a new personal bearing. Vocal music was not interdicted, being supposed to have a soothing, tranquilizing quality, and one song, sung by Man-o'-War Jack, an English sailor from Her Majesty's[10] Australian colonies, was quite popular as a lullaby. It was a lugubrious recital of the exploits of "the *Arethusa*, Seventy-four," in a muffled minor, ending with a prolonged dying fall at the burden of each verse, "On b-o-o-o-ard of the *Arethusa*." It was a fine sight to see Jack holding The Luck, rocking from side to side as if with the motion of a ship, and crooning forth this naval ditty. Either through the peculiar rocking of Jack or the length of his song—it contained ninety stanzas, and was continued with conscientious deliberation to the bitter end—the lullaby generally had the desired effect. At such times the men would lie at full length under the trees, in the soft summer twilight, smoking their pipes and drinking in the melodious utterances. An indistinct idea that this was pastoral happiness pervaded the camp. "This 'ere kind o' think," said the Cockney Simmons, meditatively re-

10. *Her Majesty*, Queen Victoria, ruler of England from 1837 to 1901.

clining on his elbow, "is 'evingly." It reminded him of Greenwich.[11]

On the long summer days The Luck was usually carried to the gulch, from whence the golden store of Roaring Camp was taken. There, on a blanket spread over pine boughs, he would lie while the men were working in the ditches below. Latterly, there was a rude attempt to decorate this bower with flowers and sweet-smelling shrubs, and generally someone would bring him a cluster of wild honeysuckles, azaleas, or the painted blossoms of Las Mariposas.[12] The men had suddenly awakened to the fact that there were beauty and significance in these trifles, which they had so long trodden carelessly beneath their feet. A flake of glittering mica, a fragment of variegated quartz, a bright pebble from the bed of the creek, became beautiful to eyes thus cleared and strengthened, and were invariably put aside for The Luck. It was wonderful how many treasures the woods and hillsides yielded that "would do for Tommy." Surrounded by playthings such as never child out of fairyland had before, it is to be hoped that Tommy was content. He appeared to be serenely happy, albeit there was an infantine gravity about him, a contemplative light in his round gray eyes, that sometimes worried Stumpy. He was always tractable and quiet, and it is recorded that once, having crept beyond his "corral"—a hedge of tessellated pine boughs, which surrounded his bed—he dropped over the bank on his head in the soft earth, and remained with his mottled legs in the air in that position for at least five minutes with unflinching gravity. He was extricated without a murmur. I hesitate to record the many other instances of his sagacity, which rest, unfortunately, upon the statements of prejudiced friends. Some of them were not without a tinge of superstition. "I crep' up the bank just now," said Kentuck one day, in a breathless state of excitement, "and dern my skin if he wasn't talking to a jay bird as was a-sittin' on his lap. There they was, just as free and sociable as anything you please, a-jawin' at each other just like two cherrybums."[13] Howbeit, whether creeping over the pine boughs or lying lazily on his back blinking at the leaves above him, to him the birds sang, the squirrels chattered, and the flowers bloomed. Nature was his nurse and playfellow. For him she would let slip between the leaves golden shafts of sunlight that fell just within his grasp; she would send wandering breezes to visit him with the balm of bay and resinous gums; to him the tall redwoods nodded familiarly and sleepily, the bumblebees buzzed, and the rooks cawed a slumberous accompaniment.

Such was the golden summer of Roaring Camp. They were flush times—and The Luck was with them. The claims had yielded enormously. The camp was jealous of its privileges and looked suspiciously on strangers. No encouragement was given to immigration, and, to make their seclusion more perfect, the land on either side of the mountain wall that surrounded the camp they duly preëmpted. This, and a reputation of singular proficiency with the revolver, kept the reserve of Roaring Camp inviolate. The expressman—their only connecting link with the surrounding world—sometimes told wonderful stories of the camp. He would say, "They've a street up there in Roaring, that would lay over any street up there in Red Dog. They've got vines and flowers round their houses, and they wash themselves twice a day. But they're mighty rough on strangers, and they worship an Injun baby."

With the prosperity of the camp came a desire for further improvement. It was proposed to build a hotel in the following spring, and to invite one or two decent families to reside there for the sake of The Luck, who might perhaps profit by female companionship. The sacrifice that this concession to the sex cost these men, who were fiercely skeptical in regard to its general virtue and usefulness, can only be accounted for by their affection for Tommy. A few still held out. But the resolve could not be carried into effect for three months, and the minority meekly yielded in

---

11. *Cockney Simmons . . . It reminded him of Greenwich* (grin′ij *or* gren′ich). To Simmons, who came from and spoke the dialect of a poor, crowded section of London, the atmosphere was like that of Greenwich, a much more green and open section of the city. 12. *the painted blossoms of Las Mariposas* (läs mar′i pō′səs), the Mariposa lily. 13. *cherrybums,* cherubim, or angels.

the hope that something might turn up to prevent it. And it did.

The winter of '51 will long be remembered in the foothills. The snow lay deep on the sierras, and every mountain creek became a river, and every river a lake. Each gorge and gulch was transformed into a tumultuous watercourse that descended the hillsides, tearing down giant trees and scattering its drift and debris along the plain. Red Dog had been twice under water, and Roaring Camp had been forewarned. "Water put the gold into them gulches," said Stumpy; "it's been here once and will be here again!" And that night the North Fork suddenly leaped over its banks, and swept up the triangular valley of Roaring Camp.

In the confusion of rushing water, crashing trees, and crackling timber, and the darkness which seemed to flow with the water and blot out the fair valley, but little could be done to collect the scattered camp. When the morning broke, the cabin of Stumpy nearest the river-bank was gone. Higher up the gulch they found the body of its unlucky owner; but the pride—the hope—the joy—The Luck—of Roaring Camp had disappeared. They were returning with sad hearts, when a shout from the bank recalled them.

It was a relief boat from down the river. They had picked up, they said, a man and an infant, nearly exhausted, about two miles below. Did anybody know them, and did they belong here?

It needed but a glance to show them Kentuck lying there, cruelly crushed and bruised, but still holding The Luck of Roaring Camp in his arms. As they bent over the strangely assorted pair, they saw that the child was cold and pulseless.

"He is dead," said one.

Kentuck opened his eyes.

"Dead?" he repeated feebly.

"Yes, my man, and you are dying, too."

A smile lit the eyes of the expiring Kentuck. "Dying!" he repeated, "he's a-taking me with him—tell the boys I've got The Luck with me now"; and the strong man, clinging to the frail babe as a drowning man is said to cling to a straw, drifted away into the shadowy river that flows forever to the unknown sea.

 TO INCREASE UNDERSTANDING

1. The "Better Reading" article on page 55 describes how setting helps develop a story. Reread this article and then explain in what ways the setting of "The Luck of Roaring Camp" is functional.

2. The first two paragraphs set the scene, and are therefore very important in this local-color story. (a) Describe in your own words the character of Roaring Camp and of its inhabitants. (b) How has the author managed to tell you what the town is like?

3. (a) Why does Roaring Camp reform? Trace the stages in its reformation. (b) Explain why the reformation does or does not seem believable to you.

4. One device Harte was famous for (perhaps he'd learned it from Dickens) was that of making characters memorable by giving them combinations of traits or a contrast between traits and appearance not usually found in the same person. For example, "The greatest scamp had a Raphael face with a profusion of blonde hair" (page 407, column 1, paragraph 4). (a) What incongruous traits do you find in Stumpy and in Kentuck? (b) Cite other examples of incongruous traits.

5. Harte once wrote of Dickens: "I observe that whenever an accident, a murder, or death is about to happen, there is something in the furniture, in the locality, in the atmosphere, that foreshadows and suggests it ...." Does this comment apply to any passages in Harte's story? If so, which ones?

6. Throughout "The Luck of Roaring Camp" Harte often says things in an overelaborate manner. Thus instead of merely stating that Cherokee Sal was buried, he writes that she "had such rude sepulture as Roaring Camp afforded" and her body was "committed to the hillside." (a) Find other examples of this type of writing. (b) How do such passages affect the tone of the story? (c) Do you like or dislike the inclusion of such passages? Why?

 WORDS!

When pioneering Americans pushed on into the Southwest and the Far West, they were in land with the Spanish tradition of hacienda and mission. From long established Spanish settlers, the westering Americans borrowed many words. Spanish loan-words such as *bonanza* and *placer* were part of the Forty-Niners' vocabulary when Mark Twain and Bret Harte were telling their mining-camp tales. Some Spanish loan-words changed in meaning as they passed into American-English. For instance, the Spaniards of the Southwest favored a broad-brimmed hat decorated with rows of braid or *galón* (gä lōn'). Americans apparently mispronounced *galón* or mistook its meaning, for a hat trimmed with ten rows of braid was a ten-*gallon* hat to them.

The following paragraph contains fifteen loan-words that passed into American-English by way of the Western frontier.

1. Identify the fifteen loan-words, consulting a dictionary to verify your identification.

2. Explain why you think these words were useful additions to the pioneers' vocabulary.

Rain was falling heavily now; Hal Thorp reined his weary pinto to a halt and slumped over the pommel. What, he wondered, was he doing playing nurse-maid to a herd of cattle? Cowboy Thorp? That wasn't the dream that had pulled *him* West. No, indeed. In the calm of a Boston winter he had dreamed of Vigilante Thorp, who rode the creamiest palomino in the territory and threw outlaws into the calaboose. He shifted in the saddle, ignoring the rain that ran down his sun-bleached sombrero and worn chaps. Hal Thorp almost longed for the cool green order of New England—for brick houses instead of adobe huts, for neat farms instead of sprawling ranches, and for hills that rolled gently and didn't claw the sky the way the sierras did. Yet here he was, the would-be hero of the West, urging cattle that nibbled mesquite, chasing strays out of twisted canyons, turning stampedes in dusty arroyos. Vigilante Thorp? Hal touched a gentle spur to his horse and fingered the lariat hung from his saddle: Well, maybe he'd lasso that dream yet.

Sarah Orne Jewett 1849-1909

A hundred years ago South Berwick, Maine, was a country village. It stood on the bank of a river which flowed through dark forests of firs and pines, past white farmhouses shaded by elms, to the ocean not many miles away. Here Sarah Orne Jewett was born, lived most of her life, and died. The village and the surrounding country became the world of her delicate and serene stories.

In her girlhood Sarah often went on the rounds with her father, a doctor. As Dr. Jewett talked with her about patients living in Berwick households, in fishermen's cottages, or on inland farms, she unconsciously acquired insights and family histories which years after would find place in her stories. Sarah attended Berwick Academy, and, encouraged by her book-loving father, read widely. One of her favorite authors was Harriet Beecher Stowe, the author of *Uncle Tom's Cabin*. Like Whittier, Mrs. Stowe had turned from writing fiery abolitionist books to picturing the New England of her childhood. While still in her teens Sarah learned from Mrs. Stowe that New England village- and farm-life was the stuff of good fiction.

Before she was twenty, Miss Jewett wrote and sold her first story. In her first book, *Deephaven* (1877), she published a series of related stories about the people of Berwick. In later stories, collected in such books as *A Country Doctor* (1884), *A White Heron and Other Stories* (1886), and *The Country of the Pointed Firs* (1896), she pictured also life on the farms and in coastal towns.

Miss Jewett's quiet tales are different indeed from the robust California mining-camp tales of Harte, the stories of Louisiana by George Washington Cable, or the stories of old Virginia by Thomas Nelson Page published during the same decades. Nevertheless, her stories were also outstanding products of the local-color movement. The played-out rocky farms, the moldering fishing shacks, the deserted shipyards of coastal towns which marked the part of Maine in which she was reared as a declining section, were accurately re-created in her stories. With affection and humor she wrote of Maine folk of the fairly recent past—their ways of living, their joys and tragedies, their speech. "A White Heron," a tender account of a little country girl's loyalty to a wild and lonely winged creature, shows Miss Jewett's fine talent.

A Maine fishing village, in the area made memorable by Miss Jewett.

A White Heron

I

The woods were already filled with shadows one June evening, just before eight o'clock, though a bright sunset still glimmered faintly among the trunks of the trees. A little girl was driving home her cow, a plodding, dilatory, provoking creature in her behavior, but a valued companion for all that. They were going away from whatever light there was, and striking deep into the woods, but their feet were familiar with the path, and it was no matter whether their eyes could see it or not.

There was hardly a night the summer through when the old cow could be found waiting at the pasture bars; on the contrary, it was her greatest pleasure to hide herself away among the huckleberry bushes, and though she wore a loud bell she had made the discovery that if one stood perfectly still it would not ring. So Sylvia had to hunt for her until she found her, and call Co'! Co'! with never an answering Moo, until her childish patience was quite spent. If the creature had not given good milk and plenty of it, the case would have seemed very different to her owners. Besides, Sylvia had all the time there was, and very little use to make of it. Sometimes in pleasant weather it was a consolation to look upon the cow's pranks as an intelligent attempt to play hide-and-seek, and as the child had no playmates she lent herself to this amusement with a good deal of zest. Though this chase had been so long that the wary animal herself had given an unusual signal of her whereabouts, Sylvia had only laughed when she came upon Mistress Moolly at the swampside, and urged her affectionately homeward with a twig of birch leaves. The old cow was not inclined to wander farther, she even turned in the right direction for once as they left the pasture, and stepped along the road at a good pace. She was quite ready to be milked now, and seldom stopped to browse. Sylvia wondered what her grandmother would say because they were so late. It was a great while since she had left home at half-past five o'clock, but everybody knew the difficulty of making this errand a short one. Mrs. Tilley had chased the horned torment too many summer evenings herself to blame any one else for lingering, and was only thankful as she waited that she had Sylvia, nowadays, to give such valuable assistance. The good woman suspected that Sylvia loitered occasionally on her own account; there never was such a child for straying about out-of-doors since the world was made! Everybody said that it was a good change for a little maid who had tried to grow for eight years in a crowded manufacturing town, but, as for Sylvia herself, it seemed as if she never had been alive at all before she came to live at the farm. She thought often with wistful compassion of a wretched geranium that belonged to a town neighbor.

" 'Afraid of folks,' " old Mrs. Tilley said to herself, with a smile, after she had made the unlikely choice of Sylvia from her daughter's houseful of children, and was returning to the farm. " 'Afraid of folks,' they said! I guess she won't be troubled no great with 'em up to the old place!" When they reached the door of the lonely house and stopped to unlock it, and the cat came to purr loudly, and rub against them, a deserted pussy, indeed, but fat with young robins, Sylvia whispered that this was a beautiful place to live in, and she never should wish to go home.

The companions followed the shady wood road, the cow taking slow steps and the child very fast ones. The cow stopped long at the brook to drink, as if the pasture were not half a swamp, and Sylvia stood still and waited, letting her bare feet cool themselves in the shoal water, while the great twilight moths struck softly against her. She waded on through the brook as the cow moved away, and listened to the thrushes with a heart that beat fast with pleasure. There was a stirring in the great boughs overhead. They were full of little birds and beasts that seemed to be wide awake, and going about their world, or else saying good night to each other in sleepy twitters. Sylvia herself felt sleepy as she walked along. However, it was not much farther to the house, and the air was soft and sweet. She was not often in the woods so late as this, and it made her feel as if she were a part of the gray shadows and the moving leaves. She was just thinking how long it seemed since she first came to the farm a year ago, and wondering if everything went on in the noisy town just the same as when she was there; the thought of the great red-faced boy who used to chase and frighten her made her hurry along the path to escape from the shadow of the trees.

Suddenly this little woods-girl is horror-stricken to hear a clear whistle not very far away. Not a bird's whistle, which would have a sort of friendliness, but a boy's whistle, determined, and somewhat aggressive. Sylvia left the cow to whatever sad fate might await her, and stepped discreetly aside into the bushes, but she was just too late. The enemy had discovered her, and called out in a very cheerful and persuasive tone, "Halloa, little girl, how far is it to the road?" and trembling Sylvia answered almost inaudibly, "A good ways."

She did not dare to look boldly at the tall young man, who carried a gun over his shoulder, but she came out of her bush and followed the cow, while he walked alongside. "I have been hunting for some birds," the stranger said kindly, "and I have lost my way, and need a friend very much. Don't be afraid," he added gallantly. "Speak up and tell me what your name is, and whether you think I can spend the night at your house, and go out gunning early in the morning."

Sylvia was more alarmed than before. Would not her grandmother consider her much to blame? But who could have foreseen such an accident as this? It did not seem to be her fault, and she hung her head as if the stem of it were broken, but managed to answer "Sylvy," with much effort when her companion again asked her name.

Mrs. Tilley was standing in the doorway when the trio came into view. The cow gave a loud moo by way of explanation.

"Yes, you'd better speak up for yourself, you old trial! Where'd she tucked herself away this time, Sylvy?" But Sylvia kept an awed silence; she knew by instinct that her grandmother did not comprehend the gravity of the situation. She must be mistaking the stranger for one of the farmer-lads of the region.

The young man stood his gun beside the door, and dropped a lumpy game bag beside it; then he bade Mrs. Tilley good evening, and repeated his wayfarer's story, and asked if he could have a night's lodging.

"Put me anywhere you like," he said. "I must be off early in the morning, before day; but I am very hungry, indeed. You can give me some milk at any rate, that's plain."

"Dear sakes, yes," responded the hostess, whose long slumbering hospitality seemed to be easily awakened. "You might fare better if you went out to the main road a mile or so, but you're welcome to what we've got. I'll milk right off, and you make yourself at home. You can sleep on husks or feathers," she proffered graciously. "I raised them all myself. There's good pasturing for geese just below here toward the ma'sh. Now step round and set a plate for the gentleman, Sylvy!" And Sylvia promptly stepped. She was glad to have something to do, and she was hungry herself.

It was a surprise to find so clean and comfortable a little dwelling in this New England wilderness. The young man had known the horrors of its most primitive housekeeping, and the dreary squalor of that level of society which does not rebel at the companionship of hens. This was the best thrift of an old-fashioned farmstead, though on such a small scale that it seemed like a hermitage. He listened eagerly to the old woman's quaint talk, he watched Sylvia's pale face and shining gray eyes with ever growing enthusiasm, and insisted that this was the best supper he had eaten for a month, and afterward the new-made friends sat down in the doorway together while the moon came up.

Soon it would be berrytime, and Sylvia was a great help at picking. The cow was a good milker, though a plaguy thing to keep track of, the hostess gossiped frankly, adding presently that she had buried four children, so Sylvia's mother, and a son (who might be dead) in California were all the children she had left. "Dan, my boy, was a great hand to go gunning," she explained sadly. "I never wanted for pa'tridges or gray squer'ls while he was to home. He's been a great wand'rer, I expect and he's no hand to write letters. There, I don't blame him, I'd ha' seen the world myself if it had been so I could."

"Sylvy takes after him," the grandmother continued affectionately, after a minute's pause. "There ain't a foot o' ground she don't know her way over, and the wild creatures counts her one o' themselves. Squer'ls she'll tame to come an' feed right out o' her hands, and all sorts o' birds. Last winter she got the jay birds to bangeing[1] here, and I believe she'd 'a' scanted herself of her own meals to have plenty to throw out amongst 'em, if I hadn't kep' watch. Anything but crows, I tell her, I'm willin' to help support—though Dan he had a tamed one o' them that did seem to have reason same as folks. It was round here a good spell after he went away. Dan an' his father they didn't hitch—but he never held up his head ag'in after Dan had dared him an' gone off."

The guest did not notice this hint of family sorrows in his eager interest in something else. "So Sylvy knows all about birds, does she?" he exclaimed, as he looked round at the little girl who sat, very demure but increasingly sleepy, in the moonlight. "I am making a collection of birds myself. I have been at it ever since I was a boy." (Mrs. Tilley smiled.) "There are two or three very rare ones I have been hunting for these five years. I mean to get them if they can be found."

"Do you cage 'em up?" asked Mrs. Tilley doubtfully, in response to this enthusiastic announcement.

"Oh no, they're stuffed and preserved, dozens and dozens of them," said the ornithologist, "and I have shot or snared every one myself. I caught a glimpse of a white heron a few miles from here on Saturday, and I have followed it in this direction. They have never been found in this district at all. The little white heron, it is," and he turned again to look at Sylvia with the hope of discovering that the rare bird was one of her acquaintances.

But Sylvia was watching a hop-toad in the narrow footpath.

"You would know the heron if you saw it," the stranger continued eagerly. "A queer tall white bird with soft feathers and long thin legs. And it would have a nest perhaps in the top of a high tree, made of sticks, something like a hawk's nest."

Sylvia's heart gave a wild beat; she knew that strange white bird, and had once stolen softly near where it stood in some bright green swamp grass, away over at the other side of the woods. There was an open place where the sunshine always seemed strangely yellow and hot, where tall, nodding rushes grew, and her grandmother had warned her that she might sink in the soft black mud underneath and never be heard of more. Not far beyond were the salt marshes just this side the sea itself, which Sylvia wondered and dreamed much about, but never had seen, whose great voice could sometimes be heard above the noise of the woods on stormy nights.

"I can't think of anything I should like so much as to find that heron's nest," the handsome stranger was saying. "I would give ten dollars to anybody who could show it to me," he added desperately, "and I mean to spend my whole vacation hunting for it. Perhaps it was only migrating, or had been chased out of its own region by some bird of prey."

Mrs. Tilley gave amazed attention to all this, but Sylvia still watched the toad, not divining, as she might have done at some calmer time, that the creature wished to get to its hole under the doorstep, and was much hindered by the unusual spectators at that hour of the evening. No amount of thought, that night, could decide how many treasures the ten dollars, so lightly spoken of, would buy.

The next day the young sportsman hovered about the woods, and Sylvia kept him company, having lost her first fear of the friendly lad, who proved to be most kind and sympathetic. He told her many things about the birds and what they knew and where they lived and what they did with themselves. And he gave her a jackknife, which she thought as great a treasure as if she were a desert islander. All day long he did not once make her troubled

---

1. *bangeing,* gathering in groups.

or afraid except when he brought down some unsuspecting singing creature from its bough. Sylvia would have liked him vastly better without his gun; she could not understand why he killed the very birds he seemed to like so much. But as the day waned, Sylvia still watched the young man with loving admiration. She had never seen anybody so charming and delightful; the woman's heart, asleep in the child, was vaguely thrilled by a dream of love. Some premonition of that great power stirred and swayed these young creatures who traversed the solemn woodlands with soft-footed silent care. They stopped to listen to a bird's song; they pressed forward again eagerly, parting the branches—speaking to each other rarely and in whispers; the young man going first and Sylvia following, fascinated, with her gray eyes dark with excitement.

She grieved because the longed-for white heron was elusive, but she did not lead the guest, she only followed, and there was no such thing as speaking first. The sound of her own unquestioned voice would have terrified her—it was hard enough to answer yes or no when there was need of that. At last evening began to fall, and they drove the cow home, and Sylvia smiled with pleasure when they came to the place where she heard the whistle and was afraid only the night before.

II

Half a mile from home, at the farther edge of the woods, where the land was highest, a great pine tree stood, the last of its generation. Whether it was left for a boundary mark, or for what reason, no one could say; the wood-choppers who had felled its mates were dead and gone long ago, and a whole forest of sturdy trees, pines and oaks and maples, had grown again. But the stately head of this old pine towered above them all and made a landmark for sea and shore miles and miles away. Sylvia knew it well. She had always believed that whoever climbed to the top of it could see the ocean; and the little girl had often laid her hand on the great rough trunk and looked up wistfully at those dark boughs that the wind always stirred, no matter how hot and still the air might be below. Now she thought of the tree with a new excitement, for why, if one climbed it at break of day could not one see all the world, and easily discover from whence the white heron flew, and mark the place, and find the hidden nest?

What a spirit of adventure, what wild ambition! What fancied triumph and delight and glory for the later morning when she could make known the secret! It was almost too real and too great for the childish heart to bear.

All night the door of the little house stood open and the whippoorwills came and sang upon the very step. The young sportsman and his old hostess were sound asleep, but Sylvia's great design kept her broad awake and watching. She forgot to think of sleep. The short summer night seemed as long as the winter darkness, and at last when the whippoorwills ceased, and she was afraid the morning would after all come too soon, she stole out of the house and followed the pasture path through the woods, hastening toward the open ground beyond, listening with a sense of comfort and companionship to the drowsy twitter of a half-awakened bird, whose perch she had jarred in passing. Alas, if the great wave of human interest which flooded for the first time this dull little life should sweep away the satisfactions of an existence heart-to-heart with nature and the dumb life of the forest!

There was the huge tree asleep yet in the paling moonlight, and small and silly Sylvia began with utmost bravery to mount to the top of it, with tingling, eager blood coursing the channels of her whole frame, with her bare feet and fingers, that pinched and held like bird's claws to the monstrous ladder reaching up, up, almost to the sky itself. First she must mount the white oak tree that grew alongside, where she was almost lost among the dark branches and the green leaves heavy and wet with dew; a bird fluttered off its nest, and a red squirrel ran to and fro and scolded pettishly at the harmless housebreaker. Sylvia felt her way easily. She had often climbed there, and knew that higher still one of the oak's upper branches chafed against the pine trunk. There, when she made the dangerous pass from one tree to the other, the great enterprise would really begin.

She crept out along the swaying oak limb at last, and took the daring step across into the old pine tree. The way was harder than she thought; she must reach far and hold fast, the sharp dry twigs caught and held her and scratched her like angry talons, the pitch made her thin little fingers clumsy and stiff as she went round and round the tree's great stem, higher and higher upward. The sparrows and robins in the woods below were beginning to wake and twitter to the dawn, yet it seemed much lighter there aloft in the pine tree, and the child knew she must hurry if the project were to be of any use.

The tree seemed to lengthen itself out as she went up, and to reach farther and farther upward. It was like a great mainmast to the voyaging earth; it must truly have been amazed that morning through all its ponderous frame as it felt this determined spark of human spirit wending its way from higher branch to branch. Who knows how steadily the least twigs held themselves to advantage this light, weak creature on her way! The old pine must have loved his new dependent. More than all the hawks, and bats, and moths, and even the sweet-voiced thrushes, was the brave, beating heart of the solitary gray-eyed child. And the tree stood still and frowned away the winds that June morning while the dawn grew bright in the east.

Sylvia's face was like a pale star, if one had seen it from the ground, when the last thorny bough was past, and she stood trembling and tired but wholly triumphant, high in the treetop. Yes, there was the sea with the dawning sun making a golden dazzle over it, and toward that glorious east flew two hawks with slow-moving pinions. How low they looked in the air from that height when one had only seen them before far up, and dark against the blue sky. Their gray feathers were as soft as moths; they seemed only a little way from the tree, and Sylvia felt as if she too could go flying away among the clouds. Westward, the woodlands and farms reached miles and miles into the distance; here and there were church steeples, and white villages, truly it was a vast and awesome world!

The birds sang louder and louder. At last the sun came up bewilderingly bright. Sylvia could see the white sails of ships out at sea, and the clouds that were purple and rose-colored and yellow at first began to fade away. Where was the white heron's nest in the sea of green branches, and was this wonderful sight and pageant of the world the only reward for having climbed to such a giddy height? Now look down again, Sylvia, where the green marsh is set among the shining birches and dark hemlocks; there where you saw the white heron once you will see him again; look, look! a white spot of him like a single floating feather comes up from the dead hemlock and grows larger, and rises, and comes close at last, and goes by the landmark pine with steady sweep of wing and outstretched slender neck and crested head. And wait! wait! do not move a foot or a finger, little girl, do not send an arrow of light and consciousness from your two eager eyes, for the heron has perched on a pine bough not far beyond yours, and cries back to his mate on the nest and plumes his feathers for the day!

The child gives a long sigh a minute later when a company of shouting catbirds comes also to the tree, and vexed by their fluttering and lawlessness the solemn heron goes away. She knows his secret now, the wild, light, slender bird that floats and wavers, and goes back like an arrow presently to his home in the green world beneath. Then Sylvia, well satisfied, makes her perilous way down again, not daring to look far below the branch she stands on, ready to cry sometimes because her fingers ache and her lamed feet slip. Wondering over and over again what the stranger would say to her, and what he would think when she told him how to find his way straight to the heron's nest.

"Sylvy, Sylvy!" called the busy old grandmother again and again, but nobody answered, and the small husk bed was empty and Sylvia had disappeared.

The guest waked from a dream, and remembering his day's pleasure hurried to dress himself that might it sooner begin. He was sure from the way the shy little girl looked once or twice yesterday that she had at least seen the white heron, and now she must really be made to tell. Here she comes now, paler than ever, and her worn old frock is torn and tattered, and smeared with pine pitch. The grandmother and the sportsman stand in the door together and question her, and the splendid moment has come to speak of the dead hemlock tree by the green marsh.

But Sylvia does not speak after all, though the old grandmother fretfully rebukes her, and the young man's kind, appealing eyes are looking straight in her own. He can make them rich with money; he has promised it, and they are poor now. He is so well worth making happy, and he waits to hear the story.

No, she must keep silence! What is it that suddenly forbids her and makes her dumb? Has she been nine years growing and now, when the great world for the first time puts out a hand to her, must she thrust it aside for a bird's sake? The murmur of the pine's green branches is in her ears, she remembers how the white heron came flying through the golden air and how they watched the sea and the morning together, and Sylvia cannot speak; she cannot tell the heron's secret and give its life away.

Dear loyalty, that suffered a sharp pang as the guest went away disappointed later in the day, that could have served and followed him and loved him as a dog loves! Many a night Sylvia heard the echo of his whistle haunting the pasture path as she came home with the loitering cow. She forgot even her sorrow at the sharp report of his gun and the sight of thrushes and sparrows dropping silent to the ground, their songs hushed and their pretty feathers stained and wet with blood. Were the birds better friends than their hunter might have been—who can tell? Whatever treasures were lost to her, woodlands and summertime, remember! Bring your gifts and graces and tell your secrets to this lonely country child!

 TO INCREASE UNDERSTANDING

1. In the biography of Bret Harte you read that the local colorists "stressed sectional backgrounds,

characters, actions, and dialect." Cite examples from "A White Heron" that illustrate these qualities.

2. (a) What methods of characterization does Sarah Orne Jewett use in describing Sylvia? (Reviewing the "Better Reading" article on page 47 will help you answer this question.) (b) What is the significance of Sylvia's jarring the bird's nest (page 418, column 2, paragraph 2)? (c) What is the force of the adjective *silly* (page 418, column 2, paragraph 3)?

3. What device does Miss Jewett use to give the reader information about Sylvia's earlier life?

4. Sylvia is described as living "heart-to-heart with nature and the dumb life of the forest." (a) Point out passages which you feel make the girl's sensitivity to nature especially vivid. (b) How does the young sportsman's interest in the white heron differ from Sylvia's?

5. (a) What is the conflict in "A White Heron"? (b) What is the technical climax? (c) What is the emotional climax? (If you are doubtful about the meaning of these terms, see the "Better Reading" article on page 37.)

6. To a greater extent than most modern short-story writers, Miss Jewett speaks directly to the reader. (a) Find examples of this. (b) What do these passages tell you about the author? (c) What effect do they have on the story itself?

 EXTENDING INTERESTS

Many of the local colorists wrote short stories that are just as entertaining to readers today as they were to their first audiences. Among such authors are George Washington Cable, Edward Eggleston, Thomas Nelson Page, Mary Noailles Murfree, Joel Chandler Harris, and Mary E. Wilkins Freeman. Plan to read one or more stories by one of these authors or by Mark Twain, Bret Harte, or Sarah Orne Jewett. Pay particular attention to the section of the country the writer represents and to the way in which he uses local color. If you can arrange with your teacher for a class period at which the stories may be discussed, you will find it interesting to exchange information about the various local-color stories that members of the class have read. You will find collections of short stories by some of the individual writers listed in the Bibliography on page 440. Others are represented in collections like the following: *Local Colorists: American Short Stories, 1857-1900*, edited by Claude M. Simpson; *The Brave and The Fair*, edited by Helen Ferris; *Golden Tales of Our America*, edited by May Lamberton Becker; and *American Short Stories*, edited by Fred Lewis Pattee.

Stephen Crane 1871-1900

Most writers in the years following the Civil War tried to be *realists;* that is, they attempted to portray scenes, characters, and actions like those in real life. But the degree of realism in their stories varied. William Dean Howells, a famous champion of realism, boasted that his novels did not show man's "heroic or occasional phases" but "his habitual moods of vacancy and tiresomeness." On the other hand, local colorists like Bret Harte and Sarah Orne Jewett were accused by some critics of making life more pleasant and men and women more admirable than they really are.

One group of writers made even more of an effort than most realists to be "unflinching" in facing up to life's coarse, brutal, or disgusting aspects. These were the *naturalists,* prominent among whom was Stephen Crane. Strongly influenced by nineteenth-century scientific studies, the naturalists believed that heredity predetermines character, and that (as Crane put it) "environment is a tremendous thing in the world and frequently shapes lives regardless." Consequently, the naturalists were fatalists, often pessimists. Believing as they did that their writing should embody their beliefs about the nature of existence, the naturalists used every possible means to express their ideas about life with stark honesty. They found symbolism especially effective for this purpose.

Crane, the son of a clergyman, was born in Newark, New Jersey. He had more schooling than most other writers of the period, attending Lafayette College and Syracuse University a year each. But he himself said, "It

Candid view of life in a New York tenement district, 1900.

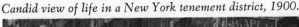

CULVER PICTURES

was on the Bowery that I got my artistic education." Fresh from college in 1891, as a New York newspaperman Crane studied at first-hand the derelicts in Bowery tenements and shelters. His first novel, *Maggie* (1893), unfolded so savage and so sordid a story of the slums that he was unable to find a publisher and had to publish it himself.

Crane's second novel, *The Red Badge of Courage* (1895), was immediately successful. It reached so large an audience that its twenty-four-year-old author became a celebrity overnight. This account of a farm boy's experiences in a battle during the Civil War was based upon reading rather than personal observation. But it pictured with compelling vividness a primal experience—a boy's exposure to horror and death and his ultimate triumph over fear. Veterans acclaimed its accuracy; and later, after serving as a war correspondent in Greece and in Cuba, Crane happily told a friend, "*The Red Badge* is all right."[1]

Crane died of tuberculosis in Germany in 1900. During the last five years of his life, the dark, intense author wrote many newspaper stories, some free-verse poems, and a number of fine short stories. Often his stories derived much of their power from the insights they gave into the minds of characters. A typical story shows a character gripped by a strong emotion. Crane conveyed that emotion by what critics have called *impressionism*. This means that he recounted the character's experiences, selected details, and described elements in the scene in such a way as to convey the character's emotions or to interpret them in naturalistic terms. Almost always he paid special attention to the effects of light, as the "impressionist" painters of his day were doing. In "The Open Boat," for example, he thus

---

1. See the discussion guide for *The Red Badge of Courage* on page 429.

The dead near Dunker Church at Antietam, after the bloodiest day of the Civil War. Photo by James Gardener, a Brady assistant.

describes the sea as it is viewed from a tiny dinghy by the survivors of a wreck: "There was a terrible grace in the move of the waves, and they came in silence, save for the snarling of the crests." Or he describes a shark hopefully following the boat at night as "a gleaming trail of phosphorescence" which "might have been made by a monstrous knife." Thus, with quick, deft touches, Crane suggests the *menace* that the survivors feel in the snarling sea and its sharp-toothed monsters. At another point he describes a tower sighted from the boat as "a giant, standing with its back to the plight of the ants." This description, which implies the indifference of Nature—indeed, of the Universe—to the struggles of men, embodies a tenet of naturalistic belief.

The following story, which has been called by Carl Van Doren "pure, concentrated Crane," shows the author in his rôle as a naturalist.

A Mystery of Heroism

The dark uniforms of the men were so coated with dust from the incessant wrestling of the two armies that the regiment almost seemed a part of the clay bank which shielded them from the shells. On the top of the hill a battery was arguing in tremendous roars with some other guns, and to the eye of the infantry the artillerymen, the guns, the caissons, the horses, were distinctly outlined upon the blue sky. When a piece was fired, a red streak as round as a log flashed low in the heavens, like a monstrous bolt of lightning. The men of the battery wore white duck trousers, which somehow emphasized their legs; and when they ran and crowded in little groups at the bidding of the shouting officers, it was more impressive than usual to the infantry.

Fred Collins, of A Company, was saying: "Thunder! I wisht I had a drink. Ain't there any water round here?"

Then somebody yelled, "There goes th' bugler!"

As the eyes of half the regiment swept in one machinelike movement, there was an instant's picture of a horse in a great convulsive leap of a death wound and a rider leaning back with a crooked arm and spread fingers before his face. On the ground was the crimson terror of an exploding shell, with fibers of flame that seemed like lances. A glittering bugle swung clear of the rider's back as fell headlong the horse and the man. In the air was an odor as from a conflagration.

Sometimes they of the infantry looked down at a fair little meadow which spread at their feet. Its long green grass was rippling gently in a breeze. Beyond it was the gray form of a house half torn to pieces by shells and by the busy axes of soldiers who had pursued firewood. The line of an old fence was now dimly marked by long weeds and by an occasional post. A shell had blown the wellhouse to fragments. Little lines of gray smoke ribboning upward from some embers indicated the place where had stood the barn.

From beyond a curtain of green woods there came the sound of some stupendous scuffle, as if two animals of the size of islands were fighting. At a distance there were occasional appearances of swift-moving men, horses, batteries, flags, and with the crashing of infantry volleys were heard, often, wild and frenzied cheers. In the midst of it all Smith and Ferguson, two privates of A Company, were engaged in a heated discussion which involved the greatest questions of the national existence.

The battery on the hill presently engaged in a frightful duel. The white legs of the gunners scampered this way and that way, and the officers redoubled their shouts. The guns, with their demeanors of stolidity and courage, were typical of something infinitely self-possessed in this clamor of death that swirled around the hill.

One of a "swing" team[1] was suddenly smitten quivering to the ground, and his maddened brethren dragged his torn body in their struggle to escape from this turmoil and danger. A young soldier astride one of the leaders swore and fumed in his saddle and furiously jerked at the bridle. An officer screamed out an order so violently that his voice broke and ended the sentence in a falsetto shriek.

The leading company of the infantry regiment was somewhat exposed, and the colonel ordered it moved more fully under the shelter of the hill. There was the clank of steel against steel.

A lieutenant of the battery rode down and passed them, holding his right arm carefully in his left hand. And it was as if this arm was not at all a part of him, but belonged to another man. His sober and reflective charger went slowly. The officer's face was grimy and perspiring, and his uniform was tousled as if he had been in direct grapple with an enemy. He smiled grimly when the men stared at him. He turned his horse toward the meadow.

Collins, of A Company, said: "I wisht I had a drink. I bet there's water in that there ol' well yonder!"

"Yes; but how you goin' to git it?"

For the little meadow which intervened was now suffering a terrible onslaught of shells. Its green and beautiful calm had vanished utterly. Brown earth was being flung in monstrous handfuls. And there was a massacre of the young blades of grass. They were being torn, burned, obliterated. Some curious fortune of the battle had made this gentle little meadow the object of the red hate of the shells, and each one as it exploded seemed like an imprecation in the face of a maiden.

The wounded officer who was riding across this expanse said to himself: "Why, they couldn't shoot any harder if the whole army was massed here!"

A shell struck the gray ruins of the house, and as, after the roar, the shattered wall fell in fragments, there was a noise which resembled the flapping of shutters during a wild gale of winter. Indeed, the infantry paused in the shelter of the bank appeared as men standing upon a shore contemplating a madness of the sea. The angel of calamity had under its glance the battery upon the hill. Fewer white-legged men labored about the guns. A shell had smitten one of the pieces, and after the flare, the smoke, the dust, the wrath of this blow were gone, it was possible to see white legs stretched horizontally upon the ground. And at that interval to the rear, where it is the business of battery horses to stand with their noses to the fight awaiting the command to drag their guns out of the destruction, or into it, or wheresoever these incomprehensible humans demanded with whip and spur—in this line of passive and dumb spectators, whose fluttering hearts yet would not let them forget the iron laws of man's control of them—in this rank of brute-soldiers there had been relentless and hideous carnage. From the ruck of bleeding and prostrate horses, the men of the infantry could see one animal raising its stricken body with its forelegs and turning its nose with mystic and profound eloquence toward the sky.

Some comrades joked Collins about his thirst. "Well, if yeh want a drink so bad, why don't yeh go git it?"

"Well, I will in a minnet, if yeh don't shut up!"

A lieutenant of artillery floundered his horse straight down the hill with as little concern as if it were level ground. As he galloped past the colonel of the infantry, he threw up his hand in swift salute. "We've got to get out of that," he roared angrily. He was a black-bearded officer, and his eyes, which resembled beads, sparkled like those of an insane man. His jumping horse sped along the column of infantry.

The fat major, standing carelessly with his sword held horizontally behind him and with his legs far apart, looked after the receding horseman and laughed. "He wants to get back with orders pretty quick, or there'll be no batt'ry left," he observed.

The wise young captain of the second company hazarded to the lieutenant-colonel that

---

1. a "swing" team, the middle pair of horses in a team of six.

the enemy's infantry would probably soon attack the hill, and the lieutenant-colonel snubbed him.

A private in one of the rear companies looked out over the meadow, and then turned to a companion and said, "Look there, Jim!" It was the wounded officer from the battery, who some time before had started to ride across the meadow, supporting his right arm carefully with his left hand. This man had encountered a shell, apparently, at a time when no one perceived him, and he could now be seen lying face downward with a stirruped foot stretched across the body of his dead horse. A leg of the charger extended slantingly upward, precisely as stiff as a stake. Around this motionless pair the shells still howled.

There was a quarrel in A Company. Collins was shaking his fist in the faces of some laughing comrades. "Dern yeh! I ain't afraid t' go. If yeh say much, I will go!"

"Of course, yeh will! You'll run through that there medder, won't yeh?"

Collins said, in a terrible voice: "You see now!"

At this ominous threat his comrades broke into renewed jeers.

Collins gave them a dark scowl, and went to find his captain. The latter was conversing with the colonel of the regiment.

"Captain," said Collins, saluting and standing at attention—in those days all trousers bagged at the knees—"Captain, I want t' get permission to go git some water from that there well over yonder!"

The colonel and the captain swung about simultaneously and stared across the meadow. The captain laughed. "You must be pretty thirsty, Collins?"

"Yes, sir, I am."

"Well—ah," said the captain. After a moment, he asked, "Can't you wait?"

"No, sir."

The colonel was watching Collins' face. "Look here, my lad," he said, in a pious sort of voice—"Look here, my lad"—Collins was not a lad—"don't you think that's taking pretty big risks for a little drink of water?"

"I dunno," said Collins uncomfortably. Some of the resentment toward his companions, which perhaps had forced him into this affair, was beginning to fade. "I dunno w'ether 'tis."

The colonel and the captain contemplated him for a time.

"Well," said the captain finally.

"Well," said the colonel, "if you want to go, why, go."

Collins saluted. "Much obliged t' yeh."

As he moved away the colonel called after him. "Take some of the other boys' canteens with you an' hurry back now."

"Yes, sir, I will."

The colonel and the captain looked at each other then, for it had suddenly occurred that they could not for the life of them tell whether Collins wanted to go or whether he did not.

They turned to regard Collins, and as they perceived him surrounded by gesticulating comrades, the colonel said: "Well, by thunder! I guess he's going."

Collins appeared as a man dreaming. In the midst of the questions, the advice, the warnings, all the excited talk of his company mates, he maintained a curious silence.

They were very busy in preparing him for his ordeal. When they inspected him carefully, it was somewhat like the examination that grooms give a horse before a race; and they were amazed, staggered, by the whole affair. Their astonishment found vent in strange repetitions.

"Are yeh sure a-goin'?" they demanded again and again.

"Certainly I am," cried Collins at last, furiously.

He strode sullenly away from them. He was swinging five or six canteens by their cords. It seemed that his cap would not remain firmly on his head, and often he reached and pulled it down over his brow.

There was a general movement in the compact column. The long animal-like thing moved slightly. Its four hundred eyes were turned upon the figure of Collins.

"Well, sir, if that ain't th' derndest thing! I never thought Fred Collins had the blood in him for that kind of business."

"What's he goin' to do, anyhow?"

"He's goin' to that well there after water."

"We ain't dyin' of thirst, are we? That's foolishness."

"Well, somebody put him up to it, an' he's doin' it."

"Say, he must be a desperate cuss."

When Collins faced the meadow and walked away from the regiment, he was vaguely conscious that a chasm, the deep valley of all prides, was suddenly between him and his comrades. It was provisional, but the provision was that he return as a victor. He had blindly been led by quaint emotions, and laid himself under an obligation to walk squarely up to the face of death.

But he was not sure that he wished to make a retraction, even if he could do so without shame. As a matter of truth, he was sure of very little. He was mainly surprised.

It seemed to him supernaturally strange that he had allowed his mind to maneuver his body into such a situation. He understood that it might be called dramatically great.

However, he had no full appreciation of anything, excepting that he was actually conscious of being dazed. He could feel his dulled mind groping after the form and color of this incident. He wondered why he did not feel some keen agony of fear cutting his sense like a knife. He wondered at this, because human expression had said loudly for centuries that men should feel afraid of certain things, and that all men who did not feel this fear were phenomena—heroes.

He was, then, a hero. He suffered that disappointment which we would all have if we discovered that we were ourselves capable of those deeds which we most admire in history and legend. This, then, was a hero. After all, heroes were not much.

No, it could not be true. He was not a hero. Heroes had no shames in their lives, and, as for him, he remembered borrowing fifteen dollars from a friend and promising to pay it back the next day, and then avoiding that friend for ten months. When at home his mother had aroused him for the early labor of his life on the farm, it had often been his fashion to be irritable, childish, diabolical; and his mother had died since he had come to the war.

He saw that, in this matter of the well, the canteens, the shells, he was an intruder in the land of fine deeds.

He was now about thirty paces from his comrades. The regiment had just turned its many faces toward him.

From the forest of terrific noises there suddenly emerged a little uneven line of men. They fired fiercely and rapidly at distant foliage on which appeared little puffs of white smoke. The spatter of skirmish firing was added to the thunder of the guns on the hill. The little line of men ran forward. A color-sergeant fell flat with his flag as if he had slipped on ice. There was hoarse cheering from this distant field.

Collins suddenly felt that two demon fingers were pressed into his ears. He could see nothing but flying arrows, flaming red. He lurched from the shock of this explosion, but he made a mad rush for the house, which he viewed as a man submerged to the neck in a boiling surf might view the shore. In the air, little pieces of shell howled and the earthquake explosions drove him insane with the menace of their roar. As he ran, the canteens knocked together with a rhythmical tinkling.

As he neared the house, each detail of the scene became vivid to him. He was aware of some bricks of the vanished chimney lying on the sod. There was a door which hung by one hinge.

Rifle bullets called forth by the insistent skirmishers came from the far-off bank of foliage. They mingled with the shells and the pieces of shells until the air was torn in all directions by hootings, yells, howls. The sky was full of fiends who directed all their wild rage at his head.

When he came to the well, he flung himself face downward and peered into its darkness. There were furtive silver glintings some feet from the surface. He grabbed one of the canteens and, unfastening its cap, swung it down by the cord. The water flowed slowly in with an indolent gurgle.

And now as he lay with his face turned away he was suddenly smitten with the terror. It came upon his heart like the grasp of claws.

All the power faded from his muscles. For an instant he was no more than a dead man.

The canteen filled with a maddening slowness, in the manner of all bottles. Presently he recovered his strength and addressed a screaming oath to it. He leaned over until it seemed as if he intended to try to push water into it with his hands. His eyes as he gazed down into the well shone like two pieces of metal, and in their expression was a great appeal and a great curse. The stupid water derided him.

There was the blaring thunder of a shell. Crimson light shone through the swift-boiling smoke and made a pink reflection on part of the wall of the well. Collins jerked out his arm and canteen with the same motion that a man would use in withdrawing his head from a furnace.

He scrambled erect and glared and hesitated. On the ground near him lay the old well bucket, with a length of rusty chain. He lowered it swiftly into the well. The bucket struck the water and then, turning lazily over, sank. When, with hand reaching tremblingly over hand, he hauled it out, it knocked often against the walls of the well and spilled some of its contents.

In running with a filled bucket, a man can adopt but one kind of gait. So, through this terrible field over which screamed practical angels of death, Collins ran in the manner of a farmer chased out of a dairy by a bull.

His face went staring white with anticipation—anticipation of a blow that would whirl him around and down. He would fall as he had seen other men fall, the life knocked out of them so suddenly that their knees were no more quick to touch the ground than their heads. He saw the long blue line of the regiment, but his comrades were standing looking at him from the edge of an impossible star. He was aware of some deep wheel ruts and hoofprints in the sod beneath his feet.

The artillery officer who had fallen in this meadow had been making groans in the teeth of the tempest of sound. These futile cries, wrenched from him by his agony, were heard only by shells, bullets. When wild-eyed Collins came running, this officer raised himself. His face contorted and blanched from pain, he was about to utter some great beseeching cry. But suddenly his face straightened and he called: "Say, young man, give me a drink of water, will you?"

Collins had no room amid his emotions for surprise. He was mad from the threats of destruction.

"I can't!" he screamed, and in his reply was a full description of his quaking apprehension. His cap was gone and his hair was riotous. His clothes made it appear that he had been dragged over the ground by the heels. He ran on.

The officer's head sank down and one elbow crooked. His foot in its brassbound stirrup still stretched over the body of his horse and the other leg was under the steed.

But Collins turned. He came dashing back. His face had now turned gray and in his eyes was all terror. "Here it is! here it is!"

The officer was as a man gone in drink. His arm bent like a twig. His head drooped as if his neck were of willow. He was sinking to the ground, to lie face downward.

Collins grabbed him by the shoulder. "Here it is. Here's your drink. Turn over. Turn over, man, for God's sake!"

With Collins hauling at his shoulder, the officer twisted his body and fell with his face turned toward that region where lived the unspeakable noises of the swirling missiles. There was the faintest shadow of a smile on his lips as he looked at Collins. He gave a sigh, a little primitive breath like that from a child.

Collins tried to hold the bucket steadily, but his shaking hands caused the water to splash all over the face of the dying man. Then he jerked it away and ran on.

The regiment gave him a welcoming roar. The grimed faces were wrinkled in laughter.

His captain waved the bucket away. "Give it to the men!"

The two genial, skylarking young lieutenants were the first to gain possession of it. They played over it in their fashion.

When one tried to drink, the other teasingly knocked his elbow. "Don't, Billie! You'll make me spill it," said the one. The other laughed.

Suddenly there was an oath, the thud of wood on the ground, and a swift murmur of astonishment among the ranks. The two lieutenants glared at each other. The bucket lay on the ground, empty.

TO INCREASE UNDERSTANDING

1. (*a*) Why does Collins make his dangerous journey? (*b*) Since Crane doesn't tell you explicitly, how does he make it possible for you to understand Collins' motives?

2. (*a*) What sort of man is Collins? (*b*) Do his particular characteristics account for his actions, or does Crane imply that forces beyond his control lead him on?

3. Read again the examples of Crane's use of "impressionism" on pages 422-423. Then reread page 423, column 1, paragraph 4 and page 424, column 1, paragraph 6, selecting descriptive passages which are noteworthy in suggesting the emotions of the spectators.

4. Reread the part of the story which describes Collins' trip to the well and his return (page 426, column 1, paragraph 4, to page 427, column 2, paragraph 9). Select the details which show Collins' emotions during this hazardous journey.

5. (*a*) What are the reactions of Collins' fellow soldiers to his dash for water? (*b*) Why does Collins himself feel he must be a hero? (*c*) Explain why you do or do not agree that Collins is a hero.

6. Crane is noted for his use of two types of irony: *verbal irony*, or saying the opposite of what is meant; and *irony of situation*, or showing a result that is the opposite of what might be appropriate. (*a*) How does the spilling of the water at the end of the story illustrate irony of situation? (*b*) What verbal irony occurs in the title itself?

BETTER READING
Contrasting romanticists and realists

Depending on the attitude with which he regards life, an author may be classified as a romanticist or a realist. But both *romanticist* and *realist* are very broad terms, allowing for great divergence. Thus Washington Irving, Edgar Allan Poe, and Nathaniel Hawthorne, dissimilar as their works are, all are regarded as romanticists. Similarly, the term *realism* embraces writers as different as Willa Cather, Sinclair Lewis, and Samuel Clemens. In some of its aspects it includes the local colorists, who stressed life in a particular section, and the naturalists, whose fatalistic philosophy resulted in works that exposed the darker aspects of living.

Among the short stories you have studied in this chronological development of American literature are three that end in death and disappointment. They are: "The Devil and Tom Walker," by Washington Irving, a romanticist; "The Luck of Roaring Camp," by Bret Harte, a local colorist; and "A Mystery of Heroism," by Stephen Crane, a naturalist. Conjecture how each of these stories would differ in tone, in characterization, in the type of details presented—even in the outcome of the plot—had it been written by an author employing a different mode. For example, how do you think Crane would have handled the story of miserly Tom Walker? What details might he have stressed? How might the tone have differed from Irving's? Could the result conceivably have been a tragedy? How do you think Bret Harte would have handled the story?

Follow the same general pattern in considering the other two stories. How important is the attitude of a writer in determining the type of fiction he produces?

WORDS!

The word *carnage*, which Stephen Crane uses to suggest the awful blood and slaughter of the battlefield, derives from the Latin word *caro*, meaning "flesh." Many other English words, some of them very different in their present meaning from the original Latin word, have been derived from some form of this word. For example, the word *carnival* was made by uniting a form of *caro*, "flesh," and *levare*, "to put away." Originally *carnival* meant the days of celebration before Lent, at which time the eating of meat was forbidden. The italicized words in the sentences below are all derived from the Latin word *caro*. Rewrite each sentence, substituting another word or group of words for the one italicized. You may use the Glossary if necessary. In a class discussion be ready to point out the connection between the original Latin word and the modern English meaning.

1. The lion is a *carnivorous* animal, but the elephant eats only plants.

2. As the man looked back on his childhood and remembered his mother's care and devotion, he thought of her as the *incarnation* of all virtues.

3. For generations the *carnelian* necklace had been the most prized family heirloom.

4. The rays of the setting sun *incarnadined* the sky.

5. The villain of the novel was a fiend *incarnate*.

DISCUSSION GUIDE

The Red Badge of Courage, by Stephen Crane

To arrive at the meaning of the novel it is necessary to consider Crane as a naturalist and as a user of impressionistic techniques.

PLOT AND CHARACTERS. *Most of Chapter I may be considered exposition.* What time order does Crane use to give the reader information about the youth? What is the youth's background? Crane tells us that the youth's mother "had disappointed him by saying nothing whatever about returning with his shield or on it." What does this statement imply about the youth's ideas of war? How has the youth's reading shaped his ideas? How have his first months in camp differed from what his reading has led him to expect?

The action proper begins when the youth's regiment moves forward. Why does the youth feel apart from the other soldiers? What is significant about the loud soldier's giving him a packet to keep? Explain the youth's actions and the changes in his attitude from the time he first hears gunfire until he meets the spectral soldier (Chapters III-IX). Who is the spectral soldier? What is the effect of his death upon the youth? What rôle does the tattered soldier play?

To the youth a wound is a red badge of courage. What circumstances cause the youth to want this badge? How does he acquire it? What effect does this badge have on his comrades? How does it ultimately affect the youth himself? What is ironic about this entire situation?

The youth is praised by his lieutenant as a wild cat and noticed by the colonel for keeping the flag up in front. Explain the incidents that bring forth these commendations and the relationship between them. What is the youth's attitude as the story ends?

CRANE'S WAY OF WRITING A NOVEL. *Stephen Crane defined a novel as a "succession of sharply outlined pictures, which pass before the reader like a panorama, leaving each its definite impression."* Can this definition be applied to *The Red Badge of Courage?* Cite examples to prove your point.

On page 422 you read that "a typical story by Crane shows a character gripped by a strong emotion." This emotion is conveyed by what critics have called impressionism. Does the youth

in *The Red Badge of Courage* fit the description quoted above? How do you learn most about the youth's emotions—through his actions, his conversation, or his thoughts? Cite examples to explain your answer. In what ways is the treatment of this character impressionistic?

Some critics claim that Crane's method of writing a novel has led him to do nothing more than set forth series of loosely related incidents. If this is true, it will be impossible for the reader to find any overall development in the story. Explain, giving specific examples, whether you agree with this critical opinion or whether you find an overall development in the novel.

STYLE AND MEANING. *Crane, as a naturalist, rediscovered a procedure which Hawthorne had used long before—that of using meaningful symbols.* After his first experience of battle, the youth feels "a flash of astonishment" that "Nature had gone tranquilly on with her golden process in the midst of so much devilment" (Chapter V, last paragraph). How does the youth's reaction "symbolize" a naturalistic concept about man's place in the universe?

In Chapter VII, troubled with having left the battle, the youth enters a forest. Explain how the following details indicate that the forest symbolizes the workings of his conscience: his going into the wood "as if resolved to bury himself"; the noise he makes as he moves; the difficulties the creepers, saplings, and bushes cause; the comparison of the woods to a chapel; the encounter with the dead man. How do the animal and the fish which he sees prove that he had been wrong in deciding that Nature's religion is a "religion of peace"?

How, in the final chapters, is the flag made to serve as a symbol of the youth's state of mind?

Throughout the novel Crane refers to his principal character as "the youth." What appellations does he use for other important characters? What concept does this use of appellations develop?

Contrast the passages in which Crane describes the youth's attitudes with passages in which the youth speaks. How does the style differ?

What is the theme of the novel? How is the style used by Crane an effective instrument for telling the story he tells and giving it the meaning he wishes to convey?

Sidney Lanier 1842-1881

A Southerner who celebrated the life and the natural beauties of his section, Sidney Lanier, a lawyer's son, was reared in Macon, Georgia. Shortly after graduating from Oglethorpe College, he enlisted as a Confederate soldier and served for the duration. The last five months of the war he was imprisoned in a Federal camp where, as a result of exposure, his health was impaired for the rest of his life.

After the war, while teaching school and working as a hotel clerk, Lanier found time to revive an earlier interest in writing. He published a novel, *Tiger-Lilies,* in 1867. But he decided that he had a greater enthusiasm for poetry than for fiction, and he worked hard to perfect his skill. Lanier was a musician as well as a poet. A flutist of great ability, he was a member of the Peabody Symphony Orchestra in Baltimore in the 1870's. During these same years he was a lecturer in literature at Johns Hopkins University.

Lanier's musical skill influenced his development as a poet. Like Whitman he revolted against what he called the "prim smugness and clean-shaven propriety" of conventional verse forms; and his musical training helped him to rebel. As he explained in *The Science of English Verse,* he came to regard verse as "in all respects a phenomenon of sound" and held that "the main distinction between music and verse is ... the difference between the scale of tones used in music and the scale of tones used by the human speaking voice." In analyzing the rhythms of poetry, accordingly, Lanier used musical notes, and he wrote his most individual poems with the melodies, cadences, and overall patterns of musical compositions in mind.

Of "The Symphony" (1875) he said, "I personify each instrument in the orchestra, and make them discuss deep social questions, in the progress of the music." Lanier believed that treating of social issues was the mission

The marshes of Glynn.

of a responsible poet. Thus in "The Symphony" he considered the materialism which he felt had besmirched American life after the Civil War. Lanier's poetry, in dealing with social and economic problems, anticipates the poetry of the modern era. It foreshadows much of today's poetry also in the rhythmical variations it employs: the shifting line lengths and the rhythms imitating musical instruments—violin, flute, oboe, horn, and others.

"The Marshes of Glynn" (1878) is typical of the poet in construction, melody, and thought. The rhythms show a great deal of freedom; the handling of alliteration, of sounds, and of rhyme produces a very musical effect. The poem may be read as a series of symphonic movements. Its delight in the beauties of the Glynn County marshes of Georgia typifies this Southern poet's affection for his boyhood surroundings. Although this particular poem touches very little on specific current problems, it deals with a lasting problem—the revelation of God in Nature. Shortly before writing the poem, Lanier had been reading both Emerson and Whitman; and what he says on this topic interestingly resembles their doctrines.

*The Marshes
of Glynn*

Glooms of the live oaks, beautiful-braided and woven
  With intricate shades of the vines that myriad-cloven
    Clamber the forks of the multiform boughs—
      Emerald twilights—
      Virginal shy lights,   5
Wrought of the leaves to allure to the whisper of vows,
When lovers pace timidly down through the green colonnades
Of the dim sweet woods, of the dear dark woods,
  Of the heavenly woods and glades,
That run to the radiant marginal sand beach within   10
      The wide sea-marshes of Glynn—

Beautiful glooms, soft dusks in the noonday fire—
Wildwood privacies, closets of lone desire,
Chamber from chamber parted with wavering arras of leaves—
Cells for the passionate pleasure of prayer to the soul that grieves, 15
Pure with a sense of the passing of saints through the wood,
Cool for the dutiful weighing of ill with good—

O braided dusks of the oak and woven shades of the vine,
While the riotous noonday sun of the June day long did shine
Ye held me fast in your heart and I held you fast in mine;   20
But now when the noon is no more, and riot is rest,
And the sun is a-wait at the ponderous gate of the West,
And the slant yellow beam down the wood aisle doth seem
Like a lane into heaven that leads from a dream—
Ay, now, when my soul all day hath drunken the soul of the oak, 25
And my heart is at ease from men, and the wearisome sound of
    the stroke
  Of the scythe of time and the trowel of trade is low,
  And belief overmasters doubt, and I know that I know,
  And my spirit is grown to a lordly great compass within,

That the length and the breadth and the sweep of the marshes of Glynn ³⁰
Will work me no fear like the fear they have wrought me of yore
When length was fatigue, and when breadth was but bitterness sore,
And when terror and shrinking and dreary unnameable pain
Drew over me out of the merciless miles of the plain—

Oh, now, unafraid, I am fain to face   ³⁵
   The vast sweet visage of space.
To the edge of the wood I am drawn, I am drawn,
Where the gray beach glimmering runs, as a belt of the dawn,
   For a mete and a mark
      To the forest dark—   ⁴⁰
          So:
Affable live oak, leaning low—
Thus—with your favor—soft, with a reverent hand
(Not lightly touching your person, Lord of the land!)
Bending your beauty aside, with a step I stand   ⁴⁵
On the firm-packed sand,
          Free
By a world of marsh that borders a world of sea.
   Sinuous southward and sinuous northward the shimmering band
   Of the sand beach fastens the fringe of the marsh to the folds
      of the land.   ⁵⁰
Inward and outward to northward and southward the beach lines
      linger and curl
As a silver-wrought garment that clings to and follows the firm sweet
      limbs of a girl.
Vanishing, swerving, evermore curving again into sight,
Softly the sand beach wavers away to a dim gray looping of light.
And what if behind me to westward the wall of the woods stands high? ⁵⁵
The world lies east: how ample, the marsh and the sea and the sky!
A league and a league of marsh grass, waist-high, broad in the blade,
Green, and all of a height, and unflecked with a light or a shade,
Stretch leisurely off, in a pleasant plain,
To the terminal blue of the main.   ⁶⁰

Oh, what is abroad in the marsh and the terminal sea?
   Somehow my soul seems suddenly free
From the weighing of fate and the sad discussion of sin,
By the length and the breadth and the sweep of the marshes of Glynn.

Ye marshes, how candid and simple and nothing-withholding and free ⁶⁵
Ye publish yourselves to the sky and offer yourselves to the sea!
Tolerant plains, that suffer the sea and the rains and the sun,
Ye spread and span like the catholic man who hath mightily won
God out of knowledge and good out of infinite pain
And sight out of blindness and purity out of a stain.   ⁷⁰

As the marsh hen secretly builds on the watery sod,
Behold I will build me a nest on the greatness of God;

I will fly in the greatness of God as the marsh hen flies
In the freedom that fills all the space 'twixt the marsh and the skies;
By so many roots as the marsh grass sends in the sod   75
I will heartily lay me a-hold on the greatness of God;
Oh, like to the greatness of God is the greatness within
The range of the marshes, the liberal marshes of Glynn.

And the sea lends large, as the marsh; lo, out of his plenty the sea
Pours fast; full soon the time of the flood tide must be: 80
Look how the grace of the sea doth go
About and about through the intricate channels that flow
            Here and there,
                Everywhere,
Till his waters have flooded the uttermost creeks and the low-lying lanes, 85
And the marsh is meshed with a million veins,
That like as with rosy and silvery essences flow
    In the rose-and-silver evening glow.
                Farewell, my lord Sun!
The creeks overflow; a thousand rivulets run   90
'Twixt the roots of the sod; the blades of the marsh grass stir;
Passeth a hurrying sound of wings that westward whirr;
Passeth, and all is still; and the currents cease to run;
And the sea and the marsh are one.

How still the plains of the waters be!   95
The tide is in his ecstasy.
The tide is at his highest height—
                And it is night.

And now from the Vast of the Lord will the waters of sleep
Roll in on the souls of men,   100
But who will reveal to our waking ken
The forms that swim and the shapes that creep
                Under the waters of sleep?
And I would I could know what swimmeth below when the tide comes in
On the length and the breadth of the marvelous marshes of Glynn.   105

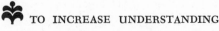 TO INCREASE UNDERSTANDING

1. (a) What particular aspect of the forest does Lanier emphasize in lines 1-20? (b) What change in his feelings does he describe in lines 21-34? (c) Describe the poet's mood as he steps to the edge of the forest and looks out over marsh and sea (lines 35-48). (d) What aspects of the marsh does Lanier describe in lines 49-60? (e) Why does the sight of the marsh and the marsh hen (lines 61-78) revive his confidence in the goodness of God? (f) What effect does the order and beauty of the flood tide (lines 79-105) have upon him?

2. What is the theme of "The Marshes of Glynn"?

3. Read aloud the first two stanzas of the poem. (a) What is the rhyme scheme? (b) What meter predominates? (c) Is the metrical pattern of stanzas 1 and 2 carried throughout the poem? Explain your answer. (d) Discuss the adaptation of the meter to the thought.

4. (a) Point out good examples of repetition, alliteration, and assonance in "The Marshes of Glynn." (b) Are these used simply to make the poetry musical, or do they have additional value? Explain.

Emily Dickinson 1830-1886

Like Sarah Orne Jewett, Emily Dickinson, one of America's great poets and our greatest woman poet, lived all her life in the New England village of her birth. Her home in Amherst, Massachusetts, was a square brown brick mansion partly hidden by great trees and a hemlock hedge and shut off from the street by three closed gates. This huge, forbidding house was an appropriate dwelling for Emily's father, Squire Dickinson—a tight-lipped, stern-looking lawyer, who ruled his family. Its half-hidden aspect and its gates excluding interlopers were apt symbols of the shyness and the reclusiveness of the poet, who at her death left her intimate poems unpublished and asked that they be burned.

She was not always withdrawn. As a girl, despite her repressive surroundings she was vivacious and fun-loving. She was educated at Amherst Academy and at nearby Mount Holyoke Female Seminary. Although she never married, she enjoyed friendships with several men whom she thought of as her tutors. The first was Benjamin F. Newton, a gentle, grave law student studying under her father. It was he, twenty-year-old Emily said, who "taught me what to read, what authors to admire, what was most grand or beautiful in nature, and . . . a faith in things unseen." He also encouraged her to write poetry.

Emily Dickinson, and a poem in her own hand. For a discussion of this poem see page 439.

The second "tutor" was the Reverend Charles Wadsworth, whom she met in 1854 on a visit to Philadelphia. They corresponded. He called on her in 1860 in Amherst and on one or two other occasions. There was no romance, since he was married; and quite probably the good minister had no idea that Emily considered him her "dearest earthly friend." Nevertheless, it was in 1860 that Miss Dickinson discovered herself as a poet, developed a professional interest in poetic techniques, and began to write "love" poems. She was devastated when Wadsworth moved to San Fran-

cisco in 1862. It was very soon after that she withdrew from village society. When visitors called, she disappeared; and even her best friends seldom saw the elusive girl, although she corresponded with them by letter.

The third of Miss Dickinson's masculine friends was the writer, Thomas Wentworth Higginson. In the *Atlantic Monthly* for April 1862 he had published "Letter to a Young Contributor," urging beginning writers to avoid high-flown language and to "charge their style with life." On April 16, Higginson found in his mailbox a brief note. "Mr. Higginson," it began, "Are you too deeply occupied to say if my verse is alive?" Enclosed were four poems and, in a separate envelope—as if the author wished to hide it—the name *Emily Dickinson*. Higginson, fascinated by the strange communication, answered at once, asking the author to send more poems and to tell him about herself. So began a long correspondence with the poet's new "preceptor," during which, despite his inability to appreciate verse so unconventional in content and form, Higginson encouraged his "scholar" to continue.

He visited her in 1870 and later told of meeting her in the dark cool parlor: "A step like a pattering child's in the entry and in glided a little plain woman with two smooth bands of reddish hair and a face with no good feature—in a very plain and exquisitely clean white piqué and blue net worsted shawl. She came to me with two white day lilies, which she put in a . . . childlike way into my hand and said, 'These are my introduction,' in a soft, frightened, breathless, childlike voice—and added under her breath, 'Forgive me if I am frightened; I never see strangers and hardly know what to say'—but she talked soon and thenceforth continuously . . . .'"

It may be that she was plain, although the best likeness of her shows a not unattractive face and great haunting eyes. But whatever her appearance, Emily Dickinson was an arresting personality. "I never was with anyone who drained my nerve power so much," Higginson wrote after his first visit. "Without touching her she drew from me." And a friend who knew the poet well said: "She was different. Emily Dick had more charm than anyone I ever knew."

Her intensity, her charm, her unique outlook all color her poetry. Like Whitman she rejected regular rhythms. Higginson thought that perhaps Whitman had influenced her, until she said she had not read his poetry, having heard "that he was disgraceful." Emerson she knew in person and as a writer; his rather rough-hewn and often cryptic verse may have encouraged her to avoid regular rhythms and perfect rhymes, and to violate grammatical rules when she wished. But the Bible was the book whose words she echoed most frequently, and the hymnal the most important source of her verse forms. These forms appear simple, but she handles them with skill to achieve the pauses and the emphases she wants. In thought also her poems are far from simple: they are packed with nimble perceptions, with humor, and with irony.

"The immediate sources of Emily Dickinson's inspiration," says Thomas H. Johnson in a fine biography, "sprang from the associations she most deeply cherished and about which she felt greatest awe. First was the world about her, the moods of nature, the creatures . . . and the buds that bloom and fade. Equally important were friends, always held in a brittle remembrance by her acute consciousness that death at any moment can occur.

And lurking behind every thought . . . was the abiding wonder, the craving for assurance, about the sempiternal." In her hundreds of poems, most of them of only a few lines and none very long, she wrote wittily, profoundly, and movingly about these topics—life, nature, love, death and immortality.

During Emily Dickinson's lifetime, only seven of her poems were published, several without her consent. Her sister Lavinia knew that she wrote poems but had no idea how many she had written until, after Emily's death, she went through her boxes, her desk, and her bureau. To her astonishment Lavinia found at that time nearly nine hundred poems, and others discovered later swelled the total to nearly eighteen hundred. These Miss Dickinson had left in packets bound with ribbons. Luckily instead of being destroyed, they were printed in a series of volumes, the first in 1890, the last in 1955. Thus practically all of Emily Dickinson's poetry came to the attention of readers long after its creation, and was still fresh and exciting when modern poets discovered it and felt its powerful influence.

I Like To See It Lap the Miles

I like to see it lap the miles,
And lick the valleys up,
And stop to feed itself at tanks;
And then, prodigious, step

Around a pile of mountains,   5
And, supercilious, peer
In shanties by the sides of roads;
And then a quarry pare

To fit its sides, and crawl between,
Complaining all the while   10
In horrid, hooting stanza;
Then chase itself down hill

And neigh like Boanerges;[1]
Then, punctual as a star,
Stop—docile and omnipotent—   15
At its own stable door.

I'll Tell You How the Sun Rose

I'll tell you how the sun rose,
A ribbon at a time.
The steeples swam in amethyst,
The news like squirrels ran.
The hills untied their bonnets,   5

The bobolinks begun.
Then I said softly to myself,
"That must have been the sun!"

   . . . . . .

But how he set, I know not.
There seemed a purple stile   10
That little yellow boys and girls
Were climbing all the while

Till when they reached the other side,
A dominie in gray
Put gently up the evening bars,   15
And led the flock away.

Hope Is the Thing With Feathers

Hope is the thing with feathers
That perches in the soul,
And sings the tune without the words,
And never stops at all,

And sweetest in the gale is heard;   5
And sore must be the storm
That could abash the little bird
That kept so many warm.

I LIKE TO SEE IT LAP THE MILES. **1.** *Boanerges* (bō′a nėr′jēz). Miss Dickinson uses this name to suggest the thundering sound of the locomotive. *Boanerges* ("sons of thunder") was the name Christ gave to James and John. (Mark 3:17)

I've heard it in the chillest land,
And on the strangest sea;   10
Yet, never, in extremity,
It asked a crumb of me.

Longing Is Like the Seed

Longing is like the seed
That wrestles in the ground,
Believing if it intercede
It shall at length be found.

The hour and the zone   5
Each circumstance unknown,
What constancy must be achieved
Before it see the sun!

Success Is Counted Sweetest

Success is counted sweetest
By those who ne'er succeed.
To comprehend a nectar
Requires sorest need.

Not one of all the purple host   5
Who took the flag today
Can tell the definition,
So clear, of victory,

As he, defeated, dying,
On whose forbidden ear   10
The distant strains of triumph
Break, agonized and clear.

Much Madness Is Divinest Sense

Much madness is divinest sense
To a discerning eye;
Much sense the starkest madness.
'Tis the majority
In this, as all, prevails.   5
Assent, and you are sane;
Demur, you're straightway dangerous,
And handled with a chain.

Alter? When the Hills Do

Alter? When the hills do.
Falter? When the sun
Question if his glory
Be the perfect one.

Surfeit? When the daffodil   5
Doth of the dew:
Even as herself, O friend!
I will of you!

A Triumph May Be of Several Kinds

A triumph may be of several kinds.
There's triumph in the room
When that old imperator, Death,
By faith is overcome.

There's triumph of the finer mind   5
When truth, affronted long,
Advances calm to her supreme,
Her God her only throng.

A triumph when temptation's bribe
Is slowly handed back,   10
One eye upon the heaven renounced
And one upon the rack.

Severer triumph, by himself
Experienced, who can pass
Acquitted from that naked bar,   15
Jehovah's countenance!

Surgeons Must Be Very Careful

Surgeons must be very careful
When they take the knife!
Underneath their fine incisions
Stirs the culprit—Life!

To Make a Prairie

To make a prairie it takes a clover and one
  bee,
And revery.
The revery alone will do
If bees are few.

Because I Could Not Stop for Death

Because I could not stop for Death,
He kindly stopped for me;
The carriage held but just ourselves
And Immortality.

We slowly drove, he knew no haste,   5
And I had put away
My labor, and my leisure too,
For his civility.

We passed the school where children played
At wrestling in a ring;   10
We passed the fields of gazing grain,
We passed the setting sun.

We paused before a house that seemed
A swelling of the ground;
The roof was scarcely visible,   15
The cornice but a mound.

Since then 'tis centuries; but each
Feels shorter than the day
I first surmised the horses' heads
Were toward eternity.   20

 TO INCREASE UNDERSTANDING

1. In "I Like To See It Lap the Miles," although she never mentions by name what she is writing about, Miss Dickinson conveys her feeling about a train in the days when the relatively new railway offered the fastest means of traveling. (*a*) What does the fact that the train stops "at its own stable door" show about the basic comparison? (*b*) How do the verbs which picture its movement enforce this comparison? (*c*) Judging from the poet's description of its performance in the valleys, on the mountains, and along the quarries, what is one of her chief impressions? (*d*) What do its complaining and chasing itself down hill add to this impression? (*e*) What *paradox*, or apparent contradiction, does the poet stress by having it stop "punctual as a star" at a "stable door"? (*f*) Relate the words *docile* and *omnipotent* (line 15) to this paradox and to the poem as a whole.

2. "I'll Tell You How the Sun Rose" represents the passage of a day, with the figures of speech not only making a vivid picture but also giving the picture emotional significance. (*a*) Relate the order in which the colors are mentioned to the progress of the day. (*b*) What elements in the first eight lines make the sunrise appear gay? (*c*) To what are the "little yellow boys and girls" in the last lines compared? (*d*) What does the comparison imply about the ending of the day? (*e*) How would the emotional effect be changed if the day were pictured ending with a blazing scarlet sunset?

3. In "Hope Is the Thing With Feathers" and "Longing Is Like the Seed" the poet uses similes and metaphors to develop the theme. (*a*) What comparison is drawn in each poem? (*b*) In each is the comparison sustained or only briefly mentioned? (*c*) How does each comparison develop an abstract idea? (*d*) What is gained by using the comparison instead of stating the idea abstractly?

4. How do the following words increase the effectiveness of "Success Is Counted Sweetest": *nectar* (line 3), *purple* (line 5), and *agonized* (line 12)?

5. Explain the paradox upon which "Much Madness Is Divinest Sense" is built.

6. (*a*) State the theme of "Alter? When the Hills Do." (*b*) Discuss its development.

7. (*a*) What are the several kinds of triumph the poet describes in "A Triumph May Be of Several Kinds"? (*b*) What does she consider the greatest triumph to be?

8. "Surgeons Must Be Very Careful" and "To Make a Prairie" are brief poems. But do they therefore express simple thoughts? Account for your answer by stating in your own words the thought of each.

9. In "Because I Could Not Stop for Death," the poet uses personification. (*a*) Who is her companion in the carriage, and what qualities are assigned to him? (*b*) In lines 9-12 the children, the grain, and the setting sun each represent a different stage on the journey the traveler is describing. What stage does each represent? (*c*) What is the house mentioned in lines 13-16? (*d*) Explain in your own words the idea the poem develops.

Imagery, or the use of words that appeal to the senses, is important in both poetry and prose. Words that cause a scene to flash before the reader's eye or summon up a sudden sound or smell give the reader a sense of reality; they help him share the experience of the poet or enter into the feelings of an imagined character in a novel or short story. The competent writer chooses words appealing to the senses with extreme care. Rather than use as many images as possible, he selects only those that help the reader interpret the poem or story, and he arranges them in such order as to convey certain attitudes and feelings.

Few poets have handled images with more artistry than Emily Dickinson. The brevity of most of her poems testifies to her skill in choosing words that have a sharp impact upon the imagination, and in arranging them so that each single detail carries a heavy load of meaning.

Printed at the right are two versions of a poem Miss Dickinson wrote about hummingbirds. She wrote "Within My Garden Rides a Bird" first, and about twenty years later rewrote it as "A Route of Evanescence." Studying these two versions in conjunction shows that even a very fine poet can refine the use and efficiency of images.

Read the first and longer version of this hummingbird poem. (*a*) What image is used in the first two stanzas to suggest the motion of the bird's wings? (*b*) Why does the poet use the word *rides* rather than *flies*? (*c*) How do you know the bird is a hummingbird? (*d*) What is a *gig* (line 10)? How is a gig related to the image developed in stanzas 1 and 2? (*e*) What question perplexes the poet and her dog after the bird has disappeared? (*f*) What is the "exquisite reply" to the question?

Note that in "A Route of Evanescence" the bird is not even mentioned. The meaning of the poem is so concentrated in eight short lines that to understand it the reader must grasp the full implication of every image. Check in your Glossary the meaning of any unfamiliar words. Then, referring to the poem as you read, study the following analysis of "A Route of Evanescence" by George Frisbie Whicher.

Here is the whole *sensation* of hummingbird: first, a dazzle of sudden sense impressions, movement, motion of wings, color, and whir (in the reiterated *r*'s), all at once; then (the bird's departure taken for granted) the emptiness emphasized by the clear picture of nodding blossoms; and finally the startled mind of the (assumed) spectator regaining its poise

with a whimsical comment. Nothing could be spared and no more is needed. Emily Dickinson was never to write a better nature-poem than this . . . .[1]

What ideas do you find in both versions? Which details do you find only in the longer one? Why does Whicher regard "A Route of Evanescence" as a better poem than "Within My Garden Rides a Bird"? Which do you prefer? Why?

Within My Garden Rides a Bird

Within my garden rides a bird
Upon a single wheel,
Whose spokes a dizzy music make
As 'twere a traveling mill.

He never stops, but slackens   5
Above the ripest rose,
Partakes without alighting,
And praises as he goes;

Till every spice is tasted,
And then his fairy gig   10
Reels in remoter atmospheres,
And I rejoin my dog.

And he and I perplex us
If positive 'twere we—
Or bore the garden in the brain   15
This curiosity?

But he, the best logician,
Refers my duller eye
To just vibrating blossoms—
An exquisite reply!   20

A Route of Evanescence

A route of evanescence
With a revolving wheel;
A resonance of emerald,
A rush of cochineal;
And every blossom on the bush   5
Adjusts its tumbled head,
The mail from Tunis, probably,
An easy morning's ride.

1. George Frisbie Whicher, *This Was a Poet*, Ann Arbor Paperback, 1957, pp. 261-262.

THE LARGER VIEW

Sarah Orne Jewett in her quiet tale of Maine mentions that Sylvia's uncle had left New England for the excitements of California. This reference suggests the extent to which interest in the lands to the West and the types of living developing there had permeated the thought of Americans everywhere. Discussing the following questions will help you evaluate the impact of this new growth in all areas of living upon American literature.

1. How do the differences between pre-Civil War writers and postwar writers help account for the interest in new themes?

2. In their writing both Mark Twain and Bret Harte display intimate knowledge of life in the West. Cite examples of this knowledge.

3. Describe how Western writers influenced the local-color movement.

4. How did the impact of the frontier on American thought contribute to the development of literary realism?

BIBLIOGRAPHY

BROOKS, VAN WYCK, *New England: Indian Summer, 1865-1915.* (Dutton) Literary figures, their works, and historical aspects of the period are excellently covered by this competent critic.

CLEMENS, SAMUEL, *The Adventures of Tom Sawyer.* (Harper •Dolphin) The story of an imaginative, mischievous boy, and its sequel, *The Adventures of Huckleberry Finn,* the story of an easy-going, irresponsible river-rat, are masterpieces of humorous fiction dealing with regional character.

CLEMENS, SAMUEL, *A Connecticut Yankee in King Arthur's Court.* (Dodd •Washington Square) Clemens burlesques conventional historical novels in an account of a Yankee of the most arrant type plumped down in the middle of King Arthur's England. The book is a series of farcical incidents.

CLEMENS, SAMUEL, *Life on the Mississippi.* (Harper •Bantam) The author's accounts of his own efforts to become a steamboat pilot on the Mississippi River are humorous and exciting.

CLEMENS, SAMUEL, *The Prince and the Pauper.* (Harper •Dolphin) Through a quirk of fate, the boy-king Edward VI changes places with a street waif. The courage and humanity of both are brought out in the adventures that follow.

CRANE, STEPHEN, *Red Badge of Courage.* (••Modern Library) Mr. Crane's great classic is a remarkable bit of imaginative writing describing the fear, confusion, and fatigue that beset a young soldier in his first battle.

DICKINSON, EMILY, *Final Harvest; Emily Dickinson's Poems,* edited by Thomas H. Johnson. (Little) Miss Dickinson writes candidly of her own state of mind and speculates on the timeless mysteries of love and death in this collection of her best and most representative poems.

GARLAND, HAMLIN, *Son of the Middle Border.* (••Macmillan) In one of the greatest biographies ever written, the author tells of his youth on a farm in Iowa and of his struggle to establish himself as a writer in Boston.

HARTE, BRET, *Best of Bret Harte.* (Houghton) Harte's works are leading examples of local-color fiction with emphasis on character study. You will enjoy these carefully chosen selections.

HOWELLS, WILLIAM DEAN, *The Rise of Silas Lapham.* (Houghton •Riverside) Mature students will enjoy this outstanding novel of Mark Twain's period. It tells the story of an honest man who unexpectedly becomes rich and moves to Boston. His contacts with the city people give rise to many thought-provoking situations.

JAMES, HENRY, *Washington Square.* (Modern Library •Bantam) Relationships between a simple, honest girl, her romantic aunt, her worldly-wise father, and a mercenary suitor are studied in this short psychological novel by a great writer.

JEWETT, SARAH ORNE, *Country of the Pointed Firs and Other Stories.* (•Anchor) These stories are a series of closely knit sketches of a Maine seaport town during the era of its decay from the grandeur of East Indian trading days.

WECTER, DIXON, *Sam Clemens of Hannibal.* (Houghton •Sentry) No major writer ever made more of his boyhood than Samuel Clemens, whose growing up has become part of our heritage. This is a definitive biography of the fun-loving lad whose youth typifies the golden age of boyhood.

•paperback   ••paperback and hard-cover

part two

TWENTIETH CENTURY AMERICAN LITERATURE

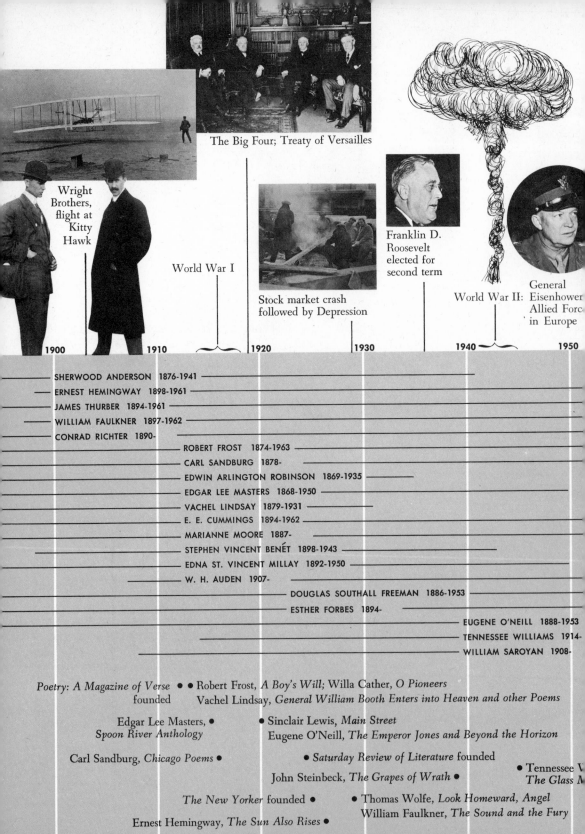

The Big Four; Treaty of Versailles

Wright Brothers, flight at Kitty Hawk

World War I

Stock market crash followed by Depression

Franklin D. Roosevelt elected for second term

World War II: General Eisenhower Allied Force in Europe

1900 1910 1920 1930 1940 1950

SHERWOOD ANDERSON 1876-1941
ERNEST HEMINGWAY 1898-1961
JAMES THURBER 1894-1961
WILLIAM FAULKNER 1897-1962
CONRAD RICHTER 1890-

ROBERT FROST 1874-1963
CARL SANDBURG 1878-
EDWIN ARLINGTON ROBINSON 1869-1935
EDGAR LEE MASTERS 1868-1950
VACHEL LINDSAY 1879-1931
E. E. CUMMINGS 1894-1962
MARIANNE MOORE 1887-
STEPHEN VINCENT BENÉT 1898-1943
EDNA ST. VINCENT MILLAY 1892-1950
W. H. AUDEN 1907-

DOUGLAS SOUTHALL FREEMAN 1886-1953
ESTHER FORBES 1894-

EUGENE O'NEILL 1888-1953
TENNESSEE WILLIAMS 1914-
WILLIAM SAROYAN 1908-

Poetry: A Magazine of Verse founded ● ● Robert Frost, *A Boy's Will*; Willa Cather, *O Pioneers*
Vachel Lindsay, *General William Booth Enters into Heaven and other Poems*

Edgar Lee Masters, ●
Spoon River Anthology
● Sinclair Lewis, *Main Street*
Eugene O'Neill, *The Emperor Jones and Beyond the Horizon*

Carl Sandburg, *Chicago Poems* ●
● *Saturday Review of Literature* founded

John Steinbeck, *The Grapes of Wrath* ●
● Tennessee W
The Glass M

The New Yorker founded ●
● Thomas Wolfe, *Look Homeward, Angel*
William Faulkner, *The Sound and the Fury*

Ernest Hemingway, *The Sun Also Rises* ●

Sinclair Lewis is first American to receive Nobel Prize in Letters ● ● Pearl Buck, *The Good Earth*

The United States entered the twentieth century a vastly different country from the sparsely settled, isolated nation it had been when the nineteenth century dawned. In the intervening hundred years its continental destiny had been realized, floods of immigrants had swelled the population, and the rise of science and industry, of the machine and the city had brought about tremendous changes in the way men lived. At the very end of the century victory in the Spanish-American War caused the United States to be recognized as a world power.

As the twentieth century progressed, the United States became more and more involved with foreign powers. During 1917 and 1918 the country joined with the allied nations in fighting World War I. The soldiers and many of the civilians who served in the war, borne on a tremendous wave of enthusiasm, hoped "to make the world safe for democracy." The following years bitterly disappointed such enthusiasts. Democracy did not triumph in Europe. Even in the United States various politicians proved to be unworthy servants of a democracy, and some profiteers used their wealth to gain special privileges.

For these reasons, many thoughtful Americans were disillusioned. Writers voiced widespread disgust. A large number of authors told of the effect of disillusionment upon American youth—their loss of faith, their tendency to become cynical, their feeling that the best thing was to forget the hopeless world and to enjoy themselves. A young man named F. Scott Fitzgerald, who had been a student at Princeton, expressed this new viewpoint in

Photographs for Graphic Chronology from Culver Pictures.

This Side of Paradise (1920), a sensationally successful book and the first of many which show the rebellion of what was called "flaming youth."

As the bitter memories of war receded, the country was plunged into the economic depression of the 1930's. Again the writers mirrored the emotions of the people—the despair of the homeless, the anxiety of the unemployed. In *The Grapes of Wrath* (1939), a novel about migratory workers, John Steinbeck protested the lack of economic opportunity that was blighting the lives of countless Americans.

Strangely enough, during the hard times of the 1930's, a belief in the essential soundness of America began to emerge side by side with concern for the underprivileged. The positive measures taken by the government to improve economic conditions caused Americans to feel more hopeful. Furthermore, the dictatorships which arose in Europe during the 1930's gave emphasis, by contrast, to the blessings of our free and democratic way of life. Carl Sandburg, who earlier had protested against the exploitation of some of the poor, in 1936 published a book-length poem voicing belief in Americans—*The People, Yes*. Eventually, when the United States was attacked in World War II, Americans solidly backed the war effort.

Two world wars, a great depression, advanced technology, and the increasing urbanization of life affected not only what men of letters wrote about but the way they wrote. Poets, novelists, short-story writers, and dramatists experimented ceaselessly with new forms and techniques. Advances in psychology, which stimulated a greater interest in the inner life of the individual, were reflected in the content as well as in the forms of fiction, poetry, and drama. Many fiction writers, finding new types of plot and new methods of characterization attractive, evolved new types of stories. Some writers attempted to capture in poetry and prose the abrupt staccato pattern of modern life. Constant experimentation, together with a high level of competence in American writers, resulted in a large body of excellent and interesting literature.

chapter seven The Modern Short Story

The short story today reflects not only the influence of the earlier masters of this form of fiction, but also the complex time in which we live and the effort of serious writers to tell the truth about life as they see and interpret it. Twentieth-century short-story writers, like their predecessors, have felt free to experiment, to develop new techniques in writing, to create stories of new types, and to adapt traditional types of stories to their own times. This means that the detective story descended from Poe's "The Purloined Letter" (page 208) is still popular, and that modern variants of "The Masque of the Red Death" (page 218) continue to create a mood of horror. Stories whose real meanings emerge only when the symbolism is understood continue the tradition of Hawthorne's "Maypole of Merry Mount" (page 300) and similar tales. Modern regionalists follow in the tradition of local-color writers like Bret Harte and Sarah Orne Jewett. Modern naturalists acknowledge a debt to Stephen Crane. In addition to these types of stories with a clear relationship to earlier American masterpieces, other kinds of stories have developed. The roots of some of these lie in the tales of other lands; others are new in concept. The purpose of this chapter is to highlight some of these important developments in the American short story and, through the study of some representative short stories, to increase both your understanding and your enjoyment of this important type of literature.

O. Henry 1862-1910

During the final years of the local-color movement, a new type of story became popular with American readers. This kind of story, which reached the height of its development between 1873 and 1910, is the story of ingenious situations whose point is revealed by a twist of plot at the very end—the story of "the surprise ending."

One of the best writers of such stories was William Sydney Porter, who achieved world-wide fame under the pen name O. Henry. He was born in Greensboro, North Carolina. After leaving school and then clerking for a time in his uncle's drugstore, he went to Texas for his health. While working as a bank teller in Austin, he was charged with embezzlement and fled to South America. The serious illness of his wife caused him to return and surrender to the authorities. He was convicted, and in 1897 was sent to the federal penitentiary at Columbus, Ohio, for three years. While there he began to write short stories under his pen name. When released, he went to New York, and within two years had signed a contract with the New York *World* for a story a week at one hundred dollars each. *Cabbages and Kings* (1904), his first volume of short stories, was followed by twelve others. No other American writer has enjoyed so widespread a reputation based on short stories alone.

Like the local colorists, O. Henry habitually set his short stories in a particular area, and he wrote of a number of locales. However, he is chiefly famous for his pictures of the lives of the ordinary folk of New York City— "the four million," as he called them in the title of one of his books to distinguish them from "the four hundred," the very exclusive list of social leaders of New York. "The Third Ingredient" (page 447) is one of the best of O. Henry's stories set in this locale.

O. Henry was a master of irony and humor—sometimes achieved by character portrayal, sometimes by dialogue, sometimes by the style itself. Above all O. Henry was skilled in unfolding his stories in such a way as to keep the reader in suspense until the end, and then to deliver a "punch line" or "twist" at the conclusion.

The Third Ingredient

The (so-called) Vallambrosa Apart[ment House¹ is not an apartment] house. It is composed of two old[-]fashioned, brownstone-front res[i]dences welded into one. The parl[or] floor of one side is gay with the wraps an[d] headgear of a modiste; the other is lugubriou[s] with the sophistical promises and grisly di[s]play of a painless dentist. You may have [a] room there for two dollars a week or you m[ay] have one for twenty dollars. Among the V[al]lambrosa's roomers are stenographers, mu[si]cians, brokers, shopgirls, space-rate writers, art students, wire tappers, and other people who lean far over the banister rail when the doorbell rings.

This treatise shall have to do with but two of the Vallambrosians—though meaning no disrespect to the others.

At six o'clock one afternoon Hetty Pepper came back to her third-floor rear $3.50 room in the Vallambrosa with her nose and chin more sharply pointed than usual. To be discharged from the department store where you have been working four years, and with only fifteen cents in your purse, does have a tendency to make your features appear more finely chiseled.

And now for Hetty's thumbnail biography, while she climbs the two flights of stairs.

She walked into the Biggest Store one morning four years before with seventy-five other girls, applying for a job behind the waist department counter. The phalanx of wage earners formed a bewildering scene of beauty, carrying a total mass of blond hair sufficient to have justified the horseback gallops of a hundred Lady Godivas.

The capable, cool-eyed, impersonal, young, bald-headed man whose task it was to engage six of the contestants, was aware of a feeling of suffocation as if he were drowning in a sea of frangipani,² while white clouds, hand-embroidered, floated about him. And then a sail hove in sight. Hetty Pepper, homely of countenance, with small, contemptuous, green eyes and chocolate-colored hair, dressed in a [...] burlap and a common-sense hat, [...]im with every one of her twenty-[...]life unmistakably in sight.

[...]" shouted the bald-headed young [...]s saved. And that is how Hetty [...]employed in the Biggest Store. [...]her rise to an eight-dollar-a-week [...]e combined stories of Hercules, [...], Una,³ Job, and Little Red Rid[...]ou shall not learn from me the [...]vas paid her as a beginner. There [...]nt growing about such things, and I want no millionaire store-proprietors climbing the fire escape of my tenement house to throw dynamite bombs into my skylight boudoir.

The story of Hetty's discharge from the Biggest Store is so nearly a repetition of her engagement as to be monotonous.

In each department of the store there is an omniscient, omnipresent, and omnivorous person carrying always a mileage book and a red necktie, and referred to as a "buyer." The destinies of the girls in his department who live on (see Bureau of Victual Statistics)—so much per week are in his hands.

This particular buyer was a capable, cool-eyed, impersonal, young, bald-headed man. As he walked along the aisles of his department, he seemed to be sailing on a sea of frangipani, while white clouds, machine-embroidered floated around him. Too many sweets bring surfeit. He looked upon Hetty Pepper's homely countenance, emerald eyes, and chocolate-colored hair as a welcome oasis of green in a desert of cloying beauty. In a quiet angle of a counter he pinched her arm kindly, three inches above the elbow. She slapped him

"The Third Ingredient" from *Options* by O. Henry. Copyright 1908, 1909 by Doubleday and Company, Inc., New York, and reprinted by their permission.
1. *Vallambrosa Apartment House.* Vallombrosa (väl'lŏmbrō'sä) or "shady valley" is a resort near Florence, Italy, noted for its beauty. O. Henry apparently misspells the name to emphasize its inappropriate use. 2. *frangipani* (fran'ji pan'i), a perfume with a jasmine fragrance. 3. *Una* (ū'na), a lovely lady who personifies Truth. She is the central figure in Book I of *The Faerie Queene*, an epic poem written by the Englishman Edmund Spenser (1552?-1599).

three feet away with one good blow of her muscular and not especially lily-white right. So, now you know why Hetty Pepper came to leave the Biggest Store at thirty minutes' notice, with one dime and a nickel in her purse.

This morning's quotations list the price of rib beef at six cents per (butcher's) pound. But on the day that Hetty was "released" by the B. S. the price was seven and one half cents. That fact is what makes this story possible. Otherwise, the extra four cents would have—

But the plot of nearly all the good stories in the world is concerned with shorts who were unable to cover, so you can find no fault with this one.

Hetty mounted with her rib beef to her $3.50 third-floor back. One hot, savory beef stew for supper, a night's good sleep, and she would be fit in the morning to apply again for the tasks of Hercules, Joan of Arc, Una, Job, and Little Red Ridinghood.

In her room she got the graniteware stew-pan out of the 2 × 4-foot china—er—I mean earthenware closet, and began to dig down in a rats' nest of paper bags for the potatoes and onions. She came out with her nose and chin just a little sharper pointed.

There was neither a potato nor an onion. Now, what kind of a beef stew can you make out of simply beef? You can make oyster soup without oysters, turtle soup without turtles, coffeecake without coffee, but you can't make a beef stew without potatoes and onions.

But rib beef alone, in an emergency, can make an ordinary pine door look like a wrought-iron gambling-house portal to the wolf. With salt and pepper and a tablespoon-ful of flour (first well stirred in a little cold water) 'twill serve—'tis not so deep as a lobster à la Newburg nor so wide as a church festi-val doughnut; but 'twill serve.

Hetty took her stewpan to the rear of the third-floor hall. According to the advertise-ments of the Vallambrosa there was running water to be found there. Between you and me and the water meter, it only ambled or walked through the faucets; but technicalities have no place here. There was also a sink where house-keeping roomers often met to dump their cof-fee grounds and glare at one another's kimonos.

At this sink Hetty found a girl with heavy, gold-brown, artistic hair and plaintive eyes, washing two large Irish potatoes. Hetty knew the Vallambrosa as well as anyone not own-ing "double hextra-magnifying eyes" could compass its mysteries. The kimonos were her encyclopedia, her *Who's What?*, her clearing house of news, of goers and comers. From a rose-pink kimono edged with Nile green she had learned that the girl with the potatoes was a miniature painter living in a kind of attic—or "studio," as they prefer to call it—on the top floor. Hetty was not certain in her mind what a miniature was; but it certainly wasn't a house; because house painters, al-though they wear splashy overalls and poke ladders in your face on the street, are known to indulge in a riotous profusion of food at home.

The potato girl was quite slim and small, and handled her potatoes as an old bachelor uncle handles a baby who is cutting teeth. She had a dull, shoemaker's knife in her right hand, and she had begun to peel one of the potatoes with it.

Hetty addressed her in the punctiliously formal tone of one who intends to be cheer-fully familiar with you in the second round.

"Beg pardon," she said, "for butting into what's not my business, but if you peel them potatoes, you lose out. They're new Bermudas. You want to scrape 'em. Lemme show you."

She took a potato and the knife, and began to demonstrate.

"Oh, thank you," breathed the artist. "I didn't know. And I *did* hate to see the thick peeling go; it seemed such a waste. But I thought they always had to be peeled. When you've got only potatoes to eat, the peelings count, you know."

"Say, kid," said Hetty, staying her knife, "you ain't up against it, too, are you?"

The miniature artist smiled starvedly.

"I suppose I am. Art—or, at least, the way I interpret it—doesn't seem to be much in de-mand. I have only these potatoes for my dinner. But they aren't so bad boiled and hot, with a little butter and salt."

"Child," said Hetty, letting a brief smile soften her rigid features. "Fate has sent me and you together. I've had it handed to me in the neck, too; but I've got a chunk of meat in my room as big as a lap dog. And I've done everything to get potatoes except pray for 'em. Let's me and you bunch our commissary departments and make a stew of 'em. We'll cook it in my room. If we only had an onion to go in it! Say, kid, you haven't got a couple of pennies that've slipped down into the lining of your last winter's sealskin, have you? I could step down to the corner and get one at old Giuseppe's stand. A stew without an onion is worse'n a matinée without candy."

"You may call me Cecilia," said the artist. "No, I spent my last penny three days ago."

"Then we'll have to cut the onion out instead of slicing it in," said Hetty. "I'd ask the janitress for one, but I don't want 'em hep just yet to the fact that I'm pounding the asphalt for another job. But I wish we did have an onion."

In the shopgirl's room the two began to prepare their supper. Cecilia's part was to sit on the couch helplessly and beg to be allowed to do something, in the voice of a cooing ring-dove. Hetty prepared the rib beef, putting it in cold salted water in the stew pan and setting it on the one-burner gas stove.

"I wish we had an onion," said Hetty, as she scraped the two potatoes.

On the wall opposite the couch was pinned a flaming, gorgeous advertising picture of one of the new ferryboats of the P. U. F. F. Railroad that had been built to cut down the time between Los Angeles and New York City one eighth of a minute.

Hetty, turning her head during her continuous monologue, saw tears running from her guest's eyes as she gazed on the idealized presentment of the speeding, foam-girdled transport.

"Why, say, Cecilia, kid," said Hetty, poising her knife, "is it as bad art as that? I ain't a critic; but I thought it kind of brightened up the room. Of course, a manicure painter could tell it was a bum picture in a minute. I'll take it down if you say so, I wish to the holy Saint Potluck we had an onion."

But the miniature miniature painter had tumbled down, sobbing, with her nose indenting the hard-woven drapery of the couch. Something was here deeper than the artistic temperament offended at crude lithography.

Hetty knew. She had accepted her rôle long ago. How scant the words with which we try to describe a single quality of a human being! When we reach the abstract, we are lost. The nearer to Nature that the babbling of our lips comes, the better do we understand. Figuratively (let us say), some people are Bosoms, some are Hands, some are Heads, some are Muscles, some are Feet, some are Backs for burdens.

Hetty was a Shoulder. Hers was a sharp sinewy shoulder; but all her life people had laid their heads upon it, metaphorically or actually, and had left there all or half their troubles. Looking at Life anatomically, which is as good a way as any, she was preordained to be a Shoulder. There were few truer collar-bones anywhere than hers.

Hetty was only thirty-three, and she had not yet outlived the little pang that visited her whenever the head of youth and beauty leaned upon her for consolation. But one glance in her mirror always served as an instantaneous painkiller. So she gave one pale look into the crinkly old looking glass on the wall above the gas stove, turned down the flame a little lower from the bubbling beef and potatoes, went over to the couch, and lifted Cecilia's head to its confessional.

"Go on and tell me, honey," she said. "I know now that it ain't art that's worrying you. You met him on a ferryboat, didn't you? Go on, Cecilia, kid, and tell your—your Aunt Hetty about it."

But youth and melancholy must first spend the surplus of sighs and tears that waft and float the bark of romance to its harbor in the delectable isles. Presently, through the stringy tendons that formed the bars of the confessional, the penitent—or was it the glorified communicant of the sacred flame—told her story without art or illumination.

"It was only three days ago. I was coming back on the ferry from Jersey City. Old Mr. Schrum, an art dealer, told me of a rich man in Newark who wanted a miniature of his daughter painted. I went to see him and showed him some of my work. When I told him the price would be fifty dollars, he laughed at me like a hyena. He said an enlarged crayon twenty times the size would cost him only eight dollars.

"I had just enough money to buy my ferry ticket back to New York. I felt as if I didn't want to live another day. I must have looked as I felt, for I saw *him* on the row of seats opposite me looking at me as if he understood. He was nice-looking, but oh, above everything else, he looked kind. When one is tired or unhappy or hopeless, kindness counts more than anything else.

"When I got so miserable that I couldn't fight against it any longer, I got up and walked slowly out the rear door of the ferryboat cabin. No one was there, and I slipped quickly over the rail and dropped into the water. Oh, friend Hetty, it was cold, cold!

"For just one moment I wished I was back in the old Vallambrosa, starving and hoping. And then I got numb, and didn't care. And then, I felt that somebody else was in the water close by me, holding me up. *He* had followed me, and jumped in to save me.

"Somebody threw a thing like a big, white doughnut at us, and he made me put my arms through the hole. Then the ferryboat backed, and they pulled us on board. Oh, Hetty, I was so ashamed of my wickedness in trying to drown myself; and besides, my hair had all tumbled down and was sopping wet, and I was such a sight.

"And then some men in blue clothes came around; and *he* gave them his card, and I heard him tell them he had seen me drop my purse on the edge of the boat outside the rail, and in leaning over to get it I had fallen overboard. And then I remembered having read in the papers that people who try to kill themselves are locked up in cells with people who try to kill other people, and I was afraid.

"But some ladies on the boat took me downstairs to the furnace-room and got me nearly dry and did up my hair. When the boat landed, *he* came and put me in a cab. He was all dripping himself, but laughed as if he thought it was all a joke. He begged me, but I wouldn't tell him my name nor where I lived, I was so ashamed."

"You were a fool, child," said Hetty kindly. "Wait till I turn the light up a bit. I wish to Heaven we had an onion."

"Then he raised his hat," went on Cecilia, "and said, 'Very well. But I'll find you anyhow. I'm going to claim my rights of salvage.' Then he gave money to the cab driver and told him to take me where I wanted to go, and walked away. What is 'salvage,' Hetty?"

"The edge of a piece of goods that ain't hemmed," said the shopgirl. "You must have looked pretty well frazzled out to the little hero boy."

"It's been three days," moaned the miniature painter, "and he hasn't found me yet."

"Extend the time," said Hetty. "This is a big town. Think of how many girls he might have to see soaked in water with their hair down before he would recognize you. The stew's getting on fine—but oh, for an onion! I'd even use a piece of garlic if I had it."

The beef and potatoes bubbled merrily, exhaling a mouth-watering savor that yet lacked something, leaving a hunger on the palate, a haunting, wistful desire for some lost and needful ingredient.

"I came near drowning in that awful river," said Cecilia, shuddering.

"It ought to have more water in it," said Hetty; "the stew, I mean. I'll go get some at the sink."

"It smells good," said the artist.

"That nasty old North River?" objected Hetty. "It smells to me like soap factories and wet setterdogs—oh, you mean the stew. Well, I wish we had an onion for it. Did he look like he had money?"

"First, he looked kind," said Cecilia. "I'm sure he was rich; but that matters so little. When he drew out his billfold to pay the cabman, you couldn't help seeing hundreds and thousands of dollars in it. And I looked over the cab doors and saw him leave the ferry station in a motorcar; and the chauffeur gave him his bearskin to put on, for he was sopping wet. And it was only three days ago."

"What a fool!" said Hetty, shortly.

"Oh, the chauffeur wasn't wet," breathed Cecilia. "And he drove the car away very nicely."

"I mean *you*," said Hetty. "For not giving him your address."

"I never give my address to chauffeurs," said Cecilia, haughtily.

"I wish we had one," said Hetty, disconsolately.

"What for?"

"For the stew, of course—oh, I mean an onion."

Hetty took a pitcher and started to the sink at the end of the hall.

A young man came down the stairs from above just as she was opposite the lower step. He was decently dressed, but pale and haggard. His eyes were dull with the stress of some burden of physical or mental woe. In his hand he bore an onion—a pink, smooth, solid, shining onion as large around as a ninety-eight-cent alarm clock.

Hetty stopped. So did the young man. There was something Joan of Arcish, Herculean, and Unaish in the look and pose of the shoplady—she had cast off the rôles of Job and Little Red Ridinghood. The young man stopped at the foot of the stairs and coughed distractedly. He felt marooned, held up, attacked, assailed, levied upon, sacked, assessed, panhandled, browbeaten, though he knew not why. It was the look in Hetty's eyes that did it. In them he saw the Jolly Roger fly to the masthead and an able seaman with a dirk between his teeth scurry up the ratlines and nail it there. But as yet he did not know that the cargo he carried was the thing that had caused him to be so nearly blown out of the water without even a parley.

"*Beg* your pardon," said Hetty, as sweetly as her dilute, acetic acid tones permitted, "but did you find that onion on the stairs? There was a hole in the paper bag; and I've just come out to look for it."

The young man coughed for half a minute. The interval may have given him the courage to defend his own property. Also, he clutched his pungent prize greedily, and, with a show of spirit, faced his grim waylayer.

"No," he said huskily, "I didn't find it on the stairs. It was given to me by Jack Bevens, on the top floor. If you don't believe it, ask him. I'll wait until you do."

"I know about Bevens," said Hetty sourly. "He writes books and things up there for the paper-and-rags man. We can hear the postman guy him all over the house when he brings them thick envelopes back. Say—do you live in the Vallambrosa?"

"I do not," said the young man. "I come to see Bevens sometimes. He's my friend. I live two blocks west."

"What are you going to do with the onion?—begging your pardon," said Hetty.

"I'm going to eat it."

"Raw?"

"Yes; as soon as I get home."

"Haven't you got anything else to eat with it?"

The young man considered briefly.

"No," he confessed; "there's not another scrap of anything in my diggings to eat. I think old Jack is pretty hard up for grub in his shack, too. He hated to give up the onion, but I worried him into parting with it."

"Man," said Hetty, fixing him with her world-sapient eyes, and laying a bony but impressive finger on his sleeve, "you've known trouble, too, haven't you?"

"Lots," said the onion owner, promptly. "But this onion is my own property, honestly come by. If you will excuse me, I must be going."

"Listen," said Hetty, paling a little with anxiety. "Raw onion is a mighty poor diet. And so is a beef stew without one. Now, if you're Jack Bevens' friend, I guess you're nearly right. There's a little lady—a friend of mine—in my room there at the end of the hall. Both of us are out of luck; and we had just potatoes and meat between us. They're stewing now. But it ain't got any soul. There's something lacking to it. There's certain things in life that are naturally intended to fit and belong together. One is pink cheesecloth and green roses, and one is ham and eggs, and one is Irish and trouble. And the other one is beef and potatoes *with* onions. And still another one is people who are up against it and other people in the same fix."

The young man went into a protracted paroxysm of coughing. With one hand he hugged his onion to his bosom.

"No doubt; no doubt," said he, at length. "But, as I said, I must be going because—"

Hetty clutched his sleeve firmly.

"Don't eat raw onions, Little Brother. Chip it in toward the dinner and line yourself inside with the best stew you ever licked a spoon over. Must two ladies knock a young gentleman down and drag him inside for the honor of dining with 'em? No harm shall befall you, Little Brother. Loosen up and fall into line."

The young man's pale face relaxed into a grin.

"Believe I'll go you," he said, brightening. "If my onion is good as a credential, I'll accept the invitation gladly."

"It's good as that, but better as seasoning," said Hetty. "You come and stand outside the door till I ask my lady friend if she has any objections. And don't run away with that letter of recommendation before I come out."

Hetty went into her room and closed the door. The young man waited outside.

"Cecilia, kid," said the shopgirl, oiling the sharp saw of her voice as well as she could, "there's an onion outside. With a young man attached. I've asked him in to dinner. You ain't going to kick, are you?"

"Oh, dear!" said Cecilia, sitting up and patting her artistic hair. She cast a mournful glance at the ferryboat poster on the wall.

"Nit," said Hetty. "It ain't him. You're up against real life now. I believe you said your hero friend had money and automobiles. This is a poor skeezicks that's got nothing to eat but an onion. But he's easy-spoken and not a freshy. I imagine he's been a gentleman, he's so low down now. And we need the onion. Shall I bring him in? I'll guarantee his behavior."

"Hetty, dear," sighed Cecilia, "I'm so hungry. What difference does it make whether he's a prince or a burglar? I don't care. Bring him in if he's got anything to eat with him."

Hetty went back into the hall. The onion man was gone. Her heart missed a beat, and a gray look settled over her face except on her nose and cheekbones. And the tides of life flowed in again, for she saw him leaning out of the front window at the other end of the hall. She hurried there. He was shouting to someone below. The noise of the street overpowered the sound of her footsteps. She looked down over his shoulder, saw whom he was speaking to and heard his words. He pulled himself in from the window sill and saw her standing over him. Hetty's eyes bored into him like two steel gimlets.

"Don't lie to me," she said, calmly. "What were you going to do with that onion?"

The young man suppressed a cough and faced her resolutely. His manner was that of one who had been bearded sufficiently.

"I was going to eat it," said he with emphatic slowness; "just as I told you before."

"And you have nothing else to eat at home?"

"Not a thing."

"What kind of work do you do?"

"I am not working at anything just now."

"Then why," said Hetty, with her voice set on its sharpest edge, "do you lean out of windows and give orders to chauffeurs in green automobiles in the street below?"

The young man flushed, and his dull eyes began to sparkle.

"Because, madam," said he, in accelerando tones, "I pay the chauffeur's wages and I own the automobile—and also this onion—this onion, madam." He flourished the onion within an inch of Hetty's nose. The shoplady did not retreat a hair's-breadth.

"Then why do you eat onions," she said, with biting contempt, "and nothing else?"

"I never said I did," retorted the young man, heatedly. "I said I had nothing else to eat where I live. I am not a delicatessen storekeeper."

"Then why," pursued Hetty, inflexibly, "were you going to eat a raw onion?"

"My mother," said the young man, "always made me eat one for a cold. Pardon my referring to a physical infirmity; but you may have noticed that I have a very, very severe cold. I was going to eat the onion and go to bed. I wonder why I am standing here and apologizing to you for it."

"How did you catch this cold?" went on Hetty, suspiciously.

The young man seemed to have arrived at some extreme height of feeling. There were two modes of descent open to him—a burst of rage or a surrender to the ridiculous. He chose wisely; and the empty hall echoed his hoarse laughter.

"You're a dandy," said he. "And I don't blame you for being careful. I don't mind telling you. I got wet. I was on a North River ferry a few days ago when a girl jumped overboard. Of course, I—"

Hetty extended her hand, interrupting his story.

"Give me the onion," she said.

The young man set his jaw a trifle harder.

"Give me the onion," she repeated.

He grinned, and laid it in her hand.

Then Hetty's infrequent, grim, melancholy smile showed itself. She took the young man's arm and pointed with her other hand to the door of her room.

"Little Brother," she said, "go in there. The little fool you fished out of the river is there

waiting for you. Go on in. I'll give you three minutes before I come. Potatoes is in there waiting. Go on in, Onions."

After he had tapped at the door and entered, Hetty began to peel and wash the onion at the sink. She gave a gray look at the gray roofs outside, and the smile on her face vanished by little jerks and twitches. "But it's us," she said, grimly, to herself, "it's *us* that furnishes the beef."

❧ TO INCREASE UNDERSTANDING

1. (*a*) At what point in "The Third Ingredient" did you begin to anticipate the surprise ending? (*b*) What clues pointed the way toward this ending?

2. Coincidence plays a large part in "The Third Ingredient," as it does in most of O. Henry's stories. The picture of the P. U. F. F. ferryboat on Hetty's wall, for example, provokes Cecilia's tearful story. (*a*) Mention other events that seem pure coincidence. (*b*) Would you classify the event that creates the surprise ending as something that might happen naturally or as a coincidence? Explain.

3. O. Henry uses irony of situation and verbal irony. (See question 6, page 428, for definitions of these terms.) (*a*) What is ironic in Hetty's securing a job at the Biggest Store? (*b*) Point out other humorous examples of irony of situation. (*c*) Why is the fact that Hetty's apartment house is named the "Vallambrosa" an example of verbal irony? (*d*) Locate other examples of verbal irony.

4. O. Henry often uses figurative language to create a humorous effect; for example, he states that the onion carried by the young man was "as large around as a ninety-eight-cent alarm clock." Point out other examples of amusing figurative language.

5. (*a*) Do Hetty, Cecilia, and the young man emerge as real individuals or as character types? (*b*) What effect does O. Henry's reliance upon coincidence have on his character development?

6. In the "Better Reading" article on page 75 you read that the "attitude of a writer as evident in his work is called tone." (*a*) Find examples in "The Third Ingredient" of comments of O. Henry in which he speaks directly to the reader. (*b*) What effect does he create by his use of irony and humorous figurative language? (*c*) What is his attitude toward his characters? (*d*) How would you describe the tone of the story?

7. (*a*) Cite details which show that this story is located in New York City. (*b*) Is the local color here as functional as it is in Bret Harte's "Luck of Roaring Camp"? Give reasons for your answer.

Sherwood Anderson 1876-1941

The new group of writers that arose as the twentieth century advanced were in revolt against both the subject matter and the form of older stories. They reflected in their works the evolving knowledge of psychology, which was causing men to view the individual and his problems in a new light. Particularly important in the thinking of these writers were the ideas advanced by Sigmund Freud (1856-1939), an Austrian psychologist who had developed new theories concerning the underlying reasons for the emotions, reactions, and behavior (often unconscious or semi-conscious) of an individual. In their preoccupation with probing the obscure causes of human behavior these twentieth-century writers were related to Stephen Crane and the nineteenth-century naturalists (see page 421).

Prominent among this new group of writers was Sherwood Anderson. His volume of short stories, *Winesburg, Ohio* (1919), marked a radical change not only in the content but also in the form of the American short story. Because their happenings differed so in form from those of earlier fiction, many readers considered Anderson's stories almost plotless. Since he felt that "the true history of life" was "the history of moments" and not a charted plan, events in his stories often are not arranged in well-defined and completed patterns. Rather they seem to be the recording of events in the frustrated lives of undistinguished people in small-town America.

Anderson knew this America well. Growing up in Clyde, Ohio, he worked at odd jobs ranging from errand boy to stable groom. His father, a wandering house painter and harness maker, never made much money but was a very entertaining storyteller and amateur actor. From him, and from a literary idol, Mark Twain, young Anderson learned to use the rhythms of the oral story, an ability that later enabled him to achieve in his writing a deceptively unstudied air of reminiscence and improvisation.

At the age of fourteen Anderson quit school. For over twenty years he worked at various jobs both in Clyde and in Chicago, served in the Spanish-American War, returned to school, became a writer of advertising copy, and finally established a manufacturing company specializing in roof paint. He was thirty-six years old when, married and the father of three children, he suddenly left his factory and departed for Chicago, determined to devote his life to writing.

Chicago, at that time, was the scene of a new ferment in the arts—the "Chicago Renaissance," led by Carl Sandburg, Edgar Lee Masters, Vachel Lindsay, and others. Although Anderson was forced to write advertising copy for a living, he became a member of this circle of writers. Here, and later in Paris, he was introduced to the psychological theories of Freud and to the experimental writing of Gertrude Stein (see page 458).

These interests and influences came to a focus in *Winesburg, Ohio.* Many readers were scandalized by the stories it contained because they frequently dealt with men and women of psychopathic tendencies. To other readers the stories seemed formless and pointless. Nevertheless, they have had a profound effect on the development of the American short story. "Sophistication," from *Winesburg, Ohio,* is an excellent example of this new type of short story.

Sophistication

I t was early evening of a day in the late fall and the Winesburg County Fair had brought crowds of country people into town. The day had been clear and the night came on warm and pleasant. On the Trunion Pike, where the road after it left town stretched away between berry fields now covered with dry brown leaves, the dust from passing wagons arose in clouds. Children, curled into little balls, slept on the straw scattered on wagon beds. Their hair was full of dust and their fingers black and sticky. The dust rolled away over the fields and the departing sun set it ablaze with colors.

In the main street of Winesburg crowds filled the stores and the sidewalks. Night came on, horses whinnied, the clerks in the stores ran madly about, children became lost and cried lustily, an American town worked terribly at the task of amusing itself.

Pushing his way through the crowds in Main Street, young George Willard concealed himself in the stairway leading to Doctor Reefy's office and looked at the people. With feverish eyes he watched the faces drifting past under the store lights. Thoughts kept coming into his head and he did not want to think. He stamped impatiently on the wooden steps and looked sharply about. "Well, is she going to stay with him all day? Have I done all this waiting for nothing?" he muttered.

George Willard, the Ohio village boy, was fast growing into manhood and new thoughts had been coming into his mind. All that day, amid the jam of people at the Fair, he had gone about feeling lonely. He was about to leave Winesburg to go away to some city where he hoped to get work on a city newspaper and he felt grown-up. The mood that had taken possession of him was a thing known to men and unknown to boys. He felt old and a little tired. Memories awoke in him. To his mind his new sense of maturity set him apart, made of him a half-tragic figure. He wanted someone to understand the feeling that had taken possession of him after his mother's death.

There is a time in the life of every boy when he for the first time takes the backward view of life. Perhaps that is the moment when he crosses the line into manhood. The boy is walking through the street of his town. He is thinking of the future and of the figure he will cut in the world. Ambitions and regrets awake within him. Suddenly something happens; he stops under a tree and waits as for a voice calling his name. Ghosts of old things creep into his consciousness; the voices outside of himself whisper a message concerning the limitations of life. From being quite sure of himself and his future he becomes not at all sure. If he be an imaginative boy a door is torn open and for the first time he looks out upon the world, seeing, as though they marched in procession before him, the countless figures of men who before his time have come out of nothingness into the world, lived their lives and again disappeared into nothingness. The sadness of sophistication has come to the boy. With a little gasp he sees himself as merely a leaf blown by the wind through the streets of his village. He knows that in spite of all the stout talk of his fellows he must live and die in uncertainty, a thing blown by the winds, a thing destined like corn to wilt in the sun. He shivers and looks eagerly about. The eighteen years he has lived seem but a moment, a breathing space in the long march of humanity. Already he hears death calling. With all his heart he wants to come close to some other human, touch someone with his hands, be touched by the hand of another. If he prefers that the other be a woman, that is because he believes that a woman will be gentle, that she will understand. He wants, most of all, understanding.

When the moment of sophistication came to George Willard his mind turned to Helen White, the Winesburg banker's daughter. Always he had been conscious of the girl growing into womanhood as he grew into manhood. Once on a summer night when he was eighteen, he had walked with her on a country road and in her presence had given way to an impulse to boast, to make himself appear big and significant in her eyes. Now he wanted to see her for another purpose. He wanted to tell her of the new impulses that had come to him. He had tried to make her think of him as a man when he knew nothing of manhood and now he wanted to be with her and to try to make her feel the change he believed had taken place in his nature.

As for Helen White, she also had come to a period of change. What George felt, she in her young woman's way felt also. She was no longer a girl and hungered to reach into the grace and beauty of womanhood. She had come home from Cleveland, where she was attending college, to spend a day at the Fair. She also had begun to have memories. During the day she sat in the grandstand with a young man, one of the instructors from the college, who was a guest of her mother's. The young man was of a pedantic turn of mind and she felt at once he would not do for her purpose. At the Fair she was glad to be seen in his company as he was well dressed and a stranger. She knew that the fact of his presence would create an impression. During the day she was happy, but when night came on she began to grow restless. She wanted to drive the instructor away, to get out of his presence. While they sat together in the grandstand and while the eyes of former schoolmates were upon them, she paid so much attention to her escort that he grew interested. "A scholar needs money. I should marry a woman with money," he mused.

Helen White was thinking of George Willard even as he wandered gloomily through the crowds thinking of her. She remembered the summer evening when they had walked together and wanted to walk with him again. She thought that the months she had spent in the city, the going to theaters and the seeing of great crowds wandering in lighted thoroughfares, had changed her profoundly. She wanted him to feel and be conscious of the change in her nature.

The summer evening together that had left its mark on the memory of both the young man and woman had, when looked at quite sensibly, been rather stupidly spent. They had walked out of town along a country road. Then they had stopped by a fence near a field of young corn and George had taken off his coat and let it hang on his arm. "Well, I've stayed here in Winesburg—yes—I've not yet gone away but I'm growing up," he had said. "I've been reading books and I've been thinking. I'm going to try to amount to something in life.

"Well," he explained, "that isn't the point. Perhaps I'd better quit talking."

The confused boy put his hand on the girl's arm. His voice trembled. The two started to walk back along the road toward town. In his desperation George boasted, "I'm going to be a big man, the biggest that ever lived here in Winesburg," he declared. "I want you to do something, I don't know what. Perhaps it is none of my business. I want you to try to be different from other women. You see the point. It's none of my business I tell you. I want you to be a beautiful woman. You see what I want."

The boy's voice failed and in silence the two came back into town and went along the street to Helen White's house. At the gate he tried to say something impressive. Speeches he had thought out came into his head, but they seemed utterly pointless. "I thought—I used to think—I had it in my mind you would marry Seth Richmond. Now I know you won't," was all he could find to say as she went through the gate and toward the door of her house.

On the warm fall evening as he stood in the stairway and looked at the crowd drifting through Main Street, George thought of the talk beside the field of young corn and was ashamed of the figure he had made of himself. In the street the people surged up and down like cattle confined in a pen. Buggies and wagons almost filled the narrow thoroughfare. A band played and small boys raced along the sidewalk, diving between the legs of men. Young men with shining red faces walked awkwardly about with girls on their arms. In a room above one of the stores, where a dance was to be held, the fiddlers tuned their instruments. The broken sounds floated down through an open window and out across the murmur of voices and the loud blare of the horns of the band. The medley of sounds got on young Willard's nerves. Everywhere, on all sides, the sense of crowding, moving life closed in about him. He wanted to run away by himself and think. "If she wants to stay with that fellow she may. Why should I care? What difference does it make to me?" he growled and went along Main Street and through Hern's grocery into a side street.

George felt so utterly lonely and dejected that he wanted to weep but pride made him walk rapidly along, swinging his arms. He came to Westley Moyer's livery barn and stopped in the shadows to listen to a group of men who talked of a race Westley's stallion, Tony Tip, had won at the Fair during the afternoon. A crowd had gathered in front of the barn and before the crowd walked Westley, prancing up and down and boasting. He held a whip in his hand and kept tapping the ground. Little puffs of dust arose in the lamplight. "Hell, quit your talking," Westley exclaimed. "I wasn't afraid, I knew I had 'em beat all the time. I wasn't afraid."

Ordinarily George Willard would have been intensely interested in the boasting of Moyer, the horseman. Now it made him angry. He turned and hurried away along the street. "Old windbag," he sputtered. "Why does he want to be bragging? Why don't he shut up?"

George went into a vacant lot and as he hurried along, fell over a pile of rubbish. A nail protruding from an empty barrel tore his trousers. He sat down on the ground and swore. With a pin he mended the torn place and then arose and went on. "I'll go to Helen White's house, that's what I'll do. I'll walk right in. I'll say that I want to see her. I'll walk right in and sit down, that's what I'll do," he declared, climbing over a fence and beginning to run.

On the veranda of Banker White's house Helen was restless and distraught. The instructor sat between the mother and daughter. His talk wearied the girl. Although he had also been raised in an Ohio town, the instructor began to put on the airs of the city. He wanted to appear cosmopolitan. "I like the chance you have given me to study the background out of which most of our girls come," he declared. "It was good of you, Mrs. White, to have me down for the day." He turned to Helen and laughed. "Your life is still bound up with the life of this town?" he asked. "There are people here in whom you are interested?" To the girl his voice sounded pompous and heavy.

Helen arose and went into the house. At the door leading to a garden at the back she stopped and stood listening. Her mother began to talk. "There is no one here fit to associate with a girl of Helen's breeding," she said.

Helen ran down a flight of stairs at the back of the house and into the garden. In the darkness she stopped and stood trembling. It seemed to her that the world was full of meaningless people saying words. Afire with eagerness she ran through a garden gate and turning a corner by the banker's barn, went into a little side street. "George! Where are you, George?" she cried, filled with nervous excitement. She stopped running, and leaned against a tree to laugh hysterically. Along the dark little street came George Willard, still saying words. "I'm going to walk right into her house. I'll go right in and sit down," he declared as he came up to her. He stopped and stared stupidly. "Come on," he said and took hold of her hand. With hanging heads they walked along the street under the trees. Dry leaves rustled under foot. Now that he had found her George wondered what he had better do and say.

At the upper end of the fairground, in Winesburg, there is a half-decayed old grandstand. It has never been painted and the boards are all warped out of shape. The fairground stands on top of a low hill rising out of the valley of Wine Creek and from the grandstand one can see at night, over a cornfield, the lights of the town reflected against the sky.

George and Helen climbed the hill to the fairground, coming by the path past Waterworks Pond. The feeling of loneliness and isolation that had come to the young man in the crowded streets of his town was both broken and intensified by the presence of Helen. What he felt was reflected in her.

In youth there are always two forces fighting in people. The warm unthinking little animal struggles against the thing that reflects and remembers, and the older, the more sophisticated thing had possession of George Willard. Sensing his mood, Helen walked beside him filled with respect. When they got to the grandstand they climbed up under the roof and sat down on one of the long benchlike seats.

There is something memorable in the experience to be had by going into a fairground that stands at the edge of a Middle Western town on a night after the annual fair has been held. The sensation is one never to be forgotten. On all sides are ghosts, not of the dead, but of living people. Here, during the day just passed, have come the people pouring in from the town and the country around. Farmers with their wives and children and all the people from the hundreds of little frame houses have gathered within these board walls. Young girls have laughed and men with beards have talked of the affairs of their lives. The place has been filled to overflowing with life. It has itched and squirmed with life and now it is night and the life has all gone away.

GERTRUDE STEIN AND THE LOST GENERATION

In Paris in the 1920's, writers and artists soon found their way to 27 Rue de Fleurus, the home of Gertrude Stein. Sherwood Anderson, Ernest Hemingway, and F. Scott Fitzgerald were her most frequent American visitors. Of them, Miss Stein remarked to Hemingway, "You are all a lost generation."

THE METROPOLITAN MUSEUM OF ART, BEQUEST OF GERTRUDE STEIN, 1946

In 1903, American-born Gertrude Stein had abandoned a promising medical career to settle in Paris where she pursued three great interests—modern painting, interesting people, and writing. The walls of her salon were hung with canvases by Picasso, Matisse, and other avant-garde artists whose work she was among the first to recognize. One might also say Miss Stein collected people, for her vibrant interest in modern art and writing drew to her side a young generation of artists whom she encouraged to paint their "new" paintings and write their "new" books.

Her own fiction, drama, and poetry broke away from nineteenth-century conventions. In *Three Lives,* her training in psychology had turned her from conventional plots to portray what went on inside her characters. In order to describe the "bottom nature" of people and their endless stream of thought, she experimented with words, rhythm, and repetitive devices. At its worst her experimentation produced the incoherence of "Paralysis why is paralysis a syllable why is it not more lively" in the five-act play *What Happened,* or the monotony of "A rose is a rose is a rose" from her play *Sacred Emily.* At her best she captured the essence of moments, relying heavily

The silence is almost terrifying. One conceals oneself standing silently beside the trunk of a tree and what there is of a reflective tendency in his nature is intensified. One shudders at the thought of the meaninglessness of life while at the same instant, and if the people of the town are his people, one loves life so intensely that tears come into the eyes.

In the darkness under the roof of the grandstand, George Willard sat beside Helen White and felt very keenly his own insignificance in the scheme of existence. Now that he had come out of town where the presence of the people stirring about, busy with a multitude of affairs, had been so irritating the irritation was all gone. The presence of Helen renewed and refreshed him. It was as though her wom-

an's hand was assisting him to make some minute readjustment of the machinery of his life. He began to think of the people in the town where he had always lived with something like reverence. He had reverence for Helen. He wanted to love and to be loved by her, but he did not want at the moment to be confused by her womanhood. In the darkness he took hold of her hand and when she crept close put a hand on her shoulder. A wind began to blow and he shivered. With all his strength he tried to hold and to understand the mood that had come upon him. In that high place in the darkness the two oddly sensitive human atoms held each other tightly and waited. In the mind of each was the same thought. "I have come to this lonely place and

---

upon varied repetitions to advance characterization or poetic themes as these lines illustrate:

We cannot retrace our steps, going forward may be the same as going backwards. We cannot retrace our steps, retrace our steps. All my long life, all my life, we do not retrace our steps, all my long life, but.[1]

Despite her best-selling *Autobiography of Alice B. Toklas,* which shows she could write conventionally, Miss Stein's experiments make her unintelligible to the general public. But she was always a writer's writer: the men who visited her salon were themselves groping for a new technique and respected her experimentations. Under her stimulus, they learned to value simple words and speech rhythms, and to develop skill in capturing the essence of the significant moment.

But who were these men and why were they writing in Paris instead of Chicago or Cincinnati? What great similarity caused them to be grouped as the "lost" generation? Most of these writers had reached maturity at the outbreak of World War I. The war uprooted, embittered, disillusioned them: they returned home unable to conform with what they felt were outmoded values. The literary

ideals of the time were also too constricting for men whose thinking had been shaped in the bloody trenches of France. They returned to Europe to find a new way to write. One by one they arrived in Paris. Anderson, Hemingway, and Fitzgerald were first to arrive; John Dos Passos came, as did E. E. Cummings, Archibald MacLeish, Stephen Benét, and Thornton Wilder. In Parisian cafés and book stores they could meet T. S. Eliot or the Irish writer James Joyce. One by one, the expatriates rediscovered the vitality of the American scene, its people, its speech.

Anderson and Hemingway were the writers most influenced by Gertrude Stein. Their stories show a parallel interest in portraying what people feel. Both are indebted to her insistence upon unadorned style and simple words. The following lines from *For Whom the Bell Tolls* show how Hemingway's prose frequently reflects her repetitive device:

Look. With a red face and blond hair and blue eyes. With no cap and his mustache is yellow. With blue eyes. With pale blue eyes. With pale blue eyes with something wrong with them. With pale blue eyes that don't focus.

1. Gertrude Stein, "The Mother of Us All" from *Last Operas and Plays* (New York: Rinehart & Co., Inc., 1949), page 87.

here is this other," was the substance of the thing felt.

In Winesburg the crowded day had run itself out into the long night of the late fall. Farm horses jogged away along lonely country roads pulling their portion of weary people. Clerks began to bring samples of goods in off the sidewalks and lock the doors of stores. In the Opera House a crowd had gathered to see a show and further down Main Street the fiddlers, their instruments tuned, sweated and worked to keep the feet of youth flying over a dance floor.

In the darkness in the grandstand Helen White and George Willard remained silent. Now and then the spell that held them was broken and they turned and tried in the dim light to see into each other's eyes. They kissed but that impulse did not last. At the upper end of the fairground a half dozen men worked over horses that had raced during the afternoon. The men had built a fire and were heating kettles of water. Only their legs could be seen as they passed back and forth in the light. When the wind blew the little flames of the fire danced crazily about.

George and Helen arose and walked away into the darkness. They went along a path past a field of corn that had not yet been cut. The wind whispered among the dry corn blades. For a moment during the walk back into town the spell that held them was broken. When they had come to the crest of Waterworks Hill they stopped by a tree and George again put his hands on the girl's shoulders. She embraced him eagerly and then again they drew quickly back from that impulse. They stopped kissing and stood a little apart. Mutual respect grew big in them. They were both embarrassed and to relieve their embarrassment dropped into the animalism of youth. They laughed and began to pull and haul at each other. In some way chastened and purified by the mood they had been in they became, not man and woman, not boy and girl, but excited little animals.

It was so they went down the hill. In the darkness they played like two splendid young things in a young world. Once, running swiftly forward, Helen tripped George and he

fell. He squirmed and shouted. Shaking with laughter, he rolled down the hill. Helen ran after him. For just a moment she stopped in the darkness. There is no way of knowing what woman's thoughts went through her mind but, when the bottom of the hill was reached and she came up to the boy, she took his arm and walked beside him in dignified silence. For some reason they could not have explained they had both got from their silent evening together the thing needed. Man or boy, woman or girl, they had for a moment taken hold of the thing that makes the mature life of men and women in the modern world possible.

TO INCREASE UNDERSTANDING

1. Check the various definitions of *sophistication* in an unabridged dictionary and select the one appropriate for its use in this story. Explain the reasons for your choice.

2. Sherwood Anderson was greatly interested in psychology, the science of the mind that tries to explain why people act, think, and feel as they do. Reread page 455, column 2, paragraph 1, which describes the moment a boy "crosses the line into manhood." (*a*) How does this passage give you deeper insight into George's mental confusion? (*b*) Would you agree that this passage also states the theme of "Sophistication"? (*c*) How does this paragraph illustrate Anderson's interest in psychology?

3. (*a*) What circumstances lead to George Willard's new sense of maturity? (*b*) Before he sees Helen, how is his new feeling reflected in his thoughts and actions?

4. Although the story is focused on George, how does the author make you sympathize with Helen too? (*b*) How does Helen react to George's new sense of maturity?

5. On page 454 you read that Anderson's *Winesburg, Ohio* marks a radical change in the content and form of the American short story. Compare "Sophistication" with "The Third Ingredient." (*a*) What radical difference in plot treatment do you find? (The "Better Reading" article on page 37 will help you answer this question.) (*b*) How does Anderson's method of characterization differ from O. Henry's? (*c*) How do these two stories differ in their effect on the reader?

6. Discuss the implications of the last sentence of "Sophistication" both in relation to the story and to your own definition of maturity.

Ernest Hemingway 1898-1961

Few writers have achieved greater international fame during their lifetimes than did Ernest Hemingway, winner of both the Nobel and Pulitzer prizes. (See articles on these prizes, page 22 and page 51.) He grew up in Oak Park, Illinois, where he won a considerable reputation as a high-school football player and boxer. During vacations, he hunted with his father, a physician, in northern Michigan. After graduation from high school, he worked as a newspaper reporter in Kansas City, where his interest in boxing and his skill as a sparring partner acquainted him with prizefighters and gunmen. Before the United States entered World War I, he served in a French ambulance unit; later he was seriously wounded while fighting in the Italian infantry. After the Armistice, Hemingway went to Paris. Here he worked as a correspondent for American newspapers and became identified with the "lost" generation. In 1924 his first volume of short stories, *In Our Time,* was published, and two years later *The Sun Also Rises,* his first successful novel, appeared.

Hemingway's entire life was filled with action. He served as a newspaper correspondent in the Spanish Civil War and World War II. He hunted big game in Africa and became an expert on bullfighting in Spain. His novels and short stories, in their settings and their plots, reflect this exciting, often hazardous life; still they differ from the tightly plotted, fast-moving adventure stories one might expect from a man of action. Like Sherwood Anderson's stories, his short stories by older standards seem plotless and they deal largely with the unpleasant aspects of life. Many of them emphasize the reactions of characters to a world which is not too kind. Some deal with the discovery by young men of the cruelty, intentional or unintentional, of human beings. Many of them are pessimistic because of Hemingway's loss of faith in usually accepted ideals —an attitude Hemingway shared with other members of the "lost" generation.

However, Hemingway did discover some values in which he believed. For one thing, he admired people who do not whine about their disillusionment, who find what joy they can in life—in physical well-being, in amusement, in companionship, in love. His typical hero is a courageous man of action who falls a tragic victim to the elements of nature, an ill-fated love affair, or the circumstances of war and political upheaval. He faces death stoically, with a certain nobility of spirit. In *For Whom the Bell Tolls* (1940), a novel based on Hemingway's experiences in the Spanish Civil War, the main character, before his inevitable death in blowing up a bridge, remarks that his life has been a good one. In *The Old Man and the Sea* (1952), in spite of age and weariness, the old man reconciles himself to the loss of his prize fish and doggedly resolves to try again. (See the discussion guide for *The Old Man and the Sea,* page 537.)

Although Hemingway's philosophy of life has undoubtedly affected the work of other modern authors, it is his artistry as a writer that has wielded the greatest influence. The poet Archibald MacLeish has called his way of writing "the one intrinsic style our century has produced." Not since Poe has an American writer mastered the "single effect" so well as Hemingway, although his "single effect" was of a very different sort. He believed that the main problem in writing is setting down what you truly feel rather than what you are supposed to feel. To get this effect he records the bare actions and thoughts of his characters. Descriptive detail is at a minimum and matter-of-fact. The language has a bare simplicity in keeping with the characters. The plain words, colloquial phrases, and simple sentences stimulate within the reader sensations like those felt by the characters.

However, Hemingway was interested in developing themes as well as in reporting emotions. Hence, his language is often symbolic and gives a significance to the story that at first reading is unsuspected. In fact, the misleading simplicity of his diction and sentence structure marks Hemingway as one of the most thoroughly painstaking and self-conscious writers of our time.

The four photographs above show Hemingway in various phases of his active life. From left to right: Hunting with his wife Martha; fishing; preparing to fly across France in 1944; reporting on World War II. Portrait at far right shows an older Hemingway in a reflective mood.

In Another Country

I n the fall the war[1] was always there, but we did not go to it any more. It was cold in the fall in Milan[2] and the dark came very early. Then the electric lights came on, and it was pleasant along the streets looking in the windows. There was much game hanging outside the shops, and the snow powdered in the fur of the foxes and the wind blew their tails. The deer hung stiff and heavy and empty, and small birds blew in the wind and the wind turned their feathers. It was a cold fall and the wind came down from the mountains.

We were all at the hospital every afternoon, and there were different ways of walking across the town through the dusk to the hospital. Two of the ways were alongside canals, but they were long. Always, though, you crossed a bridge across a canal to enter the hospital. There was a choice of three bridges. On one of them a woman sold roasted chest-

1. *the war*, World War I.   2. *Milan* (mi lan′), a city in northern Italy.

BROWN BROTHERS

HANS MALMBERG FROM BLACK STAR

nuts. It was warm, standing in front of her charcoal fire, and the chestnuts were warm afterward in your pocket. The hospital was very old and very beautiful, and you entered through a gate and walked across a courtyard and out a gate on the other side. There were usually funerals starting from the courtyard. Beyond the old hospital were the new brick pavilions, and there we met every afternoon and were all very polite and interested in what was the matter, and sat in the machines that were to make so much difference.

The doctor came up to the machine where I was sitting and said: "What did you like best to do before the war? Did you practice a sport?"

I said: "Yes, football."

"Good," he said. "You will be able to play football again better than ever."

My knee did not bend and the leg dropped straight from the knee to the ankle without a calf, and the machine was to bend the knee and make it move as in riding a tricycle. But it did not bend yet, and instead the machine lurched when it came to the bending part. The doctor said: "That will all pass. You are a fortunate young man. You will play football again like a champion."

In the next machine was a major who had a little hand like a baby's. He winked at me when the doctor examined his hand, which was between two leather straps that bounced up and down and flapped the stiff fingers, and said: "And will I too play football, captain-doctor?" He had been a very great fencer, and before the war the greatest fencer in Italy.

The doctor went to his office in the back room and brought a photograph which showed a hand that had been withered almost as small as the major's, before it had taken a machine course, and after was a little larger. The major held the photograph with his good hand and looked at it very carefully. "A wound?" he asked.

"An industrial accident," the doctor said.

"Very interesting, very interesting," the major said, and handed it back to the doctor.

"You have confidence?"

"No," said the major.

There were three boys who came each day who were about the same age I was. They were all three from Milan, and one of them was to be a lawyer, and one was to be a painter, and one had intended to be a soldier, and after we were finished with the machines, sometimes we walked back together to the Café Cova, which was next door to thé Scala.[3] We walked the short way through the communist quarter because we were four together. The people hated us because we were officers, and from a wineshop some one called out, "A basso gli ufficiali!"[4] as we passed. Another boy who walked with us sometimes and made us five wore a black silk handkerchief across his face because he had no nose then and his face was to be rebuilt. He had gone out to the front from the military academy and been wounded within an hour after he had gone into the front line for the first time. They rebuilt his face, but he came from a very old family and they could never get the nose exactly right. He went to South America and worked in a bank. But this was a long time ago, and then we did not any of us know how it was going to be afterward. We only knew then that there was always the war, but that we were not going to it any more.

We all had the same medals, except the boy with the black silk bandage across his face, and he had not been at the front long enough to get any medals. The tall boy with a very pale face who was to be a lawyer had been a lieutenant of Arditi[5] and had three medals of the sort we each had only one of. He had lived a very long time with death and was a little detached. We were all a little detached, and there was nothing that held us together except that we met every afternoon at the hospital. Although, as we walked to the Cova through the tough part of town, walking in the dark, with light and singing coming out of the wineshops, and sometimes having to walk into the street when the men and women would crowd

---

3. the Scala, La Scala (lä skä′lä), Milan's world-famous opera house.   4. A basso gli ufficiali, down with the officers. [Italian]   5. a lieutenant of Arditi (är dē′tē), a lieutenant in a picked group of volunteers which served as storm troops of the Italian infantry.

together on the sidewalk so that we would have had to jostle them to get by, we felt held together by there being something that had happened that they, the people who disliked us, did not understand.

We ourselves all understood the Cova, where it was rich and warm and not too brightly lighted, and noisy and smoky at certain hours, and there were always girls at the tables and the illustrated papers on a rack on the wall. The girls at the Cova were very patriotic, and I found that the most patriotic people in Italy were the café girls—and I believe they are still patriotic.

The boys at first were very polite about my medals and asked me what I had done to get them. I showed them the papers, which were written in very beautiful language and full of *fratellanza* and *abnegazione*,[6] but which really said, with the adjective removed, that I had been given the medals because I was an American. After that their manner changed a little toward me, although I was their friend against outsiders. I was a friend, but I was never really one of them after they had read the citations, because it had been different with them and they had done very different things to get their medals. I had been wounded, it was true; but we all knew that being wounded, after all, was really an accident. I was never ashamed of the ribbons, though, and sometimes, after the cocktail hour, I would imagine myself having done all the things they had done to get their medals; but walking home at night through the empty streets with the cold wind and all the shops closed, trying to keep near the street lights, I knew that I would never have done such things, and I was very much afraid to die, and often lay in bed at night by myself, afraid to die and wondering how I would be when I went back to the front again.

The three with the medals were like hunting hawks; and I was not a hawk, although I might seem a hawk to those who had never hunted; they, the three, knew better and so we drifted apart. But I stayed good friends with the boy who had been wounded his first day at the front, because he would never know now how he would have turned out; so he could never be accepted either, and I liked him because I thought perhaps he would not have turned out to be a hawk either.

The major, who had been the great fencer, did not believe in bravery, and spent much time while we sat in the machines correcting my grammar. He had complimented me on how I spoke Italian, and we talked together very easily. One day I had said that Italian seemed such an easy language to me that I could not take a great interest in it; everything was so easy to say. "Ah, yes," the major said. "Why, then, do you not take up the use of grammar?" So we took up the use of grammar, and soon Italian was such a difficult language that I was afraid to talk to him until I had the grammar straight in my mind.

The major came very regularly to the hospital. I do not think he ever missed a day, although I am sure he did not believe in the machines. There was a time when none of us believed in the machines, and one day the major said it was all nonsense. The machines were new then and it was we who were to prove them. It was an idiotic idea, he said, "a theory, like another." I had not learned my grammar, and he said I was a stupid impossible disgrace, and he was a fool to have bothered with me. He was a small man and he sat straight up in his chair with his right hand thrust into the machine and looked straight ahead at the wall while the straps thumped up and down with his fingers in them.

"What will you do when the war is over if it is over?" he asked me. "Speak grammatically!"

"I will go to the States."

"Are you married?"

"No, but I hope to be."

"The more of a fool you are," he said. He seemed very angry. "A man must not marry."

"Why, Signor Maggiore?"[7]

"Don't call me 'Signor Maggiore.' "

"Why must not a man marry?"

"He cannot marry. He cannot marry," he

---

6. *fratellanza* (frä tel län′zä) and *abnegazione* (äb′nä gä-tzyō′ne), brotherhood and self-denial. [Italian] 7. *Signor Maggiore* (sē′nyōr mäj jō′re), Mr. Major. In Italy it is a sign of respect to prefix an officer's rank with *Signor*.

said angrily. "If he is to lose everything, he should not place himself in a position to lose that. He should not place himself in a position to lose. He should find things he cannot lose."

He spoke very angrily and bitterly, and looked straight ahead while he talked.

"But why should he necessarily lose it?"

"He'll lose it," the major said. He was looking at the wall. Then he looked down at the machine and jerked his little hand out from between the straps and slapped it hard against his thigh. "He'll lose it," he almost shouted. "Don't argue with me!" Then he called to the attendant who ran the machines. "Come and turn this damned thing off."

He went back into the other room for the light treatment and the massage. Then I heard him ask the doctor if he might use his telephone and he shut the door. When he came back into the room, I was sitting in another machine. He was wearing his cape and had his cap on, and he came directly toward my machine and put his arm on my shoulder.

"I am so sorry," he said, and patted me on the shoulder with his good hand. "I would not be rude. My wife has just died. You must forgive me."

"Oh—" I said, feeling sick for him. "I am *so* sorry."

He stood there biting his lower lip. "It is very difficult," he said. "I cannot resign myself."

He looked straight past me and out through the window. Then he began to cry. "I am utterly unable to resign myself," he said, and choked. And then crying, his head up looking at nothing, carrying himself straight and soldierly, with tears on both his cheeks and biting his lips, he walked past the machines and out the door.

The doctor told me that the major's wife, who was very young and whom he had not married until he was definitely invalided out of the war, had died of pneumonia. She had been sick only a few days. No one expected her to die. The major did not come to the hospital for three days. Then he came at the usual hour, wearing a black band on the

sleeve of his uniform. When he came back, there were large framed photographs around the wall, of all sorts of wounds before and after they had been cured by the machines. In front of the machine the major used were three photographs of hands like his that were completely restored. I do not know where the doctor got them. I always understood we were the first to use the machines. The photographs did not make much difference to the major because he only looked out of the window.

 TO INCREASE UNDERSTANDING

1. A critic has pointed out that the opening paragraph offers a number of symbolic details which stand for the " 'other countries' which the lonely characters portrayed in the story sense but do not enter." These countries are: "the country of battle from which [the characters'] wounds have removed them; that of peace which [the characters] glimpse through lighted windows from darkened streets; country of nature symbolized by the game; and the country, finally, of death—connoted by the cold, the dark, and by the wind which blows from the mountains." How is the exclusion of the soldiers from these "countries" important in this story?

2. Not only are the soldiers, as a group, shut off from other groups; as individuals, they are separated from one another. (*a*) How do they happen to be separated? (*b*) Have their war experiences had anything to do with their loneliness? Explain.

3. (*a*) Judging from your knowledge of the characters in Hemingway's stories, to what extent is the narrator typical of the characters Hemingway admires? (*b*) Are the other characters typical?

4. (*a*) How does the major differ from the other invalids? (*b*) Why does his wife's illness cause him to quarrel with the narrator?

5. Reread the passage in which the narrator describes the major's lack of confidence (page 464, column 1, paragraphs 5-10) and that in which he describes the major's grief (page 465, column 2, paragraph 2 to page 466, column 1, paragraph 8). (*a*) Explain "the sequence of motion and fact" in each passage—in other words, what happens? (*b*) Characterize the diction and sentence structure in each passage, paying particular attention to the dialogue. (*c*) What emotional effect does each passage create? (*d*) Relate these incidents to this statement by Philip Young in *Ernest Hemingway*: "It is the major's pain that the story is about; the hero's wounds have been established, and there are now two casualties."

Katherine Anne Porter 1894-

Hemingway called bravery "grace under pressure" and in much of his writing he explored the nature of valor. Stephen Crane, whom Hemingway admired very much, had earlier investigated this same facet of human behavior and had written about it in such stories as "A Mystery of Heroism" (page 423) and *The Red Badge of Courage*. Among other writers who have shown a similar interest in courage as a theme is Katherine Anne Porter.

Born in Indian Creek, Texas, Katherine Anne Porter grew up in Texas and Louisiana. From her earliest childhood she was interested in writing stories. After graduation from a convent school, she earned a living by working as a newspaper reporter in Dallas and in Denver. Illness forced her to give up her career as a journalist. She traveled extensively, earning her living by writing reviews, critical articles, and translations of Spanish and French materials.

Miss Porter's first published volume was *Flowering Judas and Other Stories*, which appeared in 1930. In the introduction to this volume she wrote that most of the energies of her mind and spirit had been spent in an effort to grasp the meaning of the threat of world catastrophe under which her life had been lived. She wanted to understand "the logic of this majestic and terrible failure of the life of men in the Western World." In many of her stories she explores this "terrible failure." Frequently her characters are drawn into disillusionment and despair, sometimes by social, political, and natural forces beyond their control, often by their own selfishness and deceit.

Because of this emphasis on disillusionment and maladjustment, Miss Porter's stories somewhat resemble those of Sherwood Anderson. However, her characters have a stability stemming from family and regional traditions that Anderson's do not have.

Like Hemingway, Miss Porter seems to look into the minds of characters and record their thoughts or even fleeting fragments of thoughts. Thus the reader does not view the character from the outside but from within; he is so closely drawn into the character's world that he seems to be experiencing what is happening to the character.

The important place Miss Porter has won for herself among contemporary American writers is based on a comparatively small total output. A slow writer, she has produced only a few books in the more than thirty years since *Flowering Judas* was published. Her most recent book and her first novel, *Ship of Fools* (1962), followed *Through a Glass Darkly* by four years. But her technical mastery of the art of writing is undeniable. Like Hemingway, she is noted as a stylist. However, her sentence patterns and her choice of words produce an effect far different from Hemingway's crisp, often abrupt prose. Miss Porter's writing is delicate and precise, sensitive and subtle, and the effect she achieves is both eloquent and graceful.

"The Jilting of Granny Weatherall," which is taken from *Flowering Judas and Other Stories*, is the story of an old woman who is dying. As her mind floats back and forth, blending the past and the present, she reveals in bits and snatches the story of a full life.

The Jilting of Granny Weatherall

She flicked her wrist neatly out of Doctor Harry's pudgy careful fingers and pulled the sheet up to her chin. The brat ought to be in knee breeches. Doctoring around the country with spectacles on his nose! "Get along now, take your schoolbooks and go. There's nothing wrong with me."

Doctor Harry spread a warm paw like a cushion on her forehead where the forked green vein danced and made her eyelids twitch. "Now, now, be a good girl, and we'll have you up in no time."

"That's no way to speak to a woman nearly eighty years old just because she's down. I'd have you respect your elders, young man."

"Well, Missy, excuse me." Doctor Harry patted her cheek. "But I've got to warn you, haven't I? You're a marvel, but you must be careful or you're going to be good and sorry."

"Don't tell me what I'm going to be. I'm on my feet now, morally speaking. It's Cornelia. I had to go to bed to get rid of her."

Her bones felt loose, and floated around in her skin, and Doctor Harry floated like a balloon around the foot of the bed. He floated and pulled down his waistcoat and swung his glasses on a cord. "Well, stay where you are, it certainly can't hurt you."

"Get along and doctor your sick," said Granny Weatherall. "Leave a well woman alone. I'll call for you when I want you. . . . Where were you forty years ago when I pulled through milkleg and double pneumonia? You weren't even born. Don't let Cornelia lead you on," she shouted, because Doctor Harry appeared to float up to the ceiling and out. "I pay my own bills, and I don't throw my money away on nonsense!"

She meant to wave goodby, but it was too much trouble. Her eyes closed of themselves, it was like a dark curtain drawn around the bed. The pillow rose and floated under her, pleasant as a hammock in a light wind. She listened to the leaves rustling outside the window. No, somebody was swishing newspapers: no, Cornelia and Doctor Harry were whispering together. She leaped broad awake, thinking they whispered in her ear.

"She was never like this, *never* like this!" "Well, what can we expect?" "Yes, eighty years old. . . ."

Well, and what if she was? She still had ears. It was like Cornelia to whisper around doors. She always kept things secret in such a public way. She was always being tactful and kind. Cornelia was dutiful; that was the trouble with her. Dutiful and good: "So good and dutiful," said Granny, "that I'd like to spank her." She saw herself spanking Cornelia and making a fine job of it.

"What'd you say, Mother?"

Granny felt her face tying up in hard knots.

"Can't a body think, I'd like to know?"

"I thought you might want something."

"I do. I want a lot of things. First off, go away and don't whisper."

She lay and drowsed, hoping in her sleep that the children would keep out and let her rest a minute. It had been a long day. Not that she was tired. It was always pleasant to snatch a minute now and then. There was always so much to be done, let me see: tomorrow.

Tomorrow was far away and there was nothing to trouble about. Things were finished somehow when the time came; thank God there was always a little margin over for peace: then a person could spread out the plan of life and tuck in the edges orderly. It was good to have everything clean and folded away, with the hair brushes and tonic bottles sitting straight on the white embroidered linen: the day started without fuss and the pantry shelves laid out with rows of jelly glasses and brown jugs and white stone-china jars with blue whirligigs and words painted on them: coffee, tea, sugar, ginger, cinnamon, allspice: and the bronze clock with the lion on top nicely dusted off. The dust that lion could collect in twenty-four hours! The box in the attic with all those letters tied up, well, she'd have to go through that tomorrow. All those letters—George's letters and John's letters and her letters to them both—lying around for the children to find afterward made her uneasy. Yes, that would be tomorrow's business. No use to let them know how silly she had been once.

While she was rummaging around she found death in her mind and it felt clammy and unfamiliar. She had spent so much time preparing for death there was no need for bringing it up again. Let it take care of itself now. When she was sixty she had felt very old, finished, and went around making farewell trips to see her children and grandchildren, with a secret in her mind: This is the very last of your mother, children! Then she made her will and came down with a long fever. That was all just a notion like a lot of other things, but it was lucky too, for she had once and for all got over the idea of dying for a long time. Now she couldn't be worried. She hoped she had better sense now. Her father had lived to be one hundred and two years old and had drunk a noggin of strong hot toddy on his last birthday. He told the reporters it was his daily habit, and he owed his long life to that. He had made quite a scandal and was very pleased about it. She believed she'd just plague Cornelia a little.

"Cornelia! Cornelia!" No footsteps, but a sudden hand on her cheek. "Bless you, where have you been?"

"Here, Mother."

"Well, Cornelia, I want a noggin of hot toddy."

"Are you cold, darling?"

"I'm chilly, Cornelia. Lying in bed stops the circulation. I must have told you that a thousand times."

Well, she could just hear Cornelia telling her husband that Mother was getting a little childish and they'd have to humor her. The thing that most annoyed her was that Cornelia thought she was deaf, dumb, and blind. Little hasty glances and tiny gestures tossed around her and over her head saying, "Don't cross her, let her have her way, she's eighty years old," and she sitting there as if she lived in a thin glass cage. Sometimes Granny almost made up her mind to pack up and move back to her own house where nobody could remind her every minute that she was old. Wait, wait, Cornelia, till your own children whisper behind your back!

In her day she had kept a better house and had got more work done. She wasn't too old yet for Lydia to be driving eighty miles for advice when one of the children jumped the track, and Jimmy still dropped in and talked things over: "Now, Mammy, you've a good business head, I want to know what you think of this? . . ." Old. Cornelia couldn't change the furniture around without asking. Little things, little things! They had been so sweet when they were little. Granny wished the old days were back again with the children young and everything to be done over. It had been a hard pull, but not too much for her. When she thought of all the food she had cooked, and all the clothes she had cut and sewed, and all the gardens she had made—well, the children showed it. There they were, made out of her, and they couldn't get away from that. Sometimes she wanted to see John again and point to them and say, Well, I didn't do so badly, did I? But that would have to wait. That was for tomorrow. She used to think of him as a man, but now all the children were older than their father, and he would be a child beside her if she saw him now. It seemed strange and there was something wrong in the idea. Why, he couldn't possibly recognize her. She had fenced in a hundred acres once, digging the postholes herself and clamping the wires with just a Negro boy to help. That changed a woman. John would be looking for a young woman with the peaked Spanish comb in her hair and the painted fan. Digging postholes changed a woman. Riding country roads in the winter when women had their babies was another thing: sitting up nights with sick horses and sick Negroes and sick children and hardly ever losing one. John, I hardly ever lost one of them! John would see that in a minute, that would be something he could understand, she wouldn't have to explain anything!

It made her feel like rolling up her sleeves and putting the whole place to rights again. No matter if Cornelia was determined to be everywhere at once, there were a great many things left undone on this place. She would start tomorrow and do them. It was good to be strong enough for everything, even if all you made melted and changed and slipped under your hands, so that by the time you finished you almost forgot what you were working for. What was it I set out to do? she asked herself intently, but she could not remember. A fog rose over the valley, she saw it marching across the creek swallowing the trees and moving up the hill like an army of ghosts. Soon it would be at the near edge of the orchard, and then it was time to go in and light the lamps. Come in, children, don't stay out in the night air.

Lighting the lamps had been beautiful. The children huddled up to her and breathed like little calves waiting at the bars in the twilight. Their eyes followed the match and watched the flame rise and settle in a blue curve, then they moved away from her. The lamp was lit, they didn't have to be scared and hang on to mother any more. Never, never, never more. God, for all my life I thank Thee. Without Thee, my God, I could never have done it. Hail, Mary, full of grace.[1]

I want you to pick all the fruit this year and see that nothing is wasted. There's always someone who can use it. Don't let good things rot for want of using. You waste life when you waste good food. Don't let things get lost. It's bitter to lose things. Now, don't let me get to thinking, not when I am tired and taking a little nap before supper. . . .

The pillow rose about her shoulders and pressed against her heart and the memory was being squeezed out of it: oh, push down the pillow, somebody: it would smother her if she tried to hold it. Such a fresh breeze blowing and such a green day with no threats in it. But he had not come, just the same. What does a woman do when she has put on the white veil and set out the white cake for a man and he doesn't come? She tried to remember. No, I swear he never harmed me but in that. He never harmed me but in that

. . . and what if he did? There was the day, the day, but a whirl of dark smoke rose and covered it, crept up and over into the bright field where everything was planted so carefully in orderly rows. That was hell, she knew hell when she saw it. For sixty years she had prayed against remembering him and against losing her soul in the deep pit of hell, and now the two things were mingled in one and the thought of him was a smoky cloud from hell that moved and crept in her head when she had just got rid of Doctor Harry and was trying to rest a minute. Wounded vanity, Ellen, said a sharp voice in the top of her mind. Don't let your wounded vanity get the upper hand of you. Plenty of girls get jilted. You were jilted, weren't you? Then stand up to it. Her eyelids wavered and let in streamers of blue-gray light like tissue paper over her eyes. She must get up and pull the shades down or she'd never sleep. She was in bed again and the shades were not down. How could that happen? Better turn over, hide from the light, sleeping in the light gave you nightmares. "Mother, how do you feel now?" and a stinging wetness on her forehead. But I don't like having my face washed in cold water!

Hapsy? George? Lydia? Jimmy? No, Cornelia, and her features were swollen and full of little puddles. "They're coming, darling, they'll all be here soon." Go wash your face, child, you look funny.

Instead of obeying, Cornelia knelt down and put her head on the pillow. She seemed to be talking but there was no sound. "Well, are you tongue-tied? Whose birthday is it? Are you going to give a party?"

Cornelia's mouth moved urgently in strange shapes. "Don't do that, you bother me, daughter."

"Oh, no, Mother. Oh, no. . . ."

Nonsense. It was strange about children. They disputed your every word. "No what, Cornelia?"

"Here's Doctor Harry."

"I won't see that boy again. He just left five minutes ago."

---

1. *Hail, Mary, full of grace.* The opening line of a prayer.

"That was this morning, Mother. It's night now. Here's the nurse."

"This is Doctor Harry, Mrs. Weatherall. I never saw you look so young and happy!"

"Ah, I'll never be young again—but I'd be happy if they'd let me lie in peace and get rested."

She thought she spoke up loudly, but no one answered. A warm weight on her forehead, a warm bracelet on her wrist, and a breeze went on whispering, trying to tell her something. A shuffle of leaves in the everlasting hand of God, He blew on them and they danced and rattled. "Mother, don't mind, we're going to give you a little hypodermic." "Look here, daughter, how do ants get in this bed? I saw sugar ants yesterday." Did you send for Hapsy too?

It was Hapsy she really wanted. She had to go a long way back through a great many rooms to find Hapsy standing with a baby on her arm. She seemed to herself to be Hapsy also, and the baby on Hapsy's arm was Hapsy and himself and herself, all at once, and there was no surprise in the meeting. Then Hapsy melted from within and turned flimsy as gray gauze and the baby was a gauzy shadow, and Hapsy came up close and said, "I thought you'd never come," and looked at her very searchingly and said, "You haven't changed a bit!" They leaned forward to kiss, when Cornelia began whispering from a long way off, "Oh, is there anything you want to tell me? Is there anything I can do for you?"

Yes, she had changed her mind after sixty years and she would like to see George. I want you to find George. Find him and be sure to tell him I forgot him. I want him to know I had my husband just the same and my children and my house like any other woman. A good house too and a good husband that I loved and fine children out of him. Better than I hoped for even. Tell him I was given back everything he took away and more. Oh, no, oh, God, no, there was something else besides the house and the man and the children. Oh, surely they were not all? What was it? Something not given back. . . . Her breath crowded down under her ribs and grew into a monstrous frightening shape with cutting edges; it

bored up into her head, and the agony was unbelievable: Yes, John, get the Doctor now, no more talk, my time has come.

When this one was born it should be the last. The last. It should have been born first, for it was the one she had truly wanted. Everything came in good time. Nothing left out, left over. She was strong, in three days she would be as well as ever. Better. A woman needed milk in her to have her full health.

"Mother, do you hear me?"

"I've been telling you—"

"Mother, Father Connolly's here."

"I went to Holy Communion only last week. Tell him I'm not so sinful as all that."

"Father just wants to speak to you."

He could speak as much as he pleased. It was like him to drop in and inquire about her soul as if it were a teething baby, and then stay on for a cup of tea and a round of cards and gossip. He always had a funny story of some sort, usually about an Irishman who made his little mistakes and confessed them, and the point lay in some absurd thing he would blurt out in the confessional showing his struggles between native piety and original sin. Granny felt easy about her soul. Cornelia, where are your manners? Give Father Connolly a chair. She had her secret comfortable understanding with a few favorite saints who cleared a straight road to God for her. All as surely signed and sealed as the papers for the new Forty Acres. Forever . . . heirs and assigns forever. Since the day the wedding cake was not cut, but thrown out and wasted. The whole bottom dropped out of the world, and there she was blind and sweating with nothing under her feet and the walls falling away. His hand had caught her under the breast, she had not fallen, there was the freshly polished floor with the green rug on it, just as before. He had cursed like a sailor's parrot and said, "I'll kill him for you." Don't lay a hand on him, for my sake leave something to God. "Now, Ellen, you must believe what I tell you. . . ."

So there was nothing, nothing to worry about any more, except sometimes in the night one of the children screamed in a nightmare, and they both hustled out shaking and hunting for the matches and calling, "There, wait a minute, here we are!" John, get the doctor now, Hapsy's time has come. But there was Hapsy standing by the bed in a white cap. "Cornelia, tell Hapsy to take off her cap. I can't see her plain."

Her eyes opened very wide and the room stood out like a picture she had seen somewhere. Dark colors with the shadows rising toward the ceiling in long angles. The tall black dresser gleamed with nothing on it but John's picture, enlarged from a little one, with John's eyes very black when they should have been blue. You never saw him, so how do you know how he looked? But the man insisted the copy was perfect, it was very rich and handsome. For a picture, yes, but it's not my husband. The table by the bed had a linen cover and a candle and a crucifix. The light was blue from Cornelia's silk lampshades. No sort of light at all, just frippery. You had to live forty years with kerosene lamps to appreciate honest electricity. She felt very strong and she saw Doctor Harry with a rosy nimbus around him.

"You look like a saint, Doctor Harry, and I vow that's as near as you'll ever come to it."

"She's saying something."

"I heard you, Cornelia. What's all this carrying-on?"

"Father Connolly's saying—"

Cornelia's voice staggered and bumped like a cart in a bad road. It rounded corners and turned back again and arrived nowhere. Granny stepped up in the cart very lightly and reached for the reins, but a man sat beside her and she knew him by his hands, driving the cart. She did not look in his face, for she knew without seeing, but looked instead down the road where the trees leaned over and bowed to each other and a thousand birds were singing a Mass. She felt like singing too, but she put her hand in the bosom of her dress and pulled out a rosary, and Father Connolly murmured Latin in a very solemn voice and tickled her feet.[2] My God, will you stop that nonsense? I'm a married woman. What if he did run away and leave me to face the priest by myself? I found another a whole world better. I wouldn't have exchanged my husband for anybody except St. Michael himself, and you may tell him that for me with a thank you in the bargain.

Light flashed on her closed eyelids, and a deep roaring shook her. Cornelia, is that lightning? I hear thunder. There's going to be a storm. Close all the windows. Call the children in. . . . "Mother, here we are, all of us." "Is that you, Hapsy?" "Oh, no, I'm Lydia. We drove as fast as we could." Their faces drifted above her, drifted away. The rosary fell out of her hands and Lydia put it back. Jimmy tried to help, their hands fumbled together, and Granny closed two fingers around Jimmy's thumb. Beads wouldn't do, it must be something alive. She was so amazed her thoughts ran round and round. So, my dear Lord, this is my death and I wasn't even thinking about it. My children have come to see me die. But I can't, it's not time. Oh, I always hated surprises. I wanted to give Cornelia the amethyst set—Cornelia, you're to have the amethyst set, but Hapsy's to wear it when she wants, and, Doctor Harry, do shut up. Nobody sent for you. Oh, my dear Lord, do wait a minute. I meant to do something about the Forty Acres, Jimmy doesn't need it and Lydia will later on, with that worthless husband of hers. I meant to finish the altar cloth and send six bottles of wine to Sister Borgia for her dyspepsia. I want to send six bottles of wine to Sister Borgia, Father Connolly, now don't let me forget.

Cornelia's voice made short turns and tilted over and crashed. "Oh, Mother, oh, Mother, oh, Mother. . . ."

"I'm not going, Cornelia. I'm taken by surprise. I can't go."

You'll see Hapsy again. What about her? "I thought you'd never come." Granny made a long journey outward, looking for Hapsy. What if I don't find her? What then? Her heart sank down and down, there was no bottom to death, she couldn't come to the end of it. The blue light from Cornelia's lampshade drew into a tiny point in the center of her brain, it flickered and winked like an eye,

---

2. *Father Connolly . . . feet.* The priest is administering the sacrament for the dying, which includes anointing the hands and feet.

quietly it fluttered and dwindled. Granny lay curled down within herself, amazed and watchful, staring at the point of light that was herself; her body was now only a deeper mass of shadow in an endless darkness and this darkness would curl around the light and swallow it up. God, give a sign!

For the second time there was no sign. Again no bridegroom and the priest in the house. She could not remember any other sorrow because this grief wiped them all away. Oh, no, there's nothing more cruel than this— I'll never forgive it. She stretched herself with a deep breath and blew out the light.

❧ TO INCREASE UNDERSTANDING

1. (a) Describe what happens in the sickroom while Granny is reliving the past. (b) How much time do these actual events cover? (c) How is the seemingly random order in which past events come into Granny's mind related to happenings in the sickroom? (d) To what situations in the past do Granny's thoughts keep returning? Why?

2. (a) Tell in detail the story of the jilting mentioned in the title. (b) What significance do you find in Miss Porter's choice of a surname for Granny? (c) How long ago did the jilting occur? (d) What is Granny's attitude toward it? (e) Why does the author reveal the facts about the jilting as she does instead of giving the information straightforwardly and then ending her story?

3. In "The Jilting of Granny Weatherall" the style of writing suggests the vagueness and confusion as well as the moments of clarity that characterize Granny. Thus passages like ". . . Doctor Harry floated like a balloon around the foot of the bed" alternate with sharp images like ". . . white stone-china jars with blue whirligigs and words painted on them. . . ." (a) Cite passages in which the manner of writing reflects Granny's state of mind. (b) Do most of the clearly visualized scenes relate to the present or the past? Explain why this is so.

🌷 BETTER READING
Narrative point of view

The point of view from which a story is told determines the extent to which a reader is allowed to peer into the minds of the characters. Since the artistic unity of a piece of fiction may depend to a great degree on this aspect of telling a story, deciding what point of view to use is one of the first and most important considerations a writer must face.

The three following points of view, with variations, are the choices open to the writer.

1. *The personal point of view of a participant.* When a story is unfolded in the first person by one of the characters involved, the point of view is *personal.* The narrator may be merely a bystander, or like the young soldier in Hemingway's "In Another Country," he may be an important character.

Had Miss Porter chosen to use the personal point of view in a story about Granny Weatherall, she could have used Cornelia as the narrator. Cornelia then would have been able to recount what happened and to describe her own thoughts; but she could not have entered her mother's mind. Rewrite the first paragraph of the story as it might read if Cornelia were the narrator. Why would the title of the story probably have been different?

2. *The objective point of view.* When an author tells us what his characters do and say but not what they think, his narration of events is called *objective.* Had Miss Porter used the objective point of view in "The Jilting of Granny Weatherall," she could have told us what Granny, Cornelia, and Doctor Harry did in the sickroom and what they said to one another, but she could not have entered Granny's mind. Rewrite the first paragraph of the story from this point of view. Does it contain more or less information than the version you wrote using the personal point of view? Why? What types of stories are best suited to use of the objective point of view?

3. *The omniscient point of view.* When an author, writing in the third person, tells us what goes on in the minds of his characters, his point of view is *omniscient* (knowing all); if he enters the mind of only one character, his point of view is *partially omniscient.* Which of these omniscient points of view is used in "The Jilting of Granny Weatherall"?

Consider carefully all the things Miss Porter reveals to you about Granny, including what you learn about the old woman from the speeches and actions of others, from Granny's own words, and from her thoughts. Which of these sources is most important in building up your understanding of Granny? Why?

Consider your impressions of John, Cornelia, Doctor Harry, Hapsy, and George. What shaped your attitude toward Cornelia? How did you form an impression of characters who never entered the room?

Now think over the story as a whole. All our interest centers upon Granny. The time shifts from present to past and back again as Granny's mind wanders. The style changes its rhythms as the old woman lives alternately in the sickroom and in her memories. Would this artistic unity have been possible if Miss Porter had adopted another point of view in writing this particular story? Explain.

Thomas Wolfe 1900-1938

Although Thomas Wolfe reached maturity in the 1920's, his writing does not express the pessimism and futility so characteristic of his contemporaries. Wolfe had a Whitmanesque faith in America and possessed all of the vitality, exuberance, and ardor of an uninhibited romantic.

Thomas Wolfe was born and reared in Asheville, North Carolina, which he describes vividly in *Look Homeward, Angel*. Because of friction between his parents, the Wolfe family was divided; Tom and his brother Ben lived with Mrs. Wolfe in her boarding house, while Tom's father and sister occupied the old family home. Tom was a lonely child who found companionship in books. An avid reader and bright student, he entered the University of North Carolina at fifteen. During his undergraduate days, he was a member of the Carolina Playmakers, a group of students who wrote and performed their own plays, and he determined to become a playwright. When he graduated in 1920, Tom borrowed money to enroll at Harvard. He attended Harvard's intensive drama course, Workshop 47, and completed his master's degree in 1922. In the next few years Wolfe unsuccessfully tried to sell his plays, made trips abroad, taught at New York University, and completed his first novel, *Look Homeward, Angel*.

Look Homeward, Angel is a subjective and energetic novel. It is, also, largely autobiographical, for Eugene Gant, the hero, is young Tom Wolfe. Like all of Wolfe's writing, it is a curious blend of realistic, detailed reporting and romantic self-torment. When the novel was published in 1929, it produced reactions ranging from ecstatic praise to savage criticism. Readers who had been swept along by Wolfe's sensuous images and dynamic characters praised the novel's lyric power and its dramatic impact. Sinclair Lewis, in his Nobel Prize address (1930), pointed to Wolfe's promising talent. Other critics, like Bernard De Voto, acknowledged his talent—even his genius—but deplored the novel's formlessness and its lack of objective control. In Asheville, a highly indignant citizenry protested the accuracy of Wolfe's unfavorable descriptions of his old home town; they never quite forgave him. These reactions to *Look Homeward, Angel* are a summation of Wolfe's strengths and weaknesses as a writer: his characters are vivid and larger than life, and his rhapsodic language re-creates subjective experiences by piling adjective on adjective and by cataloging sights, sounds, and sensations in passages of such lyric intensity that they can be chanted like Whitman's verse. But Wolfe's compulsion to get everything he felt on paper made his writing undisciplined and almost totally autobiographical.

Wolfe continued the story of Eugene Gant in *Of Time and the River* (1935) and then followed with two more autobiographical novels, *The Web and the Rock* (1939) and *You Can't Go Home Again* (1940), both of which were published after Wolfe's untimely death from pneumonia complications in 1938.

Wolfe stated that his collection of short stories, *From Death to Morning* (1935), contained his finest writing. In this shorter form of fiction he seems to have approached the objectivity, unity, and technical mastery which critics found so lacking in his novels. "The Far and the Near" is from this collection.

The Far and the Near

On the outskirts of a little town upon a rise of land that swept back from the railway there was a tidy little cottage of white boards, trimmed vividly with green blinds. To one side of the house there was a garden neatly patterned with plots of growing vegetables, and an arbor for the grapes which ripened late in August. Before the house there were three mighty oaks which sheltered it in their clean and massive shade in summer, and to the other side there was a border of gay flowers. The whole place had an air of tidiness, thrift, and modest comfort.

Every day, a few minutes after two o'clock in the afternoon, the limited express between the two cities passed this spot. At that moment the great train, having halted for a breathing space at the town nearby, was beginning to lengthen evenly into its stroke, but it had not yet reached the full drive of its terrific speed. It swung into view deliberately, swept past with a powerful swaying motion of the engine, a low smooth rumble of its heavy cars upon pressed steel, and then it vanished in the cut. For a moment the progress of the engine could be marked by heavy bellowing puffs of smoke that burst at spaced intervals above the edges of the meadow grass, and finally nothing could be heard but the solid clacking tempo of the wheels receding into the drowsy stillness of the afternoon.

Every day for more than twenty years, as the train approached this house, the engineer had blown on the whistle, and every day, as soon as she heard this signal, a woman had appeared on the back porch of the little house and waved to him. At first she had a small child clinging to her skirts, and now this child had grown to full womanhood, and every day she, too, came with her mother to the porch and waved.

The engineer had grown old and gray in service. He had driven his great train, loaded with its weight of lives, across the land ten thousand times. His own children had grown up and married, and four times he had seen before him on the tracks the ghastly dot of tragedy converging like a cannon ball to its eclipse of horror at the boiler head—a light spring wagon filled with children, with its clustered row of small stunned faces; a cheap automobile stalled upon the tracks, set with the wooden figures of people paralyzed with fear; a battered hobo walking by the rail, too deaf and old to hear the whistle's warning; and a form flung past his window with a scream—all this the man had seen and known. He had known all the grief, the joy, the peril, and the labor such a man could know; he had grown seamed and weathered in his loyal service, and now, schooled by the qualities of faith and courage and humbleness that attended his labor, he had grown old, and had the grandeur and the wisdom these men have.

But no matter what peril or tragedy he had known, the vision of the little house and the women waving to him with a brave free motion of the arm had become fixed in the mind of the engineer as something beautiful and enduring, something beyond all change and ruin, and something that would always be the same, no matter what mishap, grief, or error might break the iron schedule of his days.

The sight of the little house and of these two women gave him the most extraordinary happiness he had ever known. He had seen them in a thousand lights, a hundred weathers. He had seen them through the harsh bare light of wintry gray across the brown and frosted stubble of earth, and he had seen them again in the green luring sorcery of April.

He felt for them and for the little house in which they lived such tenderness as a man might feel for his own children, and at length the picture of their lives was carved so sharply in his heart that he felt that he knew their lives completely, to every hour and moment of the day, and he resolved that one day, when his years of service should be ended, he would go and find these people and speak at last with them whose lives had been so wrought into his own.

That day came. At last the engineer stepped

from a train onto the station platform of the town where these two women lived. His years upon the rail had ended. He was a pensioned servant of his company, with no more work to do. The engineer walked slowly through the station and out into the streets of the town. Everything was as strange to him as if he had never seen this town before. As he walked on, his sense of bewilderment and confusion grew. Could this be the town he had passed ten thousand times? Were these the same houses he had seen so often from the high windows of his cab? It was all as unfamiliar, as disquieting as a city in a dream, and the perplexity of his spirit increased as he went on.

Presently the houses thinned into the straggling outposts of the town, and the street faded into a country road—the one on which the women lived. And the man plodded on slowly in the heat and dust. At length he stood before the house he sought. He knew at once that he had found the proper place. He saw the lordly oaks before the house, the flower beds, the garden, and the arbor, and farther off, the glint of rails.

Yes, this was the house he sought, the place he had passed so many times, the destination he had longed for with such happiness. But now that he had found it, now that he was here, why did his hand falter on the gate; why had the town, the road, the earth, the very entrance to this place he loved turned unfamiliar as the landscape of some ugly dream? Why did he now feel this sense of confusion, doubt, and hopelessness?

At length he entered by the gate, walked slowly up the path and in a moment more had mounted three short steps that led up to the porch, and was knocking at the door. Presently he heard steps in the hall, the door was opened, and a woman stood facing him.

And instantly, with a sense of bitter loss and grief, he was sorry he had come. He knew at once that the woman who stood there looking at him with a mistrustful eye was the same woman who had waved to him so many thousand times. But her face was harsh and pinched and meager; the flesh sagged wearily in sallow folds, and the small eyes peered at him with timid suspicion and uneasy doubt.

All the brave freedom, the warmth, and the affection that he had read into her gesture, vanished in the moment that he saw her and heard her unfriendly tongue.

And now his own voice sounded unreal and ghastly to him as he tried to explain his presence, to tell her who he was and the reason he had come. But he faltered on, fighting stubbornly against the horror of regret, confusion, disbelief that surged up in his spirit, drowning all his former joy and making his act of hope and tenderness seem shameful to him.

At length the woman invited him almost unwillingly into the house, and called her daughter in a harsh shrill voice. Then, for a brief agony of time, the man sat in an ugly little parlor, and he tried to talk while the two women stared at him with a dull, bewildered hostility, a sullen, timorous restraint.

And finally, stammering a crude farewell, he departed. He walked away down the path and then along the road toward town, and suddenly he knew that he was an old man. His heart, which had been brave and confident when he looked along the familiar vista of the rails, was now sick with doubt and horror as it saw the strange and unsuspected visage of an earth which had always been within a stone's throw of him, and which he had never seen or known. And he knew that all the magic of that bright lost way, the vista of that shining line, the imagined corner of that small good universe of hope's desire, was gone forever, could never be got back again.

 TO INCREASE UNDERSTANDING

1. (a) What is Thomas Wolfe's narrative point of view in this story? (b) Explain how, through use of this point of view, Wolfe's method of characterizing the man differs from the way he portrays the women. (c) How does his use of this point of view make the engineer the central figure?

2. (a) What is symbolized by the house and the waving women as viewed from the train? Cite lines to justify your answer. (b) What is symbolized by the town and the women when seen at close range?

3. (a) What is the theme of "The Far and the Near"? (b) What sentence summarizes this theme?

4. Now that you have read the story, what does the title mean to you?

John Steinbeck 1902-

While Sherwood Anderson, Ernest Hemingway, and other members of the "lost" generation voiced their disillusionment with ideals they considered outworn, another group of writers concerned themselves with the economic plight of countless Americans during the years of the Great Depression of the 1930's. Foremost among these is John Steinbeck.

Born in Salinas, California, Steinbeck grew up in a rich but strike-tormented valley where the plight of agricultural and factory workers made a deep impression on him. Between 1919 and 1925, he intermittently attended Stanford University, where he developed a lasting interest in marine biology and contributed to university magazines. After leaving Stanford, he worked for a while as a newspaper reporter in New York City. His first three books were financial failures, and he was forced to fall back on such jobs as hod-carrying, surveying, and fruit picking. His literary popularity began in 1935 with a book that is said to have been rejected by nine publishers: this was *Tortilla Flat,* a series of stories about Mexican-Americans on the Monterey Peninsula. His short novel, *Of Mice and Men,* became a best seller in 1937; his novel dealing with the plight of migratory workers, *The Grapes of Wrath* (1939), earned the Pulitzer Prize in Letters in 1940.

The social protest that characterizes much of Steinbeck's writing is only one aspect of his work. Many labels have been used to describe him. Some critics and literary historians, pointing to the way he glorifies eccentrics and simple people who live close to the soil, call him a "primitivist" or a "romantic." Others see him as primarily a "realist" who seldom shirks from describing life's rude aspects, or as a "naturalist" who emphasizes cruel impersonal forces. Still others call him a "regionalist" because his favorite setting is the rural area of central California, or a "symbolist" because he frequently uses allegory. In his novels and short stories Steinbeck shows in varying degrees some of the qualities of all these schools of literature. The strong poetic quality of his prose, one of his outstanding features as a stylist, is evident in "The Leader of the People."

The Leader of the People

On Saturday afternoon Billy Buck, the ranch hand, raked together the last of the old year's hay-stack and pitched small forkfuls over the wire fence to a few mildly interested cattle. High in the air small clouds like puffs of cannon smoke were driven eastward by the March wind. The wind could be heard whishing in the brush on the ridge crests, but no breath of it penetrated down into the ranch-cup.

The little boy, Jody, emerged from the house eating a thick piece of buttered bread. He saw Billy working on the last of the haystack. Jody tramped down scuffing his shoes in a way he had been told was destructive to good shoe leather. A flock of white pigeons flew out of the black cypress tree as Jody passed, and circled the tree and landed again. A half-grown tortoise-shell cat leaped from the bunkhouse porch, galloped on stiff legs across the road, whirled, and galloped back again. Jody picked up a stone to help the game along, but he was too late, for the cat was under the porch before the stone could be discharged. He threw the stone into the cypress tree and started the white pigeons on another whirling flight.

Arriving at the used-up haystack, the boy leaned against the barbed-wire fence. "Will that be all of it, do you think?" he asked.

The middle-aged ranch hand stopped his careful raking and stuck his fork into the ground. He took off his black hat and smoothed down his hair. "Nothing left of it that isn't soggy from ground moisture," he said. He replaced his hat and rubbed his dry leathery hands together.

"Ought to be plenty mice," Jody suggested.

"Lousy with them," said Billy. "Just crawling with mice."

"Well, maybe, when you get all through, I could call the dogs and hunt the mice."

"Sure, I guess you could," said Billy Buck. He lifted a forkful of the damp ground hay and threw it into the air. Instantly three mice leaped out and burrowed frantically under the hay again.

Jody sighed with satisfaction. Those plump, sleek, arrogant mice were doomed. For eight months they had lived and multiplied in the haystack. They had been immune from cats, from traps, from poison, and from Jody. They had grown smug in their security, overbearing and fat. Now the time of disaster had come; they would not survive another day.

Billy looked up at the top of the hills that surrounded the ranch. "Maybe you better ask your father before you do it," he suggested.

"Well, where is he? I'll ask him now."

"He rode up to the ridge ranch after dinner. He'll be back pretty soon."

Jody slumped against the fencepost. "I don't think he'd care."

As Billy went back to his work he said ominously, "You'd better ask him anyway. You know how he is."

Jody did know. His father, Carl Tiflin, insisted upon giving permission for anything that was done on the ranch, whether it was important or not. Jody sagged farther against the post until he was sitting on the ground. He looked up at the little puffs of wind-driven cloud. "Is it like to rain, Billy?"

"It might. The wind's good for it, but not strong enough."

"Well, I hope it don't rain until after I kill those damn mice." He looked over his shoulder to see whether Billy had noticed the mature profanity. Billy worked on without comment.

Jody turned back and looked at the sidehill where the road from the outside world came down. The hill was washed with lean March sunshine. Silver thistles, blue lupins, and a few poppies bloomed among the sage bushes. Halfway up the hill Jody could see Doubletree Mutt, the black dog, digging in a squirrel hole. He paddled for a while and then paused to kick bursts of dirt out between his hind legs, and he dug with an earnestness which belied the knowledge he must have had that no dog had ever caught a squirrel by digging in a hole.

Suddenly, while Jody watched, the black dog stiffened, and backed out of the hole and looked up the hill toward the cleft in the ridge where the road came through. Jody looked up too. For a moment Carl Tiflin on horseback stood out against the pale sky, and then he moved down the road toward the house. He carried something white in his hand.

The boy started to his feet. "He's got a letter," Jody cried. He trotted away toward the ranch house, for the letter would probably be read aloud and he wanted to be there. He reached the house before his father did, and ran in. He heard Carl dismount from his creaking saddle and slap the horse on the side to send it to the barn where Billy would unsaddle it and turn it out.

Jody ran into the kitchen. "We got a letter!" he cried.

His mother looked up from a pan of beans. "Who has?"

"Father has. I saw it in his hand."

Carl strode into the kitchen then, and Jody's mother asked. "Who's the letter from, Carl?"

He frowned quickly. "How did you know there was a letter?"

She nodded her head in the boy's direction. "Big-Britches Jody told me."

Jody was embarrassed.

His father looked down at him contemptuously. "He *is* getting to be a big-britches," Carl said. "He's minding everybody's business but his own. Got his big nose into everything."

Mrs. Tiflin relented a little. "Well, he hasn't enough to keep him busy. Who's the letter from?"

Carl still frowned on Jody. "I'll keep him busy if he isn't careful." He held out a sealed letter. "I guess it's from your father."

Mrs. Tiflin took a hairpin from her head and slit open the flap. Her lips pursed judiciously. Jody saw her eyes snap back and forth over the lines. "He says," she translated, "he says he's going to drive out Saturday to stay for a little while. Why, this is Saturday. The letter must have been delayed." She looked at the postmark. "This was mailed day before yesterday. It should have been here yesterday." She looked up questioningly at her husband, and then her face darkened angrily. "Now what have you got that look on you for? He doesn't come often."

Carl turned his eyes away from her anger. He could be stern with her most of the time, but when occasionally her temper rose, he could not combat it.

"What's the matter with you?" she demanded again.

In his explanation there was a tone of apology Jody himself might have used. "It's just that he talks," Carl said lamely. "Just talks."

"Well, what of it? You talk yourself."

"Sure I do. But your father only talks about one thing."

"Indians!" Jody broke in excitedly. "Indians and crossing the plains!"

Carl turned fiercely on him. "You get out, Mr. Big-Britches! Go on, now! Get out!"

Jody went miserably out the back door and closed the screen with elaborate quietness. Under the kitchen window his shamed, downcast eyes fell upon a curiously shaped stone, a stone of such fascination that he squatted down and picked it up and turned it over in his hands.

The voices came clearly to him through the open kitchen window. "Jody's right," he heard his father say. "Just Indians and crossing the plains. I've heard that story about how the horses got driven off about a thousand times. He just goes on and on, and he never changes a word in the things he tells."

When Mrs. Tiflin answered, her tone was so changed that Jody, outside the window, looked up from his study of the stone. Her voice had become soft and explanatory. Jody knew how her face would have changed to match the tone. She said quietly, "Look at it this way, Carl. That was the big thing in my father's life. He led a wagon train clear across the plains to the west coast, and when it was finished, his life was done. It was a big thing to do, but it didn't last long enough. Look!" she continued, "it's as though he was born to do that, and after he finished it, there wasn't anything more for him to do but think about it and talk about it. If there'd been any farther west to go, he'd have gone. He's told me so himself. But at last there was the ocean. He lives right by the ocean where he had to stop."

She had caught Carl, caught and entangled him in her soft tone.

"I've seen him," he agreed quietly. "He goes down and stares off west over the ocean." His voice sharpened a little. "And then he goes up to the Horseshoe Club in Pacific Grove, and he tells people how the Indians drove off the horses."

She tried to catch him again. "Well, it's everything to him. You might be patient with him and pretend to listen."

Carl turned impatiently away. "Well, if it gets too bad, I can always go down to the bunkhouse and sit with Billy," he said irritably. He walked through the house and slammed the front door after him.

Jody ran to his chores. He dumped the grain to the chickens without chasing any of them. He gathered the eggs from the nests. He trotted into the house with the wood and interlaced it so carefully in the woodbox that two armloads seemed to fill it to overflowing.

His mother had finished the beans by now.

She stirred up the fire and brushed off the stove top with a turkey wing. Jody peered cautiously at her to see whether any rancor toward him remained. "Is he coming today?" Jody asked.

"That's what his letter said."

"Maybe I better walk up the road to meet him."

Mrs. Tiflin clanged the stove lid shut.

"That would be nice," she said. "He'd probably like to be met."

"I guess I'll just do it then."

Outside, Jody whistled shrilly to the dogs. "Come on up the hill," he commanded. The two dogs waved their tails and ran ahead. Along the roadside the sage had tender new tips. Jody tore off some pieces and rubbed them on his hands until the air was filled with

Right: John Steinbeck. Below: Scene in Steinbeck country.

CULVER PICTURES

WILLIAM M. GRAHAM FROM PHOTO RESEARCHERS, INC.

the sharp wild smell. With a rush the dogs leaped from the road and yapped into the brush after a rabbit. That was the last Jody saw of them, for when they failed to catch the rabbit, they went back home.

Jody plodded on up the hill toward the ridge top. When he reached the little cleft where the road came through, the afternoon wind struck him and blew up his hair and ruffled his shirt. He looked down on the little hills and ridges below and then out at the huge green Salinas Valley. He could see the white town of Salinas far out in the flat and the flash of its windows under the waning sun. Directly below him, in an oak tree, a crow congress had convened. The tree was black with crows all cawing at once.

Then Jody's eyes followed the wagon road down from the ridge where he stood, and lost it behind a hill, and picked it up again on the other side. On that distant stretch he saw a cart slowly pulled by a bay horse. It disappeared behind the hill. Jody sat down on the ground and watched the place where the cart would reappear again. The wind sang on the hilltops and the puff-ball clouds hurried eastward.

Then the cart came into sight and stopped. A man dressed in black dismounted from the seat and walked to the horse's head. Although it was so far away, Jody knew he had unhooked the checkrein, for the horse's head dropped forward. The horse moved on, and the man walked slowly up the hill beside it. Jody gave a glad cry and ran down the road toward them. The squirrels bumped along off the road, and a road runner flirted its tail and raced over the edge of the hill and sailed out like a glider.

Jody tried to leap into the middle of his shadow at every step. A stone rolled under his foot and he went down. Around a little bend he raced, and there, a short distance ahead, were his grandfather and the cart. The boy dropped from his unseemly running and approached at a dignified walk.

The horse plodded stumble-footedly up the hill and the old man walked beside it. In the lowering sun their giant shadows flickered darkly behind them. The grandfather was dressed in a black broadcloth suit and he wore kid congress gaiters[1] and a black tie on a short, hard collar. He carried his black slouch hat in his hand. His white beard was cropped close and his white eyebrows overhung his eyes like mustaches. The blue eyes were sternly merry. About the whole face and figure there was a granite dignity, so that every motion seemed an impossible thing. Once at rest, it seemed the old man would be stone, would never move again. His steps were slow and certain. Once made, no step could ever be retraced; once headed in a direction, the path would never bend nor the pace increase nor slow.

When Jody appeared around the bend, Grandfather waved his hat slowly in welcome, and he called, "Why, Jody! Come down to meet me, have you?"

Jody sidled near and turned and matched his step to the old man's step and stiffened his body and dragged his heels a little. "Yes, sir," he said. "We got your letter only today."

"Should have been here yesterday," said Grandfather. "It certainly should. How are all the folks?"

"They're fine, sir." He hesitated and then suggested shyly, "Would you like to come on a mouse hunt tomorrow, sir?"

"Mouse hunt, Jody?" Grandfather chuckled. "Have the people of this generation come down to hunting mice? They aren't very strong, the new people, but I hardly thought mice would be game for them."

"No, sir. It's just play. The haystack's gone. I'm going to drive out the mice to the dogs. You can watch, or even beat the hay a little."

The stern, merry eyes turned down on him. "I see. You don't eat them, then. You haven't come to that yet."

Jody explained, "The dogs eat them, sir. It wouldn't be much like hunting Indians, I guess."

"No, not much—but then later, when the troops were hunting Indians and shooting children and burning tepees, it wasn't much different from your mouse hunt."

They topped the rise and started down into the ranch-cup, and they lost the sun from their

---

1. *congress gaiters*, high shoes with elastic sides, by the stretching of which they are drawn onto the feet.

shoulders. "You've grown," Grandfather said. "Nearly an inch, I should say."

"More," Jody boasted. "Where they mark me on the door, I'm up more than an inch since Thanksgiving even."

Grandfather's rich throaty voice said, "Maybe you're getting too much water and turning to pith and stalk. Wait until you head out, and then we'll see."

Jody looked quickly into the old man's face to see whether his feelings should be hurt, but there was no will to injure, no punishing nor putting-in-your-place light in the keen blue eyes. "We might kill a pig," Jody suggested.

"Oh, no! I couldn't let you do that. You're just humoring me. It isn't the time and you know it."

"You know Riley, the big boar, sir?"

"Yes, I remember Riley well."

"Well, Riley ate a hole into that same haystack, and it fell down on him and smothered him."

"Pigs do that when they can," said Grandfather.

"Riley was a nice pig, for a boar, sir. I rode him sometimes, and he didn't mind."

A door slammed at the house below them, and they saw Jody's mother standing on the porch waving her apron in welcome. And they saw Carl Tiflin walking up from the barn to be at the house for the arrival.

The sun had disappeared from the hills by now. The blue smoke from the house chimney hung in flat layers in the purpling ranch-cup. The puff-ball clouds, dropped by the falling wind, hung listlessly in the sky.

Billy Buck came out of the bunkhouse and flung a wash basin of soapy water on the ground. He had been shaving in midweek, for Billy held Grandfather in reverence, and Grandfather said that Billy was one of the few men of the new generation who had not gone soft. Although Billy was in middle age, Grandfather considered him a boy. Now Billy was hurrying toward the house too.

When Jody and Grandfather arrived, the three were waiting for them in front of the yard gate.

Carl said, "Hello, sir. We've been looking for you."

Mrs. Tiflin kissed Grandfather on the side of his beard, and stood still while his big hand patted her shoulder. Billy shook hands solemnly, grinning under his straw mustache. "I'll put up your horse," said Billy, and he led the rig away.

Grandfather watched him go, and then, turning back to the group, he said as he had said a hundred times before, "There's a good boy. I knew his father, old Mule-tail Buck. I never knew why they called him Mule-tail except he packed mules."[2]

Mrs. Tiflin turned and led the way into the house. "How long are you going to stay, Father? Your letter didn't say."

"Well, I don't know. I thought I'd stay about two weeks. But I never stay as long as I think I'm going to."

In a short while they were sitting at the white oilcloth table eating their supper. The lamp with the reflector hung over the table. Outside the dining-room windows the big moths battered softly against the glass.

Grandfather cut his steak into tiny pieces and chewed slowly. "I'm hungry," he said. "Driving out here got my appetite up. It's like when we were crossing. We all got so hungry every night we could hardly wait to let the meat get done. I could eat about five pounds of buffalo meat every night."

"It's moving around does it," said Billy. "My father was a government packer.[3] I helped him when I was a kid. Just the two of us could about clean up a deer's ham."

"I knew your father, Billy," said Grandfather. "A fine man he was. They called him Mule-tail Buck. I don't know why except he packed mules."

"That was it," Billy agreed. "He packed mules."

Grandfather put down his knife and fork and looked around the table, "I remember one time we ran out of meat—" His voice dropped to a curious low singsong, dropped into a tonal groove the story had worn for itself. "There was no buffalo, no antelope, not even rabbits.

2. *packed mules.* Billy's father was in charge of a string of mules which carried goods or provisions.   3. *government packer,* one who ran a string of mules owned by the government.

The hunters couldn't even shoot a coyote. That was the time for the leader to be on the watch. I was the leader, and I kept my eyes open. Know why? Well, just the minute the people began to get hungry they'd start slaughtering the team oxen. Do you believe that? I've heard of parties that just ate up their draft cattle. Started from the middle and worked toward the ends. Finally they'd eat the lead pair, and then the wheelers.[4] The leader of a party had to keep them from doing that."

In some manner a big moth got into the room and circled the hanging kerosene lamp. Billy got up and tried to clap it between his hands. Carl struck with a cupped palm and caught the moth and broke it. He walked to the window and dropped it out.

"As I was saying," Grandfather began again, but Carl interrupted him. "You'd better eat some more meat. All the rest of us are ready for our pudding."

Jody saw a flash of anger in his mother's eyes. Grandfather picked up his knife and fork. "I'm pretty hungry, all right," he said. "I'll tell you about that later."

When supper was over, when the family and Billy Buck sat in front of the fireplace in the other room, Jody anxiously watched Grandfather. He saw the signs he knew. The bearded head leaned forward; the eyes lost their sternness and looked wonderingly into the fire; the big lean fingers laced themselves on the black knees. "I wonder," he began, "I just wonder whether I ever told you how those thieving Piutes[5] drove off thirty-five of our horses."

"I think you did," Carl interrupted. "Wasn't it just before you went up into the Tahoe country?"[6]

Grandfather turned quickly toward his son-in-law. "That's right. I guess I must have told you that story."

"Lots of times," Carl said cruelly, and he avoided his wife's eyes. But he felt the angry eyes on him, and he said, " 'Course I'd like to hear it again."

Grandfather looked back at the fire. His fingers unlaced and laced again. Jody knew how he felt, how his insides were collapsed and empty. Hadn't Jody been called a big-britches

that very afternoon? He arose to heroism and opened himself to the term big-britches again. "Tell about Indians," he said softly.

Grandfather's eyes grew stern again. "Boys always want to hear about Indians. It was a job for men, but boys want to hear about it. Well, let's see. Did I ever tell you how I wanted each wagon to carry a long iron plate?"

Everyone but Jody remained silent. Jody said "No. You didn't."

"Well, when the Indians attacked, we always put the wagons in a circle and fought from between the wheels. I thought that if every wagon carried a long plate with rifle holes, the men could stand the plates on the outside of the wheels when the wagons were in the circle and they would be protected. It would save lives and that would make up for the extra weight of the iron. But of course the party wouldn't do it. No party had done it before, and they couldn't see why they should go to the expense. They lived to regret it, too."

Jody looked at his mother, and knew from her expression that she was not listening at all. Carl picked at a callus on his thumb and Billy Buck watched a spider crawling up the wall.

Grandfather's tone dropped into its narrative groove again. Jody knew in advance exactly what words would fall. The story droned on, speeded up for the attack, grew sad over the wounds, struck a dirge at the burials on the great plains. Jody sat quietly watching Grandfather. The stern blue eyes were detached. He looked as though he were not very interested in the story himself.

When it was finished, when the pause had been politely respected as the frontier of the story, Billy Buck stood up and stretched and hitched his trousers. "I guess I'll turn in," he said. Then he faced Grandfather. "I've got an old powder horn and a cap and ball pistol

4. *lead pair . . . wheelers.* The lead pair were the animals harnessed first in a team; the wheelers were placed immediately in front of the wheels of a wagon.   5. *Piutes* (pī′ūtz), a term applied to various Shoshone Indian tribes who were scattered from Arizona and Utah to Nevada, California, and Oregon.   6. *Tahoe* (tä′hō *or* tä′hō) *country,* the high, forested land near Lake Tahoe, a lake which lies at the base of the Sierra Nevada Mountains on the Nevada-California boundary.

down to the bunkhouse. Did I ever show them to you?"

Grandfather nodded slowly. "Yes, I think you did, Billy. Reminds me of a pistol I had when I was leading the people across." Billy stood politely until the little story was done, and then he said, "Good night," and went out of the house.

Carl Tiflin tried to turn the conversation then. "How's the country between here and Monterey? I've heard it's pretty dry."

"It is dry," said Grandfather. "There's not a drop of water in the Laguna Seca. But it's a long pull from '87. The whole country was powder then, and in '61 I believe all the coyotes starved to death. We had fifteen inches of rain this year."

"Yes, but it all came too early. We could do with some now." Carl's eye fell on Jody. "Hadn't you better be getting to bed?"

Jody stood up obediently. "Can I kill the mice in the old haystack, sir?"

"Mice? Oh! Sure, kill them all off. Billy said there isn't any good hay left."

Jody exchanged a secret and satisfying look with Grandfather. "I'll kill every one tomorrow," he promised.

Jody lay in his bed and thought of the impossible world of Indians and buffaloes, a world that had ceased to be forever. He wished he could have been living in the heroic time, but he knew he was not of heroic timber. No one living now, save possibly Billy Buck, was worthy to do the things that had been done. A race of giants had lived then, fearless men, men of a stanchness unknown in this day. Jody thought of the wide plains and of the wagons moving across like centipedes. He thought of Grandfather on a huge white horse, marshaling the people. Across his mind marched the great phantoms, and they marched off the earth and they were gone.

He came back to the ranch for a moment, then. He heard the dull rushing sound that space and silence make. He heard one of the dogs, out in the doghouse, scratching a flea and bumping his elbow against the floor with every stroke. Then the wind arose again, and the black cypress groaned, and Jody went to sleep.

He was up half an hour before the triangle sounded for breakfast. His mother was rattling the stove to make the flames roar when Jody went through the kitchen. "You're up early," she said. "Where are you going?"

"Out to get a good stick. We're going to kill the mice today."

"Who is 'we'?"

"Why, Grandfather and I."

"So you've got him in it. You always like to have someone in with you in case there's blame to share."

"I'll be right back," said Jody. "I just want to have a good stick ready for after breakfast."

He closed the screen door after him and went out into the cool blue morning. The birds were noisy in the dawn and the ranch cats came down from the hill like blunt snakes. They had been hunting gophers in the dark, and although the four cats were full of gopher meat, they sat in a semicircle at the back door and mewed piteously for milk. Doubletree Mutt and Smasher moved sniffling along the edge of the brush, performing the duty with rigid ceremony, but when Jody whistled, their heads jerked up and their tails waved. They plunged down to him, wriggling their skins and yawning. Jody patted their heads seriously, and moved on to the weathered scrap pile. He selected an old broom handle and a short piece of inch-square scrap wood. From his pocket he took a shoelace and tied the ends of the sticks loosely together to make a flail. He whistled his new weapon through the air and struck the ground experimentally, while the dogs leaped aside and whined with apprehension.

Jody turned and started down past the house toward the old haystack ground to look over the field of slaughter, but Billy Buck, sitting patiently on the back steps, called to him, "You better come back. It's only a couple of minutes till breakfast."

Jody changed his course and moved toward the house. He leaned his flail against the steps. "That's to drive the mice out," he said. "I'll bet they're fat. I'll bet they don't know what's going to happen to them today."

"No, nor you either," Billy remarked philosophically, "nor me, nor anyone."

Jody was staggered by this thought. He knew it was true. His imagination twitched away from the mouse hunt. Then his mother came out on the back porch and struck the triangle, and all thoughts fell in a heap.

Grandfather hadn't appeared at the table when they sat down. Billy nodded at his empty chair. "He's all right? He isn't sick?"

"He takes a long time to dress," said Mrs. Tiflin. "He combs his whiskers and rubs up his shoes and brushes his clothes."

Carl scattered sugar on his mush. "A man that's led a wagon train across the plains has got to be pretty careful how he dresses."

Mrs. Tiflin turned on him. "Don't do that, Carl! Please don't!" There was more of threat than of request in her tone. And the threat irritated Carl.

"Well, how many times do I have to listen to the story of the iron plates, and the thirty-five horses? That time's done. Why can't he forget it, now it's done?" He grew angrier while he talked, and his voice rose. "Why does he have to tell them over and over? He came across the plains. All right! Now it's finished. Nobody wants to hear about it over and over."

The door into the kitchen closed softly. The four at the table sat frozen. Carl laid his mush spoon on the table and touched his chin with his fingers.

Then the kitchen door opened and Grandfather walked in. His mouth smiled tightly and his eyes were squinted. "Good morning," he said, and he sat down and looked at his mush dish.

Carl could not leave it there. "Did—did you hear what I said?"

Grandfather jerked a little nod.

"I don't know what got into me, sir. I didn't mean it. I was just being funny."

Jody glanced in shame at his mother, and he saw that she was looking at Carl, and that she wasn't breathing. It was an awful thing that he was doing. He was tearing himself to pieces to talk like that. It was a terrible thing to him to retract a word, but to retract it in shame was infinitely worse.

Grandfather looked sidewise. "I'm trying to get right side up," he said gently. "I'm not being mad. I don't mind what you said, but it might be true, and I would mind that."

"It isn't true," said Carl. "I'm not feeling well this morning. I'm sorry I said it."

"Don't be sorry, Carl. An old man doesn't see things sometimes. Maybe you're right. The crossing is finished. Maybe it should be forgotten, now it's done."

Carl got up from the table. "I've had enough to eat. I'm going to work. Take your time, Billy!" He walked quickly out of the dining room. Billy gulped the rest of his food and followed soon after. But Jody could not leave his chair.

"Won't you tell any more stories?" Jody asked.

"Why, sure I'll tell them, but only when—I'm sure people want to hear them."

"I like to hear them, sir."

"Oh! Of course you do, but you're a little boy. It was a job for men, but only little boys like to hear about it."

Jody got up from his place. "I'll wait outside for you, sir. I've got a good stick for those mice."

He waited by the gate until the old man came out on the porch. "Let's go down and kill the mice now," Jody called.

"I think I'll just sit in the sun, Jody. You go kill the mice."

"You can use my stick if you like."

"No, I'll just sit here a while."

Jody turned disconsolately away, and walked down toward the old haystack. He tried to whip up his enthusiasm with thoughts of the fat juicy mice. He beat the ground with his flail. The dogs coaxed and whined about him, but he could not go. Back at the house he could see Grandfather sitting on the porch, looking small and thin and black.

Jody gave up and went to sit on the steps at the old man's feet.

"Back already? Did you kill the mice?"

"No, sir. I'll kill them some other day."

The morning flies buzzed close to the ground and the ants dashed about in front of the steps. The heavy smell of sage slipped down the hill. The porch boards grew warm in the sunshine.

Jody hardly knew when Grandfather started

to talk. "I shouldn't stay here, feeling the way I do." He examined his strong old hands. "I feel as though the crossing wasn't worth doing." His eyes moved up the sidehill and stopped on a motionless hawk perched on a dead limb. "I tell those old stories, but they're not what I want to tell. I only know how I want people to feel when I tell them.

"It wasn't Indians that were important, nor adventures, nor even getting out here. It was a whole bunch of people made into one big crawling beast. And I was the head. It was westering and westering. Every man wanted something for himself, but the big beast that was all of them wanted only westering. I was the leader, but if I hadn't been there, someone else would have been the head. The thing had to have a head.

"Under the little bushes the shadows were black at white noonday. When we saw the mountains at last, we cried—all of us. But it wasn't getting here that mattered, it was movement and westering.

"We carried life out here and set it down the way those ants carry eggs. And I was the leader. The westering was as big as God, and the slow steps that made the movement piled up and piled up until the continent was crossed.

"Then we came down to the sea, and it was done." He stopped and wiped his eyes until the rims were red. "That's what I should be telling instead of stories."

When Jody spoke, Grandfather started and looked down at him. "Maybe I could lead the people someday," Jody said.

The old man smiled. "There's no place to go. There's the ocean to stop you. There's a line of old men along the shore hating the ocean because it stopped them."

"In boats I might, sir."

"No place to go, Jody. Every place is taken. But that's not the worst—no, not the worst. Westering has died out of the people. Westering isn't a hunger any more. It's all done. Your father is right. It is finished." He laced his fingers on his knee and looked at them.

Jody felt very sad. "If you'd like a glass of lemonade, I could make it for you."

Grandfather was about to refuse, and then he saw Jody's face. "That would be nice," he said. "Yes, it would be nice to drink a lemonade."

Jody ran into the kitchen where his mother was wiping the last of the breakfast dishes. "Can I have a lemon to make a lemonade for Grandfather?"

His mother mimicked—"And another lemon to make a lemonade for you."

"No, ma'am. I don't want one."

"Jody! You're sick!" Then she stopped suddenly. "Take a lemon out of the cooler," she said softly. "Here, I'll reach the squeezer down to you."

✿ TO INCREASE UNDERSTANDING

1. In the opening paragraphs of "The Leader of the People" how does Steinbeck show you that Jody is a typical ten-year-old boy?

2. (a) How does Jody's attitude toward killing mice change between the beginning and the end of the story? (b) Trace the steps that have brought about this change. (c) Why, at the end of the story, does Jody "feel very sad"? (d) Why does Jody's mother speak to him as she does in the last paragraph?

3. (a) Both of Jody's parents call him "Big-Britches." Why is Jody's reaction to his father's use of the term different from his feeling when his mother uses it? (b) Grandfather wonders whether Jody is "turning to pith and stalk." How does Jody react to this description of himself? (c) Contrast Jody's relationship with his grandfather with his relationship with his father.

4. (a) What is the narrative point of view of "The Leader of the People"? (b) During the course of the story Jody overhears his father and mother discussing Grandfather. How does this overheard conversation illustrate the difficulties inherent in handling this point of view? (c) Later Jody is present when his father utters the criticism that Grandfather overhears. Explain why, using the point of view that Steinbeck has adopted, Jody's presence is necessary. (d) Explain the importance of each of these conversations to the development of the plot.

5. Reread Grandfather's conversation with Jody (page 485, column 2, paragraph 18 to page 486, column 1, paragraph 8). (a) What ideas about the Westward Movement does Grandfather express? (b) How does his talk here differ in substance from his narrative of the previous evening? (c) Does

Grandfather's conversation here or his earlier stories give you a better understanding of him? Explain.

6. Grandfather tells Jody that he believes "Westering has died out of the people." (a) Why do you think Grandfather has reached this conclusion? (b) Do you think Grandfather's conclusion is correct? Justify your answer.

7. (a) Because of Steinbeck's tone, the reader sympathizes with Grandfather and admires Jody's capacity for understanding. Why is this so? (b) Had you been a member of the Tiflin family seated in front of the fireplace and listening to Grandfather, what do you think your attitude toward Grandfather would have been? Why?

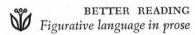

BETTER READING
Figurative language in prose

Figurative language is as essential an ingredient of prose as it is of poetry. In "The Leader of the People" John Steinbeck shows the artistry with which a writer of prose uses figures of speech to convey exact and vivid meaning to the story he has to tell.

Steinbeck uses a simile to help the reader understand just how the great overland movement appeared in Jody's young imagination: "Jody thought of the wide plains and of *the wagons moving across like centipedes.*" Later, when the author wishes you to grasp the idea about crossing the country that Grandfather has failed to convey through his stories, he has the old man speak in metaphors: "It wasn't Indians that were important, nor adventures, nor even getting out here. It was a whole bunch of people made into one big crawling beast. . . . Every man wanted something for himself, but *the big beast that was all of them* wanted only westering."

In addition to similes, metaphors, and other particular figures of speech, John Steinbeck often uses a single word or phrase figuratively to suggest a rich picture. When he introduces Grandfather, he writes: "About the whole face and figure there was a *granite* dignity." Can you grasp the idea that the figurative use of *granite* adds to the image of Grandfather? Is there any literal way of suggesting so briefly yet so clearly the simple strength, the integrity, and the unchanging quality of the old man? Why is suggesting this important?

Each of the following sentences contains figurative language. Read each sentence carefully and explain why the figurative language helps the author convey an impression briefly and clearly.

1. The hill was washed with lean March sunshine.

2. She had caught Carl, caught and entangled him in her soft tone.

3. His voice dropped into a curious low singsong, dropped into a tonal groove the story had worn for itself.

4. He wished he could have been living in the heroic time, but he knew he was not of heroic timber.

5. The birds were noisy in the dawn and the ranch cats came down from the hill like blunt snakes.

6. Then his mother . . . struck the triangle, and all thoughts fell in a heap.

WORDS!

Words similar in sound or appearance can often be confusing. For example, in sentence 1 below, which of the two words in parenthesis—*contemptible* or *contemptuous*—is correct? On a sheet of paper write the correct word after number 1. Continue in the same manner with the other sentences. You may use the Glossary or a dictionary if necessary.

1. Mr. Tiflin's reluctance to hear Grandfather's stories again seemed (contemptible, contemptuous) to Jody.

2. As leader of the people, Grandfather had suffered (incredible, incredulous) hardships.

3. Grandfather had proved himself (ingenuous, ingenious) in protecting the caravan against Indian raids.

4. Mr. Tiflin (deprecated, depreciated) Jody's habit of "minding everybody's business but his own."

Stephen Vincent Benét 1898-1943

Stephen Vincent Benét, like the writers of the "lost" generation, began his career in a mood of disillusionment and cynicism. His first novel, *The Beginning of Wisdom* (1921), like Scott Fitzgerald's *This Side of Paradise,* voiced the rebellion of "flaming youth." Similarly, his early poems dealt with his resentment of World War I and its aftermath. Several influences then combined to turn him from postwar topics to a theme which was beginning to find adherents all over the United States—the American past. It was in interpreting this theme that Benét achieved lasting fame.

In both upbringing and interests, Stephen Vincent Benét was well prepared to interpret the past. Born in Bethlehem, Pennsylvania, in 1898, he was descended from three generations of professional soldiers. The grandfather for whom he was named had translated into English a French history of the Battle of Waterloo. When Stephen was a boy, his father, an Army colonel, had argued for hours with him about the tactics used in the Civil War and had introduced him to some good histories of that war. Stephen's early reading of historical novels for boys had been supplemented by later reading from novelists, biographers, and poets who had drawn upon history for their subject matter.

Benét began to write while he was at preparatory school. His first book of poetry, *Five Men and Pompey*, was published in 1915, the year he entered Yale. Among his classmates there were several gifted young authors; three of them—Archibald MacLeish (see page 591), Thornton Wilder, and Philip Barry—were, like Benét, destined to be Pulitzer Prize winners.

In 1917 during Benét's college years, the United States entered World War I. Benét, a junior, tried to enlist, but was rejected because of his nearsightedness. He spent the war years working for the State Department. After the war he returned to Yale and received both his B.A. and M.A. degrees. Subsequently, like many other young Americans of the time, he went to Paris, where he remained for a year.

In 1926 Benét published a historical novel, *Spanish Bayonet*, which did not sell very well. He turned then to short-story writing, and his short stories, by contrast, were highly remunerative. In the same year, however, he accepted a relatively small fellowship from a foundation and set out for Paris, where he planned to write a long poem dealing with the Civil War. The resultant volume, *John Brown's Body*, won a Pulitzer Prize. (For a selection from and additional information about this poem see page 580.) It established Benét securely as a writer on the American past and indicated clearly that it was in this field his greatest gifts lay.

In his short stories about an earlier America, Benét showed a talent for mingling legend and humor with history. "In talk," wrote a friend, Basil Davenport, "he seems to 'make fun' of everything, not in the sense of ridicule, but with the humor that comes from looking at everything with a really original mind.... That is the Benét who ... can write a new legend so perfectly that it seems to have been always a part of our folklore." Benét wrote such short stories in the manner of a tall-tale narrator—a manner not unlike that of Mark Twain telling his "Jumping Frog" story (page 382). His characters were figures who had actually lived or who had been invented by the folk in the past. These tales were inventive to the point of being fantastic, but they were told in the language of common speech, and they were constantly flavored with salty humor.

"The Devil and Daniel Webster" (1937) was first published in the *Saturday Evening Post*. It was later made into an opera by Douglas Moore, and has been adapted for radio and television. Such a record shows not only the artistry of a very fine story but the importance of the historical tale as a type of American short story today.

The Devil and Daniel Webster

I t's a story they tell in the border country, where Massachusetts joins Vermont and New Hampshire.

Yes, Dan'l Webster's dead—or, at least, they buried him. But every time there's a thunderstorm around Marshfield, they say you can hear his rolling voice in the hollows of the sky. And they say that if you go to his grave and speak loud and clear, "Dan'l Webster—Dan'l Webster!" the ground'll begin to shiver and the trees begin to shake. And after a while you'll hear a deep voice saying, "Neighbor, how stands the Union?" Then you better answer the Union stands as she should, rock-bottomed and copper-sheathed, one and indivisible, or he's liable to rear right out of the ground. At least, that's what I was told when I was a youngster.

You see, for a while, he was the biggest man in the country. He never got to be President, but he was the biggest man. There were thousands that trusted in him right next to God Almighty, and they told stories about him that were like the stories of patriarchs and such. They said, when he stood up to speak, stars and stripes came right out in the sky, and once he spoke against a river and made it sink into the ground. They said, when he walked the woods with his fishing rod, Killall, the trout would jump out of the streams right into his pockets, for they knew it was no use putting up a fight against him; and when he argued a case, he could turn on the harps of the blessed and the shaking of the earth underground. That was the kind of man he was, and his big farm up at Marshfield was suitable to him. The chickens he raised were all white meat down through the drumsticks, the cows were tended like children, and the big ram he called Goliath had horns with a curl like a morning-glory vine and could butt through an iron door. But Dan'l wasn't one of your gentlemen farmers; he knew all the ways of the land, and he'd be up by candlelight to see that the chores got done. A man with a mouth like a mastiff, a brow like a mountain, and eyes like burning anthracite—that was Dan'l Webster in his prime. And the biggest case he argued never got written down in the books, for he argued it against the devil, nip and tuck and no holds barred. And this is the way I used to hear it told.

There was a man named Jabez Stone, lived at Cross Corners, New Hampshire. He wasn't a bad man to start with, but he was an unlucky man. If he planted corn, he got borers; if he planted potatoes, he got blight. He had good-enough land, but it didn't prosper him; he had a decent wife and children, but the more children he had, the less there was to feed them. If stones cropped up in his neighbor's field, boulders boiled up in his; if he had a horse with the spavins, he'd trade it for one with the staggers and give something extra. There's some folks bound to be like that, apparently. But one day Jabez Stone got sick of the whole business.

He'd been plowing that morning and he'd just broke the plowshare on a rock that he could have sworn hadn't been there yesterday. And, as he stood looking at the plowshare, the off horse[1] began to cough—that ropy[2] kind of cough that means sickness and horse doctors. There were two children down with measles, his wife was ailing, and he had a whitlow on his thumb. It was about the last straw for Jabez Stone. "I vow," he said, and he looked around him kind of desperate—"I vow it's enough to make a man want to sell his soul to the devil! And I would, too, for two cents!"

Then he felt a kind of queerness come over him at having said what he'd said; though, naturally, being a New Hampshireman, he wouldn't take it back. But, all the same, when it got to be evening and, as far as he could

1. *off horse*, the horse on the right-hand side in a team.
2. *ropy*, roupy, or hoarse.

see, no notice had been taken, he felt relieved in his mind, for he was a religious man. But notice is always taken, sooner or later, just like the Good Book says. And, sure enough, next day, about suppertime, a soft-spoken, dark-dressed stranger drove up in a handsome buggy and asked for Jabez Stone.

Well, Jabez told his family it was a lawyer, come to see him about a legacy. But he knew who it was. He didn't like the looks of the stranger, nor the way he smiled with his teeth. They were white teeth, and plentiful—some say they were filed to a point, but I wouldn't vouch for that. And he didn't like it when the dog took one look at the stranger and ran away howling, with his tail between his legs. But having passed his word, more or less, he stuck to it, and they went out behind the barn and made their bargain. Jabez Stone had to prick his finger to sign, and the stranger lent him a silver pin. The wound healed clean, but it left a little white scar.

After that, all of a sudden, things began to pick up and prosper for Jabez Stone. His cows got fat and his horses sleek, his crops were the envy of the neighborhood, and lightning might strike all over the valley, but it wouldn't strike his barn. Pretty soon, he was one of the prosperous people of the county; they asked him to stand for selectman, and he stood for it; there began to be talk of running him for state senate. All in all, you might say the Stone family was as happy and contented as cats in a dairy. And so they were, except for Jabez Stone.

He'd been contented enough, the first few years. It's a great thing when bad luck turns; it drives most other things out of your head. True, every now and then, especially in rainy weather, the little white scar on his finger would give him a twinge. And once a year, punctual as clockwork, the stranger with the handsome buggy would come driving by. But the sixth year, the stranger lighted, and after that, his peace was over for Jabez Stone.

The stranger came up through the lower field, switching his boots with a cane—they were handsome black boots, but Jabez Stone never liked the look of them, particularly the toes. And, after he'd passed the time of day, he said, "Well, Mr. Stone, you're a hummer! It's a very pretty property you've got here, Mr. Stone."

"Well, some might favor it and others might not," said Jabez Stone, for he was a New Hampshireman.

"Oh, no need to decry your industry!" said the stranger, very easy, showing his teeth in a smile. "After all, we know what's been done, and it's been according to contract and specifications. So when—ahem—the mortgage falls due next year, you shouldn't have any regrets."

"Speaking of that mortgage, mister," said Jabez Stone, and he looked around for help to the earth and the sky, "I'm beginning to have one or two doubts about it."

"Doubts?" said the stranger, not quite so pleasantly.

"Why, yes," said Jabez Stone. "This being the U.S.A. and me always having been a religious man." He cleared his throat and got bolder. "Yes, sir," he said, "I'm beginning to have considerable doubts as to that mortgage holding in court."

"There's courts and courts," said the stranger, clicking his teeth. "Still, we might as well have a look at the original document." And he hauled out a big black pocketbook, full of papers. "Sherwin, Slater, Stevens, Stone," he muttered. "I, Jabez Stone, for a term of seven years—Oh, it's quite in order, I think."

But Jabez Stone wasn't listening, for he saw something else flutter out of the black pocketbook. It was something that looked like a moth, but it wasn't a moth. And as Jabez Stone stared at it, it seemed to speak to him in a small sort of piping voice, terrible small and thin, but terrible human. "Neighbor Stone!" it squeaked. "Neighbor Stone! Help me! For God's sake, help me!"

But before Jabez Stone could stir hand or foot, the stranger whipped out a big bandanna handkerchief, caught the creature in it, just like a butterfly, and started tying up the ends of the bandanna.

"Sorry for the interruption," he said. "As I was saying—"

But Jabez Stone was shaking all over like a scared horse.

"That's Miser Stevens' voice!" he said, in a

croak. "And you've got him in your handker-chief!"

The stranger looked a little embarrassed.

"Yes, I really should have transferred him to the collecting box," he said with a simper, "but there were some rather unusual speci-mens there and I didn't want them crowded. Well, well, these little contretemps will occur."

"I don't know what you mean by conter-tan," said Jabez Stone, "but that was Miser Stevens' voice! And he ain't dead! You can't tell me he is! He was just as spry and mean as a woodchuck, Tuesday!"

" 'In the midst of life—' "[3] said the stran-ger, kind of pious. "Listen!" Then a bell began to toll in the valley and Jabez Stone listened, with the sweat running down his face. For he knew it was tolled for Miser Stevens and that he was dead.

"These long-standing accounts," said the stranger with a sigh; "one really hates to close them. But business is business."

He still had the bandanna in his hand, and Jabez Stone felt sick as he saw the cloth struggle and flutter.

"Are they all as small as that?" he asked hoarsely.

"Small?" said the stranger. "Oh, I see what you mean. Why, they vary." He measured Jabez Stone with his eyes, and his teeth showed. "Don't worry, Mr. Stone," he said. "You'll go with a very good grade. I wouldn't trust you outside the collection box. Now, a man like Dan'l Webster, of course—well, we'd have to build a special box for him, and even at that, I imagine the wing spread would astonish you. But, in your case, as I was say-ing—"

"Put that handkerchief away!" said Jabez Stone, and he began to beg and pray. But the best he could get at the end was a three years' extension, with conditions.

But till you make a bargain like that, you've got no idea of how fast four years can run. By the last months of those years, Jabez Stone's known all over the state and there's talk of running him for governor—and it's dust and ashes in his mouth. For every day, when he gets up, he thinks, "There's one more night gone," and every night when he lies down, he

thinks of the black pocketbook and the soul of Miser Stevens, and it makes him sick at heart. Till, finally he can't bear it any longer, and, in the last days of the last year, he hitches up his horse and drives off to seek Dan'l Webster. For Dan'l was born in New Hampshire, only a few miles from Cross Corners, and it's well known that he has a particular soft spot for old neighbors.

It was early in the morning when he got to Marshfield, but Dan'l was up already, talking Latin to the farm hands and wrestling with the ram, Goliath, and trying out a new trotter and working up speeches to make against John C. Calhoun. But when he heard a New Hampshireman had come to see him, he dropped everything else he was doing, for that was Dan'l's way. He gave Jabez Stone a break-fast that five men couldn't eat, went into the living history of every man and woman in Cross Corners, and finally asked him how he could serve him.

Jabez Stone allowed that it was a kind of mortgage case.

"Well, I haven't pleaded a mortgage case in a long time, and I don't generally plead now, except before the Supreme Court," said Dan'l, "but if I can, I'll help you."

"Then I've got hope for the first time in ten years," said Jabez Stone, and told him the details.

Dan'l walked up and down as he listened, his hands behind his back, now and then ask-ing a question, now and then plunging his eyes at the floor, as if they'd bore through it like gimlets. When Jabez Stone had finished, Dan'l puffed out his cheeks and blew. Then he turned to Jabez Stone and a smile broke over his face like the sunrise over Monad-nock.[4]

"You've certainly given yourself the devil's own row to hoe, Neighbor Stone," he said, "but I'll take your case."

"You'll take it?" said Jabez Stone, hardly daring to believe.

"Yes," said Dan'l Webster. "I've got about

---

3. "In the midst of life . . . ," "In the midst of life we are in death." (From "The Burial of the Dead" in *The Book of Common Prayer*.) 4. *Monadnock* (mə nad'nok), a moun-tain in southwestern New Hampshire.

seventy-five other things to do and the Missouri Compromise to straighten out, but I'll take your case. For if two New Hampshiremen aren't a match for the devil, we might as well give the country back to the Indians."

Then he shook Jabez Stone by the hand and said, "Did you come down here in a hurry?"

"Well, I admit I made time," said Jabez Stone.

"You'll go back faster," said Dan'l Webster, and he told 'em to hitch up Constitution and Constellation to the carriage. They were matched grays with one white forefoot, and they stepped like greased lightning.

Well, I won't describe how excited and pleased the whole Stone family was to have the great Dan'l Webster for a guest, when they finally got there. Jabez Stone had lost his hat on the way, blown off when they overtook a wind, but he didn't take much account of that. But after supper he sent the family off to bed, for he had most particular business with Mr. Webster. Mrs. Stone wanted them to sit in the front parlor, but Dan'l Webster knew front parlors and said he preferred the kitchen. So it was there they sat, waiting for the stranger, with a jug on the table between them and a bright fire on the hearth—the stranger being scheduled to show up on the stroke of midnight, according to specifications.

Well, most men wouldn't have asked for better company than Dan'l Webster and a jug. But with every tick of the clock Jabez Stone got sadder and sadder. His eyes roved round, and though he sampled the jug you could see he couldn't taste it. Finally, on the stroke of 11:30 he reached over and grabbed Dan'l Webster by the arm.

"Mr. Webster, Mr. Webster!" he said, and his voice was shaking with fear and a desperate courage. "For God's sake, Mr. Webster, harness your horses and get away from this place while you can!"

"You've brought me a long way, neighbor, to tell me you don't like my company," said Dan'l Webster, quite peaceable, pulling at the jug.

"Miserable wretch that I am!" groaned Jabez Stone. "I've brought you a devilish way, and now I see my folly. Let him take me if he wills. I don't hanker after it, I must say, but I can stand it. But you're the Union's stay and New Hampshire's pride! He mustn't get you, Mr. Webster! He mustn't get you!"

Dan'l Webster looked at the distracted man, all gray and shaking in the firelight, and laid a hand on his shoulder.

"I'm obliged to you, Neighbor Stone," he said gently. "It's kindly thought of. But there's a jug on the table and a case in hand. And I never left a jug or a case half finished in my life."

And just at that moment there was a sharp rap on the door.

"Ah," said Dan'l Webster, very coolly, "I thought your clock was a trifle slow, Neighbor Stone." He stepped to the door and opened it. "Come in!" he said.

The stranger came in—very dark and tall he looked in the firelight. He was carrying a box under his arm—a black, japanned box with little air holes in the lid. At the sight of the box, Jabez Stone gave a low cry and shrank into a corner of the room.

"Mr. Webster, I presume," said the stranger, very polite, but with his eyes glowing like a fox's deep in the woods.

"Attorney of record for Jabez Stone," said Dan'l Webster, but his eyes were glowing too. "Might I ask your name?"

"I've gone by a good many," said the stranger carelessly. "Perhaps Scratch will do for the evening. I'm often called that in these regions."

Then he sat down at the table and poured himself a drink from the jug. The liquor was cold in the jug, but it came steaming into the glass.

"And now," said the stranger, smiling and showing his teeth, "I shall call upon you, as a law-abiding citizen, to assist me in taking possession of my property."

Well, with that the argument began—and it went hot and heavy. At first, Jabez Stone had a flicker of hope, but when he saw Dan'l Webster being forced back at point after point, he just scrunched in his corner, with his eyes on that japanned box. For there wasn't any doubt as to the deed or the signature—that was the worst of it. Dan'l Webster twisted and turned and thumped his fist on the table, but he couldn't get away from that. He offered to compromise the case; the stranger wouldn't hear of it. He pointed out the property had increased in value, and state senators ought to be worth more; the stranger stuck to the letter of the law. He was a great lawyer, Dan'l Webster, but we know who's the King of Lawyers,[5] as the Good Book tells us, and it seemed as if, for the first time, Dan'l Webster had met his match.

Finally, the stranger yawned a little. "Your spirited efforts on behalf of your client do you credit, Mr. Webster," he said, "but if you have no more arguments to adduce, I'm rather pressed for time—" and Jabez Stone shuddered.

Dan'l Webster's brow looked dark as a thundercloud.

"Pressed or not, you shall not have this man!" he thundered. "Mr. Stone is an American citizen, and no American citizen may be forced into the service of a foreign prince. We fought England for that in '12 and we'll fight all hell for it again!"

"Foreign?" said the stranger. "And who calls me a foreigner?"

"Well, I never yet heard of the dev—of your claiming American citizenship," said Dan'l Webster with surprise.

"And who with better right?" said the stranger, with one of his terrible smiles. "When the first wrong was done to the first Indian, I was there. When the first slaver put out for the Congo, I stood on her deck. Am I not in your books and stories and beliefs, from the first settlements on? Am I not spoken of, still, in every church in New England? 'Tis true the North claims me for a Southerner and the South for a Northerner, but I am neither. I am merely an honest American like yourself—and of the best descent—for, to tell the truth, Mr. Webster, though I don't like to boast of it, my name is older in this country than yours."

"Aha!" said Dan'l Webster, with the veins standing out in his forehead, "then I stand on the Constitution! I demand a trial for my client!"

"The case is hardly one for an ordinary court," said the stranger, his eyes flickering. "And, indeed the lateness of the hour—"

"Let it be any court you choose, so it is an American judge and an American jury!" said Dan'l Webster in his pride. "Let it be the quick or the dead; I'll abide the issue!"[6]

"You have said it," said the stranger, and pointed his finger at the door. And with that, and all of a sudden, there was a rushing of wind outside and a noise of footsteps. They came, clear and distinct, through the night. And yet, they were not like the footsteps of living men.

"In God's name, who comes by so late?" cried Jabez Stone.

"The jury Mr. Webster demands," said the stranger, sipping at his boiling glass. "You must pardon the rough appearance of one or two; they will have come a long way."

And with that the fire burned blue and the door blew open and twelve men entered, one by one.

If Jabez Stone had been sick with terror before, he was blind with terror now. For there was Walter Butler, the Loyalist, who spread fire and horror through the Mohawk Valley[7] in the times of the Revolution; and there was Simon Girty, the renegade, who saw white men burned at the stake and whooped with the Indians to see them burn. His eyes were green, like a catamount's, and the stains on his hunting shirt did not come from the blood of the deer. King Philip[8] was there, wild and proud as he had been in life, with the great gash in his head that gave him his death wound, and cruel Governor Dale, who broke men on the wheel.[9] There was Morton of Merry Mount,[10] who so vexed the Plymouth Colony, with his flushed, loose, hand-

---

5. *the King of Lawyers*, the devil. 6. *I'll abide the issue*, I'll accept the verdict. 7. *the Mohawk Valley*, a valley in New York State. 8. *King Philip*, Indian chief of New England who led a war against the colonists from 1675 to 1676. 9. *Governor Dale, who broke men on the wheel*. Thomas Dale, a governor of Virginia in the first years of the colony, was noted for his cruel laws and punishments. The wheel was a contrivance on which men were bound; their bones were broken by its action. 10. *Morton of Merry Mount*. Thomas Morton incurred the displeasure of the Puritans because he fought the Puritan austerity. See the "Better Reading" article on page 314.

some face and his hate of the godly. There was Teach, the bloody pirate,[11] with his black beard curling on his breast. The Reverend John Smeet, with his strangler's hands and his Geneva gown,[12] walked as daintily as he had to the gallows. The red print of the rope was still around his neck, but he carried a perfumed handkerchief in one hand. One and all, they came into the room with the fires of hell still upon them, and the stranger named their names and their deeds as they came, till the tale of twelve was told. Yet the stranger had told the truth—they had all played a part in America.

"Are you satisfied with the jury, Mr. Webster?" said the stranger mockingly, when they had taken their places.

The sweat stood upon Dan'l Webster's brow, but his voice was clear.

"Quite satisfied," he said. "Though I miss General Arnold[13] from the company."

"Benedict Arnold is engaged upon other business," said the stranger, with a glower. "Ah, you asked for a justice, I believe."

He pointed his finger once more, and a tall man, soberly clad in Puritan garb, with the burning gaze of the fanatic, stalked into the room and took his judge's place.

"Justice Hathorne[14] is a jurist of experience," said the stranger. "He presided at certain witch trials once held in Salem. There were others who repented of the business later, but not he."

"Repent of such notable wonders and undertakings?" said the stern old justice. "Nay, hang them—hang them all!" And he muttered to himself in a way that struck ice into the soul of Jabez Stone.

Then the trial began, and, as you might expect, it didn't look anyways good for the defense. And Jabez Stone didn't make much of a witness in his own behalf. He took one look at Simon Girty and screeched, and they had to put him back in his corner in a kind of swoon.

It didn't halt the trial, though; the trial went on, as trials do. Dan'l Webster had faced some hard juries and hanging judges in his time, but this was the hardest he'd ever faced, and he knew it. They sat there with a kind of

glitter in their eyes, and the stranger's smooth voice went on and on. Every time he'd raise an objection, it'd be "Objection sustained," but whenever Dan'l objected, it'd be "Objection denied." Well, you couldn't expect fair play from a fellow like this Mr. Scratch.

It got to Dan'l in the end, and he began to heat, like iron in the forge. When he got up to speak he was going to flay that stranger with every trick known to the law, and the judge and jury too. He didn't care if it was contempt of court or what would happen to him for it. He didn't care any more what happened to Jabez Stone. He just got madder and madder, thinking of what he'd say. And yet, curiously enough, the more he thought about it, the less he was able to arrange his speech in his mind.

Till, finally, it was time for him to get up on his feet, and he did so, all ready to bust out with lightnings and denunciations. But before he started he looked over the judge and jury for a moment, such being his custom. And he noticed the glitter in their eyes was twice as strong as before, and they all leaned forward. Like hounds just before they get the fox, they looked, and the blue mist of evil in the room thickened as he watched them. Then he saw what he'd been about to do, and he wiped his forehead, as a man might who's just escaped falling into a pit in the dark.

For it was him they'd come for, not only Jabez Stone. He read it in the glitter of their eyes and in the way the stranger hid his mouth with one hand. And if he fought them with their own weapons, he'd fall into their power; he knew that, though he couldn't have told you how. It was his own anger and horror that burned in their eyes; and he'd have to wipe that out or the case was lost. He stood there for a moment, his black eyes burning like anthracite. And then he began to speak.

11. *Teach, the bloody pirate.* Edward Teach, commonly called Blackbeard, operated along the coasts of Virginia and the Carolinas. He was notorious for his cruelty. 12. *Geneva gown,* a minister's wide-sleeved black robe. 13. *General Arnold,* Benedict Arnold, an American general in the Revolutionary War, who turned traitor. 14. *Justice Hathorne,* John Hathorne, an ancestor of the author Nathaniel Hawthorne, who, as the author said, "made himself . . . conspicuous in the martyrdom of the witches of Salem."

He started off in a low voice, though you could hear every word. They say he could call on the harps of the blessed when he chose. And this was just as simple and easy as a man could talk. But he didn't start out by condemning or reviling. He was talking about the things that make a country a country, and a man a man.

And he began with the simple things that everybody's known and felt—the freshness of a fine morning when you're young, and the taste of food when you're hungry, and the new day that's every day when you're a child. He took them up and he turned them in his hands. They were good things for any man. But without freedom, they sickened. And when he talked of those enslaved, and the sorrows of slavery, his voice got like a big bell. He talked of the early days of America and the men who had made those days. It wasn't a spread-eagle speech, but he made you see it. He admitted all the wrong that had ever been done. But he showed how, out of the wrong and the right, the suffering and the starvations, something new had come. And everybody had played a part in it, even the traitors.

Then he turned to Jabez Stone and showed him as he was—an ordinary man who had had hard luck and wanted to change it. And, because he'd wanted to change it, now he was going to be punished for all eternity. And yet there was good in Jabez Stone, and he showed that good. He was hard and mean, in some ways, but he was a man. There was sadness in being a man, but it was a proud thing too. And he showed what the pride of it was till you couldn't help feeling it. Yes, even in hell, if a man was a man, you'd know it. And he wasn't pleading for any one person any more, though his voice rang like an organ. He was telling the story and the failures and the endless journey of mankind. They got tricked and trapped and bamboozled, but it was a great journey. And no demon that was ever foaled could know the inwardness of it—it took a man to do that.

The fire began to die on the hearth and the wind before morning to blow. The light was getting gray in the room when Dan'l Webster finished. And his words came back at the end to New Hampshire ground, and the one spot of land that each man loves and clings to. He painted a picture of that, and to each one of that jury he spoke of things long forgotten. For his voice could search the heart, and that was his gift and his strength. And to one, his voice was like the forest and its secrecy, and to another like the sea and the storms of the sea; and one heard the cry of his lost nation in it, and another saw a little harmless scene he hadn't remembered for years. But each saw something. And when Dan'l Webster finished he didn't know whether or not he'd saved Jabez Stone. But he knew he'd done a miracle. For the glitter was gone from the eyes of judge and jury, and, for the moment, they were men again, and knew they were men.

"The defense rests," said Dan'l Webster, and stood there like a mountain. His ears were still ringing with his speech, and he didn't hear anything else till he heard Judge Hathorne say, "The jury will retire to consider its verdict."

Walter Butler rose in his place and his face had a dark, gay pride on it.

"The jury has considered its verdict," he said, and looked the stranger full in the eye. "We find for the defendant, Jabez Stone."

With that the smile left the stranger's face, but Walter Butler did not flinch.

"Perhaps 'tis not strictly in accordance with the evidence," he said, "but even the damned may salute the eloquence of Mr. Webster."

With that, the long crow of a rooster split the gray morning sky, and judge and jury were gone from the room like a puff of smoke and as if they had never been there. The stranger turned to Dan'l Webster, smiling wryly.

"Major Butler was always a bold man," he said. "I had not thought him quite so bold. Nevertheless, my congratulations, as between two gentlemen."

"I'll have that paper first, if you please," said Dan'l Webster, and he took it and tore it into four pieces. It was queerly warm to the touch. "And now," he said, "I'll have you!" and his hand came down like a bear trap on the stranger's arm. For he knew that once you bested anybody like Mr. Scratch in fair fight, his power on you was gone. And he could see that Mr. Scratch knew it too.

The stranger twisted and wriggled, but he couldn't get out of that grip. "Come, come, Mr. Webster," he said, smiling palely. "This sort of thing is ridic—ouch!—is ridiculous. If you're worried about the costs of the case, naturally, I'd be glad to pay—"

"And so you shall!" said Dan'l Webster, shaking him till his teeth rattled. "For you'll sit right down at that table and draw up a document, promising never to bother Jabez Stone nor his heirs or assigns nor any other New Hampshireman till doomsday! For any hades we want to raise in this state, we can raise ourselves, without assistance from strangers."

"Ouch!" said the stranger. "Ouch! Well, they never did run very big to the barrel, but —ouch!—I agree."

So he sat down and drew up the document. But Dan'l Webster kept his hand on his coat collar all the time.

"And now, may I go?" said the stranger, quite humble, when Dan'l'd seen the document was in proper and legal form.

"Go?" said Dan'l, giving him another shake. "I'm still trying to figure out what I'll do with you. For you've settled the costs of the case, but you haven't settled with me. I think I'll take you back to Marshfield," he said, kind of reflective. "I've got a ram there named Goliath that can butt through an iron door. I'd kind of like to turn you loose in his field and see what he'd do."

Well, with that the stranger began to beg and plead. And he begged and he pled so humble that finally Dan'l, who was naturally kind-hearted, agreed to let him go. The stranger seemed terrible grateful for that and said, just to show they were friends, he'd tell Dan'l's fortune before leaving. So Dan'l agreed to that, though he didn't take much stock in fortunetellers ordinarily. But naturally the stranger was a little different.

Well, he pried and he peered at the lines in Dan'l's hands. And he told him one thing and another that was quite remarkable. But they were all in the past.

"Yes, that's all true, and it happened," said Dan'l Webster. "But what's to come in the future?"

The stranger grinned, kind of happily, and shook his head.

"The future's not as you think it," he said. "It's dark. You have a great ambition, Mr. Webster."

"I have," said Dan'l firmly, for everybody knew he wanted to be President.

"It seems almost within your grasp," said the stranger, "but you will not attain it. Lesser men will be made President and you will be passed over."

"And, if I am, I'll still be Daniel Webster," said Dan'l. "Say on."

"You have two strong sons," said the stranger, shaking his head. "You look to found a line. But each will die in war and neither reach greatness."

"Live or die, they are still my sons," said Dan'l Webster. "Say on."

"You have made great speeches," said the stranger. "You will make more."

"Ah," said Dan'l Webster.

"But the last great speech you make will turn many of your own against you," said the stranger. "They will call you Ichabod[15]; they will call you by other names. Even in New England, some will say you have turned your coat[16] and sold your country, and their voices will be loud against you till you die."

"So it is an honest speech, it does not matter what men say," said Dan'l Webster. Then he looked at the stranger and their glances locked.

"One question," he said. "I have fought for the Union all my life. Will I see that fight won against those who would tear it apart?"

"Not while you live," said the stranger grimly, "but it will be won. And after you are dead, there are thousands who will fight for your cause, because of words that you spoke."

"Why then, you long-barreled, slab-sided, lantern-jawed, fortune-telling note shaver!" said Dan'l Webster, with a great roar of laughter, "be off with you to your own place before I put my mark on you! For, by the thirteen

---

15. *Ichabod.* See Whittier's poem, "Ichabod," on page 290.
16. *turned your coat,* became a traitor.

original colonies, I'd go to the Pit itself to save the Union!"

And with that he drew back his foot for a kick that would have stunned a horse. It was only the tip of his shoe that caught the stranger, but he went flying out of the door with his collecting box under his arm.

"And now," said Dan'l Webster, seeing Jabez Stone beginning to rouse from his swoon, "let's see what's left in the jug, for it's dry work talking all night. I hope there's pie for breakfast, Neighbor Stone."

But they say that whenever the devil comes near Marshfield, even now, he gives it a wide berth. And he hasn't been seen in the state of New Hampshire from that day to this. I'm not talking about Massachusetts or Vermont.

 TO INCREASE UNDERSTANDING

1. Because Benét had a great "talent for mingling legend and humor with history," he cast many of his short stories as tall tales. (a) How does Benét, in the first three paragraphs of "The Devil and Daniel Webster," prepare his readers to accept the story as a tall tale? (b) How does Benét employ humorous exaggeration to suggest legend? (c) What aspects of the story are historical?

2. (a) What arguments does Webster use to persuade the devil that Jabez should be freed from his agreement? (b) On what grounds does he demand a trial by jury? (c) What is ironic about this situation?

3. Benét endows the judge and jury with a common trait. (a) What is this trait, and how does it underscore the conflict of the story? (b) Into what fatal trap does Webster almost fall as he begins to argue his case before the jury? (c) On what line of argument does he finally win it?

4. In speaking of Benét's legends, the biographical sketch says: "These tales were inventive to the point of being fantastic, but they were told in the language of common speech, and they were constantly flavored with salty humor." Cite passages in which Benét's language and humor lend realism to fantastic situations.

5. American history recognizes Daniel Webster as a lawyer of great eloquence and as a statesman devoted to the preservation of the Union. (a) How does Benét weave these elements of Webster's career into the short story? (b) Reread Whittier's poem "Ichabod" on page 290 and then compare Whittier's treatment of Webster with Benét's.

6. Compare this selection with "The Devil and Tom Walker" (page 176). (a) What similarities in plot do you find? (b) In what respect does one portrayal of the devil differ from the other? (c) How do Tom Walker's character traits differ from Jabez Stone's? (d) What folklore characteristics are common to both stories? (e) Which story do you like better and why?

 WORDS!

When you read that Daniel Webster's ram was called Goliath, you probably inferred that he was named after the Biblical giant whom David killed with a pebble from his slingshot. You probably also decided that, like the first Goliath, this Goliath was large, fierce, and immensely strong.

Over the centuries the name *Goliath* has come to be used as a synonym for "giant." Other widely used proper names have also taken on a more general, often figurative, meaning. In an unabridged dictionary, look up the italicized word in each sentence below. Determine both the original meaning of the word and its meaning in the sentence printed below. Then on a sheet of paper rewrite each sentence in such a way as to make its meaning clear without using the italicized word. Below each sentence briefly give the original meaning of the italicized word.

1. Mathematics has always been my *Waterloo*.

2. All compromise had failed and the nation waited *Armageddon*.

3. Looking back from maturity, he saw his childhood as a remote *Arcadian* time.

4. The *Lilliputian* in blue jeans advanced slowly, gravely, and fearfully toward me.

5. All through high school she had been the class *Cinderella*.

6. I object to inviting that *Jonah* to our party.

7. Although he was a *Methuselah* according to the calendar, he was young in enthusiasm.

 EXTENDING INTERESTS

Now that you have enjoyed "The Devil and Daniel Webster," you may want to read more of Benét's short stories such as "A Tooth for Paul Revere," "Johnny Pye and the Fool Killer," "The Angel Was a Yankee," "Jacob and the Indians," or "Freedom Is a Hard-Bought Thing." With your teacher's permission, arrange for a class period during which Benét's use of the American past in stories such as these is discussed.

Members of your class may also be interested in hearing Douglas Moore's operatic version of "The Devil and Daniel Webster." It is available on Westminster recording 11032.

James Thurber 1894-1961

James Thurber was a short-story writer, playwright, humorist, essayist, and cartoonist. Although "The Secret Life of Walter Mitty," like most of Thurber's stories, first appeared in the *New Yorker*, Thurber was not a typical *New Yorker* writer. In his case interest in the popular subject of psychology resulted in his becoming a humorist of the school Bernard De Voto characterized as "the Perfect Neurotics"—people nervously unable to adjust to life. Of "the Perfect Neurotics" Thurber himself wrote: "They lead . . . an existence of jumpiness and apprehension. . . . In the House of Life they have the feeling that they have never taken off their overcoats . . . [They] have a genius for getting into minor difficulties: they walk into the wrong apartments, they drink furniture polish for stomach bitters, they drive their cars into the prize tulip beds of haughty neighbors . . ."[1]

He was born in Columbus, Ohio, in 1894. In *My Life and Hard Times* (1933) he wrote amusingly of his growing up in the unpredictable Thurber household and of his difficulties as a student at Ohio State University. After several years in newspaper work, he became a staff writer for the *New Yorker* and contributed many short stories and cartoons to the magazine. These have been collected in several volumes: *The Thurber Carnival* (1945), *Fables for Our Time*, and *Famous Poems Illustrated* (1940), *Thurber Country* (1953), and others. He collaborated with Eliot Nugent in writing a successful comedy, *The Male Animal*, in 1940; and in 1960 several of his essays and stories were dramatized for the stage under the title *The Thurber Carnival*. For a time Thurber himself acted in this production.

Thurber's humor springs from the way he viewed people and events. He was able to look at life with irony and amusement and see the incongruities and inconsistencies in the actions of men. Walter Mitty is one of the most beloved and best-known Thurber characters.

TERRENCE LEGOUBIN FROM BLACK STAR

The Secret Life of Walter Mitty

"We're going through!" The Commander's voice was like thin ice breaking. He wore his full-dress uniform, with the heavily braided white cap pulled down rakishly over one cold gray eye. "We can't make it, sir. It's spoiling for a hurricane, if you ask me." "I'm not asking you, Lieutenant Berg," said the Commander. "Throw on the power light! Rev her up to 8500! We're going through!" The pounding of the cylinders increased: ta-pocketa-pocketa-*pocketa-pocketa-pocketa*. The Commander

1. James Thurber, Preface to *My Life and Hard Times*, (New York: Harper & Brothers, 1933), pages xiv-xv.

stared at the ice forming on the pilot window. He walked over and twisted a row of complicated dials. "Switch on No. 8 auxiliary!" he shouted. "Switch on No. 8 auxiliary!" repeated Lieutenant Berg. "Full strength in No. 3 turret!" shouted the Commander. "Full strength in No. 3 turret!" The crew, bending to their various tasks in the huge, hurtling eight-engined Navy hydroplane, looked at each other and grinned. "The Old Man'll get us through," they said to one another. "The Old Man ain't afraid of Hell!"

"Not so fast! You're driving too fast!" said Mrs. Mitty. "What are you driving so fast for?"

"Hmm?" said Walter Mitty. He looked at his wife, in the seat beside him, with shocked astonishment. She seemed grossly unfamiliar, like a strange woman who had yelled at him in a crowd. "You were up to fifty-five," she said. "You know I don't like to go more than forty. You were up to fifty-five." Walter Mitty drove on toward Waterbury in silence, the roaring of the SN202 through the worst storm in twenty years of Navy flying fading in the remote, intimate airways of his mind. "You're tensed up again," said Mrs. Mitty. "It's one of your days. I wish you'd let Dr. Renshaw look you over."

Walter Mitty stopped the car in front of the building where his wife went to have her hair done. "Remember to get those overshoes while I'm having my hair done," she said. "I don't need overshoes," said Mitty. She put her mirror back into her bag. "We've been all through that," she said, getting out of the car. "You're not a young man any longer." He raced the engine a little. "Why don't you wear your gloves? Have you lost your gloves?" Walter Mitty reached in a pocket and brought out the gloves. He put them on, but after she had turned and gone into the building and he had driven on to a red light, he took them off again. "Pick it up, brother!" snapped a cop as the light changed, and Mitty hastily pulled on his gloves and lurched ahead. He drove around the streets aimlessly for a time, and then he drove past the hospital on his way to the parking lot.

. . . "It's the millionaire banker, Wellington McMillan," said the pretty nurse. "Yes?" said Walter Mitty, removing his gloves slowly. "Who has the case?" "Dr. Renshaw and Dr. Benbow, but there are two specialists here, Dr. Remington from New York and Mr. Pritchard-Mitford from London. He flew over." A door opened down a long, cool corridor and Dr. Renshaw came out. He looked distraught and haggard. "Hello, Mitty," he said, "We're having the devil's own time with McMillan, the millionaire banker and close personal friend of Roosevelt. Obstreosis of the ductal tract. Tertiary.[1] Wish you'd take a look at him." "Glad to," said Mitty.

In the operating room there were whispered introductions: "Dr. Remington, Dr. Mitty. Mr. Pritchard-Mitford, Dr. Mitty." "I've read your book on streptothricosis," said Pritchard-Mitford, shaking hands. "A brilliant performance, sir." "Thank you," said Walter Mitty. "Didn't know you were in the States, Mitty," grumbled Remington. "Coals to Newcastle, bringing Mitford and me up here for a tertiary." "You are very kind," said Mitty. A huge, complicated machine, connected to the operating table, with many tubes and wires, began at this moment to go pocketa-pocketa-pocketa. "The new anesthetizer is giving way!" shouted an intern. "There is no one in the East who knows how to fix it!" "Quiet, man!" said Mitty, in a low, cool voice. He sprang to the machine, which was now going pocketa-pocketa-queep-pocketa-queep. He began fingering delicately a row of glistening dials. "Give me a fountain pen!" he snapped. Someone handed him a fountain pen. He pulled a faulty piston out of the machine and inserted the pen in its place. "That will hold for ten minutes," he said. "Get on with the operation." A nurse hurried over and whispered to Renshaw, and Mitty saw the man turn pale. "Coreopsis has set in," said Renshaw nervously. "If you would take over, Mitty?" Mitty looked at him and at the craven figure of Benbow, who drank, and at the grave, uncertain faces of the two great specialists. "If you wish," he said. They slipped a white gown on him; he adjusted a

1. *Obstreosis of the ductal tract. Tertiary.* The diagnosis that the imaginary Dr. Renshaw is giving to Walter Mitty is complete nonsense.

mask and drew on thin gloves; nurses handed him shining . . .

"Back it up, Mac! Look out for that Buick!" Walter Mitty jammed on the brakes. "Wrong lane, Mac," said the parking-lot attendant, looking at Mitty closely. "Gee. Yeh," muttered Mitty. He began cautiously to back out of the lane marked "Exit Only." "Leave her sit there," said the attendant. "I'll put her away." Mitty got out of the car. "Hey, better leave the key." "Oh," said Mitty, handing the man the ignition key. The attendant vaulted into the car, backed it up with insolent skill, and put it where it belonged.

They're so damn cocky, thought Walter Mitty, walking along Main Street; they think they know everything. Once he had tried to take his chains off, outside New Milford, and he had got them wound around the axles. A man had had to come out in a wrecking car and unwind them, a young, grinning garageman. Since then Mrs. Mitty always made him drive to a garage to have the chains taken off. The next time, he thought, I'll wear my right arm in a sling; they won't grin at me then. I'll have my right arm in a sling and they'll see I couldn't possibly take the chains off myself. He kicked at the slush on the sidewalk. "Overshoes," he said to himself, and he began looking for a shoe store.

When he came out into the street again, with the overshoes in a box under his arm,

THE MAGAZINE IN AMERICA

The New Yorker

A nineteenth-century dandy, peering through his monocle at a butterfly, graced the first cover of the New Yorker. This is Eustace Tilley, the symbol of the magazine. Like him in sophistication, the New Yorker has followed a unique way of observing the passing scene since 1925 with great success.

The New Yorker is a reflection of the urbane life of America's largest city, yet seventy per cent of its readers live far from the glimmering lights of Manhattan. How does the weekly attract such a widespread and devoted audience? If we examine the staff-written portions of the magazine, we find, first of all, that the New Yorker is informative. Week after week, its calendar of events, its letters from foreign capitals, and such timely departments as "Books," "The Current Cinema," "Onward and Upward with the Arts," "The Theatre," "Musical Events," and "Football" keep the New Yorker reader abreast of current affairs. A reader may disagree with the New Yorker's opinions and judgments, but he can trust its facts. Secondly, whatever the New Yorker has to say, it says clearly. Each word, sentence, and paragraph is written and edited, rewritten and re-edited until polished to maximum clarity. E. B. White, whom you will meet on page 633, was in charge of "The Talk of the Town" department for eleven years: many of the brief pieces featured there are carefully wrought essays in miniature. Thirdly, the New Yorker's satiric tone appeals to its readers: irony and wit, humor and whimsy, understatement and mockery sparkle from the opening sentence of "Notes and Comments" on through the cartoons and feature articles.

In the New Yorker "Profiles" we may see how these typical ingredients combine to create a different kind of biographical writing. The subject may be a businessman, an entertainer, a politician, a philosopher—or even an airplane such as the DC-3 that E. J. Kahn, Jr. describes in "The Three" (page 614). The facts, both the admirable and the ludicrous, are presented in clearly written prose and touched with irony or wit. Largely staff-written, the "Profiles" may be complete in a single issue or run to several installments. Lillian Ross' 1950 "Profile" of Ernest Hemingway has recently been published separately as Portrait of Hemingway.

The New Yorker usually relies on outside contributors for its cartoons, verse, and short stories: James Thurber was a notable excep-

Walter Mitty began to wonder what the other thing was his wife had told him to get. She had told him twice, before they set out from their house for Waterbury. In a way he hated these weekly trips to town—he was always getting something wrong. Kleenex, he thought, Squibb's, razor blades? No. Toothpaste, toothbrush, bicarbonate, carborundum, initiative and referendum? He gave it up. But she would remember it. "Where's the what's-its-name?" she would ask. "Don't tell me you forgot the what's-its-name." A newsboy went by shouting something about the Waterbury trial. ... "Perhaps this will refresh your memory." The District Attorney suddenly thrust a heavy automatic at the quiet figure on the witness stand. "Have you ever seen this before?" Walter Mitty took the gun and examined it expertly. "This is my Webley-Vickers 50.80," he said calmly. An excited buzz ran around the courtroom. The judge rapped for order. "You are a crack shot with any sort of firearms, I believe?" said the District Attorney, insinuatingly. "Objection!" shouted Mitty's attorney. "We have shown that the defendant could not have fired the shot. We have shown that he wore his right arm in a sling on the night of the fourteenth of July." Walter Mitty raised his hand briefly and the bickering attorneys were stilled. "With any known make of gun," he said evenly, "I could have killed Gregory Fitzhurst at three hundred feet *with my left*

tion, for many of his humorous cartoons and short stories were accepted for publication in the magazine while he was a member of the *New Yorker* staff.

The weekly has done a great deal to popularize the modern short story. In a typical *New Yorker* piece we find the form so characteristic of the twentieth-century story: it may or may not have an apparent beginning or end; the plot is uncontrived and the characters understated; frequently the story lacks a dramatic climax; and, more often than not, the approach is psychological. Yet most of the stories excite and interest the reader who seeks entertainment that is different, stimulating, and unpredictable. Dorothy Parker, James Thurber, Irwin Shaw, and Eudora Welty are writers appearing in this anthology who have contributed short stories to the *New Yorker*.

Eustace Tilley reappears once a year on the *New Yorker* anniversary cover and on the covers of three outstanding short-story collections: *Short Stories from The New Yorker: 1925-1940; 55 Short Stories from The New Yorker: 1940-1950;* and *Stories from The New Yorker: 1950-1960*. Make his acquaintance and you will be rewarded by hours of enjoyable reading.

DRAWING BY REA IRVIN:
COPR. © 1925 1962 THE NEW YORKER MAGAZINE, INC.

hand." Pandemonium broke loose in the court-room. A woman's scream rose above the bed-lam and suddenly a lovely, dark-haired girl was in Walter Mitty's arms. The District Attorney struck at her savagely. Without rising from his chair, Mitty let the man have it on the point of the chin. "You miserable cur!"

"Puppy biscuit," said Walter Mitty. He stopped walking and the buildings of Water-bury rose up out of the misty courtroom and surrounded him again. A woman who was passing laughed. "He said 'Puppy biscuit,'" she said to her companion. "That man said 'Puppy biscuit' to himself." Walter Mitty hurried on. He went into an A. & P., not the first one he came to but a smaller one farther up the street. "I want some biscuit for small, young dogs," he said to the clerk. "Any special brand, sir?" The greatest pistol shot in the world thought a moment. "It says 'Puppies Bark for It' on the box," said Walter Mitty.

His wife would be through at the hair-dresser's in fifteen minutes, Mitty saw in looking at his watch, unless they had trouble drying it; sometimes they had trouble drying it. She didn't like to get to the hotel first; she would want him to be there waiting for her as usual. He found a big leather chair in the lobby, facing a window, and he put the over-shoes and the puppy biscuit on the floor beside it. He picked up an old copy of *Liberty* and sank down into the chair. "Can Germany Conquer the World Through the Air?" Walter Mitty looked at the pictures of bombing planes and of ruined streets.

... "The cannonading has got the wind up in young Raleigh, sir," said the sergeant. Captain Mitty looked up at him through tousled hair. "Get him to bed," he said wearily. "With the others. I'll fly alone." "But you can't, sir," said the sergeant anxiously. "It takes two men to handle that bomber and the Archies are pounding hell out of the air. Von Richtman's circus is between here and Saulier." "Somebody's got to get that ammunition dump," said Mitty. "I'm going over. Spot of brandy?" He poured a drink for the sergeant and one for himself. War thundered and whined around the dugout and battered at the door. There was a rending of wood and

splinters flew through the room. "A bit of a near thing," said Captain Mitty carelessly. "The box barrage is closing in," said the sergeant. "We only live once, Sergeant," said Mitty, with his faint fleeting smile. "Or do we?" He poured another brandy and tossed it off. "I never see a man could hold his brandy like you, sir," said the sergeant. "Begging your pardon, sir." Captain Mitty stood up and strapped on his huge Webley-Vickers auto-matic. "It's forty kilometers through hell, sir," said the sergeant. Mitty finished one last brandy. "After all," he said softly, "what isn't?" The pounding of the cannon increased; there was the rat-tat-tatting of machine guns, and from somewhere came the menacing pocketa-pocketa-pocketa of the new flame throwers. Walter Mitty walked to the door of the dugout humming "Auprès de Ma Blonde."[2] He turned and waved to the sergeant. "Cheerio!" he said....

Something struck his shoulder. "I've been looking all over this hotel for you," said Mrs. Mitty. "Why do you have to hide in this old chair? How did you expect me to find you?" "Things close in," said Walter Mitty vaguely. "What?" Mrs. Mitty said. "Did you get the what's-its-name? The puppy biscuit? What's in that box?" "Overshoes," said Mitty. "Couldn't you have put them on in the store?" "I was thinking," said Walter Mitty. "Does it ever occur to you that I am sometimes thinking?" She looked at him. "I'm going to take your temperature when I get you home," she said.

They went out through the revolving doors that made a faintly derisive whistling sound when you pushed them. It was two blocks to the parking lot. At the drugstore on the corner she said, "Wait here for me. I forgot something. I won't be a minute." She was more than a minute. Walter Mitty lighted a ciga-rette. It began to rain, rain with sleet in it. He stood up against the wall of the drugstore, smoking.... He put his shoulders back and his heels together. "To hell with the hand-kerchief," said Walter Mitty scornfully. He took one last drag on his cigarette and snapped

2. *Auprès de Ma Blonde,* title of a French song, "Near My Blonde."

it away. Then, with that faint, fleeting smile playing about his lips, he faced the firing squad; erect and motionless, proud and disdainful, Walter Mitty the Undefeated, inscrutable to the last.

✿ TO INCREASE UNDERSTANDING

1. (a) What contrast does Thurber draw between Walter and his wife? (b) What character traits do Commander Mitty, Doctor Mitty, and Defendant Mitty have in common? (c) How does the real Walter Mitty differ from them?
2. Walter Mitty has no real knowledge of modern aircraft, medicine, or courtroom procedures. (a) Point out examples in Mitty's daydreams of how knowledge of technical details fails him. (b) What substitutions does he make?
3. Give examples of the way Thurber connects the events of Walter Mitty's real life with the events of his imaginary life.
4. (a) Point out the ways Thurber uses exaggeration and irony to create humor in this story. (b) Do you think most people escape now and again into daydreams? If so, why do you think readers do not resent Thurber's way of making fun of them?
5. Thurber once said that "humor is a kind of emotional chaos told about calmly and in retrospect." Judging from "The Secret Life of Walter Mitty," how does this statement illustrate the way Thurber adapted psychology to his own ends?

Irwin Shaw 1913-

As the twentieth century progressed, an ever greater number of first-rate short-story writers turned to the slice-of-life story in which Sherwood Anderson had pioneered. But unlike Anderson's stories, which often dwelt on the more sordid or pessimistic aspects of life, the stories of these younger writers are often light-hearted. Some of them make extensive use of symbolism; some are ironic in tone, others are nostalgic. But they are alike in avoiding contrived plots and exaggerated dramatic effects. Most of these stories are characterized by wit, sophistication, and a lightness of touch that frequently conceals the painstaking care that has gone into the writing. Because the *New Yorker* magazine has consistently featured stories of this type, they are often referred to as *New Yorker* type stories.

Irwin Shaw's stories have most frequently appeared in the *New Yorker*. Born in Brooklyn in 1913, Shaw began writing while in high school. After graduating from Brooklyn College, where he played quarterback on the varsity football team and wrote a regular column for the college newspaper, he earned his living by writing serial dramatizations of comic strips for radio. His success in this form of writing provided leisure time for writing two plays. One of these, *Bury the Dead* (1936), skyrocketed young Shaw to fame. A protest against war, it came at a time when the threat of World War II was growing more ominous throughout the world.

Shaw next went to Hollywood, where he wrote for the motion-picture industry and began to write short stories. In 1939 his first collection of stories was published under the title *Sailor Off the Bremen*. This was followed by several other collections of short stories. His best-known novel, *The Young Lions* (1948), grew out of his experiences in World War II.

The note of social protest Shaw sounded in his early play, *Bury the Dead*, continues to echo in most of his short stories. In form these stories belong to the sketch-from-life genre, and they feature city smarties, taxi drivers, hooligans, and nagging wives. In theme, form, and characters "The Dry Rock" is typical of Shaw's short stories.

The Dry Rock

We're late," Helen said, as the cab stopped at a light. "We're twenty minutes late." She looked at her husband accusingly.

"All right," Fitzsimmons said. "I couldn't help it. The work was on the desk and it had to ..."

"This is the one dinner party of the year I didn't want to be late for," Helen said. "So naturally ..."

The cab started and was halfway across the street when the Ford sedan roared into it, twisting, with a crashing and scraping of metal, a high mournful scream of brakes, the tinkling of glass. The cab shook a little, then subsided.

The cabby, a little gray man, turned and looked back, worriedly. "Everybody is all right?" he asked nervously.

"Everybody is fine," Helen said bitterly, pulling at her cape to get it straight again after the jolting.

"No damage done," said Fitzsimmons, smiling reassuringly at the cabby, who looked very frightened.

"I am happy to hear that," the cabby said. He got out of his car and stood looking sadly at his fender, now thoroughly crumpled, and his headlight, now without a lens. The door of the Ford opened and its driver sprang out. He was a large young man with a light gray hat. He glanced hurriedly at the cab.

"Why don't yuh watch where the hell yer goin'?" he asked harshly.

"The light was in my favor," said the cabby. He was a small man of fifty, in a cap and ragged coat, and he spoke with a heavy accent. "It turned green and I started across. I would like your license, Mister."

"What for?" the man in the gray hat shouted. "Yer load's all right. Get on yer way. No harm done." He started back to his car.

The cabby gently put his hand on the young man's arm. "Excuse me, friend," he said. "It is a five-dollar job, at least. I would like to see your license."

The young man pulled his arm away, glared at the cabby. "Aaah," he said and swung. His fist made a loud, surprising noise against the cabby's nose. The old man sat down slowly on the running board of his cab, holding his head wearily in his hands. The young man in the gray hat stood over him, bent over, fists still clenched. "Didn't I tell yuh no harm was done?" he shouted. "Why didn't yuh lissen t' me? I got a good mind to ..."

"Now, see here," Fitzsimmons said, opening the rear door and stepping out.

"What d'you want?" The young man turned and snarled at Fitzsimmons, his fists held higher. "Who asked for you?"

"I saw the whole thing," Fitzsimmons began, "and I don't think you ..."

"Aaah," snarled the young man. "Dry up."

"Claude," Helen called. "Claude, keep out of this."

"Claude," the young man repeated balefully. "Dry up, Claude."

"Are you all right?" Fitzsimmons asked, bending over the cabby, who still sat reflectively on the running board, his head down, his old and swollen cap hiding his face, blood trickling down his clothes.

"I'm all right," the cabby said wearily. He stood up, looked wonderingly at the young man. "Now, my friend, you force me to make trouble. Police!" he called, loudly. "Police!"

"Say, lissen," the man in the gray hat shouted. "What the hell do yuh need to call the cops for? Hey, cut it out!"

"Police!" the old cabby shouted calmly, but with fervor deep in his voice. "Police!"

"I ought to give it to yuh good." The young man shook his fist under the cabby's nose. He jumped around nervously. "This is a small matter," he shouted, "nobody needs the cops!"

"Police!" called the cabby.

"Claude," Helen put her head out the window. "Let's get out of here and let the two gentlemen settle this any way they please."

"I apologize!" The young man held the cabby by his lapels with both large hands,

---

"The Dry Rock" from *Mixed Company* by Irwin Shaw. Copyright 1941 by Irwin Shaw. Reprinted by permission of Random House, Inc., New York, and Jonathan Cape Ltd., London.

shook him, to emphasize his apology. "Excuse me. I'm sorry. Stop yelling police," he shouted.

"I'm going to have you locked up," the cabby said. He stood there, slowly drying the blood off his shabby coat with his cap. His hair was gray, but long and full, like a musician's. He had a big head for his little shoulders, and a sad, lined little face and he looked older than fifty, to Fitzsimmons, and very poor, neglected, badly nourished. "You have committed a crime," the cabby said, "and there is a punishment for it."

"Will yuh talk to him?" The young man turned savagely to Fitzsimmons. "Will yuh tell him I'm sorry?"

"It's entirely up to him," Fitzsimmons said.

"We're a half hour late," Helen announced bitterly. "The perfect dinner guests."

"It is not enough to be sorry," said the cab driver. "Police . . ."

"Say, listen, Bud," the young man said, his voice quick and confidential, "what's yer name?"

"Leopold Tarloff," the cabby said. "I have been driving a cab on the streets of New York for twenty years, and everybody thinks just because you're a cab driver they can do whatever they want to you."

"Lissen, Leopold," the young man pushed his light gray hat far back on his head. "Let's be sensible. I hit yer cab. All right. I hit you. All right."

"What's all right about it?" Tarloff asked.

"What I mean is, I admit it, I confess I did it, that's what I mean. All right." The young man grabbed Tarloff's short ragged arms as he spoke, intensely. "Why the fuss? It happens every day. Police are unnecessary. I'll tell yuh what I'll do with yuh, Leopold. Five dollars, yuh say, for the fender. All right. And for the bloody nose, another pound. What do yuh say? Everybody is satisfied. Yuh've made yerself a fiver on the transaction; these good people go to their party without no more delay."

Tarloff shook his arms free from the huge hands of the man in the gray hat. He put his head back and ran his fingers through his thick hair and spoke coldly. "I don't want to hear another word. I have never been so insulted in my whole life."

The young man stepped back, his arms wide, palms up wonderingly. "I insult him!" He turned to Fitzsimmons. "Did you hear me insult this party?" he asked.

"Claude!" Helen called. "Are we going to sit here all night?"

"A man steps up and hits me in the nose," Tarloff said. "He thinks he makes everything all right with five dollars. He is mistaken. Not with five hundred dollars."

"How much d'yuh think a clap in the puss is worth?" the young man growled. "Who d'yuh think y'are—Joe Louis?"[1]

"Not ten thousand dollars," Tarloff said, on the surface calm, but quivering underneath. "Not for twenty thousand dollars. My dignity."

"His dignity!"

"What do you want to do?" Fitzsimmons asked, conscious of Helen glooming in the rear seat of the cab.

"I would like to take him to the station house and make a complaint," Tarloff said. "You would have to come with me, if you'd be so kind. What is your opinion on the matter?"

"Will yuh tell him the cops are not a necessity!" the young man said hoarsely. "Will yuh tell the bum?"

"Claude!" called Helen.

"It's up to you," Fitzsimmons said, looking with what he hoped was an impartial, judicious expression at Tarloff, hoping he wouldn't have to waste any more time. "You do what you think you ought to do."

Tarloff smiled, showing three yellow teeth in the front of his small and childlike mouth, curved and red and surprising in the lined and weather-beaten old hackie's face. "Thank you very much," he said. "I am glad to see you agree with me."

Fitzsimmons sighed.

"Yer drivin' me crazy!" the young man shouted at Tarloff. "Yer makin' life impossible!"

"To you," Tarloff said with dignity, "I talk from now on only in a court of law. That's my last word."

The young man stood there, breathing

---

1. *Joe Louis,* American boxer, world's heavyweight champion from 1937 to 1949.

heavily, his fists clenching and unclenching, his pale gray hat shining in the light of a street lamp. A policeman turned the corner, walking in a leisurely and abstract manner, his eyes on the legs of a girl across the street.

Fitzsimmons went over to him. "Officer," he said, "there's a little job for you over here." The policeman regretfully took his eyes off the girl's legs and sighed and walked slowly over to where the two cars were still nestling against each other.

"What are yuh?" the young man was asking Tarloff, when Fitzsimmons came up with the policeman. "Yuh don't act like an American citizen. What are yuh?"

"I'm a Russian," Tarloff said. "But I'm in the country twenty-five years now, I know what the rights of an individual are."

"Yeah," said the young man hopelessly. "Yeah . . ."

The Fitzsimmonses drove silently to the police station in the cab, with Tarloff driving slowly and carefully, though with hands that shook on the wheel. The policeman drove with the young man in the young man's Ford. Fitzsimmons saw the Ford stop at the cigar store and the young man jump out and go into the store, into a telephone booth.

"For three months," Helen said, as they drove, "I've been trying to get Adele Lowrie to invite us to dinner. Now we've finally managed it. Perhaps we ought to call her and invite the whole party down to night court."

"It isn't night court," Fitzsimmons said patiently. "It's a police station. And I think you might take it a little better. After all, the poor old man has no one else to speak up for him."

"Leopold Tarloff," Helen said. "It sounds impossible. Leopold Tarloff. Leopold Tarloff."

They sat in silence until Tarloff stopped the cab in front of the police station and opened the door for them. The Ford with the policeman and the young man drove up right behind them and they all went in together.

There were some people up in front of the desk lieutenant, a dejected-looking man with long mustaches and a loud, blonde woman who kept saying that the man had threatened her with a baseball bat three times that eve-

ning. Two Negroes with bloody bandages around their heads were waiting, too.

"It will take some time," said the policeman. "There are two cases ahead of you. My name is Kraus."

"Oh, my," said Helen.

"You'd better call Adele," Fitzsimmons said. "Tell her not to hold dinner for us."

Helen held her hand out gloomily for nickels.

"I'm sorry," Tarloff said anxiously, "to interrupt your plans for the evening."

"Perfectly all right," Fitzsimmons said, trying to screen his wife's face from Tarloff by bending over to search for the nickels in his pocket.

Helen went off, disdainfully holding her long formal skirt up with her hand, as she walked down the spit- and butt-marked corridor of the police station toward a pay telephone. Fitzsimmons reflectively watched her elegant back retreat down the hallway.

"I am tired," Tarloff said. "I think I will have to sit down, if you will excuse me." He sat on the floor, looking up with a frail, apologetic smile on his red face worn by wind and rain and traffic policemen. Fitzsimmons suddenly felt like crying, watching the old man sitting there among the spit and cigarette butts, on the floor against the wall, with his cap off and his great bush of musician's gray hair giving the lie to the tired, weathered face below it.

Four men threw open the outside doors and walked into the police station with certainty and authority. They all wore the same light-gray hats with the huge flat brims. The young man who had hit Tarloff greeted them guardedly. "I'm glad you're here, Pidgear," he said to the man who, by some subtle mixture of stance and clothing, of lift of eyebrow and droop of mouth, announced himself as leader.

They talked swiftly and quietly in a corner.

"A Russian!" Pidgear's voice rang out angrily. "There are 10,000 cab drivers in the metropolitan area, you have to pick a Russian to punch in the nose!"

"I'm excitable!" the young man yelled. "Can I help it if I'm excitable? My father was the same way; it's a family characteristic."

"Go tell that to the Russian," Pidgear said. He went over to one of the three men who had come with him, a large man who needed a shave and whose collar was open at the throat, as though no collar could be bought large enough to go all the way around that neck. The large man nodded, went over to Tarloff still sitting patiently against the wall.

"You speak Russian?" the man with the open collar said to Tarloff.

"Yes, sir," Tarloff said.

The large man sat down slowly beside him, gripped Tarloff's knee confidentially in his tremendous hairy hand, spoke excitedly, winningly, in Russian.

Pidgear and the young man who had hit Tarloff came over to Fitzsimmons, leaving the other two men in the gray hats, small, dark men with shining eyes, who just stood at the door and looked hotly on.

"My name is Pidgear," the man said to Fitzsimmons, who by now was impressed with the beautiful efficiency of the system that had been put into motion by the young driver of the Ford—an obviously legal mind like Pidgear's, a man who spoke Russian, and two intense men with gray hats standing on call just to see justice done, and all collected in the space of fifteen minutes. "Alton Pidgear," the man said, smiling professionally at Fitzsimmons. "I represent Mr. Rusk."

"Yeah," said the young man.

"My name is Fitzsimmons."

"Frankly, Mr. Fitzsimmons," Pidgear said, "I would like to see you get Mr. Tarloff to call this whole thing off. It's an embarrassing affair for all concerned; nobody stands to gain anything by pressing it."

Helen came back and Fitzsimmons saw by the expression on her face that she wasn't happy. "They're at the soup by now," she said loudly to Fitzsimmons. "Adele said for us to take all the time we want, they're getting along fine."

"Mr. Rusk is willing to make a handsome offer," Pidgear said. "Five dollars for the car, five dollars for the nose . . ."

"Go out to dinner with your husband," Helen muttered, "and you wind up in a tele-phone booth in a police station. 'Excuse me for being late, darling, but I'm calling from the 8th precinct, this is our night for street fighting.'"

"Sssh, Helen, please," Fitzsimmons said. He hadn't eaten since nine that morning and his stomach was growling with hunger.

"It was all a mistake," Pidgear said smoothly. "A natural mistake. Why should the man be stubborn? He is being reimbursed for everything, isn't he? I wish you would talk to him, Mr. Fitzsimmons; we don't want to keep you from your social engagements. Undoubtedly," Pidgear said, eyeing their evening clothes respectfully, "you and the madam were going to an important dinner party. It would be too bad to spoil an important dinner party for a little thing like this. Why, this whole affair is niggling," he said, waving his hand in front of Fitzsimmons' face. "Absolutely, niggling."

Fitzsimmons looked over to where Tarloff and the other Russian were sitting on the floor. From Tarloff's face and gestures, even though he was talking in deepest Russian, Fitzsimmons could tell Tarloff was still as firm as ever. Fitzsimmons looked closely at Rusk, who was standing looking at Tarloff through narrow, baleful eyes.

"Why're you so anxious?" Fitzsimmons asked.

Rusk's eyes clouded over and his throat throbbed against his collar with rage. "I don't want to appear in court!" he yelled. "I don't want the whole damn business to start all over again, investigation, lawyers, fingerprints . . ."

Pidgear punched him savagely in the ribs, his fist going a short distance, but with great violence.

"Why don't you buy time on the National Broadcasting System?" Pidgear asked. "Make an address, coast to coast!"

Rusk glared murderously for a moment at Pidgear, then leaned over toward Fitzsimmons, pointing a large blunt finger at him. "Do I have to put my finger in your mouth?" he whispered hoarsely.

"What does he mean by that?" Helen asked loudly. "Put his finger in your mouth? Why should he put his finger in your mouth?"

Rusk looked at her with complete hatred, turned, too full for words, and stalked away, with Pidgear after him. The two little men in the gray hats watched the room without moving.

"Claude?" Helen began.

"Obviously," Fitzsimmons said, his voice low, "Mr. Rusk isn't anxious for anyone to look at his fingerprints. He's happier this way."

"You picked a fine night!" Helen shook her head sadly. "Why can't we just pick up and get out of here?"

Rusk, with Pidgear at his side, strode back. He stopped in front of the Fitzsimmonses. "I'm a family man," he said, trying to sound like one. "I ask yuh as a favor. Talk to the Russian."

"I had to go to Bergdorf Goodman,"[2] Helen said, too deep in her own troubles to bother with Rusk, "to get a gown to spend the evening in a police station. 'Mrs. Claude Fitzsimmons was lovely last night in blue velvet and silver fox at Officer Kraus' reception at the 8th precinct. Other guests were the well-known Leopold Tarloff, and the Messrs. Pidgear and Rusk, in gray hats. Other guests included the Russian ambassador and two leading Italian artillerymen, also in gray hats.'"

Pidgear laughed politely. "Your wife is a very witty woman," he said.

"Yes," said Fitzsimmons, wondering why he'd married her.

"Will yuh just *ask*?" Rusk demanded. "Can it hurt yuh?"

"We're willing to do our part," Pidgear said. "We even brought down a Russian to talk to him and clear up any little points in his own language. No effort is too great."

Fitzsimmons' stomach growled loudly. "Haven't eaten all day," he said, embarrassed.

"That's what happens," Pidgear said. "Naturally."

"Yeah," said Rusk.

"Perhaps I should go out and get you a malted milk," Helen suggested coldly.

Fitzsimmons went over to where Tarloff was sitting with the other Russian. The others followed him.

"Are you sure, Mr. Tarloff," Fitzsimmons said, "that you still want to prosecute?"

"Yes," Tarloff said promptly.

"Ten dollars," Rusk said. "I offer yuh ten dollars. Can a man do more?"

"Money is not the object." With his cap Tarloff patted his nose, which was still bleeding slowly and had swelled enormously, making Tarloff look lopsided and monstrous.

"What's the object?" Rusk asked.

"The object, Mr. Rusk, is principle."

"*You* talk to him," Rusk said to Fitzsimmons.

"All right," Officer Kraus said, "you can go up there now."

They all filed in in front of the lieutenant sitting high at his desk.

Tarloff told his story, the accident, the wanton punch in the nose.

"It's true," Pidgear said, "that there was an accident, that there was a slight scuffle after by mistake. But the man isn't hurt. A little swelling in the region of the nose. No more." He pointed dramatically to Tarloff.

"Physically," Tarloff said, clutching his cap, talking with difficulty because his nose was clogged, "physically that's true. I am not badly hurt. But in a mental sense . . ." He shrugged. "I have suffered an injury."

"Mr. Rusk is offering the amount of ten dollars," Pidgear said. "Also, he apologizes; he's sorry."

The lieutenant looked wearily down at Rusk. "Are you sorry?" he asked.

"I'm sorry," said Rusk, raising his right hand. "On the Bible, I swear I'm sorry."

"Mr. Tarloff," the lieutenant said, "if you wish to press charges there are certain steps you will have to take. A deposition will have to be taken. Have you got witnesses?"

"Here," Tarloff said with a shy smile at the Fitzsimmonses.

"They will have to be present," the lieutenant said sleepily.

"Oh, great," Helen said.

"A warrant will have to be sworn out, there must be a hearing at which the witnesses must also be present . . ."

---

2. *Bergdorf Goodman*, a specialty store in New York City.

"Oh, great," Helen said.

"Then the trial," said the lieutenant.

"Great!" Helen said loudly.

"The question is, Mr. Tarloff," said the lieutenant, yawning, "are you willing to go through all that trouble?"

"The fact is," Tarloff said unhappily, "he hit me in the head without provocation. He is guilty of a crime on my person. He insulted me. He did me an injustice. The law exists for such things. One individual is not to be hit by another individual in the streets of the city without legal punishment." Tarloff was using his hands to try to get everyone, the Fitzsimmonses, the lieutenant, Pidgear, to understand. "There is a principle. The dignity of the human body. Justice. For a bad act a man suffers. It's an important thing . . ."

"I'm excitable," Rusk shouted. "If yuh want, yuh can hit me in the head."

"That is not the idea," Tarloff said.

"The man is sorry," the lieutenant said, wiping his eyes, "he is offering you the sum of ten dollars; it will be a long, hard job to bring this man to trial; it will cost a lot of the taxpayers' money; you are bothering these good people here who have other things to do. What is the sense in it, Mr. Tarloff?"

Tarloff scraped his feet slowly on the dirty floor, looked sadly, hopefully, at Fitzsimmons. Fitzsimmons looked at his wife, who was glaring at Tarloff, tapping her foot sharply again and again. Fitzsimmons looked back at Tarloff, standing there, before the high desk, small, in his ragged coat and wild gray hair, his little worn face twisted and grotesque with the swollen nose, his eyes lost and appealing. Fitzsimmons shrugged sadly. Tarloff drooped inside his old coat, shook his head wearily, shrugged, deserted once and for all before the lieutenant's desk, on the dry rock of principle.

"OK," he said.

"Here," Rusk brought the ten-dollar bill out with magical speed.

Tarloff pushed it away. "Get out of here," he said, without looking up.

No one talked all the way to Adele Lowrie's house. Tarloff opened the door and sat, looking straight ahead, while they got out. Helen went to the door of the house and rang. Silently, Fitzsimmons offered Tarloff the fare. Tarloff shook his head. "You have been very good," he said. "Forget it."

Fitzsimmons put the money away slowly.

"Claude!" Helen called. "The door's open."

Fitzsimmons hated his wife, suddenly, without turning to look at her. He put out his hand and Tarloff shook it wearily.

"I'm awfully sorry," Fitzsimmons said. "I wish I . . ."

Tarloff shrugged. "That's all right," he said. "I understand." His face, in the shabby light of the cab, worn and old and battered by the streets of the city, was a deep well of sorrow. "There is no time. Principle." He laughed, shrugged. "Today there is no time for anything."

He shifted gears and the taxi moved slowly off, its motor grinding noisily.

"Claude!" Helen called.

"Oh, shut up!" Fitzsimmons said as he turned and walked into Adele Lowrie's house.

TO INCREASE UNDERSTANDING

1. Since "The Dry Rock" is told from the objective point of view, the speech of various individuals is extremely important in establishing character. (a) Describe the speech of Rusk, Tarloff, Fitzsimmons, and Helen. (b) With which character are you most sympathetic? Why? (c) List the other characters mentioned in order of the sympathy you feel for each, ending with the least sympathetic character. (d) Explain why recognizing sympathetic and unsympathetic characters is important in understanding a story.

2. (a) Relate the speech of each character to the details Shaw gives about the appearance, dress, and manner of each. (b) How do such details strengthen the impression created by the characters' speech?

3. (a) State the theme of "The Dry Rock." (b) Describe the conflicts developed in the story. (c) How does each conflict underscore Shaw's theme?

4. Do you think that the characters in this story are used symbolically? Explain.

5. In the biography of Shaw you read that his stories often sound a "note of social protest." (a) What is Shaw protesting against in "The Dry Rock"? (b) Explain why you approve or disapprove of this protest.

One of the outstanding characteristics of modern short stories is the indirect way they are told. To a greater extent than their predecessors, modern writers *suggest* or *imply* more than they *tell*. You will remember how earlier short-story writers like Irving and Hawthorne told you directly how their characters felt, and how they frequently interrupted their narratives to comment on the significance of events. But a modern writer, like Irwin Shaw, is more apt to *show* you how a character feels and to let events speak for themselves. This technique makes a great demand on the reader to grasp an author's *implications*. In brief and tightly written stories a reader must be able to infer character traits, conflict, and even theme from sparse details.

Reread the first three paragraphs of "The Dry Rock" (page 504). The dialogue states that a man and his wife are late for a dinner party. The characters are named; the immediate setting is a taxicab. But much more is implied. From what Helen says and how she says it, we may infer that she is an impatient social-climber. From what Fitzsimmons says, we may infer that he is a rather harried business man who attaches less importance to the dinner party than his wife does, but who, nevertheless, is anxious to placate her. We also detect the first clues to the conflict that will develop between them.

Review the characterizations of Helen and Fitzsimmons in "The Dry Rock," and trace the implications that provide important clues to their traits and to the nature of their conflict. Is the characterization of Tarloff more or less dependent upon implication than the characterization of Helen? Explain.

How much of the theme of "The Dry Rock" were you able to infer before reading that Tarloff was "deserted on the dry rock of principle"? Was this summation necessary to your understanding? Explain.

Your pleasure in reading will be greatly enhanced as your skill to draw inferences improves. You will remember, for example, how many "countries" a competent critic could infer from Hemingway's "In Another Country" (question 1, page 466). This ability to recognize implications will stand you in good stead when you read William Faulkner's short story, "The Bear" (page 521).

Ray Bradbury 1920-

The explosion of the first atomic bomb in 1945 marks the beginning of the great popularity of modern science fiction. Back in the early nineteenth century Edgar Allan Poe had introduced certain elements of this type of fiction. In the intervening years other writers occasionally turned out "thrillers" about superhuman adventures, life on other planets, and machines which developed mental faculties and threatened mankind. In the past twenty years increased scientific knowledge and the race among nations to conquer outer space have turned many writers to science fiction.

Ray Bradbury stands high among science-fiction writers. He was born in Waukegan, Illinois, in 1920, but moved with his family to Los Angeles, where he attended high school. There he joined the Science-Fantasy Society and began to write fiction. After graduation he worked at jobs that allowed sufficient spare time for writing. Soon his stories began to appear in the annual *Best American Short Stories* and *O. Henry Memorial Award Prize Stories*. His first collection of short stories, *Dark Carnival* (1947), was followed by several other collections of short stories and several novels.

Bradbury's science fiction combines fantasy with a logical or mathematical projection of reality. Blending delicate imagination with serious thought on man's probable life in an unknown future, he often produces stories with a high degree of artistic unity. Often the purpose of these stories is to show man how he can utterly destroy himself if he fails to use science and technology for the common good.

There Will Come Soft Rains

The house was a good house and had been planned and built by the people who were to live in it, in the year 1980. The house was like many another house in that year; it fed and slept and entertained its inhabitants, and made a good life for them. The man and wife and their two children lived at ease there, and lived happily, even while the world trembled. All of the fine things of living, the warm things, music and poetry, books that talked, beds that warmed and made themselves, fires that built themselves in the fireplaces of evenings, were in this house, and living there was a contentment.

And then one day the world shook and there was an explosion followed by ten thousand explosions and red fire in the sky and a rain of ashes and radioactivity, and the happy time was over.

In the living room the voice-clock sang, *Tick-tock, seven* A.M. *o'clock, time to get up!* as if it were afraid nobody would. The house lay empty. The clock talked on into the empty morning.

The kitchen stove sighed and ejected from its warm interior eight eggs, sunny side up, twelve bacon slices, two coffees, and two cups of hot cocoa. *Seven nine, breakfast time, seven nine.*

"Today is April 28th, 1985," said a phonograph voice in the kitchen ceiling. "Today, remember, is Mr. Featherstone's birthday. Insurance, gas, light, and water bills are due."

Somewhere in the walls, relays clicked, memory tapes glided under electric eyes. Recorded voices moved beneath steel needles:

Eight one, run, run, off to school, off to work, run, run, tick-tock, eight one o'clock!

But no doors slammed, no carpets took the quick tread of rubber heels. Outside, it was raining. The voice of the weather box on the front door sang quietly: "Rain, rain, go away, rubbers, raincoats for today." And the rain tapped on the roof.

At eight thirty the eggs were shriveled. An aluminum wedge scraped them into the sink, where hot water whirled them down a metal throat which digested and flushed them away to the distant sea.

Nine fifteen, sang the clock, *time to clean.*

Out of warrens in the wall, tiny mechanical mice darted. The rooms were acrawl with the small cleaning animals, all rubber and metal. They sucked up the hidden dust, and popped back in their burrows.

Ten o'clock. The sun came out from behind the rain. The house stood alone on a street where all the other houses were rubble and ashes. At night, the ruined town gave off a radioactive glow which could be seen for miles.

Ten fifteen. The garden sprinkler filled the soft morning air with golden fountains. The water tinkled over the charred west side of the house where it had been scorched evenly free of its white paint. The entire face of the house was black, save for five places. Here, the silhouette, in paint, of a man mowing a lawn. Here, a woman bent to pick flowers. Still farther over, their images burned on wood in one titanic instant, a small boy, hands flung in the air—higher up, the image of a thrown ball—and opposite him a girl, her hands raised to catch a ball which never came down.

The five spots of paint—the man, the woman, the boy, the girl, the ball—remained. The rest was a thin layer of charcoal.

The gentle rain of the sprinkler filled the garden with falling light.

Until this day, how well the house had kept its peace. How carefully it had asked, "Who goes there?" and getting no reply from rains and lonely foxes and whining cats, it had shut up its windows and drawn the shades. If a sparrow brushed a window, the shade snapped up. The bird, startled, flew off! No, not even an evil bird must touch the house.

And inside, the house was like an altar with nine thousand robot attendants, big and small, servicing, attending, singing in choirs, even though the gods had gone away and the ritual was meaningless.

A dog whined, shivering, on the front porch.

The front door recognized the dog's voice and opened. The dog padded in wearily, thinned to the bone, covered with sores. It tracked mud on the carpet. Behind it whirred the angry robot mice, angry at having to pick up mud and maple leaves, which, carried to the burrows, were dropped down cellar tubes into an incinerator which sat like an evil Baal[1] in a dark corner.

The dog ran upstairs, hysterically yelping at each door. It pawed the kitchen door wildly.

Behind the door, the stove was making pancakes which filled the whole house with their odor.

The dog frothed, ran insanely, spun in a circle, biting its tail, and died.

It lay in the living room for an hour.

One o'clock.

Delicately sensing decay, the regiments of mice hummed out of the walls, soft as blown leaves, their electric eyes blowing.

One fifteen.

The dog was gone.

The cellar incinerator glowed suddenly and a whirl of sparks leaped up the flue.

Two thirty-five.

Bridge tables sprouted from the patio walls. Playing cards fluttered onto pads in a shower of pips. Martinis appeared on an oaken bench.

But the tables were silent, the cards untouched.

At four thirty the tables folded back into the walls.

Five o'clock. The bathtubs filled with clear hot water. A safety razor dropped into a wall-mold, ready.

Six, seven, eight, nine o'clock.

Dinner made, ignored, and flushed away;

dishes washed; and in the study, the tobacco stand produced a cigar, half an inch of gray ash on it, smoking, waiting. The hearth fire bloomed up all by itself, out of nothing.

Nine o'clock. The beds began to warm their hidden circuits, for the night was cool.

A gentle click in the study wall. A voice spoke from above the crackling fireplace:

"Mrs. McClellan, what poem would you like to hear this evening?"

The house was silent.

The voice said, "Since you express no preference, I'll pick a poem at random." Quiet music rose behind the voice. "Sara Teasdale. A favorite of yours, as I recall."

*There will come soft rains and the smell
    of the ground,
And swallows circling with their shimmering
    sound;*

*And frogs in the pools singing at night,
And wild plum-trees in tremulous white.*

*Robins will wear their feathery fire
Whistling their whims on a low fence-wire;*

*And not one will know of the war, not one
Will care at last when it is done.*

*Not one would mind, neither bird nor tree,
If mankind perished utterly:*

*And Spring herself, when she woke at dawn,
Would scarcely know that we were gone.*

The voice finished the poem. The empty chairs faced each other between the silent walls, and the music played.

At ten o'clock, the house began to die.

The wind blew. The bough of a falling tree smashed the kitchen window. Cleaning solvent, bottled, crashed on the stove.

"Fire!" screamed voices. "Fire!" Water pumps shot down water from the ceilings. But the solvent spread under the doors, making fire as it went, while other voices took up the alarm in chorus.

The windows broke with heat and the wind blew in to help the fire. Scurrying water rats,

---

1. *Baal* (bā′əl or bāl), a false god worshiped by the Canaanites of the Old Testament.

their copper wheels spinning, squeaked from the walls, squirted their water, ran for more.

Too late! Somewhere, a pump stopped. The ceiling sprays stopped raining. The reserve water supply, which had filled baths and washed dishes for many silent days, was gone.

The fire crackled upstairs, ate paintings, lay hungrily in the beds! It devoured every room.

The house was shuddering, oak bone on bone, the bared skeleton cringing from the heat, all the wires revealed as if a surgeon had torn the skin off to let the red veins quiver in scalded air. Voices screamed, *"Help, help, fire, run!"* Windows snapped open and shut, like mouths, undecided. *Fire, run!* the voices wailed a tragic nursery rhyme, and the silly Greek chorus faded as the sound-wires popped their sheathings. Ten dozen high, shrieking voices died, as emergency batteries melted.

In the other parts of the house, in the last instant under the fire avalanche, other choruses could be heard announcing the time, the weather, appointments, diets; playing music, reading poetry in the fiery study, while doors opened and slammed and umbrellas appeared at the doors and put themselves away—a thousand things happening, like the interior of a clockshop at midnight, all clocks striking, a merry-go-round of squeaking, whispering, rushing, until all the film spools were burned and fell, and all the wires withered and the circuits cracked.

In the kitchen, an instant before the final collapse, the stove, hysterically hissing, could be seen making breakfasts at a psychopathic rate, ten dozen pancakes, six dozen loaves of toast.

The crash! The attic smashing kitchen down into cellar and subcellar. Deep freeze, armchairs, film tapes, beds, were thrown in a cluttered mound deep under.

Smoke and silence.

Dawn shone faintly in the east. In the ruins, one wall stood alone. Within the wall, a voice said, over and over again and again, even as the sun rose to shine upon the heaped rubble and steam:

"Today is April 29th, 1985. Today is April 29th, 1985. Today is . . ."

 TO INCREASE UNDERSTANDING

1. (*a*) How far into the future has Bradbury projected his story? (*b*) How much time elapses between the beginning and the end of the story? (*c*) In what way does the author use time to unify the story?

2. (*a*) Cite several references that point to the happy time of man before his extinction. (*b*) What changes take place during the course of the story?

3. Bradbury imagines a high degree of automation in the world of tomorrow. (*a*) Cite examples of the advanced technology he describes in future daily living. (*b*) Had the story been written in 1925, do you think it would have seemed more or less fantastical to readers then than it does to readers now? Why? (*c*) How does your answer to the previous question illustrate Bradbury's logical projection of reality in science fiction? (*d*) Why is a degree of reality necessary to successful science fiction?

4. (*a*) From what narrative point of view is the story written? (*b*) Why is this point of view appropriate to the author's purpose?

5. A strong note of irony pervades Bradbury's story. Explain why the following are ironical: (*a*) the mechanical devices that perform human functions; (*b*) the reading of the Teasdale poem; and (*c*) the title.

6. Relate the theme of "There Will Come Soft Rains" to Bradbury's concern about the way men use their scientific knowledge.

 WORDS!

Because scientific words are so much a part of our daily vocabulary, Bradbury can use *robot* and *radioactivity* without defining these words in the context of his story. Many familiar scientific words have interesting derivations. Some are derived from modern languages: *robot*, for example, comes from the Czech word *robotnik* ("serf") and retains much of its original meaning in modern usage. Other words, like *radioactivity*, combine a word element, *radio-* (from the Latin *radius*, "ray or spoke of a wheel") with another word. Still others, like *eclipse* (from the Greek *ekleipsis* "to leave out") are derived from a Latin or a Greek root.

Check a dictionary for the many words which have been derived from combinations of the word element *radio-*.

Explain also the derivation and original meaning of the following scientific words: *atom, petroleum, phosphorus, psychology, telescope, trajectory, missile, astronaut, cyclotron,* and *megaton.*

Eudora Welty 1909-

The twentieth century has been predominantly the age of mass production, the assembly line, and of all the aspects of industrialization that have tended to concentrate large masses of men in crowded cities. In reaction to this urban quality of modern life, a new school of regional writers arose in the 1920's whose chief interest was in portraying men in rural settings. In their use of regional backgrounds and local customs these writers resembled the local-color writers of the late nineteenth century. However, because of their concern with the psychological motivation of character and their tendency to let character rather than plot determine the form of a story, their stories are far different from those of Bret Harte and other writers of the local-color school.

Various parts of the United States are represented in the novels and short stories of the new regionalists. O. E. Rölvaag concerns himself with the effect upon man of hostile nature in pioneer Dakota.[1] William Saroyan (page 56) writes of the Fresno region of California. John Steinbeck rose to fame with his tales of the Salinas Valley region in the same state. It is the South, however, that has produced the greatest wealth of regional literature. William Faulkner (page 519), Robert Penn Warren (page 48), Carson McCullers, Flannery O'Connor, Eudora Welty, and others have

---

1. See the Novel Discussion Guide to *Giants in the Earth*, page 531.

portrayed the South in novels, short stories, and poetry. Many of them have concentrated on the unpleasant and sordid aspects of a society in turmoil after the social and economic upheaval of the Civil War and Reconstruction. Disturbed and angered by apparently insoluble problems, some of these writers have presented distorted and unsympathetic views of the individual and his place in society. Eudora Welty, however, has consistently looked upon her characters with sympathy and has portrayed them in such a way as to show their kinship with people everywhere.

Miss Welty was born in Jackson, Mississippi, and has spent most of her life in her native state. She attended the University of Wisconsin, then went to New York where she studied journalism at Columbia University and wrote publicity, society news, and radio scripts. After returning to Mississippi, she settled down to a career of writing, with gardening, painting, and photography as avocations. Her first volume of short stories, *A Curtain of Green*, was published in 1941. The title story won the O. Henry Memorial Award for that year. Since then she has published several other volumes of short stories and a few novels.

"A Visit of Charity" is from her first collection. It reveals her talent for vivid and unusual characterization and for seemingly effortless but always careful and exact prose. Like an impressionistic painter, she sketches with a minimum of words but grasps the essence of an experience.

A Visit of Charity

It was midmorning—a very cold, bright day. Holding a potted plant before her, a girl of fourteen jumped off the bus in front of the Old Ladies' Home, on the outskirts of town. She wore a red coat, and her straight yellow hair was hanging down loose from the pointed white cap all the little girls were wearing that year. She stopped for a moment beside one of the prickly dark shrubs with which the city had beautified the Home, and then proceeded slowly toward the building, which was of whitewashed brick and reflected the winter sunlight like a block of ice. As she walked vaguely up the steps she shifted the small pot from hand to hand; then she had to set it down and remove her mittens before she could open the heavy door.

"I'm a Campfire Girl. . . . I have to pay a visit to some old lady," she told the nurse at the desk. This was a woman in a white uniform who looked as if she were cold; she had close-cut hair which stood up on the very top of her head exactly like a sea wave. Marian,

the little girl, did not tell her that this visit would give her a minimum of only three points in her score.

"Acquainted with any of our residents?" asked the nurse. She lifted one eyebrow and spoke like a man.

"With any old ladies? No—but—that is, any of them will do," Marian stammered. With her free hand she pushed her hair behind her ears, as she did when it was time to study Science.

The nurse shrugged and rose. "You have a nice *multiflora Cineraria* there," she remarked as she walked ahead down the hall of closed doors to pick out an old lady.

There was loose, bulging linoleum on the floor. Marian felt as if she were walking on the waves, but the nurse paid no attention to it. There was a smell in the hall like the interior of a clock. Everything was silent until, behind one of the doors, an old lady of some kind cleared her throat like a sheep bleating. This decided the nurse. Stopping in her tracks, she first extended her arm, bent her elbow, and leaned forward from the hips—all to examine the watch strapped to her wrist; then she gave a loud double-rap on the door.

"There are two in each room," the nurse remarked over her shoulder.

"Two what?" asked Marian without thinking. The sound like a sheep's bleating almost made her turn around and run back.

One old woman was pulling the door open in short, gradual jerks, and when she saw the nurse a strange smile forced her old face dangerously awry. Marian, suddenly propelled by the strong, impatient arm of the nurse, saw next the sideface of another old woman, even older, who was lying flat in bed with a cap on and a counterpane drawn up to her chin.

"Visitor," said the nurse, and after one more shove she was off up the hall.

Marian stood tongue-tied; both hands held the potted plant. The old woman, still with that terrible, square smile (which was a smile of welcome) stamped on her bony face, was waiting.... Perhaps she said something. The old woman in bed said nothing at all, and she did not look around.

Suddenly Marian saw a hand, quick as a bird claw, reach up in the air and pluck the white cap off her head. At the same time, another claw to match drew her all the way into the room, and the next moment the door closed behind her.

"My, my, my," said the old lady at her side.

Marian stood enclosed by a bed, a washstand, and a chair; the tiny room had altogether too much furniture. Everything smelled wet—even the bare floor. She held onto the back of the chair, which was wicker and felt soft and damp. Her heart beat more and more slowly, her hands got colder and colder, and she could not hear whether the old women were saying anything or not. She could not see them very clearly. How dark it was! The window shade was down, and the only door was shut. Marian looked at the ceiling.... It was like being caught in a robbers' cave, just before one was murdered.

"Did you come to be our little girl for a while?" the first robber asked.

Then something was snatched from Marian's hand—the little potted plant.

"Flowers!" screamed the old woman. She stood holding the pot in an undecided way. "Pretty flowers," she added.

Then the old woman in bed cleared her throat and spoke. "They are not pretty," she said, still without looking around, but very distinctly.

Marian suddenly pitched against the chair and sat down in it.

"Pretty flowers," the first old woman insisted. "Pretty—pretty...."

Marian wished she had the little pot back for just a moment—she had forgotten to look at the plant herself before giving it away. What did it look like?

"Stinkweeds," said the other old woman sharply. She had a bunchy white forehead and red eyes like a sheep. Now she turned them toward Marian. The fogginess seemed to rise in her throat again, and she bleated, "Who—are—you?"

To her surprise, Marian could not remember her name. "I'm a Campfire Girl," she said finally.

"Watch out for the germs," said the old woman like a sheep, not addressing anyone.

"One came out last month to see us," said the first old woman.

A sheep or a germ? wondered Marian dreamily, holding onto the chair.

"Did not!" cried the other old woman.

"Did so! Read to us out of the Bible, and we enjoyed it!" screamed the first.

"Who enjoyed it," said the woman in bed. Her mouth was unexpectedly small and sorrowful, like a pet's.

"We enjoyed it," insisted the other. "You enjoyed it—I enjoyed it."

"We all enjoyed it," said Marian, without realizing that she had said a word.

The first old woman had just finished putting the potted plant high, high on the top of the wardrobe, where it could hardly be seen from below. Marian wondered how she had ever succeeded in placing it there, how she could ever have reached so high.

"You mustn't pay any attention to old Addie," she now said to the little girl. "She's ailing today."

"Will you shut your mouth?" said the woman in bed. "I am not."

"You're a story."

"I can't stay but a minute—really, I can't," said Marian suddenly. She looked down at the wet floor and thought that if she were sick in here they would have to let her go.

With much to-do the first old woman sat down in a rocking chair—still another piece of furniture!—and began to rock. With the fingers of one hand she touched a very dirty cameo pin on her chest. "What do you do at school?" she asked.

"I don't know. . . ." said Marian. She tried to think but she could not.

"Oh, but the flowers are beautiful," the old woman whispered. She seemed to rock faster and faster; Marian did not see how anyone could rock so fast.

"Ugly," said the woman in bed.

"If we bring flowers—" Marian began, and then fell silent. She had almost said that if Campfire Girls brought flowers to the Old Ladies' Home, the visit would count one extra point, and if they took a Bible with them on the bus and read it to the old ladies, it counted double. But the old woman had not listened, anyway; she was rocking and watching the other one, who watched back from the bed.

"Poor Addie is ailing. She has to take medicine—see?" she said, pointing a horny finger at a row of bottles on the table, and rocking so high that her black comfort shoes lifted off the floor like a little child's.

"I am no more sick than you are," said the woman in bed.

"Oh, yes you are!"

"I just got more sense than you have, that's all," said the other old woman, nodding her head.

"That's only the contrary way she talks when *you all* come," said the first old lady with sudden intimacy. She stopped the rocker with a neat pat of her feet and leaned toward Marian. Her hand reached over—it felt like a petunia leaf, clinging and just a little sticky.

"Will you hush! Will you hush!" cried the other one.

Marian leaned back rigidly in her chair.

"When I was a little girl like you, I went to school and all," said the old woman in the same intimate, menacing voice. "Not here—another town. . . ."

"Hush!" said the sick woman. "You never went to school. You never came and you never went. You never were anything—only here. You never were born! You don't know anything. Your head is empty, your heart and hands and your old black purse are all empty, even that little old box that you brought with you, you brought empty—you showed it to me. And yet you talk, talk, talk, talk, talk all the time until I think I'm losing my mind! Who are you? You're a stranger—a perfect stranger! Don't you know you're a stranger? Is it possible that they have actually done a thing like this to anyone—sent them in a stranger to talk, and rock, and tell away her whole long rigmarole? Do they seriously suppose that I'll be able to keep it up, day in, day out, night in, night out, living in the same room with a terrible old woman—forever?"

Marian saw the old woman's eyes grow bright and turn toward her. This old woman was looking at her with despair and calculation in her face. Her small lips suddenly dropped apart, and exposed a half circle of false teeth with tan gums.

"Come here, I want to tell you something," she whispered. "Come here!"

Marian was trembling, and her heart nearly stopped beating altogether for a moment.

"Now, now, Addie," said the first old woman. "That's not polite. Do you know what's really the matter with old Addie today?" She, too, looked at Marian; one of her eyelids drooped low.

"The matter?" the child repeated stupidly. "What's the matter with her?"

"Why, she's mad because it's her birthday!" said the first old woman, beginning to rock again and giving a little crow as though she had answered her own riddle.

"It is not, it is not!" screamed the old woman in bed. "It is not my birthday, no one knows when that is but myself, and will you please be quiet and say nothing more, or I'll go straight out of my mind!" She turned her eyes toward Marian again, and presently she said in the soft, foggy voice, "When the worst comes to the worst, I ring this bell, and the nurse comes." One of her hands was drawn out from under the patched counterpane—a thin little hand with enormous black freckles. With a finger which would not hold still she pointed to a little bell on the table among the bottles.

"How old are you?" Marian breathed. Now she could see the old woman in bed very closely and plainly, and very abruptly, from all sides, as in dreams. She wondered about her—she wondered for a moment as though there was nothing else in the world to wonder about. It was the first time such a thing had happened to Marian.

"I won't tell!"

The old face on the pillow, where Marian was bending over it, slowly gathered and collapsed. Soft whimpers came out of the small open mouth. It was a sheep that she sounded like—a little lamb. Marian's face drew very close, the yellow hair hung forward.

"She's crying!" She turned a bright, burning face up to the first old woman.

"That's Addie for you," the old woman said spitefully.

Marian jumped up and moved toward the door. For the second time, the claw almost touched her hair, but it was not quick enough. The little girl put her cap on.

"Well, it was a real visit," said the old woman, following Marian through the doorway and all the way out into the hall. Then from behind she suddenly clutched the child with her sharp little fingers. In an affected, high-pitched whine she cried, "Oh, little girl, have you a penny to spare for a poor old woman that's not got anything of her own? We don't have a thing in the world—not a penny for candy—not a thing! Little girl, just a nickel—a penny—"

Marian pulled violently against the old hands for a moment before she was free. Then she ran down the hall, without looking behind her and without looking at the nurse, who was reading *Field & Stream* at her desk. The

nurse, after another triple motion to consult her wrist watch, asked automatically the question put to visitors in all institutions: "Won't you stay and have dinner with *us*?"

Marian never replied. She pushed the heavy door open into the cold air and ran down the steps.

Under the prickly shrub she stooped and quickly, without being seen, retrieved a red apple she had hidden there.

Her yellow hair under the white cap, her scarlet coat, her bare knees all flashed in the sunlight as she ran to meet the big bus rocketing through the street.

"Wait for me!" she shouted. As though at an imperial command, the bus ground to a stop.

She jumped on and took a big bite out of the apple.

 TO INCREASE UNDERSTANDING

1. (*a*) Describe Marian's motive in visiting the Old Ladies' Home. (*b*) How does the red apple she retrieves at the conclusion symbolize her attitude during the course of her visit? (*c*) Cite details that make Marian feel she is "caught in a robbers' cave." (*d*) Do you think her attitude toward the two elderly women is typical of a fourteen-year-old girl? Why or why not?

2. (*a*) How does Miss Welty employ contrast to describe the appearance and behavior of the two old women? (*b*) From whose point of view are they described? (*c*) In the eye of the beholder, an old lady's hand is a "claw." Point out other details that show this unsympathetic point of view. (*d*) In contrast, how does the author imply the loneliness and sorry condition of the two women?

3. "A Visit of Charity," like "The Jilting of Granny Weatherall," portrays old age. Which story do you think creates the more sympathetic portrait of the elderly? Why?

4. Miss Welty makes brilliant use of figurative language and imagery to express exactly how the Home and its inhabitants appear to Marian. (*a*) Cite sentences or passages that use these devices. (*b*) Taken together, what atmosphere do they establish? (*c*) Does this atmosphere actually exist in the Home? Explain your answer.

5. What is the theme of the story? Your answer should say something about adolescence, old age, and organized charity.

6. In what way is the title ironic?

William Faulkner 1897-1962

The major influences that have shaped the American short story seem to come more nearly to a focus in the writing of William Faulkner than in that of any other writer today. For sheer horror, many of his stories rival those of Edgar Allan Poe. Like Hawthorne he made frequent use of symbolism and allegory, he probed the shadowy inner world of man, and he often explored the "one idea" which Hawthorne described as running through all his own stories "like an iron rod." Like Bret Harte and the other local colorists, he set his stories in a particular region, in his case in mythical Yoknapatawpha County in the Deep South. His interest in psychology was just as strong as that of Stephen Crane, Sherwood Anderson, and Ernest Hemingway. In fact Sherwood Anderson, with whom Faulkner lived for a while in New Orleans, is credited with encouraging Faulkner to become a writer and with helping him get his first novel published. Yet with all these influences so clearly evident in his writing, Faulkner is one of the most original of American writers—in technique, in style, and in subject matter.

For many years Faulkner's work won little recognition. Among several early novels, only two, *The Sound and the Fury* (1929) and *As I Lay Dying* (1930), won very much praise. *Intruder in the Dust* (1948) and the film version that followed attracted more readers to Faulkner. By 1950 his reputation had become world-wide. In that year he was awarded the Nobel Prize in Literature. Five years later, his novel, *The Fable*, won for him the National Book Award for Fiction and the Pulitzer Prize in Letters.

What is the quality of Faulkner's writing that wins such acclaim? He is by no means easy to read. He makes extensive use of symbolism. His sentences are long and involved. He offends many readers by writing often of degenerate people who lead violent, sordid lives. Perhaps a clue to the high esteem in which his writing is held can be found in his speech in which he accepted the Nobel Prize in 1950. On that occasion he said:

Our tragedy today is a general and universal physical fear so long sustained by now that we can even bear it. There are no longer problems of the spirit. There is only the question: .When will I be blown up? Because of this, the young man or woman writing today has forgotten the problems of the human heart in conflict with itself which alone can make good writing because only that is worth writing about, worth the agony and the sweat.

He must learn them again. He must teach himself that the basest of all things is to be afraid; and, teaching himself that, forget it forever, leaving no room in his workshop for anything but the old verities and truths of the heart, the old universal truths lacking which any story is ephemeral and doomed— love and honor and pity and pride and compassion and sacrifice. . . .

Until he relearns these things, he will write as though he stood and watched the end of man. I decline to accept the end of man . . . I believe that man will not merely endure: he will prevail. He is immortal, not because he alone among creatures has an inexhaustible voice, but because he has a soul, a spirit capable of compassion and sacrifice and endurance. The poet's, the writer's, duty is to write about these things. It is his privilege to help man endure by lifting his heart, by reminding him of the courage and honor and

*Top: Photo on the left
is of Faulkner's home;
the next two are views
of Oxford, county seat
of Lafayette County,
where Faulkner lived.
Bottom: Other scenes
in the northern
Mississippi area, which
suggested to Faulkner
his Yoknapatawpha
County.
Right: William Faulkner.*

hope and pride and compassion and pity and sacrifice which have been the glory of the past. . . .

Faulkner writes of "the problems of the human heart in conflict with itself," of "courage and honor and hope and pride and compassion and pity and sacrifice." He writes of particular people, places, and events, that, through the skill of the author, are yet universal and timeless. They are individual, yet representative. They are imaginary; yet, by virtue of their resemblance to actual people, places, and events, they take us deeper into the real world. The characters are involved in problems like our own; and in their success or failure, joy or sorrow, hope or despair, nobility or base-ness, they illuminate aspects of our own lives and give us a keener aware-ness of ourselves and of the world around us. By writing on these subjects and writing in this way, Faulkner showed how all literature uses things that are seen to make people aware of the unseeable—the things of the mind and spirit.

The following short story is a striking example of Faulkner's skill and power as a writer. He shows us how a teen-age boy relates an exciting experience of his own to one of the great truths of life. Like almost all of Faulkner's stories, it takes place in that mythical county in northern Mississippi, the fictional counterpart of Lafayette County, where Faulkner was born in 1897 and where he lived most of his life.

The Bear

He was ten. But it had already begun, long before that day when at last he wrote his age in two figures and he saw for the first time the camp where his father and Major de Spain and old General Compson and the others spent two weeks each November and two weeks again each June. He had already inherited then, without ever having seen it, the tremendous bear with one trap-ruined foot which, in an area almost a hundred miles deep, had earned for itself a name, a definite designation like a living man.

He had listened to it for years: the long legend of corncribs rifled, of shoats and grown pigs and even calves carried bodily into the woods and devoured, of traps and deadfalls overthrown and dogs mangled and slain, and shotgun and even rifle charges delivered at point-blank range and with no more effect than so many peas blown through a tube by a boy—a corridor of wreckage and destruction beginning back before he was born, through which sped, not fast but rather with the ruth-less and irresistible deliberation of a locomo-tive, the shaggy tremendous shape.

It ran in his knowledge before ever he saw it. It looked and towered in his dreams before he even saw the unaxed woods where it left its crooked print, shaggy, huge, red-eyed, not malevolent but just big—too big for the dogs which tried to bay it, for the horses which tried to ride it down, for the men and the bul-lets they fired into it, too big for the very country which was its constricting scope. He seemed to see it entire with a child's complete divination before he ever laid eyes on either— the doomed wilderness whose edges were being constantly and punily gnawed at by men with axes and plows who feared it be-cause it was wilderness, men myriad and nameless even to one another in the land where the old bear had earned a name, through which ran not even a mortal animal but an anachronism, indomitable and invincible, out of an old dead time, a phantom, epitome and apotheosis of the old wild life at which the puny humans swarmed and hacked in a fury of abhorrence and fear, like pygmies about the ankles of a drowsing elephant: the old bear solitary, indomitable and alone, widowered, childless, and absolved of mortality—old Priam[1] reft of his old wife and having outlived all his sons.

Until he was ten, each November he would watch the wagon containing the dogs and the bedding and food and guns and his father and Tennie's Jim, the Negro, and Sam Fathers, the Indian, son of a slave woman and a Chickasaw chief, depart on the road to town, to Jefferson where Major de Spain and the others would join them. To the boy, at seven, eight, and nine, they were not going into the Big Bottom to hunt bear and deer, but to keep yearly rendezvous with the bear which they did not even intend to kill. Two weeks later they would return, with no trophy, no head and skin. He had not expected it. He had not even been afraid it would be in the wagon. He believed that even after he was ten and his father would let him go too, for those two weeks in November, he would merely make another one, along with his father and Major de Spain and General Compson and the others, the dogs which feared to bay at it and the rifles and shotguns which failed even to bleed it, in the yearly pageant of the old bear's furious immortality.

Then he heard the dogs. It was in the second week of his first time in the camp. He stood with Sam Fathers against a big oak beside the faint crossing where they had stood each dawn for nine days now, hearing the dogs. He had heard them once before, one morning last week—a murmur, sourceless, echoing through the wet woods, swelling presently into separate voices which he could recognize and call by name. He had raised and cocked the gun as Sam told him and stood motionless again while the uproar, the invisible course, swept up and past and faded; it seemed to him that he could actually see the deer, the buck, blond, smoke-colored, elongated with speed, fleeing, vanishing, the woods, the gray solitude, still ringing even when the cries of the dogs had died away.

"Now let the hammers down," Sam said.

"You knew they were not coming here too," he said.

"Yes," Sam said. "I want you to learn how to do when you didn't shoot. It's after the chance for the bear or the deer has done already come and gone that men and dogs get killed."

"Anyway," he said, "it was just a deer."

Then on the tenth morning he heard the dogs again. And he readied the too-long, too-heavy gun as Sam had taught him, before Sam even spoke. But this time it was no deer, no ringing chorus of dogs running strong on a free scent, but a moiling yapping an octave too high, with something more than indecision and even abjectness in it, not even moving very fast, taking a long time to pass completely out of hearing, leaving them somewhere in the air that echo, thin, slightly hysterical, abject, almost grieving, with no sense of a fleeing, unseen, smoke-colored, grass-eating shape ahead of it, and Sam, who had taught him first of all to cock the gun and take position where he could see everywhere and then never move again, had himself moved up beside him; he could hear Sam breathing at his shoulder and he could see the arched curve of the old man's inhaling nostrils.

"Hah," Sam said. "Not even running. Walking."

"Old Ben!" the boy said. "But up here!" he cried. "Way up here!"

"He do it every year," Sam said. "Once. Maybe to see who in camp this time, if he can shoot or not. Whether we got the dog yet that can bay and hold him. He'll take them to the river, then he'll send them back home. We may as well go back, too; see how they look when they come back to camp."

When they reached the camp the hounds were already there, ten of them crouching back under the kitchen, the boy and Sam squat-

---

1. *Priam* (prī′əm), in Greek mythology, the king of Troy at the time of the Trojan War. His sons were killed defending the city against the Greeks.

ting to peer back into the obscurity where they huddled, quiet, the eyes luminous, glowing at them and vanishing, and no sound, only that effluvium of something more than dog, stronger than dog and not just animal, just beast, because still there had been nothing in front of that abject and almost painful yapping save the solitude, the wilderness, so that when the eleventh hound came in at noon and with all others watching—even old Uncle Ash, who called himself first a cook—Sam daubed the tattered ear and the raked shoulder with turpentine and axle grease, to the boy it was still no living creature, but the wilderness which, leaning for the moment down, had patted lightly once the hound's temerity.

"Just like a man," Sam said. "Just like folks. Put off as long as she could having to be brave, knowing all the time that sooner or later she would have to be brave to keep on living with herself, and knowing all the time beforehand what was going to happen to her when she done it."

That afternoon, himself on the one-eyed wagon mule which did not mind the smell of blood nor, as they told him, of bear, and with Sam on the other one, they rode for more than three hours through the rapid, shortening winter day. They followed no path, no trail even that he could see; almost at once they were in a country which he had never seen before. Then he knew why Sam had made him ride the mule which would not spook. The sound one stopped short and tried to whirl and bolt even as Sam got down, blowing its breath, jerking and wrenching at the rein, while Sam held it, coaxing it forward with his voice, since he could not risk tying it, drawing it forward while the boy got down from the marred one.

Then, standing beside Sam in the gloom of the dying afternoon, he looked down at the rotted overturned log, gutted and scored with claw marks and, in the wet earth beside it, the print of the enormous warped two-toed foot. He knew now what he had smelled when he peered under the kitchen where the dogs huddled. He realized for the first time that the bear which had run in his listening and loomed in his dreams since before he could remember to the contrary, and which, therefore, must have existed in the listening and dreams of his father and Major de Spain and even old General Compson, too, before they began to remember in their turn, was a mortal animal, and that if they had departed for the camp each November without any actual hope of bringing its trophy back, it was not because it could not be slain, but because so far they had had no actual hope to.

"Tomorrow," he said.

"We'll try tomorrow," Sam said. "We ain't got the dog yet."

"We've got eleven. They ran him this morning."

"It won't need but one," Sam said. "He ain't here. Maybe he ain't nowhere. The only other way will be for him to run by accident over somebody that has a gun."

"That wouldn't be me," the boy said. "It will be Walter or Major or—"

"It might," Sam said. "You watch close in the morning. Because he's smart. That's how come he has lived this long. If he gets hemmed up and has to pick out somebody to run over, he will pick out you."

"How?" the boy said. "How will he know—" He ceased. "You mean he already knows me, that I ain't never been here before, ain't had time to find out yet whether I—" He ceased again, looking at Sam, the old man whose face revealed nothing until it smiled. He said humbly, not even amazed, "It was me he was watching. I don't reckon he did need to come but once."

The next morning they left the camp three hours before daylight. They rode this time because it was too far to walk, even the dogs in the wagon; again the first gray light found him in a place which he had never seen before, where Sam had placed him and told him to stay and then departed. With the gun which was too big for him, which did not even belong to him, but to Major de Spain, and which he had fired only once—at a stump on the first day, to learn the recoil and how to reload it—he stood against a gum tree beside a little bayou whose black still water crept without movement out of a canebrake and crossed a small clearing and into cane again, where, invisible, a bird—the big woodpecker called Lord-to-God by Negroes—clattered at a dead limb.

It was a stand like any other, dissimilar only in incidentals to the one where he had stood each morning for ten days; a territory new to him, yet no less familiar than that other one which, after almost two weeks, he had come to believe he knew a little—the same solitude, the same loneliness through which human beings had merely passed without altering it, leaving no mark, no scar, which looked exactly as it must have looked when the first ancestor of Sam Fathers' Chickasaw predecessors crept into it and looked about, club or stone ax or bone arrow drawn and poised; different only because, squatting at the edge of the kitchen, he smelled the hounds huddled and cringing beneath it and saw the raked ear and shoulder of the one who, Sam said, had had to be brave once in order to live with herself, and saw yesterday in the earth beside the gutted log the print of the living foot.

He heard no dogs at all. He never did hear them. He only heard the drumming of the woodpecker stop short off and knew that the bear was looking at him. He never saw it. He did not know whether it was in front of him or behind him. He did not move, holding the useless gun, which he had not even had warning to cock and which even now he did not cock, tasting in his saliva that taint as of brass which he knew now because he had smelled it when he peered under the kitchen at the huddled dogs.

Then it was gone. As abruptly as it had ceased, the woodpecker's dry, monotonous clatter set up again, and after a while he even believed he could hear the dogs—a murmur, scarce a sound even, which he had probably been hearing for some time before he even remarked it, drifting into hearing and then out again, dying away. They came nowhere near him. If it was a bear they ran, it was another bear. It was Sam himself who came out of the cane and crossed the bayou, followed by the injured bitch of yesterday. She was almost at heel, like a bird dog, making no

sound. She came and crouched against his leg, trembling, staring off into the cane.

"I didn't see him," he said. "I didn't, Sam!"

"I know it," Sam said. "He done the looking. You didn't hear him neither, did you?"

"No," the boy said. "I—"

"He's smart," Sam said. "Too smart." He looked down at the hound, trembling faintly and steadily against the boy's knee. From the raked shoulder a few drops of fresh blood oozed and clung. "Too big. We ain't got the dog yet. But maybe someday. Maybe not next time. But someday."

So I must see him, he thought. *I must look at him.* Otherwise, it seemed to him that it would go on like this forever, as it had gone on with his father and Major de Spain, who was older than his father, and even with old General Compson, who had been old enough to be a brigade commander in 1865. Otherwise, it would go on so forever, next time and next time, after and after and after. It seemed to him that he could never see the two of them, himself and the bear, shadowy in the limbo from which time emerged, becoming time; the old bear absolved of mortality and himself partaking, sharing a little of it, enough of it. And he knew now what he had smelled in the huddled dogs and tasted in his saliva. He recognized fear. *So I will have to see him,* he thought, without dread or even hope. *I will have to look at him.*

It was in June of the next year. He was eleven. They were in camp again, celebrating Major de Spain's and General Compson's birthdays. Although the one had been born in September and the other in the depth of winter and in another decade, they had met for two weeks to fish and shoot squirrels and turkey and run coons and wildcats with the dogs at night. That is, he and Boon Hoggenback and the Negroes fished and shot squirrels and ran the coons and cats, because the proved hunters, not only Major de Spain and old General Compson, who spent those two weeks sitting in a rocking chair before a tremendous iron pot of Brunswick stew, stirring and tasting, with old Ash to quarrel with about how he was making it and Tennie's Jim to pour whiskey from the demijohn into the tin dipper from which he drank, but even the boy's father and Walter Ewell, who were still young enough, scorned such, other than shooting the wild gobblers with pistols for wagers on their marksmanship.

Or, that is, his father and the others believed he was hunting squirrels. Until the third day, he thought that Sam Fathers believed that too. Each morning he would leave the camp right after breakfast. He had his own gun now, a Christmas present. He went back to the tree beside the bayou where he had stood that morning. Using the compass which old General Compson had given him, he ranged from that point; he was teaching himself to be a better-than-fair woodsman without knowing he was doing it. On the second day he even found the gutted log where he had first seen the crooked print. It was almost completely crumbled now, healing with unbelievable speed, a passionate and almost visible relinquishment, back into the earth from which the tree had grown.

He ranged the summer woods now, green with gloom; if anything, actually dimmer than in November's gray dissolution, where, even at noon, the sun fell only in intermittent dappling upon the earth, which never completely dried out and which crawled with snakes—moccasins and water snakes and rattlers, themselves the color of the dappling gloom, so that he would not always see them until they moved, returning later and later, first day, second day, passing in the twilight of the third evening the little log pen enclosing the log stable where Sam was putting up the horses for the night.

"You ain't looked right yet," Sam said.

He stopped. For a moment he didn't answer. Then he said peacefully, in a peaceful rushing burst as when a boy's miniature dam in a little brook gives way, "All right. But how? I went to the bayou. I even found that log again. I—"

"I reckon that was all right. Likely he's been watching you. You never saw his foot?"

"I," the boy said—"I didn't—I never thought—"

"It's the gun," Sam said. He stood beside the fence, motionless—the old man, the Indian, in the battered faded overalls and the five-cent straw hat which in the Negro's race had been the badge of his enslavement and was now the regalia of his freedom. The camp—the clearing, the house, the barn and its tiny lot with which Major de Spain in his turn had scratched punily and evanescently at the wilderness—faded in the dusk, back into the immemorial darkness of the woods. *The gun*, the boy thought. *The gun.*

"Be scared," Sam said. "You can't help that. But don't be afraid. Ain't nothing in the woods going to hurt you unless you corner it, or it smells that you are afraid. A bear or a deer, too, has got to be scared of a coward the same as a brave man has got to be."

The gun, the boy thought.

"You will have to choose," Sam said.

He left the camp before daylight, long before Uncle Ash would wake in his quilts on the kitchen floor and start the fire for breakfast. He had only the compass and a stick for snakes. He could go almost a mile before he would begin to need the compass. He sat on a log, the invisible compass in his invisible hand, while the secret night sounds, fallen still at his movements, scurried again and then ceased for good, and the owls ceased and gave over to the waking of day birds, and he could see the compass. Then he went fast yet still quietly; he was becoming better and better as a woodsman, still without having yet realized it.

He jumped a doe and a fawn at sunrise, walked them out of the bed, close enough to see them—the crash of undergrowth, the white scut, the fawn scudding behind her faster than he had believed it could run. He was hunting right, upwind, as Sam had taught him; not that it mattered now. He had left the gun; of his own will and relinquishment he had accepted not a gambit, not a choice, but a condition in which not only the bear's heretofore inviolable anonymity but all the old rules and balances of hunter and hunted had been abrogated. He would not even be afraid, not even in the moment when the fear would take him completely—blood, skin, bowels, bones, memory from the long time before it became his memory—all save that thin, clear, immortal lucidity which alone differed him from this bear and from all the other bear and deer he would ever kill in the humility and pride of his skill and endurance, to which Sam had spoken when he leaned in the twilight on the lot fence yesterday.

By noon he was far beyond the little bayou, farther into the new and alien country than he had ever been. He was traveling now not only by the old, heavy, biscuit-thick silver watch which had belonged to his grandfather. When he stopped at last, it was for the first time since he had risen from the log at dawn when he could see the compass. It was far enough. He had left the camp nine hours ago; nine hours from now, dark would have already been an hour old. But he didn't think that. He thought, *All right. Yes. But what?* and stood for a moment, alien and small in the green and topless solitude, answering his own question before it had formed and ceased. It was the watch, the compass, the stick—the three lifeless mechanicals with which for nine hours he had fended the wilderness off; he hung the watch and compass carefully on a bush and leaned the stick beside them and relinquished completely to it.

He had not been going very fast for the last two or three hours. He went no faster now, since distance would not matter even if he could have gone fast. And he was trying to keep a bearing on the tree where he had left the compass, trying to complete a circle which would bring him back to it or at least intersect itself, since direction would not matter now either. But the tree was not there, and he did as Sam had schooled him—made the next circle in the opposite direction, so that the two patterns would bisect somewhere, but crossing no print of his own feet, finding the tree at last, but in the wrong place—no bush, no compass, no watch—and the tree not even the tree, because there was a down log beside it and he did what Sam Fathers had told him was the next thing and the last.

As he sat down on the log he saw the crooked print—the warped, tremendous, two-toed indentation which, even as he watched it, filled with water. As he looked up, the wilderness coalesced, solidified—the glade, the tree he sought, the bush, the watch and the compass glinting where a ray of sunlight touched them. Then he saw the bear. It did not emerge, appear; it was just there, immobile, solid, fixed in the hot dappling of the green and windless noon, not as big as he had dreamed it, but as big as he had expected it, bigger, dimensionless against the dappled obscurity, looking at him where he sat quietly on the log and looked back at it.

Then it moved. It made no sound. It did not hurry. It crossed the glade, walking for an instant into the full glare of the sun; when it reached the other side it stopped again and looked back at him across one shoulder while his quiet breathing inhaled and exhaled three times.

Then it was gone. It didn't walk into the woods, the undergrowth. It faded, sank back into the wilderness as he had watched a fish, a huge old bass, sink and vanish into the dark depths of its pool without even any movement of its fins.

He thought, *It will be next fall.* But it was not next fall, nor the next nor the next. He was fourteen then. He had killed his buck, and Sam Fathers had marked his face with the hot blood, and in the next year he killed a bear. But even before that accolade he had become as competent in the woods as many grown men with the same experience; by his fourteenth year he was a better woodsman than most grown men with more. There was no territory within thirty miles of the camp that he did not know—bayou, ridge, brake, landmark, tree, and path. He could have led anyone to any point in it without deviation, and brought them out again. He knew the game trails that even Sam Fathers did not know; in his thirteenth year he found a buck's bedding place, and unbeknown to his father he borrowed Walter Ewell's rifle and lay in wait at dawn and killed the buck when it walked back to the bed, as Sam had told him how the old Chickasaw fathers did.

But not the old bear, although by now he knew its footprints better than he did his own, and not only the crooked one. He could see any one of the three sound ones and distinguish it from any other, and not only by its size. There were other bears within these thirty miles which left tracks almost as large, but this was more than that. If Sam Fathers had been his mentor and the backyard rabbits and squirrels at home his kindergarten, then the wilderness the old bear ran was his college, the old male bear itself, so long unwifed and childless as to have become its own ungendered progenitor, was his alma mater. But he never saw it.

He could find the crooked print now almost whenever he liked, fifteen or ten or five miles, or sometimes nearer the camp than that. Twice while on stand during the three years he heard the dogs strike its trail by accident; on the second time they jumped it seemingly, the voices high, abject, almost human in hysteria, as on that first morning two years ago. But not the bear itself. He would remember that noon three years ago, the glade, himself and the bear fixed during that moment in the windless and dappled blaze, and it would seem to him that it had never happened, that he had dreamed that too. But it had happened. They had looked at each other, they had emerged from the wilderness old as earth, synchronized to the instant by something more than the blood that moved the flesh and bones which bore them, and touched, pledged something, affirmed something more lasting than the frail web of bones and flesh which any accident could obliterate.

Then he saw it again. Because of the very fact that he thought of nothing else, he had forgotten to look for it. He was still-hunting with Walter Ewell's rifle. He saw it cross the end of a long blowdown, a corridor where a tornado had swept, rushing through rather than over the tangle of trunks and branches as a locomotive would have, faster than he had ever believed it could move, almost as fast as a deer even, because a deer would have spent most of that time in the air, faster than he could bring the rifle sights with it. And now he knew what had been wrong during all the three years. He sat on a log, shaking and trembling as if he had never seen the woods before nor anything that ran them,

wondering with incredulous amazement how he could have forgotten the very thing which Sam Fathers had told him and which the bear itself had proved the next day and had now returned after three years to reaffirm.

And now he knew what Sam Fathers had meant about the right dog, a dog in which size would mean less than nothing. So when he returned alone in April—school was out then, so that the sons of farmers could help with the land's planting, and at last his father had granted him permission, on his promise to be back in four days—he had the dog. It was his own, a mongrel of the sort called by Negroes a fyce, a ratter, itself not much bigger than a rat and possessing that bravery which had long since stopped being courage and had become foolhardiness.

It did not take four days. Alone again, he found the trail on the first morning. It was not a stalk; it was an ambush. He timed the meeting almost as if it were an appointment with a human being. Himself holding the fyce muffled in a feed sack and Sam Fathers with two of the hounds on a piece of a plowline rope, they lay downwind of the trail at dawn of the second morning. They were so close that the bear turned without even running, as if in surprised amazement at the shrill and frantic uproar of the released fyce, turning at bay against the trunk of a tree, on its hind feet; it seemed to the boy that it would never stop rising, taller and taller, and even the two hounds seemed to take a desperate and despairing courage from the fyce, following it as it went in.

Then he realized that the fyce was actually not going to stop. He flung, threw the gun away, and ran; when he overtook and grasped the frantically pinwheeling little dog, it seemed to him that he was directly under the bear.

He could smell it, strong and hot and rank. Sprawling, he looked up to where it loomed and towered over him like a cloudburst and colored like a thunderclap, quite familiar, peacefully and even lucidly familiar, until he remembered: This was the way he had used to dream about it. Then it was gone. He didn't see it go. He knelt, holding the frantic fyce with both hands, hearing the abashed wailing of the hounds drawing farther and farther away, until Sam came up. He carried the gun. He laid it down quietly beside the boy and stood looking down at him.

"You've done seed him twice now with a gun in your hands," he said. "This time you couldn't have missed him."

The boy rose. He still held the fyce. Even in his arms and clear of the ground, it yapped frantically, straining and surging after the fading uproar of the two hounds like a tangle of wire springs. He was panting a little, but he was neither shaking nor trembling now.

"Neither could you!" he said. "You had the gun! Neither did you!"

"And you didn't shoot," his father said. "How close were you?"

"I don't know, sir," he said. "There was a big wood tick inside his right hind leg. I saw that. But I didn't have the gun then."

"But you didn't shoot when you had the gun," his father said. "Why?"

But he didn't answer, and his father didn't wait for him to, rising and crossing the room, across the pelt of the bear which the boy had killed two years ago and the larger one which his father had killed before he was born, to the bookcase beneath the mounted head of the boy's first buck. It was the room which his father called the office, from which all the plantation business was transacted; in it for the fourteen years of his life he had heard the best of all talking. Major de Spain would be there and sometimes old General Compson, and Walter Ewell and Boon Hoggenback and Sam Fathers and Tennie's Jim, too, were hunters, knew the woods and what ran them.

He would hear it, not talking himself but listening—the wilderness, the big woods, bigger and older than any recorded document of white man fatuous enough to believe he had bought any fragment of it or Indian ruthless enough to pretend that any fragment of it had been his to convey. It was of the men, not white nor black nor red, but men, hunters with the will and hardihood to endure and the humility and skill to survive, and the dogs and the bear and deer juxtaposed and reliefed against it, ordered and compelled by and within the wilderness in the ancient and unremitting contest by the ancient and immitigable rules which voided all regrets and brooked no quarter, the voices quiet and weighty and deliberate for retrospection and recollection and exact remembering, while he squatted in the blazing firelight as Tennie's Jim squatted, who stirred only to put more wood on the fire and to pass the bottle from one glass to another. Because the bottle was always present, so that after a while it seemed to him that those fierce instants of heart and brain and courage and wiliness and speed were concentrated and distilled into that brown liquor which not women, not boys and children, but only hunters drank, drinking not of the blood they had spilled but some condensation of the wild immortal spirit, drinking it moderately, humbly even, not with the pagan's base hope of acquiring the virtues of cunning and strength and speed, but in salute to them.

His father returned with the book and sat down again and opened it. "Listen," he said. He read the five stanzas aloud, his voice quiet and deliberate in the room where there was no fire now because it was already spring. Then he looked up. The boy watched him. "All right," his father said. "Listen." He read again, but only the second stanza this time, to the end of it, the last two lines, and closed the book and put it on the table beside him. "She cannot fade, though thou hast not thy bliss, for ever wilt thou love, and she be fair,"[2] he said.

"He's talking about a girl," the boy said.

"He had to talk about something," his father said. Then he said, "He was talking about truth. Truth doesn't change. Truth is one thing. It covers all things which touch the heart—honor and pride and pity and justice and courage and love. Do you see now?"

He didn't know. Somehow it was simpler than that. There was an old bear, fierce and ruthless, not merely just to stay alive, but with the fierce pride of liberty and freedom, proud enough of the liberty and freedom to see it

2. The boy's father has been reading from the poem "Ode on a Grecian Urn," written by the English Romantic poet, John Keats (1795-1821).

threatened without fear or even alarm; nay, who at times even seemed deliberately to put that freedom and liberty in jeopardy in order to savor them, to remind his old strong bones and flesh to keep supple and quick to defend and preserve them. There was an old man, son of a Negro slave and an Indian king, inheritor on the one side of the long chronicle of a people who had learned humility through suffering, and pride through the endurance which survived the suffering and injustice, and on the other side, the chronicle of a people even longer in the land than the first, yet who no longer existed in the land at all save in the solitary brotherhood of an old Negro's alien blood and the wild and invincible spirit of an old bear. There was a boy who wished to learn humility and pride in order to become skillful and worthy in the woods, who suddenly found himself becoming so skillful so rapidly that he feared he would never become worthy because he had not learned humility and pride, although he had tried to, until one day and as suddenly he discovered that an old man who could not have defined either had led him, as though by the hand, to that point where an old bear and a little mongrel of a dog showed him that, by possessing one thing other, he would possess them both.

And a little dog, nameless and mongrel and many-fathered, grown, yet weighing less than six pounds, saying as if to itself, "I can't be dangerous, because there's nothing much smaller than I am; I can't be fierce, because they would call it just noise; I can't be humble, because I'm already too close to the ground to genuflect; I can't be proud, because, I wouldn't be near enough to it for anyone to know who was casting the shadow, and I don't even know that I'm not going to heaven, because they have already decided that I don't possess an immortal soul. So all I can be is brave. But it's all right. I can be that, even if they still call it just noise."

That was all. It was simple, much simpler than somebody talking in a book about a youth and a girl he would never need to grieve over, because he could never approach any nearer her and would never have to get any farther away. He had heard about a bear, and

finally got big enough to trail it, and he trailed it four years and at last met it with a gun in his hands and he didn't shoot. Because a little dog—But he could have shot long before the little dog covered the twenty yards to where the bear waited, and Sam Fathers could have shot at any time during that interminable minute while Old Ben stood on his hind feet over them. He stopped. His father was watching him gravely across the spring-rife twilight of the room; when he spoke, his words were as quiet as the twilight, too, not loud, because they did not need to be because they would last. "Courage, and honor, and pride," his father said, "and pity, and love of justice and of liberty. They all touch the heart, and what the heart holds to becomes truth, as far as we know the truth. Do you see now?"

Sam, and Old Ben, and Nip, he thought. And himself too. He had been all right too. His father had said so. "Yes, sir," he said.

 TO INCREASE UNDERSTANDING

1. The first part of the story, up to the time the boy goes to hunt the bear (page 522, column 1, paragraph 2) may be regarded as the introduction or *exposition*. (*a*) What has the boy learned about the bear? (*b*) The boy regards the bear as "not even a mortal animal but an anachronism, indomitable and invincible, out of an old dead time, a phantom, epitome and apotheosis of the old wild life." Interpret this statement and explain what this view of the bear tells the reader about the boy. (*c*) In what way does the exposition establish the tone of the story?

2. On his initial trip to the swamp the boy has his first experience with the bear (page 522, column 2, paragraph 5 to page 524, column 2, paragraph 4). (*a*) How does he know the dogs are on the bear's trail? (*b*) Reread Sam Fathers' comment about the dog whose shoulder is raked by the bear (page 523, column 1, paragraph 1). What does it mean? (*c*) What does the boy learn from seeing the print of the bear's warped foot? (*d*) Why does Sam believe the bear can't be caught? (*e*) How does the boy discover on the next morning's hunt that the unseen bear is looking at him? (*f*) When does he realize what the effluvium under the porch where the dogs are huddled as well as the "taint as of brass" in his saliva is?

3. When the boy is eleven he visits the swamp again (page 524, column 2, paragraph 6 to page

526, column 2, paragraph 2). (*a*) How does he pass the time that the men think he is squirrel hunting? (*b*) What choice concerning the gun does Sam put up to him? (*c*) What does he find it necessary to do before he finally sees the bear? (*d*) What is the significance of his *quiet* inhaling and exhaling three times when he sees the bear?

4. The boy is fourteen when he has his next face-to-face meeting with Old Ben (page 526, column 2, paragraph 3 to page 528, column 1, paragraph 3). (*a*) Give examples of his progress as a woodsman in the intervening years. (*b*) What does he remember after he has seen the bear "cross the end of a long blowdown"? (*c*) What does his dog do when they meet the bear? (*d*) What does he do?

5. In the concluding section of the story (page 528, column 1, paragraph 4) the boy and his father discuss his adventure. (*a*) Why does his father read Keats' "Ode on a Grecian Urn" to him, emphasizing certain lines (page 528, column 2, paragraph 1)? (*b*) How does the boy explain his failure to shoot the bear? (*c*) What is the purpose of this last section of the story?

6. (*a*) What is the technical climax of the story? (*b*) Is it the same as the dramatic climax?

7. The theme of the story is the way a child gradually attains maturity. (*a*) What part does Sam Fathers play in the boy's progress toward maturity? (*b*) What part does the bear play? (*c*) What is the father's rôle?

8. Beginning with mention of the hound whose shoulder is raked by the bear (page 523, column 1, paragraph 1), references to the meaning of bravery recur throughout the story. (*a*) Locate and explain the meaning of several of these references. (*b*) What seems to be Faulkner's conception of bravery? (*c*) How is the concept of bravery related to the theme of the story?

9. (*a*) What is the narrative point of view in "The Bear"? (*b*) How does it serve as a unifying influence?

10. Faulkner gives a detailed description of the woods in which the boy hunts. (*a*) How does he convey that the woods are wild, dense, and vast? (*b*) Why is it important to the story that these woods be more than a tamed forest preserve?

11. At the conclusion of the story the boy sees that Sam Fathers, the bear, and the fyce embody certain concepts which he has begun to understand. What concept does each of these represent?

THE LARGER VIEW

A. Since mature reading is always a creative process in which the reader, in a sense, is matching his mind, experience, taste, and sense values with the writer's, there can be no absolute standards for judging the short story or any other kind of literature. But to grow in understanding, to enjoy and appreciate literature, a person needs to form some valid judgments about his reading.

Select a modern story that you have read outside of class. With the following questions to guide you, examine the story as closely as you have the stories in this chapter and exercise your critical judgment to evaluate its artistry. You may wish to refer to the "Better Reading" articles on the short story in this and preceding chapters. Their page numbers are listed in the Table of Contents.

1. Consider, first of all, the *plot*. (*a*) Does it have a well-defined beginning, middle, and end or is it closer to the sketch-from-life genre? Explain. (*b*) To what extent does the plot depend upon coincidence? (*c*) Does the story have a surprise ending? (*d*) To what degree is the plot treatment typical of twentieth-century innovations?

2. *Conflict* may be physical, moral, or emotional. (*a*) What is the nature of the conflict in the story you have selected to evaluate? (*b*) Does it grow naturally out of the characters or situations the story presents?

3. Identify the central *character* in the story and describe his traits. (*a*) Do you wish you knew more about his thoughts and feelings or more about his action, speech, and appearance? (*b*) How much must you infer about the character? How much are you told directly? (*c*) Would you say the narrative point of view unifies and lends proper emphasis to the characterization? Why?

4. A *setting* may be functional or may merely set the scene. (*a*) Determine whether the setting is or is not functional. (*b*) To what extent does the author use descriptive details to develop the setting? (*c*) Are these details realistic or romantic? Are they symbolic?

5. Does the story have a *theme*? Explain. (*a*) To what extent does this story make you think? (*b*) Does it increase your understanding of individuals, of social problems, of some facet of living?

6. A story's *tone* is often related to its theme. (*a*) Would you identify the tone of the story as comic, tragic, witty, satirical, sentimental, disillusioned, idealistic, or a combination of several of

these? (*b*) How is tone related to theme in the story?

7. On the basis of the points you have just examined, would you evaluate the story of your selection as artistically *fair, good,* or *excellent*?

B. There are short stories of horror or detection, of science fiction or local color. Some stories are humorous, historical, allegorical, psychological, naturalistic, or romantic. To which of these broad categories does the story you have selected belong? Explain.

C. To what extent does the story reflect the experimentation, attitudes, and interest in psychology typical of twentieth-century short stories?

Guides to Discussion of the Modern Novel

In your study of the modern American short story you have learned that there is no one pattern or type that covers all the short stories being written today. The same thing is true of the modern novel. The revolt against the form and subject matter of the nineteenth-century short story that produced "In Another Country," by Ernest Hemingway, and "The Jilting of Granny Weatherall," by Katherine Anne Porter, set off equally great changes in the novel. Plot became less important as the new interest in psychology led authors to concentrate on characters, sometimes almost to the exclusion of plot. Yet along with long, subjective, sometimes episodic novels, short tightly plotted novels like Edith Wharton's *Ethan Frome* continued to appear. Interest in psychology, together with the uncertainty and complexity of modern life, was also largely responsible for bringing the realistic and the naturalistic novel to a dominant position. As the years passed, few modern novelists of the first rank wrote in the romantic mode that had animated Cooper's novels of adventure. The local-color novel of the late nineteenth century also became less popular. It was succeeded by the regional novel, in which the interest in a specific locale remained but emphasis was shifted from the setting itself to the effect of that setting upon the individual.

On the following pages are discussion guides to three twentieth-century novels: *Giants in the Earth,* by O. E. Rölvaag; *Ethan Frome,* by Edith Wharton; and *The Old Man and the Sea,* by Ernest Hemingway. These novels differ greatly in length, in form, and in tone. Reading all three of them will give you a good sample of the variety and the excellence of the modern American novel.

DISCUSSION GUIDES

Giants in the Earth, by Ole Rölvaag

Plot, character, setting, and theme are all of great importance in this well-constructed novel. However, since the dominant impression on the reader is created by the characters rather than by the other elements, discussion of the novel may well begin with a consideration of Per Hansa and Beret and of their effect upon one another.

CHARACTER. *Since Per Hansa is the driving force of the story, it seems appropriate to discuss his character first.* What kind of individual is he? What is his outlook on life? What is his purpose in life? Why does it seem logical to the reader that Per Hansa chose to immigrate to the prairie? After all, he might have found a secure future for himself and his family on a farm farther east. He could have been much more easily successful in Norway as a fisherman. For evidence of the personal characteristics which made Per Hansa choose the West, and which, once he was there, made him seem so naturally suited to the land he chose, study the opening chapter. Here the family is wandering across an unmarked wilderness of grass which stretches as far as the eye can see. Does Per Hansa reveal that he is lost, or give any hint of the terrible consequences that could easily transpire if he does not soon detect signs of the advance party? From Per Hansa's behavior in this crisis, what can you reasonably expect of him throughout the remainder of the story? Note also his arrival at the Spring Creek settlement. In his conversation how does he treat the extreme peril from which he and his family have so narrowly escaped? What does his decision to build a larger house than the other settlers reveal about him? How does his plan to build the house and barn under one roof show his shrewdness? What other incidents and decisions during the course of the book reveal his resourcefulness, practical shrewdness, and adaptability to the demands of the West? Point out several and discuss the specific qualities they reveal.

Since Per Hansa's physical and emotional constitution suited him so aptly to the challenge of the prairie, this novel would have every reason to turn itself into an exuberant success story. As such, it would have been another romantic treatment of the "man against the West" situation.

Rölvaag, however, chose a tragic treatment. One way of achieving the tragic purpose would have been to set two strong and robust individuals in the West and let the forces of nature—crop failures, storms, and the like—ruin them both, which would have been quite believable. But in Giants in the Earth, even though the obstacles are formidable indeed, Per Hansa, with both luck and shrewd planning, is reasonably successful in surmounting them. The author introduces a far more subtle and interesting basis for tragedy: the emotional weakness and fatalism of a woman who should never have been subjected to the cruel ordeal of the pioneer West, Per Hansa's wife, Beret.

Discuss Beret's character as it is revealed in Chapter 1. In what way does this chapter foreshadow the development of Beret's character throughout the book? What idea is here planted that hints at the tragedy of the final outcome?

What demands in Beret's character rendered her unfit for the extreme rigors of the prairie? What events in her past played on her mind, giving her a sense of guilt? In what way does she relate her presence on the prairie to her sense of guilt? How does this finally lead to the religious zeal which is apparent toward the end of the novel? How do these factors affect her mental state? Cite incidents which show the progressive deterioration of Beret's mental state during the course of the novel.

What elements of prairie life were hardest for Beret to bear? Explain her feeling that humanity was reverting to animal existence and animal nature on the prairie. What incidents involving the children affected her thinking in this regard? What incidents involving Per Hansa?

How did the stories of Norse mythology on which Beret had been brought up intensify her hatred of the prairie? Discuss her references to the trolls. Explain how this belief in evil powers, meaningless to most native Americans, is a believable motivating force in a provincially reared Norwegian woman of the last century.

CHARACTER RELATIONSHIPS. *If Per Hansa is the driving force of the novel, Beret is the controlling character. Given the sometimes malignant forces of nature, the relationship be-*

tween these two characters is the real cause of the tragedy.

Review briefly the strong contrast between the characters of Per Hansa and Beret. Did it seem to you, at any point in the course of the story, that Per Hansa's great optimism and strength might carry Beret through and win her over to an acceptance of pioneer life? What does Per Hansa plan that he hopes will help Beret to a happier state of mind? If he had built a house to replace the hut sooner, do you think it would have had a marked influence on Beret? Would it have been enough? Why, or why not?

What effect does the change in Beret's mental condition have on Per Hansa at first? What specific instances give evidence of its growing effect on his own state of mind as time goes on? What evidence do you have that Beret's condition ages him long before his time?

When does Per Hansa first begin to realize fully the seriousness of his wife's mental condition? To what extent is he sympathetic? Could he have done more than he does to help her? Or would you say that he does more than most men would do?

The relationship between Per Hansa and Beret may be summarized as follows:

(a) Beret and Per Hansa love each other deeply.

(b) By upbringing and temperament Beret is completely unable to cope with the loneliness and isolation of prairie life.

(c) Per Hansa, a man of great physical and mental vigor, is the kind of individual who thrives on adversity and challenge. He is, therefore, naturally attracted to pioneer life. Its promise for the future becomes his life.

(d) Beret, because of her feeling that the prairie is God's punishment for her sin, feels that it is futile to explain her suffering; therefore her attempts to reach Per Hansa's understanding are feeble.

(e) Per Hansa is a long time in coming to realize Beret's condition; when he does realize it, he cannot really understand it.

(f) Thus we have a tragedy in which the "man against nature" situation is subordinated to the deeper and more complex circumstance of two unlike people in love but completely unable to understand one another.

(g) Therefore, the prairie enters, not as a force against them both, but as a third member of a triangle. Beret finds the prairie engrossing Per Hansa's attention and feels herself alone in her struggle.

On the basis of this brief analysis and your foregoing discussion, comment on the predicament of Beret. Comment on Per Hansa's position. Conjecture whether, if Per Hansa had truly understood Beret's plight, he would have continued to keep her on the prairie, or would have gone east with her. Had he left, what effect do you think the leaving would have had on him? Discuss the elements that would have set up a powerful conflict in his making a choice.

Once Beret accepted the prairie as her punishment, would it have been possible for her to try seriously to influence Per Hansa to leave with her? Explain.

Initially Beret had tried to get Per Hansa to stay farther east. Does this tragedy begin, then, with an act of willfulness on Per Hansa's part, coupled with an ignorance of his wife's limitations?

Although throughout the novel the interest of the reader is centered on Per Hansa and Beret and their troubled relationship, the other characters are skillfully drawn individuals who add color and variety. How do most of the women in the settlement react to pioneer life? In what ways are their feelings like Beret's? How does she differ from them?

What is Per Hansa's relationship to Hans Olsa? Under the circumstances is Beret justified in her feeling of jealousy toward Hans Olsa and Sorrina? Explain. What purpose do Syvert and Kjersti serve in the novel? Cite evidences of Rölvaag's attention to presenting characters different in type. What effect does this have on the atmosphere of the novel?

PLOT. *The plot is simple and straightforward in outline. There is an* exposition *giving the background of the principal characters, a long, uneventful* rising action, *a* climax, *and a* denouement.

Cite specific references in the early chapters to background information that helps the reader understand Per Hansa and Beret. Is enough data provided in the exposition to make their actions believable?

The complicating factors causing suspense in the plot are kept extremely simple. On the adventure side there is a series of crises furnished by the prairie and its weather. Closely tied to these there are the times of psychological and spiritual crisis for Beret, and, consequently, for her husband. These are triggered by simple incidents in the story; for example, the Indian episode, the first winter's confinement, Per Hansa's trips, and the christening of Peder Victorious. Point out other dramatic incidents that intensify the psychological crises of Beret and broaden the gulf between her and Per Hansa. In each case discuss the effect of the natural happenings on the characters.

Throughout the long rising action interest is sustained by the ordering of incidents and by various types of contrast. The most obvious contrast and the one most important to the plot is that between Per Hansa and Beret. How does it create the plot? Cite its effectiveness in the development of various incidents. Contrast the characters of Per Hansa and Syvert. How does this contrast provide variety in the fight with the Irish? Find other instances of contrast and discuss their dramatic effectiveness in the story.

Cite examples of the rhythmic rise and fall of action. Explain how the calm between crises adds to variety and to reader interest and dramatizes by contrast the crises themselves. Which element —the prairie adventure or the psychological states of the characters—is more absorbing as the novel reaches the last seven or eight chapters? Explain why.

The climax is centered around the illness of Hans Olsa and the blizzard that precipitates it. The tension arises over concern for him, Beret's talks with him, and the mounting pressure on Per Hansa to go for the minister. Exciting as it is, this climax would be a false one if the author had not prepared for it by developing the characters plausibly, making it impossible for them to act differently in this crisis. Had the author, for example, arranged the ending so that Hans Olsa, strictly of his own volition, had persuaded Per Hansa to go after a doctor, the emphasis in the story would have been shattered and the ending merely melodramatic. As it is, there is a sense of tragedy and of irony. Your discussion will explain why.

In what way is Per Hansa's decision to go for the minister directly the result of Beret's influence? Would he have gone on her insistence alone? Hans Olsa, his lifelong friend, also asked him to go. So did Sorinna. But what actually is behind their asking him? Explain Beret's influence in this.

Is the action of Beret at this point consistent with what you have learned of her previously? Think back to her past, her mental anguish and despair. What force has she finally been led to turn to as the only emotional relief and the only hope available to her disturbed state of mind?

How does this motivate her exhortation to Hans Olsa as she nurses him? Does the writer enable the reader to see her point of view?

Explain why you do not lose your respect for Hans Olsa, Sorinna, and especially Beret when they send Per Hansa off on a mission which they know is fraught with terrible danger. What motives impel each one of them in this action? Explain as fully as possible why this motivation leads the reader to forgive them. What would be the effect on the reader's reaction to the novel if at this climactic point the author had mishandled the motivation of his characters?

The denouement of the novel is brief but powerful. It is heavy in implication. The reader has no doubt as to who the man is that the children find dead by the haystack. In view of the vivid accounts of blizzards all through the book, it is hardly necessary to discuss whether this is a plausible ending.

One tragedy has already occurred—Beret's mental collapse. Per Hansa's death is the final one.

Under other circumstances Per Hansa's death in a blizzard might have been regarded as an accident arousing sympathy, but it would not have qualified as tragedy in the true sense of the word. Why do the circumstances under which Per Hansa dies sound a deeper tone than would his death in one of the blizzards described earlier in the novel? What element makes it tragic? How does Beret's influence add to the sense of tragedy? How is the tragedy heightened by the love of Beret for her husband? By his love for her? By the fact that there was a strong mutual bond between Hans Olsa, Sorinna, and Per Hansa? By the fact that Per Hansa seems to have begun to conquer the prairie? By Per Hansa's plans to build Beret's house in the spring?

Explain the irony of the situation. What did Beret hope to accomplish from Per Hansa's trip? What was her motive for pressing him to go? In contrast, what will she actually receive? What will be its effect on her? Why is this worse for her than it would have been for the other women had their husbands met the same fate? In the final analysis who comes out unscathed—Beret, Per Hansa, or the prairie?

SETTING. On page 514 Rölvaag is described as a "regionalist." What does this term mean? Why may Giants in the Earth be considered a regional novel? Distinguish between the new regionalists and the nineteenth-century local colorists.

Describe briefly the setting of the novel. What aspects of the setting are emphasized? If this were a romantic novel, what features might be played up? Explain why the setting may be considered functional. (See the article on setting, page 55.)

Recall various specific descriptions Rölvaag gives of the setting. What is the atmosphere conveyed by each. What effect is gained by contrasting descriptions of the prairie? In general, what is the atmosphere? Explain ways in which the atmosphere conveyed by the setting harmonizes with the story the novel tells.

THEME AND TONE. *How would you state Rölvaag's theme? It would be incorrect to say that it is man helpless before the forces of nature, since at his death Per Hansa is well on his way to conquering the wilderness. Neither can the theme be stated as simply the inevitable result of opposite personalities trying to face life together, since in another setting Per Hansa and Beret might have struck a better balance and been happy together.*

Rölvaag's theme might be stated as the harsh reality and impartiality of the forces of nature, and the human tragedy that occurs when those unsuited to meet the challenge of nature are subjected to its forces—even when supported by the very strong.

Comment on this statement of theme. Discuss its adequacy, basing your opinions on your knowledge of the plot and the characters. Draw a contrast between this novel and other more romantic novels of the frontier you have read. How do the general treatment of plot and character compare? What is the difference in atmosphere? How do they differ in the type of theme developed?

Tone, you will remember "is the attitude of an author as evident in his work." (See the article on page 75.) What is Rölvaag's attitude toward his characters? Is this attitude stated explicitly or implied? Give evidence for your answer. What words would you use to describe the dominant tone of *Giants in the Earth*?

STYLE. *Since the English version of* Giants in the Earth *is a translation from the Norwegian original, it is impossible to gain an accurate idea*

of Rölvaag's style. However, although some precision and originality in the use of words have been lost through translation, the fact that the author assisted the translator assures the reader that the English version is reasonably close to the original.

On the whole would you describe Rölvaag's use of words as simple and direct or as elaborately literary? Is the style predominantly formal or informal? What effect is created by the occasional use of terms such as *lousy* and *swell*?

Does the dialogue seem natural? Are you convinced that Per Hansa's speech is true to his character and true to life? Is the speech of various individuals a clue to character and personality?

Do the descriptions of the prairie landscape, the snow, the blizzards, the sunsets create strong, vivid images? Locate passages that present Per Hansa's attitude toward the prairie. What kinds of words are used to communicate enthusiasm and delight to the reader? Contrast these passages with ones in which the prairie is viewed through Beret's eyes. Discuss the use of words to achieve contrasting effects.

THE AUTHOR'S PURPOSE. *Ole Rölvaag was twenty years old when he left his native Norway and came to Elk Point, South Dakota. For three years he worked as a laborer on his uncle's farm at Brule Creek. He attended college in South Dakota and Minnesota. In summer he spent part of his time as a traveling salesman and part reading in small town libraries.*

What kinds of information about the Dakotas might Rölvaag have gathered merely by living in this part of the country? What could he have learned from relatives who had been among the early settlers? Cite episodes from *Giants in the Earth* which could have been based on stories he heard from such settlers. How might his travels in the area have broadened his background? Explain why his personal experiences and the stories he heard probably worked against his writing a glamorized novel of pioneer life.

Rölvaag dedicated his novel "To Those of My People Who Took Part in the Great Settling, To Them and Their Generations." What does the tone of the dedication indicate about the novel itself? What does it imply about the author's purpose in writing the novel?

Ethan Frome, by Edith Wharton

Most novels are characterized by length, various subplots, and a fairly large number of characters. Ethan Frome is extremely brief, the construction is tight, and the action involves only three characters. Discussion should center on the techniques used by the author in creating a masterpiece of form and content in a very limited space.

NARRATIVE POINT OF VIEW. Ethan Frome *is a story within a frame. In both the opening section and the very short closing section the narrator speaks in his own person.* Who is the narrator? About how old is Ethan Frome at the time the narrator meets him? What are Frome's circumstances and appearance? What arouses the narrator's curiosity about him? How does the narrator happen to learn Ethan Frome's story?

The story itself, which is based on the narrator's "vision" of the occurrences as told to him by Ethan Frome, is told in the third person from the partially omniscient point of view. (See the article on page 473.) Into which character's mind does the reader enter? What effect might this intimate knowledge of one character have on the way the reader views each of the three principal characters?

At what point does the flashback which constitutes the body of the novel end? Where do you learn what happened in the accident? What differences are apparent in Zeena as she appears in the novel proper and in the concluding section? Account for these differences.

CHARACTERS. *In her introduction to* Ethan Frome *Edith Wharton mentions that in fiction about New England "the outcropping granite" has been often overlooked. Later she speaks of the characters in her novel as "granite outcroppings; but half-emerged from the soil, and scarcely more articulate."* What is granitelike about the characters? In what way does their inarticulateness seem to increase this characteristic? Are the characters romantically or realistically drawn? Do their actions and emotions ring true? Give concrete evidence for your opinion.

Discuss the circumstances that caused the mutual attraction between Ethan and Mattie? How has Zeena unwittingly furthered this feeling between them? What are Zeena's ostensible motives for commanding Mattie to leave? Explain whether you think these are her real motives. What future does Mattie face? What is Ethan's dilemma? Which of these two suggests the desperate solution to the problems each one faces?

PLOT-CHARACTER RELATIONSHIP. *In the introduction to* Ethan Frome, *Edith Wharton said of the theme of her novel: "It must be presented as starkly and summarily as life had always presented itself to my protagonists."* How does the form of the novel represent the starkness desired by its author? In what way does the form echo the story the novel tells? In your opinion which is dominant—plot or characters? That is, do the events take the shape they do because, the characters being what they are, the happenings could be no different? Or are the characters invented to fit into a preconceived and powerful plot? Give evidence to support your opinion.

Discuss the rapid tightening of the plot from the beginning. Where does suspense first begin to develop? What factors add to suspense in the rising action? What do you consider the technical climax? What is the dramatic climax?

Edith Wharton foreshadows the direction the plot is to take and forges a dramatic continuity between the four days the story proper covers by accenting Mattie's desire to go coasting with Ethan. The subject comes up the first time the reader sees Ethan and Mattie together. How does "the big elm at the bottom" of the hill happen to be mentioned in the conversation? What does mention of the elm foreshadow? Ethan promises to take Mattie coasting the next night, "if there's a moon." Why do they not go? What is the effect of Ethan's mentioning the "ugly corner down by the big elm"? Why do Ethan and Mattie not go coasting the third night? Explain how the mentions of coasting on the three preceding nights have made the initial event of the fourth night seem plausible. Does the final and catastrophic trip also seem plausible? Why, or why not?

Why may the outcome of the novel be considered ironic? In what way is the outcome more terrible than if the two lovers had been killed? Edith Wharton herself called this novel a tragedy. What grounds does she have for this viewpoint? Why does this story qualify as a tragedy, whereas, in a literary sense, death by accident in a plane crash does not? What constitutes the difference?

STYLE AND TONE. *The introductory section serves not only as a frame for the action of the story but also sets the tone of the entire novel. Speaking of the end of the long, hard winter the narrator says: "I began to understand why Starkfield emerged from its six months siege like a starved garrison capitulating without quarter." A little later he quotes one of the inhabitants of Starkfield as saying, "Most of the smart ones get away." What significance is there in the name of the town? What is the force of the simile in the first quotation? In what way do these two quotations anticipate the tone of the story?*

Comment on the style in which the novel is written. Explain how the style generally and the descriptions of the setting in particular relate to the form of the novel, the nature of the characters, the plot, and the tone.

The Old Man and the Sea, by Ernest Hemingway

This great short novel can be read on several levels. On the literal level it tells a story that a child can understand. But underneath the simple story of an old man and a fishing expedition are profound meanings about life, death, and the human condition. It is on these deeper meanings that the discussion should focus.

PLOT. *Abstracted from the other elements of the novel, the plot of* The Old Man and the Sea *is strikingly simple in form and content.* What is the time arrangement? Describe the basic conflict? Mention several events that occur during the rising action. What is the technical climax? Does it coincide with the dramatic climax? How does the novel end? What makes it an exciting action story?

CHARACTER. *Before involving his hero—the old man—in the main action of the story, Hemingway gives the reader an idea of what sort of man this hero is through his conversations with the boy.* What do you learn about the old man from the boy's devotion to him? What sort of luck has the old man been having? Why will he not allow the boy to go fishing with him? How do the baseball references add to the picture of the old man's character? What, in addition to providing humor, is their purpose in the novel? What does DiMaggio mean to the old man? Why does the old man think of him when later he fights the big fish?

The novel is written from the point of view of the old man. Thus throughout the main portion of the story when the fisherman is alone at sea, the reader learns about him not only through what he does and what he says aloud, but also through what he thinks. Of what significance is the fact that the old man keeps his fishing lines straighter than anyone else? What character traits are emphasized by the story of the elbow-bending session the old man recalls? Cite incidents from the story that illustrate the fisherman's strength, his practical common sense, and his skill.

Of what attitudes is the old man's feeling toward the sea compounded? Why is he fond of flying fish? In what way are they his friends? Why is he sorry for turtles? How does he feel himself to be like them? What do you learn about him from the way he kills the albacore? Several times the old man refers to flying fish and other sea life as "brothers" and "friends." What do these designations tell you about the old man's nature?

During the first night after he has hooked the great fish, the old man remembers a previous expedition on which he had caught one of a pair of marlin. What had his feeling toward the marlin been? Why do you think this episode of the marlin is described in detail?

Explain the old man's mixed feelings toward the great fish that is pulling him farther and farther to sea. How does he regard the first shark, the *dentuso?* What makes him feel regret in battling both the great fish and the *dentuso?* Why does he not give in to his regret but continue to fight?

The old man has quite different feelings toward the second sharks, the *galanos,* than toward the *dentuso.* Why? Why is the old man resolved to fight off the successive attacks of sharks until his death or as long as there is anything left to fight for? What does this attitude tell you about the old man generally, not only in this particular situation?

In your own words explain how the old man rises to greatness in his battle with the sharks. What is there in his nature that causes the reader to feel admiration, love, and respect? Why is he far greater in defeat than he would have been in victory? Is *defeat* the correct word to use in speaking of the end of his adventure? Explain.

Reread the paragraph describing the values Hemingway believed in and the typical Hemingway hero (page 461). Explain ways in which the old man exemplifies these ideas.

To what extent is your understanding of the old man dependent upon the narrative point of view the author has chosen? (See the article on page 473.) What would have been lost had the objective point of view been used?

CHARACTER AND MEANINGS. *Except for the very beginning and the extreme end of the novel, one character only is present. Therefore most of the underlying meanings of the story must be sought in the thoughts and actions of the old man.*

Although the old man and the boy are given names—Santiago and Manolin—these names are used only in conversations when one addresses the other. The author habitually refers to them as "the old man" and "the boy." Does Santiago represent anything other than a single uneducated fisherman? What does the author suggest by using the general term rather than the specific name?

Hemingway explains that two Spanish words are used in referring to the sea: the feminine *la mar* and the masculine *el mar*. What different attitude toward the sea is expressed by each of these words? Which word does the old man use? He thinks of the sea as a woman who must be wooed to bestow her favors, and who is some-

times cruel—but only because she cannot help herself. What favors does she bring the old man? How does she hinder him? Compare his feeling that the sea is impersonal in her favors and her buffets with the attitude he takes toward the sea creatures he fishes for.

When the old man was the boy's age, he saw lions in Africa. Memory of the lions connects the old man with the boy he used to be, and in so doing connects the old man with Manolin. What did the old man dream of in the past? What does he dream of now? What is the significance of his present dreams? What circumstances cause him to think of the boy during his ordeal at sea? Will the boy, in time, be a great fisherman?

At the end of the struggle the old man is almost destroyed. His titanic struggle has almost cost him his life. He has had his fondest dream destroyed when it seemed near fulfillment. He seems too old and spent ever to dream again. At the end of the novel what brings him new hope? What significance is there in the fact that the boy is involved in it?

The old man believes that killing is universal and that life is interdependent with death. How do the events of the story support this view?

At the very end of the novel the tourists enter. What is their understanding of the skeleton of the great fish? Why are they introduced?

How would you state the theme of the novel? What meanings do you draw from it?

●

STYLE. Reread the analysis of Hemingway's style on pages 461-462. Do you agree that in *The Old Man and the Sea* Hemingway has recorded "the bare actions and thoughts of his characters"? Cite incidents in which this is particularly evident. Can you mention passages written in "plain words, colloquial phrases, and simple sentences"? Explain why this style is peculiarly appropriate for the characters and story of this novel.

BIBLIOGRAPHY

BENÉT, STEPHEN VINCENT, *Twenty-five Short Stories.* (Sun Dial) The versatility of Benét as a master of the short story is evident in this excellent collection of his best work.

BRADBURY, RAY, *Fahrenheit.* (Ballantine) Here is a tale as engrossing as its title suggests. Science-fiction fans will want to read about a time and a place where thinking is punishable by destruction by fire.

DALY, MAUREEN, *Seventeenth Summer.* (Dodd) Girls who have not already read this touching story of a bitter-sweet summer love should put it on their reading lists.

FAULKNER, WILLIAM, *Collected Stories.* (Random) As a chronicler of the South, Faulkner remains unsurpassed. This collection of forty-two of his best offers excellent fare for short-story enthusiasts.

FOLEY, MARTHA (editor), *Best of American Short Stories: 1915-1950.* (Houghton) Sherwood Anderson, William Faulkner, Ernest Hemingway, Irwin Shaw, and James Thurber are only a few of the outstanding writers included in this fine collection.

HAVIGHURST, WALTER (editor), *Masters of the Modern Short Story;* new edition, 1955. (••Harcourt) The writers included in this collection have one thing in common—they are all highly skilled in the art of storytelling. Among the American writers represented here you will find such masters as Edith Wharton, William Faulkner, Ernest Hemingway, John Steinbeck, William Saroyan, and Eudora Welty.

HEMINGWAY, ERNEST, *The Old Man and the Sea.* (Scribner) This story of an old man's battle with a huge creature of the sea is a story of the human will to endure, and it is told with all the austerity and compassion it deserves. No one but Hemingway could have written it.

HENRY, O., *The Four Million.* (Doubleday) If you enjoyed reading the selection in the text, you'll want to read more of O. Henry's sparkling, surprise-ending stories of the ordinary people of New York.

HYMAN, MAC, *No Time for Sergeants.* (Random •New Am. Lib.) A determined father and a barbed-wire fence are not enough to hold off the army recruiting agent, and Will Stock-dale, fun-loving Georgia cracker, is inducted into the army. His career as a soldier is a series of preposterous, wildly funny events.

NORDHOFF, CHARLES, and JAMES HALL, *Mutiny on the Bounty.* (Little •Pocket Books) Blood and thunder leap forth from the pages of this great story of adventures on the high seas. Based on actual occurrences, this book has all the drama and atmosphere of the best in fiction.

PORTER, KATHERINE ANNE, *The Leaning Tower and Other Stories.* (Harcourt) Skillfully worked out themes, rich in both aim and execution, are the mainstay of Miss Porter's short stories. This is an excellent collection.

ROLVAAG, OLE, *Giants in the Earth.* (Harper) Per Hansa, a Norwegian immigrant, struggles with the stubborn earth of the Dakota prairie; to him that earth means freedom. But to his wife, Beret, it means only nameless fears. Their very moving story will contribute greatly to your understanding of the human element in the settling of the West.

STEINBECK, JOHN, *The Pearl.* (Viking •Bantam) According to an old Mexican folk tale, there is in existence a giant pearl that will bring good luck to its finder. In a story that reads like a parable, Steinbeck tells of the effects of the pearl on a poor Mexican family.

THURBER, JAMES, *The Thirteen Clocks.* (Simon & Schuster) This fascinating fairy tale for adults is complete with romantic and sinister illustrations, as all good fairy tales should be.

WELTY, EUDORA, *Selected Stories.* (Modern Library) These sensitive, skillfully told stories of contemporary Mississippi will offer excellent fare to those who enjoy the unusual in fiction.

WEST, JESSAMYN, *The Friendly Persuasion.* (Harcourt) A stanch Quaker, Jess Birdwell, is determined to stay out of the Civil War; and he wants his son to have no part of it, either. The boy's decision is the result of a great struggle between his religious and his patriotic principles. This account of early Indiana settlers is filled with warmth and humor.

WHARTON, EDITH, *Ethan Frome.* (••Scribner) In less than two-hundred pages Edith Wharton tells a tragic and powerfully ironic story of three people's wasted lives: Ethan Frome; Zeena, his wife; and Mattie, Zeena's cousin.

•paperback ••paperback and hard-cover

Henry Rago, editor of *Poetry* (see page 593), has said that no poet in the United States has contributed as much to the teaching of young poets as Paul Engle. A widely published poet and a native Iowan, Mr. Engle heads the Writers' Workshop at the University of Iowa, where he himself received his M.A. degree. Chosen students in creative writing from all over the country meet at the workshops to write, talk, and criticize each other's work. From this school have come a remarkable number of America's best young poets. One of the leading anthologies of contemporary poetry is *New Poets of England and America,* published in 1957, just twenty years after Paul Engle began teaching at Iowa. One third of all the American poets represented have studied in the workshops! Here is living proof of Paul Engle's unique achievement.

Why modern poetry?

Paul Engle

Probably the shortest poem in the English language is the slightly irreverent one called "Fleas," which runs,

> Adam
> Had 'em.

This little absurdity not only has some of the qualities of the poetry of all ages, but it also is written in the tone of modern poetry. The little verse has a firm rhythm, with the accent on the first syllable of each line. It also has a crisp and unexpected rhyme, somewhat in the manner of Ogden Nash.[1] If the poet had said that Eve had 'em, he would have been unkind to the lady, but he would also have lost the amusing and original rhyme. The poem is ironic in the modern way, slightly mocking but without being cruel. It does not state its meaning, but hints at it, just as many poems do today. The verse is really saying: Adam was human, as is proved by the fact that he suffered from one of the irritations of life, fleas. By cutting the expression of that down to the smallest possible number of words, the poet has made each word mean more.

---

1. A brief biography of Ogden Nash and a poem by him may be found on pages 602-603.

*A day in the life of Paul Engle
finds him teaching young poets
on the University of Iowa
campus; enjoying some leisure
time with his daughter at
home on his farm; and at work
in his study, where he does
his writing and evaluates
students' work.*

Of course modern poetry differs from nineteenth-century poetry. Don't the clothes you wear differ? The houses in which you live, the words you hear spoken on those devices, the radio and television, which did not even exist then, are curiously different. The society in which you study and work, the nature of the physics and chemistry you learn, even the other countries of the world and our relationship with them, all are dramatically changed. Then why should poetry remain unchanged? In fact, in a world so altered from that of only seventy years ago, would it not be wrong if poetry failed to follow the shifts of human life?

One reason why some people resent modern poetry is that they prefer poetry which helps them forget the dreariness and the menace of daily experience. But this is not the only use of poetry; some is written not to take you away from life, but to return you to it, only with a more intense insight into its nature. Wallace Stevens wrote that "the wonder and mystery of art . . . is the revelation of something 'wholly other' by which the inexpressible loneliness of thinking is broken and enriched." The poem refreshes life, Stevens once said. It does so by making you see in the world around you things you had never seen before.

People who say, "I like only traditional poetry," should remember that in the past the very poems which they now like differed greatly from those of a preceding age. In fact, the most untraditional thing in the world is for poetry *not* to change, not to respond to life by finding its own form and attitudes, and thus make its own tradition.

Take a stanza from Longfellow's "Psalm of Life":

Tell me not, in mournful numbers,
    Life is but an empty dream!
For the soul is dead that slumbers,
    And things are not what they seem.

When this poem was first published over a hundred years ago, it spoke directly to readers of Longfellow's own time, voicing an exciting new idea about the best way to live. Sandburg's lively lines about Chicago are closer to experience today:

Come and show me another city with lifted
    head singing so proud to be alive and
    coarse and strong and cunning.
Flinging magnetic curses amid the toil of
    piling job on job, here is a tall bold slug-
    ger set vivid against the little soft cities.

Modern poetry believes in many things. It tries to use the language of ordinary speech, not anything sounding like words learned in a library or heard in a classroom lecture. Robert Frost begins a poem with deliberate simplicity: "When I see birches bend to left and right . . ." Anyone could speak that line in ordinary conversational tones and yet it has the measured sound of poetry.

The language has also been purified of archaic words, *thee* and *canst* and *wouldst*, and of words in unnatural order. Vachel Lindsay in "General William Booth Enters into Heaven" describes Salvation Army girls:

Big-voiced lasses made their banjos bang,
Tranced, fanatical they shrieked and sang. . .

This is in sharp contrast to the outworn words in many poems of the past.

The poets who called themselves Imagists[2] in the early years of this century argued for three conditions which explain much of what seems strange in verse today. They believed that poetry should treat its subject directly, without a lot of comment and moralizing; that not one word should be used which did not strengthen the poem; and that rhythm should not be exact sounds as with a metronome, but rather long phrases which were close to the voice speaking. In his poem "Spring and All" (see facing page) William Carlos Williams (a doctor in New Jersey; he delivered more babies than any other poet who ever lived) writes about the way in which bushes, trees, and vines receive their initial nudge toward new life. Notice how in lines 16-23 the poet tries to represent in words the first thrust of "dazed spring."

2. See the biography of Amy Lowell, page 52.

Spring and All
William Carlos Williams

By the road to the contagious hospital
under the surge of the blue
mottled clouds driven from the
northeast—a cold wind. Beyond, the
waste of broad, muddy fields   5
brown with dried weeds, standing and fallen

patches of standing water
the scattering of tall trees

All along the road the reddish
purplish, forked, upstanding, twiggy   10
stuff of bushes and small trees
with dead, brown leaves under them
leafless vines—

Lifeless in appearance, sluggish
dazed spring approaches—   15

They enter the new world naked,
cold, uncertain of all
save that they enter. All about them
the cold, familiar wind—
Now the grass, tomorrow   20
the stiff curl of wild carrot leaf
One by one objects are defined—
It quickens: clarity, outline of leaf

But now the stark dignity of
entrance—Still, the profound change   25
has come upon them: rooted they
grip down and begin to awaken

For biographical sketches of William Carlos Williams and
John Crowe Ransom see pages 572 and 573.

Bells for John Whiteside's Daughter
John Crowe Ransom

There was such speed in her little body,
And such lightness in her footfall,
It is no wonder her brown study
Astonishes us all.

Her wars were bruited in our high window. 5
We looked among orchard trees and beyond,
Where she took arms against her shadow,
Or harried unto the pond

The lazy geese, like a snow cloud
Dripping their snow on the green grass,   10
Tricking and stopping, sleepy and proud,
Who cried in goose, Alas,

For the tireless heart within the little
Lady with rod that made them rise
From their noon apple-dreams and scuttle   15
Goose-fashion under the skies!

But now go the bells, and we are ready,
In one house we are sternly stopped
To say we are vexed at her brown study,
Lying so primly propped.   20

odern poetry also works
against sentimentality, against
putting more emotion into a
poem than the situation demands. In his moving poem,
"Bells for John Whiteside's Daughter," John
Crowe Ransom is writing about the death of
a little girl, certainly as easy a subject to be
sentimental about as any. Yet in the modern
manner, Ransom writes with enough irony to
make the poem safe from being too soft, but
with enough feeling to move the reader. For
example, he never refers to the child's death,

but speaks of "her brown study," as if she were only withdrawn from people for a while. He describes the way in which she chased

> The lazy geese, like a snow cloud
> Dripping their snow on the green grass,
> Tricking and stopping, sleepy and proud,
> Who cried in goose, Alas . . .

The bells are those which toll for the girl's death; the friends go into the house and see her there, "Lying so primly propped." Here, the poet does not say that she is in her casket, but chooses the more detached way of referring to her as if she were merely sick, propped up, perhaps, by a pillow.

That is the modern way, and you must watch for it, and not expect the poem to come out bluntly and tell you what it is all about, but realize that much of its meaning is left for you to imagine from the hints given by the poet.

Poets have always manipulated language; when E. E. Cummings scatters the lines of his poems down the page in what may seem like a confusion, just read the poem out loud, and you will find that all of the lines fit the idea perfectly, and that the humor and the fancy become more apparent when you hear them. In "Chanson Innocente," Cummings invents new combinations which are wonderfully exact in describing the wet excitement of Spring—"mud-luscious," "puddle-wonderful." He writes the combination "Just-spring," dividing it to emphasize that it is barely the first hour of the season, just-barely. Later he writes the names of the children together, "eddieandbill . . . bettyandisbel," to suggest the simultaneous rush with which they come running. The goat is the old image for fertility, and so is Spring, and thus the balloon man is called "goat-footed," to *hint* at this reference to the new life of the season, not to tell you directly. By putting his title into French, Cummings appears to take a sly dig at William Blake's title, *Songs of Innocence*, and also to stress the fact that his own poems are not really songs, but do have some of the lyrical movement of words to be sung.

chanson innocente

e. e. cummings

in Just-
spring   when the world is mud-
luscious the little
lame balloonman

whistles   far   and wee   5

and eddieandbill come
running from marbles and
piracies and it's
spring

when the world is puddle-wonderful   10

the queer
old balloonman whistles
far   and   wee
and bettyandisbel come dancing

from hop-scotch and jump-rope and   15

it's
spring
and
        the

                goat-footed   20

balloonMan   whistles
far
and
wee

For a biographical sketch of E. E. Cummings see page 572.

"Chanson Innocente" from *Poems 1923-1954* by E. E. Cummings. Copyright 1923, 1951 by E. E. Cummings. Reprinted by permission of Harcourt, Brace & World, Inc., New York, and Faber & Faber, Ltd., London.

Modern poetry is at the same time both more intellectual and more immediately connected with actual life than the verse of the nineteenth century. For example, it would be difficult, and perhaps impossible, to find in Victorian poetry such comments as W. H. Auden's (in his "Musée des Beaux Arts") about suffering, and "how it takes place/While someone else is eating or opening a window or just walking dully along." Auden says that suffering is a natural part of our lives, and that, however terrible it may be for us when we endure it, the rest of the world cannot stop to sympathize, but has to pursue its own affairs, however trivial. Now he does not state this meaning clearly but suggests it imaginatively. Even a martyrdom, he says, takes place in some spot

Where the dogs go on with their doggy life
    and the torturer's horse
Scratches its innocent behind on a tree.

The horse is "innocent" because he does not know that his rider, the torturer, is killing an innocent man.

Auden calls his poem Museum of the Fine Arts because he ends with a paragraph describing a great painting by the Flemish artist Breughel, which shows in the foreground a farmer plowing, and in the background, a ship with sails moving over water, while a tiny figure of a young man, Icarus (who tried to fly into the sun on wings his father had made him), is falling into the sea. The ship sails on, the farmer plows, although Icarus dies, because they have their committed lives to lead and must remain indifferent.

Musée des Beaux Arts   W. H. Auden

About suffering they were never wrong,
The Old Masters: how well they understood
Its human position; how it takes place
While someone else is eating or opening a window or just walking dully
    along;
How, when the aged are reverently, passionately waiting   5
For the miraculous birth, there always must be
Children who did not specially want it to happen, skating
On a pond at the edge of the wood:
They never forgot
That even the dreadful martyrdom must run its course   10
Anyhow in a corner, some untidy spot
Where the dogs go on with their doggy life and the torturer's horse
Scratches its innocent behind on a tree.

In Breughel's *Icarus,* for instance: how everything turns away
Quite leisurely from the disaster; the ploughman may   15
Have heard the splash, the forsaken cry,
But for him it was not an important failure; the sun shone
As it had to on the white legs disappearing into the green
Water; and the expensive delicate ship that must have seen
Something amazing, a boy falling out of the sky,   20
Had somewhere to get to and sailed calmly on.

For a biographical sketch of W. H. Auden see page 592.

"Musée des Beaux Arts" reprinted from The Collected Poetry of W. H. Auden, by permission of Random House, Inc., New York, and Faber and Faber Ltd., London, publishers of Collected Shorter Poems by W. H. Auden. Copyright 1940 by W. H. Auden.

Another effort of twentieth-century poets is to get the most concentrated expression possible. T. S. Eliot often leaves out the usual connecting material in a poem, so that there will be nothing but essential images. This is one reason why his famous poem *The Waste Land* is so difficult. A movie will show a man walking down a street, thinking of some other place, and suddenly he is in that other place, with no view of the intervening landscape. You accept that in a film, why not in a poem? Robert Lowell's poem "Salem" describes an old sailor knitting in a storm, then mentions pollution of the sea by sewage, then recalls how fishing fleets from Salem used to go to Newfoundland (to the Great Banks, just off the coast there), and ends with a question which it does not answer.

This poem's theme is the decline of a once-great port, Salem, and the disappearance of the hardy sailors who went out in their frail wooden ships to defy the dangerous ocean and to fight the British navy. Nowhere in the poem will you find such a statement. In the modern method, the poet has given the reader a set of dramatic facts, and left it to him to put them together and make the final meaning. You must learn to read with greater care than you would bring to any prose, always looking for the meanings that are implied and not stated. The "oily slick" lashing about the heads of the sailors stands for their drowning in history, in the overwhelming push of life now, whose miserable sewage sickens the once clean seas. The adjective *nimble* to describe the fishing fleets is precise and original; the ships were small, quick ancestors of the beautiful clippers.

The final question, where did New England breed the men who sailed those seas (the Leviathan is a figure standing for the ocean, but the adjective *fat* also suggests the whale, from which immense quantities of oil were taken), and fought the British (symbolized as Lion) and defeated them, is to be answered: those men were bred in Salem. The poet does not tell you outright, but he gives enough information so that, with your own imagination, you can decide that of course it was Salem, and the implication is that Salem does not breed such men now.

Longfellow has a recollection of his youth and the trees he saw:

I can see the breezy dome of groves,
  The shadows of Deering's Woods;
And the friendships old and the early loves
Come back with a Sabbath sound, as of
  doves . . .

Robert Frost also remembers his youth among trees in "Birches," but his is a far more realistic scene. Note the exact image in the line describing ice on a birch bough when the wind shakes it: "As the stir cracks and crazes their enamel." The boy who lives too far from town to have any games except those he finds himself climbs a young birch almost to the top, and then swings out and rides the bending tree back to the ground. Climbing the tree symbolizes escape from the earth, and swinging back stands for the return to reality. Frost does not directly say this, but he gives you strong hints, as when (line 56) he emphasizes the word *toward* heaven. He wants to approach the abstract, to get away from earth, but not all of the way, and he always wants to return; the reason for wanting to return is that earth is where he has found love, of a sort he does not expect to find in heaven, and this satisfies him. The meaning of this poem is that, for all of its risks, "Earth's the right place for love." Frost hopes he will always remain close to it.

Salem

Robert Lowell

In Salem seasick spindrift drifts or skips
To the canvas flapping on the seaward panes
Until the knitting sailor stabs at ships
Nosing like sheep of Morpheus through his brain's
Asylum. Seaman, seaman, how the draft   5
Lashes the oily slick about your head,
Beating up whitecaps! Seaman, Charon's raft
Dumps its damned goods into the harbor-bed,
There sewage sickens the rebellious seas.
Remember, seaman, Salem fishermen   10
Once hung their nimble fleets on the Great Banks.
Where was it that New England bred the men
Who quartered the Leviathan's fat flanks
And fought the British Lion to his knees?

Birches

Robert Frost

When I see birches bend to left and right
Across the line of straighter, darker trees,
I like to think some boy's been swinging them.
But swinging doesn't bend them down to stay.
Ice storms do that. Often you must have seen them   5
Loaded with ice a sunny winter morning
After a rain. They click upon themselves
As the breeze rises, and turn many-colored
As the stir cracks and crazes their enamel.   9
Soon the sun's warmth makes them shed crystal shells
Shattering and avalanching on the snow crust—
Such heaps of broken glass to sweep away
You'd think the inner dome of heaven had fallen.
They are dragged to the withered bracken by the load,
And they seem not to break; though once they are
            bowed   15
So low for long, they never right themselves;
You may see their trunks arching in the woods
Years afterwards, trailing their leaves on the ground
Like girls on hands and knees that throw their hair
Before them over their heads to dry in the sun.   20
But I was going to say when Truth broke in
With all her matter-of-fact about the ice storm
I should prefer to have some boy bend them
As he went out and in to fetch the cows—
Some boy too far from town to learn baseball,   25

For a biographical sketch of Robert Lowell see page 573; Robert
Frost's biography appears on page 553.

Whose only play was what he found himself,
Summer or winter, and could play alone.
One by one he subdued his father's trees
By riding them down over and over again
Until he took the stiffness out of them,   30
And not one but hung limp, not one was left
For him to conquer. He learned all there was
To learn about not launching out too soon
And so not carrying the tree away
Clear to the ground. He always kept his poise   35
To the top branches, climbing carefully
With the same pains you use to fill a cup
Up to the brim, and even above the brim.
Then he flung outward, feet first, with a swish,   39
Kicking his way down through the air to the ground.
So was I once myself a swinger of birches
And so I dream of going back to be.
It's when I'm weary of considerations,
And life is too much like a pathless wood   44
Where your face burns and tickles with the cobwebs
Broken across it, and one eye is weeping
From a twig's having lashed across it open.
I'd like to get away from earth awhile
And then come back to it and begin over.
May no fate willfully misunderstand me   50
And half grant what I wish and snatch me away
Not to return. Earth's the right place for love:
I don't know where it's likely to go better.
I'd like to go by climbing a birch tree,
And climb black branches up a snow-white trunk   55
Toward heaven, till the tree could bear no more,
But dipped its top and set me down again.
That would be good both going and coming back.
One could do worse than be a swinger of birches.

Much of the modern attitude toward poetry has been put into a poem by Marianne Moore (who lives in Brooklyn and once described herself as a fan of the Dodgers). She describes poetry in the manner of the new poets, being ironical and indirect. She begins by saying about poetry, "I, too, dislike it." There are more important things in the world, she admits, and yet when it is genuine, when it moves with the honesty of "Hands that can grasp, eyes/ that can dilate, hair that can rise," then it must have some value. Gradually we see that her objection is to "half poets," the imitators, probably, of an older poetry. Her shrewd phrase for the combining of the practical and the imaginative, the raw and the genuinely original, is: "imaginary gardens with real toads in them." This is like Frost's combination in "Birches," the abstract heaven and the actual ground. This is a very powerful insight of Miss Moore's, for without the imagination, the poem is not genuinely poetic, just as with-

Poetry Marianne Moore

I, too, dislike it: there are things that are important beyond all this fiddle.
  Reading it, however, with a perfect contempt for it, one discovers in
  it after all, a place for the genuine.
     Hands that can grasp, eyes
     that can dilate, hair that can rise   5
       if it must, these things are important not because a

high-sounding interpretation can be put upon them but because they are
  useful. When they become so derivative as to become unintelligible,
  the same thing may be said for all of us, that we   10
     do not admire what
     we cannot understand: the bat
       holding on upside down or in quest of something to

eat, elephants pushing, a wild horse taking a roll, a tireless wolf under
  a tree, the immovable critic twitching his skin like a horse that feels a flea, the baseball fan, the statistician—   15
     nor is it valid
       to discriminate against 'business documents and

school-books'; all these phenomena are important. One must make a distinction
  however: when dragged into prominence by half poets, the result is not poetry,
  nor till the poets among us can be   20
     'literalists of
     the imagination'—above
       insolence and triviality and can present

for inspection, 'imaginary gardens with real toads in them,' shall we have
  it. In the meantime, if you demand on the one hand,
  the raw material of poetry in   25
     all its rawness and
     that which is on the other hand
       genuine, you are interested in poetry.

For a biographical sketch of Marianne Moore see page 576.

out the solid earth, the poem is in danger of being too remote. All good poetry has both the mind and the body in it.

The reading of an imaginative work can only be done properly if you bring some imagination of your own to it. The analyzing of a scientific problem can only be done properly if you bring some reasoning intelligence to it. You must read a line of a poem and look not only for the literal meanings of each word, but also for the whole meaning beyond the words. It is like piling up bricks; each is a single unit, but when you have put them into a shape which has height and width, then you have not just a collection of separate bricks, you have a wall, a new thing which was not there before.

I n a poem I wrote called "To Praise a Poet," I describe not only Robert Frost, but also the imaginative quality of his poetry. One stanza reads:

When he says *star,* we make a wish.
When he says *lake,* we watch live fish,
The water moving with their motion.
When he says *salt,* we taste the ocean.

This is an attempt to say that words in poetry are only the beginning of the poem. You must read the word *salt,* and then you must have a salty taste in your mouth. You must read the word *promises* in Frost's poem "Stopping by Woods on a Snowy Evening" (page 554), and then you must realize that the promises are not only to his family to come home that evening, but also the commitments of his whole life—to his job, to his friends, to the

unfinished work, and even the final promise to die.

Later in the same poem I say of Frost:

His shadow, folded like a fan
Over the pavement, casts a man.

Now why did I compare a shadow to a fan? Because Frost is walking, and when a man walks his legs alternately stretch forward; when one leg passes the other, there is a moment when the shadow is a single, fixed shape, and then as that leg moves ahead, the shadow opens out, just as a fan does. The image also suggests that Frost is not a rigid, distant form of a public poet, but a live person on the go, still moving ahead even at an advanced age.

This poem also tells about the maple tree, which gains the sweetness of its syrup from the rough New England soil, just as Frost gained the sweetness *and* the strength of his poetry from that soil. He never denied the rocks on Vermont's high green hills; he made poetry out of them. Cézanne's[3] apples in his paintings are radiant, and seem to push back the air with their own ruddy shape; this seems to be true of Frost's own ruddy and strong face. The same person who seems to hear light coming goldenly from remote stars, also hears the cricket in the grass at his feet, which is of course taken from "Birches," acknowledging both sky and earth as parts of our lives. And so for love at the end of the poem, the face of the loved one seems to bruise the air in which it is seen; in turn, the face is bruised by experience. Finally, as Frost suggested in "Birches," love is something given us as a grace, not really given because earned and deserved.

3. *Cézanne's.* Paul Cézanne (sā zan′), 1839-1906, was a French artist whose paintings are noted for glowing colors, clear, solid shapes, and deep space. His emphasis on geometrical constructions and distorted forms helped pave the way for modern schools of abstract design.

To Praise a Poet: Robert Frost   Paul Engle

You give this man the sort of praise
You give to ripened autumn days
When the air glows with radiant light
And leaf fires darken the dense night.

He reads our life. We read his book,   5
Seeing his own eyes' luminous look
Gleam from the poem, knowing behind
That inky page a shining mind.

The falling red leaf silently
Proves the standing maple tree.   10

When he says *star,* we make a wish.
When he says *lake,* we watch live fish,
The water moving with their motion.
When he says *salt,* we taste the ocean.

Independent animal,   15
Stubborn individual,
He makes his way, and has from birth,
With or against obstinate earth,
Trudging, like a man through snows,
Leaving deep footprints where he goes.   20

His shadow, folded like a fan
Over the pavement, casts a man.

Like a New Hampshire apple growing
Ripe in the sun and green winds blowing,
Or painted, and about to roll   25
Out of Cézanne's red-painted bowl,
Pushing the green air back, his face
Brings with it his own light and space.

A sugar maple, sweet and hard,
He stands up in his own back yard,   30
Taking the sunlight eagerly,
Rooted in rough integrity.

Aware, the honest poem is no
Romantic cry, because tears flow,

He lays with calloused hand each thick   35
Word on word like brick on brick.
Aware rich soil is grit ground fine,
That the same voice can sing or whine,
He knows in evil we define
Good, as tears make our eyes shine.   40

Stargazer whom no star deceives,
Shrewd skywatcher who perceives
The midnight moon bark at the prowling
Mongrel dog and send him howling;
Farmer who heard the rattler warn   45
From the stone ledge his angry scorn,
Hears from their coiling length the bright
Galaxies hiss their golden light,
And in that instant hears the high
Shrill from low grass of cricket cry.   50

Earth or sky or mortal heart
He travels without map or chart,
Or any compass but his art.

Loving the marvelous human scene
Where the absurd grins at the mean,   55

Knowing the mixed magnificence
Of all life's sensual innocence,
He mingles vision with plain sense:
On this wind-rounded world the bare
Loved face hangs like a bruise in air.   60
We lift our hands to touch it there.

If that touch brings pain with delight,
Joy so great as to give fright,
It is our life, and it is right.

Love is not wages to be earned,   65
Nor lessons to be grimly learned,
But a grace given and returned.

First Voices

Robert Frost, Carl Sandburg, Edwin Arlington Robinson, Edgar Lee Masters, and Vachel Lindsay—these five men were the first of the distinctively modern poets to gain a nation-wide audience. They came from different backgrounds and different sections of the country. The subjects they wrote about differed greatly. The verse forms they used embraced all types from rhymed stanzas in regular meter to free verse. Yet each one spoke in a voice that authentically caught the rhythm and accent of twentieth-century America.

Robert Frost

"Out, Out——"

The title of this poem is taken from a line in Shakespeare's *Macbeth* which reads "Out, out, brief candle." This line compares the shortness of man's life to a candle whose light is snuffed out suddenly—and too soon.

The buzz-saw snarled and rattled in the yard
And made dust and dropped stove-length sticks of wood,
Sweet-scented stuff when the breeze drew across it.
And from there those that lifted eyes could count
Five mountain ranges one behind the other   5
Under the sunset far into Vermont.
And the saw snarled and rattled, snarled and rattled,
As it ran light, or had to bear a load.
And nothing happened: day was all but done.
Call it a day, I wish they might have said   10
To please the boy by giving him the half hour
That a boy counts so much when saved from work.
His sister stood beside them in her apron
To tell them "Supper." At the word, the saw,
As if it meant to prove saws knew what supper meant,   15
Leaped out at the boy's hand, or seemed to leap—
He must have given the hand. However it was,
Neither refused the meeting. But the hand!
The boy's first outcry was a rueful laugh,
As he swung toward them holding up the hand   20
Half in appeal, but half as if to keep
The life from spilling. Then the boy saw all—
Since he was old enough to know, big boy
Doing a man's work, though a child at heart—
He saw all spoiled. "Don't let him cut my hand off—   25
The doctor, when he comes. Don't let him, sister!"
So. But the hand was gone already.
The doctor put him in the dark of ether.
He lay and puffed his lips out with his breath.
And then—the watcher at his pulse took fright.   30
No one believed. They listened at his heart.
Little—less—nothing!—and that ended it.
No more to build on there. And they, since they
Were not the one dead, turned to their affairs.

ROBERT FROST 1874-1963

A man who lived most of his life with great simplicity in New England where nine generations of his ancestors had lived before him, Robert Frost more than most poets was a nationally known figure. Four times winner of the Pulitzer Prize in Poetry (see the article on the Pulitzer Prize on page 51), he did much to win acceptance for modern poetry.

Frost was born in San Francisco; and it was not until his newspaper-editor father died that the ten-year-old boy moved with his Scottish-born mother and his sister to his Grandfather Frost's home in Lawrence, Massachusetts. After graduation as valedictorian from high school there, he entered Dartmouth College. But finding himself dissatisfied with college life he soon withdrew, and for the next few years he drifted from one occupation to another. He worked as a mill hand, wrote for a weekly paper, and taught school. In 1897, after marrying Elinor White, he entered Harvard University where, although deeply interested in the study of Greek, Latin, and philosophy, he chafed under the academic routine.

After two years Frost left Harvard and moved to a farm near Derry, New Hampshire, which had been given to him by his grandfather. For eleven unprofitable years he farmed, then for four more taught school. During all these years he had been writing poems and sending them to magazines. In 1911 Frost added up his accounts and discovered that in twenty years his verses had earned him about two hundred dollars.

Determined to find out once and for all whether he could make a living from his poetry, he resolved to devote several years to concentrated poetic work. According to reports, the cost of living was less in England. Frost sold his farm and in 1912 moved with his wife and four children to Gloucestershire, England.

Frost's first book, *A Boy's Will,* was published in England in 1913. Soon after the

first volume came *North of Boston*. Both were enthusiastically received by the British public and the critics, and were shortly republished in the United States.

When Frost returned to this country in 1915, he found himself famous. Lecture invitations poured in. He was appointed a professor of English at Amherst College and in 1916 elected to membership in the National Institute of Arts and Letters. But he managed to keep much of his old pattern of life, farming and teaching while continuing to produce volume after volume of excellent poetry.

Much of Frost's poetry seems to grow naturally from the changing seasons, the wooded mountains, and the rugged farms north of Boston. But although Frost often uses this New England setting, he is not primarily either a nature poet or a local colorist. His setting is usually merely background for the New Englander himself. His basic interest is man; the drama of the human situation is the hard core of his poetry.

Like the New Englanders he writes about—and like most modern poets—Frost leaves much unsaid. His apparently simple poems often turn out to be rich in hidden meanings. A fine storyteller, he often gives only the facts of an episode and leaves it to the reader to discover the significance.

Part of Frost's popularity with the general reader has no doubt stemmed from the fact that his poetry looks and sounds "like poetry." Readers respond favorably to the familiar iambic pentameter lines he often uses or to other traditional verse forms and stanza patterns. Only on careful reading is the subtly changed rhythm apparent, or the fact that every word carries a particular weight of meaning. Frost once said that art should "clean" life and "strip it to form." There is nothing superfluous in the poetry of Robert Frost.

Stopping by Woods on a Snowy Evening

Whose woods these are I think I know.
His house is in the village though;
He will not see me stopping here
To watch his woods fill up with snow.

My little horse must think it queer   5
To stop without a farmhouse near
Between the woods and frozen lake
The darkest evening of the year.

He gives his harness bells a shake
To ask if there is some mistake.   10
The only other sound's the sweep
Of easy wind and downy flake.

The woods are lovely, dark, and deep,
But I have promises to keep,
And miles to go before I sleep,   15
And miles to go before I sleep.

Nothing Gold Can Stay

Nature's first green is gold,
Her hardest hue to hold.
Her early leaf's a flower;
But only so an hour.
Then leaf subsides to leaf.   5
So Eden sank to grief,
So dawn goes down to day.
Nothing gold can stay.

Fire and Ice

Some say the world will end in fire,
Some say in ice.
From what I've tasted of desire
I hold with those who favor fire.
But if it had to perish twice,   5
I think I know enough of hate
To say that for destruction ice
Is also great
And would suffice.

To a Young Wretch

As gay for you to take your father's axe
As take his gun - rod - to go hunting - fishing.
You nick my spruce until its fiber cracks,
It gives up standing straight and goes down
    swishing.
You link an arm in its arm, and you lean   5
Across the light snow homeward smelling
    green.

I could have bought you just as good a tree
To frizzle resin in a candle flame,
And what a saving 'twould have meant to me.
But tree by charity is not the same   10
As tree by enterprise and expedition.
I must not spoil your Christmas with
    contrition.

It is your Christmases against my woods.
But even where thus opposing interests kill,
They are to be thought of as opposing
    goods   15
Oftener than as conflicting good and ill;
Which makes the war-god seem no special
    dunce
For always fighting on both sides at once.

And though in tinsel chain and popcorn
    rope,
My tree a captive in your window bay   20
Has lost its footing on my mountain slope
And lost the stars of heaven, may, or, may
The symbol star it lifts against your ceiling
Help me accept its fate with Christmas
    feeling.

"To a Young Wretch." "The Death of the Hired Man."
From *Complete Poems of Robert Frost.* Copyright 1930,
1939 by Holt, Rinehart and Winston, Inc. Copyright
1942 by Robert Frost. Reprinted by permission of Holt,
Rinehart and Winston, Inc., New York, and Jonathan
Cape Ltd., London.

The Death of the Hired Man

Mary sat musing on the lamp-flame at the
    table
Waiting for Warren. When she heard his
    step,
She ran on tip-toe down the darkened passage
To meet him in the doorway with the news
And put him on his guard. 'Silas is back.'   5
She pushed him outward with her through
    the door
And shut it after her. 'Be kind,' she said.
She took the market things from Warren's
    arms
And set them on the porch, then drew him
    down
To sit beside her on the wooden steps.   10

'When was I ever anything but kind to him?
But I'll not have the fellow back,' he said.
'I told him so last haying, didn't I?
If he left then, I said, that ended it.   14
What good is he? Who else will harbor him
At his age for the little he can do?
What help he is there's no depending on.
Off he goes always when I need him most.
He thinks he ought to earn a little pay,
Enough at least to buy tobacco with,   20
So he won't have to beg and be beholden.
"All right," I say, "I can't afford to pay
Any fixed wages, though I wish I could."
"Someone else can." "Then someone else will
    have to."
I shouldn't mind his bettering himself   25
If that was what it was. You can be certain,
When he begins like that, there's someone at
    him
Trying to coax him off with pocket-money,—
In haying time, when any help is scarce.
In winter he comes back to us. I'm done.'   30

'Sh! not so loud: he'll hear you,' Mary said.

'I want him to: he'll have to soon or late.'

'He's worn out. He's asleep beside the stove.

When I came up from Rowe's I found him
    here,
Huddled against the barn-door fast asleep, 35
A miserable sight, and frightening, too—
You needn't smile—I didn't recognize him—
I wasn't looking for him—and he's changed.
Wait till you see.'   .

        'Where did you say he'd been?'

'He didn't say. I dragged him to the house, 40
And gave him tea and tried to make him
    smoke.
I tried to make him talk about his travels.
Nothing would do: he just kept nodding off.'

'What did he say? Did he say anything?'

'But little.'

        'Anything? Mary, confess   45
He said he'd come to ditch the meadow[1] for
    me.'

'Warren!'

        'But did he? I just want to know.'

'Of course he did. What would you have him
    say?
Surely you wouldn't grudge the poor old man
Some humble way to save his self-respect. 50
He added, if you really care to know,
He meant to clear the upper pasture, too.
That sounds like something you have heard
    before?
Warren, I wish you could have heard the way
He jumbled everything. I stopped to look 55
Two or three times—he made me feel so
    queer—
To see if he was talking in his sleep.
He ran on Harold Wilson—you remember—
The boy you had in haying four years since.
He's finished school, and teaching in his
    college. 60
Silas declares you'll have to get him back.
He says they two will make a team for work:
Between them they will lay this farm as
    smooth!
The way he mixed that in with other things.

He thinks young Wilson a likely lad, though
    daft   65
On education—you know how they fought
All through July under the blazing sun,
Silas up on the cart to build the load,
Harold along beside to pitch it on.'   69

'Yes, I took care to keep well out of earshot.'

'Well, those days trouble Silas like a dream.
You wouldn't think they would. How some
    things linger!
Harold's young college boy's assurance piqued
    him.
After so many years he still keeps finding 74
Good arguments he sees he might have used.
I sympathize. I know just how it feels
To think of the right thing to say too late.
Harold's associated in his mind with Latin.
He asked me what I thought of Harold's
    saying
He studied Latin like the violin   80
Because he liked it—that an argument!
He said he couldn't make the boy believe
He could find water with a hazel prong—
Which showed how much good school had
    ever done him.
He wanted to go over that. But most of all 85
He thinks if he could have another chance
To teach him how to build a load of hay—'

'I know, that's Silas' one accomplishment.
He bundles every forkful in its place,   89
And tags and numbers it for future reference,
So he can find and easily dislodge it
In the unloading. Silas does that well.
He takes it out in bunches like big birds'
    nests.
You never see him standing on the hay
He's trying to lift, straining to lift himself.' 95

'He thinks if he could teach him that, he'd be
Some good perhaps to someone in the world.
He hates to see a boy the fool of books.
Poor Silas, so concerned for other folk,   99
And nothing to look backward to with pride,
And nothing to look forward to with hope,
So now and never any different.'

---

1. *ditch the meadow*, drain the meadow by digging ditches.

Part of a moon was falling down the west,
Dragging the whole sky with it to the hills.
Its light poured softly in her lap. She saw it
And spread her apron to it. She put out her
    hand   106
Among the harp-like morning-glory strings,
Taut with the dew from garden bed to eaves,
As if she played unheard some tenderness 109
That wrought on him beside her in the
    night.
'Warren,' she said, 'he has come home to die:
You needn't be afraid he'll leave you this
    time.'

'Home,' he mocked gently.

                  'Yes, what else but home?
It all depends on what you mean by home.
Of course he's nothing to us, any more   115
Than was the hound that came a stranger to
    us
Out of the woods, worn out upon the trail.'

'Home is the place where, when you have to
    go there,
They have to take you in.'

                'I should have called it
Something you somehow haven't to deserve.'

Warren leaned out and took a step or two, 121
Picked up a little stick, and brought it back
And broke it in his hand and tossed it by.
'Silas has better claim on us you think
Than on his brother? Thirteen little miles 125
As the road winds would bring him to his
    door.
Silas has walked that far no doubt today.
Why doesn't he go there? His brother's rich,
A somebody—director in the bank.'

'He never told us that.'

              'We know it though.' 130

'I think his brother ought to help, of course.
I'll see to that if there is need. He ought of
    right
To take him in, and might be willing to—
He may be better than appearances.

But have some pity on Silas. Do you think 135
If he had any pride in claiming kin
Or anything he looked for from his brother,
He'd keep so still about him all this time?'

'I wonder what's between them.'

                    'I can tell you.
Silas is what he is—we wouldn't mind him—
But just the kind that kinsfolk can't abide. 141
He never did a thing so very bad.
He don't know why he isn't quite as good
As anybody. Worthless though he is,
He won't be made ashamed to please his
    brother.'   145

'I can't think Si ever hurt anyone.'

'No, but he hurt my heart the way he lay
And rolled his old head on that sharp-edged
    chair-back.
He wouldn't let me put him on the lounge.
You must go in and see what you can do. 150
I made the bed up for him there tonight.
You'll be surprised at him—how much he's
    broken.
His working days are done: I'm sure of it.'

'I'd not be in a hurry to say that.'

'I haven't been. Go, look, see for yourself. 155
But, Warren, please remember how it is:
He's come to help you ditch the meadow.
He has a plan. You mustn't laugh at him.
He may not speak of it, and then he may.
I'll sit and see if that small sailing cloud 160
Will hit or miss the moon.'

                    It hit the moon.
Then there were three there, making a dim
    row,
The moon, the little silver cloud, and she.

Warren returned—too soon, it seemed to her,
Slipped to her side, caught up her hand and
    waited.   165

'Warren?' she questioned.

                'Dead,' was all he answered.

Mending Wall

Something there is that doesn't love a wall,
That sends the frozen ground swell under it,
And spills the upper boulders in the sun;
And makes gaps even two can pass abreast.
The work of hunters is another thing: 5
I have come after them and made repair
Where they have left not one stone on a stone,
But they would have the rabbit out of hiding,
To please the yelping dogs. The gaps I mean,
No one has seen them made or heard them made, 10
But at spring mending time we find them there.
I let my neighbor know beyond the hill;
And on a day we meet to walk the line
And set the wall between us once again.
We keep the wall between us as we go. 15
To each the boulders that have fallen to each.
And some are loaves and some so nearly balls
We have to use a spell to make them balance:
"Stay where you are until our backs are turned!"
We wear our fingers rough with handling them. 20
Oh, just another kind of outdoor game,
One on a side. It comes to little more:
There where it is we do not need the wall:
He is all pine and I am apple orchard.
My apple trees will never get across 25
And eat the cones under his pines, I tell him.
He only says, "Good fences make good neighbors."
Spring is the mischief in me, and I wonder
If I could put a notion in his head:
"Why do they make good neighbors? Isn't it 30
Where there are cows? But here there are no cows.
Before I built a wall I'd ask to know
What I was walling in or walling out,
And to whom I was like to give offense.
Something there is that doesn't love a wall, 35
That wants it down." I could say "Elves" to him,
But it's not elves exactly, and I'd rather
He said it for himself. I see him there
Bringing a stone grasped firmly by the top
In each hand, like an old stone savage armed. 40
He moves in darkness as it seems to me,
Not of woods only and the shade of trees.
He will not go behind his father's saying,
And he likes having thought of it so well
He says again, "Good fences make good neighbors." 45

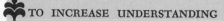

1. (*a*) Explain the relationship of the title to the story told in "Out, Out—." (*b*) Relate the details of the setting and those about the boy's thoughts in lines 1-12 to the feeling engendered by the poem. (*c*) What justification is there for describing the accident so vividly? (*d*) Compare the end of the poem with that of Auden's "Musée des Beaux Arts" (page 545).

2. In his essay Paul Engle comments on the exact images Frost uses in "Birches" (page 547). Point out some of the images in "Stopping by Woods on a Snowy Evening" and explain whether Engle's comment might also apply to them.

3. (*a*) What is the theme of "Nothing Gold Can Stay"? (*b*) How does the word *gold* help develop this theme?

4. "Fire and Ice" is *epigrammatic* in form—that is, it condenses a complex idea into a short, pithy statement. (*a*) What is Frost's idea here? (*b*) Explain the associations he sketches in for fire and ice.

5. (*a*) In "To a Young Wretch" what has the boy done? (*b*) What is the mood of the poem? How is it shown? (*c*) What does Frost mean by stating that "your Christmases against my woods" are "opposing goods"? (*d*) How do "opposing goods" differ from "conflicting good and ill"? (*e*) Relate these ideas to the statement that the war-god seems "no special dunce."

6. (*a*) What information does the opening stanza of "The Death of the Hired Man" give about Warren's attitude toward Silas? (*b*) How does Warren's attitude change? (*c*) What brings this about?

7. (*a*) Compare Warren's definition of home (lines 118-119) and Mary's (lines 119-120). (*b*) Explain how each definition fits the personality of the speaker.

8. Relate the characters and actions in "Mending Wall" to the theme.

9. In his poetry Frost often presents a conflict between two opposing views of life. Cite poems by Frost in which this is true and explain the conflicts.

Carl Sandburg

CARL SANDBURG   1878-

The genius of Carl Sandburg has shown itself in several areas. He is a greatly admired poet. He has written delightful stories for children. His multi-volumed biography of Lincoln has placed him high among modern writers of biography. (See page 690.) He has received two Pulitzer Prizes, one for his *Complete Poems* (1951) and the other for *Abraham Lincoln: The War Years* (1939). He is a noted collector of folklore, and has done much to popularize music of this type by singing folk songs and accompanying himself on the guitar.

Sandburg was born in Galesburg, Illinois, of Swedish immigrant parents. It was not until he was thirty-eight years old and had tried his hand at many different occupations that fame came to him with the publication of *Chicago Poems* (1916). Written in a free-verse style reminiscent of Walt Whitman, these poems, like those he wrote later, speak in the bold and often earthy idiom of the people. Sensitive to injustice and hypocrisy, fearful of the effect of industrialization on man, Sandburg finds hope for the future in the common people, a hope he expresses most fully in *The People, Yes* (see page 562).

The following autobiographical comments are part of Sandburg's preface to his *Complete Poems*.[1]

At the age of six, as my fingers first found how to shape the alphabet, I decided to become a person of letters. At the age of ten I had scrawled letters on slates, on paper, on boxes and walls and I formed an ambition to become a sign-painter. At twenty I was an American soldier in Puerto Rico writing letters printed in the home town paper. At twenty-one I went to West Point, being a classmate of Douglas MacArthur and Ulysses S. Grant III—for two weeks —returning home after passing in spelling, geography, history, failing in arithmetic and grammar. At twenty-three I edited a college paper and wrote many a paragraph that after a lapse of fifty years

(Continued on page 560.)

The Harbor

Passing through huddled and ugly walls
By doorways where women
Looked from their hunger-deep eyes,
Haunted with shadows of hunger-hands,
Out from the huddled and ugly walls   5
I came sudden, at the city's edge,
On a blue burst of lake,
Long lake waves breaking under the sun
On a spray-flung curve of shore;
And a fluttering storm of gulls,   10
Masses of great gray wings
And flying white bellies
Veering and wheeling free in the open.

BROWN BROTHERS

Jazz Fantasia

Drum on your drums, batter on your banjos, sob on the long cool winding saxophones. Go to it, O jazzmen.

Sling your knuckles on the bottoms of the happy tin pans, let your trombones ooze, and go husha-husha-hush with the slippery sandpaper.

Moan like an autumn wind high in the lonesome treetops, moan soft like you wanted somebody terrible, cry like a racing car slipping away from a motorcycle-cop, bang-bang! you jazzmen, bang altogether drums, traps, banjos, horns, tin cans—make two people fight on the top of a stairway and scratch each other's eyes in a clinch tumbling down the stairs.

Can the rough stuff . . . Now a Mississippi steamboat pushes up the night river with a hoo-hoo-hoo-oo . . . and the green lanterns calling to the high soft stars . . . a red moon rides on the humps of the low river hills . . . Go to it, O jazzmen.

Cool Tombs

When Abraham Lincoln was shoveled into the tombs, he forgot the copperheads and the assassin . . . in the dust, in the cool tombs.

And Ulysses Grant lost all thought of con men and Wall Street, cash and collateral turned ashes . . . in the dust, in the cool tombs.

Pocahontas' body, lovely as a poplar, sweet as a red haw in November or a pawpaw in May, did she wonder? does she remember? . . . in the dust, in the cool tombs?

Take any streetful of people buying clothes and groceries, cheering a hero or throwing confetti and blowing tin horns . . . tell me if the lovers are losers . . . tell me if any get more than the lovers . . . in the dust . . . in the cool tombs.

still seems funny, the same applying to the college yearbook I edited the following year. Across several years I wrote many odd pieces—two slim books—not worth later reprint. In a six-year period came four books of poetry having a variety of faults, no other person more keenly aware of their accomplishments and shortcomings than myself. In the two books for children in this period are a few cornland tales that go on traveling, one about "The Two Skyscrapers Who Decided to Have a Child." At fifty I had published a two-volume biography and *The American Songbag*, and there was puzzlement as to whether I was a poet, a biographer, a wandering troubadour with a guitar, a midwest Hans Christian Andersen, or a historian of current events whose newspaper re

porting was gathered into a book *The Chicago Race Riots*. . . . I am still studying verbs and the mystery of how they connect nouns. I am more suspicious of adjectives than at any other time in all my born days. I have forgotten the meaning of twenty or thirty of my poems written thirty or forty years ago. . . . All my life I have been trying to learn to read, to see and hear, and to write.

Chicago

Hog Butcher for the World,
Tool Maker, Stacker of Wheat,
Player with Railroads and the Nation's Freight Handler;
Stormy, husky, brawling,
City of the Big Shoulders: 5

They tell me you are wicked and I believe them, for I have seen your painted women
    under the gas lamps luring the farm boys.
And they tell me you are crooked and I answer: Yes, it is true I have seen the gunman
    kill and go free to kill again.
And they tell me you are brutal and my reply is: On the faces of women and children
    I have seen the marks of wanton hunger.
And having answered so I turn once more to those who sneer at this my city, and
    I give them back the sneer and say to them:
Come and show me another city with lifted head singing so proud to be alive and
    coarse and strong and cunning.   10
Flinging magnetic curses amid the toil of piling job on job, here is a tall bold slugger
    set vivid against the little soft cities;
Fierce as a dog with tongue lapping for action, cunning as a savage pitted against the
    wilderness,
        Bareheaded,
        Shoveling,
        Wrecking,
        Planning,
        Building, breaking, rebuilding,
Under the smoke, dust all over his mouth, laughing with white teeth,
Under the terrible burden of destiny laughing as a young man laughs,
Laughing even as an ignorant fighter laughs who has never lost a battle,   20
Bragging and laughing that under his wrist is the pulse, and under his ribs the heart
    of the people,
        Laughing!
Laughing the stormy, husky, brawling laughter of Youth, half-naked, sweating, proud
    to be Hog Butcher, Tool Maker, Stacker of Wheat, Player with Railroads
    and Freight Handler to the Nation.

They Have Yarns

They have yarns
Of a skyscraper so tall they had to put hinges
On the two top stories so to let the moon go by,
Of one corn crop in Missouri when the roots
Went so deep and drew off so much water   5
The Mississippi riverbed that year was dry,
Of pancakes so thin they had only one side,
Of "a fog so thick we shingled the barn and six feet out on the fog,"
Of Pecos Pete straddling a cyclone in Texas and riding it to the west coast where "it
    rained out under him,"
Of the man who drove a swarm of bees across the Rocky Mountains and the Desert
    "and didn't lose a bee,"   10
Of a mountain railroad curve where the engineer in his cab can touch the caboose
    and spit in the conductor's eye,
Of the boy who climbed a cornstalk growing so fast he would have starved to death
    if they hadn't shot biscuits up to him,
Of the old man's whiskers: "When the wind was with him his whiskers arrived a
    day before he did,"
Of the hen laying a square egg and cackling, "Ouch!" and of hens laying eggs with
    the dates printed on them,
Of the ship captain's shadow: it froze to the deck one cold winter night,   15
Of mutineers on that same ship put to chipping rust with rubber hammers,
Of the sheep counter who was fast and accurate: "I just count their feet and divide
    by four,"
Of the man so tall he must climb a ladder to shave himself,
Of the runt so teeny-weeny it takes two men and a boy to see him,
Of mosquitoes: one can kill a dog, two of them a man,   20
Of a cyclone that sucked cookstoves out of the kitchen, up the chimney flue, and on
    to the next town,
Of the same cyclone picking up wagon-tracks in Nebraska and dropping them over
    in the Dakotas,
Of the hook-and-eye snake unlocking itself into forty pieces, each piece two inches
    long, then in nine seconds flat snapping itself together again,
Of the watch swallowed by the cow—when they butchered her a year later the watch
    was running and had the correct time,
Of horned snakes, hoop snakes that roll themselves where they want to go, and rattle-
    snakes carrying bells instead of rattles on their tails,   25
Of the herd of cattle in California getting lost in a giant redwood tree that had
    hollowed out,
Of the man who killed a snake by putting its tail in its mouth so it swallowed itself,
Of railroad trains whizzing along so fast they reach the station before the whistle,
Of pigs so thin the farmer had to tie knots in their tails to keep them from crawling
    through the cracks in their pens,
Of Paul Bunyan's big blue ox, Babe, measuring between the eyes forty-two ax-
    handles and a plug of Star tobacco exactly,   30

"They Have Yarns" from *The People, Yes* by Carl Sandburg. Copyright 1936 by Harcourt, Brace & World,
Inc., New York, and reprinted by their permission.

Of John Henry's hammer and the curve of its swing and his singing of it as "a rain-
    bow round my shoulder."
                    "Do tell!"
                    "I want to know!"
                    "You don't say so!"
                    "For the land's sake!"   35
                    "Gosh all fish-hooks!"
                    "Tell me some more.
                    I don't believe a word you say
                    but I love to listen
                    to your sweet harmonica   40
                    to your chin-music.
                    Your fish stories hang together
                    when they're just a pack of lies:
                    you ought to have a leather medal:
                    you ought to have a statue   45
                    carved of butter: you deserve
                    a large bouquet of turnips."

        "Yessir," the traveler drawled,
"Away out there in the petrified forest
everything goes on the same as usual.   50
The petrified birds sit in their petrified nests
and hatch their petrified young from petrified eggs."

A high pressure salesman jumped off the Brooklyn Bridge and was saved by a police-
    man. But it didn't take him long to sell the idea to the policeman. So together
    they jumped off the bridge.

One of the oil men in heaven started a rumor of a gusher down in hell. All the other
    oil men left in a hurry for hell. As he gets to thinking about the rumor he had
    started he says to himself there might be something in it after all. So he
    leaves for hell in a hurry.

"The number 42 will win this raffle, that's my number." And when he won they
    asked him whether he guessed the number or had a system. He said he had a
    system, "I took up the old family album and there on page 7 was my grand-
    father and grandmother both on page 7. I said to myself this is easy for
    7 times 7 is the number that will win and 7 times 7 is 42."   55

Once a shipwrecked sailor caught hold of a stateroom door and floated for hours
    till friendly hands from out of the darkness threw him a rope. And he called
    across the night, "What country is this?" and hearing voices answer, "New
    Jersey," he took a fresh hold on the floating stateroom door and called back
    half-wearily, "I guess I'll float a little farther."

An Ohio man bundled up the tin roof of a summer kitchen and sent it to a motor-
    car maker with a complaint of his car not giving service. In three weeks a new
    car arrived for him and a letter: "We regret delay in shipment but your car
    was received in a very bad order."

A Dakota cousin of this Ohio man sent six years of tin can accumulations to the same works, asking them to overhaul his car. Two weeks later came a rebuilt car, five old tin cans, and a letter: "We are also forwarding you five parts not necessary in our new model."

Thus fantasies heard at filling stations in the Midwest. Another relates to a Missouri mule who took aim with his heels at an automobile rattling by. The car turned a somersault, lit next a fence, ran right along through a cornfield till it came to a gate, moved onto the road and went on its way as though nothing had happened. The mule heehawed with desolation, "What's the use?"

Another tells of a farmer and his family stalled on a railroad crossing, how they jumped out in time to see a limited express knock it into flinders, the farmer calling, "Well, I always did say that car was no shucks in a real pinch."   60

When the Masonic Temple in Chicago was the tallest building in the United States west of New York, two men who would cheat the eyes out of you if you gave 'em a chance, took an Iowa farmer to the top of the building and asked him, "How is this for high?" They told him that for $25 they would go down in the basement and turn the building around on its turntable for him while he stood on the roof and saw how this seventh wonder of the world worked. He handed them $25. They went. He waited. They never came back.

This is told in Chicago as a folk tale, the same as the legend of Mrs. O'Leary's cow kicking over the barn lamp that started the Chicago fire, when the Georgia visitor, Robert Toombs, telegraphed an Atlanta crony, "Chicago is on fire, the whole city burning down, God be praised!"

Nor is the prize sleeper Rip Van Winkle and his scolding wife forgotten, nor the headless horseman scooting through Sleepy Hollow

Nor the sunken treasure-ships in coves and harbors, the hideouts of gold and silver sought by Coronado,[1] nor the Flying Dutchman[2] rounding the Cape doomed to nevermore pound his ear nor ever again take a snooze for himself

Nor the sailor's caretaker Mother Carey[3] seeing to it that every seafaring man in the afterworld has a seabird to bring him news of ships and women, an albatross for the admiral, a gull for the deckhand   65

Nor the sailor with a sweetheart in every port of the world, nor the ships that set out with flying colors and all the promises you could ask, the ships never heard of again,

Nor Jim Liverpool, the riverman who could jump across any river and back without touching land he was that quick on his feet,

Nor Mike Fink along the Ohio and the Mississippi, half wild horse and half cock-eyed alligator, the rest of him snags and snapping turtle. "I can out-run, out-jump, out-shoot, out-brag, out-drink, and out-fight, rough and tumble, no holts barred, any man on both sides of the river from Pittsburgh to New Orleans and back again to St. Louis. My trigger finger itches and I want to go redhot. War, famine and bloodshed puts flesh on my bones, and hardship's my daily bread."

Nor the man so lean he threw no shadow: six rattlesnakes struck at him at one time and every one missed him.

---

1. *Coronado*, Spanish explorer who set out in 1540 to search for seven cities in the present southwestern area of the United States that were said to be stocked with gold and gems. 2. *Flying Dutchman*, in legend, a captain condemned to sail his ship forever and never reach port. He and his spectral ship were often seen near the Cape of Good Hope. 3. *Mother Carey*, changed form of Latin words *Mater cara* (tender Mother or dear Mother), in reference to the Virgin, Mother of Jesus.

TO INCREASE UNDERSTANDING

1. "The Harbor" is a poem built on contrasts. (*a*) What two areas are contrasted? (*b*) Contrast the dominant sound in the first six lines with that in the last lines and explain how this change in sound heightens the contrast. (*c*) What is the theme of the poem? (*d*) Is the theme stated or implied? Explain precisely how it is developed.

2. In "Jazz Fantasia" Sandburg makes extensive use of *onomatopoeia*, a device in which the sound of a word echoes its sense. (*a*) Pick out onomatopoeic words and explain how they add to the effectiveness of the poem. (*b*) Why is onomatopoeia an appropriate device to use in this particular poem?

3. (*a*) In "Cool Tombs" what is the justification for the division of the poem into four sentences? (*b*) What does the poet emphasize in picturing the burial of Lincoln and Grant? (*c*) What memories of Pocahontas does he evoke? (*d*) Can you advance any reason for his using literal speech in writing of Lincoln and Grant and figurative language in speaking of Pocahontas? (*e*) What is the theme of the poem?

4. (*a*) In the poem "Chicago" what ideas of the city is Sandburg emphasizing? (*b*) Cite images that help develop these ideas. (*c*) What is the tone of the poem?

5. When "Chicago" was first published before World War I in *Poetry* (see page 593), it created a stir of excitement. Explain what at the time was startling about this poem in (*a*) idea, (*b*) imagery, (*c*) diction, and (*d*) poetic form.

6. "They Have Yarns" is a section from *The People, Yes* (1936), a long poem affirming belief in the American people. (*a*) Select from among the yarns that Sandburg offers ones which belong to different historical epochs. (*b*) Name yarns of various geographical settings. (*c*) What are the dominant traits and interests shown in these yarns? (*d*) What image of the American people do the yarns considered collectively present?

BETTER READING
Contrasting the poetry of Frost and Sandburg

Both Robert Frost and Carl Sandburg celebrate the American, the common man; both echo in their verses the speech rhythms of ordinary Americans. Often compared because they belong to the same generation and have done much to bring poetry to the American people, they nevertheless emphasize different aspects of American life, speak for different types of people, and represent differing schools of modern poetry.

The central theme of both poets is man, but they handle this subject in different ways. Frost lived most of his life on farms and in small towns. The people he pictures in his poetry are specific individuals seen against a particular background. Sandburg, on the other hand, is keyed to the bustle of an industrial society and has made the city the setting for much of his poetry. He sees man as surrounded by the city, dwarfed by his environment, a member of a group rather than a clearly realized individual.

Glance again over the poems by Frost which you have studied. In which of them are you aware of individuals with distinct personalities? Can you describe the boy in "Out, Out—"? What sort of person is the neighbor in "Mending Wall"? The speaker? Do you find any individual portraits in the poems by Sandburg? What feeling toward men does Sandburg convey through these poems? How does he convey it?

In their diction and the rhythms of language Frost and Sandburg also differ. In his laconic and understated poetry Frost is talking as a New Hampshire farmer, an authentic New Englander. His phrases are spare, monosyllabic, often epigrammatic; sometimes they achieve a quality resembling folk speech. Midwesterner Carl Sandburg, by contrast, uses the language of the factory and the sidewalk. While he too speaks colloquially, there is a roughness, a colorful extravagance to his speech that produces a totally different effect from the habitual understatement of Frost.

Read aloud lines spoken by Mary or Warren in "The Death of the Hired Man" that catch the rhythm of New England speech. Contrast these lines with lines from "Chicago" or "They Have Yarns." What differences do you notice in diction and rhythm?

Frost and Sandburg also differ in their handling of poetic form. Behind Frost's work is the influence of his New England predecessors, Emerson and Emily Dickinson. Sandburg's vigorous free verse is in the tradition of Whitman. Each has mastered the fusion between idea and poetic form. How do the rhyme and meter of "Stopping by Woods on a Snowy Evening" relate to its laconic, controlled quality? What effect is gained by the repetition of the last line? How does the use of free verse help Sandburg create the mood of "Jazz Fantasia"?

Select some poem by Frost or Sandburg that you particularly like (not one in this anthology) and explain to the class ways in which it is typical of this poet's work.

Edwin Arlington Robinson

EDWIN ARLINGTON ROBINSON
1869-1935

During the 1920's Edwin Arlington Robinson was generally regarded as America's greatest living poet. Three times during that single decade he was awarded the Pulitzer Prize. Yet by the time he won the prize for the first time he was already fifty-three years old, and the "Tilbury" portraits upon which his fame rests most securely today were all behind him.

Robinson spent his youth in Gardiner, Maine, the fictitious "Tilbury Town," near the village of Head Tide where he was born. Financial difficulties subsequent to his father's death brought an end to his schooling after two years at Harvard. When he returned to Gardiner, he devoted his time to writing poetry. When he moved to New York City in 1897 he led a hermitlike existence, taking jobs only to enable him to live and spending his greatest efforts on his poetry. In 1916 *The Man Against the Sky* brought him sudden fame.

Robinson's poems fall roughly into two classes: the earlier Tilbury portraits, which grew out of his New England experiences, and the later narrative poems like *Lancelot* and *Tristram*, which are based on medieval legends. "Miniver Cheevy," "Richard Cory," and others of Robinson's best-known poems belong to the earlier group. This Tilbury Town gallery is composed largely of "cheated dreamers" and "bewildered mediocrities," most of whom manage in one way or another to withdraw from hard reality. But Robinson's pessimism is always tempered by wit and imagination, often by flashes of wry humor. His thorough mastery of intricate and varied poetic forms and his fine feeling for the subtler meanings of words give his poems a distinctive flavor.

Miniver Cheevy

Miniver Cheevy, child of scorn,
  Grew lean while he assailed the seasons;
He wept that he was ever born,
  And he had reasons.

Miniver loved the days of old   5
  When swords were bright and steeds were prancing;
The vision of a warrior bold
  Would set him dancing.

Miniver sighed for what was not,
  And dreamed, and rested from his labors;   10
He dreamed of Thebes and Camelot,
  And Priam's neighbors.[1]

Miniver mourned the ripe renown
  That made so many a name so fragrant;
He mourned Romance, now on the town,[2]   15
  And Art, a vagrant.

Miniver loved the Medici,[3]
  Albeit he had never seen one;
He would have sinned incessantly
  Could he have been one.   20

Miniver cursed the commonplace
  And eyed a khaki suit with loathing;
He missed the medieval grace
  Of iron clothing.

Miniver scorned the gold he sought,   25
  But sore annoyed was he without it;
Miniver thought, and thought, and thought,
  And thought about it.

Miniver Cheevy, born too late,
  Scratched his head and kept on thinking;   30
Miniver coughed, and called it fate,
  And kept on drinking.

---

1. *Priam's neighbors.* Priam (prī'əm), the last king of Troy, an ancient city in Asia Minor, was killed in the Trojan War. His neighbors were the Greeks, who, under Agamemnon, conquered Troy. 2. *on the town*, living on charity, a pauper. 3. *the Medici* (med'ə chē), the ruling family of Florence, Italy, during the fifteenth and sixteenth centuries. They were notable both for their generous patronage of art and for their lavish living and wicked lives.

Richard Cory

Whenever Richard Cory went downtown,
    We people on the pavement looked at him:
He was a gentleman from sole to crown,
    Clean-favored, and imperially slim.

And he was always quietly arrayed,   5
    And he was always human when he talked;
But still he fluttered pulses when he said,
    "Good morning," and he glittered when he walked.

And he was rich—yes, richer than a king—
    And admirably schooled in every grace: 10
In fine, we thought that he was everything
    To make us wish that we were in his place.

So on we worked, and waited for the light,
    And went without the meat, and cursed the bread;
And Richard Cory, one calm summer night,   15
    Went home and put a bullet through his head.

Cliff Klingenhagen

Cliff Klingenhagen had me in to dine
With him one day; and after soup and meat,
And all the other things there were to eat,
Cliff took two glasses and filled one with wine
And one with wormwood. Then, without a sign   5
For me to choose at all, he took the draught
Of bitterness himself, and lightly quaffed
It off, and said the other one was mine.

And when I asked him what the deuce he meant
By doing that, he only looked at me   10
And grinned, and said it was a way of his.
And though I know the fellow, I have spent
Long time a-wondering when I shall be
As happy as Cliff Klingenhagen is.

TO INCREASE UNDERSTANDING

1. In "Miniver Cheevy" the name of the character gives the reader a sly hint as to his personality. *Miniver* is a kind of fur popular during the Middle Ages; *cheevy* echoes such adjectives as *childish* and *peevish*. What is the relationship between this name and the individual who bears it?

2. Would Miniver have been happy in ancient Troy, or Camelot, or in the Florence of the Medicis? Why, or why not?

3. "Richard Cory" builds up to a surprise ending. (*a*) Cite details that make this ending a surprise. (*b*) What does the poem say about human insight?

4. (*a*) Describe the tone of "Miniver Cheevy" and explain how the verse form and the diction help create this tone. (*b*) Explain how "Richard Cory" differs from "Miniver Cheevy" in tone, and name some of the factors creating this difference.

5. "Cliff Klingenhagen" is cast in sonnet form. Review the "Better Reading" article on the sonnet (page 273) and explain whether or not this poem follows the sonnet form in its development.

6. In Miniver Cheevy, Richard Cory, and Cliff Klingenhagen, Robinson has created three distinct individuals, each of whom faces a problem. (*a*) Which problems can you identify? (*b*) How does Cliff's solution differ from those of the others?

Edgar Lee Masters

EDGAR LEE MASTERS 1868-1950

The Spoon River which runs through central Illinois is only a small stream, yet it is famous throughout the country because of the poetry of Edgar Lee Masters. This regional poet grew up in Lewistown, Illinois, and immortalized the Spoon River country by making it the setting for his perceptive and often disturbing *Spoon River Anthology*.

Lucinda Matlock

I went to dances at Chandlerville,
And played snap-out 'at Winchester.
One time we changed partners,
Driving home in the moonlight of middle June,
And then I found Davis.   5
We were married and lived together for seventy years,
Enjoying, working, raising the twelve children,
Eight of whom we lost
Ere I had reached the age of sixty.
I spun, I wove, I kept the house, I nursed the sick,   10
I made the garden, and for holiday
Rambled over the fields where sang the larks,
And by Spoon River gathering many a shell,
And many a flower and medicinal weed—
Shouting to the wooded hills, singing to the green
      valleys.   15
At ninety-six I had lived enough, that is all,
And passed to a sweet repose.
What is this I hear of sorrow and weariness,
Anger, discontent, and drooping hopes?
Degenerate sons and daughters,   20
Life is too strong for you—
It takes life to love Life.

As a young boy Masters began writing poems and stories, and during his brief sojourn at Knox College and his work in his father's law office, this remained an important interest. In 1891 he was admitted to the bar. The following year he went to Chicago, where he became in time a highly respected lawyer. With the publication of *Spoon River Anthology* in 1915 his fame as a poet overshadowed his reputation as a lawyer. A few years later he abandoned law to devote all his time to writing.

Spoon River Anthology consists of a series of epitaphs which the dead of a small Illinois community speak from their graves. In both this book and its sequel, *The New Spoon River* (1924), Masters emphasizes, often in ironic tones, the frailties, the eccentricities, and the failures of man. Although most of the speakers are embittered by life, some, like Lucinda Matlock, speak with courage and optimism.

Since their publication the Spoon River epitaphs have appealed to thousands of readers. In addition to their subject matter, which readers have found as interesting and easy to understand as fiction, the simplicity of the conversational language and the free-verse form have made the poems popular. Even the most pessimistic epitaph is sharp and clear in language, and some of the verses sparkle with a sense of humor and a keen appreciation of beauty.

George Gray

I have studied many times
The marble which was chiseled for me—
A boat with a furled sail at rest in a harbor.
In truth it pictures not my destination
But my life.   5
For love was offered me, and I shrank from its
      disillusionment;
Sorrow knocked at my door, but I was afraid;
Ambition called to me, but I dreaded the chances.
Yet all the while I hungered for meaning in my life
And now I know that we must lift the sail   10
And catch the winds of destiny
Wherever they drive the boat.
To put meaning in one's life may end in madness,
But life without meaning is the torture
Of restlessness and vague desire—   15
It is a boat longing for the sea and yet afraid.

Masters continued to write poetry and biographies, such as *Lincoln—the Man* (1931), until he died in 1950. Although his later works were interesting and readable, he never again achieved the brilliance of the Spoon River poems.

1. (a) Why does Lucinda Matlock refer to her sons and daughters as *degenerate*? (b) What does she mean by saying "Life is too strong for you/—It takes life to love life"? (c) In what ways does her own life bear out the statement?

2. The image of a boat runs through "George Gray." (a) Why does Gray begin his epitaph by speaking of it "with sail furled"? (b) What does George believe it symbolizes in his life? (c) Relate the knowledge George Gray sets forth in lines 10-12 to the tragedy of his life.

3. (a) Contrast Fiddler Jones' reaction with that of most of his neighbors to the following: a field of clover, a cloud of dust, a robin's song. (b) What do his reactions to these things show about the fiddler's philosophy of life?

4. Lines 5-14 in "Fiddler Jones" contrast ways of viewing country scenes. (a) How are the fiddler's ways peculiar? (b) Why was his life not tragic?

5. Lucinda Matlock, Fiddler Jones, and George Gray are all buried in the same graveyard, and we may assume that they knew each other while they were alive. Do you think the three would have been friendly with one another? Mention personality characteristics of the three which support your ideas.

6. In "Miniver Cheevy," "Richard Cory," and "Cliff Klingenhagen" (pages 566, 567) Edwin Arlington Robinson pictures three of the people of Tilbury Town in Maine. In "Lucinda Matlock," "Fiddler Jones," and "George Gray" Edgar Lee Masters presents three individuals of Spoon River in Illinois. (a) How does the verse form used by Robinson in creating his portraits differ from that used by Masters? (b) Contrast Robinson's point of view with Masters'. (c) Using the portraits as a basis for judgment, compare the attitudes toward small-town life of these two poets. (d) Are the Tilbury Town and Spoon River portraits criticisms of people in a certain locality or of men in general?

Fiddler Jones

The earth keeps some vibration going
There in your heart, and that is you.
And if the people find you can fiddle,
Why, fiddle you must, for all your life.
What do you see, a harvest of clover?   5
Or a meadow to walk through to the river?
The wind's in the corn; you rub your hands
For beeves hereafter ready for market;
Or else you hear the rustle of skirts
Like the girls when dancing at Little Grove.   10
To Cooney Potter a pillar of dust
Or whirling leaves meant ruinous drouth;
They looked to me like Red-Head Sammy
Stepping it off, to "Toor-a-Loor."
How could I till my forty acres   15
Not to speak of getting more,
With a medley of horns, bassoons, and piccolos
Stirred in my brain by crows and robins
And the creak of a windmill—only these?
And I never started to plow in my life   20
That some one did not stop in the road
And take me away to a dance or picnic.
I ended up with forty acres;
I ended up with a broken fiddle—
And a broken laugh, and a thousand memories,   25
And not a single regret.

BROWN BROTHERS

VACHEL LINDSAY 1879-1931

The agricultural Middle West, with its strong belief in democracy and its equally strong religious beliefs, profoundly influenced the poetry of Vachel Lindsay. He was born and brought up in Springfield, Illinois, a town rich in memories of Abraham Lincoln. After attending Hiram College in Ohio, he studied at the Art Institute of Chicago and at the New York School of Art. Believing that art and literature were necessary for all people, he began tramping across the country, a preacher in a hobo garb. Often in exchange for a meal and a night's lodging he recited verses from a collection which he published in 1912 entitled *Rhymes to Be Traded for Bread*. In his poems he used the rhythms of the pulpit, of Fourth of July oratory, and of jazz to bring his Gospel of Beauty to people who would not listen to conventional poetry. It was while he was on a walking trip from Illinois to New Mexico in 1912 that he composed "General William Booth Enters into Heaven." Published in *Poetry*, this poem brought Lindsay fame. It became the title poem in *General William Booth Enters into Heaven and Other Poems* (1913); this volume was followed by *The Congo and Other Poems* (1914), and by several other volumes of Lindsay's new and exciting poetry. In the decade preceding his death his poetry became quieter and more lyrical, but this later poetry was less popular.

The content of Lindsay's poetry was strongly influenced by the democratic ideas of Lincoln, Andrew Jackson, and Walt Whitman. From Edgar Allan Poe he learned how to vary his rhythms and to use words to create various kinds of musical effects. He saw the artistry of folk songs and caught their rhythms. All these elements he combined in what he called "the higher vaudeville"—a new kind of poetry direct in its approach, democratic in its outlook, startling in its pulsating, syncopated chants, and enlivened by humor and sharp imagery.

Vachel Lindsay

William Booth, the founder of the Salvation Army, was an Englishman with an enormous sympathy for the poor and degraded. As the leader of the "army" which strove to bring the comforts of religion to these unfortunate people, this great-hearted man became known as "General" Booth. Shortly after Booth's death in 1912, Vachel Lindsay composed this tribute. In it he visualizes the scene as General Booth enters into the presence of God, accompanied by all the unfortunates he has led to religion.

General William Booth Enters into Heaven

To be sung to the tune of THE BLOOD OF THE LAMB[1] *with indicated instruments.*

I

[*Bass drum beaten loudly.*]
Booth led boldly with his big bass drum—
(Are you washed in the blood of the Lamb?)
The saints smiled gravely, and they said: "He's come."
(Are you washed in the blood of the Lamb?)
Walking lepers followed, rank on rank,   5
Lurching bravos from the ditches dank,
Drabs from the alleyways and drug fiends pale—
Minds still passion-ridden, soul-powers frail—
Vermin-eaten saints with moldy breath,
Unwashed legions with the ways of death—   10
(Are you washed in the blood of the Lamb?)

[*Banjos.*]
Every slum had sent its half-a-score
The round world over. (Booth had groaned for more.)
Every banner that the wide world flies
Bloomed with glory and transcendent dyes.   15
Big-voiced lasses made their banjos bang!
Tranced, fanatical, they shrieked and sang—
"Are you washed in the blood of the Lamb?"
Hallelujah! It was queer to see
Bull-necked convicts with that land make free!   20
Loons with bazoos blowed a blare, blare, blare
On, on, upward through the golden air.
(Are you washed in the blood of the Lamb?)

1. *The Blood of the Lamb*, a hymn much used in the Salvation Army. "The Lamb" is Christ, and the refrain line, "Are you washed in the blood of the Lamb?" calls on the sinner to repent and receive Christ's forgiveness.

II

[*Bass drum slower and softer.*]
Booth died blind, and still by faith he trod,
Eyes still dazzled by the ways of God.   25
Booth led boldly and he looked the chief—
Eagle countenance in sharp relief,
Beard a-flying, air of high command
Unabated in that holy land.

[*Sweet flute music.*]
Jesus came from out the courthouse door,   30
Stretched His hands above the passing poor.
Booth saw not, but led his queer ones there
Round and round the mighty courthouse square.
Yet in an instant all that blear review
Marched on spotless, clad in raiment new.   35
The lame were straightened, withered limbs uncurled,
And blind eyes opened on a new, sweet world.

[*Bass drum louder.*]
Drabs and vixens in a flash made whole!
Gone was the weasel-head, the snout, the jowl!
Sages and sibyls now, and athletes clean,   40
Rulers of empires, and of forests green!

[*Grand chorus of all instruments. Tambourines to
the foreground.*]
The hosts were sandaled and their wings were fire!
(Are you washed in the blood of the Lamb?)
But their noise played havoc with the angel choir.
(Are you washed in the blood of the Lamb?)   45
Oh, shout Salvation! it was good to see
Kings and princes by the Lamb set free.
The banjos rattled and the tambourines
Jing-jing-jingled in the hands of queens!

[*Reverently sung, no instruments.*]
And when Booth halted by the curb for prayer   50
He saw his Master through the flag-filled air.
Christ came gently with a robe and crown
For Booth the soldier, while the throng knelt down.
He saw King Jesus. They were face to face,
And he knelt a-weeping in that holy place.   55
(Are you washed in the blood of the Lamb?)

TO INCREASE UNDERSTANDING

1. (*a*) What do you know about Vachel Lindsay that might explain why he would be moved to write a tribute to General Booth? (*b*) What qualities of Booth does he extol in "General William Booth Enters into Heaven"?

2. Many modern poets reveal the complexities they feel in life today by the use of *incongruity*, or the inclusion of details that are inappropriate or out of harmony with one another. In Lindsay's poems this incongruity is related to American tall tales and is based on heightened imagination. For example, in "General William Booth Enters into Heaven" the setting is part celestial and part country town. (*a*) Name specific examples of incongruity in the poem. (*b*) What purposes do these incongruities serve?

3. The poem is written in marching rhythm. (*a*) Why is this rhythm appropriate? (*b*) What devices does Lindsay use to emphasize the idea of a march? (*c*) What factors in addition to the rhythm add to the music of the poem?

4. Compare and contrast "General William Booth Enters into Heaven" with Sandburg's "Jazz Fantasia" (page 560). Consider (*a*) poetic form, (*b*) imagery, (*c*) tone, (*d*) author's purpose.

The Swelling Chorus

In the decade after World War I, many new poets found an audience. The earlier popularity of Frost, Sandburg, and Lindsay had somewhat accustomed readers to the ideas and rhythms of distinctively twentieth-century poetry. *Poetry* magazine (see page 593) was furnishing a market for experimental verse. In this atmosphere such widely different types of poetry as the idea-packed free verse of Marianne Moore, the subtle, restrained stanzas of John Crowe Ransom, and the provocative, different-looking poetry of E. E. Cummings were gradually accepted.

Of the poets who rose to fame in the 1920's, some were only a few years younger than the group which had achieved national prominence before World War I. Some of these, because of the difficulty of their poetry, had only belatedly gained recognition. Some had succeeded in other careers before turning to poetry. As the years passed, younger poets climbed to fame until, at the outbreak of World War II, the United States had a remarkable number of poets of true excellence.

E. E. CUMMINGS 1894-1962

A few years ago a student wrote to E. (Edward) E. (Estlin) Cummings (or e. e. cummings, as he signed his poems) requesting information. The student received a reply addressed and written in bold crayon colors. This unconventional mode of writing is indicative of the poet's impulse to experiment; it suggests also his sense of fun.

For an experimentalist whose poems have been referred to as "typographical oddities," Cummings was reared according to a rather traditional New England pattern, ending with study at Harvard. During World War I, he served in the ambulance corps in France. After the war, unsettled and disillusioned, like many other American writers and artists in the 1920's, he went to Paris. (See "Gertrude Stein and the Lost Generation," page 458.) Later he returned to America to live in Greenwich Village, New York, and write and paint.

Cummings experimented with a problem poets have been trying to resolve since writing first began, the task of representing sounds on paper. He tried old methods and created new ones. He worked with rhymes, assonance, alliteration. He broke compound words into parts and put explanatory words or phrases between the parts. He ran words together to increase the tempo, or separated them, putting one to a line to express slow movement. Through his experiments he created some of the most delightful lyrics in contemporary poetry.

Although Cummings is popularly known because his poetry "looks different," it was his ability to fit the form of the poem to the ideas he was expressing and to clothe the thought in fresh imagery that fostered his high reputation.

WILLIAM CARLOS WILLIAMS 1883-1963

Although for many years Dr. Williams spent much of his time seeing patients and delivering babies in and around Rutherford, New Jersey, he found time to write more than thirty-seven volumes of prose and poetry.

For Dr. Williams the everyday event had beauty, interest, and significance. His poetry deals with such common things as spring, plums, a wheelbarrow —in short, what one might see daily, yet not notice. His writing reflects the physician's experience of seeing people under all conditions of life—from when they are being born to the moment of their death. Such observation has given insight and substance to his poetry and stories. Two collections of his poetry are *Collected Later Poems* (1950) and *Collected Earlier Poems* (1951).

JOHN CROWE RANSOM 1888-

John Crowe Ransom is noted as poet, literary critic, and teacher. While teaching at Vanderbilt University in Nashville, Tennessee, he and seven other Southern writers formed "The Fugitive Group," which supported the "new poetry" and published poems and critical essays in their periodical, *The Fugitive*. In 1937 Ransom went to Kenyon College, Ohio, where he founded *The Kenyon Review*.

Among the volumes of poetry Ransom has published are *Chills and Fever* (1924), *Two Gentlemen in Bonds* (1927), and *Selected Poems* (1945). His poems are notable for their irony and lack of sentimentality. Unlike some other modern poets such as Cummings, Ransom often works within regular rhythms, rhyme schemes, and stanza forms.

ROBERT LOWELL 1917-

Robert Lowell's poetry, like that of earlier members of the Lowell family, James Russell Lowell (page 281) and Amy Lowell (page 52), often is set in New England. But he treats his subjects in a very different manner.

After he had studied at Harvard for two years, Lowell was led by his interest in writing poetry to transfer to Kenyon College for study under John Crowe Ransom. Lowell published his first volume of poetry in 1944, and in 1947 he received the Pulitzer Prize for his second volume, *Lord Weary's Castle*. Like Ransom, Lowell uses traditional stanza forms. Because of his extensive use of allusion and symbolism, and his compression of thought, his poetry requires careful reading.

SARA TEASDALE 1884-1933

Sara Teasdale was born in St. Louis. A most noteworthy event in her life was the fact that Vachel Lindsay (page 570) fell in love with her; but she rejected him. For the most part she lived quietly, writing hundreds of poems notable for their apparently effortless imagery, easy rhythm, and their personal revelations. Her best poems can be found in *The Collected Poems of Sara Teasdale* (1937).

❧ TO INCREASE UNDERSTANDING

1. What is the situation of the speaker in "Spring Night"?

2. (*a*) What is the setting of the lyric? (*b*) How does the poet convey the beauty of this setting? (*c*) How is its beauty related to her theme?

3. Compare "Spring Night" with Williams' "Spring and All" (page 543) and Cummings' "Chanson Innocente" (page 544) considering (*a*) theme, (*b*) verse form, (*c*) melody, (*d*) imagery.

Sara Teasdale

Spring Night

The park is filled with night and fog,
    The veils are drawn about the world,
The drowsy lights along the paths
    Are dim and pearled.

Gold and gleaming the empty streets,   5
    Gold and gleaming the misty lake,
The mirrored lights like sunken swords,
    Glimmer and shake.

Oh, is it not enough to be
Here with this beauty over me?   10
My throat should ache with praise, and I
Should kneel in joy beneath the sky.
O beauty, are you not enough?
Why am I crying after love,
With youth, a singing voice and eyes   15
To take earth's wonder with surprise?
Why have I put off my pride,
Why am I unsatisfied,
I for whom the pensive night
Binds her cloudy hair with light,   20
I for whom all beauty burns
Like incense in a million urns?
O beauty, are you not enough?
Why am I crying after love?

PHOTOGRAPH BY E. O. HOPPÉ, LONDON

Wallace Stevens

Domination of Black

At night, by the fire,
The colors of the bushes
And of the fallen leaves,
Repeating themselves,
Turned in the room,   5
Like the leaves themselves
Turning in the wind.
Yes: but the color of the heavy hemlocks[1]
Came striding.
And I remembered the cry of the peacocks.[2]   10

The colors of their tails
Were like the leaves themselves
Turning in the wind,
In the twilight wind.
They swept over the room,   15
Just as they flew from the boughs of the hemlocks
Down to the ground.
I heard them cry—the peacocks.
Was it a cry against the twilight
Or against the leaves themselves   20
Turning in the wind,
Turning as the flames
Turned in the fire,
Turning as the tails of the peacocks
Turned in the loud fire,   25
Loud as the hemlocks
Full of the cry of the peacocks?
Or was it a cry against the hemlocks?

Out of the window,
I saw how the planets gathered   30
Like the leaves themselves
Turning in the wind.
I saw how the night came,
Came striding like the color of the heavy hemlocks.
I felt afraid.
And I remembered the cry of the peacocks.

1. *hemlocks*, dark evergreen trees with drooping branches. There may
also be an indirect association with evil implied by another type of
hemlock which is a poisonous plant. 2. *cry of the peacocks*. In folklore
the peacock's cry is considered a bad omen.

Marianne Moore

Silence My father used to say,
"Superior people never make long visits,
have to be shown Longfellow's grave
or the glass flowers at Harvard.
Self-reliant like the cat—   5
that takes its prey to privacy,
the mouse's limp tail hanging like a shoelace from its mouth—
they sometimes enjoy solitude,
and can be robbed of speech
by speech which has delighted them.   10
The deepest feeling always shows itself in silence;
not in silence, but restraint."
Nor was he insincere in saying, "Make my house your inn."
Inns are not residences.

Robinson Jeffers

The Eye The Atlantic is a stormy moat; and the Mediterranean,
The blue pool in the old garden,
More than five thousand years has drunk sacrifice
Of ships and blood, and shines in the sun; but here the Pacific—
Our ships, planes, wars are perfectly irrelevant.   5
Neither our present blood-feud with the brave dwarfs
Nor any future world-quarrel of westering
And eastering man, the bloody migrations, greed of power, clash
        of faiths—
Is a speck of dust on the great scale-pan.
Here from this mountain shore, headland beyond stormy   10
        headland plunging like dolphins through the blue sea-smoke
Into pale sea—look west at the hill of water: it is half the planet:
        this dome, this half-globe, this bulging
Eyeball of water, arched over to Asia,
Australia and white Antarctica: those are the eyelids that never close;
        this is the staring unsleeping
Eye of the earth; and what it watches is not our wars.

WALLACE STEVENS 1879-1955

Like his friend William Carlos Williams (page 572), Wallace Stevens combined poetry with another full-time career. A law-school graduate, he was employed for most of his life by a Connecticut insurance company, in his later years as vice-president.

In 1914 Stevens submitted a few poems to a contest sponsored by *Poetry*. Not only were they published, but they also received a prize. In spite of this success, Stevens did not publish his first volume of poetry until 1923.

Stevens considered poetry the stuff that "made life palatable," since he felt that only in the world of the imagination could the true meaning of life be sensed. Consequently he sets his poetry in a fanciful world of extravagant sound and color. He seldom states an idea directly, relying rather on the implication of symbols and intricate metaphors to convey the thought.

MARIANNE MOORE 1887-

When asked what was the difference between a poet and an ordinary individual, Miss Moore answered, "Nothing, unless it is an exaggerated tendency to visualize; and on encountering manifestations of life —insects, lower animals, or human beings—to wonder if they are happy and what will become of them." This interest and sympathy are evident in Miss Moore's life and in her writing. She frequently entertains friends, students, and other writers in her Brooklyn apartment. (She keeps a bowl of subway tokens from which the Manhattan visitor may take the fare for his trip back to the city.) At the invitation of David Wallace of the Ford Motor Company, she suggested names for a projected car. *Edsel* won over her entries of *Mongoose Civique, Utopian Turtle-Top, Impeccable,* and *Andante con Motto.* Her fascination for strange animals and plants is evident in the frequency with which their names appear in her poetry. Her writing sparkles with the insights of a keen and incisive mind. Winner of many honors and awards, including the Pulitzer Prize, she was recently named Poet of Honor by *Poetry*, the magazine in which her poems first appeared. Her latest book, *A Marianne Moore Reader* (1961), contains much of her best poetry and other writing.

ROBINSON JEFFERS 1887-1962

Although Robinson Jeffers was born in Pennsylvania, his long residence in Carmel, California, identified him closely with the Pacific Coast. In fact, one of the characteristic aspects of his poetry is the sonorous and rhythmic movement in which he captures the moods and scenery of his adopted landscape.

Jeffers' poetry presents man as a being caught up in a complex of forces which he can neither understand nor control. Lacking any choice, said Jeffers, man should accept his fate and not complain.

Jeffers' works include the verse drama *Medea* (1946). *Hungerfield and Other Poems* was his last collection of poetry.

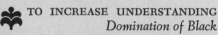 **TO INCREASE UNDERSTANDING**
Domination of Black

1. (*a*) Describe the situation of the poet sketched in lines 1-7. (*b*) What season is it? (*c*) What aspects of the scene are emphasized in these lines?
2. Mention of the hemlocks (line 8) introduces a new color and atmosphere. (*a*) What is this color? (*b*) Cite lines throughout the poem which suggest this color. (*c*) What feeling does the poet associate with the hemlocks and this color? Why?
3. The cry of the peacock is introduced at the end of the first stanza. (*a*) In the second stanza what three things do the peacocks cry against? (*b*) What do these three things have in common?
4. (*a*) Contrast the atmosphere of the first seven lines with that developed in the remainder of the poem. Which is dominant? (*b*) Does the title suggest only the domination of a color or something more of which the color is symbolic? Explain. (*c*) How is the cry of the peacock related to the atmosphere? (*d*) Explain how, setting, color imagery, and words of motion aid in developing this atmosphere.
5. Explain the relationship between the speaker's being afraid and remembering the peacocks' cry.

Silence

1. Most of the poem "Silence" consists of two quotations. (*a*) Locate these quotations and identify the speaker. (*b*) Is there any contradiction between the first quotation and the second? Explain. (*c*) What is the purpose of the last line of the poem?
2. Why is the poem entitled "Silence"?
3. Reread Miss Moore's "Poetry" (page 549). (*a*) What qualities does she insist a good poem must have? (*b*) Judged according to these standards, is "Silence" a good poem? Explain.

The Eye

1. (*a*) What is the "eye" of the title? (*b*) Explain the development of the metaphor.
2. (*a*) Explain Jeffers' descriptions of the Atlantic and the Mediterranean. (*b*) How do they differ from his picture of the Pacific?
4. (*a*) What is the theme of the poem? Cite the words that express it. (*b*) Relate the theme to Jeffers' philosophy as explained in his biography.

James Weldon Johnson

The Creation

And God stepped out on space,
And he looked around and said:
I'm lonely—
I'll make me a world.

And as far as the eye of God could see   5
Darkness covered everything,
Blacker than a hundred midnights
Down in a cypress swamp.

Then God smiled,
And the light broke,   10
And the darkness rolled up on one side,
And the light stood shining on the other,
And God said: That's good!

Then God reached out and took the light in
    his hands,
And God rolled the light around in his hands
Until he made the sun;   16
And he set that sun a-blazing in the heavens.
And the light that was left from making the
    sun
God gathered it up in a shining ball
And flung it against the darkness,   20
Spangling the night with the moon and stars.
Then down between
The darkness and the light
He hurled the world;
And God said: That's good!   25

Then God himself stepped down—
And the sun was on his right hand,
And the moon was on his left;
The stars were clustered about his head,
And the earth was under his feet.   30
And God walked, and where he trod
His footsteps hollowed the valleys out
And bulged the mountains up.

Then he stopped and looked and saw
That the earth was hot and barren.   35
So God stepped over to the edge of the world
And he spat out the seven seas—
He batted his eyes, and the lightnings flashed—
He clapped his hands, and the thunders
    rolled—
And the waters above the earth came down,
The cooling waters came down.   41

Then the green grass sprouted,
And the little red flowers blossomed,
The pine tree pointed his finger to the sky,
And the oak spread out his arms,   45
The lakes cuddled down in the hollows of the
    ground,
And the rivers ran down to the sea;
And God smiled again,
And the rainbow appeared,
And curled itself around his shoulder.   50

Then God raised his arm and he waved his
    hand
Over the sea and over the land,
And he said: Bring forth! Bring forth!
And quicker than God could drop his hand,
Fishes and fowls   55
And beasts and birds
Swam the rivers and the seas,
Roamed the forests and the woods,
And split the air with their wings.
And God said: That's good!   60

Then God walked around,
And God looked around
On all that he had made.
He looked at his sun,
And he looked at his moon,   65
And he looked at his little stars;
He looked on his world
With all its living things,
And God said: I'm lonely still.

Then God sat down— 70
On the side of a hill where he could think;
By a deep, wide river he sat down;
With his head in his hands,
God thought and thought,
Till he thought: I'll make me a man! 75

Up from the bed of the river
God scooped the clay;
And by the bank of the river
He kneeled him down;
And there the great God Almighty 80
Who lit the sun and fixed it in the sky,
Who flung the stars to the most far corner of
the night,
Who rounded the earth in the middle of his
hand;
This Great God
Like a mammy bending over her baby, 85
Kneeled down in the dust
Toiling over a lump of clay
Till he shaped it in his own image;

Then into it he blew the breath of life,
And man became a living soul. 90
Amen. Amen.

MOUNT WILSON AND PALOMAR OBSERVATORIES

JAMES WELDON JOHNSON 1871-1938

Although he will probably be longest remembered as a poet and an essayist, James Weldon Johnson was successful in many fields. Born in Jacksonville, Florida, he received his B.A. and M.A. degrees at Atlanta University; he later continued his studies for three years at Columbia University. He taught school in Jacksonville while studying law. After being admitted to the bar in Florida in 1897, he went to New York where he prospered as a writer of songs and light opera. Later he was equally successful as United States consul in Venezuela and Nicaragua.

As Johnson became older, the flair for rhythm and the feeling for words that had made him a successful song writer found more serious channels. He edited books of Negro poetry and spirituals, and in 1927 he published *God's Trombones,* his finest poetic achievement. In the last years of his life, without ceasing to write, he turned again to teaching. In 1930 he became professor of creative literature at Fisk University and in 1934 visiting professor of literature at New York University.

From boyhood Johnson had been fascinated by old-time Negro preachers who with consummate skill translated Biblical events into stories a congregation of simple people could understand. Believing that these needy and uneducated people would find comfort in a God whose characteristics were like those of men, the preachers pictured not the stern God of the Hebrew prophets but a gentle Father who Himself experienced loneliness and worried over His children. In these poetic retellings even the landscape of the Old Testament came to resemble the familiar rural South. One preacher in particular had an excellent feeling for dramatic delivery and rhythm. It was such memories along with Johnson's own talent for rhythm and expression that went into *God's Trombones,* a series of seven Negro sermons in verse in which the phraseology of the Bible is beautifully fused with the primitive poetry of an old-time preacher. "The Creation" is from *God's Trombones.*

TO INCREASE UNDERSTANDING

1. "God made man in His own image, but man also makes God in his own image." (*a*) What does this statement mean? (*b*) Cite specific lines from "The Creation" that bear out the statement.

2. (*a*) Cite images that the preacher uses to bring God close to the everyday experience of the congregation. (*b*) Which lines in their rhythm and phraseology are most like Biblical language?

3. Describe the tone of the poem.

Richard Eberhart has been poet, teacher, and vice-president of a floor-polish manufacturing firm. Commenting on his varied career he has said that a poet has to be at least two persons: he must have enough energy to live in two worlds—the present world which he doesn't believe in, and the world of becoming which he makes real through his poetry.

After receiving degrees from Dartmouth College and Cambridge University, Eberhart became tutor to the son of King Prajahhipoh of Siam. During World War II he was a lieutenant commander in the Navy.

Eberhart has published several volumes of poetry, among them *Selected Poems* and *Undercliff: Poems 1946-1953*. Although like Carl Sandburg and Vachel Lindsay he grew up in the Midwest, his poems do not suggest as theirs do the rhythms of Midwestern speech. The strength of his poetry lies in its honesty, its individualism, and in its directness. A thoughtful man, he writes simply of subjects that men of all ages have pondered: man's place in the universe, his destiny, and death.

BETTER READING
Analogy

The title of Richard Eberhart's poem and the first few stanzas suggest that this is merely a pleasant descriptive lyric about a group of boys stealing horse chestnuts from a neighbor's tree. But as we finish the poem we realize that the poet is using the boys and the tree to make us ponder about man and his place in the universe. A comparison of this sort in which a familiar object or idea is used to explain a more abstract concept is known as an *analogy*.

In which stanza of the poem does the poet begin to expand the description of the boys' prank into something else? Find counterparts in the first part of the poem for: "we, outlaws on God's property" (line 19); "Fling out imagination" (line 20); "tangible good" (line 21); "death will drive us from the scene" (line 22); "great flowering world" (line 23); and "a little handful" (line 24). Explain in your own words the analogy the poet develops.

Richard Eberhart

The Horse Chestnut Tree

Boys in sporadic but tenacious droves
Come with sticks, as certainly as Autumn,
To assault the great horse chestnut tree.

There is a law governs their lawlessness.
Desire is in them for a shining amulet   5
And the best are those that are highest up.

They will not pick them easily from the ground.
With shrill arms they fling to the higher branches,
To hurry the work of nature for their pleasure.

I have seen them trooping down the street   10
Their pockets stuffed with chestnuts shucked,
          unshucked.
It is only evening keeps them from their wish.

Sometimes I run out in a kind of rage
To chase the boys away; I catch an arm,
Maybe, and laugh to think of being the lawgiver.   15

I was once such a young sprout myself
And fingered in my pocket the prize and trophy.
But still I moralize upon the day.

And see that we, outlaws on God's property,
Fling out imagination beyond the skies   20
Wishing a tangible good from the unknown.

And likewise death will drive us from the scene
With the great flowering world unbroken yet,
Which we held in idea, a little handful.

When sixteen-year-old Stephen Vincent Benét[1] published his first volume of poetry, he had already been submitting verse to *St. Nicholas*, the children's magazine, for many years. By the time "Carol: New Style" appeared in 1924, the exuberant young contributor to *St. Nicholas* had entered a period of disillusionment. Benét patterned this poem after the meter and rhyme of the carol "I Saw Three Ships," emphasizing by the contrast between form and idea his discontent with society.

Interested from early childhood in the American past, Benét had for years wished to write a long poem about the Civil War, but the necessity of supporting a family made this impossible. In 1926 the problem was solved when he received a Guggenheim Fellowship. He took his family to Paris to live—the cost of living was lower there and the atmosphere more conducive to writing. He spent the next two years working on his proposed Civil War epic and enjoying conversations with other writers in Paris at that time. (See "Gertrude Stein and the Lost Generation," page 458.) In 1928 he finished the 350-page narrative poem, which he had entitled *John Brown's Body,* and returned home.

John Brown's Body tells the story of various individuals — Northerner and Southerner, man and woman, plantation owner, townsman, mountaineer— set against the tremendous background of the Civil War. Although the principal characters are imaginative, great historical figures of both North and South enter the story. Different verse rhythms, including short rhymed couplets, blank verse, and free verse, are used to follow the stories of various individuals.

John Brown's Body not only became a popular best seller but also won a Pulitzer Prize, an indication of its popular appeal as well as of its literary merit. "Robert E. Lee," reprinted here, is from this poem.

❦ TO INCREASE UNDERSTANDING

1. (*a*) What is the tone of "Carol: New Style"? (*b*) How does the style contribute to the tone?

2. Define the word *carol*. What does the title add to the irony of the poem?

3. Explain how the following contribute to the irony of the poem: (*a*) setting, (*b*) each of the three men's suggestions, (*c*) line 3, line 10, lines 39-40, line 47.

4. What idea is Benét trying to develop in "Carol: New Style"?

1. For additional material on Benét see page 487.

Stephen Vincent Benét

Carol: New Style

If Jesus Christ should come again,
On Christmas day, on Christmas day,
To bother the minds of gentlemen
On Christmas day in the morning?

The first one said as he passed by, 5
As he passed by, as he passed by,
"I see three thieves a-hanging high,
This Christmas day in the morning."

The second one said, "What sinful men!
What sinful men, what sinful men! 10
Hanging is too good for them,
On Christmas day in the morning."

The third one said, "Oh stay your word!
Stay your word, oh stay your word!
Do you not see that one's the Lord, 15
This Christmas day in the morning?

"I know him by his weary head,
His weary head, his weary head."
Whereat they all fell sore adread,
That Christmas day in the morning. 20

"How sad this is we all avow,
Yes indeed, we all avow!
But what shall we do about it now,
On Christmas day in the morning?"

PRIMUS[1]
"I'll run away as fast as I may, 25
As fast as I may, as fast as I may,
And pretend I haven't been out all day,
On Christmas day in the morning."

SECUNDUS
"I'll buy Him a shroud that's spick and span,

1. *Primus* (pri′məs), the Latin word meaning first. Here it means first speaker. The two other men are identified in similar manner. *Secundus* (se kun′dəs) is the second speaker, and *Tertius* (tĕr′shi əs) is the third speaker.

Spick and span, spick and span,
For I was always a generous man,
On Christmas day in the morning." 30

TERTIUS
"But what if we should cut Him down,
Cut Him down, cut Him down?"

SECUNDUS ET PRIMUS
"You fool, do you want to arouse the town, 35
On Christmas day in the morning?"

"My speech was rash," the third one said,
The third one said, the third one said.
"We're surer of God when we know He's dead,
On any day in the morning." 40

They knelt in the snow and prayed and bowed,
Prayed and bowed, prayed and bowed,
And the two dead thieves laughed out aloud
On Christmas day in the morning.

As Jesus Christ was hanging high, 45
Hanging high, hanging high,
He saw three Christians, passing by,
On Christmas day in the morning.

Robert E. Lee

And now at last,
Comes Traveller and his master. Look at them well.
The horse is an iron-grey, sixteen hands high,
Short back, deep chest, strong haunch, flat legs, small head,
Delicate ear, quick eye, black mane and tail, 5
Wise brain, obedient mouth.
                                                    Such horses are
The jewels of the horseman's hands and thighs,
They go by the word and hardly need the rein.
They bred such horses in Virginia then,
Horses that were remembered after death 10
And buried not so far from Christian ground
That if their sleeping riders should arise
They could not witch them from the earth again

*This photograph of
Lee on Traveller was
taken the year after
the surrender by
Michael Miley, a
Southern photographer
whose life's ambition
was to leave a record
of Lee. This is one
of the few portraits
that Lee expressly
desired to have made.*

And ride a printless course along the grass
With the old manage and light ease of hand.   15
The rider, now.
              He too, is iron-grey,
Though the thick hair and thick, blunt-pointed beard
Have frost in them.
              Broad-foreheaded, deep-eyed,
Straight-nosed, sweet-mouthed, firm-lipped, head cleanly set,
He and his horse are matches for the strong   20
Grace of proportion that inhabits both.
They carry nothing that is in excess
And nothing that is less than symmetry,
The strength of Jackson[1] is a hammered strength,
Bearing the tool marks still. This strength was shaped   25
By as hard arts but does not show the toil
Except as justness, though the toil was there.
—And so we get the marble man again,
The head on the Greek coin, the idol-image,
The shape who stands at Washington's left hand,   30
Worshiped, uncomprehended and aloof,
A figure lost to flesh and blood and bones,
Frozen into a legend out of life,
A blank-verse statue—
              How to humanize
That solitary gentleness and strength   35
Hidden behind the deadly oratory
Of twenty thousand Lee Memorial days,
How show, in spite of all the rhetoric,
All the sick honey of the speechifiers,
Proportion, not as something calm congealed   40
From lack of fire, but ruling such a fire
As only such proportion could contain?

The man was loved, the man was idolized,
The man had every just and noble gift.
He took great burdens and he bore them well,   45
Believed in God but did not preach too much,
Believed and followed duty first and last
With marvellous consistency and force,
Was a great victor, in defeat as great,
No more, no less, always himself in both,   50
Could make men die for him but saved his men
Whenever he could save them—was most kind
But was not disobeyed—was a good father,
A loving husband, a considerate friend:
Had little humor, but enough to play   55
Mild jokes that never wounded, but had charm,

---

1. *Jackson,* one of Lee's best officers who gained his nickname, Stonewall, during the
Battle of Bull Run. Self-educated, his stature was largely the result of his hard work and
determination.

Did not seek intimates, yet drew men to him,
Did not seek fame, did not protest against it,
Knew his own value without pomp or jealousy
And died as he preferred to live—sans phrase, 60
With commonsense, tenacity and courage,
A Greek proportion—and a riddle unread.
And everything that we have said is true
And nothing helps us yet to read the man,
Nor will he help us while he has the strength 65
To keep his heart his own.
                          For he will smile
And give you, with unflinching courtesy,
Prayers, trappings, letters, uniforms and orders,
Photographs, kindness, valor and advice,
And do it with such grace and gentleness 70
That you will know you have the whole of him
Pinned down, mapped out, easy to understand—
And so you have.
                  All things except the heart.
The heart he kept himself, that answers all.
For here was someone who lived all his life 75
In the most fierce and open light of the sun,
Wrote letters freely, did not guard his speech,
Listened and talked with every sort of man,
And kept his heart a secret to the end
From all the picklocks of biographers. 80

He was a man, and as a man he knew
Love, separation, sorrow, joy and death.
He was a master of the tricks of war,
He gave great strokes and warded strokes as great.
He was the prop and pillar of a State, 85
The incarnation of a national dream,
And when the State fell and the dream dissolved
He must have lived with bitterness itself—
But what his sorrow was and what his joy,
And how he felt in the expense of strength, 90
And how his heart contained its bitterness,
He will not tell us.
                    We can lie about him,
Dress up a dummy in his uniform
And put our words into the dummy's mouth,
Say "Here Lee must have thought," and "There, no doubt, 95
By what we know of him, we may suppose
He felt—this pang or that—" but he remains
Beyond our stagecraft, reticent as ice,
Reticent as the fire within the stone.

Yet—look at the face again—look at it well— 100
This man was not repose, this man was act.

This man who murmured "It is well that war
Should be so terrible, if it were not
We might become too fond of it—" and showed
Himself, for once, completely as he lived   105
In the laconic balance of that phrase;
This man could reason, but he was a fighter,
Skillful in every weapon of defence
But never defending when he could assault,
Taking enormous risks again and again,   110
Never retreating while he still could strike,
Dividing a weak force on dangerous ground
And joining it again to beat a strong,
Mocking at chance and all the odds of war
With acts that looked like hairbreadth recklessness   115
—We do not call them reckless since they won.
We do not see him reckless for the calm
Proportion that controlled the recklessness—
But that attacking quality was there.
He was not mild with life or drugged with justice,   120
He gripped life like a wrestler with a bull,
Impetuously. It did not come to him
While he stood waiting in a famous cloud,
He went to it and took it by both horns
And threw it down.
                    Oh, he could bear the shifts   125
Of time and play the bitter loser's game,
The slow, unflinching chess of fortitude,
But while he had an opening for attack
He would attack with every ounce of strength.
His heart was not a stone but trumpet-shaped   130
And a long challenge blew an anger through it
That was more dread for being musical
First, last, and to the end.
                    Again he said
A curious thing to life.
"I'm always wanting something."
                    The brief phrase   135
Slides past us, hardly grasped in the smooth flow
Of the well-balanced, mildly-humorous prose
That goes along to talk of cats and duties,
Maxims of conduct, farming and poor bachelors.
But for a second there, the marble cracked   140
And a strange man we never saw before
Showed us the face he never showed the world
And wanted something—not the general
Who wanted shoes and food for ragged men,
Not the good father wanting for his children,   145
The patriot wanting victory—all the Lees
Whom all the world could see and recognize
And hang with gilded laurels—but the man

Who had, you'd say, all things that life can give
Except the last success—and had, for that,   150
Such glamor as can wear sheer triumph out,
Proportion's son and Duty's eldest sword
And the calm mask who—wanted something still,
Somewhere, somehow and always.
                                    Picklock biographers,
What could he want that he had never had?   155

He only said it once—the marble closed—
There was a man enclosed within that image.
There was a force that tried Proportion's rule
And died without a legend or a cue
To bring it back. The shadow-Lees still live.   160
But the first-person and the singular Lee?

The ant finds kingdoms in a foot of ground
But earth's too small for something in our earth,
We'll make a new earth from the summer's cloud,
From the pure summer's cloud.
                                    It was not that,   165
It was not God or love or mortal fame.
It was not anything he left undone.
—What does Proportion want that it can lack?
—What does the ultimate hunger of the flesh
Want from the sky more than a sky of air?   170
He wanted something. That must be enough.

Now he rides Traveller back into the mist.

❧ TO INCREASE UNDERSTANDING

1. The opening passage (lines 1-27) serves two purposes: it suggests the past, and it introduces the idea of proportion. (a) Cite lines that evoke the past and characterize their tone. (b) Explain the type of proportion Benét sees in both horse and rider.

2. (a) What impression does Benét convey by using the term "marble man" (line 28) to describe Lee? (b) Explain other terms in lines 28-34 that reinforce this impression. (c) What difficulties does this idea of Lee create for the poet or biographer?

3. Relate each of the following lines to Benét's description of Lee: (a) "The heart he kept himself . . ." (line 74); (b) "Reticent as the fire within

the stone" (line 99); (c) "This man was not repose, this man was act" (line 101).

4. Throughout Benét's description of Lee the words *proportion* and *stone* (or *marble*) recur. (a) Which of these terms describes what the poet regards as central to Lee's character? (b) Trace the poet's development of this idea. (c) Which of the terms only apparently characterizes Lee? Explain.

5. According to Benét, Lee once said, "I'm always wanting something" (line 135). (a) Why, to the poet, does this seem an unusual remark for Lee to make? (b) What significance does he find in it? (c) Relate this remark to lines 156-171.

6. (a) To what lines is the last line related? (b) What is its function?

Léonie Adams

The Figurehead This that is washed with weed and pebblestone
Curved once a dolphin's length before the prow,
And I who read the land to which we bore
In its grave eyes, question my idol now,
What cold and marvelous fancy it may keep,   5
Since the last terror swept us from our course.
Or if a wisdom later than the storm,
For old green ocean's tinctured it so deep;
And with some reason to me on this strand
The waves, the ceremonial waves have come,   10
And stooped their barbaric heads, and all flung out
Their glittering arms before them and are gone,
Leaving the murderous tribute lodged in sand.

Elinor Wylie

Bread Alone

Let not the heart's intention
To be both brave and good
Cheat that devoted engine
Of spiritual food.

Because it is not cruel,   5
Because it is not great,
Provide it fire, and fuel
Sufficient for its state.

Ah, poor machine, and faithful,
That limps without a wing!   10
My love, be never wrathful
With this imperfect thing.

Let No Charitable Hope

Now let no charitable hope
Confuse my mind with images
Of eagle and of antelope:
I am in nature none of these.

I was, being human, born alone;   5
I am, being woman, hard beset;
I live by squeezing from a stone
The little nourishment I get.

In masks outrageous and austere
The years go by in single file;   10
But none has merited my fear,
And none has quite escaped my smile.

Edna St. Vincent Millay

Not in a Silver Casket Cool with Pearls

Not in a silver casket cool with pearls
Or rich with red corundum or with blue,
Locked, and the key withheld, as other girls
Have given their loves, I give my love to you;
Not in a lovers'-knot, not in a ring   5
Worked in such fashion, and the legend plain—
Semper fidelis,[1] where a secret spring
Kennels a drop of mischief for the brain:
Love in the open hand, no thing but that,
Ungemmed, unhidden, wishing not to hurt,   10
As one should bring you cowslips in a hat
Swung from the hand, or apples in her skirt,
  I bring you, calling out as children do:
  "Look what I have!—And these are all for you."

Euclid Alone Has Looked on Beauty Bare

Euclid alone has looked on Beauty bare.
Let all who prate of Beauty hold their peace,
And lay them prone upon the earth and cease
To ponder on themselves, the while they stare
At nothing, intricately drawn nowhere   5
In shapes of shifting lineage; let geese
Gabble and hiss, but heroes seek release
From dusty bondage into luminous air.
O blinding hour, O holy, terrible day,
When first the shaft into his vision shone   10
Of light anatomized! Euclid alone
Has looked on Beauty bare. Fortunate they
Who, though once only and then but far away,
Have heard her massive sandal set on stone.

"Not in a Silver Casket Cool with Pearls." "Euclid Alone Has Looked on Beauty Bare." Reprinted from *Collected Poems* by Edna St. Vincent Millay, by permission of Norma Millay Ellis. Copyright 1923, 1930, 1951, 1958 by Edna St. Vincent Millay and Norma Millay Ellis. Published by Harper & Bros., N.Y.

1. *semper fidelis* (sem′pər fi dē′lis), always faithful. [*Latin*]

LÉONIE ADAMS 1899-

Born and raised in Brooklyn, New York, Léonie Adams was the next youngest of six children. After being graduated from Barnard College, she taught at several colleges. She has been Consultant in Poetry to the Library of Congress, and is now a member of the faculty at Columbia University in New York City. In 1949 she received an award for lyric poetry from the National Institute of Arts and Letters.

Miss Adams writes about nature. People seldom appear in her poems, but when she talks about time's effect on growth and death, she is indirectly talking about man's brief, changing life as well. The compelling power of her poetry lies in her ability to write about subjects like the moon, a walk in the woods, or harvest in simple language, yet to retain an element of the mysterious that is inherent in nature.

ELINOR WYLIE 1885-1928

Personal charm and beauty won as much fame for Elinor Wylie during her lifetime as did her poetry and novels. This is not to say that her writing was inferior; some of her lyrics are admirable works of art. Rather it indicates what an extraordinary woman she was.

Born into a wealthy and cultured family, Elinor Wylie spent much of her childhood in Washington, D.C., where her father served as Assistant Attorney-General under Theodore Roosevelt. When she was eighteen, her grandfather took her to London and Paris for a season of parties and travel.

In the United States she made her home in New York City, where she became acquainted with most of the prominent writers of that time. She was married to William Rose Benét, brother of Stephen Vincent Benét (page 580). Her poetry was delicate, finely wrought, painstakingly intelligent. She revised continually until her poetry was as perfect as she could make it.

Elinor Wylie was only forty-three when she died, and had just finished work on her latest volume of poetry, which was soon to appear. In 1932 the volume *Collected Poems* was published.

EDNA ST. VINCENT MILLAY 1892-1950

Edna St. Vincent Millay was born in Maine. Even before the time she entered Vassar College, she had been contributing poetry to *St. Nicholas* magazine for several years. At nineteen she wrote "Renascence," a long lyric whose quiet melodic beginning is followed by an ecstatic affirmation of life.

Moving to Greenwich Village in New York City, Miss Millay was recognized in the 1920's as the poetic voice of "flaming youth." For a few years the young and optimistic outlook she had voiced in "Renascence" was submerged. In *A Few Figs from Thistles* (1921) and *Second April* (1921) she expressed the cynicism and disillusionment of the "lost generation."

Edna St. Vincent Millay frequently visited Europe both before and after her marriage in 1923. While traveling she wrote some of the poetry that, in a volume titled *The Harp-Weaver and Other Poems* (1923), won a Pulitzer Prize.

For the last twenty-five years of her life Miss Millay spent most of her time at Steepletop Farm in northern New York. Her poetry no longer possessed the serene optimism of "Renascence," nor was it the flippant, satiric verse of her Greenwich Village days. The lyrics and sonnets of this period are more subdued and less self-conscious than her earlier work. Showing genuine poetic power, they bear the mark of a striking and intense personality. In *Fatal Interview* (1931) Miss Millay produced one of the finest sonnet sequences written by an American.

TO INCREASE UNDERSTANDING
The Figurehead

1. (*a*) What is the figurehead on a ship? (*b*) What does the term mean when applied to a person?

2. (*a*) Describe the figurehead as it appears when the speaker discovers it. (*b*) What words personify the figurehead? How? (*c*) What does the word *idol* suggest about the speaker's feeling toward it?

3. In line 3 the poet speaks of *reading* "the land to which we bore"; then she questions the fancies of the figurehead "since the last terror swept us from our course" (lines 4-6). (*a*) Interpret these lines as they apply to the actual figurehead of a ship and an actual voyage. (*b*) What figurative meaning applicable to the experiences of an individual can you discover?

4. (*a*) Cite lines in which the ocean is personified. (*b*) Why does the speaker consider the figurehead "a tribute" (line 13)? (*c*) What words develop the image of the ocean as bearing tribute? (*d*) Why

is the tribute spoken of as *murderous* (line 13)? (*e*) What question does the speaker ask of the idol? (*f*) Is it answered?

Bread Alone, Let No Charitable Hope

1. In the Old Testament is the verse "Man doth not live by bread only but by every word that proceedeth out of the mouth of the Lord doth man live" (Deuteronomy 8:3). Emerson adapted the Biblical quotation as follows: "Man does not live by bread alone, but by faith, by admiration, by sympathy." (*a*) Which quotation is closer in meaning to the idea Miss Wylie develops in "Bread Alone"? (*b*) Cite specific words or lines upon which you base your answer.

2. The first stanza of "Let No Charitable Hope" may be read as the poet's denial of the good qualities attributed to her. (*a*) What impression is conveyed by using the word *Now* at the very beginning of the poem? (*b*) Why does the poet speak of hope as "charitable"? (*c*) What types of mind do the eagle and the antelope signify? (*d*) What statement does line 4 make?

3. (*a*) In stanzas 2 and 3 what qualities does the poet claim? (*b*) How would you describe her view of life? (*c*) In your opinion is she characterizing one woman (herself) or women in general? Cite lines to support your answer.

Sonnets by Millay

1. (*a*) What idea does Miss Millay present in "Not in a Silver Casket Cool with Pearls"? (*b*) Does she follow the sonnet form in her organization of the subject? (See "The Sonnet," page 273.)

2. (*a*) Cite the details which develop the images of the casket and the ring. (*b*) What impressions do these images convey? (*c*) Contrast these images with those of the cowslips and the apples. (*d*) How is this contrast of images essential to the poet's development of her idea?

3. (*a*) In "Euclid Alone Has Looked on Beauty Bare" Miss Millay describes the beauty of geometry as " . . . nothing, intricately drawn nowhere/ In shapes of shifting lineage," and calls it "light anatomized." What does this mean? (*b*) What characteristics does geometry possess that enable the poet to say that to study it is to study beauty?

4. Why does the poet speak of the day on which Euclid discovered the principles of geometry as a "blinding hour," a "holy terrible day" (line 9)?

5. (*a*) Note that the opening line "Euclid alone has looked on Beauty bare" is repeated in lines 11-12. What is the effect of this repetition? (*b*) What is the relation of the repeated line to the final lines of the poem?

Countee Cullen

Any Human to Another

The ills I sorrow at
Not me alone
Like an arrow,
Pierce to the marrow,
Through the fat   5
And past the bone.

Your grief and mine
Must intertwine
Like sea and river,
Be fused and mingle,   10
Diverse yet single,
Forever and forever.

Let no man be so proud
And confident,
To think he is allowed   15
A little tent
Pitched in a meadow
Of sun and shadow
All his little own.

Joy may be shy, unique,   20
Friendly to a few,
Sorrow never scorned to speak
To any who
Were false or true.

Your every grief   25
Like a blade
Shining and unsheathed
Must strike me down.
Of bitter aloes wreathed,
My sorrow must be laid   30
On your head like a crown.

COUNTEE CULLEN 1903-1946

The influence of the English romantic poets of the nineteenth century and of Edwin Arlington Robinson may be found in the lyrics of Countee Cullen. An adopted son of a Methodist minister, Cullen grew up in New York City, attended New York University, and received a master's degree in English literature from Harvard University. For a time he edited *Opportunity: Journal of Negro Life,* but his major occupation, in addition to writing poetry, was teaching French.

"Most things I write I do for the sheer joy of the music in them," he once said when talking about how he wrote poetry. In his lyrics he combines an understanding of the joys and sorrows of the Negro race with a thoughtful probing of the attitudes of men in relation with one another. Cullen collected what he considered to be the best verse written by Negro poets and put them in an anthology which he titled *Caroling Dusk.* His ability and careful judgment made the book a notable addition to the few collections of this type that had preceded his.

✿ TO INCREASE UNDERSTANDING

1. (*a*) What idea does the poet outline in the first stanza of "Any Human to Another"? (*b*) What does the second stanza add to the idea of the first? (*c*) Point out the images used in these stanzas and explain their function.

2. (*a*) What does the "little tent" (line 16) stand for? (*b*) What other images does the poet use to make his idea vivid?

3. The ancient Greeks and Romans crowned victors with wreaths of laurel. From early times the word *aloes* has been used to symbolize grief or bitterness. (Aloes is a bitter drug made from the leaves of the aloe.) Using this information, explain the last three lines of "Any Human to Another."

4. Four centuries ago the English poet John Donne wrote:

. . . No man is an island, entire of itself; every man is a piece of the continent, a part of the main; if a clod be washed away by the sea, Europe is the less, as well as if a promontory were, as well as if a manor of thy friends or of thine own were; any man's death diminishes me, because I am involved in mankind . . .

Relate the ideas expressed by John Donne to the theme of "Any Human to Another."

Archibald MacLeish

The End of the World

Quite unexpectedly as Vasserot
The armless ambidextrian was lighting
A match between his great and second toe
And Ralph the lion was engaged in biting
The neck of Madame Sossman while the
    drum   5
Pointed, and Teeny was about to cough
In waltz-time swinging Jocko by the thumb—
Quite unexpectedly the top blew off:

And there, there overhead, there, there,
    hung over
Those thousands of white faces, those
    dazed eyes,   10
There in the starless dark, the poise, the
    hover,
There with vast wings across the canceled
    skies,
There in the sudden blackness, the black pall
Of nothing, nothing, nothing—nothing at all.

Brave New World

But you, Thomas Jefferson,
You could not lie so still,
You could not bear the weight of stone
On the quiet hill,

You could not keep your green-grown peace 5
Nor hold your folded hand
If you could see your new world now,
Your new sweet land.

There was a time, Tom Jefferson,
When freedom made free men.   10
The new-found earth and the new-freed mind
Were brothers then.

There was a time when tyrants feared
The new world of the free.
Now freedom is afraid and shrieks   15
At tyranny.

Words have not changed their sense so soon
Nor tyranny grown new.
The truths you held, Tom Jefferson,
Will still hold true.   20

What's changed is freedom in this age.
What great men dared to choose
Small men now dare neither win
Nor lose.

Freedom, when men fear freedom's use   25
But love its useful name,
Has cause and cause enough for fear
And cause for shame.

We fought a war for freedom's name
And won it on our own.   30
We fought to free a world and raised
A wall of stone.

Your countrymen who could have built
The hill fires of the free
To set the dry world all ablaze   35
With liberty—

To burn the brutal thorn in Spain
Of bigotry and hate[1]
And the dead lie and the brittle weed
Beyond the Plate:[2]   40

Who could have heaped the bloody straw,
The dung of time, to light
The Danube[3] in a sudden flame
Of hope by night—

"The End of the World" from *Collected Poems* by Archibald
MacLeish. Copyright 1933 by Houghton Mifflin Company,
the authorized publishers, and reprinted with their permission.
"Brave New World" from *Actfive and Other Poems* by
Archibald MacLeish. Copyright 1946 by Archibald Mac-
Leish. Reprinted by permission of Random House, Inc.,
New York, and The Bodley Head Ltd., London.

1. *the brutal thorn . . . bigotry and hate*, a reference to the
dictatorship of Francisco Franco in Spain. 2. *the dead lie
. . . beyond the Plate*. These lines refer to the dictatorship of
Juan Peron (pə rōn') in Argentina (1946-1955). The Plata
(plä'tə), to which the poet gives an English pronunciation,
is Argentina's principal waterway. 3. *to light the Danube*,
to bring the hope of freedom to the eastern European countries along the Danube River. After World War II these
countries fell under Russian Communist rule.

Your countrymen who could have hurled   45
Their freedom like a brand
Have cupped it to a candle spark
In a frightened hand.

Freedom that was a thing to use
They've made a thing to save   50
And staked it in and fenced it round
Like a dead man's grave.

You, Thomas Jefferson,
You could not lie so still,
You could not bear the weight of stone   55
On your green hill,

You could not hold your angry tongue
If you could see how bold
The old stale bitter world plays new—
And the new world old.   60

W. H. Auden

The Unknown Citizen

(To JS/07/M/378 This Marble Monument Is Erected by the State)

He was found by the Bureau of Statistics to be
One against whom there was no official complaint,
And all the reports on his conduct agree
That, in the modern sense of an old-fashioned word, he was a saint,
For in everything he did he served the Greater Community.   5
Except for the War till the day he retired
He worked in a factory and never got fired,
But satisfied his employers, Fudge Motors Inc.
Yet he wasn't a scab or odd in his views,
For his Union reports that he paid his dues,   10
(Our report on his Union shows it was sound)
And our Social Psychology workers found
That he was popular with his mates and liked a drink.
The Press are convinced he bought a paper every day
And that his reactions to advertisements were normal in every way.   15
Policies taken out in his name prove that he was fully insured,
And his Health-card shows he was once in hospital but left it cured.
Both Producers Research and High-Grade Living declare
He was fully sensible to the advantages of the Installment Plan
And had everything necessary to the Modern Man,   20
A phonograph, a radio, a car, and a frigidaire.
Our researchers into Public Opinion are content
That he held the proper opinions for the time of year;
When there was peace, he was for peace; when there was war, he went.
He was married and added five children to the population,   25
Which our Eugenist says was the right number for a parent of his generation,
And our teachers report that he never interfered with their education.
Was he free? Was he happy? The question is absurd:
Had anything been wrong, we should certainly have heard.

ARCHIBALD MAC LEISH 1892-

Archibald MacLeish has managed successfully to combine academic, political, and business careers.

He was born in Glencoe, Illinois, and educated at Yale, Harvard, and Tufts. He established himself in a prosperous law practice, but gave it up because he "never could believe in it." In 1923 he left for Paris with his wife and children. Opportunity to discuss theory with contemporary writers and to write his own poetry made him say that he dated the beginning of his life from that year. He stayed in France until 1928.

After he had returned to the United States, he traveled in Mexico, following the route of Cortez. The result was the narrative poem *Conquistador,* which won the Pultizer Prize in 1933. During the Second World War, as Director of the Office of Facts and Figures, he was responsible for wartime propaganda. He has been Librarian of Congress, and has also been active in the organization of UNESCO.

Although he won a Pulitzer Prize for a narrative poem, critics consider his lyric poetry his best. In 1953 he won a second Pulitzer Prize for his volume, *Collected Poems 1917-1952.*

W. H. AUDEN 1907-

When a young Englishman, Wystan Auden, began writing, the new poetry had already emerged from the pens of its first innovators. The more important of these men, T. S. Eliot, William Butler Yeats, and Ezra Pound, had achieved eminence and were in their writing prime when Auden, a young man about London, used to meet with his fellow poets to discuss what direction their lives and their thinking were taking. His own cynicism, his wit and originality, and revolutionary times made some of the early poetry that Auden wrote an uneven mixture of expression and ideas. Nonetheless, his poetry was outstanding enough even then to be awarded the King's Poetry Medal in 1937.

In 1939 Auden left England for the United States. Since he had always been in rebellion against the age and traditions of his native land, the openness and lack of tradition in this new country appealed to him. He became a citizen. His poetry began to lose some of its personal references and obscurities, yet retained its former deft wit and brilliance.

Since he has been in the United States, Auden has taught and lectured at various universities. In 1948 he won a Pulitzer Prize for his book *The Age of Anxiety.*

❧ TO INCREASE UNDERSTANDING
Brave New World, The End of the World

1. "The End of the World" is written in sonnet form. (*a*) Point out precise uses of sonnet technique. (*b*) In what way does the poem differ from the typical sonnet?

2. (*a*) What is the subject of the octave in "The End of the World"? (*b*) What is the subject of the sestet? (*c*) How do octave and sestet differ in tone? (*d*) How are the two divisions related to the theme?

3. An *apostrophe* is a figure of speech in which an abstract quality, an absent person, or an imaginary person is addressed as though present. (*a*) Point out MacLeish's use of apostrophe in "Brave New World." (*b*) What makes the apostrophe a valuable device to use in this poem?

4. (*a*) In describing freedom what basic metaphor does MacLeish use? (*b*) Read aloud and explain the stanzas in which this figure is developed.

The Unknown Citizen

1. (*a*) According to "The Unknown Citizen," what things are necessary to Modern Man? (*b*) Contrast this idea of necessity with that expressed by Thoreau (page 236).

2. In "There Will Come Soft Rains" (page 510), Ray Bradbury pictures a civilization in which man has even more machines at his command than has Auden's Modern Man. Compare the implications about advanced technological society made by these two writers.

3. (*a*) How does the type of words Auden uses in "The Unknown Citizen" differ from the diction of much poetry? (*b*) How would you characterize the rhythm? (*c*) Compare the diction and rhythm of "The Unknown Citizen" and "Musée des Beaux Arts" (page 545). (*d*) How does the form of Auden's poetry affect the ideas he is expressing?

❧ BETTER READING
The poet as satirist

The brief biographical sketches of W. H. Auden and Archibald MacLeish are sufficient to illustrate how deeply involved these two poets have been in contemporary society. Instead of inhabiting the poet's traditional ivory tower, they have shown interest in political movements, worked at different occupations, and investigated various professions. This fascination with the currents of everyday life is reflected in their poetry, much of which is satiric commentary on twentieth-century life.

Like satirists of every age, Auden and MacLeish use poetry as a weapon to attack the facets or tendencies of which they disapprove. James Russell Lowell followed the same tradition when over a hundred years ago he used the *Biglow Papers* to attack the Mexican War. (See page 281.) Realizing that humorous exposure of an evil is often far more effective than biting sarcasm, Lowell created Hosea Biglow to state his case in homespun Yankee terms. In "Carol: New Style" (page 580), Stephen Vincent Benét used irony, a form of satire, to protest the cowardice of modern man.

What aspects of modern life is Auden protesting in "The Unknown Citizen"? Explain why statements like "he served the Greater Community" (line 5) and "He was fully sensible to the advantages of the Installment Plan" (line 19) may be considered ironic. Cite other ironic lines. What lines best summarize Auden's attitude?

Another satirist, the Englishman Aldous Huxley, has used the words "brave new world" for a title. Originally the words were written in *The Tempest,* the last play by William Shakespeare. In a moment of joyous discovery the character Miranda says:

O, wonder!
How many goodly creatures are there here!
How beauteous mankind is! O, brave new world,
That has such people in't!

Why is MacLeish's title, "Brave New World," ironic? Against what specific happenings of recent history is MacLeish's poem directed? What general tendency does he deplore? What adjectives would you use to describe his attitude?

What is satiric about "The End of the World"? What criticism of modern society is implied? How does the tone of these two poems by MacLeish differ from Auden's in "The Unknown Citizen"?

THE MAGAZINE IN AMERICA

Poetry: A Magazine of Verse

In October 1912, the first issue of *Poetry: A Magazine of Verse* appeared, the winged horse Pegasus on its cover. (Pegasus has been on every issue since then.) The press reviewed the new magazine good naturedly, generally amused that Chicago, "hog butcher" of the world, used the "proceeds of pork for the promotion of poetry," as one columnist put it. The moving spirit behind the new magazine was Harriet Monroe, an energetic woman in her fifties who felt that poetry was not so well supported as some of the other arts. A painter, for example, might receive $500 for his work. Who would think of offering $500 for a poem, or even $50? Miss Monroe felt that there were probably two reasons for the decline in the appreciation of poetry. First, poetry needed revitalizing: the quaint expressions of past centuries extolling pleasures equally quaint had little to say to people facing the problems of modern life. Secondly, poets found it financially uncomfortable to write poetry attuned to the twentieth century because few magazine editors were willing to publish experimental verse.

Harriet Monroe set about insuring the success of the projected magazine in a business-like manner. For eighteen months she talked to prominent people around Chicago, asking them to pledge $50 a year for five years to its support. Then she wrote to fifty poets inviting their contributions.

While many "little magazines" disappeared after a few years, *Poetry* never missed an issue. One reason for its success is the fact that it was established on a sound economic basis. Another reason is that its editors have always printed the best verse available. It was the only magazine, for example, that would risk printing that "radical" poem, "General William Booth Enters into Heaven," by Vachel Lindsay (page 570), or the rough-worded "Chicago" by Carl Sandburg (page 561). Almost every one of the poets represented in this chapter has had poems published in *Poetry.*

Harriet Monroe served as editor of *Poetry* until her death in 1936. Today the magazine is published monthly and has about sixty pages of poetry, criticism, and reviews. Its competitions encourage new talent. Its awards have become coveted honors.

Newer Voices

Most of the poets introduced in this section were born after the end of World War I in 1918. During World War II (1939-1945), when Stephen Vincent Benét, Archibald MacLeish, and other older poets were fighting with their pens for freedom and democracy, younger poets like Randall Jarrell and Howard Nemerov were serving in the armed forces. Strictly speaking, some of these young men did not become poets until after the war. Earlier they had toyed with writing verses. Their war experiences exposed a world in disorder and posed profound questions that set them searching for answers. The result was poetry.

While some of the younger poets write most frequently in free verse forms, many of them have returned to the disciplines of rhyme and regular meter. Thus their poems may look like the verse of older poets, and one may hear the rhymes. However, in the subtle nuances of meter, in the diction, in the handling of imagery, and in the way the theme is developed, this is twentieth-century poetry.

Randall Jarrell

The Breath of Night

The moon rises. The red cubs rolling
In the ferns by the rotten oak
Stare over a marsh and a meadow
To the farm's white wisp of smoke.

A spark burns, high in heaven.   5
Deer thread the blossoming rows
Of the old orchard, rabbits
Hop by the well-curb. The cock crows

From the tree by the widow's walk;
Two stars, in the trees to the west,   10
Are snared, and an owl's soft cry
Runs like a breath through the forest.

Here too, though death is hushed, though joy
Obscures, like night, their wars,
The beings of this world are swept   15
By the Strife that moves the stars.

RANDALL JARRELL 1914-1965

Randall Jarrell was one of a number of poets who gained recognition in the years immediately following World War II. His career followed a pattern similar to that of other poets of his generation in that after receiving his university degree he entered the armed services and afterwards taught at various colleges and wrote poetry. His teaching was interrupted for a year when he had the distinction of serving as Consultant in Poetry to the Library of Congress.

Jarrell, who was born and raised in Tennessee, first gained attention through his war poems. In these, and more especially in poems written since the war, there is a quality of fantasy, a muted, dreamlike air. This atmosphere is apparent in "The Breath of Night."

Jarrell was a prolific writer. In addition to several books of poetry, including *The Woman at the Washington Zoo*, which won the National Book Award in 1961, he wrote critical essays, short stories, and a novel.

THEODORE ROETHKE 1908-1963

Theodore Roethke (reth'kē) grew up in Saginaw, Michigan. In his spare time he worked in his father's greenhouse, and the liking for plants and flowers which he then developed crops up now and again in his poetry. Roethke left Saginaw to attend the University of Michigan and later Harvard.

Like many contemporary poets, Roethke taught literature at several colleges while continuing to write poetry of his own.

Roethke was highly praised by contemporary critics, some of them considering him one of the three or four best poets writing in the United States at mid-century. An extremely skillful technician, he manipulates rhyme and rhythm with such competence that the reader often senses the meaning of a poem emotionally before he has grasped it intellectually. In 1954 Roethke won a Pulitzer Prize for his volume of poems, *The Waking*.

Theodore Roethke

Night Journey

Now as the train bears west,
Its rhythm rocks the earth,
And from my Pullman berth
I stare into the night
While others take their rest.   5
Bridges of iron lace,
A suddenness of trees,
A lap of mountain mist
All cross my line of sight,
Then a bleak wasted place,   10
And a lake below my knees.
Full on my neck I feel
The straining at a curve;
My muscles move with steel,
I wake in every nerve.   15
I watch a beacon swing
From dark to blazing bright;
We thunder through ravines
And gullies washed with light.
Beyond the mountain pass   20
Mist deepens on the pane;
We rush into a rain
That rattles double glass.
Wheels shake the roadbed stone,
The pistons jerk and shove,   25
I stay up half the night
To see the land I love.

Elizabeth Bishop

Little Exercise at Four A.M.

Think of the storm roaming the sky uneasily
like a dog looking for a place to sleep in,
listen to it growling.

Think how they must look now, the mangrove keys   5
lying out there unresponsive to the lightning
in dark, coarse-fibred families,

where occasionally a heron may undo his head,
shake up his feathers, make an uncertain comment
when the surrounding water shines.

Think of the boulevard and the little palm trees   10
all stuck in rows, suddenly revealed
as fistfuls of limp fish-skeletons.

It is raining there. The boulevard
and its broken sidewalks with weeds in every crack,
are relieved to be wet, the sea to be freshened.   15

Now the storm goes away again in a series
of small, badly lit battle-scenes,
each in 'Another part of the field.'

Think of someone sleeping in the bottom of a row-boat
tied to a mangrove root or the pile of a bridge;   20
think of him as uninjured, barely disturbed.

Gwendolyn Brooks

The Explorer

Somehow to find a still spot in the noise
Was the frayed inner want, the winding, the frayed hope
Whose tatters he kept hunting through the din.
A velvet peace somewhere.
A room of wily hush somewhere within.   5

So tipping down the scrambled halls he set
Vague hands on throbbing knobs. There were behind
Only spiraling, high human voices,
The scream of nervous affairs,
Wee griefs,   10
Grand griefs. And choices.

He feared most of all the choices, that cried to be taken.

There were no bourns.
There were no quiet rooms.

ELIZABETH BISHOP 1911-

When Elizabeth Bishop's volume of poetry *North and South* appeared in 1946 and won a $1000 prize in a sizable competition, critics varied in their reception of the new poet. All agreed, however, that she had a gift for imagery as well as unusual facility in handling the techniques of writing poetry.

Miss Bishop's travels are reflected in her poetry. She has lived recently in Brazil, and her poem "Little Exercise" echoes an earlier sojourn in Florida. She was born, however, in Worcester, Massachusetts, far from the tropical settings of much of her poetry, and attended Vassar College. She was Consultant in Poetry to the Library of Congress in 1949-1950.

By the time Miss Bishop's second volume of poems appeared in 1955, the critics enthusiastically agreed that her poetry had managed to overcome some of its earlier faults and had retained the sharp wit and fine imagery of the earlier writing. This second volume, *Poems: North and South—A Cold Spring*, won the Pulitzer Prize in 1956. Besides these volumes of poetry, Miss Bishop has written short stories.

GWENDOLYN BROOKS 1917-

For all but one month of her life Gwendolyn Brooks has lived on the south side of Chicago. Her early attempts at writing were encouraged by her family, all of whom were interested in the arts. After being graduated from Wilson Junior College in Chicago, she did editorial work on a magazine and secretarial work. While she was working, she took a writing course, submitted one of her poems to *Poetry* magazine, and was delighted to have it accepted.

After her initial success, fame came rapidly to Gwendolyn Brooks. Her first volume of poetry, *A Street in Bronzeville* (1945), led to the award of both an American Academy of Arts and Letters award and a Guggenheim Fellowship. Her second book of poems, *Annie Allen,* won the Pulitzer Prize for poetry in 1950.

Critics have praised Miss Brooks' poetry for its directness, its naturalness, and the way in which it views commonplace situations in an original manner.

❧ TO INCREASE UNDERSTANDING
The Breath of Night

1. (*a*) What season and what time form the setting of the first three stanzas? (*b*) How would you describe the atmosphere? (*c*) Cite images that create this atmosphere.

2. (*a*) In the last stanza the words "Here too" suggest a shift in scene or subject. Explain the meaning of the stanza introduced by these words. (*b*) What relationship does the poet develop between the idea stated in this stanza and the scene sketched in the preceding three stanzas?

3. What do lines 15-16 suggest about the reality or permanence of serenity and rebirth expressed in the first three stanzas?

Night Journey

1. "Night Journey" describes the United States as seen from a Pullman berth. (*a*) Cite lines that suggest the speed of the train. (*b*) What lines or words convey the sense of the train's movement?

2. (*a*) What is the meter of "Night Journey"? (See the article on meter, page 287.) (*b*) Why is it particularly appropriate to the subject?

3. (*a*) Chart the rhyme scheme for at least ten lines of the poem. In what way is it unusual? (*b*) What other devices make the poem melodic?

4. The biographical sketch of Roethke speaks of the skill with which he manipulates rhyme and rhythm. Is that statement borne out by "Night Journey"? Explain your answer.

Little Exercise

1. "Little Exercise" is an exercise in imagination. (*a*) What words indicate this? (*b*) What is the subject of the exercise?

2. In working out her exercise, Miss Bishop makes frequent use of imagery. (*a*) Cite some images that are based on unusual similes or metaphors. (*b*) What images evoke common sights? (*c*) Why do you think the poet used both types of images?

3. In a battle scene in a Shakespearean play, a change of setting is indicated by the words "Another part of the field." With this in mind, explain the image developed in the sixth stanza.

4. (*a*) What new element in the exercise is introduced in the last stanza? (*b*) What does it add to the poem as a whole?

The Explorer

1. (*a*) What does the word *explorer* usually suggest? (*b*) How does this poem differ from what the title might lead you to expect?

2. (*a*) What words in lines 2-3 imply that the explorer believes his search is futile? (*b*) What words in the second stanza suggest disorder and indecision? (*c*) What does the explorer fear most?

3. What symbolic meaning does the poem hold? Explain the analogy.

Howard Nemerov

HOWARD NEMEROV 1920-

Howard Nemerov (nem'er off) was born in New York City and lived there until he went away to school. After being graduated from Harvard, he served in the air force from 1939 to 1945. He has contended that a college atmosphere is as good as any for a writer, and has taught at Hamilton and Bennington.

Many of his poems, especially in his volume *The Salt Garden* (1955), are analogies between elements in nature and characteristics of man. These analogies give his poetry a thoughtful quality rather than a felt lyric intensity.

TO INCREASE UNDERSTANDING

1. What apparently contradictory characteristics of trees does Nemerov mention in lines 1-7?

2. Because a tree in its properties of growth, dependence, and death suggests a comparison with certain basic aspects of the life of man, Nemerov sees an analogy between trees and men. (*a*) With this idea in mind explain lines 8-9, noting particularly the expressions "One's Being" and "One's Becoming." (*b*) Comment on the point made in lines 14-17, with emphasis on the word *exemplify*. (*c*) What basic difference between man and the rest of nature is suggested by the words "... though there has never been/A critical tree ..."?

3. State in your own words the theme of the poem.

Trees

To be a giant and keep quiet about it,
To stay in one's own place;
To stand for the constant presence of process
And always to seem the same;
To be steady as a rock and always trembling,   5
Having the hard appearance of death
With the soft, fluent nature of growth,
One's Being deceptively armored,
One's Becoming deceptively vulnerable;
To be so tough, and take the light so well,   10
Freely providing forbidden knowledge
Of so many things about heaven and earth
For which we should otherwise have no word—
Poems or people are rarely so lovely,
And even when they have great qualities   15
They tend to tell you rather than exemplify
What they believe themselves to be about,
While from the moving silence of trees,
Whether in storm or calm, in leaf and naked,
Night or day, we draw conclusions of our own,   20
Sustaining and unnoticed as our breath,
And perilous also—though there has never been
A critical tree—about the nature of things.

James Wright

Mutterings over the Crib of a Deaf Child

"How will he hear the bell at school
Arrange the broken afternoon,
And know how to run across the cool
Grasses where the starlings cry,
Or understand the day is gone?"   5

Well, someone lifting curious brows
Will take the measure of the clock.
And he will see the birchen boughs
Outside sagging dark from the sky,
And the shade crawling upon the rock.   10

"And how will he know to rise at morning?
His mother has other sons to waken,
She has the stove she must build to burning
Before the coals of the nighttime die;
And he never stirs when he is shaken."   15

I take it the air affects the skin,
And you remember, when you were young,
Sometimes you could feel the dawn begin,
And the fire would call you, by and by,
Out of the bed and bring you along.   20

"Well, good enough. To serve his needs
All kinds of arrangements can be made.
But what will you do if his finger bleeds?
Or a bobwhite whistles invisibly
And flutes like an angel off in the shade?"   25

He will learn pain. And, as for the bird,
It is always darkening when that comes out.
I will putter as though I had not heard,
And lift him into my arms and sing
Whether he hears my song or not.   30

JAMES WRIGHT 1927-

James Wright, the youngest poet represented in this chapter, was born in Martins Ferry, Ohio. After graduating from Kenyon College, he spent a year in Vienna on a Fulbright scholarship. He received his M.A. and Ph.D. degrees from the University of Washington, and now teaches at the University of Minnesota.

Wright's poetry has been published in magazines in both the United States and Europe, and he has won several awards, among them the Robert Frost Poetry Prize and the Yale Younger Poets Award. In fact, Wright's first book of poetry, *The Green Wall* (1957), was published by Yale as the first of its series of volumes by promising new poets.

Critics have compared Wright's poetry to that of Robinson and Frost. Like these older poets, he most often uses both rhyme and conventional meter. He is like them also in the compassion with which he views humanity and in the simple language in which he states his ideas.

❧ TO INCREASE UNDERSTANDING

1. Is one person or more than one speaking in this poem? Give reasons for your answer.

2. (*a*) What particular problem for the deaf child is raised in stanza 1? (*b*) How is the problem solved?

3. (*a*) What problem is posed in stanza 3? (*b*) What is the answer?

4. (*a*) How do the problems raised in stanza 5 differ from those mentioned earlier? (*b*) Is there a solution for these problems? If so, what is it?

5. In the essay which opens this chapter Paul Engle comments on various aspects of good modern poetry, including: (*a*) its use of the language of ordinary speech (page 542); (*b*) its use of natural word order (page 542); (*c*) the absence of metronomic meter (page 542); (*d*) its lack of sentimentality (page 543). Measured by these standards, is "Mutterings over the Crib of a Deaf Child" a good modern poem? Explain your answer.

Richard Wilbur is widely regarded as one of the most skillful of contemporary poets. He has been the recipient of many honors, including a Guggenheim Fellowship, the Prix de Rome Fellowship of the American Academy of Arts and Letters, and the Pulitzer Prize in poetry in 1956 for *Things of This World.*

Wilbur was born into a family which encouraged his early attempts at versifying. During his boyhood in a rural corner of New Jersey he developed the liking for the outdoor world which is apparent in much of his poetry. While he was a student at Amherst, he widened his knowledge of the United States by spending his summers bumming across country on freight cars. He served in the infantry during World War II, then took an M.A. degree at Harvard. After teaching in the English department there for several years, he became a member of the faculty at Wesleyan University.

It was not until he had seen active service during the war that Wilbur began to work seriously at his poetry, trying through poetry to bring order into his disordered world. His first book of poems, *The Beautiful Changes* (1947), showed qualities that are apparent to a greater extent in his later poetry—a strong lyric note, mastery of form, and fusion of form and idea. Because he believes in the disciplines of meter, rhyme, and other formal devices, he attempts to reconcile these adjuncts of traditional poetry with the modern modes of thought and expression. It is this tendency in his poetry that has caused him to be called "a New Formalist."

TO INCREASE UNDERSTANDING

1. The subject of "She" is the eternal feminine. (*a*) What specific woman is the subject of stanzas 1-2? (*b*) Why is she referred to as *her* in line 1 rather than by name? (*c*) What is the meaning of *estate* in line 1? (*d*) Can you describe this woman? (*e*) What is meant by "Resemblance had to wait/For separation" (lines 4-5)?

2. Lines 9-22 suggest the rôle and the appearance of woman in various ages.
(*Continued on page 601.*)

Richard Wilbur

She

What was her beauty in our first estate
When Adam's will was whole, and the least thing
Appeared the gift and creature of his king,
How should we guess? Resemblance had to wait

For separation, and in such a place   5
She so partook of water, light, and trees
As not to look like any one of these.
He woke and gazed into her naked face.

But then she changed, and coming down amid
The flocks of Abel and the fields of Cain,   10
Clothed in their wish, her Eden graces hid,
A shape of plenty with a mop of grain,

She broke upon the world, in time took on
The look of every labor and its fruits.
Columnar in a robe of pleated lawn   15
She cupped her patient hand for attributes,

Was radiant captive of the farthest tower
And shed her honor on the fields of war,
Walked in her garden at the evening hour,
Her shadow like a dark ogival door,   20

Breasted the seas for all the westward ships
And, come to virgin country, changed again—
A moonlike being truest in eclipse
And subject goddess of dreams of men.

Tree temple, valley, prow, gazelle, machine,   25
More named and nameless than the morning star,
Lovely in every shape, in all unseen,
We dare not wish to find you as you are,

Whose apparition, biding time until
Desire decay and bring the latter age,   30
Shall flourish in the ruins of our will
And deck the broken stones like saxifrage.

"She" from the *Atlantic Monthly*, November 1958. Reprinted by permission of the author.
"Juggler" from *Ceremony and Other Poems* by Richard Wilbur. Copyright 1948, 1949, 1950 by Richard Wilbur. Reprinted by permission of Harcourt, Brace & World, Inc., New York, and Faber & Faber, Ltd., London.

Juggler   A ball will bounce, but less and less. It's not
A light-hearted thing, resents its own resilience.
Falling is what it loves, and the earth falls
So in our hearts from brilliance,
Settles and is forgot.   5
It takes a sky-blue juggler with five red balls

To shake our gravity up. Whee, in the air
The balls roll round, wheel on his wheeling hands,
Learning the ways of lightness, alter to spheres
Grazing his finger ends,   10
Cling to their courses there,
Swinging a small heaven about his ears.

But a heaven is easier made of nothing at all
Than the earth regained, and still and sole within
The spin of worlds, with a gesture sure and noble   15
He reels that heaven in,
Landing it ball by ball,
And trades it all for a broom, a plate, a table.

Oh, on his toe the table is turning, the broom's
Balancing up on his nose, and the plate whirls   20
On the tip of the broom! Damn, what a show, we cry:
The boys stamp, and the girls
Shriek, and the drum booms
And all comes down, and he bows and says good-bye.

If the juggler is tired now, if the broom stands   25
In the dust again, if the table starts to drop
Through the daily dark again, and though the plate
Lies flat on the table top,
For him we batter our hands
Who has won for once over the world's weight.   30

(a) What era may be associated with lines 9-12? (b) In what age is woman often pictured as "Columnar in a robe of pleated lawn"? (c) What age do lines 17-20 indicate? (The word *ogival* is the strongest clue.) (d) What is the meaning of line 21? (e) What period of history is suggested by line 22?

3. Beginning with line 23, Wilbur describes the qualities of woman since she lost the perfection of Eden. (a) Why may she be considered "truest in eclipse"? (b) Why is the morning star nameless? (c) In what way is woman like the morning star?

4. The mention in the first stanza of the time "When Adam's will was whole" is contrasted in the last stanza with "the ruins of our will." What part does woman play in the imperfect world until "the latter age" of perfection arrives?

5. (a) In "Juggler" what two meanings does *gravity* (line 7) convey? (b) How does the poet introduce these meanings in the first stanza?

6. (a) Trace the development of the image of a heaven of five red balls in stanzas 2-3. (b) What do the lines "But a heaven is easier made of nothing at all/Than the earth regained" mean?

7. (a) Explain the two meanings of *weight* in the last line. (b) What is the theme of the poem?

8. (a) Compare the meter, rhyme scheme, and imagery in "She" and "Juggler." (b) How do these poems differ in tone? (c) To what extent is this tone determined by meter, rhyme, and type of imagery?

Light Verse

Light verse deals with all aspects of the human comedy. Its intent is often satirical, and its subject playfully nipped and teased. Even when the mood is sarcastic, however, it is never severe. The tone is conversational, the rhythms and rhymes regular and unforced, and there is a sparkle in the wit. Puns and incongruities are used just for fun. The ease of expression that is characteristic of light verse may deceive the reader into missing the subtle and thoughtful ideas the poet is expressing. Types of light verse range from light-hearted lyrics, limericks, and occasional poems to parodies and other forms of satire.

Ogden Nash

Laments for a Dying Language

What's the monster of this week?
"Mystique"—[1]
A noun that in its current arcane use leaves me frigid,
Since it is not to be found in either the O. E. D.[2] or Webster's Unabridged.
It is primarily the invention of the mystagogues of esoteric criticism, so it means
    whatever they choose,   5
But I will give you an example of what I think they think it means, only from the
    domain of a different muse.
I recently heard on the air a song in which the lover states that the loved one is his
    idea
Of a band of angels singing "Ave Maria."
This is not only a metaphor unique,
It is also an example of the songwriter's mystique at its peak.   10

II
Someone comes up with a linguistic gimmick,
And thousands flock to mimic.
This noisy age, when big loud bangs give way to bangs louder and bigger still,
And admirals, congressmen, and minor government officials pop off at will,
Gives us two gimmicks that reflect our minds' corrosion: 15
"Crash program" and "explosion."
See here the population explosion, the freedom explosion, the Broadway and off-
    Broadway incest-theme explosion, the explosion of British secretaries in offices
    of grandiose pretensions,
And there the crash program for defense, for space exploration, for a third major
    league, for nominating the candidates previous to the conventions.
With each successive bang my hopes grow limper
That the world's end will be a simple whimper.[3]   20

---

1. *mystique* (mis tēk′), a recent acquisition to the English language from the French. When Nash wrote the poem, *mystique* did not appear in Webster's unabridged dictionary. It is in the 1961 edition, however. 2. *O.E.D.*, the twelve-volume *Oxford English Dictionary*. 3. *With each . . . whimper.* T.S. Eliot's poem "The Hollow Men" ends with the line, "This is the way the world ends/Not with a bang but a whimper."

III

In the nice-minded Department of Prunes and Prisms,
It's I for you
And euphemisms.
Hence the phrase I would eagerly jettison:
"Senior citizen."   25
Let us, then, retranslate
Joel, 2, 28.[4]
To the sociologist squeamish
The words "Your old men shall dream dreams" are less than beamish,
So "Your senior citizens shall dream dreams" it shall henceforth be,   30
Along with Hemingway's "The Senior Citizen and the Sea."
I, though no Joel, prophesy that someday while the senior citizens are projecting the
    image of an age-adjusted social group,
The old men will rise up and knock them for a loop.

IV

Those authors I can never love
Who write, "It fit him like a glove."   35
Though baseballs may be hit, not "hitted,"
The past of "fit" is always "fitted."
The sole exception worth a *haricot*[5]
Is "Joshua fit de battle ob Jericho."

V

Coin brassy words at will, debase the coinage;   40
We're in an if-you-cannot-lick-them-join age,
A slovenliness-provides-its-own-excuse age,
Where usage overnight condones misusage.
Farewell, farewell to my beloved language,
Once English, now a vile orangutanguage.   45

4. *Joel*, 2:28. The Biblical passage reads: "And it shall come to pass afterward, that I will pour out my spirit upon all flesh; and your sons and your daughters shall prophesy, your old men shall dream dreams, your young men shall see visions." 5. *haricot* (är′ē kō), bean. [*French*]

OGDEN NASH 1902-

For some years Ogden Nash has been popularly regarded as the poet laureate of light verse. He has won this reputation by twisting the syntax of standard English in a bewildering manner, coining outrageous rhymes, and pricking with deft satire practically every aspect of twentieth-century living.

Nash was born in Rye, New York. After a year at Harvard, he held various positions in New York City, including a job in the advertising department of a publishing company. Here, however, according to Christopher Morley, instead of working on advertising copy "he was writing the earliest of his metrical outrages." In 1931 he joined the editorial staff of the *New Yorker* and his first book appeared. Language purists protested his handling of the language; but the public, caught in the problems of the Great Depression, was delighted. Writing in the *Saturday Review* Russell Maloney spoke of Nash as "the laureate of a generation which had to develop its own wry, none-too-joyful humor as the alternative to simply lying down on the floor and screaming." Whatever reason Nash had originally for writing his particular type of verse—and he himself has suggested that part of his productivity has always been connected with the wish to feed himself, family, and dog daily—he has continued to produce wry wit in his own inimitable verse forms. *Verses from 1929 On* is the most complete collection of his poetry.

David McCord

Gloss

I know a little man both ept and ert.
An intro-? extro-? No, he's just a vert.
Sheveled and couth and kempt, pecunious,
    ane,
His image trudes upon the ceptive brain.

When life turns sipid and the mind is
    traught,   5
The spirit soars as I would sist it ought.
Chalantly then, like any gainly goof,
My digent self is sertive, choate, loof.

Grand Tour

His glasses broke at Brokenbow,
He changed a tire at Lost Mule Flat,
He drank a Coke in Kokomo
And Bisodol in Medicine Hat.

There was no sleep at Sabbath Rest,   5
In Waterproof it rained quite hard;
Lo Lo is higher than he guessed.
You ever et at Cheesquake, pard?

He did some work in Shirkieville,
Sweated in Frozen, froze in Fry;   10
Called it a day in Half Day, Ill.,
And fled from Brave, bade Sweet good-by.

Tuesday in Monday, stranger to Strange,
Christmas for Easter, perhaps Maybee;
Zap on the map was a welcome change   15
From chowder in Clam and coffee in Tea.

Lonely in Only, sickly in Slick,
Better in Best, but down in Drain;
Soso in Oso, dead in Quick,
In Stamping Ground he's home again.   20

Morris Bishop

The Perforated Spirit

The fellows up in Personnel,
    They have a set of cards on me.
The sprinkled perforations tell
    My individuality.

And what am I? I am a chart   5
    Upon the cards of IBM;
The secret places of the heart
    Have little secrecy for them.

It matters not how I may prate,
    They punch with punishments my scroll. 10
The files are masters of my fate,
    They are the captains of my soul.[1]

Monday my brain began to buzz;
    I was in agony all night.
I found out what the trouble was: 15
    They had my paper clip too tight.

PHOTO BY CHIANG YEE

CULVER PICTURES

Richard Armour

The Ant

The ant, a prodigy of strength,
Lifts objects twice his weight and length
And never stops or sighs or glowers
Because it's after working hours.
Though underground, he bears the onus   5
And peril without thought of bonus,
And never once is heard to mention
Retiring on a tax-free pension.
Nor does he frown or look askance
At other, lighter-burdened ants.   10
Not one to bicker, blame, or sob,
Not angling for a better job,
The ant has but one flaw I see,
To wit, he doesn't work for me.

DAVID MC CORD 1897-

David McCord graduated from Harvard and took his A.M. degree there in 1922. His continued association with Harvard formed a basis for a recent book of essays, *In Sight of Sever*. McCord's first love, however, has always been poetry. He has books of serious poetry—*Old Bateau*, for example; light verse—*Odds Without Ends*; and children's verse—*Take Sky*. Among the books he has edited is *What Cheer*, one of the best anthologies of light verse. McCord delighted readers of the *New Yorker* for almost thirty years with his brilliant verses. Typical McCord wit shows in "Gloss," a poem in which he plays with "lost positive" forms of words like *inept* and *inert*.

MORRIS BISHOP 1893-

When Morris Bishop was a contributor to *St. Nicholas* magazine at the age of ten, he wrote "heavy verse," as he called it. He has since turned his talents to light verse, but his early desire to be serious is still evident in the satiric quality of his poetry.

Besides being a poet, Bishop is a critic, biographer, and professor of Romance Languages at Cornell University. He has said that his chief interest is biography, and has written the lives of Cabeza de Vaca, Champlain, and La Rochefoucauld. His work has appeared in *Life*, the *Saturday Evening Post*, and the *New Yorker*.

RICHARD ARMOUR 1906-

Richard Armour—a scholar, teacher, critic, and poet—delights the public by sitting down and composing on an average of three light verses a day. He began this avocation when he was still a student at Harvard University. In the intervening years his light verse and his other writings add up to more than twenty books.

Life's trials such as nonflowing catchup bottles, people who hum, punctuation, the foibles of women and teen-agers are jousted with in *Nights with Armour* (1958) and *Light Armour* (1954). In his preface to the latter he says that "most of the things he [the satirist] makes fun of are what he likes most . . . because he knows them best and has discovered their wonderful oddities and inconsistencies."

Another one of his likes, teaching literature, has received its share of affection in such parodies as *Twisted Tales from Shakespeare* (1957) and *The Classics Reclassified* (1960). Armour's work often appears in the *Saturday Evening Post* and the *New Yorker*.

Don Marquis

DON MARQUIS 1878-1937

About fifty years ago in the pressroom of the *New York Sun* a cockroach named Archy climbed laboriously from the floor to a typewriter which by good fortune had a piece of paper left in it, and began hurling himself, head downward, on the keys. The result was a poem explaining that his soul in a former life had belonged to a poet and he still felt the need for expression. He told about the other night inhabitants of the pressroom: Freddy the rat, an ugly fellow who ate poetry; and Mehitabel, the cat who in a former life had been Cleopatra.

Archy expressed his views about life in the daily "Sun Dial" column of the *New York Sun,* always writing in lower case because he could not operate the shift key on the typewriter.

The creator of these characters, Don Marquis (mar'kwis), remarked once that "it would be one on me if I should be remembered longest for creating a cockroach character," and, ironically, it is probably for Archy that Marquis will be remembered best. Marquis' collected pieces on Archy appeared in 1930 as *Archy and Mehitabel.*

Don Marquis was a Midwesterner who worked at various jobs—actor with a touring stock company, part-time reporter for the *Washington Times,* assistant editor of the *Uncle Remus Magazine*—until he migrated to New York in 1912 and started the "Sun Dial" column. His physical appearance suggested the typical jolly fat man, but his friends said that his wit was rather the product of cynicism. Like Archy, he found his work exhausting; he also found his labors unrewarding financially; and as he constantly struggled to meet deadlines, filling the ever-empty daily column often kept him from the rewriting he felt necessary.

The public's reaction to his writing was always a surprise to him. His novel *The Old Soak,* written in three days, was very successful, while *The Dark. Hours,* which he worked on for ten years, was a failure.

Opinion on Don Marquis as a literary artist has always been divided. While many critics scoff at the merits of *The Old Soak* and *Archy and Mehitabel,* authors like Bernard De Voto (page 15) and E. B. White (page 633) include these books among their favorites and are enthusiastic admirers of Don Marquis' work. Writers undoubtedly feel some affinity toward Archy in his exhausting efforts to express himself, and other people are delighted with his unique outlook on life.

Don Marquis

archy hears from mars

at eleven o clock
p m on last saturday evening
i received the following
message on my
own private radio set   5
good evening little archibald
and how are you
this is mars speaking
i replied at once
whom or who   10
as the case may be
do i know on mars
everyone here is familiar
with your work archy
was the answer   15
and we feel well repaid
for all the trouble we have had
in getting in touch
with your planet
thank you i replied   20
i would rather hear
mars say that
than any other planet
mars has always been
one of my favorite planets   25
it is sweet of you
to think that way about us
said mars
and so we continued to pay
each other interstellar   30
compliments
what is or are
thirty five million miles
between kindred souls
tell us all about   35
your planet said mars
well i said it is
round like an orange
or a ball
and it is all cluttered   40
up with automobiles

and politicians
it doesn t know where it is
going or why
but it is in a hurry 45
it is in charge of a
two legged animal called
man who is genuinely
puzzled as to whether
his grandfather was a god 50
or a monkey
i should think said mars
that what he is himself
would make more difference
than what his grandfather was 55
not to this animal i replied
he is the great alibi ike of
the cosmos when he raises hell
just because he feels like
raising hell 60
he wants somebody to blame it on
can t anything be done about him
said mars
i am doing the best i can
i answered 65
but after all i am only one
and my influence is limited
you are too modest archy
said mars
we all but worship you 70
here on this planet
a prophet said i is not
without honor save on his own
planet[1] wait a minute
said mars 75
i want to write that down
that is one of your best things
archy is it original
it was once i answered truthfully
and may be again 80
won t you tell us a little
something said mars
about yourself what you look like
and what you think
is the best thing you have written 85
and your favorite games
and that sort of thing
well i said i am brunette
and stand over six feet

without any shoes on 90
the best skits i have done
were some little plays
i dashed off
under the general title
of shakespeare s plays 95
and my favorite sport is theology
you must meet
a great many interesting people
said mars
oh yes i said one becomes 100
accustomed to that after a while
what is your favorite dish
said mars and do you believe
in the immortality of the soul
stew i said and yes 105
at least mine is immortal
but i could name several others that i have my
          doubts about
is there anything else
of interest about your planet
which you wish to tell your 110
many admirers on mars
asked mars
there is very little else
of any real interest i said
and now will you tune out 115
and let me do some work
you people who say you admire
my work are always butting in
and taking up my time
how the hell can i get any 120
serious literary work done
if you keep bothering me
all the time now you get off
the ether and let me do some
deep thinking 125
you might add that i am shy
and loathe publicity

      archy

1. *a prophet ... his own planet.* Matthew 8:57, reads, "A
prophet is not without honor save in his own country."

FROM *ARCHY AND MEHITABEL*

I WAS CLEOPATRA ONCE SHE SAID.

Dorothy Parker

Love Song

My own dear love he is strong and bold
    And he cares not what comes after.
His words ring sweet as a chime of gold,
    And his eyes are lit with laughter.
He is jubilant as a flag unfurled—   5
    Oh, a girl, she'd not forget him.
My own dear love, he is all my world—
    And I wish I'd never met him.

My love, he's mad, and my love, he's fleet,
    And a wild young wood-thing bore him!   10
The ways are fair to his roaming feet,
    And the skies are sunlit for him.
As sharply sweet to my heart he seems
    As the fragrance of acacia.
My own dear love, he is all my dreams—   15
    And I wish he were in Asia.

My love runs by like a day in June,
    And he makes no friends of sorrows,
He'll tread his galloping rigadoon
    In the pathway of the morrows.   20
He'll live his days where the sunbeams start,
    Nor could storm or wind uproot him.
My own dear love, he is all my heart—
    And I wish somebody'd shoot him.

PHOTO BY PETER BASCH

PHOTO BY GEORGE PLATT LYNES

DOROTHY PARKER 1893-

In 1927 Dorothy Parker became book critic for the *New Yorker* and wrote her first book of poetry, which became a best seller. She took advantage of this financial phenomenon to resign from the magazine staff and became a very successful free-lance writer. She has written poetry, short stories, and plays for the theater and the movies. In 1929 one of her short stories won the O. Henry prize (see page 451), but her plays have had only moderate success.

In spite of the fact that the public has for years regarded Miss Parker as one of its favorite humorists, she herself prefers to be known as a satirist. Her observations on life are bittersweet; her light touch and sparkling rhymes veil a critical attitude toward life.

The lyric on this page is typical of Miss Parker's light verse. It starts with an airy flight into a romantic dreamland—and ends with a swoop back to the cold, sharp world of reality. The humor of its lilting rhythm and exaggerated figurative language throws into sharp focus the disillusionment of the speaker.

In 1944 an anthology of Miss Parker's work entitled *The Portable Dorothy Parker* was published.

PHYLLIS MC GINLEY 1905-

Some years ago Phyllis McGinley's fancy was caught by a newspaper article which prompted her to write her first light verse. The *New Yorker* was so pleased with it that she was urged to write more "funny" verse, as Miss McGinley calls it. Since then she has written more than seven volumes.

Miss McGinley said in an article in the *Saturday Review* that she thinks the gulf between light and serious verse is a narrow one. Her poems, she says, are "outwardly amusing, but inwardly serious." Like most writers of light verse, she has also written serious poetry. For a while she was on the staff of *Town and Country* magazine; she is also an author of many children's books.

Two of her most popular collections of light verse have been *The Love Letters of Phyllis McGinley* published in 1954, and *Times Three* published in 1960. When she is not throwing poetic barbs at things like TV panel programs or praising the useful bobby pin, she takes care of a husband, two daughters, and a hundred-year-old Victorian home.

Phyllis McGinley

Reactionary Essay on Applied Science

I cannot love the Brothers Wright.
  Marconi[1] wins my mixed devotion.
Had no one yet discovered flight
  Or set the air waves in commotion,
Life would, I think, have been as well.
That also goes for A. G. Bell.   5

What I'm really thankful for, when I'm
      cleaning up after lunch,
Is the invention of waxed paper.

That Edison improved my lot,
  I sometimes doubt; nor care a jitney   10
Whether the kettle steamed, or Watt,[2]
  Or if the gin invented Whitney.
Better the world, I often feel,
Had nobody contrived the wheel.

On the other hand, I'm awfully indebted   15
To whoever it was dreamed up the elastic
      band.

Yes, pausing grateful, now and then,
  Upon my prim, domestic courses,
I offer praise to lesser men—
  Fultons unsung, anonymous Morses—   20
Whose deft and innocent devices
Pleasure my house with sweets and spices.

I give you, for instance, the fellow
Who first had the idea for Scotch tape.

I hail the man who thought of soap,   25
  The chap responsible for zippers,
Sun lotion, the stamped envelope,
  And screens, and wading pools for nippers,
Venetian blinds of various classes,
And bobby pins and tinted glasses.   30

DeForest[3] never thought up anything
So useful as a bobby pin.

Those baubles are the ones that keep
  Their places, and beget no trouble,
Incite no battles, stab no sleep,   35
  Reduce no villages to rubble,
Being primarily designed
By men of unambitious mind.

You remember how Orville Wright said his
      flying machine
Was going to outlaw war?   40

Let them on Archimedes[4] dote
  Who like to hear the planet rattling.
I cannot cast a hearty vote
  For Galileo[5] or for Gatling,[6]
Preferring, of the freaks of science,   45
The pygmies rather than the giants

(And from experience being wary of
Greek geniuses bearing gifts),

Deciding, on reflection calm,
  Mankind is better off with trifles: 50
With Band-Aid rather than the bomb,
  With safety match than safety rifles.
Let the earth fall or the earth spin!
A brave new world might well begin
With no invention   55
Worth the mention
Save paper towels and aspirin.

Remind me to call the repairman
About my big new automatically defrosting
      refrigerator with the built-in electric
      eye.

1. *Marconi* (mär kō'ni), 1874-1937, Italian inventor who perfected the wireless telegraph. 2. *Watt* (wot), 1736-1819, Scottish engineer and inventor who perfected the steam engine. 3. *DeForest* (di fôr'ist *or* di for'ist), 1873-, American inventor who has made improvements in radio, sound pictures, and television. 4. *Archimedes* (är'kə mē'dēz). 287?-212 B.C., Greek mathematician, physicist, and inventor. He formulated principles of specific gravity and of the lever. 5. *Galileo* (gal'ə lē'ō *or* gal'ə lā'ō), 1564-1642, Italian astronomer who propounded the theory that the earth goes round the sun. 6. *Gatling* (gat'ling), 1818-1903, American inventor of the machine gun.

Laments for a Dying Language

1. In each of the five stanzas of this poem Nash discusses some aspect of the current use of language. Explain the type of usage dealt with in each stanza. In each case cite examples to illustrate the point Nash is making.

2. Much of Nash's humor depends on word play and literary reference. (*a*) How does he play with the word *fit* in the fourth stanza? (*b*) Explain the literary reference in lines 19-20. (*c*) Cite other literary references.

3. Nash is known for his unique rhymes. Find examples of unusual rhymes in the poem.

4. (*a*) What is Nash satirizing in "Laments for a Dying Language"? (*b*) What makes the verses funny as well as satirical?

Gloss, Grand Tour

1. Cite several examples of lost positives from "Gloss" and explain their meanings.

2. One of the nineteen words McCord uses as a lost positive in "Gloss" does not belong in this class. Since this word has always been a single root rather than a root prefixed by an affix, without the initial *in-* it is not a word at all. Use a dictionary to discover which word is not a lost positive.

3. Why is "Gloss" considered light verse?

4. What makes "Grand Tour" amusing?

5. Judging from "Gloss" and "Grand Tour," what are the prime characteristics of McCord's light verse?

The Perforated Spirit

1. (*a*) What is the meaning of *spirit* as it is used in the title of Bishop's poem? (*b*) What contradiction is there in the title?

2. (*a*) Compare "The Perforated Spirit" and "The Unknown Citizen" (page 591), paying particular attention to the theme and tone of each. (*b*) Do you think "The Unknown Citizen" can be classified as light verse? Why, or why not?

The Ant

1. The first twelve lines of the poem extol the industry of the ant. In what way is this praise of the ant a criticism of human nature?

2. What is the relation of the last two lines to the remainder of the verse?

3. Comment on Armour's use of rhyme and meter in "The Ant."

Archy Hears from Mars

1. According to Archy himself, he is shy and "loathes publicity." How would *you* describe him?

2. In the biographical sketch of Don Marquis you read that his friends believed much of his wit was the product of his cynicism. (*a*) Cite passages in "Archy Hears from Mars" which exhibit a cynical or disillusioned view of human nature. (*b*) Which passages are sheer fun?

3. *Archy and Mehitabel* has remained a favorite book of light verse for over thirty years. Judging from "Archy Hears from Mars," what are some of the factors of Marquis' verse that have produced this enduring popularity?

Love Song

1. Do you consider the title ironic? Explain your answer.

2. In what way is "Love Song" a burlesque of romantic love poetry?

3. The biographical sketch of Miss Parker mentions the exaggerated figurative language and the lilting rhythm of "Love Song." (*a*) Cite examples of figurative language. (*b*) Scan a stanza of the poem. What do the combined rhythm and rhyme add to the humor of the verse? (*c*) In your opinion would the poem be equally funny if it used literal language and a free-verse form? Explain your answer.

Reactionary Essay on Applied Science

1. (*a*) Why is this a "reactionary" essay? (*b*) What is applied science?

2. (*a*) Why does Miss McGinley think "Mankind is better off with trifles"? (*b*) What are some of the trifles of which she approves?

3. (*a*) Name some of the inventions of which Miss McGinley specifically disapproves. (*b*) Are her objections facetious or serious? Explain the reasons for your answer.

4. Miss McGinley speaks of her writing as "funny" verse. Does this description fit "Reactionary Essay on Applied Science"? Explain.

THE LARGER VIEW

A. In your opinion which poem in this chapter best exemplifies Miss Moore's idea of "imaginary gardens with real toads in them"? (Be sure that you can explain what is meant by that phrase.) Give reasons for your choice and cite examples from the poem to validate your reasons. In your answer consider theme, use of imagery to emphasize the theme, appropriateness of verse form, and other poetic devices.

B. From a collection of poetry select and read a poem you like by one of the following: Robert Frost, Carl Sandburg, E. A. Robinson, Edna St. Vincent Millay, Robinson Jeffers, Elinor Wylie, Marianne Moore, Randall Jarrell, or Richard Wilbur.

1. State the theme or main purpose of the poem.
2. What features of the poem are characteristic of this poet's work?
3. What features identify it as a modern poem? (Reread Paul Engle's introduction.)

C. Dorothy Parker has said that she would prefer to be called "satirist" rather than "humorist."

1. Define *satire* and *humor*. How do they differ? In what ways may they resemble one another?
2. Review the light verse, deciding which selections are pure humor and which contain satire as well.
3. Which poem would you say best synthesizes pure humor and satire?

BIBLIOGRAPHY

BONTEMPS, ARNA WENDELL (compiler), *Golden Slippers; an Anthology of Negro Poetry for Young Readers*. (Harper) While your chief interest in this appealing volume will be the lyrics, you probably won't be able to resist entirely the narrative and humorous poetry also included. The brief biographies will add to your understanding of the poets.

CIARDI, JOHN (editor), *Mid-Century American Poets*. (Twayne) Fifteen modern American poets explain what they set out to do in their poems here printed.

DREW, ELIZABETH, *Poetry; A Modern Guide to its Understanding and Enjoyment*. (Norton) Miss Drew's approach to the study of poetry is refreshing and delightful.

ENGLE, PAUL (editor), *Reading Modern Poetry*. (Scott, Foresman) The same clarity in explaining modern poetry that is apparent in the introduction to this chapter makes *Reading Modern Poetry* outstanding. This anthology, complete with critical notes, is both entertaining and instructive.

FROST, ROBERT, *Complete Poems*. (Holt) Simplicity, humanity, and craftsmanship have made Frost the unchallenged poet laureate of New England. This magnificent volume is proof of his talents.

HUMPHRIES, ROLFE (editor), *New Poems by American Poets*. (•Ballantine) The works of both familiar and lesser-known poets can be found in this highly readable volume edited by a man with a great appreciation of poetry.

MASTERS, EDGAR LEE, *Spoon River Anthology*. (Macmillan) In this extraordinary book, written in free verse, the men and women of Spoon River speak from the cemetery where they are buried.

MC GINLEY, PHYLLIS, *Times Three*. (Viking) With amused affection toward all and malice toward none, Miss McGinley views herself and her world. This wise and witty poet is a delight to read.

The New Poets of England and America; edited and selected by Donald Hall, Robert Pack, and Louis Simpson. (•Meridian) In order to present a true picture of the poetic concepts of a generation, the editors have included only those poets born after 1917. An introduction by Robert Frost adds to the book's value and interest.

Oxford Book of American Verse; chosen and with an introduction by F. O. Matthiessen. (Oxford) This book is one of the best anthologies available. Including American poets from colonial days to the present, it contains enough of the work of each poet to enable the reader to know and understand him.

ROSENTHAL, MACHA, *The Modern Poets*. (Oxford) Do you sometimes feel you could really enjoy modern poetry, if only you knew what it was all about? If so, read this informative, fair-minded résumé of twentieth-century poets and their works.

UNTERMEYER, LOUIS (editor), *Modern American Poetry; Mid-Century Edition*. (Harcourt) The rich diversity of recent American poetry and Untermeyer's interesting biographical and critical sketches make this a first-rate book.

•paperback

chapter nine

Article and Essay

In the eighteenth century the magazine and the essay grew up together; and it is in the magazine that brief nonfiction has continued to make itself at home. This form of writing is the chief reason that magazines are highly popular today. At present there are more magazines circulated in the United States than there are people living in this country. It is safe to assume that nearly everyone in the nation who can read, reads magazines.

What is it that the modern American expects to find when he picks up a magazine? First, what he reads must be brief and interesting—something timely that can be read while going to work, during lunch hour, or while the baby is asleep. Second, it must be immediately valuable—something that will increase his knowledge, give practical help, or be inspiring or diverting. The literary type that seems to fulfill these needs best is the article, and in the reading habits of the American people the article has certainly carried the day. Forms of writing as diverse as the novel and the newspaper have felt its effects, and been changed in response to it. In fact, the popularity of the article has been so great that to seize reader interest publishers often present the familiar essay (see page 245) under the guise and name of the article.

Perhaps the best way to discover the distinguishing characteristics of the article is to contrast it with its cousin, the informal essay. Reading Franklin's letter "The First Aerial Voyage by Man" (page 138) one is aware that his purpose was to give his view of an actual, newsworthy event. Today such a piece of writing, if it appeared in a magazine, would be called an article. It is interesting, timely, factual; it is written by a scientist; and it is designed to increase the knowledge of the reader. In "The Ephemera" (page 144), it is clear, Franklin was trying to do something entirely different. Instead of simply telling us facts, "The

Ephemera" communicates a complex but distinct attitude toward what things are valuable in life, and behind it one feels the wisdom of Franklin the whole man, instead of just the keen eye of Franklin the scientist. Its personal, reflective viewpoint characterizes this piece of writing as an essay.

It is not hard to see why the article has become extremely popular in our time. In the first place, the effectiveness of scientific method in many areas has led us to look for an objective, factual approach to all aspects of life. In the second place, the complexity of the practical problems that confront us today makes us inclined to view people—even ourselves—as specialists within a small field. Consequently we are more likely to be reassured by someone approaching part of a problem as an expert than we are by someone approaching the whole problem as a whole man. Finally, in order to make intelligent decisions or even intelligent conversation in a culture in which knowledge is both complex and specialized, we demand writing that will give us up-to-date, factual information easily and quickly.

Even under the conditions of modern life, however, there is a place for the personal essay. This kind of writing provides an important means for dealing with human purposes and values—the things which alone make facts meaningful and useful. Through the essay, as some of the following selections show, a writer can sift the important from the unimportant, make evaluations, or advocate a course of action.

Indeed, as others of these selections show, the best article writers realize that our needs go beyond the acquisition of quick, sometimes superficial information. Such writers are able to combine the informative virtues of the purely factual article with the personal, reflective viewpoint of the informal essay.

The Three E. J. Kahn

When the United Nations began emergency land and air operations in the Congo, it came as no surprise to thousands of aviation authorities here and abroad that among the planes used prominently was the DC-3—a venerable, if diminutive, twin-engine monoplane, which, unless it is souped up, has a cruising speed of only a hundred and eighty miles an hour. Ever since the Douglas Aircraft Company, Inc., brought out this model, in 1936, it has been considered a uniquely serviceable creation. Its admirers point to the fact that although the last of these planes was assembled in 1946—an aeon ago, as aviation history is measured—five thousand DC-3s, or about half of all those ever turned out, are believed to be still flying. The DC-3's boosters concede that in the jet age there is no point in manufacturing more of their favorites, and they agree that some of the model's statistical achievements—such as having flown six hundred million passengers seven billion miles in less than a quarter of a century—can be attributed simply to Douglas' big-scale production of the plane, but they maintain that this hardly accounts for its astonishing tenacity. In support of their claim, they recall that in 1942 the Civil Aeronautics Board decreed that after 1947 it would no longer issue certificates of airworthiness to DC-3s as commercial passenger carriers, and that it repeatedly extended the deadline until, in 1953, it declared that the model would be rated airworthy indefinitely.

The D (for "Douglas") C (for "Commercial") -3 (for "Three")—sometimes referred to simply as "the Three"—is represented not once but twice in the collection of celebrated aircraft at the Smithsonian Institution, in Washington. Most of the planes there are enshrined because they participated in some single notable feat—Lindbergh's "Spirit of St. Louis,"[1] for example, and one of the pair of DC-3s. This DC-3, known as an R4-D—the Navy's term for the model—was the first plane of any kind to land at the South Pole. (A so far unenshrined C-47, or Army DC-3, was the first plane to land at the North Pole.) How-

ever, the national museum's second DC-3, a retired Eastern Air Lines transport, is there not because of any historic event but merely because it is a run-of-the-mill example of what the United States government, in a citation to the Douglas Company, has solemnly proclaimed a "beloved aircraft" and, emotionalism aside, "the best single airplane ever built." That last has to be qualified, of course; it was the best single plane produced for its time. The surviving members of the species, though, have shown abundantly that they are still useful in our time.

For any museum piece to be in active service is unusual. The DC-3 has been likened to the Model T Ford, but Model Ts were hardly more of a factor in automotive travel a quarter of a century after their arrival on the scene than Edsels[2] are now. The DC-3 is still very much a factor in contemporary air travel; indeed, far more DC-3s are engaged in scheduled airline service around the world than planes of any other type. The United States Air Force, for all its glittering stable of jets, has twelve hundred DC-3s in active service, and if they are not likely to make the Soviet Union throw in the towel, they are regularly called upon to perform important chores. One of them flew ahead of President Eisenhower's Boeing 707 during his 1959 tour of India and Pakistan and radioed back weather reports. A number of DC-3s are assigned to Air Force ballistic-missile teams to take them, however prosaically, from factory to launching pad. Still others are employed as flying laboratories to test new defense devices. Similarly, the parent company, Douglas, relied on several DC-3s to try out many of the mechanisms it subsequently installed in its first passenger jet, the DC-8, which made its debut last year. Douglas

---

1. "*Spirit of St. Louis*," the airplane in which, in 1927, Charles Lindbergh made the first non-stop, transatlantic solo flight. 2. *Edsels*. By December of 1960 the Edsel automobile, introduced by the Ford Motor Company only three years earlier, had been discontinued.

executive were taken aback when some aviation writers, after being given an introductory ride on the DC-8, seemed much less interested in telling their readers about the swift new giant than in reminiscing mistily about its lumbering old forebear. In their choice of emphasis, the writers were following an example set by American Airlines, which ordered the first DC-3s ever produced, and at one time had a fleet of eighty of them; American gave up the model in 1949, but with such reluctance that in one of its ads at the time, instead of crowing about the up-to-date planes it had just acquired, it dwelt on the DC-3s of its past.

Like American, the other major United States air lines have pretty much outgrown the DC-3, save for scattered local flights—a Braniff run, for instance, between Sioux City and Kansas City, Capital's Washington-Pittsburgh run, Delta's Charleston-Atlanta run, and a few others. Nevertheless, approximately three hundred and fifty of the planes are still in domestic scheduled service, not to mention scores operated by nonscheduled carriers.

Abroad, far more than here, the DC-3 is still the ubiquitous work horse it once was, being currently in harness to a hundred and seventy nations. (In the Netherlands, Hungary, and Chile, it has been depicted on airmail stamps—an honor that it has yet to win at home.) A British magazine called *Flight* calculated last year that the DC-3s operated by scheduled air lines came to a thousand six hundred and seventy-two. "It is a sobering fact that numerically about thirty per cent of the world's total transport air fleet consists of DC-3s," *Flight* said. Of eighty-six air lines, collectively using sixty-nine makes of aircraft, that recently reported on their comings and goings to the International Air Transport Association, a trade group with headquarters in Montreal, fifty-seven lines were flying some DC-3s, while two additional companies, in Poland and Czechoslovakia, were flying Russian-built copies of the DC-3.

Few ordinary air travelers brag much about, or even give much thought to, the kind of plane they ride on, unless, to use the current advertising idiom, they want to jet somewhere.

The DC-3, however, has its partisans—an extraordinary lot, who are never really happy in flight unless they are aboard one of their pet aircraft. They are also a fervent lot, as is clearly demonstrated by a sampling of the adjectives with which they have publicly hailed the plane of their choice — "stouthearted," "indomitable," "irreplaceable," "incredible," and "sophisticated." Odes have been written to the DC-3 and songs composed about it, including "The Ballad of a Bush Pilot," which reaches its climax with the words "Before I die/ I want to fly/ A Douglas DC-3." A few years ago, a long-retired pilot in Santa Monica, California, where Douglas Aircraft has its headquarters, was granted a wish of an ebbing lifetime when finally, on his eightieth birthday, he got to fly a DC-3. Some of the idolaters of the plane tend to take an anthropomorphic view of it. An American pilot who was decorated during the Korean War for evacuating some trapped Marines said of the DC-3s he had used to accomplish the task, "Their countenances seemed to smile satisfaction" and "I wondered if they didn't deserve a Medal of Honor." He did not endow the planes with sex, but most laureates have

E. J. KAHN 1916-

E. J. Kahn, baffled when he attempts to explain the success of his journalistic career, usually ends by attributing it to luck. And, indeed, it was his good fortune to get a job writing for the *New Yorker* only four months after graduating from Harvard. The job was a result of more than just luck, however. Kahn had worked on school newspapers in his native New York City and at Harvard, and the skills he had developed were evident to the editors of the *New Yorker* when they offered him the job on the basis of the one manuscript he had submitted. Since that time Kahn's reportorial skill has been a staple of that magazine.

Serving in the infantry during World War II, Kahn continued to write. In his reports to the home front he displayed a reporter's keen eye for singling out those details that made vivid to his readers a private's-eye view of the great war. After the war Kahn turned this skill to good use in writing, among other things, a number of "Profiles" for the *New Yorker*. One of these, "The Three," appeared on September 10, 1960.

viewed the DC-3—a squat craft weighing six-teen thousand five hundred pounds unloaded and unfueled, and with a normal cargo capac-ity of sixty-five hundred more—as feminine. Two Air Force lieutenant colonels who last year brought out a book-length eulogy of the plane entitled it *Grand Old Lady* and con-fessed they had been in love with her since their teens.

If the DC-3 is already a grand old lady, it is nonetheless hazardous to guess at how long its life span may turn out to be. In 1950, the magazine *Aero Digest* asked rhetorically, "Who among us is emboldened to deny that the DC-3 will go on forever?" Just what consti-tutes an airplane is arguable. Some vintage DC-3s have had over fifty changes of engine, and, except for the fuselage, little is left of their other original parts, either. (In the DC-3's defense, of course, it can be pointed out that every living creature is constantly re-newing its cells.) Last year, Southern Airways detected a cracked wing bolt in one of its DC-3s, and sent the bolt to the Douglas Com-pany, soliciting advice as to the cause of this defect. Careful examination revealed that the wing bolt had been part of the plane when it was assembled, twenty-two years earlier. By tracing the plane through its successive owners, the Douglas people established that the bolt, which, according to their engineers, had a theoretical life of sixteen thousand hours of flight, had actually stood up for sixty-four thousand eight hundred and seventy-nine hours and fifty-two minutes. "The only mes-sage we could think of to send Southern was 'Congratulations,'" a Douglas engineer said later. North Central Airlines, the largest of the United States feeders, which operates out of Minneapolis, has two DC-3s that flew fifty thousand hours each for Eastern Air Lines, for which they were built, in 1939, and that have racked up twenty thousand hours more each since being sold to their present owner. To-gether, they have flown a good twenty million miles, and both are still going strong.

The DC-3, of course, is not indestructible. Grace Moore was killed in a DC-3 crash, and so was Carole Lombard.[3] In 1949, a Canadian Pacific DC-3 earned the unsought distinction

of being the first air liner to be blown up in flight, when a man who hoped to collect in-surance on one of its passengers—his wife—planted a bomb in it. Generally, though, the DC-3 is both hardy and resourceful. In fact, one DC-3 foiled a would-be murderer when, flying across Mexico, it survived a bomb that ripped open one of its gas tanks; it landed forty-five minutes later, and no one aboard was scratched. (It was through Mexico's brac-ing skies, too, that a hitchhiker once traveled from Torreón to Mexico City, a three-hour ride, while clinging to a DC-3's tail.) The *second* plane to land at the South Pole was a fancy four-engine Navy craft; it got stuck there, and couldn't take off until a DC-3 set-tled alongside with some spare parts. A few years ago, another DC-3 landed on a frozen Quebec lake. The ice was thin, and the plane broke through and sank. The owner despair-ingly sold what he assumed was its carcass to the first bidder, who fished the plane out, drained it, started the engines, and zoomed away. In England, a DC-3 once landed on the roof of a house without appreciably damaging either the house or itself. Many pilots regard the DC-3 as an exceptionally forgiving plane. They say it has the knack of somehow compen-sating for their errors. Indeed, some of them go so far as to insist that it can fly all by itself, citing as evidence an incident that took place three years ago in Missouri. An Air Force DC-3 ran out of gas, and the pilot and crew parachuted. Presently, the plane landed gently in a field. The only damage it suffered came when, as it was rolling to a halt, one wing hit a bale of hay.

In the air, the DC-3 has weathered some remarkable wrenches and tugs, including di-rect hits by lightning bolts, sixteen-inch naval shells, and kamikaze planes. During the war, one DC-3 pilot whose plane was riddled by anti-aircraft fire decided to ditch it in a Pacific lagoon. After hitting the water, the plane bounced fifty feet into the air. Heartened by its resiliency, he changed his mind and flew on to his base. More recently, a DC-3 ferrying

3. *Grace Moore ... Carole Lombard.* Grace Moore was a celebrated opera star; Carole Lombard, a popular movie actress.

a cargo of monkeys from Pakistan to Morocco got to its destination even though several monkeys broke loose and swarmed all over the pilot's compartment, playfully pulling at the controls. When a DC-3 does crash, the reason is apt to be that the plane is not pressurized, which means that it cannot be flown comfortably over seventeen thousand feet and thus may bump into mountains. In 1957, however, a Frontier Airlines DC-3, in turbulent air over Arizona, plummeted four thousand feet and scraped a hill, which sheared twelve feet off one wing, yet the pilot was able to right the plane and get it safely home, where he laconically reported, "Aircraft settled uncontrollably, contacting west slope of mountain peak on my left wing."

The first Douglas commercial air liner, the DC-1, was an experimental twin-engine plane unveiled in the summer of 1933, when commercial air travel was more or less experimental itself. Only one DC-1 was made.

(Howard Hughes[4] bought it, and thought for a while of flying around the world in it; eventually, in other hands, it cracked up in Spain.) The DC-2, a 1934 modification of its predecessor, was reproduced a hundred and thirty-eight times. It was a fourteen-passenger plane with a wing span of eighty-five feet—ten feet less than that of the DC-3. (During the war, when a DC-3 lost a wing in India, a spare DC-2 wing was attached to it; this improvised but navigable hybrid became known, inevitably, as the DC-2½.) The DC-3 itself was designed originally as a sleeper plane for American Airlines, with fourteen berths in the main passenger section and a secluded honeymoon compartment forward. To accommodate all the berths, a longer fuselage than the DC-2's was required, and this increased the weight of the ship, necessitating a greater wing span and more powerful twin engines. (The DC-4, DC-6, and DC-7 were all four-

4. *Howard Hughes*, a well-known aviator, movie producer, and inheritor of a large and powerful corporation.

engine planes, each larger than its predecessor. The DC-5, a 1939 model, was a two-engine, fourteen-passenger throwback, which flopped.) Many air-minded observers believed that the DC-3 was too spacious to be economically practical. The Douglas Company more or less agreed, and prudently tooled up, at the outset, for a maximum production of twenty-five such planes, the first of which were launched early in 1936. It is difficult to state with assurance which DC-3 in operation today is the oldest one around, not only because planes change numbers when they change hands but because some of the air lines still flying DC-3s are reluctant to remind passengers that some of their equipment is almost twenty-five years old. But there is fairly good reason to believe that the oldest being flown commercially, which bears the Federal Aviation Agency number NC 16005, is an Ozark Air Lines plane, the second of the model ever built, and that the most ancient of all those still taking to the air is the very first of the whole lot, NC 16004, a one-time American Airlines sleeper plane that came off the Douglas assembly line on June 28, 1936, and that is now owned by the Pacific Lumber Company, of San Francisco.

When the DC-3 was new, it was the behemoth of its day, and despite its manufacturer's misgivings, it revolutionized air travel, though not as a sleeper, for it was quickly converted into a standard passenger plane. Before the DC-3 came along, air-line passengers could not take out flight insurance at terminals, and air-line pilots had to pay heavily for any kind of life insurance anywhere. The DC-3 was the first passenger plane to be equipped with an automatic pilot, a heated cabin, and soundproofing. Between 1936 and 1946, ninety-three per cent of all domestic air-line passenger service was via DC-3.

The standard capacity of a DC-3 is twenty-one passengers—fourteen in double seats on one side of the aisle, seven in single seats on the other. (Nowadays, though, in some parts of the world one side is reserved for freight.) But over the years, as the DC-3 continued to demonstrate its worth, some air lines began jamming more and more paying fares into it.

Pacific Western, of Canada, has accommodations for thirty-two passengers on a DC-3 run between Vancouver and Powell River, and Philippine Air Lines has its DC-3s fixed up to carry forty passengers in as many rather small seats. Qantas, on its New Guinea runs, handles fifty tight-squeezed passengers at a clip, using canvas slings for perches. The all-time record is believed to have been set on a non-scheduled flight in Bolivia in 1949, when a town was imperiled by rising floods. A DC-3 carried out ninety-three refugees, together with a three-man crew; most of the passengers, however, were children.

A year ago, Aerolineas Argentinas disclosed that one of its DC-3s—a souped-up one, of course—had set a new DC-3 speed record for the three-hundred-and-sixty-mile run between Buenos Aires and Santa Rosa, making it in an hour and thirty-four minutes, for an average of two hundred and thirty miles an hour, or, in current parlance, Mach .31.[5] Most of the air lines that rely on DC-3s don't give a hoot about speed records. It can be argued—and some of those air lines do argue—that an air liner's speed is a mystifying and often meaningless attribute. A DC-8 or a Boeing 707 can outfly a DC-3 by four hundred miles an hour, but considering what happens to a passenger before and after he gets up there—the long overland crawl to and from outlying airports, plus all the standing and waiting and walking and wilting and wailing—the big jets are often only a few minutes faster, if that, in terms of helping an individual move from the downtown area of City A to the downtown area of City B. Then, too, small planes can land at small airfields—like La Guardia, in New York, or Midway, in Chicago—that are closer to town than the new giant installations for jets. The Federal Aviation Agency recently announced, specifically, that a traveler from mid-Manhattan to mid-Chicago could save twenty-five minutes in total travel time by flying in a piston-engine plane instead of a jet. On short hauls—that is, between cities no

5. *Mach .31.* The Mach number is the ratio of air speed to the speed of sound. Thus, Mach .31 indicates a speed of roughly three tenths the speed of sound under normal conditions.

more than a hundred miles apart—it is undeniable that the race is seldom to the swift, for the slower planes can land not only on smaller fields but with less fuss and delay. Faucett Airlines, a Peruvian company, whose DC-3s on its Lima-Iquitos local run make eight stops in ten hours, couldn't use DC-8s for that trip even if it got them free. By the same token, MacRobertson Miller Airlines, in northwestern Australia, would find it awkward to supplant DC-3s with jets on one of its runs—a less-than-two-thousand-mile stretch in which its planes make about forty stops, some of them only eight miles apart.

When the United States went to war in December, 1941, three hundred and sixty DC-3s were in service on domestic air lines. The Air Transport Command swiftly commandeered nearly two hundred of these, and, at the behest of the armed forces, Douglas began turning out new ones as fast as it could. By 1945, it had produced over ten thousand, nearly half of them at a hastily constructed plant in Oklahoma City. A couple of thousand went to England and Canada. The Soviet Union got seven hundred, and, with plans and tools provided by Douglas, built around two thousand more for itself, calling them Lissunov-2s and neglecting to pay any royalties. Last year, when the celebrated Soviet plane designer Andrei Tupolev was in this country, Donald Douglas, who founded the Douglas Company and is now its chairman, invited him and some traveling companions to lunch at Santa Monica. During the toasts, Tupolev made a flowery speech about the DC-3. Mr. Douglas, when his turn came, responded handsomely that he'd heard the Russians had done a magnificent job building DC-3s. At this, Tupolev and his compatriots all looked stonily blank, and Douglas, deducing that they had no intention of admitting that they owed him anything, tactfully changed the subject.

While the war was on, the Douglas Company built a total of over twenty-nine thousand planes. The majority were battle weapons, but Mr. Douglas says that the DC-3s he made gave him the most satisfaction. "It was kind of nice to be making something that you didn't drop bombs out of or shoot bullets out of but that could still do a good job," he observed recently. By mid-1944, his company was churning out DC-3s at the rate of nearly two an hour, following an urgent personal appeal to its factory workers at the start of that year by General H. H. Arnold, the Air Force chief of staff, who said he desperately needed four hundred more of the transports than the production schedule called for. He got his extra four hundred in time for D Day, when the greatest fleet of DC-3s ever assembled—twelve hundred of them, flying four abreast in a column two hundred miles long—delivered parachutists and glider troops to Normandy. Meanwhile, DC-3s had been active in other theaters. They were used for flying tank parts to Montgomery's forces at El Alamein,[6] and, in the South Pacific, for flying troops across the Owen Stanley Mountains of New Guinea —the first United States combat ground forces ever air-lifted to battle. They also flew in fuel to the fighter planes based on Guadalcanal[7] during the fighting there. Stilwell, Mountbatten, and Chiang Kai-shek[8] had DC-3s equipped as command posts, and another DC-3 that participated in the war against Japan was equipped as a traveling laundry. In the course of the war, DC-3s toted disassembled fighter planes and heavy trucks to this or that destination, to be welded together again on arrival, while to the snow-shrouded Battle of the Bulge[9] they ferried two dozen dog sleds, a hundred and fifty Huskies, and twenty-five dog-handling soldiers. In all theaters of war combined, they carried a total of seven hundred and fifty thousand sick and wounded servicemen to hospitals.

6. *Montgomery's forces at El Alamein* (el alʹə mān). El Alamein is the city in Egypt at which the British forces under Montgomery finally stopped the Germans' eastward drive in the highly motorized African Campaign of World War II.   7. *Guadalcanal*, the island in the Solomons on which the United States Marines, cut off from their naval line of supply by the Japanese fleet, captured and held a key Japanese airstrip in August 1942.   8. *Stilwell, Mountbatten, and Chiang Kai-shek*, the three Allied commanders (American, British, and Chinese, respectively) involved in the Burma Campaign.   9. *Battle of the Bulge*, the last German offensive of the war, undertaken during the winter of 1944 while the weather rendered the Allied Air Force generally ineffective.

Notwithstanding Douglas' pleasure in the thought that the DC-3 was a noncombatant plane, it was used in both Europe and Asia as a bomber (the bombs were kicked out of open doors) and as a fighter, too (machine guns were mounted in the doorways). One peripatetic American interceptor pilot, who had already earned the right to paint German, Italian, and Japanese flags on the fuselage of his P-51, added the Stars and Stripes to his collection by bringing down a DC-3 when its navigator became confused and started to land, with an important cargo, on a Japanese-held island. To prevent the DC-3, its crew, and its freight from being captured, the P-51 man fired at it, forcing it to make a crash landing on friendly territory.

Between that war and the Korean War, in which the DC-3 was confined to less adventurous tasks of supply and evacuation, the model played its part on the stage of world history during the Berlin air lift.[10] In theory, the DC-3 has a payload of only slightly over three tons, but on one occasion a West German loading crew innocently stuffed into the belly of a DC-3 a seven-and-a-half-ton pile of cargo that was supposed to make the trip to the capital in a much larger plane. The crew, unaware of the mistake, climbed aboard and took off, and, though bewildered to find that they couldn't force their plane any higher than five hundred feet, made it to Berlin, where the impact of their landing flattened all their tires. When the air lift began, in June, 1948, the Allied transport fleet consisted almost entirely of DC-3s. After three months of round-the-clock flying, the Americans substituted a fleet of more commodious DC-4s. (The British continued to use DC-3s.) By the time the American DC-3s were relieved of duty, they had made more than twelve thousand round trips between West Germany and Berlin, and had delivered more than forty thousand tons of goods. In the last month of their operations, one DC-3 never missed a day and flew three hundred and twenty-seven hours and thirty minutes. For an airplane, that's working overtime.

Right after V-J Day,[11] DC-3s were a glut on the airplane market. Many of them were abandoned—and still stand rusting—on remote Pacific bases. DC-3s in good shape were sold as surplus for as little as twelve hundred dollars, and incapacitated ones for as little as two hundred and fifty. (Some of the latter were trucked off and converted into homes.) At the time, nearly everybody in aviation assumed that the DC-3 was all but washed up as a passenger plane, and it was then that Douglas stopped manufacturing it. The company tried to make the best of what seemed like a bad situation by introducing the Super DC-3—a plane two and a half feet longer than the original model, and incorporating various improvements, which increased the cruising speed to around two hundred and forty miles an hour with a load of over thirty passengers. The company promotionally acclaimed its new offering as a plane "capable of carrying on indefatigably in the noble tradition of its famous ancestor," but despite this hoopla, and a transcontinental sales tour that Donald Douglas himself made in a Super DC-3, it never proved to be all that capable. The Navy bought a hundred of the planes, but all other customers together ordered a mere ten.

In the meantime, the famous ancestor found itself in gradually mounting demand. Its relatively low purchase price made it extremely attractive to shoestring entrepreneurs offering modest nonscheduled air-coach transportation. Cargo carriers found it appealing, too—notably in the Antipodes. Before long, DC-3s were trundling emigrants from Italy and Cyprus to Australia, beef from inland Australian abattoirs to coastal ports, and sheep from Australia to grazing lands in New Guinea, and were being used to spread fertilizer in New Zealand. DC-3s were also being used to harass browntail moths in the United States, while DC-3s on skis were patrolling the DEW line,[12] and

10. *Berlin air lift*, the successful effort to supply the Western Sector of Berlin with supplies by air after Russia stopped ground traffic between that city and West Germany on June 21, 1948.   11. *V-J Day*, Victory-Japan Day, the day on which the Japanese surrendered to the Allies, August 15, 1945.   12. *DEW line*, Distant Early Warning System. This is a radar network constructed in the extreme northern part of our hemisphere to warn the United States of attack by enemy aircraft.

DC-3s on floats were wafting fishermen to remote trout-packed lakes. DC-3s were doing everything, and quite a few of them still are.

The first twenty DC-3s built cost American Airlines a hundred and ten thousand dollars each. Today, used DC-3s may sell for as much as two hundred and sixty thousand, and one that is fit and fitted for corporate use is not likely to fetch less than a hundred and fifty thousand. As for the DC-3s owned by a few Middle East sheiks, who fancy studding the paneling with precious jewels, their value is impossible to compute. Even the dowdiest old cargo-carrying DC-3 cannot be bought anywhere in the world for much under twenty-five thousand, and in this country the minimum market price is fifty thousand—a substantial appreciation since the end of the war. W. S. Shackleton, of London, a leading international dealer in used planes, who ships old Aer Lingus DC-3s from Ireland to Tanganyika and who sold a couple of DC-3s to the Sydney *Morning Herald* to deliver papers, observed recently that the DC-3 "still plays the most significant rôle of all in the used-plane market."

Ever since the war, an American DC-3 has nestled high on Mount Fujiyama, but although the United States government has announced its willingness to consider offers, no one has yet come forward to bid on it. Used-plane dealers compete eagerly, however, for more accessible DC-3s, or fragments of them, and convert the more or less whole planes into polished executive-style aircraft, relying on the bits for spare parts. A South African Air Force DC-3 that crashed in the Transvaal, in 1944, was sold for eighty pounds to a local man, who transformed it into a roadhouse, its wings ablaze with neon. Twelve years later, a traveling salesman of airplane parts came upon the odd-shaped cafe, bought it on the spot, shipped it to California, and had it reconditioned as an airplane. Of the several domestic companies that make a good thing out of this kind of salvage work, the most prominent is Remmert-Werner, in St. Louis, which since the end of the war has revivified more than two hundred DC-3s, and which a while ago sold one that it had pieced together out of a fuselage picked up in Minnesota, a wing from California, another wing from Florida, and odds and ends from other states. The fuselage of a plush DC-3 that Remmert-Werner recently sold to a large and sedate corporation for its officials to gad about in was, when the company first spotted it, a chicken house in the backwoods of Alabama. The DC-3 bought by another corporation from AiResearch Aviation Service Company, a Los Angeles salvaging firm, had previously been used in Hawaii to haul fish. The main problem AiResearch had in fixing that one up was to get the smell out of it.

The many DC-3 zealots who have never trafficked in the planes but merely ridden in them are likely to have singularly retentive memories. In England, the members of an organization called Air-Britain and subtitled the National Association of Aviation Enthusiasts can rattle off the serial numbers of long-gone DC-3s, whose peregrinations from one owner to another the enthusiasts have faithfully charted. In the columns of British aviation magazines, for instance, spirited arguments are regularly waged over whether the Nazis did or did not capture and sneakily avail themselves of certain Allied DC-3s during the war. One of the Queen's subjects, who operates out of Nairobi, wrote the following cryptic passage in a lengthy and astonishingly learned letter to a buff's magazine called *Air Pictorial*: "Regarding Mr. Bateson's comments on K.L.M. DC-3s, c/n. 1935 was PH-ALH, later becoming PC-EA in the Luftwaffe. Its earlier acquisition by D.L.H. as D-ABUG is probably accounted for by the fact that it was in Germany on the day Holland was invaded by the Nazis. His other DC-3 listed, c/n. 2036, which he claims to be another ex-K.L.M. aircraft, I cannot find listed in the 1939/40 K.L.M. fleet list in my possession. It might therefore be an ex-C.L.S. DC-3 or even one of the two Sabena DC-3s referred to in my letter." While the Berlin air lift was on, a newly arrived United States Air Force colonel, who had been flying DC-3s over the Hump[13]

---

13. *the Hump*, the name given to the dangerous route over the Himalaya Mountains flown by the American Air Force to supply the Chinese Army from bases in India.

to China five years before, was walking across a West German runway when he stopped short, arrested by the sight of a DC-3 that to most mortals would have been indistinguishable from ten thousand others. To him, though, it evoked poignant recollections. "I'll be damned!" he exclaimed. "Unless I'm having hallucinations, that's old 316051!" It was.

There can be no doubt that the DC-3 has exerted a powerful pull on man's emotions. A few years ago, Donald Douglas got a nine-page, single-spaced letter from a Canadian banker who had been a wartime wing commander in the R.A.F.[14] At the age of twenty, he wrote Douglas, he had traveled from Halifax to Montreal merely to gape at a DC-3—"a beautiful mechanical beast," he called it. He had at once fallen for the beast, and on flying aboard it as a passenger had found the experience "smooth and firm and straight and level." During the war, he had flown a DC-3 himself, and when the Japanese destroyed it on the ground, he was heartsick. "I missed her—as a person, not a piece of machinery," he wrote. "And that, to a driver who gets a 'right' plane in his hands, is the spell of the DC-3.... If ever an inanimate object earned, deserved, and received the love of a man, your DC-3 was that object. In fact, I, and probably thousands of others, consider it callous to refer to her as 'inanimate.' " Douglas was touched by this testimonial, since he, too, is fonder of the DC-3 than of any other inanimate object his company has manufactured. "The Three is certainly the best and best-loved airplane we've ever produced," he said not long ago, speaking like a father. "But the circumstances that made it great just happened. They were not of our making. I doubt whether any airplane will have the same impact, or the same opportunity, again."

TO INCREASE UNDERSTANDING

1. (a) Do you imagine that most types of airplanes would furnish interest for a selection of this type? Explain. (b) What convinces E. J. Kahn that the DC-3 is an interesting enough airplane to justify a magazine piece?

2. Explain how each of the following factors sets the DC-3 apart as an unusual airplane: (a) its being called simply "The Three"; (b) its use at the present time by the U.S. Air Force and by some U.S. air lines; (c) its various uses in other countries; (d) the way travelers and pilots feel about it; (e) the histories of individual DC-3s and their market prices since production was stopped in 1946; (f) discussions about the plane in aviation magazines and among enthusiasts.

3. Classify this selection as an article or an essay. Give your reasons.

Knacks and Crafts Paul Horgan

A frontiersman "boasted that with only hickory withes and a jackknife he could make a very good wagon."

In such a statement lay the seed of all the arts and crafts—the "practical arts" as they were called—in early America. Dr. Franklin's concern for the marriage of beauty and utility was unconsciously answered by the men and women who in successive settlements were obliged by scarcity of rich materials to equip and ornament their daily tasks with objects of their own making. It was natural that the practical arts in a democracy were first of all functional. If the conditions of their lives denied to the settlers access to the fine arts, there was also in the crochety plainness of the people a hint that the fine arts were suspect. Puritan bleakness was partly responsible for such a view. But another and overriding sense had effect too. This was a democratic suspicion that the fine arts had always been identified with aristocratic patronage. Palaces

Reprinted from *Great River: The Rio Grande In North American History*, Vol. Two by Paul Horgan. Copyright 1954 by Paul Horgan. Reprinted by permission of Holt, Rinehart and Winston, Inc., New York, and Curtis Brown, Ltd., London.

THE THREE 14. R.A.F., Royal Air Force, the combined air forces of the British Commonwealth.

crammed with splendors, artists appointed to court, prestige and expense attached to the work of master-artists—such airs of luxury seemed highfalutin, and to partake of them called for a whole world of experience, education, and allusion in which the democrat could only feel at a disadvantage. In their gnarled self-respect the people must earn their own evolvement of the arts. If at first they must be content with making a beautifully finished rake handle that felt good to the grasp, or a plain little chair that looked polite as it sat empty and felt good as it was occupied, or a wooden decoy duck carved and painted to fool a game bird in early daylight and otherwise to ornament a shelf with its sleek green, brown, gray, black, and white reminders of sport and sustenance, then what they fashioned so honestly had the authority of answering honest needs.

In the pattern of ordinary social development the settlers would have climbed through primitive generations or centuries toward a flowering of refined art based on their utilitarian creations. But there were two reasons why such a sequence was not necessary. First, the settlers were not socially primitive people, but civilized people taking new land with a new social idea; and second, to their new idea of man and to new land in which to realize it there was soon added a third newness that swept the first two along at an amazing rate of historical development. This was the discovery and spreading use of technological methods—many new means of making corporate life closer, and individual life easier, so that united to his fellows the individual was to be relatively free from toil. The frontiering and completion of the American continent took place during the first years of a world revolution in technology. The effect of this coincidence upon the people's expression in the arts was to drive home more deeply than ever the love of usefulness over beauty—if it came to a choice. The handicraft of the settler would soon exert itself in designing for machine crafts. Machine crafts would make possible through duplication of copies a widespread use of what before had been limited to an original and its user, who was so often

its maker. The spirit of the copy said, My value is in serving as many people as possible, to help in their lives. Has this work not its own beauty? The spirit of the original said, I am unique, and my beauty lies in my rarity, for the touch of my creator is on me everywhere. What matter that I serve only one?

But there the matter came to a point. For the democratic impulse sought to bring the goods and beauties of life to as many people as possible, in contrast to the aristocratic impulse that granted patronage to art forms for an élite. If traditional fine-art forms were the highest expression of creative spirit in civilization, then the Americans seemed to have forgotten the fact, and to have busied themselves with an expression of creative spirit for which the raw material was mankind itself, in a powerful belief that the arts of living together must come first. Their masterpiece of creative spirit was the forging of human liberty and equality in a coherent society. In the process they illustrated the difference between the practical arts and the fine or inutile arts, considered as historical records.

Through articles made for use, the practical arts left an uncritical likeness of the society

PAUL HORGAN 1903-

When he moved to New Mexico from Buffalo, New York, at the age of eleven, young Paul Horgan was deeply impressed by the country where familiar streets ended in the strange mesa. His fascination with the rugged Southwest did not leave him when he returned to the East to study singing and theater at the Eastman School of Music. So, after forming his experiences in Rochester into the Harper Prize Novel, *The Fault of Angels,* he began work on a long book which would express his love for the Southwest. Fourteen years of intensive research about the settlers who made the history of the Rio Grande became *The Great River,* awarded the Pulitzer and Bancroft prizes for history in 1955. In 1960 Horgan turned novelist again with the publication of *A Distant Trumpet.* Here he created a historical novel about the Southwest in the 1880's. But if it is clear that Horgan's historical studies helped him in writing *A Distant Trumpet,* it is equally clear in this excerpt from *The Great River* that his skill as a novelist has enabled him to illumine the bare facts of history.

that produced them. On the other hand, the fine, or inutile, arts always made a conscious criticism or interpretation of the life from which they grew. This was one of their chief intentions. The record they left was formal, and while it suggested the taste of the times, it suggested even more sharply the personality of the designer. The position and character of the arts in America seemed to equate utility with anonymous people, and formal beauty with the individual creator in the fine arts. And as it was the body of the people together who made the conditions of life, it was their popular expression in the arts and crafts that achieved originality, style, and freshness, while to the scattered few "fine" artists was left the task of treating American subject matter in techniques and visions imitative of European models. The universal American tinker became a maker of machines for work, the whittler became a sculptor of workaday sign, artisan and artist were one; and their genius for the practical became a national characteristic that would lead to a standard of material life new to the world.

In their conviction of purpose there could also be delight in how they worked; and in countless objects made for use they celebrated their own gaunt graces, and left a record of how, in their spirits, fancy and patience and good sense could meet.

Where color was used, they used it exuberantly, on wood, metal, or in fabrics. On the other hand, form was frugal, as the gestures of labor were frugal, with the inference of meeting a purpose with not too little, or too much, but just enough energy. The Conestoga wagon illustrated both idioms of color and form. Shaped like a great open coffer, and slung on wheels to go away, it was just a plain receptacle; but with its bright blue sides, vermilion wheels, and dazzling creamy hood of Osnabrück linen, it recalled the painting palette of the Pennsylvania Germans, who made flowers in such frank colors, and stars, fruit, doves, parrots, on their boxes, furniture, and certificates of occasion.

Wood was the commonest American material. The continent had a seemingly inexhaustible supply. The frontier American craftsman used it for most houses he built, and for most of the objects that went into a house or served business. He made all manner of chests, none exactly alike, but all sharing a common plainness. If he made a tall clockcase, it was severely plain. His benches, beautifully surfaced, remained as close as possible to their original parts of plank and branch. Such severity suggested not only that the maker was a plain man, for religious or other reasons unsympathetic toward rich ornament; but also that he was in a hurry, with many another task awaiting him. But when he came to make machines of wood, his pace of work must have been measured and easy; for what resulted sometimes were such masterpieces of functional design that their beauty would satisfy long later any interest in abstract art. Such machines were a Shaker[1] spinning wheel, with its large delicate wheel suspended above a base remarkably light on slender legs; and a fork for pitching barley and straw that extended four wooden tines in repeated tapering curves in a gesture of work that combined exquisite efficiency with elegance. Something of the same beauty brought thoughtlessly to life out of a grave concern for a good feel and a perfect usefulness could be seen in the wooden stocks made to support the cast metal parts of American rifles. Their tactile appeal, combined out of finish and shape, was so great that no man could see a good one without wanting to run his hand over it, even if he wasn't thinking directly about how a white morning came over whitening water where game must rise with the day.

Wooden crafts and painting came together in various needs for painted sculpture, and for outdoor commercial signs. Ships built in the Eastern yards were given figureheads that were portraits of real men or women, great figures out of the young national history, or idealized allegorical creations. In their proud realism, these were often heroic in scale, and carved with wonderful, wavelike freedom of scrolling design. They were brightly painted and heightened with gold leaf, and when installed under the bowsprit leaning over the

---

1. *Shaker*, an American religious sect.

The pictures on these two pages show some products of American craftsmanship described by Horgan. Note especially the graceful forms of the hay fork and Shaker spinning wheel (above), the functional simplicity of the tall clock (left) and the gunstock (right), the delight in color displayed in the decoy and the watercolor decoration of the Pennsylvania Germans (below).

Painting and woodworking were combined to
produce the sign for the Black Horse Inn
(above) and the cigar store Indian (left);
color was also used in metalworking in the
cast-iron hitching post and a weather vane
atop Faneuil Hall, Boston, done by the Drowne
on whom Hawthorne based his story (below);
woman's handicraft is illustrated by an
appliqué quilt (above, right). All pictures
on both pages (except that of the weather
vane) are from the National Gallery of Art,
Index of American Design, Washington, D. C.

bosom of the waters, they made visible the personality with which men have always endowed ships. At the stern, there was often opportunity to create carving and gilding, where the ship's name and home port were shown. In such long horizontal panels a peculiarly American style of decoration, using letters and ornaments, treated space with the balance and grace of the printer's art.

Other figures of popular sculpture were life-sized wooden Indians or Turks or Negroes to stand before tobacco stores in bright paint and arresting stare. It took twelve days to make such a figure—six for the carving at a foot a day, and six for the finishing. To produce hanging signs for inns, shops, barbers, the craftsman again allied woodworking to painting, and often called again on the serene severities of typography to govern the spacing of his symbols and letters. Many such signs were beautifully contrived, and when they called to the customer, did so calmly, offering, at inns, the one word, "Entertainment," and displaying, for shops, carved likenesses of wares in bas-relief.

Painting was allied to metal crafts in the production of such articles as tin utensils, canisters, pots, trays, and boxes; andirons and bootjacks and hitching posts that represented human or animal figures; and various toys. The metal craftsman made weather vanes in every kind of symbol. The conventional cock was joined by new designs, with certain ones recurring to reflect the interests of the public—a fish, a whale, a grasshopper, a trotting horse, a horse in extended racing stride, a frigate in full sail, a locomotive and tender. These were painted or treated entirely with gold leaf or left in the black silhouette of wrought iron. Lanterns and candlesticks and trivets; locks, hinges and latches; fire marks[2] in iron with designs that again recalled typography—all had simple grace and the occasional appealing falter whereby the hand of the originator could be detected. It was in duplicated objects of cast metal that the impersonality of the coming steam power era was suggested—rifle barrels, spread eagles for flagpole and cornice finials, plain iron kettles with their three little legs cast on the pouchlike belly.

In weaving, embroidering, rugmaking, quilting, women contributed to the idiom of American crafts. The richly colored floral and vine-like designs of crewel embroidery derived from Jacobean England were succeeded by plainer patterns in hard homespun cloth. Weaving tablecloths and bedspreads and coverlets, the housewife developed simple geometries that repeated variations based on squares and triangles, frequently in colors of blue and white. Her most personal style appeared in quilting. Here was an exercise in thrift, for she used patches of cloth saved from every which source; and in ingenuity, for her hope was to achieve symmetrical patterns out of scraps that came along with no rhyme or reason; and in patience, for a quilt was big, to fit on a man-and-wife bed, and to make only one six-inch-square patch of the ten dozen or so needed would call for thousands of stitches. But she persisted, and produced an original work whose simplicity and modesty told much about her life and the joys of her labors throughout many hours made up of a few minutes here, a few there, when in repose she was not idle.

---

2. *fire marks*, metal plates affixed to buildings in the eighteenth century to indicate that they were insured.

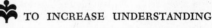 TO INCREASE UNDERSTANDING

1. In "Knacks and Crafts" Paul Horgan draws a number of distinctions between the "fine arts" and the "practical arts." (*a*) How do these arts differ? (*b*) Why did the pioneer shy away from the fine arts?

2. (*a*) How do the fine arts evolve in the normal pattern of social development from primitivism to civilization? (*b*) According to Horgan, what two factors prevented this pattern from being completed in America? (*c*) Explain exactly how these two factors operated to hinder "a flowering of refined art based on [the settlers'] utilitarian creations."

3. Horgan says, "The practical arts left an uncritical likeness of the society that produced them. On the other hand, the fine, or inutile, arts always made a conscious criticism or interpretation of the life from which they grew." (*a*) Explain this statement. (*b*) How does it help explain why people whose chief interest was making a democratic society found the practical arts more satisfying?

4. In his story "Drowne's Wooden Image" (page 306), Hawthorne makes a distinction between the

fine arts and the practical arts. (*a*) What difference does he develop between Drowne's work as a craftsman and his work as a fine artist? (*b*) Is Hawthorne's distinction between fine arts and practical arts the same as or different from Horgan's? Explain. (*c*) Do you think Hawthorne and Horgan would agree about the relative value of the fine and the practical arts? Cite passages from each text to support your statement.

5. (*a*) What did the pioneers value in the articles they made besides their practical utility? (*b*) Does the impression you gain from looking at the pictures of some of these objects agree with the impression you gained from reading about them? Explain.

BETTER READING
Fact and feeling

"A rose is a rose is a rose," said Gertrude Stein (see page 458), or, to put her meaning in another way, "a fact (such as a rose) is a fact is a fact, and that's about all you can say about it." This may be true, but as soon as a fact is put into print, strange things can happen to it.

"The Three" appears to be simply a collection of facts about the DC-3, but the reader gains more from this article than information about a particular type of airplane. E. J. Kahn expresses his attitude toward the plane as well. There are a number of ways a writer can convey his feelings toward a subject while seeming to report only facts about it. Kahn often expresses his feelings about the plane by the facts he chooses to emphasize and the facts he chooses to de-emphasize or omit. For example, he writes that the plane may "bump into mountains." How would your impression have been changed if he had written, "The plane occasionally crashes on mountains," or if he had given you statistics on how many people had been killed in such crashes, or had proceeded to describe a number of crash scenes in as detailed a way as he tells anecdotes that dwell on the airplane's merits?

Another way in which a writer can express his attitudes is by a shrewd choice of the words by which he states a fact. Paul Horgan appears to be making a simple statement of historical fact in "Knacks and Crafts" when he says, "To the scattered few 'fine' artists was left the task of treating American subject matter in techniques and visions imitative of European models." The same fact can be made to sound quite different, however, by making a few substitutions in the words used to express it: "To the scattered few *fine* artists was left the *mission* of treating American subject matter in the techniques and visions of the *grand traditions* of *western civilization*." Describe in each case how the substitution changes your attitude toward America's fine artists. What view of the arts in America is Horgan trying to persuade you to adopt?

One should not infer from this that a writer's techniques of emphasis and verbal manipulation are necessarily deceitful. On the contrary, it is by just such means that writers of articles lift their work from the level of pure fact reporting to the level on which the perspective of the writer can lend depth and meaning to the subject.

Point out places in the articles you have studied where word choice or emphasis conveys an attitude not implied by the facts themselves.

Your Oldest Heirlooms W. L. White

What are your oldest heirlooms? Not Grandfather's Civil War cavalry saber. Not even Great-Grandmother's wedding silver. Your oldest heirlooms are the words which you use for familiar things—*come, go, water, eat, sun, moon, father, mother*. They have been handed down to you from a tiny, nameless, and forgotten tribe which, five or six thousand years ago, was the ancestor of our speech.

These heirloom-words—more ancient than the Pyramids, more enduring than the walls of Troy—make us the speech-cousins of more than a billion people of all races, living today in Europe, India, South Africa, the Americas, and the Pacific Isles, for they use almost the same words and many others like them.

For centuries scholars puzzled over the striking similarity of words in different languages. *Father* in English, *vader* in Dutch, *pater* in Latin, all meant the same and sounded alike, as did *fader* in Swedish, *vater* in German, *athir* in Irish, *pidar* in Persian, and *pitr* in the

Reprinted from *The Saturday Review*, October 4, 1958, by permission of the publishers. Copyright ©1958 by Saturday Review Associates, New York.

Sanskrit of distant India. Why? How did it happen that widely separated peoples used such closely related sound symbols?

And *father* was but one of a host of such "coincidences" which baffled linguists for years. Then, toward the end of the eighteenth century it dawned on scholars that surely all were cousins, stemming maybe from some common language far back before recorded history. And at last, the brilliant German, Jacob Grimm,[1] and other scholars of his time worked out a Law of Language Changes, based on the fact that speech-sounds fall into natural groups. Their discoveries showed that the changes which took place during the history of a language were regular and consistent enough to permit comparisons between languages and to reconstruct the earlier stages of languages.

Once the law of change was clear, scholars could see that the many words for father all pointed back to an original *pater;* that *water* in English, *wasser* in German, *hydor* in Greek, *voda* in Russian (*vodka* is "little water"), *udan* in Sanskrit, and even *watar* in the language of King David's Captain Uriah the Hittite[2]—all could have come only from an original *wodor.* (Using the law, they could trace the origin of countless words.) The mother-word for English *corn,* Latin *granum,* German *korn,* and Russian *zerno* (they decided) must certainly have been *grano.*

The scholars evolved an entire ancient vocabulary. This ancient speech they labeled Indo-European, because it had both Indic and European branches. There is a Latin branch, from which stem Italian, Spanish, French, Portuguese, Rumanian; there is a Germanic branch, which includes English, German, Danish, Dutch, Swedish, Norwegian; the Celtic branch includes Welsh, Irish, Breton; the Slavic includes Russian, Polish, Czech, Bulgar, Serb. In addition, Indo-European includes Lithuanian, Persian, Greek, Armenian, and a score of dialects in India which have sprung from ancient Sanskrit.

Beyond, they discovered, were still other word families: Semitic (Hebrew, Phoenician, Arabic); Uralic (Hungarian, Finnish); and others which bore no likeness either in sound or in grammar to each other, or to the Indo-European family.

But what tribe first spoke that mother-tongue which hatched out the brood of cousin-languages that embraces both Icelandic and Armenian, and includes even the speech of the ancient Hittites—dead now these three thousand years?

For decades scholars had puzzled over inscriptions in some unknown tongue engraved in cuneiform characters by the long vanished Hittites 3,500 years ago in what is now Central Turkey. Then, in 1915, a Czech scholar Hrozny put forward the astounding theory that Hittite might be an Indo-European language. Now, using as their tools their "theoretical" Indo-European grammar and word list, scholars were able to translate Hittite out of its Babylonian cuneiform, so that today we have their history and can even sing their hymns.

---

1. *Jacob Grimm,* early German linguistic scientist whose famous collection of folk tales was actually only incidental to his study of language. 2. *King David's . . . Uriah the Hittite.* David, the second king of Israel, lived after the dissolution of the Hittite empire, which had been the third largest, after Egypt and Babylon, of its time.

W. L. WHITE 1900-

William L. White, himself a famous journalist, is the son of a famous newspaperman. His father, William Allen White, owner and editor of the Emporia, Kansas, *Gazette* until his death in 1944, had achieved national fame as a symbol of the homey, Midwestern common man through his strongly Republican editorials. Working on his father's newspaper from boyhood, William L. White was marked for a career in journalism. His years as a war correspondent in both the European and Pacific theaters furnished him with the material for some famous books. In *They Were Expendable* he reported the heroic story of a motor torpedo boat squadron. *Queens Die Proudly* was a similar book about the Flying Fortresses in the early days of the Pacific campaign.

Since the war, White has continued his journalistic career primarily as a roving editor for the *Reader's Digest.* It should come as no surprise that White, who uses the living language to report on the contemporary scene, considers the origin and history of words important. In this article he attempts to make vivid and interesting to the layman the arduous researches of linguistic scientists.

Today we know almost as much about that forgotten and nameless tribe which was the mother of our speech: how and where they lived, what they ate and wore, even what they believed. Yet archaeologists have uncovered not a single crumbling wall, nor any fragment of pottery which we can be sure was theirs. These dawn people could leave no inscriptions for they lived, we think, ten thousand years ago—five millennia before the first Egyptian devised picture writing.

By years of work—comparing Sanskrit with Greek and Gothic[3] with Latin—language students have excavated the complicated grammar of this dead mother-speech, and reconstructed lists of those old Indo-European mother-words. Just as a paleontologist puts together from a hatful of bones a long extinct reptile, these scholars have re-created languages. And with these old words as evidence, we can reconstruct that ancient civilization that existed perhaps six thousand years ago.

Using as our magic carpet those words which are ours and were theirs, let us fly back thousands of years to look at that first Indo-European tribe. We find that the family unit may well have been as strong then as now, for English *brother* comes from their word *bhrater,* as *sister* comes from their *swesor,* our word *son* from their *sunu.* English *daughter* cannot be so exactly traced, but it has close cousins: *dottir* in Icelandic, *doche* in Russian and—closest of all—*dukhtar* in distant Persia—all stemming from *dhughater.*

In culture the Indo-Europeans were far ahead of the North American Indians, who had no domestic animals although the Eskimos had tamed the dog. Our speech ancestors had bred the wild buffalo into a *cow (gwou)* which gave them *milk (melg).* From this strain they also bred *oxen (uksen)* which were joined together with a *yoke (yug).* What did they pull? Surely a *wagon,* for this word comes from their *wegh* (meaning "to carry")—and doubly sure because we know they had the wheel, a wondrous device unknown in the primitive Americas until Columbus. The ancient word for *wheel* was *qeqlo,* from which the Latins made *circus,* which later came over into English, bringing with it *circle* and *circumference.*

They also knew sheep (their *owi* became English *ewe*) which surely were tame, for from their *fleece (pleus)* they got *wool (wlana)* which they had learned to *weave (webh)* into cloth and then *sew (siw)* into garments.

We might still think them only wandering nomads had not the dictionary-detective given us their word for *plow,* which was *ara,* from which we get an English word *ear* which means "to plow," but is now seldom used. Yet because of Latin *arare* ("to plow") we speak in English of land which is *arable*—that can be cultivated.

When they plowed, using that yoke of *uksen,* what did they plant? Well, their word *grano* becomes English *grain.* Of this *grano,* one kind they planted was surely light in color, for their word for *white (kweit)* coming down through Old Germanic *hweits* has also given us English *wheat.*

Corn, planted in spring, does not ripen until fall, and this points to permanent settlements, in which each family has a home. They called it a *dom,* and, from this old word, Latin got *domus* and then gave us *domicile, domestic,* and *dome.* Was this ancient *dom* a rude tent of skins? We can be sure not, for *dom* gave us English *timber,* of which their homes were built. How was this timber cut? Certainly with an *aks* which, however, was probably of flint, for this Late Stone Age people knew little of metals, could not tell iron from gold, but called them all by a common word from which we have derived *iron.*

Did they know fire? Of course: it had been used even by Peking Man,[4] half a million years before. And these speech ancestors of ours ground their grain fine in a *mill (mel),* added *water (wodar)* and *yeast (yes)* to make a *dough (dheigh),* which they then would *bake (bhog)* in an *oven (uqno)* to make *bread (pa)*—Latin *panis,* hence English *pantry,* the place where bread is kept.

In such a home you might from a *cup (qeup)* fashioned of *clay (glei),* drink not only milk, but also a fermented *brew (bhreu)* made

3. *Gothic,* the language of the tribes of Teutonic people that settled in southern Europe and overran the Roman Empire.
4. *Peking Man,* an early type of human known through fossil remains found near Peking, China.

from grain. All this we know from those old root words, which have come down to us in a score of languages. Likewise their numerals, which were:

1. *oinos*
2. *duo*
3. *treies*
4. *qetwer*
5. *penqe*
6. *sweks*
7. *septn*
8. *okto*
9. *newn*
10. *dekm*

While each modern language has changed them a little, at least half the list would be understood by a native of ancient Greece, or by a modern native of London, Moscow, Bombay, or Manila.

Had these people, thousands of years ago, a government? Their word meaning "to rule" was *reg*, from which India got *rajah*, Latin got *rex*. Often their old root words slid into new

---

SLURVIAN SELF-TAUGHT John Davenport

Listening to a well-known Hollywood radio commentator some time back, I heard her say that she had just returned from a *Yerpeen* trip, and had had a lovely time *nittly*. I at once recognized her as an accomplished Slurvian linguist and, being a student of Slurvian, readily understood that she had just returned from a European trip, and while there (in *Yerp*) had had a lovely time in Italy.

Slurvian is coming into common use in the United States, but I am, so far as I know, the only scholar to have made a start toward recording it. There is no official written Slurvian language, but it is possible, by means of phonetic spelling, for me to offer a brief course of instruction in it. In a short time, the student can learn enough to add immeasurably to his understanding and enjoyment of conversation wherever he travels in the country.

A linguistic authority of my acquaintance, much interested in my work in Slurvian, has suggested to me the possibility that the language may be related to, or a variation of, the one still spoken in England of which such a contraction as *Chumley* for *Cholmondeley*, is a familiar example. However, I think the evidence insufficient for drawing such a conclusion. Surnames cannot be considered subject to the ordinary rules of pronunciation. In fact, the only one I have positively identified in Slurvian is *Faggot*, the name of the American admiral who won the Battle of Mobile Bay.

The name *Faggot* brings me to a discussion of what I designate as "pure" Slurvian. This includes those Slurvian words that, when spelled exactly as pronounced, also make good English words (such as *Faggot, burr,* and *claps*). The day I can add to the lexicon such a word, hitherto unrecorded, is a happy day for me. Here are some examples of pure Slurvian, alphabetically listed:

BEAN, *n.* A living creature, as in *human bean.*
CACTUS, *n. pl.* The people in a play or story.
COURSE, *n.* A group of singers.
FISCAL, *adj.* Pertaining to the body, as opposed to the *spurt.*
FORM, *n.* Gathering place of the ancient Romans.
GNOME, *n.* Contraction for *no, Ma'am. Colloq.*
LINE, *n.* The king of beasts.
LORE, *n.* The more desirable of the two berths in a Pullman section.
MYRRH, *n.* A looking glass.
PAR, *n.* An attribute of strength, as in *the par and the glory.*
PLIGHT, *adj.* Courteous.
SEARS, *adj.* Grave, intent.
SPORT, *v.t.* To hold up, to bear the weight of.
WRECKERS, *n. pl.* Discs on which music is recorded for phonographs.

I am presently engaged in compiling a dictionary of Slurvian words, which I hope will prove to be the definitive work on the subject. The help of any interested students is welcomed, but I must caution such students to be certain the words are genuine Slurvian, and not merely regional speech, such as that of Alabama, Texas, or New England.

Condensed from *The New Yorker*, June 18, 1949, by permission of the author and publisher. Copyright 1949 by The New Yorker Magazine, Inc., and Harper & Row Publishers, Inc., New York.

meanings. "To lead" was *deuk*—which has changed to *tug*.

Where did these ancestors of ours live? Now our word-detectives are ready to close in —locating from their dictionaries this homeland of our speech, from which the tribes scattered many thousand years ago.

Since all Indo-European languages lack a common word for *lion, tiger, elephant, camel,* or *palm,* the homeland could not have been far south. Their old word *sneighw* (English *snow,* Russian *sneig,* Greek *nipha,* Welsh *nyf,* Latin *nix,* French *neige*) might push this homeland far northward, even against the great Polar Ice Cap—then still melting from the last Ice Age.

Consider the animals they knew! Their old name for *dog* was *kun,* which came into English as *hound,* into Latin as *canis,* but then crossed back into English as *canine.* (Cats, however, were then unknown, and since the Arabs call them *qitt* and the Turks *kedi* [maybe our *kitty*?] it is probable that this dwarf tiger crept late into our homes from some Asian or African jungle, and its name from another speech family.)

While they knew the pig (*su*—English *sow* and *swine*) and the horse (*ekwo*—Latin *equus,* into English *equestrian*), still we cannot be sure these were tamed. Perhaps they wandered in herds and were hunted.

Wild animals we know they knew are the snake (*serp*), the beaver (*bhebhru*), the bear (*ber*), the goose, the rabbit, and the duck. Their word for *fish* went into Swedish as *fisk* and into Latin as *piscis*—hence English *piscatorial.* They had a word for small streams (*strew*), and another for little ponds, which came down into English as *marsh, mire,* and *moor,* and into Latin as *mare*—hence English *mariner* and *maritime.* But of vast salt oceans they probably knew nothing: when, fanning out, migrating branches of the tribe met the thunder of ocean surf, each gave to this new marvel a separate name.

Of trees, they knew the *birch* and the *beech,* and because, much later, the writings of North Europe were scratched on smooth *beech* boards, we get our English word *book.*

Now, almost at the end of their search for this homeland, our word-detectives must call in the biologists, who first point out that all these animals and trees are natives of the Temperate Zone. Many other signs point to one possible location in Central Europe, which has roughly the boundaries of the old Austrian Empire.

Gradually, pushed by overpopulation or invaders, the Indo-Europeans began to move. Their wanderings lasted thousands of years and led them far afield. One branch was to push Slavic up to the Polar Sea, another had brought Latin down to the Mediterranean, while still others were to carry Celtic into what is today England and France, and Germanic down to the Rhine's right bank and up into Scandinavia.

We have inherited a rich legacy, one that ties into many nations. There is yet one more: Our English word *God* comes from the ancient *ghutom,* meaning "the Being that is worshipped." And a trace of this name is found even in the Sanskrit of distant India. Their word for *God* was *dyaus,* which Greek changed to *zeus,* while Latin *divus* gave English *divinity,* French *Dieu,* and *Dio* to Spanish and Italian. The syllable *sac* meant "sacred" then as now. From *prek* ("to pray") through Latin *precari* ("to pray") comes our word *prayer.*

Be sure that these Indo-European speech ancestors of ours must have pondered the dim mysteries of their own beginnings, even as do you (*yu*)!

❧ TO INCREASE UNDERSTANDING

1. (*a*) What was the strange fact about languages that puzzled early scholars? (*b*) What did they infer from this fact?

2. (*a*) With what kind of changes did Grimm's law deal? (*b*) What were scholars able to do with the new information furnished by Grimm's discovery?

3. What does the Indo-European language source tell about where the people that spoke it lived?

4. Explain in detail how we learn some things about the way of life of these people from their language.

5. Compare "Your Oldest Heirlooms" with "Slurvian Self-Taught." (*a*) What kind of language changes is each concerned with? (*b*) How do the purposes of the writers differ? (*c*) What effect does this difference in purpose have on the tone?

Walden E. B. White

Miss Nims, take a letter to Henry David Thoreau. Dear Henry: I thought of you the other afternoon as I was approaching Concord doing fifty on Route 62. That is a high speed at which to hold a philosopher in one's mind, but in this century we are a nimble bunch.

On one of the lawns in the outskirts of the village a woman was cutting the grass with a motorized lawn mower. What made me think of you was that the machine had rather got away from her, although she was game enough, and in the brief glimpse I had of the scene it appeared to me that the lawn was mowing the lady.[1] She kept a tight grip on the handles, which throbbed violently with every explosion of the one-cylinder motor, and as she sheered around bushes and lurched along at a reluctant trot behind her impetuous servant, she looked like a puppy who had grabbed something that was too much for him. Concord hasn't changed much, Henry; the farm implements and the animals still have the upper hand.

I may as well admit that I was journeying to Concord with the deliberate intention of visiting your woods; for although I have never knelt at the grave of a philosopher nor placed wreaths on moldy poets, and have often gone a mile out of my way to avoid some place of historical interest, I have always wanted to see Walden Pond. The account which you left of your sojourn there is, you will be amused to learn, a document of increasing penitence; each year it seems to gain a little headway, as the world loses ground. We may all be transcendental yet, whether we like it or not. As our common complexities increase, any tale of individual simplicity (and yours is the best written and the cockiest) acquires a new fascination; as our goods accumulate, but not our well-being, your report of an existence without material adornment takes on a certain awkward credibility.

My purpose in going to Walden Pond, like yours, was not to live cheaply or to live dearly there, but to transact some private business with the fewest obstacles. Approaching Concord, doing forty, doing forty-five, doing fifty, the steering wheel held snug in my palms, the highway held grimly in my vision, the crown of the road now serving me (on the right-hand curves), now defeating me (on the left-hand curves), I began to rouse myself from the stupefaction which a day's motor journey induces. It was a delicious evening, Henry, when the whole body is one sense, and imbibes delight through every pore, if I may coin a phrase. Fields were richly brown where the harrow, drawn by the stripped Ford, had lately sunk its teeth; pastures were green; and overhead the sky had that same everlasting great look which you will find on Page 144 of the Oxford pocket edition.[2] I could feel the road entering me, through tire, wheel, spring, and cushion; shall I not have intelligence with

"Walden" (June 1939) from *One Man's Meat* by E. B. White. Copyright 1939 by E. B. White. Reprinted with permission of Harper & Row, Publishers, Inc., New York.
1. *it appeared to me . . . the lady.* Here White is echoing Thoreau's own words (see "Why I Went to the Woods," page 236) to make a satiric reference to modern man.
2. *the Oxford pocket edition.* White is referring to an edition of *Walden* published by the Oxford Press.

E. B. WHITE 1899-

After he had graduated from Cornell University, E. B. White took some time to find the kind of work he could enjoy. He adventured for a while in the West, but returned to his native state to work for two unsatisfying years as a production assistant and copy writer for an advertising agency in New York. During this time, however, he was sending contributions to *The New Yorker*. Through these he earned an editorial post on the magazine, where he edited "The Talk of the Town" department for many years (see page 500). Since it is this department that really sets the tone for the entire magazine, the style of *The New Yorker* became identified with that of E. B. White. Actually his style is inimitable, and has earned him widespread acclaim.

Many people believe that White is the best of modern American essayists, and some have tried to describe his unique gift. *Time* magazine has said that his style is "a sort of precocious offhand humming." As is evident in the accompanying essay, this seemingly offhand grace serves to heighten the brilliant precision of his insights.

earth too? Am I not partly leaves and vegetable mold myself?—a man of infinite horsepower, yet partly leaves.

Stay with me on 62 and it will take you into Concord. As I say, it was a delicious evening. The snake had come forth to die in a bloody S on the highway, the wheel upon its head, its bowels flat now and exposed. The turtle had come up too to cross the road and die in the attempt, its hard shell smashed under the rubber blow, its intestinal yearning (for the other side of the road) forever squashed.

There was a sign by the wayside which announced that the road had a "cotton surface." You wouldn't know what that is, but neither, for that matter, did I. There is a cryptic ingredient in many of our modern improvements—we are awed and pleased without knowing quite what we are enjoying. It is something to be traveling on a road with a cotton surface.

The civilization round Concord today is an odd distillation of city, village, farm, and manor. The houses, yards, fields look not quite

WALDEN POND

To Thoreau the primitive nature of Walden Pond was a challenge "to live deliberately"; to Emerson, who owned much of the area, it was a thing to be cherished and preserved. Emerson once told his daughter Edith, "I will keep these woods until everything else is gone." In memory of Thoreau and her father, in 1922 Edith arranged to give the pond to the Commonwealth of Massachusetts for the enjoyment of the public. Unfortunately the bequest was not explicit as to what kind of enjoyment was intended. The Middlesex County Commissioners, to whom the area was entrusted, provided a bathhouse, boat dock, and picnicking facilities, thinking of Walden as a natural place for the people of Concord to enjoy outdoor sports and recreation. Others, like E. B. White, saw in Walden a place to enjoy an unspoiled wilderness. These people were distressed at what seemed to them the intrusion of man on the natural scene.

The conflict between these two viewpoints came to a head in 1957. Responding to pressure from a growing Concord, the commissioners began to make preparations for improving the recreational facilities at Walden. For two days they worked, felling trees, bulldozing the land, building an asphalt road. At that point their activities were discovered by the Thoreau Society, about to hold its annual meeting in Concord. What the commissioners

considered improvements, the Thoreau Society saw as destruction of a valuable wilderness. Backed by legal counsel, they determined to do everything in their power to preserve Walden in its natural state.

The Thoreau Society is a modest one—there are about five hundred members—whose purpose is "to honor Henry David Thoreau, to stimulate more interest in his life and writings, and to act as a repository for Thoreauviana." The task that faced this small and scholarly society was large and practical. The litigation was to cost it nearly twelve thousand dollars and involve a three-year fight to the Massachusetts Supreme Judicial Court.

In the end, however, the battle was not won or lost by money. The practical decision had to be based on abstract opinion: Which "nature" is ultimately more valuable for men, that which man has made over for his recreation or that which man has left in its natural state for his wonder? On this abstract level of idea and attitude the Thoreau Society found it had the support of influential writers across the nation. Men who cherished Thoreau came to the defense of the land where he had found inspiration. Such men as the noted conservationist Edwin Way Teal, the New York Times theater-critic Brooks Atkinson, the famous architect Walter Gropius, and the distinguished editor Bernard De Voto (see page

suburban, not quite rural. Under the bronze beech and the blue spruce of the departed baron grazes the milch goat of the heirs. Under the porte-cochere stands the reconditioned station wagon; under the grape arbor sit the puppies for sale. (But why do men degenerate ever? What makes families run out?)

It was June and everywhere June was publishing her immemorial stanza; in the lilacs, in the syringa, in the freshly edged paths and the sweetness of moist beloved gardens, and the little wire wickets that preserve the tulips'

front. Farmers were already moving the fruits of their toil into their yards, arranging the rhubarb, the asparagus, the strictly fresh eggs on the painted stands under the little shed roofs with the patent shingles. And though it was almost a hundred years since you had taken your ax and started cutting out your home on Walden Pond, I was interested to observe that the philosophical spirit was still alive in Massachusetts; in the center of a vacant lot some boys were assembling the framework of a rude shelter, their whole mind

---

15), among others, campaigned in print to save Walden.

It is certain that the writings of these men contributed to the public "reputation" on which the Court based its final decision. Its ruling was that the Commissioners would

have to stop their "improvements" and restore the natural scene. In rendering its decision the Court explained, "The reputation of the pond grows out of Thoreau's book, of which we take judicial notice....Walden Pond is an American literary shrine."

and skill concentrated in the rather inauspicious helter-skeleton of studs and rafters. They too were escaping from town, to live naturally, in a rich blend of savagery and philosophy.

That evening, after supper at the inn, I strolled out into the twilight to dream my shapeless transcendental dreams and see that the car was locked up for the night (first open the right front door, then reach over, straining, and pull up the handles of the left rear and the left front till you hear the click, then the handle of the right rear, then shut the right front but open it again, remembering that the key is still in the ignition switch, remove the key, shut the right front again with a bang, push the tiny keyhole cover to one side, insert key, turn, and withdraw). It is what we all do, Henry. It is called locking the car. It is said to confuse thieves and keep them from making off with the lap robe. Four doors to lock behind one robe. The driver himself never uses a lap robe, the free movement of his legs being vital to the operation of the vehicle; so that when he locks the car it is a pure and unselfish act. I have in my life gained very little essential heat from lap robes, yet I have ever been at pains to lock them up.

The evening was full of sounds, some of which would have stirred your memory. The robins still love the elms of New England villages at sundown. There is enough of the thrush in them to make song inevitable at the end of day, and enough of the tramp to make them hang round the dwellings of men. A robin, like many another American, dearly loves a white house with green blinds. Concord is still full of them.

Your fellow townsmen were stirring abroad —not many afoot, most of them in their cars; and the sound which they made in Concord at evening was a rustling and a whispering. The sound lacks steadfastness and is wholly unlike that of a train. A train, as you know who lived so near the Fitchburg line, whistles once or twice sadly and is gone, trailing a memory in smoke soothing to ear and mind. Automobiles, skirting a village green, are like flies that have gained the inner ear—they buzz, cease, pause, start, shift, stop, halt,

brake, and the whole effect is a nervous polytone curiously disturbing.

As I wandered along, the toc toc of Pingpong balls drifted from an attic window. In front of the Reuben Brown house a Buick was drawn up. At the wheel, motionless, his hat upon his head, a man sat, listening to "Amos and Andy" on the radio (it is a drama of many scenes and without an end). The deep voice of Andrew Brown, emerging from the car, although it originated more than two hundred miles away, was unstrained by distance. When you used to sit on the shore of your pond on Sunday morning, listening to the church bells of Acton and Concord, you were aware of the excellent filter of the intervening atmosphere. Science has attended to that, and sound now maintains its intensity without regard for distance. Properly sponsored, it goes on forever.

A fire engine, out for a trial spin, roared past Emerson's house, hot with readiness for public duty. Over the barn roofs the martins dipped and chittered. A swarthy daughter of an asparagus grower, in culottes, shirt, and bandanna, pedaled past on her bicycle. It was indeed a delicious evening, and I returned to the inn (I believe it was your house once) to rock with the old ladies on the concrete veranda.

Next morning early I started afoot for Walden, out Main Street and down Thoreau, past the depot and the Minuteman Chevrolet Company. The morning was fresh and in a beanfield along the way I flushed an agriculturalist, quietly studying his beans. Thoreau Street soon joined Number 126, an artery of the State. We number our highways nowadays, our speed being so great we can remember little of their quality or character and are lucky to remember their number. (Men have an indistinct notion that if they keep up this activity long enough all will at length ride somewhere, in next to no time.) Your pond is on 126.

I knew I must be nearing your woodland retreat when the Golden Pheasant lunchroom came into view—Sealtest ice cream, toasted sandwiches, hot frankfurters, waffles, tonics, and lunches. Were I the proprietor, I should add rice, Indian meal, and molasses—just for old time's sake. The Pheasant, incidentally, is for sale: a chance for some nature lover who wishes to set himself up beside a pond in the Concord atmosphere and live deliberately, fronting only the essential facts of life[3] on Number 126. Beyond the Pheasant was a place called Walden Breezes, an oasis whose porch pillars were made of old green shutters sawed into lengths. On the porch was a distorting mirror, to give the traveler a comical image of himself, who had miraculously learned to gaze in an ordinary glass without smiling. Behind the Breezes, in a sun-parched clearing, dwelt your philosophical descendants in their trailers, each trailer the size of your hut, but all grouped together for the sake of congeniality. Trailer people leave the city, as you did, to discover solitude and in any weather, at any hour of the day or night, to improve the nick of time; but they soon collect in villages and get bogged deeper in the mud than ever. The camp behind Walden Breezes was just rousing itself to the morning. The ground was packed hard under the heel, and the sun came through the clearing to bake the soil and enlarge the wry smell of cramped housekeeping. Cushman's bakery truck had stopped to deliver an early basket of rolls. A camp dog, seeing me in the road, barked petulantly. A man emerged from one of the trailers and set forth with a bucket to draw water from some forest tap.

Leaving the highway I turned off into the woods toward the pond, which was apparent through the foliage. The floor of the forest was strewn with dried old oak leaves and *Transcripts*.[4] From beneath the flattened popcorn wrapper *(granum explosum)* peeped the frail violet. I followed a footpath and descended to the water's edge. The pond lay clear and blue in the morning light, as you have seen it so many times. In the shallows a man's water-logged shirt undulated gently. A few flies came out to greet me and convoy me to your cove, past the No Bathing signs on which the fellows and the girls had scrawled their names. I felt strangely excited suddenly to be snooping around your premises, tiptoeing along watchfully, as though not to tread

by mistake upon the intervening century. Before I got to the cove I heard something which seemed to me quite wonderful: I heard your frog, a full, clear *troonk,* guiding me, still hoarse and solemn, bridging the years as the robins had bridged them in the sweetness of the village evening. But he soon quit, and I came on a couple of young boys throwing stones at him.

Your frontyard is marked by a bronze tablet set in stone. Four small granite posts, a few feet away, show where the house was. On top of the tablet was a pair of faded blue bathing trunks with a white stripe. Back of it is a pile of stones, a sort of cairn, left by your visitors as a tribute I suppose. It is a rather ugly little heap of stones, Henry. In fact the hillside itself seems faded, browbeaten; a few tall skinny pines, bare of lower limbs, a smattering of young maples in suitable green, some birches and oaks, and a number of trees felled by the last big wind. It was from the bole of one of these fallen pines, torn up by the roots, that I extracted the stone which I added to the cairn—sentimental act in which I was interrupted by a small terrier from a nearby picnic group, who confronted me and wanted to know about the stone.

I sat down for a while on one of the posts of your house to listen to the bluebottles and the dragonflies. The invaded glade sprawled shabby and mean at my feet, but the flies were tuned to the old vibration. There were remains of a fire in your ruins, but I doubt that it was yours; also two beer bottles trodden into the soil had become part of earth. A young oak had taken root in your house, and two or three ferns, unrolling like the ticklers at a banquet. The only other furnishings were a DuBarry pattern sheet, a page torn from a picture magazine, and some crusts in wax paper.

Before I quit I walked clear round the pond and found the place where you used to sit on the northeast side to get the sun in the fall, and the beach where you got sand for scrub-

---

3. *live deliberately . . . facts of life.* This is another echo of Thoreau's words (see page 236). 4. *Transcripts,* a highly conservative Boston newspaper (ceased publication in 1941).

bing your floor. On the eastern side of the pond, where the highway borders it, the State has built dressing rooms for swimmers, a float with diving towers, drinking fountains of porcelain, and rowboats for hire. The pond is in fact a State Preserve, and carries a twenty-dollar fine for picking wild flowers, a decree signed in all solemnity by your fellow citizens Walter C. Wardwell, Erson B. Barlow, and Nathaniel I. Bowditch. There was a smell of creosote where they had been building a wide wooden stairway to the road and the parking area. Swimmers and boaters were arriving; bodies plunged vigorously into the water and emerged wet and beautiful in the bright air. As I left, a boatload of town boys were splashing about in midpond, kidding and fooling, the young fellows singing at the tops of their lungs in a wild chorus:

Amer-ica, Amer-ica, God shed his grace on thee,
And crown thy good with brotherhood
From sea to shi-ning sea!

I walked back to town along the railroad, following your custom. The rails were expanding noisily in the hot sun, and on the slope of the roadbed the wild grape and the blackberry sent up their creepers to the track.

The expense of my brief sojourn in Concord was:

Canvas shoes	$1.95
Baseball bat	.25
Left-handed fielder's glove	1.25
Hotel and meals	4.25
In all	$7.70

{ gifts to take back to a boy

As you see, this amount was almost what you spent for food for eight months. I cannot defend the shoes or the expenditure for shelter and food: they reveal a meanness and grossness in my nature which you would find contemptible. The baseball equipment, however, is the kind of impediment with which you were never on even terms. You must remember that the house where you practiced the sort of economy which I respect was haunted only by mice and squirrels. You never had to cope with a shortstop.

 TO INCREASE UNDERSTANDING

1. (*a*) What changes did E. B. White find had taken place at Walden since the time of Thoreau? (*b*) Why did these changes prompt him to write the article?

2. In each of the following quotations there is an implied comparison between the modern way of living and Thoreau's way of living at Walden. Show in each case how White makes a satiric criticism of modern life by means of the comparison.

(*a*) The machine had rather got away from her; . . . it appeared to me that the lawn was mowing the lady.

(*b*) I have in my life gained very little essential heat from lap robes, yet I have ever been at pains to lock them up.

(*c*) We number our highways nowadays, our speed being so great we can remember little of their quality or character and are lucky to remember their number.

(*d*) From beneath the flattened popcorn wrapper (*granum explosum*) peeped the frail violet.

3. What is unusual about the personal viewpoint expressed by White in this essay?

WORDS!

An author with as individual and distinctive a style as E. B. White will frequently make word choices that are surprising and delightful. Below you will find a number of the sentences that White used in "Walden" with some word or phrase left out of each. (1) Complete each sentence using the word or phrase you might have expected to follow in that context before you read the essay. (2) Look again at the sentence quoted to find how White actually completed it. (3) Explain how White's "surprise ending" helped him accomplish his purpose.

(*a*) The account which you left of your sojourn there is, you will be amused to learn, a document of increasing _____. (page 633, column 1, paragraph 3)

(*b*) . . . as our goods accumulate but not our well-being, your report of an existence without material adornment takes on _____. (page 633, column 1, paragraph 3)

(*c*) That evening, after supper at the inn, I strolled out into the twilight to dream my shapeless transcendental dreams and see _____. (page 636, column 1, paragraph 1)

(*d*) The floor of the forest was strewn with dried old oak leaves and _____. (page 637, column 1, paragraph 1)

On Baseball Jacques Barzun

Whoever wants to know the heart and mind of America had better learn baseball, the rules and realities of the game—and do it by watching first some high-school or small-town teams. The big league games are too fast for the beginner and the newspapers don't help. To read them with profit you have to know a language that comes easy only after philosophy has taught you to judge practice. Here is scholarship that takes effort on the part of the outsider, but it is so bred into the native that it never becomes a dreary round of technicalities. The wonderful purging of the passions that we all experienced in the fall of '51, the despair groaned out over the fate of the Dodgers, from whom the league pennant was snatched at the last minute,[1] give us some idea of what Greek tragedy was like. Baseball *is* Greek in being national, heroic, and broken up in the rivalries of city-states. How sad that Europe knows nothing like it! Its Olympics generate anger, not unity, and its interstate politics follow no rules that a people can grasp. At least Americans understand baseball, the true realm of clear ideas.

That baseball fitly expresses the powers of the nation's mind and body is a merit separate from the glory of being the most active, agile, varied, articulate, and brainy of all group games. It is of and for our century. Tennis belongs to the individualistic past—a hero, or at most a pair of friends or lovers, against the world. The idea of baseball is a team, an outfit, a section, a gang, a union, a cell, a commando squad—in short, a twentieth-century setup of opposite numbers.

Baseball takes its mystic nine and scatters them wide. A kind of individualism thereby returns, but it is limited—eternal vigilance is the price of victory. Just because they're far apart, the outfield can't dream or play she-loves-me-not with daisies. The infield is like a steel net held in the hands of the catcher. He is the psychologist and historian for the staff—or else his signals will give the opposition hits. The value of his headpiece is shown by the ironmongery worn to protect it. The pitcher, on the other hand, is the wayward man of genius, whom others will direct. They will expect nothing from him but virtuosity. He is surrounded no doubt by mere talent, unless one excepts that transplanted acrobat, the shortstop. What a brilliant invention is his rôle despite its exposure to ludicrous lapses! One man to each base, and then the free lance, the trouble-shooter, the movable feast for the eyes, whose motion animates the whole foreground.

The rules keep pace with this imaginative creation so rich in allusions to real life. How excellent, for instance, that a foul tip muffed by the catcher gives the batter another chance. It is the recognition of Chance that knows no argument. But on the other hand, how wise and just that the third strike must not be

1. *fate of the Dodgers . . . last minute.* The then Brooklyn Dodgers, who led the National League by as much as thirteen games late in the season of 1951, were tied on the last day of the season by the then New York Giants, and subsequently lost the play-off.

JACQUES BARZUN 1907-

Jacques Barzun (zhäk bär'zun) passed his boyhood in the stimulating atmosphere of the so-called "Abaye" group of French writers, to which his father belonged. At the outbreak of the first World War his family came to the United States, and Jacques subsequently became an American citizen. While attending Columbia University he became interested in scholarly history. He pursued this interest for a number of years as a professor of history at Columbia, but his later works show him turning from technical history to what he calls "studies of cultural history." This allows his keen intelligence to range the field of his wide interests, from democratic freedom to education to music. In *God's Country and Mine*, the book from which this essay was taken, he has attempted to analyze those aspects of our life, both good and bad, that he finds characteristically American.

dropped. This points to the fact that near the end of any struggle life asks for more than is needful in order to clinch success. A victory has to be won, not snatched. We find also our American innocence in calling "World Series" the annual games between the winners in each big league. The world doesn't know or care and couldn't compete if it wanted to, but since it's us children having fun, why, the world is our stage. I said baseball was Greek. Is there not a poetic symbol in the new meaning—our meaning—of "Ruth hits Homer"?

Once the crack of the bat has sent the ball skimmiting left of second between the infielder's legs, six men converge or distend their defense to keep the runner from advancing along the prescribed path. The ball is not the center of interest as in those vulgar predatory games like football, basketball, and polo. Man running is the force to be contained. His getting to first or second base starts a capitalization dreadful to think of: every hit pushes him on. Bases full and a homer make four runs, while the defenders, helpless without the magic power of the ball lying over the fence, cry out their anguish and dig up the sod with their spikes.

But fate is controlled by the rules. Opportunity swings from one side to the other because innings alternate quickly, keep up spirit in the players, interest in the beholders. So does the profusion of different acts to be performed—pitching, throwing, catching, batting, running, stealing, sliding, signaling. Blows are similarly varied. Flies, Texas Leaguers, grounders, baseline fouls—praise God the human neck is a universal joint! And there is no set pace. Under the hot sun, the minutes creep as a deliberate pitcher tries his feints and curves for three strikes called, or conversely walks a threatening batter. But the batter is not invariably a tailor's dummy. In a hundredth of a second there may be a hissing rocket down right field, a cloud of dust over first base—the bleachers all a-yell—a double play, and the other side up to bat.

Accuracy and speed, the practiced eye and hefty arm, the mind to take in and readjust to the unexpected, the possession of more than one talent and the willingness to work in har-

ness without special orders—these are the American virtues that shine in baseball. There has never been a good player who was dumb. Beef and bulk and mere endurance count for little, judgment and daring for much. Baseball is among group games played with a ball what fencing is to games of combat. But being spread out, baseball has something sociable and friendly about it that I especially love. It is graphic and choreographic. The ball is not shuttling in a confined space, as in tennis. Nor does baseball go to the other extreme of solitary whanging and counting stopped on the brink of pointlessness, like golf. Baseball is a kind of collective chess with arms and legs in full play under sunlight.

How adaptable, too! Three kids in a backyard are enough to create the same quality of drama. All of us in our tennis days have pounded balls with a racket against a wall, for practice. But that is nothing compared with batting in an empty lot, or catching at twilight, with a fella who'll let you use his mitt when your palms get too raw. Every part of baseball equipment is inherently attractive and of a most enchanting functionalism. A man cannot have too much leather about him; and a catcher's mitt is just the right amount for one hand. It's too bad the chest protector and shinpads are so hot and at a distance so like corrugated cardboard. Otherwise, the team is elegance itself in its striped knee breeches and loose shirts, colored stockings and peaked caps. Except for brief moments of sliding, you can see them all in one eyeful, unlike the muddy hecatombs of football. To watch a football game is to be in prolonged neurotic doubt as to what you're seeing. It's more like an emergency happening at a distance than a game. I don't wonder the spectators take to drink. Who has ever seen a baseball fan drinking within the meaning of the act? He wants all his senses sharp and clear, his eyesight above all. He gulps down soda pop, which is a harmless way of replenishing his energy by the ingestion of sugar diluted in water and colored pink.

Happy the man in the bleachers. He is enjoying the spectacle that the gods on Olympus contrived only with difficulty when they sent Helen to Troy[2] and picked their teams. And the gods missed the fun of doing this by catching a bat near the narrow end and measuring hand over hand for first pick. In Troy, New York, the game scheduled for 2 P.M. will break no bones, yet it will be a real fight between Southpaw Dick and Red Larsen. For those whom civilized play doesn't fully satisfy, there will be provided a scapegoat in a blue suit—the umpire, yell-proof and even-handed as justice, which he demonstrates with outstretched arms when calling "Safe!"

And the next day in the paper: learned comment, statistical summaries, and the verbal imagery of metaeuphoric experts. In the face of so much joy, one can only ask, Were you there when Dogface Joe parked the pellet beyond the pale?

---

2. *Helen to Troy.* To reward Paris, son of the king of Troy, for awarding her the apple inscribed "for the fairest," Aphrodite (af'rə di'ti) helped Paris abduct Helen, daughter of Zeus and Leda, from her husband, Menelaus (men'ə lā'əs), one of the Greek kings. This precipitated the siege of Troy by the Greeks, in which, according to Greek legend, the gods were very interested, all taking sides and sometimes fighting among themselves over the outcome.

❧ TO INCREASE UNDERSTANDING

1. (a) Why does baseball delight Jacques Barzun? (b) Do you or do you not like the same things about baseball? Explain.

2. Barzun sees baseball as expressing the "powers of the nation's mind and body." (a) Cite specific aspects of the game that Barzun uses to illustrate his point of view. (b) Explain in each case how this aspect of the game is typically American. (c) Can you think of other familiar activities from which modern Americans derive similar pleasure?

3. (a) How much could someone with no previous knowledge of the DC-3 learn about it from Kahn's article? (b) Would a person with no knowledge of baseball know how to play the game after reading Barzun's essay? Explain. (c) What would he have learned about it? (d) Compare Barzun's purposes in writing "On Baseball" with Kahn's in his article on the DC-3.

❧ WORDS!

Suppose a certain Senator X has just returned from an exhausting trip abroad, and a crowd of admirers has gathered at the airport to welcome his return.

The reactions registered by various people might be expressed in a variety of forms of usage.

Familiar (spoken between friends): "Gosh! He looked beat, the look I got of him."

Informal (spoken or written between friends): "He seemed tired when he got off the plane."

Formal (written): The Senator arrived, appearing thoroughly exhausted as a result of his extended travels.

Journalese (newspaper account): Senator X's (Dem., N.Y.) face wore a haggard look as he deplaned last night.

Shoptalk (medical report): A cursory examination of 31 March revealed that the Senator was suffering from nothing more than acute exhaustion.

The differences among these styles are partly a matter of diction (*beat, tired, exhausted, haggard, acute exhaustion*), partly a matter of tone, and partly a matter of sentence structure.

Much of the unique quality of affectionate humor communicated by this essay is achieved by Barzun's mixing of these different varieties of usage. Consider the sentence, "He gulps down soda pop, which is a harmless way of replenishing his energy by the ingestion of sugar diluted in water and colored pink." Notice the surprising and amusing contrast between the familiar diction of the first part of the sentence (*gulps down, soda pop*) and the shoptalk tone of the second part, established partly by diction (*replenishing, ingestion*) and partly by the form of the clause. Notice the formal sound of most of this sentence: "That baseball fitly expresses the powers of the nation's mind and body is a merit separate from the glory of being the most active, agile, varied, articulate, and brainy of all group games." Only near the end of the sentence does one word make an abrupt shift in tone: *brainy* rarely occurs except in informal use.

Examine each one of the following quotations. Referring to the labels used in the examples of various types of usage, decide which label best describes each quotation. Justify your decision.

1. . . . six men converge or distend their defense to keep the runner from advancing along the prescribed path.

2. . . . parked the pellet beyond the pale.

3. The world doesn't know or care and couldn't compete if it wanted to, but since it's us children having fun, why, the world is our stage.

4. . . . catching at twilight, with a fella who'll let you use his mitt.

5. Flies, Texas Leaguers, grounders, ...

War George Santayana

To fight is a radical instinct; if men have nothing else to fight over, they will fight over words, fancies, or women, or they will fight because they dislike each other's looks, or because they have met walking in opposite directions. To knock a thing down, especially if it is cocked at an arrogant angle, is a deep delight to the blood. To fight for a reason and in a calculating spirit is something your true warrior despises; even a coward might screw his courage up to such a reasonable conflict. The joy and glory of fighting lie in its pure spontaneity and consequent generosity; you are not fighting for gain, but for sport and for victory. Victory, no doubt, has its fruits for the victor. If fighting were not a possible means of livelihood, the bellicose instinct could never have established itself in any long-lived race. A few men can live on plunder, just as there is room in the world for some beasts of prey; other men are reduced to living on industry, just as there are diligent bees, ants, and herbivorous kine. But victory need have no good fruits for the people whose army is victorious. That it sometimes does so is an ulterior and blessed circumstance hardly to be reckoned upon.

Since barbarism has its pleasures it naturally has its apologists. There are panegyrists of war who say that without a periodical bleeding a race decays and loses its manhood. Experience is directly opposed to this shameless assertion. It is war that wastes a nation's wealth, chokes its industries, kills its flower, narrows its sympathies, condemns it to be governed by adventurers, and leaves the puny, deformed, and unmanly to breed the next generation. Internecine war, foreign and civil, brought about the greatest set-back which the life of reason has ever suffered; it extermi-nated the Greek and Italian aristocracies.[1] Instead of being descended from heroes, modern nations are descended from slaves; and it is not their bodies only that show it. After a long peace, if the conditions of life are propitious, we observe a people's energies bursting their barriers; they become aggressive on the strength they have stored up in their remote and unchecked development. It is the unmutilated race, fresh from the struggle with nature (in which the best survive, while in war it is often the best that perish), that descends victoriously into the arena of nations and conquers disciplined armies at the first blow, becomes the military aristocracy of the next epoch, and is itself ultimately sapped and decimated by luxury and battle and merged at last into the ignoble conglomerate beneath. Then, perhaps, in some other virgin country a genuine humanity is again found, capable of victory because unbled by war. To call war the soil of courage and virtue is like calling debauchery the soil of love.

Blind courage is an animal virtue indispensable in a world full of dangers and evils where a certain insensibility and dash are requisite to skirt the precipice without vertigo. Such animal courage seems therefore beautiful rather than desperate or cruel, and being the lowest and most instinctive of virtues it is the one most widely and sincerely admired. In the form of steadiness under risks rationally taken, and perseverance so long as there is a chance of success, courage is a true virtue; but it ceases to be one when the love of danger, a useful passion when danger is unavoidable, begins to lead men into evils which it was unnecessary to face. Bravado, provocativeness, and a gambler's instinct, with a love of hitting hard for the sake of exercise, is a temper

Reprinted from *Little Essays Drawn From The Writings of George Santayana* edited by Logan Pearsall Smith. Reprinted by permission of Constable and Company, Ltd., and the Executors of the Smith Estate. Copyright 1920 by Constable and Company, Ltd.

1. *Internecine war . . . aristocracies*, the series of interstate wars which devastated the economy of and put an end to the extraordinary Greek culture after the reign of Pericles (c. 430 B.C.); and the series of civil wars and political intrigue that continued among the fluctuating territories and city-states in Italy from the decline of the Roman empire through the Renaissance.

which ought already to be counted among the vices rather than the virtues of man. To delight in war is a merit in the soldier, a dangerous quality in the captain, and a positive crime in the statesman.

The panegyrist of war places himself on the lowest level on which a moralist or patriot can stand, and shows as great a want of refined feeling as of right reason. For the glories of war are all blood-stained, delirious, and infected with crime; the combative instinct is a savage prompting by which one man's good is found in another's evil. The existence of such a contradiction in the moral world is the original sin of nature, whence flows every other wrong. He is a willing accomplice of that perversity in things who delights in another's discomfiture or in his own, and craves the blind tension of plunging into danger without reason, or the idiot's pleasure in facing a pure chance. To find joy in another's trouble is, as man is constituted, not unnatural, though it is wicked; and to find joy in one's own trouble, though it be madness, is not yet impossible for man. These are the chaotic depths of that dreaming nature out of which humanity has to grow.

❧ TO INCREASE UNDERSTANDING

1. (*a*) What is the meaning of *radical* as used on page 642, column 1, line 1? (*b*) What does Santayana mean by calling fighting a "radical instinct"?
2. (*a*) What argument has been advanced for periodic war? (*b*) How does Santayana refute this argument?
3. (*a*) Explain Santayana's attitude toward courage, mentioning the conditions under which he regards it (1) as a virtue, (2) as a vice. (*b*) Santayana writes: "To delight in war is a merit in the soldier, a dangerous quality in the captain, and a positive crime in the statesman." How is this statement related to his views on courage?
4. This essay was written about the time of World War I. (*a*) How has the "art of war" changed since then? (*b*) Partly as a result of these changes there is very little written today about the "glories" of war. Do you think that man has grown out of his craving for the excitement of war? Explain.
5. Reread the last paragraph of the essay. Explain

exactly what Santayana means by each of the following statements, paying particular attention to the italicized parts of each sentence.

(*a*) ... the combative instinct is a savage prompting by which one man's good is found in another's evil. The existence of such a *contradiction in the moral world* is the original sin of nature. . . .

(*b*) He is a willing accomplice of *that perversity in things* who delights in another's discomfiture or *in his own*. . . .

(*c*) ... the idiot's *pleasure in* facing a pure chance.

(*d*) ... to find joy in one's own trouble, though it be madness, is not *yet* impossible for man.

(*e*) These are the chaotic depths of that *dreaming nature* out of which humanity *has to grow*.

GEORGE SANTAYANA 1863-1952

George Santayana (sän'tə yä'nə) moved to Boston from his birthplace in Madrid, Spain, at the age of eight. After studying at Harvard and the University of Berlin, he returned to the Boston area to begin a distinguished teaching career as one of Harvard's most eminent professors of philosophy. Santayana was never a highly technical philosopher, and the style of his two most important works, *The Life of Reason* and *The Sense of Beauty*, makes them good reading for the layman. His artistic genius was remarkably demonstrated when his only novel, *The Last Puritan*, finished in 1935 when he was over seventy years old, became a best seller.

Although Santayana's main concerns in his philosophy were beauty and reason, he never had any illusions about the brutal aspects of human nature. In later years his horror of the incredible stupidity of war deepened. After extensive travel in Europe between the wars, he gained asylum at a convent in Rome at the outbreak of World War II. When in 1944 he was found still at the convent by the advancing Allied armies, he told reporters, "I shall never leave here. . . . There has been so much killing and so much suffering in the world's history. In solitude it is possible to love mankind; in the world, there can be nothing but secret or open war."[1]

In the essay "War," written early in this century, Santayana was less fatalistic and more detached. Nonetheless, while he believed then that mankind could improve, he indicated clearly that man's indulgence in war was positive evidence of how far he had to grow.

---

1. *Time,* June 26, 1944, p. 42.

The Leatherstocking Saga Cleveland Amory

Who is the most famous character, the world over, in American fiction? Is it Tom Sawyer or George F. Babbitt? Tarzan or Uncle Tom? Frank Merriwell or Scarlett O'Hara?[1] The answer is easy; it is none of them. Instead, it is an 'arnest man of natur' whose chief consarn, through five books, is rascuing vartuous darters on parilous jarneys from sartain dith at the hands of Frenchmen, injuns, riptyles, and all sarts of arther inimies.

His name, of course, is Natty Bumppo, otherwise known as Deerslayer, Hawkeye, Pathfinder, or Long Rifle, and to rescue this man from sartain dith at the hands of schoolmarms, camic books, tilivision, and all sarts of arther ibscurities, Pantheon Books has published a brand-new, hair-trigger, rim-fire, single-action, five-barrel book called *The Leatherstocking Saga*. This doughty volume, containing a running version of five whole novels, was originated by Pantheon's Helen Wolff, encouraged by SR's Amy Loveman,[2] edited by Columbia's Allan Nevins,[3] illustrated by the late Reginald Marsh—and, oh yes, it was written by James Fenimore Cooper.

Starting with Mark Twain, who claimed that Cooper's characters were "corpses," his Indians "cigar-store," his dialogue "book talk," his humor "pathetic," and his pathos "funny," Cooper has for many years suffered at the hands of critics. Nonetheless, he has been the most widely translated of all American authors, and while this may give some more ammunition to the argument that the poorer a book (in the sense of refinements of the mother tongue) the better for translation, the fact remains that *The Cambridge History of American Literature* has come around to calling Natty Bumppo "the most memorable character American fiction has given the world." In *The Leatherstocking Saga* Professor Nevins has taken a brand-new tack. Scorning the verbal underbrush, he has hewed to the chronological line of Natty Bumppo's life, letting the chips of subplots and subcharacters fall where they may. Thus, *The Deerslayer*, which

was the last to be published, comes first; *The Last of the Mohicans*, which was second, second; *The Pathfinder*, which was fourth, third; *The Pioneers*, which was first, fourth; and *The Prairie*, which was third, last. Meanwhile Deerslayer himself, who is twenty-three years old in *Deerslayer*, which concerns the years 1740-1745, is thirty-six in *Mohicans*, which concerns 1757, is thirty-eight in *Pathfinder* (1759), seventy-two in *Pioneers* (1793), and finally eighty-three in *Prairie* (1804). (Actually, it isn't quite that easy. Cooper says *Prairie* was about the year 1804 but Nevins says it was about 1820, so Deerslayer, who Cooper says was eighty-three, was, Nevins says, ninety-nine.)

In any case, the rascuing job has been done, and today Deerslayer, at age 223 (both Cooper and Nevins would agree on this) is still a man to be reckoned with. Any man who in his own time was not only read but also unanimously praised by such adults as Goethe, Scott, Balzac, Victor Hugo, Francis Parkman,[4] Washington Irving, and Walt Whitman, would seem, at least, to deserve an adult hearing in his old age—whether or not one can go all the way with Professor Nevins "that those who take the pains to read the five novels at-

Reprinted from *The Saturday Review*, August 21, 1954, by permission of the publishers. Copyright 1954 by Saturday Review Associates, New York.

1. *Babbitt... Scarlett O'Hara.* Babbitt is the principal character in Sinclair Lewis' novel by that name, published in 1922. Tarzan, brought up by animals in the African jungle, is the character invented by E. R. Burroughs in 1914 and used in a series of adventure books. Uncle Tom, the old slave in *Uncle Tom's Cabin* by Harriet Beecher Stowe, became the hero of the abolitionist movement. Frank Merriwell, a college-athlete hero in a series of juvenile novels by W. B. Patten, was the idol of American boys in the early part of this century. Scarlett O'Hara is the fiery heroine of Margaret Mitchell's *Gone with the Wind*, published in 1936. 2. *Amy Loveman*, one of the original associate editors of the *Saturday Review*. 3. *Allan Nevins*, professor of history at Columbia University. 4. *Goethe... Parkman*. Goethe (gœ'tə), 1799-1832, is generally considered the greatest German poet. Sir Walter Scott, 1771-1832, was the popular developer of the historical novel in England. Balzac, 1799-1850, and Victor Hugo, 1802-1855, were famous French novelists. Francis Parkman, 1823-1893, was a well-known American historian.

tentively ... will find that they have read nothing less than the nearest approach yet made to an American epic."

Where *The Leatherstocking Saga* concerns Deerslayer himself the text is intact; in other sections the novels are bridged by brief narrative transitions written by Professor Nevins and printed in italics. Not the least interesting are the notes, both Cooper's and Nevins'; in one of these Cooper disputes what later became H. L. Mencken's[5] thesis that the word

Yankee was first used as a disparaging nickname for the Dutch freebooters—*Jan* ("John") plus *Kees* ("cheese")—then later applied by the Dutch themselves to English settlers. Nonsense, says Cooper, the word was Indian in origin; the Indians pronounced the word *English* as *Yengeese.*

Whether cheese or goose, pro-Cooper or

---

5. *H. L. Mencken,* modern American newspaperman and essayist, famous for his debunking of traditional ideals and for his scholarly linguistic study of the American language.

THE MAGAZINE IN AMERICA

The Saturday Review

When Cyrus Curtis bought the New York *Evening Post* in 1924, it was a paper written primarily for the Wall Street financiers, but it contained every Saturday, as a complement to its stock tables, a literary supplement. Mr. Curtis was distressed at the skill which his readers had acquired in flipping the literary supplement out onto the floor with a single, smooth motion as they picked up the Saturday edition of the *Post.* This habit had, in fact, given Wall Street what was known as its "Saturday book look." Curtis dropped the supplement forthwith, and so inadvertently started the *Saturday Review;* for two other business men, Thomas Lamont and Henry Luce, recognizing the quality of the editorial staff of the supplement (H. S. Canby, Amy Loveman, Christopher Morley, William Rose Benét) and sensing the need for a weekly literary review, helped salvage this part of the paper and establish it as the *Saturday Review of Literature.* Under the editorship of Henry Seidel Canby for sixteen years and that of Bernard De Voto (see page 15) for two years, the magazine presented high quality book reviews and some scholarly literary discussions. When Norman Cousins took over the editorship in 1942, the magazine began to broaden its scope. In 1952 it dropped *of Literature* from its title and took all culture for its province. *Newsweek,* commenting on

the history of this expanding magazine, called the *Saturday Review* the book worm that turned.

The turn proved popular, and the circulation of the *Saturday Review* now rivals that of the older magazines of its type, *Harper's* and the *Atlantic.* The critical book reviews remain, setting a standard of excellence. But besides reviewing books SR reviews musical and theatrical events, movies, television programs, chess games, recordings, paintings, and sculpture. The real change, however, came with SR's express intention of dealing with ideas of immediate concern in our modern culture. And now a sizable portion of each issue is devoted to SR *Ideas.* Here one may find a statement by Nobel-Prize-winning Bertrand Russell on the changes that lie ahead in science and society. Nat Hentoff may analyze a new jazz artist. Or Justice William O. Douglas may examine the problems of international law. Besides these weekly features, special sections on topics that the editors feel are of crucial importance in today's world appear at regular intervals. These include discussions of education, communication, and scientific research. And then from time to time there will appear a special issue which may be devoted to a subject ranging from "Photography" to "One Hundred Years of Italy." In short, the *Saturday Review* engages penetrating minds in lively discussion with noted writers.

No one tosses it onto the floor—any more!

pro-Twain, no present-day Yankee can read some of Deerslayer's better lines without coming to the conclusion that the man was indeed carved of epic proportions. If he can say, "Now, I come of a humble stock, though we have white gifts and a white natur'" and "Bumppo has no lofty sound, I admit, and yet men have bumped through the world with it," he can also exclaim when he first gazes at Lake Otsego, "This is grand!—'tis solemn! —'tis an edication of itself to look upon!" Again, when he gazes on the rotting corpses of the Americans and British whom the French allowed to be massacred at Fort William Henry, he can rise to heights. "What say you, Chingachgook, shall the Hurons boast of this to their women when the deep snows come?" Finally, it is a moving scene indeed, when, at the end of *The Prairie*, death comes to the Deerslayer. "A valiant, a just, and a wise warrior has gone on the path which will lead him to the blessed grounds of his people," declares the Indian chief. "Go, my children; remember the just chief of the palefaces and clear your own tracks from briers!"

 TO INCREASE UNDERSTANDING

1. (*a*) How does Nevins' edition of the Leatherstocking Series differ from Cooper's original novels? (If necessary review the information on the Leatherstocking Series, page 196.) (*b*) Why did Nevins make these changes?

2. Each of the following quotations from the review makes a different appeal to the reader. After describing what appeal each makes, explain which quotation would be most apt to lead you to read *The Leatherstocking Saga*.

(*a*) Who is the most famous character, the world over, in American fiction?

(*b*) . . . brand-new, hair-trigger, rim-fire, single-action, five-barrel book. . . .

(*c*) . . . he [Cooper] has been the most widely translated of all American authors.

(*d*) Again, when [Natty Bumppo] gazes on the rotting corpses of Americans and British whom the French allowed to be massacred at Fort William Henry. . . .

(*e*) "What say you, Chingachgook, shall the Hurons boast of this to their women when the deep snows come?"

(*f*) "[The novels are] the nearest approach yet made to an American epic."

CLEVELAND AMORY 1917-

It is not surprising that a man who was born in the fashionable resort town of Nahant, Massachusetts, of a family connected with Boston society should have written *The Proper Bostonians*. In this popular, lightly satiric book Cleveland Amory tried to recapture the faded glory of Boston society.

Prior to the success of his first book, *The Proper Bostonians*, Amory had spent a number of years writing for and editing magazines. While at Harvard he had been president of the undergraduate daily, the *Crimson*. He had been an editor for the *Saturday Evening Post*—the youngest ever hired by that magazine. And he had written many detailed articles on American institutions for various magazines.

Amory published a second book in 1952 called *The Last Resorts* in which he chronicled the exclusive resort towns of early twentieth-century "high society." In 1955 he became an editor once more, this time for the *Saturday Review*, in which the book review printed here appeared on August 21, 1954.

 EXTENDING INTERESTS

Book reviews serve many purposes. At one extreme is the publisher's "blurb," which is a candid attempt to get the reader to buy the book by showing him why he will enjoy it or find it helpful. At the other extreme is the scholarly critique, which attempts a formal, critical analysis and an objective evaluation of the merits of the book. Most book reviews in the magazines and newspapers combine these purposes. Bring to class a review that has interested you in reading a particular book. It may be from a newspaper book section, advertisement, magazine (the *Saturday Review*, the *New Yorker*, or one of the news magazines); or the preface to some literary classic. Summarize the review for the class, explain what type of review it is, and how it stimulated your interest.

As a group activity you and several of your classmates might read different reviews of the same book. Arrange to present to the class your findings as to the different purposes and appeals of reviews from different sources.

Twenty-Twenty Norman Cousins

In Rochester, New York, Whepley & Paul, a firm of opticians, ran an advertisement, which said in part: "You know, Mother, if your child is near-sighted, he needs so much of your special help. It's vitally important that he does what the other kids do. Otherwise, he could easily develop an inferiority complex and turn to books instead of healthy outdoor play . . ."

For the benefit of those mothers who may be terrified by this grim warning, some reassurance may be in order. It isn't necessarily true that only children who have inferiority complexes turn to books. Medical history is liberally sprinkled with the documented cases of children who have read books and yet remained free of serious psychic symptoms. Indeed, they have read books with the full knowledge and consent of their doctors, many of whom have been known to read books themselves without apparent ill effects. Some doctors have asserted that books not only are not harmful; they constitute a form of exercise for the brain, which is something akin to a muscle in terms of its need to be used.

We don't know what "other kids" Messrs. Whepley & Paul may have had in mind, but we assume they are supposed to represent the golden norm. As against this, it is a matter of verifiable record that some children have achieved a remarkable versatility, excelling both in athletics and reading. Even if their ambition is to be sportsmen they need not fear that books will unduly impede their careers. It is said that Mr. G. Tunney was perusing *A Midsummer Night's Dream* by Mr. Shakespeare two hours before he entered the ring where Mr. J. Dempsey, the most ferocious heavyweight hitter in history, was waiting to take a poke at him. Neither his own reading nor Mr. Dempsey's vaunted left hook did much damage to Mr. Tunney, who was still the world's heavyweight champion when the

fight ended. And in baseball, it is reported a major league catcher, Mr. M. Berg, read poems by Dante directly from the Italian between innings. In the evening he read Flaubert in the French.

Another noted sportsman whose name was synonymous for many years with outdoor life eventually became President of the United States. One day when he was asked about his interests Theodore Roosevelt replied that he put reading and outdoor sports at the top of his list.

Speaking of Presidents, it is possible that some of the mothers in Rochester who read the Whepley & Paul advertisement may cherish the hope that they may some day visit their sons in the White House. These mothers will doubtless be glad to know that a book hasn't yet kept a man from becoming President.

Thomas Jefferson had perhaps the finest private library of any American of his time; some of his books were in Latin, Greek, Hebrew, French, and Italian, and he navigated in those languages on his own. Many of Jefferson's colleagues were rather bookish fellows who found their reading most helpful in deciding how best to set up the government of the United States. It is true, of course, that Abraham Lincoln jeopardized his eyesight by insisting on reading late at night by

NORMAN COUSINS 1912-

Norman Cousins' concern with education began early. He took his degree at the Teachers College of Columbia University in 1933, but instead of going into the teaching profession, he became the education editor of the New York *Evening Post*. For five years he served as critic and then editor of *Current History* before succeeding H. S. Canby and Bernard De Voto as another distinguished editor of the *Saturday Review*. In this capacity he has served for over twenty years.

The accompanying editorial shows that Norman Cousins' interest in education has not dulled. Indeed, among the supplements which he established in the magazine, one of the most important is that on education.

flickering candlelight—a fact that may horrify Messrs. Whepley & Paul. This may not be the ideal way to maintain one's 20-20 standing, but it helped Mr. Lincoln to develop the kind of vision that a nation needed in the moment of its greatest ordeal.

We feel justified in mentioning all this not only because many of these distinguished bookmen were robust fellows but because no mother need fear that her son is even vaguely un-American if he likes to read—indoors or outdoors. Some books may even enable a youngster to have a real awareness of what America really means. These books deal with history, biography, even high adventure. The youngster who makes friends with these books will have the most valuable sight of all—he will be able to see clearly into the past in a way that will enable him to make some fairly complicated decisions about the American future.

Knowing how to put a basketball through a hoop is important, of course; but it is also important in our time to know how to keep nations from putting their neighbors through wringers. The muscles of nations have never been bigger or stronger, but the cause of the individual has never been frailer or more precarious. Indeed, we are fast approaching the point where the continuation of the human species may depend more on accident or sheer good luck than upon any far-seeing, intelligent plan or program in which things happen or don't happen because that is the way we want things to be. Books won't provide such a design all by themselves; but they may furnish a better focused view of the problem. They might also help to stimulate and nourish the kind of disciplined, sustained thought that may be even more valuable than bulging power in meeting our problems.

But we must not become too solemn. Books are fun. With each year that passes, the choice of books becomes wider—and readers that much richer. Writers have been writing for thousands of years, building up the resources on which an individual can draw—and thus enlarging the individual's choice. Indeed, one of the most meaningful choices open to a free man in the twentieth century is his choice of what to read, what to know, what to think about, what to enjoy. The youngster who learns something about the art of making such a choice has come into possession of one of the highest gifts that are accessible to the human mind.

Messrs. Whepley & Paul may be fine craftsmen in grinding a lens but they need a little refocusing in order to get a clear view of a child and what it is that gives him complexes. Nor need they fear books, which are so intimately concerned with human perception. The best sight is still insight.

❧ TO INCREASE UNDERSTANDING

1. Of what is Norman Cousins trying to convince his readers in this editorial?

2. Consider the reasoning behind each of the following arguments and the tone in which it is stated. Point out how the argument effectively opposes the position taken in the advertisement through its force as a serious argument, and its tone.

(a) Medical history is liberally sprinkled with documented cases of children who have read books and yet remained free of serious psychic symptoms.

(b) . . . it is reported a major league catcher, Mr. M. Berg, read poems by Dante directly from the Italian between innings.

(c) Thomas Jefferson had perhaps the finest private library of any American of his time.

(d) Some books may even enable a youngster to have a real awareness of what America really means.

 WORDS!

Norman Cousins carries out the satire which pervades "Twenty-Twenty" by using words in both a literal and a figurative sense. When he describes Abraham Lincoln's reading by candlelight, for example, he says, "This may not be the ideal way to maintain one's 20-20 standing, but it helped Mr. Lincoln to develop the kind of *vision* that a nation needed in the moment of its greatest ordeal." What two meanings for *vision* can you supply in this context? With which meaning are the opticians concerned? With which meaning is Cousins concerned? What device does he use to make the literal meaning seem short-sighted? Find at least three other examples in this essay of words used in both their literal and figurative senses. Show in each case how this use of certain words on two levels adds to the effectiveness of the editorial.

Each One Teach One
Frank C. Laubach

A hundred years ago, when James Russell Lowell was editing the new *Atlantic Monthly,* an interview would have seemed strange reading matter to New Englanders accustomed to the personal essays of Holmes, the poetry of Emerson, and formal essays like "The Origin of Didactic Poetry." However, when the *Atlantic* published the following interview in October 1957, it occasioned no surprise. With increasing frequency magazines are making use of the interview technique to present the views of authorities on various subjects with all the immediacy of conversation.

The following interview was originally presented over the St. Louis, Missouri, television station KETC in connection with a conference at Washington University. Professor Houston Smith asked Dr. Laubach the questions he thought all intelligent people would themselves like to ask him. The interview was recorded, then transcribed into print for readers across the nation.

SMITH. In the early sessions of this conference on science and human responsibility, we tried to sharpen up some of the momentous problems which science is posing for man: the problems of lowering the danger of war and rising to the tremendous economic challenges that face us.

Dr. Laubach, I've heard you say that your view on these things is essentially a worm's-eye view. What do you mean by that phrase?

LAUBACH. I mean that I've lived down among those people on the other side of the world who are illiterate—the three fifths of the world who cannot read and write—and I know what they are thinking about. I have lived there a great deal longer than I have lived over here. So I know how they look at you privileged people on this side of the world, and I share, to some extent, their viewpoint. A worm's-eye view is the view from down below, looking up.

SMITH. How many years have you spent among these people?

LAUBACH. Forty-one years. I went out in 1915 to the Philippine Islands, and since 1930 have been traveling all over the world. I have worked in ninety-one countries in Asia and Africa and Latin America.

SMITH. Have you noticed any changes come over these peoples through the years?

LAUBACH. Oh, titanic changes have come over them! When I first started, they had their heads down, they had no hope, they were in despair. But all that is changed now. There is a tremendous new determination on the part of all these people who represent three fourths of the human race; they are determined to come up.

SMITH. What has caused this change?

LAUBACH. There have been a great many forces playing on them. For example, our new scientific discoveries have enabled us to make the thousands of isolated communities into one world. We have swift steamships, we have automobiles, we have the airplane, we have motion pictures. Missionaries have been spreading a gospel of the dignity of every human being all over the globe. Our soldiers have gone to all parts of the world, and the natives have seen our tourists and businessmen. They have heard of Woodrow Wilson's

FRANK C. LAUBACH 1884-

Frank C. Laubach has aptly been described as a teacher to the world. Over forty years ago, in connection with his duties as a Congregational missionary to the Moro tribe in the Philippines, he began to teach reading. His enthusiastic students became so numerous that Dr. Laubach appealed to the chief of the tribe for help. The chief ordered that everyone who learned would have to teach others —or be executed! Since that time Dr. Laubach has carried the "each one teach one" program around the world, and in doing so has been responsible for teaching nearly one hundred million people to read. He has described his adventures in a book, *Thirty Years with the Silent Billions.*

Fourteen Points.[1] They have also heard about the Four Freedoms[2] and our democratic idea that all men have a right to "life and liberty and happiness." All these things, together with the Japanese slogan of "Asia for the Asiatics," have encouraged the idea of independence from Europe. And then the Communists came along and agitated these people, promising to fulfill the desires which we had inspired.

These forces were working among the masses, and suddenly, right after the Second World War, all of them seemed to explode at once. In the last eleven years we have had a new world, of which most Americans are very dimly conscious—a world in which three fourths of the human race suddenly decided to march toward progress, toward better things, out of hunger up toward the prosperity that we have.

SMITH. Is there anything that we can do to help them in this march?

LAUBACH. Not only *can* we help them, but we *must* help them. They know that we have half of the world's wealth, and if we do not help them they will hate us. They will seize the hand of anybody who offers to help them. So if we help them with their agriculture, they will be our friends. If we help them with their health and with their economic conditions and especially with their education, they will love us. They know that they are hungry and destitute because they are ignorant. They know we have secrets that enable us to get ahead, whereas they lack those secrets, and so they stay down. Therefore they want our secrets.

SMITH. Are you telling us that what they want primarily is not our food surplus—of which we have considerable—but they want instead something which will enable them to help themselves?

LAUBACH. Yes. They don't want to be paupers. They don't want to need charity. They want to come up. They won't settle for anything else. We ought to send them our surplus food and clothing as a stopgap, until we can do something more permanent for them. I believe in doing that, but it is not what they really want. They want to know

why we have so much and they have so little. They want our secrets.

SMITH. Now this, I assume, is where your world literacy program comes in. Is that right?

LAUBACH. Yes. Because, as you can see very well, the beginning of this education that they demand and are clamoring for is literacy. They not only want this for their children; they also want it for themselves. So we must teach them to read as the very first step.

In all of these countries, at least seventy per cent of the people are illiterate; in some, illiteracy is as high as ninety per cent. A little fringe of ten per cent at the top have the education. They have the money. They have the power. But there is not enough money to educate all the ninety per cent who are illiterate. They could not afford to build school buildings, or train and pay schoolteachers even for the children. But these adults who are on the march are saying, "Educate our children, but also educate us, and do it now. Or, if you don't, we will blow up!" Our American educational methods are not cheap enough for those backward areas. Indeed our own state governments are appealing for federal aid. Our highly expensive educational process is hopeless in countries with a high rate of illiteracy.

SMITH. So, a new method is required?

LAUBACH. Yes. We have got to prepare textbooks which can be taught by untrained teachers who are just barely able to read. We are making textbooks so easy to teach that the teachers do not need to go to school even for one year. If they can read our textbook, they can teach it to somebody else. The students get together and help one another. One of them knows a little more than the others, and he tells them what he knows. They can do that, you see, without any pay, and they can do it at home; so no school building is needed. For the past twenty-five years I have been

1. *Woodrow Wilson's Fourteen Points*, President Wilson's statement of the aims of the Allies, made during World War I. Included were proposals to establish equality of trade, restore former boundaries between countries, and establish a league of nations to protect the rights of small countries. 2. *Four Freedoms*, President Franklin D. Roosevelt's statement of the aims of the United States and the United Nations, made in 1941, including as one proposal freedom from want for all nations.

traveling from one country to another, working with educators and missionaries and others, making lessons that are easy to teach. Would it interest you to see what those lessons look like?

SMITH. I think it would.

LAUBACH. I can show you one of them. This is a lesson in English.

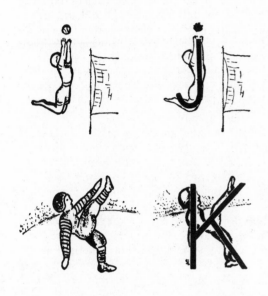

We associate the sound of a letter with a word—*Jumping*, for example. This man is jumping for a ball. He has his feet behind him. The hook on the letter *j* looks like his feet turned back. The ball over his head is the dot over *j*. *Kicking*—this man has his leg high, kicking the football, and the letter *k* has its leg high up like the football player's.

By associating every letter with a picture, we teach the sounds of the letters. After that, we have a short story using these words. The book almost teaches itself, because we go from the known to the unknown by very short steps; from the known picture to the word, and from the word to the first sound. In that way we teach the phonetics of languages. It requires only four or five days for very phonetic languages. In other languages it takes ten or twenty days, depending upon the difficulties encountered.

SMITH. Then in the course of two weeks the people might begin to get a working, reading knowledge of their language?

LAUBACH. Yes. In most languages of the world there is only one sound for a letter. In our English language we have eight sounds for *a*, and we have fifteen ways to pronounce *o*. Our vowels are maddening chaos. I don't see how anybody learns English when he is grown up without going to a madhouse. But in those languages where there is only one sound for each vowel, the moment the people know all the sounds of the letters, they can pronounce any word in their language. Where I began this work, in Mindanao among the Moros, one of the Malay languages, called Maranaw, had only sixteen sounds, and we taught them in two days—eight sounds a day. Then the people could pronounce any word in the Maranaw language without ever making a mistake. That's more than anybody in the world can do in English, I think, because you never know what to do with a new vowel. In fact, I've never really decided how to pronounce my own name!

SMITH. What about the content of what you teach?

LAUBACH. As soon as they have learned these sounds, which is in a matter of days, we try to give them something that will be helpful in their everyday life struggle.

In India, for example, we have been coöperating with what is called the Community Development Project. The Indian government, with the help of American Point Four[3] money, is training men to go out and improve conditions in the villages. I helped the government prepare lessons for those projects. We asked Indian and American experts, "What are you trying to tell the villagers? You know what they need, but they cannot understand your technical language. You tell us, and we'll write it down in simple language in a graded series, and thus we will get your knowledge across to them. We will be the bridge."

The health experts said, "Tell them they

3. *American Point Four*, the fourth point in President Truman's program to promote peace and freedom, proposed in his inaugural address of 1949. The Point Four Program was designed to give technical assistance to underdeveloped nations.

don't eat the right foods. When they eat a lopsided diet all the time, they are not strong and they are not well." So we say in our textbook, "Anand, the Wise Man, was wise because he learned to read. He knew what foods to eat in order to be strong."

SMITH. *Anand* is a man's name, isn't it?

LAUBACH. Yes. The name means "lucky." It's the most common name in India, equivalent to *John* in this country.

The first lesson that Anand read said, "You are not eating the right food." Then it told him what to eat; it says he began to eat that food and he got stronger.

In India, and all over the illiterate world, practically every illiterate has intestinal diseases like bacillary or amoebic dysentery. So the third lesson in our textbook says, "You are this way because the flies are contaminating your food. They breed out in the filth in the field, and then they fly onto your food, and their legs have these disease germs." It tells them, "Kill the flies with DDT; put it on the walls of your house; cover your food so that the flies can't get to it; cover your babies' mouths so flies cannot light on them. And bury the filth."

These illiterate people have no latrines, so the flies breed in the fields. The story says that Anand tried all this and took the medicine the book told him to take, and he and his whole village became free from dysentery. Today, as the villagers read these secrets, they say, "If Anand could do that, I can, too." Among many other diseases, I might mention one more that will make you smile. Everybody in the illiterate areas of the world is scratching. They have itch, and they don't know what to do about it. So Anand read in his book about itch. It said, "If you put gamaxene on your mat [they have no beds] and on your clothes and all over your body, the next day you won't scratch." Gamaxene cures the itch in a day.

Now, let us turn to agriculture. That's the greatest problem. Anand read in our textbook that the reason his land is not feeding him enough is that he does not feed his land; it is starving to death. In India there are millions of cattle, but the people burn their cow manure for fuel. The women and children make little cakes of cow manure, plaster them against a wall, let them dry, and then use them for cooking fuel. They have no wood and no oil and no gas; they have only cow manure for fuel to cook with. So this book says to Anand, "You should plant rapid-growing firewood along your irrigation canal, and then you should throw this manure, along with all the filth from the ground and all the leaves, into a compost pit, leave it there for three months, then put it on your land. Feed your land, and your land will feed you." Anand tried it, and you know very well what soil does when it is fertilized. The change is miraculous.

Then Anand read that you can get better seeds from the government—hybrid seeds of corn, wheat, and rice—and better fruit seedlings. So Anand goes to the government store and gets them. The crops are many times better. All the people in his village imitate him and get wonderful crops. Then Anand read that the little wooden plow he has, which goes an inch into the ground some of the time and much of the time does not penetrate at all, should have an iron point on it. So he gets an iron point for his plow from the government, and it goes three inches into the soil and strikes virgin dirt that has never been turned over before.

Then Anand reads about "green" manure. There are many leguminous plants which put nitrogen into the soil, such as beans and alfalfa and clover. Anand does not read big words in the textbook, but he gets the ideas in very easy Hindi.[4] Illiterate people need to apply only about five secrets of agriculture and they can raise just as much food on their land as we can on ours.

SMITH. And so the person reading this thinks, "If Anand can do it, I can." Is that right?

LAUBACH. Yes, that's it. When the expert comes to see the peasants who have read our secrets, he doesn't have to sell these modern ideas or explain them in his difficult vocabulary. He merely says, "What would you like

4. *Hindi*, a dialect of Hindustani, the common language spoken in northern India.

me to do for you?" And they reply, "Get that iron point for our plows; help us get those better seeds; help us to crossbreed our cattle with those better breeds that we've read about." All the expert has to do is comply, and he gets exactly the results he wants. So what seemed nearly impossible becomes easy.

SMITH. What has been the response of governments to your program?

LAUBACH. Wonderful—and I will tell you the reason. The governments in the less developed parts of the world are not so afraid of Russia and China as we are. They are afraid of their own masses, because these masses are boiling with unrest and are threatening to overthrow the governments unless they do something to help the people out of their poverty. The masses clamor for literacy and basic secrets.

The governments are very anxious for a method that is cheap enough for them to be able to teach their many illiterates, and so the governments are coming after us to learn our "each one teach one" method. I have, myself, helped the ministries of education in sixty-two countries at their official invitations.

SMITH. You've actually done this in ninety-one countries; and in sixty-two of them you have had official status?

LAUBACH. Yes. I've been with missions and other private agencies in the other countries.

SMITH. Do you have any idea how many persons, perhaps, you have been helping by this?

LAUBACH. Well, this is only a "guesstimate." Nobody can contradict it because nobody knows for certain; a campaign like this gets out of hand and becomes almost impossible to count. About every day we get letters from some place we didn't know was using our method. At least sixty million have learned to read, perhaps one hundred million.

SMITH. What could be done to facilitate a program like this?

LAUBACH. A tremendous lot could be done. You must realize that there are at least a billion adults who cannot write their own names, and a billion and a half who are unable to read books or newspapers. Our progress thus far is very small compared to the tremendous

need. Our government is doing something, and literacy organizations are doing what they can. Governments in these countries would like us to establish schools like Literacy Village in India to train their village workers. Last year Literacy Village trained eight hundred people for the Indian government, and many more for the Gandhi Movement, UNESCO,[5] Christian missions, and the Servants of India. Other countries want similar literacy schools to train their village workers to go out and supervise the "each one teach one" program, and to write books that will help their people.

One thing America can do is to send a very much larger number of people who are experts in literacy and simple journalism out where they are needed.

And then there's another thing that I hope will happen. A million American soldiers are stationed abroad. Why don't we start American troops who are in foreign lands teaching illiterates? Teach the servicemen how to use these books—they could learn in a week easily. They are now learning foreign languages. Then in their leisure hours have them put a book under their arm and go down the streets and say to somebody, "Would you like to learn to read?" These illiterate people would all go crazy with delight. It's wonderful to teach people, because they are so grateful!

Why, I ask, are we wasting the talents of young men in training for a war that must never happen? Why are we not using them in the war for these hungry multitudes who are making up their minds whether to come up by the know-how route or in a pathway of blood?

5. UNESCO, the United Nations Educational, Scientific, and Cultural Organization.

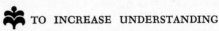 TO INCREASE UNDERSTANDING

1. (a) According to Frank Laubach, what are the people of underdeveloped nations thinking about? (b) How has the attitude of these people changed in this century? (c) What factors does Dr. Laubach feel account for the change? (d) When did the change take place?

2. (a) To what, according to Dr. Laubach, do these people attribute their low standard of living?

(b) What does he think these people demand of us?
(c) What does he think they threaten if they cannot get what they need?

3. What makes some languages easier and faster to teach than others?

4. (a) Why can the governments of the countries in which Dr. Laubach works not set up an educational system like that of the United States? (b) How does Laubach's program avoid the difficulties of a more formal educational system?

5. Many people in these countries have lived in much the same way for centuries. How does the ability to read change the lives of these people? Be specific in your answer.

6. Dr. Laubach believes that the United States should (a) "send them [these people] surplus food and clothing as a stopgap," and (b) send experts to these countries to help them institute educational systems like those he describes. What are his reasons for advocating such a program? Do you agree or disagree with his reasoning?

7. By his skillful questioning Professor Smith plays an important part in creating an interesting, informative interview. (a) Reread Smith's questions and describe the order into which he guides Dr. Laubach's information. (b) By the question "Anand is a man's name, isn't it?" the interviewer has Laubach explain something that may not be clear to the reader or the listener. Find at least two other questions which have this purpose.

The Gentleman of Culture Vannevar Bush

Since the war we have witnessed in this country a wave of anti-intellectualism. This is nothing new; in a country with a pioneering background, which prides itself on its practicality, it is normal and natural that emphasis on the manly virtues should at times carry with it a distrust of the value of aesthetics or theory. Yet the form that our national prejudice has taken this time, exemplified best perhaps by the invention of the term *egghead* as a label of opprobrium, is not only injurious to the public welfare and the true enjoyment of the finer things of life, it is also positively dangerous.

The reason for the danger is that we are in a grim contest with a skillful and ruthless antagonist who has not burdened himself with this liability. He cannot compete effectively, in a complex world of air transport and guided missiles, by being merely tough-minded and practical. It is well, therefore, that we should examine some of the reasons for the difference in attitude, and take stock of why—with of course notable exceptions—we hold forth to youth ideals which differ from those which today inspire the youth of Russia.

We can readily discern some of the causes of our own attitudes. Science, during the war, produced results which completely revolutionized the art of war—which in fact rendered obsolete the concept of great war as an implement of national policy, and did so by techniques which identified all-out war with national suicide. Radar, proximity fuses, guided missiles, the atom bomb, did not appear because some bright inventor built models in his garage; they burst into being because a long background of fundamental science, mathematical theory, and controlled basic experimentation[1] rendered it possible under the spur of war to reap results in the form of distinctly practical, though terrifying applications. Lest I be misunderstood, let me interpolate here that the result was inevitable, given the greatly accelerated march of science: had there been no A-bomb, great wars in the old sense would still have become unthinkable to any sane people, because of devastating chemical or biological weapons. But our whole people suddenly appreciated for the first time the power of man's concentrated efforts to understand and control the forces of nature. We were appalled by what we witnessed, and made afraid. The result was a mixed one. In certain circles, and in the minds of some youth, there was an urge to emulate and a

1. *basic experimentation*, that is, as opposed to "practical" research aimed only at developing a specific product.

tendency to raise the scientist on a pedestal, which he did not always occupy with grace and modesty. The overriding result, however, was a reaction against all that such things implied, and a revulsion, sometimes unconscious, from a complex existence—futile though an urge to return to the simple life was bound to be.

There was another reason, and perhaps a deeper one. This country has experienced the greatest prosperity that any people in history has ever enjoyed. It extends far beyond the availability to the great majority of the population of gadgetry—automobiles, washing machines, television. It has had its more serious side: public health has improved, disease has been conquered, new law has protected the humble and unfortunate against some of the vicissitudes of nature and even against the cruelty of his fellow men. We have acquired leisure, so that the skilled mechanic among us, if he merely knows how to use it, is more blessed in this regard than the philosopher of ancient Greece, whose great accomplishments were possible only because chance placed him at the top of the pyramid of a slave society.[2]

Just as we really began to enjoy our new-found prosperity, we were suddenly confronted with the specter of another great power armed to the teeth with modern weapons, which proclaims for all to hear that it intends to conquer the world, by subversion and infiltration, if possible, and by economic contest and the threat of war. We are told that if we hope to counter this threat, we must forgo some of the pleasant things we anticipated, and buckle down to a tough grind of competition. We do not want to do any such thing, and our reaction is to live partly in a dream world, where there are no threats and no crises. One aspect of this, on the part of many of the population, is to turn against those individuals and those ideas which exemplify the inherent nature of the struggle we face. For our contest will not be one of mere hard work and application; it will involve the most abstruse intellectual effort.

One aspect of this reaction is of especial significance. On the one hand, it has over-emphasized science, in comparison with other intellectual attributes which make up the full man. On the other hand, it has fanned the flames of bigotry, doubted the loyalty of scientists as a group of citizens, and added to the present tendency to discount and ridicule those whose contributions to our stock of knowledge are most basic and fundamental. Fear is never rational in its acts. The search for an escape from grim truth will always find excuses. When danger threatens long enough, and insistently enough, it ends by being disregarded by wishful thinkers. All this can explain the presence of anti-intellectualism among us; the wonder is that we have not had more of it.

Russia presents a paradox in this regard. On the one hand, we see the cruelty and arbitrariness of the police state, as in the recent

2. *philosopher of ancient Greece ... slave society.* The extraordinary cultural accomplishments of ancient Greece were only possible because a small segment of the population enjoyed leisure time made possible through the use of slave labor to provide the necessities of living.

VANNEVAR BUSH 1890-

The New Englander who headed the highly important Office of Scientific Research and Development during World War II became interested in mathematics and science while taking degrees at Tufts, Harvard, and Massachusetts Institute of Technology. As vice-president of M.I.T. and later as president of the Carnegie Institution in Washington, Vannevar Bush developed a number of important electronic machines. One of these was the first of the giant electronic brains. This differential analyzer solved crucial problems during the war.

Dr. Bush proved himself an extraordinary administrator as well as a scientist. Even before the war he became aware of the necessity for some nation-wide organization to coördinate the work of scientific research and to administer funds for that work. The OSRD was the result; to it was entrusted, among other activities, the administration of the early phases of the atomic bomb project. As director of this organization Dr. Bush's ability to get politicians, Army and Navy officials, and some thirty thousand scientists to work together was directly influential in the Allied victory. The style of the accompanying speech makes evident some of the persuasive skill for which Dr. Bush is justly famous.

case of Pasternak.[3] On the other hand, there is no doubt that among the youth of Russia there is a drive and an enthusiasm which is something we would immensely admire, were it only guided by a truly democratic system. For two governments really responsible to public opinion will never deliberately go to war, as the art of war now stands.

Why the enthusiasm, in Russia especially, for matters of the intellect? Why do youngsters earnestly delve into tough subjects—physics, chemistry, mathematics—while our youngsters, many of them, avoid hard intellectual work almost completely? Why is the local teacher in Russia a man of distinction in his community, while our secondary school teachers have lost much of the sincere respect that was accorded them a generation ago?

Russia is by no means a communistic state; it departed from this ideal of Marxism long ago and is simply a totalitarian state in the hands of a self-perpetuating oligarchy.[4] The old theory—from each according to his ability, to each according to his need—was thrown overboard simply because it did not work.[5] For example, a professor in Russia is paid twice as much as one in this country, if measured as a multiple of what is paid a common laborer. Russia has copied from us some of the essential elements of our system, without incurring all the liabilities which are the price we pay for freedom under democracy. To this is due the vigorous surge forward we have witnessed in such matters as winning the race to place a satellite in orbit. Some time ago there was extended to their scientists and laboratories freedom of action, in the choice and pursuance of scientific programs, fully as great as exists here. It was even extended in marked degree to essential industry.

It is hard for us to realize that the youth of Russia is basking in a new-found freedom, that its real accomplishments are the results of an exuberance of youth, yet it seems to be true. In spite of the crime of Hungary,[6] in spite of the treachery and lies, which must be witnessed and grasped by the intelligent among the Russian people, it is apparent that the taste of freedom for a people which has been ground down for centuries[7] can provide a stimulant which is unmatched. Thus the young men and women of Russia face life seriously, and with courage and determination. It is this spirit with which we compete. If the government of Russia were like our own, or like many of the governments of the free world, the competition could be a salutary one, devoted to raising standards of living and banishing disease—and lifting the level of life in the whole world in doing so. But the Russian government is a barbarous one, and it holds, and will hold for a long time, complete control of its people and their destiny, without their consent and even without their knowledge of what it does. This it is that renders the contest grim.

The outcome will not depend merely on the race to produce weapons of greater and more instantaneous destructive power, although we must indeed, for our security, strive mightily to excel in this field. It will not depend essentially upon an economic struggle, seeking to win adherence of backward peoples by catering to their needs and seeking to isolate us in

---

3. *Pasternak*, Boris Leontovitch Pasternak, 1890-1960, Russian poet and novelist. Because of his insistence that a writer should not be bound by government policy, most of his writings were suppressed in Russia. When his famous novel, *Doctor Zhivago*, was published outside of Russia, the government refused to let him accept the Nobel Prize tendered him for his novel and his poetry. By expelling him from the writers union and the Party also subjected him to a degree of personal and intellectual isolation. He died of cancer in June 1960.   4. *Russia . . . oligarchy*. The Marxist ideal, as envisioned by Karl Marx (1818-1883), called for an eventual elimination of government; but Russia today has a government of extremely broad powers vested in a small group of committees with interlocking memberships. Since election to these committees requires party membership and is several removes from the popular elections, a group of skillful politicians can remain in power almost indefinitely. 5. *The old theory . . . did not work*. Unlike Marx's political ideal, the economic ideal advocated by him was actually tried in Russia. From 1917 to 1921 the new Soviet government attempted to take all the produce of the entire country and distribute it as it was needed. Because there remained no incentive to work, the entire economy ground to a halt. Russia was thus forced to introduce graduated pay scales and other "capitalist" incentives to stimulate economic growth.   6. *crime of Hungary*, the ruthless suppression by Russian tanks and troops of the revolution attempted by the Hungarian people against their satellite government in October 1956.   7. *ground down for centuries*. Russia maintained a feudal social structure under the Czars through much of the nineteenth century. While the serfs gained their freedom during the fifteenth century in most of Europe, the Russian serfs were not freed until 1861.

world trade. It will depend, in the last analysis, upon the attitude of our people, and especially of our young men—whether they can face resolutely the threat and the challenge, whether they will strive to excel, vigorously, untiringly, skillfully. In particular, it depends upon whether our youth who are gifted with intellectual talent will develop it to the utmost, with the respect and approbation of their fellows.

Let me emphasize at once that this involves much more than merely the training of scientists and engineers, more than leadership in this country in every field of fundamental science, important though that is. In fact, I believe that one serious fault of the Russian educational system, which they will later regret, is its narrowness. We need well-rounded men as the leaders of the next generation—skilled in science, law, medicine; skilled in organization and the complex relations between men in a modern society, with an understanding of history and an appreciation of art at its best. True, we need specialists as well, and many of these, if they are to extend the boundaries of knowledge, must devote themselves so assiduously to their specialties that they will have little time for great breadth of understanding. But even these must live in an intellectual atmosphere which is both broad and deep, where true accomplishment of seasoned minds is everywhere respected, and where youth will be caused to seek to emulate the full man. In the creation of this atmosphere we can all have a part.

But just how do we move to alter the atmosphere, in particular to hold before youth sound ideals amid all the clamor of the modern age? Certainly it will help if we clarify our own thinking, and the adult approach today is far from free of prejudices and misconceptions. In the space we have, it will be impossible to examine many of these, and to be explicit I will confine myself to just one. Let us examine the term *cultured gentleman.* Just what do we mean by it? Does it hold for youth the image of true accomplishment to which he would aspire; do many of our youngsters seek to earn the title, or respect the individual who does above the popular heroes of

the screen or the playing field? And if not, what is wrong?

There are two misconceptions or fallacies in popular parlance in regard to just this one term. Let us take the last one first. Virile youth looks forward to a life of positive action; the boy, if he is normal, aims to develop his masculine qualities and to assert himself in one way or another, not crudely, if he is well guided, but certainly not weakly. He has no wish to be gentle, if that means to avoid the contests of life. But the word *gentleman* has nothing whatever to do with gentleness. It is derived from the same Latin root as is *genetics,* and its early significance was merely "of noble birth." Moreover the gentlemen of England were long those who were entitled to wear coats of arms under the rules of heraldry, and they were primarily second sons of noble families, who, under the rules of primogeniture, could not inherit estates or titles, and who hence went into the army. Their careers there were not notable for gentleness. Somewhat later the significance became altered and extended, and all those were included as gentlemen who took a lofty view of life, as opposed to the crassness of the market place, and sometimes merely those who were among the few whom chance allowed to enjoy leisure.

The gentleman is always courteous, even when annoyed, to those who cannot meet him on even terms. To those who can, he is still courteous, but in a way which signifies that he is perfectly willing to enter combat, orally or even physically, should that become necessary. In other words, he is habitually polite because he can afford to be, and because he knows enough psychology to recognize that habitual roughness or belligerency usually appears as compensation for self-doubt. Incidentally, some of the finest gentlemen, in regard to preserving outward equanimity under stress or provocation, are found on our fields of sport, and one of the great values of competitive sport is that it encourages the development of this quality in those who are inherently capable of developing it.

The term also implies pride, often concealed under a façade of formal modesty, but nevertheless genuine. It is the pride of the individual who is not afraid of the world or the men in it, and is based on a confidence that there are areas of accomplishment in which he can on occasion excel, even if it be in such minor activity as the making of a witty after-dinner speech, or the intimate knowledge of Sandwich glass.

The central characteristic of the gentleman, however, is that he embodies, or thinks he embodies, culture, however he may define it.

And this leads me to discuss the word *culture*. What do we mean by it today?

Unfortunately, it still carries an aura of smugness and conceit, and it is readily possible to realize how this came about. The evidence of a cultural group used to be, even in this country, the password which certified that an individual belonged to a privileged class. If he could turn a Latin phrase skillfully, he belonged and was admitted to the best circles. But if he violated the accepted Latin pronunciation of the day, even though that pronunciation would probably not have been understood in ancient Rome, he was promptly cast into outer darkness. And this exclusive class played into one another's hands. The son of the old family, if he adhered to a set of artificial standards of speech and manner, inherited the leadership of a business, or was rapidly advanced in the business of a friend, often quite irrespective of talent or merit. The girl who married "beneath her station" was ostracized. We must admit also that financial matters, national as well as industrial, were often manipulated to perpetuate the power of the select group. Again, before we are too harsh, let us remember that the alternative might have been worse, and that, without this stabilizer, the young democracy might well have foundered, to be succeeded by a system which would have concentrated power in a still smaller and more selfish group, or even in a dictator. But with this heritage, of which too many traces still remain, it is easy to see why culture came to have a note of exclusiveness about it, and why rugged individuals, born on the wrong side of the tracks, snorted when it was mentioned; why the pioneer, carving out a home for his family with his ax, came to regard culture as the symbol of the social constraints from which he sought to escape. No doubt it is some of this same attitude which accounts for the anti-intellectualism we have seen, and which we cannot afford.

From this history probably emerged the belief, held even today in many quarters, that knowledge to be cultural in nature must also be utterly useless. It must be aesthetic and not practical. Thus the ability to distinguish at once a genuine Sheraton chair from a recent copy would be a part of culture, and to recite the differences between Adams and Hepplewhite[8] still more so. But a knowledge of the evolution of woodworking tools, which caused the concomitant evolution of furniture styles, which in fact ushered in modern mass production, would not be considered cultural at all. To attend a symphony concert would be a cultural action, but to listen to transmitted or reproduced music would be a relatively low form of amusement. This particular prejudice has now almost entirely disappeared, for reproduced music can render a more accurate impression, free as it is from audience noise or distortion of instrument balance due to bad acoustics, than can be had by sitting in a crowded hall. The latter does give more in one way, for the enthusiasm of an audience can be contagious. But one is as cultural as the other.

True culture consists of a broad grasp of the world in which we live and of the people who inhabit it, their history, their hopes and aspirations, their joys and sorrows. It includes a broad understanding of the current scene, industrial, political, social. It is by nature interpretive, questioning, analytical. In short, it is the true basis of wisdom.

Let me illustrate by discussing science briefly, for science is emphatically an important part of culture today, as scientific knowledge and its applications are transforming the world, and conditioning every aspect of the relations between men and nations. I will take just two examples.

Can a man who is truly cultured know nothing whatever about solid state physics, about the fascinating way in which electrons

---

8. *Sheraton chair ... Adams and Hepplewhite*, furniture made by three late eighteenth-century English designers.

and holes move through a semi-conductor,[9] and the ways in which their progress can be controlled? If he is a layman, we can hardly expect him to grasp the mathematics involved. Still he can understand the fundamentals just as the pioneer grasped many of the subtleties of the flight of a bullet, although not versed in ballistics. And it is necessary that the rudiments at least be grasped, in order to view intelligently some basic trends of the time. For devices based on solid state physics promise to alter completely many of the ways in which we generate and utilize electric energy for our purposes. Man has already relegated to the machine many of the repetitive processes of his thinking to free his mind for those functions which the machine cannot perform, and which constitute the attributes by which he is distinguished from the other mammals. Moreover, the day is coming when man at his best will be far more able to cope with the complexities of life under modern civilization, by reason of the extension of his mental power, through arts which will transform human relations as thoroughly as did the advent of printing. This is a revolution in the offing far more important than the extension of automation in industry. It is a trend which it is vital to grasp if one would be alert to the probable evolution of our accelerating civilization. Yet it cannot really be understood, even in its generality, without a sound, if limited, grasp of the physics on which it is based.

The other example comes from the field of astronomy, the science of the cosmos, of matters external to our little earth. The air is full today of discussions of space projectiles and of extravagant predictions on space flight. This is certainly a subject of military significance; it even has valid scientific content, although I believe this is usually exaggerated. But why concentrate on this one aspect of the whole subject? From a practical military aspect, we must. But from the standpoint of deep intellectual interest there are other branches of astronomy which to me are far more fascinating. The sequence of stars, the process by which stars are born, grow old, disintegrate in appalling explosions, extending their life history over billions of years, is daily becoming

unfolded for our grasp and our awe. The arguments of the cosmologists, with their red shift and expanding universe, their non-Euclidian geometry, their closed but unlimited volumes, their strange interlocking of time and space,[10] their examination of galaxies whose light started toward us before the mountains were formed or the seas condensed, these are speculations and analyses which open and expand man's mind. They are far more fascinating than the gropings of the ancient philosophers, for they are subject to check by experimental observation, and to the searching test of mathematical analysis. Do they have practical implication? Well, the same conversion of mass to energy which keeps the stars radiating also now turns some wheels in our factories, and may well render it possible for man to continue his great adventure long after he has exhausted his fossil fuels.[11] Who would live today and ignore this, the most magnificent example of the power of man's thought about his position in the cosmos and his destiny that has been consummated since he first learned to dominate nature by the uniqueness of his brain?

What is a cultured gentleman? What is he at his best? He is a man who aspires to wisdom, because of his keen interest and broad knowledge of all that conditions his relations with his fellows and their relations with one another; who goes beyond this and strives to add to the sum total of human intellectual accomplishments, and to establish thinking on a higher and broader plane. He is a man who is modest and kind to the humble and the unfortunate. Above all, he is a man with a mission to minister to the welfare of the society in which he lives, and who takes a just pride in his guidance and his leadership. He is a member of that modern select group upon which the continuance and further develop-

---

9. *semi-conductor*, a crystal which permits electricity to move in one direction only. Its most familiar use is the transistor.   10. *red shift ... time and space*, a group of concepts introduced by physicists and mathematicians in this century.   11. *fossil fuels*, coal, petroleum, and gas, all thought to be formed by the decomposition of organic matter under pressure and without access to air over a period of geologic ages.

ment of our free way of life intimately depends.

To be a cultured gentleman, one does not need to wear clothes cut in the latest fashion, or to be able to judge the vintage of a choice wine. He does not need to command a nicety of language, or a superior manner at a social gathering. Basically, he needs to have a deep spirit of altruism, an urge to aid his fellow men, and especially thus to aid by his depth and breadth of thought and his skill in imparting his ideals to those about him. He may not call himself a cultured gentleman, or allow others to do so; he may dislike the term, for which there is no good equivalent, because of its historic connotations. But he must aspire to be a leader, and a leader whose eminence is not based on low cleverness, or a demagoguery, or financial power, or clannishness of any form, but which rather is based upon presenting to his fellows ideals and programs which they will recognize and be willing to follow because of their inherent merit. He needs to be a forceful individual to be heard amid the discordant clamor. Above all, he needs to be one who will have the interest, the patience, the perseverance to attain a broad and deep grasp of the current scene in all its complicated ramifications, and to ponder thereon, as the true basis for wisdom.

This is an ideal which we can honestly and emphatically hold before our gifted youth with the firm conviction that it is worthy of their steel, and that if they fully grasp it, they will then be inspired. Throughout our history we have had many citizens of this stamp; otherwise we would not now as a nation be what we are. They are all about us today, in positions of eminence and in humble stations where their influence is bounded but none the less salutary. Whether we continue to prosper, whether we remain secure, whether we develop in this country a life truly worth living, depends upon whether in the next generation there are enough such men, sufficiently articulate, sufficiently powerful in honest and admirable ways, to guide us around the rocks in our path and lead us to the heights.

 TO INCREASE UNDERSTANDING

1. Vannevar Bush states that "since the war we have witnessed in this country a wave of anti-intellectualism." Explain how he holds each of the following factors responsible for this attitude: (a) pioneering background, (b) advances in the technology of science, (c) the grim contest with Russia in a time of national prosperity.

2. (a) Explain why you agree or disagree with Dr. Bush that there is widespread anti-intellectualism in this country. (b) Do you agree that anti-intellectualism is a bad thing? Why?

3. What does Bush mean by saying that Russia is not a communist state?

4. (a) Why, according to Bush, are the Russian youth enthusiastically pro-intellectual? (b) What basic fault does Bush find in the Russian educational system?

5. Bush examines three factors that he believes will determine the outcome of our contest with Russia. (a) What are they? (b) Which does he feel is the most important? (c) Explain why you agree or disagree with his conclusions.

6. Dr. Bush attempts to redefine the concept of the cultured gentleman. (a) What is his purpose in so doing? (b) How does his concept differ from the usual concept of the gentleman? (c) What interests would such a person cultivate in order to become cultured? (d) Would your conception of the cultured gentleman differ from Bush's, include other qualities, leave out some he lists, or have a different emphasis? Explain.

7. Dr. Bush's speech is more than a detached analysis of recent social history; it is an argument aimed at getting something done. (a) What is it that Dr. Bush hopes can be achieved? (b) Explain why you do or do not think Dr. Bush's speech might prove to be effective in promoting this.

EXTENDING INTERESTS

Vannevar Bush mentions a number of mathematical and scientific concepts with which you may not be familiar—red shift, non-Euclidian geometry, closed but unlimited volumes, interlocking of time and space, conversion of mass to energy, and so forth. Prepare a report to the class on any one of these subjects, including the background material necessary for understanding. You will probably want to use some good popularization of modern science such as George Gamow's *One, Two, Three, . . . Infinity.*

THE LARGER VIEW

Today most articles and essays make their first appearance in magazines. Look through a number of recent issues of good magazines, preferably those that have been discussed earlier in the book. Read some of the articles that appeal to you particularly. Prepare one for class discussion, using the following questions as a guide.

1. How would you classify this piece of writing—informative article, formal or informal essay, or editorial?

2. What purpose did the author apparently have in mind in writing the article?

3. What do you know about the author? Does his background or reputation add weight to what he says?

4. (*Informative Article*) Do you see any evidence of the author's personal viewpoint in the way he presents the facts, as you did, for example, in "The Three"? Do you feel his viewpoint is borne out by the facts, or does it distort them? Explain.

5. (*Essay*) Do you find a personalized style—an unusual or surprising use of words that might be characteristic of this author—as you did, for example, in E. B. White's "Walden"? Demonstrate with some examples.

6. (*Editorial*) Is the issue raised controversial? Could you present arguments to defend the position the author is attacking? Does the author use any techniques besides argument to persuade the reader, as Norman Cousins did in "Twenty-Twenty"?

7. Was your initial interest sustained in reading the article? Does either of the following factors help account for this: (*a*) tone—the attitude the author adopts toward his subject, for example, serious, satiric, ironic; (*b*) style—the author's personal way of using the language? Are there other factors instead of or in addition to these that help account for your continued interest, or lack of it?

8. Is the article of value? Explain.

BIBLIOGRAPHY

AMORY, CLEVELAND, *The Last Resorts*. (Harper •Grosset) These delightful views of fashionable U.S. resort life produce at least one hearty laugh per page.

BORLAND, HAL, *American Year*. (Simon & Schuster) Anyone who has ever fallen under the gentle spell of the country will understand Hal Borland's love for the slow rhythms and quiet ways of nature. These essays capture perfectly the quality of rural America.

FADIMAN, CLIFTON, *Any Number Can Play*. (World Pub. •Avon) In a cheerfully serious manner, Fadiman discusses everything from mathematics to cheeses. You will find his style charming and refreshing.

GOLDEN, HARRY, *Only in America*. (World Pub. •Permabooks) These are read-aloud, "listen-to-this" type essays about the folkways and foibles of the American people. Mr. Golden's book is full of cracker-barrel philosophy.

GREENE, JAY (editor), *Essays for Modern Youth*. (Globe) Something to suit every taste can be found in this outstanding collection of essays by both classic and modern writers. Such topics as aeronautics, theatre, psychology, sports, and youth are covered.

KRUTCH, JOSEPH WOOD, *Twelve Seasons*. (Sloane •Apollo) A deep sense of appreciation for the beauties and wonders of nature is clearly evident in this collection. The essays were inspired by the changes the months make on the Connecticut countryside.

PARKER, ELINOR (editor), *I Was Just Thinking*. (Crowell) Subtle humor, keen observation, and calm reflection are well represented in this collection of essays by American and English writers from Francis Bacon to E. B. White. For readers who enjoy the unusual, this is a literary gem.

SKINNER, CORNELIA OTIS, *The Ape in Me*. (Houghton) Miss Skinner's two greatest assets are her marvelous sense of the ridiculous and her ability to laugh at herself. With gay unconcern she discusses her height, her stammers, her inability to stop copying accents, and other inane but delightful problems.

WHITE, E. B., *One Man's Meat*. (Harper) In this collection and *Second Tree from the Corner*, E. B. White muses in his inimitable style on a great variety of subjects.

•paperback

chapter ten Biography

"The portrait . . . speaks and lives; I have found the man!" exclaimed the French critic Sainte-Beuve when, after months of study, he understood at last the personality of a literary figure whose biography he was to write. The almost universal desire to "find the man" behind the public figure of the scientist, general, president, artist, or writer is an important reason for the great popularity of biographical writing. This desire sends the biographer delving into old records, letters, diaries, going beyond the public life of his subject into his private life. After his painstaking research reveals the individual hidden in the massive array of data, the biographer still faces an equally formidable task; he must write his account in such a way as to communicate his insight to the reader.

In his first task—that of searching out, checking, and evaluating facts—the biographer must exercise all the skill of a historian. It seems obvious today that at this stage of his work his first concern should be for accuracy, completeness, and evaluation, but it was not always so. When Mason Weems wrote his biography of Washington (see page 159), he did not hesitate to invent stories or to omit facts in order to make his subject a figure to be respected and emulated. The trouble was that since the figure Weems portrayed was not Washington, was not even believable, this procedure of "whitewashing" his hero ended by defeating its own purpose. By suppressing any faults in a subject and giving him incredible virtues, biographers like Weems also stripped the figure of his humanity. This kind of biography became prominent enough in Victorian times to move Thomas Carlyle, the Scottish historian and philosopher, to remark, "How delicate, how decent is English biography, bless its mealy mouth!"

Early in the twentieth century a reaction set in. Biographers began to realize that this method of creating an artificial image had masked most of the great figures of history, that biography had too often concealed rather than revealed the man. In their zeal for realism the new biographers now emphasized the other side—the seamy side—of the great men of whom they wrote. Washington was seen, not as a lofty-minded irreproachable patriot, but as a wealthy Virginia planter who wielded political influence unfairly for the advantage of his class. Heroes that the Victorians had puffed up beyond recognition were now "debunked" —equally beyond recognition. The hero himself remained lost somewhere between the artificial image of impossible virtue and the equally artificial image of absurd weakness.

Most biographers today try to avoid both extremes, but accuracy and fair judgment are easier to set as goals than to achieve. If the subject lived more than three hundred years ago, the facts are often too few. This requires the biographer to fill in the gaps with speculation. If the subject lived recently, or is still living, the facts sometimes are overwhelming, and the biographer has trouble deciding which are the most important. Dr. Frank Freidel, for example, who is engaged in writing the biography of Franklin D. Roosevelt, is confronted with, literally, forty tons of material!

Beyond the problem of finding and selecting information about his subject, the biographer is also faced with the problem of interpreting the facts he unearths. Almost any act can be interpreted in a number of different ways to reveal any of a host of motives. A general with an advantage over his enemy suddenly calls off the battle. Does this action reveal him as a traitor, a coward, a man who simply never should have been made a general, a victim of inaccurate information or bungling subordinates, or a great strategist who, in the interests of the larger view, has decided on a tactical retreat? The careful weighing of such alternatives calls for balanced and unprejudiced judgment.

Depending on the scope of the biography, the first phase of the biographer's task, collecting and evaluating the facts about his subject, may require from several months to many years of unremitting work. But the task of writing up his information in such a way that his insight into his subject is communicated to the reader still has to be performed. The information he has gathered must now be organized and presented in such a way as to convey the image of a living, breathing person. The techniques available for accomplishing this part of the task are many. They include narration, quoted conversation or letters, reports of contemporaries, excerpts from diaries—even attempts to probe the subconscious mind of the subject. The skillful employment of these techniques calls for the profoundest insight and sympathy and for a high degree of artistic, literary skill and judgment. At this point the months or years of scholarly research must be transmuted into a work of literary art. The researcher must turn writer, and he must do so without distorting what he has been at pains to find out. In the phrase of Desmond McCarthy, British critic and journalist, the eminent biographer is, finally, "an artist upon oath."

from

The Thread That Runs So True

JESSE STUART 1907-

Jesse Stuart's grandparents had moved to W-Hollow, an isolated valley in the Kentucky mountains, because of a deadly feud with a rival clan in eastern Kentucky. The world into which Jesse was born in 1907, as he was to discover before many years had passed, was still one in which rivals in love and politics were apt to settle their differences with fists or firearms. Being tall and powerfully built, Jesse accepted this code readily.

Because his family was very poor and Jesse was needed on the farm, he had not had much schooling, nor had he had much use for schools, before he quit going altogether at the age of fifteen. Then one day, working on a construction gang at the nearby town of Greenup, he noticed well-dressed youngsters going to the large high school there. He gave up his job on the spot, took the exams, and enrolled. (He was later to return to this school, after working his way through a few years of college, as its principal.) Interested in poetry and inspired by Robert Burns, the Scottish poet, he began to write, and, encouraged by his teachers, he continued. In 1934 his first book of poems, *Man with a Bull-Tongue Plow*, was published and widely acclaimed. While he was laying the foundations for his writing career, Jesse Stuart was fighting the county politicians to bring greater educational opportunity to the rural school children. He was finally forced out of his position in the schools, and nearly killed in the bargain, but not before he had well begun a crusade that eventually succeeded and won him great admiration in Kentucky. In 1939 Jesse Stuart bought three hundred acres of land in W-Hollow and settled down to write the poetry and books which have made him famous. *The Thread That Runs So True*, from which the accompanying selection is drawn, is the account of his life as a schoolteacher in the Kentucky mountain country.

When I had first come to Winston, I wondered what my pupils did for recreation. I wondered what I would do for recreation. I had thought reading was about the only kind of recreation. It didn't take me long to learn differently. One evening in September I was invited to Bill Madden's home. He was one of my pupils. His father had invited six or seven of the local musicians in to play for us. We sat in the yard where the grass was dying and the peach-tree leaves had turned golden and the moon was high in the sky above us. We listened to this local band play with their banjos, fiddles, guitar, mandolin, and accordion from seven until eleven. They never played the same tune twice, and often when they played a fast breakdown, one of the listeners would dance. I had never heard old-time music sound as beautiful as this, in the moonlight of the mild September evening.

There was hardly a family in this big vicinity who didn't have a musician. This was part of their recreation. People had learned to play musical instruments to furnish their own music just as they had learned to plant, cultivate, and harvest crops for their food supply. They depended upon themselves.

I went with my pupils, their parents, and neighbors to cornhuskings, apple-peelings, bean-stringings,[1] square dances, and to the

1. *cornhuskings, apple-peelings, bean-stringings*, social gatherings at which the neighbors came together to help one another get their crops ready for winter use.

belling of the bride[2] when there was a wedding. Often we rode mules many miles through darkness or moonlight to these community events.... This was the most democratic recreation I'had ever seen.

Not one of my pupils had ever seen a stage play. If one had ever seen a movie, I'd never heard of it. They didn't have to leave landlocked Winston to find recreation. They had it at home. They created it just as they created most of their necessities of life. As the autumn days wore on they popped corn over the blazing wood fires and made molasses-and-popcorn balls. There was somewhere to go every night. I couldn't accept all the invitations. Each pupil invited me to his home to spend the night. This was an old custom, for in the past years the teacher had boarded with his pupils, since his salary wasn't enough to enable him to pay his board and have anything left.

When the hunting season came, I hunted quail with my pupils. I hunted rabbits with them in the Tiber[3] weed fields. My pupils were good marksmen. But I gave them a few surprises at some of the shots I made. I had never told them about my years of hunting experience. I went to the autumn-coloring hills to hunt possums. And I taught them—as I had tried to teach them high-school subjects —a little about possum hunting: that on the still and misty, warm nights when not a leaf stirred was the time to catch possums and coons. When I learned more about the terrain of the east and west walls,[4] where the persimmons and papaws grew, I showed them where to find the possums. They—as I had once done—hunted for animal pelts, shipped them, and bought books and clothes with the money. I showed them how to take better care of their pelts. ...

When the leaves changed color in the valley and the sun was bright as a brush-pile flame, I went on long hikes with my pupils. We'd take a hike to the autumn-colored hills soon as the school day was over. We'd take food to cook over an open fire on the summit of one of the walls that enclosed the valley. Sometimes the girls would go with us. ...

Down in the valley we could see every splash of color. Green leaves were there still, for the Tiber mists had protected them against the biting frost. There were blood-red shoemake[5] leaves, golden sycamore and poplar leaves, slate-colored water-birch leaves, and the dull- and bright-gold willow leaves. And down in the valley the corn shocks stood like wigwams in an Indian village. We could see the bright knee-high corn stubble glittering in the autumn sun. We could see the brown meadow stubble, too, where the hay had been mown and piled in high mounds with poles through the center.

Often I walked alone beside the Tiber in autumn. For there was a somberness that put me in a mood that was akin to poetry. I'd watch the big sycamore leaves zigzag from the interlocking branches above to the clear blue Tiber water and drift away like tiny golden ships. I'd find the farewell-to-summer[6] in bloom along this river. Then a great idea occurred to me. It wasn't about poetry. It was about schools.

I thought if every teacher in every school in America—rural, village, city, township, church, public, or private—could inspire his pupils with all the power he had, if he could teach them as they had never been taught before to live, to work, to play, and to share, if he could put ambition into their brains and hearts, that would be a great way to make a generation of the greatest citizenry America had ever had. All of this had to begin with the little unit. Each teacher had to do his share. Each teacher was responsible for the destiny of America, because the pupils came under his influence. The teacher held the destiny of a great country in his hand as no member of any other profession could hold it. All other professions stemmed from the products of his profession. ...

When I told my pupils about a scholastic contest with Landsburgh High School, I

2. *the belling of the bride*, a shivaree (shiv ə rē′), or noisy serenade for a newly married couple. 3. *the Tiber*, the river that flows through the valley. 4. *walls*, the hills that enclose the valley in which Winston is situated. 5. *shoe-make*, sumac. 6. *farewell-to-summer*, a late blooming aster.

watched their expressions. They were willing and ready for the challenge. The competitive spirit was in them.

"We must review everything we have covered in our textbooks," I told them. "We must cover more territory in our textbooks too. Hold up your right hands if you are willing!"

Every pupil raised his hand.

Right then we started to work. In addition to regular assignments, my pupils began reviewing all of the old assignments. . . .

Despite the challenge ahead and all the reviewing and study we planned to do, we never stopped play. The Tiber River was frozen over. The ring of skates and merry laughter broke the stillness of the winter nights. We skated on the white winding ribbon of ice beneath the high, cold winter moon. . . .

Over the weekends we'd go to Tiber, where we'd cut holes in the ice and gig fish. The boys and I would rabbit-hunt up and down the Tiber Valley in the old stubble fields now covered with snow and swept by wind. . . . When we hunted, the girls didn't go with us, but when we skated, fished, and rode sleighs, they went along. There was a long gentle slope not far from the schoolhouse, we found

ideal for our sleighs. It was almost a mile to the end of our sleigh run. We went over the river bank and downstream for many yards on the Tiber ice. We rode sleighs during the noon hour, before and after school.

On winter days when the snow had melted, leaving the dark earth a sea of sloppy mud, we designed floor games for our little one-room school. They were simple games such as throwing bolts in small boxes. And we played darts. We also played a game called "fox and goose." We made our fox-and-goose boards and we played with white, yellow, and red grains of corn. We had to make our own recreation. I never saw a distracted look on a pupil's face. I never heard one complain that the short, dark winter days were boresome because there wasn't anything to do. I think each pupil silently prayed for the days to be longer. We were a united little group. We were small, but we were powerful. We played hard, and we studied hard. We studied and played while the December days passed.

That day in early January, we dismissed school. . . . This was the big day for us. It was too bad that another blizzard had swept our rugged land and that a stinging wind was

Jesse Stuart does most of his writing in the shed behind his house (below), but the ruins of Winston High School (opposite) served him for the poem at right.

smiting the valleys and the hills. But this didn't stop the boys and me from going. Leona Maddox, my best Latin pupil, couldn't go along. Her father, Alex Maddox, wouldn't let her ride a mule seventeen miles to Landsburgh to compete in a contest on a day like this. I couldn't persuade him to let her go.

On that cold blizzardy morning, Budge Waters[7] rode his mule to school very early and built a fire in the potbellied stove. When the rest of us arrived on our mules at approximately seven o'clock, Budge had the schoolroom warm. We tied our mules to the fence, stood before the fire, and warmed ourselves before we started on our journey. Then we unhitched our mules from the fence and climbed into the saddles. Little clouds of frozen snow in powdery puffs arose from the mules' hoofs as six pupils and their teacher rode down the road.

Though the force of wind in the Tiber Valley was powerful, it was at our backs. The wind was strong enough to give our mules more momentum. We made good time until we left the valley and climbed the big hill. Here, we faced the wind. It was a whipping wind—stinging, biting wind on this mountain —that made the water run from our eyes and our mules' eyes, but for us there was no turning back. We were going to Landsburgh High School. That was that. We were determined to meet this big school—big to us, for they outnumbered us twenty-six to one. Soon we were down in Hinton Valley. Then we rode to the top of the Raccoon Hill. . . .

"Mr. Stuart, I have been thinking," Budge Waters said, as we rode along together, "if you can sleep in a fodder shock when it's twelve degrees below zero, we can take this contest from Landsburgh High School! I've not forgotten how you walked seventeen miles to carry us books.[8] All of your pupils remember. We'll never let you down!"

Budge Waters thought of this because we were riding down the mountain where I had slept that night. Then we rode down into the Raccoon Valley, and Billie Leonard, only thirteen years old, complained of numbness in his

---

7. *Budge Waters*, a remarkably brilliant boy, the best student in the school.   8. *I've not forgotten . . . carry us books.* Mr. Stuart had set out on foot to walk the seventeen miles to Landsburgh to bring back some books for his pupils. On the way he lost the trail in a blinding snowstorm. Having to spend the night out, he suffered many hardships. But he brought the books back.

It is most painful now as I
Schoolmaster once return to this;
Master of learning, all they had
Until they grew and went beyond.
This barn was dear to them and me.
Only the skeleton remains;
Parts of the roof, windows and doors
And master's desk and window panes
Are gone into oblivion.

The birds and bats now carry on,
Where elm trees have reached new heights;
Young winds blow over greened-up fields
That lie in all directions here
Where fields of grass run with the winds.
These friendly winds have not erased
The memories of what has been
From those who caught fire here that spread
The flame of learning to the world.

From *The Saturday Evening Post*, July 25, 1959, by permission of the author. ©The Curtis Publishing Co., Phila.

hands, feet, and lips. He said he felt as if he was going to sleep. . . . We stopped at a home, tied our mules to the fence, and went in and asked to warm. Bert Patton, a stranger to us, piled more wood on the open fire until we were as warm as when we had left the schoolhouse. We told him who we were and where we were going.

"On a day like this!" he said, shaking his head sadly.

We climbed into the saddles again. We were over halfway now. The second hitch would put us at Landsburgh High School. We had valley all the way to Landsburgh, with walls of rugged hills on each side for windbreaks.

At eleven o'clock we rode across the Landsburgh High School yard, and hitched our mules to the fence around the athletic field. There were faces against the windowpanes watching us. Then we walked inside the high school, where Principal Ernest Charters met and welcomed us. He told us that he was surprised we had come on a day like this and that we had been able to arrive so soon.

In the principal's office my pupils and I huddled around the gas stove while we heard much laughter in the high-school corridors. The Landsburgh High School pupils thought we were a strange-looking lot. Many came inside their principal's office to take a look at us. We were regarded with curiosity, strangeness, and wonder. Never before had these pupils seen seven mules hitched to their schoolyard fence. Never before had they competed scholastically with so few in number—competitors who had reached them by muleback. The Landsburgh High School principal didn't feel about the contest the way we felt. To him, this was just a "setup" to test his pupils for the district contest which would soon be held. He told me this when he went after the sealed envelopes that held the questions. We warmed before the gas stove while he made arrangements for the contest.

"These questions were made out by the state department of education," he said when he returned. "I don't know how hard they are."

My pupils stood silently by the stove and looked at each other. We were asked to go to one of the largest classrooms. A Landsburgh High School teacher had charge of giving the tests. When the Landsburgh High School pupils came through the door to compete against my pupils, we knew why Principal Charters had selected this large classroom. My pupils looked at each other, then at their competitors.

I entered redheaded Jesse Jarvis to compete with ten of their plane-geometry pupils. I entered Billie Leonard against twenty-one of their selected algebra pupils.

"Budge, you'll have to represent us in grammar, English literature, and history," I said. "And I believe I'll put you in civil government. Is that all right?"

"Yes," he agreed. Budge had never had a course in civil government. All he knew about it was what he had read in connection with history.

"Robert Batson, you enter in history and grammar.

"Robin Baylor, you enter in algebra.

"Snookie Baylor, you enter in algebra and plane geometry.

"Sorry, Mr. Charters," I said, "we don't have anyone to enter in Latin. My best Latin pupil, Leona Maddox, couldn't make this trip."

After the contest had begun, I left the room. Miss Bertha Madden was in charge. I took our mules to Walter Scott's barn on the east end of Landsburgh, where I fed and watered them.

With the exception of an interval when the contestants ate a quick lunch, the contest lasted until 2:30 P.M. I had one pupil, Budge Waters, in four contests. I had planned to enter him in two. Just as soon as Budge had finished with civil government, we started grading the papers. All the pupils were requested to leave the room.

We graded the papers with keys. Mr. Charters, Miss Madden, and two other teachers and I did the grading. Mr. Charters read the answers on the keys, and we checked the answers. Once or twice we stopped long enough to discuss what stiff questions these were. We wondered how far we would have gotten if we—all of us, college graduates—

had taken the same test. One of the teachers asked me, while we graded these papers, if Budge Waters had ever seen these questions.

When we were through grading the papers, Mr. Charters called the contestants into the classroom.

"I want to read you the scores of this contest," he said. His voice was nervous.

"Budge Waters, winner in English literature.

"Budge Waters, winner in grammar.

"Budge Waters, winner in history with almost a perfect score.

"Budge Waters, winner in civil government.

"Why didn't you bring just this one boy?" Principal Charters asked me.

"Because I've got other good pupils," I quickly retorted.

"Billie Leonard, winner in algebra, with plenty of points to spare.

"Jesse Jarvis, second in plane geometry.

"Snookie Baylor and Robin Baylor tied for second place in algebra.

"Congratulations," said Principal Charters, "to your pupils and to you, on your success. It looks as though Winston High will represent this county in the district scholastic contest. I've never heard of such a remarkable thing."

When we left the Landsburgh High School we heard defeated pupils crying because "a little mudhole in the road like Winston beat us."

In a few minutes our mule cavalcade passed the Landsburgh High School. Faces were against the windowpanes and many pupils waved jubilantly to us as we rode by, our coattails riding the wind behind our saddles, and the ends of our scarfs bright banners on the wind. We rode victoriously down the main street of Landsburgh on our way home.

❧ TO INCREASE UNDERSTANDING

1. Describe Stuart's view of the rôle of the teacher in our society.

2. To what cause do you attribute the unusual success of the Winston pupils in the contest?

3. (a) What was the first reaction of the Landsburgh students to those from Winston? Why did they react in this way? (b) Why were some of the Landsburgh students particularly unhappy about their defeat? (c) Why was it that many of the Landsburgh students "waved jubilantly" to the group from Winston?

4. How might Stuart have used this incident to support his argument for raising the standards of educational opportunity in rural areas to match those in the towns and cities?

❧ BETTER READING
Autobiography

The biographer's difficulty in giving an unbiased account of his hero is clearly increased many times when the writer himself is the hero, as is the case in an autobiography. An individual pondering over the happenings of his life may gradually come to see himself as a more extraordinary figure than he was. Thus Captain John Smith in his first account of his adventures in Virginia did not even mention the famous Pocahontas episode; only years later, when his days of exploration in the New World were far behind him, did he include the story in his *Generall Historie* (see page 117). Whether or not the story is invented, it is certain that the Captain's account of himself grew in glory in the later version of his life. An autobiographer may also, of course, give a false impression because of modesty. When Lincoln was requested to write an autobiography for the campaign of 1860, he could not find enough material in the first fifty-one years of his life to fill three pages!

At its best an autobiography can reveal a person's goals and satisfactions as can no third-person biography. For example, John Bird, in his brief biography of Jesse Stuart, has only this to say about Stuart's motivations for teaching school at Winston High School: "Lonesome or not, he had to make a living. . . . So he became a teacher and loved it. He became convinced that it was the greatest profession in the world."[1] Jesse Stuart gives the reader a far more detailed idea of the nature of his teaching experience. What satisfaction of teaching in a rural school does he reveal in this statement: "When we left the Landsburgh High School we heard pupils crying because 'a little mudhole in the road like Winston beat us' "? How does this reveal more about Jesse Stuart's reasons for enjoying school teaching than the statement by John Bird? What other satisfactions in teaching at Winston does Stuart reveal in this selection? How many of these do you think a biographer knowing only the facts of Stuart's life could have discovered?

1. John Bird, "My Friend Jesse Stuart," *The Saturday Evening Post*, Volume 232 (July 25, 1959), page 81.

On June 13, 1953, having just penned the last paragraph of the sixth volume of his biography of George Washington, Douglas Southall Freeman died. In this dramatic way ended the career of one of America's truly distinguished biographers. Freeman's career had begun in earnest in 1914 when, as a young Ph.D. from Johns Hopkins on the staff of the Richmond *News Leader*, he began editing the confidential dispatches of General Lee to the President of the Confederate States, Jefferson Davis. That same year a publishing firm requested of him a brief biography of the General, but Freeman quickly found that nothing new could be said about Robert E. Lee without a comprehensive and exacting study. When he decided to undertake this much larger task, he launched on a monumental effort which occupied twenty years and resulted in the four-volume definitive biography of Lee—and a Pulitzer Prize.

During the period that Freeman was amassing material for this biography, he became a radio announcer as well as editor and part owner of the *News Leader*. These varied activities forced him to adhere to a rigid work schedule. He arose every morning at 2:30 A.M., sandwiching two hours of work on the biography between duties as editor and announcer which occupied him until lunch time. From 3:00 P.M. until dinner, Freeman devoted his time to the biography; by 8:00 he was in bed.

Since this unremitting activity turned up far more information about the Army of Northern Virginia than he could use in his account of Lee, he immediately turned his attention to *Lee's Lieutenants,* a three-volume work. General Omar Bradley found this work important enough to make it his major reading just prior to the liberation of Europe in World War II. After completing this six-year task, Freeman contemplated a history of the Union's Army of the Potomac, but was persuaded by the president of the Rockefeller Foundation to undertake the most difficult task in American biography—that of finding out what George Washington was really like. The remaining nine years of his life were not enough, however, and the seventh and final volume of the Washington biography had to be completed by other hands.

The following selection is taken from the fourth and final volume of *R. E. Lee.* Because this work is regarded as the "definitive" biography of Lee (*Time* magazine, October 18, 1948, said "Historians of the Civil War were agreed that the job of writing Lee's biography need never be done again"), this selection is presented exactly as it stands in the original, including Freeman's own scholarly footnotes. It must be remembered that a reader of the entire biography would see the events in this selection in the light of the preceding three volumes. Four aids are therefore provided to sketch in this background: A list of the major officers mentioned in the text appears on page 671. Immediately following that list there is a selected bibliography of works referred to in the footnotes. On page 683 a "Words!" study explains the abbreviations commonly used in footnoting. Following is an outline of the events leading up to the point at which the selection opens.

Hardly a hundred miles separated Washington, the capital of the Union, from Richmond, the capital of the Confederacy. Between these two points the Army of Northern Virginia under Robert E. Lee battled the often superior numbers of the Army of the Potomac, winning a number of remarkable engagements and suffering no decisive defeats—until March 25, 1865. Besieged for nine months, Lee's army could no longer hold Petersburg, the last line of defense before Richmond, against the Federal lines east of the city. When Grant threatened to cut off the only rail line to the city, Lee was forced to evacuate. As General Meade pursued Lee from the east, Grant cut off his intended retreat south. At last on April 8 General Sheridan's cavalry got across Lee's only remaining route to the west at the town of Appomattox Court House. Lee was virtually surrounded, and Grant called for the surrender of his army. Since Lee would not surrender until he had tried the Federal force to the west, he countered Grant's message with an offer to talk of peace, as opposed to surrender. He clearly recognized that by so delaying what he knew must be the inevitable outcome he might lose even the offer contained in Grant's message—that his men would be paroled to their homes rather than marched off to prison. Grant did not reply to the request for such a meeting that day. The next day, April 9, Lee met with his officers and concluded that he had no choice but to surrender the army. After some difficulty he obtained a temporary truce from Meade in order to send a letter to Grant asking Grant to meet him now for the purpose of surrender. At this point he retired to an apple orchard near the front, around which the engineers under Colonel Talcot had thrown a cordon so that Lee might rest undisturbed. Because the Union army was widely extended, communication by officers riding through the lines was difficult and uncertain; but at last, on the same afternoon, the memorable meeting was arranged.

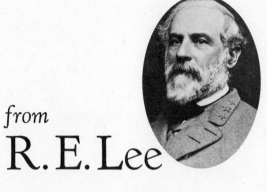

from
R. E. Lee

Douglas Southall Freeman

G rant already had offered, it will be remembered, to have the surrender arranged through officers designated for that purpose, in order that the Confederate leader might be spared humiliation, but Lee probably never thought of passing on to others this unpleasant task. He meant literally what he had said to Alexander—that he would go to General Grant and surrender himself and

Reprinted from *R. E. Lee, Volume IV* by Douglas Southall Freeman; copyright 1935 by Charles Scribner's Sons; used by permission of the publishers.

PHOTOGRAPH FROM LIBRARY OF CONGRESS

CONFEDERATE AND UNION OFFICERS

This list contains in alphabetical order only those officers that figure significantly in this selection and are not identified in the text.

Alexander, Brigadier General E. Porter, C.S.A. (Confederate States of America), chief of artillery in the corps of General James Longstreet.

Babcock, Colonel Orville E., Union officer, aide-de-camp to Grant.

Jackson, Lt. General Thomas J. ("Stonewall"), C.S.A., commander of the Second Corps, killed accidentally by his own men at Chancellorsville. (The other generals mentioned with Jackson on page 673 had also been officers under Lee.)

Marshall, Colonel Charles, Lee's military secretary.

Meade, General George, Union officer, commander of the Army of the Potomac from June 1863 to the end of the war.

Porter, Colonel Horace, Union officer.

Taylor, Lt. Colonel Walter H., Assistant Adjutant General, Army of Northern Virginia.

Venable, Colonel Charles S., one of Lee's staff officers.

BIBLIOGRAPHY

In the next column arranged in alphabetical order, are the most important texts which are referred to

in the footnotes and which are not explained there. For information about the authors refer to the list of officers on this page.

ALEXANDER. E. P. Alexander. *Military Memoirs.* ... N.Y.: 1907. Freeman considered this his most valuable single commentary on the operations of the army.

B. AND L. *Battles and Leaders of the Civil War.* ... N.Y. Freeman considered this one of the three most useful sources on military operations.

GRANT. U. S. Grant. *Personal Memoirs.* 2 vols. N.Y.: 1885.

LONGSTREET. James Longstreet. *From Manassas to Appomattox, Memoirs of the Civil War in America.* ... Philadelphia: 1896. Freeman calls this "important but inaccurate."

MARSHALL'S APPOMATTOX. Charles Marshall. *Appomattox. An Address Delivered before the Society of the Army and Navy of the Confederate States.* ... Baltimore: 1894. Freeman found this one of the major sources on the details of Appomattox.

O. R. U.S. War Department. *A Compilation of the Official Records of the Union and Confederate Armies.* 70 vols. Washington: 1880-1901. This is unquestionably the most important source of all.

S. H. S. P. *Southern Historical Society Papers.* 47 vols. Richmond, Virginia: 1876-1930. Freeman found that this contained much valuable material which had not been previously used.

TAYLOR'S FOUR YEARS. Walter H. Taylor. *Four Years with General Lee.* ... N.Y.: 1887. Taylor's position in the army gave him access to considerable information.

Babcock　Marshall　Lee　Sherman　Grant　Meade　Park

take the consequences of his acts.[1] Marshall thought that Lee subconsciously was impelled to this personal surrender by reason of his father's unfavorable reference in his *Memoirs* to Cornwallis' failure to appear on the day of the surrender at Yorktown.[2]

Making ready to proceed, Lee took from his breast pocket the folded map with which he had fought the campaign and gave it to Colonel Venable, who, a little later, burnt it. Lee questioned, also, whether the truce that had been granted would last long enough to cover the necessary interview. Babcock met this by writing in Grant's name a dispatch to Meade to continue the truce until further orders.[3]

On such a mission as he was now about to begin, Lee naturally would be accompanied by his adjutant general and by his military secretary, but Colonel Taylor had no heart for being present at a surrender. He begged off on the ground that he already had ridden twice through the lines that morning.[4] Lee excused him with his usual consideration for

the feelings of others. In the company of Marshall, Babcock, and Tucker, the daring orderly, Lee started up the road and beyond the thin and silent line of battle on the hillside.[5] At the stream, Traveller wanted to drink. Lee waited until his faithful mount had his fill.[6] Then he went on.

How often he had ridden that strong steed and in scenes how various! Up Malvern Hill, when the very earth seemed alive with the crawling wounded; over Thoroughfare Gap,

1. See *supra*, p. 123. [This refers to the place earlier in Volume IV at which Lee had answered General Alexander's suggestion that the army might simply be disbanded, hoping that most of the men could escape and reband. Lee said that the only dignified course for him would be to go to Grant and surrender himself, taking the consequences of his acts.] 2. *Marshall's Appomattox*, p. 8. 3. *Alexander*, 603 n. and 610. Alexander stated that this message was sent by Colonel Forsyth. As Forsyth proceeded, according to Taylor (*General Lee*, 290), back into his own lines, where he naturally would go at once to report to Sheridan, Alexander must have confused Forsyth's ride before Babcock's arrival with that of another officer subsequently. 4. *Taylor's Four Years*, 152. 5. *Marshall's Appomattox*, 18. 6. W. H. Palmer to W. H. Taylor, MS., June 24, 1911—*Taylor MSS*.

Above: Surrender
scene in a litho-
graph of 1867.
Right: Sketch by
Thomas Nast (see
pages 354-355).

while "Stonewall's" guns were growling, and
after the spinning wheels of the pursuing
guns at Second Manassas; across South Mountain; among the bloody ridges of the Antietam;
with the mists enveloping him at Fredericksburg; confident and calm when the cheering
thousands acclaimed him in the woods of
Chancellorsville; out on the hill at Gettysburg; along the mournful byways of the Wilderness; down the Telegraph road toward
Cold Harbor; over the James and over that
same Appomattox, sullen and tawny, at Petersburg. Jackson had ridden with him, the battle
light in his eyes, the laughing Stuart, the
nervous Hill, the diligent Pender, the gallant
Rodes—all of them dead now, and he alone,
save for those silent companions, was on his
last ride as commander of the Army of North-

ern Virginia. Thirty-nine years of devotion to
military duty had come to this . . . and this,
too, was duty.

As the little cavalcade passed toward the
village of Appomattox, Lee had to arouse himself and arrange the details: Grant had left
it to him to select the place of meeting. Would
Marshall go ahead and find a suitable house?
Obediently, the colonel trotted off; Lee remained with Babcock. They did not talk—how
could they?[7]

After a while the orderly returned to say
that Colonel Marshall had found a room for
the conference. Lee went on and, under the
soldier's guidance, drew rein beyond the courthouse in the yard of a house on the left-hand

---

7. Marshall is the only authority for this part of the
ride.

side of the road to Lynchburg. The residence belonged to Major Wilmer McLean, who, by the oddest chance, had owned the farm on Bull Run where, in the first battle of that name, the initial clash had occurred. Major McLean had removed from that exposed position and had purchased a property at Appomattox—only to find that the march of the armies he had sought to avoid was now about to end, as it had begun, at his door.[8]

Lee dismounted in the yard, and, after the orderly took Traveller, he walked toward the wide steps that led to the covered porch, which ran the whole width of the house. Entering the central hall, at the top of the steps, he turned into the front room on his left, a typical parlor of a middle-class Virginia home.[9] Colonel Marshall went with him. Colonel Babcock accompanied Lee, also, with the explanation that, as General Grant would soon arrive, the orderly could easily direct him to the place. Lee walked diagonally across the room and sat down close to a small table in the corner beyond the front window and farthest from the hall.[10] He put his hat and gauntlets on the table, and there he waited. Babcock and Marshall remained in the room and, no doubt, seated themselves at his invitation.

Half an hour passed, perhaps the longest half hour in Lee's whole life. If there was any conversation, it was in snatches and was slow, labored, and vague.[11] About 1:30 o'clock there was a clatter in the road, the sound of the approach of a large body of mounted men. They drew nearer; they halted; they dismounted. Some of them climbed the steps. Babcock went to the door and opened it. A man of middle height, slightly stooped and heavily bearded, came in alone. He was dressed for the field, with boots and breeches mud-bespattered.[12] He took off his yellow thread gloves as he stepped forward. Lee had never seen him to remember him but he knew who he was, and, rising with Marshall, he started across the room to meet General Grant. They shook hands quietly with brief greetings. Then Grant sat down at the table in the middle of the room, and Lee returned to his place. Marshall stood to the left and somewhat be-

hind him. Babcock had a few whispered words with Grant, then went from the room and out on the porch. He soon was back, followed by a full dozen Federal officers, Sheridan and Ord among them. These newcomers arranged themselves behind Grant and in sight of Lee as quietly as boots and spurs and clanking swords permitted. Grant made no reference to their coming. Lee showed no sign of resentment at their presence.

The conversation began: "I met you once before, General Lee," Grant said in his normal tones,[13] "while we were serving in Mexico, when you came over from General Scott's headquarters to visit Garland's brigade, to which I then belonged. I have always remembered your appearance, and I think I should have recognized you anywhere."

"Yes," answered Lee quietly, "I know I met you on that occasion, and I have often thought of it and tried to recollect how you looked, but I have never been able to recall a single feature."

Mention of Mexico aroused many memories. Grant pursued them with so much interest and talked of them so readily that the conversation went easily on until the Federal was almost forgetting what he was about.[14] Lee felt the weight of every moment and brought Grant back with words that seemed to come naturally, yet must have cost him anguish that cannot be measured.

"I suppose, General Grant," he said, "that the object of our present meeting is fully understood. I asked to see you to ascertain upon

8. *Marshall's Appomattox*, 18; *Alexander*, 610. Major McLean happened to be the first white civilian Colonel Marshall met in the village. When Marshall told him what was wanted, McLean first conducted him to a different house. Marshall found this vacant and in very bad repair and told McLean it would not serve the purpose. Thereupon McLean offered his own, well-furnished residence. **9.** The photograph of the house, used in the text, is perhaps the best, but one of much excellence appears, along with other good pictures of the retreat, in the *Photographic History of the Civil War*, 3, 315. The reader should be warned, however, that the legends under these particular cuts are singularly inaccurate. **10.** 4 *B. and L.*, 735. **11.** Babcock never wrote of Appomattox. **12.** Cf. A. J. McKelway in 52 *Harper's Weekly*, 411. **13.** Grant subsequently admitted that he was "much embarrassed" during the interview (J. T. Austin: *Moses Coit Tyler*, 60-61). **14.** 2 *Grant*, 490. General Ely S. Parker, on the other hand, in his *Narrative* asserted in 1893 that the conversation lagged.

what terms you would receive the surrender of my army."

Grant did not change countenance or exhibit the slightest note of exultation in his reply. "The terms I propose are those stated substantially in my letter of yesterday—that is, the officers and men surrendered to be paroled and disqualified from taking up arms again until properly exchanged, and all arms, ammunition, and supplies to be delivered up as captured property."

Lee nodded an assent that meant more than his adversary realized. The phantom of a proud army being marched away to prison disappeared as Grant spoke, and the hope Lee had first expressed to Taylor that morning was confirmed. "Those," said he, "are about the conditions I expected would be proposed."

"Yes," Grant answered, "I think our correspondence indicated pretty clearly the action that would be taken at our meeting; and I hope it may lead to a general suspension of hostilities and be the means of preventing any further loss of life."

That, of course, was a theme that Lee's conception of his duty as a soldier would not permit him to discuss. It was his to obey orders and to direct the forces in the field. The civil authorities had the sole power, he held, to make peace of the sort General Grant had in mind. So he merely inclined his head again.

Grant talked on of peace and its prospects. Lee waited, and then, courteously, but in a manifest desire to finish the business in hand, he said: "I presume, General Grant, we have both carefully considered the proper steps to be taken, and I would suggest that you commit to writing the terms you have proposed, so that they may be formally acted upon."

"Very well, I will write them out."

Lee sat in silence and looked straight ahead as Grant called for his manifold order book, opened it, lit his pipe, puffed furiously, wrote steadily for awhile with his pencil, paused, reflected, wrote two sentences, and then quickly completed the text.[15] Grant went over it in an undertone with one of his military secretaries, who interlined a few words. Lee did not follow any of this. He sat as he was until Grant rose, crossed to him, and put the manifold book in his hands, with the request that he read over the letter.

Lee probably was at his tensest then, for he busied himself with little mechanical acts as though to master his nerves. He placed the book on the table. He took his spectacles from his pocket. He pulled out his handkerchief. He wiped off the glasses, he crossed his legs, he set his glasses very carefully on his nose, and then he took up the order book for a slow, careful reading:

Appomattox C. H., Va.
Apr. 9th, 1865.

Gen. R. E. Lee,
    Comd. C.S.A.
Gen.

In accordance with the substance of my letter to you of the 8th instant I propose to receive the surrender of the Army of N. Va. on the following terms, to-wit:

Rolls of all the officers and men to be made in duplicate, one copy to be given to an officer designated by me, the other to be retained by such officer or officers as you may designate. The officers to give their individual paroles not to take up arms against the

—At this point, Lee turned the page and read on—

Government of the United States until properly and each company or regimental commander sign a like parole for the men of their command.

Lee stopped in his reading, looked up, and said to Grant: "After the words *until properly,* the word *exchanged* seems to be omitted. You doubtless intended to use that word."

"Why, yes," answered Grant. "I thought I had put in the word *exchanged.*"

"I presumed it had been omitted inadvertently, and with your permission I will mark where it should be inserted."

"Certainly."

Lee felt for a pencil, but could not find one. Colonel Horace Porter stepped forward and offered his. Lee took it, thanked him,

---

15. For the reason for Grant's pause in his writing, see *infra*, p. 679, n. 27.

Contemporary sketch of Lee leaving the McLean house, photo of which appears in inset.

placed the book on the table, inserted the caret, and resumed his reading:

The arms, artillery and public property to be parked and stacked and turned over to the officer appointed by me to receive them.

This will not embrace the side arms of the officers, nor their private horses or baggage. This done each officer and man will be allowed to return to their homes not to be disturbed by United States authority so long as they observe their paroles and the laws in force where they may reside.

> Very respectfully,
> U. S. Grant, Lt. Gl.[16]

There was a slight change in Lee's expression as he read the closing sentences, and his tone was not without warmth as now he looked up at Grant and said: "This will have a very happy effect on my army."

"Unless you have some suggestions to make in regard to the form in which I have stated the terms," Grant resumed, "I will have a copy of the letter made in ink and sign it."

Lee hesitated: "There is one thing I would like to mention. The cavalrymen and artillerists own their own horses in our army. Its organization in this respect differs from that of the United States. I would like to understand whether these men will be permitted to retain their horses."

"You will find," answered Grant, "that the

16. A reproduction of the original, with Lee's caret duly appearing, is in 2 *Grant*, 497.

terms as written do not allow this. Only the officers are allowed to take their private property."

Lee read over the second page of the letter again. For months he had agonized over his field transportation and cavalry mounts. He knew what the army's horses would mean to the South stripped as it had been of all draft animals, and he wanted those of his men who owned mounts to have them for the spring ploughing. His tongue would not go beyond a regretful "No, I see the terms do not allow it; that is clear."

Grant read his opponent's wish, and, with the fine consideration that prevailed throughout the conversation—one of the noblest of his qualities, and one of the surest evidences of his greatness—he did not humiliate Lee by forcing him to make a direct plea for a modification of terms that were generous. "Well, the subject is quite new to me. Of course, I did not know that any private soldiers owned their animals, but I think this will be the last battle of the war—I sincerely hope so—and that the surrender of this army will be followed soon by that of all the others, and I take it that most of the men in the ranks are small farmers, and, as the country has been so raided by the two armies, it is doubtful whether they will be able to put in a crop to carry themselves and their families through the next winter without the aid of the horses they are now riding, and I will arrange it this way: I will not change the terms as now written, but I will instruct the officers I shall appoint to receive the paroles to let all the men who claim to own a horse or mule take the animals home with them to work their little farms."

It could not have been put more understandingly or more generously. Lee showed manifest relief and appreciation. "This will have the best possible effect upon the men," he said. "It will be very gratifying, and will do much toward conciliating our people."

While Grant set about having his letter copied, Lee directed Marshall to draft a reply. In the wait that followed, Grant brought up and introduced the officers who had remained silent in the background. Lee shook hands with those who extended theirs and bowed to the others, but he spoke only to General Seth Williams, a warm friend during his superintendency at West Point. He talked to Williams without apparent effort, but when that officer introduced a pleasantry of the old days, Lee had no heart for it. He could not jest as his army was surrendering and his country dying. He only inclined his head ever so little at Williams' joke, and he did not smile. When Colonel Parker was presented, it seemed to Horace Porter that General Lee looked at him longer than at the others. It was Porter's belief that General Lee thought the Indian a Negro and was surprised to find an African on Grant's staff.[17]

When the introductions were over, Lee turned again to Grant. "I have a thousand or more of your men as prisoners, General Grant, a number of them officers whom we have required to march along with us for several days. I shall be glad to send them into your lines as soon as it can be arranged, for I have no provisions for them. I have, indeed, nothing for my own men. They have been living for the last few days principally upon parched corn, and are badly in need of both rations and forage. I telegraphed to Lynchburg, directing several train loads of rations to be sent on by rail from there, and when they arrive I should be glad to have the present wants of my men supplied from them."

There was a stir among the listeners at this remark, and they looked at Sheridan, for, unknown to Lee, he had the previous night captured at Appomattox Station the rations that had come down from Lynchburg. Those that had been sent up from Farmville had been found by the Federals farther down the road.[18] Grant did not add to Lee's distress by a recountal of these seizures. He merely said, "I should like to have our men within our lines as soon as possible. I will take steps at once to have your army supplied with rations, but I am sorry we have no forage for the animals. We have had to depend upon the country for

---

17. Parker, op. cit., stated that the introductions were made when Grant's officers entered the room. 18. St. John's report, Lee MSS.—L; Gibbon, 311; O. R., 46, part I, p. 1109.

our supply of forage. Of about how many men does your present force consist?"

Lee reflected for a moment: "Indeed, I am not able to say. My losses in killed and wounded have been exceedingly heavy, and besides, there have been many stragglers and some deserters. All my reports and public papers, and, indeed, my own private letters, had to be destroyed on the march to prevent them from falling into the hands of your people.[19] Many companies are entirely without officers, and I have not seen any returns for several days, so that I have no means of ascertaining our present strength."[20]

Grant had estimated Lee's numbers at 25,000 and he asked, "Suppose I send over 25,000 rations, do you think that will be a sufficient supply?"

"I think it will be ample," Lee is said by Horace Porter to have replied. "And it will be a great relief, I assure you," he added instantly. Colonel Marshall's memory of Lee's answer was that he said 25,000 rations would be "more than enough."[21]

General Sheridan then came forward and requested that he might copy two dispatches he had sent Lee that day in such a hurry that he had not written them out for his records. These dispatches were protests against alleged violations of the truce.[22] Lee took out the dispatches from his pocket and said he was sure that if the truce had been violated it was through a misunderstanding.

By this time, Marshall had finished his draft of Lee's acceptance of Grant's terms of surrender. It began with a sentence which would indicate that the agreement had been reached by correspondence. Lee modified this because he thought it would create a false impression. He made, perhaps, a few other changes, and then he had Marshall copy the document. The Federals had borrowed Marshall's ink in order to write their answer, and now, Marshall, having no paper with him, had to procure some from their stock.

The finished letter was now brought Lee and was read over by him:

Lieut-Gen. U. S. Grant,
    Commanding Armies of the United States.

General: I have received your letter of this date containing the terms of surrender of the Army of Northern Virginia as proposed by you. As they are substantially the same as those expressed in your letter of the 8th instant, they are accepted. I will proceed to designate the proper officers to carry the stipulations into effect.
Very respectfully, your obedient servant,[23]

Lee put his signature to this without a quiver. Marshall sealed it and went over to Parker, who already had Grant's letter waiting for him, duly signed and in an addressed envelope. They made the exchange and the surrender was complete.[24] It was then about 3:45 P.M.

The rest was casual and brief. Grant explained why he was without his sword.[25] Lee is said to have remarked that he usually wore his when with the army in the field.[26] Then Lee requested that Grant notify Meade of the surrender, so that firing might not break out and men be slain to no purpose. He requested also that, pending the actual surrender, the two armies be kept separate, so that personal encounters would be avoided. Grant acquiesced immediately and suggested

19. Lee left Petersburg, according to Doctor J. H. Claiborne (Seventy-Five Years in Old Virginia, 279), with his headquarters wagon, his ambulance and a carriage, the last-named probably the vehicle he had used in his illness during the last week of May 1864. In a panic, on April 7, the teamsters or clerks had destroyed all records of army headquarters (Jones, 180, quoting Lee), except probably those that were in the General's military chest. The letterbooks and a few other papers were preserved. With the documents sent Lee after the war, when he was planning to write a history of his campaigns, these form the corpus of the Lee MSS. quoted so many times in these pages. Among the papers destroyed must have been most of the reports and much of the correspondence covering the period from May 4, 1864. Apparently all headquarters' correspondence prior to that date had been sent to the archives in Richmond, whence it was shipped farther south for safety. It is now in the records of the War Department, Washington. 20. This is taken, with the rest, from Horace Porter's well-known account (4 B. and L., 735 ff.). It does not seem reasonable to accept all else that Porter said as direct quotation and to omit this. The collateral evidence, however, is against its literal accuracy. Lee would hardly have failed to take into account his losses of prisoners and, besides, he had watched as closely as he could the decline in his numbers. 21. 4 B. and L., 742; Marshall's Appomattox, 18. 22. There is no mention of these dispatches in the Official Records and no reference to them in the narratives of any of those who were near Lee that day. 23. O. R., 46, part 3, p. 666. 24. Parker, op. cit. 25. Cf. Parker, op. cit. 26. There was, however, some misunderstanding here as Lee rarely wore a sword.

that time might be saved if two of his officers rode to Meade through the Confederate lines.[27]

Lee thereupon rose, shook hands with General Grant, bowed to the spectators, and passed from the room. He went through the hall to the porch, where several Federal officers at once sprang to their feet and saluted. Putting on his hat Lee mechanically, but with manifest courtesy, returned their salute and with measured tread crossed the porch. At the head of the steps, he drew on his gauntlets, and absently smote his hands together several times as he looked into space across the valley to the hillside where his faithful little army lay. In a moment he aroused himself and, not seeing his mount, called in a voice that was hoarse and half-choked, "Orderly! Orderly!" Quickly Tucker answered from the corner of the house, where he was holding Traveller's rein as the steed grazed. Lee walked down the steps and stood in front of the animal while the man replaced the bridle. Lee himself drew the forelock from under the brow band and parted and smoothed it. Then, as Tucker stepped aside, Lee mounted slowly and with an audible sigh.[28] At that moment General Grant stepped down from the porch on his way to the gate, where his horse was waiting. Stopping suddenly, Grant took off his hat, but did not speak. The other Federals followed the courteous example of their chief. Lee raised his hat without a word, turned his horse, and rode away to an ordeal worse than a meeting with Grant—the ordeal of breaking the news to his soldiers and of telling them farewell.

By no means all the men were prepared for the surrender. The rapidity of the retreat, the failure of rations, and the dwindling of brigades to companies had spelled disaster in the minds of the intelligent. The circle of fire reflected on the clouds the night of the 8th had convinced the discerning that the army was virtually surrounded. The halt of the morning and the frequent passage of flags of truce had confirmed their fears of capitulation. Yet such was the faith of the army in itself and in its commander that many were unwilling to believe the end had come.

Lee came toward them down from the ridge, across the little valley, up the hillside through the pickets, and into the line. He was as erect as ever, but he was staring straight ahead of him, with none of the cheerfulness and composure that usually marked his countenance even in the most dreadful moments of his hardest battles.[29] The men started to cheer him, as they often did when he rode among them, but somehow their cheers froze in their throats at the sight of him.[30] They hesitated a moment as he rode fixedly on, and then without a word they broke ranks and rushed toward him.

"General," they began to cry, "are we surrendered?"

The question was like a blow in the face. He tried to go on, but they crowded about him, bareheaded. He removed his hat in acknowledgment and attempted once more to proceed. The road was too full of frenzied, famished faces. He had to halt and answer his loyal old soldiers. "Men," he said, "we have fought the war together, and I have done the best I could for you. You will all be paroled

---

27. This account, in the main, follows Horace Porter, *loc. cit.* Parker's *Narrative*, written in 1893, is substantially the same but presents what would seem to be a less logical sequence of events. The myth of a tender of Lee's sword and its return by Grant was, of course, so exploded by Grant (*op. cit.*, 2, 494) and by Marshall (29 *S. H. S. P.*, 269-73; cf. 9 *ibid.*, 139-40) that reference to it in the text has not been considered necessary. The sword, by the way, did not have a hilt "studded with jewels," as Porter thought. It was Lee's "Maryland sword," fully described by Fitz Lee (*op. cit.*, 394). It is now in the Confederate Museum, Richmond. Talking after the war with John Randolph Tucker, Lee answered in this way a question as to whether Grant had returned his sword. "No, sir," he said, "he had no opportunity of doing so. By the terms the side arms of officers were exempt from surrender, and I did not violate those terms by tendering him my sword. All that was said about swords was that General Grant apologized to me for not wearing his sword, saying it had gone off in his baggage, and he had not been able to get it in time." (J. William Jones in *Richmond Times-Dispatch*, Jan. 20, 1907). Badeau (*Grant in Peace*, 18-23) stated on Grant's authority that the Federal commander glanced at Lee's sword during the composition of the terms of surrender, reasoned that it would be a humiliation to Lee to surrender his weapon, and thereupon wrote the sentence exempting officers' side arms. 28. George A. Forsyth: "The Closing Scene at Appomattox Court House," *Harper's Magazine*, April 1898, pp. 708-10. 29. Major A. R. H. Ranson in *Harper's Monthly*, 335. 30. E. A. Moore, 290.

and go to your homes until exchanged."[31] Tears came into his eyes as he spoke. He attempted to say more but even his amazing self-mastery failed him. Moving his lips in a choking "good-bye," he again essayed to ride on to the orchard from which he had come.

"General, we'll fight 'em yet," they answered.

"General, say the word and we'll go in and fight 'em yet."[32]

Everywhere as the news spread, each soldier reacted to it in his own fashion. Some wept, openly and without abashment. Others were dazed, as though they did not understand how the Army of Northern Virginia, Lee's army, could surrender. To Field's division, which had suffered little on the retreat, it seemed incomprehensible.[33] To others, it was as the very end of the world. "Blow, Gabriel, blow!" cried one man, and threw down his musket as General Grimes told him what had happened. "My God, let him blow; I am ready to die!"[34]

Some blasphemed and some babbled, but all who could do so crowded to say farewell to Lee. Catching hold of his hands, they looked up at him and cried the more. They touched his uniform or his bridle rein, if they could not grasp his hand, and if they could not reach him, they smoothed Traveller's flank or patted his neck. And in a confused roar—half-sob, half-acclamation—they voiced their love for him, their faith in him, their goodbye to him as their commander.[35]

Passing on slowly, agonizingly, he stopped at the apple orchard, where Talcott's engineers were still doing duty, and passed the cordon they had formed around the place. Lee saw Talcott among his men, and had sufficient composure to tell the colonel what the terms were. Grant would soon send rations, he said. Talcott must keep his men together and must make them as comfortable as possible until they were paroled.[36]

Then Lee retired a short distance into the orchard away from the road, and there he began to feel the reaction. He could not sit down or rest, but kept pacing up and down under a tree. To one at least of those who watched him, Blackford of the engineers, he

seemed in "one of his savage moods." Blackford added, "When these moods were on him, it was safer to keep out of his way." The staff officers did not disturb him. He walked and turned, and walked again and turned, battling with his own emotions. Presently, through the abandoned lines, there began to arrive Federal officers, generally in groups of four or five. Some knew him and wished to greet him. Others were drawn by curiosity to gaze at the old lion, captured at last. They went to Taylor or to Venable, who had field headquarters under another tree, and asked to be presented to the General. Taylor brought them over. At their approach, Lee halted, drew himself up and stood at attention. He "glared" at them, according to Blackford, "with a look few men but he could assume."[37] They approached and took off their hats. He merely touched the rim of his hat in return and sometimes did not seem to Major Blackford to do even that. The interviews all were brief and manifestly not to his liking. In the hour of the supreme tragedy of his career as a soldier, Lee did not wish to see strangers or to be stared at, it mattered not with what deference.

He probably had halted at the apple orchard to be accessible for the necessary business of the surrender, and he waited until the

---

31. 38 S. H. S. P., 12. Of the many versions of his words, the writer has taken that of Captain Frederick M. Colston. That officer said he climbed to a wagon hub and heard Lee distinctly, though he stated that Lee added some other words which he forgot. Lawley's contemporary version (Fortnightly Review, September 1865, p. 9) is almost identical. A fuller version, Peacock's, which appears in 19 S. H. S. P., 269, may include some of Lee's remarks later in the day: "Yes, my men, you are surrendered. The odds against us were too great. I would not lead you to fruitless slaughter. Private property will be respected; officers will retain their side arms and horses. All will be paroled and transported to your homes and may you find your families and loved ones well. Good-bye, my men, good-bye." 32. Major Giles B. Cooke, quoted in 1 Macrae, 193. 33. Longstreet, 629. 34. 27 S. H. S. P., 96; Grimes, 122. 35. Gordon must have come up about this time. On the authority of Gordon, after the war, Jones quoted Lee as saying at this time, "I could wish that I were numbered among the fallen in the last battle!" But this was too rhetorical for Lee (Jones, 346; Cf. Gordon, 282). 36. 32 S. H. S. P., 72. 37. Memoirs of Life in and out of the Army in Virginia. . . . Compiled by Susan Leigh Blackford (cited hereafter as Blackford), vol. 2 Appendix, p. iv.

Federal wagons had begun to arrive with the rations.[38] It may have been while he was there that he received from Grant's headquarters a copy of the order appointing the three Federal commissioners to arrange the details of the surrender.[39] His own representatives, Longstreet, Gordon, and Pendleton, were named the same day, it is not known where or at what hour.[40]

The sun was now near its setting. The immediate duties were done. Lee mounted Traveller and started toward his headquarters, which were under a large white oak, about a mile to the rear. As he went, the scenes of his return from the interview with General Grant were repeated in heightened pathos. For now the whole army knew that the surrender had occurred, and most of the intelligent men had been given time to reflect what that act meant to him who was, in their eyes, both cause and country. "There was," Blackford wrote, "a general rush from each side of the road to greet him as he passed, and two solid walls of men were formed along the whole distance. Their officers followed; and behind the lines of men were groups of them, mounted and dismounted, awaiting his coming. . . . As soon as he entered this avenue of these old soldiers —the flower of the army, the men who had stood to their duty through thick and thin in so many battles—wild, heartfelt cheers arose which so touched General Lee that tears filled his eyes and trickled down his cheeks as he rode his splendid charger, hat in hand, bowing his acknowledgments. This exhibition of feeling on his part found quick response from the men whose cheers changed to choking sobs, as, with streaming eyes and many evidences of affection, they waved their hats as he passed. Each group began in the same way, with cheers, and ended in the same way, with sobs, all along the route to his quarters. Grim, bearded men threw themselves on the ground, covered their faces with their hands, and wept like children. Officers of all ranks made no attempt to conceal their feelings, but sat on their horses and cried aloud. . . . Traveller . . . took as much pleasure in applause as a human being, and always acknowledged the cheers of the troops by tosses of his head and the men frequently cheered him for it, to which he would answer back as often as they did. On this, Traveller's last appearance before them, his head was tossing a return to the salutes all along the line. . . . One man . . . extended his arms, and with an emphatic gesture said, 'I love you just as well as ever, General Lee!' "[41]

They thronged about him when he reached his headquarters, and when he dismounted, all who were in sight of his camp hastened up.

"Let me get in," they began to cry. "Let me bid him farewell."

Lee stood with Long and Stevens and a few other old personal friends, and he sought to keep his composure, but as man after man crowded around him, each with warm words, his eyes filled anew with tears. In broken phrases he told his veterans to go home, to plant a crop, and to obey the law; and again and again he tried to say farewell. But they would not have it so. One handsome private, a gentleman in bearing for all his dirt and rags, shook hands and said, "General, I have had the honor of serving in this army since you took command. If I thought I were to blame for what has occurred today, I could not look you in the face, but I always try to do my duty. I hope to have the honor of serving under you again. Good-bye, General; God bless you."

On the instant another gripped his fingers. "Farewell, General Lee," he said. "I wish for your sake and mine that every damned Yankee on earth was sunk ten miles in hell!"

This forthright profession relieved the strain. In the stir that followed, Lee lifted his hat once more in salute and went into his tent . . . to be alone.[42]

---

38. *Blackford,* loc. cit. 39. The copy in *Lee MSS.—N* is in Colonel Parker's handwriting, O. R., 46, part 3, p. 666. 40. O. R., 46, part 3, pp. 666-67. It is not plain whether he sent for Longstreet from the apple orchard or later in the evening from his headquarters to get his advice as to distribution of the money in the custody of the chief of ordnance (*Longstreet,* 628). 41. *Blackford,* II, Appendix, p. vi. Most of those who have written of this historic scene apparently have overlooked the fact that there were two rides through the army. Consequently the remarks Lee made when stopped on his ride through Gordon's command, on his way back to the apple orchard, are usually quoted as though spoken just before he went to his tent. 42. *Blackford,* II, Appendix, p. vi; *Frank Potts,* 14-15.

1. What does each of the following passages reveal about Lee as he faces this moment of crisis?

(a) He meant literally what he had said to Alexander—that he would go to General Grant and surrender himself and take the consequences of his acts (page 671, column 2, paragraph 1).

(b) Colonel Taylor . . . begged off on the ground that he already had ridden twice through the lines that morning. Lee excused him . . . (page 672, column 1, paragraph 2).

(c) Thirty-nine years of devotion to military duty had come to this . . . and this, too, was duty (page 673, column 2, line 1).

(d) "Yes," Grant answered, ". . . I hope it may lead to a general suspension of hostilities and be the means of preventing any further loss of life." That, of course, was a theme that Lee's conception of his duty as a soldier would not permit him to discuss (page 675, column 1, paragraphs 3-4).

(e) He placed the book on the table. He took his spectacles from his pocket. He pulled out his handkerchief. He wiped off the glasses, he crossed his legs, he set his glasses very carefully on his nose (page 675, column 2, paragraph 1).

(f) Lee stopped in his reading, looked up, and said to Grant: "After the words *until properly*, the word *exchanged* seems to be omitted. You doubtless intended to use that word" (page 675, column 2, paragraph 3).

(g) Lee walked down the steps and stood in front of the animal [Traveller] while the man replaced the bridle. Lee himself drew the forelock from under the brow band and parted and smoothed it (page 679, column 1, paragraph 1).

(h) "General, we'll fight 'em yet," they answered (page 680, column 1, paragraph 1).

(i) Catching hold of his hands, they looked up at him and cried the more. They touched his uniform or his bridle rein, if they could not grasp his hand, and if they could not reach him, they smoothed Traveller's flank or patted his neck. And in a confused roar—half-sob, half-acclamation—they voiced . . . their good-bye to him as their commander (page 680, column 1, paragraph 4).

(j) . . . there began to arrive Federal officers. . . . At their approach, Lee halted, drew himself up and stood at attention. He "glared" at them, according to Blackford, "with a look few men but he could assume" (page 680, column 2, lines 7-18).

2. What qualities of Grant's character appear in this account? Cite some instances of these qualities.

The problem of re-creating the life of an actual person in words is one that has called forth many different methods for its solution. The approach to biography that Freeman used is one. It has been variously labeled the "conservative," "historical," or "definitive" biography. These adjectives applied to Freeman's work indicate his intention to write a history of Lee's life—and nothing else; if possible to make that life vivid to the reader, but only insofar as strict adherence to well-documented facts permits. This account of the surrender has all the vividness of an on-the-spot report. Examine the description of Freeman's sources on page 671. Name at least three different kinds of sources that he used. Explain why he was able to give nearly a minute-by-minute account of this event with historical accuracy. Would his sources have enabled Freeman to give as vivid an account of events in Lee's early private life? Explain your answer.

There are three other approaches to biography which differ in principle from the conservative approach. While biographers like Freeman avoid the techniques used in these other approaches, many writers feel that only by some combination of these methods can they overcome the limitations of the strictly historical approach.

First, some biographers include the social background of the period to give the reader an insight into the subject's way of looking at things. Freeman includes no more of this background material than is necessary to show why Lee acted as he did. Nearly everyone, for example, who has written about the surrender has viewed the contrast in appearance and manners between Lee and Grant as symbolic of the kinds of societies they represented. Bruce Catton, noted historian of the Civil War, says in *This Hallowed Ground*, "Two separate versions of America met in this room, each perfectly embodied by its chosen representative." Why does Freeman not include a statement of this nature? What *facts* does Freeman include that point out the contrast between the two generals.

Second, some biographers, to round out the portrait of their subject, include events in his private life which have no bearing on his public rôle. Since the conservative biographer is primarily concerned with the way his subject has influenced history, he finds these personal details out of place in his work.

Third, some biographers feel that the gain in vividness justifies their inventing details of the subject's gestures, actions, conversations, and thoughts where this is necessary. The conservative biographer also works for a sense of realism, but since his aim is to write a history of the subject, he will not add his own invented details.

Freeman includes conversation and detailed action in this selection. To see how he is able to do this, examine the following footnotes and the text to which they refer: note 27 on page 679; note 31 on page 680; note 41 on page 681; and note 42 on page 681. Explain why in this selection Freeman is able to include direct quotations and detailed action while staying within the strict limits of his approach to biography. Examine footnote 20 on page 678, and footnote 35 on page 680. What are some of the precautions Freeman took to ensure the accuracy of his sources for these details?

Explain what facts Freeman uses to support the following insights into Lee's thinking.

(a) ... Lee subconsciously was impelled to this personal surrender by reason of his father's unfavorable reference in his *Memoirs* to Cornwallis' failure to appear on the day of the surrender at Yorktown (page 672, column 1, lines 2-6).

(b) Lee felt the weight of every moment ... (page 674, column 2, paragraph 3).

(c) Lee probably was at his tensest then ... (page 675, column 2, paragraph 1).

(d) Then Lee retired a short distance into the orchard away from the road, and there he began to feel the reaction (page 680, column 1, paragraph 6).

(e) ... Lee did not wish to see strangers or to be stared at, it mattered not with what deference (page 680, column 2, lines 25-27).

Reread the poetry selection "Robert E. Lee" by Stephen Vincent Benét on page 581. Using "Fact versus Fiction" (page 18) as a guide, explain some of the differences between Benét's poetic portrait of Lee and Freeman's factual biography. In terms of this distinction explain why Benét expresses contempt for the efforts of "picklock biographers." To what extent do you think his criticism is justified, to what extent unjustified?

❧ WORDS!

There are, basically, two different kinds of footnotes: *reference* footnotes and *content* footnotes. A *reference* footnote is one in which the author acknowledges the work from which he has quoted a passage or borrowed an idea. A *content* footnote is one in which the author explains or amplifies what he says

in the text, either by a statement of his own or by a cross reference to some other work or some other part of his own work. With both types of footnotes certain standard abbreviations are commonly used.

Reference Footnotes. The first reference to a work to appear in the footnotes is always given in complete form: (a) author, (b) title, (c) publication data, (d) page reference. When the same work is again referred to, a shortened form is used.

(1) If the second reference follows the first immediately, with no intervening footnote, it can be shortened to the single abbreviation *ibid.* followed by the page number. (*Ibid.* stands for the Latin *ibidem*, meaning "in the same place.")

(2) If a reference to another work comes between the second reference and the first, the second reference takes the following form: (a) author, (b) either *op. cit.* and the page number, or *loc. cit.* (*Op. cit.* stands for the Latin *opere citato*, meaning "in the work cited"; *loc. cit.* stands for the Latin *loco citato*, meaning "in the place cited," that is, in the same work *and on the same page.*)

1. Examine note 27 on page 679. To what work does the notation "9 *ibid.* 139-40" refer? Why can Freeman use *ibid.* here?

2. Refer again to note 27. To what work does the notation "Grant (*op. cit.*, 2, 494)" refer? Why can Freeman not use *ibid.* here?

3. Note 38 on page 681 contains the notation "*Blackford, loc. cit.*" To what work does this refer? Why is no page number necessary?

Content Footnotes. Here, in alphabetical order, is a list of abbreviations often used in content footnotes. (Some of these abbreviations are used occasionally in reference footnotes as well.)

cf., compare (for the Latin word *confer*, meaning "bring together").

f, ... and the page following (plural, ff.).

infra, (Latin) below (that is, farther on in the work).

MS., manuscript (plural MSS.).

n., note, footnote (plural nn.).

supra, (Latin) above (that is, earlier in the work).

1. Tell exactly where you would look for the cross reference "... *infra*, p. 679, n. 27."

2. What does each of the following mean: (a) B. and L., 735 ff., (b) Lee MSS., (c) Cf. Parker, *op. cit.*?

3. Examine nn. 24, 26, p. 678. Which of these is a reference footnote and which a content note? How can you tell? Find at least three reference and three content footnotes.

Catherine Drinker Bowen

from
John Adams, and the American Revolution

John Adams and Abigail Smith were engaged for more than two years, a long and trying time. Abby's mother was responsible for the delay. She did not openly oppose the marriage; she was, indeed, helpless to do so against her husband's approval. Moreover, Mrs. Smith noted that Abigail herself, usually so gentle, so sympathetic to family plans, developed a sudden assurance, a poise that seemed to have no point of vulnerability. Moving about the house, making beds, lifting the baking pans in the kitchen and thrusting them in the chimney oven, Abigail seemed encased in a new and shining armor; even the old jibes at female education could no longer reach her.[1] She read her books openly, where and when she pleased, and she had begun to study French. . . .

Not French but spinning, Mrs. Smith said irritably, should occupy the attention of an

1. *even the old jibes . . . reach her.* Mrs. Smith, who shared the generally held belief that girls needed only the most elementary education, had often taken Abigail to task for reading philosophical books. Abigail, however, continued to read them.

affianced girl. Abby only smiled, and running to her chest brought out a blanket, light and soft. She had finished it yesterday, she said. Was it not a beautiful clear yellow? She had dyed the wool with onionskins as her mother suggested. . . . She thought she would take the small quilt to Wollaston and finish it during her month's visit with Grandfather Quincy.[2]

John, as time passed, was amazed at Abby's adroitness, her unfailing patience with her mother. Mrs. Smith's excuse for the long engagement was, at first, that she could not bear to lose two daughters in one year. Mary was married in the autumn of 1762. The day after the ceremony, John approached Mrs. Smith in the little parlor at Weymouth, summoning what he considered his most persuasive manner. Unfortunately he did not, in his eagerness, notice that Mrs. Smith, in her chair facing the window, held a handkerchief to her eyes. She thought she was mourning her eldest daughter's departure. In reality she was simply recovering from the pleasurable excitement of a wedding which she was well aware had advanced her daughter's interests in a most satisfactory manner.[3]

Would it not be possible, John began deferentially, for Abigail and himself to be married after the New Year, or at least, in the

spring? His house at Braintree could be made ready in December. . . .

A veritable torrent of indignation answered him. Mrs. Smith, only too pleased to let off her feelings in some way more effectual than solitary tears, rose and faced this potential robber of her nest. Under its tight, plum-colored bodice the maternal bosom heaved, the maternal voice was shrill.

Listening, John's own anger rose until it boiled and steamed within him. His face grew fiery red. The tone of Mrs. Smith's voice was irritating beyond endurance.

"Madam!" John shouted. He raised his right arm in a dramatic gesture, forefinger extended. "Be pleased to hear me!"

At this crucial moment Abby entered the room, shook John's arm as if he were a recalcitrant child, and without the slightest hesitation or maiden reluctance pressed her other hand firmly against his lips. Mrs. Smith glared, drawn up to full height and trembling

2. *Wollaston . . . Grandfather Quincy.* Abigail's grandfather, Colonel John Quincy, owned a big white house at Mount Wollaston in Braintree. Abigail's mother, Elizabeth Quincy Smith, was proud of her descent from the distinguished Quincy family. 3. *her daughter's interests . . . satisfactory manner.* Mrs. Smith's eldest daughter, Mary, married Richard Cranch, a young man who had been born and bred in England and who already owned shares in a local industry.

in every stout limb. "Mamma dearest," Abby said quickly, gaily, moving to her mother and kissing her on the cheek—"have I not the promise of a noisy husband? Can he not roar like a very lion for love of me?"

This good-natured and merry impudence was so wholly unexpected that Mrs. Smith, in spite of herself, broke down and melted, half smiling. John, stiff as a poker, bowed his apology. Mrs. Smith loved her daughter dearly, and did not desire an open breach. She did not, indeed, know exactly what she desired in this situation, but held out rather desperately for delay, telling herself that her antagonism to John stemmed from a mother's natural ambition for her child. She had nothing against the young man's character, although his manners, certainly, were not distinguished.

At Braintree, John's mother was wholly delighted with Abigail. So were the aunts and uncles. Mrs. Adams' sister, Anne, was in open ecstasies. "You could not have done better for yourself, John," she said complacently, pressing his arm as if they were conspirators. "There is not a family in the county more distinguished than the Quincys. In every respect, the connection will be a furtherance to your career."

John, though he thought his aunt a fool— he had always thought so—was by no means displeased by this praise of his beloved. Ever since their engagement, John had himself been amazed at the qualities revealed week after week by his future bride. He had fallen in love with a young deer, a shy elusive creature that sat in corners and hung down her head—"like a bulrush," John had written one evening when they were first engaged. Now he found himself about to be united to a woman who, though under twenty, could maintain her position with the best of them, who managed a very difficult mother like a seasoned diplomat, and who even managed him, John Adams—he acknowledged it freely —with a loving skill that gave him great happiness.

John had not lived to be twenty-eight without knowing that his temper was short. Lately, he was aware that he had gained the reputa-tion, around Braintree especially, of being stubborn and headstrong. It was a tendency that had grown on him with the increase of his business. How slow people were with their responses! John thought often, in irritation. They required six sentences where one would do; their minds turned heavily, like old wagon wheels lumbering up a hill road. A man could not stand there forever, waiting, while the wheels creaked round. . . .

Since his father's death, there had been no one to check John's impatience; it rose sometimes to open arrogance. The matter of the licensed taverns should have taught him a lesson.[4] John thought it had, when he acknowledged in his diary the list of his new enemies. But listing enemies does not make friends. In Boston, Worcester, Cambridge, in the courthouse and among lawyers and politicians, John was well liked. Flattery was beyond his repertory, but when he admired a man, John let it be known instantly by his bearing. Unfortunately, this frankness extended also to those he did not like, of both sexes. Abigail remonstrated with him gently. "You frightened *me* for months, John," she said. "Even now, your manner drives me sometimes into silence. Have you not noticed?"

No, John said. He had not noticed. Abby was such a wonderfully sympathetic listener; when he was with her, his talk had the eloquence of an archangel. What was more, he could let his tongue run on with no after-worries. "How miraculous, Abby," John said, sighing, "to discover a person with whom one can make a thousand, thousand mistakes!"

As the months went by, the two contrived to meet at least once a week. Weymouth was only four miles from Braintree; John could be there in half an hour. But in the winter of 1764, they had a long separation. Smallpox broke out in Boston and Braintree. Mrs. Adams, who had lost her husband through an epidemic fever, declared herself terrified, and insisted that John go in to Boston for inoculation. Abigail's mother, on the other hand, dis-

---

4. *The matter . . . lesson.* Early in his career as a lawyer and a selectman in Braintree, John had succeeded in his efforts to close down all the taverns of the town. Much to his surprise this success won him as many enemies as friends.

approved of the treatment and would not permit any of her daughters to have it. John begged and fought, offering to take Abigail to the hospital himself and act as nurse. In the end he went off with a group of friends to be treated by a Dr. Perkins. They were shut up, five to a room, dieted, given powders, denied bread, milk, and pudding, pricked and inoculated. Their heads ached, they burned with fever, broke out triumphantly, compared scabs and pustules after the traditional manner.

At last the long quarantine was over and John, concerning whose health Abigail had greatly feared, returned to Braintree. But to John's dismay, he was no sooner settled at home than Abby was dispatched on a long visit to Boston. "My soul and body," wrote John gloomily, "have been thrown into disorder by your absence. A month or two would make me the most insufferable Cynic in the world. I see nothing but Faults, Follies, Frailties and Defects in anybody. People have lost all their good properties. But you who have always softened and warmed my heart shall restore my Benevolence as well as my Health and 'Tranquillity of mind.'"

John knew well, by now, how deeply he needed Abigail Smith. ("You are teaching me kindness, dear Abby," he had said once.) Abby was indeed kind; she had none of the dreary, virtuous piety John had learned to associate with the good women of Braintree. There was a gaiety in Abigail that delighted John's very soul. Yet, at bottom, the girl was a serious creature, who believed that men and women were placed on earth not for their enjoyment but for a purpose. Man, created in the image of God, must fulfill his promise or become a blasphemy to his Maker.

With all his heart, John agreed. He could not have married a woman who did not share this philosophy. It was a Puritan inheritance. In the long road to heaven, man was accountable to God for every moment of his time; he must therefore "improve" that time, that day, that moment. An hour wasted was an hour's sin. The conviction was part of John and Abigail, running in their veins to be transmitted to their progeny even of the fifth generation. It was a philosophy and a program that would

sustain husband and wife through long separation, through ordeal most fiery (years while John served the Congress at Philadelphia, years with an ocean between them). Separation was a decade in the future. Yet the future was implicit now in the meeting and the courtship of these two.

One morning in early autumn, Abigail took John to Wollaston to spend the day with her grandparents. The scene proved by no means so brilliant as Aunt Anne Adams had once painted it. The company, gathered in the long dining room that opened on the terrace, consisted merely of Abigail's Uncle Norton Quincy, a quiet, easygoing man of forty-odd, her grandparents and two of her married aunts who had come to view the prospective bridegroom. The aunts took their leave after dinner, about four in the afternoon. Madam Quincy, a merry, talkative old lady, handsomely dressed in voluminous, rustling lavender and a cap with ribbons, excused herself and went upstairs to rest. Colonel Quincy suggested that the three of them, Abby, John and himself, stroll about the grounds and farm.

They went out; the Colonel walked between them, his ruddy face glowing with health and pleasure, his white hair, caught at the neck in a bag and narrow black ribbon, blowing a little in the wind. At seventy-four he was upright and sturdy, though he leaned at times on his cane and took John's arm if they had to traverse a rocky place. John thought he had never met so friendly a gentleman.

In the late afternoon sunshine, with a September breeze blowing from the Bay, his cherished trees and fields about him, the old man expanded on every subject from politics to horticulture. He stopped to gesticulate with his cane, pointing at each newly planted shrub or tree, explaining whence it had come and if he had obtained it from a neighboring colony or by special shipment from England.

In perfect amity, the three wandered over the bare hills below the mansion. Always, John noted, the Colonel included Abby in his talk, asking her frequent questions, waiting for the approval of her laugh.

"Abby," said Colonel John, "let us rest here

on the bench. Do you tell the story of Mr. Josiah Quincy[5] and the Spanish frigate with the chests of gold."

The three sat down in a sheltered, sunny spot behind the orchard wall. Abby began to talk. She told her story eagerly, using her hands, moving her head and body as she spoke. John had never seen her so at ease or so delightful. Her brown fine hair blew across her face; something in her gesture when she raised a hand to her forehead enchanted John. There was a joy about her that was infectious, a nervous force he had not sensed before. Her story ranged beyond Mr. Josiah and his privateering schooner; Abby knew the history of privateering, was familiar with the Acts of Trade that made smuggling necessary. She did not hesitate to embellish her tale with pertinent historical and political details.

John was a little abashed at this skillful flow of narrative from one who had hitherto been content to let him do the talking—or content, certainly, to leave political explanation to his superior masculine intellect. More than once, Abby had tried to tell him there was something forbidding in his aspect, some lack of invitation that froze the words on her lips. "I can be more free with you in letters, John," she had said once, wistfully, "than when we are together."

John, at the time, had dismissed this as mere feminine coquetry. Only today was his mistake revealed. He knew it, uneasily, as a grave mistake. "Sir," he said to the Colonel as Abby's story was done, and the three rose to return to the house, "your presence is an inspiration to Miss Abby. I never heard her talk so well."

They were at the foot of a long flight of stone steps, leading to the garden. The old man took John's arm. "I am Abby's great admirer," he said. "I have enjoyed that rôle since she was three, and told me her first tale." He stopped to take breath. "Human beings need admiration and love," he said, "as plants need the sun."

On the twenty-fifth of October, 1764, John Adams and Abigail Smith were married from her father's house at Weymouth. All summer, week by week, the bride's belongings, her linens and blankets, her chests and furniture and modest trousseau of dresses, had been carted over the hill from Weymouth. Mr. Smith had given his daughter a handsome marriage portion; with it the two had purchased an orchard and a piece of land just down the slope from their barn. The little house itself was painted and refurnished to the last inch; John was very proud of it. It faced the highway bravely; Abigail had planted a lilac bush by the front step. It would surely bloom next year, she said. The old kitchen had been made over into an office for John, with a separate door cut in the side wall so that clients need not walk through the house.

Mrs. Adams had thrown herself into the marriage plans with all the energy of her nature. Her final act had been to purchase a superb piece of white imported satin and make her son a wedding waistcoat embroidered in gold thread. She asked John what pattern he preferred for the embroidery; John chose sprays of wheat to symbolize October and the harvest.

The twenty-fifth of October dawned clear and cold. The rooms of Weymouth parsonage were dressed for the wedding in autumn foliage, sumach and maple branches, bright red and gold. There were bowls of fruit on the tables, yellow pears and big shiny apples, little round purple country grapes in festoons, and even some oranges, rather dried up, that Mr. Josiah Quincy had saved out of a shipment from Spain. John, in the dazed condition traditional with bridegrooms, thought he had never seen so many people in such a small space: Quincys, Nortons, Smiths, Tyngs, Adamses, Basses, chattered and stared. Abigail's bridal dress was of fine white challis, sprigged with little scarlet flowers. The bodice was tight, the neck cut square and edged with lace, the skirt enormous. John's legs were splendid in white silk stockings, the buckles of his shoes shone like the moon at high tide. His breeches were fawn-colored; above them

---

5. *Mr. Josiah Quincy.* Josiah Quincy, Colonel John's cousin, had acquired a fortune by privateering during the Seven Years War between England and France. The Peace of Paris ended this profitable business.

the white satin waistcoat shimmered. His coat, long-skirted and fashionable, was of dark blue broadcloth, with silver buttons.

Altogether, people agreed, as wedding parties always agree, they made a very handsome couple. Aunt Anne Adams, surprisingly prim and speechless in the gay throng, stayed close by John's mother, noting each detail of dress, of entertainment, of food and drink and service, to carry later to a waiting Braintree world.

At last it was over. The sacred words were said, the happy vows exchanged. The bride was embraced, the groom congratulated. The bowls of punch were drained, the wedding meats devoured, the golden fruits were gone.

Mrs. Smith had alternately wept and forgotten to weep. Mrs. Adams endeavored not to crow because she was gaining a daughter while Madam Smith was losing one. John's brothers told him the horse was ready on the highway just below the lawn; he went out and waited. Abigail, in her long scarlet riding cloak and hood, ran down the stairs from her chamber and out the door of her father's house. John mounted his horse, leaned down and swung his bride to the pillion behind him.

Then, with a salute to the throng by the parsonage door, Mr. and Mrs. John Adams rode triumphantly down the highway, headed northward for Braintree and home.

---

from BERNARD DE VOTO Catherine Drinker Bowen

Once De Voto wrote a paragraph to me, about American history and his feeling toward it. (I have quoted this in my last book, but it's worth repetition.) The words came, remember, from a man tough-minded, who professed to write history from the facts and the facts alone. I was working, at the time, on our revolutionary period, and I had been challenged by a scholar who declared that my view of American history was too romantic altogether. The men who composed our United States Constitution were interested not in ideals but in property—their own property and its protection. George Washington only went into the army to recover his lands along the Shenandoah, and so on. In distress I wrote De Voto, telling my chagrin because I had not made adequate rebuttal. He wrote back at once. Here is what he said:

"Sure you're romantic about American history. What your detractor left out of the account was the fact that it is the most romantic of all histories. It began in myth and has developed through centuries of fairy stories. Whatever the time is in America it is always, at every moment, the mad and wayward hour when the prince is finding the little foot that alone fits into the slipper of glass. It is a little hard to know what romantic means to those who use the word umbrageously. But if the mad, impossible voyage of Columbus or Cartier or La Salle or Coronado or John Ledyard is not romantic, if the stars did not dance in the sky when our Constitutional Convention met, if Atlantis has any landscape stranger or the other side of the moon any lights or colors or shapes more unearthly than the customary homespun of Lincoln and the morning coat of Jackson, well, I don't know what romance is. Ours is a story mad with the impossible; it is by chaos out of dream; it began as dream and has continued as dream down to the last headlines you read in a newspaper. And of our dream there are two things above all others to be said, that only madmen could have dreamed them or would have dared to, and that we have shown a considerable faculty for making them come true. The simplest truth you can ever write about our history will be charged and surcharged with romanticism, and if you are afraid of the word you had better start practicing seriously on your fiddle."

TO INCREASE UNDERSTANDING

1. (*a*) What were some of the defects in young John Adams' character? (*b*) What aspects of his character seem admirable? (*c*) What techniques does Catherine Drinker Bowen use to make these character traits vivid? (If necessary review the introduction, page 663, paragraph 4.)

2. (*a*) What indications are given that Abigail will make a suitable wife for John? (*b*) What are some of her qualities that surprise John? (*c*) How are these qualities brought to his attention?

3. (*a*) What difference in tone do you notice between this biography and that written by Freeman? (*b*) Explain why you do or do not think the tone of each biography is appropriate to its subject. Take into account the period of each man's career which the selection covers.

4. In De Voto's letter to Mrs. Bowen (page 689) he speaks of American history as romantic. (*a*) What does he mean? (*b*) Does he give any support of this claim in his account of the crossing of the Salt Desert (page 16)? (*c*) What evidence is there in the selection by Mrs. Bowen that her view of human nature, as contrasted with that of her detractors, is romantic? (*d*) What kind of biographies would you expect Mrs. Bowen's critics to write?

5. The challenge of portraying a man of law as a vivid human being is largely responsible for Catherine Drinker Bowen's interest in writing about jurists. To meet this challenge she has employed with great success an approach to biography quite different from Freeman's. (Refer to "Approaches to Biography," page 682.) She frequently elaborates what is given in the letters and diaries that are her sources by filling in details of gesture, action, conversation, and thought. (*a*) Point out a number of details of this type which you believe are invented, and explain why you think so. (*b*) How might this selection differ if the author had adopted the conservative approach to biography? (*c*) What does the cutting gain from Mrs. Bowen's filling in of details? (*d*) To what extent do you think these details help her to accomplish her purpose of trying to bring the figure of John Adams into human terms?

6. Catherine Drinker Bowen goes to great lengths to ensure that whatever she adds to her sources does not distort the character she is portraying. As part of this effort she studies court transcripts and diaries to get the exact flavor of the style of speech of the period she is writing about. (*a*) Point out sentences quoted as conversation that are phrased quite differently from the way they would be today. (*b*) How might each be phrased now?

CARL SANDBURG 1878-

When the Pulitzer Prize committee met in 1940, one work before them had met with such acclaim the year before that it simply could not be denied a prize. Carl Sandburg had at last finished his monumental biography of Lincoln, launched thirteen years earlier with the two volumes that covered what Sandburg called Lincoln's *Prairie Years*.

Sandburg, who by 1940 was nationally known as poet and balladeer (see page 559), seemed ideally suited to write about Lincoln. He was born in Galesburg, Illinois, where Lincoln and Douglas had held a great debate twenty years before; his Middle West boyhood—like Lincoln's—was hard; and through his many years as newspaperman, lecturer, and poet he had steeped himself in information about Lincoln. Since 1932 he had buried himself in his attic, surrounded by documents on Lincoln and the Civil War, pounding out the President's life on a typewriter perched on a packing crate. The already famous result which confronted the Pulitzer Prize committee in 1940 was the four-volume *Lincoln: The War Years*. Because, according to the stipulation of Joseph Pulitzer, no prize for biography could be awarded to a work on Washington or Lincoln, the second part of Sandburg's biography was given a Pulitzer Prize for history.

Classifying Sandburg's work as history, however, is not inappropriate. As is clear in the accompanying selection from *The Prairie Years*, Lincoln's life is set in relief against the social and political history of the times in which he lived. One of Sandburg's chief methods for viewing the spirit of Lincoln is to project it against the background of his age.

from Abraham Lincoln: The Prairie Years

Sixteen-year-old Abe had worked on the farm of James Taylor, at the mouth of Anderson Creek, on that great highway of traffic, the Ohio River. Besides plowing and doing barn and field work, he ran the ferryboat across the Ohio. Two travelers wanted to get on a steamboat one day, and after Abe sculled them to it and lifted their trunks on board they threw him a half dollar apiece; it gave him a new feeling; the most he had ever earned before that was at butchering for thirty-one cents a day. And when one of the half dollars slipped from him and sank in the river, that too gave him a new feeling.

At Anderson Creek ferry, he saw and talked with settlers, land buyers and sellers, traders, hunters, peddlers, preachers, gamblers, politicians, teachers, and men shut-mouthed about their business. Occasionally came a customer who looked as if he might be one of the "half-horse, half-alligator men" haunting the Ohio watercourse those years. There was river talk about Mike Fink,[1] known on the Ohio as the "Snapping Turtle" and on the Mississippi as "The Snag," the toughest of the half-horse, half-alligator crowd; he was a famous marksman, and aiming his rifle from his keelboat floating the Ohio had shot off the tails of pigs running loose in the bottom lands; once Mike ordered his wife off his barge, covered her with autumn leaves while he threat-ened to shoot her, set fire to the leaves, so that Mrs. Fink ran with clothes and hair on fire and jumped into the river, to hear her husband saying, "Ye will make eyes at the men on other boats, will ye?"

Along the water front of Louisville, Mike Fink had backed up his claim, "I can outrun, outhop, outjump, throw down, drag out, and lick any man in the country; I'm a Salt River roarer; I love the wimming and I'm chock-full of fight." They tried him for crimes in Louisville and acquitted him for lack of sufficient evidence; he waved a red bandanna for a good-by and told them he would come back to face their other indictments.

Among the bad men of the river, rough-and-tumble fighting included gouging of eyes, thumb-chewing, knee-lifting, head-butting, the biting off of noses and ears, and the tearing loose of underlips with the teeth. "Fights was fights in them days."

Travelers had a proverb that a tavern was hardly safe if the proprietor had a nose or an ear off. It was a sign the landlord couldn't take care of himself.

Lawyers with books in their saddlebags took the ferryboat across the Ohio; law and order

---

1. *Mike Fink*, a legendary boatman of the Ohio and the Mississippi rivers.

was coming to that wild young country, they believed; they could remember only ten years back how the law of the Territory of Indiana[2] provided that a horse thief should have two hundred lashes with a whip on his bare back and stay in jail till the horse was paid for, and the second time he was caught horse-stealing he was shot or hanged; for stealing cattle or hogs the thief had his shirt taken off and was given thirty-nine lashes.

Old-timers came along who could tell how the Indians in 1809 were stealing horses, burning barns and fences, killing settlers, running off with cattle and chickens, and how General Hopkins with 1200 soldiers burned the Indian villages along the Wabash, their log cabins, gardens, orchards, stationed rangers to hunt down every Indian they found, till the time came when there was not a red man on the Wabash or south of that river in the state of Indiana.

The ferry boy at Anderson Creek watched and listened to this human drift across the Ohio River—the bushwhackers and bad men who called themselves bad, and the others who called themselves good. Civilization went by, boats and tools breaking ways. Steamboats came past in a slow and proud pageantry making their fourteen- to twenty-day passage from New Orleans to Pittsburgh; geography became fact to the boy looking on; flags on the steamboats were a sign of that long stretch of country the steamboats were crossing. Strings of flatboats passed, loaded with produce— pork, turkeys, chickens, corn meal, flour, whiskey, venison hams, hazelnuts, skins, furs, ginseng; this was farm produce for trading at river ports to merchants or to plantation owners for feeding slaves. Other trading boats carried furniture, groceries, clothes, kitchenware, plows, wagons, harness; this was from manufacturing centers, consignments to storekeepers and traders. Houseboats, arks, sleds,[3] flatboats with small cabins in which families lived and kept house, floated toward their new homesteads; on these the women were washing, the children playing. The life flow of a main artery of American civilization, at a vivid line of growth, was a piece of pageantry there at Anderson Creek.

Young Abe was out with ax, saw, and drawknife building himself a light flatboat at Bates' Landing, a mile and a half down the river from Anderson Creek. He was eighteen years old, a designer, builder, navigator; he cut down trees, hewed out planks, pegged and cleated together the bottoms and sides of his own boat, wood from end to end.

Pieces of money jingled in his pockets. Passengers paid him for sculling them from Bates' Landing out to steamboats in the middle of the Ohio River.

He studied words and figurations on pieces of money. Thirteen stars stood for the first Thirteen States of the Union. The silver print of an eagle spreading its wings and lifting a fighting head was on the half dollar. As though the eagle were crying high, important words, above its beak was inscribed *E Pluribus Unum*; this meant the many states should be One, young Abe learned.

Circled with the thirteen stars were the head and bust of a motherly looking woman. On her forehead was the word *Liberty*. Just what did *She* mean?

Waiting for passengers and looking out on the wide Ohio to the drooping trees that dipped their leaves in the water on the farther shore, he could think about money and women and eagles.

A signal came from the opposite shore one day and Lincoln rowed across the river. As he stepped out of his boat two men jumped out of the brush. They took hold of him and said they were going to "duck" him in the river. They were John and Lin Dill, brothers who operated a ferry and claimed Abe had been transporting passengers contrary to the law of Kentucky.

As they sized up Abe's lean husky arms they decided not to throw him in the river. He might be too tough a customer. Then all three went to Squire Samuel Pate, justice of the peace, near Lewisport.[4]

A warrant for the arrest of Abraham Lin-

2. *the Territory of Indiana.* Indiana had been admitted as a state in 1816, just before the Lincoln family moved there from Kentucky. 3. *arks, sleds,* types of clumsy, roughly made river boats. 4. *Lewisport,* a Kentucky town located on the Ohio River.

coln was sworn out by John T. Dill. And the trial began of the case of "The Commonwealth of Kentucky versus Abraham Lincoln," charged with violation of "An Act Respecting the Establishment of Ferries."

Lincoln testified he had carried passengers from the Indiana shore out to the middle of the river, never taking them to the Kentucky shore. And the Dill brothers, though sore and claiming the defendant Lincoln had wronged them, did not go so far as to testify he had "for reward set any person over a river," in the words of the Kentucky statute.

Squire Pate dismissed the warrant against Lincoln. The disappointed Dills put on their hats and left. Lincoln sat with Squire Pate for a long talk. If a man knows the law about a business he is in, it is a help to him, the Squire told young Abe.

They shook hands and parted friends. Afterwards on days when no passengers were in sight and it was "law day" at Squire Pate's down the river, Abe would scull over and watch the witnesses, the constables, the Squire, the machinery of law, government, justice.

The State of Indiana, he learned, was one thing, and the State of Kentucky, something else. A water line in the middle of a big river ran between them. He could ask: "Who makes state lines? What *are* state lines?"

In the year 1825, ox teams and pack horses came through Gentryville[5] carrying people on their way to a place on the Wabash River they called New Harmony.[6] A rich English businessman named Robert Owen had paid $132,-000 for land and $50,000 for live stock, tools, and merchandise, and had made a speech before the Congress at Washington telling how he and his companions were going to try to find a new way for people to live their lives together, without fighting, cheating, or exploiting each other, where work would be honorable yet there would be time for play and learning; they would share and share alike, each for all and all for each. In January 1826 Owen himself, with a party of thirty people, came down the Ohio River in what was called the "boatload of knowledge."

More ox wagons and pack horses kept coming past the Gentryville crossroads; about a thousand people were joined in Owen's scheme at New Harmony on the Wabash. The scheme lighted up Abe Lincoln's heart. His eyes were big and hungry as a hoot owl's as he told Dennis Hanks,[7] "There's a school and thousands of books there and fellers that know everything in creation." The schooling would have cost him about $100 a year and he could have worked for his board. But Tom Lincoln had other plans for his son Abe.

Across the next three years the boy grew longer of leg and arm, tougher of bone and sinew, with harder knuckles and joints. James Gentry, with the largest farms in the Pigeon Creek clearings, and a landing on the Ohio River, was looking the big boy over. He believed Abe could take his pork, flour, meal, bacon, potatoes, and produce to trade down the Mississippi River for cotton, tobacco, and sugar. Young Abe was set to work on a flatboat; he cut the oaks for a double bottom of stout planks, and a deck shelter, two pairs of long oars at bow and stern, a check-post,[8] and a setting pole for steering.

As the snow began to melt, a little before the first frogs started shrilling, in that year of 1828, they loaded the boat and pushed off.

In charge of the boat Mr. Gentry had placed his son Allen, and in charge of Allen he had placed Abe Lincoln, to hold his own against any half-horse, half-alligator bushwhackers who might try to take the boat or loot it, and leave the bones of those they took it from, at Cave-in-Rock on the Illinois shore, or other spots where the skeletons of flatboatmen had been found years after the looters sold the cargo down the river. The honesty of Abe, of course, had been the first point Mr. Gentry considered; and the next point had been whether he could handle the boat in the snags and sand bars. The two young men

---

5. *Gentryville*, a crossroads hamlet located in southern Indiana near the Pigeon Creek clearings where Lincoln lived. 6. *New Harmony.* For another reference to this town see the discussion of experimental communities in Thoreau's time on page 234. 7. *Dennis Hanks*, a cousin of Lincoln. His recollections form a very important source for biographers of the early Lincoln. 8. *check-post*, a post used to secure the boat.

pushed off on their trip of a thousand miles to New Orleans, on a wide, winding waterway, where the flatboats were tied up at night to the river bank, and floated and poled by day amid changing currents, strings of other flatboats, and in the paths of the proud white steamboats.

Whitecaps rose and broke with their foam feathers, a mile, two miles, beyond the limit of eyesight, as fresh winds blew along the Ohio River. Cave-in-Rock was passed on the Illinois shore, with its sign, "Wilson's Liquor Vault and House of Entertainment," with a doorway 25 feet high, 80 feet wide, and back of that entrance a cavern 200 feet deep, a 14-foot chimney leading to an upper room, where one time later were found 60 human skeletons, most of them rivermen lured and trapped by the Wilson gang that camped at Hurricane Island near by.

Timber-covered river bluffs stood up overlooking the river like plowmen resting big shoulders between the plow handles; twisted dumps and runs of clay banks were like squatters who had lost hope and found rheumatism and malaria; lone pine trees had silhouetted their dry arms of branches on reefs where they dissolved and reappeared in river-mist lights as if they struggled to tell some secret of water and sky before going under.

The nineteen-year-old husky from Indiana found the Mississippi River as tricky with comic twists as Aesop's fables, as mystical, boding, and promising as the family Bible. Sand bars, shoals, and islands were scattered along with the look of arithmetic numbers. Sudden rains, shifting winds, meant new handling of oars. A rising roar and rumble of noise might be rough water ahead or some whimsical current tearing through fallen tree branches at the riverside. A black form seems to be floating up-river through a gray drizzle; the coming out of the sun shows it is an island point, standing still; the light and air play tricks with it.

The bends of the river ahead must be watched with ready oars and sweeps or the flatboat naturally heads in to shore. Strong winds crook the course of the boat, sometimes blowing it ashore; one of the crew must hustle

off in a rowboat, tie a hawser to a tree or stump, while another man on the big boat has a rope at the check-post; and they slow her down. Warning signals must be given at night, by waving a lantern or firewood, to other craft.

So the flatboat, "the broadhorn," went down the Father of Waters, four to six miles an hour, the crew frying their own pork and cornmeal cakes, washing their own shirts, sewing on their own buttons.

Below Baton Rouge, among the sugar plantations known as the "Sugar Coast," they tied up at the plantation of Madame Duquesne one evening, put their boat in order, spoke their good nights to any sweet stars in the sky, and dropped off to sleep. They woke to find seven rowdies on board trying to steal the cargo and kill the crew; the long-armed Indiana husky swung a crab-tree club, knocked them galley-west, chased them into the woods, and laid a bandanna on a gash over the right eye that left a scar for life as it healed. Then they cut loose the boat and moved down the river.

At New Orleans they traded, sold the rest of their cargo of potatoes, bacon, hams, flour, apples, jeans, in exchange for cotton, tobacco, and sugar, and sold the flatboat for what it would bring as lumber. And they lingered and loitered a few days, seeing New Orleans, before taking steamer north.

On the streets and by-streets of that town, which had floated the flags of French, British, and American dominion, young Abraham Lincoln felt the pulses of a living humanity with far heartbeats in wide, alien circles over the earth: English sailors who sang "Ranzo" and "Boney," "Hangin' Johnny," and "O Fare-you-well, My Bonny Young Girls"; Dutchmen and French in jabber and exclamative; Swedes, Norwegians, and Russians with blond and reddish mustaches and whiskers; Spaniards and Italians with knives and red silk handkerchiefs; New York, Philadelphia, Boston, Rome, Amsterdam became human facts; it was London those men came from ejaculating, "Ow can ye blime me?"

Women in summer weather wearing slippers and boots; creoles with dusks of eyes;

quadroons and octoroons with elusive soft voices; streets lined with saloons where bets were laid on steamboat races; talk ran fast about the construction, then going on, of the New Orleans & Pontchartrain Railroad, to be one of the first steam railroads in America and the world; slaves passed handcuffed into gangs headed for cotton fields of one, two, six thousand acres in size; and everywhere was talk about slaves.

As young Abe Lincoln and Allen Gentry made their way back home to the clearings of Pigeon Creek, Indiana, the tall boy had his thoughts. He had crossed half the United States, it seemed, and was back home after three-months' vacation with eight-dollars-a-month pay in his pocket and a scar over the right eye.

That year Indiana University was to print its first catalogue, but Abe Lincoln didn't show up among the students who registered. He was between the plow handles or pulling fodder or sinking the ax in trees and brush, and reading between times *Pilgrim's Progress*,[9] a history of the United States, the life of Francis Marion,[10] the life of Ben Franklin, and the book he borrowed from Dave Turnham, the constable. The title page of the book said it contained "The Revised Laws of Indiana, adopted and enacted by the general assembly at their eighth session. To which are prefixed the Declaration of Independence, the Constitution of the United States, the Constitution of the State of Indiana, and sundry other documents connected with the Political History of the Territory and State of Indiana. Arranged and published by the authority of the General Assembly."

The science of government, theories of law, and schemes of administration spread themselves before the young man's mind as he crept along from page to page, wrestling with those statutes of Indiana and other documents. Crimes and punishments were listed there, in black and white; fine distinctions between murder and manslaughter, between burglary, robbery, larceny, forgery, trespass, nuisance, fraud; varied circumstances of assault and battery, affray, unlawful assembly, rout and riot. Lives of masses of people spread out before him in a panorama as he read the statutes. He read that there are crimes which shall be deemed "infamous," and any man found guilty of an infamous crime "shall thereafter be rendered incapable of holding any office of honor, trust, or profit, of voting at any election, of serving as a juror, of giving testimony within this state." He read in Section 60 on page 48, "Every person of the age of fourteen years or upwards, who shall profanely curse or damn, or shall profanely swear by the name of God, Jesus Christ, or the Holy Ghost, shall be fined not less than one, nor more than three dollars, for each offence." Sharp lines were drawn between murder and manslaughter; a murderer shall be a person "of sound memory and discretion, who shall unlawfully kill any reasonable creature in being and under the peace of this state, with malice aforethought"; a manslaughterer shall be a person "who without malice, either express or implied, shall unlawfully kill another person, either voluntarily upon a sudden heat, or involuntarily, but in the commission of some unlawful act." It seemed, too, there was a stream of people born or gone wrong, for the state to take care of, the criminals in jails and prisons, the paupers in poorhouses, the insane and feebleminded in asylums, wives with runaway husbands, and children born out of wedlock.

It was tough plowing through that book, with the satisfaction, however, that he could keep what he earned.

---

9. *Pilgrim's Progress*, a famous religious allegory telling of a man's progress through life to eternity, by John Bunyan. It was first published in England in 1678. From the time of its publication until late in the nineteenth century it was probably more widely read in America than any other book except the Bible, and was rated next to the Bible in importance as a Christian document. 10. *Francis Marion*, a Revolutionary War general noted for the skill and speed of his operations. Because he operated in the lowlands of the South, he was generally referred to as "the Swamp Fox."

 TO INCREASE UNDERSTANDING

1. (*a*) In what ways, according to Carl Sandburg, was Abe Lincoln a typical frontier youth? (*b*) What interests and qualities of character distinguished him from other frontier boys?

2. One of the factors that has made Sandburg's

Lincoln popular is its style. Perhaps the grand sweep of his style is partly explained by the fact that Sandburg was a poet before he was a biographer. (*a*) Review some of Sandburg's poems (pages 559-564). Point out passages in the biography that are similar in style to the poems. Explain wherein the similarity lies. (*b*) How is this style especially suited to the subjects treated in this biographical selection?

3. (*a*) How was Lincoln introduced to the elements of law and government? (*b*) How might this introduction to the intricacies of law and government have fitted Lincoln to become a leader during a war over some of the fundamental principles of the Constitution?

4. The passages that tell about Lincoln's activities are interspersed with passages describing the frontier life of his time that he might well have witnessed. (*a*) Point out some of these latter passages. (*b*) What impression of frontier society do they create? Why? (*c*) What aspects of Lincoln's character and his success do these sketches help a modern reader to understand?

5. (*a*) Which of the approaches to biographical writing described in "Approaches to Biography" on page 682 does Sandburg adopt? (*b*) What impression of Lincoln's youth does this approach convey beyond what would be possible in a conservative biography?

The
Great Judge

Philip Hamburger

PHILIP HAMBURGER 1914-

In his more than twenty years of journalistic writing, Philip Hamburger has written most of the forms of brief nonfiction popular in magazines today. Mr. Hamburger, who was born in Wheeling, West Virginia, prepared for his career by taking a bachelor's degree at Johns Hopkins and an M.S. degree at the Columbia University School of Journalism. After joining the staff of the *New Yorker* in 1939, he gained considerable experience in writing, among other things, the brief but detailed biographies of the type which that magazine pioneered and called "Profiles" (see page 500).

The accompanying biographical portrait is presented in its entirety as it appeared in *Life* magazine, November 4, 1946. Judge Hand (1872-1961) retired from the Circuit Court of Appeals in 1951, five years after this biography was written.

Jurists are by nature argumentative, and nothing delights them more than to consider the qualities that constitute lasting greatness on the bench. Is the important factor the literary style and grandeur of a judge's opinions? Zeal for uniting the law with the economic realities of life? Sturdy defense of the *status quo*[1]?

Debates of this nature frequently end in an atmosphere of mellow agreement at the mention of Learned Hand, senior judge of the U.S. Circuit Court of Appeals for the

Reprinted from *Life*, Nov. 4, 1946, by permission of the author. Copyright 1946 by Time, Inc.
1. *status quo*, the way things are; the existing state of affairs. [*Latin*]

Second Circuit (New York, Connecticut and Vermont), a robust, stocky man with thick eyebrows and a voice like the crackle of lightning. An impressive number of judges and lawyers consider him the outstanding member of the federal judiciary, the spiritual heir of such judicial giants as Marshall, Holmes, Brandeis, and Cardozo.[2]

Judge Hand will be seventy-five this winter, and many of his colleagues and friends, more than anxious to pay him tribute, have planned testimonial dinners and the presentation of a bust. Typically the Judge has been trying to keep one step ahead of them in an attempt to scotch their plans. It is his modest and reasoned decision that public tributes have small place in the life of a judge. Nonetheless he cannot stop thousands of lawyers and judges the world over from turning their thoughts in his direction at this time, reëxamining his opinions and papers, and evaluating his lifework. "Learned Hand is the most distinguished, living English-speaking jurist," a Supreme Court justice has remarked with deep feeling. Those who insist that a judge must write with the pen of a master will accept no substitute for his prose. "There is a lovely tune in his head," said one of his colleagues on the bench, "and somehow he translates it into words."

To Judge Hand each individual is sacred and entitled to his day in court. His roots are imbedded in the deepest and healthiest soil of American democracy. To discover the essence of that soil he has devoted a lifetime of inquiry, both on and off the bench. "The only America you can love," he once wrote, "is one whose citizens have learned the self-discipline of compliance in the face of truth, the only country which any man has a right to love is one where there is a balanced judgment, justice founded on wisdom, a free spirit and a temperate mind." He conceives of the law as a living organism and of interpretation as an imaginative exercise. Statutes are the result of legislative compromise, he holds, and judges must therefore discover what the authors had in mind while framing them.

Broad generalizations leave him in a cold intellectual fury. Lawyers who attempt to impress him by reminding the court of "those eternal principles of justice ringing down the ages" do so only once. His broad jaw drops in anguish. His bushy gray eyebrows rise in horror. His face, a moment ago as serene and inquiring as Cardozo's, becomes as fierce as Daniel Webster's at the height of a peroration. The courtroom echoes with a sharp crack as he slaps a hand to his brow and leans far back in a tall leather armchair. "Rubbish!" he shouts, almost disappearing from view behind the bench.

The casual observer, watching Judge Hand charge up the front steps of the federal courthouse in New York or preside on the bench with majestic authority, would conclude that he was a tower of self-assurance. Actually he is torn by doubts and constantly reëxamines his first principles. "What are the values? Do you know? Believe me, I do not," he will suddenly say to his law clerk during the discussion of a case. Although convinced that permanent solutions to the problems of life do not exist, he belies the thought by a ceaseless pursuit of solutions. "Shakespeare had Learned in mind when he wrote *Hamlet*," a distinguished corporation lawyer said recently. "Twenty-four hours a day he is a thinking being."

His moods are unpredictable. Some months ago he stepped into an elevator at the courthouse, deep in thought and with a dejected expression. "Pardon me, Judge Hand," said a stranger, as the elevator started up, "but I thought your opinion yesterday was wonderful." Judge Hand beamed. "Thank you, sir, thank you very much indeed," he said, stepping off at the twenty-fourth floor. Humming, he walked briskly through his suite of offices. He waved to his bailiff and Mrs. Berna Lohrman, his secretary. He stopped by the desk of his law clerk to repeat what the man in the elevator had said. "Splendid morning, splendid!" he said, entering his chambers. For the

2. *Marshall, Holmes, Brandeis, and Cardozo.* John Marshall (1755-1835) was chief justice of the Supreme Court from 1801 to 1835. Oliver Wendell Holmes (1841-1935) was an associate justice of the Supreme Court from 1902 until 1932. Louis Brandeis (1856-1941) was an associate justice from 1916 to 1939. Benjamin Cardozo (1870-1938) was an associate justice from 1932 to 1938.

next ten minutes those outside heard him gaily whistling a tune from *The Pirates of Penzance*.[3] Suddenly all sounds ceased, followed by an insistent buzz for the law clerk, who entered and found the Judge looking as though he had passed through the valley of the shadow of death. "I cannot fathom," said Judge Hand, "why I allowed myself to care *what* that fellow thought of my opinion!"

No other federal judge has been on the bench as long as Judge Hand. President Coolidge appointed him to the Circuit Court in 1924, directly from the District Court for the Southern District of New York, where he had sat for fifteen years. Since 1939 he has held the title of senior judge, a matter of seniority. In the hierarchy of the federal judiciary the ten Circuit Courts of Appeals and the Court of Appeals for the District of Columbia lie just below the Supreme Court, which rarely reviews a circuit-court decision unless it involves a constitutional problem or conflicts with decisions in another circuit. Circuit-court judges are appointed for life by the President with the consent of the Senate. Their salary is $17,500 a year.

Each morning Judge Hand walks four miles to work, leaving his home, a three-story brownstone on Manhattan's upper East Side, precisely one hour before he is due at the courthouse. This daily walk has become a ritual, to which he attributes his general robustness. "I shall continue the practice," he has told a friend, "until that final morning when, fittingly, I shall fall backward head over heels down the courthouse steps." His cousin, Judge Augustus Noble Hand, two and a half years his senior, considers the walks a species of self-torture and is given to saying, "Learned wonders why his back sometimes hurts. Why shouldn't it, walking all that distance at his age?" Several of the other judges of the Circuit Court occasionally go along on the walks, but few men can survive the sheer speed of the journey. The other judges have been known to drop out of line, one by one, and jump into cabs, while Judge Hand ploughs ahead without so much as a glance behind.

In the courtroom Judge Hand's appearance is formidable even when he is totally relaxed. Those who appear before him testify that it is a broadening intellectual experience, often with shattering overtones. Only the most hardy retain their composure, and once, during a Yale Law School moot court at which he presided, a prize student rose to address him, took one look, and promptly keeled over in a dead faint. Lawyers have a habit of in-

3. *The Pirates of Penzance*, an operetta by the famous British team of William S. Gilbert (1836-1911) and Arthur Sullivan (1842-1900). Their operettas are favorite musical productions in many high schools.

THE SPIRIT OF LIBERTY
Judge Learned Hand

We have gathered here to affirm a faith, a faith in a common purpose, a common conviction, a common devotion. Some of us have chosen America as the land of our adoption; the rest have come from those who did the same. For this reason we have some right to consider ourselves a picked group, a group of those who had the courage to break from the past and brave the dangers and the loneliness of a strange land. What was the object that nerved us, or those who went before us, to this choice? We sought liberty; freedom from oppression, freedom from want, freedom to be ourselves. This we then sought; this we now believe that we are by way of winning. What do we mean when we say that first of all we seek liberty? I often wonder whether we do not rest our hopes too much upon constitutions, upon laws, and upon courts. These are false hopes; believe me, these are false hopes. Liberty lies in the hearts of men and women; when it dies there, no constitution, no law, no court can save it; no constitution, no law, no court can even do much to help it. While it lies there it needs no constitution,

Reprinted by permission of Alfred A. Knopf, Inc., New York, from *The Spirit of Liberty: Papers and Addresses of Learned Hand*. Copyright 1952 by Alfred A. Knopf, Inc.

sisting that the case at bar either presents special aspects of the law hitherto inapplicable or is open-and-shut on the basis of established doctrine. Judge Hand resists both tendencies with the air of a tolerant schoolmaster. As long as the argument remains germane, he listens attentively, putting on and removing heavy tortoise-shell glasses and leaning across the bench. But let the argument wander or become diffused in mists of rhetoric and he begins to wriggle and twist. Experienced attorneys, recognizing the storm warnings, hurry back to the point. To an attorney who persists in rambling he will say, "May I inquire sir, what *are* you trying to tell us?" Spirited cross-questioning follows, during which the Judge attempts to reach the bedrock of the argument. Few things infuriate him more than what he calls the "meadows of easy assumptions," interruptions or attempts to flatter the bench. "I need not remind the distinguished judges of the Second Circuit of the law in this case," an attorney once began, with a broad smile. Judge Hand shot forward in his chair, cutting him short. "You impute a knowledge of the law to this bench," he said, "which it does not possess." Suffering from an attorney in love with the sound of his own voice, the Judge will occasionally scribble a note of protest and slip it to a colleague on the bench.

no law, no court to save it. And what is this liberty which must lie in the hearts of men and women? It is not the ruthless, the unbridled will; it is not freedom to do as one likes. That is the denial of liberty, and leads straight to its overthrow. A society in which men recognize no check upon their freedom soon becomes a society where freedom is the possession of only a savage few; as we have learned to our sorrow.

What then is the spirit of liberty? I cannot define it; I can only tell you my own faith. The spirit of liberty is the spirit which is not too sure that it is right; the spirit of liberty is the spirit which seeks to understand the minds of other men and women; the spirit of liberty is the spirit which weighs their interests alongside its own without bias; the spirit of liberty remembers that not even a sparrow falls to earth unheeded; the spirit of liberty is the spirit of Him who, near two thousand years ago, taught mankind that lesson it has never learned, but has never quite forgotten: that there may be a kingdom where the least shall be heard and considered side by side with the greatest. And now in that spirit, that spirit of an America which has never been, and which may never be; nay, which never will be except as the conscience and courage of Americans create it; yet in the spirit of that America

which lies hidden in some form in the aspirations of us all; in the spirit of that America for which our young men are at this moment fighting and dying; in that spirit of liberty and of America I ask you to rise and with me pledge our faith in the glorious destiny of our beloved country.

"John Marshall once said," read one of them, "that among the qualities of a great judge was the ability to look a lawyer straight in the eye and not hear one word he was saying."

Before writing a first draft of an opinion, Judge Hand calls in his law clerk and, thinking aloud, outlines the general pattern of his decision. To clerk for Learned Hand is considered a signal honor among lawyers. All but a few of his law clerks have been former editors of the *Harvard Law Review;* each spring the dean of the Law School recommends several applicants from whom the Judge selects one, who comes to him the fall after graduation. Judge Hand and his clerk plunge into a case together, the clerk looking up references and suggesting possible lines of reasoning. The relationship is highly informal. The Judge has no objection to his clerk's bringing a sandwich, say, into his chambers, but he does balk at the chewing of gum. The clerk has a private office but no phone, a contemptuous gesture on the Judge's part not toward the clerk but toward the telephone, which he considers a distracting factor in modern life. He feels that mobility tends to stimulate thought, and while discussing a case both he and the clerk pace rapidly back and forth across the room, in opposite directions, brushing past each other approximately every thirty seconds. "My feeling," the Judge will say, "is that plaintiff has suffered a grievance for which there should be a remedy, but a man's property is limited to the chattels which embody his invention." Then, as he whizzes by the clerk: "Sonny! We have come to a parting of the ways. I smell spearmint again. Throw out that gum! ... But amendment of the copyright law is not urged here. Come now, what do you think?" At the conclusion of the discussion the clerk, winded, retires to his office and orders are issued not to disturb the Judge.

Judge Hand writes three to four drafts of every decision, either hunched over his desk composing on long sheets of yellow foolscap or leaning back in his chair with a wooden writing board across his legs. "I write opinions with my life's blood," he often says. "I suffer, believe me, I suffer." He will write and re-

write steadily for hours, occasionally diverting his mind by walking to a wooden lectern in a far corner of the room and reading several pages of some nonlegal book which lies open there. For several weeks one summer he made his way, at odd intervals, through a life of Cromwell.[4] While concentrating on a point of law, he appears to be affected by extrasensory perceptions, enabling him to be jarred by noises inaudible to the normal ear. "There's a dog barking its head off down on the street," he told his secretary one afternoon. The secretary had inner doubts that anyone could hear barking twenty-four floors above the street, but she nonetheless told Sherman, his bailiff, who went downstairs and could neither see nor hear a dog. The results of his inquiry were transmitted to the Judge, who looked pained. Fifteen minutes later he buzzed for Sherman. "I tell you I can't work with that dog barking," he said. "Here's ten dollars. Find the dog and buy him." Sherman again went downstairs and walked several times around the courthouse, cocking an ear. Faintly, in the distance, he heard a dog barking. Following the sound, he trapped his quarry, howling like mad in the rear of a bar and grill on the edge of Chinatown, three blocks away. "Judge Hand can't work," said Sherman, pointing to a tiny window near the top of the courthouse. Somewhat stunned, the proprietor muzzled the dog.

When reviewing an admiralty case the Judge is not satisfied merely to study the briefs and oral arguments. He keeps a compass and magnifying glass in his top desk drawer, and his closet contains a complete set of maps of the waters adjacent to New York City. Whipping out the compass and spreading a map across his desk, he will squint for hours through his magnifying glass, checking with the compass the location of every spot mentioned. In deciding *Dauntless Towing Line v. Canal Lakes Towing Co.,* 140 Fed. 2nd

4. *Cromwell,* Oliver (1599-1658), English leader of the Puritan-controlled army that overthrew Charles I and attempted to establish full parliamentary government. Subsequently Cromwell was named Lord Protector and became a virtual dictator. With his army he kept complete control of the British Commonwealth until his death.

215, a matter of a collision between two barges, he wrote, "As usual the testimony as to the whistles is contradictory. . . . Perhaps the most reasonable estimate is that she first blew when somewhat east of buoy 3A, about 1,200 feet from the place of collision. The only testimony is that the mutual approach of the vessels was nine miles an hour; and if so, the signal must have been given nearly three minutes before collision (even if we disregard the slow bell of the *Calatco*). That was ample time for the *Dauntless* to go to starboard."

Each case presents to Judge Hand a new intellectual pursuit of freedom, admittedly an awesome task considering that liberty, as he has said, "is an essence so volatile that it will escape any vial, however corked." A lawyer once said of the Judge, "First he articulates his prejudices and then cancels them out. If he happens to reflect liberal sentiment—and he appears to a good deal of the time—it is only because he feels it to be the correct interpretation, not the popular one." These days a considerable number of the Judge's opinions deal with labor disputes. Inevitably he has been accused of being both pro- and antilabor. He would appear to be neither. "Justice, I think, is the tolerable accommodation of the conflicting interests of society," he has said, "and I don't believe there is any royal road to attain such accommodations concretely."

The first of the Hands in America, John, left Kent, England, in 1644 and landed at Southampton, Long Island. Shortly thereafter he became one of the nine original settlers of Easthampton, a windswept waste of moors and dunes. His estate consisted solely of a Bible, psalm book, pistol, and sword. In 1792 the Hands trekked to Shoreham, Vermont, on the shores of Lake Champlain. Judge Hand's grandfather Augustus attended the first law school in this country, Judge Gould's, at Litchfield, Connecticut. He subsequently served in Congress, the New York State Senate, and on the State Supreme Court. Learned Hand was born in Albany in 1872. He was christened Billings Learned Hand but before he was thirty had dropped the name Billings in favor of Learned, which is his mother's maiden name. "Nobody could possibly think of a nick-

name for Learned," he said at the time. His father, Samuel, was a prominent attorney and sat for a time on the Court of Appeals, the highest court in the state. Learned's closest childhood companion was his cousin Augustus, who lived in Elizabethtown, north of Albany in the Adirondacks. Learned spent his summers there, mostly swimming and climbing mountains. Occasionally at night the boys would sit behind the house in the light of a lantern, discussing free will and predestination. "We early decided," Augustus Noble Hand recalls, "that the problem was insoluble." During the winters Learned corresponded regularly with his cousin. "For Christmas, I got Papa a set of books by Dumas," he wrote when he was twelve, "and I have nearly finished *The Count of Monte Cristo*, which is bully, but mamma won't let me read it on Sunday which is a great privation. . . . I stood 2 in my class in the semi-annual work. The boy who stood head being 97 240/480 and I stood 97 227/480 he being 13/480 ahead of me."

Learned followed Augustus to Harvard by two years, parted his hair in the middle, sported a drooping mustache and a pointed black beard, and was known, from his appearance, as the "ancient Mongolian." He bustled through college *summa cum laude*,[5] majoring in philosophy under Santayana, Royce, and William James,[6] becoming an editor of the *Advocate*, a member of Phi Beta Kappa, and Class Day orator of the class of 1893. "We have come at last to the time when we must put away childish things and think as men," he declaimed in his oration, but he was uncertain of his next move. "I was perfectly indeterminate," he says today. "I thought of sticking to philosophy, but my cousin had moved along to the law school, and there were so many lawyers in the family—so I went, too." Although he became an editor of the

---

5. *summa cum laude* (sŭm′ə kŭm lou′də or sum′ə kum lô′di), with the highest honor, a Latin phrase added by some colleges to the diploma of a student who has excelled in his academic work. 6. *Santayana, Royce, and William James.* Josiah Royce (1855-1916) and William James (1842-1910) form with George Santayana (see page 642) Harvard's great trio of philosophers.

Harvard Law Review and graduated with honors, the law and Learned were not perfectly mated. "He had a speculative train of thought," his cousin recalls, "and thinking based to a considerable extent on precedent did not particularly interest him." Within two years after graduation from law school he had become a partner in an Albany law firm, but he was not at peace with himself. "Many times I felt like putting a gun to my head," he has said. "Nothing but foreclosures, mortgages, settlement of estates. Everything was petty and formal. Nobody wanted to get *behind* a problem."

In 1902 he took two decisive steps: he married and moved to New York. His bride was the former Frances Fincke of Utica, a graduate of Bryn Mawr. Hand joined a Wall Street firm and bought the brownstone house where he lives today. Three daughters were born to the Hands. Essentially discontented with the practice of law, Hand nonetheless prospered. Older attorneys such as C. C. Burlingham and George Wickersham, President Taft's attorney general, recognized that his talents were primarily judicial. In 1909, at their instigation, Taft appointed Hand a federal district judge for the Southern District of New York. The new judge was thirty-seven. Within three years he had become an active Bull Mooser.[7] "I knew this: we had to break away from the Hanna[8] thing—the control of the nation by big business," he says now. He ran for chief justice of the New York Court of Appeals on the Progressive ticket in 1913 and was defeated. "He just stood up," his cousin recalls, "and was knocked down." He never again went into politics.

By and large, judges lead unspectacular lives. Their careers, like broad plateaus, are unmarked by gullies and hills. Day after day across the years the struggles and triumphs of Judge Hand—his growth and influence—have been matters of the mind and spirit and therefore immeasurable. You cannot point to a judge as you would to a general and say, "He won *that* battle." Yet, as Hand once said of Cardozo, judges possess "a power greater than the power of him who ruleth a city." Many students of Judge Hand's work feel that his

public addresses and articles in law journals have been among his greatest contributions. In them he has given expression to some of his deepest feelings on law and life and more particularly to his thoughts on the meaning of freedom. "We were wrong," he told a group of lawyers some years ago, "in supposing that native intelligence or stupidity have much to do with the workings of democracy or the gift of liberty. It is a question of the habit, so hard to acquire, of detachment in forming beliefs, in the end, of the character of a people, not of its brains. A group of pretty dull men can manage fairly well, if they be disposed to suspend judgment where they do not know the facts, but nothing—I think you will agree —is more exasperating than a group of clever disputants each concealing behind his front of argument determined and uncompromising convictions which no evidence can touch."

He reiterated this theme in May 1944, when he led 150,000 newly naturalized citizens in the pledge to the flag at the "I Am An American Day" ceremonies in New York's Central Park. One million four hundred thousand persons attended, including Mrs. Hand, who sat behind the French horn of the Fire Department Band. They heard him formulate what many people still consider one of the finest definitions of liberty uttered by a living American. [It is printed here on pages 698-699.] Though not a newspaper quoted his remarks, word of the speech rapidly spread. Several months later, as the result of reprints in newspapers and magazines, it had been read by an audience conservatively estimated at 25,000,000.

In former years when the work of the court was completed, the Judge and his wife often made summer trips to Europe, the Judge racing through chateaux, libraries and museums at the rate of approximately a dozen a day. Returning to the U.S., he observed customs

---

7. *Bull Mooser.* "Bull Moose" was the popular name of the Progressive Party organized by Theodore Roosevelt in 1912. A chance remark by Roosevelt that he felt like a bull moose is supposed to be the source of the name.
8. *Hanna*, Mark (1837-1904), a successful American businessman who had considerable influence with President McKinley. Roosevelt was Vice-President at the time McKinley was assassinated.

regulations so scrupulously that he once declared an old pair of shoes on the grounds that they had been resoled and heeled in Europe. Now, at the end of court sessions, the Judge leaves promptly for Cornish, New Hampshire, where he has a summer place called Low Court. He spends his days reading or tramping through the woods. In the evenings he puts on a white apron and helps Mrs. Hand with the dishes.

His New York home is high-ceilinged and comfortable, dominated on the lower floor by a long, narrow library containing several thousand books, including a large number of highly technical volumes of chemistry, physics, and geography. Judge and Mrs. Hand have four grandsons and three granddaughters. Their youngest daughter, Constance, is married to Newbold Morris, former president of the New York City Council and a member of the City Planning Commission.

Judge Hand's children have long been astounded at the duality of his nature: self-discipline and dedication to work on one hand, ability to relax thoroughly on the other. When they were young, they waited for him to come home each evening from the court-room. Crouched on the second-floor landing, they learned to recognize his footsteps as he walked down Sixty-Fifth Street and put a heavy bronze key in the front door. "If father entered the hall quietly and came silently up the stairs we knew he had problems and promptly dispersed," one of his daughters recalls. "If he were whistling or singing, we would tumble into his room for a story." The Judge would often reward them with an episode from *Br'er Rabbit*. "Lippity-lop, lippity-lop," he would say, hopping across the room. Or he might recount a chapter in the history of a blowzy character called Marge, a figment of his imagination. Marge, who has been involved in outrageous encounters with the law for more than thirty years, is well-meaning but cannot avoid trouble. These days, she is in constant demand by the Judge's grandchildren, who also like to watch him place a wastebasket over his head and leap around the room like an Indian. "You do not see one Indian," Newbold Morris says, "but a whole

tribe." The Judge frequently performs as the Crooked Mouth Family. He lights a candle and, taking the part of each member of the family, from the largest to the smallest Crooked-Mouth, tries to blow it out. He puffs and huffs, but the candle burns brightly. Finally he wets a finger and snuffs out the flame.

Judge Hand's closest friends have profound respect for his humor and for the vocabulary that embellishes it. "When he plays the role of William Jennings Bryan[9] addressing a political meeting in Jersey City, he is simply fantastically good," Felix Frankfurter,[10] an old friend, has said. Oliver Wendell Holmes relished his repertoire. Once, during a visit to Holmes with Frankfurter, Hand was prevailed upon to sing a ribald song of the sea, entitled *The Cabin Boy*. When they left Holmes, Hand turned to Frankfurter and said, "I fear the old man thinks I am a mere vaudevillian." On the contrary, Holmes in 1923 wrote to his perennial correspondent, Sir Frederick Pollock, that Hand was a man "whom I should like to see on our bench." That Judge Hand is not on the Supreme Court is a matter of keen disappointment to a large section of the American bar.

If Judge Hand has any feelings on this subject, they lie deeply within him. "If I were to do it over again," he told a friend visiting him in his chambers not long ago, "I think perhaps I would be a physicist—open new vistas, move in step with the world. You know, I used to hope that I might be able to garner a harvest of wisdom. That has turned out to be a mistake, for I cannot see much further into the tangle of life than I could fifty years ago. I'm less disappointed than I should have thought. Indeed, there is solace in a companionship where all are groping their way equally in the same fog."

---

9. *William Jennings Bryan* (1860-1925), a popular lecturer, three times unsuccessful Democratic candidate for President, and Secretary of State under President Woodrow Wilson. His radical policies, which were supported by the agrarian reformers of the Populist Party, were very unpopular among the Eastern conservatives. 10. *Felix Frankfurter* (1882-   ), formerly law professor at Harvard University, legal adviser to Franklin D. Roosevelt, and legal author. He was made an associate justice of the Supreme Court in 1939.

1. (a) Explain the meaning of "Statutes are the result of legislative compromise . . ." (page 697, column 1, paragraph 2. (b) What relation do you find between this statement and Judge Hand's view that each case should be considered on its own grounds —as "a new intellectual pursuit of freedom"? (c) Why, then, does Hand distrust statements like "those eternal principles of justice ringing down the ages"?

2. (a) How is Hand's view of the way in which laws are made related to the fact that Hand was impatient of being a lawyer and more suited to the bench? (b) How might that view be explained in terms of his early interest in philosophy?

3. (a) What fresh insights does "The Spirit of Liberty" (page 698) bring to the nature of American freedom? (b) In what ways was this speech especially significant in view of the time at which it was delivered and of its audience?

4. The most quoted sentence from "The Spirit of Liberty" is "The spirit of liberty is the spirit which is not too sure that it is right." (a) What are some of the ways in which Philip Hamburger demonstrates that Judge Hand possessed such a spirit? (b) Explain why you do or do not believe that there is a contradiction between Hand's spirit of humility and his belief that judges like Cardozo have "a power greater than the power of him who ruleth a city."

The biography of Learned Hand, which is presented complete in this chapter, is representative of a type of biography which, like other forms of brief non-fiction, has achieved great popularity in the modern magazine. In at least two ways the purposes of the writer of the short biography differ from those of the writer of the long biography.

First, since the limited space will not permit an exhaustive study of a man's *life*, the writer instead has as his purpose presenting the man's *portrait*—a rounded impression of the man himself.

Second, contrasted with the long biography written for the enjoyment and information of a reader who already has some interest in its subject, the short biography usually makes a conscious attempt to catch and sustain the interest of the casual reader.

In the biography of Learned Hand, does the writer organize his material in the order of events in the Judge's life? What attempt does Hamburger make to arouse and sustain reader interest through the order in which he presents his topics? Which of the four approaches discussed in "Approaches to Biography" (page 682) does Hamburger adopt? Cite examples from the text to support your answer. How does this approach help him to give a rounded portrait of his subject? In your opinion does this approach also add to the interest of the piece? Explain your answer.

THE LARGER VIEW

A. The biographer is often seen as a historian as well as a literary artist. Allan Nevins, professor of history at Columbia University, in the *Saturday Review* of November 5, 1955, discussed the question "Is History Made by Heroes?" and came to the conclusion that while biographies tend to exaggerate the rôle of great men in the course of history at the expense of the rôles of lesser figures, social forces, and institutions, they do illuminate history by making it vividly dramatic.

1. Lee and Lincoln, for example, are perhaps the two most famous heroes of the Civil War. From what you read in the biographies of these two men, and from what you can suppose the remainder of those biographies to be like, how would the viewpoint on the Civil War expressed in these biographies differ from a strictly historical account? What might the biographies leave

out that a historical account would include? How would your appreciation of the Civil War be increased by reading these biographies?

2. On the basis of what you have read of the lives of John Adams and Learned Hand, do you think that one of Nevins' statements—that biography can humanize the facts of history—is justified? What did you learn about the making of legal decisions from the biography of Learned Hand that you had not learned from courses in history or civics?

3. You will recall that Jesse Stuart was politically active in bringing about improved rural education. How does his autobiographical account help make the conflicts involved in this important social change more meaningful?

B. At the end of the introduction to this chapter (page 663), Desmond McCarthy was quoted as saying that the biographer is "an artist upon oath." In that the biographer is a historian, he is upon oath; but in the methods he adopts to present his facts, he is a literary artist. Point out some of the techniques of the short-story writer—another kind of literary artist—that were employed by the biographers in this chapter.

BIBLIOGRAPHY

ALLEN, FRED, *Much Ado About Me*. (Little) This is the wry, wistful, wonderfully entertaining story of a Boston boy named John Florence Sullivan who became Fred Allen, one of the world's wittiest comedians.

BARUCH, BERNARD, *Baruch: My Own Story*. (Little •Pocket Books) In an intensely interesting autobiography Mr. Baruch, famous American financier and philanthropist, tells of political and business events in which he has taken part, world leaders with whom he has dealt, and positions he has held.

BORLAND, HAL, *High, Wide and Lonesome*. (Lippincott) The author recaptures his boyhood experiences on the unsettled plains of Colorado with freshness, spirit, and sensitivity.

BOWEN, CATHERINE, *Yankee from Olympus*. (Little) This fine biography traces the Holmes family of Massachusetts through three generations—Abiel Holmes, a minister; the senior Oliver Wendell Holmes, poet and physician; and the junior Oliver Wendell Holmes, an associate justice of the Supreme Court. The last named is the "Yankee from Olympus."

DAUGHERTY, JAMES, *Abraham Lincoln*. (Viking) In this very satisfying biography Lincoln is presented in direct relation to his time and his contemporaries, with none of the too-familiar anecdotes.

DE MILLE, AGNES, *Dance to the Piper*. (Little) The witty, stubborn, and ambitious ballerina and choreographer has written an extremely interesting autobiography as full of bounce and imagination as the dances she composes.

DOOLEY, TOM, *Dr. Tom Dooley's Three Great Books: Deliver Us from Evil; Edge of Tomorrow; The Night They Burned the Mountain*. (Farrar-Straus) The dedicated Dr. Dooley spent much of his life fighting to improve health conditions in Laos, in the Far East. With earnestness and compassion he tells of the many serious problems he faced in his work.

FREEMAN, DOUGLAS SOUTHALL, *Lee of Virginia*. (Scribner) The successive stages of Lee's life from boyhood on a Virginia plantation to his work towards Reconstruction make absorbing reading. This scholarly book is condensed from Freeman's four-volume biography of Lee.

GUNTHER, JOHN, *Death Be Not Proud*. (Harper) Mr. Gunther, a famed journalist, has written an eloquent and beautiful tribute to his son, Johnny, who died of a brain tumor at the age of seventeen. It is a profoundly moving book with no traces of morbidity or sentimentality.

HART, MOSS, *Act I*. (Random •Signet) With the same comic and satiric gifts that marked his Broadway productions, Mr. Hart gives a hilarious account of his youth and his first experiences in the theater.

JAMES, MARQUIS, *Portrait of a President*. (•Grosset) The action, the color, the turbulence, and the political fervor of the Jackson era enliven this fine biography. Andrew Jackson emerges as a real and sympathetic figure.

MIERS, EARL, *Robert E. Lee*. (Knopf •Vintage) In tracing the influences that shaped Lee, the author gives us an excellent portrait of the man and a revealing look into the dramatic events that formed his military genius.

ROOSEVELT, ELEANOR, *On My Own*. (Harper) One of the most remarkable figures of our time tells of her life in and out of politics after her husband's death. She tells her story in the same colorful manner that characterizes all she does.

SANDBURG, CARL, *Prairie-Town Boy*. (Harcourt) You will feel the special spirit of a special person in Sandburg's account of himself as a young and uncertain boy. He relates his experiences in his own inimitable style.

SANDBURG, CARL, *Abraham Lincoln: The Prairie Years and the War Years*. (Harcourt) Mr. Sandburg has very successfully condensed six volumes into one outstanding book. He has included material recently made available which did not appear in the previous books.

•paperback

chapter eleven

Modern Drama

Many of the elements the dramatist uses in writing a play are the same as those used by, for example, the short-story writer. Most writers of both literary forms make use of a *plot* of limited length acted out by a number of *characters* in a definite *setting*. Yet to the reader the differences between a short story and a play are likely to seem more striking than the resemblances. A play is, after all, almost always written for presentation in a theater, and this fact accounts, to a large extent, for those differences.

When a person picks up a book, he meets the author directly through the printed words. When a person sits in a theater, however, the contact between author and spectator is less direct, since the person is actually confronted only by the stage itself and by the actors. In reading a play it is easy to lose sight of the full effect of these two aspects of the play, since neither stage nor actor is visually present to the reader. With some practice the reader can supply with his imagination the full effect that is obvious to the person sitting in the theater. But to do this the reader must know what to look for in the author's descriptions of set, lighting, and placement of actors, and also how the playwright goes about developing and judging the characters.

STAGING   Understanding the author's use of staging is especially important today because modern playwrights have a wide variety of theatrical styles from which to choose. There are two reasons for this variety. First, since the time of the great Norwegian dramatist Henrik Ibsen (1828-1906), playwrights have frequently experimented with radically new ways of writing plays. Each of these new ways demanded its own theatrical style—a manner of staging which would complement the new literary form.

Thus, for example, the so-called *realist* drama was associated with realistic techniques of staging; the *expressionist* drama demanded techniques for going beneath the surface reality to expose mental life—devices which have come to be called *expressionistic*. Contemporary playwrights, Americans in particular, have usually not been content to follow exclusively any one of these experimental ways of writing. Instead they have often created modes of writing, and, in the matter of staging, they have used a combination of staging techniques developed by earlier schools of play writing. A second source of the variety in staging is experimentation with stage design and methods of acting by famous producers.

SCHOOLS OF
PLAY WRITING

Most persistent among the modern schools of play writing is that for which Ibsen himself was most noted: *realism*. Realists felt that pre-Ibsen drama showed men as being more noble, more beautiful, more powerful than they really are. For this they substituted a drama that shows ordinary men, struggling against the unspectacular and unpleasant problems of ordinary life, and succeeding no better than men ordinarily do. The staging that has become associated with realist drama can be described as the living room of a household in which the "fourth wall" has been turned into a one-way mirror: the audience can see in, but the characters cannot see out. In the room the audience discovers appropriate furnishings, often specified in great detail by the author. The set is not designed to dazzle the spectator with its beauty, but to imitate the worn, or vulgarly ostentatious, or dilapidated surroundings that are often encountered in reality. The set reflects the ugliness, meanness, or triviality that the typical realist believes surrounds the lives of most people. The reader is, of course, expected to recognize the kind of contribution these elements make to the play as a whole.

Playwrights who saw the basic human condition in a different light than the realists did began searching for other dramatic forms almost as soon as realism became popularly established. The *symbolists'* aim was to do justice to the beauty and deeper realities of man's life. The use of symbolic characters and, especially, symbolic settings was of primary importance in evoking feelings that could not be expressed in literal terms. Pure symbolist drama did not prove to be a lasting form, but later dramatists have found some elements of symbolist drama useful. The reader of contemporary plays must therefore be alert to the possible use of characters to symbolize whole classes of men, for example, or the use of symbolic settings or stage properties by which the author suggests things about characters which they cannot tell about themselves.

Expressionists agreed largely with the realists that in its outward aspect modern life is often empty, trivial, and oppressive; but they believed that much excitement and value could be found in modern life if one could only look inside of people. They presented this subjective life on the stage by presenting dreams, nightmares, memories—the whole internal drama of hopes, fears, and regrets common to all people. The representation of mental drama demanded special staging techniques: special lighting, exaggerated sound effects, use of scrims (a backdrop curtain that becomes transparent when lighted from behind), madly whirling stage platforms, and other appropriate nonrealistic devices. Expressionism, like symbolism, is no longer an active movement in the theater, but it has

707

shown later dramatists the possibilities of presenting on stage what is going on in the mind of one of the characters. The flashback—showing something that happened in the past as remembered by one of the characters—has become widely used, even in motion pictures. In plays that employ expressionist techniques the reader must watch for the clues that will indicate the nature of what is happening— whether it is "real" action or "mental" action. He must also bear in mind that *how* a character dreams or remembers tells something about that character.

In the 1920's still another school of play writing was developed called *epic realism.* Epic realists agree with antirealist schools that realism itself is too restricted. They believe that since a play is not life, but is really a play, anything that can be done in a theater can be of legitimate use. Epic theater is frankly theatrical: actors address the audience, stylized gestures are used. Staging often calls for carrying titles on stage or flashing them on a screen, altering sets in mid-scene, and using sets that will allow the showing of action taking place at the same time but in different locales. These complexities of time and place, which can be made obvious on stage, call for additional care on the part of the reader.

All these theatrical forms are further complicated by the experiments of producers with methods of staging. Two of the most important are (1) the *empty stage,* which centers the attention of the audience on the characters themselves, and (2) the *plastic theater,* in which lighting is used to mold the actors into something resembling moving sculpture.

Most major American dramatists of this century have combined elements of staging from more than one of these styles, depending on each to add its own characteristic effect in reinforcing the central ideas of the play. Tennessee Williams' play *The Glass Menagerie,* included in this chapter, is a good example of such a synthesis. The tenement setting, hemming in the lives of the characters, is in the *realistic* tradition. At least one of the characters, the fire escape entrance, and the collection of glass animals are explicitly *symbolic.* Nearly the whole play is the memory of one of the characters, and is to that extent *expressionistic* in form. Techniques used by the *epic realists* are included: a character addresses the audience as narrator, one scene is effective in showing simultaneous scenes in two rooms, a number of screen titles are used. And Williams uses the light-modeling of the *plastic theater* to show how memory colors the thing remembered.

CHARACTERS

However complex theatrical style may be, it remains only one aspect of the play. The center of interest remains in the characters. The dramatist must succeed in communicating two things by means of these characters: (1) the feelings and attitudes of the characters themselves, and (2) his judgment on the characters and their attitudes. This fact is obvious in the typical Western. Here there are basically two characters: the hero and the villain. The villain will do anything to gain a selfish advantage, but the hero lives and fights strictly by the code. This is most dramatically revealed in the final, crucial situation, but the attitudes of the villain and hero are made clear from the beginning, even by look, dress, and bearing. Given such clearly good and bad characters, the judgment of them for the most part is obvious.

The literary dramatist, on the other hand, must make a more complex judgment, and make it about more complex characters. If, for example, a character who demonstrates many virtues suddenly commits an act of dishonesty, the audience or reader wants to know how to feel about this character. Are the circumstances of the act such that he can be excused, or does he merely become pitiful, or laughable, or wretched, or disgusting? These judgments are not obvious; the dramatist must use every means at his disposal to communicate exactly the shade of feeling which he thinks is right. It is in his ability to communicate to an audience his judgment on the characters he has created—and to make this judgment one that the audience will accept as being in harmony with the characters—that the playwright most surely shows his mastery of drama.

EUGENE O'NEILL 1888-1953

The critical disputes that have raged about the towering figure of Eugene O'Neill have not yet subsided, but it is generally agreed that O'Neill must be ranked with the greatest of the world's modern dramatists.

O'Neill was the son of a famous romantic actor. His interest did not turn to the theater at once, however, and the most significant experience of his roving youth was his working on several ships as a merchant seaman. When, among other occupations, he tried that of a newspaper reporter, he began to develop a serious interest in writing. During a lengthy recovery from tuberculosis, he focused his interest on writing drama, and from that time on he devoted himself to tireless study, experimentation, and achievement in this field.

O'Neill's early efforts in playwriting coincided with the growth of the little-theater movement in the United States. All over the country intelligent Americans, tiring of the elaborate and hackneyed plays of the commercial theater, were forming groups to experiment in the production of original and artistic dramas. O'Neill's first dramas, three one-act plays, were produced by the Provincetown Players, one of the most successful of these groups, in 1916.

As O'Neill turned to longer plays, he experimented constantly with dramatic techniques. In successive plays he tried nearly all of the theatrical forms developed by the European experimentalists. Seeking adequate means to express his view of the human condition, he often used various techniques with great imagination. In *The Emperor Jones* (1921) he used flashbacks which appeared before the eyes of the tortured hero to show the effect of uprootedness and dislocation upon human life. In *The Hairy Ape* (1922) he used masked figures to dramatize the struggle of man seeking his rightful place in an overpowering social structure. In *Strange Interlude* (1928) he used soliloquies to unfold in nine acts (really a trilogy, three plays in one) an intense psychological drama of a very selfish woman.

The climax of his career came when, after winning three Pulitzer Prizes and producing the ambitious *Mourning Becomes Electra* (1931), he was awarded the Nobel Prize in Literature in 1936.

Ile

by Eugene O'Neill

Characters

BEN (*the cabin boy*)

THE STEWARD

CAPTAIN KEENEY

SLOCUM (*second mate*[1])

MRS. KEENEY

JOE (*a harpooner*)

Members of the crew of the steam whaler *Atlantic Queen*

"Ile" from *The Long Voyage Home*, by Eugene O'Neill. Copyright 1919 and renewed 1946 by Eugene O'Neill. Reprinted by permission of Random House, Inc., New York, and Jonathan Cape Ltd., London.

1. *second mate*, the man third in command of the ship. (The captain of the ship and the first mate are his superiors.)

*Views of a whaler,
the* Charles W. Morgan
*at Mystic Seaport,
Connecticut: the
skylight in the
captain's cabin, seen
from below (left)
and a view along
the deck (right).*

SCENE

CAPTAIN KEENEY'S *cabin on board the steam
whaling ship* Atlantic Queen—*a small, square
compartment about eight feet high with a
skylight in the center looking out on the poop
deck. On the left (the stern of the ship) a
long bench with rough cushions is built in
against the wall. In front of the bench, a table.
Over the bench, several curtained portholes.*

In the rear, left, a door leading to the CAP-
TAIN'S *sleeping quarters. To the right of the
door a small organ, looking as if it were brand-
new, is placed against the wall.*

*On the right, to the rear, a marble-topped
sideboard. On the sideboard, a woman's sewing basket. Farther forward, a doorway leading to the companionway, and past the officers'
quarters to the main deck.*

*In the center of the room, a stove. From the
middle of the ceiling a hanging lamp is suspended. The walls of the cabin are painted
white.*

*There is no rolling of the ship, and the light
which comes through the skylight is sickly and
faint, indicating one of those gray days of
calm when ocean and sky are alike dead. The
silence is unbroken except for the measured
tread of someone walking up and down on the
poop deck overhead.*

*It is nearing two bells—one o'clock—in the
afternoon of a day in the year 1895.*

*At the rise of the curtain there is a moment
of intense silence. Then the* STEWARD *enters
and commences to clear the table of the few
dishes which still remain on it after the* CAP-

TAIN'S *dinner. He is an old, grizzled man
dressed in dungaree pants, a sweater, and a
woolen cap with earflaps. His manner is sullen and angry. He stops stacking up the plates
and casts a quick glance upward at the skylight; then tiptoes over to the closed door in
rear and listens with his ear pressed to the
crack. What he hears makes his face darken
and he mutters a furious curse. There is a
noise from the doorway on the right and he
darts back to the table.*

BEN *enters. He is an overgrown, gawky boy
with a long, pinched face. He is dressed in
sweater, fur cap, etc. His teeth are chattering
with the cold and he hurries to the stove,
where he stands for a moment shivering, blowing on his hands, slapping them against his
sides, on the verge of crying.*

THE STEWARD (*in relieved tones—seeing who
it is*). Oh, 'tis you, is it? What're ye shiverin'
'bout? Stay by the stove where ye belong and
ye'll find no need of chatterin'.

BEN. It's c-c-cold. (*Trying to control his
chattering teeth—derisively.*) Who d'ye think
it were—the Old Man?

THE STEWARD (*makes a threatening move—
BEN shrinks away*). None o' your lip, young
un, or I'll learn ye. (*More kindly.*) Where was
it ye've been all o' the time—the fo'c's'tle?[2]

BEN. Yes.

THE STEWARD. Let the Captain see ye up
for'ard monkeyshinin' with the hands and

2. *the* fo'c's'tle, *the forecastle* (fōk'səl *or* fôr'kas'əl), *the
sailors' quarters in the forward part of the ship.*

ye'll get a hidin' ye'll not forget in a hurry.

BEN. Aw, he don't see nothin'. (*A trace of awe in his tones—he glances upward.*) He jest walks up and down like he didn't notice nobody—and stares at the ice to the no'th'ard.

THE STEWARD (*the same tone of awe creeping into his voice*). He's always starin' at the ice. (*In a sudden rage, shaking his fist at the skylight.*) Ice, ice, ice! Damn the ice! Holdin' us in for nigh on a year—nothin' to see but ice—stuck in it like a fly in molasses!

BEN (*apprehensively*). Ssshh! He'll hear ye.

THE STEWARD (*raging*). Aye, damn him, and damn the Arctic seas, and damn this stinkin' whalin' ship of his, and damn me for a fool to ever ship on it! (*Subsiding as if realizing the uselessness of this outburst—shaking his head—slowly, with deep conviction.*) He's a hard man—as hard a man as ever sailed the seas.

BEN (*solemnly*). Aye.

THE STEWARD. The two years we all signed up for are done this day. Two years o' this dog's life, and no luck in the fishin', and the hands half starved with the food runnin' low, rotten as it is; and not a sign of him turnin' back for home! (*Bitterly.*) Home! I begin to doubt if ever I'll set foot on land again. (*Excitedly.*) What is it he thinks he's goin' to do? Keep us all up here after our time is worked out till the last man of us is starved to death or frozen? We've grub enough hardly to last out the voyage back if we started now. What are the men goin' to do 'bout it? Did ye hear any talk in the fo'c's'tle?

BEN (*going over to him—in a half whisper*). They said if he don't put back south for home today they're goin' to mutiny.

THE STEWARD (*with grim satisfaction*). Mutiny? Aye, 'tis the only thing they can do; and serve him right after the manner he's treated them— 's if they weren't no better nor dogs.

BEN. The ice is all broke up to s'uth'ard. They's clear water s'far 's you can see. He ain't got no excuse for not turnin' back for home, the men says.

THE STEWARD (*bitterly*). He won't look nowheres but no'th'ard where they's only the ice to see. He don't want to see no clear water. All he thinks on is gettin' the ile— 's if it was

our fault he ain't had good luck with the whales. (*Shaking his head.*) I think the man's mighty nigh losin' his senses.

BEN (*awed*). D'you really think he's crazy?

THE STEWARD. Aye, it's the punishment o' God on him. Did ye ever hear of a man who wasn't crazy do the things he does? (*Pointing to the door in rear.*) Who but a man that's mad would take his woman—and as sweet a woman as ever was—on a stinkin' whalin' ship to the Arctic seas to be locked in by the rotten ice for nigh on a year, and maybe lose her senses forever—for it's sure she'll never be the same again.

BEN (*sadly*). She useter be awful nice to me before—(*His eyes grow wide and frightened.*)—she got—like she is.

THE STEWARD. Aye, she was good to all of us. 'Twould have been hell on board without her; for he's a hard man—a hard, hard man—a driver if there ever was one. (*With a grim laugh.*) I hope he's satisfied now—drivin' her on till she's near lost her mind. And who could blame her? 'Tis a God's wonder we're not a ship full of crazed people—with the ice all the time, and the quiet so thick you're afraid to hear your own voice.

BEN (*with a frightened glance toward the door on right*). She don't never speak to me no more—jest looks at me 's if she didn't know me.

THE STEWARD. She don't know no one—but him. She talks to him—when she does talk—right enough.

BEN. She does nothin' all day long now but sit and sew—and then she cries to herself without makin' no noise. I've seen her.

THE STEWARD. Aye, I could hear her through the door awhile back.

BEN (*tiptoes over to the door and listens*). She's cryin' now.

THE STEWARD (*furiously—shaking his fist*). Blast him for the devil he is!

(*There is the noise of someone coming slowly down the companionway stairs. The* STEWARD *hurries to his stacked-up dishes. He is so nervous from fright that he knocks off the top one, which falls and breaks on the floor. He stands aghast, trembling with dread.* BEN *is vio-*

lently rubbing off the organ with a piece of cloth which he has snatched from his pocket. CAPTAIN KEENEY *appears in the doorway on right and comes into the cabin, removing his fur cap as he does so. He is a man of about forty, around five-ten in height but looking much shorter on account of the enormous proportions of his shoulders and chest. His face is massive and deeply lined, with gray-blue eyes of a bleak hardness, and a tightly clenched, thin-lipped mouth. His thick hair is long and gray. He is dressed in a heavy blue jacket and blue pants stuffed into his sea-boots.*

He is followed into the cabin by the SECOND MATE, *a rangy six-footer with a lean weather-beaten face. The* MATE *is dressed about the same as the* CAPTAIN. *He is a man of thirty or so.*)

KEENEY (*comes toward the* STEWARD *with a stern look on his face. The* STEWARD *is visibly frightened and the stack of dishes rattles in his trembling hands.* KEENEY *draws back his fist and the* STEWARD *shrinks away. The fist is gradually lowered and* KEENEY *speaks slowly*). 'Twould be like hittin' a worm. It is nigh on two bells, Mr. Steward, and this truck not cleared yet.

THE STEWARD (*stammering*). Y-y-yes, sir.

KEENEY. Instead of doin' your rightful work ye've been below here gossipin' old woman's talk with that boy. (*To* BEN, *fiercely.*) Get out o' this, you! Clean up the chart room.[3] (BEN *darts past the* MATE *to the open doorway.*) Pick up that dish, Mr. Steward!

THE STEWARD (*doing so with difficulty*). Yes, sir.

KEENEY. The next dish you break, Mr. Steward, you take a bath in the Bering Sea at the end of a rope.

THE STEWARD (*tremblingly*). Yes, sir.

(*He hurries out. The* SECOND MATE *walks slowly over to the* CAPTAIN.)

MATE. I warn't 'specially anxious the man at the wheel should catch what I wanted to say to you, sir. That's why I asked you to come below.

KEENEY (*impatiently*). Speak your say, Mr. Slocum.

MATE (*unconsciously lowering his voice*). I'm afeared there'll be trouble with the hands by the look o' things. They'll likely turn ugly, every blessed one o' them, if you don't put back. The two years they signed up for is up today.

KEENEY. And d'you think you're tellin' me somethin' new, Mr. Slocum? I've felt it in the air this long time past. D'you think I've not seen their ugly looks and the grudgin' way they worked?

(*The door in rear is opened and* MRS. KEENEY *stands in the doorway. She is a slight, sweet-faced little woman, primly dressed in black. Her eyes are red from weeping and her face drawn and pale. She takes in the cabin with a frightened glance and stands as if fixed to the spot by some nameless dread, clasping and unclasping her hands nervously. The two men turn and look at her.*)

KEENEY (*with rough tenderness*). Well, Annie?

MRS. KEENEY (*as if awakening from a dream*). David, I— (*She is silent. The* MATE *starts for the doorway.*)

KEENEY (*turning to him—sharply*). Wait!

MATE. Yes, sir.

KEENEY. D'you want anything, Annie?

MRS. KEENEY (*after a pause, during which she seems to be endeavoring to collect her thoughts*). I thought maybe—I'd go up on deck, David, to get a breath of fresh air. (*She stands humbly awaiting his permission. He and the* MATE *exchange a significant glance.*)

KEENEY. It's too cold, Annie. You'd best stay below today. There's nothin' to look at on deck—but ice.

MRS. KEENEY (*monotonously*). I know—ice, ice, ice! But there's nothing to see down here but these walls. (*She makes a gesture of loathing.*)

KEENEY. You can play the organ, Annie.

MRS. KEENEY (*dully*). I hate the organ. It puts me in mind of home.

KEENEY (*a touch of resentment in his voice*). I got it jest for you.

MRS. KEENEY (*dully*). I know. (*She turns

---

3. *chart room*, place where compass, maps, etc. are kept.

away from them and walks slowly to the bench on left. She lifts up one of the curtains and looks through a porthole; then utters an exclamation of joy.) Ah, water! Clear water! As far as I can see! How good it looks after all these months of ice! *(She turns round to them, her face transfigured with joy.)* Ah, now I must go up on deck and look at it, David!

KEENEY *(frowning)*. Best not today, Annie. Best wait for a day when the sun shines.

MRS. KEENEY *(desperately)*. But the sun never shines in this terrible place.

KEENEY *(a tone of command in his voice)*. Best not today, Annie.

MRS. KEENEY *(crumbling before this command—abjectly)*. Very well, David. *(She stands there staring straight before her as if in a daze. The two men look at her uneasily.)*

KEENEY *(sharply)*. Annie!

MRS. KEENEY *(dully)*. Yes, David.

KEENEY. Me and Mr. Slocum has business to talk about—ship's business.

MRS. KEENEY. Very well, David. *(She goes slowly out, rear, and leaves the door three-quarters shut behind her.)*

KEENEY. Best not have her on deck if they's goin' to be any trouble.

MATE. Yes, sir.

KEENEY. And trouble they's goin' to be. I feel it in my bones. *(Takes a revolver from his coat pocket and examines it.)* Got your'n?

MATE. Yes, sir.

KEENEY. Not that we'll have to use 'em—not if I know their breed of dog—jest to frighten 'em up a bit. *(Grimly.)* I ain't never been forced to use one yit; and trouble I've had by land and by sea s'long as I kin remember, and will have till my dyin' day, I reckon.

MATE *(hesitatingly)*. Then you ain't goin'—to turn back?

KEENEY. Turn back? Mr. Slocum, did you ever hear o' me pointin' s'uth for home with only a measly four hundred barrel of ile in the hold?

MATE *(hastily)*. No, sir—but the grub's gittin' low.

KEENEY. They's enough to last a long time yit, if they're careful with it; and they's plenty o' water.

MATE. They say it's not fit to eat—what's left; and the two years they signed on fur is up today. They might make trouble for you in the courts when we git home.

KEENEY. Let them make what law trouble they kin! I've got to git the ile! *(Glancing sharply at the MATE.)* You ain't turnin' no sea-lawyer, be you, Mr. Slocum?

MATE *(flushing)*. Not by a sight, sir.

KEENEY. What do the fools want to go home fur now? Their share o' the four hundred barrel wouldn't keep 'em in chewin' terbacco.

MATE *(slowly)*. They wants to git back to their folks an' things, I s'pose.

KEENEY *(looking at him searchingly)*. 'N you want to turn back, too. *(The MATE looks down confusedly before his sharp gaze.)* Don't lie, Mr. Slocum. It's writ down plain in your eyes. *(With grim sarcasm.)* I hope, Mr. Slocum, you ain't agoin' to jine the men agin me.

MATE *(indignantly)*. That ain't fair, sir, to say sich things.

KEENEY *(with satisfaction)*. I warn't much afeard o' that, Tom. You been with me nigh on ten year and I've learned ye whalin'. No man kin say I ain't a good master, if I be a hard one.

MATE. I warn't thinkin' of myself, sir—'bout turnin' home, I mean. *(Desperately.)* But Mrs. Keeney, sir—seems like she ain't jest satisfied up here, ailin' like—what with the cold an' bad luck an' the ice an' all.

KEENEY *(his face clouding—rebukingly but not severely)*. That's my business, Mr. Slocum. I'll thank you to steer a clear course o' that. *(A pause.)* The ice'll break up soon to no'th'ard. I could see it startin' today. And when it goes and we git some sun Annie'll perk up. *(Another pause—then he bursts forth.)* It ain't the money what's keepin' me up in the northern seas, Tom. But I can't go back to Homeport with a measly four hundred barrel of ile. I'd die fust. I ain't never come back home in all my days without a full ship. Ain't that truth?

MATE. Yes, sir; but this voyage you been icebound, an'——

KEENEY *(scornfully)*. And d'you s'pose any of 'em would believe that—any o' them skippers I've beaten voyage after voyage? Can't you hear 'em laughin' and sneerin'—Tibbots 'n' Harris 'n' Simms and the rest—and all o' Homeport makin' fun o' me? "Dave Keeney what boasts he's the best whalin' skipper out o' Homeport comin' back with a measly four hundred barrel of ile?" (*The thought of this drives him into a frenzy, and he smashes his fist down on the marble top of the sideboard.*) I got to git the ile, I tell you. How could I figger on this ice? It's never been so bad before in the thirty year I been acomin' here. And now it's breakin' up. In a couple o' days it'll be all gone. And they's whale here, plenty of 'em. I know they is and I ain't never gone wrong yit. I got to git the ile! And I ain't agoin' home till I do git it!

(*There is the sound of subdued sobbing from the door in rear. The two men stand silent for a moment, listening. Then* KEENEY *goes over to the door and looks in. He hesitates for a moment as if he were going to enter—then closes the door softly.* JOE, *the harpooner, an enormous six-footer with a battered, ugly face, enters from right and stands waiting for the* CAPTAIN *to notice him.*)

KEENEY (*turning and seeing him*). Don't stand there like a gawk, Harpooner. Speak up!

JOE (*confusedly*). We want—the men, sir—they wants to send a depitation aft to have a word with you.

KEENEY (*furiously*). Tell 'em to go to— (*Checks himself and continues grimly.*) Tell 'em to come. I'll see 'em.

JOE. Aye, aye, sir. (*He goes out.*)

KEENEY (*with a grim smile*). Here it comes, the trouble you spoke of, Mr. Slocum, and we'll make short shift of it. It's better to crush such things at the start than let them make headway.

MATE (*worriedly*). Shall I wake up the First and Fourth,[4] sir? We might need their help.

KEENEY. No, let them sleep. I'm well able to handle this alone, Mr. Slocum.

(*There is the shuffling of footsteps from outside and five of the crew crowd into the cabin, led by* JOE. *All are dressed alike—sweaters, seaboots, etc. They glance uneasily at the* CAPTAIN, *twirling their fur caps in their hands.*)

KEENEY (*after a pause*). Well? Who's to speak fur ye?

JOE (*stepping forward with an air of bravado*). I be.

KEENEY (*eying him up and down coldly*). So you be. Then speak your say and be quick about it.

JOE (*trying not to wilt before the* CAPTAIN'S *glance and avoiding his eyes*). The time we signed up for is done today.

KEENEY (*icily*). You're tellin' me nothin' I don't know.

JOE. You ain't p'intin' fur home yit, far 's we kin see.

KEENEY. No, and I ain't agoin' to till this ship is full of ile.

JOE. You can't go no further no'th with the ice afore ye.

KEENEY. The ice is breaking up.

JOE (*after a slight pause during which the others mumble angrily to one another*). The grub we're gittin' now is rotten.

KEENEY. It's good enough fur ye. Better men than ye are have eaten worse.

(*There is a chorus of angry exclamations.*)

JOE (*encouraged by this support*). We ain't agoin' to work no more 'less you puts back for home.

KEENEY (*fiercely*). You ain't, ain't you?

JOE. No; and the law courts'll say we was right.

KEENEY. We're at sea now and I'm the law on this ship! (*Edging up toward the harpooner.*) And every mother's son of you what don't obey orders goes in irons.

(*There are more angry exclamations from the crew.* MRS. KEENEY *appears in the doorway in rear and looks on with startled eyes. None of the men notice her.*)

JOE (*with bravado*). Then we're agoin' to mutiny and take the old hooker home ourselves. Ain't we, boys?

(*As he turns his head to look at the others,* KEENEY'S *fist shoots out to the side of his jaw.* JOE *goes down in a heap*

---

4. *the First and Fourth*, the first and fourth mates.

and lies there. MRS. KEENEY *gives a shriek and hides her face in her hands. The men pull out their sheath knives and start a rush, but stop when they find themselves confronted by the revolvers of* KEENEY *and the* MATE.)

KEENEY (*his eyes and voice snapping*). Hold still! (*The men stand huddled together in a sullen silence.* KEENEY's *voice is full of mockery.*) You've found out it ain't safe to mutiny on this ship, ain't you? And now git for'ard where ye belong, and— (*He gives* JOE's *body a contemptuous kick.*) Drag him with you. And remember, the first man of ye I see shirkin' I'll shoot dead as sure as there's a sea under us, and you can tell the rest the same. Git for'ard now! Quick! (*The men leave in cowed silence, carrying* JOE *with them.* KEENEY *turns to the* MATE *with a short laugh and puts his revolver back in his pocket.*) Best get up on deck, Mr. Slocum, and see to it they don't try none of their skulkin' tricks. We'll have to keep an eye peeled from now on. I know 'em.

MATE. Yes, sir.

(*He goes out, right.* KEENEY *hears his wife's hysterical weeping and turns around in surprise—then walks slowly to her side.*)

KEENEY (*putting an arm around her shoulder—with gruff tenderness*). There, there, Annie. Don't be afeard. It's all past and gone.

MRS. KEENEY (*shrinking away from him*). Oh, I can't bear it— Oh, I can't bear it any longer!

KEENEY (*gently*). Can't bear what, Annie?

MRS. KEENEY (*hysterically*). All this horrible brutality, and these brutes of men, and this terrible ship, and this prison cell of a room, and the ice all around, and the silence. (*After this outburst she calms down and wipes her eyes with her handkerchief.*)

KEENEY (*after a pause during which he looks down at her with a puzzled frown*). Remember, I warn't hankerin' to have you come on this voyage, Annie.

MRS. KEENEY. I wanted to be with you, David, don't you see? I didn't want to wait back there in the house all alone as I've been doing these last six years since we were married—waiting, and watching, and fearing—with nothing to keep my mind occupied—not able to go back teaching school on account of being Dave Keeney's wife. I used to dream of sailing on the great, wide, glorious ocean. I wanted to be by your side in the danger and vigorous life of it all. I wanted to see you the hero they make you out to be in Homeport. And instead—(*her voice grows tremulous*)—all I find is ice and cold—and brutality! (*Her voice breaks.*)

KEENEY. I warned you what it'd be, Annie. "Whalin' ain't no ladies' tea party," I says to you, and "You better stay to home where you've got all your woman's comforts." (*Shaking his head.*) But you was so set on it.

MRS. KEENEY (*wearily*). Oh, I know it isn't your fault, David. You see, I didn't believe you. I guess I was dreaming about the old Vikings in the story books and I thought you were one of them.

KEENEY (*protestingly*). I done my best to make it as cozy and comfortable as could be. (MRS. KEENEY *looks around her in wild scorn.*) I even sent to the city for that organ for ye, thinkin' it might be soothin' to ye to be playin' it times when they was calms and things was dull-like.

MRS. KEENEY (*wearily*). Yes, you were very kind, David. I know that. (*She goes to left and lifts the curtains from the porthole and looks out—then suddenly bursts forth.*) I won't stand it—I can't stand it—pent up by these walls like a prisoner. (*She runs over to him and throws her arms around him, weeping. He puts his arm protectingly over her shoulders.*) Take me away from here, David! If I don't get away from here, out of this terrible ship, I'll go mad! Take me home, David! I can't think any more. I feel as if the cold and the silence were crushing down on my brain. I'm afraid. Take me home!

KEENEY (*holds her at arm's length and looks at her face anxiously*). Best go to bed, Annie. You ain't yourself. You got fever. Your eyes look so strange-like. I ain't never seen you look this way before.

MRS. KEENEY (*laughing hysterically*). It's the ice and the cold and the silence—they'd make anyone look strange.

KEENEY (*soothingly*). In a month or two, with good luck, three at the most, I'll have her filled with ile and then we'll give her everything she'll stand and p'int for home.

MRS. KEENEY. But we can't wait for that—I can't wait. I want to get home. And the men won't wait. They want to get home. It's cruel, it's brutal for you to keep them. You must sail back. You've got no excuse. There's clear water to the south now. If you've a heart at all, you've got to turn back.

KEENEY (*harshly*). I can't, Annie.

MRS. KEENEY. Why can't you?

KEENEY. A woman couldn't rightly understand my reason.

MRS. KEENEY (*wildly*). Because it's a stupid, stubborn reason. Oh, I heard you talking with the second mate. You're afraid the other captains will sneer at you because you didn't come back with a full ship. You want to live up to your silly reputation even if you do have to beat and starve men and drive me mad to do it.

KEENEY (*his jaw set stubbornly*). It ain't that, Annie. Them skippers would never dare sneer to my face. It ain't so much what anyone'd say—but—(*he hesitates, struggling to express his meaning*)—you see—I've always done it—since my first voyage as skipper. I always come back—with a full ship—and—it don't seem right not to—somehow. I been always first whalin' skipper out o' Homeport, and—don't you see my meanin', Annie? (*He glances at her. She is not looking at him, but staring dully in front of her, not hearing a word he is saying.*) Annie! (*She comes to herself with a start.*) Best turn in, Annie, there's a good woman. You ain't well.

MRS. KEENEY (*resisting his attempts to guide her to the door in rear*). David! Won't you please turn back?

KEENEY (*gently*). I can't, Annie—not yet awhile. You don't see my meanin'. I got to git the ile.

MRS. KEENEY. It'd be different if you needed the money, but you don't. You've got more than plenty.

KEENEY (*impatiently*). It ain't the money I'm thinkin' of. D'you think I'm mean as that?

MRS. KEENEY (*dully*). No—I don't know—I can't understand— (*Intensely.*) Oh, I want to be home in the old house once more and see my own kitchen again, and hear a woman's voice talking to me and be able to talk to her. Two years! It seems so long ago—as if I'd been dead and could never go back.

KEENEY (*worried by her strange tone and the faraway look in her eyes*). Best go to bed, Annie. You ain't well.

MRS. KEENEY (*not appearing to hear him*). I used to be lonely when you were away. I used to think Homeport was a stupid, monotonous place. Then I used to go down on the beach, especially when it was windy and the breakers were rolling in, and I'd dream of the fine, free life you must be leading. (*She gives a laugh which is half a sob.*) I used to love the sea then. (*She pauses; then continues with slow intensity.*) But now—I don't ever want to see the sea again.

KEENEY (*thinking to humor her*). 'Tis no fit place for a woman, that's sure. I was a fool to bring ye.

MRS. KEENEY (*after a pause—passing her hand over her eyes with a gesture of pathetic weariness*). How long would it take us to reach home—if we started now?

KEENEY (*frowning*). 'Bout two months, I reckon, Annie, with fair luck.

MRS. KEENEY (*counts on her fingers—then murmurs with a rapt smile*). That would be August, the latter part of August, wouldn't it? It was on the twenty-fifth of August we were married, David, wasn't it?

KEENEY (*trying to conceal the fact that her memories have moved him—gruffly*). Don't you remember?

MRS. KEENEY (*vaguely—again passes her hand over her eyes*). My memory is leaving me—up here in the ice. It was so long ago. (*A pause—then she smiles dreamily.*) It's June now. The lilacs will be all in bloom in the front yard—and the climbing roses on the trellis to the side of the house—they're budding. (*She suddenly covers her face with her hands and commences to sob.*)

KEENEY (*disturbed*). Go in and rest, Annie. You're all worn out cryin' over what can't be helped.

MRS. KEENEY (*suddenly throwing her arms around his neck and clinging to him*). You love me, don't you, David?

KEENEY (*in amazed embarrassment at this outburst*). Love you? Why d'you ask me such a question, Annie?

MRS. KEENEY (*shaking him fiercely*). But you do, don't you, David? Tell me!

KEENEY. I'm your husband, Annie, and you're my wife. Could there be aught but love between us after all these years?

MRS. KEENEY (*shaking him again—still more fiercely*). Then you do love me. Say it!

KEENEY (*simply*). I do, Annie.

MRS. KEENEY (*gives a sigh of relief—her hands drop to her sides.* KEENEY *regards her anxiously. She passes her hand across her eyes and murmurs half to herself*). I sometimes think if we could only have had a child— (KEENEY *turns away from her, deeply moved. She grabs his arm and turns him around to face her—intensely.*) And I've always been a good wife to you, haven't I, David?

KEENEY (*his voice betraying his emotion*). No man has ever had a better, Annie.

MRS. KEENEY. And I've never asked for much from you, have I, David? Have I?

KEENEY. You know you could have all I got the power to give ye, Annie.

MRS. KEENEY (*wildly*). Then do this, this once, for my sake, for God's sake—take me home! It's killing me, this life—the brutality and cold and horror of it. I'm going mad. I can feel the threat in the air. I can hear the silence threatening me—day after gray day and every day the same. I can't bear it. (*Sobbing.*) I'll go mad, I know I will. Take me home, David, if you love me as you say. I'm afraid. For the love of God, take me home!

(*She throws her arms around him, weeping against his shoulder. His face betrays the tremendous struggle going on within him. He holds her out at arm's length, his expression softening. For a moment his shoulders sag, he becomes old, his iron spirit weakens as he looks at her tear-stained face.*)

KEENEY (*dragging out the words with an effort*). I'll do it, Annie—for your sake—if you say it's needful for ye.

MRS. KEENEY (*with wild joy—kissing him*). God bless you for that, David!

(*He turns away from her silently and walks toward the companionway. Just at that moment there is a clatter of footsteps on the stairs and the SECOND MATE enters the cabin.*)

MATE (*excitedly*). The ice is breakin' up to no'th'ard, sir. There's a clear passage through the floe, and clear water beyond, the lookout says.

(KEENEY *straightens himself like a man coming out of a trance.* MRS. KEENEY *looks at the MATE with terrified eyes.*)

KEENEY (*dazedly—trying to collect his thoughts*). A clear passage? To no'th'ard?

MATE. Yes, sir.

KEENEY (*his voice suddenly grim with determination*). Then get her ready and we'll drive her through.

MATE. Aye, aye, sir.

MRS. KEENEY (*appealingly*). David!

KEENEY (*not heeding her*). Will the men turn to willin' or must we drag 'em out?

MATE. They'll turn to willin' enough. You put the fear o' God into 'em, sir. They're meek as lambs.

KEENEY. Then drive 'em—both watches. (*With grim determination.*) They's whale t'other side o' this floe and we're agoin' to git 'em.

MATE. Aye, aye, sir.

(*He goes out hurriedly. A moment later there is the sound of scuffling feet from the deck outside and the MATE's voice shouting orders.*)

KEENEY (*speaking aloud to himself—derisively*). And I was agoin' home like a yaller dog!

MRS. KEENEY (*imploringly*). David!

KEENEY (*sternly*). Woman, you ain't adoin' right when you meddle in men's business and weaken 'em. You can't know my feelin's. I got to prove a man to be a good husband for ye to take pride in. I got to git the ile, I tell ye.

MRS. KEENEY (*supplicatingly*). David. Aren't you going home?

KEENEY (*ignoring this question—commandingly*). You ain't well. Go and lay down a mite. (*He starts for the door.*) I got to git on deck.

> (*He goes out. She cries after him in anguish, "David!" A pause. She passes her hand across her eyes—then commences to laugh hysterically and goes to the organ. She sits down and starts to play wildly an old hymn.* KEENEY *reënters from the doorway to the deck and stands looking at her angrily. He comes over and grabs her roughly by the shoulder.*)

KEENEY. Woman, what foolish mockin' is this? (*She laughs wildly and he starts back from her in alarm.*) Annie! What is it? (*She doesn't answer him.* KEENEY's *voice trembles.*) Don't you know me, Annie?

> (*He puts both hands on her shoulders and turns her around so that he can look into her eyes. She stares up at him with a stupid expression, a vague smile on her lips. He stumbles away from her, and she commences softly to play the organ again.*)

KEENEY (*swallowing hard—in a hoarse whisper, as if he had difficulty in speaking*). You said—you was agoin' mad—God!

> (*A long wail is heard from the deck above, "Ah, bl-o-o-o-ow!"[5] A moment later the* MATE's *face appears through the skylight. He cannot see* MRS. KEENEY.)

MATE (*in great excitement*). Whales, sir—a whole school of 'em—off the starb'd quarter 'bout five miles away—big ones!

KEENEY (*galvanized into action*). Are you lowerin' the boats?

MATE. Yes, sir.

KEENEY (*with grim decision*). I'm acomin' with ye.

MATE. Aye, aye, sir. (*Jubilantly.*) You'll git the ile now right enough, sir.

> (*His head is withdrawn and he can be heard shouting orders.*)

KEENEY (*turning to his wife*). Annie! Did you hear him? I'll git the ile. (*She doesn't answer or seem to know he is there. He gives a hard laugh, which is almost a groan.*) I know you're foolin' me, Annie. You ain't out of your mind—(*anxiously*)—be you? I'll git the ile now right enough—jest a little while longer,

Annie—then we'll turn home'ard. I can't turn back now, you see that, don't you? I've got to git the ile. (*In sudden terror.*) Answer me! You ain't mad, be you?

> (*She keeps on playing the organ, but makes no reply. The* MATE's *face appears again through the skylight.*)

MATE. All ready, sir.

> (KEENEY *turns his back on his wife and strides to the doorway, where he stands for a moment and looks back at her in anguish, fighting to control his feelings.*)

MATE. Comin', sir?

KEENEY (*his face suddenly grown hard with determination*). Aye.

> (*He turns abruptly and goes out.* MRS. KEENEY *does not appear to notice his departure. Her whole attention seems centered in the organ. She sits with half-closed eyes, her body swaying a little from side to side to the rhythm of the hymn. Her fingers move faster and faster and she is playing wildly and discordantly as the curtain falls.*)

---

5. Ah, bl-o-o-o-ow! the lookout's cry when he sights a jet of spray showing the location of a whale.

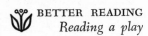

BETTER READING
Reading a play

Most plays are written primarily not to be read but to be performed. In Shakespeare's time the publication of a play after it had been produced was a rather haphazard affair carried out largely on the initiative of the publisher. The playwright, working very closely with the actors and other members of the theater, gave them instructions as they went, rather than writing out his instructions. As a result, the written version of a Shakespearian play contains little but dialogue.

In contrast to this, modern printed plays are often only half dialogue, the other half being stage directions to the director and actors. There are a number of reasons for this. First, plays of high literary quality are now acted all over the world within a few years of their initial production. Since the playwright cannot work closely with all these groups, he furnishes quite specific instructions showing how the play is to be produced. Secondly, the modern stage is a highly complex machine, providing almost infinite possibilities for imaginative use of sets and lighting. The skillful dramatist makes full use of what the theater has to offer in the way of visual impact to communicate his meaning. In the third place, it is now realized that great drama makes good reading, as well as good seeing. Indeed, like all works of literature, a play cannot be fully appreciated when it is seen only. The full enjoyment it has to offer can be gained only after studying it on the printed page. When reading a modern play one needs to study all the stage directions carefully and to reconstruct the scene imaginatively.

Describe the set used in "Ile." What is the effect of the lighting and the color of the cabin? How are the walls made symbolic of the surroundings of the ship? What effect does the setting have on Mrs. Keeney and on the action? Of which of the following stage techniques does O'Neill make use: realist, symbolist, expressionist, or epic? Support your answer by reference to the text and the chapter introduction.

What does the reader learn about the Captain, before he ever speaks a line, from the directions beginning at the bottom of page 711 that describe his entrance into the cabin?

Besides stage directions, the playwright also includes specific directions to the actors, describing how certain lines are to be read. Consider the following speeches, paying particular attention to these directions. What is the significance of the manner of speech indicated? Imagine some other way in which each speech might reasonably be read. What is the difference in meaning between the two ways?

(a) KEENEY (a tone of command in his voice). Best not today, Annie (page 713, column 1, paragraph 3).

(b) KEENEY (disturbed). Go in and rest, Annie (page 716, column 2, last paragraph).

(c) MRS. KEENEY (supplicatingly). David. Aren't you going home? (page 717, column 2, next to last paragraph).

(d) KEENEY (swallowing hard—in a hoarse whisper, as if he had difficulty in speaking). You said—you was agoin' mad—God! (page 718, column 1, paragraph 2).

The play ends, not with a dramatic speech, but with an indication of action. What is the significance of this action? Why is it more expressive than any speech could possibly be under these conditions?

TO INCREASE UNDERSTANDING

1. What kind of man does Captain Keeney seem to be to (a) the men, (b) his wife, (c) the mate, (d) himself? Explain how you know.

2. (a) What were Mrs. Keeney's reasons for wanting to go with her husband on this voyage?

(b) What does the incident with the mutineers show Mrs. Keeney about her husband and his profession? (c) What effect does this revelation have on her?

3. Describe Captain Keeney's view of the proper rôles for men and women in the family and at work. Take into account particularly the following quotations:

(a) You know you could have all I got the power to give ye, Annie (page 717, column 1, paragraph 10).

(b) Woman, you ain't adoin' right when you meddle in men's business and weaken 'em. You can't know my feelin's. I got to prove a man to be a good husband for ye to take pride in. I got to git the ile, I tell ye (page 717, column 2, paragraph 14).

4. (a) What is the effect created by an organ in the cabin of a whaling ship? (b) How does this organ act as a symbol of the relationship between Captain Keeney and his wife?

5. (a) What are the painful alternatives between which the Captain must choose? (b) Why had this problem never arisen while he had been on previous voyages? (c) Whatever way the Captain decides, something very important to him will be destroyed. Explain what this would be in each case.

6. (a) To what extent is the reader made to feel that the Captain's final decision is heroic, to what extent deplorable? (b) On what characters or on what other factors do you think the blame for the tragedy lies? Justify your answer.

EXTENDING INTERESTS

Whaling was perhaps the most romantic and dangerous of all early sailing work. Its history, from the time of its remarkable growth in the nineteenth century, through the transition period when the whales had been chased to the remote waters of the Arctic and the Indian oceans, to the nearly complete extinction of the industry with the coming of gas and petroleum, makes a fascinating study. With the permission of your teacher you may want to arrange a group project reporting on the various phases of whaling and its history. You might begin your study with an article in a good encyclopedia, following this up by reading some of the books in the bibliography at the end of the article. *Of Whales and Men* by Robert B. Robertson shows the whaling industry as it is today. Two other sources of information about whaling are ballads and novels. There are some excellent collections of whaling ballads on records, and, of course, much fascinating reading in *Moby-Dick* (see page 318).

Nobody,
not even the rain,
has such small hands
—E. E. CUMMINGS

The Glass Menagerie

by Tennessee Williams

TENNESSEE WILLIAMS 1914-

The first play of Tom ("Tennessee") Williams to appear on Broadway was a sensational flop. For four years thereafter he worked at odd jobs around the country, returning to the theater in 1945 to captivate first Chicago and then New York with *The Glass Menagerie*.

Thomas Lanier Williams was born in Columbus, Mississippi, the son of a shoe salesman and the grandson of an Episcopalian clergyman. The family moved to St. Louis when Tom's father was transferred there. Tom's one ambition was to write, and his aim when he entered college was to learn to do so. But since the elder Williams saw writing as a slow and precarious way of making a living, Tom was recalled from college after little more than a year and sent to work in the shoe factory. Determined to fulfill his dreams of becoming a writer, Tom labored over his manuscripts until two or three o'clock every night. A nervous breakdown ended his shoe-business career. Eventually he returned to college and received an A.B. degree from the University of Iowa in 1938.

In *The Glass Menagerie* Tennessee Williams drew heavily upon the impressions of his early life. The Southern background, the distasteful job, the yearning to write, the drab surroundings—all these are based on memories. The success of this drama established Williams as a playwright. The intense concentration on writing which he had developed in his youth made him a prolific writer, turning out an average of one play every two years. A remarkable number of these have been of high quality and have met with great success, both at home and abroad. They have won him two Pulitzer Prizes and three New York Drama Critics' Circle Awards. And they have established his reputation as one of the foremost playwrights of the contemporary stage.

Production Notes

Being a "memory play," The Glass Menagerie can be presented with unusual freedom of convention. Because of its considerably delicate or tenuous material, atmospheric touches and subtleties of direction play a particularly important part. Expressionism and all other unconventional techniques in drama have only one valid aim, and that is a closer approach to truth. When a play employs unconventional techniques, it is not, or certainly shouldn't be, trying to escape its responsibility of dealing with reality, or interpreting experience, but is actually or should be attempting to find a closer approach, a more penetrating and vivid expression of things as they are. The straight realistic play with its genuine frigidaire and authentic ice cubes, its characters that speak exactly as its audience speaks, corresponds to the academic landscape and has the same virtue of a photographic likeness. Everyone should know nowadays the unimportance of the photographic in art: that truth, life, or reality is an organic thing which the poetic imagination can represent or suggest, in essence, only through transformation, through changing into other forms than those which were merely present in appearance.

These remarks are not meant as a preface only to this particular play. They have to do with a conception of a new, plastic theatre which must take the place of the exhausted theatre of realistic conventions if the theatre is to resume vitality as a part of our culture.

Characters

AMANDA WINGFIELD (the mother)

A little woman of great but confused vitality clinging frantically to another time and place. Her characterization must be carefully created, not copied from type. She is not paranoiac, but her life is paranoia.[1] There is much to admire in AMANDA, and as much to love and pity as there is to laugh at. Certainly she has endurance and a kind of heroism, and though her foolishness makes her unwittingly cruel at times, there is tenderness in her slight person.

LAURA WINGFIELD (her daughter)

AMANDA, having failed to establish contact with reality, continues to live vitally in her illusions, but LAURA's situation is even graver. A childhood illness has left her crippled, one leg slightly shorter than the other, and held in a brace. This defect need not be more than suggested on the stage. Stemming from this, LAURA's separation increases till she is like a piece of her own glass collection, too exquisitely fragile to move from the shelf.

TOM WINGFIELD (her son)

And the narrator of the play. A poet with a job in a warehouse. His nature is not remorseless, but to escape from a trap he has to act without pity.

JIM O'CONNOR (the gentleman caller)

A nice, ordinary, young man.

THE SCREEN DEVICE

There is only one important difference between the original and acting version of the play *and that is the* omission *in the latter of* the device which I tentatively included in my original *script. This device was the use of a screen on which were projected magic-lantern*

SCENE:

An alley in St. Louis

PART I. *Preparation for a Gentleman Caller*
PART II. *The Gentleman calls*

TIME: *Now and the Past*

---

1. *paranoiac . . . paranoia.* Paranoia is a form of insanity characterized by elaborate delusions. Williams is saying that Amanda is not insane, but that her life is out of contact with reality.

slides bearing images or titles. I do not regret the omission of this device from the present Broadway production. The extraordinary power of Miss Taylor's performance[2] made it suitable to have the utmost simplicity in the physical production. But I think it may be interesting to some readers to see how this device was conceived. So I am putting it into the published manuscript. These images and legends, projected from behind, were cast on a section of wall between the front-room and dining-room areas, which should be indistinguishable from the rest when not in use.

The purpose of this will probably be apparent. It is to give accent to certain values in each scene. Each scene contains a particular point (or several) which is structurally the most important. In an episodic play, such as this, the basic structure or narrative line may be obscured from the audience; the effect may seem fragmentary rather than architectural. This may not be the fault of the play so much as a lack of attention in the audience. The legend or image upon the screen will strengthen the effect of what is merely allusion in the writing and allow the primary point to be made more simply and lightly than if the entire responsibility were on the spoken lines. Aside from this structural value, I think the screen will have a definite emotional appeal, less definable but just as important. An imaginative producer or director may invent many other uses for this device than those indicated in the present script. In fact the possibilities of the device seem much larger to me than the instance of this play can possibly utilize.

THE MUSIC

Another extra-literary accent in this play is provided by the use of music. A single recurring tune, "The Glass Menagerie," is used to give emotional emphasis to suitable passages. This tune is like circus music, not when you are on the grounds or in the immediate vicinity of the parade, but when you are at some distance and very likely thinking of something else. It seems under those circumstances to continue almost interminably and it weaves in and out of your preoccupied consciousness; then it is the lightest, most delicate music in the world and perhaps the saddest. It expresses the surface vivacity of life with the underlying strain of immutable and inexpressible sorrow. When you look at a piece of delicately spun glass you think of two things: how beautiful it is and how easily it can be broken. Both of those ideas should be woven into the recurring tune, which dips in and out of the play as if it were carried on a wind that changes. It serves as a thread of connection and allusion between the narrator with his separate point in time and space and the subject of his story. Between each episode it returns as reference to the emotion, nostalgia, which is the first condition of the play. It is primarily LAURA's music and therefore comes out most clearly when the play focuses upon her and the lovely fragility of glass which is her image.

THE LIGHTING

The lighting in the play is not realistic. In keeping with the atmosphere of memory, the stage is dim. Shafts of light are focused on selected areas or actors, sometimes in contradistinction to what is the apparent center. For instance, in the quarrel scene between TOM and AMANDA, in which LAURA has no active part, the clearest pool of light is on her figure. This is also true of the supper scene, when her silent figure on the sofa should remain the visual center. The light upon LAURA should be distinct from the others, having a peculiar pristine clarity such as light used in early religious portraits of female saints or madonnas. A certain correspondence to light in religious paintings, such as El Greco's,[3] where the figures are radiant in atmosphere that is relatively dusky, could be effectively used throughout

2. *Miss Taylor's performance.* Laurette Taylor (1884-1946), of a theatrical family, had a long and successful career as an actress. In spite of her extraordinary reputation, she did not accept any rôles after 1941, until *The Glass Menagerie* was produced in 1945. The praise for her interpretation of Amanda was immediate and universal. 3. *El Greco* (el grek′ō), late sixteenth-century painter who used perspective and lighting not to achieve a photographic likeness but for expressive effects.

the play. (It will also permit a more effective use of the screen.) A free, imaginative use of light can be of enormous value in giving a mobile, plastic quality to plays of a more or less static nature.　　　　　　　　　T. W.

Scene 1

The Wingfield apartment is in the rear of the building, one of those vast hive-like conglomerations of cellular living-units that flower as warty growths in overcrowded urban centers of lower middle-class population and are symptomatic of the impulse of this largest and fundamentally enslaved section of American society to avoid fluidity and differentiation and to exist and function as one interfused mass of automatism.

The apartment faces an alley and is entered by a fire escape, a structure whose name is a touch of accidental poetic truth, for all of these huge buildings are always burning with the slow and implacable fires of human desperation. The fire escape is included in the set— that is, the landing of it and steps descending from it.

The scene is memory and is therefore non-realistic. Memory takes a lot of poetic license. It omits some details; others are exaggerated, according to the emotional value of the articles it touches, for memory is seated predominantly in the heart. The interior is therefore rather dim and poetic.

At the rise of the curtain, the audience is faced with the dark, grim rear wall of the Wingfield tenement. This building, which runs parallel to the footlights, is flanked on both sides by dark, narrow alleys which run into murky canyons of tangled clotheslines, garbage cans and the sinister latticework of neighboring fire escapes. It is up and down these side alleys that exterior entrances and exits are made, during the play. At the end of TOM's opening commentary, the dark tenement wall slowly reveals (by means of a transparency) the interior of the ground floor Wingfield apartment.

Downstage is the living room, which also serves as a sleeping room for LAURA, the sofa unfolding to make her bed. Upstage, center, and divided by a wide arch or second proscenium with transparent faded portieres (or second curtain), is the dining room. In an old-fashioned what-not in the living room are seen scores of transparent glass animals. A blown-up photograph of the father hangs on the wall of the living room, facing the audience, to the left of the archway. It is the face of a very handsome young man in a doughboy's First World War cap. He is gallantly smiling, ineluctably smiling, as if to say, "I will be smiling forever."

The audience hears and sees the opening scene in the dining room through both the transparent fourth wall of the building and the transparent gauze portieres of the dining-room arch. It is during this revealing scene that the fourth wall slowly ascends, out of sight. This transparent exterior wall is not brought down again until the very end of the play, during TOM's final speech.

The narrator is an undisguised convention of the play. He takes whatever license with dramatic convention as is convenient to his purposes.

TOM enters dressed as a merchant sailor from alley, stage left, and strolls across the front of the stage to the fire escape. There he stops and lights a cigarette. He addresses the audience.

TOM. Yes, I have tricks in my pocket, I have things up my sleeve. But I am the opposite of a stage magician. He gives you illusion that has the appearance of truth. I give you truth in the pleasant disguise of illusion.

To begin with, I turn back time. I reverse it to that quaint period, the thirties, when the huge middle class of America was matriculating in a school for the blind. Their eyes had failed them, or they had failed their eyes, and so they were having their fingers pressed forcibly down on the fiery Braille alphabet of a dissolving economy.

In Spain there was revolution. Here there was only shouting and confusion.

In Spain there was Guernica.[4] Here there were disturbances of labor, sometimes pretty violent, in otherwise peaceful cities such as Chicago, Cleveland, Saint Louis. . . .

This is the social background of the play.

(MUSIC.)

The play is memory.

Being a memory play, it is dimly lighted, it is sentimental, it is not realistic.

In memory everything seems to happen to music. That explains the fiddle in the wings.

I am the narrator of the play, and also a character in it.

The other characters are my mother, Amanda, my sister, Laura, and a gentleman caller who appears in the final scenes.

He is the most realistic character in the play, being an emissary from a world of reality that we were somehow set apart from.

But since I have a poet's weakness for symbols, I am using this character also as a symbol; he is the long delayed but always expected something that we live for.

There is a fifth character in the play who doesn't appear except in this larger-than-life-size photograph over the mantel.

This is our father who left us a long time ago.

He was a telephone man who fell in love with long distances; he gave up his job with the telephone company and skipped the light fantastic out of town. . . .

The last we heard of him was a picture postcard from Mazatlan, on the Pacific coast of Mexico, containing a message of two words— "Hello— Good-bye!" and no address.

I think the rest of the play will explain itself. . . .

(AMANDA's *voice becomes audible through the portieres.*)

(LEGEND ON SCREEN: *"Ou Sont les Neiges."*[5])

(*He divides the portieres and enters the upstage area.*)

(AMANDA *and* LAURA *are seated at a drop-leaf table. Eating is indicated by gestures without food or utensils.* AMANDA *faces the audience.* TOM *and* LAURA *are seated in profile.*)

(*The interior has lit up softly and through the scrim we see* AMANDA *and* LAURA *seated at the table in the upstage area.*)

AMANDA (*calling*). Tom?

TOM. Yes, Mother.

AMANDA. We can't say grace until you come to the table!

TOM. Coming, Mother. (*He bows slightly and withdraws, reappearing a few moments later in his place at the table.*)

AMANDA (*to her son*). Honey, don't *push* with your *fingers.* If you have to push with something, the thing to push with is a crust of bread. And chew—chew! Animals have sections in their stomachs which enable them to digest food without mastication, but human beings are supposed to chew their food before they swallow it down. Eat food leisurely, son, and really enjoy it. A well-cooked meal has lots of delicate flavors that have to be held in the mouth for appreciation. So chew your food and give your salivary glands a chance to function!

(TOM *deliberately lays his imaginary fork down and pushes his chair back from the table.*)

TOM. I haven't enjoyed one bite of this dinner because of your constant directions on how to eat it. It's you that make me rush through meals with your hawk-like attention to every bite I take. Sickening—spoils my appetite—all this discussion of—animal's secretion—salivary glands—mastication!

AMANDA (*lightly*). Temperament like a Metropolitan star! (*He rises and crosses downstage.*) You're not excused from the table.

TOM. I'm getting a cigarette.

AMANDA. You smoke too much.

(LAURA *rises.*)

LAURA. I'll bring in the blancmange.

(*He remains standing with his cigarette by the portieres during the following.*)

---

4. *In Spain there was Guernica.* Guernica (ger nē′kä), a town in northern Spain, was held by the democratic faction during the Spanish Civil War. It was bombed by German and Italian airplanes in 1937 at the direction of the leader of the Fascist faction, General Franco, and thus became a symbol of the cruelty of the Fascist overthrow of the Spanish republic. 5. *"Ou Sont les Neiges"* (ü sôn lä näzh). "Ou sont les neiges d'antan?" is a famous line from one of the ballads of François Villon (frän swä′ vē yôn′), French poet of the fifteenth century. It means "Where are the snows of yesteryear?" that is, what has happened to the past.

AMANDA (*rising*). No, sister, no, sister—you be the lady this time and I'll be the servant.

LAURA. I'm already up.

AMANDA. Resume your seat, little sister—I want you to stay fresh and pretty—for gentlemen callers!

LAURA. I'm not expecting any gentlemen callers.

AMANDA (*crossing out to kitchenette. Airily*). Sometimes they come when they are least expected! Why, I remember one Sunday afternoon in Blue Mountain—(*Enters kitchenette.*)

TOM. I know what's coming!

LAURA. Yes. But let her tell it.

TOM. Again?

LAURA. She loves to tell it.

(AMANDA *returns with bowl of dessert.*)

AMANDA. One Sunday afternoon in Blue Mountain—your mother received—*seventeen!* —gentlemen callers! Why, sometimes there weren't chairs enough to accommodate them all. We had to send the servant over to bring in folding chairs from the parish house.

TOM (*remaining at portieres*). How did you entertain those gentlemen callers?

AMANDA. I understood the art of conversation!

TOM. I bet you could talk.

AMANDA. Girls in those days *knew* how to talk, I can tell you.

TOM. Yes?

(IMAGE: AMANDA *as a girl on a porch, greeting callers.*)

AMANDA. They knew how to entertain their gentlemen callers. It wasn't enough for a girl to be possessed of a pretty face and a graceful figure—although I wasn't slighted in either respect. She also needed to have a nimble wit and a tongue to meet all occasions.

TOM. What did you talk about?

AMANDA. Things of importance going on in the world! Never anything coarse or common or vulgar. (*She addresses* TOM *as though he were seated in the vacant chair at the table though he remains by portieres. He plays this scene as though he held the book.*) My callers were gentlemen—all! Among my callers were some of the most prominent young planters of the Mississippi Delta—planters and sons of planters!

(TOM *motions for music and a spot of light on* AMANDA.)

(*Her eyes lift, her face glows, her voice becomes rich and elegiac.*)

(SCREEN LEGEND: *"Ou Sont les Neiges."*)

There was young Champ Laughlin who later became vice-president of the Delta Planters Bank.

Hadley Stevenson who was drowned in Moon Lake and left his widow one hundred and fifty thousand in Government bonds.

There were the Cutrere brothers, Wesley and Bates. Bates was one of my bright particular beaux! He got in a quarrel with that wild Wainwright boy. They shot it out on the floor of Moon Lake Casino. Bates was shot through the stomach. Died in the ambulance on his way to Memphis. His widow was also well-provided for, came into eight or ten thousand acres, that's all. She married him on the rebound—never loved her—carried my picture on him the night he died!

And there was that boy that every girl in the Delta had set her cap for! That beautiful, brilliant young Fitzhugh boy from Greene County!

TOM. What did he leave his widow?

AMANDA. He never married! Gracious, you talk as though all of my old admirers had turned up their toes to the daisies!

TOM. Isn't this the first you've mentioned that still survives?

AMANDA. That Fitzhugh boy went North and made a fortune—came to be known as the Wolf of Wall Street! He had the Midas touch, whatever he touched turned to gold! And I could have been Mrs. Duncan J. Fitzhugh, mind you! But—I picked your *father!*

LAURA (*rising*). Mother, let me clear the table.

AMANDA. No, dear, you go in front and study your typewriter chart. Or practice your shorthand a little. Stay fresh and pretty!—It's almost time for our gentlemen callers to start arriving. (*She flounces girlishly toward the kitchenette.*) How many do you suppose we're going to entertain this afternoon?

(TOM *throws down the paper and jumps up with a groan.*)

LAURA (*alone in the dining room*). I don't believe we're going to receive any, Mother.

AMANDA (*reappearing, airily*). What? No one—not one? You must be joking! (LAURA *nervously echoes her laugh. She slips in a fugitive manner through the half-open portieres and draws them gently behind her. A shaft of very clear light is thrown on her face against the faded tapestry of the curtains.* MUSIC: "*The Glass Menagerie*" *under faintly. Lightly.*) Not one gentleman caller? It can't be true! There must be a flood, there must have been a tornado!

LAURA. It isn't a flood, it's not a tornado, Mother. I'm just not popular like you were in Blue Mountain. . . . (TOM *utters another groan.* LAURA *glances at him with a faint, apologetic smile. Her voice catching a little.*) Mother's afraid I'm going to be an old maid.

THE SCENE DIMS OUT WITH "GLASS MENAGERIE" MUSIC

Scene 2

"*Laura, Haven't You Ever Liked Some Boy?*"

On the dark stage the screen is lighted with the image of blue roses.

Gradually LAURA'*s figure becomes apparent and the screen goes out.*

The music subsides.

LAURA *is seated in the delicate ivory chair at the small claw-foot table.*

She wears a dress of soft violet material for a kimono—her hair tied back from her forehead with a ribbon.

She is washing and polishing her collection of glass.

AMANDA *appears on the fire escape steps. At the sound of her ascent,* LAURA *catches her breath, thrusts the bowl of ornaments away and seats herself stiffly before the diagram of the typewriter keyboard as though it held her spellbound.*

Something has happened to AMANDA. *It is written in her face as she climbs to the landing: a look that is grim and hopeless and a little absurd.*

She has on one of those cheap or imitation velvety-looking cloth coats with imitation fur collar. Her hat is five or six years old, one of those dreadful cloche hats that were worn in the late twenties and she is clasping an enormous black patent-leather pocketbook with nickel clasps and initials. This is her full-dress outfit, the one she usually wears to the D.A.R.[1]

Before entering she looks through the door.

She purses her lips, opens her eyes very wide, rolls them upward and shakes her head.

Then she slowly lets herself in the door. Seeing her mother's expression LAURA *touches her lips with a nervous gesture.*

LAURA. Hello, Mother, I was— (*She makes a nervous gesture toward the chart on the wall.* AMANDA *leans against the shut door and stares at* LAURA *with a martyred look.*)

AMANDA. Deception? Deception? (*She slowly removes her hat and gloves, continuing the sweet suffering stare. She lets the hat and gloves fall on the floor—a bit of acting.*)

LAURA (*shakily*). How was the D.A.R. meeting? (AMANDA *slowly opens her purse and removes a dainty white handkerchief which she shakes out delicately and delicately touches to her lips and nostrils.*) Didn't you go to the D.A.R. meeting, Mother?

AMANDA (*faintly, almost inaudibly*).—No. —No. (*Then more forcibly.*) I did not have the strength—to go to the D.A.R. In fact, I did not have the courage! I wanted to find a hole in the ground and hide myself in it forever! (*She crosses slowly to the wall and removes the diagram of the typewriter keyboard. She holds it in front of her for a second, staring at it sweetly and sorrowfully—then bites her lips and tears it in two pieces.*)

LAURA (*faintly*). Why did you do that, Mother? (AMANDA *repeats the same procedure with the chart of the Gregg Alphabet.*) Why are you—

AMANDA. Why? Why? How old are you, Laura?

LAURA. Mother, you know my age.

AMANDA. I thought that you were an adult;

---

1. D.A.R., Daughters of the American Revolution, a society of women who can claim descent from Americans who fought in the Revolutionary War.

it seems that I was mistaken. (*She crosses slowly to the sofa and sinks down and stares at* LAURA.)

LAURA. Please don't stare at me, Mother.

(AMANDA *closes her eyes and lowers her head. Count ten.*)

AMANDA. What are we going to do, what is going to become of us, what is the future? (*Count ten.*)

LAURA. Has something happened, Mother? (AMANDA *draws a long breath and takes out the handkerchief again. Dabbing process.*) Mother, has—something happened?

AMANDA. I'll be all right in a minute, I'm just bewildered—(*Count five.*)—by life. . . .

LAURA. Mother, I wish that you would tell me what's happened!

AMANDA. As you know, I was supposed to be inducted into my office at the D.A.R. this afternoon. (IMAGE: *A swarm of typewriters.*) But I stopped off at Rubicam's Business College to speak to your teachers about your having a cold and ask them what progress they thought you were making down there.

LAURA. Oh. . . .

AMANDA. I went to the typing instructor and introduced myself as your mother. She didn't know who you were. Wingfield, she said. We don't have any such student enrolled at the school!

I assured her she did, that you had been going to classes since early in January.

"I wonder," she said, "if you could be talking about that terribly shy little girl who dropped out of school after only a few days' attendance?"

"No," I said, "Laura, my daughter, has been going to school every day for the past six weeks!"

"Excuse me," she said. She took the attendance book out and there was your name, unmistakably printed, and all the dates you were absent until they decided that you had dropped out of school.

I still said, "No, there must have been some mistake! There must have been some mix-up in the records!"

And she said, "No—I remember her perfectly now. Her hands shook so that she couldn't hit the right keys! The first time we gave a speed-test, she broke down completely—was sick at the stomach and almost had to be carried into the wash-room! After that morning she never showed up any more. We phoned the house but never got any answer"—while I was working at Famous and Barr, I suppose, demonstrating those— Oh!

I felt so weak I could barely keep on my feet!

I had to sit down while they got me a glass of water!

Fifty dollars' tuition, all of our plans—my hopes and ambitions for you—just gone up the spout, just gone up the spout like that.

(LAURA *draws a long breath and gets awkwardly to her feet. She crosses to the victrola and winds it up.*)

What are you doing?

LAURA. Oh! (*She releases the handle and returns to her seat.*)

AMANDA. Laura, where have you been going when you've gone out pretending that you were going to business college?

LAURA. I've just been going out walking.

AMANDA. That's not true.

LAURA. It is. I just went walking.

AMANDA. Walking? Walking? In winter? Deliberately courting pneumonia in that light coat? Where did you walk to, Laura?

LAURA. All sorts of places—mostly in the park.

AMANDA. Even after you'd started catching that cold?

LAURA. It was the lesser of two evils, Mother. (IMAGE: *Winter scene in park.*) I couldn't go back up. I—threw up—on the floor!

AMANDA. From half past seven till after five every day you mean to tell me you walked around in the park, because you wanted to make me think that you were still going to Rubicam's Business College?

LAURA. It wasn't as bad as it sounds. I went inside places to get warmed up.

AMANDA. Inside where?

LAURA. I went in the art museum and the bird-houses at the Zoo. I visited the penguins every day! Sometimes I did without lunch and went to the movies. Lately I've been spending most of my afternoons in the Jewel-box, that big glass house[2] where they raise the tropical flowers.

AMANDA. You did all this to deceive me, just for deception? (LAURA *looks down.*) Why?

LAURA. Mother, when you're disappointed, you get that awful suffering look on your face, like the picture of Jesus' mother in the museum!

AMANDA. Hush!

LAURA. I couldn't face it.

(*Pause. A whisper of strings.*)

(LEGEND: *"The Crust of Humility."*)

AMANDA (*hopelessly fingering the huge pocketbook*). So what are we going to do the rest of our lives? Stay home and watch the parades go by? Amuse ourselves with the glass menagerie, darling? Eternally play those worn-out phonograph records your father left as a painful reminder of him?

We won't have a business career—we've given that up because it gave us nervous indigestion! (*Laughs wearily.*) What is there left but dependency all our lives? I know so well what becomes of unmarried women who aren't prepared to occupy a position. I've seen such pitiful cases in the South—barely tolerated spinsters living upon the grudging patronage of sister's husband or brother's wife!—stuck away in some little mouse-trap of a room—encouraged by one in-law to visit another—little birdlike women without any nest—eating the crust of humility all their life!

Is that the future that we've mapped out for ourselves?

I swear it's the only alternative I can think of!

It isn't a very pleasant alternative, is it?

Of course—some girls *do marry.*

(LAURA *twists her hands nervously.*)

Haven't you ever liked some boy?

LAURA. Yes. I liked one once. (*Rises.*) I came across his picture a while ago.

AMANDA (*with some interest*). He gave you his picture?

LAURA. No, it's in the yearbook.

AMANDA (*disappointed*). Oh—a high-school boy.

(SCREEN IMAGE: *Jim as high-school hero bearing a silver cup.*)

LAURA. Yes. His name was Jim. (LAURA *lifts the heavy annual from the claw-foot table.*) Here he is in *The Pirates of Penzance.*[3]

AMANDA (*absently*). The what?

LAURA. The operetta the senior class put on. He had a wonderful voice and we sat across the aisle from each other Mondays, Wednesdays and Fridays in the Aud. Here he is with the silver cup for debating! See his grin?

AMANDA (*absently*). He must have had a jolly disposition.

LAURA. He used to call me—Blue Roses.

(IMAGE: *Blue roses.*)

AMANDA. Why did he call you such a name as that?

LAURA. When I had that attack of pleurosis—he asked me what was the matter when I came back. I said pleurosis—he thought that I said Blue Roses! So that's what he always called me after that. Whenever he saw me, he'd holler, "Hello, Blue Roses!" I didn't care for the girl that he went out with. Emily Meisenbach. Emily was the best-dressed girl at Soldan. She never struck me, though, as being sincere . . . It says in the Personal Section—they're engaged. That's—six years ago! They must be married by now.

AMANDA. Girls that aren't cut out for business careers usually wind up married to some nice man. (*Gets up with a spark of revival.*) Sister, that's what you'll do!

(LAURA *utters a startled, doubtful laugh. She reaches quickly for a piece of glass.*)

LAURA. But, Mother—

AMANDA. Yes? (*Crossing to photograph.*)

LAURA (*in a tone of frightened apology*). I'm—crippled!

(IMAGE: *Screen.*)

AMANDA. Nonsense! Laura, I've told you never, never to use that word. Why, you're not crippled, you just have a little defect—hardly noticeable, even! When people have some slight disadvantage like that, they cultivate other things to make up for it—develop charm—and vivacity—and—*charm!* That's all

2. *big glass house,* conservatory at the St. Louis zoo. Williams emphasizes the identification of Laura with the delicate flowers and the fragile, glass building. 3. *The Pirates of Penzance,* an operetta by the famous English team of William S. Gilbert (1836-1911) and Sir Arthur Sullivan (1842-1900).

you have to do! (*She turns again to the photograph.*) One thing your father had *plenty of* —was *charm!*

(TOM *motions to the fiddle in the wings.*)
THE SCENE FADES OUT WITH MUSIC

Scene 3

LEGEND ON SCREEN: *"After the fiasco—"*

TOM *speaks from the fire escape landing.*

TOM. After the fiasco at Rubicam's Business College, the idea of getting a gentleman caller for Laura began to play a more and more important part in Mother's calculations.

It became an obsession. Like some archetype of the universal unconscious,[1] the image of the gentleman caller haunted our small apartment. . . .

(IMAGE: *Young man at door with flowers.*)

An evening at home rarely passed without some allusion to this image, this spectre, this hope. . . .

Even when he wasn't mentioned, his presence hung in Mother's preoccupied look and in my sister's frightened, apologetic manner— hung like a sentence passed upon the Wingfields!

Mother was a woman of action as well as words.

She began to take logical steps in the planned direction.

Late that winter and in the early spring— realizing that extra money would be needed to properly feather the nest and plume the bird—she conducted a vigorous campaign on the telephone, roping in subscribers to one of those magazines for matrons called *The Home-maker's Companion,* the type of journal that features the serialized sublimations of ladies of letters who think in terms of slim, tapering waists, eyes like wood-smoke in autumn, fingers that soothe and caress like strains of music, bodies as powerful as Etruscan sculpture.

(SCREEN IMAGE: *Glamor magazine cover.*)
(AMANDA *enters with phone on long extension cord. She is spotted in the dim stage.*)

AMANDA. Ida Scott? This is Amanda Wingfield!

We *missed* you at the D.A.R. last Monday!

I said to myself: She's probably suffering with that sinus condition! How is that sinus condition?

Horrors! Heaven have mercy!—You're a Christian martyr, yes, that's what you are, a Christian martyr!

Well, I just now happened to notice that your subscription to the *Companion's* about to expire! Yes, it expires with the next issue, honey!—just when that wonderful new serial by Bessie Mae Hopper is getting off to such an exciting start. Oh, honey, it's something that you can't miss! You remember how *Gone With the Wind* took everybody by storm? You simply couldn't go out if you hadn't read it. All everybody *talked* was Scarlett O'Hara. Well, this is a book that critics already compare to *Gone With the Wind.* It's the *Gone With the Wind* of the post-World War generation!—What?—Burning?—Oh, honey, don't let them burn, go take a look in the oven and I'll hold the wire! Heavens—I think she's hung up!

DIM OUT
(LEGEND ON SCREEN: *"You think I'm in love with continental shoemakers?"*)
(*Before the stage is lighted, the violent voices of* TOM *and* AMANDA *are heard.*)
(*They are quarreling behind the portieres. In front of them stands* LAURA *with clenched hands and panicky expression.*)
(*A clear pool of light on her figure throughout this scene.*)

TOM. What in God's name am I—
AMANDA (*shrilly*). Don't you use that—

1. *archetype of the universal unconscious,* a key portion of the psychological theory of Carl G. Jung (1875-1961), eminent German medical psychologist. It was his belief that everyone inherits images of experiences that are typical for all mankind. According to Jung's theory, these images are what give people their idea, for example, of what a mother or father should be, and they exert a powerful influence on behavior. Tom satirically suggests that the image of the "typical gentleman caller" began to dominate his mother's thinking in the manner of one of these universal archetypes.

TOM. Supposed to do!

AMANDA. Expression! Not in my—

TOM. Ohhh!

AMANDA. Presence! Have you gone out of your senses?

TOM. I have, that's true, *driven* out!

AMANDA. What is the matter with you, you —big—big—IDIOT!

TOM. Look!—I've got *no thing,* no single thing—

AMANDA. Lower your voice!

TOM. In my life here that I can call my OWN! Everything is—

AMANDA. Stop that shouting!

TOM. Yesterday you confiscated my books! You had the nerve to—

AMANDA. I took that horrible novel back to the library—yes! That hideous book by that insane Mr. Lawrence.[2] (TOM *laughs wildly.*) I cannot control the output of diseased minds or people who cater to them— (TOM *laughs still more wildly.*) BUT I WON'T ALLOW SUCH FILTH BROUGHT INTO MY HOUSE! No, no, no, no, no!

TOM. House, house! Who pays rent on it, who makes a slave of himself to—

AMANDA (*fairly screeching*). Don't you DARE to—

TOM. No, no, *I* mustn't say things! *I've* got to just—

AMANDA. Let me tell you—

TOM. I don't want to hear any more! (*He tears the portieres open. The upstage area is lit with a turgid smoky red glow.*)

(AMANDA'S *hair is in metal curlers and she wears a very old bathrobe, much too large for her slight figure, a relic of the faithless Mr. Wingfield.*)

(*An upright typewriter and a wild disarray of manuscripts is on the drop-leaf table. The quarrel was probably precipitated by* AMANDA'S *interruption of his creative labor. A chair lying overthrown on the floor.*)

(*Their gesticulating shadows are cast on the ceiling by the fiery glow.*)

AMANDA. You *will* hear more, you—

TOM. No, I won't hear more, I'm going out!

AMANDA. You come right back in—

TOM. Out, out, out! Because I'm—

AMANDA. Come back here, Tom Wingfield! I'm not through talking to you!

TOM. Oh, go—

LAURA (*desperately*). —Tom!

AMANDA. You're going to listen, and no more insolence from you! I'm at the end of my patience!

(*He comes back toward her.*)

TOM. What do you think I'm at? Aren't I supposed to have any patience to reach the end of, Mother? I know, I know. It seems unimportant to you, what I'm *doing*—what I *want* to do—having a little *difference* between them! You don't think that—

AMANDA. I think you've been doing things that you're ashamed of. That's why you act like this. I don't believe that you go every night to the movies. Nobody goes to the movies night after night. Nobody in their right minds goes to the movies as often as you pretend to. People don't go to the movies at nearly midnight, and movies don't let out at two A.M. Come in stumbling. Muttering to yourself like a maniac! You get three hours' sleep and then go to work. Oh, I can picture the way you're doing down there. Moping, doping, because you're in no condition.

TOM (*wildly*). No, I'm in no condition!

AMANDA. What right have you got to jeopardize your job? Jeopardize the security of us all? How do you think we'd manage if you were—

TOM. Listen! You think I'm crazy *about* the warehouse? (*He bends fiercely toward her slight figure.*) You think I'm in love with the Continental Shoemakers? You think I want to spend fifty-five *years* down there in that—*celotex interior!* with—*fluorescent—tubes!* Look! I'd rather somebody picked up a crowbar and battered out my brains—than go back mornings! I *go!* Every time you come in yelling that damn *"Rise and Shine!" "Rise and Shine!"* I say to myself, "How *lucky dead* people are!" But I get up. I *go!* For sixty-five dollars a month I give up all that I dream of doing and being *ever!* And you say self—

---

2. *Mr. Lawrence,* D. H. Lawrence (1885-1930), English novelist and poet. Some of his works aroused considerable protest on moral grounds. The artistic merit of much of his work, however, is unquestioned.

self's all I ever think of. Why, listen, if self is what I thought of, Mother, I'd be where he is—GONE! (*Pointing to father's picture.*) As far as the system of transportation reaches! (*He starts past her. She grabs his arm.*) Don't grab at me, Mother!

AMANDA. Where are you going?

TOM. I'm going to the *movies!*

AMANDA. I don't believe that lie!

TOM (*crouching toward her, overtowering her tiny figure. She backs away, gasping*). I'm going to opium dens! Yes, opium dens, dens of vice and criminals' hang-outs, Mother. I've joined the Hogan gang, I'm a hired assassin, I carry a tommy-gun in a violin case! They call me Killer, Killer Wingfield, I'm leading a double-life, a simple, honest warehouse worker by day, by night a dynamic *czar* of the *underworld, Mother.* I go to gambling casinos, I spin away fortunes on the roulette table! I wear a patch over one eye and a false mustache, sometimes I put on green whiskers. On those occasions they call me —*El Diablo!*[3] Oh, I could tell you things to make you sleepless! My enemies plan to dynamite this place. They're going to blow us all sky-high some night! I'll be glad, very happy, and so will you! You'll go up, up on a broomstick, over Blue Mountain with seventeen gentlemen callers! You ugly—babbling old—*witch.* . . . (*He goes through a series of violent, clumsy movements, seizing his overcoat, lunging to the door, pulling it fiercely open. The women watch him, aghast. His arm catches in the sleeve of the coat as he struggles to pull it on. For a moment he is pinioned by the bulky garment. With an outraged groan he tears the coat off again, splitting the shoulder of it, and hurls it across the room. It strikes against the shelf of* LAURA's *glass collection, there is a tinkle of shattering glass.* LAURA *cries out as if wounded.*)

(MUSIC. LEGEND: "*The Glass Menagerie.*")

LAURA (*shrilly*). My glass!—menagerie. . . . (*She covers her face and turns away.*)

(*But* AMANDA *is still stunned and stupefied by the "ugly witch" so that she barely notices this occurrence. Now she recovers her speech.*)

AMANDA (*in an awful voice*). I won't speak to you—until you apologize! (*She crosses through portieres and draws them together behind her.* TOM *is left with* LAURA. LAURA *clings weakly to the mantel with her face averted.* TOM *stares at her stupidly for a moment. Then he crosses to shelf. Drops awkwardly on his knees to collect the fallen glass, glancing at* LAURA *as if he would speak but couldn't.*)

"*The Glass Menagerie*" *steals in as* THE SCENE DIMS OUT

Scene 4

The interior is dark. Faint light in the alley. A deep-voiced bell in a church is tolling the hour of five as the scene commences.

TOM *appears at the top of the alley. After each solemn boom of the bell in the tower, he shakes a little noise-maker or rattle as if to express the tiny spasm of man in contrast to the sustained power and dignity of the Almighty. This and the unsteadiness of his advance make it evident that he has been drinking.*

As he climbs the few steps to the fire escape landing light steals up inside. LAURA *appears in night-dress, observing* TOM's *empty bed in the front room.*

TOM *fishes in his pockets for door-key, removing a motley assortment of articles in the search, including a perfect shower of movie-ticket stubs and an empty bottle. At last he finds the key, but just as he is about to insert it, it slips from his fingers. He strikes a match and crouches below the door.*

TOM (*bitterly*). One crack—and it falls through!

(LAURA *opens the door.*)

LAURA. Tom! Tom, what are you doing?

TOM. Looking for a door-key.

LAURA. Where have you been all this time?

TOM. I have been to the movies.

---

3. *El Diablo* (el di ab'lō), the devil. [*Spanish*]

LAURA. All this time at the movies?

TOM. There was a very long program. There was a Garbo picture and a Mickey Mouse and a travelogue and a newsreel and a preview of coming attractions. And there was an organ solo and a collection for the milk-fund —simultaneously—which ended up in a terrible fight between a fat lady and an usher!

LAURA (innocently). Did you have to stay through everything?

TOM. Of course! And, oh, I forgot! There was a big stage show! The headliner on this stage show was Malvolio the Magician. He performed wonderful tricks, many of them, such as pouring water back and forth between pitchers. First it turned to wine and then it turned to beer and then it turned to whiskey. I know it was whiskey it finally turned into because he needed somebody to come up out of the audience to help him, and I came up— both shows! It was Kentucky Straight Bourbon. A very generous fellow, he gave souvenirs. (He pulls from his back pocket a shimmering rainbow-colored scarf.) He gave me this. This is his magic scarf. You can have it, Laura. You wave it over a canary cage and you get a bowl of gold-fish. You wave it over the gold-fish bowl and they fly away canaries. . . . But the wonderfullest trick of all was the coffin trick. We nailed him into a coffin and he got out of the coffin without removing one nail. (He has come inside.) There is a trick that would come in handy for me—get me out of this 2 by 4 situation! (Flops onto bed and starts removing shoes.)

LAURA. Tom—Shhh!

TOM. What're you shushing me for?

LAURA. You'll wake up Mother.

TOM. Goody, goody! Pay 'er back for all those "Rise an' Shines." (Lies down, groaning.) You know it don't take much intelligence to get yourself into a nailed-up coffin, Laura. But who in hell ever got himself out of one without removing one nail?

(As if in answer, the father's grinning photograph lights up.)

SCENE DIMS OUT

(Immediately following: The church bell is heard striking six. At the sixth stroke the alarm clock goes off in AMANDA'S room, and after a few moments we hear her calling: "Rise and Shine! Rise and Shine! Laura, go tell your brother to rise and shine!")

TOM (sitting up slowly). I'll rise—but I won't shine.

(The light increases.)

AMANDA. Laura, tell your brother his coffee is ready.

(LAURA slips into front room.)

LAURA. Tom!—It's nearly seven. Don't make Mother nervous. (He stares at her stupidly. Beseechingly.) Tom, speak to Mother this morning. Make up with her, apologize, speak to her!

TOM. She won't to me. It's her that started not speaking.

LAURA. If you just say you're sorry she'll start speaking.

TOM. Her not speaking—is that such a tragedy?

LAURA. Please—please!

AMANDA (calling from kitchenette). Laura, are you going to do what I asked you to do, or do I have to get dressed and go out myself?

LAURA. Going, going—soon as I get on my coat! (She pulls on a shapeless felt hat with nervous, jerky movement, pleadingly glancing at TOM. Rushes awkwardly for coat. The coat is one of AMANDA'S, inaccurately made-over, the sleeves too short for LAURA.) Butter and what else?

AMANDA (entering upstage). Just butter. Tell them to charge it.

LAURA. Mother, they make such faces when I do that.

AMANDA. Sticks and stones can break our bones, but the expression on Mr. Garfinkel's face won't harm us! Tell your brother his coffee is getting cold.

LAURA (at door). Do what I asked you, will you, will you, Tom?

(He looks sullenly away.)

AMANDA. Laura, go now or just don't go at all!

LAURA (rushing out). Going—going! (A second later she cries out. TOM springs up and crosses to door. AMANDA rushes anxiously in. TOM opens the door.)

TOM. Laura?

LAURA. I'm all right. I slipped, but I'm all right.

AMANDA (*peering anxiously after her*). If anyone breaks a leg on those fire escape steps, the landlord ought to be sued for every cent he possesses! (*She shuts door. Remembers she isn't speaking and returns to other room.*)

(*As* TOM *enters listlessly for his coffee, she turns her back to him and stands rigidly facing the window on the gloomy gray vault of the areaway. Its light on her face with its aged but childish features is cruelly sharp, satirical as a Daumier print.[1]*)

(MUSIC UNDER: *"Ave Maria."*)

(TOM *glances sheepishly but sullenly at her averted figure and slumps at the table. The coffee is scalding hot; he sips it and gasps and spits it back in the cup. At his gasp,* AMANDA *catches her breath and half turns. Then catches herself and turns back to window.*)

(TOM *blows on his coffee, glancing sidewise at his mother. She clears her throat.* TOM *clears his. He starts to rise. Sinks back down again, scratches his head, clears his throat again.* AMANDA *coughs.* TOM *raises his cup in both hands to blow on it, his eyes staring over the rim of it at his mother for several moments. Then he slowly sets the cup down and awkwardly and hesitantly rises from the chair.*)

TOM (*hoarsely*). Mother. I—I apologize, Mother. (AMANDA *draws a quick, shuddering breath. Her face works grotesquely. She breaks into childlike tears.*) I'm sorry for what I said, for everything that I said, I didn't mean it.

AMANDA (*sobbingly*). My devotion has made me a witch and so I make myself hateful to my children!

TOM. No, you *don't*.

AMANDA. I worry so much, don't sleep, it makes me nervous!

TOM (*gently*). I understand that.

AMANDA. I've had to put up a solitary battle all these years. But you're my right-hand bower! Don't fall down, don't fail!

TOM (*gently*). I try, Mother.

AMANDA (*with great enthusiasm*). Try and you will SUCCEED! (*The notion makes her breathless.*) Why, you—you're just *full* of natural endowments! Both of my children—they're *unusual* children! Don't you think I know it? I'm so—*proud!* Happy and—feel I've —so much to be thankful for but— Promise me one thing, Son!

TOM. What, Mother?

AMANDA. Promise, son, you'll—never be a drunkard!

TOM (*turns to her grinning*). I will never be a drunkard, Mother.

AMANDA. That's what frightened me so, that you'd be drinking! Eat a bowl of Purina!

TOM. Just coffee, Mother.

AMANDA. Shredded wheat biscuit?

TOM. No. No, Mother, just coffee.

AMANDA. You can't put in a day's work on an empty stomach. You've got ten minutes—don't gulp! Drinking too-hot liquids makes cancer of the stomach. . . . Put cream in.

TOM. No, thank you.

AMANDA. To cool it.

TOM. No! No, thank you, I want it black.

AMANDA. I know, but it's not good for you. We have to do all that we can to build ourselves up. In these trying times we live in, all that we have to cling to is—each other. . . . That's why it's so important to— Tom, I— I sent out your sister so I could discuss something with you. If you hadn't spoken I would have spoken to you. (*Sits down.*)

TOM (*gently*). What is it, Mother, that you want to discuss?

AMANDA. *Laura!*

(TOM *puts his cup down slowly.*)

(LEGEND ON SCREEN: *"Laura."*)

(MUSIC: *"The Glass Menagerie."*)

TOM. —Oh.—Laura . . .

AMANDA (*touching his sleeve*). You know how Laura is. So quiet but—still water runs deep! She notices things and I think she—broods about them. (TOM *looks up.*) A few days ago I came in and she was crying.

TOM. What about?

AMANDA. You.

TOM. Me?

---

1. *Daumier print.* Honoré Daumier (ô nô rā′ dō myā′) was a nineteenth-century French painter whose fame rests primarily on his thousands of merciless, satirical lithographs.

AMANDA. She has an idea that you're not happy here.

TOM. What gave her that idea?

AMANDA. What gives her any idea? However, you do act strangely. I—I'm not criticizing, understand *that*! I know your ambitions do not lie in the warehouse, that like everybody in the whole wide world—you've had to—make sacrifices, but—Tom—Tom—life's not easy, it calls for—Spartan endurance! There's so many things in my heart that I cannot describe to you! I've never told you but I—*loved* your father. . . .

TOM (*gently*). I know that, Mother.

AMANDA. And you—when I see you taking after his ways! Staying out late—and—well, you *had* been drinking the night you were in that—terrifying condition! Laura says that you hate the apartment and that you go out nights to get away from it! Is that true, Tom?

TOM. No. You say there's so much in your heart that you can't describe to me. That's true of me, too. There's so much in my heart that I can't describe to *you*! So let's respect each other's—

AMANDA. But, why—*why*, Tom—are you always so *restless*? Where do you *go* to, nights?

TOM. I—go to the movies.

AMANDA. Why do you go to the movies so much, Tom?

TOM. I go to the movies because—I like adventure. Adventure is something I don't have much of at work, so I go to the movies.

AMANDA. But, Tom, you go to the movies *entirely* too *much*!

TOM. I like a lot of adventure.

(AMANDA *looks baffled, then hurt. As the familiar inquisition resumes he becomes hard and impatient again.* AMANDA *slips back into her querulous attitude toward him.*)

(IMAGE ON SCREEN: *Sailing vessel with Jolly Roger.*)

AMANDA. Most young men find adventure in their careers.

TOM. Then most young men are not employed in a warehouse.

AMANDA. The world is full of young men employed in warehouses and offices and factories.

TOM. Do all of them find adventure in their careers?

AMANDA. They do or they do without it! Not everybody has a craze for adventure.

TOM. Man is by instinct a lover, a hunter, a fighter, and none of those instincts are given much play at the warehouse!

AMANDA. Man is by instinct! Don't quote instinct to me! Instinct is something that people have got away from! It belongs to animals! Christian adults don't want it!

TOM. What do Christian adults want, then, Mother?

AMANDA. Superior things! Things of the mind and the spirit! Only animals have to satisfy instincts! Surely your aims are somewhat higher than theirs! Than monkeys—pigs—

TOM. I reckon they're not.

AMANDA. You're joking. However, that isn't what I wanted to discuss.

TOM (*rising*). I haven't much time.

AMANDA (*pushing his shoulders*). Sit down.

TOM. You want me to punch in red at the warehouse, Mother?

AMANDA. You have five minutes. I want to talk about Laura.

(LEGEND: *"Plans and Provisions."*)

TOM. All right! What about Laura?

AMANDA. We have to be making some plans and provisions for her. She's older than you, two years, and nothing has happened. She just drifts along doing nothing. It frightens me terribly how she just drifts along.

TOM. I guess she's the type that people call home girls.

AMANDA. There's no such type, and if there is, it's a pity! That is unless the home is hers, with a husband!

TOM. What?

AMANDA. Oh, I can see the handwriting on the wall as plain as I see the nose in front of my face! It's terrifying!

More and more you remind me of your father! He was out all hours without explanation!—then *left*! Good-bye!

And me with the bag to hold. I saw that letter you got from the Merchant Marine. I know what you're dreaming of. I'm not standing here blindfolded.

Very well, then. Then *do* it!

But not till there's somebody to take your place.

TOM. What do you mean?

AMANDA. I mean that as soon as Laura has got somebody to take care of her, married, a home of her own, independent—why, then you'll be free to go wherever you please, on land, on sea, whichever way the wind blows you!

But until that time you've got to look out for your sister. I don't say me because I'm old and don't matter! I say for your sister because she's young and dependent.

I put her in business college—a dismal failure! Frightened her so it made her sick at the stomach.

I took her over to the Young People's League at the church. Another fiasco. She spoke to nobody, nobody spoke to her. Now all she does is fool with those pieces of glass and play those worn-out records. What kind of a life is that for a girl to lead?

TOM. What can I do about it?

AMANDA. Overcome selfishness!

Self, self, self is all that you ever think of!

(TOM *springs up and crosses to get his coat. It is ugly and bulky. He pulls on a cap with earmuffs.*)

Where is your muffler? Put your wool muffler on!

(*He snatches it angrily from the closest and tosses it around his neck and pulls both ends tight.*)

Tom! I haven't said what I had in mind to ask you.

TOM. I'm too late to—

AMANDA (*catching his arm—very importunately. Then shyly*). Down at the warehouse, aren't there some—nice young men?

TOM. No!

AMANDA. There *must* be—some . . .

TOM. Mother—

(*Gesture.*)

AMANDA. Find out one that's clean-living—doesn't drink and—ask him out for sister!

TOM. What?

AMANDA. For *sister!* To *meet!* Get acquainted!

TOM (*stamping to door*). Oh, my go-osh!

AMANDA. Will you? (*He opens door. Imploringly.*) Will you? (*He starts down.*) Will you? *Will* you, dear?

TOM (*calling back*). Yes!

(AMANDA *closes the door hesitantly and with a troubled but faintly hopeful expression.*)

(SCREEN IMAGE: *Glamor magazine cover.*)

(*Spot* AMANDA *at phone.*)

AMANDA. Ella Cartwright? This is Amanda Wingfield!

How are you, honey?

How is that kidney condition?

(*Count five.*)

Horrors!

(*Count five.*)

You're a Christian martyr, yes, honey, that's what you are, à Christian martyr!

Well, I just now happened to notice in my little red book that your subscription to the *Companion* has just run out! I knew that you wouldn't want to miss out on the wonderful serial starting in this new issue. It's by Bessie Mae Hopper, the first thing she's written since *Honeymoon for Three.*

Wasn't that a strange and interesting story? Well, this one is even lovelier, I believe. It has a sophisticated, society background. It's all about the horsey set on Long Island!

FADE OUT

Scene 5

LEGEND ON SCREEN: *"Annunciation." Fade with music.*

It is early dusk of a spring evening. Supper has just been finished in the Wingfield apartment. AMANDA *and* LAURA *in light-colored dresses are removing dishes from the table, in the upstage area, which is shadowy, their movements formalized almost as a dance or ritual, their moving forms as pale and silent as moths.*

TOM, *in white shirt and trousers, rises from the table and crosses toward the fire escape.*

AMANDA (*as he passes her*). Son, will you do me a favor?

TOM. What?

AMANDA. Comb your hair! You look so pretty when your hair is combed! (TOM *slouches on sofa with evening paper. Enormous caption "Franco Triumphs."*[1]) There is only one respect in which I would like you to emulate your father.

TOM. What respect is that?

AMANDA. The care he always took of his appearance. He never allowed himself to look untidy. (*He throws down the paper and crosses to fire escape.*) Where are you going?

TOM. I'm going out to smoke.

AMANDA. You smoke too much. A pack a day at fifteen cents a pack. How much would that amount to in a month? Thirty times fifteen is how much, Tom? Figure it out and you will be astounded at what you could save. Enough to give you a night-school course in accounting at Washington U! Just think what a wonderful thing that would be for you, Son!

(TOM *is unmoved by the thought.*)

TOM. I'd rather smoke. (*He steps out on landing, letting the screen door slam.*)

AMANDA (*sharply*). I know! That's the tragedy of it.... (*Alone, she turns to look at her husband's picture.*)

(DANCE MUSIC: *"All the World is Waiting for the Sunrise!"*)

TOM (*to the audience*). Across the alley from us was the Paradise Dance Hall. On evenings in spring the windows and doors were open and the music came outdoors. Sometimes the lights were turned out except for a large glass sphere that hung from the ceiling. It would turn slowly about and filter the dusk with delicate rainbow colors. Then the orchestra played a waltz or a tango, something that had a slow and sensuous rhythm. Couples would come outside, to the relative privacy of the alley. You could see them kissing behind ash-pits and telephone poles.

This was the compensation for lives that passed like mine, without any change or adventure.

Adventure and change were imminent in this year. They were waiting around the corner for all these kids.

Suspended in the mist over Berchtesgaden, caught in the folds of Chamberlain's umbrella—[2]

In Spain there was Guernica!

But here there was only hot swing music and liquor, dance halls, bars, and movies, and sex that hung in the gloom like a chandelier and flooded the world with brief, deceptive rainbows....

All the world was waiting for bombardments!

(AMANDA *turns from the picture and comes outside.*)

AMANDA (*sighing*). A fire escape landing's a poor excuse for a porch. (*She spreads a newspaper on a step and sits down, gracefully and demurely as if she were settling into a swing on a Mississippi veranda.*) What are you looking at?

TOM. The moon.

AMANDA. Is there a moon this evening?

TOM. It's rising over Garfinkel's Delicatessen.

AMANDA. So it is! A little silver slipper of a moon. Have you made a wish on it yet?

TOM. Um-hum.

AMANDA. What did you wish for?

TOM. That's a secret.

AMANDA. A secret, huh? Well, I won't tell mine either. I will be just as mysterious as you.

TOM. I bet I can guess what yours is.

AMANDA. Is my head so transparent?

TOM. You're not a sphinx.

AMANDA. No, I don't have secrets. I'll tell you what I wished for on the moon. Success and happiness for my precious children! I wish for that whenever there's a moon, and when there isn't a moon, I wish for it, too.

TOM. I thought perhaps you wished for a gentleman caller.

1. *Franco Triumphs*, another reference to the Spanish general (see note 4, page 724). 2. *Berchtesgaden* (bĕrH′təs-gä′dən) . . . *Chamberlain's umbrella.* Adolf Hitler was visited at Berchtesgaden, his mountain retreat, by Britain's Conservative Prime Minister, Neville Chamberlain, in 1938. Here Chamberlain, in an effort to avoid war, decided that Hitler should be allowed to annex part of Czechoslovakia in return for a pledge by Hitler to make no further aggression. Hitler's breaking of this pledge brought on World War II.

AMANDA. Why do you say that?

TOM. Don't you remember asking me to fetch one?

AMANDA. I remember suggesting that it would be nice for your sister if you brought home some nice young man from the warehouse. I think that I've made that suggestion more than once.

TOM. Yes, you have made it repeatedly.

AMANDA. Well?

TOM. We are going to have one.

AMANDA. *What?*

TOM. A gentleman caller!

(*The Annunciation* IS CELEBRATED WITH MUSIC.)

(AMANDA *rises.*)

(IMAGE ON SCREEN: *Caller with bouquet.*)

AMANDA. You mean you have asked some nice young man to come over?

TOM. Yep. I've asked him to dinner.

AMANDA. You really did?

TOM. I did!

AMANDA. You did, and did he—*accept?*

TOM. He did!

AMANDA. Well, well—well, well! That's—lovely!

TOM. I thought that you would be pleased.

AMANDA. It's definite, then?

TOM. Very definite.

AMANDA. Soon?

TOM. Very soon.

AMANDA. For heaven's sake, stop putting on and tell me some things, will you?

TOM. What things do you want me to tell you?

AMANDA. *Naturally* I would like to know when he's *coming!*

TOM. He's coming tomorrow.

AMANDA. *Tomorrow?*

TOM. Yep. Tomorrow.

AMANDA. But, Tom!

TOM. Yes, Mother?

AMANDA. Tomorrow gives me no time!

TOM. Time for what?

AMANDA. Preparations! Why didn't you phone me at once, as soon as you asked him, the minute that he accepted? Then, don't you see, I could have been getting ready!

TOM. You don't have to make any fuss.

AMANDA. Oh, Tom, Tom, Tom, of course I have to make a fuss! I want things nice, not sloppy! Not thrown together. I'll certainly have to do some fast thinking, won't I?

TOM. I don't see why you have to think at all.

AMANDA. You just don't know. We can't have a gentleman caller in a pig-sty! All my wedding silver has to be polished, the monogrammed table linen ought to be laundered! The windows have to be washed and fresh curtains put up. And how about clothes? We have to *wear* something, don't we?

TOM. Mother, this boy is no one to make a fuss over!

AMANDA. Do you realize he's the first young man we've introduced to your sister? It's terrible, dreadful, disgraceful that poor little sister has never received a single gentleman caller! Tom, come inside! (*She opens the screen door.*)

TOM. What for?

AMANDA. I want to ask you some things.

TOM. If you're going to make such a fuss, I'll call it off, I'll tell him not to come!

AMANDA. You certainly won't do anything of the kind. Nothing offends people worse than broken engagements. It simply means I'll have to work like a Turk! We won't be brilliant, but we will pass inspection. Come on inside. (TOM *follows, groaning.*) Sit down.

TOM. Any particular place you would like me to sit?

AMANDA. Thank heavens I've got that new sofa! I'm also making payments on a floor lamp I'll have sent out! And put the chintz covers on, they'll brighten things up! Of course I'd hoped to have these walls repapered.... What is the young man's name?

TOM. His name is O'Connor.

AMANDA. That, of course, means fish—tomorrow is Friday! I'll have that salmon loaf—with Durkee's dressing! What does he do? He works at the warehouse?

TOM. Of course! How else would I—

AMANDA. Tom, he—doesn't drink?

TOM. Why do you ask me that?

AMANDA. Your father *did!*

TOM. Don't get started on that!

AMANDA. He *does* drink, then?

TOM. Not that I know of!

AMANDA. Make sure, be certain! The last thing I want for my daughter's a boy who drinks!

TOM. Aren't you being a little bit premature? Mr. O'Connor has not yet appeared on the scene!

AMANDA. But will tomorrow. To meet your sister, and what do I know about his character? Nothing! Old maids are better off than wives of drunkards!

TOM. Oh, my God!

AMANDA. Be still!

TOM (*leaning forward to whisper*). Lots of fellows meet girls whom they don't marry!

AMANDA. Oh, talk sensibly, Tom—and don't be sarcastic! (*She has gotten a hairbrush.*)

TOM. What are you doing?

AMANDA. I'm brushing that cowlick down! What is this young man's position at the warehouse?

TOM (*submitting grimly to the brush and the interrogation*). This young man's position is that of a shipping clerk, Mother.

AMANDA. Sounds to me like a fairly responsible job, the sort of a job *you* would be in if you just had more *get-up*.

What is his salary? Have you any idea?

TOM. I would judge it to be approximately eighty-five dollars a month.

AMANDA. Well—not princely, but—

TOM. Twenty more than I make.

AMANDA. Yes, how well I know! But for a family man, eighty-five dollars a month is not much more than you can just get by on....

TOM. Yes, but Mr. O'Connor is not a family man.

AMANDA. He might be, mightn't he? Some time in the future?

TOM. I see. Plans and provisions.

AMANDA. You are the only young man that I know of who ignores the fact that the future becomes the present, the present the past, and the past turns into everlasting regret if you don't plan for it!

TOM. I will think that over and see what I can make of it.

AMANDA. Don't be supercilious with your mother! Tell me some more about this—what do you call him?

TOM. James D. O'Connor. The D. is for Delaney.

AMANDA. Irish on *both* sides! *Gracious!* And doesn't drink?

TOM. Shall I call him up and ask him right this minute?

AMANDA. The only way to find out about those things is to make discreet inquiries at the proper moment. When I was a girl in Blue Mountain and it was suspected that a young man drank, the girl whose attentions he had been receiving, if any girl *was*, would sometimes speak to the minister of his church, or rather her father would if her father was living, and sort of feel him out on the young man's character. That is the way such things are discreetly handled to keep a young woman from making a tragic mistake!

TOM. Then how did you happen to make a tragic mistake?

AMANDA. That innocent look of your father's had everyone fooled!

He *smiled*—the world was *enchanted!*

No girl can do worse than put herself at the mercy of a handsome appearance!

I hope that Mr. O'Connor is not too good-looking.

TOM. No, he's not too good-looking. He's covered with freckles and hasn't too much of a nose.

AMANDA. He's not right-down homely, though?

TOM. Not right-down homely. Just medium homely, I'd say.

AMANDA. Character's what to look for in a man.

TOM. That's what I've always said, Mother.

AMANDA. You've never said anything of the kind and I suspect you would never give it a thought.

TOM. Don't be so suspicious of me.

AMANDA. At least I hope he's the type that's up and coming.

TOM. I think he really goes in for self-improvement.

AMANDA. What reason have you to think so?

TOM. He goes to night school.

AMANDA (*beaming*). Splendid! What does he do, I mean study?

TOM. Radio engineering and public speaking!

AMANDA. Then he has visions of being advanced in the world!

Any young man who studies public speaking is aiming to have an executive job some day!

And radio engineering? A thing for the future!

Both of these facts are very illuminating. Those are the sort of things that a mother should know concerning any young man who comes to call on her daughter. Seriously or—not.

TOM. One little warning. He doesn't know about Laura. I didn't let on that we had dark ulterior motives. I just said, why don't you come and have dinner with us? He said okay and that was the whole conversation.

AMANDA. I bet it was! You're eloquent as an oyster.

However, he'll know about Laura when he gets here. When he sees how lovely and sweet and pretty she is, he'll thank his lucky stars he was asked to dinner.

TOM. Mother, you mustn't expect too much of Laura.

AMANDA. What do you mean?

TOM. Laura seems all those things to you and me because she's ours and we love her. We don't even notice she's crippled any more.

AMANDA. Don't say crippled! You know that I never allow that word to be used!

TOM. But face facts, Mother. She is and—that's not all—

AMANDA. What do you mean "not all"?

TOM. Laura is very different from other girls.

AMANDA. I think the difference is all to her advantage.

TOM. Not quite all—in the eyes of others—strangers—she's terribly shy and lives in a world of her own and those things make her seem a little peculiar to people outside the house.

AMANDA. Don't say peculiar.

TOM. Face the facts. She is.

(*The dance-hall music changes to a tango that has a minor and somewhat ominous tone.*)

AMANDA. In what way is she peculiar—may I ask?

TOM (*gently*). She lives in a world of her own—a world of—little glass ornaments, Mother.... (*Gets up.* AMANDA *remains holding brush, looking at him, troubled.*) She plays old phonograph records and—that's about all— (*He glances at himself in the mirror and crosses to door.*)

AMANDA (*sharply*). Where are you going?

TOM. I'm going to the movies. (*Out screen door.*)

AMANDA. Not to the movies, every night to the movies! (*Follows quickly to screen door.*) I don't believe you always go to the movies! (*He is gone.* AMANDA *looks worriedly after him for a moment. Then vitality and optimism return and she turns from the door. Crossing to portieres.*) Laura! Laura! (LAURA *answers from kitchenette.*)

LAURA. Yes, Mother.

AMANDA. Let those dishes go and come in front! (LAURA *appears with dish towel. Gaily.*) Laura, come here and make a wish on the moon!

(SCREEN IMAGE: *Moon.*)

LAURA (*entering*). Moon—moon?

AMANDA. A little silver slipper of a moon. Look over your left shoulder, Laura, and make a wish!

(LAURA *looks faintly puzzled as if called out of sleep.* AMANDA *seizes her shoulders and turns her at an angle by the door.*)

Now!

Now, darling, *wish!*

LAURA. What shall I wish for, Mother?

AMANDA (*her voice trembling and her eyes suddenly filling with tears*). Happiness! Good fortune!

(*The violin rises and the stage dims out.*)

CURTAIN

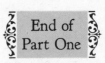

End of
Part One

✦ TO INCREASE UNDERSTANDING
Part I, Scene 1

1. Reread the description of the setting at the beginning of Scene 1 (page 723). (*a*) What do you learn about the condition of the Wingfield family from this setting? (*b*) What feeling does it convey?

2. (*a*) What two functions does Tom have in the play? (*b*) What difference in temperament do you notice between Tom as Narrator and Tom as Character? (*c*) What is meant by Tom's remark, "The play is memory"?

3. How is the fact that there is tension in the family revealed at the outset?

4. (*a*) What do you learn about Amanda's past in this scene? (*b*) How does she view her past? (*c*) What indications are there that her past was not exactly as she remembers it?

Scene 2

1. What do you learn about Laura in this scene?

2. (*a*) In what ways does it appear Amanda has been trying to help Laura? (*b*) Why have her efforts failed? (*c*) What alternative does Amanda decide upon toward the end of this scene? (*d*) What are the prospects, at this point, for the success of her plan? Explain.

Scene 3

1. (*a*) What is the source of the fight between Tom and his mother? (*b*) Why is Tom discontented?

2. (*a*) Amanda calls Tom selfish. To what extent is her accusation fair, to what extent unfair? (*b*) Tom apparently thinks that his mother is making unfair demands upon him. To what extent is this true, to what extent untrue?

Scene 4

1. How does Amanda go about implementing the plan she has formed?

2. (*a*) What is the effect of Amanda's attempt to sell magazines by telephone? (*b*) Why is she doing it? (*c*) What does this show about her character?

Scene 5

1. Humor is much more obvious when a play is performed than when it is read. There is humor throughout *The Glass Menagerie*, but in this scene it predominates. (*a*) Point out how Tom teases his mother with his announcement. (*b*) How might the actors point up the humor of this scene? (*c*) Quote some lines that are particularly funny.

2. (*a*) How does this scene advance the action? (*b*) What indication is there of the fate of Amanda's plan?

Part I in Review

1. In the first part of a play, the dramatist's objective must usually be to make his characters introduce themselves. To do this without seeming awkward, he must involve them in events in which they will naturally reveal enough of their past and of their personalities so that the audience can understand their present situation and their attitudes toward it. Look back over the first three scenes, and, taking them one at a time, tell (*a*) which character is most fully revealed in each scene; (*b*) what dramatic situation the author creates to make the character reveal himself; and (*c*) why the situation is or is not plausible.

2. The basic situation in which all the characters are placed is simply the Wingfield family. (*a*) What special conditions exist in the Wingfield family that make it an especially trying situation for these characters? (*b*) How are these conditions revealed early in the play? (*c*) Discuss the relations among the members of the entire family as they are revealed in the first three scenes.

3. Each of the characters has a private world into which he sometimes retreats when the real world becomes unbearable. (*a*) Describe the kinds of situations that each character finds unpleasant. (*b*) What is the private world into which each retreats?

4. Tell from what theatrical style each of the following elements in part I is derived, and what contribution it makes to the effect of the scene.
   (*a*) The fact that the play is Tom's memory
   (*b*) The use of a narrator
   (*c*) The scene at the rise of the curtain
   (*d*) The lighting on Laura in Scene 3
   (*e*) The fire escape entrance

5. It has been said that Williams has a symbolist's sensibility. Find at least three symbolic elements in part I, explain the meaning of each, and describe its effect on the scene.

✿ BETTER READING
Tone in the drama

The means for communicating tone are as infinite as are shades of feeling. Drama shares a number of these with other literary forms. By causing a character to bear himself in a certain way or use a certain manner of speech, the writer can make the

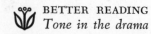

character seem despicable. In doing so the author effectively communicates his own attitude toward the character. By the same means the writer can make a character pitiful, noble, whimsical, and so forth. The author's attitude toward a character can also be communicated by the behavior of other characters toward him, or by showing what happens to the character as a result of his attitude.

Describe Williams' attitude toward each of the characters in *The Glass Menagerie* as revealed in the first part of the play. What are some of the means that Williams uses to communicate this?

Beyond the means common to literature in general, there are a number of distinctively dramatic means for expressing tone, many of which were developed by the various schools of realism and antirealism. The stage setting and lighting may be "realistically" dingy or oppressive, or "expressionistically" gay or dreamlike, creating a visible atmosphere that acts as an effective commentary on the characters and their activities. As the play moves from one scene to the next, a pattern of time and place sequences develops. One play may contain wide time lapses, sometimes jumping into the future, or back into the past. Its scenes may take place in widely separated locales. By these means a playwright can place disastrous events in a perspective of time that softens their harsh outlines. On the other hand, by making all the action take place in the same room over a short period of time, he is able to project the feeling that whatever happens here and now is decisive and will not be changed.

Explain what tone is established by Williams' uses of the following theatrical methods: (1) the presentation of Tom's comments upon the scene, characters, and actions; (2) the setting; (3) the techniques of lighting, music, and images on the screen.

Laurette Taylor as Amanda and Julie Haydon as Laura in the first Broadway production of The Glass Menagerie.

Scene 6

IMAGE: *High school hero.*

TOM. And so the following evening I brought Jim home to dinner. I had known Jim slightly in high school. In high school Jim was a hero. He had tremendous Irish good nature and vitality with the scrubbed and polished look of white chinaware. He seemed to move in a continual spotlight. He was a star in basketball, captain of the debating club, president of the senior class and the glee club and he sang the male lead in the annual light operas. He was always running or bounding, never just walking. He seemed always at the point of defeating the law of gravity. He was shooting with such velocity through his adolescence that you would logically expect him to arrive at nothing short of the White House by the time he was thirty. But Jim apparently ran into more interference after his graduation from Soldan. His speed had definitely slowed. Six years after he left high school he was holding a job that wasn't much better than mine.

(IMAGE: *Clerk.*)

He was the only one at the warehouse with whom I was on friendly terms. I was valuable to him as someone who could remember his former glory, who had seen him win basketball games and the silver cup in debating. He knew of my secret practice of retiring to a cabinet of the wash-room to work on poems when business was slack in the warehouse. He called me Shakespeare. And while the other boys in the warehouse regarded me with suspicious hostility, Jim took a humorous attitude toward me. Gradually his attitude affected the others, their hostility wore off and they also began to smile at me as people smile at an oddly fashioned dog who trots across their path at some distance.

I knew that Jim and Laura had known each other at Soldan, and I had heard Laura speak admiringly of his voice. I didn't know if Jim remembered her or not. In high school Laura had been as unobtrusive as Jim had been astonishing. If he did remember Laura, it was not as my sister, for when I asked him to dinner, he grinned and said, "You know, Shakespeare, I never thought of you as having folks!"

He was about to discover that I did....

(*Light up stage.*)

(LEGEND ON SCREEN: *"The Accent of a Coming Foot."*)

(*Friday evening. It is about five o'clock of a late spring evening which comes "scattering poems in the sky."*)

(*A delicate lemony light is in the Wingfield apartment.*)

(AMANDA *has worked like a Turk in preparation for the gentleman caller. The results are astonishing. The new floor lamp with its rose-silk shade is in place, a colored paper lantern conceals the broken light fixture in the ceiling, new billowing white curtains are at the windows, chintz covers are on chairs and sofa, a pair of new sofa pillows make their initial appearance.*)

(*Open boxes and tissue paper are scattered on the floor.*)

(LAURA *stands in the middle with lifted arms while* AMANDA *crouches before her, adjusting the hem of the new dress, devout and ritualistic. The dress is colored and designed by memory. The arrangement of* LAURA's *hair is changed; it is softer and more becoming. A fragile, unearthly prettiness has come out in* LAURA: *she is like a piece of translucent glass touched by light, given a momentary radiance, not actual, not lasting.*)

AMANDA (*impatiently*). Why are you trembling?

LAURA. Mother, you've made me so nervous!

AMANDA. How have I made you nervous?

LAURA. By all this fuss! You make it seem so important!

AMANDA. I don't understand you, Laura. You couldn't be satisfied with just sitting home, and yet whenever I try to arrange something for you, you seem to resist it.

(*She gets up.*)

LAURA. You make it seem like we were setting a trap.

AMANDA. All pretty girls are a trap, a pretty trap, and men expect them to be.

(LEGEND: *"A Pretty Trap."*)

Now look at yourself, young lady. This is the prettiest you will ever be!

I've got to fix myself now! You're going to be surprised by your mother's appearance! (*She crosses through portieres, humming gaily.*)

> (LAURA *moves slowly to the long mirror and stares solemnly at herself.*)
>
> (*A wind blows the white curtains inward in a slow, graceful motion and with a faint, sorrowful sighing.*)

AMANDA (*off stage*). It isn't dark enough yet. (*She turns slowly before the mirror with a troubled look.*)

> (LEGEND ON SCREEN: *"This is My Sister: Celebrate Her with Strings!"* MUSIC.)

AMANDA (*laughing, off*). I'm going to show you something. I'm going to make a spectacular appearance!

LAURA. What is it, Mother?

AMANDA. Possess your soul in patience—you will see!

Something I've resurrected from that old trunk! Styles haven't changed so terribly much after all. . . .

> (*She parts the portieres.*)

Now just look at your mother!

> (*She wears a girlish frock of yellowed voile with a blue silk sash. She carries a bunch of jonquils—the legend of her youth is nearly revived. Feverishly.*)

This is the dress in which I led the cotillion. Won the cakewalk twice at Sunset Hill, wore one spring to the Governor's ball in Jackson!

See how I sashayed around the ballroom, Laura?

> (*She raises her skirt and does a mincing step around the room.*)

I wore it on Sundays for my gentlemen callers! I had it on the day I met your father—

I had malaria fever all that spring. The change of climate from East Tennessee to the Delta—weakened resistance—I had a little temperature all the time—not enough to be serious—just enough to make me restless and giddy!—Invitations poured in—parties all over the Delta!—"Stay in bed," said Mother, "you have fever!"—but I just wouldn't.—I took quinine but kept on going, going!—Evenings, dances!—Afternoons, long, long rides! Picnics—lovely!—So lovely, that country in May.—All lacy with dogwood, literally flooded with jonquils!—That was the spring I had the craze for jonquils. Jonquils became an absolute obsession. Mother said, "Honey, there's no more room for jonquils." And still I kept on bringing in more jonquils. Whenever, wherever I saw them, I'd say, "Stop! Stop! I see jonquils!" I made the young men help me gather the jonquils! It was a joke, Amanda and her jonquils! Finally there were no more vases to hold them, every available space was filled with jonquils. No vases to hold them? All right, I'll hold them myself! And then I—(*She stops in front of the picture.* MUSIC.) met your father!

Malaria fever and jonquils and then—this—boy. . . .

> (*She switches on the rose-colored lamp.*)

I hope they get here before it starts to rain.

> (*She crosses upstage and places the jonquils in bowl on table.*)

I gave your brother a little extra change so he and Mr. O'Connor could take the service car home.

LAURA (*with altered look*). What did you say his name was?

AMANDA. O'Connor.

LAURA. What is his first name?

AMANDA. I don't remember. Oh, yes, I do. It was—Jim!

> (LAURA *sways slightly and catches hold of a chair.*)
>
> (LEGEND ON SCREEN: *"Not Jim!"*)

LAURA (*faintly*). Not—Jim!

AMANDA. Yes, that was it, it was Jim! I've never known a Jim that wasn't nice!

> (MUSIC: *Ominous.*)

LAURA. Are you sure his name is Jim O'Connor?

AMANDA. Yes. Why?

LAURA. Is he the one that Tom used to know in high school?

AMANDA. He didn't say so. I think he just got to know him at the warehouse.

LAURA. There was a Jim O'Connor we both knew in high school—(*Then, with effort.*) If that is the one that Tom is bringing to dinner—you'll have to excuse me, I won't come to the table.

AMANDA. What sort of nonsense is this?

LAURA. You asked me once if I'd ever liked a boy. Don't you remember I showed you this boy's picture?

AMANDA. You mean the boy you showed me in the yearbook?

LAURA. Yes, that boy.

AMANDA. Laura, Laura, were you in love with that boy?

LAURA. I don't know, Mother. All I know is I couldn't sit at the table if it was him!

AMANDA. It won't be him! It isn't the least bit likely. But whether it is or not, you will come to the table. You will not be excused.

LAURA. I'll have to be, Mother.

AMANDA. I don't intend to humor your silliness, Laura. I've had too much from you and your brother, both!

So just sit down and compose yourself till they come. Tom has forgotten his key so you'll have to let them in, when they arrive.

LAURA (panicky). Oh, Mother—you answer the door!

AMANDA (lightly). I'll be in the kitchen—busy!

LAURA. Oh, Mother, please answer the door, don't make me do it!

AMANDA (crossing into kitchenette). I've got to fix the dressing for the salmon. Fuss, fuss—silliness!—over a gentleman caller!

(Door swings shut. LAURA is left alone.)

(LEGEND: "Terror!")

(She utters a low moan and turns off the lamp, sits stiffly on the edge of the sofa, knotting her fingers together.)

(LEGEND ON SCREEN: "The Opening of a Door!")

(TOM and JIM appear on the fire escape steps and climb to landing. Hearing their approach, LAURA rises with a panicky gesture. She retreats to the portieres.)

(The doorbell. LAURA catches her breath and touches her throat. Low drums.)

AMANDA (calling). Laura, sweetheart! The door!

(LAURA stares at it without moving.)

JIM. I think we just beat the rain.

TOM. Uh-huh. (He rings again, nervously. JIM whistles and fishes for a cigarette.)

AMANDA (very, very gaily). Laura, that is your brother and Mr. O'Connor! Will you let them in, darling?

(LAURA crosses toward kitchenette door.)

LAURA (breathlessly). Mother—you go to the door!

(AMANDA steps out of kitchenette and stares furiously at LAURA. She points imperiously at the door.)

LAURA. Please, please!

AMANDA (in a fierce whisper). What is the matter with you, you silly thing?

LAURA (desperately). Please, you answer it, please!

AMANDA. I told you I wasn't going to humor you, Laura. Why have you chosen this moment to lose your mind?

LAURA. Please, please, please, you go!

AMANDA. You'll have to go to the door because I can't!

LAURA (despairingly). I can't either!

AMANDA. Why?

LAURA. I'm sick!

AMANDA. I'm sick, too—of your nonsense! Why can't you and your brother be normal people? Fantastic whims and behavior!

(TOM gives a long ring.)

Preposterous goings on! Can you give me one reason—(Calls out lyrically.) COMING! JUST ONE SECOND!—why you should be afraid to open a door? Now you answer it, Laura!

LAURA. Oh, oh, oh . . . (She returns through the portieres. Darts to the victrola and winds it frantically and turns it on.)

AMANDA. Laura Wingfield, you march right to that door!

LAURA. Yes—yes, Mother!

(A faraway, scratchy rendition of "Dardanella" softens the air and gives her strength to move through it. She slips to the door and draws it cautiously open.)

(TOM enters with the caller, JIM O'CONNOR.)

TOM. Laura, this is Jim. Jim, this is my sister, Laura.

JIM (stepping inside). I didn't know that Shakespeare had a sister!

LAURA (*retreating stiff and trembling from the door*). How—how do you do?

JIM (*heartily extending his hand*). Okay!

(LAURA *touches it hesitantly with hers.*)

JIM. Your hand's *cold*, Laura!

LAURA. Yes, well—I've been playing the victrola. . . .

JIM. Must have been playing classical music on it! You ought to play a little hot swing music to warm you up!

LAURA. Excuse me—I haven't finished playing the victrola. . . . (*She turns awkwardly and hurries into the front room. She pauses a second by the victrola. Then catches her breath and darts through the portieres like a frightened deer.*)

JIM (*grinning*). What was the matter?

TOM. Oh—with Laura? Laura is—terribly shy.

JIM. Shy, huh? It's unusual to meet a shy girl nowadays. I don't believe you ever mentioned you had a sister.

TOM. Well, now you know. I have one. Here is the *Post Dispatch*. You want a piece of it?

JIM. Uh-huh.

TOM. What piece? The comics?

JIM. Sports! (*Glances at it.*) Ole Dizzy Dean[1] is on his bad behavior.

TOM (*disinterest*). Yeah? (*Lights cigarette and crosses back to fire escape door.*)

JIM. Where are *you* going?

TOM. I'm going out on the terrace.

JIM (*goes after him*). You know, Shakespeare—I'm going to sell you a bill of goods!

TOM. What goods?

JIM. A course I'm taking.

TOM. Huh?

JIM. In public speaking! You and me, we're not the warehouse type.

TOM. Thanks—that's good news. But what has public speaking got to do with it?

JIM. It fits you for—executive positions!

TOM. Awww.

JIM. I tell you it's done a helluva lot for me.

(IMAGE: *Executive at desk.*)

TOM. In what respect?

JIM. In every! Ask yourself what is the difference between you an' me and men in the office down front? Brains?—No!—Ability? —No! Then what? Just one little thing—

TOM. What is that one little thing?

JIM. Primarily it amounts to—social poise! Being able to square up to people and hold your own on any social level!

AMANDA (*off stage*). Tom?

TOM. Yes, Mother?

AMANDA. Is that you and Mr. O'Connor?

TOM. Yes, Mother.

AMANDA. Well, you just make yourselves comfortable in there.

TOM. Yes, Mother.

AMANDA. Ask Mr. O'Connor if he would like to wash his hands.

JIM. Aw, no—no—thank you—I took care of that at the warehouse. Tom—

TOM. Yes?

JIM. Mr. Mendoza was speaking to me about you.

TOM. Favorably?

JIM. What do you think?

TOM. Well—

JIM. You're going to be out of a job if you don't wake up.

TOM. I am waking up—

JIM. You show no signs.

TOM. The signs are interior.

(IMAGE ON SCREEN: *The sailing vessel with Jolly Roger again.*)

TOM. I'm planning to change. (*He leans over the rail speaking with quiet exhilaration. The incandescent marquees and signs of the first-run movie houses light his face from across the alley. He looks like a voyager.*) I'm right at the point of committing myself to a future that doesn't include the warehouse and Mr. Mendoza or even a night-school course in public speaking.

JIM. What are you gassing about?

TOM. I'm tired of the movies.

JIM. Movies!

TOM. Yes, movies! Look at them— (*A wave toward the marvels of Grand Avenue.*) All of those glamorous people—having adventures— hogging it all, gobbling the whole thing up! You know what happens? People go to the

---

1. *Ole Dizzy Dean*, Jerome Hanna "Dizzy" Dean (1911-   ), rather eccentric in his life outside of baseball and a brilliant pitcher for the St. Louis Cardinals.

movies instead of *moving!* Hollywood characters are supposed to have all the adventures for everybody in America, while everybody in America sits in a dark room and watches them have them! Yes, until there's a war. That's when adventure becomes available to the masses! *Everyone's* dish, not only Gable's! Then the people in the dark room come out of the dark room to have some adventures themselves—Goody, goody!—It's our turn now, to go to the South Sea Island—to make a safari—to be exotic, far-off!—But I'm not patient. I don't want to wait till then. I'm tired of the *movies* and I am *about to move!*

JIM (*incredulously*). Move?

TOM. Yes.

JIM. When?

TOM. Soon!

JIM. Where? Where?

(*Theme three music seems to answer the question, while Tom thinks it over. He searches among his pockets.*)

TOM. I'm starting to boil inside. I know I seem dreamy, but inside—well, I'm boiling!—Whenever I pick up a shoe, I shudder a little thinking how short life is and what I am doing!—Whatever that means, I know it doesn't mean shoes—except as something to wear on a traveler's feet! (*Finds paper.*) Look—

JIM. What?

TOM. I'm a member.

JIM (*reading*). The Union of Merchant Seamen.

TOM. I paid my dues this month, instead of the light bill.

JIM. You will regret it when they turn the lights off.

TOM. I won't be here.

JIM. How about your mother?

TOM. I'm like my father. See how he grins? And he's been absent going on sixteen years!

JIM. You're just talking, you drip. How does your mother feel about it?

TOM. Shhh!—Here comes Mother! Mother is not acquainted with my plans!

AMANDA (*enters portieres*). Where are you all?

TOM. On the terrace, Mother.

(*They start inside. She advances to them.*

TOM *is distinctly shocked at her appearance. Even* JIM *blinks a little. He is making his first contact with girlish Southern vivacity and in spite of the night-school course in public speaking is somewhat thrown off the beam by the unexpected outlay of social charm.*)

(*Certain responses are attempted by* JIM *but are swept aside by* AMANDA'S *gay laughter and chatter.* TOM *is embarrassed but after the first shock* JIM *reacts very warmly. Grins and chuckles, is altogether won over.*)

(IMAGE: *Amanda as a girl.*)

AMANDA (*coyly smiling, shaking her girlish ringlets*). Well, well, well, so this is Mr. O'Connor. Introductions entirely unnecessary. I've heard so much about you from my boy. I finally said to him, Tom—good gracious!—why don't you bring this paragon to supper? I'd like to meet this nice young man at the warehouse!—Instead of just hearing him sing your praises so much!

I don't know why my son is so stand-offish—that's not Southern behavior!

Let's sit down and—I think we could stand a little more air in here! Tom, leave the door open. I felt a nice fresh breeze a moment ago. Where has it gone to?

Mmm, so warm already! And not quite summer, even. We're going to burn up when summer really gets started.

However, we're having—we're having a very light supper. I think light things are better fo' this time of year. The same as light clothes are. Light clothes an' light food are what warm weather calls fo'. You know our blood gets so thick during th' winter—it takes a while fo' us to *adjust* ou'selves!—when the season changes. . . .

It's come so quick this year. I wasn't prepared. All of a sudden—heavens! Already summer!—I ran to the trunk an' pulled out this light dress—Terribly old! Historical almost! But feels so good—so good an' co-ol, y' know. . . .

TOM. Mother—

AMANDA. Yes, honey?

TOM. How about—supper?

AMANDA. Honey, you go ask Sister if supper

is ready! You know that Sister is in full charge of supper!

Tell her you hungry boys are waiting for it. (*To* JIM.)

Have you met Laura?

JIM. She—

AMANDA. Let you in? Oh, good, you've met already! It's rare for a girl as sweet an' pretty as Laura to be domestic! But Laura is, thank heavens, not only pretty but also very domestic. I'm not at all. I never was a bit. I never could make a thing but angel-food cake. Well, in the South we had so many servants. Gone, gone, gone. All vestige of gracious living! Gone completely! I wasn't prepared for what the future brought me. All of my gentlemen callers were sons of planters and so of course I assumed that I would be married to one and raise my family on a large piece of land with plenty of servants. But man proposes—and woman accepts the proposal!—To vary that old, old saying a little bit—I married no planter! I married a man who worked for the telephone company!—That gallantly smiling gentleman over there! (*Points to the picture.*) A telephone man who—fell in love with long-distance!—Now he travels and I don't even know where!—But what am I going on for about my—tribulations?

Tell me yours—I hope you don't have any! Tom?

TOM (*returning*). Yes, Mother?

AMANDA. Is supper nearly ready?

TOM. It looks to me like supper is on the table.

AMANDA. Let me look—(*She rises prettily and looks through portieres.*) Oh, lovely!—But where is Sister?

TOM. Laura is not feeling well and she says that she thinks she'd better not come to the table.

AMANDA. What?—Nonsense!—Laura? Oh, Laura!

LAURA (*off stage, faintly*). Yes, Mother.

AMANDA. You really must come to the table. We won't be seated until you come to the table!

Come in, Mr. O'Connor. You sit over there, and I'll—

Laura? Laura Wingfield!

You're keeping us waiting, honey! We can't say grace until you come to the table!

(*The back door is pushed weakly open and* LAURA *comes in. She is obviously quite faint, her lips trembling, her eyes wide and staring. She moves unsteadily toward the table.*)

(LEGEND: *"Terror!"*)

(*Outside a summer storm is coming abruptly. The white curtains billow inward at the windows and there is a sorrowful murmur and deep blue dusk.*)

(LAURA *suddenly stumbles—she catches at a chair with a faint moan.*)

TOM. Laura!

AMANDA. Laura!

(*There is a clap of thunder.*)

(LEGEND: *"Ah!"*)

(*Despairingly.*)

Why, Laura, you *are* sick, darling! Tom, help your sister into the living room, dear!

Sit in the living room, Laura—rest on the sofa.

Well!

(*To the gentleman caller.*)

Standing over the hot stove made her ill!—I told her that it was just too warm this evening, but—

(TOM *comes back in.* LAURA *is on the sofa.*)

Is Laura all right now?

TOM. Yes.

AMANDA. What *is* that? Rain? A nice cool rain has come up!

(*She gives the gentleman caller a frightened look.*)

I think we may—have grace—now . . .

(TOM *looks at her stupidly.*)

Tom, honey—you say grace!

TOM. Oh . . .

"For these and all thy mercies—"

(*They bow their heads,* AMANDA *stealing a nervous glance at* JIM. *In the living room* LAURA, *stretched on the sofa, clenches her hands to her lips, to hold back a shuddering sob.*)

God's Holy Name be praised—

THE SCENE DIMS OUT

Scene 7

A Souvenir.

Half an hour later. Dinner is just being finished in the upstage area which is concealed by the drawn portieres.

As the curtain rises LAURA *is still huddled upon the sofa, her feet drawn under her, her head resting on a pale blue pillow, her eyes wide and mysteriously watchful. The new floor lamp with its shade of rose-colored silk gives a soft, becoming light to her face, bringing out the fragile, unearthly prettiness which usually escapes attention. There is a steady murmur of rain, but it is slackening and stops soon after the scene begins; the air outside becomes pale and luminous as the moon breaks out.*

A moment after the curtain rises, the lights in both rooms flicker and go out.

JIM. Hey, there, Mr. Light Bulb!

(AMANDA *laughs nervously.*)

(LEGEND: *"Suspension of a Public Service."*)

AMANDA. Where was Moses when the lights went out? Ha-ha. Do you know the answer to that one, Mr. O'Connor?

JIM. No, Ma'am, what's the answer?

AMANDA. In the dark!

(JIM *laughs appreciatively.*)

Everybody sit still. I'll light the candles. Isn't it lucky we have them on the table? Where's a match? Which of you gentlemen can provide a match?

JIM. Here.

AMANDA. Thank you, sir.

JIM. Not at all, Ma'am!

AMANDA. I guess the fuse has burnt out. Mr. O'Connor, can you tell a burnt-out fuse? I know I can't and Tom is a total loss when it comes to mechanics.

(SOUND: *Getting up: Voices recede a little to kitchenette.*)

Oh, be careful you don't bump into something. We don't want our gentleman caller to break his neck. Now wouldn't that be a fine howdy-do?

JIM. Ha-ha!

Where is the fuse-box?

AMANDA. Right here next to the stove. Can you see anything?

JIM. Just a minute.

AMANDA. Isn't electricity a mysterious thing? Wasn't it Benjamin Franklin who tied a key to a kite? We live in such a mysterious universe, don't we? Some people say that science clears up all the mysteries for us. In my opinion it only creates more!

Have you found it yet?

JIM. No, Ma'am. All these fuses look okay to me.

AMANDA. Tom!

TOM. Yes, Mother?

AMANDA. That light bill I gave you several days ago. The one I told you we got the notices about?

(LEGEND: *"Ha!"*)

TOM. Oh.—Yeah.

AMANDA. You didn't neglect to pay it by any chance?

TOM. Why, I—

AMANDA. Didn't! I might have known it!

JIM. Shakespeare probably wrote a poem on that light bill, Mrs. Wingfield.

AMANDA. I might have known better than to trust him with it! There's such a high price for negligence in this world!

JIM. Maybe the poem will win a ten-dollar prize.

AMANDA. We'll just have to spend the remainder of the evening in the nineteenth century, before Mr. Edison made the Mazda lamp!

JIM. Candlelight is my favorite kind of light.

AMANDA. That shows you're romantic! But that's no excuse for Tom.

Well, we got through dinner. Very considerate of them to let us get through dinner before they plunged us into everlasting darkness, wasn't it, Mr. O'Connor?

JIM. Ha-ha!

AMANDA. Tom, as a penalty for your carelessness you can help me with the dishes.

JIM. Let me give you a hand.

AMANDA. Indeed you will not!

JIM. I ought to be good for something.

AMANDA. Good for something? (*Her tone is rhapsodic.*)

You? Why, Mr. O'Connor, nobody, *nobody's* given me this much entertainment in years—as you have!

JIM. Aw, now, Mrs. Wingfield!

AMANDA. I'm not exaggerating, not one bit! But Sister is all by her lonesome. You go keep her company in the parlor!

I'll give you this lovely old candelabrum that used to be on the altar at the church of the Heavenly Rest. It was melted a little out of shape when the church burnt down. Lightning struck it one spring. Gypsy Jones was holding a revival at the time and he intimated that the church was destroyed because the Episcopalians gave card parties.

JIM. Ha-ha.

AMANDA. And how about you coaxing Sister to drink a little wine? I think it would be good for her! Can you carry both at once?

JIM. Sure. I'm Superman!

AMANDA. Now, Thomas, get into this apron!

(*The door of kitchenette swings closed on* AMANDA's *gay laughter; the flickering light approaches the portieres.*)

(*LAURA sits up nervously as he enters. Her speech at first is low and breathless from the almost intolerable strain of being alone with a stranger.*)

(*THE LEGEND: "I don't suppose you remember me at all!"*)

(*In her first speeches in this scene, before* JIM's *warmth overcomes her paralyzing shyness,* LAURA's *voice is thin and breathless as though she has just run up a steep flight of stairs.*)

(*JIM's attitude is gently humorous. In playing this scene it should be stressed that while the incident is apparently unimportant, it is to* LAURA *the climax of her secret life.*)

JIM. Hello, there, Laura.

LAURA (*faintly*). Hello. (*She clears her throat.*)

JIM. How are you feeling now? Better?

LAURA. Yes. Yes, thank you.

JIM. This is for you. A little dandelion wine. (*He extends it toward her with extravagant gallantry.*)

LAURA. Thank you.

JIM. Drink it—but don't get drunk!

(*He laughs heartily.* LAURA *takes the glass uncertainly; laughs shyly.*)
Where shall I set the candles?

LAURA. Oh—oh, anywhere . . .

JIM. How about here on the floor? Any objections?

LAURA. No.

JIM. I'll spread a newspaper under to catch the drippings. I like to sit on the floor. Mind if I do?

LAURA. Oh, no.

JIM. Give me a pillow?

LAURA. What?

JIM. A pillow!

LAURA. Oh . . . (*Hands him one quickly.*)

JIM. How about you? Don't you like to sit on the floor?

LAURA. Oh—yes.

JIM. Why don't you, then?

LAURA. I—will.

JIM. Take a pillow! (*LAURA does. Sits on the other side of the candelabrum.* JIM *crosses his legs and smiles engagingly at her.*) I can't hardly see you sitting way over there.

LAURA. I can—see you.

JIM. I know, but that's not fair, I'm in the limelight. (*LAURA moves her pillow closer.*) Good! Now I can see you! Comfortable?

LAURA. Yes.

JIM. So am I. Comfortable as a cow! Will you have some gum?

LAURA. No, thank you.

JIM. I think that I will indulge, with your permission. (*Musingly unwraps it and holds it up.*) Think of the fortune made by the guy that invented the first piece of chewing gum. Amazing, huh? The Wrigley Building is one of the sights of Chicago.—I saw it summer before last when I went up to the Century of Progress.[1] Did you take in the Century of Progress?

LAURA. No, I didn't.

JIM. Well, it was quite a wonderful exposition. What impressed me most was the Hall

---

1. *Century of Progress*, the world's fair held in Chicago in 1933-1934.

of Science. Gives you an idea of what the future will be in America, even more wonderful than the present time is! (*Pause. Smiling at her.*) Your brother tells me you're shy. Is that right, Laura?

LAURA. I—don't know.

JIM. I judge you to be an old-fashioned type of girl. Well, I think that's a pretty good type to be. Hope you don't think I'm being too personal—do you?

LAURA (*hastily, out of embarrassment*). I believe I *will* take a piece of gum, if you—don't mind. (*Clearing her throat.*) Mr. O'Connor, have you—kept up with your singing?

JIM. Singing? Me?

LAURA. Yes. I remember what a beautiful voice you had.

JIM. When did you hear me sing?

(*Voice off stage in the pause.*)

VOICE (*off stage*).

O blow, ye winds, heigh-ho,
A-roving I will go!
  I'm off to my love
  With a boxing glove—
Ten thousand miles away!

JIM. You say you've heard me sing?

LAURA. Oh, yes! Yes, very often . . . I—don't suppose—you remember me—at all?

JIM (*smiling doubtfully*). You know I have an idea I've seen you before. I had that idea soon as you opened the door. It seemed almost like I was about to remember your name. But the name that I started to call you—wasn't a name! And so I stopped myself before I said it.

LAURA. Wasn't it—Blue Roses?

JIM (*springs up. Grinning*). Blue Roses!—My gosh, yes—Blue Roses!

That's what I had on my tongue when you opened the door!

Isn't it funny what tricks your memory plays? I didn't connect you with high school somehow or other.

But that's where it was; it was high school. I didn't even know you were Shakespeare's sister!

Gosh, I'm sorry.

LAURA. I didn't expect you to. You—barely knew me!

JIM. But we did have a speaking acquaintance, huh?

LAURA. Yes, we—spoke to each other.

JIM. When did you recognize me?

LAURA. Oh, right away!

JIM. Soon as I came in the door?

LAURA. When I heard your name I thought it was probably you. I knew that Tom used to know you a little in high school. So when you came in the door—

Well, then I was—sure.

JIM. Why didn't you *say* something, then?

LAURA (*breathlessly*). I didn't know what to say, I was—too surprised!

JIM. For goodness' sakes! You know, this sure is funny!

LAURA. Yes! Yes, isn't it, though . . .

JIM. Didn't we have a class in something together?

LAURA. Yes, we did.

JIM. What class was that?

LAURA. It was—singing—Chorus!

JIM. Aw!

LAURA. I sat across the aisle from you in the Aud.

JIM. Aw.

LAURA. Mondays, Wednesdays and Fridays.

JIM. Now I remember—you always came in late.

LAURA. Yes, it was so hard for me, getting upstairs. I had that brace on my leg—it clumped so loud!

JIM. I never heard any clumping.

LAURA (*wincing at the recollection*). To me it sounded like—thunder!

JIM. Well, well, well, I never even noticed.

LAURA. And everybody was seated before I came in. I had to walk in front of all those people. My seat was in the back row. I had to go clumping all the way up the aisle with everyone watching!

JIM. You shouldn't have been self-conscious.

LAURA. I know, but I was. It was always such a relief when the singing started.

JIM. Aw, yes, I've placed *you* now! I used to call you Blue Roses. How was it that I got started calling you that?

LAURA. I was out of school a little while with pleurosis. When I came back you asked me what was the matter. I said I had pleurosis

—you thought I said Blue Roses. That's what you always called me after that!

JIM. I hope you didn't mind.

LAURA. Oh, no—I liked it. You see, I wasn't acquainted with many—people. . . .

JIM. As I remember you sort of stuck by yourself.

LAURA. I—I—never have had much luck at —making friends.

JIM. I don't see why you wouldn't.

LAURA. Well, I—started out badly.

JIM. You mean being—

LAURA. Yes, it sort of—stood between me—

JIM. You shouldn't have let it!

LAURA. I know, but it did, and—

JIM. You were shy with people!

LAURA. I tried not to be but never could—

JIM. Overcome it?

LAURA. No, I—I never could!

JIM. I guess being shy is something you have to work out of kind of gradually.

LAURA (sorrowfully). Yes—I guess it—

JIM. Takes time!

LAURA. Yes—

JIM. People are not so dreadful when you know them. That's what you have to remember! And everybody has problems, not just you, but practically everybody has got some problems.

You think of yourself as having the only problems, as being the only one who is disappointed. But just look around you and you will see lots of people as disappointed as you are. For instance, I hoped when I was going to high school that I would be further along at this time, six years later, than I am now— You remember that wonderful write-up I had in The Torch?

LAURA. Yes! (She rises and crosses to table.)

JIM. It said I was bound to succeed in anything I went into! (LAURA returns with the annual.) Holy gee! The Torch! (He accepts it reverently. They smile across it with mutual wonder. LAURA crouches beside him and they begin to turn through it. LAURA's shyness is dissolving in his warmth.)

LAURA. Here you are in The Pirates of Penzance!

JIM (wistfully). I sang the baritone lead in that operetta.

LAURA (raptly). So—beautifully!

JIM (protesting). Aw—

LAURA. Yes, yes—beautifully—beautifully!

JIM. You heard me?

LAURA. All three times!

JIM. No!

LAURA. Yes!

JIM. All three performances?

LAURA (looking down). Yes.

JIM. Why?

LAURA. I—wanted to ask you to—autograph my program.

JIM. Why didn't you ask me to?

LAURA. You were always surrounded by your own friends so much that I never had a chance to.

JIM. You should have just—

LAURA. Well, I—thought you might think I was—

JIM. Thought I might think you was— what?

LAURA. Oh—

JIM (with reflective relish). I was beleaguered by females in those days.

LAURA. You were terribly popular!

JIM. Yeah—

LAURA. You had such a—friendly way—

JIM. I was spoiled in high school.

LAURA. Everybody—liked you!

JIM. Including you?

LAURA. I—yes, I—I did, too— (She gently closes the book in her lap.)

JIM. Well, well, well!—Give me that program, Laura. (She hands it to him. He signs it with a flourish.) There you are—better late than never!

LAURA. Oh, I—what a—surprise!

JIM. My signature isn't worth very much right now.

But some day—maybe—it will increase in value!

Being disappointed is one thing and being discouraged is something else. I am disappointed but I am not discouraged.

I'm twenty-three years old.

How old are you?

LAURA. I'll be twenty-four in June.

JIM. That's not old age!

LAURA. No, but—

JIM. You finished high school?

LAURA (*with difficulty*). I didn't go back.

JIM. You mean you dropped out?

LAURA. I made bad grades in my final examinations. (*She rises and replaces the book and the program. Her voice strained.*) How is—Emily Meisenbach getting along?

JIM. Oh, that kraut-head!

LAURA. Why do you call her that?

JIM. That's what she was.

LAURA. You're not still—going with her?

JIM. I never see her.

LAURA. It said in the Personal Section that you were—engaged!

JIM. I know, but I wasn't impressed by that —propaganda!

LAURA. It wasn't—the truth?

JIM. Only in Emily's optimistic opinion!

LAURA. Oh—

(LEGEND: *"What have you done since High School?"*)

(JIM *lights a cigarette and leans indolently back on his elbows smiling at* LAURA *with a warmth and charm which lights her inwardly with altar candles. She remains by the table and turns in her hands a piece of glass to cover her tumult.*)

JIM (*after several reflective puffs on a cigarette*). What have you done since high school? (*She seems not to hear him.*) Huh? (LAURA *looks up.*) I said what have you done since high school, Laura?

LAURA. Nothing much.

JIM. You must have been doing something these six long years.

LAURA. Yes.

JIM. Well, then, such as what?

LAURA. I took a business course at business college—

JIM. How did that work out?

LAURA. Well, not very—well—I had to drop out, it gave me—indigestion—

(JIM *laughs gently.*)

JIM. What are you doing now?

LAURA. I don't do anything—much. Oh, please don't think I sit around doing nothing! My glass collection takes up a good deal of time. Glass is something you have to take good care of.

JIM. What did you say—about glass?

LAURA. Collection I said—I have one— (*She clears her throat and turns away again, acutely shy.*)

JIM (*abruptly*). You know what I judge to be the trouble with you?

Inferiority complex! Know what that is? That's what they call it when someone low-rates himself!

I understand it because I had it, too. Although my case was not so aggravated as yours seems to be. I had it until I took up public speaking, developed my voice, and learned that I had an aptitude for science. Before that time I never thought of myself as being outstanding in any way whatsoever!

Now I've never made a regular study of it, but I have a friend who says I can analyze people better than doctors that make a profession of it. I don't claim that to be necessarily true, but I can sure guess a person's psychology, Laura! (*Takes out his gum.*) Excuse me, Laura. I always take it out when the flavor is gone. I'll use this scrap of paper to wrap it in. I know how it is to get it stuck on a shoe.

Yep—that's what I judge to be your principal trouble. A lack of confidence in yourself as a person. You don't have the proper amount of faith in yourself. I'm basing that fact on a number of your remarks and also on certain observations I've made. For instance that clumping you thought was so awful in high school. You say that you even dreaded to walk into class. You see what you did? You dropped out of school, you gave up an education because of a clump, which as far as I know was practically non-existent! A little physical defect is what you have. Hardly noticeable even! Magnified thousands of times by imagination!

You know what my strong advice to you is? Think of yourself as *superior* in some way!

LAURA. In what way would I think?

JIM. Why, man alive, Laura! Just look about you a little. What do you see? A world full of common people! All of 'em born and all of 'em going to die!

Which of them has one-tenth of your good points! Or mine! Or anyone else's, as far as that goes—Gosh!

Everybody excels in some one thing. Some in many!

(*Unconsciously glances at himself in the mirror.*)

All you've got to do is discover in *what!*

Take me, for instance.

(*He adjusts his tie at the mirror.*)

My interest happens to lie in electrodynamics. I'm taking a course in radio engineering at night school, Laura, on top of a fairly responsible job at the warehouse. I'm taking that course and studying public speaking.

LAURA. Ohhhh.

JIM. Because I believe in the future of television!

(*Turning back to her.*)

I wish to be ready to go up right along with it. Therefore I'm planning to get in on the ground floor. In fact I've already made the right connections and all that remains is for the industry itself to get under way! Full steam—

(*His eyes are starry.*)

Knowledge—Zzzzzp! Money—Zzzzzzp! Power!

That's the cycle democracy is built on!

(*His attitude is convincingly dynamic. LAURA stares at him, even her shyness eclipsed in her absolute wonder. He suddenly grins.*)

I guess you think I think a lot of myself!

LAURA. No—o-o-o, I—

JIM. Now how about you? Isn't there something you take more interest in than anything else?

LAURA. Well, I do—as I said—have my— glass collection—

(*A peal of girlish laughter from the kitchen.*)

JIM. I'm not right sure I know what you're talking about.

What kind of glass is it?

LAURA. Little articles of it, they're ornaments mostly!

Most of them are little animals made out of glass, the tiniest little animals in the world. Mother calls them a glass menagerie!

Here's an example of one, if you'd like to see it!

This one is one of the oldest. It's nearly thirteen.

(MUSIC: *"The Glass Menagerie."*)

(*He stretches out his hand.*)

Oh, be careful—if you breathe, it breaks!

JIM. I'd better not take it. I'm pretty clumsy with things.

LAURA. Go on, I trust you with him!

(*Places it in his palm.*)

There now—you're holding him gently!

Hold him over the light, he loves the light! You see how the light shines through him?

JIM. It sure does shine!

LAURA. I shouldn't be partial, but he is my favorite one.

JIM. What kind of a thing is this one supposed to be?

LAURA. Haven't you noticed the single horn on his forehead?

JIM. A unicorn, huh?

LAURA. Mmm-hmmm!

JIM. Unicorns, aren't they extinct in the modern world?

LAURA. I know!

JIM. Poor little fellow, he must feel sort of lonesome.

LAURA (*smiling*). Well, if he does he doesn't complain about it. He stays on a shelf with some horses that don't have horns and all of them seem to get along nicely together.

JIM. How do you know?

LAURA (*lightly*). I haven't heard any arguments among them!

JIM (*grinning*). No arguments, huh? Well, that's a pretty good sign!

Where shall I set him?

LAURA. Put him on the table. They all like a change of scenery once in a while!

JIM (*stretching*). Well, well, well, well—

Look how big my shadow is when I stretch!

LAURA. Oh, oh, yes—it stretches across the ceiling!

JIM (*crossing to door*). I think it's stopped raining. (*Opens fire escape door.*) Where does the music come from?

LAURA. From the Paradise Dance Hall across the alley.

JIM. How about cutting the rug a little, Miss Wingfield?

LAURA. Oh, I—

JIM. Or is your program filled up? Let me have a look at it. (*Grasps imaginary card.*) Why, every dance is taken! I'll just have to scratch some out. (WALTZ MUSIC: *"La Golondrina."*) Ahhh, a waltz! (*He executes some sweeping turns by himself then holds his arms toward* LAURA.)

LAURA (*breathlessly*). I—can't dance!

JIM. There you go, that inferiority stuff!

LAURA. I've never danced in my life!

JIM. Come on, try!

LAURA. Oh, but I'd step on you!

JIM. I'm not made out of glass.

LAURA. How—how—how do we start?

JIM. Just leave it to me. You hold your arms out a little.

LAURA. Like this?

JIM. A little bit higher. Right. Now don't tighten up, that's the main thing about it—relax.

LAURA (*laughing breathlessly*). It's hard not to.

JIM. Okay.

LAURA. I'm afraid you can't budge me.

JIM. What do you bet I can't? (*He swings her into motion.*)

LAURA. Goodness, yes, you can!

JIM. Let yourself go, now, Laura, just let yourself go.

LAURA. I'm—

JIM. Come on!

LAURA. Trying!

JIM. Not so stiff—Easy does it!

LAURA. I know but I'm—

JIM. Loosen th' backbone! There now, that's a lot better.

LAURA. Am I?

JIM. Lots, lots better! (*He moves her about the room in a clumsy waltz.*)

LAURA. Oh, my!

JIM. Ha-ha!

LAURA. Oh, my goodness!

JIM. Ha-ha-ha! (*They suddenly bump into the table.* JIM *stops.*) What did we hit on?

LAURA. Table.

JIM. Did something fall off it? I think—

LAURA. Yes.

JIM. I hope that it wasn't the little glass horse with the horn!

LAURA. Yes.

JIM. Aw, aw, aw. Is it broken?

LAURA. Now it is just like all the other horses.

JIM. It's lost its—

LAURA. Horn!

It doesn't matter. Maybe it's a blessing in disguise.

JIM. You'll never forgive me. I bet that that was your favorite piece of glass.

LAURA. I don't have favorites much. It's no tragedy, Freckles. Glass breaks so easily. No matter how careful you are. The traffic jars the shelves and things fall off them.

JIM. Still I'm awfully sorry that I was the cause.

LAURA (*smiling*). I'll just imagine he had an operation.

The horn was removed to make him feel less—freakish!

(*They both laugh.*)

Now he will feel more at home with the other horses, the ones that don't have horns . . .

JIM. Ha-ha, that's very funny!

(*Suddenly serious.*)

I'm glad to see that you have a sense of humor.

You know—you're—well—very different!

Surprisingly different from anyone else I know!

(*His voice becomes soft and hesitant with a genuine feeling.*)

Do you mind me telling you that?

(LAURA *is abashed beyond speech.*)

I mean it in a nice way . . .

(LAURA *nods shyly, looking away.*)

You make me feel sort of—I don't know how to put it!

I'm usually pretty good at expressing things, but—

This is something that I don't know how to say!

(LAURA *touches her throat and clears it— turns the broken unicorn in her hands.*)
(*Even softer.*)

Has anyone ever told you that you were pretty?

(*Pause: music.*)

(LAURA *looks up slowly, with wonder. and shakes her head.*)

Well, you are! In a very different way from anyone else.

And all the nicer because of the difference, too.

(*His voice becomes low and husky.* LAURA *turns away, nearly faint with the novelty of her emotions.*)

I wish that you were my sister. I'd teach you to have some confidence in yourself. The different people are not like other people, but being different is nothing to be ashamed of. Because other people are not such wonderful people. They're one hundred times one thousand. You're one times one! They walk all over the earth. You just stay here. They're common as—weeds, but—you—well, you're— Blue Roses!

(IMAGE ON SCREEN: *Blue Roses.*)

(*Music changes.*)

LAURA. But blue is wrong for—roses . . .

JIM. It's right for you!—You're—pretty!

LAURA. In what respect am I pretty?

JIM. In all respects—believe me! Your eyes—your hair—are pretty! Your hands are pretty!

(*He catches hold of her hand.*)

You think I'm making this up because I'm invited to dinner and have to be nice. Oh, I could do that! I could put on an act for you, Laura, and say lots of things without being very sincere. But this time I am. I'm talking to you sincerely. I happened to notice you had this inferiority complex that keeps you from feeling comfortable with people. Somebody needs to build your confidence up and make you proud instead of shy and turning away and—blushing—

Somebody—ought to—

Ought to—*kiss* you, Laura!

(*His hand slips slowly up her arm to her shoulder.*)

(*Music swells tumultuously.*)

(*He suddenly turns her about and kisses her on the lips.*)

(*When he releases her,* LAURA *sinks on the sofa with a bright, dazed look.*)

(JIM *backs away and fishes in his pocket for a cigarette.*)

(LEGEND ON SCREEN: "*Souvenir.*")

Stumble-john!

(*He lights the cigarette, avoiding her look.*)

(*There is a peal of girlish laughter from* AMANDA *in the kitchen.*)

(LAURA *slowly raises and opens her hand. It still contains the little broken glass animal. She looks at it with a tender, bewildered expression.*)

Stumble-john!

I shouldn't have done that— That was way off the beam.

You don't smoke, do you?

(*She looks up, smiling, not hearing the question.*)

(*He sits beside her a little gingerly. She looks at him speechlessly—waiting.*)

(*He coughs decorously and moves a little farther aside as he considers the situation and senses her feelings, dimly, with perturbation.*)

(*Gently.*)

Would you—care for a—mint?

(*She doesn't seem to hear him but her look grows brighter even.*)

Peppermint—Life-Saver?

My pocket's a regular drug store—wherever I go . . .

(*He pops a mint in his mouth. Then gulps and decides to make a clean breast of it. He speaks slowly and gingerly.*)

Laura, you know, if I had a sister like you, I'd do the same thing as Tom. I'd bring out fellows and—introduce her to them. The right type of boys of a type to—appreciate her.

Only—well—he made a mistake about me.

Maybe I've got no call to be saying this. That may not have been the idea in having me over. But what if it was?

There's nothing wrong about that. The only trouble is that in my case—I'm not in a situation to—do the right thing.

I can't take down your number and say I'll phone.

I can't call up next week and—ask for a date.

I thought I had better explain the situation in case you—misunderstood it and—hurt your feelings. . . .

(*Pause.*)

(*Slowly, very slowly,* LAURA'S *look*

changes, her eyes returning slowly from his to the ornament in her palm.)

(AMANDA *utters another gay laugh in the kitchen.*)

LAURA (*faintly*). You—won't—call again?

JIM. No, Laura, I can't.

(*He rises from the sofa.*)

As I was just explaining, I've—got strings on me.

Laura, I've—been going steady!

I go out all of the time with a girl named Betty. She's a home-girl like you, and Catholic, and Irish, and in a great many ways we—get along fine.

I met her last summer on a moonlight boat trip up the river to Alton, on the *Majestic.*

Well—right away from the start it was— love!

(LEGEND: *Love!*)

(LAURA *sways slightly forward and grips the arm of the sofa. He fails to notice, now enrapt in his own comfortable being.*)

Being in love has made a new man of me!

(*Leaning stiffly forward, clutching the arm of the sofa,* LAURA *struggles visibly with her storm. But* JIM *is oblivious, she is a long way off.*)

The power of love is really pretty tremendous!

Love is something that—changes the whole world, Laura!

(*The storm abates a little and* LAURA *leans back. He notices her again.*)

It happened that Betty's aunt took sick, she got a wire and had to go to Centralia. So Tom —when he asked me to dinner—I naturally just accepted the invitation, not knowing that you—that he—that I—

(*He stops awkwardly.*)

Huh—I'm a stumble-john!

(*He flops back on the sofa.*)

(*The holy candles in the altar of* LAURA's *face have been snuffed out. There is a look of almost infinite desolation.*)

(JIM *glances at her uneasily.*)

I wish that you would—say something. (*She bites her lip which was trembling and then bravely smiles. She opens her hand again on*

the broken glass ornament. Then she gently takes his hand and raises it level with her own. She carefully places the unicorn in the palm of his hand, then pushes his fingers closed upon it.) What are you—doing that for? You want me to have him?—Laura? (*She nods.*) What for?

LAURA. A—souvenir . . .

(*She rises unsteadily and crouches beside the victrola to wind it up.*)

(LEGEND ON SCREEN: *"Things have a way of turning out so badly!"*)

(OR IMAGE: *"Gentleman caller waving good-bye!—gaily."*)

(*At this moment* AMANDA *rushes brightly back in the front room. She bears a pitcher of fruit punch in an old-fashioned cut-glass pitcher and a plate of macaroons. The plate has a gold border and poppies painted on it.*)

AMANDA. Well, well, well! Isn't the air delightful after the shower?

I've made you children a little liquid refreshment.

(*Turns gaily to the gentleman caller.*)

Jim, do you know that song about lemonade?

"Lemonade, lemonade
Made in the shade and stirred with a spade—
Good enough for any old maid!"

JIM (*uneasily*). Ha-ha! No—I never heard it.

AMANDA. Why, Laura! You look so serious!

JIM. We were having a serious conversation.

AMANDA. Good! Now you're better acquainted!

JIM (*uncertainly*). Ha-ha! Yes.

AMANDA. You modern young people are much more serious-minded than my generation. I was so gay as a girl!

JIM. You haven't changed, Mrs. Wingfield.

AMANDA. Tonight I'm rejuvenated! The gaiety of the occasion, Mr. O'Connor!

(*She tosses her head with a peal of laughter. Spills lemonade.*)

Oooo! I'm baptizing myself!

JIM. Here—let me—

AMANDA (*setting the pitcher down*). There

now. I discovered we had some maraschino cherries. I dumped them in, juice and all!

JIM. You shouldn't have gone to that trouble, Mrs. Wingfield.

AMANDA. Trouble, trouble? Why, it was loads of fun!

Didn't you hear me cutting up in the kitchen? I bet your ears were burning! I told Tom how outdone with him I was for keeping you to himself so long a time! He should have brought you over much, much sooner! Well, now that you've found your way, I want you to be a very frequent caller! Not just occasional but all the time.

Oh, we're going to have a lot of gay times together! I see them coming!

Mmm, just breathe that air! So fresh, and the moon's so pretty!

I'll skip back out—I know where my place is when young folks are having a—serious conversation!

JIM. Oh, don't go out, Mrs. Wingfield. The fact of the matter is I've got to be going.

AMANDA. Going, now? You're joking! Why, it's only the shank of the evening, Mr. O'Connor!

JIM. Well, you know how it is.

AMANDA. You mean you're a young workingman and have to keep workingmen's hours. We'll let you off early tonight. But only on the condition that next time you stay later.

What's the best night for you? Isn't Saturday night the best night for you workingmen?

JIM. I have a couple of time-clocks to punch, Mrs. Wingfield. One at morning, another one at night!

AMANDA. My, but you *are* ambitious! You work at night, too?

JIM. No, Ma'am, not work but—Betty! (*He crosses deliberately to pick up his hat. The band at the Paradise Dance Hall goes into a tender waltz.*)

AMANDA. Betty? Betty? Who's—Betty!

(*There is an ominous cracking sound in the sky.*)

JIM. Oh, just a girl. The girl I go steady with! (*He smiles charmingly. The sky falls.*)

(LEGEND: "The Sky Falls.")

AMANDA (*a long-drawn exhalation*). Ohhhh ...Is it a serious romance, Mr. O'Connor?

JIM. We're going to be married the second Sunday in June.

AMANDA. Ohhhh—how nice!

Tom didn't mention that you were engaged to be married.

JIM. The cat's not out of the bag at the warehouse yet.

You know how they are. They call you Romeo and stuff like that.

(*He stops at the oval mirror to put on his hat. He carefully shapes the brim and the crown to give a discreetly dashing effect.*)

It's been a wonderful evening, Mrs. Wingfield. I guess this is what they mean by Southern hospitality.

AMANDA. It really wasn't anything at all.

JIM. I hope it don't seem like I'm rushing off. But I promised Betty I'd pick her up at the Wabash depot, an' by the time I get my jalopy down there her train'll be in. Some women are pretty upset if you keep 'em waiting.

AMANDA. Yes, I know— The tyranny of women!

(*Extends her hand.*)

Good-bye, Mr. O'Connor.

I wish you luck—and happiness—and success! All three of them, and so does Laura!—Don't you, Laura?

LAURA. Yes!

JIM (*taking her hand*). Good-bye, Laura. I'm certainly going to treasure that souvenir. And don't you forget the good advice I gave you.

(*Raises his voice to a cheery shout.*)

So long, Shakespeare!

Thanks again, ladies— Good night!

(*He grins and ducks jauntily out.*)

(*Still bravely grimacing,* AMANDA *closes the door on the gentleman caller. Then she turns back to the room with a puzzled expression. She and* LAURA *don't dare to face each other.* LAURA *crouches beside the victrola to wind it.*)

AMANDA (*faintly*). Things have a way of turning out so badly.

I don't believe that I would play the victrola.

Well, well—well—

Our gentleman caller was engaged to be married!

Tom!

TOM (*from back*). Yes, Mother?

AMANDA. Come in here a minute. I want to tell you something awfully funny.

TOM (*enters with macaroon and a glass of the lemonade*). Has the gentleman caller gotten away already?

AMANDA. The gentleman caller has made an early departure.

What a wonderful joke you played on us!

TOM. How do you mean?

AMANDA. You didn't mention that he was engaged to be married.

TOM. Jim? Engaged?

AMANDA. That's what he just informed us.

TOM. I'll be jiggered! I didn't know about that.

AMANDA. That seems very peculiar.

TOM. What's peculiar about it?

AMANDA. Didn't you call him your best friend down at the warehouse?

TOM. He is, but how did I know?

AMANDA. It seems extremely peculiar that you wouldn't know your best friend was going to be married!

TOM. The warehouse is where I work, not where I know things about people!

AMANDA. You don't know things anywhere! You live in a dream; you manufacture illusions!

(*He crosses to door.*)

Where are you going?

TOM. I'm going to the movies.

AMANDA. That's right, now that you've had us make such fools of ourselves. The effort, the preparations, all the expense! The new floor lamp, the rug, the clothes for Laura! All for what? To entertain some other girl's fiancé!

Go to the movies, go! Don't think about us, a mother deserted, an unmarried sister who's crippled and has no job! Don't let anything interfere with your selfish pleasure!

Just go, go, go—to the movies!

TOM. All right, I will! The more you shout about my selfishness to me the quicker I'll go, and I won't go to the movies!

AMANDA. Go, then! Then go to the moon—you selfish dreamer!

(TOM *smashes his glass on the floor. He plunges out on the fire escape, slamming the door.* LAURA *screams—cut by door.*)

(*Dance-hall music up.* TOM *goes to the rail and grips it desperately, lifting his face in the chill white moonlight penetrating the narrow abyss of the alley.*)

(LEGEND ON SCREEN: *"And so Goodbye...."*)

(TOM's *closing speech is timed with the interior pantomime. The interior scene is played as though viewed through soundproof glass.* AMANDA *appears to be making a comforting speech to* LAURA *who is huddled upon the sofa. Now that we cannot hear the mother's speech, her silliness is gone and she has dignity and tragic beauty.* LAURA's *dark hair hides her face until at the end of the speech she lifts it to smile at her mother.* AMANDA's *gestures are slow and graceful, almost dance-like, as she comforts the daughter. At the end of her speech she glances a moment at the father's picture —then withdraws through the portieres. At close of* TOM's *speech,* LAURA *blows out the candles, ending the play.*)

TOM. I didn't go to the moon, I went much further—for time is the longest distance between two places—

Not long after that I was fired for writing a poem on the lid of a shoe-box.

I left Saint Louis. I descended the steps of this fire escape for a last time and followed, from then on, in my father's footsteps, attempting to find in motion what was lost in space—

I traveled around a great deal. The cities swept about me like dead leaves, leaves that were brightly colored but torn away from the branches.

I would have stopped, but I was pursued by something.

It always came upon me unawares, taking me altogether by surprise. Perhaps it was a familiar bit of music. Perhaps it was only a piece of transparent glass—

Perhaps I am walking along a street at night, in some strange city, before I have found companions. I pass the lighted window of a shop where perfume is sold. The window is filled with pieces of colored glass, tiny transparent bottles in delicate colors, like bits of a shattered rainbow.

Then all at once my sister touches my shoulder. I turn around and look into her eyes . . .

Oh, Laura, Laura, I tried to leave you behind me, but I am more faithful than I intended to be!

I reach for a cigarette, I cross the street, I run into the movies or a bar, I buy a drink, I speak to the nearest stranger—anything that can blow your candles out!

(LAURA *bends over the candles.*)
—for nowadays the world is lit by lightning! Blow out your candles, Laura—and so goodbye. . . .

(*She blows the candles out.*)
THE SCENE DISSOLVES

 TO INCREASE UNDERSTANDING
Part II, Scenes 6 and 7

1. Explain how Laura feels and why she reacts as she does at each of the following points: (*a*) her mother tells her to let Jim in; (*b*) she starts to join Jim and the family at dinner; (*c*) Jim joins Laura in the parlor; (*d*) Jim dances with her and kisses her; (*e*) Jim explains that he is engaged.

2. Describe Jim O'Connor, paying particular attention to: (*a*) Tom's description of him (page 724, column 1, paragraph 8) as "an emissary from a world of reality that we were somehow set apart from"; (*b*) Jim's reaction to Amanda; (*c*) his view of himself; (*d*) his reasons for liking Tom and Laura; (*e*) the fairness of his treatment of Laura.

3. (*a*) What is Amanda's reaction to the failure of her plan? (*b*) How does this affect your attitude toward her?

4. Why has Laura's image haunted Tom since his leaving home?

The Play in Review

1. In the final part of the play the dramatist usually presents the main characters in a climactic situation. This situation is one in which he can best reveal the strength and weakness of the characters and of their ways of looking at things. It is here that the author's judgment is fully revealed. In this play Jim's visit brings about the climactic situation. Because he is an up-and-coming employee of the shoe company, because Laura was in love with him at school, and because he is the "gentleman caller," Jim represents a typically threatening situation to each of the other characters. Explain exactly how Jim's visit to the Wingfield home brings about a situation that is trying to (*a*) Tom, (*b*) Laura, and (*c*) Amanda.

2. Williams has said that what happens to a person is not so important as the attitude with which he meets it. (*a*) How does each character react to the threat that Jim represents—to what extent does each retreat into his private world, to what extent does each try to face the situation realistically? (*b*) What attitude does the author communicate toward the reaction of each character (including Jim)? To what extent does he make each character's reaction seem (1) blameworthy, (2) pitiable, (3) sympathetic, (4) laudable?

3. Discuss the function of the following symbols, emphasizing what each shows about a character or characters, their problems, and the author's attitude toward them.
(*a*) Amanda's dress
(*b*) The glass menagerie
(*c*) The candelabrum and its history
(*d*) Blue roses

THE LARGER VIEW

In the introduction to this chapter (page 706) you studied some of the typical features of realist plays and some of the means that were used in antirealist plays to achieve a wider range of expression.

1. In writing *Ile* did O'Neill use mainly techniques associated with realist drama or antirealist drama? Justify your answer by considering specifically (*a*) the setting, (*b*) the kind of speech used by the characters, (*c*) the extent to which the characters observe the imaginary "fourth wall" between them and the audience, (*d*) lighting, (*e*) time and place sequence (see pages 708 and 741).

2. (*a*) What realistic techniques does Williams use in *The Glass Menagerie*? What nonrealist techniques does he use? (*b*) What effect do the realist techniques have on the tone of the play? What effect do the nonrealist techniques have? (*c*) What is the effect of combining realist and nonrealist techniques in the same play?

BIBLIOGRAPHY

ANDERSON, MAXWELL, *Eleven Verse Plays, 1929-1939*. (Harcourt) The fine poetry combined with the dramatic action of these plays will provide rewarding reading for the discriminating student.

CERF, BENNETT, and VAN H. CARTMELL, (editors), *Sixteen Famous American Plays*. (Modern Library) The names of the authors of these plays — Marc Connelly, Eugene O'Neill, Robert Sherwood, Thornton Wilder, and others—read like a roll call of the most prominent modern American dramatists. The plays are worthy of the playwrights.

CONNELLY, MARCUS, *Green Pastures*. (••Rinehart) This great classic of the American stage presents a Negro interpretation of the Bible; it shows God's dealing with His sinning and suffering earth-people from the creation to the redemption.

GOODRICH, FRANCES, and ALBERT HACKET, *Diary of Ann Frank*. (Random) The horrors of war as seen through the naïve and hopeful eyes of a fifteen-year-old girl and recorded in her diary are here turned into a tense and forceful drama.

HART, MOSS, and GEORGE KAUFMAN, *Six Plays*. (Modern Library) Here are six hilarious comedies by a famous team of collaborators. Be sure to read the very funny *You Can't Take It with You* and the equally amusing *The Man Who Came to Dinner*.

MAC LEISH, ARCHIBALD, *J. B.* (Houghton •Sentry) This discussion of good and evil is a modern version of the book of Job. Written in verse, it is a highly intelligent and moving play.

MILLER, ARTHUR, *The Crucible*. (•Bantam) Children's lies spread until a whole town becomes aroused and nineteen men and women go to the gallows for being possessed by the devil in this tense drama about the Puritan purge of witchcraft.

O'NEILL, EUGENE, *Nine Plays*. (Modern Library) The mature student will find extremely absorbing reading in these plays which O'Neill chose as being representative of his best work.

PATRICK, JOHN, and VERN SNEIDER, *Teahouse of the August Moon*. (Putnam) This Pulitzer prize-winning play handles the problems U.S. occupation troops faced in trying to introduce democracy into Okinawa. The play, an excellent blending of comedy and satire, is highly entertaining.

RODGERS, RICHARD, and OSCAR HAMMERSTEIN II, *Six Plays*. (Modern Library) The Rodgers and Hammerstein name on a musical is assurance of good entertainment. This enjoyable collection includes such famous plays as *Oklahoma!* and *South Pacific*.

SCHARY, DORE, *Sunrise at Campobello*. (Random •Signet) The courage and stamina of Franklin Delano Roosevelt during his bout with polio are shown in this fine play.

SHERWOOD, ROBERT, *Abe Lincoln in Illinois*. (Scribner) The critical years of Lincoln's early manhood from his legendary meeting with Ann Rutledge up to the moment of his election as President are told in this great American drama.

VAN DRUTEN, JOHN, *I Remember Mama*. (Harcourt) Humor and pathos abound in this fond recollection of Mama and her efforts to bring up the family.

WILDER, THORNTON, *Three Plays*. (Harper) Included in this book are *Our Town*, a deeply moving study of life in a small New England community; *The Skin of Our Teeth*, a fantastic comedy about a family who manages to survive the world upheavals from prehistoric times until the present; and *The Matchmaker*, an amusing but understanding look at a spinster's efforts to find a husband.

WOUK, HERMAN, *The Caine Mutiny Court-Martial*. (Doubleday) This powerful psychological drama tells of court-martial proceedings against a young lieutenant who relieved his captain of command in the midst of a harrowing typhoon on the grounds that he was directing the ship and its crew to destruction.

•paperback only ••paperback and hardcover

Composition Guide

Don Otto

The purpose of this composition guide is to help you develop skill in handling various types of writing. And since the authors you are studying in this textbook are all masters of the techniques of writing, it seems only sensible to learn from the models they furnish whenever possible.

This composition guide contains sixteen lessons, each of which is divided into two assignments. Many of the lessons also contain a third optional assignment for ambitious students or students particularly interested in writing. In most lessons Assignment 1 is for a short paper ranging from one to three paragraphs; Assignment 2 calls for a longer paper of from 300 to 500 words. Lesson Fifteen lists ideas for a research paper. Since in the greater number of lessons both the first and second assignments cover the same type of writing, it is possible to use only one part of a lesson without altogether omitting practice in a particular area of writing if time does not permit working out all the compositions suggested.

The lessons make use of the material in the textbook both in the type of writing practice offered and in the suggestions for compositions. For example, the lesson on writing the formal essay is planned to follow the reading of Emerson's "Self-Reliance." Thus when you are asked to write a formal essay, you will have the form clearly in mind from studying one. And the subjects about which you are asked to write will draw on the information you have gained in reading.

Printed below are the titles of the lessons in the composition guide and the chapters in the text which they are designed to accompany.

LESSON ONE: Sentence Variety

ASSIGNMENT 1. *Based on "Early Marriage" and "Crossing the Great Salt Desert," pages 5-19.*

As competent professional writers, Bernard De Voto and Conrad Richter consciously avoid monotony through the use of variety in sentence structure. Not only do they vary the lengths of sentences, but they also use variation in sentence word order. In addition to achieving interesting, effective rhythmic patterns by such methods, the writers are able to place just the right emphasis on important ideas.

A study of the opening paragraphs of "Early Marriage" and "Crossing the Great Salt Desert" will reveal the skillful use these writers have made of normal and inverted word order in sentences. One paragraph may begin with a sentence in normal word order; the next paragraph may open with words in an inverted order. Within the sentence patterns of each paragraph, added shifting of structure may occur. The rhythmic effect is calculated and successful.

Consult your language text for more information about sentence word order and sentence variety. When you have done so, choose one of the statements below as a topic sentence and develop it into a good paragraph (one hundred words or more) in which you use a variety of word orders.

1. Asa Putman lived a dangerous life.
2. Religion was a part of Nancy Belle's strength.
3. The Donner party had problems that the modern motorist does not have to face.
4. Morale was the key to the success or failure of a wagon train.
5. When circumstances turn against them, only the truly heroic fail to seek a scapegoat.
6. Danger and difficulty promote early maturity.

ASSIGNMENT 2. *Based on "Auto Wreck," "The Enemy," "The Sculptor's Funeral," "Court-Martial," pages 20-51.*

Good writers pay close attention to sentence length in developing rhythmic patterns. Some of the free rhythms of such poems as Shapiro's "Auto Wreck" and Warren's "Court-Martial" derive from the lengths of thought units in the poems. Prose writers like Pearl Buck and Willa Cather develop rhythms through variation in the length of both sentences and paragraphs. For instance, the numbers below indicate the word counts in sentences in the opening paragraphs of Buck's "The Enemy."

Paragraph 1 (four sentences): 22-20-29-39
Paragraph 2 (one sentence): 10
Paragraph 3 (three sentences): 6-5-7
Paragraph 4 (six sentences): 35-10-21-26-22-37

If you compare the opening paragraphs of "The Sculptor's Funeral" with the patterns above, you can see the skill of two of America's finest women writers in the use of prose patterns.

Beginning with one of the topic sentences that follow, develop an opening paragraph and two or three additional paragraphs, providing your own topic sentences for the other paragraphs if they need them. Remember to use variety in both sentence and paragraph length and in sentence word order. Use such patterns to emphasize dramatic or climactic points in your essay.

1. Each of us is guilty when another traffic victim dies.
2. A physician must place the welfare of the sick before all else.
3. Sadao was (was not) guilty of treason.
4. Jim Laird's idea of success differed from that of his fellow townsmen.
5. Depending on his purpose, a guerrilla may be regarded with favor or censure.

Can you think of illustrations for these sentences from the literature that you have read?

OPTIONAL ASSIGNMENT

This is the time to begin keeping a "writer's notebook," jottings of ideas that may later be expanded into poems, essays, articles, short stories, or research papers.

Later this year you may be assigned a research report on literature. Begin now to compile a list of authors in whom you might be interested. When you discover a problem that interests you, write a summary of it in your notebook for future reference. State the question involved and indicate some possible sources of answers. Such information can be of real help when you are asked to choose a research topic.

LESSON TWO: Emphasizing Important Ideas

ASSIGNMENT 1. *Based on "Patterns," "The Oyster and the Pearl," "One Star Fell and Another," pages 52-69.*

Amy Lowell's "Patterns" suggests among other things that much of life is made up of patterns. Certainly planned patterns are important in good writing. A writer needs to know how to use them for variety, for emphasis, for rhythmic effects.

The most important job of prose patterns is to give emphasis to principal thoughts. A writer may choose to draw the reader's particular attention to a single statement by placing it by itself in a short, simple sentence. Again, he may link several ideas together in a longer sentence, either compound or complex in structure. Such longer combinations may join closely related independent clauses, subordinate (dependent) clauses, phrases, and single words. (You may need to review the meanings of some of these terms in your language text before working with them.) By means of the many structural possibilities available to him, the writer is able to give varying degrees of emphasis to ideas.

Review the "Better Reading" article on theme (page 67). Then practice your skill at emphasizing important ideas and subordinating less important ones by writing a paragraph on one of the topics listed below. Remember to use variety in sentence structure. Make up your own topic sentence.

1. The theme of "The Oyster and the Pearl."
2. The theme of "Patterns."
3. The theme of "One Star Fell and Another."
4. The theme of a novel read outside of class.
5. The "theme" of a personal experience. (*What meaning did a memorable experience in your own life have for you, beyond the incidents and place and people involved? You can "read" meaning into personal experiences as well as into stories and poems.*)

ASSIGNMENT 2. *Based on "The Hack Driver" and "Paul Revere and the Alarum," pages 71-87.*

Prose rhythms become most evident when an article is read aloud. Many writers read their work aloud a number of times to make sure that the total effect of sentence patterns and paragraphing is just right. The prepared speech, then, is obviously a good form in which to practice rhythmic effects, long and short sentences, normal and inverted word order, subordination and emphasis, and so forth.

After reviewing the implications of "The Hack Driver," "Paul Revere and the Alarum," and other selections you have read, you should have material for a good short talk on one of the topics below. Reduce the scope of the topic, if you wish. Write a draft of your talk—it should be no longer than three to five paragraphs. Pay particular attention to the way your sentences sound when spoken. Read your talk over often enough that a few notes will be all the prompting you need when you give your talk before the class.

1. Beware of Hack Drivers! (And similar confidence men!)
2. Flattery Is Youth's Temptation.
3. Paul Revere's Ride Is an Example for Modern Youth.
4. Our Generation Needs the Spirit of '75.
5. There Are Still Pearls in Oysters.

OPTIONAL ASSIGNMENT

Many writers keep notebooks or journals in which they record brief descriptions of people and places and summaries of incidents which they may use later. However disguised they may be when they appear in print, at least some of the elements of most good stories stem from real life.

In your writer's notebook include a separate section for notes suggesting the germs of essays, poems, and short stories. While the subject of *theme* is fresh in your mind, record short summaries of incidents from your own life or from the lives of those around you that might be used to illustrate certain themes. Follow the summary with a brief statement of the meaning each of these incidents has left in your consciousness. Such a list of creative ideas is sure to be useful later this year, when, perhaps, leafing through your notebook will bring back a significant incident that has slipped your memory.

LESSON THREE: Exposition

ASSIGNMENT 1. *Based on biographies of and selections by William Byrd and Jonathan Edwards, pages 100-114.*

The men of colonial times wrote for different purposes than did Conrad Richter, Sinclair Lewis, Pearl Buck, and other twentieth-century writers you studied in the preceding chapter. William Byrd, like many other writers of early America, wrote principally to give information about life in a new land. In *A Progress to the Mines* and *History of the Dividing Line*, as well as in his diaries, he explains in great detail various aspects of the country, the inhabitants, and the way of life. Writing of this type is often referred to as *exposition*.

Exposition is simply an explanation of something or a presentation of information about a subject. It is usually distinguished from such other broad classifications of nonfiction as *narrative, description,* and *argument* (or *persuasion*). In actual practice, however, these four types of writing may appear in combination in a single essay. Your composition text explains these types of writing more fully.

The best way to attack writing an expository essay is to jot down notes that will suggest more ideas than you will need to use. Then organize these notes into an outline. If the first outline does not accomplish your aim in writing, revise it. It takes far less time to revise an outline than to make several futile attempts at writing the entire composition without a satisfactory plan.

Suppose you are writing an exposition or analysis of a character typical of a particular group or profession. Your first job would be to organize your notes in an outline. Before writing your outline, it would be wise to review in your composition text the way a good outline is constructed. Your completed outline might include the following main and subordinate points:

The Prospector

I. The most eccentric, strangely motivated, tenacious individual in American history was the prospector. (*The remainder of the introduction would explain just what kind of prospector you are writing about and what periods of history saw his development.*)

II. A. In appearance he was often something quite apart from the crowd. (*In this paragraph you would present details about his appearance, selecting typical characteristics.*)

B. The reasons for his choice of life were various. (*In this paragraph you would explain his motivation, citing different possible reasons for his choice of life.*)

C. His most distinguishing characteristic was his tenacity. (*You would cite examples of lengths to which a prospector might go in order to pursue his goal.*)

III. Although the prospector led no armies and governed no territories, he was an important phenomenon in American history. (*In your conclusion you would assess the importance of the prospector in history.*)

Using the outline above as a guide, write a composition of from three to five paragraphs on one of the following topics:

1. A Typical Virginia Planter.
2. A Puritan Minister.
3. A Puritan Man (or Woman).

ASSIGNMENT 2. *Based on "Planters and Puritans," pages 96-127.*

Since an expository article may require far more information than your memory has retained from past reading and study, you will need to consult reference books in preparing to write an article of this type. In order to handle properly the mass of information you obtain from such sources, you will find it worth while to use a more complex outline than that given in the previous assignment. Your composition text supplies detailed information on how to construct such an outline as well as information on writing longer themes.

After you have studied these references, choose one of the topics listed below as the subject for a theme of from 300 to 500 words. Consult as many sources as necessary. Then select the most significant facts and construct an outline, arranging topics in logical order. Use the outline as a guide in writing your paper.

1. The Causes of Migration to America.
2. The Hardships of Colonial Life.
3. How Puritan Religious Ideas Affected Everyday Life.
4. How Frontier Americans Dealt with Indians.

LESSON FOUR: Argument

ASSIGNMENT 1. *Based on biography of and selections by Franklin, pages 131-146.*

Few writers have surpassed Benjamin Franklin in the art of *argument*, or *persuasion*. He realized the power of an anecdote to put across a philosophical concept; and in his rôle of commonsense philosopher he often used an everyday experience to explain his ideas. Thus in "The Whistle" he used analogy to argue that people often pay an exorbitant price for something that momentarily seems desirable.

Can you use an anecdote, either real or imaginary, to defend a point of view? Choose one of the statements below, or propose one of your own, and use an anecdote to persuade the reader of the truth of the statement. You may be able to do this in a single paragraph; in any case, confine your anecdote to no more than three or four short paragraphs. Make sure the anecdote you choose is really pertinent to the statement you are defending. Unless the application of the anecdote is obvious, your argument may not be convincing.

1. A "whistle" is sometimes worth any price. (*Can you think of a personal experience that would seem to prove this statement? Franklin found one to show the opposite to be true.*)
2. My pride exacts high taxes from me. (*Tell the story of an instance in your own life in which you "paid" for your pride.*)
3. Prosperity can bring corruption. (*Can you use an anecdote to demonstrate this possibility?*)
4. Adolescents are sometimes more dependable than adults. (*Not every adult would accept this statement. Can you find a true story to offer as evidence?*)
5. Freedom automatically carries with it responsibilities. (*Can you tell a story illustrating the relationship between freedom and responsibility?*)

ASSIGNMENT 2. *Based on "Founders of the Nation," pages 128-163.*

Obviously you would seldom persuade anyone of the merit of your opinion on any subject if you were to offer only a single argument. An analogy may present your side of the case in a clear light, but you need other forms of persuasion if you are to win your case. You may use arguments from authority, arguments from logic, arguments from statistics or other scientific results, or arguments from single examples. Decide how each of these types of persuasion might be used most effectively. Remember that you seldom have space to present all the evidence in support of a good thesis; your job is to list all you can find, then select for use in your paper the evidence that is most persuasive. Outline before you write:

I.   State your thesis or position and, if necessary, define your terms.
II. Present your arguments in separate paragraphs according to kind, for example:
     A. Cite authorities who agree with you.
     B. Furnish statistical or scientific evidence and interpret its meaning for your position.
     C. Point out the logic of your case and the illogic of the alternative points of view.
     D. Cite in some detail a particularly vivid example or anecdote to support your position.
III. Summarize your most significant arguments in one paragraph.
IV. Restate your thesis and suggest its implications for the reader.

Choose one of the statements below or form one of your own based on the literature you have been studying and write a theme of 300 to 500 words that attempts to prove the truth of the statement.

1. A young nation should avoid foreign alliances until it is strong and secure in its government.
2. A modern nation, however new and small, must participate in world affairs.
3. All men are (are not) created equal.
4. It is the duty of each citizen to guard against the establishment of despotism.
5. "Common sense" is not the same for all men.

In concentrating your attention on planning and outlining, be careful not to neglect sentence variety and precise language in your essay. You will need to revise carefully, checking all mechanical problems in your language text and in your dictionary.

LESSON FIVE: Description

ASSIGNMENT 1. *Based on selections by Irving and Bryant, pages 169-194.*

Much of writing involves the description of objects, people, places, or ideas. The reader often is unaware of the multiple rôle description plays in creating excitement, foreshadowing significant action, and establishing an attitude toward various characters. The article on setting (page 55) summarizes the importance of description in fictional writing.

Choose one of the following scenes and describe it in a paragraph as you recall it from your reading. Do not open your book until you have finished writing.

1. The house and farm of Tom Walker.
2. The place where Tom Walker met Old Scratch.
3. Evening at the Camp of the Wild Horse.
4. The waterfowl, as seen by Bryant.

When you have finished writing, compare the details of your description with those presented by the author. Did you supply details that did not exist in the original? Did you omit significant elements? How does your description compare with the author's in style, language, unity, and vividness?

ASSIGNMENT 2. *Based on selections by Cooper and Poe, pages 198-223.*

Occasionally description is used to create a mood that dominates an entire piece of literature. In Poe's "Masque of the Red Death" description plays such an important part that the action seems minor; yet the description makes the action, when it does come, highly effective. In "The Purloined Letter" Poe's detailed description of the Prefect's examination of a room is essential to understanding his shortcomings as a detective. Cooper used description to acquaint readers in the towns along the seaboard with the magnificent wilderness in which Deerslayer adventured.

List several ideas that might serve as settings for short stories—settings that will create moods and will almost establish plots for any characters that wander into them. Choose settings with

which you are actually familiar. After you have recalled details about each of the settings on your list, choose the one you believe would be most interesting as the background for a short story. Review in your composition text the various ways of arranging details in descriptive paragraphs. Then, in three or four paragraphs or fewer, write your description, including concrete details that suggest the atmosphere your story should have. Read your paper to your classmates to see whether they obtain from it the same feeling of mood and atmosphere that you recall from actually having been on the scene.

OPTIONAL ASSIGNMENT

You may wish to try capturing a mood in another description of a scene. Think of an exciting event in your life that was fraught with emotion. A graduation, a party, an accident, or a moment of sorrow might be used. Recall the specific impressions made on you by remembered details—a blood stain in the street, bright lights glaring on the stage, an advertising sign or another object that seemed out of place in the surrounding atmosphere. Imagine that you are writing a short story built around such a happening; assume that you have introduced your principal character and his problem. Now describe that scene as your chief character would have been aware of it, searching out the details that would leave the sharpest impression on him at the time. Before beginning your description, make notes and arrange them in outline form. The following suggestions may help you:

I. Present your character's first impression of the scene.
II. Describe objects and details that catch his attention during the event in the order in which he notices them.
III. Summarize the total impression of the scene.

OPTIONAL ASSIGNMENT

You may wish to complete a short story from one of the descriptions you have written. If you don't have time to write the complete story, jot down in an outline the form the plot will take. Such a brief will help you finish the story later.

LESSON SIX: The Formal Essay

ASSIGNMENT 1. *Based on selections by Thoreau and Emerson, pages 232-266.*

Ralph Waldo Emerson stands high among writers of the formal essay in the United States. His essays are tightly organized; one idea develops logically from another; the tone is serious. Although most of Emerson's essays, like "Self-Reliance," are long, this is not a requisite of the formal essay. The great English essayist Francis Bacon often compressed his thoughts on a subject into a single idea-packed paragraph.

Review the "Better Reading" article on the essay on page 245. Then write a single paragraph developing the idea expressed in one of the following quotations:

1. We do not ride on the railroad; it rides upon us (Thoreau, *Walden*, page 237).
2. They only can force me who obey a higher law than I (Thoreau, "Civil Disobedience," page 242).
3. Nothing is at last sacred but the integrity of your own mind (Emerson, "Self-Reliance," page 252).
4. An institution is the lengthened shadow of one man (Emerson, "Self-Reliance," page 255).
5. . . . if eyes were made for seeing,
   Then Beauty is its own excuse for being (Emerson, "The Rhodora," page 265).
6. All are needed by each one;
   Nothing is fair or good alone (Emerson, "Each and All," page 265).

ASSIGNMENT 2. *Based on prose by Thoreau and Emerson, poetry by Longfellow and Holmes, pages 232-277.*

An outline is essential for logical organization in a longer formal essay. Not only does it make tight organizational patterns possible; it also helps the writer apportion the space to be devoted to various aspects of the subject. For example, an essay on the topic "Courage" may be a challenge to a writer who has never before written 500 words on a single subject. The outline permits him to divide this topic into five or more subtopics; each of these subtopics can then be approached almost as though it were a separate assignment.

If you are given a choice of length in writing a paper, you may find it better not to decide how long your paper is to be until you see how the theme naturally develops. On college writing assignments and on composition examinations, however, you will seldom have a choice of length. It will then be your job to plan your paper to fit definite wordage requirements.

Each of the topics below is given in the form of a question. Your essay will be the answer to the question. Choose a topic in which you are interested, study the information necessary, and write a formal essay of from 300 to 500 words. Breaking your big topic into little topics and treating each of these as a separate but related problem will make your job relatively simple. This technique will also be useful in developing even longer papers—from 1000 to 5000 words, for instance. Practice in the technique now will help you in writing a research paper later.

1. Are Thoreau's arguments in "Civil Disobedience" logically developed? (*Use concrete examples from the essay to prove your point.*)
2. What similarities of idea, either stated or implied, can be noted in the works of Thoreau and Emerson? (*Review the material in the text; make notes as you read. Preparatory to making your outline, organize the material according to idea.*)
3. In the selections thus far studied in "America's Golden Day" what indications are there that the writers were familiar with literature and legend of the past? (*Review material in the text, make notes as you read, then organize examples into groups before outlining and writing.*)
4. Why is Longfellow considered a master of the sonnet? (*Study the sonnets in the text and, if possible, additional sonnets by Longfellow. Organize your material with regard to sonnet patterns, word choice, and development of ideas.*)

OPTIONAL ASSIGNMENT

You may wish to do some research to determine whether one of the topics above might be expanded to serve as a research paper. Make a preliminary outline of the subject now to help keep your ideas in mind.

LESSON SEVEN: The Informal Essay

ASSIGNMENT 1. *Based on selections in "America's Golden Day," exclusive of Hawthorne and Melville, pages 232-296.*

Like the man who was impressed to find he had been speaking prose, you may have been writing informal essays for years without being aware of it. In fact, the informal essay is the type of writing you have more reason to use than any other. A bit of reflection will tell you why.

The informal essay may be either humorous or serious, but it must be personal or subjective in approach. (See the "Better Reading" article on the essay, page 245.) Oliver Wendell Holmes was a master of the humorous essay. In "My Last Walk with the Schoolmistress" he exhibits the informality, the personal tone, the wealth of anecdote, and the sense of talking to the reader that characterize this form at its best.

You will find that the humorous essay challenges the writer to give most of his attention to qualities that make for entertainment: unusual approaches to subject matter, clever phrases, informal handling of anecdote and example. The personality of the writer is important; he must present those sides of his personality that would make him most interesting in conversation. And, as in conversation, the writer must make his "talk" attractive to the reader.

Remembering to concentrate on the personal point of view and to be as entertaining as possible, write an informal essay on one of the following topics. Limit yourself to three or four paragraphs.

1. My Experiences in Being Self-Reliant.
2. Snowstorms I Have Known.
3. Why I Stay Away from the Woods.
4. Uncivil Disobedience, and How I Was Punished.
5. The Battle of the Aunts, and Uncles.

You may use another topic of your own choosing, if you wish, but try to use some sort of reverse twist on an essay in your literature book.

ASSIGNMENT 2. *Based on selections in "America's Golden Day," pages 232-327.*

An informal essay, whether serious or humorous, reflects the personality of the writer. Oliver Wendell Holmes differed in manner from other informal essayists partly because he was a different person. Your informal essays will be more interesting if your personality shows through.

Listed below are several suggestions for informal essays. If you prefer, you may write on a subject of your own choosing. You may use either a humorous or a serious approach, but be consistent in your tone throughout the essay. Let your subject determine length.

1. My Impressions of the Sea at Night.
2. A "Last Leaf" I've Known Well.
3. The First Snow.
4. Reflections on "The Chambered Nautilus."
5. On Figureheads.
6. Sailing.

When you have completed your final draft, ask yourself whether your essay would really be interesting to someone else. Are the ideas clearly stated? Have you used vivid and concrete words? Do your sentences have variety? Is the tone sustained throughout? Does your personality give the essay individuality?

OPTIONAL ASSIGNMENT

Most good essays, whether formal or informal, depend a good deal for their interest on anecdotes and examples used to heighten the major points of the essays. Collect in your notebook a list of anecdotes that might be used for such a purpose. They will be helpful in future writing assignments when you are barren of ideas.

There are many essay and story contests open to high-school students. Your teacher probably has information about them. If you enjoy writing essays and short stories, a contest may be your chance to win for your school.

LESSON EIGHT: Interpreting Poetry

ASSIGNMENT 1. *Based on poetry by Whitman, pages 338-351.*

Probably the most basic form of evaluation of a poem is involved in answering the question, "What does this poem mean to me?" Just as the shell of a rocket would mean little to a savage in a land cut off from the modern world, so a poem may at first mean little to a reader who has never encountered such an object before. You, however, are not in the position of the hypothetical savage—you have encountered poetry before. Nevertheless, the surest way of finding out whether or not you really understand a poem is to write your own interpretation of it.

Choose a poem by Whitman, either one from your text that has been discussed in class or one that is new to you. Read the poem silently once or twice, then aloud a few times, trying to capture both the theme and the tone. Think about the poem, relating its statement to your own experience and reading. How would you communicate the idea developed in the poem?

Write a brief essay entitled "What (*Title of Poem*) Means to Me."

ASSIGNMENT 2. *Based on "When Lilacs Last in the Dooryard Bloomed" (page 341) and "Ode" (page 361).*

Whitman's "When Lilacs Last in the Dooryard Bloomed" is an elegy mourning the death of Lincoln; Timrod's "Ode" mourns the fallen heroes of the South. Although the poems are somewhat similar in certain aspects, a careful study will show that they differ in many ways.

In an essay of five or more paragraphs compare and contrast these two poems. You may use the following outline or another method of organization.

Paragraph 1. State your subject and define its limits.
Paragraph 2. Compare the two poems.
Paragraph 3. Contrast the poems in content.
Paragraph 4. Contrast the verse technique.
Paragraph 5. Summarize.

LESSON NINE: Description and Exposition

ASSIGNMENT 1. *Based on selections by Clemens, Harte, and Jewett, pages 377-420.*

Because Samuel Clemens had a seeing eye, a retentive memory, and a magnificent way with words, millions of people all over the world today have a vivid picture of how a Mississippi River town looked over a hundred years ago. Bret Harte in his stories of the gold rush may have heightened the drama and exaggerated the characters; but he did capture in words the flavor of the California gold-mining camps. Similarly, Sarah Orne Jewett in her quiet prose recorded the details of life in a remote part of Maine many years ago.

The area in which you live may not seem particularly interesting to you; but probably neither did Hannibal, Missouri, to the people living there a hundred years ago. Imagine a visitor from Norway or Italy or Brazil visiting your community. What features would probably catch his attention? Write a short composition describing as a local-color writer might do the noteworthy features of your community.

ASSIGNMENT 2. *Based on "New Outlooks," pages 372-440.*

Regional differences in the United States today are not so distinct as they were in the period of Clemens, Harte, and Lanier. Yet some distinctions remain. The climate, the physical features of the landscape, the size and national origins of the population, the principal industry, and other factors have their influence. For example, December recreation patterns in Minnesota may be quite different from those in California; social events may have different characteristics in a town of two thousand and a city of almost a million; Christmas customs in Massachusetts may differ from those in New Mexico. If you observe and reflect carefully, you can identify the regional differences characteristic of your area.

Prepare to write a paper of no more than 500 words on features which have shaped life in your section of the country. Before beginning to write, jot down notes and organize your material in outline form.

LESSON TEN: Short Story

ASSIGNMENT 1. *Based on selections by O. Henry, Sherwood Anderson, Ernest Hemingway, and Katherine Anne Porter, pages 447-473.*

A professional magazine writer once remarked that he spent more time in writing the first page of a short story than he gave to the rest of the piece. When you recall the many functions that the opening of a story must perform, you will understand his reasons.

Study carefully the first page or so of the short stories in this book by O. Henry, Sherwood Anderson, Ernest Hemingway, and Katherine Anne Porter. Each is a master of the technique of the short story, and each handles the short story in a different way. Yet at various points in the opening sections of the stories by these writers you will find one or more of the important characters introduced, the scene and time established, the mood suggested, and the problem of the chief character initiated. In the hands of a skillful writer such information is so subtly revealed that the reader is seldom aware of the pattern. Emphasis on different elements will differ from story to story, as in each case the author chooses a vital portion of the story's make-up for introductory emphasis. However, he presents all of the other necessary information early enough to alert the reader to the principal problem of the story.

In no more than three paragraphs write a good opening for a short story. In this space you should probably introduce the chief character (yourself with another name), explain the setting (a scene you know well), and what the chief character is about to do. Give the reader all he needs to know about the past and the personality of the chief character. Preferably, the reader should sympathize with the character's problem. Know in advance how the plot should be worked out, even if you do not intend to finish the story. The best story plots spring from problems that would naturally face the kind of character you are presenting. See whether your story beginning will cause readers to want to know what else happens in the story.

ASSIGNMENT 2. *Based on selections by O. Henry, Sherwood Anderson, Ernest Hemingway, Katherine Anne Porter, Thomas Wolfe, and John Steinbeck, pages 447-487.*

Your assignment now is to write a complete short story. You may use the opening you wrote for Assignment 1; if you prefer, choose another character, another situation, and write a new opening. You will invariably do a better job if you write about yourself (disguised) and your own problems rather than about an eighty-year-old Martian. How many real Martians have you known! Before you begin writing, fill in the following outline:

I. Opening (who, when, where, what problem, why).
II. Steps to solve problem.
   A. First Trial (how). Result: failure or partial failure.
   B. Second Trial (how). Result: failure or partial failure.
   C. Third Trial (how). Result: failure or partial failure.
   D. Fourth Trial (how). Result: probably success after a close scrape with failure.
III. Conclusion: what happens to everyone after final attempt succeeds in solving problem.

The outline above is one formula for writing a short story. Some of the best writers seldom use a formula, but most beginners are wise to use one. For information on how to construct dialogue, ways of describing characters, and other points, refer to your language text.

LESSON ELEVEN: Book Review

ASSIGNMENT 1. *Based on selections by Stephen Vincent Benét, James Thurber, and Irwin Shaw, pages 489-509.*

If you recall the article on the essay (page 245), you understand the difference between the informal and the formal essay. The same sort of difference generally exists between the major categories of book reviews or reports. One kind may deal almost exclusively with the reviewer's personal impressions of the book; the other will probably involve a systematic, detailed attempt to relate the various elements of the book to certain more or less objective standards for books of a particular type.

For an informal or impressionistic review, choose one of the novels you have read recently and jot down the characters, incidents, qualities, and impressions you remember best. If you have time, glance through the book again to verify your first impressions. Then arrange your thoughts according to the following outline:

I. State your impression of the total meaning of the book.
II. Cite the elements of writing that seemed to be most effective in producing your reactions. (*You might note a particular suggestion of character, a twist of plot, a setting establishing a mood, a believable presentation of a minor character.*)
III. Summarize the qualities of the book that seem best to you; mention elements that seem to be inadequately handled. (*What characters seem unbelievable, for instance; what scene seems a replay of a story you have read before?*) Then evaluate the author's degree of success or failure in satisfying you as a reader.

ASSIGNMENT 2. *Based on selections by Ray Bradbury, Eudora Welty, and William Faulkner, pages 511-529.*

The most formal kind of book report requires the writer to judge elements in the novel according to a set of standards for good novels. References will help you learn more about such standards; your reading experience with other novels will help if you have read critically. A formal book report will be a good proving ground for writing scientific studies and research papers.

The following outline may help you plan your book report. As you read it through now, try to decide what you would write for each item in the outline if you were reviewing Faulkner's "The Bear."

I. Introduction. (*Explain the title of the book, the name of the author and key facts about him, the type of book, when it was published, and other general comments.*)
II. Record your estimate of the success of the author in dealing with each of the following elements:
   A. Thesis. (*Is it clear and valid?*)
   B. Chief characters. (*Are they adequately presented and believably motivated?*)
   C. Setting. (*Is it important to the story? Is it effectively presented?*)
   D. Plot. (*Is it clear, believable, fresh, and pertinent to the thesis of the novel?*)
   E. Language. (*Is it fresh or trite? Are rhythms skillfully patterned? Does the style fit the story?*)
   F. Symbols. (*Are symbols a natural part of the story? Are they given adequate emphasis?*)
   G. Moral considerations. (*Is the author both honest and honorable? Does he exaggerate immoral situations for cheap effects?*)
III. Summarize your observations and evaluate the total effectiveness of the novel.
IV. Offer conclusions as to the merits of this novel, of the author, and of this kind of writing.

Using a pattern similar to that presented above, write a careful, objective report on a novel you have read. Adapt the individual items in the list to suit the novel and your own interests in the analysis of novels.

OPTIONAL ASSIGNMENT

You may decide later to study a single novelist or a school of novelists for your research paper. If you are inclined toward a paper of this type, it is wise to begin doing the necessary reading. A paper that requires the reading of several novels demands more time than some kinds of research papers. Keep careful notes as you read; this will cut later rereading to a minimum.

LESSON TWELVE: Paraphrase and Analysis

ASSIGNMENT 1. *Based on "Modern American Poetry," pages 540-571.*

There are different degrees in the understanding of a poem. We may grasp the general idea, we may be able to trace the poet's thought loosely as it is developed throughout a poem, or through study we may arrive at the meaning and importance in the poem of each single word. One of the best ways to uncover the deeper meanings of a poem and to appreciate the skill with which it is constructed is to write a *paraphrase*.

A paraphrase is a restatement of poetry (or of prose) in such a way that the meaning is retained while the diction and form are changed. Before beginning to write a paraphrase, read the poem several times to determine what central thought the lines convey. Then go through the poem line by line, restating in your own words the thought developed by the poet. Studying Paul Engle's introduction to the poetry chapter has doubtless made you aware that in modern poetry an idea is often suggested rather than clearly stated. Since a good paraphrase explains ideas that the poet merely implies, it involves interpretation. Remember, however, that for every expanded thought in your paraphrase you must be able to cite a specific reference in the poem.

Write a paraphrase of one of the poems accompanying Paul Engle's essay or of a poem in the section of the chapter entitled "First Voices." Don't be disappointed if your paraphrase, no matter how long you work on it, fails to convey all the meaning suggested by the poem. Certain qualities are always lost when poetry is "translated" into prose—this fact suggests one of the essential differences between poetry and prose.

ASSIGNMENT 2. *Based on "Modern American Poetry," pages 540-609.*

Paul Engle, in the introduction to this chapter, explains some of the ways in which modern poetry differs from poetry written in the past. He writes of the various techniques poets use, of differences in tone, and of the necessity to read between the lines. From a thoughtful reading of this essay you can learn not only that modern poetry is in several respects different from that of the past, but also that the poems of one poet may differ in many ways from those of another.

In "Salem" Robert Lowell relies heavily on symbols to explain the decline of the port from which the clipper ships sailed. Satire is the weapon Archibald MacLeish uses in "Brave New World" to mourn the eclipse of the ideals Jefferson stood for. Edna St. Vincent Millay in "Not in a Silver Casket Cool with Pearls" uses images to tell of love. Stephen Vincent Benét writes in "Robert E. Lee" of a great American. Poets differ in the subjects they write about, in the different ways they approach the same subject, in the techniques they use, and in the tone they establish.

Write a theme on one of the topics listed below, or, with your teacher's approval, select a topic of your own. Let the length of your paper be determined by your subject, but do not write over 500 words. Be sure to construct an outline before you begin writing.

1. The Poetry of _____. (*Do not write on this subject unless you have read quite a number of poems by the poet you choose. Consider typical subject matter, verse form, language, melody, tone, and any other aspects that seem significant.*)
2. Nature in Some Modern Poems. (*What is the function of nature in poems like Frost's "Birches" and "Stopping by Woods," Sara Teasdale's "Spring Night," E. E. Cummings' "Chanson Innocente," William Carlos Williams' "Spring and All," Randall Jarrell's "The Breath of Night," and others? Can you classify any of these as "nature" poems?*)
3. Analogy in Modern Poetry. (*Reread the article on analogy on page 579. Select and analyze other poems based on an analogy. Why is analogy very popular with modern poets?*)
4. An Analysis of Benét's Portrait of Robert E. Lee. (*Pick out and discuss important ideas Benét develops in describing the character of Lee. Give your own reaction to the soundness of Benét's conclusions.*)
5. Light Verse with a Purpose. (*What is behind Nash's "Laments for a Dying Language"? Is there any criticism of humankind in "archy hears from mars"? Is "The Perforated Spirit" anything more than pure fun? In what ways may light verse be serious?*)
6. The Poet and Society. (*What poems have you read in which the poet shows himself aware of problems facing the modern world? What is the poet's attitude?*)

LESSON THIRTEEN: Article and Essay

ASSIGNMENT 1. *Based on "The Three," "Knacks and Crafts," and "Your Oldest Heirlooms," pages 614-632.*

The "Better Reading" article on page 628 points up the fact that an article about an airplane need not be merely a random collection of facts. The skillful writer adds interest to facts by selection, by arrangement, and by the attitude he expresses toward the subject he is discussing. In "The Three," E. J. Kahn speaks with affection of a certain type of airplane. In "Knacks and Crafts," Paul Horgan extols the beauty and utility of the articles made by pioneer craftsmen. The very title of "Your Oldest Heirlooms" conveys W. L. White's feeling for the beauty of language.

Suppose you decide to write an article about the family car. There are certain facts that must be included, but it is not necessary to throw them all helter-skelter into the first paragraph. Glance again over the articles by E. J. Kahn, Paul Horgan, and W. L. White. How much of the article may be considered introduction? How rapidly are facts introduced? How soon does the tone make you aware of the author's attitude?

Using one of the articles in your text as a guide, plan an article on a subject with which you are acquainted from personal experience. Some topics are listed below, but you may prefer to write on another subject of the same type. Outline your paper carefully; eliminate facts that are not pertinent; arrange those you keep with unity and coherence in mind. Write only the first two or three paragraphs of the article, even if this is not enough space to finish your discussion. In this assignment the important consideration is not to cover the subject rapidly but to write a few well-planned paragraphs.

1. The Family Car.
2. The Car I Would Like to Buy.
3. Our Street.
4. My Grandmother's Heirlooms.
5. Our Kitchen.
6. Our Boat.
7. Planning a Vacation.

ASSIGNMENT 2. *Based on "Slurvian Self-Taught," "Walden," "On Baseball," and "War," pages 631-643.*

An examination of anthologies of modern American essays will repeatedly discover the names of E. B. White, James Thurber, Jacques Barzun, Norman Cousins, Santayana, and a few others. All of these writers have possessed in different forms a kind of magical quality that turns words of information, argument, description, and narration into writing that possesses distinctive grace and charm and that differs in its rhythms and its use of words from the patterns of all other writers. For want of a more definite descriptive word we call this quality *style*.

Whatever style may be, it seems to stem a great deal from the personality of the writer. Some critics have simply identified the two; style is personality on paper. Though such an equation is more nearly true of the informal essay than of the formal, personality seems to affect good formal essays as well.

Think about some of the informal essays you have read. Often the factor that gave them their distinctive flavor was the emotional feeling the authors had for the incidents recounted or the idea presented. Is there any doubt in your mind how E. B. White felt about the appearance of Walden Pond? Do you question Jacques Barzun's appreciation of baseball?

Write an informal essay on one of the following topics or on some experience whose emotions you can recapture. Remember you are writing in the first person—let the flavor of your personality assert itself. Be conscious of the style of your writing.

1. My First Hour on My First Job.
2. The Keys to the Car.
3. Getting Ready for the Prom.
4. High Heels and Nylons. (*Can you remember the day?*)
5. The New Suit.
6. The Day I Made the Team.
7. Getting Lost. (*It happens to everyone!*)

LESSON FOURTEEN: Classification

ASSIGNMENT 1. *Based on "Slurvian Self-Taught," page 631, and "Leatherstocking Saga," "Twenty-Twenty," "Each One Teach One," and "The Gentleman of Culture," pages 644-660.*

In "Slurvian Self-Taught" John Davenport presents what is apparently an exercise in purely humorous writing. Yet a close examination of the essay reveals that a good deal of thought, research, and organization of facts has been necessary to produce the humorous results. One of the jobs Davenport must have committed himself to in the planning process was the *classification* of the kinds of Slurvians. Where does he find Slurvians, for instance? What kinds of mistakes in pronunciation do they make?

Classification of ideas, of examples, of facts, and of methods of convincing the reader is a part of the planning of most good essays. Can you classify accurately? You will need to test yourself in this respect in most of the more formal papers you write.

Prepare to write a brief composition on one of the topics listed below. First draw up an outline which takes into account the various classifications into which the subject can be divided. Be as scientific as you can in your determination of categories, but be prepared to invent your own names for classifications, if necessary. Begin your composition with a topic sentence that states what your classifications concern. Then develop a paragraph or more in which you name and define each category in a separate sentence.

1. How I Spend the Hours of a School Day. (*This is not a narrative but an analysis.*)
2. The Kinds of Essays in this Chapter. (*Invent your own categories.*)
3. The Students in Our Class. (*Be careful, scientific, and impersonal.*)
4. The Cars on the Road Today. (*Avoid brand names.*)
5. The Ages of Man. (*Forget Shakespeare; invent your own.*)

If you choose to write a longer theme on one of these topics, you may use each of the sentences that name and define categories as the topic sentence for a paragraph to be developed with examples and comments.

ASSIGNMENT 2. *Based on "Article and Essay," pages 614-660.*

An outline can be extremely useful in writing a paragraph involving classifications; it is essential in developing a longer theme of this type. The more detailed you make the outline, the more clearly the various classifications will stand out in your paper and the better organized your paper will be.

Choose one of the two topics below for a longer paper in which you state what you are classifying and name and define the categories as before. In addition, you are to present examples, details, or additional information.

1. My Rating of the Selections in this Book. (*There are several different ways in which you may classify the literature: its interest to you, its suitability for students of different types, its literary quality, or some other standard you determine. Be sure to explain your method of classification and define standards as you interpret them.*)
2. My Reading Recommendations for Others. (*This topic assumes that you have read numerous books. Again, various types of classification are open to you: you may group the books according to the type of reader for whom they are suitable; you may classify them according to subject matter as sea stories, romance, historical novels, etc.; or you may devise a classification of your own.*)

The following framework may help you organize your thinking:

I. Introduction. (*State the purpose of your classification and the general nature of the divisions you are making.*)
II. Body. (*List categories under A., B., etc.*)
 A. First Category. (*Name the category, define the standards for admission to the group, and list the items that belong here.*)
 B. Second Category.
 C. Third Category (etc.).
III. Summary. (*Review the proportion of examples in each category and summarize the implications of these proportions.*)
IV. Conclusion. (*Present your evaluation and explain why you consider it accurate.*)

LESSON FIFTEEN: The Research Paper

ASSIGNMENT 1. *Based on "Biography," pages 662-703.*

In a little book called *The Writing of Biography,* Catherine Drinker Bowen describes in some detail the writing of her book *John Adams and the American Revolution.* This book is worth reading by any student about to embark on a research paper. It tells of the years of research and note taking that were necessary before Mrs. Bowen could even begin to give final form to her outline for the biography of John Adams. She estimates that fifty per cent of the biographer's job is research; fifty per cent is planning and writing the book. The final fifty per cent may distinguish a prize-winning biography from a forgotten doctoral dissertation, but the first fifty per cent of research is essential. It may be surprising to some that such interesting biographies as Sandburg's *Lincoln* and Freeman's *Lee* represent the results of long years of careful attention to details gleaned from the study of other books and records. Yet that is the case.

A good biographer or historian frequently must summarize accurately in a short space the facts presented by another historian at some length. Such ability to summarize accurately, with due care for proportion as well as fact, is a necessary quality in a research paper.

To test your ability to summarize, write a simple factual account of the facts pertaining to one of the following topics; use only the biographical selections in the text as sources. Confine yourself to one paragraph if you can.

1. Young Abe Lincoln's Educational Experiences.
2. The Men Present at Appomattox.
3. Relatives Involved in John Adams' Wedding.
4. Lincoln's Early Contacts with the Law.
5. Lee's Movements on April 9, 1865.

SUGGESTED SUBJECTS FOR A RESEARCH PAPER

Every college student has to write one or more research papers. Learning the techniques of such writing now will help you later, when you will have more than enough new ideas to absorb. Consult your language text and other references for details about research-paper techniques. If your teacher assigns a research paper, one of the following suggestions may be helpful to you in choosing a topic. Your teacher will suggest the proper length; in most cases you will have to reduce the scope of the suggested area of study. (Review previous composition lessons for other suggestions.)

1. Critical Analyses. (*You may write a critical analysis of one of the following: a single poet, novelist, short-story writer, essayist, biographer, or historian; a group of writers related to a single school of writing; four or five comparable novels, by the same author or by different authors; principal American realists; principal American romanticists; American narrative poems.*)
2. Comparisons. (*Two novelists, two poets, etc.; romantic and realistic fiction; two widely separated periods in American literature.*)
3. Historical Summaries. (*Of types of literature: nature poetry in America, the American historical novel, the detective story, the Western, the drama; of American magazines or newspapers; of American slang.*)
4. Technical Analyses. (*Studies in the prose styles or verse techniques of selected authors.*)
5. Defense of a Proposition. (*You may wish to write a paper in which you assemble statements of authorities, facts, and other evidence to defend a proposition. Such a topic can be developed from the general suggestions above. A few examples are offered below.*)
   (a) No true literature was produced in America before 1800. (*A definition of terms would be essential in such a paper.*)
   (b) Rhyme was not an asset in the poetry of Longfellow. (*He did not always use rhyme; focus on a few logical choices from his poetry.*)
   (c) Whitman's verse needed discipline.
   (d) Cooper is one of the most underrated of American writers.
   (e) Poe's influence has been world wide.
   (f) Crane's war stories are not true to life.
   (g) Thoreau's ideas continue to influence men.
   (h) Katherine Anne Porter's stories lack plot.
   (i) Poetry is less read today than it was a hundred years ago.

The reverse of most of the statements above might also be argued. You can probably discover clashes of literary opinion in your own class discussions that will furnish propositions for research analysis.

LESSON SIXTEEN: Interpretation

ASSIGNMENT 1. *Based on "Ile," pages 710-719.*

When you see a play presented on the stage, the lighting, stage settings, and actions of the characters all help you understand the meaning of the drama. But when you read a play, you must rely primarily on the dialogue.

How much can you tell about a character in a play after you have read the play? Naturally, you will supply a certain amount of detail from your imagination, just as actors do, but a close study of the lines themselves will often reveal more than you think.

Below are listed several subjects for compositions in which a character from "Ile" is compared with a character in a novel or short story. Reread "Ile" carefully to see how much the dialogue tells you about the character; then reread passages in the novel or short story bearing on the character to be compared with the character in "Ile." Write one paragraph, or at most two, pointing out specific similarities and differences.

1. Captain Keeney and Jackson in *Redburn* (page 319).
2. Captain Keeney and Sadao in "The Enemy" (page 25).
3. Mrs. Keeney and Hana in "The Enemy" (page 25).
4. Mrs. Keeney and Granny in "The Jilting of Granny Weatherall" (page 468).
5. The Steward and Grandfather in "The Leader of the People" (page 477).
6. Mr. Slocum and Fitzsimmons in "The Dry Rock" (page 504).
7. Mr. Slocum and Fred Collins in "A Mystery of Heroism" (page 423).

ASSIGNMENT 2. *Based on* The Glass Menagerie, *pages 721-759.*

As you learned in studying the introduction to the chapter on modern drama, today's playwright depends to a great extent on staging and lighting to help him set the tone of a play and bring out the underlying meanings. Consequently many modern playwrights write detailed stage directions to suggest how these elements are to be handled in the actual production of a play. Tennessee Williams prefaces *The Glass Menagerie* with production notes which deal with a visual device, music, and lighting; he also gives a detailed description of the stage setting.

The following statements are taken from this preliminary material. Choose one of them as the subject of a composition in which you relate the statement, which gives the playwright's design for the handling of some aspect of the play, to the play itself. Williams, for example, has chosen the music to express certain themes. Explain how these themes run through the play. Where do you find vivacity? Is the underlying strain one of sorrow? Does the play bear out the idea that Williams believes the music suggests?

1. It [the recurring tune, "The Glass Menagerie"] expresses the surface vivacity of life with the underlying strain of immutable and inexpressible sorrow (page 722).
2. When you look at a piece of delicately spun glass you think of two things: how beautiful it is and how easily it can be broken (page 722).
3. The light upon LAURA should be distinct from the others, having a peculiar pristine clarity such as light used in early religious portraits of female saints or madonnas (page 722).
4. The scene is memory . . . (page 723).

OPTIONAL ASSIGNMENT

You might try your hand at writing an original one-act play. If you want to simplify matters, try to adapt to drama form a story you have previously written or one you have read. Remember that every line of dialogue must be characteristic of the person speaking, must reflect his emotional state toward the particular scene in which he is involved, must reflect his attitude toward the person or persons he is addressing, and must have something to do with either revealing his character or moving the plot forward. Quite an order! Try it!

Glossary and Index of Literary Terms

Words in italics indicate other entries in the glossary. Numbers after an entry refer to the pages in the text on which additional information can be found.

ACCENT, stress on a syllable. Accent is one of the basic elements of *rhythm* in English. 22, 287-288.

ACTION, the happenings in a narrative. The action of a story is one of the basic elements of the *plot*. 37.

ALLEGORY, a narrative in which characters, action, and sometimes setting represent abstract concepts or moral qualities. 314.

ALLITERATION, repetition of consonant sounds at the beginnings of words or accented syllables. 224.

ALLUSION, a brief, often indirect reference to a person, place, event, or work of art which the author assumes the reader will recognize.

ANALOGY, a comparison of points of likeness between two otherwise dissimilar things. An analogy uses the more familiar to explain or enforce the less familiar. 579.

ANAPEST, three-syllable metrical *foot*, consisting of two unaccented syllables, followed by an accented syllable. 288.

ANTAGONIST, the character, if there is one, that opposes the *protagonist*, or hero.

ANTIREALISM, any school of writing that opposes the aims of realist writers. 707-708.

APHORISM, a short, pithy saying. An aphorism differs from an *epigram* in that it is not necessarily witty.

APOSTROPHE, a figure of speech in which an absent person, an abstract concept, or an inanimate object is addressed directly. 592.

ARTICLE, short piece of nonfiction, like the *essay* but usually intended primarily to inform rather than to present a personal viewpoint.

ASSONANCE, strictly, a repetition of vowel sounds. Often, however, the term is used to refer to any repetition of sounds not exact enough to be called *rhyme*. 224.

ATMOSPHERE, a pervading emotional quality developed by the handling of the *setting*. The atmosphere of a work is *functional* in establishing *tone*.

AUTOBIOGRAPHY, a biographical account of at least a part of the writer's own life. 669.

BALLAD, a narrative song handed down in oral tradition, or a composed poem of similar nature. The traditional ballad stanza is a quatrain, alternating lines of *iambic tetrameter* and *trimeter*, rhyming *abcb*.

BIOGRAPHY, the full account of a man's life and character. Another form of biography, the short biography or *profile*, does not attempt to relate the history of a person but to give the reader a sharp impression of him. 662-663, 682-683, 704.

BLANK VERSE, unrhymed *iambic pentameter*, often written in sections of varying length, without regular *stanzaic* form.

CADENCE, rhythm based not on metrical form but on natural speech rhythms.

CARICATURE, a character development which ludicrously exaggerates prominent features of appearance or character. 405.

CHARACTER, a fictional personality created by an author. 47-48, 708, 759.

CHARACTERIZATION, techniques used by the writer in creating a *character*.

CLIMAX. The technical climax is the decisive point in a series of happenings. The climactic event largely determines what will happen in the rest of the plot. (See *dramatic climax*.) 37.

CONFLICT, the interplay between opposing forces. Conflict is usually one of the central elements in a *plot*. 37.

CONNOTATION, the feeling or attitude associated with a word, related to but quite distinct from its literal meaning, or *denotation*. 21.

CONTENT, a somewhat relative term used in opposition to *form* to designate the materials used by the author, such as words, images, characters.

CONVENTION, any *nonrealistic* technique which is commonly used in a particular type of literature.

CRITIC, a judge of defects and merits in literature or other arts. 217.

CRITICISM, a specialized form of formal essay writing in which literature is analyzed and evaluated.

DACTYL, three-syllable metrical *foot*, consisting of one accented syllable followed by two unaccented syllables. 288.

DENOTATION, the literal meaning of words.

DENOUEMENT, last part of the *plot*, following the *climax*. (See *falling action*.)

DIALECT, the imitation of regional speech in print, using altered, phonetic spelling.

DIALOGUE, the direct presentation of conversation between two or more characters.

DICTION, the particular words chosen for use in a work, or the plan that seems to govern that choice.

DIMETER, line of verse containing two accented syllables. 288.

DOGGEREL, very poor verse.

DRAMA, the literary form designed for presentation in a theater by actors representing the characters. 706-708, 718-719.

DRAMATIC, a term used to describe an action presented directly, rather than told about, often implying conflict and excitement.

DRAMATIC CLIMAX, the point of most intense excitement in a narrative. (See *climax*.) 37.

ELEGY, a traditional poetic form treating of the death of a person in a formal, philosophic way. 341.

EMBLEM, a visual illustration for an abstract, often moral, idea.

END RHYME, the *rhyming* of words at the ends of lines of verse. (See *internal rhyme*.) 224.

EPIC, long narrative poem—originally handed down in oral tradition, later a traditional literary form—dealing with national heroes, having a world-wide or cosmic setting, and written in a deliberately ceremonial style. By extension *epic* may refer to any writing with similar qualities.

EPIC REALISM, a specific school of modern drama aimed at capturing the broad scope and ceremonial style of *epic* writing. 708.

EPIGRAM, originally, an inscription; later any very short, highly polished verse or saying, usually ending with a witty turn.

EPISODE, an event in a narrative.

EPISODIC, a narrative largely composed of loosely related *episodes*.

ESSAY, a brief piece of nonfiction which presents a personal point of view either through informal discourse or formal analysis and argument. (See *article* and *criticism*.) 245, 612-613.

EXPOSITION, that part of a narrative, usually at the beginning, that sketches in the background of the characters and the action.

EXPRESSIONISM, a mode of writing that makes use of psychological rather than *realistic* representation.

FACT, writing intended to inform rather than to engage directly the emotions and imagination. 18-19.

FALLING ACTION, the action in a narrative which follows the *climax*, and represents the working out of the decisive action of the climax. (Also called the *denouement*.) 37.

FEATURE ARTICLE, in a magazine, an *article* which is prominently presented as the most important or most appealing of a given issue.

FICTION, in contrast to *fact*, an imaginative work of literary art designed to communicate values and interpret life. 18-19.

FIGURATIVE LANGUAGE, language used in such a way as to force words out of their literal meanings and, by emphasizing their *connotations*, bring new insight to the subject described. 21-22, 487.

FIGURES OF SPEECH, specific devices, such as *metaphors* and *similes*, for achieving the effects of *figurative language*. 21-22, 487.

FLASHBACK, interruption of the narrative to show an episode that happened before the story opens. 37.

FOLKLORE, the customs, legends, songs, tales of a people or nation.

FOLK SONG, a song handed down in oral tradition. (See *ballad*.)

FOOT, a metrical division consisting of one accented syllable and all unaccented syllables associated with it. (Exception: the *spondee*.) 287-288.

FORESHADOWING, implication by the author of events to come later in a literary work.

FORM, a somewhat relative term used in contrast to *content* to indicate the techniques by which the writer has shaped his material.

FOURTH-WALL CONVENTION, the *realist* stage *convention* that actors are to behave naturally, as if they were surrounded by four walls, though the audience, of course, sees through the "fourth wall." 707.

FREE VERSE, poetry written with *rhythm* and other poetic devices, but without *meter* or regular *rhyme scheme*. 353.

FUNCTIONAL, a term applied to elements in a work which are effectively related to other elements or to the unity of the work as a whole. 55.

GOTHIC, a term referring to a type of fiction which aims at evoking terror through a gloomy, medieval setting, and sensational, supernatural action.

HEROIC COUPLET, a pair of rhymed verse lines in *iambic pentameter*.

IAMB, two-syllable metrical *foot* consisting of one unaccented syllable followed by one accented syllable. 287-288.

IDYL, in modern usage, any narrative dealing with an idealized picture of rural life.

IMAGERY, the use of vivid, concrete, sensory details. 439.

IMAGIST, a member of a twentieth-century school of poetry writing that advocated poetry which expressed the exact impression made on the poet at a given time through the use of small, sharp *images*. 52, 542.

IMPLICATION, communication by other means than a direct statement. 510.

IMPRESSIONISM, the mode of writing in which the author describes an experience, not directly as he knows it is, but in terms of his immediate, momentary sensory reaction to it. 422-423.

INTERNAL RHYME, rhyming of words within, rather than at the end of, lines. 224.

IRONY. An ironic tone is one in which the author seems superficially to mask his real intention. In a more restricted sense *irony* refers to a statement which says the opposite of what is meant in such a way as to reveal the true meaning by implication. This form of irony is sometimes called *verbal irony* in order to distinguish it from *irony of situation* and other types of irony. 75, 428, 543-544.

IRONY OF SITUATION, a happening contrary to that which is appropriate. 428.

LEGEND, a traditional story about a particular person, place, or deity, often popularly accepted as history.

LETTERS, literary culture as a whole. 51.

LOCAL COLOR, use in fiction of the speech, customs, and setting of a particular region for their own interest. 406, 413-414.

LOCAL COLORISTS, fiction writers who make much use of *local color*. 404-406, 413-414, 420.

LYRIC, any short poem expressing a state of mind. The term is used especially in contrast to *narrative* poetry, which tells a story, *epic* poetry, and *epigrammatic* verse.

METAPHOR, a figure of speech involving an implied comparison. (See also, *simile*.) 487.

METER, any regular pattern of *rhythm*. 287-288.

MONOMETER, metrical line of one *foot*. 288.

MYTH, a traditional story connected with the religion of a people, usually attempting to account for something in nature.

MYTHOLOGY, a complete body of interrelated *myths*.

NARRATIVE, any writing which concerns a series of happenings.

NARRATIVE POINT OF VIEW, the relation assumed between the author (or the character who is telling the story) and the characters. This includes specifically the extent to which the narrator shows himself to be aware of what each character thinks and feels. 473.

NATURALISM, a form of realism that takes a fatalistic view of man. 421-423, 428.

NONREALIST, a term applied to any movement which does not accept the viewpoint of realism. 707-708.

NOVEL, an extended piece of narrative prose fiction which usually explores the values of a large segment of society. 531.

OBJECTIVE POINT OF VIEW, a *narrative point of view* in which the author does not presume to know the thoughts and feelings of the characters; he simply reports what can be seen and heard. 473.

OCCASIONAL VERSE, poetry written specifically for a memorable occasion. 275.

OCTAVE, first eight lines of a *sonnet*, particularly the Italian *sonnet*. 273.

ODE, a long *lyric* poem, formal in style and complex in form, often written for a special occasion.

OMNISCIENT POINT OF VIEW, *narrative point of view* in which the author may tell anything he wishes about the characters' thoughts and feelings. 473.

ONOMATOPOEIA, words used in such a way that the sound of the words imitates the sound of the thing spoken about. 565.

PARADOX, a statement that is self-contradictory on the surface, but which reveals a subtler meaning on reflection. 352, 438.

PATHOS, writer's tone which expresses pity and sorrow for the subject.

PENTAMETER, metrical line of five feet, the most common line length in English verse. 287-288.

PERSONAL POINT OF VIEW, *narrative point of view* in which the person telling the story is one of the characters. 473.

PLASTIC THEATER, nonrealistic use of lighting in the theater to achieve the effect of sculpture. 708.

PLOT, the pattern of happenings in a narrative. 37.

POETRY, the communication of thought and feeling, through the careful arrangement of words for their sound, rhythm, and connotation, as well as their sense. 21-22, 540-551.

POINT OF VIEW, relation assumed by the author toward his characters. (See *narrative point of view*.) 473.

PROFILE, a short biography in which the intent is to give a picture of the subject rather than an account of his entire life. (See *biography*.) 500.

PROTAGONIST, the hero, or most appealing character of a story.

QUATRAIN, verse *stanza* of four lines.

REALISM, in literature, the tendency to emphasize the limitations that real life imposes on humanity, and to show how those limitations affect life. 421, 428, 454, 461-462, 467.

REFRAIN, the repetition of one or more lines in each stanza of a poem.

REGIONALISM, the emphasis in fiction on the environment of a specific region. It is sometimes distinguished from *local color* in that it is applied to fiction that emphasizes the effect of the setting on the characters.

REPETITION, the deliberate repeating of any element in a literary work for expressive effect. 224.

REVERSAL, a point in a plot at which a force which had been dominant yields to another force. 37.

REVIEW, an article in a periodical which gives a summary of a book and usually a general evaluation, but which does not make an analysis as deep and thorough as that of a *critical* essay. 646.

RHYME, the exact or nearly exact repetition of sounds in at least the final accented syllables in two or more words. 224.

RHYME SCHEME, any pattern of rhymes in a stanza which is a conventional pattern or which is repeated in another stanza.

RHYTHM, a series of stresses or emphases in a group of words, arranged so that the reader expects a similar series to follow. These emphases may be of grammatical structure, meaning, imagery, or feeling, as well as of sound.

RISING ACTION, the first part of many narratives during which the tension between opposing characters or forces builds toward a *climax*. 37.

ROMANTICISM, a broad, often vague term which may refer to a work that shows any of the following tendencies: (*a*) choice of form and subject which is not dictated by convention or tradition; (*b*) determination to deal with nature or the writer's own subjective emotions, rather than with society; (*c*) determination to deal with the exotic, the supernatural, or the ideal rather than the commonplace, the familiar, or the real. 189, 191-192, 207-208, 428.

SARCASM, the use of exaggerated praise to imply dispraise. Similar to *irony*, but more specific in form and heavier, less subtle in tone. 146.

SATIRE, an extended work, or portion of a work, that by witty techniques of various types makes its subject ridiculous. *Irony* and *sarcasm* are common methods of satire. 146, 592.

SCANSION, marking off of a line of verse into *feet*, indicating the stressed and unstressed syllables. 287-288.

SCENE, the specific setting for a given event in a narrative; or the shortest major division of a play, which may indicate (*a*) a stage in the action, (*b*) a shift in time or place, (*c*) a change in the number of actors on stage.

SENTIMENTALISM, the attempt of an author to arouse more emotion in a work than the situation calls for. 543.

SESTET, the concluding six lines of a *sonnet*, particularly the Italian *sonnet*. 273.

SETTING, the represented place and time of an event in a literary work. 55.

SHORT STORY, a brief, highly unified piece of narrative prose fiction. 37, 47-48, 67-68, 75, 211, 445.

SIMILE, a *figure of speech* involving a comparison made explicit by the use of the word *like* or *as*. (See *metaphor*.) 21-22.

SONNET, a lyric poem with a traditional form of fourteen lines, written in *iambic pentameter*. 273.

SPONDEE, metrical *foot* of two accented syllables only. 288.

STAGE DIRECTIONS, a dramatist's written directions as to how scenes are to be set and how the play is to be produced. 718-719.

STAGE SETS, whatever is used on the stage in a play as a "background" for the actors. 718-719.

STAGING, the method used in lighting the stage, designing the sets, and placing the actors in a play. 706-708.

STANZA, the smallest division of a poem having a pattern of rhyming lines which is either conventional or repeated in another stanza. The word *stanza* is sometimes extended to refer to similar divisions in *blank verse* or *free verse*, even though in these there is no rhyme scheme. 353.

STOCK CHARACTER, a definite type of character conventionally used in a particular literary form. The villain in a Western is a familiar example. 406.

STYLE, the distinctive handling of the language by a given author. 638.

SUBSTITUTE FOOT, a metrical *foot* different from the one prevailing in a line or stanza. 288.

SYMBOL, something relatively concrete, such as an object, action, character, or scene, which signifies something relatively abstract, such as a concept or an idea. 87, 546.

SYMBOLISM, the use of symbols. *Symbolism* also refers to a specific literary movement which attempted to penetrate to a deeper reality through suggestive symbols. 707.

TECHNICAL CLIMAX, the main turning point in a narrative. (See *climax*.) 37.

TECHNIQUE, the conscious methods used by an author to shape his material.

TEMPO, degree of speed and intensity.

TETRAMETER, metrical line of four feet. 288.

THEATRICAL, any nonrealistic mode of play writing that makes obvious use of the conventions of the theater. 708.

THEME, the idea of a literary work. 67-68.

TIME SEQUENCE, pattern developed by the times at which the various episodes of a narrative take place. 740-741.

TONE, author's attitude toward his material. 75, 740-741.

TRAGEDY, in its most general sense, a term referring to any narrative writing in which the *protagonist* suffers disaster after a serious and significant struggle, but faces his downfall in such a way as to attain heroic stature. In its more restricted sense, *tragedy* refers to a play of this nature.

TRANSCENDENTALISM, a mystical philosophy which holds that individuals can penetrate to the ultimate realities of the world by intuition. 230-231, 247-250.

TRIMETER, metrical line of three feet. 288.

TROCHEE, metrical *foot* made up of one accented syllable followed by an unaccented syllable. 288.

UNITY, the quality achieved by an artistic work when all its elements are so interrelated as to form a complete whole. 37.

VERSE. In its most general sense verse is a synonym for *poetry*. *Verse* also may be used to refer to poetry carefully composed as to rhythm and rhyme scheme, but of inferior literary value. Finally, *verse* may mean a single line of poetry.

VERSE FORM, a specific pattern of rhythm and rhyme.

WESTERN, a highly conventional type of fiction using the early American West as its setting. 406, 708.

Glossary

The pronunciation of each word is shown just after the word, in this way: **ab bre vi ate** (ə brē′vi āt). The letters and signs used are pronounced as in the words below. The mark ′ is placed after a syllable with primary or strong accent, as in the example above. The mark ′ after a syllable shows a secondary or lighter accent, as in **ab bre vi a tion** (ə brē′vi ā′shən).

Some words, taken from foreign languages, are spoken with sounds that otherwise do not occur in English. Symbols for these sounds are given at the end of the table as "Foreign Sounds."

a	hat, cap	o	hot, rock	ə represents:	
ā	age, face	ō	open, go		a in about
ã	care, air	ô	order, all		e in taken
ä	father, far	oi	oil, voice		i in pencil
		ou	house, out		o in lemon
					u in circus
b	bad, rob				
ch	child, much				
d	did, red	p	paper, cup		
		r	run, try		
		s	say, yes	FOREIGN SOUNDS	
e	let, best	sh	she, rush		
ē	equal, see	t	tell, it	Y	as in French du. Pronounce
ėr	term, learn	th	thin, both		ē with the lips rounded as
		ŦH	then, smooth		for English ü in **rule**.
f	fat, if				
g	go, bag				
h	he, how	u	cup, butter	œ	as in French peu. Pronounce
		u̇	full, put		ā with the lips rounded as
i	it, pin	ü	rule, move		for ō.
ī	ice, five	ū	use, music		
				N	as in French bon. The N is
j	jam, enjoy				not pronounced, but shows
k	kind, seek	v	very, save		that the vowel before it is
l	land, coal	w	will, woman		nasal.
m	me, am	y	young, yet		
n	no, in	z	zero, breeze	H	as in German ach. Pro-
ng	long, bring	zh	measure, seizure		nounce k without closing
					the breath passage.

ETYMOLOGY KEY

<	from, derived from, taken from	*dial.*	dialect	*neut.*	neuter
		dim.	diminutive	*pp.*	past participle
?	possibly	*fem.*	feminine	*ppr.*	present participle
abl.	ablative	*gen.*	genitive	*pt.*	past tense
accus.	accusative	*lang.*	language	*ult.*	ultimately
cf.	compare	*masc.*	masculine	*var.*	variant

782

LANGUAGE ABBREVIATIONS

AF	Anglo-French (= Anglo-Norman, the dialect of French spoken by the Normans in England, esp. 1066-c. 1164)	Med.	Medieval
		Med.Gk.	Medieval Greek (700-1500)
		Med.L	Medieval Latin (700-1500)
		MF	Middle French (1400-1600)
		MHG	Middle High German (1100-1450)
Am.E	American English (word originating in the United States)	MLG	Middle Low German (1100-1450)
Am.Ind.	American Indian	NL	New Latin (after 1500)
Am.Sp.	American Spanish	O	Old
E	English	OE	Old English (before 1100)
F	French	OF	Old French (before 1400)
G	German	OHG	Old High German (before 1100)
Gk.	Greek (from Homer to 300 A.D.)	Pg.	Portuguese
Gmc.	Germanic (parent language of Gothic, Scandinavian, English, Dutch, German)	Scand.	Scandinavian (one of the languages of Northern Europe before Middle English times; Old Norse unless otherwise specified)
HG	High German (speech of Central and Southern Germany)		
Hindu.	Hindustani (the commonest language of India)	Skt.	Sanskrit (the ancient literary language of India, from the same parent language as Persian, Greek, Latin, Germanic, Slavonic, and Celtic)
Ital.	Italian		
L	Latin (Classical Latin 200 B.C.-300 A.D.)	Sp.	Spanish
LG	Low German (speech of Northern Germany)	VL	Vulgar Latin (a popular form of Latin, the main source of French, Spanish, Italian, Portuguese, and Rumanian)
LGk.	Late Greek (300-700)		
LL	Late Latin (300-700)		
M	Middle		
ME	Middle English (1100-1500)		

OTHER ABBREVIATIONS

adj.	adjective	*E*	Eastern	*pron.*	pronoun
adv.	adverb	*esp.*	especially	*sing.*	singular
Anat.	anatomy	*interj.*	interjection	*SW*	Southwestern
Ant.	antonym	*n.*	noun	*Syn.*	synonym
Brit.	British	*pl.*	plural	*U.S.*	United States
conj.	conjunction	*prep.*	preposition	*v.*	verb

The pronunciation key and language abbreviations are from the *Thorndike-Barnhart High School Dictionary*, copyright, 1962, by Scott, Foresman and Company.

ab a lo ne (ab'ə lō'ni), *n.* an edible shellfish, with a large, rather flat shell.

a bash (ə bash'), *v.* embarrass and confuse; make uneasy and somewhat ashamed. —**a bash'ment,** *n.*

a bate (ə bāt'), *v.* **1.** make less in amount, intensity, etc.: *The medicine abated his pain.* **2.** become less violent, intense, etc.: *The storm has abated.* [< OF *abatre* beat down < *a*- to (<L *ad*-) + *batre* beat < L *batuere*]

ab at toir (ab'ə twär or ab'ə twôr), *n.* slaughter-house. [< F]

a ble-bod ied sea man (ā'bəl bod'id sē'mən), *n.* experienced sailor who can perform all the ordinary duties of a sailor. Also, **able-seaman.**

ab lu tion (ab lü'shən), *n.* **1.** a washing of one's person. **2.** cleansing as a religious ceremony of purification. [< L *ablutio, -onis* < *abluere* < *ab*- away + *luere* wash]

a bom i nate (ə bom'ə nāt), *v.* **1.** feel disgust for; abhor; detest. **2.** dislike. [< L *abominari* deplore as an ill omen < *ab*- off + *ominari* prophesy < *omen* omen] —**a bom'i na ble,** *adj.*

a bom i na tion (ə bom'ə nā'shən), *n.* **1.** a revolting thing. **2.** a shamefully wicked action or custom. **3.** hate.

ab o rig i nal (ab'ə rij'ə nəl), *adj.* **1.** first; original; native: *aboriginal inhabitants.* **2.** of the earliest known inhabitants. —*n.* any one of the earliest known inhabitants.

a bor tion (ə bôr'shən), *n.* **1.** birth that occurs before the embryo has developed enough to live; miscarriage. **2.** failure to develop properly. **3.** imperfectly developed thing.

ab ro gate (ab'rə gāt), *v.* **1.** abolish or annul (a law or custom) by an authoritative act; repeal. **2.** do away with. [< L *abrogare* < *ab*- away + *rogare* demand]

ab solve (ab solv' or ab zolv'), *v.* **1.** declare (a person) free from sin, guilt, or blame. **2.** set free (from a promise or duty).

ab struse (ab strüs'), *adj.* hard to understand; profound.

ac a dem ic (ak'ə dem'ik), *adj.* **1.** having to do with schools and their studies. **2.** *U.S.* concerned with general education rather than commercial, technical, or professional education. **3.** scholarly. **4.** theoretical. **5.** formal; following rules and traditions.

ac cel er an do (ak sel'ər an'dō), *adv., adj.* in music, gradually increasing in speed. [< Ital.]

ac co lade (ak'ə lād' or ak'ə lād), *n.* praise; recognition; award.

ac cou ter ments (ə kü'tər mənts), *n. pl.* **1.** a soldier's equipment with the exception of his weapons and clothing. **2.** personal equipment; outfit.

a ce tic a cid (ə sē'tik a'sid), a very sour, colorless acid, present in vinegar.

a cros tic (ə krôs'tik or ə kros'tik), *n.* an arrangement of words in which the first, last, or certain other letters in each line spell a word or phrase.

ad duce (ə düs' or ə düs'), *v.* offer as a reason.

a do be (ə dō'bi), *n.* **1.** sun-dried clay or mud. **2.** a brick of such material, used in building. —*adj.* built or made of sun-dried bricks. [Am.E; < Sp. *adobe* < *adobar* to daub < Gmc.]

a droit (ə droit'), *adj.* skillful: *A good teacher is adroit in asking questions.* [< F *adroit* < *à droit* rightly < L *ad* to, *directus* straight] —**a droit'ly,** *adv.* —**a droit'ness,** *n.*

ad vert (ad vèrt'), *v.* direct attention; refer (to).

Ae ne id (ē nē'id)

ae on (ē'ən or ē'on), *n.* a very long period of time; many thousands of years. Also, **eon.**

aer o stat (ār'ə stat), *n.* any lighter-than-air aircraft, such as a balloon or dirigible. —**aer'o stat'ic,** *adj.*

aes thet ics (es thet'iks), *n.* study of beauty in art and nature; theory of the fine arts.

af fa ble (af'ə bəl), *adj.* easy to talk to; pleasant.

af fin i ty (ə fin'ə ti), *n.* **1.** natural attraction to a person or liking for a thing: *an affinity for dancing.* **2.** person to whom one is attracted. **3.** relation; connection. [< F *af(f)inité* < L *affinitas* < *ad*- on + *finis* boundary]

af fray (ə frā'), *n.* a noisy quarrel; fight in public.

af front (ə frunt'), *n.* a word or act that openly expresses intentional disrespect. —*v.* **1.** insult openly. **2.** meet face to face; confront.

a gape (ə gāp' or ə gap'), *adv., adj.* **1.** gaping; with the mouth wide open in wonder or surprise. **2.** wide open.

ag gre gate (*v.* ag'rə gāt; *n., adj.* ag'rə git or ag'rə gāt), *v.* collect. —*n.* total. —*adj.* total.

a lac ri ty (ə lak'rə ti), *n.* brisk and eager action.

al be it (ôl bē'it), *conj.* although; even though.

a light (ə līt'), *v.* **1.** get down; get off; *alight from a horse.* **2.** come down from the air and settle.

al ka line (al'kə līn or al'kə lin), *adj.* **1.** of or like an alkali, a chemical substance that is the opposite of an acid. **2.** containing this substance.

al lay (ə lā'), *v.* **1.** put at rest; quiet: *His fears were allayed by the news of the safety of his family.* **2.** relieve.

al oe (al'ō), *n., pl.* **-oes. 1.** plant having a long spike of flowers and thick, narrow leaves, that grows in warm, dry climates. **2. aloes,** *pl.* a bitter drug made from the dried juice of the leaves of certain aloes.
→ **Aloes,** the drug, is plural in form and singular in use: *Aloes is sometimes used as a tonic.*

al tru ism (al'trü iz əm), *n.* unselfishness; unselfish devotion to the interests and welfare of others.

Am a zon (am'ə zon or am'ə zən), *n.* **1.** river in S America. **2.** in Greek legend, one of a legendary race of women warriors supposed to live near the Black Sea. **3.** Also, **amazon.** a tall, strong, masculine woman.

am bi dex tri an (am'bə dek'stri ən), *n.* **1.** person able to use both hands equally well. **2.** deceitful person.

a mel io rate (ə mēl'yə rāt or ə mē'li ə rāt), *v.* make better; become better; improve. [< F *améliorer,* ult. < LL *meliorare* < L *melior* better] —**a mel'io ra'tion,** *n.*

am i ty (am'ə ti), *n.* peace and friendship; friendly relations. [< MF *amitie,* ult. < L *amicus* friend]

am phib i ous (am fib'i əs), *adj.* **1.** able to live both on land and in water. **2.** suited for use on land or water: *an amphibious tank.* **3.** having two qualities or parts. [< Gk. *amphibios* living a double life < *amphi*- both + *bios* life]

am u let (am'ū lit), *n.* some object worn as a magic charm against evil [< L *amuletum*]

a nach ro nism (ə nak'rə niz əm), *n.* **1.** act of putting a person, thing, or event in some time where it does not belong: *It would be an anachronism to speak of George Washington riding in an automobile.* **2.** something placed or occurring out of its proper time. [< F < Gk. *anachronismos* < *ana*- backwards + *chronos* time]

a nat o mize (ə nat'ə mīz), *v.* **1.** divide into parts to study the structure. **2.** examine the parts of; analyze.

< = from, taken from;   cf., compare;   dial., dialect;   dim., diminutive;   pp., past participle; ppr., present participle;   pt., past tense;   ult., ultimately;   var., variant;   ?=possibly.

An da lu sia (an′də lü′zhə or an′də lü′shə), *n.* region in S Spain. —**An′da lu′sian,** *adj., n.*

and i ron (and′ī′ərn), *n.* one of a pair of metal supports for wood burned in a fireplace.

an nal ist (an′əl ist), *n.* writer of annals, written accounts of events year by year.

an nu i ty (ə nü′ə ti or ə nū′ə ti), *n.* **1.** sum of money paid every year. **2.** investment that provides a fixed yearly income during one's lifetime.

an nun ci a tion (ə nun′si ā′shən), *n.* **1.** announcement. **2. the Annunciation,** the angel Gabriel's announcement to Mary that she was to be the mother of Christ.

a non (ə non′), *adv.* **1.** in a little while; soon. **2.** again.

an tag o nis tic (an tag′ə nis′tik), *adj.* acting against each other: *Cats and dogs are antagonistic.* —**an tag′o nis′ti cal ly,** *adv.* —**Syn.** hostile.

an thro po mor.phic (an′thrə pə môr′fik), *adj.* attributing human form or qualities to gods or things. [< Gk. *anthropomorphos* < *anthropos* man + *morphe* form]

an tip o des (an tip′ə dēz), *n.pl.* **1.** two places on directly opposite sides of the earth: *The North Pole and the South Pole are antipodes.* **2.** place on the opposite side of the earth. **3.** two opposites.
→ **Antipodes** is plural in form and plural or singular in use for def. 2.

A pach e plume (ə pach′i plüm′), *n.* an evergreen shrub of the SW United States and Mexico.

ap o logue (ap′ə lôg or ap′ə log), *n.* fable with a moral: *Aesop's fables are apologues.*

a poth e car y (ə poth′ə ker′i), *n.* druggist.

a poth e o sis (ə poth′i ō′sis or ap′ə thē′ə sis), *n., pl.* -ses (-sēz). **1.** raising of a human being to the rank of a god. **2.** glorification. **3.** a glorified ideal. [< L < Gk. *apotheosis,* ult. < *apo-* + *theos* god]

Ap pa ma tuck (ap′ə mat′ək; *Indian,* äp′pä mä′-tuk)

ap pend (ə pend′), *v.* add to a larger thing; attach.

ap pend age (ə pen′dij), *n.* thing attached; addition.

ap pre ci a tion (ə prē′shi ā′shən), *n.* **1.** a valuing highly; sympathetic understanding. **2.** a rise in value.

ap pro ba tion (ap′rə bā′shən), *n.* **1.** approval; favorable opinion. **2.** sanction.

ar a besque (ar′ə besk′), *n.* an elaborate and fanciful design. —*adj.* **1.** carved or painted in arabesque. **2.** elaborate; fanciful.

ar bi trar y (är′bə trer′i), *adj.* **1.** based on one's own wishes, notions, or will; not going by any particular rule or law. **2.** tyrannical.

ar cane (är kān′), *adj.* secret; hidden.

arch (ärch), *adj.* playfully mischievous: *The little girl gave her mother an arch look.*

Ar e thu sa (ar′i thü′zə or ar′i thü′sə)

ar rant (ar′ənt), *adj.* thoroughgoing; downright.

ar ras (ar′əs), *n.* curtain or tapestry.

ar roy o (ə roi′ō), *n.* in the SW United States: **1.** the dry bed of a stream; gully. **2.** a small river. [Am.E; < Sp. < L *arrugia* mine shaft]

ar tic u late (*adj.* är tik′ū lit; *v.* är tik′ū lāt), *adj.* **1.** uttered in distinct syllables or words. **2.** able to put one's thoughts into words. **3.** jointed. —*v.* **1.** speak distinctly. **2.** fit together in a joint. [< L *articulatus,* pp. of *articulare* divide into single joints < *articulus*]

ar tif i cer (är tif′ə sər), *n.* **1.** skilled workman; craftsman. **2.** maker; inventor.

as cend an cy (ə sen′den si), *n.* controlling influence; rule.

as cribe (əs krīb′), *v.* **1.** assign; attribute. **2.** consider as belonging.

a skance (ə skans′), *adv.* **1.** with suspicion or disapproval. **2.** sideways; to one side.

a skant (ə skant′), *adv.* askance.

a skew (ə skū′), *adv., adj.* to one side; out of the proper position; turned the wrong way.

as say (ə sā′ or as′ā), *v.* **1.** analyze (an ore, alloy, etc.) to find out the quantity of gold, silver, or other metal in it. **2.** try; test; examine. **3.** *Archaic.* attempt.

as sid u ous (ə sij′ü əs), *adj.* careful and attentive; diligent. —**as sid′u ous ly,** *adv.*

as sign (ə sīn′), *v.* **1.** give as a task, lesson. **2.** name definitely. **3.** transfer or hand over (property, a right, etc.) legally. —*n.* person to whom property, a right, etc., is legally transferred.

as suage (ə swāj′), *v.* **1.** make easier or milder: *assuage pain.* **2.** appease; quench: *assuage thirst.*

a the ism (ā′thi iz əm), *n.* belief that there is no God. [< F *athéisme* < Gk. *atheos* denying the gods < *a-* without + *theos* a god]

at om ize (at′əm īz), *v.* **1.** separate into atoms. **2.** break up into small units.

at trac tion (ə trak′shən), *n.* **1.** act or power of attracting. **2.** thing that attracts people. **3.** charm. **4.** in physics, the force exerted by molecules on one another, tending to draw or hold them together.

at trib ute (*v.* ə trib′ūt; *n.* at′rə būt), *v.* consider (something) as belonging or appropriate (to a person or thing); think of as caused by: *We attribute Edison's success to intelligence and hard work.* —*n.* **1.** a quality considered as belonging to a person or thing.

au di tor (ô′də tər), *n.* **1.** hearer; listener. **2.** person who officially examines business accounts.

aught¹ (ôt), *n.* anything: *You may go for aught I care.* —*adv.* in any way; to any degree; at all. [OE *āwiht* < *ā-* ever + *wiht* a thing]

aught² (ôt), *n.* zero; nothing. [< *naught; a naught* taken as *an aught; naught,* OE *nāwiht* < *nā* no + *wiht* a thing]

au gust (ô gust′), *adj.* inspiring reverence and admiration; majestic; venerable.

au ra (ô′rə), *n., pl.* **au ras, au rae** (ô′rē), something supposed to come from a person or thing and surround him or it as an atmosphere.

Au ro ra (ô rô′rə or ô rō′rə), *n.* **1.** Roman goddess of the dawn. **2. aurora, a.** dawn. **b.** streamers or bands of light appearing in the sky at night.

au then tic (ô then′tik), *adj.* **1.** reliable. **2.** genuine.

au to crat ic (ô′tə krat′ik), *adj.* absolute in authority; ruling without checks or limitations.

au tom a tism (ô tom′ə tiz əm), *n.* action not controlled by the will; involuntary action; automatic action.

a vail (ə vāl′), *v.* **1.** be of use or value to. **2.** help: *Talk will not avail without work.* **3. avail oneself of,** take advantage of; profit by; make use of. —*n.* use; help; benefit.

a vant-garde (ä′väN gärd′ or ä′vänt gärd′), *n.* [Fr., *lit.,* advance guard] a group, especially artists or writers, who are untraditional and produce or apply original or experimental ideas, designs, techniques.

a vast (ə vast′ or ə väst′), *interj.* stop! stay! *"Avast there!" shouted the sailor.* [probably < Dutch *houd vast* hold fast]

av a tar (av′ə tär′), *n.* **1.** descent of a god to earth in bodily form; incarnation. **2.** manifestation in bodily form. [Skt. *avatāra* descent < *ava* down + *tar-* pass over]

---

hat, āge, cãre, fär; let, ēqual, tèrm; it, īce; hot, ōpen, ôrder; oil, out; cup, pùt, rüle, ūse;
th, thin; ŦH, then; zh, measure; ə represents *a* in about, *e* in taken, *i* in pencil, *o* in lemon, *u* in circus.

a ver (ə vėr′), *v.* state to be true; assert.

a ver sion (ə vėr′zhən or ə vėr′shən), *n.* **1.** a strong or fixed dislike; antipathy. **2.** thing or person disliked.

a wry (ə rī′), *adv., adj.* with a twist or turn to one side: *Her hat was blown awry by the wind.*

Bab y lo ni a (bab′ə lō′ni ə), *n.* an ancient empire in SW Asia, from 2800 to 1000 B.C.

Bab y lo ni an (bab′ə lō′ni ən), *adj.* of or having to do with Babylon, the capital, or Babylonia. —*n.* **1.** inhabitant of Babylonia. **2.** language of Babylonia.

bal dric (bôl′drik), *n.* belt for a sword, horn, etc., hung from one shoulder to the opposite side of the body.

bale ful (bāl′fəl), *adj.* evil; harmful. —**bale′ful ly,** *adv.* —**bale′ful ness,** *n.*

ba nal (bā′nəl, bə nal′, or ban′əl), *adj.* commonplace; trite; trivial.

bard (bärd), *n.* **1.** a poet and singer of long ago. Bards sang their own poems to the music of their harps. **2.** poet.

bark[1] (bärk), *n.* the tough outside covering of trees and plants. —*v.* **1.** strip the bark from (a tree, etc.). **2.** scrape the skin from (shins, knuckles, etc.). [< Scand. *börkr*]

bark[2] (bärk), *n.* **1.** sound that a dog makes. **2.** a sound like this. [< v.] —*v.* **1.** make this sound or one like it. **2.** shout sharply. [OE *beorcan*]

bark[3] (bärk), *n.* **1.** ship with three masts.

basque (bask), *n.* a woman's garment consisting of a close-fitting waist extending over the hips.

bas tion (bas′chən or bas′ti ən), *n.* **1.** a projecting part of a fortification. **2.** defense; fortification.

bat tle ment (bat′əl mənt), *n.* **1.** wall for defense at the top of a tower or wall, with indentations through which soldiers could shoot. **2.** wall built like this.

bay[1] (bā), *n.* **1.** the long, deep bark of a dog. **2.** stand made by a hunted animal to face pursuers when escape is impossible. [ME *bay, abay* < OF *abai* a barking]

bay[2] (bā), *n.* a small evergreen tree with smooth, shiny leaves; laurel tree. [< OF *baie* < L *baca* berry]

bay ou (bī′ü), *n., pl.* **-ous.** *U.S.* a marshy inlet or outlet of a lake, river, or gulf in the southern United States. [Am.E; < Louisiana F < Choctaw *bayuk* small stream]

ba zoo (bə zü′), *n.* a toy musical instrument which consists of a tube containing a piece of paper that vibrates and produces a buzzing sound when one hums into the tube.

beard (bėrd) *n.* **1.** hair growing on a man's face. **2.** something resembling or suggesting this. —*v.* face boldly; defy.

Be atte (bā ät′)

be girt (bi gėrt′), *adj.* surrounded; encircled.

be grimed (bi grimd′), *v.* made grimy; soiled and dirty.

be guile (bi gīl′), *v.* **1.** deceive; cheat. **2.** take away from deceitfully. **3.** entertain; amuse. **4.** while away (time) pleasantly.

be he moth (bi hē′məth or bē′ə məth), *n.* a huge and powerful animal mentioned in the Bible. It may have been the hippopotamus.

be lea guer (bi lē′gər), *v.* **1.** besiege. **2.** surround.

be lie (bi lī′), *v.* **1.** give a false idea of; misrepresent. **2.** prove to be mistaken.

bel li cose (bel′ə kōs), *adj.* warlike; fond of fighting.

bel lows (bel′ōz or bel′əs), *n. sing. or pl.* instrument for producing a strong current of air, used for blowing fires or sounding an organ.

Be nét (bi nā′)

be night ed (bi nīt′id), *adj.* **1.** not knowing right and wrong; ignorant. **2.** overtaken by night; being in darkness.

be reave (bi rēv′), *v.*, **be reaved** or **be reft, be reav-ing. 1.** deprive (of) ruthlessly; rob: *bereave of hope.* **2.** leave desolate. [OE *berēafian* < *be-* away + *rēafian* rob]

be times (bi tīmz′), *adv.* **1.** early: *He rose betimes in the morning.* **2.** soon; before it is too late.

bev y (bev′i), *n.* a group: *a bevy of girls.*

big ot (big′ət), *n.* intolerant, prejudiced person. [<F]

big ot ry (big′ət ri), *n.* intolerance in conduct or attitude. —**Syn.** prejudice; narrow-mindedness.

bit tern (bit′ərn), *n.* a small kind of heron that lives in marshes and has a peculiar booming cry. [< OF *butor*]

biv ou ac (biv′ü ak or biv′wak), *n., v.,* **-acked, -acking.** camp outdoors without tents. [<F, probably < Swiss G *biwache* < *bī* by + *wache* watch]

blanch (blanch or blänch), *v.* turn white or pale.

blanc mange (blə mänzh′), *n.* a sweet dessert made of milk thickened with gelatin, cornstarch, etc. [< OF *blanc-manger* white food]

blear (blėr), *adj.* dim; blurred. —*v.* make dim, blurred.

bod ing (bōd′ing), *adj.* threatening; ominous.

Bo he mi an (bō hē′mi ən or bō hēm′yən), *adj.* **1.** of Bohemia. **2.** free and easy; unconventional. —*n.* **1.** native of Bohemia. **2.** Often, **bohemian.** artist, writer, etc., who lives in an unconventional way.

bole (bōl), *n.* trunk of a tree. [< Scand. *bolr*]

boot jack (büt′jak′), *n.* device to help in pulling off boots.

bore (bôr or bōr), *n.* inside a pipe, tube, or gun barrel.

bor er (bôr′ər or bōr′ər), *n.* **1.** tool for boring holes. **2.** insect or worm that bores into wood, fruit, etc.

bou quet (bō kā′ or bü kā′ *for* 1; bü kā′ *for* 2), *n.* **1.** bunch of flowers. **2.** fragrance; aroma. [< F *bouquet* little wood, dim. of OF *bosc* wood]

bourn[1] or **bourne**[1] (bôrn or bōrn), *n.* a small stream; brook. [OE *burna*]

bourn[2] or **bourne**[2] (bôrn, bōrn, or bürn), *n.* **1.** *Archaic.* boundary; limit. **2.** goal. [< F *borne*]

bow (bou), *n.* the forward part of a ship, boat, or airship.

bow ie knife (bō′i or bü′i nīf′), a long, single-edged hunting knife carried in a sheath. [Am.E; named after Col. J. *Bowie,* American pioneer]

bow sprit (bou′sprit or bō′sprit), *n.* pole projecting forward from the bow of a ship. Ropes from it help to steady sails and masts. [probably < LG or Dutch]

boy (boi), *n.* **1.** a male child from birth to about eighteen. **2.** a male servant, especially a native servant in India, China, etc. **3.** In business, an attendant who performs errands and odd jobs: *messenger boy.* **4.** inexperienced seaman.

brack en (brak′ən), *n.* growth of ferns.

brake (brāk), *n.* thicket. [cf. MLG *brake*]

brand (brand), *n.* **1.** a certain kind, grade, or make: *brand of coffee.* **2.** mark of disgrace. **3.** piece of wood that is burning or partly burned. **4.** *Archaic and Poetic.* sword.

brav er y (brāv′ər i or brāv′ri), *n. Obsolete.* showy dress; finery.

bra zier (brā′zhər), *n.* a metal container to hold burning charcoal or coal. Braziers are used for heating rooms. Also, **brasier.** [< F *brasier* < *braise* hot coals]

breach (brēch), *n.* **1.** gap. **2.** a breaking (of a law, promise, duty, etc.); neglect.

< = from, taken from;   cf., compare;   dial., dialect;   dim., diminutive;   pp., past participle;   ppr., present participle;   pt., past tense;   ult., ultimately;   var., variant;   ?=possibly.

br'er (brėr), *n.* *Dialect.* brother.

Bret on (bret'ən), *n.* **1.** native or inhabitant of Brittany, region in NW France. **2.** language of Brittany. —*adj.* having to do with Brittany, its people, or their language.

Breu ghel (brü'gəl)

brief (brēf), *adj.* **1.** lasting only a short time. **2.** using few words. —*n.* **1.** summary. **2.** statement of the facts and the points of law of a case to be pleaded in court. —*v.* **1.** summarize. **2.** furnish with a brief. **3.** give a briefing to. [< OF *bref* < L *brevis* short]

Bril lon (brē yoN')

Bri tan ni a (bri tan'i ə or bri tan'yə), *n.* **1.** Britain; Great Britain. **2.** the British Empire. **3.** woman symbolizing Britain or the British Empire.

brock le (brok'əl), *adj.* spotted, especially referring to the spotted skin of an animal.

bro ker (brō'kər), *n.* person who buys and sells stocks, grain, etc., for other people; agent.

brook¹ (brúk), *n.* a small natural stream of water. [OE *brōc*] —*Syn.* creek, rivulet.

brook² (brúk), *v.* put up with; endure; tolerate: *Her pride would not brook such insults.* [OE *brūcan* use]

bruit (brüt), *v.* spread a report or rumor of: *Rumors of the princess' engagement were bruited about.* [< *n.*] —*n.* *Archaic.* report; rumor.

Brus sels car pet (brus'əlz cär'pit), *n.* carpet with a pattern made of small loops of yarn having various colors.

buck board (buk'bôrd' or buk'bōrd'), *n.* an open, four-wheeled carriage having the seat fastened to a platform of long, springy boards.

buck ler (buk'lər), *n.* **1.** a small, round shield. **2.** protection; defense.

buff (buf), *n.* *Slang.* devotee; follower; enthusiast.

bul ly rag (búl'i rag'), *v.* *Informal.* bully; tease; abuse.

bul wark (búl'wərk), *n.* **1.** defense; protection. **2.** wall for defense against an enemy. **3.** Usually, **bulwarks,** *pl.* a ship's side above the deck. —*v.* **1.** defend; protect. **2.** provide with a bulwark or bulwarks.

bur den (bėr'dən), *n.* **1.** the main idea. **2.** chorus; refrain.

burgh er (bėr'gər), *n.* citizen of a burgh or town; citizen.

bur lesque (bėr lesk'), *n.* a literary or dramatic composition in which a serious subject is treated ridiculously, or with mock seriousness.

bur row (bėr'ō), *n.* **1.** hole dug in the ground by an animal for refuge or shelter. **2.** a similar passage for shelter or refuge. —*v.* **1.** dig a hole in the ground. **2.** live in burrows. **3.** hide. **4.** dig. **5.** search.

bush whack er (búsh'hwak'ər), *n.* *U.S.* **1.** person accustomed to go about among bushes. **2.** scythe for cutting bushes. **3.** a guerrilla fighter. [Am.E]

bus kin (bus'kin), *n.* boot reaching to the calf or knee.

butte (būt), *n.* in western United States, a steep hill standing alone. [Am.E < F]

Cain (kān), *n.* **1.** in the Bible, the oldest son of Adam and Eve, who killed his brother Abel. As punishment, a curse was laid upon Cain, and he was forced to be a fugitive and a vagabond. **2.** murderer.

cairn (kärn), *n.* pile of stones heaped up as a memorial, tomb, or landmark. [< Scotch Gaelic *carn* heap of stones]

cais son (kā'sən or kā'son), *n.* **1.** box for ammunition. **2.** wagon to carry ammunition.

Cal houn (kal hün'), *n.* **John Caldwell,** 1782-1850, American statesman, vice-president of the United States from 1825 to 1832.

Cam e lot (kam'ə lot), *n.* a legendary place in England where King Arthur had his palace and court.

cane brake (kān'brāk'), *n.* thicket of cane plants.

ca non i cal (kə non'ə kəl), *adj.* having to do with church law; prescribed by the church.

cant (kant), *n.* **1.** insincere talk; moral and religious statements that many people make, but few really believe or follow out. **2.** the peculiar language of a special group: *thieves' cant.* —*adj.* referring to cant: *a cant phrase.* —*v.* use cant. [< L *cantus* song]

Ca pa ho wo sick (kä'pä hō wō'sik)

cap i tal i za tion (kap'ə təl ə zā'shən), *n.* **1.** a capitalizing or being capitalized. **2.** capital stock of a business. **3.** a using to one's own advantage.

ca pit u la tion (kə pich'ú lā'shən), *n.* **1.** a surrender on certain terms or conditions. **2.** agreement; condition. **3.** statement of the main facts of a subject.

car bo run dum (kär'bə run'dəm), *n.* **1.** an extremely hard compound of carbon and silicon, used for grinding, polishing, etc. **2.** Carborundum, trademark for this compound.

car bun cle (kär'bung kəl), *n.* **1.** a painful, inflamed swelling under the skin. **2.** a deep-red jewel.

car et (kar'ət), *n.* mark (∧) to show where something should be put in, used in writing and in correcting proof.

car nage (kär'nij), *n.* slaughter of a great number of people. [< F < Ital. *carnaggio* < L *caro* flesh]

car nel ian (kär nēl'yən), *n.* a red stone used in jewelry. It is a kind of quartz. Also, **cornelian.** [alteration of *cornelian;* influenced by L *caro* flesh]

car niv o rous (kär niv'ə rəs), *adj.* flesh-eating. [< L *carnivorus* < *caro* flesh + *vorare* devour]

Car ra ra (kə rä'rə), *n.* city in NW Italy, famous for its fine white marble.

car ri on (kar'i ən), *adj.* feeding on dead flesh.

case ment (kās'mənt), *n.* **1.** window opening on hinges like a door. **2.** *Poetic.* any window. **3.** a casing; covering.

cas tel lat ed (kas'tə lāt'id), *adj.* **1.** like a castle, having turrets and battlements. **2.** having many castles.

cat a mount (kat'ə mount), *n.* wildcat, such as a puma or lynx.

cat a ract (kat'ə rakt), *n.* **1.** a large, steep waterfall. **2.** a violent rush or downpour of water. **3.** an opaque condition of the eye that causes partial or total blindness.

catch (kach), *n.* a short song sung by several persons or groups, beginning one after another.

cath o lic (kath'ə lik or kath'lik), *adj.* having sympathies with all; universal; broad-minded; liberal.

cav il (kav'əl), *v.,* **-iled, -il ing** or *esp. Brit.* **-illed, -il ling,** *n.* —*v.* find fault unnecessarily; raise trivial objections. —*n.* a petty objection. [<F < L *cavillari* jeer] —**cav'il er,** *esp. Brit.* **cav'il ler,** *n.*

ca vort (kə vôrt'), *v.* *U.S. Informal.* prance about; jump around.

cel i ba cy (sel'ə bə si), *n.* unmarried state.

cel o tex (sel'ə teks'), *n.* **1.** a composition board used for insulating buildings. **2.** Celotex, trademark for this board.

Celt ic (sel'tik; *esp. Brit.* kel'tik), *adj.* of the Celts or their language. —*n.* the group of languages spoken by the Celts. Also, **Keltic.**

---

hat, āge, cãre, fär; let, ēqual, tėrm; it, īce; hot, ōpen, ôrder; oil, out; cup, pút, rüle, ūse; th, thin; ŦH, then; zh, measure; ə represents *a* in about, *e* in taken, *i* in pencil, *o* in lemon, *u* in circus.

cen trif u gal (sen trif′ə gəl or sen trif′ū gəl), *adj.* **1.** moving, or being forced away, from a central core of action. [< NL *centrifugus* < L *centrum* center + *fugere* flee]

cere ment (sēr′mənt), *n.* Usually, **cerements,** *pl.* cloth or garment in which a dead person is wrapped for burial.

cha grin (shə grin′), *n.* a feeling of disappointment, failure, or humiliation. —*v.* cause to feel chagrin.

chaise (shāz), *n.* a lightweight carriage. One kind usually has a folding top.

chal lis or **chal lie** (shal′i), *n.* a lightweight woolen, woolen and cotton, or rayon cloth, used for dresses.

cha mi so (chə mē′sō), *n.* a semidesert shrub of the SW United States.

chan cel lor (chan′sə lər or chan′slər), *n.* **1.** a very high official who is the secretary of a nobleman, king, or embassy. **2.** *U.S.* the chief judge of certain courts. **3.** title of the president in certain universities.

chap let (chap′lit), *n.* **1.** wreath worn on the head. **2.** string of beads. **3.** string of beads for keeping count in saying prayers. **4.** prayers said with such beads.

Char on (kār′ən), *n.* in Greek mythology, the boatman who ferried the spirits of the dead across the river Styx to Hades.

chaste (chāst), *adj.* **1.** pure; virtuous. **2.** decent; modest. **3.** simple in taste or style.

chas ten (chās′ən), *v.* **1.** punish to improve. **2.** restrain from excess. [< obsolete v. *chaste* < F < L *castigare* make pure < *castus* pure]

chat tel (chat′əl), *n.* a movable possession; piece of property that is not real estate. Furniture, automobiles, slaves, and animals are chattels.

Chick a ha ma ni a (chik′ä hä mä′ni ä)

cho re og ra phy (kō′ri og′rə fi or kō′ri og′rə fi), *n.* **1.** art of planning the dances in a ballet. **2.** dancing; ballet dancing. [< Gk. *choreia* dance + E -*graphy* writing < Gk. *graphein* write] —**cho′re o graph′ic,** *adj.*

churl ish (chėr′lish), *adj.* rude; surly: *a churlish reply.*

cir cu i tous (sər kū′ə təs), *adj.* roundabout; not direct: *We took a circuitous route home to avoid poor roads.* —**Syn.** indirect.

cleat (klēt), *n.* **1.** strip of wood or iron fastened across anything for support or for sure footing. **2.** a small, wedge-shaped block fastened to a pole, etc., as a support, check, etc. **3.** piece of wood or iron used for securing ropes or lines. —*v.* fasten to or with a cleat.

cleave¹ (klēv), *v.,* **cleft** or **cleaved** or **clove, cleft** or **cleaved** or **clo ven, cleav ing.** **1.** split; divide. **2.** pierce; penetrate. **3.** make by cutting. [OE *clēofan*]

cleave² (klēv), *v.* hold fast (*to*); cling; be faithful (*to*): *cleave to an idea.* [OE *cleofian*]

cleft (kleft), *adj.* split; divided. —*n.* space or opening made by splitting; crack.

clime (klīm), *n. Poetic.* country; region; climate.

clock (klok), *n.* an ornamental pattern sewn or woven on the side of a stocking, extending up from the ankle.

clout (klout), *n. Informal.* a hit with the hand.

clo ven (klō′vən), *adj.* split; divided.

cloy (kloi), *v.* **1.** weary by too much, too sweet, or too rich food. **2.** weary by too much of anything pleasant.

co a lesce (kō′ə les′), *v.* **1.** grow together. **2.** unite into one mass, party, etc.: *The colonies coalesced to form a nation.* [< L *coalescere* < *co-* together + *alescere* grow]

coch i neal (koch′ə nēl′ or koch′ə nēl′), *n.* a bright-red dye made from the dried bodies of the females of a scale insect that lives on cactus plants of tropical America.

cock ade (kok ād′), *n.* knot of ribbon or a rosette worn on the hat as a badge.

cock ney (kok′ni), *n.* **1.** native or inhabitant of the poorer section of London who speaks a particular dialect of English. **2.** this dialect. —*adj.* **1.** of or like the dialect of cockneys. **2.** of or like cockneys.

cof fer (kôf′ər or kof′ər), *n.* **1.** box, chest, or trunk, especially one used to hold money or other valuables. **2. coffers,** *pl.* treasury. [<OF *cofre* < L *cophinus* basket]

co her ent (kō hēr′ənt), *adj.* **1.** logically connected; consistent in structure and thought. **2.** sticking together; holding together.

co hort (kō′hôrt), *n.* **1.** group; band; company. **2.** an associate or colleague.

col lat er al (kə lat′ər əl), *adj.* **1.** parallel. **2.** related but less important. **3.** secured by stocks, bonds, etc. —*n.* stocks, bonds, etc., pledged as security for a loan. [< Med.L *collateralis* < *com-* + L *lateralis* lateral]

col on nade (kol′ə nād′), *n.* series of columns set the same distance apart.

co los sus (kə los′əs), *n., pl.* **-los si** (-los′i) or **-los sus es, 1.** a huge statue. **2.** anything huge; gigantic person or thing.

come ly (kum′li), *adj.* **1.** having a pleasant appearance; attractive. **2.** suitable; proper. —**come li ness,** *n.*

Two colossi of ancient Egypt

com man deer (kom′ən dēr′), *v.* **1.** seize (private property) for military or public use: *All automobiles in the town were commandeered by the army.* **2.** force (men) into military service.

com mis er ate (kə miz′ər āt), *v.* feel or express sorrow for; sympathize with; pity.

com mis sar y (kom′ə ser′i), *n.* **1.** store handling food and supplies in a lumber camp, army camp, etc. **2.** an army officer in charge of food and daily supplies.

com mon (kom′ən), *adj.* **1.** belonging equally to each or all of a group. **2.** of all; general. **3.** belonging to the community at large. **4.** usual; familiar. **5.** below ordinary; inferior; coarse; vulgar. —*n.* land owned or used by all the people of a town, village, etc.

com mu ni cant (kə mū′nə kənt), *n.* **1.** person who receives Holy Communion. **2.** person who gives information by talking, writing, etc. —*adj.* communicating.

com mun ion (kə mūn′yən), *n.* **1.** act of sharing; a having in common. **2.** exchange of thoughts and feelings; fellowship. **3.** a close spiritual relationship.

com pan ion way (kəm pan′yən wā′), *n.* **1.** stairway from the deck of a ship down to the rooms below. **2.** space where such a stairway is.

com pass (kum′pəs), *n.* **1.** instrument for showing directions, consisting of a needle that points to the magnetic north. **2.** space within limits; extent; range: *The old sailor had many adventures within the compass of his lifetime.* —*v.* **1.** surround. **2.** imagine; plot; devise. **3.** grasp with the mind.

com pla cent (kəm plā′sənt), *adj.* pleased with oneself; self-satisfied: *The winner's complacent smile annoyed some people.* [< L *complacens, -entis,* ppr. of *complacere* < *com-* + *placere* please] —**com pla′cent ly,** *adv.* —**com pla′cen cy,** *n.*

< = from, taken from;   cf., compare;   dial., dialect;   dim., diminutive;   pp., past participle; ppr., present participle;   pt., past tense;   ult., ultimately;   var., variant;   ?=possibly.

com port (kəm pôrt′ or kəm pōrt′), *v.* behave: *A judge should comport himself with dignity.* [< F < L *comportare* < *com-* together + *portare* carry]

com post (kom′pōst), *n.* **1.** mixture. **2.** mixture of leaves, manure, etc., for fertilizing land.

con ceit (kən sēt′), *n.* **1.** too high an opinion of oneself or of one's ability, importance, etc. **2.** a fanciful notion; witty thought or expression, often far-fetched.

con cert ed (kən sėr′tid), *adj.* **1.** planned or made together; combined: *a concerted attack.* **2.** in music, arranged in parts for several voices or instruments.

con clave (kon′klāv or kong′klāv), *n.* a private meeting. [< L *conclave* a room that can be locked < *com-* with + *clavis* key]

con com i tant (kon kom′ə tənt or kən kom′ə-tənt), *adj.* accompanying; attending: *a concomitant result.* —*n.* an accompanying thing or circumstance. [< L *concomitans, -antis,* ppr. of *concomitari* < *com-* + *comitari* accompany]

con course (kon′kôrs or kon′kōrs), *n.* **1.** a running, flowing, or coming together. **2.** crowd.

Con es to ga wagon (kon′is tō′gə wag′ən), *n.* a covered wagon with broad wheels, formerly used for traveling on soft ground or on the prairie. [from *Conestoga,* Pa.]

con found (kon found′ or kən found′), *v.* **1.** confuse; mix up: *The shock confounded her.* **2.** be unable to tell apart: *He confounds "deprecate" and "depreciate."* **3.** surprise and puzzle.

con geal (kən jēl′), *v.* **1.** freeze. **2.** thicken; stiffen.

con gen i tal (kən jen′ə təl), *adj.* inborn; present at birth. [< L *congenitus* born with < *com-* with + *genitus* born]

con jec ture (kən jek′chər), *n.* **1.** formation of an opinion admittedly without sufficient evidence for proof. **2.** a guess. —*v.* guess. [< L *conjectura* < *conjicere* < *com-* together + *jacere* throw]

con jure (kun′jər or kon′jər *for 1-3;* kən jür′ *for 4*), *v.* **1. conjure up, a.** cause to appear in a magic way. **b.** cause to appear in the mind. **2.** compel (a spirit, devil, etc.) to appear or disappear by magic words. **3.** cause to or happen by magic or as if by magic. **4.** make a solemn appeal to; request earnestly: *I conjure you not to betray your country.* —**con′ju ra′tion,** *n.*

con san guin i ty (kon′sang gwin′ə ti), *n.* **1.** relationship by descent from the same parent or ancestor. **2.** any close relation or connection.

con sign ment (kən sīn′mənt), *n.* **1.** act of consigning. **2.** shipment sent for safekeeping or sale. **3. on consignment,** consigned to a person or company with the understanding that the goods will not be paid for until sold.

con spir a tor (kən spir′ə tər), *n.* person who plans secretly to do something wrong; plotter: *Conspirators planned to kill the king.*

con stit u ent (kən stich′ü ənt), *adj.* **1.** forming a necessary part. **2.** appointing; electing. **3.** having the power to make or change a political constitution. —*n.* **1.** a necessary part of a whole. **2.** person who votes or appoints; voter: *The congressman received many letters from his constituents.*

con strain (kən strān′), *v.* **1.** force; compel. **2.** confine; imprison. **3.** repress; restrain. [< OF *constreindre* < L *constringere* < *com-* together + *stringere* pull tightly]

con strained (kən strānd′), *adj.* **1.** forced. **2.** restrained; stiff; unnatural: *a constrained smile.*

con sum mate (*v.* kon′sə māt; *adj.* kən sum′it), *v.* complete; fulfill: *His ambition was consummated when he* won the first prize. —*adj.* complete; perfect; in the highest degree: *The paintings show consummate skill.*

con temn (kən tem′), *v.* treat with contempt; scorn.

con tempt i ble (kən temp′tə bəl), *adj.* deserving contempt or scorn; held in contempt; mean; low; worthless: *Cowards and cheats are contemptible.* —**con tempt′-i ble ness,** *n.* —**con tempt′i bly,** *adv.*

con temp tu ous (kən temp′chü əs), *adj.* showing contempt; scornful: *a contemptuous look.* —**con temp′-tu ous ly,** *adv.* —**con temp′tu ous ness,** *n.*
→ **Contemptuous** and **contemptible** are sometimes confused. The distinction will be clear if one observes that in *contemptible* the suffix *-ible,* as often, means deserving.

con tort (kən tôrt′), *v.* twist or bend out of shape. [L *contortus,* pp. of *contorquere* < *com-* + *torquere* twist]

con tre temps (kôN′trə täN′), *n.* an unlucky accident; embarrassing or awkward happening.

con verge (kən vėrj′), *v.* **1.** tend to meet in a point. **2.** come together; center. **3.** cause to converge. [< LL *convergere* < L *com-* together + *vergere* incline]

co pi ous (kō′pi əs), *adj.* **1.** plentiful; abundant. **2.** containing much matter. **3.** containing many words.

cop per head (kop′ər hed′), *n.* **1.** a poisonous North American snake with a copper-colored head. **2.** Copperhead, person in the North who sympathized with the South during the Civil War. [Am.E]

copse (kops), *n.* a thicket of small trees, bushes, shrubs.

co quet ry (kō′kə tri or kō ket′ri), *n.* **1.** flirting. **2.** trifling.

cor don (kôr′dən), *n.* **1.** line or circle of soldiers, policemen, forts, etc., placed at intervals to guard a place. **2.** cord, braid, or ribbon worn as an ornament or badge of honor. [< F *cordon* < *corde* cord]

cord wain er (kôrd′wān ər), *n.* *Obsolete.* shoemaker.

cor nice (kôr′nis), *n.* **1.** an ornamental molding that projects along the top of a wall, pillar, building, etc. **2.** molding around the walls of a room just below the ceiling. —*v.* finish with a cornice.

cor po rate (kôr′pə rit or kôr′prit), *adj.* **1.** having to do with a corporation. **2.** united; combined; in a group. [< L *corporatus,* pp. of *corporare* form into a body < *corpus* body]

cor pu lent (kôr′pū lənt), *adj.* fat. [< L *corpulen-tus* < *corpus* body]

co run dum (kə run′dəm), *n.* an extremely hard mineral. The dark-colored variety is used for polishing and grinding. Transparent varieties are sapphires, rubies, etc.

cos mos (koz′məs or koz′mos), *n.* **1.** the universe thought of as an orderly, harmonious system; opposite of chaos. **2.** any complete system that is orderly and harmonious. [< NL < Gk. *kosmos* order, world]

co til lion (kə til′yən), *n.* *Esp. U.S.* a dance with complicated steps and much changing of partners, led by one couple.

couch ant (kouch′ənt), *adj.* lying down, but with the head raised. [< F *couchant,* ppr. of *coucher* lie]

coun ter pane (koun′tər pān′), *n.* an outer covering for a bed; bedspread. [alteration of *counterpoint* quilt < OF]

cours er (kôr′sər or kōr′sər), *n.* *Poetic.* a swift horse. [< OF *coursier* < *cours* a running < L *cursus*]

cov e nant (kuv′ə nənt), *n.* **1.** a solemn agreement between two or more persons or groups to do or not to do a certain thing; compact. **2.** a legal contract; formal agreement that is legal. —*v.* solemnly agree (to do certain things).

---

hat, āge, cāre, fär; let, ēqual, tėrm; it, īce; hot, ōpen, ôrder; oil, out; cup, pu̇t, rüle, ūse;
th, thin; ᴛн, then; zh, measure; ə represents *a* in about, *e* in taken, *i* in pencil, *o* in lemon, *u* in circus.

cow (kou), *v.* frighten. —**Syn.** scare, bully.

cra ven (krā′vən), *adj.* cowardly. —*n.* coward.

Cre ole or **cre ole** (krē′ōl), *n.* **1.** a white person who is a descendant of the French who settled in Louisiana. **2.** the French language as spoken in Louisiana. **3.** a French or Spanish person born in Spanish America or the West Indies. **4.** **creole,** person who is part Negro and part Creole.

cre o sote (krē′ə sōt), *n.* **1.** an oily liquid with a penetrating odor, obtained by distilling wood tar, used to preserve wood and in cough medicine. **2.** a similar substance obtained from coal tar. —*v.* treat with creosote.

crew el (krü′əl), *n.* a loosely twisted, woolen yarn, used for embroidery.

crone (krōn), *n.* a withered old woman. [< MDutch *croonje* < OF *carogne* carcass, hag]

crypt (kript), *n.* an underground room or vault.

cryp tic (krip′tik), *adj.* having a hidden meaning; secret; mysterious: *a cryptic message, a cryptic reply.* [< LL *crypticus* < Gk. *kryptikos* < *kryptos* hidden]

C.S.A., **1.** Confederate States of America. **2.** Confederate States Army.

Cul len, Coun teé (koun′tē kul′ən)

cu lottes (kū lots′), *n.pl.* a woman's skirt divided and sewn like trousers, but cut so full as to appear much like an ordinary skirt; divided skirt. [< F]

cul vert (kul′vərt), *n.* a small channel for water crossing under a road, railroad, canal, etc.

cu mu la tive (kū′mū lā′tiv or kū′mū lə tiv), *adj.* heaped up; accumulated; increasing or growing in amount, force, etc., by additions.

cu ne i form (kū nē′ə fôrm or kū′ni ə fôrm′), *adj.* wedge-shaped. —*n.* the wedge-shaped characters used in the writing of ancient Babylonia, Assyria, Persia, etc.

cu po la (kū′pə lə), *n.* **1.** a rounded roof; dome. **2.** a small dome or tower on a roof.

cu ri os i ty (kūr′i os′ə ti), *n.* **1.** an eager desire to know. **2.** a strange, rare, or novel object.

cur lew (kėr′lü), *n., pl.* **-lews** or (*esp. collectively*) **-lew,** a wading bird with a long, thin bill.

cur ri cle (kėr′ə kəl), *n.* a two-wheeled carriage drawn by two horses.

cus tom (kus′təm), *n.* the regular business given by a customer.

cyn ic (sin′ik), *n.* **1.** person inclined to believe that the motives for people's actions are insincere and selfish. **2.** **Cynic,** member of a group of ancient Greek philosophers who taught that self-control is the essential part of virtue. They despised pleasure, money, and personal comfort. —*adj.* **1.** cynical. **2.** **Cynic,** of the Cynics or their doctrines.

dam (dam), *n.* **1.** the female parent of four-footed animals. **2.** mother. [var. of *dame*]

dank (dangk), *adj.* unpleasantly damp; moist; wet.

D'Ar landes, Mar quis (mär kē′ där länd′)

dead fall (ded′fôl′), *n.* **1.** trap for animals made so that a heavy weight falls upon the animal. **2.** mass of fallen trees and underbrush.

dearth (dėrth), *n.* **1.** scarcity; lack; too small a supply. **2.** scarcity of food; famine.

de bauch er y (di bôch′ər i or di bôch′ri), *n.* excessive indulgence in sensual pleasures.

de bris (də brē′ or dā′brē), *n.* **1.** scattered fragments; ruins; rubbish: *The street was covered with debris from the explosion.* **2.** in geology, a mass of fragments of rock, etc.

dec i mate (des′ə māt), *v.* destroy much of; kill a large part of: *War had decimated the tribe.*

dec o rous (dek′ə rəs or di kô′rəs), *adj.* well-behaved; acting properly; in good taste. —**dec′o rous ly,** *adv.* —**dec′o rous ness, de co′rum,** *n.*

de cry (di krī′), *v.* condemn; underrate; run down.

de fault (di fôlt′), *n.* **1.** failure to do something or to appear somewhere when due; neglect. **2.** failure to pay when due. **3.** lack; absence.

def er ence (def′ər əns), *n.* **1.** a yielding to the judgment or opinion of another; courteous submission. **2.** great respect. —**def′er en′tial,** *adj.*

de file[1] (di fīl′), *v.* **1.** make filthy or dirty; make disgusting in any way. **2.** destroy the purity or cleanness of; corrupt. [alteration of *defoul* (< OF *defouler* trample down, violate) after obsolete *file* befoul < OE *fȳlan* < *ful* foul]

de file[2] (di fīl′ or dē′fīl), *v.* march in a line. —*n.* a narrow way or passage through which troops can march only in narrow columns; steep and narrow valley. [< F *défilé*, special use of pp. of *défiler* march by files < *dé-* off + *file* file]

de fin i tive (di fin′ə tiv), *adj.* **1.** conclusive; final; complete. **2.** limiting; defining.

de funct (di fungkt′), *adj.* dead; no longer existing.

deign (dān), *v.* **1.** condescend; think fit: *So great a man would never deign to notice us.* **2.** condescend to give (an answer, a reply, etc.).

delft (delft), *n.* kind of glazed earthenware made in Holland, usually decorated in blue.

dem a gogu er y (dem′ə gôg′ər i or dem′ə gog′ər i), *n. Esp. U.S.* methods or principles of a demagogue, a popular leader who stirs up the people by appealing to their emotions and prejudices. [Am.E]

de mean[1] (di mēn′), *v.* lower in dignity or standing; humble. [< *de-* down + *mean* low in quality]

de mean[2] (di mēn′), *v.* behave or conduct (oneself). [< OF *demener* < *de-* (< L) + *mener* lead < L *minare* drive]

dem i john (dem′i jon), *n.* a large bottle of glass or earthenware enclosed in wicker.

de mur (di mėr′), *v.* object: *The clerk demurred at working overtime without extra pay.* —*n.* an objection.

de nun ci a tion (di nun′si ā′shən or di nun′shi ā′shən), *n.* **1.** expression of strong disapproval. **2.** accusation. **3.** declaration of a curse, revenge, etc.; warning; threat.

dep o si tion (dep′ə zish′ən or dē′pə zish′ən), *n.* **1.** act of putting out of office or a position of authority. **2.** testimony. **3.** a sworn statement in writing: *A deposition was made before the witness left town.*

dep re cate (dep′rə kāt), *v.* express strong disapproval of: *Lovers of peace deprecate war.*

→ deprecate, depreciate. Do not confuse *deprecate*, meaning to express strong disapproval of, with *depreciate*, meaning to lessen in value or price. Contrast these sentences: *I feel I must deprecate the course the club is following. Naturally the car depreciates after a number of years of service.*

de pre ci ate (di prē′shi āt), *v.* lessen the value or price of. → See **deprecate** for usage note.

de range (di rānj′), *v.* **1.** disturb the order or arrangement of; throw into confusion. **2.** make insane.

der e lic tion (der′ə lik′shən), *n.* **1.** failure in one's duty; negligence. **2.** abandonment; desertion; forsaking.

de ride (di rīd′), *v.* make fun of; ridicule.

de ri sive (di rī′siv), *adj.* mocking; ridiculing. —**de ri′sive ly,** *adv.*

de riv a tive (di riv′ə tiv), *adj.* derived; coming from a source; not original. —*n.* something derived.

< = from, taken from; cf., compare; dial., dialect; dim., diminutive; pp., past participle; ppr., present participle; pt., past tense; ult., ultimately; var., variant; ?=possibly.

der rin ger (der′ən jər), *n.* *U.S.* a short pistol that has a large inside diameter. [Am.E; named after H. *Derringer*, Am. inventor]

des e crate (des′ə krāt), *v.* treat or use without respect; disregard the sacredness of: *The enemy desecrated the church by using it as a stable.* [< *de-* + (*con*) *secrate*]

dev o tee (dev′ə tē′), *n.* person devoted to something.

De Vo to (də vō′tō)

di a pa son (dī′ə pā′zən or dī′ə pā′sən), *n.* 1. harmony. 2. melody; strain. 3. a swelling musical sound. 4. the whole range of a voice or instrument.

di late (dī lāt′ or də lāt′), *v.* make or become larger or wider: *The pupils of John's eyes dilated when the light got dim.* [< L *dilatare* < *dis-* apart + *latus* wide]

dil a to ry (dil′ə tô′ri or dil′ə tō′ri), *adj.* 1. tending to delay; not prompt. 2. causing delay.

din ghy (ding′gi), *n.* 1. a small rowboat. 2. a small boat used as a tender by a large boat.

dint (dint), *n.* force: *By dint of hard work he succeeded.*

dirge (dėrj), *n.* a funeral song or tune.

dirk (dėrk), *n.* dagger. —*v.* stab with a dirk.

dis ap pro ba tion (dis′ap rə bā′shən), *n.* disapproval.

dis a vow (dis′ə vou′), *v.* deny that one knows about, approves of, or is responsible for.

dis cern (də zėrn′ or də sėrn′), *v.* perceive; see clearly; distinguish; recognize: *He could not discern any difference between the original and the copy.*

dis com fi ture (dis kum′fi chür or dis kum′fi chər), *n.* 1. a complete overthrow; defeat; rout. 2. defeat of plans or hopes; frustration. 3. confusion.

dis com pose (dis′kəm pōz′), *v.* make uneasy.

dis con cert (dis kon′sėrt), *n.* lack of concert, harmony, simultaneous action, etc.; disorder.

dis con so late (dis kon′sə lit), *adj.* without hope; forlorn; unhappy; cheerless.

dis coun te nance (dis koun′tə nəns), *v.* 1. refuse to approve; discourage: *This school discountenances secret societies.* 2. abash.

dis crim i nate (*v.* dis krim′ə nāt; *adj.* dis krim′ə-nit), *v.* 1. make or see a difference: *It is often difficult to discriminate between a mere exaggeration and a deliberate falsehood.* 2. make a difference in treatment or favor: *The law does not discriminate against any race, creed, or color.* 3. make or see a difference between; distinguish: *discriminate good books from poor ones.* —*adj.* having discrimination. —**dis crim′i nate ly**, *adv.* —**dis-crim′i na′tor, dis crim′i na′tion,** *n.*

dis crim i nat ing (dis krim′ə nāt′ing), *adj.* able to distinguish or see differences in: *She was discriminating in her choice of friends.*

dis dain (dis dān′), *v.* look down on; consider beneath oneself; scorn: *The honest official disdained the offer of a bribe.* —*n.* act of disdaining; feeling of scorn.

dis ha bille (dis′ə bēl′), *n.* 1. informal dress. 2. garment worn in dishabille. 3. condition of being only partly dressed. [< F *déshabillé*, pp. of *déshabiller* < *dés-* (< L *dis-*) + *habiller* dress]

dis in ter est ed (dis in′tər is tid, dis in′tris tid, or dis in′tər es′tid), *adj.* free from selfish motives; impartial.

→ **Disinterested** and **uninterested** should not be confused. *Disinterested* means having no selfish interest or personal feelings in a matter and therefore having no reason or desire to be anything but strictly impartial and fair: *A judge should be disinterested. Uninterested* means not interested in any way, having no concern or feelings about the matter and paying no attention: *An uninterested boy can spoil a class.*

dis par age ment (dis par′ij mənt), *n.* 1. act of disparaging, belittling, speaking slightingly of. 2. something that lowers a thing or person in worth or importance.

dis po si tion (dis′pə zish′ən), *n.* 1. habitual ways of acting toward others or of thinking about things; nature: *a selfish disposition.* 2. tendency; inclination: *a disposition to argue.* 3. act of putting in order or position. 4. management; settlement: *the satisfactory disposition of a difficult problem.*

dis pu tant (dis′pū tənt or dis pūt′ənt), *n.* person who takes part in a dispute or debate.

dis sem i nate (di sem′ə nāt), *v.* scatter widely; spread abroad: *Missionaries disseminate Christian beliefs.*

dis si pa tion (dis′ə pā′shən), *n.* 1. a scattering or being scattered. 2. amusement; diversion, especially harmful amusements. 3. too much indulgence in evil or foolish pleasures; intemperance.

dis so lute (dis′ə lüt), *adj.* living an evil life.

dis so lu tion (dis′ə lü′shən), *n.* 1. a breaking up. 2. ruin; destruction. 3. death.

dis tem per (dis tem′pər), *n.* a disease of animals, accompanied by a loss of strength.

dis tend (dis tend′), *v.* stretch out; swell out; expand. [< L *distendere* < *dis-* apart + *tendere* stretch]

dis traught (dis trôt′), *adj.* 1. in a state of mental conflict and confusion. 2. crazed.

di ver gent (də vėr′jənt or dī vėr′jənt), *adj.* diverging; different.

di vers (dī′vərz), *adj.* several different; various.

di verse (də vėrs′ or dī vėrs′), *adj.* 1. different; unlike. 2. varied: *A person of diverse interests can talk on many subjects.* —**di ver′si ty,** *n.*

di vert (də vėrt′ or dī vėrt′), *v.* 1. turn aside. 2. amuse; entertain. —**di ver′sion,** *n.*

di vest (də vest′ or dī vest′), *v.* 1. strip; rid. 2. force to give up.

div i na tion (div′ə nā′shən), *n.* 1. act of foreseeing the future. 2. a skillful guess or prediction.

doff (dof or dôf), *v.* 1. take off; remove. 2. get rid of; throw aside. [contraction of *do off*]

dog i ron (dôg ī′ərn), *n.* andiron.

dom i nie (dom′ə ni *for 1;* dom′ə ni or dō′mə ni *for 2*), *n.* 1. *Esp. Scottish.* schoolmaster. 2. *Informal.* clergyman.

Dor ic (dôr′ik or dor′ik), *adj.* of or having to do with the oldest and simplest of the Greek kinds of architecture.

dou bloon (dub lün′), *n.* a former Spanish gold coin.

douche (düsh), *n.* 1. jet of water applied on or into any part of the body: *A douche of salt water up my nose helped relieve my cold in the head.* 2. application of a douche. 3. spray or other device for applying a douche. —*v.* 1. apply a douche to. 2. take a douche.

dough ty (dou′ti), *adj.* *Archaic* or *Humorous.* brave; valiant; strong: *doughty knights.*

drab (drab), *n.* 1. a dirty, untidy woman. 2. prostitute.

draught (draft or dräft), *n.* amount taken in one drink. —**draught′er,** *n.*

draw (drô), *n.* a small land basin into or through which water drains; valley.

dray (drā), *n.* a low, strong cart for hauling heavy loads.

droll (drōl), *adj.* amusingly odd; humorously quaint; laughable: *We smiled at the monkey's droll tricks.* [< F *drôle* (originally n.) good fellow < Dutch *drol* little fat fellow]

---

hat, āge, cãre, fär; let, ēqual, tėrm; it, īce; hot, ōpen, ôrder; oil, out; cup, pút, rüle, ūse; th, thin; ᴛн, then; zh, measure; ə represents *a* in about, *e* in taken, *i* in pencil, *o* in lemon, *u* in circus.

drove (drōv), *n.* **1.** group of cattle, sheep, hogs, etc., moving or driven along together; herd; flock. **2.** many people moving along together; crowd.

du al ism (dü′əl iz əm or dū′əl iz əm), *n.* **1.** dual condition; duality. **2.** doctrine that all the phenomena of the universe can be explained by two separate substances or principles, such as mind and matter.

du cal (dü′kəl or dū′kəl), *adj.* of a duke or dukedom.

dul cet (dul′sit), *adj.* soothing, especially to the ear; sweet; pleasing. [< F *doucet*, dim. of *doux* sweet < L *dulcis*]

Du pin, C. Au guste (sā ō gYst′ dY paN′)

Dutch ov en (duch′ uv′ən), *n.* **1.** a metal box that opens in front, used for roasting meat, etc., before an open fire or on top of a stove. **2.** a heavy iron kettle with a close-fitting cover. **3.** a brick oven in which the walls are first heated, and food is put in to cook after the fire goes out or is removed.

dys pep si a (dis pep′si ə or dis pep′shə), *n.* poor digestion; indigestion. [< L < Gk. *dyspepsia* < *dys*-bad + *pep*- cook, digest]

é clat (ā klä′), *n.* **1.** a brilliant success. **2.** glory. **3.** burst of applause or approval.

ed i fi ca tion (ed′ə fə kā′shən), *n.* moral improvement; spiritual benefit; instruction.

ef fect (ə fekt′), *n.* **1.** whatever is produced by a cause; result. **2.** power to produce results; force. **3.** influence: *The medicine had an immediate effect.* **4.** impression produced. **5. effects,** *pl.* personal property; belongings; goods. —*v.* **1.** make happen; get done; bring about. **2.** make; construct. [< L *effectus* < *efficere* < *ex*- out + *facere* make]

ef fi ca cy (ef′ə kə si), *n.* power to produce a desired effect or result; effectiveness. [< L *efficacia* < *efficere* accomplish] —**ef′fi ca′cious,** *adj.*

ef flu vi um (i flü′vi əm), *n., pl.* **-vi a** or **-vi ums. 1.** an unpleasant vapor or odor. **2.** vapor; odor. [< L *effluvium* a flowing out < *effluere*]

e gress (ē′gres), *n.* **1.** a going out: *The enemy blocked the narrow pass so that no egress was possible.* **2.** way out; exit. **3.** right to go out. [< L *egressus* < *egredi* < *ex*- out + *gradi* step, go]

El do ra do or **El Do ra do** (el′də rä′dō), *n., pl.* **-dos. 1.** a legendary city of very great wealth sought by early explorers in South America. **2.** any fabulously wealthy place. [< Sp. *El Dorado,* literally, the gilded]

el e gi ac (el′ə jī′ak or i lē′ji ak), *adj.* **1.** of or suitable for an elegy, a poem which mourns the dead. **2.** sad; mournful; melancholy.

el e men tal (el′ə men′təl), *adj.* **1.** of the four elements—earth, water, air, and fire. **2.** of the forces of nature. **3.** as found in nature; simple but powerful: *Hunger is an elemental feeling.* **4.** being a necessary part. **5.** elementary.

e lu sive (i lü′siv), *adj.* **1.** hard to describe or understand; baffling. **2.** tending to elude: *an elusive enemy.*

em bar go (em bär′gō), *n.* **1.** order of a government forbidding ships to enter or leave its ports. **2.** restriction; restraint; hindrance. —*v.* lay an embargo on.

em bel lish (em bel′ish), *v.* **1.** decorate; adorn; ornament. **2.** make more interesting by adding real or imaginary details; elaborate: *He embellished the old stories, so that they sounded new.*

em brace (em brās′), *v.* **1.** hug. **2.** hug one another: *The two girls embraced.* **3.** take up; accept. **4.** include; contain: *The cat family embraces lions, tigers, and similar animals.* —*n.* an embracing.

em i nence (em′ə nəns), *n.* **1.** rank or position above all or most others; high standing; greatness; fame. **2.** a high place; lofty hill.

em is sar y (em′ə ser′i), *n.* **1.** person sent on a mission or errand. **2.** a secret agent; spy.

e mit (i mit′), *v.* give off; send out; discharge.

em u late (em′ū lāt), *v.* try to equal or excel.

en join (en join′), *v.* **1.** order; direct; urge: *Parents enjoin good behavior on their children.* **2.** in law, issue an authoritative command.

en mi ty (en′mə ti), *n.* the feeling that enemies have for each other; hate. —**Syn.** hostility.

en nui (än′wē), *n.* boredom. [< F]

en sign (en′sīn or en′sən *for 1, 3, and 4;* en′sən *for 2*), *n.* **1.** flag; banner. **2.** *U.S.* a navy officer ranking next below a lieutenant, junior grade. **3.** a former British army officer whose duty was carrying the flag. **4.** sign of one's rank, position, or power.

en sue (en sü′), *v.* come after; happen as a result; follow.

en tre pre neur (än′trə prə nėr′), *n.* person who organizes and manages a business or industrial enterprise, taking the risk of not making a profit and getting the profit when there is one. [< F *entrepreneur* < *entreprendre* undertake]

e phem er a (i fem′ər ə), *n., pl.* **-ae. 1.** May fly, a type of insect that lives only a day or two after reaching its adult form. **2.** something which lasts or lives for a very short time. —**e phem′er al,** *adj.*

ep i thet (ep′ə thet), *n.* a descriptive expression; adjective or noun, or even a clause, expressing some quality or attribute: *In "crafty Ulysses" and "Richard the Lion-Hearted" the epithets are "crafty" and "the Lion-Hearted."*

e qui nox (ē′kwə noks), *n.* either of the two times in the year when the center of the sun crosses the celestial equator, and day and night are of equal length all over the earth, occurring about March 21 (**vernal equinox**) and September 22 (**autumnal equinox**). [< Med.L *equinoxium* < L *aequinoctium* < *aequus* equal + *nox* night]

eq ui page (ek′wə pij), *n.* **1.** carriage. **2.** carriage with its horses, driver, and servants. **3.** equipment; outfit.

es cri toire (es′krə twär′), *n.* a writing desk.

es o ter ic (es′ə ter′ik), *adj.* **1.** understood only by the select few; intended for an inner circle of disciples, scholars, etc. **2.** private; secret.

es pouse (es pouz′), *v.* **1.** marry. **2.** take up or make one's own: *He espoused a new religion.*

e the re al (i thēr′i əl), *adj.* **1.** light; airy; delicate: *Her ethereal beauty made her seem more like a spirit than a human being.* **2.** not of the earth; heavenly.

e the re al ize (i thēr′i əl īz), *v.* make ethereal.

eth no gen e sis (eth′nə jen′ə sis), *n.* origin or creation of a race or nation.

E trus can (i trus′kən), *adj.* of or having to do with Etruria, its people, their language, art, and customs. —*n.* **1.** native or inhabitant of Etruria. **2.** language of Etruria.

ABOUT 14 A.D.

Eu clid (ū′klid), *n.* Greek mathematician who wrote a book on geometry about 300 B.C.

eu gen ics (ū jen′iks), *n. sing.* or *pl.* **1.** science of improving the human race by a careful selection of parents

---

< = from, taken from; cf., compare; dial., dialect; dim., diminutive; pp., past participle; ppr., present participle; pt., past tense; ult., ultimately; var., variant; ?=possibly.

in order to develop healthier, more intelligent, and better children. **2.** science of improving offspring.

eu ge nist (ū′jə nist), *n.* a specialist in eugenics.

eu lo gy (ū′lə ji), *n.* speech or writing in praise of a person, action, etc.; high praise. [< Gk. *eulogia* < *eu-* well + *legein* speak]

eu phe mism (ū′fə miz əm), *n.* **1.** use of a mild or indirect expression instead of one that is harsh or unpleasantly direct. **2.** a mild or indirect expression used in this way. "Pass away" is a common euphemism for "die." [< Gk. *euphemismos* < *euphemizein* speak with fair words < *eu-* good + *pheme* speaking]

ev a nes cence (ev′ə nes′əns), *n.* **1.** gradual disappearance; fading away. **2.** tendency to disappear or fade away; inability to last long. —**ev′a nes′cent**, *adj.*

e vince (i vins′), *v.* show clearly.

ev i ta ble (ev′ə tə bəl), *adj.* avoidable.

ex ac tion (eg zak′shən), *n.* **1.** a demanding and getting; a forcing to be paid: *The ruler's exactions of money left the people very poor.* **2.** thing exacted.

ex co ri ate (eks kô′ri āt), *v.* **1.** strip or rub off the skin of; make raw and sore. **2.** denounce violently.

ex cru ci at ing (eks krü′shi āt′ing), *adj.* very painful; torturing; causing great suffering.

ex hort (eg zôrt′), *v.* advise or warn earnestly. [< L *exhortari* < *ex-* + *hortari* urge strongly] —**ex hort′er**, *n.*

ex pe di ent (eks pē′di ənt), *adj.* **1.** fit for bringing about a desired result; desirable or suitable under the circumstances. **2.** giving or seeking personal advantage; based on self-interest. —*n.* means of bringing about a desired result: *Having no ladder or rope, the prisoner tied sheets together and escaped by this expedient.* —**ex pe′di ent ly**, *adv.* —**ex pe′di en cy**, *n.*

ex pi ate (eks′pi āt), *v.* make amends for (a wrong, sin, etc.); atone for: *The thief expiated his theft by giving back the amount stolen.* —**ex′pi a′tion**, *n.*

ex ple tive (eks′plə tiv), *adj.* oath or meaningless exclamation.

ex plic it (eks plis′it), *adj.* definite; exact. —**Ant.** vague, indefinite.

ex pos tu la tion (eks pos′chù lā′shən), *n.* earnest reasoning with a person to protest against something he means to do or has done.

ex qui site (eks′kwi zit or eks kwiz′it), *adj.* **1.** very lovely; delicate. **2.** sharp; intense: *exquisite pain.* **3.** of highest excellence. **4.** keenly sensitive.

ex tem po ra ne ous (eks tem′pə rā′ni əs), *adj.* **1.** spoken or done without preparation; offhand. **2.** made for the occasion: *an extemporaneous shelter against a storm.* [< LL *extemporaneus* < L *ex tempore* according to the moment]

ex tem po re (eks tem′pə ri), *adv.* offhand. —*adj.* made, done, or said on the spur of the moment.

ex tort (eks tôrt′), *v.* obtain (money, a promise, etc.) by threats, force, fraud, or illegal use of authority.

ex tra sen so ry (eks′trə sen′sə ri), *adj.* outside the realm of the senses.

ex tri cate (eks′trə kāt), *v.* set free (from entanglements, difficulties, etc.); release.

ex u ber ant (eg zü′bər ənt), *adj.* very abundant; overflowing; lavish: *exuberant health, good nature, or joy.* —**ex u′ber ant ly**, *adv.* —**ex u′ber ance**, *n.*

ex ult ant (eg zul′tənt), *adj.* rejoicing greatly; exulting; triumphant. —**ex′ul ta′tion**, *n.*

fa ce tious (fə sē′shəs), *adj.* said in fun; not to be taken seriously. —**fa ce′tious ly**, *adv.* —**fa ce′tious ness**, *n.*

fa cil i tate (fə sil′ə tāt), *v.* make easy; lessen the labor of; help forward.

fa cil i ty (fə sil′ə ti), *n.* **1.** absence of difficulty; ease. **2.** power to do anything easily, quickly, and smoothly. **3.** aid; convenience. —**Syn. 1.** easiness. **2.** knack, readiness.

fac tion (fak′shən), *n.* **1.** group of people in a political party, church, club, etc., acting together or having a common end in view. **2.** a selfish or unscrupulous group. **3.** strife or quarreling among the members of a political party, church, club, etc.

fac ul ty (fak′əl ti), *n.* **1.** power of the mind or body: *the faculty of memory.* **2.** power to do some special thing, especially a power of the mind: *Nell has a great faculty for arithmetic.* **3.** teachers of a school or college. —**Syn. 1.** capacity, capability.

fag ot (fag′ət), *n.* bundle of sticks or twigs tied together: *He built the fire with fagots.*

fain (fān), *Archaic* and *Poetic.* —*adv.* by choice; willingly. —*adj.* **1.** willing, but not eager. **2.** glad; willing. **3.** eager.

fal la cious (fə lā′shəs), *adj.* **1.** deceptive; misleading. **2.** logically unsound; erroneous: *It is fallacious reasoning to base a general rule on just two or three instances.* —**fal la′cious ly**, *adv.* —**fal la′cious ness**, *n.*

fal set to (fôl set′ō), *n.* **1.** an unnaturally high-pitched voice, especially in a man. **2.** person who sings with a falsetto. —*adj.* of or for a falsetto. —*adv.* in a falsetto. [< Ital. *falsetto*, dim. of *falso* false < L *falsus*]

fa nat ic (fə nat′ik), *n.* person who is carried away beyond reason by his feelings or beliefs. —*adj.* enthusiastic or zealous beyond reason.

fa nat i cal (fə nat′ə kəl), *adj.* unreasonably enthusiastic; extremely zealous. —**fa nat′i cal ly**, *adv.*

fat u ous (fach′ü əs), *adj.* stupid but self-satisfied; foolish; silly. [< L *fatuus* foolish]

faun (fôn), *n.* a minor Roman deity that helped farmers and shepherds. A faun is represented as looking like a man, but with the ears, horns, tail, and sometimes the legs, of a goat. [< L *Faunus* a pastoral deity]

fea si ble (fē′zə bəl), *adj.* **1.** capable of being done or carried out easily. **2.** suitable. —**fea′si bil′i ty**, *n.*

fe do ra (fi dô′rə or fi dō′rə), *n.* a man's soft felt hat with a curved brim. The crown is creased lengthwise. Also, **Fedora.**

feign (fān), *v.* **1.** pretend: *Some animals feign death when in danger.* **2.** make up to deceive; invent falsely.

feint (fānt), *n.* **1.** a false appearance; pretense: *The boy made a feint of studying hard.* **2.** movement intended to deceive; pretended blow. —*v.* make a pretended blow. [< F *feinte* < *feindre* feign]

feld spar (feld′spär′), *n.* any of several crystalline minerals found in certain kinds of rocks, such as granite.

fe lic i ty (fə lis′ə ti), *n.* **1.** happiness. **2.** good fortune; blessing. **3.** a pleasing aptness in expression; appropriateness; grace. [< L *felicitas* < *felix* happy]

fer vor (fėr′vər), *n.* great warmth of feeling; intense emotion. —**fer′vent**, *adj.*

fes toon (fes tün′), *n.* **1.** a hanging curve of flowers, leaves, ribbons, etc. **2.** a carved or molded ornament like this on furniture, pottery, etc. —*v.* **1.** decorate with festoons. **2.** form into festoons.

fi as co (fi as′kō), *n., pl.* **-cos** or **-coes.** complete or ridiculous failure.

fich u (fish′ü), *n.* a three-cornered piece of soft material worn by women about the neck, with the ends drawn together or crossed on the breast.

---

hat, āge, cãre, fär; let, ēqual, tėrm; it, īce; hot, ōpen, ôrder; oil, out; cup, pút, rüle, ūse; th, thin; ŦH, then; zh, measure; ə represents *a* in about, *e* in taken, *i* in pencil, *o* in lemon, *u* in circus.

fig ure head (fig′yər hed′), *n.* **1.** person who is the head in name only, and has no real authority or responsibility. **2.** statue or carving decorating the bow of a ship.

fil i al (fil′i əl), *adj.* of a son or daughter; due from a son or daughter: *The children treated their parents with filial respect.* [< LL *filialis* < L *filius* son, *filia* daughter]

fil i gr ee (fil′ə grē), *n.* lacy, delicate, or fanciful patterns in any material. —*adj.* ornamented with filigree.

fine (fīn), *n.* sum of money paid as a punishment. —*adv.* **in fine, a.** finally. **b.** in a few words.

fi nesse (fə nes′), *n.* delicacy of execution; skill. **2.** the skillful handling of a delicate situation to one's advantage: *A shrewd diplomat must be a master of finesse.*

fin i al (fin′i əl or fī′ni əl), *n.* **1.** ornament on top of a roof, corner of a tower, end of a pew in church, etc. **2.** the highest point.

fir ma ment (fėr′mə mənt), *n.* arch of the heavens; sky.

flail (flāl), *n.* **1.** instrument for threshing grain by hand. **2.** weapon. —*v.* beat; thrash.

flam beau (flam′bō), *n.* **1.** a flaming torch. **2.** a large, decorated candlestick.

flay (flā), *v.* **1.** strip off the skin. **2.** scold severely. **3.** rob.

flor id (flôr′id or flor′id), *adj.* **1.** highly colored; ruddy: *a florid complexion.* **2.** elaborately ornamented; flowery; showy; ornate. [< L *floridus* < *flos* flower]

flue (flü), *n.* tube, pipe, or other enclosed passage for conveying smoke, hot air, etc.

flume (flüm), *n.* **1.** a deep, narrow valley with a stream running through it. **2.** a large, inclined trough or chute for carrying water. Flumes are used to transport logs or to furnish water for power.

foal (fōl), *n.* a young horse, donkey, etc. —*v.* give birth to (a foal).

fo'c's'le (fōk′səl), *n.* forecastle.

fod der (fod′ər), *n.* coarse food for horses, cattle, etc. Hay and cornstalks with their leaves are fodder.

fo li o (fō′li ō), *n.* **1.** book of the largest size. A folio is usually any book more than 11 inches in height. **2.** book made of sheets each folded once, making four pages to a sheet.

fools cap (fülz′kap′), *n.* **1.** writing paper in sheets from 12 to 13½ inches wide and 15 to 17 inches long. **2.** fool's cap.

foot pad (fut′pad′), *n.* a highway robber who goes on foot only.

fop (fop), *n.* a vain man who is very fond of fine clothes and has affected manners; empty-headed dandy.

fore cas tle (fōk′səl or fôr′kas′əl), *n.* **1.** the upper deck in front of the foremast. **2.** the sailors' quarters in a merchant ship, formerly in the forward part.

fore world (fôr′wėrld′), *n.* the world in its earliest stages.

for mi da ble (fôr′mə də bəl), *adj.* hard to overcome; hard to deal with; to be dreaded. [< L *formidabilis* < *formidare* dread] —**Syn.** appalling, fearful.

foun der (foun′dər), *v.* **1.** fill with water and sink. **2.** break down; go lame; stumble: *His horse foundered.* **3.** become worn out; fail.

fowl er (foul′ər), *n.* person who hunts, shoots, catches, or traps wild birds.

fra cas (frā′kəs), *n.* a noisy fight; disturbance; uproar. [< F < Ital. *fracasso* < *fracassare* smash]

fra ter nal (frə tėr′nəl), *adj.* **1.** brotherly. **2.** having to do with a fraternal organization. [< L *fraternus* brotherly < *frater* brother]

fraught (frôt), *adj.* loaded; filled: *A battlefield is fraught with horror.*

free boot er (frē′büt′ər), *n.* pirate; buccaneer.

free will (frē′ wil′), *n.* will free from outside restraints; voluntary choice; freedom of decision.

fresh et (fresh′it), *n.* **1.** flood caused by heavy rains or melted snow. **2.** rush of fresh water flowing into the sea.

frig ate (frig′it), *n.* a fast, three-masted, sailing warship of medium size, much used from 1750 to 1850.

fru gal (frü′gəl), *adj.* **1.** avoiding waste; saving. **2.** costing little; barely sufficient. [< L *frugalis* < *frugi* temperate] —**fru′gal ly,** *adv.* —**fru gal′i ty,** *n.*

func tion ar y (fungk′shən er′i), *n.* official.

furl (fėrl), *v.* roll up; fold up. [< F *ferler* < OF *ferlier* < *fer* firm (< L *firmus*) + *lier* bind < L *ligare*]

fur tive (fėr′tiv), *adj.* **1.** secret: *a furtive glance into the forbidden room.* **2.** sly; stealthy. —**fur′tive ly,** *adv.*

fu se lage (fü′zə lazh or fü′zə lij), *n.* framework of the body of an airplane that holds passengers, cargo, etc. The wings and tail are fastened to it.

ga ble (gā′bəl), *n.* **1.** end of a ridged roof, with the three-cornered piece of wall that it covers. **2.** a triangular ornament or canopy over a door, window, etc.

gall (gôl), *v.* **1.** make or become sore by rubbing: *The rough strap galled the horse's skin.* **2.** annoy; irritate. —*n.* **1.** a sore spot on the skin caused by rubbing. **2.** cause of annoyance or irritation.

Gal lic (gal′ik), *adj.* **1.** of or having to do with Gaul, an ancient country in W Europe which included what is now France. **2.** French. [< L *Gallicus* < *Gallus* a Gaul]

gal li gas kins (gal′ə gas′kinz), *n.pl.* **1.** loose breeches. **2.** leggings.

gal lows (gal′əs iz), *n.pl. Dialect.* pair of suspenders.

gal va nize (gal′və nīz), *v.* **1.** apply an electric current to. **2.** arouse suddenly; startle. **3.** cover (iron or steel) with a thin coating of zinc to prevent rust.

gam bit (gam′bit), *n.* **1.** way of opening a game of chess by purposely sacrificing a pawn or a piece to gain some advantage. **2.** a calculated maneuver or device. [< F < Provençal *cambi* an exchange]

gam boge (gam bōj′ or gam büzh′), *n.* a gum resin from certain tropical trees, used as a yellow pigment.

gar goyle (gär′goil), *n.* **1.** spout for carrying off rain water, ending in a grotesque head that projects from the gutter of a building. **2.** projection or ornament on a building resembling a gargoyle.

gar ru lous (gar′ə ləs or gar′ü ləs), *adj.* **1.** talking too much about trifles. **2.** using too many words.

gas con ade (gas′kən ād′), *n.* extravagant boasting. —*v.* boast extravagantly.

gas ket (gas′kit), *n.* **1.** ring or strip of rubber, metal, etc., packed around a piston, pipe joint, etc., to keep steam, gas, etc., from escaping. **2.** cord or small rope used to secure a furled sail on a yard.

gauche (gōsh), *adj.* awkward; clumsy; tactless. [< F *gauche* left] —**gauche′ly,** *adv.* —**gauche′ness,** *n.*

gauge (gāj), *n., v.,* **gauged, gaug ing.** —*n.* **1.** standard measure; scale of standard measurements; measure. **2.** instrument for measuring. A **steam gauge** measures the pressure of steam. **3.** means of estimating or judging. **4.** size; capacity; extent. —*v.* **1.** measure accurately; find out the exact measurement of with a gauge. **2.** estimate; judge: *It is difficult to gauge the character of a stranger.*

< = from, taken from; cf., compare; dial., dialect; dim., diminutive; pp., past participle; ppr., present participle; pt., past tense; ult., ultimately; var., variant; ?=possibly.

gaunt let (gônt′lit or gänt′lit), *n.* **1.** a stout, heavy glove, usually of leather covered with plates of iron or steel, that was part of a knight's armor. **2.** a stout, heavy glove with a wide, flaring cuff. **3.** the wide, flaring cuff. **4. take up the gauntlet, a.** accept a challenge. **b.** take up the defense of a person, opinion, etc. **5. throw down the gauntlet,** challenge. Also, **gantlet.** [< OF *gantelet,* dim. of *gant* glove < Gmc.]

ga zette (gə zet′), *n.* **1.** newspaper. **2.** an official government journal containing lists of appointments, promotions, etc. —*v.* publish, list, or announce in a gazette. [< F < Ital. *gazzetta,* originally, coin; from price of paper]

gen der (jen′dər), *n.* **1.** in many languages, the grouping of nouns into a series of classes, such as masculine, feminine, neuter, etc. **2.** one of such classes. **3.** *Informal.* sex. —*v. Archaic.* engender; produce. [< OF *gendre* < L *genus* kind, sort]

gen e sis (jen′ə sis), *n., pl.* **-ses** (sēz). origin; creation; coming into being. [< L < Gk.]

gen re (zhäN′rə), *n.* kind; sort; style: *Poe was the originator of a genre of detective story.* [<F<L *genus* kind]

gen u flect (jen′ū flekt), *v.* bend the knee as an act of reverence or worship. [< Med.L *genuflectere* < L *genu* knee + *flectere* bend]

ger mane (jər mān′), *adj.* closely connected; to the point; pertinent.

ges tic u late (jes tik′ū lāt), *v.* **1.** make or use gestures. **2.** make or use many vehement gestures.

ges tic u la tion (jes tik′ū lā′shən), *n.* **1.** act of gesticulating. **2.** gesture.

gig¹ (gig), *n.* **1.** a light, two-wheeled carriage drawn by one horse. **2.** a long, light ship's boat moved by oars or sails. [origin uncertain]

gig² (gig), *n.* a fish spear; harpoon. —*v.* spear (fish) with a gig. [short for *fishgig,* ult. < Sp. *fisga* harpoon]

gill (jil), *n.* measure for liquids, equal to one fourth of a pint. [< OF *gille* wine measure]

gim let (gim′lit), *n.* a small tool with a screw point, for boring holes.

gin ger bread (jin′jər bred′), *n.* **1.** cake flavored with ginger and sweetened with molasses. **2.** something showy and elaborate, but not in good taste; tasteless ornamentation of a building. —*adj.* showy; gaudy.

gin seng (jin′seng), *n.* **1.** a low plant with a thick root. **2.** this root, used in medicine by the Chinese.

glut (glut), *v.* **1.** fill full; feed or satisfy fully. **2.** fill too full; supply too much for: *The prices for wheat dropped when the market was glutted with it.* —*n.* **1.** a full supply. **2.** too great a supply. [< obsolete *glut,* n., glutton < OF]

Go di va (gə dī′və), *n.* wife of an English nobleman, who lived in the 11th century. According to legend she rode naked through the town of Coventry to win relief for the people from a burdensome tax. She is usually pictured with long, flowing hair.

gour met (gür′mā), *n.* person who is expert in judging and choosing fine foods, wines, etc. [< F < OF *groumet* wine tester]

graft (graft or gräft), *v.* **1.** insert (a shoot, bud, etc.) from one tree or plant into a slit in another so that it will grow there permanently. **2.** transfer (a piece of skin, bone, etc.) from one part of the body to another so that it will grow there permanently. —*n.* **1.** shoot, bud, etc., used in grafting. **2.** tree or plant that has had a shoot, bud, etc., grafted on it.

gran di ose (gran′di ōs), *adj.* **1.** grand in an imposing or impressive way; magnificent. **2.** grand in an affected or pompous way; trying to seem magnificent.

graph ic (graf′ik), *adj.* **1.** lifelike; vivid: *a graphic account of a battle.* **2.** of or about diagrams and their use. **3.** shown by a graph. **4.** of or about drawing, painting, etc.: *the graphic arts.* **5.** of handwriting.

Green wich (grin′ij, grin′ich, gren′ij, or gren′ich *for 1;* gren′ich or grēn′wich *for 2),* *n.* **1.** borough in SE London, England. **2.** city in SW Connecticut.

Gregg (greg), *n.* a system of shorthand.

grid i ron (grid′ī′ərn), *n.* **1.** a cooking utensil consisting of a framework of parallel iron bars. **2.** a football field.

gri mace (grə mās′ or grim′is), *n.* a twisting of the face; ugly or funny smile. —*v.* make grimaces.

griz zled (griz′əld), *adj.* **1.** grayish; gray. **2.** grayhaired. [< *grizzle* gray hair, (adj.) gray < OF *grisel,* dim. of *gris* gray < Gmc.]

grov el (gruv′əl or grov′əl), *v.* lie face downward; crawl at someone's feet; humble oneself.

gui don (gī′dən or gī′don), *n.* **1.** a small flag or streamer carried as a guide by soldiers, or used for signaling. **2.** in the United States army, a flag, streamer, or pennant of a company, regiment, etc. **3.** soldier who carries the guidon.

guile (gīl), *n.* crafty deceit; craftiness; sly tricks.

ha bil i ment (hə bil′ə mənt), *n.* **1. habiliments,** *pl.* articles of clothing. **2.** dress; attire.

hack (hak), *n.* **1.** *U.S.* carriage for hire. **2.** *Informal.* taxi.

hake (hāk), *n., pl.* **hakes** or *(esp. collectively)* **hake.** a sea fish related to the cod but inferior as food.

hale (hāl), *adj.* strong and well; healthy. —**Syn.** sound, robust. —**Ant.** sickly.

ham a dry ad (ham′ə drī′əd or ham′ə drī′ad), *n.* in Greek mythology, a wood nymph supposed to live and die with the tree she dwelt in; dryad.

hand spike (hand′spīk′), *n.* bar used as a lever, especially on a ship.

hap ly (hap′li), *adv. Archaic.* perhaps; by chance.

har le quin (här′lə kwin or här′lə kin), *n.* **1.** Often, **Harlequin.** character in comedy and pantomime who is usually masked, has a costume of varied colors, and carries a wooden sword. **2.** a mischievous person. —*adj.* varied in color; many-colored.

har row (har′ō), *v.* **1.** hurt; wound. **2.** arouse uncomfortable feelings in; distress; torment.

har ry (har′i), *v.* **1.** raid and rob with violence. **2.** keep troubling; worry; torment.

hav oc (hav′ək), *n.* **1.** very great destruction or injury. **2. play havoc with,** injure severely; ruin; destroy. —**Syn. 1.** devastation, ruin.

haw (hô), *n.* **1.** the red berry of the hawthorn. **2.** hawthorn. [OE *haga*]

haw ser (hô′zər or hô′sər), *n.* a large rope or small cable. Hawsers are used for mooring or towing ships.

haz ard (haz′ərd), *n.* **1.** risk; danger. —*v.* **1. take** a chance with; risk; venture: *I would hazard my life on his honesty.* **2.** expose to risk.

heave (hēv), *v.,* **heaved** or *(esp. Naut.)* **hove, heaving,** *n.* —*v.* **1.** lift with force or effort. **2.** lift and throw. **3.** pull with force or effort; haul. **4.** rise; swell; bulge. **5. heave to,** stop a ship; stop. —*n.* act or fact of heaving.

hec a tomb (hek′ə tōm, hek′ə tüm, or hek′ə tom), *n.* **1.** sacrifice of 100 oxen at one time. **2.** any great slaughter. [< L < Gk. *hekatombe* sacrifice of 100 oxen < *hekaton* hundred + *bous* ox]

heif er (hef′ər), *n.* a young cow that has not had a calf.

---

hat, āge, cāre, fär; let, ēqual, tėrm; it, īce; hot, ōpen, ôrder; oil, out; cup, pùt, rüle, ūse; th, thin; ᵺH, then; zh, measure; ə represents *a* in about, *e* in taken, *i* in pencil, *o* in lemon, *u* in circus.

herbage   incantation

herb age (èr′bij or hèr′bij), *n.* **1.** herbs collectively. **2.** grass. **3.** the green leaves and soft stems of plants.

her biv o rous (hèr biv′ə rəs), *adj.* feeding on grass or other plants. Cattle are herbivorous animals.

Her cu les (hèr′kū lēz), *n.* **1.** in Greek and Roman mythology, a hero famous for his great strength. **2.** a northern constellation.

he red i ty (hə red′ə ti), *n.* **1.** the fact that one generation of plants and animals produces the next. **2.** the transmission of physical or mental characteristics from parent to offspring. **3.** tendency of offspring to be like the parents. [< L *hereditas* < *heres* heir] —**he red′i-tar′y,** *adj.*

her mit age (hèr′mə tij), *n.* **1.** home of a hermit. **2.** place to live away from other people.

her on (her′ən), *n.* a wading bird with a long neck, long bill, and long legs. [< OF *hairon* < Gmc.]

hi er o glyph ic (hī′ər ə glif′ik), *n.* **1.** picture, character, or symbol standing for a word, idea, or sound. **2.** any writing that uses hieroglyphics. **3.** a secret symbol. **4. hieroglyphics,** *pl.* writing that is hard to read. —*adj.* **1.** of or written in hieroglyphics. **2.** symbolical. [< LL *hieroglyphicus* < Gk. *hieroglyphikos* < *hieros* sacred + *glyphe* carving]

hire ling (hīr′ling), *n.* person who works only for money, without interest or pride in the task.

Hit tite (hit′īt), *n.* **1.** member of an ancient people in Asia Minor and Syria. **2.** language of the Hittites. —*adj.* of or having to do with the Hittites or their language.

hoar y (hôr′i or hōr′i), *adj.* **1.** white or gray. **2.** white or gray with age. **3.** old; ancient.

hob gob lin (hob′gob′lən), *n.* **1.** goblin; elf. **2.** person or thing that is feared.

hod (hod), *n.* trough or tray with a long handle, used for carrying bricks, mortar, etc., on the shoulder.

home ly (hōm′li), *adj.* **1.** suited to home life; simple; everyday: *homely pleasures.* **2.** of plain manners; unpretending: *a simple, homely man.* **3.** *U.S.* not good-looking; ugly; plain.

hos tler (os′lər or hos′lər), *n.* person who takes care of horses at an inn or stable.

how be it (hou bē′it), *adv.* nevertheless.

hoy den (hoi′dən), *n.* a boisterous, romping girl; tomboy. —*adj.* rude; ill-bred.

Hroz ny (hrôz′nē)

hum ming bird (hum′ing bèrd′), *n.* a very small, brightly colored American bird with a long narrow bill and narrow wings that move so rapidly they make a humming sound. [Am.E]

hus band (huz′bənd), *n.* **1.** man who has a wife. **2.** *Archaic.* manager. —*v.* **1.** manage carefully: *husband one's resources.* **2.** marry. **3.** *Archaic.* till (soil); cultivate (plants). [OE *húsbónda* < *hús* house + *bónda* head of family (< Scand. *bóndi*)]

hus band ry (huz′bənd ri), *n.* **1.** farming. **2.** management of one's affairs. **3.** careful management; thrift.

hy brid (hī′brid), *n.* **1.** offspring of two animals or plants of different species, varieties, etc. **2.** anything of mixed origin. —*adj.* **1.** bred from two different species, varieties, etc. **2.** of mixed origin.

hy per ob tru sive (hī′pər əb trü′siv), *adj.* exceedingly obtrusive.

id i om (id′i əm), *n.* **1.** phrase or expression whose meaning cannot be understood from the ordinary mean-

ings of the words in it: *"How do you do?"* and *"I have caught cold"* are English idioms. **2.** a people's way of expressing themselves: *A French idiom is "of a rapidity" for "rapid."* **3.** individual manner of expression in music, art, etc.

i dle (ī′dəl), *adj.* **1.** doing nothing. **2.** lazy. **3.** useless. **4.** without any good reason, cause, or foundation.

ig no ble (ig nō′bəl), *adj.* **1.** mean; base; without honor: *To betray a friend is ignoble.* **2.** of low birth. [< L *ignobilis* < *in-* not + OL *gnobilis* noble] —**ig no′ble ness,** *n.* —**ig no′bly,** *adv.*

ig no min i ous (ig′nə min′i əs), *adj.* **1.** shameful; disgraceful; dishonorable; humiliating. **2.** contemptible. —**ig′no min′i ous ly,** *adv.*

ill-got ten (il′got′ən), *adj.* dishonestly obtained.

im bibe (im bīb′), *v.* **1.** drink; drink in. **2.** absorb. **3.** take into one's mind. [< L *imbibere* < *in-* in + *bibere* drink]

im bue (im bū′), *v.* fill; inspire.

im mi nent (im′ə nənt), *adj.* likely to happen soon; about to occur.

im mit i ga ble (i mit′ə gə bəl), *adj.* that cannot be mitigated, or made milder.

im mu ta ble (i mū′tə bəl), *adj.* never changing; unchangeable. —**Syn.** unalterable, permanent.

im pair (im pār′), *v.* make worse; damage; weaken.

im pas sive (im pas′iv), *adj.* **1.** without feeling or emotion. **2.** not feeling pain or injury; insensible.

im pel (im pel′), *v.* **1.** drive; force; cause: *Hunger impelled the lazy man to work.* **2.** cause to move; drive forward; push along.

im pend ing (im pen′ding), *adj.* **1.** likely to happen soon; threatening; about to occur. **2.** overhanging.

im per a tive (im per′ə tiv), *adj.* **1.** urgent; necessary: *It is imperative that a very sick child stay in bed.* **2.** expressing a command. —*n.* a command: *The great imperative is "Love thy neighbor as thyself."* [< L *imperativus* < *imperare* command]

im pe ra tor (im′pə rā′tər), *n.* **1.** an absolute or supreme ruler. **2.** a Roman military commander. **3.** the Roman emperor.

im pe ri al (im pēr′i əl), *adj.* **1.** of or having to do with an empire or its ruler. **2.** of or having to do with the rule or authority of one country over other countries and colonies. **3.** supreme; majestic; magnificent. [< L *imperialis* < *imperium* empire] —**im pe′ri al ly,** *adv.*

im pla ca ble (im plā′kə bəl or im plak′ə bəl), *adj.* that cannot be placated, pacified, or appeased.

im plic it (im plis′it), *adj.* **1.** without doubting, hesitating, or asking questions; absolute: *implicit obedience.* **2.** meant, but not clearly expressed or distinctly stated; implied: *Her silence gave implicit consent.* **3.** involved as a necessary part or condition.

im por tune (im′pôr tün′, im′pôr tūn′, or im pôr′-chən), *v.* ask urgently or repeatedly.

im pre ca tion (im′prə kā′shən), *n.* a curse.

im preg na ble (im preg′nə bəl), *adj.* that cannot be overthrown by force: *an impregnable fortress.*

im pute (im pūt′), *v.* consider as belonging; attribute; charge (a fault, etc.) to a person: *I impute his success to hard work.*

in ad vert ent (in′əd vèr′tənt), *adj.* **1.** not attentive; heedless; negligent. **2.** not done on purpose; caused by oversight. —**in′ad vert′ent ly,** *adv.* —**Syn. 1.** thoughtless. **2.** unintentional, accidental.

in al ien a ble (in āl′yən ə bəl or in ā′li ən ə bəl), *adj.* that cannot be given away or taken away.

in can ta tion (in′kan tā′shən), *n.* **1.** set of words

< = from, taken from; cf., compare; dial., dialect; dim., diminutive; pp., past participle; ppr., present participle; pt., past tense; ult., ultimately; var., variant; ?=possibly.

spoken as a magic charm or to cast a magic spell. **2.** use of such words. [< L *incantatio, -onis* < *incantare* chant a magic formula against < *in-* against + *cantare* chant]

in car na dine (in kär′nə din, in kär′nə dīn, or in- kär′nə dēn), *v.* make blood-red or flesh-colored. [< F < Ital. *incarnadino*, ult. < L *in-* + *caro* flesh]

in car nate (*adj.* in kär′nit or in kär′nāt; *v.* in kär′- nāt), *adj.* embodied in flesh, especially in human form: *The girl was an angel incarnate.* —*v.* **1.** make incar- nate; embody. **2.** put into an actual form; realize: *The sculptor incarnated his vision in a beautiful statue.* [< L *incarnatus*, pp. of *incarnare* < *in-* + *caro* flesh]

in car na tion (in′kär nā′shən), *n.* **1.** embodiment. **2.** person or thing that represents some quality or idea.

in cest (in′sest), *n.* crime of sexual intercourse be- tween persons so closely related that their marriage is prohibited by law.

in con gru ous (in kong′grü əs), *adj.* **1.** not appro- priate; out of place: *Heavy walking shoes would be incon- gruous with a party dress.* **2.** not consistent.

in cred i ble (in kred′ə bəl), *adj.* seeming too ex- traordinary to be possible; unbelievable: *The hero fought with incredible bravery.* —**in cred′i bly,** *adv.*
→ incredible, incredulous. *Incredible* means unbelievable; *incredulous* means not ready to believe or showing a lack of belief: *His story of having seen a ghost seemed incredible to his family. If they look incredulous, show them the evidence.*

in cred u lous (in krej′u ləs), *adj.* **1.** not ready to believe; doubting. **2.** showing a lack of belief. —**in- cred′u lous ly,** *adv.* →See **incredible** for usage note.

in de fat i ga ble (in′di fat′ə gə bəl), *adj.* never getting tired or giving up; tireless. [< L *indefatigabilis* < *in-* not + *defatigare* tire out < *de-* completely + *fatigare* tire] —**in′de fat′i ga bly,** *adv.*

in dict ment (in dīt′mənt), *n.* **1.** a formal, legal accusation. **2.** accusation.

in duce (in düs′ or in dūs′), *v.* **1.** lead on; influence; persuade: *Advertising induces people to buy.* **2.** cause.

in ef fa ble (in ef′ə bəl), *adj.* **1.** too great to be de- scribed in words. **2.** that must not be spoken.

in e luc ta ble (in′i luk′tə bəl), *adj.* not to be es- caped or avoided; inevitable. —**in′e luc′ta bly,** *adv.*

in ert (in ėrt′), *adj.* **1.** having no power to move or act; lifeless: *A stone is an inert mass of matter.* **2.** in- active; slow; sluggish. [< L *iners, inertis* idle, unskilled < *in-* without + *ars* art, skill]

in fal li bil i ty (in fal′ə bil′ə ti), *n.* absolute free- dom from error.

in fal li ble (in fal′ə bəl), *adj.* **1.** free from error; that cannot be mistaken. **2.** absolutely reliable.

in fe lic i tous (in′fə lis′ə təs), *adj.* **1.** unsuitable. **2.** unfortunate.

in fer no (in fėr′nō), *n., pl.* **-nos.** **1.** hell. **2.** a hell- like place or thing. **3. Inferno.** The first part of Dante's *Divine Comedy*, where hell is a huge pit of circles, each lower one involving a more severe punishment.

in fi del (in′fə dəl), *n.* **1.** person who does not be- lieve in religion. **2.** person who does not accept a par- ticular faith. Mohammedans call Christians infidels. **3.** person who does not accept Christianity. —*adj.* not believing in religion. [< L *infidelis* < *in-* not + *fidelis* faithful < *fides* faith]

in flex i ble (in flek′sə bəl), *adj.* **1.** firm; unyielding; steadfast: *Neither threats nor promises could change his inflexible determination.* **2.** that cannot be changed; un- alterable. **3.** not easily bent; stiff; rigid.

in fuse (in fūz′), *v.* **1.** pour in; put in: *The captain infused his own courage into his soldiers.* **2.** inspire.

in gen ious (in jēn′yəs), *adj.* **1.** clever; good at in- venting. **2.** cleverly planned and made. [< L *ingeniosus* < *ingenium* natural talent]

in gé nue (aN′zhə nü; *French* aN zhā nY′), *n.* sim- ple, innocent girl or young woman, especially as repre- sented on the stage. [< F *ingénue*, originally fem. adj., ingenuous]

in ge nu i ty (in′jə nü′ə ti or in′jə nū′ə ti), *n.* skill in planning, inventing, etc.; cleverness. [< L *ingenuitas* frankness < *ingenuus* ingenuous; influenced by associa- tion with *ingenious*]

in gen u ous (in jen′ū əs), *adj.* **1.** frank; open; sin- cere. **2.** simple; natural; innocent. [< L *ingenuus*, origi- nally, native, free born] —**Syn.** **1.** candid. **2.** naïve.

in ges tion (in jes′chən), *n.* act of taking food, etc., into the body for digesting.

in gress (in′gres), *n.* **1.** a going in: *A high fence pre- vented ingress to the field.* **2.** entrance. **3.** right to go in.

in no va tion (in′ə vā′shən), *n.* **1.** change made in the established way of doing things. **2.** making changes; bringing in new things or new ways of doing things.

in qui si tion (in′kwə zish′ən), *n.* **1.** a thorough in- vestigation; searching inquiry. **2.** an official investiga- tion; judicial inquiry. **3. the Inquisition, a.** court appointed by the Roman Catholic Church to discover and suppress heresy and to punish heretics. **b.** activities of this court.

in scru ta ble (in skrü′tə bəl), *adj.* that cannot be understood; so mysterious or obscure that one cannot make out its meaning. [< LL *inscrutabilis* < L *in-* not + *scrutari* examine, ransack < *scruta* trash]

in sen si bil i ty (in sen′sə bil′ə ti), *n.* **1.** lack of feeling. **2.** lack of consciousness.

in sin u ate (in sin′ū āt), *v.* **1.** suggest indirectly; hint. **2.** push in or get in by an indirect, twisting way.

in sol vent (in sol′vənt), *adj.* not able to pay one's debts; bankrupt. —*n.* an insolvent person.

in stant (in′stənt), *adj.* of the present month; pres- ent: *"The 10th instant" means "the tenth day of the present month."*

in stinct[1] (in′stingkt), *n.* **1.** natural feeling, knowl- edge, or power; unlearned tendency: *An instinct leads birds to fly.* **2.** a natural bent, tendency, or gift; talent. [< L *instinctus*, n. < *instinctus*, pp. of *instinguere* impel]

in stinct[2] (in stingkt′), *adj.* charged or filled with something: *The picture is instinct with life and beauty.* [< L *instinctus*, pp. of *instinguere* impel]

in sur gent (in sėr′jənt), *n.* **1.** person who rises in revolt; rebel. **2.** *U.S.* rebel within a political party. —*adj.* rising in revolt; rebellious.

in sur rec tion (in′sə rek′shən), *n.* a rising against established authority; revolt. [< LL *insurrectio, -onis* < L *insurgere* to rise. —Syn. see INSURGENT.]

in te grate (in′tə grāt), *v.* **1.** make into a whole; complete. **2.** bring together (parts) into a whole. **3.** *U.S.* make all schools, parks, etc., available to white and Negro citizens on an equal basis.

in teg ri ty (in teg′rə ti), *n.* **1.** honesty; sincerity; uprightness. **2.** wholeness; completeness. **3.** perfect con- dition; soundness. [< L *integritas* < *integer* whole]

in ter dict (in′tər dikt′), *v.* prohibit.

in ter line (in′tər līn′), *v.* **1.** insert (words, etc.) be- tween the lines of. **2.** write, print, or mark between the lines.

in ter mi na ble (in tėr′mə nə bəl), *adj.* endless; so long as to seem endless. [< LL *interminabilis*, ult. < L *in-* not + *terminare* to end] —**in ter′mi na bly,** *adv.*

---

hat, āge, cãre, fär;   let, ēqual, tėrm;   it, īce;   hot, ōpen, ôrder;   oil, out;   cup, pùt, rüle, ūse; th, thin; ŦH, then; zh, measure; ə represents *a* in about, *e* in taken, *i* in pencil, *o* in lemon, *u* in circus.

in ter ne cine (in′tər nē′sin or in′tər nē′sīn), *adj.*
1. destructive to both sides. **2.** deadly; destructive.

in ter po late (in tèr′pə lāt), *v.* **1.** alter (a book, passage, etc.) by putting in new words or groups of words. **2.** put in (new words, passages, etc.).

in trin sic (in trin′sik), *adj.* belonging to a thing by its very nature; essential; inherent: *The intrinsic value of a dollar bill is only that of a piece of paper.*

in tu i tion (in′tü ish′ən or in′tū ish′ən), *n.* **1.** perception of truths, facts, etc., without reasoning. **2.** something so perceived. [< LL *intuitio, -onis* a gazing at < L *intueri* < in- at + *tueri* look] —**in tu′i tive,** *adj.*

in un da tion (in′un dā′shən), *n.* an overflowing; flood.

in u tile (in ū′təl), *adj.* useless; unprofitable.

in vest (in vest′), *v.* **1.** use (money) to buy something that is expected to produce a profit, or income, or both. **2.** clothe; cover; surround: *Darkness invests the earth at night.* **3.** give power to.

in vet er ate (in vet′ər it), *adj.* habitual.

in vi o late (in vi′ə lit or in vi′ə lāt), *adj.* uninjured; unbroken.

in voke (in vōk′), *v.* **1.** call on in prayer; appeal to for help or protection. **2.** ask earnestly for; beg for.

i ron mon ger y (i′ərn mung′gər i), *n.* hardware; iron goods.

Is ra el ite (iz′ri əl īt), *n.* Jew; Hebrew; descendant of Israel. —*adj.* of or having to do with Israel or the Jews.

is sue (ish′ü), *v.* **1.** send out; put forth. **2.** come out; go out. **3.** result or end. —*n.* **1.** something sent out. **2.** a sending out. **3.** a coming forth. **4.** result; outcome: *the issue of the battle.* [< OF *issue,* earlier *eissue* < *issir,* earlier *eissir* go out < L *exire* < *ex-* out + *ire* go]

Ja bez (jā′bez)
Jac o be an (jak′ə bē′ən), *adj.* **1.** of King James I of England. **2.** of the period of his reign from 1603 to 1625. [< NL *Jacobaeus* < LL *Jacobus* James]

Ja cob's lad der (jā′kəbz lad′ər), *n.* **1.** in the Bible, a ladder to heaven that Jacob saw in a dream. **2.** a rope ladder used on ships.

ja pan (jə pan′), *n.* a hard, glossy varnish. —*v.* put japan on. [from *Japan*]

jeal ous (jel′əs), *adj.* **1.** full of envy; envious. **2.** watchful in guarding something. **3.** watchful.

jerk y (jèr′ki), *n.* meat preserved by drying.

jet ti son (jet′ə sən or jet′ə zən), *v.* **1.** throw (goods) overboard to lighten a ship in distress. **2.** throw away; discard. [< n.] —*n.* **1.** act of throwing goods overboard to lighten a ship in distress. **2.** goods thrown overboard.

jol ly boat (jol′i bōt′), *n.* a small boat carried on a ship.

Jo nah (jō′nə), *n.* **1.** in the Bible, a Hebrew prophet who was thrown overboard during a storm, swallowed by a large fish, and later cast up on land. **2.** person whose presence is supposed to bring bad luck.

jowl[1] (joul or jōl), *n.* **1.** part under the jaw; jaw. **2.** cheek. [OE *ceafl*]

jowl[2] (joul or jōl), *n.* fold of flesh hanging from the jaw. [? related to OE *ceole* throat]

ju di ci ar y (jü dish′i er′i), *n.* branch of government that administers justice. —*adj.* of or having to do with courts, judges, or the administration of justice.

ju rist (jür′ist), *n.* **1.** expert in law. **2.** a learned writer on law. [< Med.L *jurista* < L *jus* law]

---

jux ta pose (juks′tə pōz′), *v.* put close together; place side by side. [< F *juxtaposer* < L *juxta* beside + F *poser* place]

Kam chat ka (kam chat′kə), *n.* peninsula of NE Asia between the Sea of Okhotsk and Bering Sea.

ka mi ka ze (kä′mi kä′zē), *n.* a pilot who dives an airplane loaded with explosives into the target he seeks to destroy. [< Japanese *kamikaze,* literally, divine wind]

Ka na ka (kə nak′ə or kan′ək ə)

keel boat (kēl′bōt), *n.* a shallow freight boat having a keel, a main timber or steel piece that extends the whole length of the bottom of the boat.

ken (ken), *n.* **1.** range of sight. **2.** range of knowledge.

key (kē), *n.* a low island; reef. There are keys south of Florida. [< Sp. *càyo,* ? < F *quai* < Celtic]

kine (kīn), *n.pl.* *Archaic* or *Dialect.* cows; cattle.

knav er y (nāv′ər i or nāv′ri), *n.* tricky, dishonest behavior, characteristic of a knave.

la con ic (lə kon′ik), *adj.* using few words; brief in speech or expression; concise.

La Mu ette (lä mY et′)

lan cet (lan′sit or län′sit), *n.* a small, sharp-pointed surgical knife, usually having two sharp edges.

lan guor (lang′gər), *n.* **1.** lack of energy; weariness. **2.** lack of interest or enthusiasm; indifference. **3.** softness or tenderness of mood. **4.** quietness; stillness: *the languor of a summer afternoon.* **5.** lack of activity.

La nier (lə nir′ or lə nēr′)

Lap land (lap′land), *n.* region in northern Norway, Sweden, Finland, and northwestern Russia.

lar ce ny (lär′sə ni), *n.* **1.** theft. **2.** the unlawful taking, carrying away, and using of the personal property belonging to another person without his consent.

la tent (lā′tənt), *adj.* present but not active; hidden; concealed: *latent germs of disease, latent ability.*

lathe (lāᴛн), *n.* machine for holding articles of wood, metal, etc., and turning them against a cutting tool.

la trine (lə trēn′), *n.* toilet in a camp, factory, etc.

laud a ble (lôd′ə bəl), *adj.* worthy of praise.

lau da tion (lô dā′shun), *n.* praise.

lau re ate (lô′ri it), *adj.* **1.** crowned with a laurel wreath as a mark of honor. **2.** honored; distinguished. —*n.* poet laureate, the official poet of any country, state, etc.

lau rel (lô′rəl or lor′əl), *n.* **1.** a small evergreen tree with smooth, shiny leaves. **2.** the leaves. The ancient Greeks and Romans crowned victors with wreaths of laurel. **3.** Usually, **laurels,** *pl.* **a.** honor; fame. **b.** victory. **4. look to one's laurels,** guard one's reputation or record from rivals. **5. rest on one's laurels,** be satisfied with the honors that one has already won.

lave (lāv), *v.* *Poetic.* **1.** wash; bathe. **2.** wash or flow against: *The stream laves its banks.*

lay[1] (lā), *adj.* **1.** not of the clergy. A lay sermon is one preached by a person who is not a clergyman. **2.** not of lawyers, doctors, or those learned in the profession in question. [< OF *lai* < L *laicus.*]

lay[2] (lā), *n.* **1.** a short poem to be sung; poem. **2.** song; tune. [< OF *lai,* ? < Celtic]

league (lēg), *n.* measure of distance, usually about 3 miles.

lee (lē), *n.* **1.** shelter. **2.** side or part sheltered from the wind. **3.** direction toward which the wind is blowing. —*adj.* **1.** sheltered from the wind. **2.** in the direction toward which the wind is blowing.

< = from, taken from; cf., compare; dial., dialect; dim., diminutive; pp., past participle; ppr., present participle; pt., past tense; ult., ultimately; var., variant; ?=possibly.

lees

lees (lēz), *n.pl.* dregs; sediment.

leg a cy (leg/ə si), *n.* **1.** money or other property left to a person by a will. **2.** something handed down.

le gu mi nous (li gū/mə nəs), *adj.* of or bearing legumes, plants having seeds in a pod, many of which can absorb nitrogen from the air. Peas and beans are leguminous.

Le on i das (lē on/ə dəs)

let (let), *v.*, **let ted** or **let**, **let ting**, *n.* —*v. Archaic.* prevent; hinder. —*n.* **1.** prevention; hindrance. **2. without let or hindrance**, with nothing to prevent or obstruct.

lev ee¹ (lev/i), *n.* **1.** *U.S.* bank built to keep a river from overflowing. **2.** a landing place for boats. [Am.E; < F *levée* < *lever* raise < L *levare*]

lev ee² or **lev ée** (lev/i or le vē/), *n.* reception. French kings used to hold levees in the morning while they were getting up and dressing. [< F *levé, lever* a rising from bed, reception held while rising < *lever* raise. See LEVEE¹.]

le vi a than (lə vī/ə thən), *n.* **1.** in the Bible, a huge sea animal thought of as a reptile or a whale. **2.** a huge ship. **3.** any great and powerful person or thing.

lev i ty (lev/ə ti), *n.* lightness of mind; lack of proper seriousness; frivolity.

lex i con (lek/sə kən or lek/sə kon), *n.* dictionary, especially of Greek, Latin, or Hebrew. [< Gk. *lexikon* (*biblion*) wordbook < *lexis* word < *legein* say]

Ley den jar (lī/dən jär/), *n.* device for accumulating frictional electricity, consisting essentially of a glass jar lined inside and outside, for most of its height, with tin foil. [from *Leyden, Leiden,* Holland]

lib er al (lib/ər əl or lib/rəl), *adj.* **1.** generous. **2.** plentiful; abundant. **3.** broad-minded; not narrow in one's ideas: *a liberal thinker.* **4.** favoring progress and reforms. —*n.* person favorable to progress and reforms.

lib er ty pole (lib/ər ti pōl/), *n.* a high flagpole with a flag or some other symbol of liberty at the top.

li cense (lī/səns), *n.* **1.** permission given by law to do something. **2.** card, plate, etc., showing such permission. **3.** condition of being permitted to do something. **4.** freedom of action, speech, thought, etc., that is permitted or conceded. Poetic license is the freedom from rules that is permitted in poetry and art. **5.** too much liberty; disregard of what is right and proper. —*v.* give a license to. [< OF *licence* < L *licentia* < *licere* be allowed]

lien (lēn), *n.* a legal claim on the property of another for payment of a debt: *The garage owner has a lien on my automobile until I pay his bill.*

lig a ture (lig/ə chŭr or lig/ə chər), *n.* **1.** anything used to bind or tie up; bandage, cord, etc. **2.** thread, string, etc., used to tie up a bleeding artery or vein. **3.** a binding or tying up. —*v.* bind or tie up with a ligature. [< LL *ligatura* < L *ligare* bind]

lim bo (lim/bō), *n.* **1.** Often, **Limbo.** in Catholic theology, a place for those who have not received the grace of Christ and yet have not deserved the punishments of impenitent sinners. **2.** place for people and things forgotten or out of date: *The belief that the earth is flat belongs to the limbo of outworn ideas.*

lin age (līn/ij), *n.* **1.** alignment; formation in a line. **2.** the number of printed lines on a page. Also, **lineage.**

lin e a ment (lin/i ə mənt), *n.* part or feature; part or feature of a face with attention to its outline.

lin guist (ling/gwist), *n.* **1.** person skilled in several languages besides his own. **2.** person who studies the history and structure of language. [< L *lingua* tongue]

macaroni

lin guis tic (ling gwis/tik), *adj.* having to do with language or the study of languages.

lin tel (lin/təl), *n.* a horizontal beam or stone over a door, window, etc., to support the structure above it.

list (list), *v. Archaic* and *Poetic.* **1.** listen. **2.** listen to.

lit er al ist (lit/ər əl ist), *n.* **1.** person who adheres to the exact literal meaning. **2.** person who represents or portrays without idealizing.

li thog ra phy (li thog/rə fi), *n.* art or process of making lithographs, pictures, prints, etc., made from a flat, specially prepared stone or a metal plate.

lit i gant (lit/ə gənt), *n.* person engaged in a lawsuit. —*adj.* engaging in a lawsuit.

liv er y (liv/ər i or liv/ri), *n.* **1.** any special uniform provided for servants or adopted by any group or profession. **2.** the feeding, stabling, and care of horses for pay; the hiring out of horses and carriages. **3.** the keeping of cars, boats, etc., for hire. **4.** *U.S.* livery stable.

loath (lōth), *adj.* unwilling; reluctant: *The little girl was loath to leave her mother.* Also, **loth.**

lob ber (lob/ər), *v.* to thicken by souring; to curdle.

lo gi cian (lō jish/ən), *n.* expert in logic, the science of reasoning.

long boat (lông/bōt/ or long/bōt/), *n.* the largest and strongest boat carried by a sailing ship.

long horn (lông/hôrn/ or long/hôrn/), *n.* one of a breed of cattle that has very long horns.

lon gi tu di nal (lon/jə tü/də nəl or lon/jə tū/də-nəl), *adj.* **1.** of length; in length. **2.** running lengthwise.

loon¹ (lün), *n.* a large, web-footed diving bird that has a loud wild cry. [earlier *loom* < Scand. *lōmr*]

loon² (lün), *n.* a worthless or stupid person. [origin uncertain]

loth (lōth), *adj.* loath.

love lock (luv/lok/), *n.* **1.** any conspicuous lock of hair, especially a curl worn on the forehead. **2.** formerly, a long, flowing lock dressed separately from the rest of the hair.

lub ber (lub/ər), *n.* **1.** a big, clumsy, stupid fellow. **2.** a clumsy sailor. —**Syn.** **1.** dolt, bumpkin.

lu cid (lü/sid), *adj.* **1.** easy to understand. **2.** shining; bright. **3.** sane. **4.** clear; transparent. —**lu cid/i ty,** *n.*

lu di crous (lü/də krəs), *adj.* amusingly absurd; ridiculous. [< L *ludicrus* < *ludus* sport]

Luft waf fe (lúft/väf/ə), *n. German.* the German air force, especially under the Nazis in World War II.

lu gu bri ous (lü gü/bri əs or lü gū/bri əs), *adj.* sad; mournful. —**Syn.** dismal, melancholy.

lu mi nar y (lü/mə ner/i), *n.* **1.** the sun, moon, or other light-giving body. **2.** a famous person.

lu mi nous (lü/mə nəs), *adj.* **1.** shining by its own light: *The sun and stars are luminous bodies.* **2.** full of light; bright. **3.** easily understood. [< L *luminosus* < *lumen* light]

lust y (lus/ti), *adj.* strong and healthy; full of vigor.

ly ce um (lī sē/əm or lī/si əm), *n.* **1.** lecture hall. **2.** *U.S.* association for instruction and entertainment through lectures, debates, and concerts. **3. Lyceum,** an ancient outdoor grove and gymnasium near Athens, where Aristotle taught.

lynx (lingks), *n.* wildcat that has a short tail and rather long legs. It is traditionally considered to have sharp eyesight.

mac a ro ni (mak/ə rō/ni), *n., pl.* **-nis** or **-nies.** a fashionable English dandy of the 18th century.

hat, āge, cãre, fär; let, ēqual, tėrm; it, īce; hot, ōpen, ôrder; oil, out; cup, pŭt, rüle, ūse; th, thin; ᵗн, then; zh, measure; ə represents *a* in about, *e* in taken, *i* in pencil, *o* in lemon, *u* in circus.

magic lantern

mag ic lan tern (maj′ik lan′tərn), *n.* device with a lamp and lenses for throwing a picture upon a screen, in magnified form, from a glass slide.

mag na nim i ty (mag′nə nim′ə ti), *n.* nobility of soul or mind; generosity in forgiving.

mag ni tude (mag′nə tüd or mag′nə tūd), *n.* **1.** size. **2.** importance. [< L *magnitudo* < *magnus* large]

main (mān), *adj.* most important; largest. —*n.* **1.** a large pipe for water, gas, etc. **2.** *Poetic.* the open sea; ocean.

main mast (mān′mast′ or mān′mäst′; *Nautical* mān′məst), *n.* the principal mast of a ship.

main top mast (mān′top′mast′ or mān′top′mäst′; *Nautical* mān′top′məst), *n.* the second section of the mainmast above the deck.

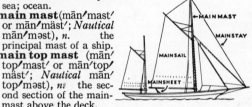

make weight (māk′wāt′), *n.* **1.** anything added to make up for some lack. **2.** anything added to a scale to make up the required weight.

ma lev o lent (mə lev′ə lənt), *adj.* wishing evil to happen to others; showing ill will; spiteful. [< L *malevolens, -entis*, ult. < *male* ill + *velle* wish] —**ma lev′o lent ly,** *adv.* —**ma lev′o lence,** *n.*

man i fest (man′ə fest), *adj.* apparent to the eye or to the mind; plain; clear. —*v.* show plainly; reveal.

man i fold (man′ə fōld), *adj.* **1.** of many kinds; many and various. **2.** having many parts or forms. **3.** doing many things at the same time.

marge (märj), *n. Poetic.* edge; border. [< F]

mar riage por tion (mar′ij pôr′shən), *n.* dowry; money, property, etc., that a woman brings to her husband when she marries.

masque (mask or mäsk), *n.* **1.** an amateur dramatic entertainment in which fine costumes, scenery, music, and dancing are more important than the story. **2.** play written for such an entertainment. **3.** a masked ball; masquerade.

mast (mast or mäst), *n.* **1.** a long pole of wood or steel set upright on a ship to support the sails and rigging. **2.** any upright pole.

mast head (mast′hed′ or mäst′hed′), *n.* top of a ship's mast. A crow's-nest near the masthead of the lower mast is used as a lookout.

mas tiff (mas′tif or mäs′tif), *n.* a large, strong dog with drooping ears and hanging lips.

ma tric u late (mə trik′ū lāt), *v.* **1.** enroll as a student in college. **2.** enroll as a candidate for a degree.

mau gre (mô′gər), *prep. Archaic.* in spite of; notwithstanding. [< OF *maugre*, originally n., ill will, spite]

max im (mak′səm), *n.* a short rule of conduct; statement of a general truth.

may hem (mā′hem or mā′əm), *n.* crime of intentionally maiming a person or injuring him so that he is less able to defend himself.

Mc Cutch eon (mə kuch′ən)

mead (mēd), *n. Poetic.* meadow. [OE *mǣd*]

mean (mēn), *adj.* small-minded; stingy.

me di ate (*v.* mē′di āt; *adj.* mē′di it), *v.* **1.** be a go-between. **2.** settle by intervening. **3.** be the medium for effecting (a result) or for communicating (knowledge). —**me′di a to′ri al,** *adj.*

me di e val (mē′di ē′vəl or med′i ē′vəl), *adj.* having to do with the Middle Ages (from about 500 A.D. to about 1450 A.D.).

mizzen-top

meer schaum (mēr′shəm or mēr′shôm), *n.* a tobacco pipe made of a very soft, light stone.

mel an chol y (mel′ən kol′i), *n.* **1.** sadness. **2.** sober thoughtfulness. —*adj.* **1.** sad; gloomy. **2.** depressing. **3.** soberly thoughtful; pensive.

me nag er ie (mə naj′ər i or mə nazh′ər i), *n.* **1.** collection of wild animals kept in cages for exhibition. **2.** place where such animals are kept.

men di cant (men′də kənt), *adj.* begging. Mendicant friars ask alms for charity. —*n.* beggar.

Men tor (men′tər), *n.* **1.** in Greek legend, a faithful friend of Ulysses. He was the teacher and adviser of Ulysses' son Telemachus. **2. mentor,** a wise and trusted adviser.

mer ce nar y (mėr′sə ner′i), *adj.* working for money only. —*n.* soldier serving for pay in a foreign army. [< L *mercenarius* < *merces* wages]

Mer o no co mo co (mer′ō nō kō mō′kō)

me sa (mā′sə), *n.* a small, high plateau with steep sides. [Am.E; < Sp. < L *mensa* table]

mes sieurs (mes′ərz; *French* mā syœ′), *n.* pl. of **monsieur.**

Messrs. (mes′ərz), *n.* messieurs.

met a eu phor ic (met′ə ū fôr′ik), *adj.* having a very great or excessive feeling of well-being.

met a phys ics (met′ə fiz′iks), *n.* branch of philosophy that tries to explain reality and knowledge; the philosophical study of the real nature of the universe.

mete (mēt), *n.* **1.** boundary. **2.** a boundary stone.

mi ca (mī′kə), *n.* mineral that divides into thin, partly transparent layers. Mica is used in stove doors, electric fuses, etc., where the heat might break glass.

Mi chael (mī′kəl), *n.* Saint, in the Bible, the archangel who led the loyal angels in defeating the revolt of Lucifer, the Devil.

Mi das (mī′dəs), *n.* in Greek legend, a king whose touch turned everything to gold.

milch (milch), *adj.* giving milk; kept for the milk it gives: *a milch cow.*

milk leg (milk′ leg′), *n.* a painful swelling of the leg caused by clots in the veins.

mil len ni um (mə len′i əm), *n., pl.* **mil len ni ums, mil len ni a** (mə len′i ə). **1.** period of a thousand years: *The world is many millenniums old.* **2.** a period of righteousness and happiness. [< NL < L *mille* thousand + *annus* year]

Mil ton (mil′tən), *n.* John, 1608-1674, English poet who wrote *Paradise Lost.*

Min da na o (min′də nä′ō), *n.* the second largest island in the Philippines. 1,828,000 pop.; 36,537 sq. mi.

min i a ture (min′i ə chŭr or min′ə chər), *n.* **1.** anything represented on a small scale. **2.** a very small painting, usually a portrait.

min is tra tion (min′is trā′shən), *n.* help; aid.

mi nute (mī′nūt′ or mī′nūt′), *adj.* **1.** very small. **2.** concerned with very small details: *a minute observer, minute instructions.* —**mi nute′ly,** *adv.*

mi nu ti a (mi nū′shi ə or mi nū′shi ə), *n., pl.* **-ae** (ē) or **-a.** very small matter; trifling detail.

mis sive (mis′iv), *n.* a written message; letter.

miz zen (miz′ən), *n.* **1.** a fore-and-aft sail on the mizzenmast. **2.** mizzenmast. [< F < Ital. *mezzana* < L *medianus* in the middle < *medius* middle]

miz zen mast (miz′ən mast′ or miz′ən mäst′; *Nautical* miz′ən məst), *n.* mast nearest the stern in a two-masted or three-masted ship.

miz zen-top (miz′ən top′), *n.* platform around the top of the mizzenmast.

< = from, taken from; cf., compare; dial., dialect; dim., diminutive; pp., past participle; ppr., present participle; pt., past tense; ult., ultimately; var., variant; ?=possibly.

mo diste (mō dēst′), *n.* maker of or dealer in women's gowns, hats, etc.; dressmaker. [<F]

moil (moil), *v.* work hard; drudge. —*n.* 1. hard work; drudgery. 2. trouble; confusion.

mold er (mōl′dər), *v.* turn into dust by natural decay; crumble; waste away.

mol li fy (mol′ə fī), *v.* soften; appease: *mollify his wrath.* [< F < LL *mollificare* < *mollis* soft + *facere* make]

mon sieur (mə syœ′), *n., pl.* **mes sieurs** (mā syœ′). Mr.; sir.

Mont gol fier (môN gôl fyā′)

moot court (müt′ côrt′), *n.* mock court held in a law school to give students practice.

mo rass (mə ras′), *n.* piece of low, soft, wet ground; swamp.

Mor mon (môr′mən), *n.* member of the Church of Jesus Christ of Latter-day Saints, founded in 1830 by Joseph Smith. —*adj.* of or having to do with the Mormons or their religion.

Mor phe us (môr′fi əs or môr′fūs), *n.* the Greek god of dreams; popularly, the god of sleep.

mor ti fy (môr′tə fī), *v.* make ashamed; humiliate. —**mor′ti fi ca′tion,** *n.* —**Syn.** chagrin, embarrass.

Mo ses (mō′ziz or mō′zis), *n.* in the Bible, the great leader and lawgiver of the Israelites who led them out of Egypt.

mot ley (mot′li), *adj.* 1. of different colors like a clown's suit. 2. made up of units not alike: *a motley collection.*

mot tle (mot′əl), *v.* mark with spots or streaks of different colors. —*n.* a mottled coloring or pattern.

mu lat to (mə lat′ō or mū lat′ō), *n., pl.* **-toes.** person having some white and some Negro blood.

mum mer (mum′ər), *n.* 1. person who wears a mask, fancy costume, or disguise for fun. 2. actor.

mum mer y (mum′ər i), *n.* 1. performance of mummers. 2. any useless or silly ceremony.

murk (mėrk), *n.* darkness; gloom.

Muse (mūz), *n.* 1. one of the nine Greek goddesses of the fine arts and sciences. 2. Sometimes, **muse.** spirit that inspires a poet or composer.

musk y (mus′ki), *adj.* having a strong, lasting odor.

mu ta tion (mū tā′shən), *n.* 1. change; alteration. 2. a new feature that appears suddenly in animals or plants and can be inherited. 3. a new variety of animal or plant formed in this way. [< L *mutatio, -onis* < *mutare* change]

myr i ad (mir′i əd), *n.* 1. ten thousand. 2. a very great number: *There are myriads of stars.* —*adj.* 1. ten thousand. 2. countless.

nai ad (nā′ad or nī′ad), *n., pl.* **-ads, -a des** (-ə dēz). 1. Also, **Naiad.** in Greek and Roman mythology, a nymph guarding a stream or spring. 2. a girl swimmer.

Nai ro bi (nī rō′bi), *n.* capital of Kenya, in Africa.

Nan ta quoud (nän′tä kwoud)

nape (nāp or nap), *n.* the back of the neck.

naught (nôt), *n.* 1. nothing. 2. zero; 0. Also, **nought.**

nau ti lus (nô′tə ləs), *n., pl.* **-luses, -li** (-lī). either of two kinds of sea animal with a soft body and a hard shell. The **pearly nautilus** has a spiral shell, pearly inside. The **paper nautilus** has saillike arms and a very thin shell.

nec tar (nek′tər), *n.* 1. in Greek mythology, the drink of the gods. 2. any delicious drink. 3. a sweet liquid found in many flowers. Bees gather nectar and make it into honey.

Nep tune (nep′tün or nep′tūn), *n.* 1. the Roman god of the sea. 2. a large planet so far from the earth that it cannot be seen with the naked eye.

neu rot ic (nü rot′ik or nū rot′ik), *adj.* 1. suffering from a nervous disease. 2. emotionally disturbed. —*n.* a neurotic person.

noi some (noi′səm), *adj.* 1. offensive; disgusting; smelling bad: *a noisome slum.* 2. harmful; injurious.

no to ri e ty (nō′tə rī′ə ti), *n.* 1. a being famous for something bad; ill fame. 2. being widely known. —**no to′ri ous,** *adj.* —**no to′ri ous ly,** *adv.*

nov ice (nov′is), *n.* beginner.

nymph (nimf), *n.* 1. one of the lesser Greek and Roman goddesses of nature, who lived in seas, rivers, springs, hills, woods, or trees. 2. *Poetic.* a beautiful or graceful young woman. [< OF < L < Gk. *nymphe*]

ob du rate (ob′dú rit or ob′dū rit), *adj.* 1. stubborn; unyielding: *an obdurate refusal.* 2. hardened in feelings or heart; not repentant.

ob lique (əb lēk′; *military* əb lĭk′), *adj.* 1. not straight up and down; not straight across; slanting. 2. not straightforward; indirect: *She made an oblique reference to her illness.*

ob lit er ate (əb lit′ər āt), *v.* remove all traces of; blot out; destroy: *The rain obliterated the footprints.*

ob se qui ous (əb sē′kwi əs), *adj.* polite or obedient from hope of gain or from fear: *Obsequious courtiers greeted the king.* [< L *obsequiosus*, ult. < *ob-* after + *sequi* follow] —**Syn.** slavish.

ob ses sion (əb sesh′ən), *n.* 1. influence of a feeling, idea, or impulse that a person cannot escape. 2. the feeling, idea, or impulse itself.

ob trude (əb trüd′), *v.* 1. put forward unasked and. unwanted; force: *Don't obtrude your opinions on others.* 2. force oneself; intrude. 3. push out; thrust forward.

ob tru sive (əb trü′siv), *adj.* inclined to obtrude

oc cult (o kult′ or ok′ult), *adj.* 1. beyond the bounds of ordinary knowledge; mysterious. 2. outside the laws of the natural world; magical.

oc to roon (ok′tə rün′), *n.* person having one eighth Negro blood or ancestry. [Am.E; < *octo-* eight + (*quad*)-*roon*]

o gi val (ō jī′vəl), *adj.* having the form of an ogive, or pointed arch.

O lym pus (ō lim′pəs), *n.* 1. **Mount,** mountain in NE Greece, where the greater Greek gods were supposed to live. 2. heaven.

om i nous (om′ə nəs), *adj.* of bad omen; unfavorable; threatening. [< L *ominosus* < *omen* omen]

om nip o tent (om nip′ə tənt), *adj.* having all power; almighty. —*n.* **the Omnipotent,** God.

om nis cient (om nish′ənt), *adj.* knowing everything; having complete or infinite knowledge.

om niv o rous (om niv′ə rəs), *adj.* 1. eating every kind of food. 2. eating both animal and vegetable food. 3. taking in everything; fond of all kinds: *An omnivorous reader reads all kinds of books.* [< L *omnivorus* < *omnis* all + *vorare* eat greedily]

o nus (ō′nəs), *n.* burden; responsibility: *The onus of housekeeping fell upon the daughters.* [< L]

O pe chan ka nough (ō′pə chän kä′nôн)

op pro bri um (ə prō′bri əm), *n.* disgrace or reproach caused by shameful conduct or status; scorn.

or a cle (ôr′ə kəl or or′ə kəl), *n.* 1. answer of a god to some question. It often had an obscure meaning.

---

hat, āge, cāre, fär;   let, ēqual, tėrm;   it, īce;   hot, ōpen, ôrder;   oil, out;   cup, pút, rüle, ūse;
th, thin;   ₮H, then;   zh, measure;   ə represents *a* in about, *e* in taken, *i* in pencil, *o* in lemon, *u* in circus.

2. place where the god gives answers. **3.** priest, priestess, or other means by which the god's answer was given. **4.** a very wise person. **5.** a very wise answer.

O ra paks (ō rä′päks)

orb (ôrb), *n.* **1.** sphere; globe. **2.** sun, moon, planet, or star. **3.** *Esp. Poetic.* eyeball or eye. —*v.* **1.** form into a circle or sphere. **2.** *Poetic.* encircle; enclose.

or gy (ôr′ji), *n.* **1.** a wild, drunken revel. **2.** period of uncontrolled indulgence.

or tho dox (ôr′thə doks), *adj.* **1.** generally accepted, especially in religion. **2.** approved by custom; usual.

os ten ta tious (os′ten tā′shəs), *adj.* **1.** done for display; intended to attract notice. **2.** showing off. —**os ten ta′tion,** *n.* —**Syn.** **1.** showy, gaudy.

o vert (ō′vėrt or ō vėrt′), *adj.* open; evident; not hidden; public: *Hitting someone is an overt act.*

pack et (pak′it), *n.* a boat that carries mail, passengers, and goods.

pale (pāl), *n.* **1.** a long, narrow board, pointed at the top, used for fences. **2.** boundary: *outside the pale of civilized society.* —*v.* enclose with pales.

pa le on tol o gist (pā′li on tol′ə jist), *n.* person skilled in paleontology, the science of the forms of life existing long ago, as represented by fossils.

pal ing (pāl′ing), *n.* **1.** fence of pales. **2.** pale in a fence.

pall (pôl), *n.* **1.** a heavy cloth of black, purple, or white velvet spread over a coffin, a hearse, or a tomb. **2.** a dark, gloomy covering.

pal pa ble (pal′pə bəl), *adj.* **1.** readily seen or heard and recognized; noticeable. **2.** that can be touched or felt. **3.** clear to the mind; evident.

pal sy (pôl′zi), *n.* paralysis, sometimes accompanied with trembling. —*v.* paralyze.

Pa maun kee (pə môn′kē; *Indian* pä moun′kā)

pan e gyr ist (pan′ə jir′ist or pan′ə jir′ist), *n.* person who praises enthusiastically or extravagantly.

pan o ply (pan′ə pli), *n.* **1.** a complete suit of armor. **2.** complete equipment or covering.

pan o ram a (pan′ə ram′ə or pan′ə rä′mə), *n.* **1.** a wide, unbroken view of a surrounding region. **2.** a complete survey of some subject. **3.** picture unrolled a part at a time and made to pass continuously before the spectators. —**pan′o ram′ic,** *adj.*

pa paw (pô′pô), *n.* **1.** a small North American tree bearing oblong, yellowish, edible fruit with many bean-like seeds. **2.** this fruit. Also, **pawpaw.**

par a gon (par′ə gon), *n.* model of excellence or perfection.

par al lax (par′ə laks), *n.* the change or amount of change in the direction in which an object is seen or photographed, caused by a change in the position of the observer or camera. Seen from A, star S is in direction AS. Seen from B, it is in direction BS. The parallax is the difference between these two directions, or the angle ASB. [< Gk. *parallaxis* alternation, ult < *para-* + *allassein* to change]

Parallax

Par i an (pãr′i ən), *adj.* of Paros, a Greek island noted for its beautiful white marble.

par lance (pär′ləns), *n.* way of speaking; talk; language. [< OF *parlance* < *parler* speak]

par ley (pär′li), *n.* **1.** conference. **2.** an informal discussion with an enemy about terms of surrender, etc.

par ox ysm (par′ək siz əm), *n.* **1.** a severe, sudden attack. **2.** fit; convulsion: *a paroxysm of rage.*

par si mo ni ous (pär′sə mō′ni əs), *adj.* too economical; stingy. —**par′si mo′ny,** *n.* —**Ant.** generous.

par take (pär tāk′), *v.,* **-took, -tak en, -tak ing.** **1.** eat or drink some; take some. **2.** take or have a share. **3. partake of,** have a share in.

par ti al i ty (pär′shi al′ə ti or pär shal′ə ti), *n.* **1.** a favoring of one more than another or others. **2.** fondness.

par ti san (pär′tə zən), *n.* a strong supporter of a person, party, or cause; one whose support is based on feeling rather than on reasoning. —*adj.* **1.** of a partisan. **2.** unreasonably devoted.

par took (pär túk′), *v.* pt. of **partake.**

pas sel (pas′əl), *n.* *Dialect.* **parcel.** **1.** package. **2.** lot; pack.

Pas sy (pä sē′)

pa tri arch (pā′tri ärk), *n.* **1.** father and ruler of a family or tribe. **2.** an old man deserving respect. [< L < Gk. *patriarches* < *patria* family + *archos* leader] —**pa tri ar′chal,** *adj.*

pa tron age (pā′trən ij or pat′rə nij), *n.* **1.** regular business given by customers. **2.** favor, encouragement, or support, especially for an art, cause, or undertaking. **3.** condescending favor.

Paul (pôl), *n.* **Saint,** died 67? A.D., Apostle who started Christian groups in many countries and wrote parts of the New Testament.

pea jack et (pē′ jak′it), *n.* a short coat of thick woolen cloth worn by sailors.

pe cu ni ar y (pi kū′ni er′i), *adj.* of or having to do with money; in the form of money.

pe dan tic (pi dan′tik), *adj.* **1.** displaying one's knowledge more than is necessary. **2.** tediously learned; scholarly in a dull and narrow way.

pel let (pel′it), *n.* **1.** a little ball of mud, paper, food, medicine, etc.; pill. **2.** bullet.

pen ance (pen′əns), *n.* punishment borne to show sorrow for sin, to make up for a wrong done, and to obtain pardon.

pend ant (pen′dənt), *n.* **1.** a hanging ornament. **2.** ornament hanging from ceiling or roof. —*adj.* hanging.

pen du lous (pen′jù ləs or pen′dū ləs), *adj.* **1.** hanging loosely. **2.** swinging.

pen i tence (pen′ə təns), *n.* sorrow for sinning or doing wrong; repentance.

pen sive (pen′siv), *adj.* **1.** thoughtful in a serious or sad way. **2.** melancholy. [< OF *pensif* < *penser* think < L *pensare* weigh, ponder < *pendere* weigh] *n.* —**Syn.** **1.** meditative, reflective. **2.** sober, grave, sad.

pent (pent), *adj.* closely confined; penned.

per e gri nate (per′ə grə nāt), *v.* travel; journey. —**per′e gri na′tion,** *n.*

per fi dy (pėr′fə di), *n.* a breaking faith; base treachery. —**per fid′i ous,** *adj.*

per force (pər fôrs′ or pər fōrs′), *adv.* necessarily.

per i pa tet ic (per′ə pə tet′ik), *adj.* walking about; traveling from place to place.

per o ra tion (per′ə rā′shən), *n.* last part of an oration or discussion. It sums up what has been said.

per pet u ate (pər pech′ü āt), *v.* make perpetual; cause to continue; keep from being forgotten.

per plex (pər pleks′), *v.* **1.** trouble with doubt; puzzle; bewilder. **2.** make difficult to understand or settle.

per se vere (pėr′sə vėr′), *v.* continue steadily in doing something hard; persist.

< = from, taken from; cf., compare; dial., dialect; dim., diminutive; pp., past participle; ppr., present participle; pt., past tense; ult., ultimately; var., variant; ?=possibly.

per son al i ty (pèr′sə nal′ə ti), *n.* 1. qualities of a person. 2. remark made about or against some person: *Personalities are not in good taste in general conversation.*

per ti nac i ty (pèr′tə nas′ə ti), *n.* great persistence; holding firmly to a purpose, action, or opinion.

per turb (pər tėrb′), *v.* disturb greatly; make uneasy or troubled. [< L *perturbare* < *per-* thoroughly + *turbare* confuse] —**per′tur ba′tion**, *n.* —Syn. trouble, distress.

pe rus al (pə rüz′əl), *n.* a reading.

per vade (pər vād′), *v.* go or spread throughout; be throughout: *The odor of pines pervades the air.* [< L *pervadere* < *per-* through + *vadere* go]

per verse (pər vėrs′), *adj.* 1. contrary and willful; stubborn. 2. persistent in wrong. [< L *perversus* turned away, pp. of *pervertere*. See PERVERT.] —**per verse′ly**, *adv.* —**per verse′ness, per ver′si ty,** *n.* —Syn. 1. obstinate.

per vert (*v.* pər vėrt′; *n.* pėr′vėrt), *v.* 1. lead or turn from the right way or from the truth. 2. give a wrong meaning to. 3. use for wrong purposes or in a wrong way: *A clever criminal perverts his talents.* —*n.* a perverted person. [< L *pervertere* < *per-* to destruction + *vertere* to turn]

pes ti lence (pes′tə ləns), *n.* disease that spreads rapidly, causing many deaths. —Syn. epidemic.

pe tite (pə tēt′), *adj.* of small size; tiny, especially with reference to a woman or girl. [< F *petite*, fem. of *petit* little]

pet ri fy (pet′rə fī), *v.* 1. turn into stone; become stone. 2. harden; stiffen; deaden. 3. paralyze with fear or surprise. [< F *pétrifier*, ult. < L *petra* stone < Gk.]

pet ty (pet′i), *adj.* 1. having little importance or value; small: *She insisted on telling me all her petty troubles.* 2. mean; narrow-minded. 3. lower; subordinate.

pet u lance (pech′ù ləns), *n.* peevishness; bad humor; being irritated by trifles.

pha lanx (fā′langks or fal′angks), *n., pl.* **pha lanx es, pha lan ges** (fə lan′jēz). 1. in ancient Greece, a special battle formation of infantry fighting in close ranks with their shields joined and long spears overlapping each other. 2. a compact body of persons, animals, or things. 3. people united for a common purpose.

phan tasm (fan′taz əm), *n.* 1. thing seen only in one's imagination; unreal fancy: *the phantasms of a dream.* 2. a supposed appearance of an absent person, living or dead. 3. a deceiving likeness (of something).

phan tom (fan′təm), *n.* 1. image of the mind: *phantoms of a dream.* 2. a vague, dim, or shadowy appearance; ghost. 3. mere show; appearance without material substance. —*adj.* like a ghost; unreal.

Phar aoh (fār′ō), *n.* title given to the kings of ancient Egypt.

phe nom e non (fə nom′ə non), *n., pl.* **-na** or (*esp. for def. 2*) **-nons.** 1. fact, event, or circumstance that can be observed: *Lightning is an electrical phenomenon.* 2. something or someone extraordinary or remarkable. —**phe nom e nal,** *adj.*

Phi Be ta Kap pa (fī′ bā′tə kap′ə), an honorary society composed of American college students and graduates who have ranked high in scholarship.

phi lan thro pist (fə lan′thrə pist), *n.* person who shows his love for mankind by practical kindness and helpfulness to humanity.

phi lan thro py (fə lan′thrə pi), *n.* 1. love of mankind shown by practical kindness and helpfulness to humanity: *The Red Cross appeals to philanthropy.* 2. thing that benefits humanity: *A hospital is a useful philanthropy.* —Syn. 1. benevolence, charity.

phil o soph ic (fil′ə sof′ik), *adj.* wise; calm; reasonable. —**phil′o soph′i cal ly,** *adv.*

Phoe ni cian (fə nish′ən), *adj.* of or having to do with Phoenicia, an ancient country in W Syria, its people, or their language. —*n.* 1. one of the people of Phoenicia. 2. language of Phoenicia.

pho net ic (fə net′ik), *adj.* 1. of or having to do with speech sounds: *phonetic laws.* 2. representing speech sounds: *phonetic symbols, phonetic spelling.* [< NL < Gk. *phonetikos*, ult. < *phone* sound]

pho net ics (fə net′iks), *n.* 1. science dealing with speech sounds and the art of pronunciation. 2. system of speech sounds.

phos pho res cence (fos′fə res′əns), *n.* 1. a giving out light without burning or by very slow burning that seems not to give out heat. 2. such light.

phys i ol o gist (fiz′i ol′ə jist), *n.* expert in physiology.

phys i ol o gy (fiz′i ol′ə ji), *n.* 1. science dealing with the normal functions of living things or their organs: *animal physiology, plant physiology.* 2. all the functions and activities of a living thing or of one of its organs. [< L < Gk. *physiologia* < *physis* nature + *-logos* treating of] —**phys′i o log′i cal,** *adj.*

pick et (pik′it), *n.* 1. a small body of troops, or a single man, posted at some place to watch for the enemy.

pier glass (pēr′ glas′), *n.* a tall mirror.

pil lage (pil′ij), *v.* rob with violence, plunder: *Pirates pillaged the towns along the coast.* —*n.* plunder; robbery.

pil lion (pil′yən), *n.* pad attached behind a saddle for a person to sit on.

pin fold (pin′fōld′), *n.* place where stray animals are kept. —*v.* confine in a pinfold.

pin ion (pin′yən), *n.* 1. the last joint of a bird's wing. 2. wing. 3. any one of the stiff flying feathers of the wing. —*v.* 1. cut off or tie the pinions of (a bird) to prevent flying. 2. bind. [< OF *pignon*, ult. < L *pinna* feather]

pi quan cy (pē′kən si), *n.* piquant quality.

pi quant (pē′kənt), *adj.* 1. stimulating to the mind, interest, etc. 2. pleasantly sharp; stimulating to the taste: *a piquant sauce.* [< F *piquant* pricking, stinging]

pique (pēk), *n.* a feeling of anger at being slighted; wounded pride. —*v.* 1. cause a feeling of anger in; wound the pride of: *It piqued her that they should have a secret she did not share.* 2. arouse; stir up.

pitch (pich), *n.* 1. a black, sticky substance made from tar or turpentine, used to cover the seams of ships, to cover roofs, to make pavements, etc. 2. a sticky yellow or brown substance that flows from certain evergreen trees. —*v.* cover with pitch.

pith (pith), *n.* 1. the central, spongy tissue in the stems of certain plants. 2. a similar soft tissue: *the pith of an orange.*

plain tiff (plān′tif), *n.* person who begins a lawsuit.

plash y (plash′i), *adj.* marshy; wet.

Pla to (plā′tō), *n.* 427?-347? B.C., Greek philosopher who was the pupil of Socrates and the teacher of Aristotle.

plau si ble (plô′zə bəl), *adj.* 1. appearing true, reasonable, or fair. 2. apparently worthy of confidence but often not really so. [< L *plausibilis* deserving applause, pleasing < *plaudere* applaud] —**plau′si bly,** *adv.* —**plau′si bil′i ty,** *n.*

ple be ian (pli bē′ən), *n.* 1. one of the common people of ancient Rome. 2. one of the common people. 3. a common, vulgar person. —*adj.* 1. of the plebeians. 2. common; vulgar. [< L *plebeius* < *plebs* the common people]

---

hat, āge, cāre, fär; let, ēqual, tėrm; it, ĭce; hot, ōpen, ôrder; oil, out; cup, pùt, rüle, ūse; th, thin; ᴛн, then; zh, measure; ə represents *a* in about, *e* in taken, *i* in pencil, *o* in lemon, *u* in circus.

pli ant (plī′ənt), *adj.* **1.** bending easily; flexible. **2.** easily influenced; yielding. —**Syn. 1.** pliable, limber. —**Ant. 1.** rigid.

plun der (plun′dər), *v.* rob by force; rob. —*n.* **1.** things taken in plundering; booty; loot. **2.** act of robbing by force. [< G *plündern* < *plunder* household goods]

ply (plī), *v.* **1.** work with; use. **2.** keep up work on; work away at or on: *We plied the water with our oars.*

pol i tic (pol′ə tik), *adj.* **1.** wise in looking out for one's own interests: *A politic person tries not to offend people.* **2.** scheming; crafty. **3.** political.

poll tax (pōl′ taks′), *n.* a tax on every person, or on every person of a specified class, especially as a prerequisite to the right to vote in public elections.

pol troon (pol trün′), *n.* a wretched coward. [< F < Ital. *poltrone* < *poltro* lazy, originally, bed]

pol y tone (pol′i tōn′), *n.* sound having varied tones.

pom mel (pum′əl or pom′əl), *n.* part of a saddle that sticks up at the front.

pon der ous (pon′dər əs), *adj.* **1.** very heavy. **2.** heavy and clumsy. **3.** dull; tiresome: *The speaker talked in a ponderous way.* [< L *ponderosus* < *pondus* weight] —**pon′der ous ly,** *adv.* —**pon′der ous ness,** *n.* —**Syn. 1.** weighty, massive. **2.** unwieldy.

pon iard (pon′yərd), *n.* dagger.

poop (püp), *n.* **1.** deck at the stern above the ordinary deck, often forming the roof of a cabin. **2.** stern of a ship. [< OF < Ital. *poppa* < L *puppis* stern]

port[1] (pôrt or pōrt), *n.* the left side of a ship, when facing the bow. —*adj.* on the left side of a ship.

port[2] (pôrt or pōrt), *n.* porthole.

porte-co chere or **porte-co chère** (pôrt′kō shãr′ or pōrt′kō shãr′), *n.* **1.** porch at the door of a building under which carriages and automobiles stop so that persons getting in or out are sheltered. **2.** entrance for carriages, leading into a courtyard. [< F *porte-cochère* coachgate]

por tent (pôr′tent or pōr′tent), *n.* sign; omen.

por tiere or **por tière** (pôr tyãr′ or pōr tyãr′), *n.* curtain hung at a doorway. [< F *portière* < *porte* door]

port man teau (pôrt man′tō or pōrt man′tō), *n.,* *pl.* **-teaus** or **-teaux** (-tōz). *Esp. Brit.* a stiff, oblong traveling bag with two compartments opening like a book.

pos ter i ty (pos ter′ə ti), *n.* **1.** generations of the future. **2.** all of a person's descendants.

pos ture (pos′chər), *n.* **1.** way of holding the body. **2.** condition; situation; state: *In the present posture of public affairs it is difficult to invest money safely.* **3.** mental or spiritual attitude. —*v.* **1.** take a certain posture. **2.** put in a certain posture. **3.** pose for effect.

Pow ha tan (pou′hə tan′)

prate (prāt), *v.* talk a great deal in a foolish way. —*n.* empty or foolish talk.

pre cious (presh′əs), *adj.* **1.** worth much; valuable. **2.** much loved; dear. **3.** too nice; overrefined.

pre cur sor (pri kėr′sər), *n.* forerunner: *A severe cold may be the precursor of pneumonia.* [< L *praecursor,* ult. < *prae-* before + *currere* run]

pred a to ry (pred′ə tô′ri or pred′ə tō′ri), *adj.* **1.** of or inclined to plundering or robbery. **2.** preying upon other animals. [< L *praedatorius,* ult. < *pareda* prey]

pre des ti na tion (prē′des tə nā′shən), *n.* **1.** an ordaining beforehand; destiny; fate. **2.** action of God in deciding beforehand what shall happen. **3.** doctrine that by God's decree certain souls will be saved and others lost.

pre ëmpt (pri empt′), *v.* **1.** secure before someone else can: *The cat had prëempted the comfortable chair.* **2.** settle on (land) with the right to buy it before others.

pre fect (prē′fekt), *n.* **1.** title of various military and civil officers in ancient Rome and elsewhere. **2.** the chief administrative official of a department of France.

pre mo ni tion (prē′mə nish′ən or prem′ə nish′ən), *n.* a forewarning.

pre pos ses sion (prē′pə zesh′ən), *n.* favorable feeling or opinion formed beforehand; bias.

pre sen ti ment (pri zen′tə mənt), *n.* a feeling or impression that something is about to happen; vague sense of approaching misfortune; foreboding. [< MF *presentiment,* ult. < L *prae-* before + *sentire* to sense]

pre ter nat u ral (prē′tər nach′ə rəl or prē′tər nach′rəl), *adj.* **1.** out of the ordinary course of nature; abnormal. **2.** due to something above or beyond nature; supernatural. [< Med.L *praeternaturalis,* ult. < L *praeter-* beyond + *natura* nature]

prev a lent (prev′ə lənt), *adj.* widespread; in general use; common: *Colds are prevalent in the winter.*

pri me val (prī mē′vəl), *adj.* **1.** of or having to do with the first age or ages, especially of the world. **2.** ancient. [< L *primaevus* early in life < *primus* first + *aevum* age]

pri mo gen i ture (prī′mə jen′ə chür or prī′mə jen′ə chər), *n.* **1.** state or fact of being the firstborn of the children of the same parents. **2.** right of inheritance or succession by the first-born, especially the inheritance of a family estate by the eldest son. [< Med.L *primogenitura,* ult. < L *primus* first + *gignere* beget]

pri mor di al (prī môr′di əl), *adj.* **1.** existing at the very beginning; primitive. **2.** original; elementary.

pris tine (pris′tēn, pris′tən, or pris′tīn), *adj.* as it was in its earliest time or state; original; primitive.

prod i gal (prod′ə gəl), *adj.* **1.** spending too much; wasteful. **2.** abundant; lavish. —*n.* person who is wasteful or extravagant. —**Syn.** *adj.* **1.** extravagant. —**Ant.** *adj.* **1.** frugal, saving, stingy.

pro di gious (prə dij′əs), *adj.* **1.** very great; huge: *The sea contains a prodigious amount of water.* **2.** wonderful.

prod i gy (prod′ə ji), *n.* **1.** marvel; wonder. An infant prodigy is a child remarkably brilliant in some respect. **2.** a marvelous example.

pro fane (prə fān′), *adj.* **1.** not sacred; worldly: *profane literature.* **2.** with contempt or disregard for God or holy things. —*v.* **1.** treat (holy things) with contempt or disregard. **2.** put to wrong or unworthy use. [< F < L *profanus* not sacred < *pro-* in front (outside) of + *fanum* shrine]

pro fan i ty (prə fan′ə ti), *n.* **1.** use of profane language; swearing. **2.** being profane; lack of reverence.

pro fi cien cy (prə fish′ən si), *n.* knowledge; expert skill.

pro fu sion (prə fū′zhən), *n.* great abundance.

pro gen i tor (prō jen′ə tər), *n.* ancestor in the direct line; forefather. [< L *progenitor* < *pro-* forth + *gignere* beget]

prog e ny (proj′ə ni), *n.* children; descendants.

pro lif ic (prə lif′ik), *adj.* **1.** producing offspring abundantly. **2.** producing much: *a prolific tree or imagination.*

pro mis cu ous (prə mis′kū əs), *adj.* **1.** mixed and in disorder: *a promiscuous heap of clothing.* **2.** making no distinctions; not discriminating: *promiscuous friendships.* [< L *promiscuus* < phrase *pro miscuo* as common < *miscere* mix]

pro pen si ty (prə pen′sə ti), *n.* a natural inclina-

< = from, taken from; cf., compare; dial., dialect; dim., diminutive; pp., past participle; ppr., present participle; pt., past tense; ult., ultimately; var., variant; ?=possibly.

tion or bent; inclination: *Most boys have a propensity for playing with machinery.*

pro pi ti ate (prə pish′i āt), *v.* prevent or reduce the anger of; win the favor of; appease. —**pro pi′ti a′tion,** *n.*

pro pi ti a to ry (prə pish′i ə tô ri or prə pish′i ə-tō′ri), *adj.* intended to propitiate; making propitiation: *a propitiatory offering.*

pro pi tious (prə pish′əs), *adj.* favorable.

pro sa ic (prō zā′ik), *adj.* like prose; matter-of-fact; ordinary; not exciting. —**pro sa′i cal ly,** *adv.* —**Syn.** commonplace, humdrum, dull, tedious.

pro sce ni um (prō sē′ni əm), *n.,* *pl.* **-ni a** (-ni ə). **1.** part of the stage in front of the curtain. **2.** curtain and framework that holds it.

pros pect (pros′pekt), *n.* **1.** thing expected or looked forward to. **2.** act of looking forward; expectation: *The prospect of a vacation is pleasant.*

pro spec tive (prə spek′tiv), *adj.* **1.** probable; expected. **2.** looking forward to the future.

pros trate (pros′trāt), *v.* **1.** lay down flat; cast down: *The captives prostrated themselves before the conqueror.* **2.** make very weak or helpless; exhaust: *Sickness often prostrates people.* —*adj.* **1.** lying flat with face downward. **2.** lying flat. **3.** overcome; helpless.

pro to type (prō′tə tīp), *n.* the first or primary type of anything; the original or model: *A modern ship has its prototype in the hollowed log used by savages.*

pro tract (prō trakt′), *v.* **1.** lengthen in time: *protract a visit.* **2.** thrust out; extend. [< L *protractus,* pp. of *protrahere* < *pro-* forward + *trahere* drag] —**pro-tract′ed,** *adj.*

prov i dence (prov′ə dəns), *n.* **1.** God's care and help. **2.** instance of God's care and help. **3.** care for the future; good management. **4. Providence,** God.

pro vi sion al (prə vizh′ən əl), *adj.* for the time being; temporary.

prov o ca tion (prov′ə kā′shən), *n.* **1.** act of provoking. **2.** something that provokes. [< L *provocatio, -onis* < *provocare.* See PROVOKE.]

pro voc a tive (prə vok′ə tiv), *adj.* **1.** irritating. **2.** tending or serving to call forth action, thought, laughter, anger, etc.: *a remark provocative of mirth.* —**pro voc′a tive ly,** *adv.* —**pro voc′a tive ness,** *n.*

pro voke (prə vōk′), *v.* **1.** make angry. **2.** stir up; excite. **3.** call forth; bring about; start into action; cause. [< L *provocare* < *pro-* forth + *vocare* to call]

prov ost (prov′əst), *n.* person appointed to superintend or preside; official in charge.

prow (prou), *n.* **1.** the pointed front part of a ship or boat; bow. **2.** something like it: *the prow of an airship.*

prox im i ty (proks im′ə ti), *n.* nearness; closeness.

pru dence (prü′dəns), *n.* **1.** wise thought before acting; good judgment. **2.** good management; economy.

pru den tial (prü den′shəl), *adj.* of, marked by, or showing prudence.

Psy che (sī′ki), *n* **1.** in Greek and Roman mythology, the human soul or spirit pictured as a beautiful young girl, usually with butterfly wings. Psyche was loved by Cupid and was made immortal. **2. psyche, a.** the human soul or spirit. **b.** the mind.

psy chic (sī′kik), *adj.* **1.** of the soul or mind; mental: *illness due to psychic causes.* **2.** supernatural. **3.** especially susceptible to psychic influences.

psy chol o gist (sī kol′ə jist), *n.* person skilled or trained in psychology.

psy chol o gy (sī kol′ə ji), *n.* the science of mind. Psychology tries to explain why people act, think, and feel as they do. [< NL *psychologia* < Gk. *psyche* soul, mind + *-logos* treating of]

psy cho path ic (sī′kə path′ik), *adj.* **1.** of or having to do with mental diseases. **2.** having a mental disease. **3.** likely to become insane.

pu ber ty (pū′bər ti), *n.* the physical beginning of manhood and womanhood. Puberty comes at about 14 in boys and about 12 in girls. [< L *pubertas* < *pubes* adult]

pu er ile (pū′ər əl), *adj.* foolish for a grown person to say or do; childish. [< L *puerilis* < *puer* boy]

pule (pūl), *v.* cry in a thin voice, as a sick child does; whimper; whine. [? imitative]

Pu litz er Prize (pū′lit sər or púl′it sər prīz′), *n.* U.S. any one of various prizes given each year for the best American drama, novel, biography, history, book of verse, editorial, and cartoon, established by Joseph Pulitzer and first awarded in 1917.

pun cheon (pun′chən), *n.* **1.** a large cask for liquor. **2.** slab of timber with the face roughly smoothed.

punc til i ous (pungk til′i əs), *adj.* **1.** very careful and exact. **2.** paying strict attention to details of conduct and ceremony. —**punc til′i ous ly,** *adv.* —**punc-til′i ous ness,** *n.*

pun gent (pun′jənt), *adj.* **1.** sharply affecting the organs of taste and smell. **2.** sharp; biting.

pur loin (pėr loin′), *v.* steal.

purs lane (pėrs′lān or pėrs′lən), *n.* a common plant that has small, yellow flowers and small, thick leaves.

pus tule (pus′chül), *n.* **1.** pimple containing pus. **2.** any swelling like a pimple or blister, such as the pustules of chicken pox. [< L *pustula* < *pus* pus]

pu ta tive (pū′tə tiv), *adj.* supposed; reputed.

put cha min (pə chä′min), *n.* yellow, plumlike fruit.

Qan tas (kwon′təs), an Australian air line.

quad rant (kwod′rənt), *n.* **1.** quarter of a circle or of its circumference. **2.** instrument used in astronomy, navigation, etc., for measuring altitudes.

quad roon (kwod rün′), *n.* person having one fourth Negro blood; child of a mulatto and a white person.

quaff (kwäf, kwaf, or kwôf), *v.* drink in large draughts; drink freely. —*n.* a quaffing.

quag mire (kwag′mīr′ or kwog′mīr′), *n.* soft, muddy ground; boggy place.

quer u lous (kwer′ủ ləs or kwer′ū ləs), *adj.* **1.** complaining; faultfinding. **2.** fretful. —**Syn. 2.** petulant.

queue (kū), *n.* **1.** braid of hair hanging down from the back of the head. **2.** a long line or people, cars, etc.

rack (rak), *n.* instrument once used for torturing people by stretching them.

rad i cal (rad′ə kəl), *adj.* **1.** going to the root; fundamental. **2.** favoring extreme changes or reforms; extreme. —*n.* person who favors extreme changes or reforms. [< LL *radicalis* < L *radix* root] —**rad′i-cal ly,** *adv.*

ram i fi ca tion (ram′ə fə kā′shən), *n.* **1.** dividing or spreading out into branches or parts. **2.** branch; part.

ram part (ram′pärt), *n.* **1.** a wide bank of earth, often with a wall on top, built around a fort to help defend it. **2.** anything that defends; defense; protection.

---

hat, āge, cãre, fär; let, ēqual, tėrm; it, īce; hot, ōpen, ôrder; oil, out; cup, pút, rüle, ūse; th, thin; ŦH, then; zh, measure; ə represents *a* in about, *e* in taken, *i* in pencil, *o* in lemon, *u* in circus.

rancor — roundabout

ran cor (rang′kər), *n.* bitter resentment or ill will; extreme hatred or spite. [< OF < LL *rancor* rankness < L *rancere* be rank] —**Syn.** malice, animosity.

rank (rangk), *adj.* **1.** large and coarse. **2.** growing richly. **3.** having a strong, bad smell or taste. **4.** strongly marked; extreme: *rank ingratitude.*

ran sack (ran′sak), *v.* **1.** search thoroughly through. **2.** rob; plunder.

rapt (rapt), *adj.* **1.** lost in delight. **2.** completely absorbed in thought, delight, etc. **3.** carried away in body or spirit from earth, life, or ordinary affairs. —*v.* carry away in body or spirit from earth, life, or ordinary affairs.

rar e fy (rãr′ə fī), *v.* **1.** make less dense. **2.** become less dense. **3.** purify.

rat tan (ra tan′), *n.* **1.** kind of palm with a very long stem. **2.** stems of such palm trees, used for wickerwork, canes, etc. **3.** cane made from a piece of such a stem.

re cal ci trant (ri kal′sə trənt), *adj.* resisting authority or control; disobedient.

rec re ant (rek′ri ənt), *adj.* **1.** cowardly. **2.** disloyal; traitorous. —*n.* **1.** coward. **2.** traitor.

rec ti fy (rek′tə fī), *v.* make right; put right; adjust.

rec ti tude (rek′tə tüd or rek′tə tūd), *n.* upright conduct or character; honesty; righteousness.

re dress (*v.* ri dres′; *n.* rē′dres or ri dres′), *v.* set right; repair; remedy. —*n.* a setting right; reparation; relief: *Any man deserves redress if he has been injured unfairly.*

reef (rēf), *n.* part of a sail that can be rolled or folded up to reduce its size. —*v.* **1.** reduce the size of (a sail) by rolling or folding up a part of it. **2.** reduce the length of (a mast, etc.) by lowering, etc.

reel (rēl), *v.* **1.** sway, swing, or rock under a blow, shock, etc. **2.** sway in standing or walking. **3.** be in a whirl; be dizzy.

re fer (ri fėr′), *v.,* **-ferred, -fer ring. 1.** direct attention: *The minister often refers to the Bible.* **2.** relate; apply: *The rule refers only to special cases.* **3.** turn for information or help. [< L *referre* < *re-* back + *ferre* take]

ref er en dum (ref′ər en′dəm), *n., pl.* **-dums, -da** (-də). **1.** process of submitting a law already passed to a direct vote of the citizens for approval or rejection. **2.** the submitting of any matter to a direct vote.

reft (reft), *v.* pt. and pp. of **reave.** deprived by force.

ref use (ref′ūs), *n.* useless stuff; waste; rubbish. —*adj.* rejected as worthless or of little value; discarded.

re ga li a (ri gā′li ə or ri gāl′yə), *n.pl.* **1.** the emblems of royalty. Crowns, scepters, etc., are regalia. **2.** the emblems or decorations of any society, order, etc.

re gen er ate (ri jen′ər āt), *v.* **1.** give a new and better spiritual life to. **2.** improve the moral condition of; put new life and spirit into. **3.** reform. —**re gen′er a′tion,** *n.*

re lin quish ment (ri ling′kwish mənt), *n.* giving up; abandonment; surrender.

re mote (ri mōt′), *adj.,* **-mot er, -mot est. 1.** far away; far off: *a remote country.* **2.** out of the way; secluded: *a remote village.* **3.** distant: *a remote relative.* **4.** slight; faint.

ren dez vous (rän′də vü), *n., pl.* **-vous** (-vüz). **1.** an appointment or engagement to meet at a fixed place or time; meeting by agreement. **2.** a meeting place; gathering place. —*v.* meet at a rendezvous. [< F *rendezvous* < *rendez-vous* betake or present yourself!]

ren e gade (ren′ə gād), *n.* traitor.

ren o vate (ren′ə vāt), *v.* make new again; make like new; restore to good condition.

rep ro bate (rep′rə bāt), *n.* an unprincipled scoundrel. —*adj.* morally abandoned; unprincipled. —*v.* disapprove; condemn. —**Syn.** *adj.* depraved, corrupt.

re sil i ence (ri zil′i əns or ri zil′yəns), *n.* **1.** power of springing back; elasticity: *Rubber has resilience.* **2.** buoyancy; cheerfulness. Also **resiliency.**

res in (rez′ən), *n.* a sticky yellow or brown substance that flows from certain plants and trees, especially the pine and fir. It is used in medicine and varnish. The harder portion remaining after heating is called rosin. —**res′in ous,** *adj.*

re solved (ri zolvd′), *adj.* **1.** firm in purpose. **2.** broken up into its original parts.

res o nance (rez′ə nəns), *n.* **1.** resounding quality; being resonant: *the resonance of an organ.* **2.** a reinforcing and prolonging of sound by reflection or by vibration of other objects. The sounding board of a piano gives it resonance.

res tive (res′tiv), *adj.* **1.** restless; uneasy. **2.** hard to manage. **3.** refusing to go ahead. —**res′tive ness,** *n.*

ret i cent (ret′ə sənt), *adj.* disposed to keep silent or say little; not speaking freely; reserved in speech. [< L *reticens, -entis,* ppr. of *reticere* keep silent < *re-* back + *tacere* be silent] —**Syn.** reserved, taciturn.

ret i cule (ret′ə kūl), *n.* a woman's small handbag.

re trieve ment (ri trēv′mənt), *n.* thing retrieved, recovered, or brought back.

ret ro spect (ret′rə spekt), *n.* survey of past time, events, etc.; thinking about the past. [ult. < L *retrospectus* < *retro-* back + *specere* to look]

ret ro spec tion (ret′rə spek′shən), *n.* act of looking back on things past; survey of past events or experiences.

re vert (ri vėrt′), *v.* go back; return: *If a man dies without heirs, his property reverts to the State.*

re vile (ri vīl′), *v.* call bad names; abuse with words.

rhet o ric (ret′ə rik), *n.* **1.** art of using words in speaking or writing. **2.** book about this art. **3.** mere display in language.

rhe tor i cal (ri tôr′ə kəl or ri tor′ə kəl), *adj.* **1.** of or having to do with rhetoric. **2.** intended especially for display; artificial. **3.** oratorical. **4.** used for rhetorical effect: *a rhetorical question.* —**rhe tor′i cal ly,** *adv.*

rhom boid (rom′boid), *n.* parallelogram with equal opposite sides that is not a rectangle. —*adj.* shaped like a rhombus or rhomboid.

rib ald (rib′əld), *adj.* offensive in speech; irreverent; indecent; obscene. —**Syn.** *adj.* indelicate.

rig a doon (rig′ə dün′), *n.* **1.** a lively dance with a jumping step. **2.** the music for this dance.

rig ger (rig′ər), *n.* **1.** person who gets sails, ropes, etc., ready on ships, or works with hoisting tackle, etc. **2.** person who manipulates something fraudulently.

rig ging (rig′ing), *n.* **1.** ropes, chains, etc., used to support and work the masts, yards, sails, etc., on a ship. **2.** tackle; equipment.

rip rap (rip′rap′), *n.* wall or foundation of broken stones thrown together irregularly. —*v.* build or strengthen with loose, broken stones.

road run ner (rōd′ run′ər), *n.* a long-tailed bird of the deserts of the SW United States that is related to the cuckoo. It usually runs instead of flying.

rook (rúk), *n.* **1.** a crow that often nests in trees near buildings. **2.** person who cheats at cards, dice, etc. —*v.* cheat.

rote (rōt), *n.* **1.** a set, mechanical way of doing things. **2. by rote,** by memory without thought of the meaning.

round a bout (round′ə bout′), *n.* **1.** an indirect

< = from, taken from; cf., compare; dial., dialect; dim., diminutive; pp., past participle; ppr., present participle; pt., past tense; ult., ultimately; var., variant; ?=possibly.

806

rout   sensual

way, course, or speech. **2.** a short, tight jacket for men or boys.
rout (rout), *n.* **1.** flight of a defeated army in disorder. **2.** a complete defeat. **3.** *Archaic.* crowd; band. **4.** group of followers. **5.** a noisy disorderly crowd. **6.** riot; disturbance. —*v.* **1.** put to flight. **2.** defeat completely.
roy al (roi′əl), *adj.* **1.** of kings and queens: *the royal family.* **2.** of a kingdom. **3.** appropriate for a king; splendid. —*n.* a small mast or sail set just below the skysail.
ruck (ruk), *n.* crowd; the great mass of common or inferior people, animals, or things.
rude (rüd), *adj.* **1.** impolite. **2.** roughly made or done: *a rude cabin.* **3.** rough in manner or behavior. **4.** not having learned much; rather wild; barbarous. **5.** belonging to the poor or to uncultured people; simple; without luxury or elegance.
rue ful (rü′fəl), *adj.* **1.** sorrowful; unhappy; mournful: *a rueful expression.* **2.** causing sorrow or pity: *a rueful sight.*
ruse (rüz or rüs), *n.* trick; stratagem.
rus tic (rus′tik), *adj.* **1.** belonging to the country; rural. **2.** simple; plain. **3.** rough; awkward. —*n.* a country person. [< L *rusticus* < *rus* country]
rust y (rus′ti), *adj.* **1.** covered with rust. **2.** faded.

sa chem (sā′chəm), *n.* chief of an American Indian tribe. [Am.E; < Algonquian]
sad i ron (sad′ī′ərn), *n.* a heavy flatiron for pressing clothes.
sa ga cious (sə gā′shəs), *adj.* **1.** wise in a keen, practical way; shrewd. **2.** intelligent. —**sa ga′cious ly,** *adv.* —**sa ga′cious ness, sa ga′ci ty,** *n.*
sage[1] (sāj), *adj.* **1.** wise. **2.** showing wisdom: *a sage reply.* —*n.* a very wise man. [< OF *sage,* ult. < L *sapere* be wise] —**Syn.** *adj.* **1, 2.** judicious, prudent.
sage[2] (sāj), *n.* **1.** plant whose leaves are used as seasoning and in medicine. **2.** sagebrush.
sal ly (sal′i), *n.* **1.** a sudden attack on an enemy made from a defensive position. **2.** a sudden rushing forth. **3.** a going forth; trip; excursion. **4.** a sudden start into activity. **5.** outburst. —*v.* **1.** go suddenly from a defensive position to attack an enemy. **2.** rush forth suddenly. **3.** set out briskly. **4.** go on an excursion or trip. **5.** of things, issue forth.
sa lu bri ous (sə lü′bri əs), *adj.* healthful. [< L *salubris* < *salus* good health] —**sa lu′bri ous ly,** *adv.*
sal u tar y (sal′ū ter′i), *adj.* **1.** beneficial: *The teacher gave the boy salutary advice.* **2.** good for the health.
sal vage (sal′vij), *n.* **1.** act of saving a ship or its cargo from wreck, capture, etc. **2.** payment for saving it. **3.** rescue of property from fire, etc. **4.** property salvaged. —*v.* save from fire, shipwreck, etc.
sanc tion (sangk′shən), *n.* **1.** permission with authority; support. **2.** action by several nations toward another, such as a blockade, economic restrictions, etc., intended to force it to obey international law.
san guine (sang′gwin), *adj.* **1.** naturally cheerful and hopeful: *a sanguine disposition.* **2.** confident; hopeful: *sanguine of success.* **3.** having a healthy red color; ruddy: *a sanguine complexion.* [< L *sanguineus* < *sanguis* blood] —**Syn.** **1.** optimistic.
sans (sanz; *French* säN), *prep.* *Archaic* or *French.* without.
San skrit or **San scrit** (san′skrit), *n.* the ancient literary language of India.

sa pi ent (sā′pi ənt), *adj.* wise; sage. [< L *sapiens, -entis,* ppr. of *sapere* be wise]
sar don ic (sär don′ik), *adj.* bitter; scornful; mocking: *a fiend's sardonic laugh.*
sa vor y (sā′vər i), *adj.* **1.** pleasing in taste or smell. **2.** giving a relish. **3.** morally pleasing; agreeable. [< OF *savoure,* ult. < L *sapor* taste] —**sa′vor i ness,** *n.*
saw (sô), *n.* a wise saying; proverb: *"A stitch in time saves nine" is a familiar saw.* [OE *sagu.* Related to *say.*]
saw log (sô′lôg′ or sô′log′), *n.* a log large enough to be sawed into lumber.
sax i frage (sak′sə frij), *n.* any of several low, spreading plants, most of which have clusters of thick leaves with silvery, toothed edges.
scab (skab), *n.* *Slang.* workman who will not join a labor union or who takes a striker's place.
scape goat (skāp′gōt′), *n.* person or thing made to bear the blame for the mistakes or sins of others. The ancient Jewish high priests used to lay the sins of the people upon a goat (called the scapegoat) which was then driven out into the wilderness.
Scip i o (sip′i ō), *n.* **1.** 237?-183? B.C., Roman general who defeated Hannibal in 202 B.C. at the battle of Zama. He is called "Scipio the Elder." **2.** 185?-129 B.C., Roman general who destroyed Carthage in 146 B.C. He is called "Scipio the Younger."
scourge (skėrj), *n.* **1.** a whip. **2.** any means of punishment. **3.** some thing or person that causes great trouble or misfortune. —*v.* **1.** whip; punish. **2.** trouble very much.
scow (skou), *n.* a large, flat-bottomed boat used to carry freight, sand, etc.
scrim (skrim), *n.* a loosely woven cotton or linen material, much used for window curtains.
scru ti ny (skrü′tə ni), *n.* close examination; careful inspection. —**scru′ti nize,** *n.*
scud (skud), *v.* run or move swiftly: *Clouds scudded across the sky driven by the high wind.* —*n.* **1.** a scudding. **2.** clouds or spray driven by the wind.
scull (skul), *n.* **1.** oar worked with a side twist over the end of a boat to make it go. **2.** one of a pair of oars used, one on each side, by a single rower. **3.** act of propelling by sculls. —*v.* propel (a boat), by a scull or by sculls. [ME; origin unknown]
scup per (skup′ər), *n.* an opening in the side of a ship to let water run off the deck. [origin uncertain]
scut (skut), *n.* a short tail, especially that of a rabbit or deer. [< Scand. *skutr* stern]
scut tle[1] (skut′əl), *v., n.* scamper; scurry.
scut tle[2] (skut′əl), *n.* **1.** an opening in the deck or side of a ship, with a lid or cover. **2.** opening in a wall or roof, with a lid or cover. **3.** the lid or cover for any such opening. —*v.* cut a hole or holes through the bottom or sides of (a ship) to sink it or to salvage the cargo.
sect (sekt), *n.* **1.** group of people having the same principles, beliefs, or opinions: *Each religious sect in the town had its own church.* **2.** a religious group separated from an established church.
se date (si dāt′), *adj.* quiet; calm; serious: *She is very sedate for a child.*
seer (sēr), *n.* person who foresees or foretells future events.
se lect man (si lekt′mən), *n., pl.* **-men.** one of a board of town officers in New England, chosen each year to manage certain public affairs. [Am.E]
sen su al (sen′shü əl), *adj.* **1.** having to do with the bodily senses rather than with the mind or soul: *sensual*

---

hat, āge, cāre, fär; let, ēqual, tėrm; it, īce; hot, ōpen, ôrder; oil, out; cup, pùt, rüle, ūse; th, thin; ℠H, then; zh, measure; ə represents *a* in about, *e* in taken, *i* in pencil, *o* in lemon, *u* in circus.

pleasures. **2.** caring too much for the pleasures of the senses. **3.** lustful; lewd.

sep ul cher (sep′əl kər), *n.* place of burial; tomb; grave. —*v.* bury (a dead body) in a sepulcher.

sep ul ture (sep′əl chər), *n. Archaic.* **1.** burial. **2.** place of burial; tomb.

se ragl io (sə ral′yō or sə räl′yō), *n., pl.* **-ragl ios. 1.** the women's quarters of a Mohammedan house or palace; harem. **2.** a Turkish palace. [< Ital. *serraglio*, ult. < L *serare* lock up; influenced by Turkish *serāi* palace]

ser aph (ser′əf), *n., pl.* **-aphs** or **-a phim.** one of the highest order of angels. [< *seraphim*, pl., < LL < Hebrew]

Se ra phis (sə rā′pəs)

Serb (sėrb) *n.* **1.** native or inhabitant of Serbia, district in SE Yugoslavia, formerly a country. **2.** language of Serbia. —*adj.* of Serbia, its people, or their language.

ser pen tine (sėr′pən tēn or sėr′pən tīn), *adj.* **1.** of or like a serpent. **2.** winding; twisting: *the serpentine course of a creek.*

shank (shangk), *n.* **1.** the part of the leg between the knee and the ankle. **2.** the whole leg. **3.** any part like a leg, stem, or shaft. **4. shank of the evening,** *Colloq.* the beginning or early part of the evening.

share (shãr), *n.* plowshare. [OE *scear*]

sheath ing (shēᴛн′ing), *n.* casing; covering. The first covering of boards on a house is sheathing.

sheet (shēt), *n.* rope that controls the angle at which a sail is set.

shoal (shōl), *n.* **1.** place where the water is shallow. **2.** sandbank or sand bar that makes the water shallow.

shoat (shōt), *n.* a young pig able to feed itself. Also, **shote.** [origin uncertain]

shock (shok), *n.* group of cornstalks or bundles of grain set up on end together. —*v.* make into shocks.

short shrift (shôrt′ shrift′), *n.* **1.** short time for confession and absolution. **2.** little mercy, rest, or delay. **3. make short shrift of,** make short work of.

shrive (shrīv), *v.,* **shrove** or **shrived, shriv en** or **shrived, shriv ing.** *Archaic.* make confession and be granted forgiveness. [OE *scrīfan* < L *scribere* write]

shriv en (shriv′ən), *v.* a pp. of **shrive.**

shroud (shroud), *n.* **1.** cloth or garment in which a dead person is wrapped for burial. **2.** something that covers, conceals, or veils. **3.** Usually, **shrouds,** *pl.* rope from a mast to the side of a ship. Shrouds help support the mast. —*v.* **1.** wrap for burial. **2.** cover; conceal; veil.

shy ster (shī′stər), *n.* *U.S. Informal.* lawyer or other person who uses improper or questionable methods in his business or profession. [Am.E; origin uncertain]

sib i lant (sib′ə lənt), *adj.* hissing. —*n.* a hissing sound, letter, or symbol. *S* and *sh* are sibilants.

sib yl (sib′əl), *n.* **1.** any of several prophetesses that the ancient Greeks and Romans consulted about the future. **2.** prophetess; fortuneteller; witch.

si er ra (si er′ə), *n.* chain of mountains with jagged peaks. [Am.E; < Sp. *sierra*, literally, a saw < L *serra*]

sig nal (sig′nəl), *n.* sign giving notice of something. —*v.* make a signal or signals (to). —*adj.* **1.** used in signaling. **2.** remarkable; striking; notable.

sil la bub (sil′ə bub), *n.* dessert made of cream, eggs, and wine sweetened and flavored.

sin gu lar (sing′gū lər), *adj.* extraordinary; unusual. —*sin′gu lar ly, adv.*

sin u ous (sin′ū əs), *adj.* **1.** having many curves or turns; winding. **2.** indirect; morally crooked.

sire (sīr), *n.* a male ancestor; father.

skid (skid), *n.* timber, frame, etc., on which something rests, or on which something heavy may slide.

sky sail (skī′sāl′; *Nautical* skī′səl), *n.* in a square-rigged ship, a light sail set at the top of the mast.

slack en (slak′ən), *v.* **1.** make slower. **2.** become slower: *Work slackens on a hot day.* **3.** become less active, vigorous, brisk, etc. **4.** loosen.

slat tern ly (slat′ərn li), *adj.* of a woman, slovenly; untidy. —**slat′tern li ness,** *n.*

sleep er (slēp′ər), *n.* **1.** person or thing that sleeps. **2.** a horizontal beam. **3.** tie to support a railroad track.

sloth (slōth or slôth), *n.* **1.** unwillingness to work or exert oneself; laziness; idleness. **2.** *Archaic.* slowness. **3.** a very slow-moving mammal of South and Central America that lives in trees. —**Syn. 1.** sluggishness.

slough (slou), *n.* a soft, deep muddy place; mud hole.

slug gard (slug′ərd), *n.* a lazy, idle person. —*adj.* lazy; idle.

small clothes (smôl′klōz′ or smôl′klōᴛнz′), *n.pl.* knee breeches, especially, close-fitting ones.

smi lax (smī′laks), *n.* a twining, trailing plant or vine, much used by florists in decoration.

snare (snãr), *n.* **1.** noose for catching small animals and birds. **2.** trap: *Popularity is a snare in which fools are caught.* —*v.* **1.** catch with a snare. **2.** trap.

snub (snub), *v.* **1.** treat coldly, scornfully, or with contempt. **2.** check or stop (a boat, horse, etc.) suddenly. **3.** check or stop (a rope or cable running out) suddenly.

so bri quet (sō′brə kā), *n.* nickname.

so journ (*v.* sō jėrn′ or sō′jėrn; *n.* sō′jėrn), *v.* stay for a time. —*n.* a brief stay. —**so journ′er,** *n.*

so lic i tude (sə lis′ə tüd or sə lis′ə tūd), *n.* anxious care; anxiety; concern.

so lil o quy (sə lil′ə kwi), *n.* **1.** a talking to oneself. **2.** speech made by an actor to himself when alone on the stage. It reveals his thoughts and feelings to the audience, but not to the other characters in the play [< LL *soliloquium* < L *solus* alone + *loqui* speak]

sol stice (sol′stis), *n.* either of the two times in the year when the sun is at its greatest distance from the celestial equator. In the Northern Hemisphere, June 21 or 22, the **summer solstice,** is the longest day of the year and December 21 or 22, the **winter solstice,** is the shortest. [< OF < L *solstitium*, ult. < *sol* sun + *sistere* stand still]

so no rous (sə nô′rəs or sə nō′rəs), *adj.* **1.** giving out or having a deep, loud sound. **2.** full and rich in sound. **3.** having an impressive sound; high-sounding: *sonorous phrases, a sonorous style.* [< L *sonorus*, ult. < *sonus* sound]

so phis ti cal (sə fis′tə kəl), *adj.* clever but misleading; based on false or unsound reasoning.

so phis ti ca tion (sə fis′tə kā′shən), *n.* a lessening or loss of naturalness, simplicity, or frankness; worldly experience or ideas.

sor cer y (sôr′sər i), *n.* magic performed with the aid of evil spirits; witchcraft.

sore (sôr or sōr), *adj.* **1.** painful. **2.** sad; distressed: *The suffering of the poor makes her heart sore.* **3.** irritable. **4.** *Informal.* angered. **5.** causing misery or anger. **6.** severe; distressing.

sot (sot), *n.* person made stupid and foolish by drinking too much alcoholic liquor; drunkard.

spark (spärk), *v.* *Informal.* court; woo.

Spar tan (spär′tən), *adj.* **1.** of Sparta or its people. **2.** like the Spartans; simple, frugal, severe, sternly dis-

---

< = from, taken from;   cf., compare;   dial., dialect;   dim., diminutive;   pp., past participle; ppr., present participle;   pt., past tense;   ult., ultimately;   var., variant;   ?=possibly.

808

ciplined, brave, brief, and concise. —*n.* **1.** native or inhabitant of Sparta. The Spartans were noted for their simplicity of life, severity, courage, and brevity of speech. **2.** person who is like the Spartans.

spasm (spaz′əm), *n.* **1.** a sudden, abnormal, involuntary contraction of a muscle or muscles. **2.** any sudden, brief fit or spell of unusual energy or activity.

spas mod ic (spaz mod′ik), *adj.* **1.** having to do with spasms; resembling a spasm: *a spasmodic cough.* **2.** sudden and violent, but brief; occurring very irregularly.

spav in (spav′ən), *n.* disease of horses, causing lameness.

spe cif ic (spi sif′ik), *adj.* **1.** definite; precise. **2.** characteristic (of); peculiar (to). **3.** curing some particular disease. —*n.* **1.** any specific statement, quality, etc. **2.** a cure for some particular disease: *Quinine is a specific for malaria.*

spe cious (spē′shəs), *adj.* seeming desirable, reasonable, or probable, but not really so; apparently good or right, but without real merit: *The teacher saw through John's specious excuse.*

spec ter (spek′tər), *n. Esp. Brit.* **spectre.** **1.** ghost. **2.** thing causing terror or dread. [< L *spectrum* appearance] —**spec′tral,** *adj.*

spec u late (spek′ū lāt), *v.* **1.** meditate; form opinions without sufficient evidence. **2.** buy or sell when there is a large risk, with the hope of making a profit from future price changes.

spec u la tist (spek′ū lā′tist), *n.* one who tries to discover explanations.

spec u la tive (spek′ū lā′tiv or spek′ū lə tiv), *adj.* **1.** thoughtful; reflective. **2.** theoretical rather than practical. **3.** risky. **4.** of or involving speculation in land, stocks, etc.

spec u la tor (spek′ū lā′tər), *n.* person who speculates, usually in business.

sphinx (sfingks), *n.* **1.** statue of a lion's body with the head of a man, ram, or hawk. **2. Sphinx,** a huge statue with a man's head and a lion's body, near Cairo, Egypt. **3. Sphinx,** in Greek mythology, a monster with the head of a woman, the body of a lion, and wings. The Sphinx proposed a riddle to every passer-by and killed those unable to guess it. **4.** a puzzling or mysterious person.

spin drift (spin′drift′), *n.* spray blown or dashed up from the waves.

spit (spit), *n.* a sharp-pointed, slender rod or bar on which meat is roasted.

spon ta ne i ty (spon′tə nē′ə ti), *n.* **1.** state, quality, or fact of being spontaneous. **2.** a spontaneous action, movement, etc.

spon ta ne ous (spon tā′ni əs), *adj.* **1.** caused by natural impulse or desire; not planned beforehand: *Both sides burst into spontaneous cheers at the skillful play.* **2.** taking place without external cause or help; caused entirely by inner forces. [< LL *spontaneus* < L *sponte* of one's own accord] —**spon ta′ne ous ly,** *adv.* —**spon ta′ne ous ness,** *n.*

spo rad ic (spə rad′ik), *adj.* **1.** appearing or happening at intervals in time: *sporadic outbreaks.* **2.** being or occurring singly or widely apart.

spread-ea gle (spred′ē′gəl), *adj.* **1.** having the form of an eagle with wings spread out. **2.** *U.S.* boastful: *spread-eagle oratory.*

squat ter (skwot′ər), *n.* **1.** person who settles on another's land without right. **2.** person who settles on public land to acquire ownership of it.

squeam ish (skwēm′ish), *adj.* **1.** easily shocked. **2.** too particular. **3.** easily turned sick.

stag ger (stag′ər), *v.* **1.** sway or reel (from weakness, a heavy load, or drunkenness). **2.** become unsteady. —*n.* **1.** a swaying; reeling. **2. staggers,** a nervous disease of horses, cattle, etc., that makes them stagger or fall suddenly.

stalk (stôk), *v.* **1.** approach (wild animals) without being seen or heard by them: *The hunters stalked the lion.* **2.** pursue (an animal or a person) without being seen or heard. **3.** walk with slow, stiff, or haughty strides. —*n.* **1.** a haughty gait. **2.** a stalking. [OE *-stealcian,* as in *bestealcian* steal along]

stanch[1] (stänch or stanch), *v.* **1.** stop or check the flow of (blood, etc.). **2.** cease flowing. Also, **staunch.** [< OF *estanchier* < VL *extanicare* press together, literally, un-thin < L *ex-* un- + Celtic *tan-* thin]

stanch[2] (stänch or stanch), *adj.* **1.** firm; strong: *a stanch defense.* **2.** loyal; steadfast. Also, **staunch.** [< OF *estanche,* fem. < *estanchier.* See STANCH[1].] —**stanch′ly,** *adv.* —**stanch′ness,** *n.*

stan chion (stan′shən), *n.* an upright bar, post, or support (in a window, in a stall for cattle, on a ship, etc.). [< OF *estanchon,* ult. < L *stare* stand]

stark (stärk), *adj.* **1.** downright; complete: *That fool is talking stark nonsense.* **2.** stiff: *The dog lay stark in death.* **3.** harsh; stern. **4.** *Archaic.* strong; sturdy. —*adv.* completely. —**stark′ly,** *adv.*

stat ic (stat′ik), *adj.* **1.** at rest; standing still: *Civilization does not remain static, but changes constantly.* **2.** having to do with bodies at rest.

sta tion (stā′shən), *n.* **1.** a regular stopping place: *a railroad station.* **2.** social position; rank.

steer age (stēr′ij), *n.* part of a passenger ship occupied by passengers traveling at the cheapest rate.

ste ril i ty (stə ril′ə ti), *n.* **1.** inability to produce offspring. **2.** inability to produce results.

stern (stėrn), *n.* the hind part of a ship or boat.

stern sheets (stėrn′ shēts′), *n.* space at the stern of an open boat.

stile (stīl), *n.* **1.** step or steps for getting over a fence or wall. **2.** turnstile [OE *stigel;* related to *stīgan* climb]

still hunt (stil′ hunt′), *n.* quiet or secret pursuit.

stol id (stol′id), *adj.* hard to arouse; not easily excited; showing no emotion —**sto lid′i ty,** *n.*

strait (strāt), *n.* **1.** narrow channel connecting two larger bodies of water. **2. straits,** *pl.* difficulty; need; distress. —*adj.* *Archaic.* **1.** narrow. **2.** strict.

stud ding sail (stud′ing sāl; *Nautical* stun′səl), *n.* a light sail set at the side of a square sail. Also **stunsail.**

stu pe fy (stü′pə fī or stū′pə fī), *v.* **1.** make stupid, dull, or senseless. **2.** overwhelm with amazement; astound. [< L *stupefacere* < *stupere* be amazed + *facere* make] —**stu′pe fi′er, stu′pe fac′tion,** *n.*

sub li mate (sub′lə māt), *v.* **1.** purify; refine. **2.** change (an undesirable impulse or trait) into a desirable activity.

sub li ma tion (sub′lə mā′shən), *n.* **1.** act or process of sublimating. **2.** the resulting product or state.

sub sist ence (səb sis′təns), *n.* **1.** existence. **2.** living. **3.** means of keeping alive; livelihood.

sub tle (sut′əl), *adj.* **1.** delicate; thin; fine: *a subtle odor of perfume.* **2.** faint; mysterious: *a subtle smile.* **3.** having a keen, quick mind; discerning; acute: *She is a subtle observer of slight differences in things.* **4.** sly; crafty; tricky. **5.** skillful; clever; expert. —*Syn.* **1.** rare. **3.** discriminating. **4.** cunning.

---

hat, āge, cãre, fär; let, ēqual, tėrm; it, īce; hot, ōpen, ôrder; oil, out; cup, pùt, rüle, ūse; th, thin; ͭн, then; zh, measure; ə represents *a* in about, *e* in taken, *i* in pencil, *o* in lemon, *u* in circus.

809

sub vert (səb vėrt′), v. **1.** ruin; overthrow: *Dictators subvert democracy.* **2.** undermine the principles of; corrupt. [< L *subvertere* < *sub-* up from under + *vertere* turn]

suc cu lent (suk′ū lənt), adj. **1.** juicy: *a succulent fruit.* **2.** interesting; not dull. **3.** of plants, etc., having thick, fleshy leaves and stems.

suf fer (suf′ər), v. **1.** have pain, grief, injury, etc. **2.** allow; permit: *"Suffer the little children to come unto me."* **3.** bear with patiently; endure: *I will not suffer such insults.* [< L *sufferre* < *sub-* up + *ferre* bear]

suf fer ance (suf′ər əns or suf′rəns), n. **1.** permission given only by a failure to object. **2.** patient endurance.

suf frage (suf′rij), n. **1.** a vote. **2.** the right to vote. **3.** casting of votes. **4.** approval; consent. [< L *suffragium* supporting vote < *sub-* nearby + *frag-* applause (related to *fragor* din, crash, originally, a breaking)]

sum mar y (sum′ə ri), n. a brief statement giving the main points. —adj. **1.** concise; brief. **2.** direct and prompt; without delay or formality: *The Indian took summary vengeance by killing his enemies.*

su per cil i ous (sü′pər sil′i əs), adj. showing scorn or indifference because of a feeling of superiority. [< L *superciliosus* < *supercilium* eyebrow]

su per flu ous (sü pėr′flü əs), adj. **1.** more than is needed. **2.** needless.

su per nal (sú pėr′nəl), adj. **1.** heavenly; divine. **2.** lofty; exalted. [< L *supernus* < *super* above]

su per nu mer ar y (sü′pər nü′mər er′i or sü′pər-nū′mər er′i), adj. more than the usual or necessary number.

su per scrip tion (sü′pər skrip′shən), n. **1.** a writing above, on, or outside of something. **2.** something written above or on the outside. **3.** address on a letter or parcel.

su pra ra tion al (sü′prə rash′ə nəl), adj. above or beyond reasoning.

sur cease (sėr sēs′), n. *Archaic.* end; ceasing.

sur feit (sėr′fit), n. too much; excess: *A surfeit of food makes one sick. A surfeit of advice annoys me.* —v. overfeed. —Syn. v. gorge.

sur name (sėr′nām′), n. **1.** a last name. **2.** name added to a person's real name: *William I of England had the surname "the Conqueror."* —v. give an added name to. [< F *surnom* < *sur-* over (< L *super-*) + *nom* name < L *nomen*; influenced by E *name*]

sur plice (sėr′plis), n. a broad-sleeved, white gown worn by clergymen and choir singers over their other clothes. [< OF *surpelice* < *sur-* over (< L *super-*) + *pelice* fur garment, ult. < L *pellis* hide]

sus cep ti bil i ty (sə sep′tə bil′ə ti), n. **1.** quality or state of being easily influenced by feelings or emotions. **2.** quality of being open to certain treatment.

swain (swān), n. *Archaic* or *Poetic.* **1.** lover. **2.** young man who lives in the country. [< Scand. *sveinn* boy]

swarth y (swôr′ᵵᴴi or swôr′thi), ‐adj. having a dark skin. [earlier *swarfy* < *swarf* grit, OE *geswearf*]

swath (swoth or swôth), n. **1.** space covered by one cut of a scythe or mowing machine. **2.** row of cut grass, grain, etc. **3.** a strip. **4. cut a wide swath,** make a showy display; splurge. [OE *swæth* track, trace]

swathe (swāᵵᴴ), v. wrap up closely or fully.

sweep (swēp), n. **1.** dignified motion: *the sweep of verse.* **2.** a curve, bend. **3.** a long oar.

syc o phan tic (sik′ə fan′tik), adj. having to do with a sycophant, a servile, self-seeking flatterer.

sym me try (sim′ə tri), n. **1.** a regular, balanced arrangement on opposite sides of a line or plane, or around a center or axis: *A swollen cheek spoiled the symmetry of his face.* **2.** pleasing proportions between the parts of a whole. [< L < Gk. *symmetria* < *syn-* together + *metron* measure] —sym met′ri cal, adj.

tab leau (tab′lō), n., pl. -leaux or -leaus. **1.** a striking scene; picture. **2.** representation of a picture, statue, scene, etc., by a person or group posing in appropriate costume. [< F *tableau*, dim. of *table* table]

tac it (tas′it), adj. **1.** unspoken; silent. **2.** implied or understood without being openly expressed. [< L *tacitus*, pp. of *tacere* be silent] —tac′it ly, adv.

tac i turn (tas′ə tėrn), adj. speaking very little. [< L *taciturnus* < *tacitus* tacit. See TACIT.] —tac′ i tur′-ni ty, n. —Syn. reserved, reticent. —Ant. garrulous.

tack (tak), n. **1.** a zigzag course against the wind. **2.** direction in which a ship moves in regard to the position of her sails. When on port tack, a ship has the wind on her left. —v. **1.** sail in a zigzag course against the wind. **2.** change from one tack to another.

tac tile (tak′təl), adj. **1.** of or having to do with touch. **2.** having the sense of touch.

taff rail (taf′rāl′), n. a rail around a ship's stern.

tal ly (tal′i), n. anything corresponding to a certain other thing; duplicate; counterpart. —v. agree; correspond (to another thing) as a duplicate or counterpart: *Your account tallies with mine.*

tan dem (tan′dəm), adv. one behind the other. —adj. having animals, seats, parts, etc., arranged one behind the other. —n. **1.** two horses harnessed tandem. **2.** a carriage drawn by two horses so harnessed. **3.** a bicycle with two seats, one behind the other.

tan gi ble (tan′jə bəl), adj. **1.** capable of being touched or felt by touch. **2.** that can be understood; real; actual; definite. —n. tangibles, pl. things whose value is easily appraised; material assets. [< LL *tangibilis* < *tangere* touch]

tank ard (tangk′ərd), n. a large drinking mug with a handle and a hinged cover.

tan ta lize (tan′tə līz), v. torment or tease by keeping something desired in sight but out of reach, or by holding out hopes that are repeatedly disappointed. [< *Tantalus*, a legendary Greek king who was punished in Hades by having to stand in high water, over which were fruit-laden branches. Whenever he tried to drink or eat, the water or fruit withdrew from his reach.]

tar (tär), n. sailor.

tat ter de mal ion (tat′ər di māl′yən or tat′ər di-mal′yən), n. person in tattered clothes; ragamuffin.

taw ny (tô′ni), adj. brownish yellow.

tax (taks), v. **1.** put a tax on. **2.** lay a heavy burden on. **3.** accuse: *The teacher taxed Tom with having neglected his work.*

tech ni cal i ty (tek′nə kal′ə ti), n. a matter, point, detail, term, expression, etc., that has to do with the special facts of science, art, etc.

tech nol o gy (tek nol′ə ji), n. **1.** the science of the industrial arts. **2.** technical words, terms, or expressions used in an art, science, etc. **3.** applied science. —tech′no log′i cal, adj.

te mer i ty (tə mer′ə ti), n. reckless boldness; rashness.

te na cious (ti nā′shəs), adj. **1.** holding fast. **2.** stubborn; persistent: *a tenacious salesman.* **3.** that retains well. **4.** holding fast together. [< L *tenax, -acis* < *tenere* hold] —te na′cious ly, adv. —te nac′i ty, n.

ten et (ten′it; *esp. Brit.* tē′nit), n. doctrine, principle, belief, or opinion held as true. [< L *tenet* he holds]

< = from, taken from; cf., compare; dial., dialect; dim., diminutive; pp., past participle; ppr., present participle; pt., past tense; ult., ultimately; var., variant; ?=possibly.

ten u ous (ten′ū əs), *adj.* 1. thin; slender. 2. not dense: *Air ten miles above the earth is very tenuous.* 3. having slight importance; not substantial.

ten ure (ten′yər), *n.* 1. a holding; possessing. 2. length of time of holding or possessing. 3. conditions, terms, etc., on which anything is held or occupied.

ter ma gent (tėr′mə gənt), *n.* a violent, quarreling, scolding woman.

ter mi nal (tėr′mə nəl), *adj.* 1. forming the end part. 2. coming at the end: *a terminal examination.* 3. marking a boundary, limit, or end. [< L *terminalis* <*terminus* end]

tes sel late (*v.* tes′ə lāt; *adj.* tes′ə lit or tes′ə lāt), *v.* make of small squares or blocks, or in a checkered pattern. —*adj.* made in small squares or blocks or in a checkered pattern.

tes ty (tes′ti), *adj.* easily irritated; impatient.

teth er (teᵀH′ər), *n.* rope or chain for fastening an animal so that it can graze only within certain limits. —*v.* fasten with a tether.

Thames (temz), *n.* river flowing from SW England into the North Sea. London is on the Thames. 210 mi.

Than a top sis (than′ə top′sis)

thatch (thach), *n.* 1. straw, rushes, palm leaves, etc., used as a roof or covering. 2. roof or covering of thatch. —*v.* roof or cover with thatch.

Thebes (thēbz), *n.* an important city in ancient Greece.

Tho reau (thə rō′ or thō′rō)

thwart (thwôrt), *v.* oppose and defeat; keep from doing something. —**Syn.** baffle, balk, foil.

tim or ous (tim′ər əs), *adj.* easily frightened; timid. [< Med.L *timorosus* < L *timor* fear] —**tim′or ous ly,** *adv.* —**tim′or ous ness,** *n.*

tinc ture (tingk′chər), *n.* 1. solution of medicine in alcohol: *tincture of iodine.* 2. trace; tinge. 3. color; tint. —*v.* 1. give a trace or tinge to. 2. color; tint.

tin type (tin′tīp′), *n.* photograph taken on a sheet of enameled tin or iron. [Am.E]

Ti tan ic (tĭ tan′ik), *adj.* 1. of or like the Titans, a family of giants in Greek mythology. 2. Also, **titanic.** having great size, strength, or power; gigantic; huge: *titanic energy.*

tit u lar (tich′ù lər or tit′ū lər), *adj.* 1. in title or name only: *He is a titular prince without any power.* 2. having a title. 3. having to do with a title. [< L *titulus* title]

tod dy (tod′i), *n.* drink made of whiskey, brandy, etc., with hot water and sugar.

top mast (top′mast′ or top′mäst′; *Nautical* top′-məst), *n.* the second section of a mast above the deck.

top sail (top′sāl′; *Nautical* top′səl), *n.* the second sail above the deck on a mast.

To rre ón (tô rä ōn′), city in Mexico.

tor tu ous (tôr′chü əs), *adj.* full of twists, turns, or bends; twisting; winding; crooked. [< L *tortuosus*, ult. < *torquere* twist]

tour ni quet (tür′nə ket, tür′nə kā, tėr′nə ket, or tėr′nə kā), *n.* device for stopping bleeding by compressing a blood vessel, such as a bandage tightened by twisting with a stick, or a pad pressed down by a screw.

tract (trakt), *n.* 1. a little book or pamphlet on a religious subject. 2. any little book or pamphlet.

trac ta ble (trak′tə bəl), *adj.* easily managed or controlled; easy to deal with.

tran scend (tran send′), *v.* 1. go beyond the limits or powers of; exceed; be above. 2. be higher or greater than; surpass; excel. 3. be superior or extraordinary. [< L *transcendere* < *trans-* beyond + *scandere* climb]

tran scend ent (tran sen′dənt), *adj.* surpassing ordinary limits; excelling; superior; extraordinary.

tran scen den tal (tran′sen den′təl), *adj.* 1. transcendent. 2. supernatural. 3. obscure; incomprehensible; fantastic. 4. explaining matter and objective things as products of the mind that is thinking about them; idealistic.

tran scen den tal ism (tran′sen den′təl iz əm), *n.* 1. transcendental quality, thought, language, or philosophy. 2. any philosophy based upon the doctrine that the principles of reality are to be discovered by a study of the processes of thought, not from experience. 3. the religious and philosophical doctrines of Emerson and others in New England about 1840. It emphasized the importance of individual inspiration and had an important influence on American thought and literature.

trans fix (trans fiks′), *v.* 1. pierce through. 2. fasten by piercing through with something pointed. 3. make motionless (with amazement, terror, etc.). [< L *transfixus,* pp. of *transfigere* < *trans-* through + *figere* fix]

tran sient (tran′shənt), *adj.* 1. fleeting; not lasting. 2. passing through and not staying long.

trap (trap), *n.* 1. thing or means for catching animals. 2. trick or other means for catching someone off guard. 3. **traps,** *pl.* drums, cymbals, bells, gongs, etc.

tree (trē), *n.* 1. a large perennial plant with a woody trunk, branches, and leaves. 2. piece or structure of wood for some special purpose: *clothes tree, shoe tree.*

treen (trēn), *n.* *Archaic. pl.* of **tree.**

trel lis (trel′is), *n.* frame of light strips of wood or metal crossing one another with open spaces in between; lattice, especially one supporting growing vines. —*v.* furnish with a trellis. 2. cross as in a trellis.

tres tle (tres′əl), *n.* 1. frame used as a support. 2. a supporting framework for carrying railroad tracks across a gap. [< OF *trestel* crossbeam, ult. < L *transtrum*]

tri dent (trī′dənt), *n.* a three-pronged spear. —*adj.* three-pronged. [< L *tridens, -entis* < *tri-* three + *dens* tooth]

Trin i ty (trin′ə ti), *n.* 1. the union of Father, Son, and Holy Ghost in one divine nature. 2. **trinity,** group of three. [< OF < L *trinitas* < *trinus* triple]

triv et (triv′it), *n.* a stand or support with three legs or feet. Trivets are used over fires and under platters.

Troy (troi), *n.* 1. an ancient city in NW Asia Minor. The Greeks laid siege to Troy for ten years. 2. city in E New York State, on the Hudson River.

truck (truk), *n.* a wooden disk at the top of a flagstaff or mast with holes for the ropes.

trump er y (trump′ər i or trump′ri), *n.* something showy but without value. —*adj.* showy but without value; trifling. [< F *tromperie* < *tromper* deceive]

tu i tion (tü ish′ən or tū ish′ən), *n.* 1. teaching; instruction. 2. money paid for instruction.

Tu nis (tü′nis or tū′nis), *n.* 1. seaport and capital of Tunisia, in N Africa. 365,000. 2. Tunisia. 3. a former state in N Africa.

tur gid (tėr′jid), *adj.* 1. swollen; bloated. 2. using big words and elaborate comparisons; bombastic; inflated; pompous. [< L *turgidus* < *turgere* swell]

twain (twān), *n., adj.* *Archaic* or *Poetic.* two. [OE *twēgen*]

u biq ui tous (ū bik′wə təs), *adj.* being everywhere at the same time; present everywhere.

ul ster (ul′stər), *n.* a long, loose, heavy overcoat.

um bra geous (um brā′jəs), *adj.* 1. shady. 2. likely to take offense.

---

hat, āge, cãre, fär; let, ēqual, tėrm; it, īce; hot, ōpen, ôrder; oil, out; cup, pùt, rüle, ūse; th, thin; ᵀH, then; zh, measure; ə represents *a* in about, *e* in taken, *i* in pencil, *o* in lemon, *u* in circus.

un der bred (un′dər bred′), *adj.* of inferior breeding or manners; vulgar.

un du late (*v.* un′jů lāt or un′dū lāt; *adj.* un′jů lit, un′jů lāt, un′dū lit, or un′dū lāt), *v.* **1.** move in waves. **2.** have a wavy form or surface. —*adj.* wavy.

u ni corn (ū′nə kôrn), *n.* an imaginary animal like a horse, but having a single long horn in the middle of its forehead. [< L *unicornis* < *unus* one + *cornu* horn]

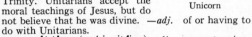

Unicorn

U ni tar i an (ū′nə tãr′i ən), *n.* person who maintains that God exists as one being, in opposition to the doctrine of the Trinity. Unitarians accept the moral teachings of Jesus, but do not believe that he was divine. —*adj.* of or having to do with Unitarians.

un re mit ting (un′ri mit′ing), *adj.* never stopping; not slackening; maintained steadily.

un seem ly (un sēm′li), *adj.* not suitable; improper.

U ra lic (ū rä′lik)

U ra nus (ūr′ə nəs), *n.* **1.** a Greek god. **2.** one of the larger planets, seventh in order from the sun.

u su rer (ū′zhə rər), *n.* person who lends money at an extremely high or unlawful rate of interest.

u surp (ū zėrp′ or ū sėrp′), *v.* seize and hold (power, position, authority, etc.) by force or without right. —**u surp′er, u′sur pa′tion,** *n.*

u su ry (ū′zhə ri), *n.* **1.** the lending of money at an extremely high or unlawful rate of interest. **2.** an extremely high or unlawful interest. —**u su′ri ous,** *adj.*

u til i tar i an (ū til′ə tãr′i ən), *adj.* **1.** having to do with utility. **2.** aiming at usefulness rather than beauty, style, etc. —*n.* adherent of utilitarianism.

ux o ri ous (uks ô′ri əs or uks ō′ri əs), *adj.* excessively or foolishly fond of one's wife. [< L *uxorius* < *uxor* wife]

van[1] (van), *n.* the leading position in any procession or movement. [< *vanguard*]

van[2] (van), *n.* a covered truck or wagon. [< *caravan*]

Van Du sen (van dū′sən)

var i e gat ed (vãr′i ə gāt′id or vãr′i gāt′id), *adj.* **1.** varied in appearance; marked with different colors: *variegated pansies.* **2.** having variety.

vast (vast or väst), *adj.* very great; immense. —*n.* boundless space.

vau de ville (vô′də vil or vōd′vil), *n.* theatrical entertainment consisting of a variety of acts. Vaudeville consists of songs, dances, acrobatic feats, short plays, trained animals, etc.

vault ed (vôl′tid), *adj.* **1.** in the form of a vault; arched. **2.** built or covered with a vault: *a vaulted room.*

vaunt (vônt or vänt), *v., n.* boast. [< F < LL *vanitare* < *vanus* vain] —**vaunt′ing ly,** *adv.*

ve dette (vi det′), *n.* **1.** a mounted sentry stationed in advance of the outposts of an army. **2.** a small naval vessel used for scouting. [< F < Ital. *vedetta,* ult. < L *videre* see]

ven er a ble (ven′ər ə bəl), *adj.* worthy of reverence; deserving respect because of age, character, or associations: *venerable customs.*

ven er ate (ven′ər āt), *v.* regard with deep respect: *He venerates his father's memory.* [< L *venerari* < *Venus,* originally, love] —**ven′er a′tion,** *n.*

ver dure (vėr′jər), *n.* **1.** fresh greenness. **2.** a fresh growth of green grass, plants, or leaves. [< OF *verdure,* ult. < L *viridis* green]

ver mil ion (vər mil′yən), *n.* **1.** a bright red. **2.** a bright-red coloring matter. —*adj.* bright-red.

ver ti go (vėr′tə gō), *n., pl.* **ver ti goes, ver tig i nes** (ver tij′ə nēz). dizziness; giddiness.

ves per (ves′pər), *adj.* of evening.

ves try man (ves′tri mən), *n., pl.* **-men.** member of a committee that helps manage church business.

ves ture (ves′chər), *n.* **1.** clothing; garments. **2.** covering. [< OF *vesture,* ult. < L *vestis* garment]

vi al (vī′əl), *n.* a small glass bottle for holding medicines or the like; bottle.

vi cis si tude (və sis′ə tüd or və sis′ə tūd), *n.* **1.** change in circumstances, fortune, etc.: *The vicissitudes of life may suddenly make a rich man poor.* **2.** change; variation. **3.** regular change.

vict ual (vit′əl), *n.* Usually, **victuals,** *pl. Informal or Dialect.* food.

vin di ca tion (vin′də kā′shən), *n.* a vindicating or being vindicated; defense; justification.

vir gin (vėr′jən), *n.* a maiden; a pure, unmarried woman. *adj.* **1.** of or having to do with a virgin. **2.** pure; spotless: *Virgin snow is newly fallen snow.* **3.** not yet used: *virgin soil.*

vir gin al (vėr′jən əl), *adj.* of or suitable for a virgin; maidenly; pure. [< L *virginalis* < *virgo* maiden]

vir ile (vir′əl), *adj.* **1.** manly; masculine. **2.** full of manly strength or masculine vigor. **3.** vigorous; forceful. [< L *virilis* < *vir* man]

vir tu al (vėr′chü əl), *adj.* being something in effect, though not so in name; actual; real: *The battle was won with so great a loss of soldiers that it was a virtual defeat.*

vir tu os i ty (vėr′chü os′ə ti), *n.* character or skill of a virtuoso, an expert.

vis age (viz′ij), *n.* **1.** face. **2.** appearance.

vis ta (vis′tə), *n.* **1.** view seen through a narrow opening or passage. **2.** such an opening or passage itself: *a shady vista of elms.* **3.** a mental view: *Education should open up new vistas.* [< Ital. *vista.* ult. < L *videre* see]

vi tal (vī′təl), *adj.* **1.** necessary to life. **2.** very important; essential. —*n.* **vitals,** *pl.* **a.** parts or organs necessary to life. The brain, heart, lungs, and stomach are vitals. **b.** essential parts or features. [< L *vitalis* < *vita* life]

vix en (vik′sən), *n.* **1.** a female fox. **2.** a bad-tempered or quarrelsome woman. [OE *fyxen* < *fox* fox]

vo cif er a tion (vō sif′ər ā′shən), *n.* noisy oratory; clamor.

vol a tile (vol′ə təl), *adj.* **1.** evaporating rapidly; changing into vapor easily: *Gasoline is volatile.* **2.** changing rapidly from one mood or interest; fickle. [< L *volatilis* flying < *volare* fly]

vol ley (vol′i), *n.* **1.** shower of stones, bullets, arrows, words, oaths, etc. **2.** the discharge of a number of guns at once. —*v.* discharge or be discharged in a volley.

vol u ble (vol′ū bəl), *adj.* **1.** tending to talk much; fond of talking. **2.** having a smooth, rapid flow of words.

vo lu mi nous (və lü′mə nəs), *adj.* **1.** forming, filling, or writing a large book or many books. **2.** of great size; very bulky; large.

vo lup tu ous (və lup′chü əs), *adj.* **1.** caring much for the pleasures of the senses. **2.** giving pleasure to the

< = from, taken from;   cf., compare;   dial., dialect;   dim., diminutive;   pp., past participle; ppr., present participle;   pt., past tense;   ult., ultimately;   var., variant;   ?=possibly.

812

senses: *voluptuous music or beauty.* [< L *voluptuosus* < *voluptas* pleasure < *volup(e)*, neut., agreeable] **—volup′tu ous ly,** *adv.*

vo ta ry (vō′tə ri), *n.* **1.** person devoted to something; devotee: *He was a votary of golf.* **2.** person bound by vows to a religious life. [< L *votum* vow]

vul ner a ble (vul′nər ə bəl), *adj.* **1.** capable of being wounded or injured; open to attack. **2.** sensitive to criticism, temptations, influences, etc.: *Most people are vulnerable to ridicule.* [< LL *vulnerabilis* wounding, ult. < *vulnus* wound] **—vul′ner a bly,** *adv.* **—vul′ner a bil′i ty,** *n.*

wag (wag), *n.* person who is fond of making jokes.

wane (wān), *v.* **1.** become smaller gradually: *The moon wanes after it has become full.* **2.** decline in power, influence, importance, etc. **3.** decline in strength, intensity, etc.

want (wont or wônt), *v.* **1.** wish for; wish. **2.** be without; lack. **3.** need: *Plants want water.* **4.** be lacking: *It wants an hour until dinner.*

want ing (won′ting or wôn′ting), *adj.* **1.** lacking; missing: *One volume of the set is wanting.* **2.** not coming up to a standard or need. **—prep.** without; less; minus: *a year wanting three days.*

wan ton (won′tən), *adj.* **1.** reckless; heartless. **2.** without reason or excuse: *a wanton attack, wanton mischief.* **3.** not moral; not chaste. **4.** *Poetic.* frolicsome; playful. **—n.** a wanton person. **—v.** act in a wanton manner. [ME *wantowen* < OE *wan-* not (related to *wane*) + *togen* brought up, pp. of *tēon* bring]

war lock (wôr′lok), *n.* a long tuft of hair on the top of the head. Many warriors shaved their heads except for this lock.

warp (wôrp), *v.* **1.** bend or twist out of shape. **2.** bend. **3.** mislead; pervert: *Prejudice warps our judgment.* **—n.** **1.** a bend or twist; distortion. **2.** the threads running lengthwise in a fabric. The warp is crossed by the woof. [OE *weorpan* throw]

war ren (wôr′ən or wor′ən), *n.* **1.** piece of ground filled with burrows, where rabbits live or are raised. **2.** a crowded district or building.

wax (waks), *v.,* **waxed, waxed** or *(Poetic)* **wax en, waxing. 1.** grow bigger or greater; increase: *The moon waxes till it becomes full, and then wanes.* **2.** become: *The party waxed merry.* [OE *weaxan*]

way (wā), *n.* **1.** manner; style. **2.** method; means. **3.** road; path; street; course. **4. ways,** *pl.* timbers on which a ship is built and launched.

weal (wēl), *n. Archaic.* well-being; prosperity; happiness: *Good citizens act for the public weal.* [OE *wela*]

well sweep (wel′ swēp′), *n.* a tapering or weighted pole swung on a pivot and having a bucket hung on the smaller end.

wench (wench), *n.* **1.** girl or young woman. **2.** a woman servant. [< *wenchel* child, OE *wencel*]

whale bone (hwāl′bōn′), *n.* **1.** an elastic, horny substance growing in place of teeth in the upper jaw of certain whales and forming a series of thin, parallel plates. **2.** a thin strip of this used for stiffening corsets, dresses, etc.

whet (hwet), *v.* **1.** sharpen by rubbing. **2.** make keen or eager; stimulate. **—n.** **1.** act of whetting. **2.** something that whets. **3.** appetizer.

Whig (hwig), *n.* **1.** member of a former political party in Great Britain that favored reforms and progress. The Whig Party became the Liberal Party. **2.** an American who favored the Revolution against England. **3.** member of a political party in the United States that was formed about 1834 in opposition to the Democratic Party. **—adj.** composed of Whigs; having to do with Whigs; like Whigs.

whim si cal (hwim′zə kəl), *adj.* having many odd notions or fancies; fanciful; odd. **whim′si cal ly,** *adv.*

whit low (hwit′lō), *n.* abscess on a finger or toe.

wind ward (wind′wərd; *Nautical* win′dərd), *adj.* on the side toward the wind.

win now (win′ō), *v.* **1.** blow off the chaff from (grain); drive or blow away (chaff). **2.** blow chaff from grain. **3.** sort out; sift: *winnow truth from falsehood.* **4.** fan (with wings); flap (wings). [OE *windwian* < *wind* wind]

with al (wiᴛʜ ôl′ or with ôl′), *Archaic.* **—adv.** with it all; as well; besides; also: *The lady is rich and fair and wise withal.* **—prep.** with. [< *with* + *all*]

withe (wiᴛʜ, with, or wiᴛ̄ʜ), *n.* **1.** a willow twig. **2.** any tough, easily bent twig suitable for binding things together.

with ers (wiᴛʜ′ərz), *n.pl.* the highest part of a horse's or other animal's back, behind the neck. [origin uncertain]

wont (wunt or wōnt), *adj.* accustomed: *He was wont to read the paper at breakfast.* **—n.** custom; habit. [originally pp., ult. < OE *wunian* be accustomed]

woof (wüf), *n.* **1.** the threads running from side to side across a woven fabric. **2.** fabric; cloth; texture.

worm wood (wėrm′wůd′), *n.* **1.** a bitter plant used in medicine, certain bitter drinks, etc. **2.** something bitter or extremely unpleasant. [< OE *wermōd*, influenced by *worm, wood*]

wreak (rēk), *v.* **1.** give expression to; work off (feelings, desires, etc.): *The boy wreaked his temper on his dog.* **2.** inflict (vengeance, punishment, etc.). **3.** *Archaic.* avenge.

wrought (rôt), *v.* a pt. and a pp. of **work.** **—adj.** **1.** made. **2.** formed with care; not rough or crude. **3.** manufactured or treated; not in a raw state. **4.** of metals, formed by hammering.

wry (rī), *adj.* turned to one side; twisted: *She made a wry face to show her disgust.* **—wry′ly,** *adv.*

Ya hoo (yä′hü or yä hü′), *n.* **1.** in Swift's *Gulliver's Travels,* a brute in human shape who works for a race of intelligent horses. **2. yahoo,** a rough, coarse person.

yard (yärd), *n.* **1.** measure of length; 36 inches; 3 feet. **2.** a long, slender beam or pole fastened across a mast, used to support a sail. [OE *gierd* rod]

yaw (yô), *v.* **1.** turn from a straight course; go unsteadily. **2.** of an aircraft, turn from a straight course by a motion about its vertical axis. **—n.** movement from a straight course. [origin uncertain]

yeo man (yō′mən), *n.* **1.** in the United States Navy, a petty officer who has clerical duties. **2.** a person who owns land, but not a large amount.

zeal ot (zel′ət), *n.* person who shows too much zeal; fanatic. [< L *zelotes* < Gk. *zelotes* < *zelos* zeal]

Ze kle (zē′kəl)

---

hat, āge, cãre, fär;   let, ēqual, tėrm;   it, īce;   hot, ōpen, ôrder;   oil, out;   cup, pùt, rüle, ūse; th, thin; ᴛʜ, then; zh, measure;   ə represents *a* in about, *e* in taken, *i* in pencil, *o* in lemon, *u* in circus.

Index of Types of Literature

General Index

Names of authors represented in the text appear in capital letters; titles of selections printed in the text are italicized. General topics, including names of authors and selections discussed but not represented in the text, are printed in regular type.

5 6 7 8 9 10 11 12 13 14 15 16 17 18 19 20 21 22 23 24 25 D 72 71 70 69 68 67 66